WEBSTER'S
DICTIONARY

D1178483

WEBSTER'S
DICTIONARY

OF THE
ENGLISH LANGUAGE

Illustrated

Handy School and Office Edition

BOOK CRAFT GUILD, INC.
NEW YORK, N. Y.

PREFACE

Every word listed in this all new, self pronouncing dictionary, has been completely reviewed and edited in order to offer the most modern reference, based on the foundation laid by the famous Noah Webster and many others.

In addition to containing words in general usage, many new words have been included that have only recently come into use, including the more difficult words that are of foreign derivation. The pronounciation of each word is clearly shown together with the most concise and accurate definitions, in accordance with current usage.

This highly informative book also contains basic rules of English Usage, including a Pronunciation Key, Spelling Of Sounds and Abbreviations Used In Definitions, as a constant guide to proper speech and writing. Also included throughout the book are helpful illustrations that further contribute to a greater understanding of the accompanying definitions.

This new concise edition is designed as a speedy reference for words in most common usage and is especially compiled for convenience at Home, School and Office. Special quality standards have been maintained in producing this book in order to offer a dictionary that can be frequently referred to and that can provide many years of valuable service.

THE EDITORS

PRONUNCIATION KEY

ā	as in fate, age	ŏ	as in hot, box
ă	as in fat, map	ô	as in dog, law, fought
â	as in dare, air	ô	as in more, roar, door, four
ä	as in father, pa, barn	oi	as in oil, boy
ē	as in be, equal	ou	as in out, loud
ĕ	as in bet, ebb	ōō	as in too, rule
ê	as in mere, near	ŏŏ	as in book, put
ī	as in bite, ice, ride	ŭ	as in fun, up
ĭ	as in bit, if	û	as in fur, term
ō	as in note, boat, low		

ə stands for the sound of: "a" in ago, Senate; "e" in open, hopeless, fairness; "i" in peril,
trellis; "o" in lemon; "u" in minus, argument;
"ou" in famous; "ai" in mountain; "oi" in tortoise.

b	as in bed (bĕd), tub (tŭb)
ch	as in chill (chĭl), batch (băch)
d	as in deed (dēd)
f	as in fate (fāt), huff (hŭf)
g	as in get (gĕt), leg (lĕg)
h	as in hop (hŏp)
hw	for "wh" as in what (hwŏt), wheel (hwēl)
j	as in jam (jăm), job (jŏb); and for "g" in gentle (jĕn'təl) and range (rānj)
k	as in kin (kĭn), smoke (smōk); for "c" in coal (kōl); and for "ck" in rack (răk)
l	as in let (lĕt), bell (bĕl)
m	as in men (mĕn), him (hĭm)
n	as in not (nŏt), ran (răn)
ng	as in song (sông); and for "n" in think (thĭngk)
p	as in pup (pŭp)
r	as in ride (rīd), very (vĕr'ē)

r	as in fur (fûr), tar (tär) (This r is not pronounced in some sections of the country.)
s	as in sod (sŏd), must (mŭst) and for "c" as in cent (sĕnt), price (prīs)
sh	as in she (shē), rush (rŭsh)
t	as in tea (tē), hot (hŏt)
th	as in thin (thĭn), bath (băth), breath (brĕth)
th	as in then (thĕn), bathe (bāth), breathe (brēth)
v	as in vat (văt), dove (dŭv); and for "f" in of (ŏv)
w	as in we (wē)
y	as in yet (yĕt)
z	as in zero (zēr'ō), buzz (bŭz); and for "s" in wise (wīz)
zh	for "s" as in usual (yōō'zhōō əl), vision (vĭzh'ən); also for some "g's" as in mirage (mə räzh')

VOWELS

The fact that most of the symbols in the table above are modified with some kind of mark indicates the problem of distinguishing vowel sounds. In general, these modifying marks, called *diacritical marks,* are of three kinds: the long mark or *macron* /¯/, the short mark or *breve* /˘/, and the *circumflex* ^ /. The macron is used to indicate the "long" sound of a vowel—the sound used in naming the vowels. The breve /˘/ indicates the "short" sound of vowels:

ă	the sound spelled a in fat
ĕ	the sound spelled e in bet
ĭ	the sound spelled i in bit
ŏ	the sound spelled o in hot
ŭ	the sound spelled u in fun

The circumflex /ˆ/ indicates the distinctive sound a vowel sometimes has before an r: dare, mere, more, fur.

The vowels â, ê, and ô are pronounced differently in different parts of the country. The vowel /â/ varies from the /ā/ in "sale" to the /ĕ/ in "ferry." The vowel /ê/ varies from /ē/ in "deed" to the /ĭ/ in "his." The vowel /ô/ is between the o in "rote" and the o in "dog" and may be very close to either. However, if you always pronounce /â/ as in "dare," the /ê/ as in "mere," and the /ô/ as in "more," you will be pronouncing them correctly for your region.

UNUSUAL SPELLINGS OF SOUNDS

You often hear the word "psychology," and you probably know its general meaning and how to spell it. But when you first heard it, you didn't think to look for it among the p's in your dictionary. You might have had the same trouble with "chord" and "phrase." If you try to find the word "account" and look for only one "c," you will be two pages away from where "account" is actually listed.

Everyone who uses a dictionary sometimes has trouble in finding a word he doesn't know how to spell. Having homophones shown, as in this dictionary, often helps. But for unusual spellings that are not homophones, we just have to try various spellings for the same sound. The following table will help you do this. You should consult it when you need it.

Some people play a game, in which one person writes a common word with unusual spellings for its sounds and asks others to guess the word. For example, one might spell "sick": ps as in "psychology"; ie as in "sieve"; and lk as in "talk"—PSIELK. Can you guess PHYSCH? If you want to try this game with your friends, it will help you grow accustomed to many of the unusual spellings in English.

COMMON SPELLINGS FOR THE SOUNDS OF AMERICAN ENGLISH

Sound		Spellings	Examples
b	as in bed	b, bb	tub, lobby
ch	as in chill	ch, tch, te, ti, tu	church, catch, righteous, bastion, naturally
d	as in deed	d, dd, ed, ld	dog, fodder, moved, could
f	as in fate	f, ff, gh, ph, lf	frog, huff, rough, physical, calf
g	as in get	g, gg, gh, gu, gue	leg, egg, ghost, guarantee, rogue
h	as in hop	h, wh	hat, whole
hw	as the "wh" in what	wh	what, wheel
j	as in jam	j, g, gg, dj, di, du, dge, dg	job, gentle, exaggeration, adjoin, soldier, gradual, badge, judgment
k	as in kin, quill [kw]	k, lk, c, cc, ch, ok, cqu, cq, qu, que, cu, q	smoke, yolk, canary, accordion, chorus, sack, lacquer, acquire, liquor, antique, biscuit, antiquity
l	as in let	l, ll, sl	lot, bell, islet
m	as in men	m, mm, mb, mn, lm, gm	him, mommy, dumb, hymn, salmon, paradigm
n	as in not	n, nn, gn, kn, pn, mn	ran, running, gnu, knight, pneumonia, mnemonic
ng	as in song	ng, ngue, n	song, tongue, think
p	as in pup	p, pp	pink, pepper
r	as in ride	r, rr, rh, wr	very, merry, rhinoceros, wrist
r	as in fur	r, rps	tar, liar, marble, order, corps
sh	as in she	sh, s, ss, sch, sci, si, ssi, ce, ch, ci, ti, se, chsi, xi	rush, sugar, fissure, schwa, conscience, mansion, fission, ocean, machine, racial, ration, nauseous, fuchsia, inflexion
s	as in sod	s, ss, sci, c, ps, sch, ce, sse	sat, miss, science, cent, psalm, schism, price, finesse
t	as in tea	t, th, tt, ed, phth, pt	hot, Theresa, matter, camped, phthisic, pterodactyl
th	as in thin	th	bath, width
th	as in then	th, the	that, bathe
v	as in vat	v, lve, f, ph, vv	dove, salve, of, Stephen, flivver
w	as in we	w, o, u	we, choir, acquire
y	as in yet	y, i, j, gn	you, onion, hallelujah, chignon
z	as in zero	z, zz, se, ss, s, x	zero, buzz, wise, scissors, dogs, xylophone
zh	as the "s" in usual or the "g" in mirage	z, g, s, si, zi	azure, loge, leisure, division, glazier

Sound		Spellings	Examples
ā	as in fate	a, ai, au, ay, ea, ei, eigh, ey, uet, et	age, maid, gauge, bay, break, veil, weight, hey, bouquet, buffet
ă	as in fat	a, ai, au	map, plaid, laugh
å	as in dare	a, ai, ay, e, ea, ei, ae	fare, air, prayer, where, wear, their, aerogram
ä	as in father	a, ea, au, e	art, heart, laugh, sergeant
ē	as in be	e, ee, ea, ei, eo, ey, i, ie, ae, oe, ay	equal, free, beam, perceive, people, key, machine, belief, caesium, phoebe, quay
ĕ	as in bet	e, ea, eo, a, ae, ie, ai, ay, u, ei	ebb, ferry, heavy, jeopardy, anyway, aesthetic, friend, said, says, bury, heifer
ê	as in mere	e, ea, ie, ee	mere, near, pier, peer
ī	as in bite	i, igh, ye, ie, uy, y, ai, eye, aye	ice, nigh, rye, die, buy, by, Kaiser, eye, aye
ĭ	as in bit	i, e, ee, ie, o, y, ui, u, a	if, enclose, been, sieve, women, hymn, build, busy, courage
ō	as in note	o, oa, au, oe, oh, eau, ew, eo, oo, ou, ough, au, ow	low, boat, hauteur, toe, oh, beau, sewing, yeoman, brooch, soul, though, gauche, grow
ŏ	as in hot	o, a	box, watt
ò	as in dog	o, aw, au, augh, a, o, ah, ough, oa	bog, law, laud, caught, ball, order, Utah, ought, broad
ô	as in more	o, oa, oo, ou	sore, roar, door, four
oi	as in oil	oi, oy	oil, boy
ou	as in out	ou, ow, ough	out, loud, plow, bough
ōō	as in too	oo, u, ew, eu, oe, ough, ou, ue, ui, ooh, ioux	too, rule, brew, pneumatic, canoe, through, croup, blue, suit, pooh, Sioux
ŏŏ	as in book	oo, u, ou, o	look, put, could, wolf
ŭ	as in fun	u, o, oo, oe, ou	fun, ton, blood, does, trouble
û	as in fur	u, e, i, ea, ou, o, y	fur, term, sir, learn, journey, worm, myrrh
ə	as in above, opinion		The schwa sound may be spelled by any vowel letter or almost any combination of vowel letters, but at the beginning of words it is most often spelled "a" or "o."

ABBREVIATIONS USED IN DEFINITIONS

Abbr.	abbreviation	fem.	feminine	p.t.	past tense
A.D.	Anno Domini (after Christ)	Fr.	French	SE	southeastern
adj—	adjective	ft.	foot, feet	sing.	singular
adv—	adverb	Hom—	homophone	Span.	Spanish
At. No.	atomic number	in.	inch, inches	S.S.R	Soviet Socialist Republic (constituent republic)
At.Wt.	atomic weight	interj.	interjection		
B.C.	before Christ	m.	mile, miles	St.	Saint
Brit.	British	n—	noun	superl.	superlative of adjective
C.	Celsius (Centigrade)	NE	northeastern	SW	southwestern
CCD	Confraternity of Christian Doctrine	NW	northwestern	U.S.	United States
compar.	comparative of adjective	pl.	plural	U.S.S.R.	Union of Soviet Socialist Republics
conj—	conjunction	p.p.	past participle	vi—	intransitive verb
etc.	et cetera	prep.	preposition	vt—	transitive verb
F.	Fahrenheit	pres. p.	present participle		
		pron—	pronoun		

WEBSTER'S
Illustrated
DICTIONARY

A

A, a (ā) *n-* [*pl.* **A's, a's**] **1** the first letter of the English alphabet. **2 A** (1) *Music* the sixth note of the C-major scale. (2) a rating of first in order or class.

a or **an** (ə or ən when unstressed; ā or ăn when stressed) *indefinite article* (a is used before words beginning with consonant sounds: *quite a man, a youth, a unit, a horse;* an is used before words beginning with vowel sounds: *just an ounce, an uncle, an hour.*) **1** one (of an indefinite number): *He entered a room.*

aard·vark (ärd' värk') *n-* a burrowing nocturnal animal of southern and central Africa, with a long snout, sharp claws, and a very long sticky tongue used to catch ants and termites, its only food.

Aardvark, 4—6 ft. from snout to tail

Aar·on (ăr' ən, âr' -) *n-* brother of Moses; first high priest of the Hebrews.

ab- *prefix* from; away from: *an abnormal thirst.* [from Latin ab meaning "from; away from."]

ab·a·cus (ăb' ə kəs) *n-* [*pl.* **ab·a·ci** (-sī) or **ab·a·cus·es**] a frame with beads sliding on rods, used in America and Europe for teaching arithmetic and in the Far East for calculating.

Abacus

a·baft (ə băft') *adv-* at or toward the stern of a ship: *to go abaft. prep-* behind: *The sailor stood abaft the bridge.*

a·ba·lo·ne (ăb' ə lō' nē) *n-* a large oysterlike Pacific shellfish, valued both for food and for its single saucer-like shell lined with mother-of-pearl. [American word from American Spanish abulón, from American Indian aulun.]

a·ban·don (ə băn' dən) *vt-* **1** to give up completely: *to abandon all hope.* **2** to leave (a place) for good: *They abandoned ship.* **3** to desert; to leave in a heartless way: *to abandon one's family. n-* a letting oneself go: *She danced with abandon.* —*n-* **a·ban'don·ment.**
abandon (oneself) to to give oneself over to: *He abandoned himself to despair.*

a·base (ə bās') *vt-* [**a·based, a·bas·ing**] to lower (a person or persons) in dignity, character, reputation, etc.; degrade: *He abased himself by his cowardly behavior.* —*n-* **a·base' ment.**

a·bash (ə băsh') *vt-* to embarrass; shame; disconcert: *The rebuke abashed him.*

a·bate (ə bāt') *vi-* [**a·bat·ed, a·bat·ing**] to become less: *After the storm, the wind abated. vt-* **1** to lessen; reduce: *The City administration abated local taxes.* **2** in law, to put an end to: *to abate a nuisance.*

a·bate·ment (ə bāt' mənt) *n-* a lessening or diminishing; reduction: *an abatement of a storm; an abatement of a debt.*

ab·at·toir (ăb' ə twär') *n-* slaughterhouse.

ab·bé (ăb' ā') *n-* in France, a title of respect for a priest or another man wearing religious dress.

ab·bess (ăb' əs) *n-* head of a religious community of women.

ab·bey (ăb' ē) *n-* **1** one or more buildings used as a monastery or convent, governed by an abbot or abbess. **2** church that is or was once part of a monastery.

ab·bot (ăb' ət) *n-* head of a religious community of men.

ab·bre·vi·ate (ə brē' vē āt') *vt-* [**ab·bre·vi·at·ed, ab·bre·vi·at·ing**] to make shorter by omitting letters or words: *to abbreviate "Mister" to "Mr.";* to abbreviate a speech.

ab·bre·vi·a·tion (ə brē' vē ā' shən) *n-* a shortened form: *The accepted abbreviation for "inch" is "in."*

Ab·di·a (ăb dī' ə) *n-* the CCD Bible name for Obadiah.

ab·di·cate (ăb' də kāt') *vt-* [**ab·di·cat·ed, ab·di·cat·ing**] to give up (a position of power, a throne, or a serious responsibility); renounce; resign: *to abdicate a throne. vi-:* *The King abdicated.* —*n-* **ab'di·ca'tion.**

HEAD
THORAX
ABDOMEN
Abdomen

ab·do·men (ăb' də mən, ăb dō'-) *n-* **1** the part of the human body containing the stomach, intestines, etc.; belly. **2** the rear section of the body of an insect.

ab·dom·i·nal (əb dŏm' ə nəl, ăb-) *adj-* having to do with the abdomen: *an abdominal pain; an abdominal operation.* —*adv-* **ab·dom' i·nal·ly.**

ab·duct (əb dŭkt', ăb-) *vt-* to kidnap. —*n-* **ab·duc' tion.**

ab·duc·tor (əb dŭk' tər) *n-* kidnaper.

A·bel (ā' bəl) *n-* in the Bible, the second son of Adam. He was slain by his brother Cain. *Hom-* able.

Ab·er·deen An·gus (ăb' ər dēn' ăng' əs) *n-* a breed of black hornless beef cattle first raised in Scotland and bred for their high-grade meat.

ab·er·rance (ə bĕr' əns) or **ab·er·ran·cy** (ə bĕr' ən sē) *n-* [*pl.* **ab·er·ran·ces** or **ab·er·ran·cies**] a straying or deviation from what is expected.

ab·er·rant (ə bĕr' ənt) *adj-* straying or deviating from the standard or normal course: *an aberrant curvature of a line;* aberrant *behavior. n-* person, thing, or group that deviates from the normal or usual.

ab·er·ra·tion (ăb' ə rā' shən) *n-* **1** a straying or deviation from the normal or usual: *His speech was full of* aberrations *from his main theme.* **2** degree of mental illness not serious enough to be considered insanity. **3** apparent change in the position of a celestial body because of change in the position of the observer as the earth moves through space.

a·bet (ə bĕt') *vt-* [**a·bet·ted, a·bet·ting**] **1** to encourage or aid: *Foreign countries abetted both parties in the Civil War.* **2** to assist; incite; connive at, especially in a crime: *By handling stolen goods they abetted thieves.*
aid and abet in law, to help someone willfully in committing a crime.

a·bey·ance (ə bā' əns) *n-* **1** temporary inactivity or disuse: *His interest in stamps has been in abeyance for weeks.* **2** suspension or postponement: *The President held in abeyance his decision to name a running mate.*

ab·hor (əb hôr', ăb hôr', ăb-) *vt-* [**ab·horred, ab·hor·ring**] to shrink from with disgust; detest; loathe.

ab·hor·rent (əb hôr' ənt, əb hôr' ənt, ăb-) *adj-* hateful; detestable; loathesome: *Treachery is abhorrent.* —*n-* **ab·hor' rence:** *his abhorrence of treachery.*

a·bide (ə bīd') *vi-* [**a·bid·ed, a·bid·ing**] **1** to remain; last; endure: *Even after disappointment, hope still abides.* **2** to dwell; live. *vt-* **1** to await: *Who will abide the day of His coming?* **2** to put up with; tolerate: *She can't abide his rudeness.*

a·bid·ing (ə bī' dĭng) *adj-* never-ending; lasting: *an abiding devotion to his country;* abiding *faith.*

a·bil·i·ty (ə bĭl′ə tē) *n*- [*pl.* **a·bil·i·ties**] **1** mental or physical power to do something: *the ability to reason.* **2** intelligence; skill; talent: *his ability as a plumber.* **3** abilities general mental powers or gifts: *a man of many abilities.*

to the best of (one's) ability as well as (one) can: *I'll do the job to the best of my ability.*

-ability or **-ibility** *suffix* (used to form nouns from adjectives by substitution for the adjective suffixes -able or -ible) state or condition of being. *"Approachability"* is tne condition of being *"approach*able.*"

ab·ject (ăb′jĕkt′) *adj*- fallen as far as one could; mean and low; wretched; miserable: *an abject liar; in abject poverty; in abject submission.* —*adv*- **ab′ject′ly.** *n*- **ab′ject′ness.**

ab·jure (ăb jŏŏr′, ăb-) *vt*- [**ab·jured, ab·jur·ing**] to promise solemnly to give up; renounce: *to abjure one's religion.* —*n*- **ab′ju·ra′tion.** *n*- **ab·jur′er.**

ab·la·tive (ăb′lə tĭv) *adj*- in the grammar of certain languages, such as Latin, pertaining to a case which expresses "from" or "by" used with or without the preposition.

a·blaze (ə blāz′) *adj*- **1** on fire; burning: *logs ablaze in the fireplace.* **2** shining brightly; flashing: *a house ablaze with lights; a face ablaze with anger.*

a·ble (ā′bəl) *adj*- [**a·bler, a·blest**] **1** capable through power, skill, or money; with the ability or means (to): *When I'm not tired, I'm able to work faster. The President is able to declare war.* **2** talented; skillful: *an able speaker.* **3** showing skill: *an able speech.* Hom- Abel. —*adv*- **a′bly:** *He spoke ably in defense of his plan.*

ab·lu·tion (ə blōō′shən, ăb lōō′-) *n*- **1** a washing, especially the ceremonial cleansing of the hands or other parts of the body as a purifying rite in the Mass, baptism, etc. **2** ablutions washing of the body or any part of it.

ab·ne·ga·tion (ăb′nə gā′shən) *n*- **1** the act of denying oneself something; self-denial. **2** self-sacrifice.

ab·nor·mal (ăb nòr′məl, ăb nôr′-) *adj*- not normal; different from the ordinary or the average; unusual: *an abnormal situation.* —*adv*- **ab·nor′mal·ly.**

ab·nor·mal·i·ty (ăb′nòr măl′ə tē) *n*- [*pl.* **ab·nor·mal·i·ties**] **1** abnormal thing; irregularity: *a speech abnormality.* **2** abnormal condition or quality.

a·board (ə bôrd′) *adv*- into or on a ship, bus, train, or airplane. *prep*- on board.

¹**a·bode** (ə bōd′) *Archaic p.t. & p.p.* of **abide.** [from Middle English ăbŏd, from Old English ăbād, past tense of **ābīdan** meaning "to abide; wait for."]

²**a·bode** (ə bōd′) *n*- home or dwelling, especially a fixed and permanent residence. [from Middle English ăbŏd meaning "a stay; a delay," related to Old English **ābīdan** and to **abide.**]

a·bol·ish (ə bŏl′ĭsh) *vt*- to do away with; put an end to.

ab·o·li·tion (ăb ə lĭsh′ən) *n*- a doing away with or a putting an end to; an abolishing: *the abolition of poverty; the abolition of slavery.*

A-bomb (ā′bŏm′) *n*- atom bomb.

a·bom·i·na·ble (ə bŏm′ə nə bəl) *adj*- **1** very hateful: *the abominable cruelties of Nero.* **2** very bad or unpleasant: *an abominable winter.* —*adv*- **a·bom′i·na·bly.**

abominable snowman *n*- mysterious, hairy, apelike or bearlike creature said to live in the Himalayas. Its existence has never been proved.

a·bom·i·nate (ə bŏm′ə nāt′) *vt*- [**a·bom·i·nat·ed, a·bom·i·nat·ing**] to hate; detest; loathe: *He abominates militarism.*

a·bom·i·na·tion (ə bŏm′ə nā′shən) *n*- **1** anything vile, hateful, or wicked; a shameful vice: *The man's cruelty is an abomination.* **2** a feeling of disgust or loathing: *an abomination for cruelty to animals.*

ab·o·rig·i·ne (ăb′ə rĭj′ə nē) *n*- **1** person whose people have inhabited a region from their beginnings. **2** aborigines the original plant and animal life of a region.

a·bort (ə bôrt′, -bôrt′) *vt*- **1** to give birth to a fetus that has not developed enough to live. **2** *Biology* to fail to develop completely or properly, as an embryo.

a·bor·tion (ə bôr′shən, ə bôr′-) *n*- **1** the birth of a fetus that has not developed fully enough to live; miscarriage. **2** *Biology* incomplete or improper development, as of an embryo.

a·bound (ə bound′) *vi*- to be plentiful; be in abundance: *Trout abound here.*

a·bout (ə bout′) *adv*- **1** near; nearby, especially on every side: *Are there any wild animals about?* **2** here and there; around, also moving around: *They drove about in search of antiques. He is up and about.* **3** in a turn or to a reversed direction or position: *He whirled his partner about. Let's change about for the next game.* **4** approximately: *I found about a hundred people there.*

¹**a·bove** (ə bŭv′) *adv*- **1** overhead; directly overhead: *the sky above.* **2** farther up; in a higher place: *a deer on the hill above.* **3** higher on the page or on a page before this one: *See the picture above.* *prep*- **1** over; higher than: *one brick above another; above the clouds.* **2** uphill from; also upstream from: *We walked above the tree line.*

a·bove·board (ə bŭv′bôrd′) *adv*- openly; without trickery: *He acted aboveboard. adj*- honest: *His actions were aboveboard.*

ab·ra·ca·dab·ra (ăb′rə kə dăb′rə) *n*- **1** an expression once used as a charm against disease, now used as a conjuring word in magic. **2** any meaningless or foolish talk; gibberish; nonsense.

a·brade (ə brād′) *vt*- [**a·brad·ed, a·brad·ing**] **1** to rub or scrape off; chafe: *John abraded the skin of his elbow when he fell.* **2** to wear away or wear down: *A moving glacier abrades the rocks along its path.*

A·bra·ham (ā′brə hăm′) *n*- in the Bible, the first great patriarch of the Hebrews.

a·bra·sion (ə brā′zhən) *n*- **1** a wearing away: *the abrasion of a cliff by wind.* **2** an injury to the skin from scraping or rubbing: *cuts and abrasions.*

a·bra·sive (ə brā′sĭv, -zĭv) *adj*- capable of scraping, rubbing, or wearing away: *Some cleansing powders are abrasive. n*- a substance, such as pumice, emery, etc., used for polishing and grinding.

a·bridge (ə brĭj′) *vt*- [**a·bridged, a·bridg·ing**] **1** to lessen, reduce, or deprive of: *to abridge one's liberties.* **2** to shorten or cut (a book, speech, etc.) while keeping the sense; condense.

a·broad (ə brôd′) *adv*- **1** in or to a foreign country: *to live abroad; to travel abroad.* **2** widely: *Spread the news abroad.* **3** outside the house: *to be abroad early.*

ab·ro·gate (ăb′rə gāt′) *vt*- [**ab·ro·gat·ed, ab·ro·gat·ing**] to repeal or cancel (a law or privilege). —*n*- **ab′ro·ga′tion.**

a·brupt (ə brŭpt′) *adj*- **1** sudden; unexpected: *an abrupt stop.* **2** steep: *an abrupt incline.* **3** curt in speech; short and blunt. —*adv*- **a·brupt′ly.**

Ab·sal·om (ăb′sə lŏm′) *n*- in the Bible, David's favorite son, slain in rebellion against his father.

ab·scess (ăb′sĕs′) *n*- mass of pus at an infected point in the body; a boil; carbuncle. —*adj*- **ab′scessed′:** *an abscessed tooth.*

ab·scis·sa (ăb sĭs′ə) *n*- [*pl.* **ab·scis·sae** (-sē) or **ab·scis·sas**] **1** in Cartesian coordinates, the distance of a point from the y axis, measured parallel to the x axis. **2** the number, term, or line segment that represents this distance.

ab·scond (əb skŏnd′, ăb-) *vi*- to flee suddenly and secretly and go into hiding to avoid arrest; decamp: *The clerk absconded with the store's money.*

ab·sence (ăb′səns) *n*- **1** a being away: *His absence was noted.* **2** a being without; lack: *an absence of humor.*

¹**ab·sent** (ăb′sənt) *adj*- **1** not present; away; missing. **2** lost in thought; not paying attention: *She was daydreaming, and answered in an absent manner.*

ab·sinthe (ăb′ sĭnth′) *n-* a bitter, green alcoholic liquor containing wormwood, now generally outlawed. Also **ab′ sinth′**.

ab·so·lute (ăb′ sə lōōt′) *adj-* 1 complete; perfect: *the* absolute *truth*. 2 not limited or restricted in any way: *Very few rulers nowadays have absolute power.* 3 certain; positive: *to have absolute proof.*

absolute value *Mathematics n-* the distance of a number on a number line in either direction, from zero to the point representing the number.

absolute zero *n-* theoretically, the lowest temperature matter can have; the temperature point at which molecules have no motion and, hence, no heat. It is the zero of the Kelvin temperature scale and is equal to − 273.16° C. (− 459.72° F.).

ab·so·lu·tion (ăb′ sə lōō′ shən) *n-* 1 a formal forgiveness of sins: *The priest pronounced* absolution. 2 a release from any obligation, charge, or penalty.

ab·solve (əb zŏlv′, -sŏlv′) *vt-* [ab·solved, ab·solv·ing] 1 to grant (a person) a formal forgiveness of sins. 2 to clear of guilt or blame: *The jury absolved him of all the charges.* 3 to free (someone) from a promise, obligation, etc.: *He absolved me from the promise I made.*

ab·sorb (əb sôrb′, -zôrb′) *vt-* 1 to take in; soak up; swallow up: *A towel absorbs water. A bright child absorbs knowledge easily.* 2 to occupy all one's attention; interest deeply; engross: *Stamp collecting absorbs John now.* 3 to make part of a greater whole; assimilate: *The city absorbed its suburbs.*

ab·sorb·ing (əb sôr′ bĭng, əb zôr′-) *adj-* taking up all one's attention; very interesting: *an absorbing tale.* —*adv-* **ab·sorb′ ing·ly.**

ab·sorp·tion (əb sôrp′ shən, əb zôrp′-) *n-* 1 the act of absorbing something: *the absorption of knowledge*; *the absorption of water.* 2 the passing of substances from one part of the body into another, as from the blood into the cells, or from the digestive system into the blood and body fluids.

absorption spectrum *n-* spectrum in which dark lines appear where certain wavelengths have been absorbed by a gas or vapor through which the light or other electromagnetic radiation has passed.

ab·stain (əb stān′, ăb-) *vi-* to hold oneself back (from an action); refrain: *Vegetarians abstain from eating meat. Five persons voted for the measure, two voted against, and one abstained.*

ab·ste·mi·ous (əb stē′ mē əs, ăb-) *adj-* moderate and sparing in the use of food and drink; temperate: *an abstemious use of tobacco; an abstemious man.* —*adv-* **ab·ste′ mi·ous·ly.** *n-* **ab·ste′ mi·ous·ness.**

ab·sten·tion (əb stĕn′ shən, ăb-) *n-* an abstaining or refraining; also, an act of abstaining, often officially recorded as a kind of vote: *his abstention from alcohol; three votes in favor, two against, and three abstentions.* —*adj-* **ab′ sti·nent.**

ab·sti·nence (ăb′ stĭ nəns) *n-* a refraining from something; a giving up of certain foods, alcoholic drinks, etc. —*adj-* **ab′ sti·nent.**

¹**ab·stract** (ăb′ străkt′, əb străkt′) *adj-* 1 concerned with or based on theory more than facts or real situations: *to speak of abstract justice; an abstract subject; an* abstract *thinker.* 2 *Grammar* describing a noun that expresses a quality or characteristic but does not name the person or thing possessing it: *"Strength" is an* abstract *noun.* 3 in art, describing a style that, either wholly or in part, avoids representing natural objects: *an abstract painting.*

²**ab·stract** (əb străkt′, ăb-) *vt-* 1 to separate: *to abstract gold from ore.* 2 to make a summary of: *to abstract a book.* 3 to take out or away, often dishonestly: *George slyly abstracted a dollar from his sister's purse when she wasn't looking.*

ab·struse (əb strōōs′, ăb-) *adj-* hard to understand; obscure in meaning: *an abstruse remark.* —*adv-* **ab·struse′ ly.** *n-* **ab·struse′ ness.**

ab·surd (əb sûrd′, -zûrd′) *adj-* ridiculous; silly; contrary to reason or sense. —*adv-* **ab·surd′ ly.**

ab·surd·i·ty (əb sûr′ də tē, əb zûr′-) *n-* [*pl.* **ab·surd·i·ties**] 1 foolishness, as of dress, speech, or conduct: *the absurdity of her hat.* 2 something contrary to reason or sense; something absurd: *His remark was a gross absurdity.*

a·bun·dance (əbŭn′ dəns) *n-* quantity that is more than enough; overflowing supply; great plenty: *an abundance of food.*

¹**a·buse** (ə byōōz′) *vt-* [a·bused, a·bus·ing] 1 to treat badly or harshly: *to abuse a pet; to abuse one's eyes by reading in dim light.* 2 to make improper use of; misuse: *The manager abused his authority. He abused his host's hospitality.* 3 to use insulting language to or about: *The candidates abused each other during the campaign.*

²**a·buse** (ə byōōs′) *n-* 1 wrong or harsh treatment. 2 wrong use; misuse: *the abuse of power.* 3 corrupt custom or practice: *Such abuses as bribery or graft are punishable by law.* 4 insulting language.

a·but (ə bŭt′) *vi-* [a·but·ted, a·but·ting] 1 to border (on, upon, or against): *The house abuts on the hill.* 2 to be in contact: *The two houses abut.*

a·but·ment (ə bŭt′ mənt) *n-* the supporting structure at either end of an arch or bridge, or a wedge-shaped piece on the upstream side of a bridge pier to resist pressure from water or ice.

Abutments of an arched bridge

a·bys·mal (ə bĭz′ məl) *adj-* so deep as to be without limit or end; bottomless; measureless: *the abysmal gloom; his abysmal ignorance.* —*adv-* **a·bys′ mal·ly.**

a·byss (ə bĭs′) *n-* 1 deep natural cut in the earth; gorge; chasm. 2 anything of limitless depth: *the abyss of space; the abyss of misery.*

ac·a·dem·ic (ăk′ ə dĕm′ ĭk) *adj-* 1 of an academy, school, or college: *an academic degree; academic studies.* 2 having to do with theory rather than practice; without practical effect; idle: *Whether or not to have a monarchy in this country is now an academic question.*

a·cad·e·my (ə kăd′ ə mē) *n-* [*pl.* **a·cad·e·mies**] 1 private high school. 2 school for special study: *a military* academy. 3 a society of learned men organized to encourage arts, letters, or sciences.

a cap·pel·la (ä′ kə pĕl′ə) *Music adv-* without instrumental accompaniment: *to sing a cappella.* *adj-: the* a cappella *choir.*

ac·cede (ăk sēd′) *vi-* [ac·ced·ed, ac·ced·ing] 1 to agree or yield (to): *He acceded to my request.* 2 to succeed or attain (to a position, throne, etc.): *She acceded to the chairmanship.*

ac·cel·e·rate (ăk sĕl′ ə rāt′) *vt-* [ac·cel·e·rat·ed, ac·cel·e·rat·ing] 1 to increase the speed of: *to accelerate the motor by stepping on the pedal.* 2 to bring about sooner; hasten: *The dictator's harsh measures accelerated his fall.*

ac·cel·e·ra·tion (ăk sĕl′ ə rā′ shən) *n-* 1 increase of speed; a hastening: *an acceleration in the pulse rate of a runner.* 2 *Physics* rate at which the speed of an object changes for each unit of time. Gravity subjects a body to an acceleration of 32 feet per second per second. See also *deceleration.*

¹**ac·cent** (ăk′ sĕnt′) *n-* 1 special or regional way of pronouncing: *a foreign accent; a Southern accent.* 2 stress on a syllable in a word or a note of music. 3 accent mark.

²**ac·cent** (ăk′ sĕnt′, ăk sĕnt′) *vt-* 1 to pronounce with special stress or emphasis, as with the second syllable of the word "relation." 2 to indicate by an accent mark. 3 to emphasize or stress; accentuate: *Her scarf accented her blue eyes.*

ac·cen·tu·ate (ăk sĕn′ chōō āt′) *vt-* [ac·cen·tu·at·ed, ac·cen·tu·at·ing] 1 to emphasize or stress in speech, writing, or music. 2 to heighten; make prominent: *Her youth accentuated her beauty.*

ac·cept (ăk sĕpt′) *vt-* (in senses 1, 2, and 3 considered intransitive when the direct object is implied but not expressed) 1 to take (what is offered): *to accept a gift.* 2 to answer yes to: *to accept an invitation.*

ac·cept·a·ble (ăk sĕp′ tə bəl) *adj-* 1 worth accepting; welcome: *The plan was acceptable to everyone.* 2 fitting or satisfactory: *quite acceptable behavior.*

ac·cess (ăk′ sĕs′) *n-* **1** entrance or approach: *They gained* access *through a back window.* **2** way or right of admittance or approach: *The avalanche cut off* access *to the mountain village. He had* access *to the records.* **3** an attack; fit: *an* access *of coughing.*

ac·ces·si·ble (ăk sĕs′ ə bol) *adj-* easy to get at, reach, obtain, talk to, etc.: *an* accessible *mountain village;* accessible *public documents; an* accessible *man.* —*adv-* **ac·ces′ si·bly.**

ac·ces·so·ry (ăk sĕs′ə rē) *adj-* aiding in a secondary way; contributory; additional: *an* accessory *fund; an* accessory *act. n-* [*pl.* **ac·ces·so·ries**]

ac·ci·dent (ăk′ sə dənt) *n-* **1** something unexpected or unplanned: *Meeting him yesterday was a lucky accident.* **2** unintentional happening resulting in loss, injury, or death: *The road accident took several lives. The bridge was completed without accident.*

ac·claim (ə klām′) *vt-* to praise; shout approval; pay tribute to: *All the newspapers acclaimed the explorers for their bravery. n-* applause; show of approval or praise: *They greeted the winner with loud acclaim.*

ac·cli·mate (ăk′lə māt′, ə klī′mət) *vi-* [**ac·cli·mat·ed, ac·cli·mat·ing**] to become accustomed (to) or physically able to live in an unfamiliar place, climate, etc.; adapt (to): *The dogs acclimated quickly to the colder country. vt-: Tom acclimated himself readily to the new town. The botanists acclimated the wheat to the drier region.*

ac·co·lade (ăk′ə lād′) *n-* **1** something that shows praise, recognition, or respect; an honor; award: *The highest accolade in the American movies is the Oscar.* **2** the ceremony for admitting to knighthood, formerly an embrace or a kiss, now a light tap on the shoulder with the flat of a sword.

ac·com·mo·date (ə kŏm′ə dāt′) *vt-* [**ac·com·mo·dat·ed, ac·com·mo·dat·ing**] **1** to have room for: *The hotel room will accommodate two guests.* **2** to oblige; help out: *He will accommodate me with the use of his car.* **3** to adjust (oneself to): *He accommodated himself to his circumstances. vi-* to become adjusted: *The eye accommodates to light.*

ac·com·pa·ny (ə kŭm′ pə nē) *vt-* [**ac·com·pa·nied, ac·com·pa·ny·ing**] **1** to go along with; escort: *Father will accompany us to the concert.* **2** to be or to happen together with: *Wind accompanied the rain.* **3** to play or sing accompaniment to another: *Ted accompanied the singer on the guitar.*

ac·com·plice (ə kŏm′ plĭs) *n-* person who aids another in a crime or wrongdoing.

ac·com·plish (ə kŏm′ plĭsh) *vt-* to carry out; complete; finish: *to accomplish a task.*

ac·cord (ə kôrd′, -kôrd′) *vi-* to agree or be in harmony (with): *He gets along with them because his ideas accord with theirs. vt-* to grant: *We accord praise to those who deserve it. n-* agreement showing harmony of ideas, especially between nations: *France and England reached an accord over certain tariffs.*

ac·cord·ing·ly (ə kôr′ dĭng lē, ə kôr′ -) *adv-* **1** in agreement with what is expected; correspondingly: *Observe the situation carefully and act accordingly.* **2** therefore; so: *He felt unwell and, accordingly, left.*

ac·cor·di·on (ə kôr′ dē ən, ə kôr′ -) *n-* portable musical instrument having a keyboard, bellows, and metal reeds. The bellows are stretched and squeezed to force air through reeds selected by pressing the right keys. *adj-* folded or pleated like the bellows of an accordion: *a skirt's accordion pleats.*

Accordion

ac·cost (ə kôst′) *vt-* to speak to first; address: *A beggar accosted me.*

ac·count (ə kount′) *n-* **1** a written or oral report (of an event, person, etc.), especially a factual and objective report; record; narrative: *an account of the accident; an account of animal life in Africa.* **2** a reason or cause for an event, etc.; explanation: *Give me an account for your behavior.*

ac·count·ant (ə kount′ ənt) *n-* **1** person who is employed to keep or examine financial records for a business or

in a public office. **2** certified public accountant.

ac·cou·ter (ə kōō′ tər) *vt-* to supply with dress and equipment, especially for military service; equip; outfit: *The regiment was accoutered for battle.* Also **ac·cou′ tre.**

ac·cred·it (ə krĕd′ ət) *vt-* **1** to send with letters of authority: *to accredit an ambassador to Spain.* **2** to accept or approve as true, up to standard, etc.: *to accredit a report: to accredit a college.*

ac·crue (ə krōō′) *vi-* [**ac·crued, ac·cru·ing**] **1** to come or happen as a result of something: *Benefits accrue to society from better education.* **2** to increase in amount; accumulate: *Interest will accrue on my savings account.*

ac·cu·mu·late (ə kyōō′ myə lāt′) *vt-* [**ac·cu·mu·lat·ed, ac·cu·mu·lat·ing**] to pile up; collect; gather: *Boys accumulate many things in their pockets. vi-* to become greater in amount; increase: *Dust accumulated in every corner.*

ac·cu·rate (ăk′ yə rət) *adj-* correct; exact: *an accurate report.* —*adv-* **ac′ cu·rate·ly.**

ac·curs·ed (ə kûr′ səd) or **ac·curst** (ə kûrst′) *adj-* **1** under a curse; ill-fated; doomed: *The poor man felt himself accursed.* **2** miserable; wretched; hateful: *his accursed poverty.*

ac·cuse (ə kyōōz′) *vt-* [**ac·cused, ac·cus·ing**] to blame for wrongdoing or crime; bring a charge against.

ac·cus·tom (ə kŭs′ təm) *vt-* to habituate (someone); make (someone) accept something as ordinary and routine (followed by "to"): *The job accustomed him to meeting many new people.*

ace (ās) *n-* **1** card with a single mark indicating the suit; also the side of one of a pair of dice having a single spot. **2** flyer in an air force who has brought down at least five enemy planes. **3** an expert. **4** in tennis and some other sports, a point made on an unreturned serve. *adj-* first-class: *an ace athlete.*

Ace

a·cer·bi·ty (ə sûr′ bə tē) *n-* **1** sharpness of speech, manner, temper, etc.; bitterness; harshness: *the acerbity of his remarks.* **2** acid taste; sourness.

ac·e·tate (ăs′ə tāt′) *n-* **1** *Chemistry* a salt or ester of acetic acid: *sodium acetate.* **2** cellulose acetate or any of its products, including acetate rayon and cellophane.

ache (āk) *n-* steady pain. *vi-* [**ached, ach·ing**] **1** to be in pain; suffer pain: *His back ached all day.* **2** *Informal* to wish very strongly; yearn; long: *He ached for his freedom.*

a·chieve (ə chēv′) *vt-* [**a·chieved, a·chiev·ing**] **1** to accomplish; complete; carry out; do: *He achieved much in a short time.* **2** to attain; win; gain: *to achieve success.*

ac·id (ăs′ əd) *n- Chemistry* sour substance that reacts with bases to form water and a salt, and turns blue litmus paper red. *adj-* **1** sour: *the acid taste of vinegar.* **2** biting; sarcastic: *an acid comment.*
►Should not be confused with ACRID.

ac·knowl·edge (ĭk nŏl′ ŏj, ăk-) *vt-* [**ac·knowl·edged, ac·knowl·edg·ing**] **1** to admit or recognize as being true, genuine, legal, etc.: *I acknowledge my faults. The court acknowledged his claim to the property.* **2** to recognize and honor (a person) publicly: *The nation acknowledged him their leader.*

ac·ne (ăk′ nē) *n-* pimples caused by swollen and infected oil glands under the skin.

ac·o·lyte (ăk′ə līt′) *n-* **1** one who assists a minister or priest in a church service; altar boy. **2** in the Roman Catholic Church, a member of an order next below a subdeacon.

a·corn (ā′ kôrn′, -kôrn′) *n-* the fruit of the oak, a nut with its base set in a woody cup.

Acorn

a·cous·ti·cal (ə kōō′ stĭ kəl) *adj-* **1** relating to sound. **2** having special qualities for transmitting or absorbing sound: *an acoustical panel.* Also **a·cous′ tic.** —*adv-* **a·cous′ ti·cal·ly.**

a·cous·tics (ə kōō′ stĭks) *n-* **1** (takes singular verb) the science of sound. **2** (takes plural verb) the properties of auditoriums, concert halls, etc., that determine how well sound is heard in them.

ac·quaint (ə kwānt′) *vt-* to make familiar: *I acquainted the new clerk with his duties.*

ac·qui·esce (ăk′ wē ĕs′) *vi-* [ac·qui·esced, ac·qui·esc·ing] to give consent by remaining silent: *He acquiesced in our plans.* —*n-* ac′qui·es′cence. *adj-* ac′qui·es′cent. *adv-* ac′qui·es′cent·ly.

ac·quire (ə kwīər′) *vt-* [ac·quired, ac·quir·ing] to get; gain; come by: *to acquire land; to acquire skill in running; to acquire good taste.*

ac·qui·si·tion (ăk′ wə zĭsh′ ən) *n-* 1 a receiving or gaining, especially of material possessions: *the acquisition of wealth.* 2 that which is received or gained, as money, land, etc.: *This land is a recent acquisition.*

ac·quit (ə kwĭt′) *vt-* [ac·quit·ted, ac·quit·ting] 1 to set free from a charge of crime; declare (someone) not guilty: *The jury acquitted the man.* 2 to behave or conduct (oneself); to do one's part: *The new player acquitted himself well in the football game.*

a·cre (ā′ kər) *n-* unit used in measuring land. An acre is about the area of a square field 208 feet on each side.

ac·rid (ăk′ rĭd) *adj-* sharp, bitter, or biting in taste, smell, tone, manner, etc.: *the acrid smell of wood smoke; the acrid tone of the debate.* —*adv-* ac′rid·ly.

ac·ri·mo·ny (ăk′ rə mŏ′ nē) *n-* bitterness or sharpness, as of temper or speech.

ac·ro·bat (ăk′ rə băt) *n-* person who does daring and skillful exercises or stunts requiring great physical agility, such as walking a tightrope.

ac·ro·bat·ic (ăk′ rə băt′ ĭk) *adj-* of or suggesting an acrobat. —*adv-* ac′ro·bat′i·cal·ly.

ac·ro·nym (ăk′ rə nĭm′) *n-* word formed from the initial letters or syllables of other words. "Radar" is an acronym of *ra*dio *d*etection *a*nd *r*anging.

a·crop·o·lis (ə krŏp′ ə lĭs) *n-* 1 highest part of an old Greek city, used as a fortress; citadel. 2 **the Acropolis** the citadel of Athens.

a·cross (ə krôs′) *prep-* (in sense 1 considered an adverb when the object is clearly implied but not expressed) 1 from one side to the other side of: *We walked across the park.* 2 lying along the short dimension of; crosswise on: *A tree was across the path.*

act (ăkt) *n-* 1 a thing done; deed; action: *an act of kindness; an act of mercy.* 2 one of the main divisions of a play or opera: *the third act of "Othello."* 3 one of the segments of a variety show, circus, etc.: *a dog act.* 4 a show of false behavior; pretense: *He isn't really friendly; it's all an act. He put on an act to get out of work.*

ACTH (ā′ sē′ tē′ āch′) *n-* hormone secreted by the pituitary gland. It stimulates the secretion of cortisone by the adrenal glands.

ac·tion (ăk′ shən) *n-* 1 the doing of something; a deed: *a kind action.* 2 energetic motion or activity: *The adventure story was packed with action.* 3 the effect of one body or substance upon another: *the action of sunlight on plants.* 4 lawsuit. 5 the effective or acting part of a mechanism: *the action of a rifle.* 6 the progress of events, as in a play. 7 battle: *injured in action.*

ac·tive (ăk′ tĭv) *adj-* 1 lively; vigorous: *an active mind.* 2 energetic; moving about a good deal: *Children are more active in the morning than at night.* 3 capable of action; not dormant: *an active chemical; an active volcano.* 4 in present use: *an active file.* 5 taking full part in: *an active member of an organization.*

ac·tu·al (ăk′ chōō əl) *adj-* real; not imaginary: *Davy Crockett was an actual person.*

ac·tu·al·i·ty (ăk′ chōō ăl′ ə tē) *n-* [*pl.* ac·tu·al·i·ties] 1 real existence; reality; fact: *In actuality, the battle never took place.* 2 a real thing or condition: *The plan never became an actuality.*

ac·tu·al·ly (ăk′ chōō ə lē) *adv-* really; in fact: *Did you actually build this beautiful table?*

ac·tu·ar·y (ăk′ chōō ĕr′ ē) *n-* [*pl.* ac·tu·ar·ies] person who calculates risks and premiums for an insurance company.

ac·tu·ate (ăk′ chōō āt′) *vt-* [ac·tu·at·ed, ac·tu·at·ing] 1 to put into motion or action; to start: *to actuate a mechanism.* 2 to influence or incite; motivate; impel: *He was actuated by ambition.*

a·cu·men (ə kyōō′ mən) *n-* keenness of understanding or insight; mental sharpness: *His business acumen*

made him rich.

a·cute (ə kyōōt′) *adj-* 1 keen; alert: *an acute sense of hearing; an acute observer of facts.* 2 sharp and intense: *an acute pang of hunger; an acute sense of pleasure.* 3 of a disease, coming on suddenly and reaching a crisis quickly: *an attack of acute appendicitis.* 4 very important; critical; crucial: *an acute stage of an illness; an acute shortage.* —*adv-* a·cute′ ly. *n-* a·cute′ ness.

acute accent *n-* accent mark [′] that is placed over a vowel to indicate its sound, as in French "café."

acute angle *n-* angle whose measure is less than 90° and greater than 0°. For picture, see *angle.*

ad·age (ăd′ ĭj) *n-* a pointed and well-known saying; a proverb. "Waste not, want not" is an adage.

a·da·gio (ə dä′ zhō, -jē ō) *Music adj-* & *adv-* slow; faster than lento but slower than andante.

ad·a·mant (ăd′ ə mənt, -mănt′) *n-* mythical rock as hard as the diamond and assumed to be magnetic. *adj-* hard; unyielding: *Once he had made his decision, he was adamant.* —*adv-* ad′ a·mant·ly.

a·dapt (ə dăpt′) *vt-* to change (a person or thing) so as to fit new conditions or uses; make suitable; adjust: *to adapt oneself to new circumstances; to adapt a novel to the movies.* *vi-* of living things, to undergo a change in physical structure or habit in adjustment to a change in the environment.

ad·ap·ta·tion (ăd′ əp tā′ shən) *n-* 1 a changing to fit different conditions: *He found adaptation to the hot climate difficult.* 2 something produced by a process of changing and arranging: *The play was a successful adaptation of the novel.*

add (ăd) *vt-* 1 to sum up (numbers). 2 to join or unite (to): *to add water to flour; to add books to a library; to add insult to injury.* 3 to say or write further: *"And don't go swimming alone," she added.* *vi-* 1 in arithmetic, to sum up numbers; total: *He adds correctly, but he cannot divide.* 2 to be or make an addition (to): *His father's illness added to his troubles.* *Hom-* ad.

ad·dend (ăd′ ĕnd′, ə dĕnd′) *n-* number added to another number. In the example 2 + 5 = 7, both 2 and 5 are addends.

ad·der (ăd′ ər) *n-* any of various snakes of different parts of the world, including the common European adder and the puff adder of Africa, both poisonous, and several harmless American snakes.

ad·dict (ăd′ ĭkt) *n-* person completely given over to a habit: *a drug addict.*

ad·di·tion (ə dĭsh′ ən) *n-* 1 process involving two or more numbers which produces their sum. Examples: 5 + 7 = 12; 3 + 3 + 6 = 12; 24 + 35 + 53 = 112. 2 the adding or joining of one thing to another: *the addition of a gymnasium to the school.*

ad·dle (ăd′ əl) *vt-* [ad·dled, ad·dling] 1 to confuse (one's mind); muddle. 2 to spoil (an egg). *vi-:* *His mind addles whenever he faces that subject. Those eggs have addled.*

¹ad·dress (ăd′ drĕs′) *n-* place in which a person or group lives, works, etc.; also, the name and destination written on a letter or package.

²ad·dress (ə drĕs′) *vt-* 1 to speak or write to: *She addressed the man politely.* 2 to place the destination on (a letter, package, etc.). *n-* 1 a speech, especially a formal one: *The President delivered an address to Congress.*

ad·duce (ə dōōs′, -dyōōs′) *vt-* [ad·duced, ad·duc·ing] to present or offer as a reason, proof, or evidence; cite as an example: *To prove his point, the lawyer adduced a previous decision.*

ad·e·noids (ăd′ ə noidz′) *n- pl.* an abnormal swelling of the spongy glandular tissue (**adenoid tissue**) in the passage leading from the nose to the throat. Adenoids often make breathing difficult.

Adenoids

¹a·dept (ə dĕpt′) *adj-* highly skilled; expert: *John is adept at repairing things about the house.* —*adv-* a·dept′ ly. *n-* a·dept′ ness.

²a·dept (ăd′ ĕpt′) *n-* one who is fully proficient or skilled in an art.

ad·e·qua·cy (ăd′ə kwə sē) *n-* the condition of being sufficient or suitable for what is needed: *We doubt the* adequacy *of his training.*

ad·e·quate (ăd′ə kwət) *adj-* sufficient; suitable; fit: *The lawyer presented* adequate *proof of his client's innocence.* —*adv-* ad′e·quate·ly. *n-* ad′e·quate·ness.

ad·here (əd hēr′, ăd-) *vi-* [ad·hered, ad·her·ing] 1 to stick fast, as if glued: *Gum* adheres *to your fingers.* 2 to be attached or devoted (to); give steady support (to): *to* adhere *to a political party; to* adhere *to a religious creed.* 3 to follow closely; hold firmly (to): *to* adhere *to the blueprints.*

ad·i·pose (ăd′ə pōs′) *adj-* fatty; having to do with fat.

ad·ja·cent (ə jā′sənt) *adj-* 1 lying close (to); next (to); near; adjoining: *a house* adjacent *to the church.* 2 *Mathematics* designating either or both of two angles with a common vertex and a common side between. —*adv-* ad·ja′cent·ly.

ad·jec·tive (ăj′ək tĭv′) *Grammar n-* 1 a word that can modify a noun and may be used in the blank spaces in both the following patterns:

The book seems————.
I want the————book.

The words "red," "heavy," "easy," "beautiful," "exciting," etc., can be used in both spaces.

ad·join (ə join′) *vt-* to be so near as to touch; be next to: *Canada* adjoins *the United States.* *vi-:* *Canada and the United States* adjoin.

ad·journ (ə jûrn′) *vt-* 1 to put off or suspend (a meeting, session, decision, etc.) to a later time or to another place: *The judge* adjourned *the court until the following day. The chairman* adjourned *the meeting to the large conference room.* 2 to end (a meeting or session) officially.

ad·journ·ment (ə jûrn′mənt) *n-* 1 a putting off or suspension of a meeting, session, decision, etc., to a later time or another place. 2 the time or period during which this is in effect.

ad·judge (ə jŭj′) *vt-* [ad·judged, ad·judg·ing] 1 to decide (a dispute) according to law; hence, to declare or sentence by law: *The defendant was* adjudged *insane.* 2 to award or grant by law: *The estate was* adjudged *to him.*

ad·junct (ăj′ŭngkt′) *n-* something added to another thing, but not a necessary part of it: *A lean-to is an* adjunct *of a house.*

ad·jure (ə joor′) *vt-* [ad·jured, ad·jur·ing] to charge solemnly, as if under oath; entreat earnestly: *I* adjure *you to tell the truth.* —*n-* ad′ju·ra′tion.

ad·just (ə jŭst′) *vt-* 1 to make mechanical changes so that parts fit or work together properly; regulate: *The mechanic* adjusted *the fuel pump in the engine.* 2 to make or become suitable; fit: *to* adjust *the length of a coat.* 3 to adapt: *to* adjust *oneself to new circumstances.*

ad·ju·tant (ăj′ə tənt) *n-* an assistant; especially, in the army, a regimental staff officer who assists the commanding officer.

ad-lib (ăd′lĭb′) *vt-* [ad-libbed, ad-lib·bing] to improvise (remarks, songs, etc.): *He* ad-libbed *a clever dance.*

ad·min·is·ter (əd mĭn′əs tər, ăd-) *vt-* 1 to manage; look after; direct: *Mr. Perez* administers *the accounting department.* 2 to put (a law) into effect; execute. 3 to give, supply, or dispense in a formal or official way: *to* administer *an oath; to* administer *a drug; to* administer *the last rites.*

ad·min·is·tra·tion (əd mĭn′əs strā′shən, ăd-) *n-* 1 act of administering. 2 direction; management: *His* administration *of the government was honest.*

ad·min·is·tra·tor (əd mĭn′əs trā′tər, ăd-) *n-* 1 one who manages, directs, or governs affairs. 2 one appointed legally to administer an estate; an executor.

ad·mi·ra·ble (ăd′mər ə bəl) *adj-* worthy of wonder and approval; excellent: *His behavior during the emergency was* admirable. —*adv-* ad′mi·ra·bly. *n-* ad′mi·ra·ble·ness.

ad·mi·ral (ăd′mər əl) *n-* 1 in the U.S. Navy and Coast Guard, a commissioned officer ranking next below an Admiral of the Fleet and next above a vice admiral. 2 a shortened form of address for a rear admiral, vice admiral, and Admiral of the Fleet.

ad·mi·ra·tion (ăd′mə rā′shən) *n-* 1 a feeling of wonder, delight, and approval: *our* admiration *for a great violinist.* 2 person or thing that is the object of such feelings: *He was the* admiration *of many young violinists.*

ad·mire (əd mīər′, ăd-) *vt-* [ad·mired, ad·mir·ing] 1 to look at with pleasure and wonder: *to* admire *a fine painting.* 2 to have a high opinion of; esteem: *to* admire *someone's good sense.*

ad·mis·si·ble (əd mĭs′ə bəl, ăd-) *adj-* 1 worthy of being permitted to enter. 2 allowable; permissible: *This form of argument is not* admissible. —*adv-* ad·mis′si·bly. *n-* ad·mis′si·bil′i·ty.

ad·mis·sion (əd mĭsh′ən, ăd-) *n-* 1 permission to enter: *Free* admission *is limited to certain days.* 2 price paid in order to enter. 3 acceptance or appointment to a profession, group, etc.: *his* admission *to the bar.* 4 a saying that something is true; acknowledgment; confession: *an* admission *of his guilt.*

ad·mit (əd mĭt′) *vt-* [ad·mit·ted, ad·mit·ting] 1 to allow to enter; grant entrance to; let in: *The guard* admitted *Tom to the vault.. The club* admitted *Bob last week.* 2 to accept as true, valid, genuine, etc; acknowledge; concede: *He* admitted *his guilt.*

ad·mit·tance (əd mĭt′əns, ăd-) *n-* 1 an entering or letting in; entrance: *They gained* admittance *through a back window.* 2 right or permission to enter: *Tom was denied* admittance *to the meeting.*

ad·mix (ăd mĭks′) *vt-* to mix into or with; blend.

ad·mix·ture (ăd mĭks′chər) *n-* 1 the act of mixing; mingling. 2 something added to a mixture: *an* admixture *of common sense in a confused situation.*

ad·mon·ish (əd mŏn′ĭsh, ăd-) *vt-* 1 to take to task; to reprove mildly: *The boys were* admonished *for their misbehavior.* 2 to warn; caution: *Ben* admonished *us not to sail far.*

ad·mo·ni·tion (ăd′mə nĭsh′ən) *n-* an admonishing; warning.

a·do (ə dōō′) *n-* fuss; bustle; stir: *There was much* ado *over the new baby.* *Hom-* adieu.

a·do·be (ə dō′bē) *n-* 1 unburnt brick dried in the sun, used in southwestern United States and Mexico. 2 structure made of such brick. *as modifier:* *an* adobe *hut.*

Adobe house

ad·o·les·cence (ăd′ə lĕs′əns) *n-* the change from childhood to manhood or womanhood; also, the period of years when this happens; youth.

ad·o·les·cent (ăd′ə lĕs′ənt) *n-* person in the process of changing from a child into an adult. *adj-:* *his* adolescent *years.*

a·dopt (ə dŏpt′) *vt-* 1 to take by choice as one's own: *to* adopt *a child; to* adopt *a name.* 2 to approve; accept: *The committee* adopted *the chairman's plan.*
▶Should not be confused with ADAPT.

a·dop·tion (ə dŏp′shən) *n-* 1 a taking as one's own: *the* adoption *of the child.* 2 approval; acceptance: *the* adoption *of a law.*

a·dor·a·ble (ə dôr′ə bəl) *adj-* 1 worthy of deep love or worship. 2 lovely; charming: *an* adorable *baby.* —*adv-* a·dor′a·bly.

ad·o·ra·tion (ăd′ə rā′shən) *n-* 1 worship of God or of a person or thing regarded as holy. 2 devoted love.

a·dore (ə dôr′) *vt-* [a·dored, a·dor·ing] 1 to love and worship. 2 to regard with deep affection and respect: *She* adored *her family.* 3 *Informal* to like very much: *I* adore *swimming.*

a·dorn (ə dôrn′, -dôrn′) *vt-* to add beauty to; decorate: *to* adorn *a hat with flowers.*

ad·re·nal (ə drē′nəl) *adj-* 1 located in the area near the kidneys. 2 having to do with the adrenal glands or their secretions.

ad·ren·al·ine or **ad·ren·al·in** (ə drĕn′ə lən) *n-* hormone secreted by the adrenal glands to brace the body for danger and stress, as for flight or violence.

a·drift (ə drĭft′) *adj-* floating about at random; without moorings or means of propulsion: *The boat was* adrift.

a·droit (ə droit´) *adj-* clever; skillful: *We admired the lawyer's* adroit *questioning of the witness.* —*adv-* a·droit´ly. *n-* a·droit´ness.

ad·sorb (ăd sòrb´, -zòrb´) *vt-* to take up a gas, liquid, or solid by the process of adsorption. See also *absorb*.

ad·u·la·tion (ăj´ə lā´shən) *n-* uncritical and excessive praise; flattery: *Mussolini inspired* adulation *among his followers. adj-* ad´u·la·tor´y (ăj´ə lə tôr´ē): *an* adulatory *speech about a leader*.

a·dult (ə dŭlt´, ăd´ŭlt´) *n-* 1 full-grown plant, animal, or person. 2 mature person; man or woman. *adj-* 1 grown to full size. 2 made by or for a mature person: *an* adult *decision; an* adult *drama.*

a·dul·ter·ant (ə dŭl´tər ənt) *n-* any substance used to adulterate another substance.

a·dul·ter·ate (ə dŭl´tə rāt´) *vt-* [a·dul·ter·at·ed, a·dul·ter·at·ing] to make poorer or thinner by mixing in some other substance: *to* adulterate *milk with water.*

a·dul·ter·a·tion (ə dŭl´tə rā´shən) *n-* 1 the adding of something inferior to a substance or mixture. 2 the product so adulterated, such as milk thinned with water.

a·dul·ter·y (ə dŭl´tə rē) *n-* [*pl.* a·dul·ter·ies] the act of breaking the marriage vow of sexual fidelity. —*adj-* a·dul´ter·ous.

ad·vance (əd văns´) *vt-* [ad·vanced, ad·vanc·ing] 1 to move (persons or things) forward or upward: *to* advance *a cause; to* advance *a person to a higher position; to* advance *prices or costs; to* advance *a meeting to a later date.* 2 to offer; propose: *to* advance *a plan.*

ad·vance·ment (əd văns´mənt, ăd-) *n-* 1 a moving forward. 2 promotion in rank or standing: *to have hopes of* advancement.

ad·van·tage (əd văn´tĭj, ăd-) *n-* thing or condition that gives one help, superiority, benefit, etc.: *His early training was clearly an* advantage. *Jack's weight gave him the* advantage *over the other fighter.*

take advantage of 1 to make the best use of: *He* took advantage *of the lull in the fighting to rest.* 2 to impose upon or treat (someone) unfairly: *Don't let him* take advantage *of you.* **to (one's) advantage** to (one's) benefit or gain: *It is to his* advantage *to study.*

ad·van·ta·geous (ăd´vən tā´jəs) *adj-* favorable; useful; profitable: *an* advantageous *position.* —*adv-* ad´van·ta´geous·ly. *n-* ad´van·ta´geous·ness.

ad·vent (ăd´vĕnt´) *n-* 1 a coming into place or being; arrival: *the* advent *of spring.* 2 **Advent** the coming of Jesus Christ into the world; also, the season (including four Sundays) of preparation for Christmas.

ad·ven·ti·tious (ăd´vən tĭsh´əs) *adj-* 1 coming from the outside, and, hence, unexpected: *an* adventitious *development in the trial.* 2 *Biology* growing in an unusual location in a plant or animal: *An* adventitious *bud appeared on the plant's leaf.* —*adv-* ad·ven·ti´tious·ly. *n-* ad´ven·ti´tious·ness.

ad·ven·ture (əd vĕn´chər) *n-* 1 bold and difficult undertaking in which risks are run: *Climbing any high mountain is an* adventure. 2 an exciting or unexpected experience: *Exploring the old castle was a pleasant* adventure. 3 activity filled with danger, excitement, etc.: *his love of* adventure; *the spirit of* adventure.

ad·ven·tur·ous (əd vĕn´chər əs) *adj-* 1 inclined to seek exciting experiences. 2 risky and requiring courage: *an* adventurous *undertaking.* *Hom-* adventuress. —*adv-* ad·ven´tur·ous·ly.

ad·verb (ăd´vûrb´) *Grammar n-* a modifier that is not an adjective, a determiner, or a noun. Adverbs usually relate with respect to time, place, manner, or degree, and may be found in various positions in sentences.

ad·ver·sar·y (ăd´vər sĕr´ē) *n-* [*pl.* ad·ver·sar·ies] 1 enemy. 2 opponent; rival.

ad·verse (ăd´vûrs, ăd vûrs´) *adj-* 1 unfavorable: *The judge gave an* adverse *decision.*

ad·ver·si·ty (əd vûr´sə tē, au-) *n-* [*pl.* ad·ver·si·ties] great trouble or trial; misfortune; hardship: *He knew many days of* adversity.

ad·ver·tise (ăd´vər tīz´) *vt-* [ad·ver·tised, ad·ver·tis·ing] 1 to give public notice of: *to* advertise *the hour of the town meeting.* 2 to call attention to in the newspapers,

over the radio, on television, etc., in order to arouse a desire to buy: *to* advertise *a sale of shoes.*

ad·ver·tise·ment (ăd´vər tīz´mənt, əd vûr´təz mənt) *n-* public notice about things that are sold, needed, lost, or found.

ad·vice (əd vīs´, ăd-) *n-* opinion about what ought to be done; counsel; guidance.

ad·vis·a·ble (əd vī´zə bəl) *adj-* worth taking as good advice; sensible; wise: *It is* advisable *to cross streets only at corners.* —*n-* ad·vis´a·bil´i·ty. *adv-* ad·vis´a·bly.

ad·vise (əd vīz´, ăd-) *vt-* [ad·vised, ad·vis·ing] 1 to give advice to: *He* advised *me to go.* 2 to notify: *He* advised *me of my promotion. vi-* to seek counsel; consult: *He* advised *with me about his trip.* —*n-* ad·vis´er or ad·vi´sor.

ad·vised (əd vīzd´, ăd-) *adj-* informed; notified: *He was kept* advised *of the latest developments.*

ad·vis·ed·ly (əd vī´zəd lē, ăd-) *adv-* after careful consideration; deliberately: *He used the word* advisedly.

ad·vise·ment (əd vīz´mənt, ăd-) *n-* consideration; deliberation: *Keep the matter under* advisement.

ad·vi·so·ry (əd vī´zə rē, ăd-) *adj-* having power to suggest or to give advice: *an* advisory *board.*

ad·vo·ca·cy (ăd´və kə sē) *n-* an urging or supporting: *his* advocacy *of a strong navy.*

¹**ad·vo·cate** (ăd´və kāt´) *vt-* [ad·vo·cat·ed, ad·vo·cat·ing] to recommend publicly; favor; urge: *The senator* advocates *careful spending of our country's money.*

²**ad·vo·cate** (ăd´və kət) *n-* 1 person who speaks in favor of any cause; defender; supporter: *Mahatma Gandhi was an* advocate *of passive resistance.*

adz or **adze** (ădz) *n-* cutting tool for shaping and finishing timber.

Adz

ae·des (ā ē´dēz) *n-* a tropical and subtropical mosquito, carrier of yellow fever, dengue, and some other diseases.

ae·gis (ē´jəs) *n-* 1 (also egis) protecting power or influence; support; backing: *He acted under the* aegis *of the federal government.* 2 in Greek mythology, the shield of Zeus or the breastplate of Athena.

ae·on (ē´ŏn´) *n-* eon.

aer·ate (âr´āt´) *vt-* [aer·at·ed, aer·at·ing] 1 to expose to the action of air: *Water is purified by* aerating *it in a fine spray.* 2 to dissolve or mix air or another gas in a liquid under pressure. 3 to supply (the blood) with oxygen: *Blood is* aerated *in the lungs.* —*n-* aer´a´tion.

aer·i·al (âr´ē əl) *adj-* 1 having to do with, or taking place in the air: *an* aerial *photograph.* 2 high; lofty: *the city's* aerial *towers.* 3 lacking substance; imaginary: *an* aerial *flight of fancy.* 4 growing in air without roots in the ground as does Spanish moss. *Hom-* Ariel. —*adv-* aer´i·al·ly.

aer·ie (âr´ē, ĕr´ē) *n-* the nest of an eagle or other bird of prey that builds high among the rocks. Also **eyrie** or **eyry.** *Hom-* airy or eerie.

aer·o·dy·nam·ics (âr´ō dī năm´ĭks) *n-* the science that deals with the flow of air and its effects, especially on aircraft.

aer·o·nau·tics (âr´ə nô´tĭks) *n-* (takes singular verb) the science of aviation, or of operating aircraft. —*adj-* aer´o·nau´tic or aer´o·nau´ti·cal.

aer·o·sol (âr´ə sŏl´, -sôl´) *n-* suspension of fine particles of a solid or liquid in a gas, as mist, smoke, or fog.

aer·o·space (âr´ō spās´) *n-* 1 region consisting of the earth's atmosphere and outer space. 2 the study of this region, especially in connection with rockets and other spacecraft.

aes·thet·ic (ĕs thĕt´ĭk) *adj-* esthetic. —*adj-* aes·thet´i·cal. *adv-* aes·thet´i·cal·ly.

aes·thet·ics (ĕs thĕt´ĭks) *n-* esthetics.

aes·ti·vate (ĕs´tə vāt´) *vi-* [aes·ti·vat·ed, aes·ti·vat·ing] estivate.

a·far (ə fär´) *adv-* far away; far off; from a distance.

af·fa·ble (ăf´ə bəl) *adj-* courteous in speech and manner; friendly. —*n-* af´fa·bil´i·ty. *adv-* af´fa·bly.

af·fair (ə fâr´) *n-* 1 any matter of interest, concern, or duty; business; job: *an* affair *of state; a difficult* affair *to handle.* 2 *Informal* an object; thing: *The hut was* *a crude* affair. **3** *Informal* social gathering or celebration. **4** a romance, usually a temporary one. **5 affairs** business of any sort: *He put his affairs in order before he left.*

af·fect (ə fĕkt′) *vt-* **1** to influence; have an effect on: *Edison's inventions have greatly affected modern civilization.* **2** to move the feelings of; stir the emotions of: *The story of his escape and wanderings affected me deeply.* [from Latin *affectus* meaning "an influence."]

af·fec·ta·tion (ăf′ĕk tā′shən) *n-* the assuming of a manner merely to create an impression; also, an instance of this: *His affectations of speech made us laugh.*

af·fect·ed (ə fĕk′ təd) *adj-* **1** not natural; assumed: *her affected manners; an affected accent.* **2** moved; stirred: *He seemed much affected by the news.*

af·fec·tion (ə fĕk′ shən) *n-* **1** fondness; love: *Although he teased her sometimes, he had a great affection for his sister.* **2** disease or complaint: *an affection of the lung.*

af·fec·tion·ate (ə fĕk′shən ət) *adj-* having or expressing affection; loving; tender: *She has an affectionate nature.* —*adv-* **af·fec′tion·ate·ly.** *n-* **af·fec′tion·ate·ness.**

af·fi·ance (ə fī′əns) *vt-* [af·fi·anced, af·fi·anc·ing] to promise (oneself or another) in marriage.

af·fi·da·vit (ăf′ə dā′ vət) *n-* a sworn statement in writing, especially one made before a court or a notary public.

¹**af·fil·i·ate** (ə fĭl′ ē āt′) *vt-* [af·fil·i·at·ed, af·fil·i·at·ing] to join or become associated (with): *The local refused to affiliate with the new union.* *vt-* to associate (oneself with). —*n-* **af·fil′i·a′tion.**

af·fin·i·ty (ə fĭn′ə tē) *n-* [*pl.* **af·fin·i·ties**] **1** a close relationship: *an affinity between two tribes; an affinity between two languages.* **2** mutual understanding and attraction, based on similarity of temperament. **3** *Chemistry* the force of attraction by which the atoms of different elements enter into and remain in combination.

af·firm (ə fûrm′) *vt-* **1** to assert strongly; declare positively: *He affirmed his innocence.* **2** to give formal approval to; confirm; ratify: *to affirm the decision of a lower court.*

af·firm·a·tion (ăf′ ər mā′shən) *n-* an affirming.

af·firm·a·tive (ə fûr′mə tĭv) *adj-* declaring assent or agreement; saying yes; affirming: *Some affirmative expressions are "OK," "all right," "certainly." Fred was on the affirmative side in the debate.* *n-* **1** word or expression indicating assent or agreement.

af·fix (ə fĭks′) *vt-* to attach or add: *I affixed my signature to the letter.*

af·flict (ə flĭkt′) *vt-* to cause great pain or trouble to; make miserable; distress: *War has long afflicted mankind.*

af·flic·tion (ə flĭk′shən) *n-* **1** a state of pain or distress: *She was brave in her affliction.* **2** anything that causes suffering or grief: *Some diseases are terrible afflictions.*

af·flu·ence (ăf′ lōō əns) *n-* abundant supply, as of riches, words, ideas, etc.; especially, material wealth.

af·flu·ent (ăf′ lōō ənt) *adj-* having abundance; wealthy: *an affluent man; affluent times.* —*adv-* **af′flu·ent·ly.**

af·ford (ə fôrd′) *vt-* **1** to give; furnish: *Swimming affords enjoyment and muscular training.* **2** to have the resources to pay for, compensate for, or expend: *Is he able to afford a new car? I can't. Can you afford such carelessness? Can you afford the time?*

af·fray (ə frā′) *n-* noisy quarrel; brawl.

af·front (ə frŭnt′) *vt-* to insult openly and on purpose: *He affronted me by walking out in the middle of my speech.* *n-* open insult: *The speech is an affront to us.*

a·fraid (ə frād′) *adj-* full of fear; frightened.

a·fresh (ə frĕsh′) *adv-* again; anew: *He had to start afresh because of his mistakes.*

aft (ăft) *adv-* toward the stern of a ship: *The sailor went aft. adj-:* *the aft funnel.*

af·ter (ăf′tər) *prep-* (in sense 1 becomes an adverb when the object is clearly implied but not expressed) **1** following in time, place, rank, etc.: *Please come after three o'clock. The supplies trailed after the troops.* **2** in search or pursuit of.

aft·er·math (ăf′tər măth′) *n-* **1** that which follows; result: *Misery is an aftermath of war.* **2** a second mowing in a season.

af·ter·ward (ăf′tər wərd′) or **af·ter·wards** (ăf′tər wərdz′) *adv-* at a later time.

a·gain (ə gĕn′) *adv-* **1** a second time; once more: *Do it again.* **2** (used for emphasis): *Give the book back again.* **3** further; on the other hand: *George is both intelligent and sensible.* Again, *he knows how to get what he wants.*

a·gainst (ə gĕnst′) *prep-* **1** in an opposite direction to: *They tried to row against the tide.* **2** upon; in contact with; touching: *He leaned against the fence.* **3** in contrast with: *black against gold.* **4** in opposition to: *There were twenty votes against the increase in club dues.* **5** in preparation for: *to save money against a rainy day.*

a·gape (ə gāp′) *adj-* having the mouth wide open, as in wonder.

ag·ate (ăg′ ət) *n-* **1** a kind of quartz with colored bands or cloudy spots, used in jewelry. **2** child's playing marble made to look like this.

Agate

a·ga·ve (ə gä′ vē) *n-* any of several tropical American plants of the amaryllis family, including the century plant or maguey, having fleshy, spiny-edged leaves, and yielding commercial fiber.

age (āj) *n-* **1** length of life or existence: *the age of a man; the age of a star.* **2** point of time in life or existence: *the age of ten.* **3** period in life or history: *the age of childhood; the age of space travel; the age of reptiles.* **4** *Informal* (also **ages**) a long time.

aged (ājd) *adj-* **1** of the age of: *a boy aged five.* **2** matured; ripened: *an aged wine.*

a·gen·cy (ā′ jən sē) *n-* [*pl.* **a·gen·cies**] **1** business or office of a person or company that acts for another: *an employment agency; advertising agency.* **2** an administrative, often regulatory, department of the government, such as the FTC (Federal Trade Commission). **3** means; operation; action: *the agency of friends; the agency of Providence.*

a·gen·da (ə jĕn′də) *n- pl.* [*sing.* **a·gen·dum**] list or outline of things to be done or discussed; schedule: *The secretary read the agenda of the meeting.*

a·gent (ā′ jənt) *n-* **1** person or company that acts for another: *a real estate agent; a press agent.* **2** official or representative of a government, company, etc.: *an agent of the FBI.* **3** substance or power that produces a result, reaction, change, etc.: *Water and wind are natural agents of erosion.*

ag·glom·er·ate (ə glŏm′ ə rət) *n-* **1** a piled or heaped collection of things; an agglomeration. **2** in geology, a kind of rock made up of volcanic fragments fused together without order. *adj-* **1** heaped up, mixed up, or clustered. **2** of a flower, composite.

ag·glom·er·a·tion (ə glŏm′ ə rā′ shən) *n-* **1** act of piling or gathering things together, especially things of different sizes and shapes. **2** heap or collection of things so formed.

ag·glu·ti·na·tion (ə glōō′ tə nā′shən) *n-* **1** a uniting or sticking together; adhesion. **2** *Biology* process in which bacteria or living cells collect or clump together, usually because of the presence of an antibody.

ag·gran·dize (ə grăn′dīz′, ăg′ grən dīz′) *vt-* [ag·gran·dized, ag·gran·diz·ing] to enlarge or increase (a thing); also, to increase the power, rank, or wealth of (a person or state): *He aggrandized himself at the expense of others.* —*n-* **ag·gran′dize·ment** (ə grăn′dəz mənt). *n-* **ag′gran·diz′ er.**

ag·gra·vate (ăg′ rə vāt′) *vt-* [ag·gra·vat·ed, ag·gra·vat·ing] **1** to make worse: *Scratching a mosquito bite aggravates it.* **2** *Informal* to irritate: *He aggravated his parents by staying out late at night.*

ag·gra·va·tion (ăg′ rə vā′shən) *n-* **1** a making worse: *the aggravation of a cold by neglect.* **2** *Informal* irritation; exasperation; also the cause of this: *Her son's stubbornness caused her much aggravation.*

¹**ag·gre·gate** (ăg′ rə gāt′) *vt-* [ag·gre·gat·ed, ag·gre·gat·ing] **1** to bring into a whole mass; collect: *He aggregated*

ag·gre·gate (ăg′ rə gət) *n-* 1 the total; entire number: *The aggregate of all his debts was $1,000.* 2 the rocky material such as sand, pebbles, etc., added to cement to make concrete. *as modifier: the aggregate amount.*
in the aggregate taken all together.

ag·gre·ga·tion (ăg′ rə gā′ shən) *n-* a collection of people or things; mass; whole; group: *an aggregation of visiting delegates; an* aggregation *of boulders in a riverbed.*

ag·gres·sion (ə grĕsh′ ən) *n-* 1 unprovoked attack or assault, especially by one nation against another. 2 in psychology, a feeling of intense hostility.

ag·gres·sive (ə grĕs′ ĭv) *adj-* 1 first to attack; quick to pick a quarrel: *an aggressive boy.* 2 energetic; enterprising: *an aggressive salesman.* —*adv-* **ag·gres′ sive·ly.** *n-* **ag·gres′ sive·ness.**

ag·gres·sor (ə grĕs′ ər) *n-* one who attacks another; one who begins a quarrel.

a·ghast (ə găst′) *adj-* struck with sudden surprise, horror, or terror: *He was* aghast *at the damage he had caused.*

ag·ile (ăj′ əl) *adj-* quick, light, and nimble in movement or thought: *an agile dancer; an* agile *mind.* —*adv-* **ag′ ile·ly.** *n-* **a·gil′ i·ty** (ə jĭl′ ə tē): *a dancer's* agility.

ag·i·tate (ăj′ ə tāt′) *vt-* [**ag·i·tat·ed, ag·i·tat·ing**] 1 to disturb; excite: *The bad news* agitated *him.* 2 to stir up violently: *The wind* agitated *the lake.* *vi-* to stir up public opinion: *The paper* agitated *for better housing.*

ag·i·ta·tion (ăj′ ə tā′ shən) *n-* 1 anxiety; worry: *to show* agitation *over a friend's safety.* 2 excited discussion; energetic activity to promote a cause: *There was general* agitation *for lower taxes.* 3 a moving to and fro: *an* agitation *of air.*

ag·i·ta·tor (ăj′ ə tā′ tər) *n-* 1 one who makes a political or industrial disturbance. 2 an implement for stirring.

a·glow (ə glō′) *adj-* bright; flushed: *cheeks* aglow *with pleasure.*

ag·nos·tic (ăg nŏs′ tĭk) *n-* one who, without denying the existence of God, believes that there is no evidence in man's experience to prove that God exists. *adj-* relating to such a belief.

a·gog (ə gŏg′) *adj-* aroused; alive with interest; excited; eager: *We are* agog *with curiosity.*

ag·o·nize (ăg′ ə nīz′) *vi-* [**ag·o·nized, ag·o·niz·ing**] to suffer extreme pain or grief: *Even though he was right, he* agonized *over his decision for weeks.* *vt-* to torment or torture: *His decision* agonized *him for weeks.*

ag·o·ny (ăg′ ə nē) *n-* [*pl.* **ag·o·nies**] 1 intense suffering of body or mind: *An earache is* agony. *She suffered* agonies *of remorse for her carelessness.* 2 the last struggle of a dying person or animal.

a·gou·ti (ə gōō′ tē) *n-* any of several rabbitlike rodents of tropical American forests. Also **a·gou′ ty.**

Agouti, 16 1/2—25 1/2 in.

a·grar·i·an (ə grâr′ ē ən) *adj-* relating to land, or to the right or manner of holding land: *our* agrarian *laws.* *n-* one who is in favor of a redistribution of land.

a·gree (ə grē′) *vi-* [**a·greed, a·gree·ing**] 1 to consent (to): *They* agreed *to buy it.* 2 to be of the same mind or opinion; concur , also, to harmonize or correspond.

a·gree·a·ble (ə grē′ ə bəl) *adj-* 1 pleasant: *A good dinner and agreeable talk go together.* 2 willing to agree: *Are you* agreeable *to this plan?* —*adv-* **a·gree′ a·bly.**

a·gree·ment (ə grē′ mənt) *n-* 1 a being of the same opinion; an understanding: *The two countries came to* agreement *on the terms of the treaty.* 2 harmony; accord: *There was complete* agreement *between the stories of the two witnesses.*

ag·ri·cul·ture (ăg′ rə kŭl′ chər) *n-* 1 the cultivation of land and the breeding and raising of farm animals; farming. 2 the art or science of farming.

a·gue (ā′ gyōō′) *n-* disease marked by regularly recurring chills and fever.

a·head (ə hĕd′) *adv-* (sometimes considered an adjective when used after a form of the verb "to be") 1 beyond or in advance of something or someone else; in or to the front: *The red car raced* ahead. *We started together,*

but she is now far ahead. 2 to or toward a more advanced place, position, or time; forward.

a·hoy (ə hoi′) *interj-* call used by sailors to hail a ship: *Ship,* ahoy!

aid (ād) *vt-* (considered intransitive when the direct object is implied but not expressed) to help or assist. *n-* 1 person or thing that helps or assists: *Books are an* aid *to learning.* 2 help: *with the* aid *of a doctor.* *Hom-* aide.

aide (ād) *n-* 1 helper or assistant: *a nurse's* aide; *a diplomatic* aide; *a military* aide. 2 aide-de-camp. *Hom-* aid.

aide-de-camp (ād′ də kămp′) *n-* [*pl.* **aides-de-camp**] military officer who acts as a personal assistant to a superior; aide. [from French, meaning literally "aide or assistant for the camp."]

ail (āl) *vt-* to cause pain or discomfort to; be the matter with; trouble: *What* ails *the man? Hom-* ale.

ai·ler·on (ā′ lə rŏn′) *n-* hinged part on the rear edge of each wing of an airplane to steady it in flight. For picture. see airplane.

ail·ment (āl′ mənt) *n-* sickness; illness.

aim (ām) *vt-* 1 to point or sight a weapon, or direct a blow, remark, etc.: *to* aim *at a target; to* aim *for an opponent's chin.* 2 to have in mind or intend: *He* aims *to become an engineer.*

air (âr) *n-* 1 mixture of gases, mostly nitrogen and oxygen, surrounding the earth and making up the earth's atmosphere. 2 tune or melody: *an old English* air. 3 general appearance or manner; look or feeling of a person or thing: *The old gentleman maintained an* air *of dignity. The hotel had an* air *of luxury.* 4 **airs** manners or appearance put on to impress people; affected attitudes: *Jane's city* airs *annoyed her friends at home.*

air-con·di·tion (âr′ kən dĭsh′ ən) *vt-* to equip with air-conditioning machinery or to supply with air treated by such machinery. —*adj-* **air′-con·di′ tioned.**

air·i·ness (âr′ ē nəs) *n-* 1 openness to the air. 2 delicacy; lightness. 3 sprightliness.

air·ing (âr′ ĭng) *n-* 1 an exposure to the air, for freshening, drying, etc.: *They gave the winter clothes an* airing. 2 a walk or ride in the outdoors. 3 a public display or discussion (of ideas, opinions, etc.): *an* airing *of his grievances.*

air·line (âr′ līn′) *n-* company that owns and operates airplanes to carry passengers and freight.

air·plane (âr′ plān′) *n-* flying machine heavier than air, driven by engines and having fixed wings.

air·tight (âr′ tīt′) *n-* 1 closed or sealed so that no air can get in or out. 2 without a flaw or weakness: *an* airtight *legal case; an* airtight *alibi.*

air·wor·thy (âr′ wûr′ thē) *adj-* fit or prepared for safe flight. *n-* **air′ wor′ thi·ness.**

air·y (âr′ ē) *adj-* [**air·i·er, air·i·est**] 1 in or of the air; high up: *the* airy *flight of the monarch butterfly.* 2 with air moving freely; breezy: *an* airy *room.* 3 light-hearted; graceful; gay: *an* airy *manner;* airy *laughter.* 4 unreal; imaginary; visionary: *his* airy *schemes. Hom-* aerie. —*adv-* **air′ i·ly.**

aisle (īl) *n-* 1 passageway between seats, as in a church, theater, or courtroom. 2 passageway between counters in a store. *Hom-* I'll, isle.

al·a·bas·ter (ăl′ ə băs′ tər) *n-* stone of fine texture, usually white and translucent, often carved into vases or other ornaments. *adj-: an* alabaster *lamp.*

a·lack (ə lăk′) *Archaic interj-* an exclamation expressing sorrow, surprise, or regret.

a·lac·ri·ty (ə lăk′ rə tē) *n-* eager readiness to do something: *He accepted the invitation with* alacrity.

a·larm (ə lärm′) *n-* 1 a warning of danger: *He gave the* alarm. 2 device to warn or awaken persons: *a fire* alarm. 3 the fear of danger: *As the waves increased,* alarm *seized the passengers.* 4 *Archaic* a call to arms. *vt-* to arouse to a sense of danger; startle: *The smell of smoke* alarmed *the campers.*

a·larm·ist (ə lär′ mĭst) *n-* one who exaggerates bad news or foretells calamities.

a·las (ə läs′) *interj-* exclamation showing sorrow, pity, or regret.

al·ba·tross (ăl′ bə trôs′) *n-* very large web-footed sea bird of southern waters, capable of remarkably long flights from land.

al·be·it (ôl′ bē′ ət) *conj-* although; even though.

al·bi·no (ăl bī′ nō) *n-* [*pl.* **al·bi·nos**] person or animal with unusually light skin, pink eyes, and nearly white hair, all due to partial or complete lack of natural pigment.

al·bum (ăl′ bəm) *n-* **1** book with blank pages in which to keep photographs, stamps, autographs, etc. **2** holder, in the form of a book, for phonograph records. **3** set of one or more phonograph records sold as a unit.

al·bu·men (ăl byoo′ mən) *n-* **1** white of an egg. **2** albumin.

al·che·my (ăl′ kə mē) *n-* the chemistry of the Middle Ages, the chief purposes of which were to turn common metals into gold and to find a method of prolonging life.

al·co·hol (ăl′ kə hôl′) *n-* **1** colorless, volatile, flammable liquid (C₂H₅OH) produced in the fermentation of fruit, grain, or other sugary or starchy substances; ethanol; ethyl alcohol; grain alcohol; spirits. **2** wood alcohol. **3** *Chemistry* any hydrocarbon whose molecules include one or more hydroxyl groups (OH⁻).

al·co·hol·ism (ăl′ kə hô′ lĭz əm) *n-* **1** uncontrollable addiction to alcohol. **2** the poisoning and deterioration of the body caused by such addiction.

al·cove (ăl′ kōv′) *n-* small room opening out of a larger room; nook.

al·der (ôl′ dər) *n-* any of several trees and shrubs related to the birches, often growing thickly in moist or swampy places. The bark is used in tanning and dyeing.

Alcove

al·der·man (ôl′ dər mən) *n-* [*pl.* **al·der·men**] member of the governing body of a ward, district, or city, or of a church.

ale (āl) *n-* a fermented drink similar to beer, made from malt and hops. *Hom-* ail.

a·lee (ə lē′) *adv-* at or toward the lee.

a·lert (ə lûrt′) *adj-* **1** mentally quick in perception and action: *an alert mind.* **2** attentive; wide-awake; watchful; bright: *an alert student.* *vt-* to warn of coming danger: *The commander alerted the troops before the enemy attack.*

al·fal·fa (ăl făl′ fə) *n-* plant resembling clover and having purple flowers and very deep roots. It is grown for hay, often yielding several cuttings a year.

al·ge·bra (ăl′ jə brə) *n-* branch of mathematics which represents quantities and relations between them by the use of letters, numerals, and other symbols. *—adj-* **al′ge·bra′ic** (ăl′ jə brā′ ĭk) or **al′ge·bra′i·cal.** *adv-* **al′ge·bra′i·cal·ly.**

a·li·as (ā′ lē əs) *n-* [*pl.* **a·li·as·es**] an assumed name: *The forger had two aliases.* *adv-* otherwise called: *Max, alias Slinky Sam.*

a·li·bi (ăl′ ə bī) *n-* **1** claim made by a person accused of a crime or wrongdoing that he was somewhere else when the crime was committed. **2** *Informal* an excuse for failure: *Tom has a ready alibi each time he's late.*

al·i·en (ā′ lǐ ən or āl′ yən) *n-* foreigner; person who is not a citizen of the country in which he is living. *adj-* foreign: *an alien people; an alien land.*

alien to strange to; not characteristic of: *Dishonesty is alien to his nature.*

al·i·en·ate (ā′ lǐ ə nāt′) *vt-* [**al·i·en·at·ed, al·i·en·at·ing**] to cause (a person) to withdraw his affections, trust, etc.; make hostile or indifferent: *His selfish habits soon alienated his friends.* *—n-* **al′i·en·a′tion.**

¹**a·light** (ə lĭt′) *adj-* **1** kindled or burning: *The fire is alight on the hearth.* **2** bright: *The bride's face was alight with happiness.* [from a combination of Old English **ən,** "on," and **lēoht** meaning "light."]

²**a·light** (ə lĭt′) *vi-* **1** to get down from a train, airplane, etc.; step down (from): *They alighted and went into the terminal.* **2** to land or settle on the earth: *The plane alighted.* [from Old English **alīhtan** meaning "make light; take weight off," from Old English **līht** meaning "light (in weight)."]

a·lign (ə līn′) *vt-* **1** to bring (the parts of a machine or electronic device) into proper relationship

cause: *The three nations aligned themselves against the common enemy.* *vi-* to be adjusted or in line: *This wheel aligns with the other.* Also **aline.** *—n-* **a·lign′ ment** or **a·line′ ment.**

a·like (ə līk′) *adj-* similar: *The two brothers are alike in their interests.* *adv-* similarly; in the same way: *The two sisters dress alike, walk alike, talk alike, and even think alike.*

al·i·men·ta·ry (ăl′ ə měn′ tə rē) *adj-* pertaining to food and nutrition.

alimentary canal *n-* the whole digestive tract, including the esophagus, stomach, and intestines.

al·i·mo·ny (ăl′ ə mō′ nē) *n-* an allowance for support paid to a woman by her former husband, by court order, after a divorce.

a·live (ə lǐv′) *adj-* **1** having life. **2** lively; animated: *John is one of the most alive boys we know.* **3** attentive; sensitive: *He is alive to his opportunities.* **4** full of living things; swarming: *The stream is alive with fish.*

al·ka·li (ăl′ kə lǐ′) *n-* [*pl.* **al·ka·lis** or **al·kal·ies**] **1** a mixture of soluble salts, such as sodium carbonate or sodium sulfate, often occurring in the soil and water of deserts. **2** *Chemistry* a strong base that dissolves in water, such as sodium or potassium hydroxide.

all (ôl) *determiner* (traditionally called adjective or pronoun) **1** the whole of: *in all the world.* **2** each and every one of; *to all men.* **3** as much as possible: *with all speed.* **4** nothing but: *This is all work and no play.* **5** everyone: *All agreed.* *All are coming.*

al·lay (ə lā′) *vt-* to quiet; calm; make less or reduce: *The doctor allayed his fears.*

all clear *n-* signal indicating that an air raid or air-raid drill is over.

al·le·ga·tion (ăl′ ə gā′ shən) *n-* assertion, whether or not supported by proof.

al·lege (ə lěj′) *vt-* [**al·leged, al·leg·ing**] **1** to offer as an argument, plea, or excuse: *He alleged illness as the reason for his failure to come.* **2** to assert: *He alleges his innocence.*

al·le·giance (ə lē′ jəns) *n-* loyalty and devotion, especially to one's country.

al·le·go·ry (ăl′ ə gôr′ ē) *n-* [*pl.* **al·le·gor·ies**] story in which the characters and happenings stand for ideas or qualities, such as truth, loyalty, virtue, etc. Examples: the parables of the Bible; "Aesop's Fables." *—adj-* **al′ le·gor′ i·cal:** *an allegorical tale.* *adv-* **al′ le·gor′ i·cal·ly.**

al·ler·gy (ăl′ ər jē) *n-* [*pl.* **al·ler·gies**] sensitivity of the body to certain foods, chemicals, pollens, insect bites, etc. *—adj-* **al·ler′ gic** (ə lûr′ jĭk): *He is allergic to strawberries.*

al·le·vi·ate (ə lē′ vē āt′) *vt-* [**al·le·vi·at·ed, al·le·vi·at·ing**] to lighten; lessen; make easier: *a medicine to alleviate pain.* *—n-* **al·le′ vi·a′ tion:** *the alleviation of severe pain.*

¹**al·ley** (ăl′ ē) *n-* [*pl.* **al·leys**] **1** narrow street or passage, especially one at the rear of buildings. **2** formal pathway in a garden, usually lined with trees. **3** bowling alley. **4** a strip on each side of a tennis court that is part of the playing area when four persons play but not when two persons play (for picture, see *tennis court*). [from Old French *alee* meaning "passage," from *aller,* "to go."]

al·li·ance (ə lī′əns) *n-* union or joining together by agreement of two or more persons, families, groups, or nations: *an alliance by marriage; an alliance for war; an international alliance.*

al·li·ga·tor (ăl′ ə gā′ tər) *n-* **1** large, lizardlike, flesh-eating animal related to the crocodile, with a short, broad head and blunt snout. One kind, growing to about twelve feet, lives in the fresh waters of southern United States. **2** leather made from the skin of this animal. *as modifier: an alligator belt.* [from Spanish **el lagarto** meaning "the lizard."]

al·lit·er·a·tion (ə lĭt ə rā′ shən) *n-* use of the same consonant sound at the beginning of words throughout a line or passage. Example: "In a summer season when soft was the sun . . ." *—adj-* **al·lit′er·a′tive:** *an alliterative expression.* *adv-* **al·lit′er·a′tive·ly.**

al·lo·cate (ăl′ ə kāt′) *vt-* [al·lo·cat·ed, al·lo·cat·ing] to set aside or distribute for a special purpose; assign; allot: *He allocated part of his income for a vacation trip.* *n-* **al′lo·ca′tion:** *the allocation of materials for a project.*

al·lot (ə lŏt′) *vt-* [al·lot·ted, al·lot·ting] to distribute (amounts or shares); assign: *to allot an hour to the work.*

al·low (ə lou′) *vt-* **1** to permit; let: *The doctor allowed the patient to sit up.* **2** to permit the presence of: *This hotel does not allow dogs.* **3** to acknowledge as right or valid: *The court allowed his claim to the property.*

al·low·ance (ə lou′ əns) *n-* **1** an accepting or admitting; concession: *the judge's allowance of a claim.* **2** definite amount or quantity, especially of money, given for a particular purpose: *a travel allowance.* **3** amount added to or subtracted from a price: *a $200 trade-in allowance.*
make allowance(s) for to take into consideration or account: *We made allowance for Jack's inexperience.*

¹**al·loy** (ăl′ oi) *n-* **1** a metal usually made by the fusion of two or more metallic elements: *Bronze is an alloy of tin and copper.* **2** something that takes away from the perfection or full enjoyment of another thing: *pleasure without alloy.*

²**al·loy** (ə loi′, *also* ăl′ oi) *vt-* **1** to combine (two or more metals). **2** to lessen (perfection, enjoyment, etc.): *His hope was alloyed by fear.*

al·lude (ə lōōd′) *vi-* [al·lud·ed, al·lud·ing] to refer to indirectly or in passing.
►Should not be confused with ELUDE.

al·lure (ə lōōr′) *n-* the power to attract; enticement: *the allure of mountain climbing.* *vt-* [al·lured, al·lur·ing] to attract; entice: *The sea allured him.*

al·lu·sion (ə lōō′ zhən) *n-* **1** a passing reference: *Do not make any allusion to his loss.* **2** a reference to something generally familiar, used by way of illustration: *a literary allusion.*
►Should not be confused with ELUSION or ILLUSION.

al·lu·vi·um (ə lōō′ vē əm) *n-* [*pl.* al·lu·vi·a (-vē ə)] materials, such as clay, sand, and gravel, carried and deposited by running water; also, any one of these materials.

¹**al·ly** (ăl′ ī′) *n-* [*pl.* al·lies] person or group of persons, especially a nation, united with another for a common purpose: *They were natural allies and agreed perfectly.*

²**al·ly** (ə lī′) *vt-* [al·lied, al·ly·ing] to join (oneself, a nation, etc.) with or to another for a special purpose: *The United States allied itself with England and France in World War I.*

al·ma·nac (ŏl′ mə năk′) *n-* **1** a book arranged according to the days, weeks, and months of the year, giving information about the weather, time of sunrise and sunset, tides, etc. **2** a book compiled annually, giving useful facts and statistics.

al·might·y (ŏl′ mī′ tē) *adj-* all-powerful. *n-* **the Almighty** God.

al·mond (ä′ mənd, ä′-, ăl′-) *n-* **1** nut of a small tree somewhat like the peach tree. **2** the tree itself.

al·most (ŏl′ mōst′) *adv-* nearly.
►For usage note see MOST.

Almond, shell and kernel

alms (ämz) *n-* [*pl.* alms] money given to the poor; charity: *to give alms to a beggar.*

al·oe (ăl′ ō) *n-* **1** garden plant whose thick, fleshy leaves have spiny edges and grow in a cluster from the base of the plant. **2** (usually aloes) a bitter drug made from the juice of its leaves. **3** the century plant or American aloe. **4** the fragrant wood or resin of an East Indian tree.

a·loft (ə lŏft′) *adj-* above the earth; high up: *The planes were aloft at the time of the air raid.* *adv-* high above the deck of a ship in the upper rigging: *The sailor nimbly climbed aloft.*

a·lo·ha (ä lō′ hä) *interj-* **1** hello; you are welcome. **2** goodbye; farewell. [from Hawaiian, meaning literally "love."]

a·lone (ə lōn′) *adj-* **1** without anyone or anything else;

solitary: *He was alone with his thoughts.* **2** and no other; only: *Mr. Jones alone has the solution to the problem.* *adv-* with no assistance; singly: *She can do it alone.*

a·long (ə lòng′) *prep-* **1** over the length of: *to walk along the beach.* **2** at the edge of: *the trees along the path.* *adv-* **1** onward: *to move along.* **2** with someone: *They brought him along.*

a·loof (ə lōōf′) *adj-* distant in position, manner, or feeling (often used with "stand," "keep," or "hold"): *Their leader stood aloof throughout the crisis.* *—n-* **a·loof′ness.**

a·loud (ə loud′) *adv-* **1** in a voice one can hear; not in a whisper: *He read the story aloud to the class.* **2** loudly: *She cried aloud for help.*

al·pac·a (ăl păk′ ə) *n-* **1** domesticated grazing animal of South America, related to the llama and vicuña, and valued for its long silky wool. **2** yarn or cloth of this wool. **3** thin, wiry silk cloth with a fine texture. *as modifier: an alpaca coat.*

al·pha·bet (ăl′ fə bět′) *n-* the system of letters or characters used in writing the words or indicating the sounds of a language, arranged in order, such as A, B, C, etc.

al·read·y (ŏl′ rĕd′ ē) *adv-* **1** some time before now; by this (or that) time: *He has already left.* **2** (often ŏl′ rĕd′ ē) so soon: *Are you here already?*

al·so (ŏl′ sō) *adv-* in addition; as well; too.
not only . . . but also both . . . and: *He was not only a good student, but also an outstanding athlete.*

al·tar (ŏl′ tər) *n-* **1** raised place or structure on which religious sacrifices are offered, or at which religious ceremonies are performed. **2** in many Christian churches, the communion table. *Hom-* alter.

al·ter (ŏl′ tər) *vt-* **1** to change; make or become different: *to alter a suit; to alter plans; to alter one's views.* **2** to castrate or spay (an animal). *Hom-* altar.

al·ter·a·tion (ŏl′ tə rā′ shən) *n-* **1** a change: *a necessary alteration in design.* **2** the act of changing or modifying anything: *I had to pay for the alteration of this dress.*

al·ter·ca·tion (ŏl′ tər kā′ shən) *n-* a quarrel or dispute; wrangle: *The conference ended in a stormy altercation between the two chief delegates.*

¹**al·ter·nate** (ŏl′ tər nət, ăl′-) *adj-* **1** every other of a series: *The boys and girls used the gymnasium on alternate days of the week.* **2** first one and then the other; by turns: *the child's alternate tears and laughter.* *n-* a substitute: *When the juror fell ill, an alternate took his place.* *—adv-* **al′ter·nate·ly.**

²**al·ter·nate** (ŏl′ tər nāt′, ăl′-) *vi-* [al·ter·nat·ed, al·ter·nat·ing] **1** to take turns: *The workmen alternate in running the machine.* **2** to take place or appear by turns: *White tiles alternated with black.* *vt-* to cause to take place or appear by turns: *The farmer alternated corn and soybeans.*

al·ter·na·tion (ŏl′ tər nā′ shən, ăl′-) *n-* a following in succession, one after the other: *the alternation of day and night.*

al·ter·na·tive (ŏl tər′ nə tĭv′, ăl′-) *n-* **1** one of two or more things to choose from: *Our choice is between slavery or resistance, and we choose the second alternative.* **2** *Informal* a choice between two or more things. *adj-* **1** offering a choice between two or more things: *He was presented with alternative plans.* **2** substitute: *an alternative menu.* *—adv-* **al·ter′na·tive′ly.**

al·though (ŏl thō′) *conj-* even though; in spite of the fact that: *I don't know him well, although he lives next door.* Also **al·tho′.**

al·tim·e·ter (ăl tĭm′ə tər, ăl′tə mē′ tər) *n-* radio or barometric instrument used to measure altitude; especially, a barometric device used in airplanes.

al·ti·tude (ăl′ tə tōōd′, -tyōōd′) *n-* **1** vertical distance above the earth, especially above sea level; height. **2** in geometry, the perpendicular distance from the base of a figure or solid to its highest point.

al·to (ăl′ tō) *Music n-* [*pl.* al·tos] musical range of the lowest female or boy's singing voice; contralto; also, a singer having this range, or a part composed for it, especially in four-part choral works. *adj-* having this or a similar range: *an alto voice; an alto flute.*

al·to·geth·er (ŏl′ tə gĕth′ ər) *adv-* **1** entirely; wholly;

completely: *He missed the target altogether. Her composition was not altogether bad.* 2 all told: *There were five pieces of luggage altogether.*

al·tru·ism (ăl′trōō ĭz əm) *n-* unselfish regard for the interests of others. —*n-* al′tru·ist.

al·um (ăl′əm) *n-* transparent, whitish mineral salt, used as a medicine either externally to stop bleeding or internally to cause vomiting. It is also used in dyeing and in the purification of water.

a·lu·mi·num (ə lōō′mə nəm) *n-* very lightweight silver-white metallic element that does not corrode in air. Symbol Al, At. No. 13, At. Wt. 26.9815.

a·lum·na (ə lŭm′nə) *n-* [*pl.* a·lum·nae (-nē)] woman graduated from a school, college, or university.

a·lum·nus (ə lŭm′nəs) *n-* [*pl.* a·lum·ni (-nī)] man or woman graduated from a school, college, or university.

al·ways (ôl′wăz, -wēz) *adv-* at all times; on all occasions; without exception: *My father is always generous.*

a·mal·gam (ə măl′gəm) *n-* 1 an alloy consisting of any metal dissolved in mercury, especially the alloy of silver and mercury that is used to fill dental cavities. 2 any mixture or combination: *In our Southwest we find an amalgam of American and Mexican cultures.*

a·mal·ga·mate (ə măl′gə māt′) *vt-* [a·mal·ga·mat·ed, a·mal·ga·mat·ing] 1 to dissolve (a metal) in mercury. 2 to unite, combine, or merge: *to amalgamate two publishing companies.* *vi-* to mix and blend completely; to become one (with): *In the past, one culture has often amalgamated with another.*

a·mass (ə măs′) *vt-* to collect into a heap; gather; accumulate: *He amassed great wealth.*

am·a·teur (ăm′ə chər, -chōōr′, -tər) *n-* 1 one who engages in any art, study, or sport for pleasure, and not for money: *a golf amateur.* 2 one whose work lacks professional finish. *adj-* nonprofessional: *a play suitable for amateur dramatics.*

am·a·to·ry (ăm′ə tôr′ē) *adj-* relating to, or expressive of, love: *Robert Burns wrote much amatory poetry.*

a·maze (ə māz′) *vt-* [a·mazed, a·maz·ing] to surprise greatly; overwhelm with astonishment: *The magician amazed the children when he lifted a rabbit out of his hat.*

am·bas·sa·dor (ăm băs′ə dər, əm-) *n-* 1 government agent of highest rank representing his country's interests at a foreign capital. 2 any representative or agent charged with a special mission.

am·ber (ăm′bər) *n-* 1 a hard, yellow or yellow-brown gum that can be polished and made into jewelry and pipe stems. Amber is actually fossil resin. 2 a yellow or yellowish-brown color. *adj-: a string of* amber *beads; the* amber *glow of a lamp.*

am·bi·dex·trous (ăm′bə dĕk′strəs) *adj-* able to use both hands with equal skill. —*adv-* am′bi·dex′trous·ly.

am·bi·gu·i·ty (ăm′bə gyōō′ə tē) *n-* [*pl.* am·bi·gu·i·ties] 1 vagueness or uncertainty of meaning; doubtfulness: *a statement full of* ambiguity. 2 something that has more than one meaning or is otherwise ambiguous: *His "no" is an* ambiguity, *since it also means "yes."*

am·big·u·ous (ăm big′yōō əs) *adj-* doubtful; having two or more possible meanings: *the speaker's* ambiguous *words; his* ambiguous *actions.* —*adv-* am·big′u·ous·ly. *n-* am·big′u·ous·ness: *The* ambiguousness *of his remarks puzzled me.*

am·bi·tion (ăm bĭsh′ən) *n-* 1 an eager desire or strong drive to gain or do something: *an ambition to be an explorer; a man of ambition.* 2 the thing desired: *It is her ambition to be the first woman President.*

am·bi·tious (ăm bĭsh′əs) *adj-* 1 full of ambition; determined to succeed. 2 eager; aspiring: *a student ambitious for knowledge.* 3 requiring great skill or effort for success: *an ambitious plan.* —*adv-* am·bi′tious·ly.

am·ble (ăm′bəl) *vi-* [am·bled, am·bling] 1 of horses, to pace, or go at a gait in which the animal lifts the two feet on the same side together. 2 to walk at an easy pace. *n-* 1 the ambling gait of a horse. 2 any easy gait. —*n-* am′bler.

am·bro·si·a (ăm′brō′zhə, -zhē ə) *n-* 1 in mythology, the food of the gods. 2 anything extremely pleasing to taste or smell. —*adj-* am·bro′si·al: *an ambrosial fragrance.*

am·bush (ăm′bŏŏsh′) *n-* 1 a surprise attack from a concealed place; also, the attackers. 2 the concealed place itself. *vt-* to waylay; attack from a concealed place: *to ambush troops.*

a·me·ba (ə mē′bə) *n-* microscopic water animal having only one cell and no definite shape. It represents one of the simplest forms of life. Also **amoeba.**

Ameba,
magnified
100 times

a·mel·io·rate (ə mēl′yə rāt′, ə mēl′ē ə rāt′) *vt-* [a·mel·io·rat·ed, a·me·lio·rat·ing] to make better; cause to improve: *laws to ameliorate living conditions.* *vi-: Our living conditions will ameliorate soon.* —*n-* a·mel′io·ra′tion. *adj-* a·mel′io·ra′tive.

a·men (ā′mĕn′, ä′mĕn′) *interj-* 1 may it be so; may God will it so (used at the end of prayers). 2 I agree; you are right: *When I said it was cold, he said "Amen."* *n-* an uttering of this word: *They all shouted an amen.*

a·me·na·ble (ə mē′nə bəl, ə mĕn′-) *adj-* 1 open or disposed to; readily accepting or yielding; responsive: *He is not amenable to her way of life.* 2 liable; answerable: *We are all amenable to the law.* —*n-* a·me′na·bil′i·ty or a·me′na·ble·ness. *adv-* a·me′na·bly.

a·mend (ə mĕnd′) *vt-* 1 to change formally: *to amend a law.* 2 to change for the better; correct.

a·mend·ment (ə mĕnd′mənt) *n-* 1 formal change, as in a legal document: *an amendment to the Constitution.* 2 a change (of one's ways) for the better.

a·mends (ə mĕndz′) **make amends** to make up for harm or injury: *His letter made amends for his rudeness.*

a·men·i·ty (ə mĕn′ə tē) *n-* [*pl.* a·men·i·ties] 1 pleasantness; agreeableness. 2 amenities agreeable or polite actions or manners: *the amenities of life.*

am·e·thyst (ăm′ə thəst, -thĭst′) *n-* 1 kind of purple or violet quartz used as a gem. 2 a deep purple color. *adj-: an amethyst ring; an amethyst velvet.*

a·mi·a·ble (ā′mē ə bəl) *adj-* friendly; pleasant; good-natured: *She is too amiable to lose her temper.* —*n-* a′mi·a·bil′i·ty also a′mi·a·ble·ness. *adv-* a′mi·a·bly.

am·i·ca·ble (ăm′ə kə bəl) *adj-* friendly; peaceable: *an amicable discussion.* —*n-* am′i·ca·bil′i·ty. *adv-* am′i·ca·bly.

a·mid (ə mĭd′) *prep-* in the middle of; among: *Only one column stood amid the ruins.*

a·miss (ə mĭs′) *adj-* wrong; out of order: *The doctor examined him and found nothing amiss.*

take amiss to have one's feelings hurt: *Don't take it amiss if I criticize your work.*

am·i·ty (ăm′ə tē) *n-* [*pl.* am·i·ties] friendship; peaceful relations: *The United States and Canada have lived in amity for many years.*

am·me·ter (ăm′mē′tər) *n-* instrument that measures, in amperes, the amount of electric current flowing through a circuit.

am·mo·ni·a (ə mōn′yə) *n-* 1 a colorless gas with a sharp, irritating odor. 2 (also **ammonia water** or **household ammonia**) a water solution of this gas used in cleaning.

am·mu·ni·tion (ăm′yə nĭsh′ən) *n-* 1 cartridges, shells, etc., used to load weapons for fighting or hunting. 2 anything usable as a weapon: *The discovery gave him ammunition in his campaign.*

am·ne·si·a (ăm nē′zhə) *n-* loss of memory caused by brain injury or emotional shock.

am·nes·ty (ăm′nəs tē) *n-* [*pl.* am·nes·ties] general pardon for offenses against the government.

a·mong (ə mŭng′) *prep-* 1 in the midst of; surrounded by: *You are among friends.* 2 in the number or group of: *Tom is a great favorite among the fans. He was listed among the wounded. Embalming was a practice among the ancient Egyptians.* 3 between (more than two): *They discussed the matter among themselves.*

am·o·rous (ăm′ər əs) *adj-* inclined to love; having to do with love: *an amorous nature; amorous letters.* —*adv-* am′o·rous·ly. *n-* am′o·rous·ness.

a·morph·ous (ə môr′fəs, ə môr′-) *adj-* 1 without definite form, shape, or character: *On the potter's wheel, the wet,* amorphous *clay became a vase.* 2 *Chemistry* of a solid, lacking a definite crystalline structure, as glass or tar. —*adv-* a·morph′ous·ly. *n-* a·morph′ous·ness.

am·or·tize (ăm′ər tīz′) *vt-* [am·or·tized, am·or·tiz·ing] to pay off gradually (a debt, mortgage, charge, etc.) in installments. —*n-* am′or·ti·za′tion (-tə zā′shən).

A·mos (ā′məs) *n-* 1 in the Bible, a Hebrew prophet of the eighth century B.C. 2 a book of the Old Testament containing his prophecies.

a·mount (ə mount′) *n-* quantity or sum: *an amount of money; a small amount of sand.*

am·per·age (ăm′ pər ĭj) *n-* the strength of an electric current, measured in amperes.

am·pere (ăm′ pêr′) *n-* unit for measuring the rate at which electricity flows. One ampere equals a flow of one coulomb of electricity per second.

am·phib·i·ous (ăm fĭb′ē əs) *adj-* 1 able to live on land or in water: *an amphibious animal; an amphibious plant.* 2 able to operate on land or water: *an amphibious vehicle.* 3 carried out by the use of land, sea, and air military forces: *an amphibious attack.*

am·phi·the·a·ter or **am·phi·the·a·tre** (ăm′ fĭ thē′ə tər) *n-* 1 any round or oval theater with a central stage or arena around which rows of seats slope upward. 2 classroom or surgical operating room of this form. 3 a clearing closely surrounded by hills; a natural arena.

am·ple (ăm′ pəl) *adj-* 1 of large size or amount: *The ample rooms held all of the furniture.* 2 enough: *He has ample money on which to live comfortably.* 3 abundant; more than enough: *We have ample food for the trip and can easily share it with you.* —*adv-* am′ply.

am·pli·fi·ca·tion (ăm′ plə fə kā′shən) *n-* 1 an enlarging, extending, or supplementing: *an amplification of a report.* 2 the material or details so added. 3 in electronics, an increasing of the strength of an electric signal or current.

am·pli·fi·er (ăm′ plə fī′ər) *n-* 1 in electronics, an electrical circuit that magnifies an electrical impulse. 2 a component, as in a sound reproduction system, that contains such a circuit.

am·pli·fy (ăm′ plə fī′) *vt-* [am·pli·fied, am·pli·fy·ing] 1 to increase the strength of (sound or an electric current). 2 to add fuller details to; enlarge on: *Will you please amplify that statement?*

am·pli·tude (ăm′ plə tōōd′, -tyōōd′) *n-* 1 fullness and richness; abundance: *the amplitude of his generosity.* 2 *Physics* the perpendicular distance from the highest or lowest point in a wave to its center line; also, a similar distance from the highest to the lowest point in the swing of a pendulum.

Amplitude

am·pu·tate (ăm′ pyə tāt′) *vt-* [am·pu·tat·ed, am·pu·tat·ing] to cut off; especially, to remove (an arm, leg, etc.) surgically. —*n-* am′pu·ta′tion.

a·muck (ə mŭk′, -mŏk′) **run amuck** to rush about wildly, especially with intent to kill or destroy. Also **amok.**

am·u·let (ăm′ yə lət) *n-* charm or token worn as a protection against evil or harm.

a·muse (ə myōōz′) *vt-* [a·mused, a·mus·ing] to cause (a person or persons) to laugh and feel pleasure; entertain.

an (ən, ăn) *indefinite article-* used before vowel sounds. See *a.*

an·a·con·da (ăn′ə kŏn′də) *n-* very large tropical South American snake, sometimes 40 feet long, which crushes and kills its prey in its coils before swallowing it.

an·a·gram (ăn′ə grăm′) *n-* 1 word or phrase obtained by changing the order of the letters of another word or phrase. Example: "Live" is an anagram of "evil."

an·al·ge·sia (ăn′ əl jē′zē ə, -zhə) *n-* absence of pain, produced by a drug without loss of consciousness.
▶Should not be confused with ANESTHESIA.

an·al·ge·sic (ăn′ əl jē′ zĭk) *adj-* dulling or removing pain: *the analgesic effect of aspirin. n-* drug that does this: *Aspirin is an analgesic.*

a·nal·o·gous (ə năl′ ə gəs) *adj-* having resemblance;

corresponding in certain ways: *A bird's wing and a human arm are* analogous. —*adv-* a·nal′o·gous·ly.

a·nal·o·gy (ə năl′ ə jē′) *n-* [*pl.* a·nal·o·gies] partial agreement or likeness between two different things: *the analogy between an eye and a camera.*

a·nal·y·sis (ə năl′ ə səs) *n-* [*pl.* a·nal·y·ses (-sēz′)] 1 the division of anything into its parts to study it carefully: *An analysis of the plan proved that it was impractical.* 2 the testing of anything by laboratory methods to learn its nature or composition: *an analysis of drinking water; an analysis of a poison.* 3 psychoanalysis.

an·a·lyt·ic (ăn′ ə lĭt′ĭk) or **an·a·lyt·i·cal** (-ĭ kəl) *adj-* using or related to analysis: *an analytic mind; a course in analytical chemistry.* —*adv-* an·a·lyt′i·cal·ly.

an·a·lyze (ăn′ ə līz′) *vt-* [an·a·lyzed, an·a·lyz·ing] 1 to separate into parts or elements: *to analyze a chemical compound.* 2 to examine critically: *to analyze evidence; to analyze someone's character.* Also an′a·lyse′.

an·a·pest (ăn′ ə pĕst′) *n-* 1 measure or foot of poetry made up of two unaccented syllables followed by one accented syllable. 2 line of poetry made up of such measures. Example: "I am mon′/arch of all′/ I sur vey′." Also an′a·paest′. —*adj-* an′a·pes′tic.

an·arch·ist (ăn′ ər kĭst) *n-* 1 one who regards all government as evil and believes, as a political ideal, in living without any government. 2 any person who stirs up violent revolt against established rule. —*adj-* an′ar·chis′tic. *adv-* an′ar·chis′ti·cal·ly.

an·ar·chy (ăn′ ər kē) *n-* 1 absence of law and government. 2 confusion; disorder: *complete anarchy in the hall.* —*adj-* an·ar′chic (ăn är′ kĭk) or an·ar′chi·cal: *the anarchic life of the forty-niners. adv-* an·ar′chi·cal·ly.

a·nath·e·ma (ə năth′ ə mə) *n-* 1 solemn curse of the church, accompanied by expulsion from the church. 2 any strong denunciation or curse. 3 person or thing regarded with extreme dislike or loathing.

an·a·tom·i·cal (ăn′ ə tŏm′ ĭ kəl) or **an·a·tom·ic** (-tŏm′ ĭk) *adj-* relating to anatomy. —*adv-* an′a·tom′i·cal·ly.

a·nat·o·my (ə năt′ ə mē) *n-* [*pl.* a·nat·o·mies] 1 the physical structure of living things. 2 the science dealing with the physical structure of living things, especially involving the dissection of animals and plants to determine the location and relation of their various organs.

an·ces·tor (ăn′ sĕs tər) *n-* person from whom one is directly descended and who is usually of a generation before that of one's grandparents; forefather; forebear.

an·ces·try (ăn′ sĕs′ trē) *n-* [*pl.* an·ces·tries] line of one's descent traced back through parents, grandparents, etc.; also, one's ancestors.

an·chor (ăng′ kər) *n-* 1 any of various devices attached by a line to a ship, boat, buoy, float, etc., and lowered to the bottom to prevent drifting or other movement.

an·cho·rite (ăng′ kə rīt′) *n-* one who forsakes the world and lives alone for study, religious meditation, etc.; recluse; hermit.

an·cho·vy (ăn′ chō′ vē) *n-* [*pl.* an·cho·vies] very small Mediterranean herring, used in sauces and as an appetizer.

an·cient (ān′ shənt) *adj-* 1 belonging to times long past, especially to the times of the Greeks and the Romans: *an ancient coin bearing the profile of Alexander.* 2 very old: *an ancient tree.* 3 (as a humorous term) old-fashioned; out-of-date: *Where did you get that ancient hat?*

and (ən when unstressed; ănd when stressed) *conj-* (used to connect words, phrases, or clauses that have exactly the same function in a sentence or other construction): *I said once, and I repeat, that I will not go.*

an·ec·dote (ăn′ ək dōt′) *n-* brief story intended to amuse or instruct, often told about a famous person.

a·ne·mi·a (ə nē′ mē ə) *n-* physical condition in which there are too few red blood cells in the blood, caused by disease, diet deficiency, or bleeding. Also **anaemia.**

an·es·the·si·a (ăn′ əs thē′ zhə) *n-* partial or complete loss of feeling in the body or a part of it, caused by injury, disease, or an anesthetic; numbness. Also an′aes·the′si·a.

an·es·the·tize (ə nĕs′thə tīz′) *vt-* [**an·es·the·tized, an·es·the·tiz·ing**] to make incapable of feeling pain, usually by means of drugs, in preparation for surgery. Also **anaesthetize.**

a·new (ə nōō′, -nyōō′) *adv-* a second time; over again: *She had to learn to walk anew after the accident.*

an·gel (ān′ jəl) *n-* 1 spiritual being that is an attendant or messenger of God. 2 person thought of as very kind, good, or beautiful. 3 *Informal* person who provides the money to produce a play; financial backer.

an·ger (ăng′ gər) *n-* strong, hostile feeling stirred up by wrong or injury to oneself or to others; emotion that makes a person want to quarrel or fight; rage; wrath. *vt-* to make angry: *The nasty remark angered her.*

¹**an·gle** (ăng′ gəl) *vi-* [**an·gled, an·gling**] 1 to fish with hook and line. 2 to use tricks in obtaining something: *to angle for compliments.*
[from Old English **angul** meaning "fishhook."]

²**an·gle** (ăng′ gəl) *n-* 1 *Mathematics* geometric figure formed by two rays that have a common endpoint. Its size is measured in degrees. 2 corner; sharp edge. 3 *Informal* point of view. [from French **angle** of the same meaning, from Latin **angulus.**]

ACUTE RIGHT OBTUSE
Angles

an·gli·cize (ăng′ glə sīz′) *vt-* [**an·gli·cized, an·gli·ciz·ing**] to make (a word, phrase, pronunciation, etc.) seem natural or at home in the English language: *English has anglicized the French "chauffeur."*

an·gry (ăng′ grē) *adj-* [**an·gri·er, an·gri·est**] 1 feeling or showing rage or resentment: *an angry beast; an angry look.* 2 inflamed; red: *an angry wound.* —*adv-* **an′ gri·ly.**

an·guish (ăng′ gwish′) *n-* extreme suffering, especially of mind: *a mother's anguish over the death of her child.*

an·gu·lar (ăng′ gyə lər) *adj-* 1 having angles or points; sharp-cornered; not smooth or rounded: *an angular structure; an angular face.* 2 of or relating to a geometric angle or angles. 3 measured by a geometric angle: *an angular motion.*

an·hy·drous (ăn hī′ drəs) *adj-* not containing water, especially water of crystallization.

a·ni·line or **an·i·lin** (ăn′ ə lən) *n-* colorless, oily, liquid compound of carbon, nitrogen, and hydrogen derived from coal tar and used in the synthesis of dyes, medicines, and many other organic chemicals.

an·i·mal (ăn′ ə məl) *n-* 1 living being that can feel and move about spontaneously, as a man, dog, sparrow, fish, snake, fly, or the like. 2 any mammal other than man, such as a dog, monkey, or horse. *adj-* 1 relating to animals: *the animal kingdom.* 2 like or characteristic of an animal: *the child's animal spirits.*

¹**an·i·mate** (ăn′ ə māt′) *vt-* [**an·i·mat·ed, an·i·mat·ing**] to give life to; inspire with energy or activity; enliven: *Joy animates his face.*

²**an·i·mate** (ăn′ ə mət) *adj-* alive: *Biology deals with animate beings.*

an·i·mat·ed (ăn′ ə mā′ təd) *adj-* 1 full of life; lively; vivacious. 2 made to seem alive and moving: *an animated doll.* —*adv-* **an′ i·mat′ ed·ly.**

an·i·ma·tion (ăn′ ə mā′ shən) *n-* 1 liveliness; spirit; life. 2 the process of preparing drawings to be filmed as animated cartoons.

an·i·mos·i·ty (ăn′ ə mŏs′ ə tē) *n-* [*pl.* **an·i·mos·i·ties**] hostility; hatred; enmity.

an·i·mus (ăn′ ə məs) *n-* feeling of dislike; ill will; enmity; animosity: *He displayed considerable animus toward his rival.*

an·i·on (ăn′ ī′ ən) *n-* ion with a negative electrical charge due to the gain of one or more electrons.

an·ise (ăn′ əs) *n-* 1 plant cultivated for its spicy seeds, which are used in medicine and as flavoring. 2 (also **an′ i·seed**) the seed of this plant.

an·kle (ăng′ kəl) *n-* 1 the joint connecting the foot with the leg. 2 slender part of the leg just above this joint.

an·klet (ăng′ klət) *n-* 1 a sock which reaches just above the ankle. 2 bracelet worn around the ankle.

an·nal·ist (ăn′ ə list) *n-* person who records events as they occur year by year. *Hom-* analyst.

an·nals (ăn′ əlz) *n- pl.* 1 an account or history of events as they happen, written or issued year by year: *The annals of the academy are published regularly.* 2 records; history: *the annals of ancient Rome.*

an·neal (ə nēl′) *vt-* 1 to heat and then cool slowly, so as to make less brittle: *to anneal glass; to anneal steel.* 2 to toughen or temper: *to anneal the mind against hardships.*

¹**an·nex** (ə nĕks′) *vt-* to unite, as a smaller thing to a greater: *to annex a province to a kingdom.*

²**an·nex** (ăn′ ĕks) *n-* an extra building, or addition to a building, that is used for a related purpose: *the annex of a library.*

an·nex·a·tion (ăn′ ĭk sā′ shən) *n-* act of adding or attaching; addition: *the annexation of Gaul to the Roman Empire.*

an·ni·hi·late (ə nī′ ə lāt′) *vt-* [**an·ni·hi·lat·ed, an·ni·hi·lat·ing**] to destroy completely; wipe out: *to annihilate an army.* —*n-* **an·ni′ hi·la′ tion.**

an·ni·ver·sa·ry (ăn′ ə vûr′ sə rē) *n-* [*pl.* **an·ni·ver·sa·ries**] yearly occurrence of the date on which something happened in some previous year, especially a marriage. *as modifier:* *an anniversary gift.*

an·no·tate (ăn′ ə tāt′, ăn′ ō-) *vt-* [**an·no·tat·ed, an·no·tat·ing**] to make notes upon, by way of comment or criticism: *to annotate a book.*

an·nounce (ə nouns′) *vt-* [**an·nounced, an·nounc·ing**] 1 to give formal notice of; make known: *to announce an engagement; to announce a guest.* 2 on radio and television, to act as an announcer for (a program, commercial, etc.): *He announces ball games.* *vi-* to be a radio or television announcer.

an·nounce·ment (ə nouns′ mənt) *n-* 1 act of announcing or declaring. 2 public notice or advertisement: *an announcement in a newspaper.*

an·noy (ə noi′) *vt-* to vex or bother; irritate.

an·noy·ance (ə noi′ əns) *n-* 1 feeling of being bothered or vexed: *to express annoyance because of noise.* 2 thing that annoys: *The buzzing of the mosquito is an annoyance.* 3 act of bothering or vexing: *The annoyance of mosquitoes kept me awake.*

an·nu·al (ăn′ yōō əl) *adj-* 1 done, happening, etc., once a year; yearly: *an annual banquet; an annual bulletin.* 2 in or for the year: *an annual wage of $7,000; an average annual rainfall of 20 inches.* 3 taking a year to complete: *the annual course of the sun.*

an·nu·i·ty (ə nōō′ ə tē, ə nyōō′-) *n-* [*pl.* **an·nu·i·ties**] money paid out periodically to a person for life or for a certain number of years.

an·nul (ə nŭl′) *vt-* [**an·nulled, an·nul·ling**] to abolish or do away with (a law, decree, or compact): *to annul a marriage.* —*n-* **an·nul′ ment:** *the annulment of a contract.*

an·nu·lar (ăn′ yə lər) *adj-* made of rings or shaped like a ring.

an·o·dyne (ăn′ ə dīn′) *n-* 1 a drug that relieves pain. 2 something that calms or soothes: *Her calm voice was an anodyne to the frightened child.*

a·noint (ə noint′) *vt-* 1 to cover with oil or an oily substance: *to anoint one's body with suntan lotion.* 2 to apply oil to, especially as a sacred rite: *to anoint a king; to annoint a sick man.* —*n-* **a·noint′ ment.**

a·nom·a·ly (ə nŏm′ ə lē) *n-* [*pl.* **a·nom·a·lies**] anything differing from the usual or normal; irregularity; abnormality: *A winter thunderstorm is an anomaly.* —*adj-* **a·nom′ a·lous:** *She has anomalous tastes.*

a·non (ə nŏn′) *adv-* 1 soon; in a little while. 2 at another time; again: *About that, more anon.*

an·o·nym·i·ty (ăn′ ə nĭm′ ə tē) *n-* condition of being anonymous: *the anonymity of many kindly deeds.*

a·non·y·mous (ə nŏn′ ə məs) *adj-* 1 not known by name; an anonymous author. 2 without the doer's name; of unknown origin: *an anonymous poem; an anonymous phone call.* 3 lacking individuality; not identifiable with an individual: *rows of anonymous houses.* —*adv-* **a·non′ y·mous·ly.** *n-* **a·non′ y·mous·ness.**

an·oth·er (ə nŭth′ ər) *determiner* (traditionally called adjective or pronoun) 1 one more; an additional: *He took another sip, and then another.*

an·swer (ăn′sər) *n-* 1 response or reply: *I'll give him my answer tomorrow.* 2 solution to any problem: *an answer in subtraction; an answer to a person's dilemma.* *vt-* 1 to speak, write, or act in reply to: *to answer a question; to answer a telephone; to answer a threat.* 2 to be suitable for; fulfill: *This tool answers the purpose.*

an·swer·a·ble (ăn′sər ə bəl) *adj-* 1 accountable; responsible: *An adult should be answerable for his conduct.* 2 such as can be answered or disproved: *an answerable argument.*

ant (ănt) *n-* any of a group of small winged or wingless insects that live in organized communities in underground tunnels, decayed logs, or nests.

Ant

ant·ac·id (ănt′ăs′əd) *n-* remedy for an acid stomach.

an·tag·o·nism (ăn tăg′ə nĭz′ əm) *n-* 1 strong feeling of dislike expressed in some way. 2 active opposition.

an·tag·o·nist (ăn tăg′ə nĭst) *n-* one who fights or competes with another for the same object, in sports, politics, battle, etc.; an opponent; adversary.

an·tag·o·nize (ăn tăg′ə nĭz′) *vt-* [an·tag·o·nized, an·tag·o·niz·ing] to make unfriendly or hostile: *Her rudeness antagonizes everyone she meets.*

ant·arc·tic (ănt′ är′ tĭk, -ärk′ tĭk) *adj-* 1 opposite to the north polar, or arctic, regions. 2 located in, or relating to, the south polar regions.

ant·eat·er (ănt′ ēt′ ər) *n-* 1 any of several toothless Central and South American mammals with long slender snouts and very long sticky tongues used to feed on ants and termites. 2 any ant-eating animal.

an·te·ced·ent (ăn′ tə sē′ dənt) *n-* 1 someone or something that goes before or precedes: *the antecedents of war.* 2 *Grammar* a noun, pronoun, etc., later referred to by a pronoun. In the sentence, "James played football until he hurt his leg," "James" is the antecedent of "he."

an·te·cham·ber (ăn′ tĭ chăm′ bər) *n-* room leading into a principal room or apartment; waiting room.

an·te·date (ăn′ tə dāt′) *vt-* [an·te·dat·ed, an·te·dat·ing] 1 to occur at an earlier time than: *Sailing ships antedated steamships.* 2 to mark with an earlier date than the correct one: *to antedate a check.*

an·te·di·lu·vi·an (ăn′ tə dĭ lōō′ vē ən) *adj-* belonging to or having to do with the time before the Flood; hence, ancient; antiquated: *an antediluvian idea.* *n-* old or old-fashioned person.

Antelope, about 2 1/2 ft high at shoulder

an·te·lope (ăn′ tə lōp′) *n-* 1 any of a group of deerlike animals of Africa and Asia, including the gazelle, impala, kudu, and eland. 2 pronghorn of western North America, though not a true antelope.

an·ten·na (ăn tĕn′ ə) *n-* 1 [*pl.* an·ten·nae (-tĕn′ ē)] one of the pair of long, fragile, sensitive feelers on the heads of insects and crustaceans. 2 [*pl.* an·ten·nas] a metallic device, such as a coil of wire or a metal framework, for transmitting or receiving radio, television signals.

1 Television antenna
2 Antennae of insect

an·te·pe·nult (ăn′ tĭ pē′ nŭlt′) *n-* the syllable before the penult; the third syllable from the end of a word. In the word "al ter a tion," the antepenult is "ter."

an·te·ri·or (ăn tēr′ ē ər) *adj-* 1 fore; toward the front: *an anterior lobe of the brain.* 2 prior; occurring earlier: *The American Revolution was anterior to the French Revolution.*

an·te·room (ăn′ tĭ rōōm′) *n-* a room leading into another; antechamber.

an·them (ăn′ thəm) *n-* 1 piece of sacred music, usually

a passage from the Bible set to music. 2 song of praise or triumph: *a national anthem.*

an·ther (ăn′ thər) *n-* in a flower, the part of the stamen which produces the pollen.

ant hill *n-* mound of earth piled up by ants at the entrances to their tunnels.

an·thol·o·gist (ăn thŏl′ ə jĭst) *n-* one who gathers the material for an anthology.

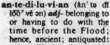

ANTHER
STAMEN
FILAMENT
Anther

an·thol·o·gy (ăn thŏl′ ə jē) *n-* [*pl.* an·thol·o·gies] collection of poems or prose passages from various authors.

an·thra·cite (ăn′ thrə sīt′) *n-* a very hard coal that burns with little smoke or flame; hard coal.

an·thrax (ăn′ thrăks′) *n-* a highly infectious, usually fatal, disease of cattle and sheep, in which boils form on their skin and lungs. It may also infect people who have worked with diseased animals or their hides.

an·thro·poid (ăn′ thrə poid′) *adj-* manlike; resembling man: *The chimpanzee is an anthropoid ape.* *n-* one of the higher apes resembling man, such as the gorilla.

an·thro·pol·o·gy (ăn′ thrə pŏl′ ə je) *n-* the science that deals with man, his origin, physical and cultural development, ways of living, language, customs, beliefs, etc. —*adj-* an·thro·po·log′ic (-pə lŏj′ĭk) or an′ thro·po·log′ical. *adv-* an′ thro·po·log′i·cal·ly.

an·ti·air·craft (ăn′ tē âr′ krăft′, ăn′ tī-) *adj-* used in defense against attack by enemy aircraft: *an anti-aircraft gun.*

an·tic (ăn′ tĭk) *adj-* odd and comical; fantastic: *an antic disposition.* *n-* (usually antics) comical trick; prank; caper: *the antics of a puppy.*

an·tic·i·pate (ăn tĭs′ ə pāt′) *vt-* [an·tic·i·pat·ed, an·tic·i·pat·ing] 1 to look forward to: *We anticipate a good time at the picnic.* 2 to foresee (a desire, question, etc.) and act or be ready to act: *I had anticipated the questions and was ready for them.* 3 to be ahead of (someone in some attempt): *The Vikings anticipated Columbus in the discovery of America.*

an·ti·cli·max (ăn′ tĭ klī′ măks′) *n-* an abrupt falling from the important or dignified to the trivial or absurd; a sudden letdown after a point of high interest or excitement: *The villain's reform in the last scene of the play was an anticlimax.* —*adj-* an′ ti·cli·mac′ tic: *an anticlimactic last scene.*

an·ti·dote (ăn′ tə dōt′) *n-* 1 medicine which counteracts a poison. 2 any remedy: *Work is an antidote to trouble.*

an·ti·mo·ny (ăn′ tə mō′ nē) *n-* dense, brittle, silvery-white metallic element used in alloys, especially in printers' type metal and in pewter. Symbol Sb, At. No. 51, At. Wt. 121.75.

an·ti·quat·ed (ăn′ tə kwā′ təd) *adj-* old-fashioned; out-of-date: *the woman's antiquated clothes; antiquated ideas.*

an·tique (ăn tēk′) *adj-* belonging to an earlier period: *an antique vase; an antique car.* *n-* art object or piece of furniture of a former period; especially, in the United States, something made before 1830. *vt-* [an·tiqued, an·ti·quing] to give the appearance of being old: *to antique a chair.*

an·tiq·ui·ty (ăn tĭk′ wə tē) *n-* [*pl.* an·tiq·ui·ties] 1 the early ages, especially before the Middle Ages: *The pyramids are a relic of antiquity.* 2 great age: *the antiquity of the castle.* 3 antiquities relics that throw light upon ancient times: *Chinese antiquities in a museum.*

an·ti·sep·tic (ăn′ tə sĕp′ tĭk) *n-* substance or preparation used to destroy harmful germs; disinfectant. *adj-* 1 having the power to destroy harmful germs. 2 free of harmful germs; sterile. —*adv-* an′ ti·sep′ ti·cal·ly.

an·ti·so·cial (ăn′ tĭ sō′ shəl, ăn′ tī′-) *adj-* 1 opposed to the good of society: *Robbery is an antisocial act.* 2 unwilling or unable to get along with one's fellows; not sociable: *He's a good citizen, but somewhat antisocial.*

an·tith·e·sis (ăn tĭth′ ə sĭs) *n-* [*pl.* an·tith·e·ses (-sēz′)] 1 exact opposite: *Hope is the antithesis of despair.* 2 opposition; contrast: *an antithesis of ideas.* 3 expression that emphasizes contrast. Example: "Give me liberty, or give me death."

an·ti·tox·in (ăn′ tĭ tŏk′ sĭn) *n-* substance produced by the body to neutralize a poison (toxin) from a disease germ; also, a serum made from the blood of animals that have been injected with germ poison.

an·to·nym (ăn′ tə nĭm′) *n-* word that means the opposite of another word. The antonym of "hard" is "soft."

a·nus (ā′ nəs) *n-* opening at the lower end of the large intestine, through which waste passes from the body.

an·vil (ăn′ vĭl) *n-* **1** block of iron on which metals are hammered and shaped. **2** the middle one of three tiny, sound-transmitting bones in the middle ear (for picture, see ¹*ear*).

Anvil

anx·i·e·ty (ăng zī′ə tē) *n-* [*pl.* **anx·i·e·ties**)] **1** feeling of uncertainty or uneasiness about the future; worry: *The anxiety of the sailors increased as the wind rose.* **2** something that causes this: *His illness is one of my anxieties.* **3** eager desire tinged with fear: *his anxiety to play music well.*

anx·ious (ăngk′ shəs, ăng′ shəs) *adj-* **1** worried; deeply troubled: *to be anxious about money.* **2** eager; wishing very strongly. —*adv-* **anx′ ious·ly.** *n-* **anx′ ious·ness.**
►EAGER has a positive force. *He was eager to go,* means that he wanted very much to go.

an·y (ĕn′ ē) *determiner* (traditionally called adjective or sometimes pronoun) **1** one of several, but no matter which: *You may have any book here.* **2** some (used with a negative or in a question): *I haven't any time. Do you have any ginger ale? No, I haven't any.* **3** every: *I did what any man would do.*

an·y·thing (ĕn′ ē thĭng′) *pron-* a thing of any sort. *adv-* in any way; at all: *Is this anything like yours?* **anything but** *Informal* certainly not.

an·y·way (ĕn′ ē wā′) *adv-* nevertheless; in any case: *I know I shouldn't spend that money, but I'll do it anyway.*

an·y·where (ĕn′ ē hwâr′) *adv-* **1** in or at any place: *Put the book anywhere.* **2** in or to any degree: *I haven't anywhere near a hundred dollars.* *n-* any place: *tourists from anywhere and everywhere.*

a·or·ta (ā ôr′ tə) *n-* main artery of man and other mammals. It arches backward from the top of the heart to the lower body, carrying blood everywhere except to the lungs. For picture, see *heart.*

a·part (ə pärt′) *adv-* **1** separately in time or place: *They live apart.* **2** in or into pieces: *It fell apart.*

a·part·ment (ə pärt′ mənt) *n-* room or group of rooms for a single household and, generally, located in a large building.

ap·a·thet·ic (ăp′ ə thĕt′ ĭk) *adj-* without interest; indifferent: *The child was apathetic toward all attempts to amuse him.* —*adv-* **ap·a·thet′ i·cal·ly.**

ap·a·thy (ăp′ ə thē) *n-* [*pl.* **ap·a·thies**] lack of feeling or interest; indifference: *to arouse a person from apathy.*

ape (āp) *n-* **1** long-armed tailless monkey such as the chimpanzee, gibbon, gorilla, or orang-utan. **2** person who mimics or imitates. *vt-* [**aped, ap·ing**] to mimic or imitate: *The boys aped the circus clown's actions.* —*adj-* **ape′ like′.**

ap·er·ture (ăp′ ər chər) *n-* **1** hole; gap: *an aperture in the stone wall.* **2** opening through which light passes into a camera or other optical instrument.

a·pex (ā′ pĕks′) *n-* [**a·pex·es** or **a·pi·ces** (ā′ pə sēz′)] peak or summit: *the apex of a triangle; the apex of his career.*

a·pha·si·a (ə fā′ zhə, -zē ə) *n-* loss of the ability to speak, read, write, or to understand, usually caused by brain injury.

a·phe·lion (ă fēl′ yən, -ē ən) *n-* the farthest point from the sun in the orbit of a planet or planetoid.

a·phid (ā′ fĭd, ăf′ ĭd) *n-* tiny green insect that infests plants and sucks their sap; plant louse. Also called **a′ phis** [*pl.* **a·phid·es** (ā′ fə dēz′)].

Aphid

a·phor·ism (ăf′ ə rĭz′ əm) *n-* short, concise statement expressing a truth; proverb; maxim; adage. Example: A penny saved is a penny earned.

a·pi·ar·y (ā′ pē ĕr′ē) *n-* [*pl.* **a·pi·ar·ies**] place where bees are kept; also, a collection of beehives.

a·piece (ə pēs′) *adv-* for each one; each: *The pencils cost five cents apiece. Give them an orange apiece.*

a·plomb (ə plŏm′, -plŭm′) *n-* assurance; self-confidence; poise: *He faced the crisis with his usual aplomb.*

a·poc·a·lypse (ə pŏk′ ə lĭps′) *n-* **1** any disclosure or revelation of the future; prophecy. **2** **Apocalypse** the last book of the New Testament; Revelation. —*adj-* **a·poc′ a·lyp′ tic:** *an apocalyptic vision.*

ap·o·gee (ăp′ ə jē′) *n-* farthest point from the earth in the orbit of a satellite.

a·pol·o·gize (ə pŏl′ ə jīz′) *vi-* [**a·pol·o·gized, a·pol·o·giz·ing**] **1** to express regret for something; say one is sorry: *I apologize for troubling you.* **2** to offer an excuse: *There's no need to apologize for a hearty appetite.*

a·pol·o·gy (ə pŏl′ ə jē) *n-* [*pl.* **a·pol·o·gies**] **1** an excuse or expression of regret for something one has said or done: *He made an apology for being noisy.* **2** something spoken, written, or offered in defense: *an apology for communism.* **3** poor substitute; makeshift: *This drawing is only an apology for a map.*

ap·o·plex·y (ăp′ ə plĕk′ sē) *n-* sudden loss of consciousness and the power to feel or move caused by the breaking of a blood vessel in the brain; a stroke.

a·pos·tate (ə pŏs′ tāt′) *n-* one who has forsaken his faith or party: *a Republican apostate.*

a·pos·tle (ə pŏs′ əl) *n-* **1** one of the twelve men chosen by Jesus to teach his gospel to the world. **2** leader of any movement: *an apostle of nonviolence.*

¹a·pos·tro·phe (ə pŏs′ trə fē′) *n-* punctuation mark (′) used to show: (1) contraction of two words. Example: I'll for I will. (2) omission of one or more letters from a word. Example: ev'r for ever; '49 for 1849. (3) the possessive case of nouns.

a·pos·tro·phize (ə pŏs′ trə fīz′) *vt-* [**a·pos·tro·phized, a·pos·tro·phiz·ing**] to address an apostrophe to: *The mayor apostrophized freedom in his Fourth of July speech.* *vi-: He apostrophized for forty minutes.*

apothecaries′ weight *n-* system of weights used to weigh drugs.

a·poth·e·car·y (ə pŏth′ə kĕr′ ē) *n-* [*pl.* **a·poth·e·car·ies**] one who prepares and sells medicines and drugs; pharmacist; druggist.

ap·o·thegm (ăp′ ə thĕm′) *n-* short, pointed saying or proverb; aphorism; maxim. Example: Haste makes waste.

ap·pall or **ap·pal** (ə pôl′) *vt-* [**ap·palled, ap·pal·ing**] to frighten; shock; dismay: *The danger of war appalled us.*

ap·pal·ling (ə pôl′ ĭng) *adj-* causing, or filling with, terror and dismay; terrifying; shocking: *an appalling number of victims.* —*adv-* **ap·pal′ ing·ly.**

ap·pa·ra·tus (ăp′ ə răt′ əs, ăp′ ə rā′ təs) *n-* [*pl.* **ap·pa·ra·tus** or **ap·pa·ra·tus·es**] **1** equipment, instruments, etc., put together for a special purpose: *laboratory apparatus; gymnasium apparatus.* **2** group of bodily organs: *our digestive apparatus.*

ap·par·el (ə pâr′ əl) *n-* clothing; dress: *boys′ apparel.* *vt-* to clothe; fit out.

ap·par·ent (ə pâr′ ənt, ə pâr′ ənt) *adj-* **1** easily understood; evident; obvious: *It is quite apparent that he is sick.* **2** appearing or seeming rather than true or real: *His apparent remorse fooled us.* —*adv-* **ap·par′ ent·ly.**

ap·pa·ri·tion (ăp′ ə rĭsh′ ən) *n-* **1** ghost or phantom: *He does not believe in apparitions.* **2** something startling or unusual that suddenly appears: *the apparition of the black ship as the fog lifted.*

ap·peal (ə pēl′) *vi-* **1** to make a plea (for); request: *The committee appealed for funds.* **2** to be interesting or attractive (to): *Both classical music and jazz appeal to me.* *vt-* to transfer or refer to a superior court or judge: *to appeal a case.*

ap·pear (ə pēr′) *vi-* **1** to come into sight: *The first flowers appeared above the snow.* **2** to seem: *The book appears to have been used many times.* **3** to come before the public: *That actor appeared in a new play.*

ap·pear·ance (ə pēr′ əns) *n-* **1** a coming into view; appearing: *A bear made a sudden appearance.* **2** outward aspect; look; bearing: *He has the appearance of a good runner.* **3** outward show; semblance: *to keep up an appearance of wealth; an appearance of modesty.*

ap·pease (ə pēz′) *vt-* [ap·peased, ap·peas·ing] 1 to make calm or peaceful; quiet: *His gentle words appeased the angry crowd.* 2 to satisfy: *to appease hunger; to appease curiosity.* 3 to pacify with concessions, usually contrary to one's principles.

ap·pel·late (ə pěl′ ət) *adj-* dealing with appeals from lower court decisions: *an appellate court*; *appellate judge*; *appellate jurisdiction.*

ap·pel·la·tion (ăp′ ə lā′ shən) *n-* name or title by which a person or thing is described or known: *One appellation of Pennsylvania is the "Keystone State."*

ap·pend (ə pěnd′) *vt-* to add to; attach: *to append a signature; to append a seal.*

ap·pend·age (ə pěn′ dĭj) *n-* 1 something added or attached to, hanging from, or accompanying a greater or more important thing. 2 *Biology* a limb, tail, horn, or other secondary part attached to the head or body of an animal.

ap·pen·di·ci·tis (ə pěn′ də sī′ təs) *n-* inflammation of the vermiform appendix.

ap·pen·dix (ə pěn′ dĭks) *n-* [*pl.* ap·pen·dix·es or ap·pen·dic·es (-də sēz′)] 1 section of additional related information at the end of a book or other writing. 2 appendage.

ap·per·tain (ăp′ ər tān′) *vi-* 1 to belong by right, nature, or custom: *These lands appertain to the abbey. The right to vote appertains to all citizens.* 2 to relate (to): *These experiments appertain to biochemistry.*

ap·pe·tite (ăp′ ə tīt′) *n-* 1 desire for food. 2 strong and active liking or desire: *an appetite for reading.*

ap·pe·tiz·er (ăp′ ə tī′ zər) *n-* 1 food or drink served before a meal to stimulate the desire for food. 2 anything that arouses interest in things to follow.

ap·pe·tiz·ing (ăp′ ə tī′zĭng) *adj-* exciting or pleasing the appetite: *a buffet of appetizing dishes.*

ap·plaud (ə plôd′) *vt-* 1 to express approval or enjoyment of, especially by clapping the hands: *The audience applauded the pianist's performance.* 2 to admire: *I applaud your courage. vi-:* *Everyone applauded.*

ap·plause (ə plôz′) *n-* 1 a clapping of the hands to show approval or appreciation. 2 admiration: *courage worthy of applause.*

ap·ple (ăp′ əl) *n-* 1 the rounded fleshy fruit of a tree common throughout the middle latitudes. 2 the tree itself. 3 (also ap′ple·wood′) the wood of this tree.

Apple

ap·pli·ance (ə plī′ əns) *n-* article or device for some special use or purpose, such as an electric iron or a washing machine.

ap·pli·ca·ble (ăp′ lĭ kə bəl, *also* ə plĭk′-) *adj-* of a nature that permits using or applying; relevant; appropriate: *That rule is not applicable in this case.* —*n-* ap′pli·ca·bil′ i·ty.

ap·pli·cant (ăp′ lə kənt) *n-* one who asks or applies for something; candidate: *an applicant for a position.*

ap·pli·ca·tion (ăp′ lə kā′ shən) *n-* 1 request made personally or in writing: *an application for a job; a letter of application.* 2 a putting something to use: *the application of astronomy to navigation.* 3 connection; relationship (to); relevance (to): *The preceding witness's testimony has no application to the case.*

ap·plied (ə plīd′) *adj-* 1 put to practical use; utilitarian as distinct from theoretical or abstract: *a textbook of applied mathematics; applied religion.* 2 having been put on or over: *a newly applied coat of paint.*

ap·ply (ə plī′) *vt-* [ap·plied, ap·ply·ing] 1 to cover with; put on: *to apply a bandage.* 2 to put into use or practice: *to apply one's training to a task.* 3 to devote (oneself) to a particular purpose: *You should apply yourself to your studies. vi-* 1 to make a request: *to apply for a job; to apply for a loan.* 2 to have reference; be suitable or fit: *The new law does not apply to this case.*

ap·point (ə point′) *vt-* 1 to name or choose for an office or position: *The basketball team appointed him captain.* 2 to fix by agreement; decide on: *The judge appointed Tuesday as the day of the trial.*

ap·point·ment (ə point′ mənt) *n-* 1 a naming or appointing to an office; a choosing: *The appointment of a city manager was delayed.* 2 the office or position itself:

He held a key appointment in the government. 3 agreement to be at a certain place or to meet someone; engagement: *an appointment with the dentist at 5 o'clock.*

ap·por·tion (ə pôr′ shən) *vt-* to divide and distribute; allot: *to apportion the profits among the partners.*

ap·prais·al (ə prā′ zəl) *n-* 1 the setting of a value or price. 2 the value assigned; valuation: *The appraisal of the painting was too high.*

ap·praise (ə prāz′) *vt-* [ap·praised, ap·prais·ing] to estimate or fix the value or price of: *to appraise a man's worth; to appraise land for taxation.* —*n-* ap·prais′ er. ►Should not be confused with APPRISE (APPRIZE).

ap·pre·cia·ble (ə prē′ shə bəl) *adj-* large or important enough to be seen or felt; noticeable: *an appreciable improvement.* —*adv-* ap·pre′ cia·bly.

ap·pre·ci·ate (ə prē′ shē āt′) *vt-* [ap·pre·ci·at·ed, ap·pre·ci·at·ing] 1 to realize the worth of; hold in high regard; value; enjoy: *I really appreciate a hot drink on a cold night.* 2 to be grateful for: *We appreciate your help.* 3 to judge the worth of; enjoy intelligently: *to appreciate music or poetry.*

ap·pre·ci·a·tion (ə prē′ shē ā′ shən) *n-* 1 understanding and approval: *the appreciation of music.* 2 an increasing, especially of money value: *the appreciation of his government bonds.* 3 a critical judgement; critique: *We asked the expert for an appreciation of our work.*

ap·pre·hend (ăp′ rĭ hěnd′) *vt-* 1 to arrest; seize. 2 to grasp with the mind; understand thoroughly: *He fully apprehended what he read.* 3 to forsee with fear: *Mother apprehended the danger of driving on icy roads.*

ap·pre·hen·sive (ăp′ rĭ hěn′ sĭv) *adj-* fearful; worried; uneasy about an outcome, a person's safety, etc.: *Jerry was apprehensive about his test marks.* —*adv-* ap·pre·hen′sive·ly. *n-* ap′pre·hen′sive·ness: *The apprehensiveness of a wild animal.*

ap·pren·tice (ə prěn′ təs) *n-* 1 person who is learning a trade or craft by practical experience under a skilled worker. 2 formerly, one bound by an agreement to work for a definite length of time in return for his training. 3 novice, or one slightly versed in anything.

ap·prise (ə prīz′) *vt-* [ap·prised, ap·pris·ing] to give notice to; warn; inform: *I apprised him of danger.* Also **ap·prize**′. ►Should not be confused with APPRAISE.

ap·proach (ə prōch′) *vi-* to come or draw near: *Winter is approaching. vt-* 1 to come near to; to move toward: *We are approaching the city.* 2 to come close to but never reach; approximate: *to approach perfection.* 3 to deal with or treat. 4 to make proposals to: *When is the best time to approach him?*

ap·proach·a·ble (ə prō′ chə bəl) *adj-* 1 located so that it can be approached; accessible: *a mountain peak approachable from the north side.* 2 easy to approach: *a friendly, approachable man.* —*n-* ap·proach′ a·bil′ i·ty.

ap·pro·ba·tion (ăp′ rə bā′ shən) *n-* the expressing of a favorable opinion; approval: *She found it difficult to earn her aunt's approbation.*

¹**ap·pro·pri·ate** (ə prō′ prē ət) *adj-* fitting; suitable: *That dress is hardly appropriate for a formal dance.* —*adv-* ap·pro′ pri·ate·ly. *n-* ap·pro′ pri·ate·ness: *Its appropriateness is highly questionable.*

²**ap·pro·pri·ate** (ə prō′ prē āt′) *vt-* [ap·pro·pri·at·ed, ap·pro·pri·at·ing] 1 to set aside for a particular use: *The government appropriated money for road improvement.* 2 to take and use for onself: *The escaped convicts appropriated the farmer's car.*

ap·prov·al (ə prōō′ vəl) *n-* 1 favorable acceptance or agreement: *News of the extra holiday was hailed with approval.* 2 official consent: *The governor gave his approval to the bill.*

ap·prove (ə prōōv′) *vt-* [ap·proved, ap·prov·ing] to speak or think well (of): *I cannot approve of his new friends. vt-* to agree or give official consent to: *Congress approved the bill after heated debate.*

¹**ap·prox·i·mate** (ə prŏk′ sə mət) *adj-* not exact but nearly so; almost correct: *The approximate weight of a pint of milk is one pound.* —*adv-* ap·prox′ i·mate·ly.

²**ap·prox·i·mate** (ə prŏk′ sə māt′) *vt-* [ap·prox·i·mat·ed, ap·prox·i·mat·ing] to come near to; approach.

a·pri·cot (ăp′rə kŏt′, ā′ prə-) *n-* 1 small, round, orange-colored fruit with downy skin somewhat like a peach. 2 tree which bears this fruit. 3 a pale yellow-orange color. *adj-: an* apricot *pie; an* apricot *silk.*

a·pron (ā′ prən) *n-* 1 piece of wearing apparel, made of cloth, rubber, leather, etc., worn over the front of the body to protect clothing. 2 the area that lies in front: *the apron of a hangar; the apron of the stage.*

apt (ăpt) *adj-* 1 suitable; appropriate: *The "space age" is an apt name for the period we are living in.* 2 quick to learn: *He is an apt student of arithmetic.* 3 likely: *When in a hurry, anyone is apt to be careless.*

ap·ti·tude (ăp′ tə tōōd′, -tyōōd′) *n-* 1 talent; flair: *an* aptitude *for painting.* 2 natural ability, skill, or quickness to learn: *an aptitude for mathematics.*

aq·ua (ăk′ wə, äk′ -) *n-* 1 *Latin* water. 2 pale blue-green color; aquamarine.

a·quar·i·um (ə kwâr′ ē əm) *n-* [*pl.* a·quar·i·ums or a·quar·i·a] 1 tank, bowl, or artificial pond in which living water plants and water animals are kept. 2 place devoted to the care and exhibition of large collections of water plants and animals.

ar·bi·trar·y (är′ bə trĕr′ ē) *adj-* 1 ruled only by one's own wishes or ideas in making decisions; despotic: *He is an intelligent, but arbitrary, ruler.* 2 based on one's own opinions and wishes, not on any rule or law: *an arbitrary decision.* **—*adv-* ar′ bi·trar′ i·ly.**

ar·bi·tra·tion (är′ bə trā′ shən) *n-* way of settling a dispute in which the two sides submit their arguments to a third person or group for decision.

ar·bor (är′ bər) *n-* 1 bower formed by vines trained over a lattice: *a grape arbor.* 2 shaded nook or walk.

arc (ärk) *n-* 1 in geometry, a part of a circle. 2 in electronics, a band of light, often arched, produced by the flow of electricity across a gap separating two electrodes.

¹arch (ärch) *n-* 1 curved structure used in buildings, bridges, etc., for supporting a load over an open space by transferring the downward thrust of the load to the sides. 2 monument consisting of such a structure, and usually erected to celebrate a victory. 3 anything resembling such a structure.

Arches

ar·cha·ic (är kā′ ĭk) *adj-* 1 of language, no longer in use, except for a special purpose. Examples: methinks, thou, in sooth. 2 of ancient times: *He studied* archaic *Roman customs.*

ar·che·ol·o·gy (är′ kē ŏl′ ə jē) *n-* scientific study of the life of earlier peoples, based on the remains of their towns or villages, and on relics, such as weapons, utensils, or ornaments, found in these remains. Also **ar′ chae·ol′ o·gy.**

ar·chi·tec·ture (är′ kə tĕk′ chər) *n-* 1 the art and work of designing buildings and supervising their construction. 2 manner or style of building: *modern architecture; Greek architecture.*

ar·chive (är′ kīv′) *n-* 1 record preserved as evidence. 2 archives (1) the place in which public records or documents of historical value are kept. (2) these documents or records.

arc·tic (är′ tĭk, ärk′ tĭk) *adj-* having to do with the north polar regions: *white* arctic *animals; cold* arctic *winds.* *n-* 1 a high, warmly lined, waterproof overshoe. 2 **Arctic** the north polar region.

ar·dent (är′ dənt) *adj-* eager; enthusiastic; warm: *an* ardent *lover of music.* **—*adv-* ar′ dent·ly.**

ar·dor (är′ dər) *n-* great eagerness; passion; intensity of feeling: *an ardor for knowledge.*

ar·du·ous (är′ jōō əs) *adj-* difficult; hard to do; strenuous: *an arduous task.* **—*adv-* ar′ du·ous·ly.**

¹are (är) form of *be* used with "you," "we," "they," or plural noun subjects in the present tense.

ar·e·a (âr′ ē ə) *n-* 1 any surface, of land, a floor, etc. 2 measure of the surface of a piece of land or of a geometric figure or solid: *the area of the United States; the area of a sphere.* 3 region or district: *a mountainous area; an industrial area.* 4 range or scope of a subject, activity, etc.: *Tom's major area of study is physics.*

a·re·na (ə rē′ nə) *n-* 1 the enclosed space of a Roman amphitheater, in which fights between gladiators took place. 2 any scene or field where men compete: *the arena of politics.*

ar·got (är′ gŏt′, är′ gō′) *n-* the special slang of any group, especially in the underworld. [from French **argot,** the dialect of the Parisian underworld.]

ar·gue (är′ gyōō) *vi-* [ar·gued, ar·gu·ing] 1 to give reasons for or against something: *I argued for disarmament, and he argued against it.* 2 to dispute: *He and his brother always argued over politics.* *vt-* to persuade by giving reasons: *You've argued me into going.*

ar·gu·ment (är′ gyə mənt) *n-* 1 discussion in which reasons are given for or against something; debate: *an argument over whether movies should be censored or not.* 2 a dispute; verbal quarrel: *an argument about money.*

ar·id (ăr′ ĭd) *adj-* 1 dry; parched; having little or no rain: *the arid regions in the western United States.* 2 uninteresting: *an arid subject; an arid personality.*

a·rise (ə rīz′) *vi-* [a·rose (ə rōz′), a·ris·en (ə rĭz′ ən), a·ris·ing] 1 to rise; get up: *The spectators arose when the judge entered the courtroom.* 2 to move upward; ascend: *Clouds of smoke arose above the forest fire.* 3 to begin; start up.

ar·is·toc·ra·cy (ăr′ ə stŏk′ rə sē) *n-* [*pl.* ar·is·toc·ra·cies] 1 class of persons of high rank or noble birth; the nobility. 2 class of persons superior in ability, culture, or wealth. 3 government in which the nobles rule. 4 a state so governed.

¹a·rith·me·tic (ə rĭth′ mə tĭk′) *n-* branch of mathematics dealing with the properties and relationships of numbers and the computations with them; the art of using numbers to add, subtract, multiply, divide, etc.

¹arm (ärm) *n-* 1 in men, apes, and monkeys, one of the two upper limbs; especially, that part between shoulder and hand. 2 forelimb of any animal having a backbone. 3 any part extending from a main body: *the arms of a chair; an arm of the sea; an arm (ray) of a starfish.*

²arm (ärm) *vt-* 1 to equip with weapons: *In wartime the navy arms all cargo ships.* 2 to set (a fuse, detonator, etc.) to explode under certain conditions: *Pull this pin to arm the grenade.* *vi-* to prepare for war or other conflict:

ar·mor (är′ mər) *n-* 1 a covering to protect the body while fighting: *Battle armor used to be made of metal or leather.* 2 the steel plating of a warship. 3 any protective covering: *the armor of a turtle.* 4 military tank forces. *vt-* to provide with a protective covering: *The king armored them with shields and helmets.* *Faith armors him against fear.*

Chain and plate armor

ar·my (är′ mē) *n-* [*pl.* ar·mies] 1 the branch of a nation's military force that is responsible for warfare on land. 2 large number of persons or things; multitude: *an army of insects.*

a·ro·ma (ə rō′ mə) *n-* pleasant odor; fragrance.

a·round (ə round′) *prep-* (in senses 1, 2, 3, and 4, considered an adverb when the object is clearly implied but not expressed) 1 in a circle about: *They walked around the tree.* 2 on every side of; surrounding: *The police were stationed around the house.*

a·rouse (ə rouz′) *vt-* [a·roused, a·rous·ing] 1 to awaken: *The singing of the birds aroused her early this morning.* 2 to stir up; excite: *His troubles aroused our sympathy.*

ar·raign (ə rān′) *vt-* to summon (a prisoner) into court to answer a charge; accuse.

ar·range (ə rānj′) *vt-* [ar·ranged, ar·rang·ing] 1 to put in order: *The librarian arranged the books on the shelf.* 2 to come to an agreement about: *I am sure we can arrange a compromise.*

ar·ray (ə rā′) *n-* 1 orderly or formal arrangement: *troops in battle array.* 2 fine or imposing collection or display: *an array of silver; an array of talent.* 3 clothing, especially fine clothing: *The crowds were in holiday array.*

ar·rest (ə rĕst′) *vt-* to sieze or hold a person by authority

of the law: *The sheriff* arrested *him for stealing horses.*
2 to stop; bring to a stop: *to arrest a flow of water.* **n-**
1 seizure or holding of a person by authority of the law.
2 the act of checking or stopping: *the arrest of decay.*

ar·rive (ə rīv′) *vi-* [ar·rived, ar·riv·ing] to reach or come
to a place or condition: *to arrive in a city; to arrive at
a conclusion.*

ar·ro·gant (ăr′ə gənt) *adj-* overestimating one's importance or ability; haughty and overbearing. **—adv-**
ar′ro·gant·ly.

ar·row (ăr′ō) *n-* 1 slender
stick or shaft made to be
shot from a bow, usually
pointed at one end and having feathers at the other end
to guide it.

Arrow

ar·se·nal (ăr′sə nəl) *n-* 1 a building for storing, making,
or repairing military equipment of all kinds. 2 any
collection of weapons intended for use.

ar·se·nic (ăr′sə nĭk′) *n-* 1 poisonous, brittle, gray
metallic element. Its compounds are much used as
insect and pest killers. Symbol As, At. No. 33, At. Wt.
74.9216. 2 poison formed from arsenic compounds.

ar·son (ăr′sən) *n-* the intentional, and usually malicious,
act of setting fire to a building or other property.

¹**art** (ărt) *n-* 1 the study or creation of beautiful things, as
in painting, sculpture, music, etc.; fine art. 2 the work
produced by painters, sculptors, musicians, etc.

ar·te·ry (ăr′tə rē) *n-* [*pl.* ar·te·ries] 1 any of the tubes
in the body that carry blood from the heart to any part
of the body. 2 any main road or important channel:
The new highway is the main artery *of travel across the
state.*

ar·thri·tis (ăr thrī′təs) *n-* a disease in which the joints
of the body become inflamed and painful. **—adj-** ar-
thrit′ic (ăr thrĭt′ĭk).

ar·ti·choke (ăr′tə chōk′) *n-* 1 tall plant,
the flowering head of which is used as a
vegetable. 2 the vegetable itself.

ar·ti·cle (ăr′tə kəl) *n-* 1 prose composition, complete in itself, in a newspaper,
magazine, etc. 2 thing belonging to a
particular class of things: *an article of
clothing.* 3 single section of a written
document, as a clause of a contract, treaty,
creed, or the like.

Artichoke

²**ar·tic·u·late** (ăr tĭk′yə lət) *adj-* 1 spoken with distinct-
ness: *an articulate sentence.* 2 able to express oneself
clearly: *an articulate person.* 3 jointed. **—adv-** ar·tic′u·
late·ly. **n-** ar·tic′u·late·ness.

ar·ti·fact (ăr′tə făkt′) *n-* product of human skill or
workmanship, especially a simple product of primitive
art.

ar·ti·fi·cial (ăr′tə fĭsh′əl) *adj-* 1 made by man; not
occurring naturally: *a bouquet of* artificial *flowers;*
artificial *pearls.* 2 not natural; affected: *an artificial
way of speaking.* **—adv-** ar′ti·fi′cial·ly.

ar·til·ler·y (ăr tĭl′ə rē) *n-* 1 mounted guns, together with
their ammunition. 2 the branch of an army using these
guns. **—n-** ar·til′ler·y·man.

ar·ti·san (ăr′tə zən) *n-* man specially trained to work with
his hands, such as a bricklayer or carpenter.

art·ist (ăr′tĭst) *n-* 1 person who practices one of the fine
arts, especially a painter or sculptor. 2 in any field, a
person who shows creative power in his work.

art·less (ărt′ləs) *adj-* 1 without guile; natural; sincere:
the artless grace of her movements. 2 lacking skill or
art; clumsy: *That painting is an artless daub!* **—adv-**
art′less·ly. **n-** art′less·ness.

as (ăz) *adv-* 1 to the same degree or extent; equally: *This
paper is as good.* 2 for example; typically: *Some birds,
such as chickadees and crows, do not fly south for the
winter.*

as·bes·tos (ăs bĕs′təs, ăz-) *n-* a fibrous, unburnable
mineral, used in making fireproof materials.

as·cend (ə sĕnd′) *vt-* to climb or go up: *They ascended
a hill.* *vi-: They ascended slowly.*

as·cer·tain (ăs′ər tān′) *vt-* to find out definitely: *to

ascertain *the truth.* **—adj-** as′cer·tain′a·ble: *The truth
is not easily ascertainable.*

as·cet·ic (ə sĕt′ĭk) *n-* person who renounces the comforts
and pleasures of life and devotes himself to religious
duties; also, any person who practices self-denial.

²**ash** (ăsh) *n-* 1 what remains of a substance that has been
burned: *wood* ash; *volcanic* ash.

a·shamed (ə shāmd′) *adj-* 1 feeling shame, guilt,
embarrassment, etc.: *He didn't speak because he was
ashamed.* 2 fearing or reluctant to do something that
may bring about such feelings.

a·side (ə sīd′) *adv-* 1 to one side: *Pull the curtain* aside.
Step aside. 2 out of mind or consideration: *to put* aside
worries; all joking aside. 3 in reserve: *Please set these
books* aside *for me.*

ask (ăsk) *vt-* 1 to seek an answer to; also, to put a question
to: *He asked a question. The doctor asked her how old
she was.* 2 to beg or request: *to ask a favor.* 3 to inquire
about: *to ask the way.* 4 to invite: *I was asked to the
party.* 5 to claim; demand: *What price do you ask?*

a·skance (ə skăns′) *adv-* sidelong; to one side.

a·sleep (ə slēp′) *adj-* 1 sleeping: *He was asleep by nine
o'clock.* 2 without feeling; numb: *His foot was asleep.*

as·per·sion (ə spûr′zhən) *n-* 1 a damaging or untrue
remark about a person: *They cast* aspersions *on us.*
2 a sprinkling with holy water, in a religious service.

as·phalt (ăs′fôlt′) *n-* a sticky, black, petroleum tar used
for making roofs waterproof and, mixed with crushed
rock or gravel, for making road surfaces.

as·phyx·i·ate (ăs fĭk′sē āt′) *vt-* [as·phyx·i·at·ed, as-
phyx·i·at·ing] to kill or make unconscious by cutting
off the supply of air, replacing air with a harmful
substance, or the like; suffocate.

¹**as·pi·rate** (ăs′pə rāt′) *vt-* [as·pi·rat·ed, as·pi·rat·ing]
1 to pronounce with the sound of the letter "h": *We
aspirate the "h" in "horse" but not in "honor."* 2 to draw
(blood, fluids, or gases) from a body cavity by suction
with an aspirator.

as·pi·ra·tion (ăs′pə rā′shən) *n-* 1 strong desire; ambition: *He has* aspirations *to be a doctor.* 2 act of breathing;
also, a breath. 3 pronunciation of the letter "h," as in
"horse."

as·pire (ə spīər′) *vi-* [as·pired, as·pir·ing] to desire
eagerly; be filled with ambition for a particular thing:
Many politicians aspire *to be president.*

as·pi·rin (ăs′pə rĭn) *n-* a medicine for easing the pain
of colds, headaches, etc.

as·sail·ant (ə săl′ənt) *n-* person who makes an attack
or assault.

as·sas·sin (ə săs′ĭn) *n-* person who commits a sudden
and treacherous murder, usually for political reasons.

as·sault (ə sôlt′) *n-* violent attack, by physical force or
by force of words: *an assault on the enemy's camp; an
assault on the character of an opponent.* *vt-* to attack
violently; assail.

¹**as·say** (ăs′ā′) *n-* 1 act or process of analyzing a metallic
compound, ore, or alloy; especially the testing of gold
or silver coin or bullion to see if it is of standard purity.
2 the substance tested.

as·sem·ble (ə sĕm′bəl) *vt-* [as·sem·bled, as·sem·bling]
1 to bring together: *to assemble members of the party.*
2 to put together the parts of: *to assemble a motor.*
vi- to come together; meet: *The students assembled.*

as·sem·bly (ə sĕm′blē) *n-* [*pl.* as·sem·blies] 1 company
or people gathered together for a common purpose:
a student Assembly. 2 a legislative body: *the United
Nations* Assembly.

as·sent (ə sĕnt′) *n-* agreement; an accepting: *The
governor's assent is needed before the bill becomes law.*
vi- to agree; consent: *She assented to my request.*
Hom- ascent.

as·sert (ə sûrt′) *vt-* 1 to declare; state positively: *The
lawyer asserted that his client was innocent of the crime.*
2 to insist upon: *By revolting, the colonies asserted their
right to govern themselves.* 3 to put in force; enforce:
The tyrant asserted his authority over most of Europe.

as·sess (ə sĕs′) *vt-* 1 to fix or determine the amount of:
to assess the damages. 2 to fix or set (a tax), as on

as·set (ăs′ĕt) *n*- 1 anything of value that belongs to a person, business, etc.: *A good reputation is an asset.* 2 assets all the property of a person, business, or estate that may be changed into cash.

as·sign (ə sīn′) *vt*- 1 to allot; give out. 2 to appoint, as to a duty. 3 to settle definitely: *to assign a time for meeting.* 4 to transfer (property) to another. —*n*- **as·sign′er** or **as·sign′or**.

as·sign·ment (ə sīn′mənt) *n*- 1 a setting apart for some particular person or use; allotment. 2 thing given out or alloted, as a lesson. 3 a legal transfer, as of property.

as·sim·i·late (ə sĭm′ə lāt′) *vt*- [as·sim·i·lat·ed, as·sim·i·lat·ing] to take in and make a part of oneself; absorb: *Plants assimilate nourishment through their roots. He assimilated the customs of his new country.*

as·sist (ə sĭst′) *vt*- to help; to aid: *Our government assisted them by sending a team of doctors.* *vi*- 1 to give help or aid. 2 to be present: *to assist at a birth.*

as·so·ci·a·tion (ə sō′sē ā′shən) *n*- 1 group of persons organized for a common purpose: *a trade association.* 2 a joining together; an associating: *an association of ideas.* 3 an idea connected with another idea: *What are the associations of the word "good"?* 4 companionship.

as·sort (ə sòrt′, -sôrt′) *vt*- to separate into classes; sort; classify. *vi*- to agree (with): *His actions assort well with his character.*

as·sort·ment (ə sòrt′mənt, ə sôrt′-) *n*- a collection of different kinds: *an assortment of candy.*

as·suage (ə swāj′) *vt*- [as·suaged, as·suag·ing] to make easier; relieve; to make less painful; calm.

as·sume (ə sōōm′, -syōōm′) *vt*- [as·sumed, as·sum·ing] 1 to take for granted: *We assume that you will be home for dinner.* 2 to take on as a task or duty; become responsible for; undertake: *Mr. Wilkins assumed the president's duties during his absence.*

as·sur·ance (ə shŏŏr′əns) *n*- 1 statement to inspire confidence or certainty: *We had his assurance that he would take care of the matter.* 2 certainty; confidence: *We had every assurance our team would win.* 3 self-confidence: *The actor played the part with assurance.*

as·sure (ə shŏŏr′) *vt*- [as·sured, as·sur·ing] 1 to say positively: *They assured us that there would be no delay.* 2 to make certain: *Practice can assure better playing.*

as·ter (ăs′tər) *n*- 1 plant related to the daisy, with white, pink, blue, or purple flower heads. 2 its flower. Some asters have large, many-flowered heads that look like chrysanthemums.

as·ter·isk (ăs′tə rĭsk′) *n*- figure of a star [*], used in printing or writing as a reference mark, or to show an omission. *vt*- to mark with such a star.

Aster

asth·ma (ăz′ mə) *n*- disease marked by wheezing, coughing, and short breath.

as·ton·ish (ə stŏn′ĭsh) *vt*- to surprise greatly; amaze: *His boldness astonished us.*

as·tound (ə stound′) *vt*- to strike with amazement; astonish greatly: *Achievements of science astound us.*

a·stray (ə strā′) *adv*- in the wrong direction; to the wrong place: *The letter went astray.* *adj*- wandering; confused: *Her thoughts are astray.*

as·trin·gent (ə strĭn′jent) *adj*- sharply contracting and tightening the skin, leaving a feeling of freshness. *n*- substance, such as alum, that shrinks or contracts body tissues. —*adv*- **as·trin′gent·ly.** *n*- **as·trin′gen·cy:** *the astringency of a lotion.*

as·trol·o·gy (ə strŏl′ə jē) *n*- the practice which claims to predict events by the position and mysterious influence on human affairs of the sun, moon, and planets. —*adj*- **as·tro·log′i·cal** (ăs′trə lŏj′ə kəl). *n*- **as·trol′o·ger.**

as·tro·naut (ăs′trə nòt′) *n*- one of the crew of a spaceship.

as·tro·nom·i·cal (ăs′trə nŏm′ĭ kəl) *adj*- 1 having to do with astronomy. 2 immensely or unimaginably large: *an astronomical price.* —*adv*- **as′tro·nom′i·cal·ly.**

as·tute (ə stōōt′, -styōōt′) *adj*- 1 keen of mind; *an astute man.* 2 showing keenness of mind; shrewd: *an astute appraisal of foreign policy.* —*adv*- **as·tute′ly.**

n- **as·tute′ness.**

a·sun·der (ə sŭn′dər) *adv*- in or into two or more parts; apart: *The tree was split asunder by lightning. They were driven asunder by the war.*

a·sy·lum (ə sī′ləm) *n*- 1 institution or hospital for the care of the helpless or the insane. 2 refuge: *The rebel found asylum in a neighboring country.*

at (ăt) *prep*- 1 in the place, time, or condition of: *Tom is waiting at home. The plant operates at night. Please come at your convenience. The nation was at peace.* 2 in the manner of: *The horse came toward us at a trot.*

a·the·ist (ā′thē ĭst) *n*- one who believes that there is no God.

ath·let·ics (ăth lĕt′ĭks) *n*- (takes singular or plural verb) games and sports requiring strength, agility, and stamina.

at·las (ăt′ləs) *n*- bound volume of maps or charts.

at·mos·phere (ăt′ məs fêr′) *n*- 1 the air that surrounds the earth. 2 air in a particular place: *the damp atmosphere of the cellar.* 3 surrounding influence: *the quiet atmosphere of the library.*

at·om (ăt′əm) *n*- 1 the smallest particle of an element that can take part in a chemical change without being permanently changed itself. Atoms contain protons, electrons, and (except for ordinary hydrogen) neutrons. 2 a tiny bit: *not an atom of sense.*

at·om·iz·er (ăt′ə mī′zər) *n*- device for changing a liquid to a fine spray.

a·tone·ment (ə tōn′mənt) *n*- a making amends for a wrong, crime, sin, etc.

a·tro·cious (ə trō′shəs) *adj*- 1 extremely cruel or wicked: *an atrocious crime.* 2 ridiculously ugly or poorly made: *an atrocious hat.* —*adv*- **a·tro′cious·ly.**

at·ro·phy (ă′trə fē′) *Biology n*- a wasting and shrinking, or an arrest in development: *Poliomyelitis can cause atrophy in muscles.*

at·tach (ə tăch′) *vt*- 1 to fasten to or upon; join: *He attached the label to the suitcase.* 2 to assign to a military company: *Please attach Corporal Smith to Company G.* 3 to affix or append (a signature, comment, etc.).

at·ta·ché (ăt′ə shā′, ă′tă′shā′) *n*- member of a staff, especially a subordinate attached to the staff of a foreign minister or ambassador.

at·tack (ə tăk′) *vt*- 1 to set upon forcefully; assault: *The enemy attacked us from the rear. The enemy attacked the hill.* 2 to criticize sharply: *The newspapers attacked the senator's speech.* 3 to have a harmful effect upon: *Some insects attack our garden plants.* 4 to begin on: *to attack a job with vigor.*

at·tain (ə tān′) *vt*- 1 to achieve or gain by effort: *He attained his goal by hard work.* 2 to reach; arrive at: *Grandfather attained the age of ninety.*

at·tempt (ə tĕmpt′) *vt*- to try; make an effort at: *The pilot attempted a landing in the fog.* *n*- effort; trial: *His second attempt at skating was more successful.*

at·tend (ə tĕnd′) *vt*- 1 to be present at: *to attend school; to attend church.* 2 to accompany; escort: *A company of nobles attended the king.* 3 to serve or wait upon: *The maid attends her mistress.*

at·tend·ance (ə tĕn′dəns) *n*- 1 fact of being present, as at school. 2 state of looking after or waiting upon some person or thing: *The nurse is in attendance.* 3 the number of persons present; also, the record of this number: *to take the attendance at school.*

at·ten·tion (ə tĕn′shən) *n*- 1 a looking, listening, or thinking carefully and steadily: *The students gave their full attention to the experiment.* 2 care; consideration: *Give attention to this request.*

at·test (ə tĕst′) *vt*- 1 to bear witness to; affirm the truth of, especially by signing one's name or by oath. 2 to give proof of: *Your work attests your ability.* *vi*- to bear witness (to): *to attest to a truth.*

at·tic (ăt′ĭk) *n*- space in a house directly under the roof; garret. *as modifier: an attic studio.*

at·tire (ə tīər′) *vt*- [at·tired, at·tir·ing] to dress or adorn; especially for formal occasions: *The queen was attired in her robe.* *n*- clothes or apparel: *formal attire.*

at·ti·tude (ăt′ə tōōd, -tyōōd′) *n*- 1 way of thinking, feeling, or acting: *What accounts for his hostile attitude* *toward us?* 2 position of the body to show feeling, mood, or purpose: *He jumped to his feet in a threatening attitude.*

at·tor·ney (ə tûr′nē) *n-* [*pl.* **at·tor·neys**] lawyer; one legally appointed by another to act for him in any legal matter. Also called **attorney at law.**

at·tract (ə trăkt′) *vt-* to draw to oneself or itself: *A magnet attracts iron. He shouted to attract attention.*

at·trac·tive (ə trăk′tĭv) *adj-* 1 appealing; charming; pleasing. 2 having the power to attract: *the attractive force of a magnet.* —*adv-* **at·trac′tive·ly.**

²**at·trib·ute** (ă′trə byŏŏt′) *n-* 1 a quality or trait considered as belonging to a person or thing; characteristic: *His chief attributes are honesty and courage.* 2 mark or object regarded as a symbol: *The crown is an attribute of royalty.*

at·tri·tion (ə trĭsh′ən) *n-* 1 a wearing away by rubbing, scraping, etc. 2 a wearing down or weakening by constant harassment, attack, etc.: *a war of attrition.*

auc·tion (ôk′shən) *n-* public sale at which property or goods are sold to the highest bidder. *vt-* to sell to the highest bidder.

au·da·cious (ô dā′shəs) *adj-* 1 bold; daring: *an audacious rescue attempt.* 2 intolerant or impatient of custom, restraint, etc.; impudent: *Jane's hosts were shocked at her audacious manner.*

au·di·ble (ô′də bəl) *adj-* loud enough to be heard: *a barely audible whisper.* —*adv-* **au′di·bly.**

au·di·ence (ô′dē əns) *n-* 1 group of people gathered to hear or see something. 2 people within hearing range; listeners: *a television audience.* 3 interview with a person of high rank: *an audience with the king.*

au·dit (ô′dət) *vt-* 1 to examine or adjust (a business record, claim, etc.) 2 to attend (a college course) as a listener without getting credit. *n-* official examination or adjustment of an account or claim.

au·di·tion (ô dĭsh′ən) *n-* trial or test at which a musician, actor, dancer, etc., gives a sample performance in hope of being hired or accepted. *vi-* to perform in such a trial: *She auditioned for the new play. vt-*: *They auditioned five singers today.*

au·di·tor (ô′də tər) *n-* 1 a listener. 2 person who examines accounts, records, and claims.

au·di·tor·i·um (ô′də tôr′ē əm) *n-* 1 building or large room used for public gatherings. 2 the part of a church, theater, etc., where the audience sits.

aug·ment (ôg měnt′) *vt-* to make larger; increase: *He augmented his income by taking an additional job.*

au·gust (ô gŭst′) *adj-* 1 having great dignity; majestic. 2 inspiring great respect: *an august personage.*

aunt (ănt, änt) *n-* 1 sister of one's father or mother. 2 wife of one's uncle. **Hom-** ant.

au·ra (ôr′ə) *n-* character which a person or thing has in the mind or feelings of a beholder: *an aura of calm.*

aus·pi·cious (ô spĭsh′əs) *adj-* favorable; promising success: *Our team made an auspicious beginning by winning the first game.* —*adv-* **aus·pi′cious·ly.** *n-* **aus·pi′cious·ness:** *the auspiciousness of the circumstances.*

aus·tere (ô stêr′) *adj-* 1 severe and stern in manner or appearance: *the austere look on the old judge's face.* 2 strict and severely simple in manner of living or behaving: *the austere life of the first pioneers.*

au·then·tic (ô thĕn′tĭk) *adj-* 1 genuine; not falsified: *an authentic signature.* 2 true; trustworthy: *Is this an authentic account of what happened?* —*adv-* **au·then′ti·cal·ly.**

au·thor·i·ty (ə thôr′ə tē, ə thŏr′-) *n-* [*pl.* **au·thor·i·ties**] 1 power or right (to command, direct, or act): *The general had authority to start the attack.* 2 accepted source of information.

au·thor·ize (ô′thə rīz′) *vt-* [**au·thor·ized, au·thor·iz·ing**] 1 to give the right or power to do something; empower: *He was authorized to buy supplies for the office.* 2 to allow by law; approve: *The legislature authorized funds for roads.*

au·to·bi·og·ra·phy (ô′tō bī ŏg′rə fē) *n-* [*pl.* **au·to·bi·og·ra·phies**] life history of a person, written by himself. —*n-* **au′to·bi·og′ra·pher.**

au·to·graph (ôt′ə grăf′) *n-* person's own signature or handwriting. *vt-* to write one's name on or in: *to autograph one's picture.*

au·to·mat·ic (ôt′ə măt′ĭk) *adj-* 1 self-operating; self-acting; capable of being run or worked without an operator: *an automatic elevator; an automatic washing machine.* 2 done unconsciously or from habit: *Breathing is automatic.*

au·to·mo·bile (ôt′ə mō bēl′) *n-* four-wheeled passenger vehicle having an engine by which it is propelled; motorcar. *as* **modifier:** *an automobile engine.*

au·top·sy (ô′tŏp′sē) *n-* [*pl.* **au·top·sies**] examination and dissection of a dead body to find the cause of death or the effects of a disease or injury. See also *biopsy.*

au·tumn (ôt′əm) *n-* the season of the year between summer and winter, in the Northern Hemisphere usually from September 22 to December 21; fall. *as* **modifier:** *the autumn leaves.*

aux·il·i·a·ry (ôg zĭl′yə rē, -lə rē) *adj-* helping; assisting: *The fire department called out auxiliary forces.* *n-* [*pl.* **aux·il·i·a·ries**] 1 helper; ally; aid of any kind. 2 an auxiliary verb.

a·vail (ə vāl′) *vt-* 1 to help or profit: *The money did not avail him.* 2 to give: *His fame availed him little happiness.* *vi-* to be of use or value; help: *Nothing can avail.*

a·vail·a·ble (ə vā′lə bəl) *adj-* 1 at hand and ready for use or service: *My assistants are available if you need them.* 2 obtainable by hire, purchase, etc.: *Is this available in blue?* —*n-* **a·vail′a·bil′i·ty** *adv-* **a·vail′a·bly.**

av·a·lanche (ăv′ə lănch′) *n-* 1 large mass of snow, ice, or earth suddenly sliding or falling down a mountain. 2 anything that overwhelms by speed and volume: *an avalanche of words.*

av·a·rice (ăv′ə rəs) *n-* greed for money.

a·venge (ə vĕnj′) *vt-* [**a·venged, a·veng·ing**] to inflict punishment in return for or in behalf of: *to avenge an insult; to avenge one's brother.* —*n-* **a·veng′er.**

av·e·nue (ăv′ə nōō′, -nyōō′) *n-* 1 wide street. 2 road with trees on each side. 3 way of reaching; approach: *Hard work is a sure avenue to success.*

a·ver (ə vûr′) *vt-* [**a·verred, a·ver·ring**] to state positively; assert: *The man averred that he had not slept.*

av·er·age (ăv′ər ĭj) *n-* 1 the number that is the result of dividing the sum of several addends by the number of addends; arithmetic mean. Example: The average of 5, 8, and 14 is 27/3, or 9. See also *mean* and *median.*

a·verse (ə vûrs′) *adj-* opposed; not inclined: *Tom Sawyer was averse to hard work.* —*adv-* **a·verse′ly.** *n-* **a·verse′ness:** *His averseness to hard work is well known.*

a·ver·sion (ə vûr′zhən) *n-* 1 dislike; disgust: *She has an aversion to snakes.* 2 thing or person disliked: *One of her pet aversions was mosquitoes.*

a·vert (ə vûrt′) *vt-* 1 to turn away: *He averted his eyes from the sight of the accident.* 2 to avoid: *to avert danger by quick thinking.* 3 to prevent: *to avert a strike.*

av·id (ăv′ĭd) *adj-* 1 eager: *an avid reader.* 2 desirous of; greedy for: *to be avid of praise; to be avid for food.* —*adv-* **av′id·ly.** *n-* **a·vid′i·ty** or **av′id·ness.**

av·o·ca·do (ăv′ə kä′dō, äv′-) *n-* [*pl.* **av·o·ca·dos**] 1 pear-shaped tropical American fruit, green to black in color, with a very large, hard pit; alligator pear. 2 the tree that it grows on.

Avocado

a·vo·ca·tion (ăv′ō kā′shən) *n-* an interest or occupation outside one's regular work: *The lawyer's avocation was painting.*

a·void (ə void′) *vt-* to keep away from; shun.

a·vouch (ə vouch′) *vt-* to declare positively; maintain; affirm: *The spectators avouched the man was injured.*

a·vow (ə vou′) *vt-* to admit; confess; declare directly and openly: *He avowed his faults.*

a·wake (ə wāk′) *vt-* [**a·woke** or **a·waked, a·waked, a·wak·ing**] 1 to rouse from sleep. 2 to rouse from inactivity; stimulate: *to awake interest.* *vi-* 1 to cease to sleep. 2 to rouse oneself; become alert: *He awoke suddenly to his danger.* **adj-** not asleep.

a·ward (ə wôrd′) *vt-* 1 to give or assign, as does a judge or an umpire, after careful consideration. 2 to bestow, as a prize. *n-* 1 a careful and deliberate decision. 2 that which is given or bestowed.

a·ware (ə wâr′) *adj-* realizing; knowing; being conscious of: *to be aware of danger.* —*n-* **a·ware′ ness.**

a·wash (ə wŏsh′, -wôsh′) *adj-* covered with water: *The street was awash after the sudden downpour.*

a·way (ə wā′) *adv-* 1 from a place; off: *to go away.* 2 aside: *to look away.* 3 at a distance; distant: *ten miles away.* 4 absent: *to be away from home.* 5 out of one's possession: *to give money away.*

aw·ful (ô′ fəl) *adj-* 1 dreadful; inspiring awe: *the awful power of a lightning bolt.* 2 *Informal* very bad; very ugly: *His handwriting is awful.* *Hom-* offal. —*n-* **aw′ ful·ness:** *the awfulness of the hurricane.*

a·while (ə hwīl′) *adv-* for a short time.

awk·ward (ôk′ wərd) *adj-* 1 ungainly in action or bearing; clumsy: *an awkward carpenter; an awkward child.* 2 difficult to handle: *an awkward situation; an awkward turn in the road.*

ax or **axe** (ăks) *n-* a chopping tool now chiefly used for felling and trimming trees and chopping wood.

¹**ax·es** (ăk′ səz) *n- pl.* of **ax** or **axe.**

²**ax·es** (ăk′ sēz′) *n- pl.* of **axis.**

ax·il (ăk′ səl, -sĭl′) *n-* 1 in anatomy, the armpit. 2 in botany, the angle formed by the upper side of a leaf or its stem and the stem or branch it grows from. *Hom-* axle.

ax·il·la·ry (ăk′ sə lĕr′ ē) *adj-* 1 in anatomy, having to do with the armpit. 2 in botany, in or near an axil of a plant: *an axillary bud between a leaf and a branch.*

ax·i·om (ăk′ sē əm) *n-* statement or principle that is accepted without proof, often because it seems obvious. Example: The whole is greater than any of its parts.

ax·i·o·mat·ic (ăk′ sē ə măt′ ĭk) *adj-* like an axiom; self-evident; accepted as true without proof.

ax·is (ăk′ sĭs) *n-* [*pl.* **ax·es** (ăk′ sēz′)] 1 straight line about which a body or figure rotates: *The earth's axis runs*

from the North Pole to the South Pole. 2 (also **axis of symmetry**) similar line which divides a body, figure, or object into symmetrical parts. 3 *Mathematics* vertical or horizontal scale or number line used in a graph. 4 **Axis** alliance of Germany, Japan, and Italy during World War II.

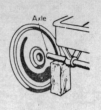

Axle

ax·le (ăk′ səl) *n-* 1 shaft on which a wheel turns. 2 shaft that connects two opposite wheels of a vehicle and turns with them. 3 axletree. *Hom-* axil.

ax·le·tree (ăk′ səl trē′) *n-* bar connecting two opposite wheels of a vehicle and forming the axle of both.

ax·on (ăk′ sŏn′) *n-* the threadlike extension of a nerve cell that carries impulses away from the cell body.

¹**ay** or **aye** (ā) *adv-* always; ever: *forever and* ay. [from Old Norse *ei* meaning "ever; always."]

²**ay** or **aye** (ī) *adv-* yes. *n-* a vote in favor of something: *The* ayes *have it.* [of unknown origin.] *Hom-* eye, I.

a·zal·ea (ə zāl′ yə) *n-* 1 any of a group of shrubs of the rhododendron family. 2 trumpet-shaped flower of this shrub, growing in clusters.

az·i·muth (ăz′ ə məth) *n-* angle between a line (such as the centerline of a road or a line of sight toward an object) and north or any other fixed direction.

STAR ★   Azimuth
HORIZON

Az·tec (ăz′ tĕk′) *n-* member of a highly civilized Indian tribe of central Mexico, destroyed at its height by Cortes (1519). *adj-: the* Aztec *calendar.* —*adj-* **Az·tec′ an.**

az·ure (ăzh′ ər) *n-* the blue color of the clear sky in daytime. *adj-: an* azure *silk.*

B

B, b (bē) *n-* [*pl.* **B's, b's**] 1 the second letter of the alphabet. 2 *Music* the seventh note of the C-major scale.

bab·ble (băb'əl) *vi-* [**bab·bled, bab·bling**] 1 to make indistinct or meaningless sounds, like a baby; prattle. 2 to talk idly, foolishly, or excessively; chatter.

ba·by (bā'bē) *n-* [*pl.* **ba·bies**] 1 young child or infant. 2 youngest member of a family. *vt-* [**ba·bied, ba·by·ing**] to treat (someone) as a baby.

ba·by·sit (bā'bē sĭt') *vi-* [**ba·by·sat, ba·by·sit·ting**] to care for a young child, usually in the evening, while the parents are away. —*n-* baby sitter.

bac·ca·lau·re·ate (băk'ə lôr'ē ət) *n-* 1 the bachelor's degree given by colleges and universities. 2 sermon given to a graduating class at commencement.

bac·cha·nal (băk'ə năl', -năl') *n-* 1 follower of Bacchus. 2 dance or song in honor of Bacchus. 3 drunken reveler. 4 wild drinking party; orgy.

bach·e·lor (băch'ə lər) *n-* 1 man who has never married. 2 one who has taken the first degree at a college or university: *a bachelor of arts or of science.* 3 (also **bachelor-at-arms**) young knight who served under the banner of another.

back (băk) *n-* 1 in man and animals having a spine, the rear or upper part of the body from the neck to the end of the spine; in other animals, the upper part of the body. 2 the part opposite the front or part normally used: *the back of the house; the back of his head; the back of the hand.* 3 the part of a chair or bench against which one leans.

back·bit·er (băk'bī'tər) *n-* one who speaks evil of a person who is absent. —*n-* back'bit'ing: *His backbiting and hypocrisy are too much for me to bear.*

back·fire (băk'fīər') *n-* 1 in a gasoline engine, a noisy explosion of gas that occurs at the wrong time. 2 a controllable fire started to check a prairie fire by burning a space in its path. *vi-* [**back·fired, back·fir·ing**] 1 to have an explosion in a gasoline engine at the wrong time. 2 to have a result opposite to the intended result: *The scheme backfired.*

back·gam·mon (băk'găm'ən) *n-* game played with dice by two persons with fifteen pieces each, on a specially marked board.

back·ground (băk'ground') *n-* 1 parts of a view, picture, etc., that lie farthest from the eye of the viewer: *There were mountains in the background of the picture.* 2 surface on which patterns or designs are placed: *The stars of the flag are sewn on a blue background.*

back·ward (băk'wərd) *adj-* 1 toward the rear: *a backward stroke with the hand.* 2 lacking average intelligence or growth; retarded: *a backward young man; a backward region.* *adv-* (also **back'wards**) 1 in the opposite or reverse direction: *to spell backward; to run a machine backward.* 2 to the back or rear: *to glance backward.*

ba·con (bā'kən) *n-* salted and smoked meat from the back and sides of a hog.

bring home the bacon *Informal* 1 to provide, as for a family; to earn a salary. 2 to succeed in what one has set out to do.

bac·te·ri·a (băk tēr'ē ə) *n- pl.* [*sing.* **bac·te·ri·um**] large class of microscopic, one-celled organisms considered to be plants, but also having animal characteristics. Their action is the cause of a number of diseases and of many processes, including decay, fermentation, and soil enrichment. —*adj-* bac·te'ri·al: *a bacterial disease.*

Bacteria, magnified 1,000 times

bad (băd) *adj-* [**worse, worst**] 1 immoral; wicked: *Theft is bad.* 2 unfavorable to one's purposes, health, taste, etc.: *a bad time to call; a weekend of bad weather; a bad odor; a bad movie.* 3 below a certain standard; incorrect; faulty: *her bad grammar; his bad table manners.* 4 not working properly; defective: *a bad watch.*

badge (băj) *n-* a mark, token, or something worn to show membership, authority, or achievement: *a policeman's badge; a badge for perfect attendance.*

bad·min·ton (băd'mĭn tən) *n-* a game, similar to tennis,

played by hitting a round, feathered cork, called a shuttlecock, with a light racket over a net five feet high.

baf·fle (băf'əl) *vt-* [**baf·fled, baf·fling**] 1 to confuse or puzzle very much: *The fox baffled the hounds. This algebra problem baffles me.* 2 to slow up or change the flow of liquids or gases with a grid, vane, or other obstruction, or to deflect or absorb sound by the use of a partition, as in loud-speaker enclosures.

bag (băg) *n-* 1 sack for holding anything; container made of paper, cloth, etc., that can be closed at the top. 2 purse; handbag. 3 suitcase; valise. 4 game killed on a hunting trip: *The day's bag was eight ducks.*

bag·gage (băg'ĭj) *n-* 1 bags, trunks, suitcases, and boxes a person takes on a trip; luggage. 2 movable army equipment. 3 (usually humorous) saucy young woman.

²bail (bāl) *n-* container used as a dipper for removing water from a boat; also, a small pump used for the

bait (bāt) *n-* 1 food, real or sham, used to attract or catch fish or other animals. 2 anything that attracts or tempts; allurement; enticement; especially in the phrase **fall for the bait.** *vt-* 1 to put food or other objects on a fishhook or in a trap to catch animals: *He baited his hook with minnows.* 2 to torment or worry a chained animal with dogs: *It was once thought a sport to bait bears.* 3 to torment or worry (a defenseless person)

bake (bāk) *vt-* [**baked, bak·ing**] 1 to cook by dry heat in an oven or on heated stones, etc.: *to bake bread.* 2 to dry or harden by heat; to heat through.

baking powder *n-* powder used to make cake or biscuits rise and become light. Baking powder contains baking soda.

baking soda *n-* bicarbonate of soda, used to make bread or cakes rise.

bald (bôld) *adj-* [**bald·er, bald·est**] 1 bare of hair. 2 without the natural or usual covering of hair, feathers, fur, or foliage upon the head, top, or summit: *a bald mountaintop.*

bale (bāl) *n-* large and closely pressed package of merchandise, prepared for storage or transportation: *a bale of cotton.* *vt-* [**baled, bal·ing**]: *Modern farm machines bale hay.* Homs- bail, Baal.

balk (bôk) *vi-* 1 to stop short and refuse to go on: *The horse balked at the high jump.* 2 in baseball, of a pitcher, to make an illegal motion, especially to fail to complete a throw he has started.

¹ball (bôl) *n-* 1 any round body; sphere; *the flaming ball of the sun.* 2 round, or nearly round, object used in a game: *a golf ball; a croquet ball; a tennis ball.* 3 game using such an object, especially baseball: *to play ball.*

bal·lad (băl'əd) *n-* 1 simple song, especially one with several verses sung to the same melody. 2 poem that tells a story, written in four-line stanzas.

bal·let (băl'ā, bă lā') *n-* 1 story or idea acted out in dance form; also, the music for it. 2 a group that performs such dances. *as modifier:* *a ballet dancer.*

ballistic missile *n-* self-propelled projectile, such as a rocket, aimed before firing and not guided in flight.

bal·lis·tics (bə lĭs'tĭks) *n-* (takes singular verb) 1 study of the flight of projectiles. 2 study of the firing process inside guns, especially the motion of the bullet or shell in the gun and the force of the exploding gunpowder. 3 study of the impact and penetration of projectiles.

bal·loon (bə lōōn') *n-* 1 an airtight bag filled with a gas that is lighter than air, used to lift passengers or scientific instruments into the air. 2 a child's toy, which consists of a rubber bag that can be blown up. *vi-* to swell up.

bal·lot (băl'ət) *n-* 1 system of secret voting in which the choice of candidates is shown on a paper form or a voting machine. 2 written or printed form used in secret voting. 3 total number of votes cast. 4 the right to vote: *Women won the ballot in 1920.* *vi-* to vote.

Balloon

balm·y (bä′mē, bäl′mē) *adj-* [balm·i·er, balm·i·est] 1 soft and gentle; soothing: *the* balmy *weather.* 2 sweet-smelling; fragrant. —*adv-* balm′i·ly. *n-* balm′i·ness.

bam·boo (băm′bōō′) *n-* [*pl.* bam·boos] 1 treelike, tropical plant related to the grasses. 2 its hollow, jointed stems, used in building in tropical climates, and in making furniture, fishing poles, canes, etc. *as modifier:* a bamboo *screen.*

Bamboo

bam·boo·zle (băm bōō′zəl) *Informal vt-* [bam·boo·zled, bam·boo·zling] to trick or cheat by misleading or confusing completely: *He* bamboozled *us with his fast talk.*

ban (băn) *n-* 1 the formal forbidding of an act, as by law: *a* ban *on lotteries.* 2 condemnation, as by public opinion. 3 decree of excommunication by the church.

ba·nan·a (bə nǎn′ə) *n-* 1 long slightly curved fruit with soft, sweet, starchy flesh and thick yellow or red skin.

¹band (bǎnd) *n-* 1 thin, flat, flexible strip used for binding, supporting, trimming, etc. 2 bar or stripe: *a* band *of white around a pole.*

²band (bǎnd) *n-* 1 group of persons or animals: *a* band *of robbers; a* band *of sheep.* 2 company of musicians, especially one having chiefly wind and percussion instruments.

band·age (bǎn′dǐj) *n-* strip of cloth used in dressing and binding wounds, sprains, etc. *vt-* [band·aged, band·ag·ing] to dress, cover, or bind an injury with a strip of any soft material.

ban·dit (bǎn′dǐt) *n-* outlaw or robber.

band·wag·on (bǎnd′wǎg′ən) *n-* 1 a large wagon for carrying a band in a parade. 2 great and noisy enthusiasm for a person or cause.

bane (bǎn) *n-* 1 originally, poison; still used in names of plants: *henbane.* 2 a cause of ruin or destruction; curse:

¹bang (bǎng) *n-* 1 heavy, noisy blow; whack: *I gave the pan a* bang. 2 loud, sudden noise; an explosive sound. 3 *Informal* sudden burst of energy: *The game started with a* bang. 4 *Slang* sudden pleasure; thrill.

ban·ish (bǎn′ĭsh) *vt-* 1 to condemn to leave; send from a country by legal decree; expel: *The former dictator was* banished *from the country.* 2 to drive out; send away: *The doctor's talk* banished *his fears of illness.*

¹bank (bǎngk) *n-* 1 long pile or heap: *a* bank *of sand;* banks *of clouds.* 2 steep slope. 3 ridge of earth bordering a river, stream, etc. 4 submerged mass of earth in the sea or at the mouth of a river over which the water is shallow; shoal: *the* banks *off Newfoundland.*

³bank (bǎngk) *n-* 1 place of business which takes care of money for its depositors, lends money at interest, and often helps in the transfer of money. 2 any reserve supply: *a blood* bank; *soil* bank. *as modifier:* a bank *employee.*

ban·ner (bǎn′ər) *n-* 1 flag. 2 piece of cloth with a design, picture, or writing on it. *adj-* outstanding; exceptional: *a* banner *year.*

ban·quet (bǎng′kwət) *n-* elaborate, often formal, dinner for many people. *vt-* to treat (a person) to such a dinner: *The townspeople* banqueted *the returning hero. vi-: They* banqueted *at the hotel.*

ban·ter (bǎn′tər) *n-* good-natured teasing. *vt-* to tease in a friendly, joking way; make fun of. *vi-* to exchange joking remarks.

bar (bär) *n-* 1 piece of wood, metal, etc., that is longer than it is wide or thick. 2 any barrier or obstacle; obstruction: *a* bar *to one's success.* 3 band or stripe: *a* bar *of red across the painting.*

bar·bar·ic (bär bär′ĭk, bär bär′-) *adj-* 1 uncivilized; primitive: *The music was* barbaric *and wild.* 2 savage: *their* barbaric *cruelty.*

bar·be·cue (bär′bə kyōō′) *n-* 1 outdoor party at which meat, originally a whole carcass, is roasted over an open fire. 2 the roasted meat. 3 the pit, grill, or spit used for roasting the meat.

barbed (bärbd) *adj-* 1 having sharp points as some fence wires, or barbs as some fishhooks. 2 sharp; cutting; biting: *a* barbed *remark.*

bar·ber (bär′bər) *n-* person who makes a business of cutting hair and shaving or trimming beards.

bar·bi·tu·rate (bär blch′ə rət, -rǎt′) *n-* any of a group of chemicals that are powerful, sleep-producing drugs.

¹bare (bâr) *adj-* [bar·er, bar·est] 1 not covered, especially, not covered with clothing: *a* bare *hillside; the child's* bare *arms.* 2 unadorned; simple; plainly or scantily furnished: *the* bare *truth;* bare *lodgings.* 3 scanty; mere: *He earned a* bare *living.*

bare·ly (bâr′lē) *adv-* 1 hardly; scarcely: *We* barely *had time to escape the flood.* 2 in a bare way; poorly; scantily: *a* barely *furnished room.*

bar·gain (bär′gən) *n-* 1 agreement on the terms of a deal: *He made a* bargain *to deliver the coal weekly.* 2 something bought cheap or offered for sale at a low price.

¹bark (bärk) *n-* outer covering of trees and other woody plants. *vt-* to damage the surface of by abrasion; abrade: *to* bark *a shin on a chair; to* bark *a shoe on a rock.* [from Scandinavian *börkr.*] *Hom-* barque.

²bark (bärk) *n-* 1 sharp, explosive sound made by a dog, fox, seal, etc. 2 any similar sound.

barn (bärn) *n-* farm building used for storing grain, hay, etc., and for housing livestock. *as modifier:* a barn *door.*

bar·o·graph (bär′ō grǎf′) *n-* barometer that automatically traces pressure readings on a graph.

bar·racks (bär′əks) *n- pl.* large building or group of buildings for lodging soldiers.

bar·rage (bə räzh′, -räj′) *n-* 1 volley of bursting shells, fired so as to fall just in front of advancing troops, in order to screen and protect them. 2 an overwhelming number of anything sent or received: *a* barrage *of letters; a* barrage *of phone calls.*

bar·rel (băr′əl) *n-* 1 round, usually bulging cask greater in length than in width, usually of wood, with flat ends. 2 quantity which such a cask contains; especially, a standard U.S. measure, such as 31.5 gallons for oil. 3 part or case of something in the shape of a tube: *a gun* barrel. *vt-* to put or pack in a cask.
Barrel

bar·ren (băr′ən) *adj-* 1 not fertile or productive: *a stretch of* barren *land.* 2 not bearing young or fruit: *a* barren *mare; a* barren *pear tree.* 3 without profit; empty: *a* barren *victory;* barren *labor.*

bar·ri·cade (băr′ə kād′) *n-* crude wall or barrier, especially one hastily put in place to keep back an enemy. *vt-* [bar·ri·cad·ed, bar·ri·cad·ing] to block with a makeshift wall or barrier: *They* barricaded *the road to the fort with logs.*

bar·ri·er (băr′ē ər) *n-* 1 something built to bar or prevent passage: *The Great Wall of China was a* barrier *against invasion.* 2 anything that prevents progress or creates difficulty: *a language* barrier; *a* barrier *to trade; a* barrier *to success.*

bar·tend·er (bär′tĕn′dər) *n-* man who serves alcoholic drinks at a bar.

bar·ter (bär′tər) *vt-* to exchange or trade (one thing for another) without the use of money: *Indians used to* barter *furs for guns. vi-: Eskimos* barter *at the trading post every spring. n-* the trade or exchange of one thing for another without the use of money.

bas·al (bā′səl) *adj-* 1 having to do with a foundation; used as a base: *the* basal *parts of a column.* 2 fundamental; basic. *Hom-* basil.

¹base (bās) *n-* 1 lowest part of something, on which it stands or rests: *a lamp* base. 2 the main part of a mixture; foundation: *Beef stock is the* base *of many soups.* 3 starting place for an operation; headquarters: *the* base *of an exploring party; a naval* base. 4 a station or goal in some games, such as baseball.

base·ball (bās′bôl′) *n-* 1 game played with a ball and bat by teams of nine players on a side. The game is played on a field with four bases at the corners of a square called a diamond. **2** ball used in this game. *as modifier: a baseball bat.*

base·ment (bās' mənt) *n-* bottom story of a building, partly or completely underground.

bash·ful (băsh' fəl) *adj-* very shy and easily embarrassed. —*adv-* bash' ful·ly. *n-* bash' ful·ness.

ba·sic (bā' sĭk) *adj-* **1** chief or main; essential; fundamental: *He cited his basic reasons for the decision.* **2** *Chemistry* being a base or having its properties.

ba·sin (bā' sən) *n-* **1** wide, shallow vessel, usually round or oval, for holding water or other liquids; a bowl. **2** the quantity held by such a vessel. **3** hollow or enclosed area containing water: *a yacht* basin. **4** all the land drained by a river and its tributaries.

Basin

ba·sis (bā' sĭs) *n-* [*pl.* **ba·ses** (bā' sēz′)] **1** part on which anything rests or depends; foundation: *Common interests form a good basis for friendship.* **2** fundamental facts or reasons: *What* basis *do you have for that statement?* **3** fundamental ingredient or mixture: *The basis of a cake is flour and eggs.*

bask (băsk) *vi-* to lie in comfortable warmth; warm oneself pleasantly: *to bask in the sun.* *Hom-* basque.

bas·ket (băs' kət) *n-* **1** container made of thin strips of wood, straw, twigs, reeds, etc., woven together: *Easter basket; clothes basket.*

²**bass** (băs) *Music n-* **1** tones of low pitch: *Turn up the bass and lower the treble on the phonograph.* **2** musical range of the lowest male singing voice; also, a singer having this range, or a musical part written for it.

¹**baste** (bāst) *vt-* [bast·ed, bast·ing] to sew temporarily with long stitches. [from Old French bastir, "to sew loosely," originally from an Old High German word meaning "to sew up with a bast."]

²**baste** (bāst) *vt-* [bast·ed, bast·ing] to moisten with fat, gravy, or other liquid while roasting: *She basted the turkey with melted butter.* [from Old French basser, "to soak," altered from bassiner, from bassin "basin."]

¹**bat** (băt) *n-* wooden stick or club, especially one used in baseball or cricket. *vt-* [bat·ted, bat·ting] to strike with such a stick or club: *to bat a ball. vi-: John bats next.* [from Old English batt.]

²**bat** (băt) *n-* small, flying, nocturnal mammal with a furry body like that of a mouse and large wings of thin, hairless skin. [greatly changed form of a Middle English word bakke from Old Norse.]

Brown bat

batch (băch) *n-* **1** amount baked at one time; a baking: *a batch of cookies.* **2** quantity of material to be used or made at one time: *a batch of cement.* **3** group of similar things: *a batch of letters.*

bath (băth) *n-* **1** a cleansing or washing of all the body. **2** water for bathing: *He drew a bath.* **3** room equipped for bathing; bathroom: *There are two baths on the second floor.* **4** (usually baths) building for bathing or steam bathing: *the public baths of Rome.*

bathe (bāth) *vt-* [bathed, bath·ing] **1** to immerse in water to clean or refresh; give a bath to: *to bathe a child; to bathe sore feet.* **2** to wash with water or other liquid: *to bathe a wound.*

bath·room (băth' room′) *n-* room with a bathtub and basin, and usually a toilet.

ba·ton (bă tŏn′) *n-* **1** stick used by the leader of a band or orchestra for beating time. **2** staff used as a badge of office or symbol of authority.

bat·tal·ion (bə tăl′ yən) *n-* an army unit of two or more companies that forms part of a regiment.

bat·ten (băt′ ən) *n-* a light strip of wood used for covering joints between boards or for fastening canvas over a ship's hatch.

¹**bat·ter** (băt′ ər) *vt-* **1** to strike with heavy, repeated blows: *The sea battered the wall.* **2** to damage; bruise; subject to rough usage: *The champion battered his opponent. vi-: The stranger battered at the door.*

²**bat·ter** (băt′ ər) *n-* thin mixture of flour, liquid, and other ingredients: *pancake* batter. [from Old French bature, from battre, "to beat," from Latin battuere.]

bat·ter·y (băt′ ə rē) *n-* [*pl.* **bat·ter·ies**] **1** a device that uses chemicals to produce or store electricity; also, two or more electric cells connected together: *a flashlight battery; a storage battery.* **2** number of like things used as a unit: *a battery of lights.*

bat·tle (băt′ əl) *n-* **1** fight between opposing armies, fleets, or air forces. **2** any fight or struggle: *a battle between the two gangs; a battle against the jungle.*

bat·ty (băt′ ē) *Slang adj-* [bat·ti·er, bat·ti·est] crazy.

bau·ble (bô′ bəl) *n-* cheap ornament; a thing that is showy, but of little value: *This bracelet is just a bauble.*

bawl (bôl) *vi-* to cry or wail loudly: *The child is bawling with rage. vt-* to utter by shouting: *The sergeant bawled his orders. n-: a bawl of rage. Hom-* ball.

bawl out *Informal* to scold; reprimand.

¹**bay** (bā) *n-* body of water partly surrounded by land, formed by a recess in the shoreline. [from Old French baie, from Spanish bahia, from Latin baia.] *Hom-* bey.

bay·o·net (bā′ ə nĕt′) *n-* dagger that can be attached to the muzzle of a rifle and used for stabbing or slashing. *vt-* **1** to stab with such an instrument. **2** to impale on something long and sharp.

Bayonet on rifle

bay window *n-* **1** window which projects outward from the line of the building. **2** *Slang* big belly.

ba·zaar (bə zär′) *n-* **1** sale of various kinds of articles for some special purpose: *a charity bazaar.* **2** place for the sale of a variety of goods. **3** in Oriental countries, a marketplace or street lined with shops.

be (bē) *vi-* [*pres. tense:* I **am**, he (she, it) **is**, you, (we, they) **are**; *p.t.:* I (he, she, it) **was**, you (we, they) **were**; *p.p.:* **been**; *pres. p.:* **be·ing**] **1** to exist: *There is a strong feeling against war.* **2** to occupy a position, condition, etc.: *He is on the chair.*

beach (bēch) *n-* sandy or pebbly shore of the ocean washed by waves; also, a similar place on a lake or river. *vt-* to bring or drive onto a shore. *Hom-* beech.

beach·head (bēch′ hĕd′) *n-* part of an enemy shore first captured by an invading army and used as a base for further operations.

bea·con (bē′ kən) *n-* fire, light, or radio signal used for guiding or warning, especially in the navigation of ships and airplanes; also, the structure bearing this signal.

bead (bēd) *n-* **1** small ball or piece of wood, glass, stone, or the like, pierced through to be strung together with others. **2** any small, round body: *a bead of dew; skin glistening with beads of sweat.*

beak (bēk) *n-* **1** the bill of a bird. **2** anything pointed or shaped like the bill of a bird, such as the lip of a pitcher or the prow of an ancient warship.

Beak

beak·er (bē′ kər) *n-* **1** cup or glass with a pouring lip, used in laboratories. **2** large drinking cup or vessel with a wide mouth.

bean (bēn) *n-* **1** the seed or the seed pod, or both, of various plants of the pea family, such as the kidney bean, soybean, and string bean; also, the plants themselves. **2** any of various seeds of a similar shape, such as cacao beans and coffee beans.

¹**bear** (bâr) *n-* **1** large animal with long shaggy hair and a very short tail. **2** rough surly person. **3** on the stock exchange, one who tries to lower prices for his own advantage (see also ¹bull). [from Old English bera.] *Hom-* bare. *-adj-* bear′like′.

²**bear** (bâr) *vt-* [bore, borne, bear·ing] **1** to support; hold up; sustain: *The pillars bear the weight of the roof.* **2** to carry or convey; transport: *The letter bears good news.* **3** to stand up under; endure; abide: *He has borne much pain. That will not bear scrutiny.*

Black bear
about 5 ft long

bear·a·ble (bâr′ ə bəl) *adj-* of a nature that allows being endured or borne; tolerable: *a bearable ache.*

beard (bērd) *n-* 1 growth of hair on the cheeks, chin, and throat. 2 any similar appendage of fishes or birds. 3 hairlike tuft on the heads of some grains, such as wheat or barley. *vt-* to confront with daring; defy: *to beard the lion in his den.* —*n-* beard' less: *a beardless youth.*

bear·er (bâr' ər) *n-* 1 person or thing that carries, supports, or gives birth. 2 one who presents a check or other order for the payment of money.

beast (bēst) *n-* 1 any four-footed animal, especially a large or ferocious animal. 2 a coarse or brutal person.

beat (bēt) *vt-* [beat, beat·en, beat·ing] 1 to strike or hit repeatedly: *to beat a drum; to beat a donkey.* 2 to flap repeatedly: *A bird beats its wings.* 3 to stir vigorously: *to beat eggs.* 4 to defeat; conquer: *We can beat their team if the field isn't muddy.* 5 *Music* to measure (time) by tapping, waving a baton, etc. *vi-* 1 to throb: *The heart beats.* 2 to strike repeatedly upon or against: *The waves beat upon the rocks.*

beat·en (bē' tən) *adj-* 1 hammered; shaped by hammering: *a bowl made of beaten brass.* 2 worn by many footsteps: *a beaten path.* 3 conquered; overcome.

beau·ti·ful (byōō' tə fəl) *adj-* delighting the ear, eye, or mind; lovely. —*adv-* beau' ti·ful·ly.

beau·ti·fy (byōō' tə fī´) *vt-* [beau·ti·fied, beau·ti·fy·ing] to make beautiful; adorn: *to beautify a yard with flowers.*

be·cause (bĭ kóz', -kŭz´) *conj-* for the reason that; since; for: *We didn't stay outside long because it was too cold.*

beck·on (bĕk' ən) *vt-* to signal (someone) to approach with a movement of the head or hand. *vi-* to attract or call: *The sea beckoned.*

be·come (bĭ kŭm', bē-) *vi-* [be·came, be·come, be·com·ing] to come or grow to be: *A lamb becomes a sheep.* *vt-* to suit; be suitable to; look well on: *That new pink dress becomes her. Childish behavior does not become you.*

bed (bĕd) *n-* 1 anything used for resting or sleeping, especially an article of furniture consisting of a frame and mattress. 2 plot of ground in which things are grown: *a bed of tulips; a bed of oysters.* 3 bottom or base: *the bed of a lake; a bed of gravel under a road.*

bed·ding (bĕd' ĭng) *n-* 1 bedclothes. 2 materials for a bed: *Straw is used as bedding for horses.*

be·deck (bĭ dĕk', bē-) *vt-* to adorn; decorate.

be·dev·il (bĭ dĕv' əl, bē-) *vt-* 1 to trouble or worry; harass; bother: *A lack of money constantly bedeviled him.* 2 to gain power over by magic; bewitch. —*n-* be·dev' il·ment.

be·drag·gled (bĭ drăg' əld) *adj-* wet, limp, and dirty: *My dress was bedraggled when I came in from the rain.*

bed·rock (bĕd' rŏk´) *n-* 1 the solid rock underlying the looser upper crust of the earth. 2 the lowest state or bottom of a thing: *My savings account has reached bedrock.*

bee (bē) *n-* 1 small insect that sucks nectar and gathers pollen from flowers; especially, the honeybee, a kind that stores honey and lives in the strictly ordered society of a beehive. 2 social gathering for work, competition, or amusement: *a quilting bee; a spelling bee.* Hom- be.

beef (bēf) *n-* [pl. beeves (bēvz)] 1 flesh of an ox, cow, or steer used for food. 2 a fully-grown ox, bull, steer, or cow that is raised for its meat. 3 *Slang* [pl. beefs] complaint.

beer (bēr) *n-* 1 an alcoholic beverage usually made from malted barley and flavored with hops. 2 drink made from roots or plants: *root beer.* Hom- bier.

beet (bēt) *n-* plant with a thick, fleshy root. The root and leaves of one variety, the red beet, are eaten as vegetables. The white root of the sugar beet is an important source of sugar. Hom- beat.

be·fit (bĭ fĭt') *vt-* [be·fit·ted, be·fit·ting] to be suited to; be suitable or appropriate for: *a dress to befit the occasion.* —*adv-* be·fit' ting·ly: *Zoe was befittingly respectful to her aunt.*

be·fore (bĭ fôr') *prep-* (in senses 1 through 4 considered

an adverb when the object is clearly implied but not expressed) 1 in front of: *She stopped before the gate. A new life lay before us.* 2 at the head of; in advance of: *He rode before his troops.* 3 earlier or sooner than: *They arrived before dinner.*

be·foul (bĭ foul', bē-) *vt-* to make dirty; pollute.

be·friend (bĭ frĕnd') *vt-* to act as a friend toward; help: *to befriend a stranger in town.*

be·fud·dle (bĭ fŭd' əl) *vt-* [be·fud·dled, be·fud·dling] to confuse: *The liquor he drank befuddled him.*

beg (bĕg) *vt-* [begged, beg·ging] 1 to ask for as charity: *to beg food.* 2 to ask for humbly; ask for as a favor; entreat: *to beg forgiveness; to beg one's pardon.* *vi-:* *He begs on the streets. She begged for a part in the play.*

beg·gar (bĕg' ər) *n-* 1 person who lives by asking for food, money, etc. 2 any very poor person; pauper.

be·gin (bĭ gĭn') *vi-* [be·gan, be·gun, be·gin·ning] 1 to come into existence; arise; commence: *Life began many million years ago. The stream begins up in the hills. The story begins on page 30.* 2 to take the first step or do the first act; start: *I'll begin tomorrow.*

be·grudge (bĭ grŭj') *vt-* [be·grudged, be·grudg·ing] 1 to envy (a person) the possession of something: *I don't begrudge him the honor.* 2 to give reluctantly: *I begrudge the money it cost me.* 3 to regard with displeasure; disapprove of: *He begrudged the pleasures of others.*

be·guile (bĭ gīl') *vt-* [be·guiled, be·guil·ing] 1 to deceive: *They beguiled the enemy into an ambush.* 2 to amuse; charm; delight: *He beguiled us with stories.* 3 to pass pleasantly: *to beguile the time.*

be·half (bĭ hăf') *n-* interest; support; favor.

in (or on) behalf of for; in the interest of: *He spoke in behalf of the plan.*

be·have (bĭ hāv') *vi-* [be·haved, be·hav·ing] 1 to act; conduct oneself: *He behaved like a fool.* 2 to act properly; do what is right (often with "oneself," "himself," etc.): *Please let me go and I'll behave myself.*

be·hav·ior (bĭ hāv' yər) *n-* way of acting; conduct; actions: *good behavior.* —*adj-* be·hav' ior·al.

be·hind (bĭ hīnd') *prep-* (in senses 3, 4, and 5 considered an adverb when the object is clearly implied but not expressed) 1 in or at the rear of; at the back: *The children are behind the house.* 2 to or on the other side of; beyond: *They hid behind some rocks.*

be·hold (bĭ hōld') *vt-* [be·held, be·hold·ing] to look at; gaze upon; see: *At last they beheld the Promised Land.* —*n-* be·hold' er.

be·ing (bē' ĭng) *n-* 1 living creature: *a human being.* 2 existence: *The airplane did not come into being until gasoline engines were invented.* 3 that which makes a thing or person what it is; essence: *His very being rebelled at the suggestion.* 4 the Supreme Being God.

be·lat·ed (bĭ lā' təd) *adj-* delayed: *a belated birthday greeting; a belated arrival.* —*adv-* be·lat' ed·ly. *n-* be·lat' ed·ness.

belch (bĕlch) *vi-* 1 to discharge gas noisily from the stomach through the mouth. 2 to throw out its contents violently: *The volcano rumbled and belched.* *vt-* to throw out with force: *The volcano belched molten rock and ashes.* *n-:* *He stifled a belch with his hand.*

be·lief (bĭ lēf') *n-* 1 acceptance of something as existing or true; faith; trust: *Nothing will shake my belief in his honesty.* 2 that which is accepted as existing or true; creed; doctrine: *His beliefs were based on reason.*

be·lieve (bĭ lēv') *vt-* [be·lieved, be·liev·ing] 1 to accept as true: *We believe her story.* 2 to trust the word of; have confidence in: *I believe him.*

¹bell (bĕl) *n-* 1 hollow metal instrument, usually cup-shaped, which makes a ringing sound when struck with a clapper or hammer. 2 anything shaped like a bell: *the bell of a horn; a diving bell.*

Bell

bell·boy (bĕl' boi´) *n-* boy or man who carries suitcases, runs errands, etc., in a hotel.

bel·li·cose (bĕl' ə kōs´) *adj-* inclined to fight; quarrelsome: *a bellicose disposition; a* bellicose *nation.*

bel·lig·er·ent (bə lĭj' ər ənt) *adj-* 1 waging war: *a* belligerent *nation.* 2 quarrelsome; warlike: *the speaker's* belligerent *words; a* belligerent *person.* *n-* nation or person at war. —*adv-* bel·lig´er·ent·ly.

bel·low (bĕl' ō) *n-* 1 the loud, deep roar of a bull. 2 any loud, deep cry. *vi-* 1 to make a loud, roaring cry: *The bulls* bellowed *when they saw each other.* 2 to cry out in a loud, deep voice; roar; bawl: *The movie director* bellowed *at the cameraman.*

bel·lows (bĕl' ōz) *n-* instrument for blowing air into a fire, the pipes of an organ, etc.

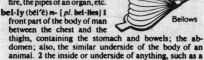
Bellows

bel·ly (bĕl' ē) *n- [pl.* bel·lies] 1 front part of the body of man between the chest and the thighs, containing the stomach and bowels; the abdomen; also, the similar underside of the body of an animal. 2 the inside or underside of anything, such as a ship or plane.

be·long (bĭ lóng') *vi-* to have a proper, suitable, or rightful place: *This tool* belongs *in the drawer. Small children* belong *in bed after dinner.*

be·long·ings (bĭ lòng' ĭngz) *n- pl.* personal property; possessions, especially those that can be moved, such as clothes, furniture, etc.

be·lov·ed (bĭ lŭv' əd, -lŭvd') *adj-* greatly loved. *n-* person who is greatly loved.

be·low (bĭ lō') *prep-* (in senses 1 and 2 considered an adverb when the object is clearly implied but not expressed) 1 lower than, in place, rank, excellence, price, etc.; underneath: *He has the locker* below *mine.*

belt (bĕlt) *n-* 1 band of leather, cloth, or other material worn around the waist as an ornament or as a support for a garment or weapon.

be·mused (bĭ myōōzd', bē-) *adj-* 1 bewildered; confused. 2 lost in thought; absent-minded.

bench (bĕnch) *n-* 1 a long seat. 2 the seat judges sit on in court. 3 position of judge: *He was chosen for the* bench *by the President.* 4 judges as a group. 5 a strong work table at which craftsmen work. *vt-* in sports, to keep (a player) out of a game.

be·neath (bĭ nēth') *prep-* (in sense 1 considered an adverb when the object is clearly implied but not expressed) 1 under: *The great fish lurked* beneath *the rock.* 2 under the power or weight of: *to sink* beneath *troubles.* 3 lower than: *a rank* beneath *captain.*

ben·e·dic·tion (bĕn' ə dĭk' shən) *n-* a blessing, such as the one pronounced at the end of a church service.

ben·e·fac·tor (bĕn' ə făk' tər) *n-* person who helps another, either with service or with money; patron.

ben·e·fi·cial (bĕn' ə fĭsh' əl) *adj-* helpful; producing good results: *Food and sleep are* beneficial *to health.* —*adv-* ben·e·fi´cial·ly.

ben·e·fi·ci·ar·y (bĕn' ə fĭsh' ə rē, -fĭsh' ē er' ē) *n- [pl.* ben·e·fi·ci·ar·ies] one who receives anything as a gift or benefit; especially, the person named on an insurance policy to receive part or all of the insurance.

ben·e·fit (bĕn' ə fĭt') *n-* 1 anything that is of help; advantage. 2 act of kindness. 3 public entertainment to raise money for a worthy cause. *vt-* to do good to; help: *The rest* benefited *his health. vi-* to get good (from); receive help; profit: *He* benefited *from his past experience.*

be·nev·o·lent (bə nĕv' ə lənt) *adj-* wanting and promoting good for others; kind and helpful. —*adv-* be·nev´o·lent·ly.

be·nign (bĭ nīn') *adj-* 1 of a kind or gentle disposition. 2 favorable; healthful: *a* benign *sea breeze.* 3 *Medicine* not malignant; harmless. —*adv-* be·nign´ly.

bent (bĕnt) *p.t. & p.p.* of **bend**. *adj-* 1 curved; crooked: *a* bent *twig.* 2 determined; set: *He is* bent *on becoming a doctor.* *n-* a natural ability or inclination: *He has a* bent *for painting.*

be·queath (bĭ kwēth', bĭ kwēth') *vt-* 1 to give or leave by will: *He* bequeathed *his money to his sons.* 2 to hand down: *Our forefathers* bequeathed *us a love of liberty.*

be·quest (bĭ kwĕst') *n-* something given or left by will; a legacy: *Small* bequests *went to the grandchildren.*

be·rate (bĭ rāt') *vt-* [be·rat·ed, be·rat·ing] to scold; upbraid: *The mother* berated *him for losing his skates.*

be·reave·ment (bĭ rēv' mənt) *n-* 1 the condition of being left desolate. 2 the loss of a relative or friend by death.

be·reft (bĭ rĕft') *adj-* stripped (of): *He was* bereft *of happiness. She is* bereft *of good sense.*

be·ret (bə rā') *n-* round, close-fitting cap of wool or other soft material, without a brim.

berg (bûrg) *n-* iceberg.

be·rib·boned (bĭ rĭb' ənd) *adj-* covered or adorned with many ribbons: *a* beribboned *general.*

Man wearing beret

ber·i·ber·i (bĕ' rē bĕ' rē) *n-* disease of the nervous system, caused by lack of vitamin B₁.

ber·ry (bĕr' ē) *n- [pl.* ber·ries] 1 any small juicy and stoneless fruit, such as a strawberry. 2 *Biology* a fleshy, many-seeded fruit such as the tomato, currant, or cranberry.

ber·serk (bər sûrk', -zûrk', bûr' sûrk') *adj-* in a violent or destructive rage; frenzied; frantic.
go (or **run**) **berserk** to go into an uncontrollable, often violent, rage.

be·seech (bĭ sēch') *vt-* [be·sought, be·seech·ing] 1 to implore; entreat: *We* beseech *you, O King, to hear our plea.* 2 to beg for; plead strongly for: *We* beseech *your mercy.*

be·seem (bĭ sēm') *vt-* to be suitable or becoming to; befit: *It hardly* beseems *you to bully your sister.*

be·set (bĭ sĕt') *vt-* [be·set, be·set·ting] 1 to attack from all sides; assail: *Many doubts* beset *him.* 2 to surround; hem in: *Danger* beset *his path.*

be·side (bĭ sīd') *prep-* 1 at or by the side of; nearby: *He stood* beside *me.* 2 in comparison with: *My foot is small* beside *yours.* 3 away from: *a case* beside *the point.*

be·sides (bĭ sīdz') *adv-* in addition; also; as well: *There will be hunting, fishing, and hiking, and swimming* besides. *prep-* in addition to; over and above: *The book club is giving a record album* besides *its book dividend.*

be·siege (bĭ sēj') *vt-* [be·sieged, be·sieg·ing] 1 to lay siege to; to surround in order to capture: *For nine weeks the enemy* besieged *the castle.* 2 to pester or harass: *They* besieged *the actor for autographs.*

best (bĕst) *adj-* (*superl.* of **good**) 1 good in the highest degree; most excellent; finest: *Jane's work is good, but Ralph's is* better, *and Stan's is* best. 2 largest: *The job took the* best *part of a week to finish.* *n-* 1 the finest: *You deserve the* best. 2 height of excellence: *I am at my* best *early in the morning.*

bes·tial (bĕs' chəl, bēs'-) *adj-* like the beasts; brutish; savage: *The fighting was carried on with* bestial *cruelty.* —*n-* bes·ti·al·i·ty (bĕs´chē ăl' ə tē). *adv-* bes´ti·al·ly.

be·stow (bĭ stō') *vt-* to give or confer: *to bestow a medal on a hero.*

bet (bĕt) *vt-* [bet or bet·ted, bet·ting] to stake, risk, or wager (money or the like) that something will or will not happen, or on the victory of a chosen competitor: *I* bet *a dollar that it will rain today. I* bet *ten dollars on the home team.* *vi-* 1 to lay a wager: *to bet on a horse.* 2 to guess with some conviction: *I'll* bet *Danny was there yesterday.*

be·tray (bĭ trā') *vt-* 1 to give into the hands of an enemy by deceit: *A disloyal soldier* betrayed *the army.* 2 to be disloyal to: *Would you* betray *a friend?* 3 to reveal (something intended to be hidden): *to betray a secret; to betray one's nervousness by stammering.* —*n-* be·tray´al: *a dastardly* betrayal *of my confidence.* *n-* be·tray´er.

be·troth (bĭ trŏth', -trŏth') *vt-* to promise to give (a daughter) in marriage.

bet·ter (bĕt' ər) *adj-* (*compar.* of **good**) 1 more excellent; of higher quality: *Apples are* better *in the fall. My work is* better *now. His swimming stroke is* better *than mine.* 2 larger; greater: *The walk takes the* better *part of an* *hour.* **3** improved in health: *The patient is* better *today.* **adv-** (*compar.* of *²well*) **1** in a finer way: *He swims better than I do.*

be·tween (bĭ twēn′) *prep-* (in senses 1-5 and 7, considered an adverb when the object is clearly implied but not expressed) **1** in the space which separates two objects or things: *There is a narrow lane between the two houses.* **2** in the time which separates one thing from another: *The accident happened between dusk and dark.*

bev·el (bĕv′ əl) *n-* **1** slanted face or faces cut along the edge of a table, mirror, piece of crystal, etc.; also, the slanted edge of a cutting tool, such as a chisel. **2** the acute angle of such slanted edges. **3** an instrument used to draw the angles for cutting such an edge.

Bevel

bev·er·age (bĕv′ ər ĭj) *n-* any kind of drink, as coffee, lemonade, wine, etc.

bev·y (bĕv′ ē) *n-* [*pl.* **bev·ies**] **1** group, especially of women or girls. **2** flock of birds, especially of quail.

be·ware (bĭ wâr′, bĕ-) *vt-* (now used only as an imperative or infinitive) to be on guard against: Beware *the dog!* *vi-* to be on guard against the hazards (of): *He cautioned me to beware of the dangerous crossing.*

be·wil·der (bĭ wĭl′ dər) *vt-* to confuse and perplex, especially by too many figures, ideas, directions, etc. *—n-* be′ wil′ der·ment: *His bewilderment was obvious, so I spoke more slowly.*

be·witch (bĭ wĭch′) *vt-* **1** to cast a magic spell over: *The bad fairy* bewitched *the princess.* **2** to fascinate or delight; charm: *Her beauty* bewitched *the audience.*

be·yond (bĭ yŏnd′) *prep-* (in senses 1 and 2 considered an adverb when the object is clearly implied but not expressed) **1** on the farther side of: *My house is* beyond *the hill.* **2** farther than; past: *He dashed well* beyond *the finish line. We talked till well* beyond *five o'clock.*

bi·an·nu·al (bī ăn′ yōō əl) *adj-* occurring twice a year. *—adv-* bi·an′ nu·al·ly.

bi·ased (bī′ əst) *adj-* willing to see only one side; prejudiced: *a biased editorial; a biased speaker.*

bib·li·cal (bĭb′ lĭ kəl) *adj-* having to do with the Bible or with times, persons, and events connected with the Bible: *the biblical wars; biblical scholars; biblical geography.*

bib·li·og·ra·phy (bĭb′ lē ŏg′ rə fē) *n-* [*pl.* **bib·li·og·ra·phies**] **1** the study of books, authors, style of printing, dates, editions, and the like. **2** list of books relating to a given subject or author. *—adj-* bib′ li·o·graph′ i·cal (bĭb′ lē ə grăf′ ĭ kəl). *adv-* bib′ li·o·graph′ i·cal·ly.

bi·cen·ten·ni·al (bī′ sĕn tĕn′ē əl) *adj-* occurring every 200 years. *n-* a 200th anniversary or its celebration.

bi·ceps (bī′ sĕps′) *n-* [*pl.* **bi·ceps**] **1** the large muscle on the front of the upper arm. **2** a similar leg muscle that flexes the knee.

bick·er (bĭk′ ər) *vi-* to quarrel; squabble: *The girls* bickered *over which TV program to turn on. n-* angry or petty dispute: *to get into a bicker.*

bi·cy·cle (bī′ sĭ kəl) *n-* light vehicle with two wheels, one behind the other, a saddlelike seat, foot pedals for propelling it, and handlebars for steering. *vi-* [bi·cy·cled, bi·cy·cling]: *Let's* bicycle *over to the park. — n- bi′ cy·cler or bi′ cy·clist.*

bid (bĭd) *vt-* [bade (băd) or bid, bid·den or bid, bid·ding] **1** to command; order; request: *The captain* bade *us to halt.* **2** to invite: *The host* bade *us make ourselves at home.* **3** to say as a greeting or farewell: *Let's* bid *them good-by.*

bid·ding (bĭd′ ĭng) *n-* **1** an offering of prices on something: *The* bidding *at the auction was brisk.* **2** request; command; order: *He came and went at his master's* bidding.

bide (bīd) *vt-* [bode or bid·ed, bid·ing] to wait. **bide one's time** to wait for the right time.

bier (bêr) *n-* frame on which a dead person or a coffin is placed or carried. *Hom-* beer.

bi·fo·cal (bī fō′ kəl, bĭ′-) *adj-* having two focal points, as a lens. *n-* **1** lens ground to form a combination of two lenses, one for near and the other for distant objects. **2** bifocals eyeglasses with this type of lens.

big (bĭg) *adj-* [big·ger, big·gest] **1** great in size, amount, extent, or volume, etc.: *a big city; a big sum; a big ranch; a big voice.* **2** full grown; tall; mature: *Her children are* big *now.* **3** full of; bursting (with): *Her eyes were* big *with tears.*

big·ot·ed (bĭg′ ət əd) *adj-* obstinately attached to one's own beliefs and opinions; intolerant.

bi·ki·ni (bə kē′ nē) *n-* very scanty two-piece woman's bathing suit.

bile (bīl) *n-* **1** bitter, yellow or greenish fluid produced by the liver to aid in digestion. **2** ill-humor; resentment.

bilge (bĭlj) *n-* **1** bulging part of a cask. **2** the bottom of a ship up to the point where the sides become vertical.

¹bill (bĭl) *n-* **1** statement of charges for goods or services: *a garage bill; a restaurant bill.* **2** printed advertisement or notice; poster; placard: "*Post no bills.*" **3** any paper listing items or events, such as a playbill, bill of fare, etc.

²bill (bĭl) *n-* **1** beak of a bird. **2** similar beak in other animals, such as some turtles. *vi-* to join beaks; show affection: *Doves* bill *and coo.* [from Old English bile.]

Bill of hummingbird

bill·board (bĭl′ bôrd′) *n-* large panel, usually set up outdoors to display public notices or advertising.

bil·lion (bĭl′ yən) *n-* **1** in the United States, a thousand million (1,000,000,000); in Great Britain, a million million (1,000,000,000,000).

bil·low·y (bĭl′ ō ē) *adj-* surging; swelling: *the* billowy *ocean; the* billowy *sails.*

bin (bĭn) *n-* box or enclosed place used for storing things: *a coal* bin*; a grain* bin. *Hom-* been.

bind (bīnd) *vt-* [bound, bind·ing] **1** to tie together or fasten with a cord, strap, etc.; make fast; tie up: *to* bind *a captive's arms and legs.* **2** to wrap around: *to* bind *one's waist with a girdle; to* bind *a wound with gauze.* **3** to cause to stick together: *to* bind *loose soil with grass; to* bind *one's life to another.* **4** to finish or protect (a seam, edge, etc.) with a band or border.

bin·go (bĭng′ gō) *n-* game played by covering numbers on a card as they are called out. The winner is the first person to cover all the numbers in a row.

bi·o·chem·is·try (bī′ ō kĕm′ əs trē) *n-* science dealing with the chemistry of living things.

bi·og·ra·phy (bī ŏg′ rə fē) *n-* [*pl.* **bi·og·ra·phies**] **1** the story of a person's life. **2** the branch of literature dealing with the lives of people.

bi·ol·o·gy (bī ŏl′ ə jē) *n-* science of living things and life processes, including such branches as botany, zoology, ecology, etc.

bi·op·sy (bī′ ŏp′ sē) *Medicine n-* [*pl.* **bi·op·sies**] the taking of a specimen of tissue from a living person or animal; also, the examination of this tissue for signs of disease. See also *autopsy.*

bi·ped (bī′ pĕd′) *n-* animal with two feet. Men and birds are bipeds.

bi·plane (bī′ plān′) *n-* airplane with two sets of wings, one above the other.

Biplane

birch (bûrch) *n-* **1** any of several trees with smooth outer bark which in some varieties may be removed in thin, papery sheets. **2** wood of these trees.

bird (bûrd) *n-* **1** any member of a class of warm-blooded, feathered, winged, egg-laying animals. **2** any small game bird, as distinguished from a waterfowl. **3** shuttlecock. **4** *Slang* fellow, chap: *He is an odd bird.*

birth (bûrth) *n-* **1** a coming into the world from the body of the mother. **2** beginning: *The birth of a nation.*

bis·cuit (bĭs′kət) *n-* 1 kind of bread baked in small, flat cakes. 2 cracker or cooky.

bi·sect (bī′sĕkt′) *vt-* to cut or divide into two equal parts. —*n-* **bi·sec′tion.**

bish·op (bĭsh′əp) *n-* 1 clergyman of high rank, the head of a diocese or church district. 2 piece used in chess.

¹bit (bĭt) *n-* 1 small piece of anything: *a bit of bread.* 2 a little while: *Please wait a bit.*

²bit (bĭt) *n-* 1 a replaceable tool for drilling, boring, driving screws, etc., that is gripped and turned by another tool such as a brace or electric drill. 2 the cutting part of a tool. 3 the metal mouthpiece of a bridle.

Bit for horse

bite (bīt) *vi-* [bit, bit·ten or bit, bit·ing] 1 to cut into or cut off with the teeth. 2 to pierce the skin for food as do certain blood-sucking insects: *A mosquito bites.* 3 to take the bait: *Fish are biting today.* *vt-* 1 to seize or grasp with the teeth; wound with the teeth: *The police dog bit the thief.* 2 to cause pain to: *The icy wind was biting my face.*

bit·ter (bĭt′ər) *adj-* [bit·ter·er, bit·ter·est] 1 sharp and unpleasant to the taste. 2 sharp; painful; stinging: *the bitter cold.* 3 hard to bear or receive: *a bitter lesson.* 4 severe; harsh: *the exchange of bitter words.*

bi·zarre (bə zär′) *adj-* odd in manner or appearance; fantastic; grotesque. *Hom-* bazaar.

blab (blăb) *vt-* [blabbed, blab·bing] to tell thoughtlessly. *vi-* to tell tales; talk too much and unwisely. *n-* 1 one who lets out secrets, or tells tales. 2 silly chatter.

black (blăk) *n-* 1 the darkest of all colors, that of materials like coal, soot, and tar that reflect no light whatever. It is not strictly a color, but the total absence or absorption of color or light. 2 a dye of this color. 3 clothes of this color; mourning.

black·ball (blăk′bôl′) *vt-* 1 to exclude from a club by adverse votes, formerly recorded by the placing of black balls in a ballot box. 2 to exclude from society in general; ostracize. *n-* an adverse vote.

black·jack (blăk′jăk′) *n-* 1 small club with a weighted head and a flexible handle. 2 small, scrubby oak tree with black bark, common in southern United States. 3 a card game; twenty-one. *vt-* to strike with a small heavy club.

black·mail (blăk′māl′) *n-* 1 an attempt to get money from a person by threatening to say something bad about him. 2 the money thus collected. *vt-* to make, or try to make, a person pay in this way. —*n-* **black′·mail′er.**

black·list (blăk′lĭst′) *n-* list of persons or organizations to be punished, denied approval, refused work, etc.; black book. *vt-: to blacklist an actor.*

black magic *n-* magic used for evil ends; witchcraft.

black widow *n-* kind of small spider that looks like a small black bead. The female is poisonous and has a red hourglass-shaped mark on the underside of its abdomen.

Black widow.
about 1 1.2 m long
underside view

blad·der (blăd′ər) *n-* 1 a small bag or sac in the body which receives and temporarily holds urine from the kidneys. 2 any similar inside bag or sac: *a football bladder; the air bladder of a fish.* —*adj-* **blad′der·like′.**

blade (blād) *n-* 1 cutting part of a knife, sword, tool, instrument, or machine. 2 flat, narrow leaf: *a blade of grass; a blade of wheat.* 3 broad flat object or part: *shoulder blade; blade of an oar.* For picture, see ¹*paddle.*

blame (blām) *vt-* [blamed, blam·ing] 1 to hold responsible (for); attribute guilt to: *The truck driver blamed the bus driver for the accident.* 2 to find fault with: *I don't blame you.*

blanch (blănch) *vt-* 1 to whiten by taking out color. 2 to put in boiling water and then into cold water to remove skins: *to blanch almonds.* *vi-* to turn pale from shame or fear.

bland (blănd) *adj-* [bland·er, bland·est] 1 mild and soft; not irritating: *a bland food; a bland manner.* 2 lacking character or emphasis; flat; undistinguished: *a bland speech.* —*adv-* **bland′ly.** *n-* **bland′ness.**

blan·dish·ment (blăn′dĭsh mənt) *n-* 1 flattery; cajolery. 2 flattering act or expression: *He could not resist her gentle blandishments.*

blank (blăngk) *adj-* [blank·er, blank·est] having nothing on or in it; lacking or empty of marks, decorations, feelings, ideas, etc.: *a blank sheet of paper; a blank look; a blank mind.* *n-* 1 empty space or condition: *He left blanks for the unanswered questions.*

blan·ket (blăng′kət) *n-* 1 covering of soft cloth, such as wool, cotton, etc., used to keep people or animals warm. 2 any thick covering: *a blanket of fog.* *vt-: Snow blanketed the earth.*

blare (blâr) *n-* loud sound like that of a trumpet. *vi-* [blared, blar·ing] to give forth a loud, brassy sound like that of a trumpet. *vt-: He blared his instructions over the public-address system.*

blas·phe·my (blăs′fə mē) *n-* [*pl.* blas·phe·mies] words that show contempt for God or sacred things. —*adj-* **blas′phe·mous:** *a blasphemous remark.* *adv-* **blas′phe·mous·ly.**

blast (blăst) *n-* 1 strong gust of wind. 2 forcible stream of air or gas from an opening: *a blast of heat from a furnace.* 3 a sudden sound, as from a wind instrument.

blast-off (blăst′ôf′) *n-* the firing of a space rocket.

bla·tant (blā′tənt) *adj-* 1 conspicuous or obvious, often in a vulgar way: *a blatant display of wealth.* 2 noisy. —*adv-* **bla′tant·ly.**

¹blaze (blāz) *n-* 1 bright flame; fire. 2 strong direct light; *the blaze of noon.* 3 brilliant display: *a blaze of color from the sunset.* 4 sudden outburst: *He reached the finish line in a blaze of energy.* *vi-* [blazed, blaz·ing] 1 to burn with a bright flame. 2 to burst into flame; flare up: *The signal fires suddenly blazed along the hills.*

bleach (blēch) *vt-* to remove color from or to whiten, by exposure to the sun or by a chemical process. *vi-* to lose color. *n-* substance that whitens or removes color.

bleach·ers (blē′chərz) *n- pl.* plank seats built in tiers for spectators at an outdoor sports event. *as modifier* (**bleach′er**): *a bleacher ticket.*

bleak (blēk) *adj-* [bleak·er, bleak·est] 1 unsheltered; exposed to wind and cold. 2 dismal; cold: *The weather was bleak.* 3 cheerless; gloomy: *a bleak outlook on life.* —*adv-* **bleak′ly.** *n-* **bleak′ness.**

blear·y (blêr′ē) *adj-* [blear·i·er, blear·i·est] 1 of the eyes, sore or watery. 2 dim; blurred.

bleat (blēt) *n-* the cry of a sheep, goat, or calf; also, any similar cry. *vi-* to utter any such cry.

bleed (blēd) *vi-* [bled (blĕd), bleed·ing] 1 to lose or shed blood. 2 of a plant, to lose sap or juice from a cut surface: *The tree bled where the branch was trimmed.* 3 of wet dyes, to run. 4 to suffer wounds or die.

blem·ish (blĕm′ĭsh) *n-* a mark that spoils the appearance; a flaw. *vt-* to put a bad mark on; mar; stain: *One bad mistake can blemish a man's reputation.*

blend (blĕnd) *vt-* to mix so thoroughly that the ingredients can no longer be separated or told apart. *vi-* to shade into each other: *The colors in the sunset blend well.*

bless (blĕs) *vt-* [blessed or blest, bless·ing] 1 to make holy: *to bless an altar.* 2 to call down the favor of God upon (a person, thing, or event). 3 to favor (with a blessing, happiness, success, etc.): *Fortune blessed him with a good disposition.*

blight (blīt) *n-* 1 a disease that withers and kills plants or trees, especially over large areas; also, the fungus, bacterium, or virus that causes the disease. 2 anything that ruins or destroys: *War is the blight of mankind.*

blind (blīnd) *adj-* [blind·er, blind·est] 1 unable to see; sightless. 2 unable or unwilling to understand: *He was blind to his own weaknesses.* 3 unthinking; heedless; rash; without reason: *in blind haste; a blind panic.* 4 hidden: *a blind curve.* 5 with no outlet: *a blind alley.*

blind·fold (blīnd′fōld′) *vt-* to cover the eyes of, as

with a bandage. *n-* the bandage or covering over the eyes. *adj-* with the eyes covered and unable to see.

blink (blĭngk) *vi-* 1 to wink quickly. 2 of a light, to twinkle; also, to go on and off rapidly. *vt-* 1 to wink (the eyes) rapidly. 2 to turn (lights) off and on rapidly.

bliss (blĭs) *n-* great happiness; perfect joy; ecstasy.

blis·ter (blĭs'tər) *n-* 1 a little swollen pocket of watery liquid under the surface of the skin, caused by a burn or other injury. 2 bubble formed beneath the surface of a layer of paint or within a slab of glass.

blithe (blĭth, blĭth) *adj-* [blith·er, blith·est] gay; glad; cheerful: *a blithe tune.* —*adv-* blithe'ly. *n-* blithe'ness.

bliz·zard (blĭz'ərd) *n-* a storm with snow, strong winds, and bitter cold.

bloat (blōt) *vt-* to cause to swell; puff up: *All that food has really bloated me! vi-: The cow bloated.*

blob (blŏb) *n-* soft, shapeless mass of anything, especially of a thick liquid: *a blob of paint.*

bloc (blŏk) *n-* political group, often of different parties, who unite for a time in order to promote some common interest: *the farm bloc.* *Hom-* block.

block (blŏk) *n-* 1 solid piece of wood, stone, metal, etc. 2 form for molding or shaping articles, such as hats. 3 stand on which articles are put up for sale by an auctioneer. 4 grooved pulley in a frame.

block·ade (blŏ kād') *n-* 1 the shutting off of a place, especially a port, by ships or troops to keep anything or anybody from coming in or going out. 2 any barrier or obstruction: *The barrels piled at the entrance made an effective blockade.* *vt-* [block·ad·ed, block·ad·ing]: *to* blockade *the enemy's ports.*

block·head (blŏk'hĕd') *n-* stupid person; dunce.

block·house (blŏk'hous') *n-* 1 fortified building, usually of concrete and steel, with loopholes in the walls for shooting at the enemy. 2 similar building that is the control center for a rocket launching. 3 fort built of logs or heavy timber, with a projecting upper story.

Blockhouse

blond (blŏnd) *adj-* [blond·er, blond·est] 1 having light skin and hair: *Many Swedish people are blond.* 2 light in color: *They bought blond furniture. n-* person with skin and hair of light color. —*n-* blond'ness.

blood (blŭd) *n-* 1 a red fluid which circulates through the bodies of men and animals. It carries food, oxygen, and hormones to all parts of the body and removes waste.

blood pressure *n-* pressure of the blood against the walls of the arteries.

blood vessel *n-* an artery, vein, or capillary.

bloom (blōōm) *n-* 1 the flower of a plant: *The violet has a delicate bloom.* 2 a time of flowering. 3 time when one is at the peak of health, beauty, etc.; prime: *the bloom of youth.* 4 a fine white coating, as on some fruit or leaves: *the bloom on a grape.*

blos·som (blŏs'əm) *n-* 1 the flower of a plant, especially a plant which bears fruit: *apple blossom; peach blossom.* 2 stage of bearing flowers: *The trees are in blossom. vi-* to bloom: *The cherry trees are about to blossom.*

blot (blŏt) *n-* 1 a spot or stain: *The ink left a blot on the paper.* 2 something against a person's reputation or character: *His bad marks left a blot on his record. vt-* [blot·ted, blot·ting] 1 to make a spot or stain on.

blotch (blŏch) *n-* 1 a large irregular spot: *There is a big blotch of ink on the curtain.* 2 an ugly, often inflamed spot or mark on the skin: *He had a large blotch on his neck from poison ivy.*

blouse (blous) *n-* 1 a kind of loose outer garment or shirt extending to the waist or below, worn by women and children; shirtwaist. 2 in parts of Europe, a loose smock worn by workmen and farmers to protect their clothes. 3 coat or jacket of military uniforms.

¹**blow** (blō) *vt-* [blew, blown, blow·ing] 1 of wind or air, to be in motion: *The wind blew all afternoon.* 2 to be moved or carried along by the wind: *The papers blew*

all over the room. 3 to make a sound by having air or steam forced through: *The whistle blew and the workers went to lunch.*

²**blow** (blō) *n-* 1 a hard stroke from a hand, fist, stick, or weapon. 2 sudden shock or upset: *The bad news was quite a blow*

blow·out (blō'out') *n-* explosive escape of air from a punctured automobile tire or any other inflated object.

blow·pipe (blō'pīp') *n-* 1 small tube for blowing air into a flame to direct it properly, and to increase its heat. 2 primitive gun of cane, from which a dart is blown by the breath; blowgun. 3 long metal tube used

blub·ber (blŭb'ər) *vi-* to weep noisily; sob. *vt-* to utter with chokes and sobs: *He blubbers his miseries to everyone. n-* 1 noisy sob. 2 layer of fat under the skin of whales, seals, and walruses, used as a source of oil.

bludg·eon (blŭj'ən) *n-* short, heavy-headed stick used as a weapon. *vt-* to strike with, or as with, a club.

blue (blōō) *n-* 1 the color of the clear daytime sky, cornflowers, and forget-me-nots. Blue is between green and indigo on the spectrum. 2 pigment of this color. 3 **the blue** (1) the sea. (2) the sky.

blue·grass (blōō'grăs') *n-* a pasture grass with bluish green stems.

blue·print (blōō'prĭnt') *n-* 1 a photographic print, white on blue paper, used as a plan in building operations, etc. 2 a precise plan of action: *a blueprint for success.*

¹**bluff** (blŭf) *n-* bold, flat headland (as opposed to a sharp, overhanging cliff). *adj-* 1 rising steeply: *the bluff headlands that rose along the shore.* 2 rough but hearty and full of good humor: *a bluff greeting.*

blaf meaning "flat."]

²**bluff** (blŭf) *vt-* 1 to mislead or overawe by assuming a bold or pretentious manner or speech: *He bluffed the guard into admitting him.* 2 to try to get by (something) by pretense: *to bluff a test.*

blu·ing or **blue·ing** (blōō'ĭng) *n-* blue coloring substance used in laundering white clothes to keep them from yellowing.

blun·der (blŭn'dər) *n-* stupid or careless mistake. *vi-* 1 to make a mistake from stupidity, ignorance, or lack of attention. 2 to move clumsily; stumble: *The boy blundered around in the dark room.* —*n-* blun'der·er. **blunder upon** to find or discover by accident.

blun·der·buss (blŭn'dər bŭs') *n-* old-time gun with a bell-shaped muzzle that spreads a quantity of shot at close range.

Blunderbuss

blunt (blŭnt) *adj-* [blunt·er, blunt·est] 1 without a sharp edge or point; not sharp; dull: *a blunt knife.* 2 frank and plain-spoken; abrupt: *a blunt answer. vt-* to make less sharp or keen: *He blunted his knife on a stone. Fatigue blunts one's wits.* —*adv-* blunt'ly. *n-* blunt'ness.

blur (blŭr) *vt-* [blurred, blur·ring] to make indistinct or obscure; dim: *The fog blurred the outlines of the buildings. Time had blurred her memory.*

blurt (blŭrt) *vt-* to speak suddenly and without thinking: *He rushed in and blurted out the bad news.*

blush (blŭsh) *vi-* 1 to become red in the face from shame or embarrassment. 2 to feel shame or embarrassment: *I blush for your mistake. n-* 1 a reddening of the face from shame or embarrassment. 2 rosy color: *the first blush of dawn.*

blus·ter (blŭs'tər) *vi-* 1 to blow gustily, as wind; to be rough and windy, as a storm. 2 to talk in a noisy, threatening style. *n-* 1 the noise and violence of a storm, or of a high wind. 2 noisy talk; empty threats. —*blus'ter·er. adj-* blus'ter·y: *a cold, blustery day.*

bo·a (bō'ə) *n-* 1 any of a large group of nonpoisonous snakes, ranging from 2 to 25 feet in length. Various kinds are found in North and South America, southern Asia, and northern Africa. Boas are constrictors, killing their prey by squeezing it in their coils before swallowing it. 2 a woman's long scarf of feathers or fur.

boar (bôr) *n-* 1 male pig or hog. 2 wild hog. *Hom-* bore.

board (bôrd) *n-* 1 flat piece of sawed timber, longer or wider than it is thick. 2 flat piece of wood or other material prepared for a definite use: *a cutting* board.

Wild boar

board·er (bôr'dər) *n-* person who regularly gets meals, or meals and lodging, at a fixed charge. *Hom-* border.

board·walk (bôrd'wôk') *n-* wide walk or promenade along a beach, usually made of boards.

boast (bōst) *vi-* to brag; praise loudly and rashly oneself and one's belongings or actions. *vt-* to pride oneself on: *The city* boasted *a fifteen-story hotel.* *n-* 1 bragging statement: *His* boasts *about his own cleverness bored everyone.*

boat (bōt) *n-* 1 any kind of small open watercraft, named according to the power by which it moves, such as *row*boat, *sail*boat, *motor*boat; also, a ship. 2 long, narrow dish.

boat·swain (bō'sən) *n-* an under officer of a ship in charge of the crew and of the rigging and anchors.

¹bob (bŏb) *n-* 1 quick jerking movement up and down or to and fro. 2 weight attached to the end of a line: *a pendulum* bob. 3 a float on a fish line. 4 short haircut for girls or women.

bob·bin (bŏb'ən) *n-* spool or reel for thread, used in making fabrics or in sewing machines.

bob·o·link (bŏb'ə lĭngk') *n-* common songbird of the New World related to the oriole and the blackbird and named for its call; ricebird; reedbird.

bob·sled (bŏb'slĕd') *n-* 1 long racing sled having two pairs of runners, a steering wheel, and brakes. 2 long sled made by joining two shorter sleds; also, either of the two sleds so joined. *vi-* [bob·sled·ded, bob·sled·ding]: *The children* bobsledded *all morning.*

bob·tail (bŏb'tāl') *n-* 1 a short tail or a tail cut short. 2 an animal with such a tail. *adj-* (also bob'tailed'): *a bobtail cat.*

¹bode (bōd) *vt-* [bod·ed, bod·ing] to be a sign of; foretell: *The frequent mishaps* boded *disaster.* [from Old English *bodian,* from *boda* meaning "a messenger."]
bode ill (or well) to be a good (or bad) sign or omen: *This* bodes *well for his political success.*

bod·ice (bŏd'əs) *n-* 1 the part of a woman's dress above the waist. 2 wide belt or girdle, laced and tight-fitting.

bod·y (bŏd'ē) *n-* [*pl.* bod·ies] 1 whole physical form of a living thing: *His body ached.* 2 dead person or animal: *The body was taken home for burial.* 3 main or central part of anything: *the body of a car; the body of a book.*

bog (bŏg) *n-* wet, spongy ground made up of partly decayed plants; marsh; swamp; quagmire.

bo·gus (bō'gəs) *adj-* fake; counterfeit; not genuine: *to pass* bogus *money.*

Bo·he·mi·an (bō hē'mē ən) *n-* 1 a native of Bohemia. 2 bohemian someone with artistic or literary leanings who is indifferent to the conventions of social life. *adj-: a* Bohemian *costume; his* bohemian *manners.*

¹boil (boil) *vi-* 1 of a liquid, to give off vapor so fast that the surface bubbles. 2 to be stirred up as if boiling: *The water* boiled *through the canyon.* 3 to be very angry: *He* boiled *with rage.*

²boil (boil) *n-* a painful, pus-filled swelling in the skin, caused by infection in a hair follicle or a skin gland. [from Old English *bȳle.*]

boil·er (boi'lər) *n-* 1 large metal vessel in which steam is produced for heating buildings and driving engines. 2 tank for storing hot water. 3 vessel in which things are boiled: *a wash* boiler. *as modifier: a* boiler *factory.*

bois·ter·ous (boi'stər əs) *adj-* 1 stormy; rough: *a* boisterous *sea.* 2 noisily cheerful: *a burst of* boisterous *laughter.* *—adv-* bois'ter·ous·ly. *n-* bois'ter·ous·ness.

bold (bōld) *adj-* [bold·er, bold·est] 1 showing or demanding courage: *a bold fighter for freedom.* 2 daring; auda-

cious: *a bold remark.* 3 strongly, sharply marked: *a bold signature.* 4 boldface. *—adv-* bold' ly. *n-* bold' ness.

bole (bōl) *n-* trunk of a tree. *Hom-* boll, bowl.

boll (bōl) *n-* the seed pod of a plant such as cotton or flax. *Hom-* bole, bowl.

boll weevil *n-* grayish beetle, about one quarter of an inch long, which lays its eggs in cotton bolls. The larvae cause serious damage to the cotton crop.

Boll weevil.

bo·lo (bō'lō) *n-* [*pl.* bo·los] large, heavy, swordlike knife used in the Philippines.

bo·lo·gna (bə lō'nē, -nə) *n-* a large sausage filled with a mixture of smoked meats.

bol·ster (bōl'stər) *n-* 1 long pillow that extends across a bed. 2 cushioned pad or support. *vt-* to support; brace: *The song* bolstered *our courage.*

¹bolt (bōlt) *n-* 1 short, heavy-headed arrow for a crossbow; dart. 2 anything coming dartingly or suddenly: *a bolt of lightning.* 3 metal pin or rod for fastening together parts of machinery, furniture, etc., threaded to hold a nut. 4 sliding catch for a door or gate; also, that part of a lock which is shot or drawn back by the key. 5 roll of cloth, usually containing about 40 yards.

BOLT   NUT
Door bolt and machine bolt

bomb (bŏm) *n-* 1 war weapon, usually a metal casing containing explosives or incendiary materials, dropped from aircraft to explode upon impact or at a certain altitude over its target. 2 any package of explosive materials equipped with a fuse or detonating mechanism: *a time* bomb; *a gasoline* bomb.

bom·bast (bŏm'băst') *n-* high-sounding or pompous language. *—adj-* bom·bas'tic: *a bombastic speech.* *adv-* bom·bas'ti·cal·ly.

bomb·sight (bŏm'sīt') *n-* instrument in a bomber for aiming bombs at targets below.

bo·nan·za (bə nǎn'zə) *n-* 1 rich vein of ore in a gold or silver mine. 2 anything which brings great wealth. [from Spanish *bonanza* meaning "prosperity; good weather," from Latin *bonus,* "good."]

bond (bŏnd) *n-* 1 anything that fastens or connects; band; tie: *The prisoner broke his* bonds *and escaped. The treaty strengthened the* bond *between the two nations.* 2 certificate issued by a government or business to a lender, promising to pay back the money borrowed plus interest at a specified time.

bond·age (bŏn'dĭj) *n-* slavery; servitude: *The Jews were held in* bondage *in Egypt.*

bone (bōn) *n-* 1 the hard, white, calcified material forming the internal skeleton. 2 any similar substance, such as the tusks of an elephant or walrus, the horns of a deer, whalebone, etc. 3 any one of the separate parts of the internal skeleton.

bon·fire (bŏn'fïar') *n-* outdoor fire for a celebration or for burning rubbish, leaves, etc.

bon·net (bŏn'ət) *n-* 1 head covering for women and children, with ribbons or strings which tie under the chin. 2 cap worn by men and boys in Scotland. 3 ceremonial headdress of feathers worn by American Indians. 4 protective cover for a machine or one of its parts.

bon·ny or **bon·nie** (bŏn'ē) *Chiefly Scot. adj-* [bon·ni·er, bon·ni·est] handsome or pretty: *a bonny lass.*

Bonnet

bo·nus (bō'nəs) *n-* something extra; a sum paid in addition to what is usual or due: *a Christmas* bonus.

boob (boob) *Slang n-* stupid person; dunce.

booby trap *n-* 1 hidden bomb that explodes when a harmless-looking object attached to it is touched. 2 any device for taking someone by surprise.

book (book) *n-* 1 a work of prose, poetry, pictures, etc., printed on sheets of paper that are bound together

bookish 38 **bounteous**

between covers. 2 bound set of blank or ruled sheets, used for taking notes, keeping financial records, etc.: *an account book.*

book·ish (bŏŏk′ĭsh) *adj-* 1 fond of study. 2 thoroughly acquainted with books; learned. 3 making a display of learning: *the student's bookish talk.* —*adv-* **book′ish·ly.** *n-* **book′ish·ness.**

book·keep·ing (bŏŏk′kē′pĭng) *n-* the work of keeping business accounts.

book·worm (bŏŏk′wûrm′) *n-* 1 person who is very fond, sometimes too fond, of reading and studying books. 2 insect larva that eats book bindings and pages.

¹boom (bōōm) *n-* deep, rumbling sound: *the boom of a cannon. vi-* to make or utter such a sound: *His voice boomed out in the empty room.* [from a Dutch word which was probably the imitation of a sound.]

²boom (bōōm) *n-* 1 long pole or beam attached to a ship's mast to hold out the bottom edge of a sail. 2 the lifting arm of a derrick.

³boom (bōōm) *vi-* to increase or develop swiftly: *Business boomed. n-* a great increase: *the business boom.* [apparently an American use of **¹boom.**]

¹boon (bōōn) *n-* a favor, gift, or blessing: *Grant me a boon, O King.* [from Old Norse **bōn** meaning "wish; petition."]

²boon (bōōn) *adj-* cheerful and congenial; jovial: *a boon companion.* [from Old French **bon,** from Latin **bonus** meaning "good."]

boor (bŏŏr) *n-* crude person with bad manners.

boost (bōōst) *vt-* 1 to lift by pushing up from underneath: *If you boost me I can climb that tree.* 2 in electricity, to increase the voltage of (an electric circuit).

¹boot (bōōt) *n-* rubber or leather footwear extending above the ankle, often above the calf. *vt-* to kick: *He booted the ball.* [from Old French **bote,** from an early Germanic language.]

hunting boot

booth (bōōth) *n-* 1 small compartment: *a telephone booth; a toll booth; a voting booth.* 2 restaurant compartment containing facing benches with a table between them. 3 stall at a fair or bazaar, or in a market.

boot·leg (bōōt′lĕg′) *Informal vt-* [**boot·legged, boot·leg·ging**] to make, sell, transport, or communicate (liquor, cameras, information, etc.) illegally. *n-* liquor, etc., made, sold, or transported illegally. *adj-: He had a bottle of bootleg whiskey.* —*n-* **boot′leg′ger.**

bor·ax (bôr′ăks) *n-* white, crystalline compound of sodium, boron, and oxygen. It is used as a cleaning agent, antiseptic, water softener, or the like.

bor·der (bôr′dər, bŏr′-) *n-* 1 edge: *reeds along the border of a stream.* 2 narrow strip along or around something: *a border of flowers along a walk.* 3 frontier of a country; boundary: *to patrol the border.*

¹bore (bôr) *vt-* [**bored, bor·ing**] 1 to make a circular hole in by twisting a screwlike tool with a cutting edge: *The drill bores the ground.* 2 to make (a tunnel, hole, etc.) by, or as by, drilling: *They plan to bore a tunnel through a mountain.*

²bore (bôr) *vt-* [**bored, bor·ing**] to make weary: *His old jokes bore us. n-* tiresome person or thing: *That tune is a bore.* [probably **¹bore** in a later and different meaning.] *Hom-* boar. —*adv-* **bor′ing·ly.**

bo·ric acid (bôr′ĭk) *n-* white powder (H₃BO₃), used as a mild antiseptic.

born (bôrn) *p.p.* of **²bear,** used only for the passive meaning "brought into life": *John was born in May. adj-* natural; so disposed from birth: *a born writer.*
be born to to be brought into life by: *Twins were born to the Smiths.*

borne (bôrn) *p.p.* of **²bear,** used in all meanings except the passive meaning "brought into life."

bo·ron (bôr′ŏn′) *n-* a yellowish-brown solid element used in steels and heat-resistant glass. Symbol B, At. No. 5, At. Wt. 10.811.

bor·ough (bûr′ō) *n-* 1 in some U.S. states, an incor-

porated town that is smaller than a city. 2 one of the five political divisions of New York City.

bor·row (bŏr′ō, bôr′-) *vt-* (considered intransitive when the direct object is implied but not expressed) 1 to get something to use for a while with the understanding that it must be returned: *to borrow a book from the library.*

bos·om (bŏŏz′əm, bōō′zəm) *n-* 1 the breast of a human being. 2 the part of a garment which covers the breast.

¹boss (bôs) *n-* 1 person in charge, especially of workmen; foreman; employer. 2 politician who controls a large number of votes.

bot·a·ny (bŏt′ə nē) *n-* the scientific study of plant life.

botch (bŏch) *vt-* to spoil by poor work; bungle: *He botched the letter and had to write it over. n-* a bungled or poor piece of work; clumsy job. —*adj-* **botch′y.**

both (bōth) *determiner* (traditionally called adjective or pronoun) the two; one and the other (of): *I know both girls. Are both here? n-: Both of his automobiles are red and white.*

both·er (bŏth′ər) *vt-* to give trouble to; worry; pester: *The ringing telephone bothers the busy doctor. vi-* to take trouble: *Don't bother to do that now. n-* source of worry; nuisance: *This broken zipper is a bother.*

both·er·some (bŏth′ər səm) *adj-* annoying; troublesome: *a bothersome cold.*

bot·tle (bŏt′əl) *n-* 1 hollow container with a narrow neck or mouth, usually made of glass. 2 contents of such a container: *a bottle of milk. vt-* [**bot·tled, bot·tling**] to put into bottles: *Milk is bottled by machines.*
bottle up to shut in or hold back: *to bottle up feelings; to bottle up an enemy fleet in port.*

Bottle

bot·tle·neck (bŏt′əl nĕk′) *n-* 1 narrow or crowded route or passageway. 2 anything that obstructs or slows progress.

bot·tom (bŏt′əm) *n-* 1 lowest part of anything: *the bottom of a hill.* 2 underside: *the bottom of a plate.* 3 the ground under water: *the bottom of the lake.* 4 the part of a ship below the water line; also, the ship. 5 important part; foundation: *Let's get to the bottom of the matter.*

bouf·fant (bōō′fănt′, Fr. bōō fä°′) *adj-* puffed out: *a bouffant hairdo; a bouffant sleeve.*

bough (bou) *n-* limb or branch of a tree. *Hom-* **²bow, ³bow.**

bouil·lon (bŏŏl′yŏn′, -yən Fr. bōōyŏn°′) *n-* a clear soup or broth usually made from beef. *Hom-* bullion.

boul·der (bōl′dər) *n-* large piece of loose rock rounded or worn smooth by water, weather, or moving ice. *Hom-* bolder.

boul·e·vard (bŏŏl′ə värd′, bōō′lĕ-) *n-* a broad avenue, often landscaped.

bounce (bouns) *vi-* [**bounced, bounc·ing**] 1 to spring back when thrown against something; rebound: *How far did the ball bounce?* 2 to leap up suddenly; bound: *He bounced out of his chair.*

¹bound (bound) *vi-* 1 to leap or spring; jump: *The dancer bounded onto the stage. Her heart bounded with joy.* 2 to rebound.

²bound (bound) *p.t. & p.p.* of **bind.** *adj-* 1 morally or legally obliged (to): *You are bound to obey.* 2 certain (to); sure (to): *You're bound to be tired if you hike all day.*

³bound (bound) *n-* (usually **bounds**) 1 anything that outlines or encloses a region or area; boundary: *the bounds of a ranch.* 2 area within a boundary or limit: *the bounds of propriety; the outermost bounds of the kingdom.*

bound·a·ry (boun′də rē) *n-* [*pl.* **bound·a·ries**] 1 anything that limits or marks a limit: *The Rio Grande is part of the boundary of Texas.* 2 a dividing line: *The United States-Canada boundary was fixed by treaties.*

bound·less (bound′ləs) *adj-* unlimited; vast: *the boundless ocean; a man of boundless energy.* —*adv-* **bound′less·ly.** *n-* **bound′less·ness.**

boun·te·ous (boun′tē əs) *adj-* 1 giving freely; generous: *a bounteous nature.* 2 plentiful: *a bounteous harvest.* —*adv-* **boun′te·ous·ly.** *n-* **boun′te·ous·ness.**

boun·ty (boun′tē) *n-* [*pl.* **boun·ties**] 1 generosity in giving; also, generous gifts: *This hospital is supported by the bounty of one man.* 2 money offered or paid by a government as a reward for killing harmful animals.

bou·quet (bōō kā′) *n-* 1 (*also* bō kā′) bunch of flowers. 2 pleasant odor; aroma.

bour·geois (bōōrzh′ wā′) *n-* [*pl.* **bour·geois** (-wā, -wāz)] member of the middle class of society. *adj-* belonging to the middle class; having the characteristics and outlook of the middle class. [from French.]

bourn (bôrn, bōōrn) *Archaic n-* 1 a boundary; limit. 2 a destination; goal. Also **bourne.**

bout (bout) *n-* 1 a contest; test of strength or skill: *a wrestling bout; a boxing bout.* 2 period of time; spell: *a long bout of fever.*

bo·vine (bō′vīn) *adj-* 1 relating to, or like, the ox or cow. 2 sluggish; stolid.

¹bow (bō) *n-* 1 anything curved, as a rainbow. 2 weapon for shooting arrows. It is usually a strip of wood bent by a cord tightly stretched between its two ends. 3 slender stick strung with horsehairs for playing the violin or other stringed instruments.

²bow (bou) *n-* a bending of the head, body, or knee expressing greeting, farewell, thanks, or respect. *vi-* 1 to make this motion: *The singer bowed in response to the applause.* 2 to give in; yield: *I bow to your wishes.*

³bow (bou) *n-* front end of a boat, ship, or aircraft. [of uncertain origin.] *Hom-* bough.

bow·el (bou′əl, boul) *n-* 1 intestine. 2 **bowels** innermost, hidden part of anything: *the bowels of the earth.*

bow·er (bou′ər) *n-* shelter of tree branches or vines; arbor.

bow·ie knife (bōō′ē, *also* bō′ē) *n-* strong, single-edged hunting knife, about a foot long, with a curved point.

Bowie knife

¹bowl (bōl) *n-* 1 hollow, rounded dish. 2 contents of such a dish; bowlful: *She ate a bowl of rice.* 3 rounded, hollow part of something: *the bowl of a spoon; the bowl of a pipe.* 4 round or oval stadium. [from Old English **bolla.**] *Hom-* bole, boll.

Bowls

²bowl (bōl) *n-* round ball used in some games. *vi-* 1 to play the game of bowling. 2 to move rapidly and smoothly as if rolling: *The huge truck bowled down the mountain road.*

¹box (bŏks) *vt-* to fight (another) with fists as a sport, usually with gloves. *vi-*: *The champions boxed for five rounds.* *n-* light slap or cuff. [of unknown origin.] **box (someone's) ears** to slap or cuff about the head.

²box (bŏks) *n-* 1 case or container, usually rectangular and furnished with a lid. 2 contents of a box: *a box of crackers.* 3 enclosure for one or more persons: *a jury box; a theater box; a sentry box.*

boy (boi) *n-* 1 male child from the time he is a baby until he is a young man. 2 lad who does errands: *messenger boy.* 3 *Informal* fellow. *Hom-* buoy.

boy·cott (boi′kŏt′) *vt-* 1 to refuse, in agreement with others, to buy from, sell to, or have dealings with (a person, firm, nation, etc.). 2 to refuse as a group to use or purchase (a thing).

brace (brās) *n-* 1 something that holds parts together or in place; something that supports or steadies, as in the framework of a building or machine, or a device to support or straighten a part of the body. 2 a pair: *a brace of ducks.* 3 a curved line [{] or [}] connecting two or more lines of print, staffs of music, or the like.

brace·let (brā′slət) *n-* ornamental band for the wrist or arm.

brack·et (brăk′ət) *n-* 1 triangular or L-shaped support attached to a wall to hold up a shelf, etc. 2 similar support for a machine part. For picture, see *collar.* 3 one of a pair of punctuation marks [ ] used to enclose a part of a text. 4 classification or grouping, usually of wage earners or taxpayers.

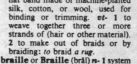

Brackets

brack·ish (brăk′ish) *adj-* slightly salty: *a pond of brackish water.*

brad (brăd) *n-* small, thin nail.

brag (brăg) *vi-* [**bragged, brag·ging**] to boast. *n-* boastful talk.

brag·gart (brăg′ərt) *n-* person given to bragging; a boaster. *adj-* boastful: *his braggart manner.*

braid (brād) *n-* 1 a woven length of three or more strands of hair. 2 a flat band made of machine-plaited silk, cotton, or wool, used for binding or trimming. *vt-* 1 to weave together three or more strands of (hair or other material). 2 to make out of braids or by braiding: *to braid a rug.*

Braid in mat making

braille or **Braille** (brāl) *n-* 1 system of printing for the blind, in which raised dots on a surface represent letters and punctuation. These dots are read by the fingers.

brain (brān) *n-* 1 the soft mass of gray nerve tissue in the skull; the center of thought, emotion, and sensation. 2 mind; intelligence: *You have a good brain; use it.* 3 **brains** intelligence.

brain·wash (brān′wŏsh′, -wôsh′) *vt-* to change the political beliefs and habits of (a person) by intense, mandatory, often hypnotic indoctrination. —*n-* **brain′wash′ing.**

braise (brāz) *vt-* [**braised, brais·ing**] to brown (meat or vegetables) lightly in a little fat and then simmer slowly with a little moisture in a covered pot.

¹brake (brāk) *n-* device for slowing or stopping the motion of a wheel, vehicle, etc. *vt-* [**braked, brak·ing**]: *He braked the car to a stop.* *vi-*: *Always brake before a curve.* [probably from early Dutch **braecke** meaning "a rakelike device."] *Hom-* break.

bran (brăn) *n-* outer coat or husk of ground grain.

branch (brănch) *n-* 1 limb of a tree that grows out of the trunk or out of another limb. 2 any limb; a part or division of a main body: *a branch of the family; the three branches of government.* *vi-* to divide into separate parts: *The road branches in three directions.*

brand (brănd) *n-* 1 a mark, name, or label given a product by the company that makes it; trade name. 2 the make of product so labeled. 3 any identifying mark, especially one made by burning the skin with a hot iron: *The rancher put his brand on the cattle.* 4 a bad reputation; stigma: *He wears the brand of a traitor.*

bran·dish (brăn′dish) *vt-* to wave about or shake as a threat: *The guards brandished their rifles.*

bran·dy (brăn′dē) *n-* [*pl.* **bran·dies**] a strong alcoholic beverage distilled from wine or other fermented fruit juice.

brash (brăsh) *adj-* [**brash·er, brash·est**] 1 rudely bold; impudent; insolent: *His brash manners offend us.* 2 recklessly quick; impetuous; rash: *a brash cavalry officer.* —*adv-* **brash′ly.** *n-* **brash′ness:** *He apologized for his brashness.*

brass (brăs) *n-* 1 yellow alloy made by melting copper and zinc together. 2 musical instrument made of this alloy, such as the trumpet or horn; also, the section of an orchestra or band made up of these instruments. 3 *Informal* bold impudence: *He had the brass to tell me he wouldn't pay.*

brat (brăt) *n-* spoiled or naughty child.

bra·va·do (brə vä′dō, *also* -vā′dō) *n-* [*pl.* **bra·va·does** or **bra·va·dos**] pretense of courage or indifference; boastful defiance: *He assumed an air of bravado.*

brave (brāv) *adj-* [**brav·er, brav·est**] having or showing courage: *The brave soldiers attacked.*

brav·er·y (brā′ və rē) *n-* courage; fearlessness.

¹**bra·vo** (brā′ vō, -vō′) *interj-* well done! *n-* [*pl.* bra·vos] a shout of applause. [from Italian **bravo** meaning literally "brave; good."]

brawl (brôl) *n-* noisy quarrel or fight. *vi-: The rowdies* brawled *in the street.*

brawn (brôn) *n-* **1** firm, strong muscles. **2** muscular strength: *The boxer had more* brawn *than skill.*

brawn·y (brô′ nē) *adj-* [brawn·i·er, brawn·i·est] muscular; strong: *his* brawny *arms.*

bray (brā) *n-* **1** a harsh, loud cry made by a donkey. **2** any sound like it. *vi-* to utter a loud, harsh sound.

braze (brāz) *vt-* [brazed, braz·ing] to weld with a solder that melts only at high temperatures.

bra·zen (brā′ zən) *adj-* **1** made of brass; like brass. **2** bold and shameless: *a* brazen *lie.* —*adv-* bra′ zen·ly. *n-* bra′ zen·ness: *The* brazenness *of the girl, lying about her age!*

¹**bra·zier** (brā′ zhər) *n-* open pan for holding burning charcoal or live coals. [from French **brasier,** from **braise** meaning "live coals."]

breach (brēch) *n-* **1** an opening made by breaking through; a gap: *a* breach *in a wall.* **2** the action of breaking (a law, a promise, etc.); violation: *a* breach *of contract; a* breach *of duty; a* breach *of friendship.* *vt-* to make a break, opening, or gap in: *to* breach *the enemy's defenses.* *Hom-* breech.

bread (brĕd) *n-* **1** article of food made from flour or meal which is moistened, raised, kneaded, and baked.

breadth·ways (brĕdth′ wāz′) or **breadth·wise** (-wīz′) *adv-* in the direction of the breadth or width.

break (brāk) *vt-* [broke, brok·en, break·ing] **1** to knock apart by a blow or strain; fracture; burst: *to* break *a dish; to* break *a bone; to* break *the skin.* **2** to put out of working order; damage; ruin: *to* break *a watch.* **3** to stop the course, order, or regularity of; interrupt: *to* break *the monotony; to* break *formation; to* break *an electrical circuit.*

break·age (brā′ klj) *n-* **1** the act of breaking. **2** things broken. **3** loss or damage caused by breaking, or an equivalent in money for such loss or damage.

break·down (brāk′ doun′) *n-* **1** mental or physical collapse. **2** a sudden failure to work properly: *A* breakdown *of machinery stopped production.*

break·er (brā′ kər) *n-* **1** wave which hits the rocks or the shore and breaks into foam. **2** person or thing that breaks.

break·fast (brĕk′ fəst) *n-* first meal of the day. *vi-: We* breakfast *at eight.*

break·neck (brāk′ nĕk′) *adj-* reckless; rash; dangerous: *Wallace rode his bicycle at* breakneck *speed.*

breast (brĕst) *n-* **1** upper front part of the body between the neck and the abdomen; chest. **2** either of the milk glands of a woman. **3** the heart; feelings. *vt-* to oppose; struggle with: *to* breast *waves.*

make a clean breast of to confess fully.

breast·bone (brĕst′ bōn′) *n-* sternum.

breast·plate (brĕst′ plāt′) *n-* a piece of armor to protect the chest.

Breastplate

breast·work (brĕst′ wûrk′) *n-* hastily constructed wall for defense, usually chest high.

breath (brĕth) *n-* **1** air drawn into and forced out of the lungs. **2** a drawing in or a forcing out of air: *Take a deep* breath. **3** the power to breathe easily: *Wait until I get my* breath.

breathe (brĕth) *vi-* [breathed, breath·ing] **1** to draw air into the lungs and force it out. **2** to stop to rest after action or strain: *The worst is over; we can* breathe *again.* *vt-* **1** to whisper: *Don't* breathe *a word of this.* **2** to inspire: *The pitcher* breathed *new life into the team.*

breech (brēch) *n-* **1** the hinder part of anything, especially of firearms. **2** buttocks; rump. *Hom-* breach.

breed (brēd) *vt-* [bred, breed·ing] **1** to give birth to: *The cat has* bred *four litters.* **2** to mate

or raise, in order to maintain or improve the stock: *The ranch owner* breeds *cattle for beef.* **3** to train; rear: *The prince was* bred *to be a king.* **4** to be a fertile place for; give rise to: *Swamps* breed *mosquitoes.*

breed·ing (brē′ dĭng) *n-* **1** the training or bringing up of young; especially, the results of training; good manners: *a man of* breeding. **2** a producing of plants and animals to get better kinds: *the* breeding *of livestock.*

breeze (brēz) *n-* a gentle wind.

breez·y (brē′ zē) *adj-* [breez·i·er, breez·i·est] **1** fanned by light winds: *a large,* breezy *porch.* **2** lively; jolly; gay and cheerful: *a* breezy *manner.* —*adv-* breez′ i·ly. *n-* breez′ i·ness.

brew·ing (brōō′ ĭng) *n-* **1** the making of beer and other malt liquors. **2** the quantity of such made at one time.

bribe (brīb) *n-* gift made or promised to a person to influence him to decide or act dishonestly: *The man tried to give the policeman a* bribe *to let him go.* *vt-* [bribed, brib·ing]: *The man tried to* bribe *the policeman.*

brib·er·y (brī′ bo rē) *n-* [*pl.* brib·er·ies] the giving or taking of bribes; also, an instance of this.

bric-a-brac (brĭk′ ə brăk′) *n-* small articles of artistic or sentimental value put on display; knicknacks.

brick (brĭk) *n-* **1** oblong block of clay hardened by baking in the sun or in an oven; also, such blocks used as building material: *a pile* of bricks; *a* house *of brick.* **2** something shaped like such a block. **3** *Informal* a good fellow. *as modifier: a* brick *wall.*

bride (brīd) *n-* woman newly married or about to be married.

bride·groom (brīd′ grōōm′) *n-* man newly married or about to be married.

¹**bridge** (brĭj) *n-* **1** structure built across a river, valley, etc., to allow passage for men or vehicles. **2** raised platform on a ship, from which the ship is navigated and controlled. **3** the upper, bony part of the nose. **4** the arched support for the strings on a violin, cello, etc. **5** one or more false teeth with a mounting for holding in place.

²**bridge** (brĭj) *n-* card game for four players. One of the most common types is **contract bridge.** [apparently from Russian **biritch,** an old card game.]

bri·dle (brī′ dəl) *n-* **1** head harness of a horse, including the bit and reins. **2** a check; restraint: *a* bridle *on one's tongue.* *vt-* [bri·dled, bri·dling] **1** to put a bit and reins on: *Saddle and* bridle *the horses.* **2** to hold; check; control: *You must learn to* bridle *your temper.*

Bridle

brief (brēf) *adj-* [brief·er, brief·est] not long in time; short: *The train made a* brief *stop. The speech was* brief. *n-* a summary, especially a lawyer's outline of a case. *vt-* to give a detailed summary of instructions to: *The captain* briefed *his officers.* —*adv-* brief′ ly. *n-* brief′ ness.

brief·case (brēf′ kās′) *n-* leather or plastic case with handles, for carrying papers and books.

¹**bri·er** or **bri·ar** (brī′ ər) *n-* **1** a thorny shrub, such as one of the rose family. **2** a thorn, as of a rose. **3** a patch of thorny shrubs. [from Old English **brēr.**] —*adj-* bri′ e·ry or bri′ a·ry.

¹**brig** (brĭg) *n-* prison cell on a warship. [a special use of ²**brig,** probably an American word.]

²**brig** (brĭg) *n-* a two-masted square-rigged vessel. [short for **brigantine,** from French **brigantine,** from Italian **brigantino,** "fighting ship."]

Brig. **1** brigade. **2** brigadier.

bri·gade (brĭ gād′) *n-* **1** in the U.S. Army, a unit consisting of two or more regiments, usually under the command of a brigadier general.

Brig

brig·and (brĭg′ ənd) *n-* member of a gang of robbers; bandit.

bright (brīt) *adj-* [**bright·er, bright·est**] 1 giving or reflecting light; shining: *Rub the silver to a bright polish.* 2 vivid; intense: *to wear bright colors.* 3 cheerful; happy: *They tried to be bright and gay.* 4 clever: a bright *idea*; a bright *student.* 5 favorable; hopeful: *The future looks bright.* —*adv-* **bright′ ly.** *n-* **bright′ ness.**

bril·liant (brĭl′ yənt) *adj-* 1 shining brightly; sparkling: *The lake looked brilliant in the sunlight.* 2 splendid; magnificent: *a brilliant celebration.* 3 having outstanding ability: *a brilliant scholar.* 4 in music, having a bright and clear sound.

brim (brĭm) *n-* 1 edge or rim: *the brim of a cup.* 2 edge that stands out from the crown of a hat. *vi-* [**brimmed, brim·ming**] to be full to the very edge: *Her eyes brimmed with tears.* —*adj-* **brim′ less.**

brine (brīn) *n-* 1 strong salt solution. 2 the ocean or its water.

bring (brĭng) *vt-* [**brought, bring·ing**] 1 to cause (a person or thing) to come along with one by leading, carrying, driving, etc.: *to bring home a friend; to bring lunch to school; to bring horses to the corral.* 2 to be accompanied by; result in: *Springtime brings flowers.*

brink (brĭngk) *n-* 1 edge or margin of a steep place: *the brink of a pit.* 2 verge: *the brink of disaster.*

brisk (brĭsk) *adj-* 1 active; lively; swift; nimble: *a brisk walker.* 2 keen; bracing: *a brisk wind.* —*adv-* **brisk′ ly.** *n-* **brisk′ ness.**

bris·ket (brĭs′ kət) *n-* the breast or lower chest of an animal used for food.

bris·tle (brĭs′ əl) *n-* a short, stiff, coarse hair. *vi-* [**bris·tled, bris·tling**] 1 to stand up in a stiff, prickly way: *The cat's hair bristled when the dog barked.* 2 to show signs of anger or defiance: *The witness bristled at the rude*

brit·tle (brĭt′ əl) *adj-* [**brit·tler, brit·tlest**] easily broken; apt to break: *a brittle glass.* —*n-* **brit′ tle·ness.**

broach (brōch) *vt-* 1 to begin to talk about; introduce: *How do you broach an unpleasant subject?* 2 to pierce or tap: *to broach a keg of cider.* *n-* 1 a spit for roasting meat. 2 a tool for boring or reaming, especially one used to tap a cask. *Hom-* **brooch.**

broad (brôd) *adj-* [**broad·er, broad·est**] 1 wide from side to side. 2 spacious; large.

broad·cast (brôd′ kăst′) *vt-* [**broad·cast or broad·cast·ed, broad·cast·ing**] 1 to send out over radio or television. 2 to spread around: *Don't broadcast the secret I just told you.* 3 to scatter: *The seed was broadcast rather than sown in rows.* *adv-* so as to scatter widely: *to sow broadcast.* *n-* act of sending a radio or television program.

broad·cloth (brôd′ klŏth′, klôth′) *n-* 1 a fine grade of cotton or silk cloth used for shirts, skirts, dresses, blouses, etc. 2 fine woolen cloth with a smooth surface.

broad·en (brôd′ ən) *vi-* to grow wider: *The river broadens at this point.* *vt-* to make broader or more tolerant.

broad jump *n-* in athletics, a jump made for distance, either from a standing position or from a running start.

broad·side (brôd′ sīd′) *n-* 1 entire side of a ship that shows above the water. 2 a firing of all the guns on one side of a ship. 3 *Informal* a printed or verbal attack on some person. *adv-* with the widest side turned toward an object: *The barge bore down broadside upon the tug.*

bro·cade (brō kād′) *n-* cloth woven with gold and silver threads or ornamented with raised designs of flowers, etc. *vt-* [**bro·cad·ed, bro·cad·ing**] to weave with a raised pattern.

broc·co·li (brŏk′ ə lē) *n-* plant related to the cauliflower, having stalks and tight clusters of green buds, eaten as a vegetable.

bro·chure (brō shŏŏr′) *n-* printed booklet or pamphlet.

bro·gan (brō′ gən) *n-* heavy, coarse work shoe, usually having a hobnailed sole, formerly worn in Ireland and Scotland.

Broccoli

¹brogue (brōg) *n-* 1 oxford shoe decorated with stitching, pinking, and perforations. 2 brogan. [from Gaelic brōg meaning "shoe."]

²brogue (brōg) *n-* a pronunciation characteristic of a dialect of English, especially Irish or Scottish. [of uncertain origin.]

broil (broil) *vt-* 1 to cook by exposing to radiant heat, as in an oven broiler or on a grid over coals: *to broil a steak.* 2 to subject to great heat; make very hot: *The sun broiled the men on the raft.*

bro·ken (brō′ kən) *p.p.* of **break.** *adj-* 1 having breaks or gaps; discontinuous: *a broken line.* 2 having a rough surface; uneven: *a stretch of broken ground.* 3 lacking parts; incomplete: *a broken set of chessmen.*

bro·ker (brō′ kər) *n-* person who buys or sells for another person as his agent: *a cotton broker; a real estate broker.*

bro·ker·age (brō′ kər ĭj) *n-* the business of a broker; also, his fee or commission.

bro·mide (brō′ mīd′, -mĭd) *n-* compound in which bromine is combined with another element or a radical, especially such a compound used as a sedative drug.

bro·mine (brō′ mēn′, -mĭn) *n-* reddish-brown liquid chemical element with irritating fumes. Symbol Br, At. No. 35, At. Wt. 79.91.

bron·chi·al tubes (brŏng′ kē əl) *n-* the larger air tubes of the lungs, including the bronchi and bronchia.

bron·chi·tis (brŏng kī′ tĭs) *n-* inflammation of the bronchial tubes.

bronze (brŏnz) *n-* 1 hard and durable alloy of copper and tin, sometimes containing small amounts of other metals. 2 work of art cast or wrought in this alloy. 3 a paint that looks like this alloy. 4 a metallic golden-brown color. *adj-: a bronze statue*; bronze *skin.*

brooch (brōch, brōōch) *n-* ornamental pin fastened with a clasp. *Hom-* **broach.**

brood (brōōd) *n-* 1 all the young hatched by a bird at one time: *a brood of chickens.* 2 all the children of one mother: *a brood of ten children.* *vi-* 1 to sit on eggs: *The hen brooded.* 2 to think long and moodily.

¹brook (brŏŏk) *n-* small, natural stream of water; creek. [from Old English brōc, related to **break.**]

²brook (brŏŏk) *vt-* to bear; tolerate: *I will brook no interference with my plans.* [from Old English brūcan meaning "to enjoy."]

broom (brōōm, brŏŏm) *n-* 1 long-handled brush used for sweeping. 2 shrub related to the clover, with stiff, slender branches and yellow flowers. *Hom-* **brougham.**

broth (brŏth, brôth) *n-* thin soup made by boiling meat in water.

broth·er (brŭth′ ər) *n-* [*pl.* **broth·ers or breth·ren**] 1 boy or man having the same parents as another person. 2 male fellow member of a race, nation, profession, lodge, union, or other group. 3 member of a male religious order who is not a priest; friar.

brow (brou) *n-* 1 the forehead. 2 arch of hair over an eye; eyebrow. 3 the edge of a steep place: *the brow of a hill.*

brow·beat (brou′ bēt′) *vt-* [**brow·beat, brow·beat·en, brow·beat·ing**] to frighten by stern looks or words; bully.

brown (broun) *n-* the color of chocolate, coffee, and most tree trunks. *adj-* [**brown·er, brown·est**] of this color: *the brown autumn leaves.* *vt-* to cause to have this color by cooking, roasting, etc.: *to brown a chicken in the oven.* *vi-: The chicken browned in the oven.* —*n-* **brown′ ness.**

browse (brouz) *vi-* [**browsed, brows·ing**] 1 to nibble on grass or young shoots; graze: *The cattle browsed in the fields.* 2 to look over various objects idly and at random.

bruise (brōōz) *n-* 1 an injury, caused by a blow or fall, which does not break the skin but discolors it. 2 an injury to the outside of a fruit, vegetable, or plant. *vt-* [**bruised, bruis·ing**] 1 to injure and produce a black-and-blue mark: *I fell and bruised my leg.* 2 to hurt (someone's feelings). *vi-* to become bruised: *Tomatoes bruise easily.*

brunt (brŭnt) *n-* heaviest part of a shock or strain.

¹brush (brŭsh) *n-* 1 implement made of bristles, hairs, or wire, set in a stiff back or fastened to a handle, and used for scrubbing, cleaning, painting, smoothing, etc.

2 electrical conductor, often a spring-loaded carbon block, that delivers current to the commutator of an electric motor or takes it from that of a generator.

brusque (brŭsk) *adj-* [**brusqu·er, brusqu·est**] rough or abrupt in speech or manner: *Bruce gave a brusque reply.* —*adv-* **brusque′ly.** *n-* **brusque′ness.**

bru·tal (brōō′ təl) *adj-* cruel; savage. —*adv-* **bru′tal·ly.**

bru·tal·i·ty (brōō tăl′ ə tē) *n-* [*pl.* **bru·tal·i·ties**] 1 violent and inhuman cruelty. 2 inhuman act.

brute (brōōt) *n-* 1 beast; animal without reasoning power. 2 a cruel, inhuman person. *as modifier:* *His* brute *strength enabled him to go on. Hurricanes and floods show nature's* brute *forces.* **Hom-** bruit.

bub·ble (bŭb′ əl) *n-* 1 a thin, globelike film of liquid filled with air or gas: *a soap* bubble. 2 a small, globelike ball of air or gas rising to the surface of water or liquid, or held within a solid such as ice or glass. 3 plan or scheme that seems promising but collapses for lack of substance or practicality.

buc·ca·neer (bŭk′ ə nēr′) *n-* pirate; sea robber.

buck (bŭk) *n-* 1 the male of certain animals, especially the deer, antelope, and rabbit. The female is called a doe. 2 young man, especially a jaunty, dapper fellow. 3 a sudden jump upward, as of an untamed or unruly horse. 4 *Slang* a dollar. *vi-* to jump upward with the back arched, as a horse does to throw off a rider. *vt-* 1 to charge or push one's way through: *The quarterback* bucked *the line of the opposing team.* 2 to struggle against; oppose: *to* buck *the crowds during the rush hour.*

pass the buck *Informal* to shift responsibility.

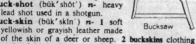
Bucking horse

buck·board (bŭk′ bôrd′) *n-* light wagon with the seat set on a long, flexible board without springs.

buck·et (bŭk′ ət) *n-* 1 container to hold or carry water, milk, etc.; a pail. 2 bucketful.

buck·et·ful (bŭk′ ət fōol′) *n-* the amount held by any bucket.

Buckboard

¹buck·le (bŭk′ əl) *n-* 1 a clasp for holding together the ends of a strap or belt. 2 a clasplike ornament for shoes, etc. *vt-* [**buck·led, buck·ling**] to fasten with such a clasp: *to* buckle *a seat belt.*

²buck·le (bŭk′ əl) *vi-* [**buck·led, buck·ling**] to bend or twist from heat or strain: *The bridge* buckled *as the armored tanks crossed it.* *vt-*: *The weight* buckled *the bridge.*

buck·saw (bŭk′ sò′) *n-* narrow saw set in a deep, H-shaped frame, used with both hands for sawing wood.

buck·shot (bŭk′ shŏt′) *n-* heavy lead shot used in a shotgun.

buck·skin (bŭk′ skĭn′) *n-* 1 soft yellowish or grayish leather made of the skin of a deer or sheep. 2 **buckskins** clothing made of this leather. *as modifier:* *a* buckskin *jacket.*

Bucksaw

buck·wheat (bŭk′ hwēt′) *n-* 1 cereal plant with black, triangular seeds used for flour. 2 the flour itself.

bud (bŭd) *n-* 1 a flower or leaf that is not yet open, such as a lily bud; also, anything in an early stage of development. 2 an undeveloped shoot on the stem of a plant, seen as a small bulge or swelling. 3 in primitive animals, a small outgrowth that develops into a new animal.

budge (bŭj) *vt-* [**budged, budg·ing**] (usually in a negative sentence) to move slightly: *The box was so heavy that no one could* budge *it.* *vi-*: *The mule wouldn't* budge.

bud·get (bŭj′ ət) *n-* a listing or plan that shows how much money is available and how it is to be divided up and spent for various purposes: *a family* budget; *a government* budget.

¹buff (bŭf) *n-* 1 pale yellowish-tan color. 2 soft, yellowish leather formerly made from the skin of a buffalo and now from that of an ox. 3 wheel or other tool covered with this leather, used for polishing.

²buff (bŭf) *Informal n-* a fan; enthusiast; amateur expert: *a racing* buff. [American word of uncertain origin.]

buf·fa·lo (bŭf′ ə lō′) *n-* [*pl.* **buf·fa·loes, buf·fa·los,** or **buf·fa·lo**] 1 any of several kinds of oxen, such as the water buffalo of Eastern Asia or the Cape buffalo of South Africa. 2 the bison of North America.

Cape buffalo

¹buff·er (bŭf′ ər) *n-* 1 anything that absorbs or cushions the shock of a blow, tension, strain, etc. 2 chemical that keeps the pH of a solution at a constant level by reacting with excess acid or base.

¹buf·fet (bŭf′ ət) *n-* 1 a blow struck by the hand or fist. 2 a knock or stroke. *vt-* 1 to strike with the hand or fist. 2 to beat; knock about: *The waves* buffeted *the boat.* [from an Old French word **buffe** meaning "a blow."]

²buf·fet (bə fā′, bōō fā′) *n-* 1 sideboard or low cabinet for dishes, silver, and table linen. 2 refreshment counter, or restaurant with such a counter. 3 a meal put out on a sideboard or table, at which guests help themselves.

buf·foon (bə fōōn′) *n-* one who amuses others by jokes, antics, etc.; a clown.

bug (bŭg) *n-* 1 any crawling insect. 2 a flattened insect with a sucking mouth, with or without wings: *a water* bug. 3 *Informal* a disease germ. 4 *Informal* person who is overly enthusiastic about a subject, hobby, etc.

bug·gy (bŭg′ ē) *n-* [*pl.* **bug·gies**] a light carriage with a single seat and a removable top.

bu·gle (byōō′ gəl) *n-* a trumpetlike, brass wind instrument for sounding military calls.

build (bĭld) *vt-* [**built, build·ing**] to make by putting materials or parts together; construct: *Men* build *houses and ships. Birds* build *nests.* *n-* way, form, or shape in which the body is put together: *a heavy* build.

Bugle

bulb (bŭlb) *n-* 1 rounded underground bud of some plants, such as the lily, onion, tulip, and narcissus, from which the plant grows. 2 anything shaped like such a bud: *the* bulb *of a thermometer.* 3 small glass globe containing a fine wire that gives off light when electricity passes through it: *light* bulb. —*adj-* **bulb′like′.**

Electric bulb

Onion bulb

bul·bous (bŭl′ bəs) *adj-* 1 in botany, growing from and producing bulbs, as tulips. 2 like a bulb; somewhat round; swollen: *The clown had a* bulbous *red nose.*

bulge (bŭlj) *n-* a rounded swelling which stands out; a protuberance. *vi-* [**bulged, bulg·ing**] to swell outward: *His schoolbag* bulged *with books.* *vt-*: *The books* bulged *his schoolbag.* —*adj-* **bulg′y** [**bulg·i·er, bulg·i·est**]: *his* bulgy *pockets.*

bulk (bŭlk, bōōlk) *n-* size; mass; great size: *In spite of its* bulk, *the elephant can move quickly.*

bulk·head (bŭlk′ hĕd′, bōōlk′-) *n-* 1 an upright partition in a ship, separating watertight compartments. 2 any structure built to resist the pressure of water, air, or earth, such as a sea wall.

bulk·y (bŭl′ kē, bōōlk′-) *adj-* [**bulk·i·er, bulk·i·est**] massive; big; broad; of large volume. —*adv-* **bulk′i·ly.** *n-* **bulk′i·ness:** *the* bulkiness *of a mohair sweater.*

BULKHEAD

Bulkhead of a ship

¹bull (bōol) *n-* 1 the male of any animal of the ox family. 2 any of several other large male animals, such as the whale or elephant. 3 on the stock exchange, a person who tries to raise prices for his own advantage

bullet 43 **bury**

bul·let (bŏŏl′ət) *n-* small piece of metal shaped to be fired from a rifle, pistol, machine gun, etc.

Bulldozer

bul·le·tin (bŏŏl′ə tən) *n-* 1 a brief report on some matter of public interest: *The doctor released a bulletin on his famous patient's condition.*

bul·lion (bŏŏl′yən) *n-* uncoined gold or silver in a mass, lumps, or bars. *Hom-* bouillon.

bull's-eye (bŏŏl′ zī′) *n-* 1 center point of a target, or a shot that hits it; hence anything especially successful. 2 a bulging lens used to focus the light from a lantern upon a small spot; also, a lantern having such a lens.

bul·ly (bŏŏl′ē) *n-* [*pl.* **bul·lies**] quarrelsome person who teases, threatens, or torments a smaller or weaker person. *vt-* [**bul·lied, bul·ly·ing**]: *He is always bullying his employees.* *adj- Informal* excellent.

bul·rush (bŏŏl′rush′) *n-* tall plant with slender stalks that grows in wet places.

bul·wark (bŏŏl′wərk) *n-* 1 a barrier or wall built for defense or protection. Earthworks, ramparts, and breakwaters are bulwarks. 2 anything that protects: *The Bill of Rights is a bulwark of our freedom.*

Bulwark of a ship

¹bump·er (bŭm′pər) *n-* something that protects against shock or collision; especially, one of the thick metal strips in the front or rear of a car. [from **bump.**]

bump·y (bŭm′pē) *adj-* [**bump·i·er, bump·i·est**] 1 having bumps: *a bumpy road.* 2 jolting; jarring: *a bumpy ride.* —*adv-* **bump′i·ly.** *n-* **bump′i·ness.**

bun (bŭn) *n-* 1 a raised rounded roll of bread or cake. 2 knot of hair usually worn at the nape of the neck.

bunch (bŭnch) *n-* 1 a number of things growing together; a cluster: *a bunch of grapes.* 2 a collection of similar things fastened or grouped together: *a bunch of flowers; a bunch of keys.* *vt-* to gather or consider together. *vi-: The dress bunches at the waist.*

bun·dle (bŭn′dəl) *n-* 1 a number of things bound or tied together: *a bundle of rags.* 2 a package. *vt-* [**bun·dled, bun·dling**] to tie or wrap: *Will you please bundle these shirts together?*

bun·ion (bŭn′yən) *n-* an inflamed swelling on the foot, usually on the first joint of the great toe.

¹bunk (bŭngk) *n-* 1 a bed built as a shelf on a wall or built into a recess in a wall. 2 a narrow bed or cot. *vi-* to sleep in a makeshift bed: *You can bunk on the sofa.* [perhaps short for **bunker,** "a ship's bin," itself of uncertain origin.]

bunk·er (bŭng′kər) *n-* 1 large bin, usually for coal on a ship. 2 natural obstacle on a golf course, such as a sandy hollow or mound of earth. 3 strong defensive fortification, such as a deep trench protected by logs or an underground chamber made of reinforced concrete and steel.

²bun·ting (bŭn′tĭng) *n-* 1 coarse cotton material used for flags. 2 long pieces of this material with flaglike patterns.

buoy (bŏŏ′ē, *also* boi) *n-* 1 a float carrying a whistle, light, bell, or marker, anchored to show the position of rocks, shoals, or a channel or anchorage. 2 device to keep a person afloat: *a life buoy.* *vt-* to support or raise in the water or as if in water (usually followed by "up"): *to buoy up a swimmer; to buoy one's spirits.*

buoy·an·cy (boi′ən sē) *n-* 1 the ability of something to float: *Cork has more buoyancy than iron.* 2 the upward force a liquid exerts on an object partly or entirely submerged in the liquid. 3 the process of floating. 4 cheerfulness.

Conical and spar buoys

bur *or* **burr** (bûr) *n-* prickly, clinging seedcase, or a plant bearing such seedcases.

¹bur·den (bûr′dən) *n-* 1 something carried; a load. 2 weight or load on the mind or spirit: *a burden of grief, sorrow, or care.* *vt-* to weary; put too much upon. [from Old English *brythan,* related to **²bear.**]

bur·den·some (bûr′dən səm) *adj-* hard to bear; weighty; troublesome: *a burdensome chore.*

bur·dock (bûr′dŏk′) *n-* coarse weed with broad leaves and prickly burs that stick to clothing and animals.

bu·reau (byŏŏr′ō) *n-* [*pl.* **bu·reaus** *or* **bu·reaux** (-ōz)] 1 chest of drawers for holding clothing. 2 office for special business: *a travel bureau.* 3 government office or department: *Federal Bureau of Investigation.*

bu·reauc·ra·cy (byŏŏr′ŏk′rə sē) *n-* [*pl.* **bu·reauc·ra·cies**] 1 government by an organized system of bureaus or departments. 2 officials of such a government, spoken of as a group.

bur·geon (bûr′jən) *vi-* 1 to bud or sprout with new growth: *Plants burgeon in the spring.* 2 to grow and prosper; expand; flourish; boom: *The town burgeoned overnight.*

bur·glar (bûr′glər) *n-* person who breaks into a building to steal.

bur·glar·y (bûr′glə rē) *n-* [*pl.* **bur·glar·ies**] crime of breaking into a building to steal.

Bur·gun·dy (bûr′gən dē) *n-* red or white wine from the province of Burgundy; also, any similar wine.

bur·i·al (bĕr′ē əl) *n-* the placing of a body in a grave. *as modifier: a burial ground.*

bur·lap (bûr′lăp′) *n-* coarse cloth of hemp or other fiber, used mostly in making bags and wrappings.

bur·lesque (bûr′lĕsk′) *n-* 1 a ridiculous imitation; a parody. 2 composition or play in which a trifling subject is treated with mock dignity, or a dignified subject with irreverence.

bur·ley *or* **Bur·ley** (bûr′lē) *n-* [*pl.* **bur·leys**] a fine, light-colored tobacco grown chiefly in Kentucky.

bur·ly (bûr′lē) *adj-* [**bur·li·er, bur·li·est**] big and strong; muscular. —*n-* **bur′li·ness.**

¹burn (bûrn) *vt-* [**burned** *or* **burnt, burn·ing**] 1 to cause to be consumed or destroyed by fire: *They burned the secret papers.* 2 to injure or damage by fire, heat, chemicals, steam, etc.: *The match burned my finger.* 3 to use as fuel: *The furnace burns gas.* 4 to cause by fire, heat, chemicals, etc.: *The acid burned a hole in his coat.* 5 *Chemistry* to cause (something) to undergo combustion.

burn·er (bûr′nər) *n-* part of a lamp, stove, or furnace from which the flame or heat comes.

bur·nish (bûr′nĭsh) *vt-* to polish by rubbing; give a shiny finish to: *Mother burnished the copper pots.*

bur·ro (bûr′ō *or* bŏŏr′ō) *n-* [*pl.* **bur·ros**] in Mexico and southwestern United States, a small donkey used as a pack animal. [from Spanish *burro,* from an earlier word *burrico* meaning "little horse."] *Homs-* borough, burrow.

bur·row (bûr′ō) *n-* 1 hole in the ground, such as is dug by a fox, rabbit, or other animal as a refuge or nest. 2 a secluded dwelling place or place of retreat. *vi-* 1 to dig a hole in the earth, as for shelter.

Burro. 3—3 1/2 ft high at shoulder

burst (bûrst) *vi-* [**burst, burst·ing**] 1 to break open violently; explode: *Bombs burst in the air.* 2 to come, go, begin, or do something suddenly: *The boy burst into the room. The storm burst.* 3 to start or break out,(into) some action or expression of feeling: *The birds burst into song. She burst into tears.*

bur·y (bĕr′ē) *vt-* [**bur·ied, bur·y·ing**] 1 to put in a grave; inter. 2 to cover, especially with earth. 3 to sink; embed: *He buried his sword in the boar.* 4 to put nearly out of reach: *They've buried themselves in the coutry.* 5 to absorb; engross: *He buried himself in his work to forget his troubles.* *Hom-* berry.

bus (bŭs) n- [pl. bus·es or bus·ses] large automobile with several rows of seats; omnibus. vt- [bused or bussed, bus·ing or bus·sing] to convey by bus: The children were bused to school. vi-: to bus to school. Hom- buss.

bush (boosh) n- 1 any low shrub with many branches. 2 (also bush country) land that is not cleared; especially, a region covered with brushwood, shrubs, and trees in Australia and Africa. vt- Slang to tire out.

beat around the bush to talk around the subject.

bush·el (boosh' əl) n- measure used for grains, fruits, vegetables, or other dry products. A bushel is equal to four pecks or eight gallons. as modifier: a bushel basket.

bush·ing (boosh' ing) n- 1 in machinery, a hollow metal cylinder used as a replaceable bearing around a rotating shaft or axle. 2 liner placed around an electrical connection to insulate it or to protect it from abrasion.

busi·ness (bĭz' nəs) n- 1 a buying and selling of goods; trade: My father is in the clothing business. 2 commercial enterprise, such as a factory, store, etc.: Their small business has been handed down from father to son.

bus·kin (bŭs' kĭn) n- 1 high, laced boot. 2 thick-soled boot worn in ancient times by tragic actors and used as a symbol of tragedy.

bus·man (bŭs' mən) n- [pl. bus·men] man who drives a bus.

busman's holiday n- holiday passed in doing something similar to one's regular job, as a postman taking a long walk.

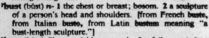
Buskins

¹bust (bŭst) n- 1 the chest or breast; bosom. 2 a sculpture of a person's head and shoulders. [from French buste, from Italian busto, from Latin bustum meaning "a bust-length sculpture."]

²bust (bŭst) Slang n- 1 blow; punch. 2 a failure. vt- 1 to hit; punch. 2 to burst or break. 3 to ruin financially. 4 to reduce in rank; demote. [variant form of burst.]

bus·tard (bŭs'tərd) n- large, swift-running game bird of the Old World, related to the cranes and plovers.

¹bus·tle (bŭs' əl) vi- [bus·tled, bus·tling] to hurry in a noisy or fussy way: He bustled about the room. n- noisy flurry of activity. [of uncertain origin.]

²bus·tle (bŭs' əl) n- pad or framework of wire, formerly worn by women under the skirt at the back, to shape the dress. [perhaps a special use of ¹bustle.]

bus·y (bĭz' ē) adj- [bus·i·er, bus·i·est] 1 at work; not idle; active. 2 crowded with activity: a busy day; a busy street. 3 of a telephone line, in use. 4 cluttered with detail: a busy print or design.

bus·y·bod·y (bĭz' ē bŏd' ē) n- [pl. bus·y·bod·ies] a meddling person who interferes in other people's affairs.

but (bŭt) conj- 1 in comparison or contrast; on the contrary; He is young, but I am old. 2 contrary to expectation; yet: I planted the seed, but it didn't grow. 3 (often after a negative statement) that: I do not doubt but he will go.

butch·er (booch' ər) n- 1 person whose job is killing animals and preparing their meat for food. 2 person who cuts and sells meat. 3 person who kills men or animals needlessly. vt- 1 to slaughter. 2 to spoil; ruin.

butch·er·y (booch' ə rē) n- [pl. butch·er·ies] brutal killing; unnecessary slaughter; also, an instance of this.

but·ler (bŭt' lər) n- the chief male servant of a household.

¹butt (bŭt) vt- to strike with the lowered head: A goat butts people who annoy him.

²butt (bŭt) n- 1 the thicker or heavier end of something: the butt of a rifle stock. 2 an unused end of something; remaining part; stub: a cigarette butt.

³butt (bŭt) n- target; especially, a person who is the target for ridicule, jokes, criticism, etc. [from French but meaning "goal," related to ²butt.] Hom- but.

⁴butt (bŭt) n- large cask or barrel, as for wine, ale, or beer. [from Old French botte, from Late Latin butta, from Greek bytinē meaning "flask."] Hom- but.

butte (byoot) n- steep, flat-topped hill standing alone. [American word from French butte.]

Butte

but·ter·cup (bŭt' ər kŭp') n- 1 common meadow plant

but·ter·fly (bŭt' ər flī') n- [pl. but·ter·flies] 1 day-flying insect with a long sucking beak, two long, knobbed antennae, and four wings, usually brightly colored. 2 a racing stroke in swimming.

Butterfly

butterfly weed n- kind of milkweed with bright orange flowers that attract butterflies.

but·ter·milk (bŭt' ər mĭlk') n- liquid left after butter has been removed from churned milk.

but·ter·nut (bŭt' ər nŭt') n- 1 the oily nut of the American white walnut tree. For picture, see husk. 2 the tree that bears this nut.

but·ter·scotch (bŭt' ər skŏch') n- candy or flavoring made with brown sugar, corn syrup, butter, etc. adj-: a butterscotch pudding.

but·ter·y (bŭt' ə rē) adj- 1 like butter: a buttery mixture. 2 containing or smeared with butter: a buttery sauce. 3 Informal overly flattering: a buttery speech.

but·ton (bŭt' ən) n- 1 small, usually disk-shaped piece of plastic, shell, bone, metal, etc., sewn to one side of a garment and slipped through a buttonhole or loop on an opposite side to hold the garment closed. Buttons are also often used for decoration. 2 disk that is pushed to operate a switch: elevator button.

but·ton·wood (bŭt' ən wood') n- sycamore.

but·tress (bŭt' trəs) n- a supporting structure built against a wall or building to brace it. vt- to support or strengthen; to brace: to buttress a wall; to buttress an argument with facts.

Buttress

bux·om (bŭk' səm) adj- of women, plump and healthy; also, full-bosomed. —n- bux' om·ness.

buy (bī) vt- [bought (bôt, bŏt), buy·ing] 1 to get by paying a price; purchase: We'll buy a new chair. Money cannot buy happiness. 2 Informal to bribe. vi-: I cannot buy without money. n- Informal a bargain: We got a good buy on the furniture. Hom- by, bye.

buzz (bŭz) n- a steady humming sound; a prolonged sound of "z": the buzz of flies; a buzz of conversation.

by (bī) prep- 1 close to; near; beside: The lamp is by the bed.

by·gone (bī' gŏn', -gôn') adj- past; gone by: in bygone days. n- thing of the past: Let bygones be bygones.

by·law (bī' lô') n- rule or law made by an organization to govern its own activities.

by·line (bī' līn') n- a line at the head of a newspaper or magazine article giving the writer's name.

by·pass (bī' păs') n- road, path, or channel that can be used as a substitute or alternate for the main route, especially, a time-saving route around a city. vt- to go around: We bypassed Pittsburgh this trip.

by·path (bī' păth') n- a side path.

by·play (bī' plā') n- action, often in pantomime, not directly connected with the main situation, especially on the stage.

by·prod·uct (bī' prŏd' əkt) n- product that is not the main product of a manufacturing process, but has a value.

by·road (bī' rōd') n- side road.

by·stand·er (bī' stăn' dər) n- person who looks on, but does not take part.

by·way (bī' wā') n- road that is not much used.

by·word (bī' wûrd') n- 1 familiar saying or proverb. 2 person or thing that becomes widely known in an unfavorable way; object of scorn or mocking.

C

C, c (sē) *n-* [*pl.* **C's c's**] 1 the third letter of the English alphabet. 2 Roman numeral for 100. 3 *Music* the first and eighth notes of the C-major scale.

cab (kăb) *n-* 1 taxicab. 2 one-horse carriage for hire with a driver. 3 the compartment of a locomotive, truck, crane, etc., where the operator sits. *as modifier: a cab driver.*

Hansom cab

ca·bal (kə băl´) *n-* 1 secret scheme. 2 a few people closely united in some secret scheme or plot.

ca·ba·ña (kə băn´yə) *n-* 1 beach shelter, often a tent, with an open, canopied side facing the water. 2 small building of light construction, used for recreation. Also **ca·ba·na** (kə băn´ə). [American word from Spanish *cabaña*, from Late Latin *capanna* meaning "hut."]

cab·a·ret (kăb´ ə rā´) *n-* 1 restaurant in which guests are entertained with dancing and vaudeville acts. 2 the entertainment itself.

cab·bage (kăb´ĭj) *n-* plant having broad, thick leaves that curl together to form a hard, round head eaten as a vegetable.

Cabbage

cabbage butterfly *n-* any of several white butterflies whose green wormlike larvae feed on cabbage.

cab·in (kăb´ən) *n-* 1 small hut or house. 2 room on a ship, used as quarters for officers or passengers. 3 enclosed part of an airplane occupied by the passengers.

cab·i·net·mak·er (kăb´ə nət māˊkər) *n-* a maker of fine woodwork, especially of fine household furniture.

cab·i·net·work (kăb´ə nət wûrk´) *n-* fine woodwork.

ca·ble (kā´ bəl) *n-* 1 thick, heavy rope of hemp or wire, used for supporting suspension bridges, towing automobiles, mooring ships, etc. 2 insulated, waterproof rope of wires used to carry electric current. 3 message sent by telegraph wires laid under the sea.

Cable

ca·boose (kə bōōs´) *n-* 1 small car, usually at the end of a train, in which railroad workers can rest or sleep. 2 *Brit.* ship's galley.

cack·le (kăk´əl) *n-* sharp, broken sound that a hen or goose makes after laying an egg. *vi-* [**cack·led, cack·ling**] to make such a sound; also, to chatter or laugh.

ca·coph·o·ny (kă kŏf´ə nē) *n-* [*pl.* **ca·coph·o·nies**] harsh, disagreeable sound; dissonance: *the cacophony of an unrehearsed orchestra.* —*adj-* **ca·coph´o·nous:** *the cacophonous street noises.* —*adv-* **ca·coph´o·nous·ly.**

cac·tus (kăk´təs) *n-* [*pl.* **cac·tus·es** or **cac·ti** (-tī)] leafless, desert plant with sharp spines or prickles along a fleshy stem and branches.

cad (kăd) *n-* a dishonorable, ungentlemanly man.

ca·dav·er (kə dăv´ ər) *n-* dead body, especially of a human being.

ca·dav·er·ous (kə dăv´ ər əs) *adj-* corpselike; pale; gaunt.

cad·die or **cad·dy** (kăd´ē) *n-* [*pl.* **cad·dies**] 1 person hired by a golf player to carry his clubs. 2 (also **caddie cart**) small two-wheeled cart for carrying things, especially for golf bag and clubs.

Fishhook cactus

ca·dence (kā´ dəns) *n-* 1 rhythm; beat: *the steady cadence of my heart.* 2 rhythmic rise and fall of a sound, especially of a voice: *the cadences of her speech.* 3 notes forming the conclusion of a musical passage.

ca·det (kə dĕt´) *n-* student in a naval or military academy.

ca·fé (kə fā´) *n-* restaurant.

cage (kāj) *n-* 1 boxlike container, usually made of wires or bars, for keeping birds or other animals. 2 any similar container or car: *an elevator cage.* 3 in basket-

ball, the basket through which the ball is thrown. 4 in hockey, the net-covered structure behind the goal line.

ca·jole (kə jōl´) *vt-* [**ca·joled, ca·jol·ing**] to coax or deceive by flattery or promises; wheedle: *He cajoled me into signing the note.*

cake (kāk) *n-* 1 mixture of flour, milk, sugar, egg, etc., usually baked as a loaf or in layers, often covered with frosting. 2 small, shaped mass of cooked batter, ground meat, fish, potatoes, etc. 3 any small, solid mass that is shaped or flattened: *a cake of soap.*

ca·lam·i·ty (kə lăm´ ə tē) *n-* [*pl.* **ca·lam·i·ties**] 1 event causing widespread destruction and misery; disaster.

cal·ci·fy (kăl´sə fī´) *vi-* [**cal·ci·fied, cal·ci·fy·ing**] to undergo calcification. *vt-* to produce calcification in.

cal·ci·um (kăl´sē əm) *n-* very active, silver-white, metallic chemical element common in limestone, marble, sea shells, and bones and teeth. Symbol Ca, At. No. 20, At. Wt. 40.08.

cal·cu·late (kăl´kyə lāt´) *vt-* [**cal·cu·lat·ed, cal·cu·lat·ing**] 1 to determine or figure out by mathematics; compute: *to calculate the speed of light.* 2 to estimate by various methods of judgment: *to calculate the benefits of atomic energy.*

cal·en·dar (kăl´ ən dər) *n-* 1 way of reckoning time by days, weeks, months, and years. See also *Gregorian calendar, Julian calendar.* 2 table showing the arrangement of days, weeks, and months of a year. 3 list or schedule of things to be done or that happen at certain times: *a church calendar of festivals.* Hom- **calender.**

Calendar

¹calf (kăf) *n-* [*pl.* **calves** (kăvs)] 1 the young of the domestic cow. 2 the young of certain other large mammals, such as the whale, elephant, or moose. 3 calfskin, the leather. [from Old English *cealf* of the same meaning.]

cal·i·brate (kăl´ə brāt´) *vt-* [**cal·i·brat·ed, cal·i·brat·ing**] 1 to graduate or mark off the scale of (a measuring instrument) into appropriate units. 2 to correct or check (a measuring scale).

cal·i·pers or **cal·li·pers** (kăl´ə pərz) *n-* (takes plural verb) instrument with two adjustable curved legs, used to measure an inside or outside diameter, thickness, etc. 2 caliper rule.

cal·is·then·ics or **cal·lis·then·ics** (kăl´ əs thĕn´ĭks) *n- pl.* simple gymnastic exercises. —*adj-* **cal´is·then´ic** or **cal´lis·then´ic:** *a calisthenic exercise.*

calk·ing (kò´ kĭng) *n-* substance, such as hemp fiber, used to caulk joints or cracks.

call (kòl) *vt-* 1 to summon; send for: *to call a policeman.* 2 to telephone: *I called him, but the line was busy.* 3 to give a name to; name; specify: *They called him "Deerslayer." He who pays the piper calls the tune.*

call·ing (kò´ lĭng) *n-* 1 profession; occupation; vocation: *It is important to find the right calling.* 2 strong inner feeling or impulse to undertake a particular duty or follow a certain way of life.

cal·lous (kăl´ əs) *adj-* lacking sympathy and affection; unfeeling; insensitive: *a callous disregard for the welfare of others.* *vt-* 1 to form calluses on: *Rough work will callous your hands.* 2 to make insensitive or unfeeling: *His hard life calloused his heart.* Hom- **callus.** —*adv-* **cal´lous·ly.** *n-* **cal´lous·ness.**

cal·low (kăl´ ō) *adj-* 1 young and inexperienced: *a callow youth.* 2 of a bird, not yet feathered; unfledged. —*adv-* **cal´low·ly.** *n-* **cal´low·ness.**

calm (kăm) *adj-* [**calm·er, calm·est**] quiet and peaceful. *n-* condition or period of quiet and peacefulness: *The sea was motionless during the calm.* *vt-* to quiet (often with "down"): *to calm a crying child.* *vi-* *The sea calmed.* —*n-* **calm´ness.** *adv-* **calm´ ly.**

cal·o·rie (kăl´ ə rē) *n-* 1 (also **small calorie, gram calorie**) unit of energy equal to the amount of heat needed to raise the temperature of one gram of water one degree centigrade. *Abbr.* **cal.** 2 (also **large calorie, great calorie, kilocalorie**) energy unit, equal to 1000 small calories, used to measure the amount of energy the body gets from food.

cal·um·ny (kăl′ əm nē) *n-* [*pl.* **cal·um·nies**] the making of a false statement harmful to someone's character or reputation; also, the statement itself; slander.

cam (kăm) *n-* movable machine part, usually an irregularly shaped wheel or shaft, that gives back-and-forth motion to another part resting against it.

cam·el (kăm′ əl) *n-* large, cud-chewing mammal well suited to desert life. The swift, single-humped **Arabian camel**, or dromedary, of Africa and the Middle East is used for riding and as a beast of burden. (For picture, see *dromedary*.) The double-humped **Bactrian camel** of Central Asia is chiefly a beast of burden.

Camel, 7 1/2 ft. high

cam·e·o (kăm′ ē ō) *n-* [*pl.* **cam·e·os**] gem or ornament with a raised design, carved from agate, shell, etc. Usually the design color contrasts with the background.

cam·er·a (kăm′ rə, -ər ə) *n-* 1 lightproof box with a lens that focuses light on a film or plate to make photographs or motion pictures. 2 piece of electronic equipment that changes visual images into electrical impulses for television broadcasting.

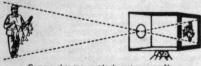

Camera, showing upside-down image on film

cam·ou·flage (kăm′ ə flăzh′) *n-* disguise or concealment, especially by means of colors, patterns, or materials that blend with the background or surroundings. *vt-* [**cam·ou·flaged, cam·ou·flag·ing**] to conceal or disguise by a deceptive appearance or manner: *to camouflage guns with green paint*; *to camouflage uneasiness.*

camp (kămp) *n-* 1 place where people live temporarily in tents, cabins, or other informal shelters: *a summer camp*; *a military camp*; *a hunter's camp.* 2 side or faction: *He abandoned his old beliefs and joined the opposing camp.*

cam·paign (kăm pān′) *n-* 1 series of military operations carried on for a particular purpose: *The general planned a campaign to capture the city.* 2 organized activity for a particular purpose: *a political campaign.* *vt-*: *to campaign for a candidate's election.* —*n-* **cam·paign′ er.**

cam·phor (kăm′ fər) *n-* whitish, crystalline substance with a strong odor, obtained chiefly from the **camphor tree** of eastern Asia, used in medicines, mothballs, etc.

¹can (kăn) *auxiliary verb* [*p.t.* **could**] 1 am, is, or are physically or mentally able to. 2 may possibly; might; could: *Do you think that can be the way it happened?*

²can (kăn) *n-* 1 metal container, usually with straight sides and a cover or sealed top: *a coffee can*; *a garbage can.* 2 amount such a container holds: *We ate two cans of beets for dinner.*

ca·nal (kə năl′) *n-* 1 man-made water channel used for navigation, irrigation, or drainage. 2 tubelike part of the body, such as the alimentary canal.

can·a·pe (kăn′ ə pā′, -pē′) *n-* cracker or small piece of toast or bread topped with a tasty spread, bit of fish or cheese, etc., and served as an appetizer.

ca·na·ry (kə nâr′ē) *n-* [*pl.* **ca·nar·ies**] 1 small, usually yellow, bird popular as a caged pet because of its song. 2 (also **canary yellow**) a light, bright yellow.

can·cel (kăn′ səl) *vt-* 1 to call off; abolish; annul: *to cancel a magazine subscription*; *to cancel a debt*; *to cancel an appointment.* 2 to mark, cross out, etc., especially so as to prevent use or reuse: *to cancel a stamp*; *to cancel a numeral.*

can·did (kăn′ dĭd) *adj-* 1 honest and frank; sincere: *a candid opinion.* 2 of photographs, informal and unposed —*adv-* **can′ did·ly.**

can·di·date (kăn′ də dāt′) *n-* person who is a contestant for an office or honor.

can·dle (kăn′ dəl) *n-* 1 stick of wax or tallow with a wick inside it, burned to give light. 2 *Physics* unit of strength or intensity of a light source.

can·dle·stick (kăn′ dəl stĭk′) *n-* holder for a candle.

can·dle·wick (kăn′ dəl wĭk′) *n-* 1 wick of a candle. 2 (also **can′ dle·wick′ ing**) thick cotton thread used to make embroidered or tufted designs on bedspreads, curtains, etc. *adj-*: *a candlewick bedspread.*

can·dor (kăn′ dər) *n-* outspoken honesty; frankness: *her embarrassing candor.*

can·dy (kăn′ dē) *n-* [*pl.* **can·dies**] sweet food, usually in the form of small pieces, made chiefly from sugar or sugar syrup to which flavoring, fruits, nuts, etc., are often added; also, a single piece of such food.

Candlestick

cane (kān) *n-* 1 stick used as an aid in walking; walking stick. 2 any of various plants having jointed, hollow, woody stems, such as the bamboo and sugar cane; also, the stem of such a plant. 3 narrow strips of rattan, wicker, etc., used in making furniture.

can·ti·le·ver (kăn′ tə lĕv′ ər, -lē′ vər) *n-* 1 bracket or block projecting from the wall of a house to support a

ca·nine (kā′ nīn′) *adj-* of, like, or characteristic of a dog. *n-* 1 any of a family of animals including the dog, wolf, etc. 2 (also **canine tooth**) one of the sharp, pointed teeth located next to the outer incisors in the upper and lower jaw; cuspid (for picture, see *tooth*).

can·is·ter (kăn′ ə stər) *n-* box or small container, usually metal, with a tightly fitting lid, for flour, coffee, etc.

can·ker (kăng′ kər) *n-* 1 open sore inside the mouth, related to cold sores. 2 disease which destroys the hooves of horses. 3 disease of the lining of a dog's or cat's ear. 4 anything that causes evil or corruption.

can·ni·bal (kăn′ ə bəl) *n-* 1 human being who eats human flesh. 2 any animal that eats its own kind.

can·non (kăn′ ən) *n-* [*pl.* **can·nons** or **can·non**] large gun mounted on wheels or a fixed base; artillery piece. *Hom-* canon.

can·non·ade (kăn′ ən ād′) *n-* a continuous firing of cannon.

Cannon

can·tan·ker·ous (kăn tăng′ kər əs) *adj-* hard to get along with; fault-finding; cranky: *a cantankerous old man.* —*adv-* **can·tan′ ker·ous·ly.** *n-* **can·tan′ ker·ous·ness.**

can·ta·ta (kən tä′ tə) *Music n-* short musical drama intended to be sung but not acted.

can·teen (kăn tēn′) *n-* 1 metal or plastic bottle for carrying drinking water. 2 shop in a camp, factory, etc., selling refreshments and tobacco. 3 place where recreation and refreshments are provided for servicemen.

can·ter (kăn′ tər) *n-* slow, easy gallop. *vi-* to ride or run at such a gallop: *He cantered across the field.* *vt-*: *He cantered his horse for half a mile.*

ca·noe (kə nōō′) *n-* light, narrow boat moved through the water by people using paddles. *vi-* [**ca·noed, ca·noe·ing**] to travel in or paddle such a boat.

Canoe

can·oe·ist (kə nōō′ ĭst) *n-* person who paddles a canoe.

¹can·on (kăn′ ən) *n-* 1 official rule or code of a church, especially the Roman Catholic Church. 2 principle or standard by which things are judged: *the canons of good conduct.*

can·o·py (kăn′ ə pē) *n-* [*pl.* **can·o·pies**] 1 covering of cloth or other material fixed above a bed or a throne.

²cant (kănt) *n-* 1 a slant or tilt; slope: *the cant of a roof.* 2 sudden, forceful push that moves something to a diagonal position.

can·vass (kǎn′ vəs) *vt-* 1 to visit (a district, house, or person) in order to get information, votes, or contributions, or to make sales. 2 to discuss in detail: *We canvassed the topic of skiing.*

can·yon (kǎn′ yən) *n-* deep valley with steep sides, usually with a stream flowing through it; a gorge. [American word from Spanish *cañon* meaning literally "tube," from Late Latin **canna** meaning "reed; cane."]

cap (kǎp) *n-* 1 a small covering for the head: *a baseball cap; a nurse's cap.* 2 anything circular suggesting or used as a cover: *a mushroom cap; a bottle cap.* 3 small explosive charge in a wrapper, such as one used in toy pistols or one used as a primer to set off a larger amount of explosive.

ca·ble (kā′ pə bəl) *adj-* gifted or skillful; able; competent: *a capable surgeon.* —*adv-* **ca′ pa·bly.**

capable of 1 having the ability or skill to do something: *He's capable of great things.* 2 susceptible to; open to: *a novel capable of many interpretations,*

ca·pa·cious (kə pā′ shəs) *adj-* able to hold much; roomy: *a capacious handbag.* —*adv-* **ca·pa′ cious·ly:** *a man capaciously endowed with courage.* *n-* **ca·pa′ cious·ness:** *the capaciousness of his understanding.*

ca·pac·i·ty (kə pǎs′ ə tē) *n-* [*pl.* **ca·pac·i·ties**] 1 ability or capability: *his capacity for learning; to work to full capacity.* 2 maximum or indicated limit to what can be received or held: *a seating capacity of twenty; a·per·colator of six-cup capacity; a bridge with a ten-ton capacity.*

¹**cape** (kāp) *n-* loose outer garment without sleeves, worn over the shoulders. [from Spanish **capa** meaning "hood," from Late Latin **cappa,** from Latin **caput** "head."]

²**cape** (kāp) *n-* point of land jutting out into a body of water; headland. [from French **cap,** from Spanish **cabo,** from Latin **caput** meaning "head."]

Cape buffalo *n-* large, black, wild ox found in swampy areas in South Africa and having two curved horns that nearly join at their base. For picture, see *buffalo.*

Policeman wearing cape

¹**ca·per** (kā′ pər) *vi-* to skip or leap about playfully: *Clowns capered about the circus ring.* *n-* 1 playful leap or jump. 2 a prank; antic. [from French **capriole,** "a leap," from Latin **capreolus** meaning "a young goat."] **cut a caper** to caper.

cap·il·lar·y (kǎp′ ə lěr′ ē) *n-* [*pl.* **cap·il·lar·ies**] a very minute blood vessel. *adj-* 1 fine as a hair; slender; having a tiny bore. 2 relating to the minute blood vessels of the body.

cap·i·tal (kǎp′ ə təl) *n-* 1 city which is the seat of government of a country or State: *Washington, D.C. is the capital of the United States.* 2 capital letter. 3 wealth and property that can be used in business and industry to make more money.

cap·i·tal·ism (kǎp′ ə tə lǐz′ əm) *n-* economic system based on private ownership of the means of production and distribution, and characterized by profit, a free market, and open competition.

cap·i·tal·ize (kǎp′ ə tə līz′) *vt-* [**cap·i·tal·ized, cap·i·tal·iz·ing**] 1 to put (a word or the first letter of a word) in capital letters. 2 to furnish (a business, project, etc.) with capital. *They capitalized the firm at $100,000.*

ca·pit·u·late (kə pǐch′ ə lāt′) *vi-* [**ca·pit·u·lat·ed, ca·pit·u·lat·ing**] to surrender to an enemy, usually on certain conditions: *The town capitulated to the enemy.*

ca·price (kə prēs′) *n-* 1 sudden, unreasoning change of mind or conduct; whim: *Her refusal to go is a mere caprice.* 2 tendency to change suddenly and unpredictably: *the caprice of fortune.*

cap·tain (kǎp′ tən) *n-* 1 in the Army, Air Force, and Marine Corps, a commissioned officer who ranks next below a major and next above a first lieutenant. 2 in the Navy and Coast Guard, a commissioned officer who ranks next below a rear admiral and next above a commander. 3 master of any ship.

cap·tion (kǎp′ shən) *n-* 1 title or explanation of a picture. 2 brief title for an article, chapter, etc., set above it in large type; heading.

cap·ti·vate (kǎp′ tə vāt′) *vt-* [**cap·ti·vat·ed, cap·ti·vat·ing**] to charm by beauty, intelligence, etc.; fascinate: *She captivated us with her songs.* —*n-* **cap′ ti·va′ tion.**

cap·tive (kǎp′ tǐv) *adj-* not free; captured: *a captive nation; a captive deer.* *n-* person or animal taken into captivity; prisoner.

cap·ture (kǎp′ chər) *vt-* [**cap·tured, cap·tur·ing**] to take, seize, or win by force, skill, surprise, trickery, charm or other means: *to capture a thief; to capture attention.* *n-* 1 person or thing seized: *Our first capture was a lion.* 2 a seizing or being seized: *the capture of a criminal.*

car (kär) *n-* 1 automobile. 2 vehicle running on rails: *a trolley car; a railway car.* 3 the cage of an elevator. 4 the part of an airship or balloon which carries people and freight.

car·a·mel (kǎr′ ə məl, kär-) *n-* 1 sugar, slowly melted and browned, used for coloring and flavoring. 2 soft chewy candy cut in small cubes and flavored with this sugar, and vanilla or chocolate.

car·at (kǎr′ ət) *n-* unit of weight for precious stones, equal to 200 milligrams. *Hom-* caret, carrot, karat.

car·a·van (kǎr′ ə vǎn′) *n-* 1 company of merchants, pilgrims, etc., traveling together for safety, as across a desert or through dangerous country. 2 a train of pack animals or vehicles. 3 *Brit.* wagon equipped for living.

car·bine (kär′ bīn′) *n-* a short, light rifle.

car·bo·hy·drate (kär′ bō hī′ drāt′) *n-* any of a class of compounds of carbon, hydrogen, and oxygen, such as sugars, starches, and cellulose, which are manufactured by plants and are the ultimate source of animal food.

car·bon (kär′ bən) *n-* chemical element which is the main element in coal and is found pure in two distinct forms, diamond and graphite. It is the basic element of all living matter. Symbol C, At. No. 6, At. Wt. 12.

car·bun·cle (kär′ bŭng′ kəl) *n-* 1 painful, inflamed swelling of the skin, more serious than a boil. 2 a deep-red garnet.

car·bu·ret·or or **car·bu·ret·tor** (kär′ bə rā′ tər) *n-* apparatus used to mix air with gasoline in the engine of an automobile.

car·cass (kär′ kəs) *n-* 1 dead body of an animal. 2 contemptuously, the living or dead body of a human being.

¹**card** (kärd) *n-* 1 piece of thin, stiff paper or pasteboard. 2 playing card. 3 in sports, a list of events. 4 **cards** any game played with playing cards. [from Old French **carte,** ultimately from Greek **chartēs,** "layer of papyrus."]

car·di·gan (kär′ də gən) *n-* collarless sweater or jacket that opens down the front.

care (kâr) *n-* 1 troubled state of mind caused by fear, doubt, etc.; anxiety; trouble; concern. 2 a cause of this: *The cares of the war years weighed heavily on the President.* 3 close and serious attention; heed; watchfulness: *work done with care.*

ca·reen (kə rēn′) *vt-* 1 to tilt (a ship) in order to clean or repair its bottom. *vi-* to lurch or sway while moving: *The car hit the pole and careened across the road.*

ca·reer (kə rêr′) *n-* 1 course or progress of one's life: *He had a checkered career.* 2 occupation or calling: *a scientific career.* 3 rushing course; full speed: *a horse in full career.* *vi-* to move with a rush; dash along: *The truck careered down the road.*

ca·ress (kə rěs′) *n-* affectionate or gentle touch or stroke. *vt-:* *The little girl caressed her kitten.*

car·et (kǎr′ ət) *n-* mark [∧], used in writing or correcting to indicate an insertion. *Hom-* carat, caret, karat.

care·tak·er (kâr′ tā′ kər) *n-* person who takes care of a place or property: *the caretaker of a cemetery.*

car·i·ca·ture (kǎr′ kə chər, -chŏŏr′) *n-* picture or description of a person or thing, in which the defects or peculiarities are so exaggerated as to appear ridiculous. *vt-* [**car·i·ca·tured, car·i·ca·tur·ing**]: *The cartoonist caricatured the actor.*

car·nal (kär′ nəl) *adj-* fleshly; sensual: *man's carnal interests.*

car·ol (kǎr′ əl) *n-* song of joy or praise, especially a Christmas song. *vt-* to sing joyfully: *We caroled hymns.*

vi-: We caroled in the snow. —n- **car′ol·er.**

car·om (kăr′ əm) n- in billiards, a shot in which the cue ball hits two or more balls, one after the other. **vi-** to strike and rebound (off): The handball caromed off the wall.

ca·rouse (kə rouz′) n- wild, noisy drinking party. **vi-** [ca·roused, ca·rous·ing]: They'll carouse all night long. —n- **ca·rous′er.**

1carp (kärp) vi- to find fault; complain: You're always carping about my work. [probably from Old Norse karpa meaning "to boast," plus Latin carpere meaning "to pluck."] —n- **carp′er.**

car·pen·ter (kär′ pən tər) n- person who builds or repairs the woodwork of houses, ships, cabinets, etc.

car·pet (kär′ pət) n- 1 large piece of heavy fabric for covering floors. 2 any continuous covering on the floor or ground: a carpet of pine needles. **vt-:** to carpet a room.

car·riage (kăr′ ĭj) n- 1 wheeled vehicle for carrying people, usually drawn by horses. 2 light, often folding, vehicle for a baby, pushed by a person on foot. 3 a carrying or transporting of goods; also, the charge for this.

Carriages baby carriage. Concord buggy

car·ri·on (kăr′ ē ən) n- dead and decaying flesh.

car·rot (kăr′ ət) n- cultivated plant related to the parsley, with an edible, orange-yellow tapering root. **Hom-** carat, caret, karat. —adj- **car′rot·y.**

car·rou·sel or **car·ou·sel** (kăr′ ə sĕl′, -zĕl′) n- merry-go-round.

car·ry (kăr′ ē) vt- [car·ried, car·ry·ing] 1 to transport or convey, especially as the load of a vehicle, person, or animal; bear: I carried the box upstairs. Railroads carry both passengers and freight. 2 to have on one's person: I always carry my driver's license. 3 to transfer or add (a number, bookkeeping entry, etc.) to the next column.

cart (kärt) n- 1 two-wheeled vehicle for carrying heavy loads: a farm cart. 2 light delivery wagon, often moved by hand. 3 light two-wheeled carriage. **vt-** 1 to transport by wagon: Please cart my baggage out to the plane. 2 Informal to take away: They carted him off to jail.

car·tel (kär tĕl′) n- combination of industrial groups, usually international, formed to fix prices, regulate output, control a market, etc.

car·ti·lage (kär′ tə lĭj) n- tough, rubbery tissue that forms much of the skeleton of young animals and infants and usually develops into bone; gristle.

car·ton (kär′ tən) n- 1 pasteboard or cardboard box. 2 amount held by such a box: a carton of tea.

car·toon (kär tōōn′) n- 1 a drawing, especially in a newspaper or magazine, that deals with well-known people or public events in a humorous or critical way 2 animated cartoon. 3 comic strip.

carve (kärv) vt- [carved, carv·ing] 1 to make or design by cutting: to carve a statue out of marble; to carve a panel with floral patterns. 2 to cut into parts or slices: to carve a turkey. **vi-:** My father always carves.

1case (kăs) n- 1 state of affairs; set of circumstances: If that's the case, you must pay. 2 matter or problem for investigation or solution: The police finally closed the case of the missing heiress.

case·ment (kăs′ mənt) n- window built to open on hinges like a door.

case·work·er (kăs′ wûr′ kər) n- social worker assigned to gather information about, and advise, a person or family that is in difficulty and needs assistance.

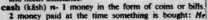

Casement

cash (kăsh) n- 1 money in the form of coins or bills. 2 money paid at the time something is bought: He

paid cash for the rug, but bought the car on credit. 3 bank deposits, certain notes, etc., easily exchangeable for coins and bills.

cas·ing (kā′ sĭng) n- 1 something that covers or encloses, such as a membrane into which sausage is packed, or a pipe lining an oil well. 2 frame of a window or door.

cask (kăsk) n- barrel-shaped wooden container for liquids; large keg; also, the amount this holds when full.

cask·et (kăs′ kət) n- 1 small chest or box, such as one used for jewels. 2 coffin.

cas·sa·ba (kə să′ bə) casaba.

Cas·san·dra (kə săn′ drə) n- in Greek legend, a daughter of King Priam of Troy.

Cask

cas·se·role (kăs′ ə rōl′) n- 1 deep glass or earthenware dish in which food is baked and served. 2 food cooked and served in such a dish.

cas·sock (kăs′ ək) n- long, close-fitting, usually black gown worn by clergymen, choir singers, etc.

cast (kăst) vt- [cast, cast·ing] 1 to throw: to cast a fishing lure; to cast stones; to cast a glance; to cast a shadow. 2 to make (a part, statue, etc.) by pouring liquid material into a mold; also, to make molded objects of: That foundry casts bronze.

caste (kăst) n- 1 any of the rigid, hereditary social classes of the Hindus. 2 any system of social divisions based on birth, wealth, and rank. **Hom-** cast.

cast·er or **cas·tor** (kăs′ tər) n- 1 small roller or wheel on a swivel, used under furniture or other heavy articles to permit easy moving. 2 a cruet; also, a stand for a number of cruets. 3 (caster only) person or thing that casts.

cas·ti·gate (kăs′ tə gāt′) vt- [cas·ti·gat·ed, cas·ti·gat·ing] to criticize severely; rebuke: He was castigated by the newspapers.

cas·tle (kăs′ əl) n- 1 building or group of buildings fortified for defense, especially the feudal fortress. 2 any large, imposing house of a person of wealth or title. 3 a piece used in chess; rook.

castles in Spain or **castles in the air** very impractical schemes; daydreams.

Castle

cast·off (kăst′ ôf′) adj- discarded as worthless; thrown away: a castoff pair of shoes.

cas·trate (kăs′ trāt′) vt- [cas·trat·ed, cas·trat·ing] to remove the sex glands of (an animal, especially a male). —n- **cas·tra′tion.**

cas·u·al (kăzh′ ōō əl) adj- 1 happening by chance; accidental: a casual meeting on the street. 2 happening irregularly or occasionally: a casual profit.

cas·u·al·ty (kăzh′ ōō əl tē) n- [pl. cas·u·al·ties] someone or something hurt or destroyed by a misfortune, especially someone killed, wounded, or lost in war: C Company had six casualties.

cat (kăt) n- 1 small fur-covered animal often kept as a household pet or to catch rats and mice. 2 any of a family of animals including lions, tigers, leopards, pumas, etc.; feline. as modifier: the cat family; cat fur.

Siamese and Persian cats

cat·a·log or **cat·a·logue** (kăt′ ə lòg, -lŏg′) n- list of names, books, things, places, etc., often arranged alphabetically: the catalog of a library. **vt-** [cat·a·loged or cat·a·logued, cat·a·log·ing or cat·a·logu·ing]: to catalog books in a library.

cat·a·pult (kăt′ ə pŭlt′) n- 1 in ancient and medieval times, a military device for hurling stones, arrows, or the like.

cat·a·ract (kăt′ ə răkt′) n- 1 large waterfall. 2 series of steep rapids. 3 disease of the eye in which the lens becomes cloudy, causing partial or total blindness.

catch (kăch, kĕch) vt- [caught, catch·ing] 1 to get hold of (a thing in motion); grasp and stop; grab: *to catch a ball and run.* 2 to capture (a person, thing, idea, etc.): *to catch a thief; to catch a trout; to catch one's meaning; to catch one's eye.*

catch·ing (kăch' ĭng, kech'-) *adj-* likely to be carried from one person to another; contagious; infectious: *Measles is a catching disease. Her laughter is catching.*

cat·e·chism (kăt' ə klz' əm) *n-* 1 small book of instruction in the Christian religion in the form of questions and answers. 2 any method of teaching by questions and answers. 3 set of questions to be answered.

cat·e·go·ry (kăt' ə gôr' ē) *n-* [*pl.* **cat·e·go·ries**] any broad class or division.

ca·ter (kā' tər) *vi-* 1 to supply someone or something with what is wanted: *This novel caters to popular tastes.* 2 to supply and serve food, as for a party or banquet. *vt-: to cater a banquet.*

eat·er-cor·ner (kăt' ē kôr' nər) catty-corner. Also **kitty-corner.**

ca·ter·er (kā' tər ər) *n-* one whose business is to supply and serve food for banquets, weddings, etc.

cat·er·pil·lar (kăt' ər pĭl' ər) *n-* the worm-like larva that hatches from the eggs of such insects as the moth or butterfly.

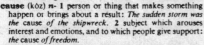

Caterpillar

ca·the·dral (kə thē' drəl) *n-* 1 resident church of a bishop, and chief church of a diocese. 2 any large and important church.

cat·tle (kăt' əl) *n- pl.* livestock, especially cows, bulls, and steers kept on a farm or ranch.

eau·cus (kô' kəs) *n-* a meeting of political party leaders to discuss party policies or choose party candidates.

caul·dron (kôl' drən) *n-* large kettle or boiler.

cau·li·flow·er (kô' lǐ flou' ər, kŏl'ǐ-) *n-* plant related to the cabbage, having a head of tiny, tightly-packed, whitish flowers eaten as a vegetable.

caulk or **calk** (kôk) *vt-* to fill (seams, joints, or cracks in a ship, building, etc.) with any of various substances called **caulking** or **calking** so as to make watertight.

Cauliflower

cause (kôz) *n-* 1 person or thing that makes something happen or brings about a result: *The sudden storm was the cause of the shipwreck.* 2 subject which arouses interest and emotions, and to which people give support: *the cause of freedom.*

caus·tic (kôs' tĭk) *adj-* 1 able to eat away or destroy by chemical action; corrosive: *Lye is caustic.* 2 sarcastic; biting: *a caustic remark. n-* substance which by chemical action burns or eats away animal tissues.

cau·ter·ize (kô' tər ĭz') *vt-* [cau·ter·ized, cau·ter·iz·ing] to sear with a hot iron or caustic, especially to prevent infection or stop bleeding: *to cauterize a wound.* —**cau'ter·i·za'tion.**

cau·tion (kô' shən) *n-* 1 act, word, etc., that warns, as against danger; warning: *He heeded my brother's numerous cautions to drive carefully.* 2 heedfulness; care in avoiding danger: *Handle chemicals with caution.*

cave (kāv) *n-* natural hollow beneath the earth. *vi-* [caved, cav·ing] to fall in; collapse: *Look out, the wall is caving!*

cav·ern·ous (kăv' ər nəs) *adj-* 1 hollow and deep like a cavern. 2 containing caverns: *a cavernous mountain.*

cav·i·ar (kăv' ē är') *n-* the eggs of certain large fishes, especially the sturgeon, prepared as an appetizer. Also **cav'i·are'.**

cav·il (kăv' əl) *vi-* to find fault without good reason; raise foolish or frivolous objections; carp: *to cavil at a proposed plan. n-* petty objection. —**cav'il·er.**

cav·i·ty (kăv' ə tē) *n-* [*pl.* **cav·i·ties**] hollow place; hole: *a cavity in a tooth.*

ca·vort (kə vôrt', -vôrt') *vi-* to prance or leap about playfully: *The colts cavorted in the meadow.*

cease (sēs) *vi-* [ceased, ceas·ing] to come to an end: *The rain ceased. vt-: They ceased firing.*

cede (sēd) *vt-* [ced·ed, ced·ing] to give up; surrender to another: *to cede land; to cede a point.* **Hom-** seed.

ceil·ing (sē' lǐng) *n-* 1 inner overhead covering of a room.

cel·e·brate (sĕl' ə brāt') *vt-* [cel·e·brat·ed, cel·e·brat·ing] 1 to perform publicly with suitable ceremonies, such as a Mass. 2 to make known with praise; honor: *We celebrate the names of great men.*

ce·les·ti·al (sə lĕs' chəl) *adj-* 1 of or related to the heavens: *The stars are celestial bodies.* 2 heavenly; divine: *a celestial joy.* —**adv- ce·les' ti·al·ly.**

cell (sĕl) *n-* 1 tiny living body, the smallest unit of an animal or plant able to carry on the basic functions of life, such as growing and reproducing. 2 small room in a prison, monastery, or convent. 3 small, enclosed space.

cel·lar (sĕl' ər) *n-* underground room or group of rooms, generally under a building and often used for storage.

cel·lo or **'cel·lo** (chĕl' ō) *n-* [*pl.* **cel·los**] stringed musical instrument, deeper and larger in tone than a viola or violin; violoncello.

cem·e·ter·y (sĕm' ə tĕr' ē) *n-* [*pl.* **cem·e·ter·ies**] burial ground; graveyard.

ce·ment (sǐ mĕnt') *n-* 1 fine gray powder made from limestone, clay, gypsum, and iron oxide which, when mixed with water, dries to the hardness of rock. It is mixed with sand or gravel to make concrete.

cen·ser (sĕn' sər) *n-* container in which incense is burned, especially one carried and swung on chains. **Hom-** censor.

Censer

cen·sor (sĕn' sər) *n-* 1 official who examines books, motion pictures, etc., to keep out anything that is thought wrong or undesirable. 2 official who, in time of war, examines letters and printed matter to keep out anything that might help the enemy.

cen·sure (sĕn' shər) *n-* expression of disapproval or condemnation: *A man in public office often receives censure from all sides. vt-* [cen·sured, cen·sur·ing]: *The Senate censured Mr. Doe for slandering people.*

cen·sus (sĕn' səs) *n-* official count of the population, including information about age, sex, employment, etc.

cent (sĕnt) *n-* 1 the hundredth part of a dollar. 2 coin of this value; penny. **Hom-** scent, sent.

cen·ter (sĕn' tər) *n-* 1 middle point of a circle or sphere. 2 point about which something turns: *the center of a wheel.* 3 place where people gather for a particular purpose: *a shopping center.* 4 principal object: *She is the center of attention.* 5 the middle: *the center of the road.*

cen·ti·pede (sĕn' tə pēd') *n-* any of a group of small wormlike animals with a long, flattened body made up of many segments, each bearing a pair of legs. The foremost pair of legs is a set of claws for grasping prey and injecting venom.

Centipede

cen·tral (sĕn' trəl) *adj-* 1 in, at, or near the middle: *the central part of the city.* 2 main; leading: *the central idea of the book.*

cen·tri·fuge (sĕn' trə fyŏŏj') *n-* device for separating substances by whirling them at high speed. The heavier material gathers near the outside wall, and the lighter remains near the center.

cen·tu·ry (sĕn' chə rē) *n-* [*pl.* **cen·tu·ries**] 1 a period of 100 years. 2 each group of 100 years before or after some fixed date, such as the birth of Christ: *the 20th century A.D.*

ce·ram·ic (sə răm' ĭk) *adj-* 1 relating to pottery and the making of pottery. 2 consisting of fired or baked clay or similar material: *a ceramic vase; a ceramic insulator.*

ce·re·al (sēr' ē əl) *n-* 1 any grass that yields a grain or seed used for food, such as rice, wheat, oats, or the like. 2 any of these grains, in a natural state or as put on the market. 3 a prepared food, especially a breakfast food, made from any of these grains.

cer·e·mo·ny (sĕr' ə mō' nē) *n-* [*pl.* **cer·e·mo·nies**] 1 formal rite or observance: *a wedding ceremony; the inauguration ceremony.*

cer·tain (sûr′tən) *adj-* **1** beyond doubt or question; indisputable; sure: *We have* certain *proof of his guilt.* **2** positive; confident; sure: *I am* certain *of victory.* **3** sure to happen; inevitable: *You are going to* certain *death.*

cer·tif·i·cate (sûr tǐf′ǐ kət) *n-* **1** official document stating the truth of some fact, fitness for some work, etc.: *a birth* certificate; *a health* certificate; *a teacher's* certificate. **2** any solemn signed statement, often sworn to under oath.

cer·ti·fy (sûr′tə fī′) *vt-* [cer·ti·fied, cer·ti·fy·ing] **1** to state, confirm, or verify by a signed statement or official document: *to* certify *the date of one's birth.* **2** to guarantee: *to* certify *a check.* —*n-* cer′ti·fi′er.

ces·sa·tion (sě sā′shən) *n-* a ceasing or halting; stopping: *a* cessation *of pain; the* cessation *of hostilities.*

chafe (chāf) *vt-* [chafed, chaf·ing] **1** to restore warmth or sensation to by rubbing: *to* chafe *numb hands.* **2** to wear away or irritate by rubbing: *A starched collar may* chafe *the neck. The pulley* chafed *the rope.*

¹chaff (chǎf) *n-* **1** the husks of grain, separated by threshing and winnowing. **2** anything worthless: *to separate the wheat from the* chaff. [from Old English word ceaf.]

cha·grin (shə grǐn′) *n-* feeling of annoyance because of disappointment, failure, or humiliation; mortification; embarrassment. *vt-: It* chagrined *him that he lost.*

chain (chān) *n-* **1** series of links or rings, usually metal, joined one after another. **2** anything that binds or restrains. **3** connected series or succession: *a* chain *of events.* **4** set of hotels, stores, banks, etc., under one management.

chair (châr) *n-* **1** a movable single seat, usually with four legs and a back. **2** office or position, especially of a professor: *the* chair *of history at the university.*

chalk (chôk) *n-* **1** soft, powdery limestone made mostly of tiny seashells. **2** white or colored marker or crayon made of this limestone or a similar material: *tailor's* chalk. *vt-* **1** to mark, draw, or write with such a crayon

chal·lenge (chǎl′ənj) *vt-* [chal·lenged, chal·leng·ing] **1** to dare (a person, group, team, etc.) to fight or compete: *I* challenge *anyone to race me.* **2** to call forth or excite the energies, interests, or talents of; arouse: *Science* challenges *today's young people.*

cham·ber (chām′bər) *n-* **1** a room, especially a bedroom. **2** a room for official occasions: *the judge's* chamber; *the Senate* chamber; *the* chamber *where the Pope meets his guests.* **3** division or house of a legislature.

cham·pi·on (chăm′pē ən) *n-* **1** winner of first place in a competition: *a tennis* champion; *a heavyweight boxing* champion. **2** person who defends another person or a cause: *a* champion *of liberty.*

chance (chǎns) *n-* **1** opportunity; suitable occasion: *I'll go when I get a* chance. **2** luck; fortune; accident: *We met by* chance. *It was* chance, *not skill, that decided the winner.* **3** a risk; gamble; hazard: *You are taking a* chance *to drive in this weather.* **4** likelihood; probability: *What is the* chance *that it will rain?*

chan·cel (chǎn′səl) *n-* the space surrounding the altar of a church, reserved for the clergy and the choir.

chan·de·lier (shǎn′də lêr′) *n-* fixture that hangs from the ceiling, with branches for holding lights.

chan·dler (chǎnd′lər) *n-* **1** person who makes or sells candles. **2** dealer in ship's supplies.

change (chānj) *vt-* [changed, chang·ing] (in senses 2 and 3 considered intransitive when the direct object is implied but not expressed) **1** to make different; alter; modify; transform: *to* change *one's habits; to* change *color; to* change *a dull story into an interesting one.*

Chandelier

channel (chǎn′əl) *n-* **1** the course through which a stream, river, or brook passes; also, a tubular passage for liquids. **2** way or course for anything: *the* channels *of communication.*

chant (chănt) *n-* **1** a song, especially a solemn, measured song. **2** any measured and repetitious singing or shouting.

cha·os (kā′ŏs) *n-* **1** great confusion; utter disorder: *The city was in* chaos *after the hurricane.* **2** (also Chaos) in some mythologies, the formless and disordered condition of matter from which the universe evolved.

¹chap (chăp) *vt-* [chapped, chap·ping] to cause to crack or become rough: *Cold* chaps *the skin. vi-: My hands* chap *quickly. n-* a roughened spot or crack in the skin. [from earlier English chappen, related to ¹chop and chip.]

²chap (chăp) *Informal n-* fellow; man or boy; guy. [once meaning "one who buys," it is a short form of the older English chapman, "one who buys or sells," and is related to cheap.]

chap·er·on or **chap·er·one** (shăp′ə rōn′) *n-* older woman who accompanies an unmarried girl in public; also, anyone who supervises the social activities of young people to maintain proper behavior.

char·ac·ter (kăr′ĭk tər) *n-* **1** combination of qualities typical of a thing; individual nature: *the dry and barren* character *of the desert.* **2** personal qualities by which others judge one; moral nature: *a man of heroic character; the weak* character *of a coward.* **3** moral excellence: *The President must be a man of* character.

char·ac·ter·is·tic (kăr′ĭk tər ĭs′tĭk) *adj-* showing the distinctive qualities or traits of a person or thing; typical: *her* characteristic *kindness.*

cha·rade (shə rād′) *n-* **1** the acting out of a word, phrase, etc., to be guessed, usually by showing each syllable in pantomime. The word "persuaded" might be shown by acting out "purr," "sway," and "dead."

charge (chärj) *vt-* [charged, charg·ing] (in senses 1 and 3 considered intransitive when the direct object is implied but not expressed) **1** to require as payment: *He* charged *a dime for a candy bar. How much did they* charge *you for that hat? Do you* charge *for this service?*

char·i·ty (chăr′ə tē) *n-* [*pl.* char·i·ties] **1** love of one's fellow men; good will, especially in judging the faults of others: *"With malice toward none, with charity for all . . ."* **2** assistance given voluntarily to the poor, the sick, and other needy people.

char·la·tan (shär′lə tən) *n-* person who deceives others by claiming to have special skill or knowledge that he does not possess; quack.

charm (chärm) *n-* **1** power to attract and please; fascination: *Paris has great* charm *for tourists.* **2** trait that attracts and pleases: *Her friendly smile is her chief charm.* **3** word, verse, object, etc., supposed to have magic power or to bring good luck.

chart (chärt) *n-* **1** map, especially one for use by mariners, showing depths of water, rocks and islands, currents, etc. **2** sheet of paper giving information in the form of graphs, diagrams, or other illustrations: *a weather* chart; *an anatomy* chart.

char·ter (chär′tər) *n-* **1** official document giving certain rights and privileges: *The king granted William Penn a* charter *to form the colony of Pennsylvania.* **2** declaration giving the aims or principles of a group or organization: *the* charter *of the United Nations.* **3** a leasing or renting of (a plane, bus, boat, etc.) for private use.

char·y (châr′ē) *adj-* [char·i·er, char·i·est] **1** careful; cautious; wary: *She is* chary *of talking to strangers.* **2** not free or extravagant; sparing: *to be* chary *in giving.*

¹chase (chās) *vt-* [chased, chas·ing] **1** to go after and try to catch; pursue: *to* chase *a rabbit.* **2** to get rid of by or as if by driving away: *to* chase *chickens out of the garden; to* chase *a child's fears away.*

chasm (kăz′əm) *n-* deep opening in the earth; gorge.

chas·sis (chăs′ē, chăs′-) *n-* [*pl.* chas·sis (-ēz)] **1** steel frame, engine, springs, wheels, etc., on which the body of a motor vehicle is mounted.

chaste (chāst) *adj-* **1** pure and virtuous. **2** simple and restrained in style or taste. —*adv-* chaste′ly. *n-* chaste′ ness.

chas·ten (chā′sən) *vt-* **1** to punish for the purpose of correcting; discipline. **2** to curb; tame; subdue: *Ex-*

chat (chăt) *vi-* [**chat·ted, chat·ting**] to converse in an easy, friendly way. *n-* 1 an informal, friendly talk or conversation. 2 any of various songbirds, especially a North American warbler, the **yellow-breasted chat.**

chat·ter (chăt′ər) *vi-* 1 to make short, rapid sounds, as some monkeys and birds do. 2 to talk fast and foolishly; jabber. 3 to make a rattling or clacking sound: *My teeth chattered from the cold.*

chau·vin·ism (shō′və nĭz′əm) *n-* blind, exaggerated, and uncritical pride in one's own group or nation, associated with militarism and, often, racism. —*n-* **chau′vin·ist.** *adj-* **chau′vin·is′tic.**

cheap (chēp) *adj-* [**cheap·er, cheap·est**] 1 low in cost: *a cheap car; a cheap victory.* 2 of poor quality; in bad taste; mean and low: *a cheap novel; his cheap remarks.* 3 charging low prices or rates: *a cheap department store.* 4 selfish about spending money; ungenerous; stingy. *Hom-* cheep. —*adv-* **cheap′ly.** *n-* **cheap′ness.**

cheat (chēt) *vi-* to act dishonestly or use trickery to gain an advantage: *to cheat on a test. vt-* to deceive, trick, or swindle: *to cheat a customer. n-* (also **cheat′er**) person who acts dishonestly or deceitfully.

check (chĕk) *n-* 1 person or thing that controls or limits: *Contour plowing acts as a check on soil erosion.* 2 test or investigation; verification: *a check on his figures; a check on the pupil's progress; a loyalty check.* 3 mark (√) used to show that something has been examined or verified.

²check·er (chĕk′ər) *n-* 1 one of the squares of a pattern marked in squares of alternating colors. 2 the pattern itself. 3 one of the pieces used in playing checkers.

cheek (chēk) *n-* 1 either side of the face below the eyes and above the level of the mouth. 2 impudence; insolence: *He had the cheek to disobey orders.*

cheer (chēr) *n-* 1 shout of joy, approval, or encouragement: *a cheer for our team.* 2 encouragement; comfort: *The doctor's report gave us some cheer.* 3 high spirits; gaiety: especially in the phrase **be of good cheer.**

cheer·ful (chēr′fəl) *adj-* 1 in good spirits; gay: *a cheerful person.* 2 bringing cheer: *a cheerful fire.* 3 willing; eager: *a cheerful worker.* —*adv-* **cheer′ful·ly.**

chee·tah (chē′tə) *n-* swift leopardlike cat found in parts of Africa and, formerly, Persia and India. It is often trained to hunt.

Cheetah, about 3 ft

chef (shĕf) *n-* 1 head cook of a hotel or restaurant. 2 any male cook.

chem·is·try (kĕm′ə strē′) *n-* 1 the science that deals with the characteristics and composition of substances, how they are formed, how they change, and how they react. 2 chemical composition, properties, and reactions of substances: *the chemistry of rubber.*

cher·ish (chĕr′ĭsh) *vt-* 1 to love; care for tenderly: *She cherishes her children.* 2 to hold dear; keep in mind; treasure: *Grandmother cherished her childhood memories.* 3 to cling to: *He cherished the hope of being famous.*

cher·ry (chĕr′ē) *n-* [*pl.* **cher·ries**] 1 tree related to the plum, bearing a small, smooth, fleshy fruit with a stone in the center. 2 the fruit or the wood of this tree. 3 a bright red like that of a red variety of this fruit.

cher·ub (chĕr′əb) *n-* [*pl.* **cher·u·bim** (-ə blm′)] an angel of the second rank of the nine orders, often represented in art as a beautiful winged child or head of a child. 2 [*pl.* **cher·ubs**] a lovely, sweet child.

chess (chĕs) *n-* a game played by two persons, each having 16 pieces called **chess′men,** which are moved about on a **chess′** board of 64 squares.

chest (chĕst) *n-* 1 upper front part of a human body, enclosed by the ribs and containing the heart and lungs. 2 large box with a lid, used for storage or shipping; also, the amount contained in it:

Chessboard

chew (chōō) *vt-* to crush and grind (food, gum, etc.) with the teeth; masticate. *n-* piece of gum, tobacco, or the like, held in the mouth and chewed.

chick·en (chĭk′ən) *n-* 1 hen or rooster, especially a young one. 2 any young bird. 3 the flesh of hen or rooster, used as food.

chide (chīd) *vt-* [**chid·ed** or **chid** (chĭd), **chid·ed** or **chid** or **chid·den** (chĭd′ən), **chid·ing**] to scold; rebuke: *The teacher chided him for being rude.*

chief (chēf) *n-* the head or leader of a group, organization, department, etc.: *an Indian chief; a chief of police. adj-* 1 highest in rank or authority; head: *the chief clerk.* 2 most important; leading; principal: *the chief crop.*

child (chīld) *n-* [*pl.* **chil·dren** (chĭl′drən)] 1 baby. 2 young boy or girl. 3 son or daughter. 4 offspring.

chill (chĭl) *n-* 1 coldness: *an autumn chill in the air.* 2 sudden cold feeling in the body, accompanied by shivering. 3 a check upon enthusiasm: *She put a chill on the party. adj-* 1 very cool: *In the evening a chill breeze blew across the lake.*

chime (chīm) *n-* 1 set of bells tuned to a musical scale. 2 the sound of such bells. *vi-* [**chimed, chim·ing**] to ring: *The bells chimed at noon. vt-* to indicate or announce (the hour) by ringing.

chim·ney (chĭm′nē) *n-* 1 an outlet for smoke from a fireplace, furnace, etc., especially the part extending above the roof of a house. 2 the glass tube shielding the flame of a lamp or lantern.

chim·pan·zee (chĭm′păn′zē′, chĭm păn′zē) *n-* highly intelligent ape of equatorial Africa, somewhat smaller than the gorilla.

chin (chĭn) *n-* the part of the face below the mouth. *vt-* [**chinned, chin·ning**] to pull (oneself) up by the hands on a horizontal bar until the level of the chin is just above the bar.

Chimpanzee.
4 1/2 to 5 ft tall

chi·na (chī′nə) *n-* 1 fine porcelain with a white background, made of clay baked in a special way, originally produced in China.

¹chink (chĭngk) *n-* a narrow crack or opening. *vt-* to fill the cracks of: *The walls of the log cabin were* chinked *with earth.* [probably from Old English **cinu** also meaning "a crack."]

chip (chĭp) *n-* 1 small bit or piece cut or broken off wood, stone, metal, or china. 2 gap left when a small piece is broken from something. 3 small, thin slice of a food: *a potato* chip.

chip·munk (chĭp′mŭngk′) *n-* small, striped, burrowing animal related to squirrels and gophers. [American word from American Indian **atchitamon** meaning "(he who descends from trees) head first."]

chipped beef *n-* dried smoked beef cut in very thin slices. Also called **dried beef.**

chi·ro·prac·tor (kī′rō prăk′tər) *n-* one who treats bodily diseases by manipulating the joints, especially of the spine.

chirp (chûrp) *n-* short, sharp sound made by birds and insects. *vi-* to make such a sound.

chis·el (chĭz′əl) *n-* tool with a sharp steel edge for cutting, shaping, or engraving. *vi-* 1 to cut or shape with such a tool. 2 *Slang* to cheat; to get something by shrewd, deceitful means: *He chisels from his friends. vt-:* *to* chisel *a statue out of marble. vt-:* *to* **chis′el·er.**

Wood chisel

Stone chisel

chiv·al·ry (shĭv′əl rē) *n-* 1 the ideal qualities of a knight, such as courage, honor, and courtesy. 2 the system of knighthood. 3 a body of knights; hence, a company of gallant gentlemen.

chlo·rine (klô' rēn') *n-* greenish-yellow, irritating gas with a strong odor, used for bleaching and in purifying water. Chemical element, symbol Cl, At. No. 17, At. Wt. 35.46.

chlo·ro·phyll or **chlo·ro·phyl** (klôr' ə fĬl) *n-* the green coloring matter of plants that uses light to combine carbon dioxide and water into the food needed by the plants.

choc·o·late (chŏk' lət, chŏk'-) *n-* 1 food substance made by roasting and grinding cacao beans. 2 a candy made from this substance. 3 hot chocolate drink made of chocolate and milk or water. *adj-:* a chocolate pie.

choice (chois) *n-* 1 act of choosing: I will leave the choice of a movie to you. 2 power to choose: We had a choice between the mountains and the seashore for vacation.

choir (kwī' ər) *n-* 1 a group of trained singers, usually in a church. 2 the part of a church in which the choir sings. Hom- quire.

choke (chōk) *vt-* [choked, chok·ing] 1 to stop or almost stop the breath or speech by blocking, pressing, or irritating the windpipe; stifle: A bone choked the dog. Smoke choked the firemen. 2 to block or check by clogging or crowding: Leaves choked the drain.

choose (chōōz) *vt-* [chose (chōz), chos·en (chō' zən), choos·ing] 1 to select from among others; pick out: to choose a heavier bat. 2 to decide; see fit: He chose to leave.

¹**chop** (chŏp) *vt-* [chopped, chop·ping] 1 to cut by blows with an ax or similar tool: to chop down a tree. 2 to cut into small pieces: to chop vegetables. 3 to cut short, as one's speech.

¹**chord** (kôrd, kōrd) *n-* 1 straight line segment joining any two points on a circle or an arc. For picture, see circle. 2 (also cord) stringlike part of the body, such as one of the vocal chords.

chore (chôr) *n-* 1 routine job, especially a daily task around the house or farm. 2 an odd job, especially an irksome or disagreeable one.

cho·re·og·ra·phy (kôr' ē ŏg' rə fē) *n-* art of composing or performing dances for ballet, opera, TV shows, etc.

chor·tle (chôr' təl, chôr'-) *vi-* [chor·tled, chor·tling] to laugh with chuckling sounds or in a snorting fashion.

cho·rus (kôr' əs) *n-* [pl. cho·rus·es] 1 group of people organized to sing or recite together. 2 group of singers and dancers in a musical show. 3 piece of music arranged for a number of voices.

chrom·i·um (krō' mē əm) *n-* shiny, silver-colored metal element used for plating other metals and in alloys; chrome. Symbol Cr, At. No. 24, At. Wt. 52.01.

chro·mo·some (krō' mə sōm') *n-* threadlike structure formed by the chromatin in the nucleus of a plant or animal cell just before the cell divides.

chron·ic (krŏn' Ĭk) *adj-* 1 lasting over a long period of time: He has a chronic cough. 2 habitual: She is a chronic complainer. —adv- chron'i·cal·ly.

chron·i·cle (krŏn' Ĭ kəl) *n-* record of events in the order in which they happened; a history. *vt-* [chron·i·cled, chron·i·cling] to record. —n- chron'i·cler.

²**chuck** (chŭk) *n-* 1 cut of beef including most of the neck and the shoulder blade. 2 clamp for holding a tool or piece of work in a lathe or drill. [apparently from French choque meaning "log."]

chuck-full (chŭk' fŏŏl') chock-full.

chuck-hole (chŭk' hōl') *n-* hole or rut in a road.

chuck·le (chŭk' əl) *vi-* [chuck·led, chuck·ling] to laugh quietly to oneself, expressing satisfaction. *n-* low, quiet laugh.

church (chûrch) *n-* 1 building for religious worship, especially Christian worship.

ci·der (sī' dər) *n-* 1 (also sweet cider) partially fermented juice of apples. 2 (also hard cider) fully fermented apple juice.

ci·gar (sĬ găr') *n-* roll of tobacco leaves for smoking.

cig·a·rette (sĬg' ə rět') *n-* shredded tobacco rolled in a thin paper for smoking. [from French cigarette meaning "little cigar."]

cin·der (sĬn' dər) *n-* 1 small piece of partly burned coal or wood that has ceased to flame but is not yet ash. 2 a piece of ash.

Cir·ce (sûr' sē) *n-* in the "Odyssey," an enchantress who changed the companions of Odysseus (Ulysses) into swine by means of a magic drink.

cir·cle (sûr' kəl) *n-* 1 Mathematics a closed plane curve, every point of which is the same distance from the center. 2 disk. 3 a ring: They made a circle for the folk dance. 4 group of people held together by common interests.

Circle

cir·cuit (sûr' kət) *n-* 1 a going around; revolution: Every year the earth completes its circuit of the sun. 2 route regularly traveled by a judge who holds court in different towns, or by a preacher who serves a number of widely scattered churches.

cir·cu·lar (sûr' kyə lər) *adj-* 1 round: a circular table. 2 moving in a circle; revolving: The turning of a phonograph record is a circular motion. *n-* printed letter or notice for circulation among the public.

cir·cu·late (sûr' kyə lāt') *vi-* [cir·cu·lat·ed, cir·cu·lat·ing] 1 to move round in a course leading back to the starting place: Hot water circulates in a heating system. Blood circulates in the body. 2 to go or send from place to place or person to person.

cir·cum·stance (sûr' kəm stăns') *n-* 1 condition, fact, or event surrounding and usually affecting another fact or event: Good weather and other circumstances favored the polar expedition.

cir·cus (sûr' kəs) *n-* 1 a traveling show of acrobats, clowns, horses, wild animals, etc.; also, the performance. 2 large level space surrounded by tiers of seats, usually within a tent, for putting on such shows.

cite (sīt) *vt-* [cit·ed, cit·ing] 1 to quote or refer to as an example, proof, or authority: He cited a poem as an illustration. The lawyer cited the evidence. 2 to summon to appear in court.

cit·i·zen (sĬt' ə zən) *n-* 1 member of a state or nation who has political rights and privileges, and gives in return his allegiance to the government.

cit·y (sĬt' ē) *n-* [pl. cit·ies] 1 a large or important town having local self-government. 2 all the people of such a town.

civil (sĬv' əl) *adj-* 1 having to do with citizens or the state: our civil rights; a civil war. 2 not connected with the church or military: a civil marriage ceremony.

ci·vil·ian (sə vĬl' yən) *n-* any person not a member of the armed services or of the police force.

civ·i·li·za·tion (sĬv' ə lə zā' shən) *n-* 1 condition of people who have advanced far beyond a primitive level in government, arts, religion, sciences, etc.

civil rights *n-* a citizen's rights in the areas of employment, housing, education, suffrage, etc., established by the thirteenth and fourteenth Constitutional amendments and reinforced by a series of other laws.

clad (klăd) *adj-* covered, sheathed, clothed, or plated (often used in compound adjectives): tin-clad copper-clad. *vt-* [clad, clad·ding] to cover, sheath, or plate (a metal) with a layer of another metal: to clad copper with tin.

claim (klām) *vt-* 1 to demand or assert as one's own or one's due: to claim an inheritance. 2 to call for; deserve: This matter claims our attention. 3 to state as a fact; assert: I claim this to be true.

clair·voy·ant (klâr voi' ənt) *adj-* 1 having the power to see things beyond the natural range of vision. 2 unusually perceptive or discerning. **n-** 1 person claiming the supernatural power of clairvoyance. 2 person who is unusually perceptive. **—adv-** clair·voy′ant·ly.

clam (klăm) **n-** mollusk with a hinged double shell, living partly or wholly buried in sand or mud, and used as food. **vi-** [clammed, clam·ming] to gather or dig for clams.

Clam

clamor (klăm′ər) **n-** loud and continued outcry or demand; uproar. **vi-:** *The people* clamored *for more.*

clamp (klămp) **n-** a brace, band, clasp, or other device for holding things tightly together; cramp. **vt-** to fasten or strengthen with such a device.

Clamp

clan (klăn) **n-** 1 group of families, the heads of which claim common ancestry and have the same surname, especially in the Scottish Highlands: *He wears the tartan of the Macleod* clan.

clap (klăp) **vt-** [clapped, clap·ping] 1 to strike together with a quick, sharp sound: *The teacher* clapped *her hands for attention.* 2 to strike or slap, usually in a friendly way: *to* clap *one on the back.*

clap·per (klăp′ər) **n-** 1 tongue of a bell. 2 person or thing that claps.

clap·trap (klăp′trăp′) *Informal* **n-** any showy device, especially in speech, for making an impression; trash: *The candidate's talk was mostly* claptrap.

Clapper

claque (klăk) **n-** 1 group of hired applauders at a performance, especially in the theater. 2 group of self-seeking followers. **Hom-** clack.

clar·i·fy (klăr′ə fī′) **vt-** [clar·i·fied, clar·i·fy·ing] 1 to make clear, transparent, or pure, as with a liquid, butter, or air. 2 to make plain or intelligible: *to* clarify *a statement.* **vi-:** *The syrup* clarified *as it heated.*

clash (klăsh) **vi-** 1 to make a loud, metallic, reverberating sound by striking together: *The cymbals* clashed. 2 to come into conflict; be in opposition or discord: *The armies* clashed *on the plain. Pink and orange* clash.

clasp (klăsp) **n-** 1 fastening device that grips or hooks two parts or things together: *a tie* clasp. 2 a firm hold or grasp, as in shaking hands; close embrace.

class (klăs) **n-** 1 group of persons or things similar in various ways; sort; kind. 2 section of society having the same social or economic level; rank: *the middle* class.

claw (klô) **n-** 1 a sharp, hooked, horny nail on a toe of an animal or bird; also, the toe and the nail. 2 the pincers of a shellfish such as a crab or lobster. 3 any hooked or pointed tool, such as the curved end of some hammer heads.

Bird's claw

clean (klēn) *adj-* [clean·er, clean·est] 1 free from dirt; not filthy; unsoiled: *A food handler must have clean hands.* 2 free from guilt, sin, wrong, etc.; morally pure: *a clean life; a clean record.*

clear (klēr) *adj-* [clear·er, clear·est] 1 free of clouds, mud, or any other obstacle that blocks or reduces vision: *a clear day; clear water; clear glass.* 2 free of any obstacle to physical passage: *a clear road.*

cleat (klēt) **n-** 1 one of the blocks or spikes put on the soles of some athletes' shoes to prevent slipping.

¹cleave (klēv) **vt-** [cleft (klĕft) or cleaved or clove (klōv), cleft or cleaved or cloven (klō′vən), cleav·ing] 1 to split or cut open: *The lightning* cleft *the tree.*

clem·en·cy (klĕm′ən sē) **n-** 1 mercy; leniency: *The court showed* clemency *toward the young prisoner.* 2 mildness, as of the weather or climate.

clench (klĕnch) **vt-** 1 to press closely together: *He* clenched *his teeth.* 2 to grasp firmly: *He* clenched *the sword in his hand.*

clerk (klûrk) **n-** 1 salesman or saleswoman in a store. 2 person who does the routine work of an office, especially keeping records: *a file* clerk. 3 public official

who keeps records and does routine business.

clev·er (klĕv′ər) *adj-* [clev·er·er, clev·er·est] 1 mentally quick or alert: *A clever fox can escape the hounds.* 2 skillfull: *I wish I were* clever *enough to make my own clothes.* 3 showing skill or mental quickness

cli·ent (klī′ənt) **n-** 1 person who engages the professional services of another, especially of a lawyer. 2 a good customer: *an antique dealer's* clients.

cli·mate (klī′mət) **n-** 1 the weather conditions of a place over a period of time: *the warm* climate *of Florida in the winter.* 2 the prevailing outlook or attitude: *a favorable* climate *of opinion.*

cli·max (klī′măks′) **n-** 1 highest and most important point in the development of events, ideas, etc.; turning point; culmination: *the* climax *of a play.*

climb (klīm) **vt-** 1 to go up or over (something) by using hands and feet; scale: *to* climb *a cliff; to* climb *a tree.* 2 to mount; ascend: *The car easily* climbed *the hill.*

cling (kling) **vi-** [clung (klŭng), cling·ing] to hold fast or stick to someone or something: *to* cling *to a rope.*

clin·ic (klĭn′ĭk) **n-** 1 an institution where specialists help people with a particular type of medical or personal problem: *heart* clinic; *dental* clinic; *reading* clinic.

¹clip (klĭp) **vt-** [clipped, clip·ping] to hold tightly together with a clasp. **n-** 1 a clasp, especially for holding papers: *a paper* clip. 2 ornament which is held by a clasp: *She wore a diamond* clip.

Clip

²clock (klŏk) **n-** long, narrow design extending upward from the ankle of a sock or stocking. [of unknown origin.] **—adj-** clocked.

clog (klŏg) **vt-** [clogged, clog·ging] 1 to obstruct; stop up; block: *Leaves* clogged *the drain.* 2 to hinder the movement of by blocking or obstructing: *Lint* clogged *the gears of the machine.*

Bath clog

²close (klōs) *adj-* [clos·er, clos·est] 1 without much space between; narrow; snug; fitting tightly: *a close weave; a* close *fit.* 2 stuffy: *The air was* close *in the room.*

cloth (klôth) **n-** 1 fabric made from wool, cotton, silk, linen, etc. 2 piece of such fabric used for a special purpose: *a dust* cloth. 3 **the cloth** the clergy.

clothe (klōth) **vt-** [clothed or clad (klăd), cloth·ing] 1 to dress; put clothes on. 2 to provide clothing for: *The poor man could not feed and* clothe *his family properly.* 3 to cover with, or as with, a garment.

cloud (kloud) **n-** 1 visible mass of condensed water floating above the earth. 2 similar mass of smoke or dust. 3 anything that moves in or like a mass, such as a large number of arrows, insects, horsemen, etc.

clout (klout) **n-** 1 strong blow. 2 in archery, a white cloth target used in long-distance shooting. 3 arrow that hits such a target. 4. *Archaic* a patch; rag. **vt-** to hit; strike: *to* clout *a home run.*

clown (kloun) **n-** 1 comedian, often dressed in an outlandish costume, who performs in a circus or other entertainment. 2 person who frequently acts like a fool and plays pranks: *the school* clown. 3 *Archaic* rude, clumsy man; boor.

coat (kōt) **n-** 1 outer garment with sleeves, especially one for winter wear reaching to or below the knees. 2 the hair or fur of an animal: *Collies have a long* coat, *dachshunds a short* coat.

club (klŭb) **n-** 1 heavy stick, usually thick at one end, especially one used as a weapon. 2 any of certain sticks or bats for hitting a ball: *a golf* club.

clue (klōō) **n-** something that helps solve a problem or a mystery: *The footprints were a* clue. Also **clew**.

clump (klŭmp) **n-** 1 thick cluster: *a* clump *of bushes.* 2 thick mass; lump: *a* clump *of earth.* **vi-** to tread heavily: *The horses* clumped *along.* **—adj-** clump′y.

clum·sy (klŭm′zē) *adj-* [clum·si·er, clum·si·est] 1 lacking in ease or grace; awkward: *a* clumsy *fellow; a* clumsy *excuse.* 2 hard to handle; unwieldy: *a* clumsy *rake.* **—adv-** clum′si·ly. **n-** clum′si·ness.

clus·ter (klŭs′tər) **n-** group of persons or things

clut·ter (klŭt′ər) *n-* disorderly state; confusion; jumble: *Please tidy up the* clutter *in your room.* *vt-*: *Heaps of books* cluttered *her room.*

coach (kōch) *n-* 1 large, enclosed, horse-drawn vehicle with four wheels. 2 formerly, a two-door sedan.

co·ag·u·late (kō ăg′yə lāt′) *vi-* [co·ag·u·lat·ed, co·ag·u·lat·ing] to become clotted; to change from a liquid to a pasty solid: *When the blood from a cut* coagulates, *the bleeding stops.* *vt-* to cause such a change.

coal (kōl) *n-* 1 a hard, black mineral fuel formed deep in the earth from buried vegetable matter by the action of heat and great pressure. 2 a glowing or charred bit of solid fuel; an ember.

co·a·li·tion (kō′ə lĭsh′ən) *n-* in politics, a temporary alliance of persons, parties, or countries for a special purpose. *as modifier*: *a* coalition *government.*

coarse (kôrs) *adj-* [coars·er, coars·est] 1 lacking in refinement; crude; vulgar: *a* coarse *manner*; *his* coarse *language.* 2 lacking fineness of texture or shape; composed of large or rough particles, features, etc..

coast (kōst) *n-* the land or region next to the sea; seashore. *vi-* 1 to ride along by the force of gravity or by the force of one's momentum after power has been cut off.

coax (kōks) *vt-* 1 to persuade or influence by gentleness, flattery, etc.: *Tom* coaxed *his father to let him borrow the car.* 2 to obtain by such means: *to* coax *a smile from the baby.*

co·bra (kō′brə) *n-* any of various closely related poisonous snakes of Africa and Asia, including the spectacled or Indian cobra, the Egyptian cobra, and the king cobra of southeastern Asia. Cobras flatten their necks into a hood when alarmed.

King cobra.

cob·web (kŏb′wĕb′) *n-* 1 web spun by a spider. 2 something flimsy or entangling, like a spider's web.

cock·tail (kŏk′tāl′) *n-* 1 chilled, mixed drink made of alcoholic liquors or fruit or vegetable juices. 2 shellfish or mixed fruit, served as an appetizer: *a shrimp* cocktail.

cock·y (kŏk′ē) *adj-* [cock·i·er, cock·i·est] arrogantly sure of oneself; conceited: *Jim was very* cocky *about his chances of winning first prize in the contest.* *—adv* cock′i·ly.

code (kōd) *n-* 1 system of symbols, letters, words, numbers, etc. used to stand for the letters and words of messages. Codes are used for secret messages or for brevity.

co·erce (kō ûrs′) *vt-* [co·erced, co·erc·ing] to compel by force or threats: *He* coerced *the prisoner into confessing.*

cof·fee (kô′fē, kŏf′-) *n-* 1 a drink brewed from the roasted and ground seeds (called beans) of the coffee tree. 2 the seeds themselves, whole or ground.

cof·fin (kô′fən) *n-* a box or case in which a dead person is buried; casket.

cog (kŏg) *n-* one of a series of teeth on the rim of a wheel that mesh with teeth on another wheel to transmit or receive motion.

COG
Cogwheel and cog

co·gent (kō′jənt) *adj-* compelling; forceful; convincing: *a* cogent *reason.* *—n-* co′gen·cy *of his reasons demands action.*

cog·ni·zant (kŏg′nə zənt) *adj-* having knowledge; aware.

co·here (kō hēr′) *vi-* [co·hered, co·her·ing] to stick together in a mass, as mud; to hold together, as cement and stone.

co·her·ent (kō hēr′ənt) *adj-* 1 sticking together: *a* coherent *mass of mud, gravel, and straw.* 2 logically connected and developed; consistent: *a* coherent *speech.* *—adv-* co·her′ent·ly.

coil (koil) *n-* 1 anything wound in a series of circles or spirals: *a* coil *of rope.* 2 one of the circles of a spiral, or a series of circles.

Coil

coin (koin) *n-* 1 piece of metal, stamped by a government, used for money. 2 metal money: *Change the dollar bill for* coin. 3 any stamped piece of metal: *Souvenir* coins *were given away to advertise the new store.* *vt-* 1 to make metal into money.

co·in·ci·dence (kō ĭn′sə dəns) *n-* 1 a remarkable occurrence of events, ideas, etc., at the same time by mere chance: *By* coincidence *the dress my cousin wore was exactly like mine.*

cold (kōld) *adj-* [cold·er, cold·est] 1 having or feeling little or no warmth; chilly: *The night is* cold *and stormy. I'm* cold *in this room.* 2 having little or no feeling: *a* cold *greeting; a* cold, *calculated scheme.*

Colander

col·lab·o·rate (kə lăb′ər āt′) *vi-* [col·lab·o·rat·ed, col·lab·o·rat·ing] 1 to work or cooperate with another in some activity: *to* collaborate *in the writing of a book.* 2 to aid or cooperate with an enemy that is occupying one's country. *—n-* col·lab′o·ra′tion.

col·lapse (kə lăps′) *vi-* [col·lapsed, col·laps·ing] 1 to fall down or in; cave in: *The roof* collapsed *under the weight of the snow.* 2 to fold, deflate, or otherwise assume a less bulky form: *The tripod* collapses *when you fold its legs. The rubber life raft* collapses *for storage.*

col·league (kŏl′ēg′) *n-* fellow member of a profession, committee, etc.; associate.

col·lect (kə lĕkt′) *vt-* 1 to bring together; gather: *They* collected *the scraps into a heap.* 2 to pick up and remove: *to* collect *the test papers, to* collect *the trash.* 3 to gather and keep for study or as part of a hobby: *to* collect *stamps.*

col·lege (kŏl′ĭj) *n-* 1 educational institution more advanced than the high school and giving bachelor degrees to its students when they have finished certain courses of study; also, a unit of a university.

col·lide (kə lĭd′) *vi-* [col·lid·ed, col·lid·ing] 1 to meet and strike together with force; crash: *The cars* collided. 2 to clash: *He* collided *with me over politics.*

col·lo·qui·al (kə lō′kwē əl) *adj-* used in ordinary conversation or other circumstances where formal language is less appropriate; informal: *"Movies" is a* colloquial *word for "moving pictures."*

co·lo·ni·al (kə lō′nē əl) *adj-* 1 relating to a colony or colonies. 2 relating to the thirteen British colonies which eventually became the United States, or to that period of our history.

col·o·ny (kŏl′ə nē) *n-* [*pl.* col·o·nies] 1 territory settled or conquered by people of a distant country and then governed by it.

col·or (kŭl′ər) *n-* 1 property of the light reaching the eyes which determines whether an individual with normal vision sees something as red, blue, green, etc. Color depends upon the wavelength of the light.

co·los·sal (kə lŏs′əl) *adj-* like a colossus; huge; immense; vast; tremendous: *a* colossal *city; the* colossal *expanse of the ocean.* *—adv-* co·los′sal·ly.

co·ma (kō′mə) *n-* a state of unconsciousness and insensibility, produced by disease, injury, or poison.

comb (kōm) *n-* 1 a thin piece of hard rubber, plastic, metal, or the like, cut so as to have many thin projections, and used to smooth, arrange, or hold the hair. 2 a similar metal instrument used to separate and clean the fibers of flax or wool. 3 a currycomb. 4 the fleshy, red growth on the head of a hen, rooster, or other fowl; crest.

COMB
Comb of rooster

¹com·bat (kəm băt′) *vt-* [com·bat·ed or com·bat·ted, com·bat·ing or com·bat·ting] to fight; oppose: *Vaccines help* combat *disease.*

²com·bat (kŏm′băt′) *n-* 1 conflict or struggle, especially a direct physical struggle: *a fierce* combat *between two swordsmen; the* combat *of ideas.* 2 military engagement with an enemy; action. *as modifier*: *the* combat *zone.*

¹com·bine (kəm bīn′) *vt-* [com·bined, com·bin·ing]

1 to join; unite: *The two boys* combined *their efforts to solve the problem.* **2** to mix: *to* combine *ingredients to make a cake.*

com·bus·ti·ble (kəm bŭs′ tə bəl) *adj-* **1** able to catch fire and burn: *Wood is* combustible. **2** excitable: *a* combustible *temper.* *n-* a flammable substance.

come (kŭm) *vi-* [**came** (kăm), **come, com·ing**] **1** to draw near; approach: *Cold weather is* coming. **2** to arrive: *He will* come *tomorrow.* **3** to reach (to a certain point): *Her hair* comes *to her shoulders.*

com·e·dy (kŏm′ ə dē) *n-* [*pl.* **com·e·dies**] **1** a play, situation, or other happening that is funny. **2** in dramatic literature, a work which has a happy ending for the main characters.

com·et (kŏm′ ət) *n-* an immense body of matter, loosely held together, that travels in a long parabolic or, sometimes, elliptical path and develops a glowing fuzzy head and long tail when it comes near the sun.

Comet

com·fort (kŭm′ fərt) *vt-* to console, soothe, or cheer (a person, pet, etc.) in pain, grief, or trouble. *n-* **1** state of mental or spiritual ease; contentment: *Good health is a source of* comfort. *Serenity is a sign of* comfort.

com·ic (kŏm′ ĭk) *adj-* **1** funny; humorous; comical: *a* comic *song.* **2** of or having to do with comedy: *a* comic *writer.* *n-* **1** a comedian. **2** comics comic strips.

com·mand (kə mănd′) *vt-* (in senses 1, 2, and 3 considered intransitive when the direct object is implied but not expressed) **1** to have authority and control over; rule; govern: *to* command *an army; to* command *a ship.*

com·mem·o·rate (kə mĕm′ ə rāt′) *vt-* [**com·mem·o·rat·ed, com·mem·o·rat·ing**] to honor or keep alive the memory of: *The names of many cities* commemorate *men who built our country.*

com·mence (kə mĕns′) *vt-* [**com·menced, com·menc·ing**] to begin; start: *to* commence *work.* *vi-* : *We'll* commence *tomorrow.*

com·mend (kə mĕnd′) *vt-* **1** to praise; express approval of: *I* commend *you for being on time.* **2** to entrust: *to* commend *one's soul to God.* **3** to convey greetings and regards of: *Please* commend *me to your aunt.*

com·ment (kŏm′ ĕnt) *n-* **1** written or spoken remark, especially one that gives a personal reaction or opinion. **2** talk; gossip: *His unexpected departure caused* comment.

com·merce (kŏm′ ərs) *n-* the buying and selling of goods; trade; business transactions.

com·mis·er·ate (kə mĭz′ ə rāt′) *vt-* [**com·mis·er·at·ed, com·mis·er·at·ing**] to feel and express pity for: *to* commiserate *someone who is ill.* *vi-* to feel or express sympathy (with): *to* commiserate *with a beaten man.*

com·mis·sion (kə mĭsh′ ən) *n-* **1** the doing or performing (of some illegal, immoral, or inept act): *a* commission *of a crime.* **2** part of a selling price, paid as a fee to a salesman or agent: *The* commission *on the sale was $25.*

com·mit (kə mĭt′) *vt-* [**com·mit·ted, com·mit·ting**] **1** to do or perform (something illegal, immoral, or inept): *to* commit *a crime; to* commit *an error.* **2** to give (someone) into another's care, custody, etc.: *to* commit *a criminal to jail; to* commit *a mental patient to an asylum.*

com·mit·tee (kə mĭt′ ē) *n-* group of persons appointed or elected for a special purpose: *the finance* committee.

com·mo·di·ous (kə mō′ dē əs) *adj-* roomy; spacious: *a* commodious *house.* —*adv-* **com·mo′di·ous·ly.** *n-* **com·mo′di·ous·ness:** *The* commodiousness *of the house.*

com·mod·i·ty (kə mŏd′ ə tē) *n-* [*pl.* **com·mod·i·ties**] article of commerce, such as wheat, copper, silk, etc.

com·mon (kŏm′ ən) *adj-* [**com·mon·er, com·mon·est**] **1** frequently seen, heard, etc.; usual; familiar: *Snow is a* common *sight in northern countries.* **2** shared by or usual for many or all people; general: *That law is a matter of* common *knowledge.*

com·mo·tion (kə mō′ shən) *n-* disturbance or disorder; confusion; turmoil: *The news caused a* commotion.

com·mu·nal (kə myōō′ nəl, kŏm′ yə nəl) *adj-* **1** of property, shared in common: *a plot of* communal *land.* **2** of or relating to a commune.

com·mu·ni·ca·ble (kə myōō′ nĭ kə bəl) *adj-* liable to be transmitted from person to person: *a* communicable *disease.* —*adv-* **com·mu′ni·ca·bly.**

com·mu·ni·cate (kə myōō′ nə kāt′) *vt-* [**com·mu·ni·cat·ed, com·mu·ni·cat·ing**] to pass on to another; convey; impart; transmit: *to* communicate *a message; to* communicate *a disease.*

com·mu·nism (kŏm′ yə nĭz′ əm) *n-* **1** economic and political idea, advanced by Karl Marx and modified by Nikolai Lenin and others, that the community as a whole should own all property and run all business and industry, and that this can be brought about only by armed revolution.

com·mu·ni·ty (kə myōō′ nə tē) *n-* [*pl.* **com·mu·ni·ties**] **1** all the people living in one place, such as a town or district, and subject to the same laws; also, the place itself: *a small New England* community. **2** group of persons bound together by common beliefs or interests.

com·mu·ta·tion (kŏm′ yə tā′ shən) *n-* a commuting of a payment or penalty: *the* commutation *of the death sentence to life imprisonment.*

com·mute (kə myōōt′) *vi-* [**com·mut·ed, com·mut·ing**] to travel regularly back and forth over a distance, usually from one's home to work in another city.

¹com·pact (kəm păkt′, kŏm′ păkt′) *adj-* **1** tightly packed; dense; compressed: *soil too* compact *for growing anything; a* compact *sentence.* **2** taking up relatively little space; small and solid; not bulky: *a* compact *bundle; a* compact *body.*

¹com·pan·ion (kəm păn′ yən) *n-* **1** person who regularly shares the work, play, interests, etc., of another; comrade: *He was my close* companion *all through school.*

com·pa·ny (kŭm′ pə nē) *n-* [*pl.* **com·pan·ies**] **1** guest or guests: *My* company *came for dinner.* **2** business or commercial firm. **3** group of people gathered together: *She guided a* company *of tourists.*

com·pa·ra·ble (kŏm′ pə rə bəl) *adj-* **1** of a nature that permits comparison: *Airplanes and birds are* comparable *because both fly.* **2** worthy or fit to be compared: *Rhinestones are hardly* comparable *to diamonds.*

com·pare (kəm pâr′) *vt-* [**com·pared, com·par·ing**] **1** to examine in order to find out, or show, likeness or difference in: *Before buying, she* compared *the two watches.*

com·part·ment (kəm pärt′ mənt) *n-* a separate part, division, or section of an enclosed space: *a separate* compartment *for paper clips; a glove* compartment *in a car.* —*adj-* **com·part′ment·ed.**

com·pass (kŭm′ pəs, kŏm-) *n-* **1** instrument used for determining direction, such as a free-swinging magnetic needle that always points to the north magnetic pole, or a gyrocompass that always points to the true north.

com·pas·sion (kəm păsh′ ən) *n-* sympathy for the sorrow or suffering of others, with a desire to help.

Drawing compass

com·pat·i·ble (kəm păt′ ə bəl) *adj-* able to exist together; harmonious; not inimical: *a* compatible *couple; a lamp* compatible *with the style of the room.* —*n-* **com·pat′i·bil′i·ty.** *adv-* **com·pat′i·bly.**

com·pel (kəm pĕl′) *vt-* [**com·pelled, com·pel·ling**] **1** to force; oblige: *The bandit's conscience* compelled *him to return.* **2** to get or exact by force: *to* compel *obedience.*

com·pen·sate (kŏm′ pən sāt′) *vt-* [**com·pen·sat·ed, com·pen·sat·ing**] to pay: *to* compensate *employees for overtime.* *vi-* to be a remedy (for); make up (for): *Glasses* compensate *for weak eyes.*

com·pete (kəm pēt′) *vi-* [**com·pet·ed, com·pet·ing**] to oppose or strive against another in a contest, business, etc.; contend; vie: *Three runners will* compete *in the race. The two companies* competed *for the contract.*

com·pe·tence (kŏm′ pə təns) *n-* **1** fitness; capability; ability: *No one questions her* competence *as a teacher.* **2** enough money for comfort; adequate means: *Income from investments assured him a lifelong* competence. Also **com′pe·ten·cy.**

com·pile (kəm pīl′) *vt-* [**com·piled, com·pil·ing**] 1 to put together (facts, articles, etc.) into a collection. 2 to compose from various sources: *to compile a history.*

com·pla·cen·cy (kəm plā′ sən sē) *n-* feeling of well-being and satisfaction, so strong as to be without any awareness of danger or the problems of others; self-satisfaction: *Lee's early victories jarred the North out of its complacency.* Also **com·pla′ cence.**

com·plain (kəm plān′) *vi-* 1 to express dissatisfaction or discontent because of a pain, sorrow, nuisance, etc.: *He complained of a headache.* 2 to report a wrong or injury: *He complained to the landlord about the noise.*

com·pos·ite (kəm pŏz′ ət) *adj-* 1 made up of different parts that form a whole: *a composite picture made from several photographs.*

com·po·si·tion (kŏm′ pə zĭsh′ ən) *n-* 1 an artistic work, especially a piece of music. 2 story, essay, etc., written as a school assignment, especially for practice in a language.

¹**com·pound** (kŏm′ pound′) *n-* 1 substance formed by the chemical combination of elements: *Salt (sodium chloride) is a compound of chlorine and sodium.* 2 a combination of two or more parts, ingredients, characteristics, etc.; mixture.

com·pre·hend (kŏm′ prĭ hĕnd′) *vt-* 1 to understand: *I heard his speech but did not comprehend his meaning.* 2 to include; take in: *Science comprehends the study of chemistry, physics, and biology.*

com·pre·hen·sive (kŏm′ prĭ hĕn′ sĭv) *adj-* including or covering much; full; complete: *a comprehensive description*; comprehensive studies. —*adv-* **com′ pre·hen′ sive·ly.** *n-* **com′ pre·hen′ sive·ness.**

¹**com·press** (kəm prĕs′) *vt-* to press, squeeze, or force tightly together or into a confined space: *to compress cotton into bales*; *to compress ideas into a paragraph.*

²**com·press** (kŏm′ prĕs′) *n-* pad of gauze or other cloth, applied to a wound, sprain, etc.

com·prise (kəm prīz′) *vt-* [**com·prised, com·pris·ing**] to consist of; include: *This volume comprises all his work.* ►For usage note see COMPOSE.

com·pro·mise (kŏm′ prə mīz′) *n-* settlement of differences in which each side yields something: *The strike was settled by compromise.*

com·pul·sion (kəm pŭl′ shən) *n-* 1 a compelling by force, fear, custom, etc.: *to govern by compulsion*; *to act under compulsion.* 2 very strong and usually unreasonable impulse: *a compulsion to avoid stepping on cracks in the pavement.*

com·pute (kəm pyōōt′) *vt-* [**com·put·ed, com·put·ing**] to determine by mathematics; calculate: *Scientists can compute the distance from the earth to distant stars.*

com·rade (kŏm′ răd′) *n-* friend or companion, especially one who shares one's interests and activities.

con·cave (kŏn′ kāv′) *adj-* curved inward like the inside of a saucer. —*adv-* **con′ cave′ ly.**

Concave

con·cav·i·ty (kŏn′ kăv′ ə tē) *n-* [*pl.* **con·cav·i·ties**] 1 the condition of being concave. 2 the inner surface of a rounded, hollow body.

con·ceal (kən sēl′) *vt-* to hide or keep secret: *to conceal a book*; *to conceal one's anger.*

con·cede (kən sēd′) *vt-* [**con·ced·ed, con·ced·ing**] 1 to admit the truth of; acknowledge: *to concede a point in a debate.* 2 to give up or grant, often reluctantly: *to concede a raise in wages.*

con·ceit (kən sēt′) *n-* excessive or flattering belief in oneself; vanity: *The star was puffed up with conceit.*

con·ceive (kən sēv′) *vt-* [**con·ceived, con·ceiv·ing**] 1 to form (a plan, project, etc.) in the mind: *They conceived a plot to overthrow the king.* 2 to form a mental picture of; imagine: *I cannot conceive his owning all that property.*

con·cen·tra·tion (kŏn′ sən trā′ shən) *n-* 1 fixed attention on one object: *It requires concentration to study during a thunderstorm.* 2 group or mass brought together in one place or thing: *a concentration of enemy troops along the border.*

con·cept (kŏn′ sĕpt′) *n-* a mental image; general idea or notion: *a concept of the solar system*; *a concept of a word's meaning.*

con·cern (kən sûrn′) *vt-* 1 to be of interest or importance to; have to do with; relate to; affect: *This doesn't concern the schedule.* 2 to make anxious or uneasy; worry; trouble: *His poor health concerns me.*

con·cert (kŏn′ sərt) *n-* musical performance by singers, or players, or both. *as modifier:* a concert hall. **in concert** in agreement; together.

con·cert·ed (kən sûr′ təd) *adj-* planned, agreed upon, or carried out together; combined; joint: *a concerted effort.*

con·cil·i·ate (kən sĭl′ ē āt′) *vt-* [**con·cil·i·at·ed, con·cil·i·at·ing**] to gain the good will of; overcome the hostility of; placate: *The boy's apology conciliated his angry father.* —*n-* **con·cil′ i·a′ tion.**

con·cise (kən sīs′) *adj-* expressing much in few words; short and to the point; terse: *a concise and witty remark.* —*adv-* **con·cise′ ly.** *n-* **con·cise′ ness.**

con·clave (kŏn′ klāv′) *n-* 1 private meeting of cardinals, especially for the election of a pope. 2 the rooms in which such a meeting is held. 3 any private or secret meeting: *a political conclave.*

con·clude (kən klōōd′) *vt-* [**con·clud·ed, con·clud·ing**] 1 to end; finish: *As he concluded his speech, there was loud applause.* 2 to settle; arrange after discussion or argument: *The two nations concluded a trade agreement.*

con·coct (kən kŏkt′, kŏn′-) *vt-* 1 to make out of various parts or things: *Wanda concocted a salad of fruit and nuts.* 2 to make up; invent: *to concoct a story.*

con·cord·ance (kən kôr′ dəns, -kôr′ dəns) *n-* 1 agreement; harmony: *a concordance of aims.* 2 book consisting of an alphabetical list giving the location of all the important words in a single work or in the collected works of an author: *a concordance to Shakespeare.*

con·course (kŏn′ kôrs) *n-* 1 a running, flowing, or coming together; confluence: *St. Louis is located at the concourse of the Mississippi and Missouri.* 2 crowd or assembly. 3 open place where crowds gather, as in a railroad station.

¹**con·crete** (kŏn′ krēt) *n-* a hardened mixture of cement, sand, gravel, and water, used in building and paving. *adj-:* a concrete walk.

²**con·crete** (kən krēt′, kŏn′ krēt′) *adj-* 1 of a nature such that it can be seen, heard, touched, measured, etc.; belonging to the physical world; real: *A table is a concrete object.* 2 relating to actual things or events: *a concrete discussion of the effects of a tax.*

con·cur (kən kûr′) *vi-* [**con·curred, con·cur·ring**] 1 to agree: *All the judges concurred in the decision.* 2 to happen or work together; coincide: *Careful planning and good luck concurred to bring about victory.*

con·cus·sion (kən kŭsh′ ən) *n-* 1 a violent jarring; shock: *the concussion of an explosion.* 2 brain injury due to a blow or fall.

con·demn (kən dĕm′) *vt-* 1 to express strong disapproval of; censure: *The board condemned his harsh measures.* 2 to declare guilty in court; also, to sentence: *The judge condemned him to five years at hard labor.*

con·den·sa·tion (kŏn′ dĕn sā′ shən) *n-* 1 the change from vapor into a liquid: *Rain forms by the condensation of water vapor.* 2 the liquid so formed: *the condensation ran down the window pane.*

con·de·scend (kŏn′ də sĕnd′) *vi-* 1 to stoop or come down willingly to the level of one's inferiors: *The king condescended to eat with the people.* 2 to do something with a superior or patronizing air: *Though she thought it beneath her, she condescended to clean the house.*

con·di·tion (kən dĭsh′ ən) *n-* 1 state in which a person or thing is: *to be in a healthy condition*; *to be in working condition.* 2 something that must exist before something else can happen or exist: *Hard work is a condition of success.*

con·du·cive (kən dōō′ sĭv, kən dyōō′-) *adj-* tending to bring about; promoting; contributory (to): *Regular exercise is said to be conducive to good health.*

¹con·duct (kən dŭkt´) *vt-* (in senses 1, 2, and 3 considered intransitive when the direct object is implied but not expressed) 1 to guide. 2 to manage; direct, as an orchestra. 3 to transmit (electricity, heat, etc.). 4 to carry: *The canal conducts water.*

con·duc·tor (kən dŭk´tər) *n-* 1 guide; leader: *the conductor of an orchestra.* 2 person in charge of passengers on a train, bus, or street car. 3 a material that transmits sound, electricity, etc.

con·duit (kŏn´dōō it) *n-* 1 canal or pipe for carrying water, etc. 2 a tube or other enclosed passage for electric wires.

cone (kōn) *n-* 1 solid body or figure which narrows evenly to a point from a flat base of circular or elliptical cross section. 2 anything having such a shape: *an ice-cream cone; the nose cone of a rocket.* 3 seed case of pine, fir, or some other evergreens.

Cones

con·fec·tion (kən fĕk´shən) *n-* 1 something very sweet, such as candy or crystallized fruit; sweetmeat. 2 frilly or elaborate article of woman's clothing.

¹con·fed·er·ate (kən fĕd´ər ət) *n-* an ally, especially an accomplice in a plot, conspiracy, crime, etc.: *The bank robber and his confederates escaped.*

con·fer (kən fûr´) *vi-* [con·ferred, con·fer·ring] to consult; have a conference: *The two umpires conferred.* *vt-* to bestow: *to confer a medal.*

con·fess (kən fĕs´) *vt-* 1 to admit or acknowledge (a fault, crime, debt, etc.): *to confess a robbery.* 2 to hear a telling of sins from: *The priest confessed my sister.* *vi-* 1 to make an acknowledgement or admission; admit (to): *He confessed to the robbery.* 2 to disclose the state of one's conscience to a priest.

con·fide (kən fīd´) *vt-* [con·fid·ed, con·fid·ing] 1 to tell as a secret: *She confided her problems to her mother.* 2 to entrust; commit: *We confided the children to their grandmother's care.*

con·fi·dent (kŏn´fə dənt) *adj-* 1 self-assured; self-confident; bold: *The boxer had a jaunty, confident air.* 2 sure; convinced: *We are confident of victory.* —*adv-* **con´fi·dent·ly.**

con·fi·den·tial (kŏn´fə dĕn´shəl) *adj-* 1 secret; private: *The agent turned in a confidential report.* 2 trusted with secret matters: *A confidential secretary must have good judgment.* —*adv-* **con´fi·den´tial·ly.**

con·fig·u·ra·tion (kən fĭg´yə rā´shən) *n-* 1 shape; outline; contour: *the configuration of the American continent.* 2 relative arrangement and spacing of parts: *the configuration of a molecule.*

con·fine (kən fīn´) *vt-* [con·fined, con·fin·ing] 1 to restrict within limits: *The banks could not confine the swollen river.* 2 to keep indoors; imprison: *Illness confined him to his room.*

con·firm (kən fûrm´) *vt-* 1 to assure the truth of; verify: *The doctor confirmed the reports about the polio vaccine.* 2 to approve formally: *The Senate confirmed his appointment as a judge.* 3 to establish more firmly; strengthen: *The book confirms my belief.*

con·fis·cate (kŏn´fĭs kāt´) *vt-* [con·fis·cat·ed, con·fis·cat·ing] to seize (property), especially for public use: *The police confiscated the smuggled goods.* —*n-* **con´fis·ca´tion.** *adj-* **con·fis´ca·tor´y** (kən fĭs´kə tôr´ē): *He said that the new tax is confiscatory.*

con·fla·gra·tion (kŏn´flə grā´shən) *n-* large and destructive fire.

¹con·flict (kŏn´flĭkt´) *n-* 1 a battle; fight; struggle. 2 a clash; failure to be in agreement or harmony: *a conflict between the two accounts of the accident.*

²con·flict (kən flĭkt´) *vi-* to be in opposition; clash (with): *One account of the accident conflicts with the other. The two accounts conflict.*

con·flu·ence (kŏn´flōō´əns) *n-* a flowing together of streams; also, the place where they join. Also **con´flux´** (kŏn´flŭks´). —*adj-* **con´flu´ent:** *two confluent streams.*

con·form (kən fôrm´, -fôrm´) *vi-* 1 to be in agreement with a set pattern or form; correspond (to): *These measurements conform to the blueprints.* 2 to act in accordance with rules, customs, etc.; obey; comply: *The army conformed to the rules of war.* *vt-:* *Should I conform my habits to yours?*

con·found (kən found´) *vt-* 1 to bewilder or perplex; amaze: *The child's answers confounded the experts.* 2 to throw into disorder; make chaotic: *Their demands confounded the situation even more.* 3 to mistake for something else: *to confound dreams with reality.*

con·front (kən frŭnt´) *vt-* 1 to meet boldly and squarely; face up to: *to confront the enemy.* 2 to present (a person, group, etc.) squarely (with): *This confronts me with the need to make a quick decision.*

con·fuse (kən fyōōz´) *vt-* [con·fused, con·fus·ing] 1 to throw into disorder; make chaotic: *Don't confuse the issue.* 2 bewilder; perplex: *Don't let all those questions confuse you.* 3 to mix up in the mind; mistake one thing for another: *The announcer confused the dates of the two events.* —*adv-* **con·fus´ing·ly.**

con·geal (kən jēl´) *vi-* 1 to change from a fluid to a solid by cooling or freezing. 2 to thicken or coagulate; become viscous: *The oil congealed.* *vt-:* *The cold air congealed the liquid.*

con·gen·ial (kən jēn´yəl) *adj-* 1 having the same tastes and interests: *a congenial roommate.* 2 suited to one's nature; agreeable: *a congenial job.* 3 sociable; genial: *a congenial host.* —*n-* **con·ge´ni·al´i·ty** (kən jēn´ē ăl´ə tē). *adv-* **con·gen´ial·ly.**

con·gen·i·tal (kən jēn´ə təl) *adj-* existing at birth and not caused by later influences. —*adv-* **con·gen´i·tal·ly.**

con·gest (kən jĕst´) *vt-* 1 to cause (an organ or part of the body) to become too full of blood or other fluid. 2 to make too crowded; clog: *Parades congest traffic.* *vi-:* *His lungs congested overnight.*

con·ges·tion (kən jĕs´chən) *n-* 1 overcrowded condition: *traffic congestion.* 2 excessive accumulation of blood or other fluid in an organ of the body: *a congestion of the lungs.*

¹con·glom·er·ate (kən glŏm´ə rāt´) *vt-* [con·glom·er·at·ed, con·glom·er·at·ing] to gather into a mass. *vi-:* *These rocks conglomerated during millions of years.*

con·grat·u·late (kən grăch´ə lāt´) *vt-* [con·grat·u·lat·ed, con·grat·u·lat·ing] to express sympathetic pleasure to (a person or persons) on account of an achievement of his, an honor, or a happy event.

con·gre·gate (kŏng´grə gāt´) *vi-* [con·gre·gat·ed, con·gre·gat·ing] to come together; assemble: *People congregated to watch the inauguration.*

con·gress (kŏng´grəs) *n-* 1 a meeting of representatives to discuss a particular thing; conference. 2 chief lawmaking body of some republics. 3 **Congress** national lawmaking body of the United States, made up of the Senate and the House of Representatives.

con·gru·ent (kən grōō´ənt, kŏng´grōō-) *adj-* 1 agreeing; harmonizing; in accordance; congruous (with): *The plan is congruent with our aims.* 2 of geometric figures, coinciding exactly when placed one upon another. —*n-* **con·gru´ence.** *adv-* **con·gru´ent·ly.**

con·jec·ture (kən jĕk´chər) *n-* 1 the forming of an opinion with little or no evidence; guesswork: *a book based on conjecture rather than research.* 2 a guess. *vt-* [con·jec·tured, con·jec·tur·ing]: *Columbus conjectured that the earth was round.* —*n-* **con·jec´tur·er.**

con·ju·ga·tion (kŏn´jə gā´shən) *n-* 1 *Grammar* a conjugating of a verb; also, a class of verbs that are conjugated in the same way. 2 *Biology* (1) the act or process of joining together; the temporary uniting or fusing of two cells. (2) result of this process; union.

con·junc·tion (kən jŭngk´shən) *n-* 1 a joining or occurring together; combination; union: *The conjunction of fog and icy roads made driving impossible.* 2 *Grammar* word, such as *and, but, or, if, when,* etc., that connects two other words, phrases, or clauses. Conjunctions also show the intended relationships between parts of a sentence.

con·jure (kŭn´jər, kŏn´-) *vt-* [con·jured, con·jur·ing] to make appear or disappear as if by magic: *The magician conjured a rabbit out of a hat.* *vi-* to perform magic: *The stranger claimed he could conjure.*

con·nect (kə nĕkt´) **vt-** 1 to join, link, or fasten together; unite: *A bus line connects the two towns. Twist the wires to* connect *them.* 2 to place in relationship; associate: *to* connect *names with faces.*

con·nec·tive (kə nĕk´ tǐv) **adj-** serving to join or connect. **n-** 1 something that joins or connects. 2 *Grammar* a connecting word, such as a conjunction. —**adv-** **con·nec´ tive·ly:** *a phrase used* connectively.

connective tissue **n-** tough, fibrous white tissue that connects and supports the organs, muscles, bones, and other tissues of the body.

conn·ing tower (kŏn´ ĭng) **n-** 1 tall structure on a submarine deck, used for observation and as entrance to the interior. 2 armored pilothouse on a battleship.

con·niv·ance (kə nī´ vəns) **n-** silent assent to secret co-operation in a wrongdoing.

con·nive (kə nīv´) **vi-** [con·nived, con·niv·ing] 1 to permit or condone a wrongdoing by remaining silent and inactive: *The jailer* connived *at the prisoner's escape.* 2 to co-operate secretly; conspire: *He* connived *with others to force the chairman out of office.* —**n-** **con·niv´ er.**

con·nois·seur (kŏn´ ə sûr´) **n-** person who knows enough about an art, food, etc., to be a judge of it.

con·no·ta·tion (kŏn´ ə tā´ shən, kŏn´ ō-) **n-** meaning added to the literal or dictionary meaning of a word or phrase by frequent association with other ideas, the feelings of the user, etc.: *"Gluttony" and "filth" are* connotations *of "pig."* See also *denotation.*

con·no·ta·tive (kŏn´ ə tā´ tǐv) **adj-** 1 connoting. 2 having to do with connotation. —**adv-** **con´ no·ta´ tive·ly.**

con·note (kə nōt´) **vt-** [con·not·ed, con·not·ing] to imply or suggest in addition to the simple or literal meaning: *The word "equator" often* connotes *heat.*

con·nu·bi·al (kə nōō´ bē əl) **adj-** relating to marriage: *their* connubial *happiness.* —**adv-** **con·nu´ bi·al·ly.**

con·quer (kŏng´ kər) **vt-** to overcome or defeat: *to* conquer *a country; to* conquer *one's fear.* **vi-:** *The strongest do not always* conquer.

con·quer·or (kŏng´ kər ər) **n-** person who conquers, especially one who subdues a country by war.

con·quest (kŏng´ kwĕst´) **n-** 1 a winning or conquering, especially by war: *the conquest of Mexico by the Spanish.* 2 that which is won or conquered.

con·quis·ta·dor (kŏn kwĭs´ tə dôr´, -dôr´) **n-** [*pl.* con·qui·sta·dors *or* con·qui·sta·do·res] one of the Spanish conquerors of parts of North and South America in the sixteenth century.

con·san·guin·i·ty (kŏn´ săng gwĭn´ ə tǐ) **n-** relationship by common ancestry.

con·science (kŏn´ shəns) **n-** sense of the rightness or wrongness of one's own acts: *Trust your* conscience.

con·sci·en·tious (kŏn´ shē ĕn´ shəs) **adj-** 1 careful and diligent; painstaking: *a* conscientious *worker.* 2 following one's conscience or sense of right; scrupulous: *a* conscientious *objection to war.* —**adv-** **con´ sci·en´ tious·ly.** **n-** **con´ sci·en´ tious·ness.**

conscientious objector **n-** person who refuses to serve in an armed force as a combatant because of religious or moral principles.

con·scious (kŏn´ shəs) **adj-** 1 able to feel and understand what is happening; in possession of one's senses; awake: *Is the patient* conscious *now?* 2 aware: *He was* conscious *of being watched.* 3 deliberate; intentional: *He made a* conscious *effort to be kind.* —**adv-** **con´ scious·ly.**

con·scious·ness (kŏn´ shəs nəs) **n-** 1 a being conscious; possession of one's senses: *A person who faints loses* consciousness. 2 awareness: *a* consciousness *of impending danger.* 3 total of one's thoughts and feelings; mind: *A new idea entered his* consciousness.

¹**con·script** (kən skrĭpt´) **vt-** to draft or force (a person) into service, especially into military service.

²**con·script** (kŏn´ skrĭpt´) **n-** person drafted into service; especially, one drafted into the army or navy. *as modifier:* a conscript *army.*

con·se·crate (kŏn´ sə krāt´) **vt-** [con·se·crat·ed, con·se·crat·ing] 1 to set apart or dedicate as sacred: *to* consecrate *a chapel.* 2 to devote to some worthy purpose: *She* consecrated *her life to the care of the sick.*

con·sec·u·tive (kən sĕk´ yə tǐv) **adj-** following without a break; coming in order; successive: *Four, five, and six are* consecutive *numbers.* —**adv-** **con·sec´ u·tive·ly.** **n-** **con·sec´ u·tive·ness.**

con·sen·sus (kən sĕn´ səs) **n-** general agreement; collective opinion: *The* consensus *was for adjournment of the meeting.*

con·sent (kən sĕnt´) **vi-** to give assent or approval; agree: *They* consented *to let him drive the car.* **n-:** *He asked his parents'* consent *to use their car.*

con·se·quence (kŏn´ sə kwĕns´) **n-** 1 outcome; result: *The* consequences *were not foreseen.* 2 importance: *a person of no* consequence.

con·serv·a·tive (kən sûr´ və tǐv) **adj-** 1 inclined to keep things as they are; opposed to change.

con·serv·a·to·ry (kən sûr´ və tôr´ ē) **n-** [*pl.* con·serv·a·tor·ies] 1 greenhouse or glassed-in room; especially, a private one for the display of plants. 2 school for study of one of the fine arts, especially music.

¹**con·serve** (kən sûrv´) **vt-** [con·served, con·serv·ing] to keep from decay, destruction, loss, waste, or depletion; preserve: *Scientific farming* conserves *the soil.*

²**con·serve** (kŏn´ sûrv´) **n-** mixture of fruits, sugar, and usually nuts, cooked until thick: *plum* conserve.

con·sid·er (kən sĭd´ ər) **vt-** (in sense 1 considered intransitive when the direct object is implied but not expressed.) 1 to think over carefully: *to* consider *an offer.* 2 to bear in mind; allow for: *We should* consider *the traffic and start early.* 3 to be thoughtful of: *The selfish boy never* considered *his brother's feelings.* 4 to regard as: *I* consider *him our best player.*

con·sid·er·a·ble (kən sĭd´ ər ə bəl) **adj-** 1 fairly large: *a* considerable *sum of money.* 2 much: *He had* considerable *trouble.* —**adv-** **con·sid´ er·a·bly:** *Her game has improved* considerably *since she took lessons.*

con·sign (kən sīn´) **vt-** 1 to hand over; deliver formally: *They* consigned *her to a guardian.* 2 to send or address (a shipment, merchandise, etc.). 3 to set apart; devote: *The host* consigned *the room to our use.* —**n-** **con·sign´ or** or **con·sign´ er.**

con·sign·ee (kŏn´ sī´ nē´, kən sī´ nē´) **n-** person to whom goods are shipped or addressed.

con·sign·ment (kən sīn´ mənt) **n-** 1 a consigning or delivering. 2 something consigned: *The trucker lost a* consignment *of pots.*

on consignment to be paid for by the retailer only when sold: *He took a load of baseballs* on consignment.

con·sist (kən sĭst´) **vi-** 1 to be made up or composed (of): *Water* consists *of hydrogen and oxygen.* 2 to have as foundation or source (in): *The success of democracy* consists *in our responsibility as citizens.*

con·sist·en·cy (kən sĭs´ tən sē) **n-** [*pl.* con·sist·en·cies] 1 degree of density or thickness: *the* consistency *of molasses.* 2 steadiness and uniformity; evenness: *the* consistency *of his taste in music.* 3 agreement; harmony: *a* consistency *between words and actions.* Also **con·sist´ ence.**

con·sist·ent (kən sĭs´ tənt) **adj-** 1 continuing without change; constant; uniform: *bread of consistent quality.* 2 in agreement; in accord (with): *His last report was not* consistent *with his usual good work.* —**adv-** **con·sist´ ent·ly.**

¹**con·sole** (kən sōl´) **vt-** [con·soled, con·sol·ing] to comfort; solace; cheer up. [from Latin **consolari** meaning "to comfort greatly."]

²**con·sole** (kŏn´ sōl) **n-** 1 floor-model radio or television cabinet. 2 the desklike part of an organ, containing the keyboard and pedals. 3 table supported on a wall by brackets, or designed to stand against a wall. [from French **console** meaning "self-supporting," from an original meaning "wall bracket; support," from the same source as ¹**console**.

con·sol·i·date (kən sŏl´ ə dāt´) **vt-** [con·sol·i·dat·ed, con·sol·i·dat·ing] 1 to unite; combine; merge: *to* consolidate *several schools; to* consolidate *packages for shipment.*

TV console

con·spic·u·ous (kən spĭk′ yōō əs) *adj-* 1 plainly visible: *a conspicuous spot.* 2 attracting attention; striking: *to be conspicuous for bad manners; a conspicuous success.* —*adv-* con·spic′u·ous·ly. *n-* con·spic′u·ous·ness.

con·spir·a·cy (kən spĭr′ə sē) *n-* [*pl.* con·spir·a·cies] 1 secret agreement to do something unlawful or evil; a plot: *a conspiracy to rob a bank.* 2 group of conspirators.

con·spir·a·tor (kən spĭr′ə tər) *n-* person who takes part in a secret plot.

con·spire (kən spĭr′) *vi-* [con·spired, con·spir·ing] 1 to plan together secretly to do something unlawful or evil; plot. 2 to act or work together: *All things conspired for a happy day.*

con·sta·ble (kŏn′ stə bəl, kŭn′ stə bəl) *n-* 1 public peace officer with some minor judicial duties. 2 *Brit.* policeman of the lowest rank; patrolman.

con·stant (kŏn′ stənt) *adj-* 1 always present; continual: *the constant noise of the street traffic.* 2 unchanging; invariable; uniform: *to walk at a constant pace.* 3 steadfast; faithful: *a constant friend.* *n-* 1 something which never changes. 2 *Mathematics* (1) a quantity that has a fixed value, such as as pi (π). (2) a quantity whose value does not change throughout a problem and its solution. —*adv-* con·stant·ly.

con·stel·la·tion (kŏn′ stə lā′ shən) *n-* 1 *Astronomy* group of stars, often named for a mythological person or thing whose outline it suggests; also, the region in the heavens occupied by such a group. 2 group of distinguished persons or things.

con·ster·na·tion (kŏn′ stər nā′ shən) *n-* terrified astonishment; paralyzing amazement; dismay: *To my consternation my wallet had disappeared.*

con·sti·pate (kŏn′ stə pāt′) *vt-* [con·sti·pat·ed, con·sti·pat·ing] to cause constipation in.

con·sti·pa·tion (kŏn′ stə pā′ shən) *n-* condition in which the bowels do not move freely enough.

con·stit·u·en·cy (kən stĭch′ōō ən sē) *n-* [*pl.* con·stit·u·en·cies] body of voters which elects a representative, as to Congress; also, the district represented.

con·stit·u·ent (kən stĭch′ōō ənt, -tyōōt′) *vt-* [con·sti·tut·ed, con·sti·tut·ing] 1 to make up or form: *Twelve eggs constitute a dozen.* 2 to appoint: *The will constituted him guardian.*

con·sti·tu·tion (kŏn′ stə tōō′ shən, -tyōō′ shən) *n-* 1 the basic law and principles of a nation, state, or other organized body. 2 composition or makeup, especially physical makeup: *to have a healthy constitution.* 3 an establishing or setting up: *to urge the constitution of a peace commission.*

con·strain (kən strān′) *vt-* 1 to urge; force; compel: *to constrain a child to eat.* 2 to imprison; confine. 3 to hold in check; restrain: *to constrain one's temper.*

con·straint (kən strānt′) *n-* 1 force; compulsion: *to keep silent under constraint.*

con·strict (kən strĭkt′) *vt-* to squeeze tightly; compress; cramp: *to constrict a vein.*

con·stric·tion (kən strĭk′ shən) *n-* 1 a tightening or narrowing; contraction; compression: *the constriction of a blood vessel.* 2 anything that binds or cramps.

con·stric·tor (kən strĭk′ tər) *n-* 1 anything that constricts, especially certain surgical instruments and body muscles. 2 snake that kills its prey by strangling or crushing it in its coils.

con·struct (kən strŭkt′) *vt-* 1 to build; put together: *to construct a house;* 2 to construct *a short story.* 2 *Mathematics* to draw geometric figures with such instruments as compass, protractor, straightedge, etc.

con·strue (kən strōō′) *vt-* [con·strued, con·stru·ing] 1 to explain the meaning of; interpret: *They construed his shyness as snobbery.* 2 *Grammar* to analyze or explain (a sentence, clause, etc.) gramatically; parse.

con·sul (kŏn′ səl) *n-* 1 official appointed by a government to live in a foreign country, look after trade, and help any citizens of his own country who live or travel there. 2 either of two chief officials of the ancient Roman republic.

con·sult (kən sŭlt′) *vt-* to seek advice or information from: *to consult a lawyer; to consult a dictionary.* *vi-* to exchange opinions; confer: *The doctors consulted*

con·sume (kən sōōm′, -syōōm′) *vt-* [con·sumed, con·sum·ing] 1 to eat or drink up; devour. 2 to destroy: *Fire consumed the barn.* 3 to spend; exhaust; use up, often wastefully: *The job consumes all his energy. Television consumes his spare time.*

con·tact (kŏn′ tăkt) *n-* 1 a touching; touch: *the contact of two wires.* 2 connection: *The pilot made contact with the tower.* 3 *Informal* person who is in a position to be helpful: *a good business contact.* 4 metal point, strip, etc., through which an electrical connection is made and broken in a switch or other device.

con·tain (kən tān′) *vt-* 1 to hold within itself: *The box contained candy.* 2 to include as a part: *Some paints contain lead.* 3 to hold in check; keep within bounds: *to contain one's excitement.* 4 to equal: *A quart contains two pints.* —*adj-* con·tain′a·ble.

con·temp·tu·ous (kən tĕmp′ chōō əs) *adj-* feeling or expressing contempt; scornful: *a contemptuous answer.* —*adv-* con·temp′tu·ous·ly. *n-* con·temp′tu·ous·ness.

con·tend (kən tĕnd′) *vi-* 1 to strive; compete; vie: *to contend for the prize.* 2 to struggle (with); put up (with): *to contend with rain and insects.* *vt-* 1 to argue; maintain: *He contended his innocence.* 2 to contest: *He contended every point raised.*

¹**con·tent** (kŏn′ tĕnt) *n-* 1 the subject matter or thought of a speech, book, etc. 2 capacity: *The content of the jar is six ounces.* 3 contents all that is contained: *the contents of a box; the table of contents of a book.* [from Latin contentum, from continere meaning "contain."]

con·ti·nence (kŏn′ tən əns) *n-* self-control; self-restraint, especially as to passions and desires. Also con′ti·nen·cy.

¹**con·ti·nent** (kŏn′ tən ənt) *adj-* temperate; exercising self-restraint. —*adv-* con′ti·nent·ly. [from Latin continens, a specialized use of ²continent.]

con·tin·ue (kən tĭn′ yōō) *vt-* [con·tin·ued, con·tin·u·ing] (considered intransitive when the direct object is implied but not expressed) 1 to keep up or go on with; persist in: *He continued working far into the night.* 2 to begin again after stopping: *We will continue the discussion after lunch.*

contour line *n-* line on a map connecting points that are equal in elevation.

contour map *n-* map showing the surface features of an area of land by means of contour lines.

contour plowing *n-* plowing across the slope so that the furrows follow the contours of the land, in order to reduce soil erosion.

contra- *prefix* against; opposite: *to contradict.*

con·tra·band (kŏn′ trə bănd′) *n-* 1 anything that may not legally be brought into or sent out of a country, especially in time of war.

Contour map

con·trac·tion (kən trăk′ shən) *n-* 1 a drawing together; shrinking; shortening: *the contraction of a muscle; the contraction of a word.* 2 a word that has been contracted. 3 an entering into; incurring: *the contraction of a debt.* 4 a catching or getting: *the contraction of a disease.*

con·trac·tor (kŏn′ trăk tər) *n-* person who agrees to supply something or do work for a certain price: *a building contractor.*

con·trac·tu·al (kən trăk′ chōō əl) *adj-* of, like, or included in a contract: *a contractual agreement.* —*adv-* con·trac′tu·al·ly.

con·tra·dict (kŏn′ trə dĭkt′) *vt-* 1 to assert the opposite of: *He contradicted his own story.* 2 to deny the words of.

con·tra·dic·tion (kŏn′ trə dĭk′ shən) *n-* 1 a statement that contradicts another; also, a statement containing facts, ideas, etc., that contradict each other. 2 a saying the opposite or contrary: *He hates any contradiction of his views.* 3 disagreement; opposition: *There is no contradiction between my words and my actions.*

con·tra·dic·to·ry (kŏn′ trə dĭk′ tə rē) *adj-* opposing; contrary: *a contradictory statement.* —*adv-* con′tra·dic′to·ri·ly. *n-* con′tra·dic′to·ri·ness.

¹**con·trast** (kən trăst′) *vt-* to compare in order to show unlikeness or difference: *to contrast black and white; to*

contrast *his joy with my sorrow.* **vi-** to be distinct; be clearly different in comparison (with): *Black and white contrast. Black contrasts with white.*

►For usage note see COMPARE.

²con·trast (kŏn′ trăst′) **n-** 1 a comparing to show up differences; a contrasting: *By contrast with Ed, Tom is well-behaved.* 2 difference or unlikeness between things: *a sharp* contrast *of tone.*

con·trib·ute (kən trĭb′ byōōt′) **vt-** [con·trib·ut·ed, con·trib·ut·ing] (considered intransitive when the direct object is implied but not expressed) to give or provide; furnish: *to contribute one's time to a cause.* **vi-** to help or aid; be of benefit (to): *Exercise contributes to one's health.*

con·tri·bu·tion (kŏn′trə byōō′ shən) **n-** a giving or bestowing of something; also, the thing given.

con·trib·u·tor (kən trĭb′ yə tər) **n-** 1 person who gives to a cause: *a contributor to a building fund.* 2 person who writes an article for a newspaper or magazine.

con·trib·u·to·ry (kən trĭb′ yə tôr′ē) **adj-** 1 helping to produce a result: *a contributory factor.* 2 giving aid; assisting: *a contributory grant of money.*

con·trite (kən trīt′, kŏn′ trīt′) **adj-** showing sorrow or regret for faults or wrongs; repentant; remorseful: *He shed* contrite *tears.* **—adv- con·trite′ly. n- con·trite′ness.**

con·tri·tion (kən trĭsh′ ən) **n-** sorrow for faults or wrongs; sincere repentance.

con·triv·ance (kən trī′ vəns) **n-** 1 invention; device: *The electric eye is a contrivance for opening the door automatically.* 2 a contriving or planning; scheming: *a plan of his own contrivance.* 3 plan or scheme: *What contrivance was used to get Alice to her surprise party?*

con·trive (kən trīv′)′ **vt-** [con·trived, con·triv·ing] 1 to plan or create by some clever means; devise; invent: *to contrive a scheme; to contrive an underwater breathing device.* 2 to bring about; manage: *to contrive escape.*

con·trol (kən trōl′) **vt-** [con·trolled, con·trol·ling] 1 to command or regulate; direct: *to control a business.* 2 to hold back; restrain; check: *to control one's temper.* **n-** 1 effective authority to direct or regulate: *to have control over a group.* 2 means of holding steady or in check: *I am in favor of price controls.*

con·tro·ver·sial (kŏn′ trə vûr′shəl) **adj-** likely to cause disagreement or discussion: *a controversial issue.* **—adv- con′tro·ver′sial·ly.**

con·tro·ver·sial·ist (kŏn′trə vur′shə lĭst) **n-** person who likes to carry on controversies or debates.

con·tro·ver·sy (kŏn′ trə vûr′ sē) **n-** [pl. con·tro·ver·sies] argument; dispute; disagreement.

con·tro·vert (kŏn′ trə vûrt′) **vt-** to oppose in an argument; contradict; dispute: *to controvert an opinion.* **—adj- con′tro·vert′i·ble.**

con·tu·ma·cious (kŏn′ tyōō mā′ shəs) **adj-** stubbornly refusing to obey authority; insubordinate; rebellious: *a contumacious prisoner.* **—adj- con′tu·ma′cious·ly. n- con′tu·ma·cy** (-mə sē) the contumacy *of a hardened criminal.*

con·tu·me·ly (kən tyōō′ mə lē, kŏn′ təm lē) **n-** [pl. con·tu·me·lies] 1 scornful rudeness in speech or action; insolence: *One must often bear the contumely of lesser men.* 2 an insult. **—adj- con′tu·me′li·ous** (kŏn′ tyə mē′ lē əs). **adv- con′tu·me′li·ous·ly.**

con·tu·sion (kən tōō′ zhən, -tyōō′ zhən) **n-** a bruise.

co·nun·drum (kə nŭn′ drəm) **n-** 1 riddle or puzzle whose answer often involves a humorous play on words. Example: What has four wheels and flies? A garbage truck. 2 any difficult or perplexing problem.

con·va·lesce (kŏn′ və lĕs′) **vi-** [con·va·lesced, con·va·lesc·ing] to get better after sickness; to recover strength and health: *He is in Florida to convalesce.*

con·va·les·cence (kŏn′ və lĕs′ əns) **n-** 1 a returning to good health after disease or injury. 2 period of time this takes.

con·va·les·cent (kŏn′ və lĕs′ ənt) **adj-** 1 getting better after sickness; recovering: *He is convalescent, but still in the hospital.* 2 having to do with recovery from illness: *a convalescent diet.* **n-** person who is getting well.

con·vene (kən vēn′) **vi-** [con·vened, con·ven·ing] to

come together; to assemble for a meeting: *The legislature convened.* **vt-:** *The mayor* convened *the council.*

con·ven·ience (kən vēn′ē əns) **n-** 1 ease in using, getting, changing, etc.; suitability: *the convenience of a telephone; the convenience of paperback books.* 2 ease or comfort: *to provide a car for one's convenience.* 3 something that adds to one's comfort and ease.

at one's convenience at a time, place, etc., that is suitable to one; at one's pleasure.

con·ven·ient (kən vēn′ē ənt) **adj-** 1 easy to use, reach, change, etc.: *a convenient appliance.* 2 suited to one's comfort or needs: *a convenient time and place.* **— adv- con·ven′ient·ly.**

con·ver·sion (kən vûr′ zhən) **n-** 1 a changing from one form or use to another: *the conversion of a vacant lot into a playground.* 2 a change from one religion, belief, etc., to another: *the conversion of heathens.*

¹con·vert (kən vûrt′) **vt-** 1 to change (something) from one form, use, or purpose to another: *A boiler converts water into steam.* 2 to cause (a person) to believe in a religion, a point of view, etc.

²con·vert (kŏn′ vûrt′) **n-** person who has changed from one religion to another, or is led to accept someone else's opinions, ideas, etc., that had not been his own.

con·vert·er (kən vûr′ tər) **n-** 1 device for changing AC electricity into DC or vice versa. 2 device for changing radio signals from one range into another in a receiver. 3 device for enabling a television set to receive broadcasts in the ultrahigh-frequency range. 4 furnace used in the Bessemer process; Bessemer converter.

con·vert·i·ble (kən vûr′ tə bəl) **adj-** of a nature that allows changing or adapting: *a convertible raincoat.* **n-** automobile with a top that can be raised and lowered. **—n- con·vert′ i·bil′ i·ty. adv- con·vert′ i·bly.**

con·vert·i·plane (kən vûr′ tə plăn′) **n-** airplane that changes in midair from the vertical flight of a helicopter to fixed-wing flight.

con·vex (kŏn′ vĕks′) **adj-** curved outward like the outside of a ball. **—adv- con′vex′ly. n- con·vex′ness.**

Convex

con·vic·tion (kən vĭk′ shən) **n-** 1 a declaring, proving, or finding that someone is guilty: *The trial ended in the conviction and imprisonment of the thief.* 2 firm belief; definite opinion: *We hold strong convictions.*

con·vince (kən vĭns′) **vt-** [con·vinced, con·vinc·ing] to make (someone) certain; cause (someone) to believe: *I convinced him that he was wrong.* **—adv- con·vinc′ing·ly. n- con·vinc′ing·ness.**

con·viv·i·al (kən vĭv′ē əl) **adj-** 1 fond of merry-making with friends; jovial; gay. 2 like a feast; festive. **—n- con·viv·i·al′ i·ty** (kən vĭv′ē ăl′ ə tē). **adv- con·viv′i·al·ly.**

con·vo·ca·tion (kŏn′ vō kā′ shən) **n-** a calling together of persons for a meeting or assembly; also, the meeting itself: *a convocation of clergymen.*

con·voke (kən vōk′) **vt-** [con·voked, con·vok·ing] to call together for a meeting: *to convoke Congress.*

con·vo·lute (kŏn′ və lōōt′) **adj-** rolled up or folded upon itself; coiled: *a convolute seashell.* **—adv- con′vo·lute′ly.**

con·vo·lu·tion (kŏn′ və lōō′ shən) **n-** 1 a coiling or winding together. 2 coil or fold, especially any of the folds on the surface of the brain.

con·voy (kŏn′ voi′) **n-** 1 group (of ships, vehicles, etc.) led or guarded by an armed escort: *a convoy of troop-ships.* 2 the escort itself. **vt-** (*also* kən voi′): *Two destroyers* convoyed *the supply ship.*

co·op·er·a·tion *or* **co·öp·er·a·tion** (kō ŏp′ə rā′shən) **n-** a working together for the same end; mutual help; joint effort: *We would appreciate your co-operation.*

co·op·er·a·tive *or* **co·öp·er·a·tive** (kō ŏp′ər ə tĭv, -ə rā′ tĭv) **adj-** 1 working or willing to work with others for the same ends: *The project was successful because everyone was co-operative.* 2 of or having to do with co-operation: *a co-operative effort.* **n-** apartment house, store, or other facility collectively owned by its users. **—adv- co·op′er·a·tive·ly** *or* **co·öp′er·a·tive·ly. n- co·op′er·a·tive·ness** *or* **co·öp′er·a·tive·ness.**

¹co·or·di·nate *or* **co·ör·di·nate** (kō ôr′də năt′) **vt- [co·or·di·nat·ed** *or* **co·ör·di·nat·ed, co·or·di·nat·ing**

cop·y (kŏp′ē) *vt-* [**cop·ied, cop·y·ing**] (considered intransitive when the direct object is implied but not expressed) 1 to make or produce something that is exactly like something else or contains the same words, ideas, details, etc.: *to copy a drawing; to copy a letter.* 2 to imitate; mimic: *to copy a dancer's movements. n-* [*pl.* **cop·ies**] 1 duplicate, imitation, or reproduction of the contents of something else: *a copy of a picture; a neat copy of a manuscript.* 2 a single one of a number of identically printed books, magazines, pictures, etc. 3 typed or written material to be set in type and printed.

co·quette (kō kĕt′) *n-* woman or girl who tries to attract men by insincerely affectionate behavior; flirt. —*adj-* **co·quet′tish:** *a coquettish glance. adv-* **co·quet′tish·ly.**

cor·a·cle (kôr′ə kəl, kŏr′-) *n-* small, wide boat made of waterproof cloth or hide stretched over a frame.

cor·al (kôr′əl, kŏr′-) *n-* 1 hard substance, somewhat like limestone, built up of the skeletons of great numbers of tiny sea animals called polyps. Coral is found in a great variety of shapes and colors. Some kinds are used in making jewelry. 2 one of the tiny animals forming this substance, or the distinctively shaped mass formed by them. 3 a deep, yellowish pink. *adj-: a coral necklace; a coral dress.*

POLYP
Coral

coral snake *n-* any of several small American poisonous snakes having bright bands of red, yellow, and black. They are related to the cobras.

cord (kôrd, kŏrd) *n-* 1 string or narrow rope made of strands twisted together. 2 thin, flexible cable of insulated wires connecting electrical equipment to a source of electricity: *a lamp cord.* 3 stringlike part of the body, such as the spinal cord. 4 measure of cut firewood, equal to a pile 4 feet high, 4 feet wide, and 8 feet long.

cor·dial (kôr′jəl, kŏr′-) *adj-* warm and sincere; hearty: *a cordial welcome. n-* 1 sweet alcoholic drink; liqueur. 2 stimulating medicine; tonic. —*adv-* **cor′dial·ly.**

cor·di·al·i·ty (kôr′jē ăl′ə tē, kôr′-) *n-* friendly sincerity; warmth: *the cordiality of her smile.*

cor·dil·ler·a (kôr′ dĬl yâr′ə, kôr′-) *n-* large system of mountain ranges.

cor·don (kôr′dən, kôr′-) *n-* 1 line or circle of persons, ships, forts, etc., surrounding and guarding something: *A cordon of detectives protected the bank.* 2 band or cord worn as a decoration of honor.

cor·do·van (kôr′də vən, kôr′-) *n-* fine leather, now made chiefly from split horsehide, originally tanned at Cordova, Spain. Also **cordovan leather.**

cor·du·roy (kôr′də roi′, kôr′-) *n-* 1 sturdy cotton fabric with a surface of velvety ridges. 2 corduroys trousers made of this material. *adj-: a corduroy jacket.* [probably adapted from French *corde du roi*, to mean "king's cord (corded material)."]

core (kôr) *n-* 1 tough or fibrous central part that contains the seeds of certain fruits, such as apples and pears. 2 central or essential part: *the core of an argument.* 3 bar of soft iron or steel forming the central part of an electromagnet. *vt-* [**cored, cor·ing**] to remove the seeds and central part from (fruit). *Hom-* **corps.**

cor·mo·rant (kôr′mər ənt, kôr′-) *n-* sea bird with dark feathers, webbed feet, and an elastic pouch under its bill in which it can hold fish.

[1]corn (kôrn, kŏrn) *n-* 1 widely cultivated cereal plant native to America, which produces large ears of grain on tall stalks; Indian corn; maize. 2 ears or kernels of this plant, used for food. 3 *Brit.* any food grain, especially wheat. 4 *Slang* trite, outmoded humor, sentiment, etc. *vt-* to preserve in spiced brine: *to corn beef.* [from Old English **corn** meaning "wheat; grain."]

Ear of corn

[2]corn (kôrn, kŏrn) *n-* a horny thickening of the skin, especially on a toe. [from Latin **cornu** meaning "horn." "Corn" and "horn" have a common origin.]

cor·nered (kôr′nərd, kôr′-) *adj-* 1 having a stated number of corners: *a three-*cornered *hat.* 2 having a stated kind of corner or corners: *a sharp-*cornered *frame.* 3 driven or hemmed into a corner: *a cornered animal.*

cor·o·nar·y (kôr′ə nĕr′ē, kôr′-) *adj-* of or relating to the arteries or veins of the heart, especially to one of two arteries that rise from the aorta and supply blood to the heart. *n-* [*pl.* **cor·o·nar·ies**] coronary thrombosis.

coronary thrombosis *n-* a blocking by a blood clot of one of the two arteries that supply the blood to heart muscles.

cor·o·na·tion (kôr′ə nā′shən, kôr′-) *n-* act or ceremony of crowning a king, queen, or other ruler.

cor·o·ner (kôr′ə nər, kôr′-) *n-* public officer who investigates death by unnatural or unknown causes.

cor·o·net (kôr′ə nĕt′, kôr′-) *n-* 1 small crown worn by nobles of a rank just below that of a king. 2 any band or ornament resembling this: *a coronet of braids.*

Coronet

Corp. 1 corporal. 2 corporation.

[1]cor·po·ral (kôr′pər əl, kôr′-) *adj-* of the body; physical: *harsh corporal punishment.* [from Latin **corporalis**, from Latin **corpus** meaning "body." From this Latin word we also get "corpse" and "corps."]

[2]cor·po·ral (kôr′pər əl, kôr′-) *n-* noncommissioned officer ranking next above private first class and next below sergeant. [from Italian **caporale** from Latin **caput** meaning "head." "[2]corporal" has no connection whatever with "[1]corporal."]

cor·po·ra·tion (kôr′pə rā′shən, kôr′-) *n-* group of persons acting under law as one person to carry on a business, perform a public service, etc.

cor·por·e·al (kôr pôr′ē əl, kôr-) *adj-* bodily; physical: *to have corporeal existence.* —*adv-* **cor·por′e·al·ly.**

corps (kôr) *n-* [*pl.* **corps** (kôrs)] 1 large unit of an army, made up of two or more divisions. 2 body of troops trained for special duties: *the medical corps.* 3 group of persons working together: *the diplomatic corps. Hom-* **core.**

cor·rect (kə rĕkt′) *vt-* 1 to remove errors from or indicate errors in; make or set right: *to correct a composition; to correct a watch that runs fast.* 2 to get rid of by curing or setting right: *to correct errors; to correct a bad habit. adj-* 1 right; exact; accurate: *Is this the correct answer?* 2 right according to a standard of judgment, taste, etc.: *to know correct manners.* —*adv-* **cor·rect′ly.** *n-* **cor·rect′ness.**

cor·rec·tion (kə rĕk′shən) *n-* 1 a correcting or setting right. 2 a change, addition, etc., made in correcting something. 3 discipline or punishment intended to correct faults.

cor·rec·tion·al (kə rĕk′shən əl) *adj-* for correction.

cor·rec·tive (kə rĕk′tĬv) *adj-* tending or aiming to correct or cure faults, defects, etc.: *to offer corrective criticism. n-* something that corrects or tends to correct. —*adv-* **cor·rec′tive·ly.** *n-* **cor·rec′ tive·ness.**

cor·re·late (kôr′ə lāt′, kôr′-) *vt-* [**cor·re·lat·ed, cor·re·lat·ing**] to show or establish a relationship or likeness between: *to correlate literature and history. vi-* have a connection or relationship with one another.

cor·re·la·tion (kôr′ə lā′shən, kôr′-) *n-* 1 relationship or connection. 2 act or process of correlating.

cor·rel·a·tive (kə rĕl′ə tĬv) *adj-* dependent upon or naturally related to something else: *The size and the weight of a stone are correlative qualities. n-* 1 either of two things related to each other. 2 correlative conjunction. —*adv-* **cor·rel′a·tive·ly.**

cor·re·spond (kôr′ə spŏnd′, kôr′-) *vi-* 1 to agree; match: *My answer corresponds with yours.* 2 to be like or similar to in position, use, character, or amount: *The wings of a bird correspond to the arms of a man.* 3 to exchange letters: *Do you correspond with her?*

cor·ri·dor (kôr′ə dər, kôr′ə dər, -dôr′) *n-* long hallway onto which rooms open: *a school corridor.*

cor·rob·o·rate (kə rŏb′ə rāt′) *vt-* [**cor·rob·o·rat·ed, cor·rob·o·rat·ing**] to add to the certainty or reliability of; confirm.

cor·rode (kə rōd′) *vt-* [**cor·rod·ed, cor·rod·ing**] to eat away or destroy gradually by or as if by chemical action: *Some acids* corrode *metal. vi-* to be eaten away by chemical action: *Iron corrodes when exposed to air and water.*

cor·ro·sion (kə rō′ zhən) *n-* a corroding or eating away.

cor·ro·sive (kə rō′ sĭv, -zĭv) *adj-* 1 corroding or tending to corrode other substances. 2 bitter and cruel; cutting: *harsh, corrosive satire. n-* something that corrodes other substances. —*adv-* **cor·ro′ sive·ly**. *n-* **cor·ro′ sive·ness**.

corrosive sublimate *n-* mercuric chloride.

cor·ru·gate (kôr′ə gāt′, kŏr′-) *vt-* [**cor·ru·gat·ed, cor·ru·gat·ing**] to shape in wrinkles or alternate ridges and grooves. *vi-* to contract into wrinkles or folds.

corrugated paper *n-* cardboard pressed into narrow grooves and ridges, often with a layer of paper pasted over one or both surfaces, and used to make cartons, to pack merchandise, etc. Also **corrugated board.**

cor·ru·ga·tion (kôr′ə gā′ shən, kŏr′-) *n-* 1 a shaping into wrinkles or regular grooves. 2 ridge or groove.

cor·rupt (kə rŭpt′) *adj-* 1 deviating from true or proper conduct; dishonest; depraved: *a corrupt government;* corrupt *morals.* 2 not accurate; full of errors: *a corrupt translation. vt-:* to cause to become dishonest or evil, especially by bribery or other improper influences: *to corrupt a witness.* —*adv-* **cor·rupt′ ly**. *n-* **cor·rupt′ ness**.

cor·rupt·i·ble (kə rŭp′ tə bəl) *adj-* likely to be corrupted; open to bribery or bad influences: *a corruptible witness.* —*n-* **cor·rupt′ i·bil′ i·ty**. *adv-* **cor·rupt′ i·bly**.

cor·rup·tion (kə rŭp′ shən) *n-* 1 a making, being, or becoming corrupt. 2 change that spoils or makes wrong: *a corruption of the original meaning.* 3 rottenness.

cor·rup·tive (kə rŭp′ tĭv) *adj-* tending or likely to corrupt: *a corruptive influence.* —*adv-* **cor·rup′ tive·ly**.

cor·sage (kôr säzh′, kôr′-) *n-* flower or cluster of flowers worn by a girl or woman, usually for a festive occasion.

cor·sair (kôr′ sâr′, kôr′-) *n-* pirate or privateer, especially one who marauded along the Barbary Coast.

¹**corse·let** or **cors·let** (kôrs′ lĕt, kôrs′-) *n-* armor worn by a knight or soldier in earlier times; also, the breastplate of such armor. [from French, from cor(p)s meaning "body," related to **corpse** and **corps**.]

²**cor·se·let** or **cor·se·lette** (kôr′sə lĕt′) *n-* woman's undergarment similar to a corset but less confining. [from ¹**corselet**.]

cor·set (kôr′ sət, kôr′-) *n-* tight-fitting undergarment extending from the thighs to the chest, worn chiefly by women to support or shape the figure. *vt-* to clothe or confine in such a garment.

cor·tege or **cor·tège** (kôr tĕzh′, kôr-) *n-* train or procession of followers, attendants, etc.

cost (kôst) *n-* 1 price charged or paid for something: *the cost of a purchase.* 2 expense; loss; sacrifice: *to be successful at the cost of one's health.* 3 **costs** the expenses of a lawsuit.

cos·tume (kŏs′ tōōm′, -tyōōm′) *n-* 1 clothes worn for a particular occasion, especially for a party or for performing on the stage: *a Halloween costume; the costumes for Hamlet.* 2 clothing or style of dress of a certain people or period: *Eskimo costume; medieval costume. vt-* [**cos·tumed, cos·tum·ing**]: *to costume actors.*

cos·tum·er (kŏs′ tōō′ mər, -tyōō′ mər) *n-* person who makes or provides costumes for actors, masqueraders, etc.

co·sy (kō′ zē) cozy.

¹**cot** (kŏt) *n-* narrow bed, especially one made of canvas stretched over a frame. [from Hindi **khat**.] *Hom-* caught.

Cot

²**cot** (kŏt) *n-* 1 cottage. 2 shelter for birds or small animals; cote. [from Old English **cot**.] *Hom-* caught.

cote (kōt) *n-* coop, shed, or pen for birds or other small animals: *a dove cote. Hom-* coat.

co·ter·ie (kō′ tə rē′) *n-* intimate group of people who share an interest; clique: *an art coterie.*

co·til·lion (kō tĭl′ yən) *n-* 1 in earlier times, a lively social dance. 2 formal ball.

cot·ton (kŏt′ ən) *n-* 1 a plant with soft white fibers

attached to its seeds. 2 the fibers of this plant; also thread made from them. 3 cloth made from such thread. *adj-:* *a cotton shirt.* —*adj-* **cot′ ton·like**.

cotton gin *n-* machine for separating cotton fibers from seeds, hulls, and other material in the boll.

cot·ton·mouth (kŏt′ ən mouth′) *n-* water moccasin; so called because the inside of its mouth is white.

Cotton

cough (kôf) *n-* 1 spasmodic forcing of air from the lungs with a sharp or wheezing noise. 2 habit or illness accompanied by this: *He has a bad cough. vi-:* *The child coughed all night. vt-:* *to cough blood.*

could (kŏŏd) *p.t.* of **can**. *auxiliary verb* 1 were able to; had the power or freedom to: *If he could buy them all, he would.* 2 would be able to; has the power or ability to under certain conditions: *He could climb the tower if they would let him.*

could·n't (kŏŏd′ ənt) could not.

couldst (kŏŏdst) *Archaic* could (used only with *thou*).

cou·lee (kōō′ lē) *n-* in the western United States, a deep gulch with sloping sides, usually the valley of a stream that is dry in summer. *Hom-* coolie.

cou·lomb (kōō′ lŏm, -lōm′) *n-* electrical unit equal to the electric charge carried by 6.25×10^{18} electrons.

coun·cil (koun′səl) *n-* 1 group of persons called together to discuss and settle problems, give advice, etc: *a council of teachers.* 2 lawmaking or governing body, as of a city or town. 3 the deliberation of such a body: *to be deep in council. Hom-* counsel.

¹**count** (kount) *vt-* 1 to find the total number or amount of (a group of separate things) by adding; sum up; tally: *Please count your change.* 2 to say the numbers in order up to: *You should count ten before answering.* 3 to take into account; include: *If we count me, there are ten of us.*

coun·te·nance (koun′ tən əns) *n-* 1 the face: *a wrinkled countenance.* 2 expression of the face showing feeling or character: *a happy countenance.* 3 approval; encouragement: *I won't give aid or countenance to such a scheme. vt-* [**coun·te·nanced, coun·te·nanc·ing**] to give approval to; condone: *to countenance dishonesty.*

¹**coun·ter** (koun′ tər) *n-* 1 narrow table or flat surface at which goods are sold and money is handled. 2 small disk or other object used in games for keeping score. [from Old French **counteour**, from **counter** "to count."]

count·less (kount′ ləs) *adj-* too many to be counted; innumerable: *the countless stars.*

coun·tri·fied (kŭn′ trĭ fīd′) *adj-* of or like country people in manners or appearance; rustic.

coun·try (kŭn′ trē) *n-* [*pl.* **coun·tries**] 1 state having its own government and definite boundaries and, usually, a single language and common customs; nation: *France and England are* countries. 2 the territory occupied by such a state: *The country of Switzerland is small.*

cou·ple (kŭp′ əl) *n-* 1 two things of the same kind; pair: *a couple of dimes.* 2 two persons of the opposite sex who are joined in some way: *a married couple; a dancing couple. vt-* [**cou·pled, cou·pling**] to join; connect: *to couple railroad cars. vi-: The tractor and trailer couple.*

coup·ler (kŭp′ lər) *n-* 1 device on a keyboard instrument that links two or more keys or keyboards to be played together. 2 device that connects railroad cars; coupling. 3 transformer, resistor, or other device for transferring electrical energy from one circuit to another.

coup·let (kŭp′ lət) *n-* two successive lines of verse which rhyme. Example: "Know then thyself, presume not God to scan;/The proper study of mankind is man."

cou·pling (kŭp′ lĭng) *n-* 1 a joining; a connection. 2 device that joins things together, especially one that joins railroad cars, one that joins pipes or hoses, or one that joins electronic circuits.

Car coupling

cou·pon (kyōō′ pŏn′, kōō′-) n- 1 ticket or part of a printed advertisement that can be exchanged for prizes.

cour·age (kûr′ ĭj) n- strength of mind and spirit that enables one to control fear when facing danger; bravery.

cou·ra·geous (kə rā′ jəs) adj- having courage; brave. —adv- cou·ra′ geous·ly.

cour·i·er (kŏŏr′ ē ər, kûr′-) n- messenger, especially one carrying military or diplomatic material intended for quick delivery and for certain persons only.

course (kôrs) n- 1 onward motion; progress: the course of history. 2 direction; path: the course of a ship; the course of a river. 3 way of proceeding: Your only proper course is to write the paper over. 4 set of things in a series: a course of X-ray treatments. 5 lessons and classes in a certain subject: a three-year course in nursing.

court (kôrt) n- 1 courtyard. 2 place marked and fitted for a game: a tennis court. 3 place for administering justice or holding trials; courtroom: The witness was brought to court. 4 judge or group of judges and officials who administer justice, hold trials, etc : The court is now in session.

cour·te·ous (kûr′ tē əs) adj- polite: a courteous reply. —adv- cour′ te·ous·ly.

cour·te·san or **cour·te·zan** (kôr′ tə zən, kûr′-) n- a prostitute, especially at a royal court.

cour·te·sy (kûr′ tə sē) n- [pl. cour·te·sies] 1 politeness. 2 act of politeness or respect. 3 kindness or generosity: Ice cream was given through the courtesy of the dairy.

court·house (kôrt′ hous′) n- building where courts of law are held.

cour·ti·er (kôr′ tē ər) n- attendant at a royal court.

court·ly (kôrt′ lē) adj- [court·li·er, court·li·est] very courteous and dignified. —n- court′ li·ness.

court-mar·tial (kôrt′ mär′ shəl) n- [pl. courts-mar·tial] court made up of military or naval personnel to try offenses against military or naval law; also, a trial by such a court. vt-: They court-martialed Sgt. Jones.

Court of St. James n- royal court of Great Britain.

court plaster n- adhesive tape.

court·room (kôrt′ rōōm′) n- room where law cases are tried.

court tennis See tennis.

court·ship (kôrt′ shĭp′) n- a courting; wooing.

court·yard (kôrt′ yärd′) n- open place enclosed by buildings or walls; court.

cous·in (kŭz′ ən) n- son or daughter of one's aunt or uncle. Hom- cozen.

cou·ture (kōō tōōr′) n- art and business of designing and making fashionable clothes for women, usually to order. [from French.]

cov·er (kŭv′ ər) vt- 1 to put or lay over: Use this cloth to cover the table. 2 to spread over: Water slowly covered the basement floor. 3 to lie or be placed over: A lid covers a box. 4 to hide: to cover a mistake. 5 to include: That book covers the geography of America.

covered wagon n- large wagon with a canvas top, used by pioneers traveling westward to the central and western parts of the United States; Conestoga wagon; prairie schooner.

Covered wagon

cov·er·ing (kŭv′ ər ĭng) n- something that covers.

cov·er·let (kŭv′ ər lət) n- bedspread.

cov·ert (kŭv′ ərt) adj- secret; hidden: I took a covert glance at the note. n- 1 protected place; shelter. 2 underbrush, thicket, etc., where animals may hide. —adv- cov′ ert·ly. n- cov′ ert·ness.

cov·et (kŭv′ ət) vt- to desire eagerly (something, especially that which belongs to someone else).

cov·et·ous (kŭv′ ə təs) adj- desiring too greatly something that belongs to another; avaricious; greedy: a covetous glance. —adv- cov′ et·ous·ly. n- cov′ et·ous·ness.

cov·ey (kŭv′ ē) n- brood or flock of game birds: a covey

cow·ard (kou′ ərd) n- person who lacks courage; one who is shamefully timid.

cow·ard·ice (kou′ ər dəs) n- lack of courage; shameful timidity.

cowl (koul) n- 1 monk's hood that covers the head and shoulders; also, a long robe with a hood. 2 forward section of an automobile to which the dashboard and instrument panel are connected.

Cowl

cow·lick (kou′ lĭk′) n- tuft of hair growing upright, often above the forehead.

cowl·ing (kou′ lĭng) n- removable metal cover to streamline an airplane engine; also, a similar engine cover.

co-work·er (kō′ wûrk′ ər) n- fellow worker.

cow·pea (kou′ pē′) n- 1 widely cultivated vine closely related to the bean and producing seed pods up to two feet long. 2 the seed of this plant, eaten as a vegetable; black-eyed pea.

cow·poke (kou′ pōk′) Slang n- cowboy.

cow·pox (kou′ pŏks′) n- contagious disease of cows. Its germs are used in vaccinating people against smallpox.

cow·punch·er (kou′ pŭn′ chər) Informal n- cowboy.

cow·rie or **cow·ry** (kou′ rē) n- [pl. cow·ries] 1 the glossy, smooth, and often beautifully marked shell of any of a group of mollusks found in warm seas, especially the money cowry, used as money in parts of Africa and Asia. 2 the mollusk itself.

cow·slip (kou′ slĭp′) n- 1 marsh marigold. 2 any of various other flowering plants, especially, in England, a wild plant with fragrant yellow flowers.

cox·comb (kŏks′ kōm′) n- 1 the red peaked crest on a jester's hat; also, the hat itself. 2 vain, conceited, and foolish fellow; fop. 3 cockscomb.

cox·swain (kŏk′ sən) n- man who steers a boat, especially a racing shell.

coy (koi) adj- [coy·er, coy·est] 1 bashful; shy. 2 pretending to be shy; coquettish. —adv- coy′ ly. n- coy′ ness.

coy·ote (kī′ ōt′, kī ō′ tē) n- small wolf of western North America; prairie wolf. [American word from Mexican Spanish coyote, from Mexican Indian koyotl.]

Coyote, about 3 1/2 ft. long

coy·pu (koi′ pōō′) n- [pl. coy·pus] a South American aquatic rodent that closely resembles the beaver and is valued for its fur; nutria.

coz (kŭz) Informal n- cousin.

coz·en (kŭz′ ən) Archaic vt- to cheat or deceive in a petty way. Hom- cousin. —n- coz′ en·age.

co·zy (kō′ zē) adj- [co·zi·er, co·zi·est] comfortable; snug: a cozy corner by the fire. n- padded cover for a teapot to keep the tea warm. Also cosy. —adv- co′ zi·ly. n- co′ zi·ness.

cp. compare.

c.p. candle power.

CPA or **C.P.A.** Certified Public Accountant.

cpd. compound.

Cpl. Corporal.

cps or **c.p.s.** cycles per second.

Cr symbol for chromium.

Crab

¹crab (krăb) n- any of various crustaceans having a flattened body, four pairs of legs, a pair of grasping claws, and a small abdomen, or so-called tail, curled under the body. vi- [crabbed, crab·bing] to fish for these crustaceans. [from Old English crabbe.]

²crab (krăb) Informal vi- [crabbed, crab·bing] to find fault; be irritable; gripe; complain. [from ¹crab, probably influenced by ³crab in the sense of "sour."]

³crab (krăb) n- crab apple. [of uncertain origin.]

crab apple n- 1 kind of small, sour apple. 2 thorny tree that bears this apple.

crab·bed (krăb′ əd) adj- 1 of handwriting, tiny, stiff, and hard to read. 2 crabby. —adv- crab′ bed·ly. n- crab′ bed·ness.

crab·by (krăb′ ē) Informal adj- [crab·bi·er, crab·bi·est] surly; irritable; crabbed. —adv- crab′ bi·ly.

crab grass n- any of several coarse grasses considered lawn pests because of their unsightly appearance and rapid growth and spread.

crack (krăk) **n-** 1 thin line showing a break without separation of parts: *a long* crack *in the wall.* 2 long, narrow opening between parts; crevice. 3 sharp, snapping sound: *the* crack *of a pistol.* 4 sharp blow: *a* crack *on the cheek.* **vt-** 1 to break or split without completely separating: *I* cracked *the cup.* 2 to cause to make a sharp, snapping sound: *He* cracked *the whip.* 3 *Chemistry* to break the molecules of (a compound, especially a petroleum compound) into simpler molecules by means of heat and, sometimes, a catalyst. **vi-:** *The* cup cracked *when she dropped it, but did not break. The* whip cracked *loudly.* **adj-** *Informal* excellent; first-rate; elite: *a* crack *company of marines.*

crack a joke to tell or make a joke.

crack up 1 to have a nervous breakdown. 2 to crash.

crack·brained (krăk′ brānd′) **adj-** crazy; senseless; crackpot: *a* crackbrained *scheme.*

crack·down (krăk′ doun′) **n-** a swift disciplinary action.

cracked (krăkt) **adj-** 1 broken without separation of parts: *He drank from a* cracked *glass.* 2 *Slang* crazy.

crack·er (krăk′ ər) **n-** 1 a dry, crisp, baked wafer made chiefly of flour and water. 2 disparaging term applied to a poor white person of the rural southeastern United States. 3 firecracker.

crack·er·jack (krăk′ ər jăk) *Informal* **n-** person or thing that is remarkably good; humdinger: *The skipper was a* crackerjack. **adj-:** *a* crackerjack *team.*

crack·ing (krăk′ Ĭng) **n-** process for breaking (by heat, pressure, and catalysis) the large molecules of compounds containing hydrogen and carbon, such as petroleum, into the smaller, lighter molecules of substances such as gasoline. *as* **modifier:** *a* cracking *tower.*

crack·le (krăk′ əl) **vi-** [**crack·led, crack·ling**] to make repeated sharp, snapping, cracking noises: *The fire* crackled. **n-** 1 a repeated sharp, snapping, cracking noise. 2 finely cracked glaze of a kind of ceramic ware; also, the ware itself. 3 crackling.

crack·ling (krăk′ lĭng) **n-** crisp, browned skin of roast pork; crackle.

crack·ly (krăk′ lē) **adj-** likely to crackle; crisp.

crack·pot (krăk′ pŏt′) *Slang* **n-** person with wild or strange ideas. **adj-:** *They dismissed her* crackpot *schemes.*

crack-up (krăk′ ŭp′) **n-** 1 a crash; smash; collision. 2 *Informal* mental breakdown.

-cracy *combining form* government or rule by: demo*cracy* (rule by the people); pluto*cracy* (rule by the wealthy). [from Latin *-cratia,* from Greek *-krateia,* from **kratos** meaning "strength."]

cra·dle (krā′ dəl) **n-** 1 small bed on rockers, for a baby or doll. 2 birthplace: *the* cradle *of liberty.* 3 period of infancy: *insurance from the* cradle *to the grave.* 4 frame or jig for holding something being built or repaired. 5 curved, forklike frame attached to a scythe so that cut grain can be laid down in small bundles; also, a scythe with such an attachment. 6 in placer mining, a trough on rockers used to wash the metal-bearing earth. **vt-** [**cra·dled, cra·dling**] 1 to hold or keep (something) in or as if in a baby's bed on rockers. 2 to mow (grain, a field, etc.) with a cradle scythe. 3 to wash (metal-bearing earth) in a trough fitted with rockers.

BABY'S
MOWER'S
Cradles

cradle scythe **n-** scythe fitted with a cradle.

craft (krăft) **n-** 1 art or trade requiring personal skill: *the* craft *of fine printing.* 2 craftsmanship. 3 [*pl.* **craft**] boat, ship, or aircraft. 4 deceit; cunning.

crafts·man (krăfts′ mən) **n-** [*pl.* **crafts·men**] skilled workman, especially at a craft; artisan.

crafts·man·ship (krăfts′ mən shĭp′) **n-** skill in a craft; also, the quality of a product resulting from such skill.

craft·y (krăf′ tē) **adj-** [**craft·i·er, craft·i·est**] skillful at planning and carrying out underhanded schemes; cunning; wily; tricky. **—adv-** **craft′ i·ly.** **n-** **craft′ i·ness.**

crag (krăg) **n-** a steep, jagged rock. **—adj-** **crag′ gy.**

crake (krāk) **n-** any of various short-billed, long-legged European birds of the rail family, especially the **corn crake,** which frequents grain fields.

cram (krăm) **vt-** [**crammed, cram·ming**] 1 to stuff (something) forcibly with more than it has space for: *to* cram *a room with desks.* 2 to stuff (something) into too small a space: *to* cram *desks into the room.* **vi-** *Informal* to study intensively, especially at the last minute, for an examination.

¹cramp (krămp) **n-** 1 iron bar bent at the ends, used to hold together blocks of stone, timber, or the like. 2 clamp. **vt-** to restrict or confine; hem in: *I don't want to* cramp *his enthusiasm.* [from early Dutch **kramp(e).**]

²cramp (krămp) **n-** 1 sudden, sharp, painful contraction of the muscles; muscle spasm. 2 **cramps** sharp abdominal pains. **vi-:** *His leg* cramped *and he was in agony.* **vt-:** *Fear* cramped *his stomach.* [from Old French, from early Dutch **kramp(e),** and related to **¹cramp.**]

cram·pon (krăm′ pŏn′) **n-** 1 spiked iron plate strapped to boots to aid in climbing or walking on ice. 2 one of a pair of metal grappling hooks to raise heavy objects.

cran·ber·ry (krăn′ bĕr′ ē) **n-** [*pl.* **cran·ber·ries**] 1 a small, tart, red berry that grows in bogs. 2 the trailing vine it grows on. **adj-:** *We had turkey with* cranberry *sauce.*

crane (krān) **n-** 1 a wading bird with very long legs, a long straight bill, and a long neck. 2 machine for raising and moving heavy weights. 3 mechanical arm or support that swings on a pivot.

crank (krăngk) **n-** 1 lever used to give rotary motion to some machine part and usually consisting of an arm with a handle at right angles on one end. 2 grouchy or cross person. 3 *Informal* person with odd ideas or one fixed idea: *This strange letter came from a* crank. **vt-** to start or operate with a rotary motion: *to* crank *an engine; to* crank *a windlass.*

Crank

crank·y (krăng′ kē) **adj-** [**crank·i·er, crank·i·est**] ill-tempered; easily annoyed; surly; irritable. **—adv-** **crank′ i·ly.** **n-** **crank′ i·ness.**

¹crash (krăsh) **vi-** 1 to fall down with great noise and usually with damage: *The vase* crashed *to the floor.* 2 to break one's way noisily (through something): *to* crash *through a wall.*

crass (krăs) **adj-** stupid; insensitive; dense: *his* crass *ignorance.* **—adv-** **crass′ ly.** **n-** **crass′ ness.**

cra·ter (krā′ tər) **n-** 1 bowl-shaped depression at the mouth of a volcano. 2 gaping hole in the ground, such as one made by a bomb or meteorite.

crawl (krôl) **vi-** 1 to move on hands and knees or by dragging the body along on the ground: *The baby* crawls. 2 to move or progress very slowly: *The cars* crawled *along. Time* crawled *that afternoon.*

craze (krāz) **n-** strong but passing interest; fad: *Large hats are the* craze *this year.* **vt-** [**crazed, craz·ing**] to make insane: *He was* crazed *by money troubles.*

creak (krēk) **vi-** to make a sharp squeaking or grating sound, especially because of age or unfit condition: *That old gate* creaks *in the wind.* **n-** a harsh, squeaky sound. **Hom-** creek.

cream (krēm) **n-** 1 the rich, fatty part of milk that rises to the top; hence, the best part; elite: *the* cream *of the crop; the* cream *of society.* 2 dessert or food made of this substance: *a butter* cream.

crease (krēs) **n-** mark or line left by folding; a fold; ridge: *a* crease *in trousers.* **vt-** [**creased, creas·ing**] to make a fold or wrinkle in: *to* crease *trousers with an iron; to* crease *a dress.* **vi-:** *The dress* creased *in the suitcase.*

cre·ate (krē āt′) **vt-** [**cre·at·ed, cre·at·ing**] 1 to bring into being; cause to come into existence: *A painter* creates *art.* 2 to cause; bring about: *to* create *trouble.*

cre·a·tion (krē ā′ shən) **n-** 1 a creating; an originating: *The* creation *of a great poem requires inspiration and hard work.* 2 anything created or brought into being: *Shakespeare's plays are great* creations. 3 the universe, the world, and its creatures; all created things

crea·ture (krē′chər) *n-* 1 any animal or human being.

cre·dence (krē′dəns) *n-* belief: *This rumor is not worthy of* credence.

cre·den·tials (krə dĕn′shəlz) *n- pl.* 1 documents that prove one's identity, authority, professional status, etc..

cred·i·ble (krĕd′ə bəl) *adj-* 1 trustworthy: *a* credible *witness.* 2 believable: *a* credible *story.* —*n-* cred′i·bil′i·ty. *adv-* cred′i·bly.

cred·it (krĕd′ət) *n-* 1 acknowledgement of achievement, merit, etc.; recognition: *The Wright brothers get* credit *for inventing the airplane.* 2 honor; good reputation: *to be of good* credit *in the community.* 3 belief; credence: *I gave* credit *to her statements.*

cre·do (krē′dō, krā′-) *n-* [*pl.* **cre·dos**] 1 creed; set o beliefs; statement of faith. 2 (also **Credo**) the Nicene Creed or the Apostle's Creed; also, a musical setting for either.

cre·du·li·ty (krə dyōō′lə tē, krə dōō′-) *n-* readiness to believe what one is told without proof.

creed (krēd) *n-* 1 a set of beliefs or principles on any subject; credo: *a soldier's* creed. 2 a brief, summarizing statement of religious belief; credo: *the Apostle's* Creed.

creek (krēk, krĭk) *n-* 1 stream smaller than a river, to which it is often tributary; brook. 2 *chiefly Brit.* narrow inlet or bay. *Hom-* creak or crick.

creel (krēl) *n-* 1 wicker basket used for carrying fish. 2 wicker trap used for catching lobsters or fish.

Creel

creep (krēp) *vi-* [**crept** (krĕpt), **creep·ing**] 1 to move with the body close to the ground; crawl: *The baby has just learned to* creep. 2 to move

cre·mate (krē′māt′) *vt-* [**cre·mat·ed, cre·mat·ing**] to burn (a dead body) to ashes. —*n-* cre·ma′tion.

cres·cent (krĕs′ənt) *n-* 1 figure shaped like the moon in its first or last quarter. 2 part of the moon visible at this time.

crev·ice (krĕv′əs) *n-* narrow crack or split; fissure.

¹crew (krōō) *n-* 1 the persons manning a ship or aircraft, rowing a boat, etc. 2 all the men, except officers, manning a ship or aircraft: *The officers and* crew *of the submarine.*

crime (krīm) *n-* 1 an act forbidden by law, or omission of an act required by law.

crim·i·nal (krĭm′ə nəl) *n-* person guilty of crime. *adj-* 1 involving guilt for crime: *a* criminal *record; a* criminal *act.* 2 relating to crime: *the study of* criminal *law.*

cringe (krĭnj) *vi-* [**cringed, cring·ing**] 1 to crouch down or shrink back in fear: *The pup* cringed *at the noise.* 2 to act in a humble timid manner; abase oneself.

crip·ple (krĭp′əl) *n-* person or animal handicapped by bodily injury, deformity, or the loss of a part; lame person.

cri·sis (krī′səs) *n-* [*pl.* **cri·ses** (-sēz′)] 1 time of unusual difficulty or danger. 2 event that is a turning point; decisive moment: *Lincoln's election was a* crisis *in the struggle over slavery.* 3 turning point toward life or death in an illness.

crisp (krĭsp) *adj-* [**crisp·er, crisp·est**] 1 stiff, dry, and brittle: *a sandwich of* crisp *bacon and toast.* 2 fresh; firm, and crunchy: *a salad of* crisp *vegetables.*

cri·te·ri·on (krī tēr′ē ən) *n-* [*pl.* **cri·te·ri·a**] standard or rule by which to form a judgment; test: *A person's acts are* criteria *of his character.*

crit·ic (krĭt′ĭk) *n-* 1 person who makes a reasoned judgment of the worth of anything, especially of literary, artistic, or scholarly works: *Jones is a professional art* critic. 2 person who finds fault or judges harshly; caviler; carper.

crit·i·cism (krĭt′ə sĭz əm) *n-* 1 the occupation and judgments of critics: *literary* criticism. 2 a particular critical opinion or review; evaluation: *His* criticism *is in today's paper.* 3 faultfinding; disapproval; blame.

croc·o·dile (krŏk′ə dīl) *n-* a tough-skinned, flesh-eating aquatic reptile with a long tail, a long narrow head, and a pointed snout, found in warm regions of Africa, Asia, Australia, and North America.

crook (krŏok) *n-* 1 the bent, curved, or hooked part of anything: *the* crook *of the elbow.* 2 a stick with a bent or curved end: *shepherd's* crook. 3 *Informal* thief or swindler. *vt-* to bend or curve: *to* crook *a finger.* *vi-*: *The stem of the flower* crooked *to the left.*

Crook

crook·ed (krŏok′əd) *adj-* 1 not straight; bent; curved: *a* crooked *road; a* crooked *buck.* 2 *Informal* not honest: *a* crooked *business.* —*adv-* crook′ed·ly. *n-* crook′ed·ness.

crop (krŏp) *n-* 1 amount of produce grown or gathered: *We had a big* crop *of potatoes this year.* 2 a lot of people or things thought of together as if they were harvested: *a* crop *of new writers.* 3 short haircut.

cro·quette (krō kĕt′) *n-* small ball of minced meat, fish, or other cooked food dipped in egg and crumbs and fried.

cro·sier or **cro·zier** (krō′zhər) *n-* ornate shepherd's crook that is the symbol of office of a bishop, archbishop, or abbot.

Crosier

¹cross (krŏs) *n-* 1 upright stake bearing a horizontal bar near the top, a form of which was used by the ancient Romans as an instrument of torture and execution. 2 **the Cross** (1) the instrument of this type upon which Christ was crucified.

²cross (krŏs) *adj-* [**cross·er, cross·est**] ill-tempered; peevish; grumpy; cranky. —*adv-* cross′ly. *n-* cross′ness. [from **¹cross** in the sense of "athwart" or "contrary."]

crotch (krŏch) *n-* point of separation into parts, branches, or legs; fork.

Crotch

crotch·et (krŏch′ət) *n-* 1 whim or fancy; eccentricity. 2 kind of small hook or hooklike instrument.

crotch·et·y (krŏch′ə tē) *adj-* full of odd whims or fancies; eccentric.

crouch (krouch) *vi-* 1 to stoop or bend low, as if ready to spring. 2 to cringe, as if in fear. *n-*: *The leopard went into a* crouch, *ready to attack.*

²crow (krō) *vi-* [*p.t.* sometimes in sense 1, **crew** (krōō); otherwise **crowed**] 1 to make the shrill cry of a rooster. 2 to boast in triumph: *to* crow *over a victory.*

crowd (kroud) *n-* 1 number of persons or things collected closely together. 2 people in general; the masses. 3 set; clique: *the college* crowd.

crown (kroun) *n-* 1 headdress of gold and jewels, worn by kings or queens on ceremonial occasions. 2 the monarch himself, or his power.

crude (krōod) *adj-* [**crud·er, crud·est**] 1 in a natural state; unrefined: *a barrel of* crude *oil;* crude *rubber.* 2 done or made without special skill; rough: *a* crude *drawing; a* crude *effort.*

cru·el (krōo′əl) *adj-* [**cru·el·er, cru·el·est**] 1 willing or inclined to cause suffering and pain to others; merciless: *a* cruel *tyrant.* 2 causing suffering, grief, or pain; harsh: *a* cruel *disease; a* cruel *winter.* —*adv-* cru′el·ly.

crum·ble (krŭm′bəl) *vt-* [**crum·bled, crum·bling**] to break into small pieces: *He* crumbled *bread to feed to the birds.*

crunch (krŭnch) *n-* a noisy chewing or grinding; also, the sound this produces. *vt-* to chew, grind, or crush noisily: *to* crunch *celery.*

crush (krŭsh) *vt-* 1 to press out of shape; crumple; squash: *The car* crushed *the ball.* 2 to break into small or very fine pieces: *to* crush *ice; to* crush *rocks.*

crust (krŭst) *n-* 1 hard outer layer of bread, or of rolls, biscuits, etc. 2 a piece of this or of stale bread. 3 the pastry forming the outside of a pie.

crutch (krŭch) *n-* 1 wooden or metal staff usually fitting under the armpit and used by lame or injured persons in walking. 2 anything that serves as a mental or emotional support or partial remedy: *Eating is a* crutch *to him during his unhappy periods.*

crux (krŭks) *n-* 1 the important point on which something depends; the pivotal point. 2 hard point to settle;

Crutches

cry (krī) *vi-* [**cried, cry·ing**] 1 to shout or call loudly: *to cry out in pain*; *to cry for help.* 2 to weep; shed tears. 3 of an animal or bird, to call loudly.

crypt (krīpt) *n-* underground vault, especially one under a church. Crypts are often used for tombs.

cryp·tic (krīp′tĭk) *adj-* puzzling; mysterious. *—adv-* **cryp′ti·cal·ly:** *to speak cryptically.*

crys·tal (krĭs′təl) *n-* 1 clear, transparent type of quartz; rock crystal. 2 jewel or other ornament cut from this quartz or from fine glass. 3 very fine glass containing lead to increase its brilliance; also, tableware made from this glass. 4 transparent cover of a watch dial. 5 *Physics* solid object having flat sides and a symmetrical form due to the arrangement of its atoms and molecules.

SNOW

cube (kyōōb) *n-* 1 solid body with six square faces. 2 any block having six sides: *ice cube*; *sugar cube.*

cu·bi·cle (kyōō′bĭ kəl) *n-* very small room or walled off area: *a telephone cubicle*; *a voter's cubicle.*

cud·dle (kŭd′əl) *vt-* [**cud·dled, cud·dling**] to hold close and tenderly: *to cuddle a baby.* *vi-* to lie close together; nestle. *n-* a close embrace; a hug.

¹cue (kyōō) *n-* 1 on the stage, a word or an action that indicates the time for the next actor to speak, act, or enter. 2 signal; hint: *That's my cue to leave.*

²cue (kyōō) *n-* 1 long tapering stick used to strike the ball in playing pool or billiards. 2 queue. *vt-* [**cued, cu·ing**] to strike (a pool or billiard ball) with a long, tapering stick.

¹cuff (kŭf) *n-* 1 the part of a glove or sleeve, or any wide band, covering the wrist. 2 the hem or fold of cloth on the bottom of a trouser leg.

cul·mi·nate (kŭl′mĭ nāt′) *vi-* [**cul·mi·nat·ed, cul·mi·nat·ing**] 1 to reach the highest point; end at the top (in): *The tower culminated in a cupola. His career culminated in the presidency.*

cul·pa·ble (kŭl′pə bəl) *adj-* deserving blame: *Reckless driving is a culpable offense.* *—n-* **cul′pa·bil′i·ty** or **cul′pa·ble·ness.** *adv-* **cul′pa·bly.**

cul·prit (kŭl′prĭt) *n-* guilty person; offender: *I caught the culprit who robbed the cookie jar.*

cul·ti·vate (kŭl′tə vāt′) *vt-* [**cul·ti·vat·ed, cul·ti·vat·ing**] 1 to prepare (soil) for the planting and care of crops. 2 to raise (plants): *to cultivate roses.* 3 to loosen the soil around (plants).

cul·ture (kŭl′chər) *n-* 1 result of improving the mind, tastes, and manners: refinement. 2 a training and developing of the mind or body: *a class in physical culture.*

cum·ber·some (kŭm′bər səm) *adj-* heavy, bulky, or unwieldy: burdensome: *a cumbersome package.* *—adv-* **cum′ber·some·ly.** *n-* **cum′ber·some·ness.**

cu·mu·la·tive (kyōō′myə lə tĭv) *adj-* growing in number, volume, strength, etc., by repeated additions; increasing steadily: *a cumulative effort.*

cup (kŭp) *n-* 1 small container, often bowl-shaped and with a handle, used for drinking, measuring, etc. 2 the amount such a container holds; cupful.

curb (kŭrb) *vt-* 1 to keep within bounds; restrain: *to curb one's temper.* 2 to walk (a dog) along the edge of a street to keep him from soiling the sidewalk.

cure (kyōōr) *vt-* [**cured, cur·ing**] 1 to make well; remedy or heal: *This medicine will cure your cough. The doctor cured him.* 2 to get rid of or rid (someone) of; correct: *to cure one's fear of the dark*; *to cure someone of a bad habit.*

cur·few (kŭr′fyōō′) *n-* 1 officially set hour or signal at which persons, usually children, must be indoors and at home for the night.

cu·ri·ous (kyōōr′ē əs) *adj-* 1 eager to know or find out: *a child's curious mind.* 2 odd; strange; unusual: *a collection of* curious *old coins*; *a curious accident.*

curl (kŭrl) *n-* 1 coiled or curved lock of hair; ringlet. 2 something resembling this: *a curl of smoke*; *wood shavings twisted into curls.*

cur·ren·cy (kŭr′ən sē) *n-* [*pl.* **cur·ren·cies**] 1 coins, bills, etc., generally used as money: *Dimes and dollars are* among the currency *of the United States.* 2 general acceptance or circulation: *The rumor quickly gained* currency.

cur·rent (kŭr′ənt) *n-* 1 a flow in one direction; stream: *an ocean* current; *an air* current. 2 flow of electricity in a circuit: *a weak* current *in a poor conductor.*

cur·ric·u·lum (kə rĭk′yə ləm) *n-* [*pl.* **cur·ric·u·lums** or **cur·ric·u·la** (-lə)] the subjects or course of study regularly taught at a school, college, etc.: *Music and French are included in our* curriculum.

curse (kŭrs) *vt-* [**cursed, curs·ing**] 1 to call down evil or harm on: *The witch cursed her tormentors.*

cur·sive (kŭr′sĭv) *adj-* joined together by flowing lines as the letters in handwriting. *n-* handwriting so joined; script. *—adv-* **cur′sive·ly.**

cur·so·ry (kŭr′sə rē) *adj-* hasty; careless: *He gave the book a* cursory *reading.* *—adv-* **cur′so·ri·ly.**

curt (kŭrt) *adj-* [**curt·er, curt·est**] short and offhand, often with the effect of seeming rude: *a curt nod*; *a curt answer.* *—adv-* **curt′ly.** *n-* **curt′ness.**

cur·tail (kər tāl′) *vt-* to make shorter or less; cut down; reduce: *to curtail a speech because of lack of time*; *to curtail expenses.* *—n-* **cur·tail′ment.**

cur·tain (kŭr′tən) *n-* 1 hanging drapery or screen, usually of cloth, used to cover or decorate, or to separate one place from another: *the curtains at a window*; *the curtain across the stage in a theater.*

curt·sy (kŭrt′sē) *n-* [*pl.* **curt·sies**] respectful bow which girls and women make by bending the knees and lowering the body.

curve (kŭrv) *n-* 1 a line no part of which is straight. 2 rounded shape, bend, etc.: *the curve of her cheek*; *a curve in the road.* 3 in baseball, ball pitched so it swerves from a straight course.

Curves

cush·ion (kōōsh′ən) *n-* 1 pillow or soft pad to sit, lie, or rest on. 2 any covering resembling such a pillow or pad: *a cushion of pine needles.* 3 anything serving as a safeguard against harm; buffer.

cus·to·dy (kŭs′tə dē) *n-* protective care; guardianship: *The children were in their grandmother's* custody.

take into custody to arrest and put under guard.

cus·tom (kŭs′təm) *n-* 1 habit or generally accepted way of doing things: *It is her custom to get up at dawn.* 2 regular buying of goods or services from a store or business: *Most of our custom is with that store.*

cut (kŭt) *vt-* [**cut, cut·ting**] (in senses 1, 4, 6, and 9 considered intransitive when the direct object is implied but not expressed) 1 to divide, separate, shorten, or make an opening in with a knife or sharp tool: *to cut a ribbon in two*; *to cut the grass.*

cu·ti·cle (kyōō′tĭ kəl) *n-* outer layer of skin, especially the thickened skin around the base of the fingernails or toenails.

cut·ler·y (kŭt′lə rē) *n-* cutting instruments, especially implements used in cutting or serving food.

cy·a·nide (sī′ə nīd′) *n-* extremely poisonous compound of the cyanogen radical (CN) and a metallic element or radical, especially potassium cyanide (KCN).

cy·cle (sī′kəl) *n-* 1 series of events, processes, actions, etc., that occur over and over again in regular order: *the cycle of the seasons.* 2 series of poems or stories about a central person or event: *the cycle of legends about King Arthur.* 3 a bicycle, tricycle, or motorcycle.

cyl·in·der (sĭl′ən dər) *n-* 1 solid geometric figure described by the circumference of a circle as it moves along a straight line. The ends of this figure are equal parallel circles. 2 any body having this form, such as a piston chamber of a gasoline or steam engine, a barrel of a pump, or a roller used

Cylinder

cyst (sĭst) *n-* 1 liquid-filled sac or pouch that forms in both plants and animals, especially a sac in the body containing diseased matter.

cyn·i·cism (sĭn′ə sĭz′ əm) *n-* 1 the attitude or beliefs of a cynic. 2 cynical statement, opinion, etc.

czar (zär) *n-* 1 (also **tsar**) the title of the former emperors of Russia. 2 person in a position of highest authority.

D

D, d (dē) *n-* [*pl.* **D's, d's**] 1 the fourth letter of the English alphabet. 2 Roman numeral for 500. 3 *Music* the second note of the C-major scale.

d. 1 died; dead. 2 in British currency, penny or pence (from Latin **denarius, denarii**).

dab (dăb) *vt-* [**dabbed, dab·bing**] 1 to pat or brush (something) without great care, usually in applying some material: *She dabbed her face with powder.* 2 to pat, brush, or smear (some material), usually in applying it to a surface: *He dabbed paint on the wall.* *vi-:* *He dabbed lazily at the table with his brush.* *n-* 1 light brushing or patting stroke: *Give it a dab with the sponge.* 2 small amount or mass; bit: *a dab of butter; a dab of grease; a dab of color.* [from Middle English **dabben**, of unknown origin.]

²dab (dăb) *n-* any of various flatfish, including some soles, plaices, and flounders. [apparently same as ¹**dab.**]

dab·ble (dăb′ əl) *vt-* [**dab·bled, dab·bling**] to dip (the hands or feet) lazily in and out: *He dabbled his feet in the sand.* *vi-* 1 to paddle and splash about in water: *The children dabbled in the brook.* 2 to do something in a lazy or casual way: *He dabbled in art. Edward dabbled at gardening.*

dace (dās) *n-* [*pl.* **dace; dac·es** (kinds of dace)] 1 small European fresh-water fish, like the chub. 2 a related North American fish.

dachs·hund (dăks′ hŏŏnt′, -hŏŏnd′) *n-* small hound with very short legs, long body, pointed nose, and drooping ears.

Da·cron (dā′ krŏn′, dăk′ rŏn′) *n-* trademark name of a strong man-made fiber and of cloth woven from it.

dac·tyl (dăk′ təl) *n-* 1 measure or foot in poetry made up of one accented syllable followed by two unaccented syllables. 2 line of poetry made up of such measures. Example: "Take′ her up/ tend′ er ly." —*adj-* **dac·tyl′ ic** (dăk tĭl′ ĭk): *a dactylic line.*

Dachshund about 18 in long

dad (dăd) *Informal n-* father.

dad·dy (dăd′ ē) *Informal n-* father.

dad·dy-long·legs (dăd′ ē lông′ lĕgz′) *n-* [*pl.* **dad·dy-long·legs**] spiderlike animal with very long legs and a small, round body; harvestman.

Daddy-long legs

da·do (dā′ dō) *n-* [*pl.* **da·does**] 1 face of a pedestal between the base and the cornice. 2 (also **dado head**) set of circular blades fitted to a power saw to cut out a rectangular groove. 3 (also **dado plane**) narrow woodworking plane for the same purpose. 4 a rectangular groove. *vt-* to cut such a groove in.

Daed·a·lus (dĕd′ ə ləs) *n-* in Greek legend, a great creator and inventor who devised, among other things, the Labyrinth in Crete and the wings of Icarus.

daf·fo·dil (dăf′ ə dĭl′) *n-* garden plant that blossoms in spring with showy, usually yellow flowers; also, the flower.

daf·fy (dăf′ ē) *Informal adj-* [**daf·fi·er, daf·fi·est**] 1 crazy; daft. 2 foolish; silly.

daft (dăft) *chiefly Brit. adj-* 1 weak-minded or simple; foolish. 2 insane; crazy. —*adv-* **daft′ ly.** *n-* **daft′ ness.**

dag·ger (dăg′ ər) *n-* 1 short, pointed, double-edged sword or knife, used to stab. 2 in printing, a reference mark (†).

Daffodil

dain·ty (dān′ tē) *adj-* [**dain·ti·er, dain·ti·est**] 1 pretty in a delicate or graceful way: *a thin, dainty dress of pink.* 2 having delicate feelings or tastes; fastidious: *one's dainty eating habits.* 3 delicious: *a dainty morsel.* *n-* [*pl.* **dain·ties**] bit of delicious food: *a box of dainties from the bakery.* —*adv-* **dain′ ti·ly.** *n-* **dain′ ti·ness.**

dair·y (dâr′ ē) *n-* [*pl.* **dair·ies**] 1 building or room in which milk and cream are kept and made into butter and cheese; creamery. 2 shop or company that sells or serves milk and milk products; creamery. *as modifier:* *a dairy farm; a dairy restaurant.*

---

dam·age (dăm′ ĭj) *n-* 1 injury; harm: *How much damage did the fire cause?* 2 **damages** in law, amount that is claimed or allowed in court for harm or injury. *vt-* [**dam·aged, dam·ag·ing**]: *The fire damaged the building.*

dam·a·scene (dăm′ ə sēn′) *vt-* [**dam·a·scened, dam·a·scen·ing**] to decorate (metal) with etching or inlaid designs. *n-* decorative inlaid or etched work in iron or steel. *as modifier:* *a damascene sword.*

Da·mas·cus steel (də măs′ kəs) *n-* hard, elastic steel, formerly made in Damascus for sword blades.

dam·ask (dăm′ əsk) *n-* 1 patterned fabric, usually linen or silk, used for table linens, draperies, dresses, etc. 2 deep, rose-pink color. 3 Damascus steel. 4 damascene. *as modifier:* *a damask tablecloth; damask cheeks.*

dame (dām) *n-* 1 in earlier times, the mistress of a household; lady. 2 an old woman; beldam. 3 *Slang* woman. 4 **Dame** *Brit.* (1) lady member of a British honorary order; also, her title. (2) title of a knight's or baronet's wife.

damn (dăm) *vt-* 1 to judge and condemn as bad, faulty, or as a failure: *The critics damned the book.* 2 to doom to eternal punishment. 3 to curse; swear at; call down a curse upon. *Hom-* dam.

dam·na·ble (dăm′ nə bəl) *adj-* deserving to be condemned; detestable: *a damnable lie.* —*adv-* **dam′ na·bly.** *n-* **dam′ na·ble·ness.**

Dane (dān) *n-* 1 person who was born in, or is a citizen of, Denmark. 2 person of Danish descent. *Hom-* deign.

dan·ger (dān′ jər) *n-* 1 chance of harm; risk; peril: *A fireman faces danger every day.* 2 possible cause of loss, injury, or death; hazard: *Ice is a danger to ships.*

dan·ger·ous (dān′ jər əs) *adj-* 1 unsafe; risky; perilous: *Handling explosives is dangerous work.* 2 likely to do harm: *A mad dog is dangerous.* —*adv-* **dan′ ger·ous·ly.** *n-* **dan′ ger·ous·ness.**

dan·gle (dăng′ əl) *vi-* [**dan·gled, dan·gling**] to hang or swing loosely: *The puppet dangled on a string.* *vt-:* *The boy dangled his legs over the edge of the pool.*

Dan·iel (dăn′ yəl) *n-* 1 in the Bible, a Hebrew prophet, captive in Babylon. 2 a book of the Old Testament containing the story of this prophet.

Dan·ish (dā′ nĭsh) *adj-* of or relating to Denmark, its people, or their language: *a Danish custom.* *n-* the Germanic language of the Danes.

dank (dăngk) *adj-* [**dank·er, dank·est**] unpleasantly damp; sodden: *a dank cellar.* —*adv-* **dank′ ly.** *n-* **dank′ ness.**

dan·seuse (dän sōōz′) *n-* female ballet dancer.

Daph·ne (dăf′ nē) *n-* in Greek mythology, a nymph who escaped from Apollo by changing into a laurel tree.

daph·ni·a (dăf′ nē ə) *n-* tiny, insectlike, fresh-water crustacean with a transparent shell; water flea.

dap·per (dăp′ ər) *adj-* neat and smart in appearance; trim; spruce: *a dapper dresser.*

dap·ple (dăp′ əl) *n-* 1 spotted or mottled marking, such as one on the skin of an animal. 2 animal with such marking. *adj-:* *a dapple cow.* *vt-* [**dap·pled, dap·pling**]: *The sunlight dappled the grass.*

D.A.R. Daughters of the American Revolution.

dare (dâr) *auxiliary verb-* to have enough courage to: *He didn't dare jump from a height.* *vt-* [**dared, dar·ing**] 1 to have courage for; meet boldly: *Columbus dared the perils of an uncharted ocean.* 2 to challenge: *He dared me to climb the pole.* *vi-* to have enough courage: *When courage was needed, he dared.* *n-* a challenge. **take a dare** to do what one is dared to do.

dare·dev·il (dâr′ dĕv′ əl) *n-* person who takes great risks recklessly. *as modifier:* *a daredevil driver.*

dar·ing (dâr′ ĭng) *n-* bravery; boldness. *adj-:* *a daring deed; a daring attempt; a daring aviator.* —*adv-* **dar′ ing·ly.** *n-* **dar′ ing·ness.**

dark·room (därk′ rŏŏm′) *n-* room that has been darkened and protected from outside light and is used for developing and handling photographic films, plates, etc.

dar·ling (där′ lĭng) *n-* much loved person; object of deep affection: *the darling of her father's heart.* *adj- Informal* very attractive: *a darling dress.*

darn (därn) *vt-* to mend by weaving thread or yarn back and forth across a hole. *n-* a place thus mended.

dash (dăsh) *vi-* to rush violently: *to dash outside. vt-* 1 to throw violently: *to dash a cup to the floor.* 2 to destroy; ruin: *She dashed all my hopes.* 3 splatter; splash: *They dashed him with cold water. n-* 1 sudden rush or run: *a dash for freedom.* 2 short race: *a hundred-yard dash.* 3 little bit: *a dash of pepper.* 4 spirited energy; éclat: *a man of great dash and vigor.* 5 punctuation mark [—], used to show a pause or break in a sentence. A shorter form [-] is used to show a span of pages (1-15), years (1732-1799), etc. 6 dashboard. 7 the longer of the two sounds used in Morse Code.
dash off to do with haste: *to dash off a letter.*
dash·board (dăsh' bôrd') *n-* 1 instrument panel of an automobile; dash. 2 screen at the front of a carriage, boat, etc., used as protection against splashing.
dash·ing (dăsh' ĭng) *adj-* 1 lively; bold: *a dashing knight.* 2 showy; bright: *a dashing costume.*
das·tard (dăs' tərd) *n-* a sneaking and malicious coward.
das·tard·ly (dăs' tərd lē) *adj-* cowardly, sly, and evil: *His betrayal of his comrades was a dastardly act.*
da·ta (dā' tə, dăt' ə) *n- pl.* [*sing.* **da·tum**] facts and figures; information: *The data for a report.*
►DATA is now often used with a singular verb.
¹**date** (dāt) *n-* 1 a particular time expressed as the day of the month, or the year, or both: *Today's date is March 30, 1965. The date of Shakespeare's birth is 1564.* 2 statement on a letter, coin, etc., giving such a time: *The date of a building is often on the cornerstone.* 3 period of time to which something belongs: *an invention of early date.* 4 *Informal* appointment or social engagement; also, the person with whom one has such an engagement. *vt-* [**dat·ed, dat·ing**] 1 to mark with the day of the month, etc.: *to date a letter.* 2 to find out or fix the time of: *Can you date that castle?* 3 *Informal* to escort socially (a person of the opposite sex). *vi- Informal* to have or keep social appointments as a couple. [from Old French, from Latin **data** meaning "(a letter or document) given (at a certain time)."] —*adj-* **date' less.**
out of date no longer in use or style; old-fashioned. **up to date** 1 in fashion. 2 (also **to date**) up to now.
date from to belong to the time of; have origin in.
²**date** (dāt) *n-* 1 kind of palm tree which bears clusters of oblong, one-seeded fruit. 2 the sweet fruit, usually dried, of this tree. *adj-: a loaf of date bread; a date palm.* [from Old French (through Latin), from Greek *daktylos* meaning "finger."]
dat·ed (dā' tǝd) *adj-* 1 having a date: *a dated letter.* 2 old-fashioned: *a dated custom.*
Da·vid (dā' vǝd) *n-* in the Bible, a son of Jesse and father of Solomon. David killed the giant Goliath, charmed Saul with a harp, and reigned over Israel for more than 40 years.
da·vit (dăv' ǝt, dā' vǝt) *n-* one of a pair of cranes for lowering boats into the water and recovering them, usually from a ship's deck.
Da·vy Jones (dā' vē jōnz') *n-* the spirit of the sea; the sailors' devil.
Davy Jones's locker *n-* the bottom of the sea, regarded as the grave of the drowned.

Davits holding a boat

daw (dô) *n-* jackdaw.
daw·dle (dô' dǝl) *vi-* [**daw·dled, daw·dling**] to loiter; waste time; be lazy and casual: *He dawdled all day.*
dawn (dôn) *n-* 1 the coming of daylight in the morning. 2 the beginning or earliest appearance of something. *The invention of the airplane marked the dawn of a new age. vi-* 1 to begin to grow light in the morning: *The day dawns in the east.* 2 to begin to appear or develop. **dawn on** to begin to be understood by; become clear to.
day (dā) *n-* 1 the period of light between sunrise and sunset. 2 period of 24 hours. 3 period in which a planet or other celestial body makes one complete rotation about its axis. 4 particular age or period: *in the days of hoop skirts.* 5 particular 24-hour period on which some special event takes place: *Thanksgiving Day; a wedding day.* 6 the number of hours given to work or school: *the eight-hour day.*

D.C. District of Columbia.
D.D. Doctor of Divinity.
D-day (dē' dā') *n-* day set for the beginning of a military or other carefully planned operation; especially, June 6, 1944, when the Allies invaded France.
D.D.S. Doctor of Dental Surgery.
DDT (dē' dē' tē') *n-* powerful chemical insect killer.
de- *prefix* 1 the opposite or the reverse: *decompress; devitalize; desensitize.* 2 an undoing: *decode; deform.* 3 removal or removal from: *defrost; derail; dehorn; dethrone.* 4 down: *devalue; demote.* [from Middle English **de-**, from Old French **de-**, **des**, from Latin **de-**, "down; away" and **dis-**, "from."]
dea·con (dē' kǝn) *n-* 1 church officer who does not preach but assists in certain ceremonies, in caring for the poor, etc. 2 in some churches, an ordained member of the clergy next below a priest in rank. —*n- fem.* **dea' con·ess.**
dead (dĕd) *adj-* [**dead·er, dead·est**] 1 no longer living: *a dead animal.* 2 without any life; inorganic: *A rock is dead matter.* 3 without force, motion, etc.; inactive: *a dead tennis ball; a dead party.* 4 no longer used; extinct: *a dead language.* 5 complete; entire: *a dead silence; a dead loss.* 6 exact: *at dead center. adv-* 1 *Informal* completely: *He's dead right.* 2 exactly; directly: *Steer dead ahead. n-* the time of the greatest quietness, inactivity, etc.: *the dead of night.* —*n- dead' ness.*
dead·beat (dĕd' bēt') *Slang n-* loafer or sponger.
dead·en (dĕd' ǝn) *vt-* 1 to make less forceful or active; damp: *to deaden a sound;* deaden *a spring.* 2 to take away feeling or keenness from; numb: *The drug deadened his pain. Grief deadened her mind.*
dead end *n-* street, alley, etc., that is closed off at one end. *as modifier* (**dead-end**): *a dead-end street.*
deaf (dĕf) *adj-* [**deaf·er, deaf·est**] unable or partly unable to hear. —*adv-* **deaf' ly.** *n-* **deaf' ness.**
deaf to unwilling to listen: *She was deaf to his pleas.*
deaf·en (dĕf' ǝn) *vt-* 1 to make unable to hear. 2 to overpower or stun with noise: *Shrieks deafened me.*
deaf-mute (dĕf' myōōt') *n-* deaf person who cannot speak, usually as a result of deafness from early childhood. *as modifier: a deaf-mute boy.*
¹**deal** (dēl) *vt-* [**dealt, deal·ing**] 1 to be concerned (with): *History deals with the past.* 2 to behave; act: *He deals fairly with his partner.* 3 to trade; do business: *That jewelry store deals mainly in watches. vt-* 1 to give out; distribute: *Please deal the cards.* 2 to give; deliver: *We dealt the enemy a hard blow. n-* 1 a single passing out of playing cards. 2 *Informal* an instance of luck or of treatment by other persons: *to get a raw deal.* 3 *Informal* transaction or arrangement, especially in business or politics. 4 fairly large number or amount. [from Old English **dælan**] —*n-* **deal' er.**
²**deal** (dēl) *n-* a board of pine or fir. *adj-: a deal table.* [probably from early Dutch **dele**, "board; plank."]
deal·ings (dē' lĭngs) *n-* relations or connections, especially in commerce: *honest dealings.*
dean (dēn) *n-* 1 official of a college or university, often head of the faculty and in charge of instruction. 2 member of a college or school faculty in charge of student affairs and discipline. 3 the member of a group or organization who has served the longest: *the dean of newspaper columnists.* 4 head of a group of clergymen connected with a cathedral.
dean·er·y (dē' nə rē) *n-* [*pl.* **dean·er·ies**] 1 position or authority of a dean. 2 residence of a dean.
de·bate (dĭ bāt') *vt-* [**de·bat·ed, de·bat·ing**] to discuss or argue by giving reasons for and against: *We debated several questions. vi-: The boys debated all night. n-* 1 argument; discussion: *after much debate, Congress passed the bill.* 2 formal contest in argumentation: *Our school team won the debate.* —*n- de·bat' er.*
de·bauch (dĭ bôch') *vt-* to lead (someone) away from virtue; corrupt; seduce. *vi-* to overindulge in eating, drinking, etc; dissipate. *n-* drunken orgy; also, any excessive indulgence in sensual pleasures. —*n- de·bauch' er·y: the debauchery of many Roman emperors.*

dec·ade (dĕk′ ād′) *n-* period of ten years.

de·ca·dent (dĭ kā′ dənt, dĕ-) *adj-* declining; deteriorating: *a decadent society.* *n-* person in a state of intellectual or moral decay. —*adv-* **de′ca·dent·ly** or **de·ca′ dent·ly.** *n-* **de′ca·dence** or **de·ca′ dence.**

de·caf·fein·at·ed (dē kăf′ ə nā′ təd) *adj-* having the caffeine removed.

dec·a·gon (dĕk′ ə gŏn′) *n-* polygon with ten sides and ten angles.

dec·a·he·dron (dĕk′ ə hē′ drən) *n-* geometric solid having ten plane faces.

dec·a·li·ter or **dec·a·li·tre** (dĕk′ ə lē′ tər) *n-* unit of volume equal to ten liters.

Dec·a·logue (dĕk′ ə lóg′, -lóg′) *n-* the Ten Commandments. Also **Dec′ alog′.**

Decahedron

de·camp (dĭ kămp′, dē-) *vi-* 1 to leave a camp; break camp. 2 to depart quickly or secretly; run away. —*n-* **de·camp′ ment.**

de·cant (dĭ kănt′, dē-) *vt-* to pour liquid, especially wine, carefully from one vessel into another without disturbing the sediment.

de·cant·er (dĭ kăn′ tər) *n-* ornamental glass bottle with a stopper, used for wine or liquor.

de·cap·i·tate (dē kăp′ ə tāt′) *vt-* [de·cap·i·tat·ed, de·cap·i·tat·ing] to cut off the head of; behead. —*n-* **de·cap′ i·ta′ tion.**

dec·a·pod (dĕk′ ə pŏd′) *n-* 1 a crustacean, such as a lobster or crab, with five pairs of legs. 2 one of a group of mollusks which resemble octopuses and have ten arms, such as the squid and the cuttlefish.

de·cath·lon (dĭ kăth′ lŏn′) *n-* athletic contest consisting of ten different track or field events in which the contestant having the highest total score is the winner. The events are the 100, 400, and 1500 meter runs, 110 meter high hurdles, broad jump, high jump, discus throw, javelin throw, pole vault, and shot-put.

de·cay (dĭ kā′) *vi-* 1 to rot or decompose: *Plants that have died* decay *and make the soil rich.* 2 to lose strength or quality gradually; fail; waste away. *n-* 1 decomposition; rotting. 2 loss of strength or quality by degrees; decline: *the decay of a business; the decay of health with age.* 3 *Physics* disintegration of radioactive material.

de·cease (dĭ sēs′) *n-* death.

de·ceased (dĭ sēst′) *adj-* dead. *n-* **the deceased** dead person or persons.

Declaration of Independence *n-* document of July 4, 1776, by which the 13 American colonies declared themselves to be free and independent of Great Britain.

de·clar·a·tive (dĭ klăr′ ə tĭv, dĭ klĕr′-) *adj-* making a statement; declaring, rather than asking or ordering: *"The cat is black."* is a declarative *sentence.*

de·clare (dĭ klâr′) *vt-* [de·clared, de·clar·ing] 1 to proclaim; announce publicly: *The President* declared *a holiday.* He declared *that he would not surrender.* 2 to affirm solemnly before a witness: *The prisoner* declared *his innocence.* 3 to list (goods on which duty is to be paid). *vi-* to make a declaration: *It was the first newspaper to* declare *for the senator.*

declare (oneself) to state one's belief or one's position in an argument or on a question.

de·clen·sion (dĭ klĕn′ shən) *Grammar n-* 1 all the forms showing the cases of a certain noun, pronoun, or adjective; paradigm. 2 group of words with the same or similar case forms.

de·clin·a·ble (dĭ klīn′ nə bəl) *adj-* such as can be gramatically declined as a noun, pronoun, or adjective.

dec·li·na·tion (dĕk′ lə nā′ shən) *n-* 1 the deviation of the needle of a magnetic compass from true north. 2 a refusal. 3 a downward slope.

de·cline (dĭ klīn′) *vt-* [de·clined, de·clin·ing] 1 (considered intransitive when the direct object is implied but not expressed) to refuse: *to decline an invitation.* 2 *Grammar* to give the declension of (nouns, pronouns, or adjectives). *vi-* 1 to slope, bend, or lean downward. 2 to decay; fail: *His vigor began to* decline. 3 to go down; diminish: *The stock market* declined. *n-* 1 downward slope. 2 a lessening; deterioration: *a decline of prices; a decline in health.*

deep·en (dē′ pən) *vt-* to make (something) deeper: *to* deepen *a well;* to deepen *a color;* to deepen *one's understanding.* *vi-* to become darker or deeper: *The shadows* deepened. *The water* deepened *offshore.*

deep-root·ed (dēp′ rōō′ təd) *adj-* firmly planted or set; deeply implanted; profound: *a deep-rooted loyalty.*

deep-sea (dēp′ sē′) *adj-* of or in the deeper parts of the sea: *a deep-sea fisherman.*

deep-seat·ed (dēp′ sē′ təd) *adj-* found or planted deep within; firm and lasting: *a deep-seated hatred; a deep-seated tradition.*

deep-set (dēp′ sĕt′) *adj-* deeply placed or fixed: *She had deep-set blue eyes.*

deer (dēr) *n-* [*pl.* **deer**] any of several hoofed, cud-chewing mammals, the males of which have antlers. *Hom-* **dear.** —*adj-* **deer′ like′.**

deer·hound (dēr′ hound′) *n-* large dog with long, coarse coat, related to the Irish wolfhound and formerly used in deer hunting.

deer mouse *n-* any of a group of very common North American mice with buff-colored coat and white feet; white-footed mouse.

White-tail deer. 3 1/2 ft high at shoulder

deer·skin (dēr′ skĭn′) *n-* 1 the skin of a deer. 2 leather made from this. *adj-* : *a deerskin jacket.*

def. definition.

de·face (dĭ fās′) *vt-* [de·faced, de·fac·ing] to spoil the appearance of (something) by marking or damaging: *to* deface *a wall with crayon marks.* —*n-* **de·face′ ment.**

de fac·to (dē făk′ tō, dā-) *Latin* actually existing, whether legally or not; in actual fact: *a de facto ruler.*

de·fal·cate (dĭ făl′ kāt′, dĭ fŏl′-) *vi-* [de·fal·cat·ed, de·fal·cat·ing] to steal or misuse money entrusted to one's charge; embezzle. —*n-* **de·fal·ca′ tion.**

def·a·ma·tion (dĕf′ ə mā′ shən) *n-* malicious injuring of a person's reputation. In law, defamation is called slander if spoken, and libel if written.

de·fam·a·tor·y (dĭ făm′ ə tôr′ ē) *adj-* slanderous; libelous.

de·fame (dĭ fām′) *vt-* [de·famed, de·fam·ing] to injure or destroy the good name of; speak evil of; slander; libel: *This article defames me.*

de·fault (dĭ fólt′) *n-* failure to do something required; especially, failure to appear for a game or contest in which one is scheduled to play. *vi-* to fail to fulfill a contract, agreement, or obligation: *He* defaulted *in his payments on the loan.* *vt-* : *He* defaulted *his contract.* —*n-* **de·fault′ er.**

in default in the condition of having failed to meet some obligation: *He was in* default *by two payments.*

de·feat (dĭ fēt′) *vt-* 1 to overthrow; overcome; win a victory over: *to* defeat *an enemy.* 2 to cause to fail; bring to nothing: *to* defeat *a purpose;* to defeat *one's hopes.* *n-* failure; condition of being overthrown.

def·e·cate (dĕf′ ə kāt′) *vi-* [def·e·cat·ed, def·e·cat·ing] to expel waste matter from the intestines; move the bowels.

de·fect (dē′ fĕkt′, dĭ fĕkt′) *n-* lack of a thing necessary to completeness; imperfection; flaw: *a defect in character; a physical defect; a defect in a tile floor.*

de·fect (dĭ fĕkt′) *vi-* to desert a party or cause, especially to join another: *He* defected *to the enemy.*

de·fec·tion (dĭ fĕk′ shən) *n-* a renouncing of allegiance, duty, loyalty, etc.; desertion: *the defection of a general.*

de·fec·tive (dĭ fĕk′ tĭv) *adj-* 1 imperfect; incomplete; faulty: *a defective switch; a defective copy; defective hearing.* 2 below normal in mental or physical growth; retarded: *a defective child.* 3 *Grammar* lacking one or more inflectional forms. "Must" and "ought" are defective because they lack infinitives and participles. *n-* person who is below normal in mental or physical growth. —*adv-* **de·fec′ tive·ly.** *n-* **de·fec′ tive·ness.**

de·fend·ant (dĭ fĕn′ dənt) *n-* person accused or sued in a law court.

deficiency disease *n-* illness, such as beriberi, caused by the lack of certain vitamins or other nutrients in the diet.

de·fi·cient (dǐ fǐsh′ ənt) *adj-* 1 not having enough of something; insufficient: *an army deficient in supplies.* 2 below standard; imperfect; defective: *to be mentally deficient.* —*adv-* **de·fi′ cient·ly.**

def·i·cit (děf′ ə sǐt) *n-* 1 amount of money by which a required or expected sum falls short; shortage: *a $10 deficit in the cash register.* 2 loss in business operation: *The store had a deficit last year.* 3 any deficiency in amount.

de·for·ma·tion (děf′ ər mā′ shən, dē′ fôr′-) *n-* a deforming or being deformed; also, an instance of this.

de·form·i·ty (dǐ fôr′ mə tē, dǐ fôr′-) *n-* [*pl.* **de·form·i·ties**] 1 part of a human or animal body not properly shaped. 2 condition of being disfigured. 3 moral defect.

de·fraud (dǐ frôd′) *vt-* to cheat; commit a fraud against; swindle: *To make a false tax return is to defraud the government.*

de·fray (dǐ frā′) *vt-* to pay (cost or expenses): *Each camper must defray his own expenses.* —*n-* **de·fray′ al.**

de·frost (dǐ frôst′, dē-) *vt-* 1 to remove frost from: *to defrost a refrigerator.* 2 to thaw: *to defrost frozen foods.* —*n-* **de·frost′ er.**

deft (děft) *adj-* skillful and clever: *a deft dressmaker; a deft phrase.* —*adv-* **deft′ ly.** *n-* **deft′ ness.**

de·funct (dǐ fŭngkt′) *adj-* no longer living or active; dead; extinct: *a defunct idea; a defunct business.*

de·fy (dǐ fī′) *vt-* [**de·fied, de·fy·ing**] 1 to challenge or dare openly and boldly: *This store defies all others to beat its prices.* 2 to treat as of no account or with contempt; scorn: *to defy the law;* to defy *a parent's wishes.* 3 to resist successfully: *The door defies attempts to open it.*

deg. degree.

de·gen·er·a·cy (dǐ jěn′ ər ə sē) *n-* 1 very low and inferior condition, especially of moral behavior; rottenness; depravity. 2 degeneration.

¹**de·gen·er·ate** (dě jěn′ ə rāt′) *vi-* [**de·gen·er·at·ed, de·gen·er·at·ing**] to sink into a lower or worse condition; grow inferior.

²**de·gen·er·ate** (dǐ jěn′ ər ət) *adj-* very much below a former level or standard; inferior; worse: *Are these degenerate times?* *n-* morally debased person. —*adv-* **de·gen′ er·ate·ly.**

de·gen·er·a·tion (dǐ jěn′ ə rā′ shən) *n-* a growing worse or inferior; also, an instance of this; degeneracy: *the degeneration of muscles through long disuse.*

de·gen·er·a·tive (dǐ jěn′ ər ə tǐv) *adj-* showing, causing, or tending to cause degeneration: *a degenerative influence;* degenerative *disease.*

deg·ra·da·tion (děg′ grə dā′ shən) *n-* 1 a lowering in rank, morals, reputation, etc.; act of degrading. 2 very low moral condition; disgrace; dishonor; shame.

de·grade (dǐ grād′) *vt-* [**de·grad·ed, de·grad·ing**] to lower the character of; debase: *Anyone who cheats degrades himself.*

de·grad·ed (dǐ grā′ dəd) *adj-* morally corrupt; weak and sinful. —*adv-* **de·grad′ ed·ly.** *n-* **de·grad′ ed·ness.**

de·gree (dǐ grē′) *n-* 1 one of the equal unit divisions on a temperature scale: *Water boils at 212 degrees (212°) Fahrenheit.* 2 unit used in measuring angles and parts of circles. 3 title of bachelor, master, or doctor given by a college or university for passing a certain course of study, or as a mark of honor.

Degrees

de·i·fi·ca·tion (dē′ ə fə kā′ shən) *n-* a deifying or being deified: *the deification of a king;* the deification *of money.*

de·i·fy (dē′ ə fī′) *vt-* [**de·i·fied, de·i·fy·ing**] to make into or worship as a god: *to deify a man;* to deify *success.*

deign (dān) *vt-* 1 to think (some action) worthy of one's dignity; condescend: *The governor deigned to grant us an audience.* 2 to give; grant. **Hom-** Dane.

de·i·ty (dē′ ə tē) *n-* [*pl.* **de·i·ties**] 1 god or goddess: *Many ancient peoples worshipped the sun as a* deity. 2 **the** Deity God.

de·ject·ed (dǐ jěk′ təd) *adj-* depressed; low-spirited; downcast: *The coach was dejected after the defeat.* —*adv-* **de·ject′ ed·ly.** *n-* **de·ject′ ed·ness.**

de·jec·tion (dǐ jěk′ shən) *n-* lowness of spirits; depression; sadness.

Del. Delaware.

Del·a·ware (děl′ ə wâr′) *n-* [*pl.* **Del·a·wares,** also **Del·a·ware**] member of a group of American Indians who formerly lived in the forests of the Delaware River valley and now live with the Cherokees in Oklahoma. *adj-: the* Delaware *treaties.*

de·li·cious (dǐ lǐsh′ əs) *adj-* pleasing; delightful, especially to taste and smell. —*adv-* **de·li′ cious·ly.** *n-* **de·li′ cious·ness.**

de·light (dǐ līt′) *vt-* to please greatly; give enjoyment and pleasure to: *Toys delight a child.* *n-* 1 a great amount of pleasure; joy: *A vacation is a time of ease and delight.* 2 something that causes pleasure.

delight in to take great pleasure in.

de·light·ed (dǐ lī′ təd) *adj-* highly pleased; gratified: *I am delighted to meet you.* —*adv-* **de·light′ ed·ly.**

de·light·ful (dǐ līt′ fəl) *adj-* giving enjoyment; pleasing; charming: *a delightful evening.* —*adv-* **de·light′ ful·ly.** *n-* **de·light′ ful·ness.**

De·li·lah (də lī′ lə) *n-* Philistine woman who betrayed Samson to the Philistines by cutting off his hair, thereby depriving him of his strength.

de·lim·it (dǐ lǐm′ ət) *vt-* to mark the limits or bounds of; demarcate: *to delimit a topic for discussion.*

de·lin·e·ate (dǐ lǐn′ ē āt′) *vt-* [**de·lin·e·at·ed, de·lin·e·at·ing**] 1 to draw with lines; sketch. 2 to describe carefully and accurately in words; depict: *The reporter delineated every detail of the fire.*

dem·on·strate (děm′ ən strāt′) *vt-* [**dem·on·strat·ed, dem·on·strat·ing**] 1 to teach or show (a way of doing something) by actual performance: *Mary will demonstrate how to solve the problem by working it on the board.* 2 to indicate or reveal: *These figures demonstrate a need for caution.* 3 to prove: *An experiment will demonstrate that wood cannot burn without oxygen.* 4 to exhibit and explain the good points of (a product): *The salesman demonstrated the sewing machine.* *vi-* to hold a meeting, parade, etc., to show public feelings: *The people demonstrated for a cleaner government.*

Den. Denmark.

de·na·ture (dē nā′ chər) *vt-* [**de·na·tured, de·na·tur·ing**] 1 to change the natural qualities or properties of (a substance). 2 to make (something) unfit for eating or drinking without affecting its other properties. —*adj-* **de·na′ tured.**

denatured alcohol *n-* alcohol made unfit for drinking by adding some poisonous or obnoxious liquid.

den·ture (děn′ chər) *n-* false tooth or a set of false teeth; dental bridge or plate.

de·nude (dǐ nōōd′, -nyōōd′) *vt-* [**de·nud·ed, de·nud·ing**] to strip all covering from; make bare: *to denude a hillside of trees.* —*n-* **de′ nu·da′ tion.**

de·nun·ci·a·tion (dǐ nŭn′ sē ā′ shən, dē′-) *n-* public accusation or condemnation: *the candidate's denunciation of his opponent.* —*adj-* **de·nun′ ci·a·to′ ry** (dǐ nŭn′ sē ə tôr′ ē): *a denunciatory speech.*

de·ny (dǐ nī′) *vt-* [**de·nied, de·ny·ing**] 1 to refuse to admit or believe; say that (something) is not true; contradict: *I denied his accusation.* 2 to withhold; refuse to give: *to deny aid.* 3 to refuse; turn down: *to deny a request.*

de·o·dor·ant (dē ō′ də rənt) *n-* substance that destroys or disguises unpleasant odors, especially body odors. *as modifier: a cake of* deodorant *soap.*

de·o·dor·ize (dē ō′ də rīz′) *vt-* [**de·o·dor·ized, de·o·dor·iz·ing**] to remove or disguise the unpleasant odors of. —*n-* **de·o′ dor·iz′ er.**

de·ox·i·dize (dē ŏk′ sə dīz′) *Chemistry vt-* [**de·ox·i·dized, de·ox·i·diz·ing**] 1 to remove oxygen from (a compound). 2 to cause (an oxide) to undergo reduction. —*n-* **de·ox′ i·diz′ er.**

dep·u·ty (dĕp′yə tē) *n-* [*pl.* **dep·u·ties**] 1 person who is appointed to act for, or in the place of, another: *The sheriff has six deputies.* 2 in some countries, a member of a legislative body. *as modifier*: *a deputy marshal.*

de·rail (dĭ rāl′, dē-) *vt-* to force off a rail or rails: *A stone on the track derailed the train. vi-* to go off the rails: *The train derailed on a sharp curve.* **—*n-* de·rail′ ment.**

de·range (dĭ rānj′) *vt-* [**de·ranged, de·rang·ing**] 1 to upset the normal state or functioning of; cause to act abnormally: *The magnetic rock deranged the compass. Shell shock deranged his mind.* 2 disorganize; disarrange.

de·ranged (dĭ rānjd′) *adj-* 1 mentally disturbed; insane; psychotic. 2 upset; disordered.

de·range·ment (dĭ rānj′ment) *n-* 1 a putting out of order; also, a condition of disorder. 2 insanity.

der·by (dûr′bē) *n-* [*pl.* **der·bies**] 1 man's hat of stiffened felt, having a narrow rolled brim and a rounded crown; bowler. 2 Derby (*Brit.* där′ bē) championship race for three-year-old horses.

der·e·lict (dĕr′ə lĭkt′) *adj-* 1 abandoned; run-down. 2 negligent; neglectful: *to be derelict in one's duty. n-* 1 anything cast away or forsaken; especially, a ship abandoned at sea. 2 person sunk to the lowest depths of degradation; tramp; bum.

Man wearing derby

der·e·lic·tion (dĕr′ə lĭk′shən) *n-* an abandoning or failure of responsibility; delinquency: *His failure to investigate was a serious dereliction of duty.*

de·ride (dĭ rīd′) *vt-* [**de·rid·ed, de·rid·ing**] to mock; laugh at; jeer: *The boys derided him for his vanity.*

de·ri·sion (də rĭzh′ən) *n-* ridicule; scorn; mockery.

de·ri·sive (də rī′sĭv, -zĭv) *adj-* expressing ridicule or scorn; jeering; mocking: *an outburst of derisive laughter.* **—*adv-* de·ri′ sive·ly. *n-* de·ri′ sive·ness.**

der·i·va·tion (dĕr′ə vā′ shən) *n-* 1 origin; source: *a tune of Turkish derivation.* 2 an obtaining of one thing from another by change or development: *the derivation of French law from Roman law.* 3 a recording or tracing of the development of a word from its original form and first meaning; etymology: *This dictionary gives the derivation of many words.* 4 *Grammar* a deriving of words from other words by adding prefixes and suffixes. The noun "darkness" may be derived from the adjective "dark" by adding the suffix "-ness"; the adjective "enjoyable" may be derived from the verb "enjoy" by adding the suffix "-able."

de·riv·a·tive (də rĭv′ə tĭv) *adj-* obtained from an earlier or primary source: *a list of derivative words; derivative products; the derivative benefits of a job abroad. n-*: *The word "canal" is a derivative of a Latin word (canalis) meaning "channel." Paper is a derivative of wood.*

de·rive (dĭ rīv′) *vt-* [**de·rived, de·riv·ing**] 1 to get or obtain (from): *to derive pleasure from a hobby.* 2 to trace the history of (a word) as far back as possible. *vi-*: *The word derives from French.*

der·mal (dûr′məl) *adj-* of or relating to the skin, especially to the dermis; cutaneous.

der·ma·tol·o·gist (dûr′mə tŏl′ə jĭst) *n-* doctor specializing in skin diseases.

de·scend (dĭ sĕnd′) *vi-* 1 to go or come down from a higher to a lower level: *The rain descended. The lawn descended to the lake.* 2 to come in force: *Relatives descended upon us Saturday.* 3 to pass by inheritance: *The estate descended from father to son.* 4 to come or be derived: *This custom descends from the ancient Greeks. vt-*: *We descended the stairs.*
be descended from to have as an ancestor or ancestry.

de·scend·ant (dĭ sĕn′dənt) *n-* person who is descended from a certain ancestor or family line.

de·scent (dĭ sĕnt′) *n-* 1 a going or coming down; movement to a lower level: *The airplane made a rapid descent.* 2 downward slope: *That hill was a sharp descent that is good for sledding.* 3 sudden attack or visit: *a descent by the hordes of locusts; a descent of week-end guests.* 4 ancestry: *She was of Spanish descent.* *Hom-* dissent.

dhow (dou) *n-* sailboat, usually having one mast and a lateen sail, used along the east coast of Africa.

di- *combining form* two; double: *a dioxide; dicotyledon.* [from Greek **di-**, from dis meaning "twice."]

dia- *combining form* (di- before vowels) through or across: *diathermy* (heating through); *diameter* (measurement through or across). [from a Greek prefix meaning "through (and through); across."]

di·a·be·tes (dī′ə bē′ tēz, -təs) *n-* disease characterized by an inability of the body to use carbohydrates, and due to the failure of the pancreas to produce sufficient insulin. Abnormally high amounts of unused sugar appear in the blood and the urine.

di·a·bet·ic (dī′ ə bĕt′ ĭk) *adj-* 1 of or relating to diabetes: *a diabetic symptom.* 2 having diabetes: *a diabetic child. n-* person having diabetes.

di·a·bol·ic (dī′ ə bŏl′ ĭk) or **di·a·bol·i·cal** (-ĭ kəl) *adj-* like a devil or his work; fiendish and inhuman: *a diabolic murder.* **—*adv-* di′ a·bol′ i·cal·ly.**

di·a·crit·ic (dī′ ə krĭt′ ĭk) *n-* diacritical mark. *adj-* diacritical.

di·a·crit·i·cal (dī′ ə krĭt′ ĭ kəl) *adj-* of a mark or sign, serving to indicate the sound value of a letter in the pronunciation of a word; diacritic. *n-* diacritical mark; diacritic. **—*adv-* di′ a·crit′ i·cal·ly.**

diacritical mark *n-* mark or sign that indicates the sound value of a letter in the pronunciation of a word; diacritic; diacritical. In the pronunciation of "cat," the diacritical mark [˘] over the "a" indicates a sound value similar to that in "fat," "sat," etc.

di·a·dem (dī′ ə dĕm′) *n-* 1 crown. 2 ornamental headband worn by royalty.

di·aer·e·sis (dī ĕr′ ə səs) *n-* dieresis.

di·ag·nose (dī′ əg nōs′) *vt-* [**di·ag·nosed, di·ag·nos·ing**] to identify or find out the nature of (a disease or other harmful condition) on the basis of certain signs or symptoms: *to diagnose measles; to diagnose an emotional difficulty.* **—*adj-* di′ ag·nos′ tic (-nŏs′ tĭk.)**

di·ag·no·sis (dī′ əg nō′ səs) *n-* [*pl.* **di·ag·no·ses** (-sēz′)] 1 investigation of the nature of a disease or other trouble: *According to the doctor's diagnosis it was mumps.* 2 the report of such an investigation: *The doctor sent his diagnosis of his patient's condition to a surgeon.*

di·ag·nos·ti·cian (dī′ əg nŏs tĭsh′ ən) *n-* person who makes diagnoses, especially a doctor skilled in this.

di·ag·o·nal (dī ăg′ ə nəl) *n-* in a polygon or polyhedron, a straight line that connects any two corners that are not adjacent or consecutive. *adj-* from corner across to corner; slanting; oblique: *Fay took a diagonal course across the field.* **—*adv-* di·ag′ o·nal·ly.**

DIAGONAL

dic·ta·tion (dĭk tā′ shən) *n-* 1 a speaking of words to be written down; also, the words that are written down: *The stenographer read the dictation back to him.* 2 a telling someone what to do; a commanding.

dic·ta·tor (dĭk′ tā tər, dĭk tā′-) *n-* 1 ruler who has unlimited power; absolute head of a government: *Caesar made himself dictator.* 2 person whose authority is accepted in some special field: *a dictator of fashion.*

dic·ta·tor·i·al (dĭk′ tə tôr′ ē əl) *adj-* of or like a dictator or his practices; autocratic; absolute: *a dictatorial policy.* **—*adv-* dic′ ta·tor′ i·al·ly.**

dic·ta·tor·ship (dĭk′ tā tər shĭp′, dĭk tā′-) *n-* 1 rule by a dictator or in the absolute manner of a dictator. 2 country, organization, etc., so ruled.

dic·tion (dĭk′ shən) *n-* 1 pronunciation and rhythm in speaking or singing; enunciation. 2 one's choice of words in speaking and writing; wording.

dic·tion·ar·y (dĭk′ shə nĕr′ ē) *n-* [*pl.* **dic·tion·ar·ies**] 1 book that lists words of a language in alphabetical order and explains them in the same language. A dictionary tells what words mean, how to pronounce them, and how to spell them, and may also show how words are used and where they come from. 2 book that lists words of one language and explains them in another language: *a French-English dictionary.*

dif·fer·en·ti·ate (dĭf′ ə rĕn′ shē āt′) vt- [dif·fer·en·ti·at·ed, dif·fer·en·ti·at·ing] 1 to mark off; single out as unlike: *Aging differentiates a really good cheese from an ordinary one.* 2 to observe an unlikeness or difference between; distinguish between; discriminate: *to differentiate the warbles of various birds.* vi- 1 to see or discover a difference; distinguish: *to differentiate between two similar colors.* 2 to become different: *Boys and girls differentiate more and more as they grow older.*

dif·fer·en·ti·a·tion (dĭf′ ə rĕn′ shē ā′ shən) n- 1 act of differentiating; a causing, observing, or marking out of difference between things. 2 change from likeness to unlikeness between things.

dif·fi·cult (dĭf′ ĭ kəlt, -kŭlt′) adj- 1 not easy; hard to do or understand: *a difficult problem; a difficult language.* 2 arduous; rigorous; trying: *Weather conditions were difficult.* 3 hard to get along with; not easily managed: *a difficult child; a difficult situation.*

dif·fi·cul·ty (dĭf′ ə kŭl′ tē) n- [pl. dif·fi·cul·ties] 1 hardness of doing; lack of easiness; rigor: *the difficulty of learning German; a task of great difficulty.* 2 source of trouble; unfortunate circumstance; obstacle: *The difficulty is that he's too small.* 3 conflict; trouble: *He's in difficulty with the law.* 4 **difficulties** disagreement; friction; quarrels.

be in difficulties to be short of money. **make difficulties** to raise objections; cause trouble. **with difficulty** only with great effort or hard work: *to read with difficulty.*

dif·fi·dence (dĭf′ ə dəns) n- lack of self-confidence; shyness; timidity: *Her diffidence makes her hard to talk with.*

dif·fi·dent (dĭf′ ə dənt) adj- lacking self-confidence; shy; timid: *a diffident smile.* —adv- **dif′ fi·dent·ly.**

dif·fract (dĭ frăkt′) vt- 1 to separate or break into parts. 2 to cause (light rays, X rays, etc.) to undergo diffraction.

dif·frac·tion (dĭ frăk′ shən) *Physics* n- 1 the bending or spreading of light or other radiation as it passes through a narrow slit or around the edges of an object. 2 a similar phenomenon of sound waves.

diffraction grating *Physics* n- device for diffracting light, X rays, and other electromagnetic waves. It is a glass or metal plate etched with many parallel grooves.

¹dif·fuse (dĭ fyōōz′) vt- [dif·fused, dif·fus·ing] to spread out or abroad from a source; send widely. vi-: *The dye diffused slowly through the water.*

²dif·fuse (dĭ fyōōs′) adj- 1 long and wordy: *a diffuse speech.* 2 spread thinly out or about; scattered: *a diffuse gas.* —adv- **dif·fuse′ ly.** n- **dif·fuse′ ness.**

dif·fu·sion (dĭ fyōō′ zhən) n- 1 a spreading: *the diffusion of knowledge by means of low-priced books; the diffusion of pollen by wind and insects.* 2 a natural spreading of one substance through another; the intermingling of molecules. 3 diffuseness. —adj- **dif·fu′ si·ble.**

di·gress (dĭ grĕs′, dī-) vi- to turn aside or get away from the main subject or line of argument.

di·gres·sion (dĭ grĕsh′ ən) n- a turning aside or wandering from the main subject: *a long digression on fate.*

di·gres·sive (dĭ grĕs′ ĭv) adj- tending to wander or turn aside from the main subject. —adv- **di·gress′ive·ly.** n- **di·gress′ ive·ness.**

dike (dīk) n- wall or bank built to hold back water and protect land from flooding: *In Holland, dikes hold back the sea.* vt- [diked, dik·ing] to protect from floods with a wall or bank: *Farmers along a river often dike their fields.*

Dike

di·lap·i·dat·ed (dĭ lăp′ ə dā′ təd) adj- run-down from neglect or hard use; fallen into ruin: *a dilapidated house; a dilapidated car.*

di·lap·i·da·tion (dĭ lăp′ ə dā′ shən) n- ruined or neglected condition; disrepair: *the dilapidation of an old house.*

di·lute (dĭ lōōt′, dī-) vt- [di·lut·ed, di·lut·ing] to weaken or thin by adding or mixing with something, especially water: *to dilute grape juice with water; to dilute the force of an argument.* adj-: *a dilute solution of soda.*

di·lu·tion (dĭ lōō′ shən, dī-) n- 1 a diluting or becoming diluted. 2 something that has been diluted.

dim (dĭm) adj- [dim·mer, dim·mest] 1 not bright or clear; having or giving little light: *the dim light of evening;* dim *headlights.* 2 not clearly or sharply seen; hazy; faint: *a dim figure in the shadows; to have only a dim idea of the truth.* 3 not seeing or perceiving clearly: *eyes dim with tears.* vt- [dimmed, dim·ming] to make less bright, clear, distinct, etc.: *The driver dimmed his headlights. Tears dimmed her eyes.* vi-: *The stars dimmed as dawn approached.* —adv- **dim′ ly.** n- **dim′ ness.**

dim. diminuendo.

dime (dīm) n- small silver coin of the United States or Canada, worth ten cents. [American word from French dime, from Old French *disme* meaning "a tithe," from Latin meaning "a tenth."]

di·men·sion (dĭ mĕn′ shən) n- 1 size in a particular direction; also, its measurement in linear units. 2 any of the three properties associated with length, area, and volume. Anything having length only is said to be of one dimension. Anything having area and not volume is said to be of two dimensions. Anything having volume is said to be of three dimensions, corresponding to the length, width, and depth of a rectangular box. 3 (also **dimensions**) importance; scope: *a plan of vast dimensions.*

di·nette (dī nĕt′) n- small room or area near a kitchen, used for eating meals.

ding (dĭng) n- high or tinkly sound made by a bell or chime. vi- to ring or chime shrilly.

ding-dong (dĭng′ dòng′, -dòng′) n- the sound of repeated strokes of a bell.

din·ghy (dĭng′ gē) n- [pl. din·ghies] any of various types of small boats, especially a small rowboat.

din·gle (dĭng′ gəl) n- small wooded valley; dell.

din·go (dĭng′ gō) n- [pl. din·goes] wild dog of Australia.

din·gy (dĭn′ jē) adj- [din·gi·er, din·gi·est] not bright, fresh, or clean; dull; dirty: *a dingy house; dingy colors.* —adv- **din′ gi·ly.** n- **din′ gi·ness.**

dining car n- railroad car in which meals are served.

dining room n- room in which meals are usually served in a home, or in a hotel or other public place.

dink·ey (dĭng′ kē) n- [pl. din·keys] small locomotive used in logging, in railroad yards, etc. *Hom-* dinky.

din·ky (dĭng′ kē) *Informal* adj- [din·ki·er, din·ki·est] small and insignificant. *Hom-* dinkey.

din·ner (dĭn′ ər) n- 1 main meal of the day, generally the evening meal on weekdays but the midday meal on holidays and among country·people. 2 formal meal given in honor of some person or occasion. *as modifier: a dinner table; dinner dress.*

di·no·saur (dī′ nə sòr′) n- any of several kinds of reptiles that lived millions of years ago, especially certain giant reptiles, the largest land animals that ever lived.

dint (dĭnt) *Archaic* vt- to dent. n- a dent.

by dint of by force or exertion of: *We finished the task on time by dint of great effort.*

di·o·cese (dī′ ə səs, -sēs′) n- the church district under the authority of a bishop.

di·ode (dī′ ōd′) n- 1 electron tube that has two electrodes (a cathode and an anode) and is used especially to change alternating current into direct current. 2 rectifier or other device using a semiconductor that operates like a two-electrode electron tube.

Di·o·ny·sus (dī′ ə nī′ səs) n- in Greek mythology, a son of Zeus and god of wine and fertility. He is identified with the Roman Bacchus.

di·o·ra·ma (dī′ ə răm′ ə) n- an arrangement, usually for exhibit, of lifelike models of plants, animals, human figures, etc., shown in a setting that blends into a realistic painted background.

di·ox·ide (dī ŏk′ sīd′) n- oxide containing two atoms of oxygen per molecule.

dip·lo·mat (dĭp′ lə măt′) n- 1 person trained in and usually engaged in handling problems and relations between nations. 2 tactful and persuasive person. Also **di·plo′ ma·tist** (dĭ plō′ mə tĭst′).

dip·so·ma·ni·ac (dĭp′ sə mā′ nē ăk′) n- an alcoholic.

dip·ter·ous (dĭp′ tər əs) adj- of or belonging to an order (Diptera) of insects having a single pair of wings, including the flies, mosquitoes, and gnats.

dip·tych (dĭp'tĭk') *n-* set of paintings, carvings, etc., made on two panels hinged together.

dire (dīər) *adj-* [dir·er, dir·est] extremely bad; dreadful; grave: *in dire need.* —*adv-* dire'ly. *n-* dire'ness.

di·rect (dĭ rĕkt', dī-) *vt-* 1 to manage the work or operation of; control; conduct: *to direct the affairs of a nation; to direct traffic; to direct a play.* 2 to order or instruct; command: *to direct the troops to advance.* 3 to show or tell the way to; lead or guide: *Can you direct me to the post office?* 4 to aim or address: *to direct one's energies toward one's work; to direct one's remarks to the class.* 5 to write the address on (a letter, package, etc.). *adj-* 1 straight; not roundabout: *a direct route.* 2 straightforward; frank; honest: *a direct answer.* 3 not through an intervening medium or source: *in direct contact; to have direct knowledge; a direct quotation.* 4 absolute; complete; exact: *the direct opposite.* 5 in an unbroken line of descent: *the direct heir to the throne.* *adv-* without intervening stops; directly: *This plane flies direct to Chicago.* — *n-* di·rect'ness.

direct current *n-* electric current, such as that from batteries and certain generators, that flows continuously in the same direction. *Abbr.* D.C. See also *alternating current.*

direct discourse *n-* exact quotation of what has been said or written. Example: She said, "I am going to the park." See also *indirect discourse.*

directed number *n-* any member of the set of integers.

direct evidence *n-* evidence that deals with the main facts to be proved, given by a witness who testifies directly of his own knowledge. An eye-witness account is direct evidence. See also *circumstantial evidence.*

di·rec·tion (dĭ rĕk'shən, dī-) *n-* 1 course or line of motion, attention, purpose, etc.: *to travel in an easterly direction; much progress in many directions.* 2 a directing or controlling; management; guidance: *to work under another's direction.* 3 (usually **directions**) instruction; order: *Read the directions.* 4 address on a letter, package, etc.

di·rec·tion·al (dĭ rĕk'shən əl, dī-) *adj-* 1 having to do with or indicating direction. 2 sending or receiving sound or radio signals in a specified direction only: *a directional antenna; a directional microphone.*

direction finder *n-* receiving device for finding the direction toward radio transmitters.

di·rec·tive (dĭ rĕk'tĭv, dī-) *n-* an order, regulation, instruction, etc.: *a military directive.*

di·rect·ly (dĭ rĕkt'lē, dī-) *adv-* 1 in a direct line or manner; straight: *Travel directly north.* 2 *Informal* immediately; at once: *I'll take the medicine directly.*

direct object See ²*object.*

di·rec·tor (dĭ rĕk'tər, dī-) *n-* 1 person who directs or manages. 2 person who guides and controls the performance of a play, motion picture, etc. 3 member of the board that controls a business corporation. 4 device that points or aims a gun, telescope, etc.

di·rec·to·rate (dĭ rĕk'tər ət, dī-) *n-* 1 group of directors. 2 the position or authority of a director.

di·rec·to·ry (dĭ rĕk'tə rē, dī-) *n-* [*pl.* di·rec·to·ries] list or collection of names, addresses, etc., usually in alphabetical order: *a telephone directory.*

direct primary *n-* primary election at which the nominees of a political party are chosen directly by the voters instead of by delegates to a nominating convention.

direct proportion *n-* relation between two variables such that their ratio always remains the same.

direct tax *n-* tax, such as one on income or inherited property, that must be paid directly by the taxpayer to the government. See also *indirect tax.*

direct variation *n-* the keeping of a constant ratio between the values of two variables; the variation that satisfies the equation $y = kx$, where k is a constant; variation in direct proportion.

dis- *prefix* 1 not; the opposite of: *a disobedient child; sharp disagreement.* 2 fail to; cease to; refuse to: *to dissatisfy; to disagree; to disobey.* 3 do the reverse of: *to disentangle.* 4 lack of: *a disunion.* [from Latin *dis-* meaning "apart; away; opposite."]

dis·al·low (dĭs'ə lou') *vt-* to refuse to admit or allow the truth, reliability, etc., of; reject: *to disallow his claim.* —*n-* dis'al·low'ance: *the disallowance of his claim.*

dis·ap·pear (dĭs'ə pêr') *vi-* 1 to go out of sight; become invisible; vanish: *The ship disappeared over the horizon.* 2 to cease to exist: *Many old customs have disappeared.*

dis·ap·pear·ance (dĭs'ə pêr'əns) *n-* a passing from sight or existence; a vanishing.

dis·ap·point (dĭs'ə point') *vt-* 1 to fail to satisfy the hopes or expectations of: *The bad performance disappointed his admirers.* 2 to thwart or put an end to (hopes, aims, etc.). —*adv-* dis'ap·point'ing·ly.

dis·ap·point·ed (dĭs'ə point'təd) *adj-* 1 saddened or disturbed because one's hopes or expectations have not been fulfilled: *a disappointed suitor.* 2 not fulfilled; thwarted.

dis·ap·point·ment (dĭs'ə point'mənt) *n-* 1 a disappointing; *his disappointment of their hopes.* 2 a feeling of being disappointed: *They couldn't hide their disappointment.* 3 person or thing that disappoints.

dis·ap·pro·ba·tion (dĭs'ăp'rə bā'shən) *n-* disapproval.

dis·ap·prov·al (dĭs'ə prōō'vəl) *n-* the act of disapproving; dislike; unfavorable feeling.

dis·ap·prove (dĭs'ə prōōv') *vi-* [dis·ap·proved, dis·ap·prov·ing] to refuse to approve; have a bad or unfavorable opinion (of) someone or something: *She disapproved of his new necktie.* *vt-:* to disapprove *a request.* —*adv-* dis'ap·prov'ing·ly.

dis·arm (dĭs ärm') *vt-* 1 to take a weapon or weapons from: *He disarmed the bandit.* 2 to remove doubts or unfriendly feelings of; win over: *He disarmed me with his smile.* *vi-* to reduce one's armed forces and weapons. —*adv-* dis·arm'ing·ly: *He smiled disarmingly.*

dis·ar·ma·ment (dĭs är'mə mənt) *n-* a ceasing to use or a putting aside of weapons, especially the reduction of weapons and men in the armed forces.

dis·ar·range (dĭs'ə rānj') *vt-* [dis·ar·ranged, dis·ar·rang·ing] to disturb the arrangement of; put in disorder. —*n-* dis'ar·range'ment.

dis·ar·ray (dĭs'ə rā') *n-* condition of disorder, untidiness, or confusion. *vt-* to throw into disorder.

dis·as·sem·ble (dĭs'ə sĕm'bəl) *vt-* [dis·as·sem·bled, dis·as·sem·bling] to take apart; separate into component parts: *to disassemble a machine.*

►Should not be confused with DISSEMBLE.

dis·as·so·ci·ate (dĭs'ə sō'sē ăt', -shē ăt') *vt-* [dis·as·so·ci·at·ed, dis·as·so·ci·at·ing] to dissociate. —*n-* dis'as·so'ci·a'tion.

dis·as·ter (dĭ zăs'tər) *n-* something that causes great trouble or suffering; great misfortune; calamity.

dis·as·trous (dĭ zăs'trəs) *adj-* causing great misfortune, destruction, trouble, etc.: *a disastrous flood; a disastrous accident.* —*adv-* dis·as'trous·ly. *n-* dis·as'trous·ness.

dis·a·vow (dĭs'ə vou') *vt-* to refuse to claim or accept as one's own; deny; disown: *to disavow a belief.*

dis·a·vow·al (dĭs'ə vou'əl) *n-* a disavowing; denial.

dis·band (dĭs bănd') *vt-* to break up and dismiss (an organized group of people): *to disband a regiment.* *vi-:* *The marchers disbanded after the parade.*

dis·bar (dĭs bär') *vt-* [dis·barred, dis·bar·ring] to deprive (a lawyer) of the right to practice his profession. —*n-* dis·bar'ment.

disc jockey *Informal n-* person who broadcasts a program of music from records.

dis·claim (dĭs klām') *vt-* to refuse to claim or accept; deny; disown: *to disclaim responsibility for an action.*

dis·claim·er (dĭs klā'mər) *n-* statement denying responsibility, knowledge, connection, etc.; denial.

dis·close (dĭs klōz') *vt-* [dis·closed, dis·clos·ing] 1 to uncover and make visible; bring to light: *Their digging disclosed a buried treasure.* 2 to make known; reveal: *to disclose secret information.*

dis·clo·sure (dĭs klō'zhər) *n-* 1 a revealing or disclosing; also, an instance of this: *The disclosure of the epidemic frightened many.* 2 means of disclosing: *The speech was a disclosure of bribery.*

dis·col·or (dĭs kŭl'ər) *vt-* to change or spoil the color of; stain: *The acid discolored his skin.* *vi-:* *cloth guaranteed not to discolor in strong sunlight.*

dis·crep·an·cy (dĭs krĕp′ ən sē) *n-* [*pl.* **dis·crep·an·cies**] difference; variance; lack of agreement: *the discrepancy between the two stories*. Also **dis·crep′ance.**

dis·crep·ant (dĭs krĕp′ ənt) *adj-* differing; disagreeing; at variance: *two discrepant explanations*.

dis·crete (dĭs krēt′) *adj-* separate and distinct: *When sugar is melted, its discrete grains melt into a mass.* Hom- discreet.

dis·cre·tion (dĭs krĕsh′ ən) *n-* 1 ability or habit of being discreet; good judgement; prudence; tact. 2 freedom of choice or action: *Let's leave that to his discretion.*

dis·cre·tion·ar·y (dĭs krĕsh′ ən ĕr′ ē) *adj-* meant to be used by choice when needed: *In some matters the police have discretionary powers.*

dis·crim·i·nate (dĭs krĭm′ ə nāt′) *vt-* [**dis·crim·i·nat·ed, dis·crim·i·nat·ing**] 1 to note small differences; distinguish or make a distinction: *to discriminate between good and inferior writers.* 2 to treat people differently and often badly because of race, religion, etc.; apply prejudice: *to discriminate against minority groups. vt-: to discriminate good books from bad.*

dis·crim·i·nat·ing (dĭs krĭm′ ə nā′ tĭng) *adj-* 1 able to make small distinctions; discerning: *a discriminating taste in music.* 2 serving to identify or single out; differentiating. —*adv-* **dis·crim′ i·nat′ ing·ly.**

dis·crim·i·na·tion (dĭs krĭm′ ə nā′ shən) *n-* 1 a noting of fine differences; discernment: *to buy without discrimination.* 2 a distinction made or noted: *I agree with that discrimination.* 3 ability to discriminate. 4 difference in treatment or attitude: *without discrimination as to creed or color.*

dis·crim·i·na·tive (dĭs krĭm′ ə nə tĭv′) *adj-* making or noting distinctions. —*adv-* **dis·crim′ i·na·tive·ly.**

dis·crim·i·na·tor (dĭs krĭm′ ə nā′ tər) *n-* 1 person who discriminates. 2 radio circuit used in FM receivers to change variations of frequency into variations in the strength of a current.

dis·crim·i·na·to·ry (dĭs krĭm′ ə nə tôr′ ē) *adj-* making distinctions, especially unfair ones based on prejudice.

dis·cus (dĭs′ kəs) *n-* heavy metal and wood disk that is thicker at the center than at the rim. It is thrown for distance in athletic contests.

dis·cuss (dĭs′ kŭs′) *vt-* to talk over thoughtfully; consider; debate: *He will discuss the political situation.*

dis·cus·sant (dĭs kŭs′ ənt) *n-* person who takes part in a discussion, especially as an authority on a particular subject.

dis·cus·sion (dĭs kŭsh′ ən) *n-* 1 exchange of ideas among persons: *The article stimulated a discussion.* 2 a handling or presentation of a subject; lecture: *His discussion was illustrated by charts.*

dis·dain (dĭs dān′) *vt-* to show contempt for; look down upon: *She disdained everyone outside her set. n-* a looking down upon; contempt; scorn: *to treat with disdain.*

dis·dain·ful (dĭs dān′ fəl) *adj-* showing disdain; haughty: *His disdainful attitude made many enemies.* —*adv-* **dis·dain′ ful·ly.** *n-* **dis·dain′ ful·ness.**

dis·ease (dĭ zēz′) *n-* 1 disorder of mind or body marked by definite symptoms; illness; sickness. 2 any particular instance or kind of such disorder: *Measles and tuberculosis are diseases.*

dis·eased (dĭ zēzd′) *adj-* 1 suffering from a disease. 2 showing the effects of a disease.

dis·em·bark (dĭs′ ĕm bärk′) *vi-* to leave a ship or aircraft; to land; debark: *The students disembarked at New York. vt-: We shall disembark the passengers at Pier 23.* —*n-* **dis·em′ bar·ka′ tion.**

dis·hon·or·a·ble (dĭs ŏn′ ər ə bəl) *adj-* not honorable. —*n-* **dis·hon′ or·a·ble·ness.** *adv-* **dis·hon′ or·a·bly.**

dis·il·lu·sion (dĭs′ ə lōō′ shən) *vt-* to set free from a mistaken belief in the goodness or value of some person or thing: *We were disillusioned by his dishonesty.* —*n-* **dis′ il·lu′ sion·ment.**

dis·in·clined (dĭs′ ĭn klīnd′) *adj-* not feeling like or wanting to; loath; unwilling: *A lazy person is disinclined to work.* —*n-* **dis·in′ cli·na′ tion** (-klə nā′shən).

dis·in·fect (dĭs′ ĭn fĕkt′) *vt-* to make free from harmful germs. —*n-* **dis′ in·fec′ tion.**

dis·join (dĭs join′) *vt-* to part, separate, or detach (some· thing). *vi-: We watched the two cells disjoin.*

dis·joint (dĭs joint′) *vt-* 1 to separate at the joints: *to disjoint a turkey.* 2 to put out of joint; dislocate.

dis·joint·ed (dĭs joint′ təd) *adj-* 1 unconnected; incoherent: *a disjointed speech.* 2 dislocated. 3 taken apart at the joints. —*adv-* **dis·joint′ ed·ly.**

disk (dĭsk) *n-* 1 circular object, usually thin and flat. 2 *Astronomy* the flat appearance of a heavenly body when viewed from the earth: *the sun's disk.* 3 central part of the flower head of the daisy, aster, etc. bearing tiny, tubular flowers. 4 *Informal* a phonograph record. Also **disc.**

Disk

disk harrow *n-* farm implement having rows of disks which cut up the soil. For picture, see *harrow*.

dis·like (dĭs līk′) *vt-* [**dis·liked, dis·lik·ing**] to have a feeling against; not like: *She dislikes visiting the dentist. n-* a feeling against someone or something; distaste.

dis·lo·cate (dĭs′ lō kāt′) *vt-* [**dis·lo·cat·ed, dis·lo·cat·ing**] 1 to force out of place; especially, to put (a bone) out of joint. 2 to upset; throw into confusion: *The depression dislocated the normal workings of the economy.*

dis·lo·ca·tion (dĭs′ lō kā′shən) *n-* a dislocating; a forcing out of place; also, the result of this: *a dislocation of the shoulder.*

dis·lodge (dĭs lŏj′) *vt-* [**dis·lodged, dis·lodg·ing**] to move or force out of position: *The earthquake dislodged massive boulders.*

dis·loy·al (dĭs loi′ əl) *adj-* not loyal: *to be disloyal to one's friends.* —*adv-* **dis·loy′ al·ly.**

dis·loy·al·ty (dĭs loi′ əl tē) *n-* [*pl.* **dis·loy·al·ties**] falseness to duty, government, friends etc.; faithlessness.

dis·mal (dĭz′ məl) *adj-* 1 gloomy; dreary; cheerless: *a dismal swamp.* 2 depressed; sad: *a dismal mood.* —*adv-* **dis′ mal·ly.**

dis·man·tle (dĭs măn′ təl) *vt-* [**dis·man·tled, dis·man·tling**] 1 to strip of furniture, equipment, etc.: *to dismantle a house.* 2 to take apart: *to dismantle a machine.*

dis·may (dĭs mā′) *vt-* to take away the courage of; frighten; dishearten; daunt: *The surprise attack dismayed them. n-* sudden loss of courage; frightened amazement: *our dismay at finding our car missing.*

dis·mem·ber (dĭs mĕm′ bər) *vt-* 1 to cut or tear off one part from another, especially limb from body. 2 to sever into parts and distribute; divide: *to dismember a country.* —*n-* **dis·mem′ ber·ment.**

dis·miss (dĭs mĭs′) *vt-* 1 to send away; direct or allow to leave: *to dismiss a class.* 2 to discharge; remove from office or employment: *to dismiss a clerk.* 3 to refuse to consider further: *The judge dismissed the case.*

dis·miss·al (dĭs mĭs′ əl) *n-* a dismissing: *the dismissal of the class; a dismissal from employment; the judge's dismissal of the case.*

dis·mount (dĭs mount′) *vi-* to get off or down (from) something: *to dismount from a horse. vt-* 1 to remove (something) from its setting, mounting, support, etc.: *to dismount a cannon.* 2 to take apart; dismantle: *to dismount a watch.*

dis·o·be·di·ence (dĭs′ ə bē′ dē əns) *n-* refusal to obey; failure to follow a rule or command.

dis·o·be·di·ent (dĭs′ ə bē′ dē ənt) *adj-* not obedient: *a disobedient child.* —*adv-* **dis′ o·be′ di·ent·ly.**

dis·o·bey (dĭs′ ə bā′) *vt-* to refuse or fail to obey: *to disobey parents; to disobey rules. vi-: He often disobeys.*

dis·o·blige (dĭs′ ə blīj′) *vt-* [**dis·o·bliged, dis·o·blig·ing**] to refuse or neglect to help or please (someone): *I hate to disoblige you, but I must leave now.*

dis·qui·et (dĭs kwī′ ət) *vt-* to make uneasy, anxious, or restless; disturb: *The sudden silence disquieted him. n-* uneasiness; anxiety: *A feeling of disquiet spread through the waiting crowd.*

dis·qui·e·tude (dĭs kwī′ ə tōōd′, -tyōōd′) *n-* uneasiness of mind; anxiety; restlessness: *Her disquietude increased when she found she was alone in the house.*

dis·qui·si·tion (dĭs′ kwə zĭsh′ ən) *n-* a formal and thorough discussion; dissertation.

dis·re·gard (dĭs′ rĭ gärd′) *vt-* to pay no attention to; ignore: *He* disregarded *the traffic lights. n-* **1** refusal to pay attention: *his* disregard *for traffic lights.* **2** lack of respect: *his* disregard *of my feelings.*

dis·re·mem·ber (dĭs′ rĭ mĕm′ bər) *Informal vt-* to forget; be unable to recall. *vi-*: *He told me his name, but I* disremember.

dis·re·pair (dĭs′ rĭ pâr′) *n-* poor or unmended condition: *The century-old house was in* disrepair.

dis·rep·u·ta·ble (dĭs rĕp′ yə tə bəl) *adj-* **1** of bad reputation; shady: *Not all* disreputable *people are in jail.* **2** not respectable: *a* disreputable *old coat.* —*n-* **dis·rep′ u·ta·ble·ness.** *adv-* **dis·rep′ u·ta·bly.**

dis·re·pute (dĭs′ rĭ pyōōt′) *n-* bad reputation; discredit: *Imperialism is now in* disrepute.

dis·re·spect (dĭs′ rĭ spĕkt′) *n-* lack of respect; rudeness.

dis·re·spect·ful (dĭs′ rĭ spĕkt′ fəl) *adj-* rude; lacking in respect. —*adv-* **dis·re·spect′ ful·ly.** *n-* **dis·re·spect′ ful·ness.**

dis·robe (dĭs rōb′) *vi-* [dis·robed, dis·rob·ing] to take one's clothes off: *He slowly* disrobed. *vt-*: *She* disrobed *the child.*

dis·rup·tive (dĭs rŭp′ tĭv) *adj-* tending to disrupt; causing disruption. —*adv-* **dis·rup′ tive·ly.** *n-* **dis·rup′ tive·ness.**

dis·sat·is·fac·tion (dĭs′ săt′ əs făk′ shən) *n-* discontent; lack of satisfaction: *a* dissatisfaction *with one's life.*

dis·sat·is·fied (dĭs săt′ əs fīd′) *adj-* not pleased; discontented: *He is a* dissatisfied *man.*

dis·sat·is·fy (dĭs săt′ əs fī′) *vt-* [dis·sat·is·fied, dis·sat·is·fy·ing] to displease or cause discontent to (someone), especially by the lack of something: *The layout of the house* dissatisfied *her.*

dis·sect (dĭ sĕkt′, dī′-) *vt-* **1** to cut (an animal or plant) in pieces in order to study or examine the inner parts: *The biology class* dissected *frogs last week.* **2** to study or analyze part by part: *The teacher* dissected *my report.*

dis·sem·ble (dĭ sĕm′ bəl) *vt-* [dis·sem·bled, dis·sem·bling] to hide under a false appearance: *to* dissemble *one's feelings. vi-*: *Some people cannot* dissemble. —*n-* **dis·sem′ bler.**

►Should not be confused with DISASSEMBLE.

dis·sem·i·nate (dĭ sĕm′ ə nāt′) *vt-* [dis·sem·i·nat·ed, dis·sem·i·nat·ing] to scatter; diffuse; give out; spread abroad: *to* disseminate *news.* —*n-* **dis·sem′ i·na′ tion.**

dis·sen·sion (dĭ sĕn′ shən) *n-* quarreling; angry disagreement because of difference of opinion; ill feeling: *A border dispute caused lasting* dissension.

dis·sent (dĭ sĕnt′) *vi-* to disagree; to have a different opinion: *Only one person* dissented *from the agreement. n-* difference in opinion: *a* dissent *from the majority.* *Hom-* descent.

dis·sent·er (dĭ sĕn′ tər) *n-* **1** one who disagrees with the majority or with established ideas, especially in religion or politics. **2 Dissenter** in Great Britain, a person not in conformity with the state church.

dis·ser·ta·tion (dĭ′ sər tā′ shən) *n-* formal, spoken, or written discourse on a subject; especially, a thesis written by a candidate for the Ph.D. degree.

dis·ser·vice (dĭs sûr′ vəs) *n-* harm; injury: *to do someone a great* disservice.

dis·sev·er (dĭ sĕv′ ər) *vt-* to sever completely.

dis·si·dent (dĭs′ ə dənt) *adj-* dissenting; differing; disagreeing: *a* dissident *voice. n-* one who differs from, or agrees: *a* dissenter. —*n-* **dis′ si·dence.**

dis·sim·i·lar (dĭ sĭm′ ə lər) *adj-* different; unlike: *two brothers with* dissimilar *tastes.* —*adv-* **dis·sim′ i·lar·ly.**

dis·so·nant (dĭs′ ə nənt) *adj-* not harmonious; discordant: *the* dissonant *sounds from my brother's battered trumpet; our* dissonant *views.* —*adv-* **dis′ so·nant·ly.**

dis·suade (dĭ swād′) *vt-* [dis·suad·ed, dis·suad·ing] to persuade or advise (someone) against doing something: *We* dissuaded *him from going.* —*n-* **dis·sua′ sion.**

dis·sua·sive (dĭ swā′ sĭv, -zĭv) *adj-* tending to dissuade: *a* dissuasive *argument.* —*adv-* **dis·sua′ sive·ly.** *n-* **dis·sua′ sive·ness.**

dis·taff (dĭs′ stăf′) *n-* a stick around which wool, flax, etc., is wound for use in spinning.

distaff side *n-* female side of a family.

dis·til·late (dĭs′ tə lāt′, -lət) *n-* product obtained by the process of distillation.

dis·til·la·tion (dĭs′ tə lā′ shən) *n-* **1** the process of heating a liquid or a solid until it forms a vapor, leading the vapor into a separate vessel, and condensing it by cooling. **2** a distillate.

dis·till·er (dĭ stĭl′ ər) *n-* person or thing that distills, especially an individual or company that makes liquors by distillation.

dis·till·er·y (dĭ stĭl′ ə rē) *n-* [pl. dis·till·er·ies] **1** industrial plant designed to carry out distillation. **2** factory for making and distilling alcoholic liquors.

dis·tinct (dĭ stĭngkt′) *adj-* **1** different; separate: *two* distinct *kinds of animals.* **2** clear; plain: *a* distinct *pronunciation.* **3** very definite; unmistakable: *a* distinct *improvement.* —*adv-* **dis·tinct′ ly:** *a* distinctly *helpful suggestion.* *n-* **dis·tinct′ ness.**

dis·tinc·tion (dĭ stĭngk′ shən) *n-* **1** the making of a difference: *to treat everybody alike without* distinction *as to race or creed.* **2** difference; point of difference: *to note the* distinction *between mice and rats.* **3** excellence; superiority: *a writer of* distinction. **4** mark of favor or honor: *A Nobel Prize is among his* distinctions.

dis·tinc·tive (dĭ stĭngk′ tĭv) *adj-* marking a difference from others: *They wore* distinctive *uniforms.* —*adv-* **dis·tinc′ tive·ly.** *n-* **dis·tinc′ tive·ness.**

dis·tin·guish (dĭ stĭng′ gwĭsh) *vt-* **1** to mark as different; to set apart: *Their uniforms* distinguish *soldiers, sailors, and marines from each other.* **2** to see clearly the difference between (two things): *He could not* distinguish *right from wrong.* **3** to perceive; recognize: *The captain could* distinguish *a lighthouse through the fog.* **4** to bring fame or honor on (oneself): *He* distinguished *himself by his courage on the battlefield. vi-* to note or make differences (between or among): *Can you* distinguish *between the two sets of instructions?* —*adj-* **dis·tin′ guish·a·ble.** *adv-* **dis·tin′ guish·a·bly.**

dis·tin·guished (dĭ stĭng′ gwĭsht) *adj-* **1** famous for outstanding achievement; celebrated; eminent: *a* distinguished *statesman.* **2** showing distinction.

dis·tort (dĭ stôrt′, -stôrt′) *vt-* **1** to change the shape of; twist: *Pain* distorted *his face.* **2** to twist the original meaning of; misrepresent: *They* distorted *my speech.*

dis·tor·tion (dĭ stôr′ shən, dī stôr′-) *n-* **1** a distorting or being distorted: *a* distortion *of the truth.* **2** something distorted: *a newspaper filled with* distortions.

dis·tract (dĭ străkt′) *vt-* **1** to draw away the mind or attention of; divert: *Music* distracts *her from troubles.* **2** to confuse or bewilder; perplex: *All my directions serve only to* distract *him.* **3** to make crazy; drive mad: *That constant noise must stop before it* distracts *me entirely.*

dis·tract·ed (dĭ străk′ təd) *adj-* **1** harassed; confused. **2** insane; mad. —*adv-* **dis·tract′ ed·ly.**

dis·trac·tion (dĭ străk′ shən) *n-* **1** something that turns the attention from something: *Television is a* distraction *when you are also trying to read.* **2** amusement; diversion: *Alice needed some* distraction *after her examinations.* **3** confusion; perplexity: *In his* distraction *after the accident, he forgot his name.* **4** madness; frenzy: *That noise drives me to* distraction. —*adj-* **dis·trac′ tive.**

dis·trait (dĭ strā′) *adj-* absent-minded.

dis·traught (dĭ strôt′) *adj-* **1** deeply troubled and confused; distressed; agitated: *a* distraught *mother.* **2** insane; mad. —*adv-* **dis·traught′ ly.**

dis·tress (dĭ strĕs′) *n-* **1** misery; sorrow; pain: *She is in great* distress *over the illness of her son.* **2** danger; —*adv-* **dis·turbed** (dĭ stûrbd′) *adj-* mentally troubled or ill.

dis·ul·fide or **di·sul·phide** (dī sŭl′ fīd′) *n-* a sulfide that contains two atoms of sulfur in each molecule: *carbon* disulfide (CS_2).

dis·un·ion (dĭs yōōn′ yən) *n-* **1** lack of agreement or union. **2** a breaking apart; separation.

dis·u·nite (dĭs′ yōō nīt′) *vt-* [dis·u·nit·ed, dis·u·nit·ing] to break up the unity of; separate; divide.

dis·u·ni·ty (dĭs yōō′ nə tē) *n-* [pl. dis·u·ni·ties] lack of unity or agreement; disunion.

dis·use (dĭs yōōs′) *n-* condition of not being used or practiced; neglect: *a custom that has fallen into* disuse.

dith·er (dith'ər) *n-* condition of nervous excitement or confusion; agitation: *I'm in a dither about the party.*

dit·to (dit'ō) *n-* [*pl.* dit·tos] 1 the same as before, represented in writing by ditto marks. *Abbr.* do. 2 any duplicate.

ditto marks *n- pl.* two marks ["] placed under something written or printed to indicate that it is to be repeated. Example: Add 5 and 10
3   4

dit·ty (dit'ē) *n-* [*pl.* dit·ties] short, light song.

di·ur·nal (dī ûr'nəl) *adj-* 1 occurring every day; daily: *the diurnal rotation of the earth*; diurnal *chores.* 2 occurring or active in the daytime: *a diurnal insect.* 3 opening in the daytime and closing at night: *a diurnal flower.* —*adv-* di·ur'nal·ly.

di·van (dī'van, di vān') *n-* long, low, cushioned seat, usually having no back or ends.

dive (dīv) *vi-* [dived *or* dove (dōv), div·ing] 1 to plunge headfirst: *She dived from the prow of the boat into the waves.* 2 to go under water; submerge: *to dive seven fathoms; to dive for coins.* 3 to go quickly and deeply into something: *to dive into one's pocket; to dive into a book; to dive into a hallway. vt-: to dive a plane n-* sudden downward plunge: *The market took a dive.*

dive bomber *n-* type of warplane that releases its bombs while diving at the target.

div·er (dī'vər) *n-* 1 person or animal who dives into the water; especially, a person who dives in diving competitions. 2 person who makes a living by going beneath water for pearls, sponges, treasure, etc.

di·verge (dī vûrj', di-) *vi-* [di·verged, di·verg·ing] 1 to go out from a point; branch out: *The road diverges around the lake.* 2 to differ: *Our opinions diverge on politics.*

di·ver·gence (dī vûr'jəns, di-) *n-* 1 a branching out from a common point: *the divergence of two roads.* 2 a turning aside from a main course or standard: *a divergence from one's principles.* 3 difference: *a divergence of opinion.*

di·ver·gent (dī vûr'jənt, di-) *adj-* 1 diverging from a point: *the two divergent forks of a stream.* 2 differing: *two divergent opinions.* —*adv-* di·ver'gent·ly.

di·vers (dī'vərz) *adj-* several or various: *He has lived in divers places in the world.*

di·verse (di vûrs', dī'-) *adj-* 1 clearly different: *They have diverse views.* 2 varied; diversified: *She has diverse interests.* —*adv-* di·verse'ly. *n-* di·verse'ness.

di·ver·si·fi·ca·tion (dī vûr'sə fə kā'shən) *n-* a diversifying: *the diversification of a business.*

di·ver·si·fy (dī vûr'sə fī') *vt-* [di·ver·si·fied, di·ver·si·fy·ing] to give variety to; vary: *to diversify one's reading. vi-* in business, to invest in several different lines or products.

di·ver·sion (dī vûr'zhən, di-) *n-* 1 pastime; recreation; amusement: *Her favorite diversion was dancing.* 2 a turning something aside or in a different direction: *the diversion of a stream from its original course.* 3 a turning of attention in a different direction: *A diversion was created by a surprise attack from another point.*

di·ver·sion·a·ry (dī vûr'zhə nĕr'ē, di-) *adj-* turning the attention in a different direction: *a diversionary enemy attack.*

di·ver·si·ty (dī vûr'sə tē, di-) *n-* [*pl.* di·ver·si·ties] variety or difference: *a diversity of opinion; a diversity of color.*

di·vert (dī vûrt', di-) *vt-* 1 to turn aside or in a different direction: *Traffic was diverted until the highway was repaired. The band diverted our attention from the game.* 2 to amuse; entertain: *The movie diverted us.*

div·i·na·tion (div'ə nā'shən) *n-* 1 act or process of divining: *his divination of my purpose.* 2 something divined; a prophecy or guess.

¹di·vine (di vīn') *adj-* 1 of, coming from, or having to do with God: *His divine purpose; divine worship.* 2 seemingly more than human; godlike. 3 *Informal* delightful; divine: *What divine weather! n-* clergyman; priest. [from Old French *divin*, from Latin *divinus* meaning "godlike."] —*adv-* di·vine'ly: *a divinely planned universe.*

di·vi·sion·al (di vizh'ə nəl) *adj-* of or related to a division, especially a military division.

di·vi·sor (di vī'zər) *n-* number by which another number is divided: *In 96 ÷ 3, the divisor is 3.*

di·vorce (di vôrs') *n-* 1 legal ending of a marriage: *to sue for divorce.* 2 complete separation: *a divorce between intentions and acts. vt-* [di·vorced, di·vorc·ing]: *to divorce one's wife; to divorce the two subjects entirely.*

di·vor·cée (də vôr'sā', -sē', *also* də vôr'sā') *n-* a divorced woman.

div·ot (div'ət) *n-* small piece of turf torn up by a golf stroke.

di·vulge (di vŭlj') *vt-* [di·vulged, di·vulg·ing] to make known; reveal; disclose: *to divulge a secret.*

Dix·ie (dĭk'sē) *n-* 1 those States that made up the Confederacy during the Civil War; southern United States. 2 song about the South written in 1859, popular especially in the Confederate States.

Dix·ie·land (dĭk'sē lănd') *n-* 1 style of jazz that originated in New Orleans. 2 southern United States; Dixie.

diz·zy (dĭz'ē) *adj-* [diz·zi·er, diz·zi·est] 1 feeling as if one were whirling and falling; giddy. 2 causing or seeming to cause giddiness: *a dizzy height; a dizzy pace. vt-* [diz·zied, diz·zy·ing]: *Heights dizzy her.* —*adv-* diz'zi·ly. *n-* diz'zi·ness.

DNA (dē'ĕn·ā') *n-* deoxyribonucleic acid, a complex substance that controls the activities of chromosomes. Genes form a part of the DNA molecule, which is found in the nuclei of living cells.

¹do (dōō) *vt-* [did (did), done (dŭn), do·ing] 1 to perform or carry out; accomplish: *to do a job.* 2 to produce; execute: *to do a painting; to do a play.* 3 to give; grant: *to do a favor.* 4 to work on; set in order: *to do one's hair; to do one's room.* 5 to reach or cover (a speed, distance, etc.); achieve: *to do 60 miles an hour; to do 300 miles in a day. vi-* 1 to fare: *to do well in business.* 2 to be good enough; be satisfactory: *Those shoes won't do for hiking. auxiliary verb* (1) used as in intensifier: *I do like that color!* (2) used with "not" to make a negative statement: *I did not say that.* (3) used to ask a question: *Do you need these papers?* (4) used to replace a verb or verbal statement instead of repeating it: *Who owns this jacket? I do. He walks as his father does.* [from Old English *don*.] *Horns-* dew, due.

do away with to kill; also, to put an end to: *to do away with unnecessary expenses.*

do in *Informal* to kill.

do (someone) out of *Informal* to cheat someone of.

do up to wrap or tie up: *to do up a parcel.*

do without to proceed in spite of not having.

dock·et (dŏk'ət) *n-* 1 list of cases to be tried by a court; also, any list or calendar of matters to be acted on: *The problem of raising more money is on the docket for March.* 2 a list of legal decisions. 3 label or tag attached to a package and listing its contents. *vt-* 1 to enter on a list of matters for consideration. 2 to mark or label.

dock·yard (dŏk'yärd') *n-* place where ships are built, repaired, or outfitted; shipyard.

doc·tor (dŏk'tər) *n-* 1 person who is licensed to practice medicine or surgery. 2 person who holds the highest degree given by a university. *vt-* 1 to try to cure: *to doctor a cold.* 2 *Informal* to tamper with: *to doctor an account.*

doc·tor·al (dŏk'tər əl) *adj-* related to or studying for a doctorate: *a doctoral thesis; a doctoral candidate.*

doc·tor·ate (dŏk'tər ət) *n-* university degree or rank of doctor: *to study for a doctorate in English.*

doc·tri·naire (dŏk'trə nâr') *adj-* typical of a person who has theoretical ideas on politics or other matters, and disregards facts and practical considerations.

doc·trine (dŏk'trĭn) *n-* something taught as the deeply held belief or principles of a church, political party, or other group: *the doctrines of the church; the doctrine of states' rights.* —*adj-* doc'trin·al: *a doctrinal sermon.*

doc·u·ment (dŏk'yə mənt) *n-* official paper that gives information or proof of something; a record: *Birth and marriage certificates are documents of importance. vt-* to support or prove (a point, theory, etc.) with facts or evidence.

Diver

¹dod·der (dŏd′ər) *vi-* to move feebly and unsteadily, as a person weakened by old age does; tremble or totter. [of uncertain origin, but perhaps related to **dither**.]

²dod·der (dŏd′ər) *n-* leafless plant with tiny flowers and threadlike, twining stems that attach themselves to and weaken or destroy other plants. [perhaps from early German **doder**.]

do·dec·a·gon (dō′dĕk′ə gŏn) *n-* polygon with 12 sides.

do·dec·a·he·dron (dō′dĕk′ə hē′drən) *n-* polyhedron with 12 faces.

dodge (dŏj) *vt-* [**dodged, dodg·ing**] 1 to avoid by moving aside quickly: *to dodge a blow.* 2 to avoid by deception or cunning; evade: *to dodge an issue.* *vi-:* *to dodge through traffic.* *n-* 1 sudden move aside; twist or turn. 2 a trick: *I know that old dodge.*

dodge·ball (dŏj′bôl′) *n-* game in which a group of players throw a large ball at another group, who try to avoid being hit by it.

dodg·er (dŏj′ər) *n-* 1 person who uses trickery and evasion to avoid doing something: *a draft dodger.* 2 (usually **corn dodger**) small cake made from corn meal.

do·do (dō′dō) *n-* [*pl.* **do·does** or **do·dos**] large, extinct bird with very short legs, a large hooked beak, and wings too small for flight.

doe (dō) *n-* the female of the deer, antelope, rabbit, and some other animals. *Homs-* ²**do, dough.**

Doe, John (dō) See *John Doe.*

do·er (dōō′ər) *n-* person who does something, especially a person of action and energy: *a doer, not a thinker.*

Dodo

does (dŭz) form of ¹**do** used with "he," "she," "it," or singular noun subjects, in the present tense.

doe·skin (dō′skĭn′) *n-* 1 fine, soft leather made from the skin of a female deer, or from the skin of a sheep or lamb. 2 closely-woven cloth, usually of wool, with a soft, napped surface.

does·n't (dŭz′ənt) does not.

doff (dŏf) *vt-* to take off (clothing, especially a hat).

dog (dôg) *n-* 1 four-footed animal of which there are many domesticated breeds used as pets, for hunting, police work, etc. 2 the male of this animal or of the fox, wolf, etc. 3 *Informal* fellow: *He's a gay dog.* *vt-* [**dogged, dog·ging**] to follow closely; trail: *to dog someone's footsteps.* *—adj-* dog′ **like′.**

do·main (dō mān′) *n-* 1 lands owned by one person or family; estate. 2 region under the control of one ruler or government; dominion; realm. 3 field or sphere of thought or action: *the domain of natural science.*

dome (dōm) *n-* 1 large rounded roof on a circular base. 2 something high and rounded: *the dome of the sky.* *vt-* [**domed, dom·ing**] to top or form with a high, rounded roof or similar part.

Dome

do·mes·tic (də mĕs′tĭk) *adj-* 1 relating to home or household affairs: *busy with domestic chores.* 2 fond of home and household affairs: *a domestic type of woman.* 3 relating to or made in one's own country; not foreign: *a domestic product; domestic trade.* 4 living with and cared for by man; not wild; tame: *Household pets and cattle are domestic animals.* *n-* a household servant. *—adv-* do·mes′ **ti·cal·ly.**

do·ry (dôr′ē) *n-* [*pl.* **do·ries**] deep, flat-bottomed rowboat with a sharp prow and a narrow stern. [American word from a Central American Indian language.]

dos·age (dō′sĭj) *n-* 1 the amount of medicine, radiation, etc., to be given at one time. 2 the giving of medicine in doses. 3 process of adding one or more ingredients to a product to improve it.

dot (dŏt) *n-* property which a bride brings to her husband; dowry. [from French **dot**, from Latin *dos,* "a dowry."]

dote (dōt) *vi-* [**dot·ed, dot·ing**] 1 to lavish great or excessive love or fondness (on or upon) a person, pet, etc.: *to dote on a grandchild.* 2 to be weak and childish from old age.

doth (dŭth) *Archaic* form of ¹**do** used with "he," "she," "it," or singular noun subjects, in the present tense.

dotted swiss *n-* fine cotton or similar fabric with a pattern of small, raised dots.

dou·ble (dŭb′əl) *adj-* 1 having or forming two identical or similar parts; paired: *the double "t" in "butter"; a double door.* 2 twice the usual size, amount, value, etc.; multiplied by two: *a double portion; a solution of double strength.* 3 having two uses, applications, intentions, etc.: *a double meaning; to serve a double purpose.* 4 of a flower, having more than a single row of petals: *a double rose.* *vt-* [**dou·bled, dou·bling**] 1 to make twice as much; multiply by two: *to double one's income.* 2 to fold over so as two form two layers or thicknesses: *to double a piece of paper.* 3 of a ship, to pass around (a projecting piece of land): *to double a cape.* *vi-* 1 to increase to twice as much: *Prices have doubled.* 2 to be a replacement or substitute: *He doubles for the star.* 3 to turn sharply and trace the same or a similar course:

dou·ble-head·er (dŭb′əl hĕd′ər) *n-* two games played in succession on the same day for the price of one.

double jeopardy *n-* the subjection of a person to a second trial for an offense for which he has already been tried and judged.

dou·ble-joint·ed (dŭb′əl join′təd) *adj-* having extremely flexible joints that enable the limbs, fingers, spine, etc., to bend in unusual ways.

double negative *n-* occurrence in the same statement of two negative words or expressions. *Example:* I don't never go there.

►DOUBLE NEGATIVES are not considered proper in English.

dou·ble-park (dŭb′əl pärk′) *vt-* to park (a motor vehicle) in the street alongside another already parked parallel to the curb. *vi-:* *Please don't double-park.*

double play *n-* in baseball, the putting out of two base runners in one connected series of plays.

doubt (dout) *vt-* to be uncertain or undecided about; distrust or question: *I doubt his honesty. I doubt whether it will rain.* *vi-:* *He who doubts may learn the truth for himself.* *n-* 1 feeling of disbelief or mistrust: *I have some doubt about that.* 2 a state or condition of uncertainty: *Their fate is still in doubt.* *—n-* doubt′ **er. no doubt** or **without doubt** certainly; without question.

dough (dō) *n-* thick, spongy mixture of flour and other ingredients, such as butter, eggs, or milk, used for making bread or pastry. *Homs-* ²**do, doe.**

¹down (doun) *adv-* 1 from a higher to a lower place, position, etc.: *to look down from a height; to fall down.* 2 from a greater to a lesser state, condition, degree, quantity etc.: *to bring one's price down; to slow down; to boil syrup down.* 3 from an earlier to a later time: *Heirlooms are handed down.* 4 heavily and thoroughly; weighted down with cares. 5 as part of a price, in cash: *Pay ten dollars down, and the rest later.* 6 on paper: *Write down this address.* *adj-* 1 descending: *a down elevator.* 2 in a lowered position: *the curtain is down.* 3 ill, disabled, or depressed: *to be down with a cold; down in the dumps.* *prep-* from a higher to a lower place or position on or in: *to row down the stream; to fall down a staircase.* *vt-* 1 to defeat; subdue: *to down an enemy.* 2 *Informal* to eat or drink; swallow: *to down a hearty meal.* *n-* 1 in football, one of a series of four plays, during which the team in possession of the ball attempts to advance ten or more yards. 2 **downs** unfavorable changes of fortune, health, etc.: *to have one's ups and downs.* [from Old English **adūne,** from a joining of *af* **dune** meaning literally "from the hill," from Celtic **dūn,** "high place." Related to ³**down** and **dune.**] **down and out** penniless and friendless. **down on** bearing a grudge against: *Why are you down on him?* **Down with (someone)!** Throw (someone) out of office!

²down (doun) *n-* 1 soft, fluffy feathers: *a pillow stuffed with down.* 2 any similar soft fuzz or hair: *the down on a peach.* [from an earlier Old Norse word **dūnn.**]

doz. dozen.

doze (dōz) *vi-* [dozed, doz·ing] to sleep lightly: *Father dozed in his chair.* *n-* a light sleep; nap.
  doze off to begin to fall asleep.

doz·en (dŭz′ ən) *n-* 1 [*pl.* doz·en] set of twelve: *Give me a dozen of those brown eggs. I want three dozen of the red roses.* 2 **dozens** *Informal* a large number: *I have dozens of reasons. as determiner* (always preceded by another determiner): *There are a dozen boxes here and two dozen there.*

doz·enth (dŭz′ ənth) *adj-* twelfth.

DP displaced person.

dpt. department.

D.P.W. Department of Public Works.

Dr. 1 Doctor. 2 Drive.

drab (drăb) *adj-* [drab·ber, drab·best] 1 dull; cheerless; monotonous: *a drab existence.* 2 having a dull, grayish brown color: *wispy, drab hair. n-* 1 dull, grayish brown

draft or **draught** (drăft) *n-* 1 sketch, outline, or version of something: *the first draft of a speech.* 2 written order for the payment or drawing out of money: *a bank draft.* 3 method of selecting men for compulsory military service; conscription. 4 group of men so selected. 5 stream of air: *to feel a draft around the shoulders.* 6 device for controlling the air stream in a stove, furnace, etc. 7 line drawing or plan, as for an engine or building. 8 the pulling of a load by beasts: *to use oxen for draft.* 9 depth of a floating ship's bottom beneath the surface of the water, especially when the ship is loaded. 10 (usually **draught**) the hauling in of a net of fish; also, a catch of fish. 11 (usually **draught**) a drink: *a draught of water. adj-* 1 used for pulling loads: *a team of draft horses.* 2 (usually **draught**) drawn from a keg: *cold draught beer. vt-* 1 to write or draw the outlines or plan of. 2 to select for some special purpose: *to draft men into the army.*

draft·ee (drăf tē′) *n-* person who has been drafted for military service; conscript.

drafts·man (drăfts′ mən) *n-* [*pl.* drafts·men] one who draws mechanical drawings, building plans, etc. Also, *chiefly Brit.,* **draughts′ man.** *—n-* drafts′ man·ship.

draft·y (drăf′ tē) *adj-* [draft·i·er, draft·i·est] exposed to or admitting currents of air: *a drafty place; a drafty room.* Also, *chiefly Brit.,* **draugh′ ty.** *—n-* draft′ i·ness.

drag (drăg) *vt-* [dragged, drag·ging] 1 to draw along by force; haul. 2 to search the bottom of with a grapnel or similar device: *They dragged the lake for the sunken motor.* 3 to harrow (a field). *vi-* 1 to trail along the ground: *Her skirt dragged.* 2 to move or go too slowly: *The speech dragged. n-* 1 device for searching the bottom of a river or lake. 2 sledge for hauling loads. 3 harrow for breaking up soil. 4 anything that hinders or slows down. 5 *Slang* influence; pull. 6 *Physics* combination of forces such as friction and turbulence that retard the motion of an object (such as a plane or missile) through a fluid.
  drag (one's) feet to fail to act promptly.

drag·gle (drăg′ əl) *vi-* [drag-
gled, drag·gling] to become
wet or soiled by trailing in
the mud or along damp
ground: *The clothes draggled
in the wet grass. vt-* to wet or
soil by dragging on the
ground.

drag·net (drăg′ nĕt′) *n-* 1 a
net drawn along a river or
sea bottom to catch fish, or along the ground to catch
small game. 2 police hunt in which every resource is used.

Dragon

drag·on (drăg′ ən) *n-* imaginary animal, usually thought
of as a large, winged reptile
that breathes fire and has
terrible fangs and claws.

drag·on·fly (drăg′ ən flī′) *n-*
[*pl.* drag·on·flies] slender
insect with four gauzy wings
and a long green, blue, or
brown body, usually found
near water; darning needle.

Dragonfly

drain (drān) *vt-* 1 to draw off (a liquid) gradually: *to drain water from a reservoir.* 2 to make empty: *to drain the bathtub.* 3 to use up; exhaust: *The operation drained the doctor's energy. vi-* 1 to discharge a liquid: *The street drains into the sewer.* 2 to become dry or empty: *She left the dishes to drain. n-* 1 channel, pipe, sewer, etc., for carrying away unwanted liquids. 2 a continuous demand: *a drain on one's time.*

draw (drô) *vt-* [drew (drōō), drawn, draw·ing] (in senses 1, 2, 4, 6, 10, and 15, considered intransitive when the object is implied but not expressed) 1 to pull or drag: *to draw a cart.* 2 to pull out; haul up: *to draw water from a well.* 3 to steer or lead in some direction: *I drew him aside.* 4 to attract: *The game drew a crowd.* 5 to arouse: *to draw criticism; to draw applause.* 6 to extract; bring out: *to draw a cork; to draw a gun.* 7 to take out: *to draw money from a bank; to draw facts from a book.* 8 to get; gain; win: *to draw a salary; to draw interest; to draw a prize.* 9 to reach by reasoning: *to draw a conclusion.* 10 to form (a picture, likeness, or diagram) with pen or pencil, chalk, etc. 11 to write out in suitable form: *to draw a will.* 12 to close: *to draw the curtains.* 13 to inhale: *to draw fresh air into the lungs.* 14 to cause to come forth: *to draw blood; to draw bath water.* 15 to cause to shrink; pucker, or contract: *Hot water draws wool. The burn drew the skin.* 16 to require a certain depth in which to float: *The boat draws fifteen feet.* 17 to disembowel: *to draw a chicken. vi-* 1 to approach or recede; move: *Morning draws near. He drew back suddenly.* 2 to cause or allow a current of air to pass: *The chimney draws well.* 3 to contract or pucker: *The astringent made her skin draw.* 4 to take a chance, as in a lottery: *to draw for a prize. n-* 1 act of bringing out and aiming a gun: *The bandit had a fast draw.* 2 a chance or turn to take a playing card, slip, straw, etc., where the outcome depends on chance; also, the thing taken: *That was a lucky draw.* 3 contest left undecided; tie; toss-up. 4 movable section of a draw-bridge. 5 gully into which water drains.
  draw a blank to be unsuccessful; get no response.
  draw away to move ahead: *The horse drew away from the others and won the race.*
  draw off 1 to withdraw; depart. 2 to drain off.
  draw on to make a demand on; use as a source: *to draw on one's memory for an answer.*
  draw out 1 to prolong: *to draw out a speech.* 2 to persuade someone to talk about himself: *to draw out a shy new student.*
  draw the line to set a limit.
  draw up 1 to write in suitable form: *to draw up a contract.* 2 to bring or come to a halt: *He drew up his horse and dismounted. The carriage drew up at the inn.* 3 to straighten up; bring oneself up to full height: *He drew himself up in indignation as he denied the charge.* 4 to arrange: *The colonel drew the regiment up in battle order.*

dread (drĕd) *vt-* to look forward to with fear: *He dreads going to the dentist. n-* fear, especially of harm to come: *his dread of storms. adj-* causing fear, terror, or awe: *a dread ruler; dread omens.*

dread·ful (drĕd′ fəl) *adj-* 1 terrible; causing fear or awe: *a dreadful hurricane.* 2 very bad; unpleasant: *a dreadful error.* **—adv-** dread′ ful·ly. *n-* dread′ ful·ness.

dread·nought or **dread·naught** (drĕd′ nôt′) *n-* large battleship heavily armed with big guns.

dream (drēm) *n-* 1 thoughts, emotions, or pictures experienced or seen during sleep. 2 something fancied while awake; daydream. 3 state of mind during which a person fancies; reverie: *He mowed the grass in a dream.* 4 something more perfect than could be hoped for: *a dream of a day.* 5 goal; hope: *His dream is to buy an island. vt-* [dreamed or dreamt (drĕmt), dream·ing] 1 to have ideas or mental images during sleep: *She dreamed all night.* 2 to think hopefully and habitually (of) something one desires keenly: *He dreamed of glory.* 3 to have idle fancies while awake: *He dreamed as he mowed the lawn. vt-: Did you dream anything? —n-* dream′ er.

dried (drīd) *p.t.* & *p.p.* of **dry.** *adj-* with the moisture removed: *sweet dried prunes.*

drip (drĭp) *vi-* [**dripped, drip·ping**] to fall in drops: *Rain dripped from the roof.* *vt-* (considered intransitive when the direct object is implied but not expressed) to let fall in drops: *The roof dripped rain. The spigot drips.* *n-* 1 a falling of a liquid in drops; also, the drops themselves: *a steady drip from the roof.* 2 a projecting part, as in a window sill, shaped to throw off rain.

drive (drīv) *vt-* [**drove** (drōv), **driven** (drĭv' ən), **driving**] 1 to urge forward; make move: *to drive cattle.* 2 to put in motion and guide; steer; also, to carry in a vehicle: *to drive a car; to drive a friend home.* 3 to move by hitting: *to drive a golf ball; to drive a nail.* 4 to make by digging: *to drive a well.* 5 to set or keep in motion: *Steam drives the engine.* 6 to urge along by force; overwork: *He drives his employees.* 7 to carry through forcefully; conclude: *to drive a bargain.* 8 to force into a particular state or action: *The noise drives me mad. Ambition drove him to run for office.* *vi-* 1 to press, aim, or be moved forward steadily or with violence: *The waves drove toward the shore.* 2 to travel in a carriage or motor car. 3 in golf, to strike the ball from a tee. *n-* 1 swift hard blow or hit: *a drive to left field.* 2 trip in an automobile or carriage: *a Sunday drive.* 3 road for vehicles: *a winding drive to the house.* 4 effort to carry out some purpose; campaign: *a clothing drive.* 5 forceful effort; energy: *a man of drive and ambition.* 6 a gathering together, or rounding up, as of cattle for branding, logs for floating, etc. 7 mechanism that sets something in motion or transmits motion: *an electric drive for a telescope; chain drive on a truck.*
drive at to mean; intend: *What is he driving at?*

drop (drŏp) *vi-* [**dropped, drop·ping**] 1 to fall to a lower position, rank, degree, price, etc.: *The sun dropped out of sight. He dropped to fifth place. Prices dropped.* 2 to grow lower in sound or pitch: *Her voice dropped to a whisper.* 3 to cease or end: *There the matter dropped.* 4 to become less; slacken: *Book sales dropped.* *vt-* 1 to let fall in tiny masses: *to drop medicine from a spoon.* 2 to let fall: *to drop a book.* 3 to lower: *to drop the eyes; to drop a blind.* 4 to fell with a blow or weapon: *to drop a deer.* 5 of animals, to give birth to: *to drop a calf.* 6 to have done with; end: *to drop an argument.* 7 to send, deliver, or set down: *to drop a note; to drop a passenger.* 8 to utter casually: *to drop a suggestion.* 9 to omit: *to drop a letter from a word.* 10 to demote to a lower class, or remove from an organization: *to drop a student from the football squad.* *n-* 1 small rounded mass of liquid: *a drop of water.* 2 anything shaped or hanging like a small rounded mass of liquid: *a crystal drop on an earring.* 3 any very small quantity: *a drop of truth.* 4 sudden descent or fall: *a drop in prices.* 5 something arranged to fall or be lowered: *the drop in a gallows; a curtain drop.* 6 receptacle or slot for mail.
a drop in the bucket tiny portion of what is needed.
let (something) drop to let (a secret, remark, etc.) slip out.
drop behind to fall behind; lag behind; fail to keep up.
drop in, over, or **by** to visit informally.
drop off to fall asleep: *Timmy dropped off right away.*
drop out withdraw; quit: *He dropped out of the contest.*

dry (drī) *adj-* [**dri·er, dri·est**] 1 not wet or moist: *the dry air; dry eyes.* 2 having little or no rainfall: *India has a dry season and a rainy season.* 3 not under or in water: *They pulled the boat onto dry land.* 4 empty of its water supply; drained away: *a dry river; a dry well.* 5 thirsty: *He felt dry after working in the sun.* 6 quiet but shrewd: *The joke was made funnier by the dry manner in which he told it.* 7 not sweet: *a dry wine.* 8 uninteresting; dull: *a dry book.* 9 of solid, rather than liquid, substances: *a dry measure.* 10 forbidding the sale of intoxicants: *a dry city.* *n-* person who favors the prohibition of alcoholic beverages. *vt-* [**dried, dry·ing**] *to dry dishes.* *vi-*: *The ink dried quickly.* —*n-* **dry′ness.**

D.S.T. or **DST** Daylight Saving Time.

du·al (dōō′ əl, dyōō′-) *adj-* having two parts; twofold; double: *a dual purpose.* **Hom-** duel. —*adv-* **du′ al·ly.**

du·cal (dōō′ kəl, dyōō′-) *adj-* of or related to a duke or dukedom: *a ducal estate.*

duc·at (dŭk′ ət) *n-* 1 in earlier times, any of various gold or silver coins used in Europe, especially a coin of Venice. 2 *Slang* ticket of admission.

duch·ess (dŭch′ əs) *n-* 1 wife or widow of a duke. 2 woman with the rank or authority of a duke.

duch·y (dŭch′ ē) *n-* [*pl.* **duch·ies**] land governed by or associated with the title of a duke or duchess; dukedom.

¹duck (dŭk) *n-* 1 any of several wild and tame waterfowl smaller than a goose and having a shorter neck. 2 female of one of these waterfowl. 3 their flesh, used as food. [from English *dūce* meaning "a bird that dives."]
be a sitting duck to be a target one can hardly miss.

Mallard duck, about 2 ft long

²duck (dŭk) *vi-* to move or crouch quickly to avoid being hit: *When the shots were fired, everybody ducked.* *vt-* 1 to avoid; evade: *to duck a blow; to duck a question.* 2 to lower or bend (the head, shoulder, etc.) to avoid being hit. 3 to plunge or thrust under water: *The winning team ducked their captain.* *n-* 1 a brief plunging into water. 2 quick movement made to avoid something: *a duck to the right.* [from Old English **douken.**]

³duck (dŭk) *n-* 1 coarse linen or cotton cloth, used for outer clothing, tents, sails, and awnings. 2 **ducks** trousers made of this material. [from Dutch **doek,** "cloth."]

duck·bill (dŭk′ bĭl′) *n-* 1 beak or implement shaped like the bill of a duck. 2 (also **duck′ billed′ platypus**) platypus. 3 paddlefish.

ducking stool *n-* in earlier times, a stool used for ducking persons in water as a form of punishment.

duck·ling (dŭk′ lĭng) *n-* young duck.

duck·pins (dŭk′ pĭnz′) *n- pl.* 1 (takes singular verb) bowling game similar to tenpins but using smaller balls and pins. 2 pins used in this game.

duck soup *Slang n-* something that is easy to do.

duck·weed (dŭk′ wēd′) *n-* any of various water plants floating on ponds and having no stems or true leaves.

duct (dŭkt) *n-* 1 tube or canal for carrying a liquid or gas, especially a tube in the body that carries glandular secretions. 2 pipe through which electric wires or cables are led.

duc·tile (dŭk′ təl) *adj-* such as can be drawn out thin without breaking: *Heated glass becomes ductile before it melts.* —*n-* **duc′til′i·ty** (dŭk′ tĭl′ ə tē).

duct·less gland (dŭkt′ ləs) *n-* endocrine gland.

dud (dŭd) *n-* 1 bomb or shell that fails to explode when it should. 2 *Slang* person or thing that is a failure.

dude (dōōd) *n-* 1 man who is too concerned with his clothing or appearance. 2 in western United States, a tourist, especially one from the East who visits a ranch. [American word, perhaps from **dud up,** "dress up."]

dude ranch *n-* ranch at which vacationers ride horseback and play at ranching.

dudg·eon (dŭj′ ən) *n-* anger; displeasure.

duds (dŭdz) *Informal n- pl.* clothing.

due (dōō, dyōō) *adj-* 1 owed; payable: *a fine is due on the library book.* 2 proper or fit; appropriate: *They showed due respect to the distinguished visitor.* 3 required or expected to arrive: *The plane is due in ten minutes.* *adv-* directly; exactly: *The ship traveled due north.* *n-* 1 that which is owed; that which must be given to another: *Pay the man his due.* 2 **dues** fee or charge, as for membership in a club. **Hom-** dew, do.
due to owing to; caused by: *The poor harvest was due to lack of rain.* **fall due** to become payable: *The bill falls due the first of each month.* **in due course** in the natural course of events: *He will decide in due course.*
►Some traditionalists object to the use of DUE TO to introduce adverbial phrases of cause. In the sentence *The game was canceled due to rain* they would prefer "because of," "owing to," or "on account of." Nevertheless, many good writers now use DUE TO in this way. Traditionalists have never objected to DUE TO in phrases that modify nouns: *The cancellation was due to rain.*

du·ly (dōō′lē, dyōō′-) *adv-* in a suitable and proper way; at the proper time and place: *He was duly sworn in.*

dumb (dŭm) *adj-* [dumb·er, dumb·est] 1 unable to speak; mute: *a deaf and dumb person; our dumb animal friends.* 2 not speaking; silent: *He remained dumb with grief.* 3 *Informal* stupid. —*adv-* dumb′ ly. *n-* dumb′ ness.

dumb·bell (dŭm′ bĕl′) *n-* 1 exercising device consisting of two wooden or metal balls connected by a bar. 2 *Slang* stupid person.

dumb·found or **dumb·found** (dŭm′ found′) *vt-* to make speechless with surprise, fear, etc.; amaze.

dumb show *n-* gestures that express meaning without sounds; pantomime.

dumb-wait·er (ŭm′ wā′ tər) *n-* small elevator for conveying dishes, garbage, etc., from floor to floor.

dum·dum bullet (dŭm′ dŭm′) *n-* bullet with a soft nose or with its jacket stripped back so that the lead beneath will spread on hitting.

dum·my (dŭm′ ē) *n-* [*pl.* dum·mies] 1 copy or imitation, especially of the human figure, made to resemble or work like the real object: *a ventriloquist's dummy; a football dummy; a wooden dummy of a rifle.* 2 *Slang* stupid or thick-witted person. 3 in bridge, a person whose cards are laid on the table and played by his partner. 4 model of a page or book to be printed. *as modifier: a dummy door on a stage.*

dump (dŭmp) *vt-* 1 to let fall or throw away in a mass; unload: *to dump sand from a truck.* 2 to put up (goods, stock, etc.) for sale in large amounts and below the market price. *n-* 1 a place where trash may be thrown out: *the city dump.* 2 a place where military supplies are kept: *an ammunition dump.*

dump·ling (dŭmp′ lĭng) *n-* 1 dough boiled or steamed and served with meat: *stew with dumplings.* 2 shell of dough wrapped around a piece of fruit which is then boiled or baked: *apple dumplings.*

dumps (dŭmps) **down in the dumps** gloomy; low in spirits; depressed.

dump·y (dŭm′ pē) *adj-* [dump·i·er, dump·i·est] short and stout; squat. —*adv-* dump′ i·ly. *n-* dump′ i·ness.

¹dun (dŭn) *adj-* dull grayish brown. [from Old English dunn, apparently from Celtic.] *Hom-* done.

²dun (dŭn) *n-* 1 repeated demand for the payment of a debt. 2 person who continually demands the payment of a debt. *vt-* [dunned, dun·ning]: *The restaurant dunned him for the bill.* [a form of **din**.] *Hom-* done.

dunce (dŭns) *n-* 1 stupid person. 2 backward pupil.

dunce cap *n-* in earlier times, a cone-shaped paper cap put on the head of a slow or lazy pupil. Also **dunce's cap.**

dun·der·head (dŭn′ dər hĕd′) *n-* stupid or dull person; blockhead. —*adj-* dun′ der·head′ ed.

dune (dōōn, dyōōn) *n-* low sand hill formed by the wind, especially near a shore.

dung (dŭng) *n-* excrement from animals; manure.

dun·ga·ree (dŭng′ gə rē′) *n-* 1 coarse, durable cotton material; denim. 2 **dungarees** trousers or work clothes made from this material; jeans.

Dunes

dung beetle *n-* any of various beetles that breed in and feed upon dung.

dun·geon (dŭn′ jən) *n-* dark, underground prison. *Hom-* donjon.

dung·hill (dŭng′ hĭl′) *n-* heap of manure.

duplex apartment *n-* apartment whose rooms are on two floors.

duplex house *n-* house designed for two families.

du·pli·cate (dōō′ plə kāt′, dyōō′) *vt-* [du·pli·cat·ed, du·pli·cat·ing] 1 to make an exact or nearly exact copy of: *She duplicated the dress she had admired at the fashion show.* 2 to repeat exactly or nearly so: *He duplicated his former triumphs.* —*n-* du′ pli·ca′ tion.

du·pli·cate (dōō′ plə kət, dyōō′-) *n-* something exactly like something else; twin: *This print is a duplicate of the original. as modifier: a duplicate key.*

in duplicate with an original and one copy; double.

du·ra·ble (dŏŏr′ ə bəl, dyŏŏr′-) *adj-* lasting; not breaking down or wearing out easily: *a durable pair of shoes; a durable friendship.* —*adv-* du′ ra·bly. *n-* du′ ra·bil′ i·ty.

du·ra ma·ter (dŏŏr′ ə mā′ tər) *n-* outermost membrane that covers the brain and the spinal cord. It is tougher and more fibrous than either of the other two membranes.

dur·ance (dŏŏr′ əns, dyŏŏr′-) *Archaic n-* imprisonment.

du·ra·tion (dŏŏr ā′ shən, dyŏŏr′-) *n-* amount of time during which anything lasts: *a storm of short duration.*

du·ress (dŏŏr ĕs′, dyŏŏr′-) *n-* 1 force used to get someone to do something; compulsion; coercion: *The prisoner signed a confession under duress.* 2 *Law* unlawful confinement or imprisonment.

dur·ing (dŏŏr′ ĭng, dyŏŏr′-) *prep-* 1 throughout the time of: *We do not go to school during the summer.* 2 in the course of: *He called sometime during the evening.*

dur·ra (dŏŏr′ ə) *n-* canelike grass grown for its grain.

durst (dûrst) *Archaic* form of **dare** used in the past tense.

du·rum wheat (dŏŏr′ əm, dûr′ əm) *n-* a hard wheat widely used in making flour for macaroni, spaghetti, etc.

dusk (dŭsk) *n-* 1 the time of day when darkness comes on; twilight. 2 darkness; gloom: *in the dusk of the forest.*

dusk·y (dŭs′ kē) *adj-* [dusk·i·er, dusk·i·est] 1 somewhat dark in color. 2 lacking light; shadowy. —*adv-* dusk′ i·ly. *n-* dusk′ i·ness.

dust (dŭst) *n-* fine, dry particles of earth or other powder-like material: *a cloud of dust. vt-* 1 (considered intransitive when the direct object is implied but not expressed) to brush or wipe away such particles from: *Susie dusted*

du·ty (dōō′ tē, dyōō′-) *n-* [*pl.* du·ties] 1 what one ought to do; obligation: *a sense of duty; a man's duty to his country.* 2 service required by one's work or position: *the duties of a secretary.* 3 a tax, especially on goods brought into a country; tariff: *a duty on perfume.*

dwarf (dwôrf) *n-* 1 person, animal, or plant greatly below normal size, often deformed in some way. 2 in fairy tales, a tiny person with unusual or magical powers. 3 dwarf star. *as modifier: a dwarf rose. vt-* 1 to prevent from growing to natural size: *The lack of rain dwarfed the flowers.* 2 to make look small by comparison.

dwarf·ish (dwôrf′ ĭsh) *adj-* like a human dwarf.

dwarf star *Astronomy n-* star of average or less than average brightness and mass. The sun is a dwarf star. See also *white dwarf.*

dwell (dwĕl) *vi-* [dwelled or dwelt, dwell·ing] to live in a place; reside: *The princess dwells in yonder castle.* —*n-* dwell′ er.

dwell on to think, speak, or write about at length; linger on: *His mind dwells on unhappy memories.*

dwell·ing (dwĕl′ ĭng) *n-* house; place of residence: *a two-story dwelling.*

dwin·dle (dwĭn′ dəl) *vi-* [dwin·dled, dwin·dling] to become smaller or less; to shrink: *The water supply dwindled from lack of rain.*

Dy symbol for dysprosium.

Dy·ak (dī′ ăk′) *n-* Dayak.

dyb·buk (dĭb′ ək) *n-* in Jewish legend, a demon or spirit of a dead person that was believed to take control of and dwell in a living man or woman.

dye (dī) *vt-* [dyed, dye·ing] to give color to, usually by dipping into a liquid containing coloring matter: *She dyed her dress blue. n-* 1 coloring matter; dyestuff. 2 color produced by dyeing. *Hom-* die. —*n-* dy′ er.

dyed-in-the-wool (dīd′ ĭn thə wŏŏl′) *adj-* complete; thorough: *a dyed-in-the-wool political conservative.*

dye·ing (dī′ ĭng) *n-* act or process of using dye to give color to yarn, cloth, hair, etc. *Hom-* dying.

dye·stuff (dī′ stŭf′) *n-* any coloring matter; dye.

dy·ing (dī′ ĭng) *adj-* 1 passing from life: *the last wish of the dying man.* 2 said or done at the time of death: *a dying wish.* 3 becoming weaker. *Hom-* dyeing.

dyke (dīk) dike.

dy·nam·ic (dī năm′ ĭk) *adj-* 1 full of energy; forceful. 2 having to do with the energy of motion: *a dynamic current of air.* —*adv-* dy·nam′ i·cal·ly.

dy·nam·ics (dī năm′ ĭks) *n-* (takes singular verb) branch of physics that deals with the motion of particles or objects in relation to the forces that cause the motion.

E

, e (ē) *n-* [*pl.* **E's, e's**] 1 the fifth letter of the English alphabet. 2 **E** *Music* the third note of the C-major scale.

ach (ĕch) *determiner* (traditionally called adjective or pronoun) 1 every separate: *We allowed each student to take his turn.* 2 all, but one by one: *They each took turns.* *n-* every one: *Each of the cities had a power plant.*

a·ger (ē′ gər) *adj-* full of keen desire: *He was eager to play football.* —*adv-* **ea′ ger·ly.** *n-* **ea′ ger·ness.**

a·gle (ē′ gəl) *n-* any of various large, sharp-sighted birds of prey. For picture, see *bald eagle.*

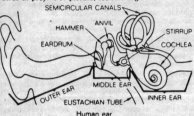

Human ear

ar (ēr) *n-* 1 the entire organ of hearing. 2 the outer, visible part of this organ: *A cat has pointed ears that stand up.* 3 sense of hearing: *George has a sharp ear.* 4 particular ability to hear and understand various sounds in music, poetry, etc.: *A good singer must have a good ear.* 5 attention; heed: *Give ear to what I say.*

ar·ly (ûr′ lē) *adv-* [**ear·li·er, ear·li·est**] 1 before the usual or required time: *Snow fell early this year. He arrived at school early.* 2 at or near the beginning: *These events occurred early in his career.*

ar·mark (ēr′ märk′) *n-* mark, such as a slit in the ear of a sheep, cow, etc., used to identify it; hence, any distinguishing mark or characteristic: *Your remark has all the earmarks of an insult.*

arn (ûrn) *vt-* 1 to receive as payment for labor, service, etc.: *He earns a large salary.* 2 to gain as a result of one's behavior, efforts, etc.; deserve: *to earn someone's praise.* 3 to produce (interest, dividends, etc.). *Hom-* urn.

ar·nest (ûr′ nəst) *adj-* filled with deep and sincere feeling, intentions, or purpose; serious: *an earnest apology; an earnest student.* [from Old English *eornost.*] —*adv-* **ear′ nest·ly.** *n-* **ear′ nest·ness.**

in earnest with sincere or serious intent.

ar·nest (ûr′ nəst) *n-* 1 token or pledge of something: *an earnest of my good will.* 2 (also **earnest money**) money given in advance to show honest intentions.

arn·ings (ûr′ nĭngz) *n- pl.* 1 payment received for work, services, etc. 2 profits.

arth (ûrth) *n-* 1 (usually **Earth**) our planet, fifth largest in the solar system, and the third in order of distance from the sun. 2 the world we inhabit: *Peace on earth, good will to men.* 3 the people who inhabit it: *All the earth rejoices.*

arth·quake (ûrth′ kwāk′) *n-* sudden trembling or shaking of the ground, usually caused by a shifting of rock layers along a fault or fissure under the earth's surface.

arth·worm (ûrth′ wûrm′) *n-* worm with a ringed or segmented body that burrows in the soil and eats decaying organic matter; angleworm.

arth·y (ûrth′ ē) *adj-* [**earth·i·er, earth·i·est**] 1 resembling or containing earth or soil: *dull, earthy colors.* 2 natural, simple, and often crude or vulgar.

ase (ēz) *n-* 1 freedom from pain, toil, effort, or worry; comfort: *a life of ease.* 2 freedom from strain; naturalness: *the ease of his manner.* *vt-* [**eased, eas·ing**] 1 to relieve; lighten: *medicine that eases pain.* 2 to make less tight; loosen: *to ease a snug waistband.*

ast (ēst) *n-* 1 the direction halfway between north and south and generally toward the rising sun.

ast·er·ly (ēs′ tər lē) *adj-* 1 generally toward the east: *an easterly direction.* 2 of winds, generally from the east: *an easterly breeze.* *adv-* generally eastward: *a ship going easterly.* *n-* [*pl.* **eas·ter·lies**] wind from the east.

east·ern (ēs′ tərn) *adj-* 1 in or toward the east: *an eastern port; an eastern view.* 2 characteristic of or from the east: *an eastern custom.*

eas·y (ē′ zē) *adj-* [**eas·i·er, eas·i·est**] 1 requiring little effort; not difficult: *an easy task; an easy book to read.* 2 free from trouble or worry: *an easy life; to be easy in one's mind.* 3 permitting ease and relaxation; comfortable: *an easy seat.*

eat (ēt) *vt-* [**ate** (āt), **eat·en, eat·ing**] 1 to take into the mouth and swallow, usually after chewing: *to eat a peach; to eat a meal.* 2 to use habitually as food: *Seals eat fish.* *vi-* 1 to have a meal: *We eat at noon.* 2 to wear (away).

eaves (ēvz) *n-* (takes plural verb) overhanging edge of a sloping roof.

eaves·drop (ēvz′ drŏp′) *vi-* [**eaves·dropped, eaves·drop·ping**] to listen secretly to the private conversation of others. —*n-* **eaves′ drop′ per.**

ebb (ĕb) *n-* 1 the going out of the tide. 2 low state: *His courage was at its ebb.* *vi-* 1 to flow back; recede: *The tide ebbed.* 2 to weaken; decline: *Hope ebbed.*

eb·on·y (ĕb′ ə nē) *n-* [*pl.* **eb·on·ies**] hard, black wood of various tropical trees, used chiefly for decorative work, piano keys, etc.; also, any of the trees from which this wood is obtained. *adj-* 1 made of this wood: *an ebony table.* 2 black: *her ebony hair.*

e·bul·lient (ĭ bool′ yənt, ĭ bŭl′-) *adj-* full of enthusiasm and high spirits; bubbling. —*n-* **e·bul′ lience** or **e·bul′ lien·cy.** *adv-* **e·bul′ lient·ly.**

eb·ul·li·tion (ĕ′ bə lĭ′ shən) *n-* 1 a bubbling or boiling up. 2 a sudden surge or outburst of feeling.

ec·cen·tric (ĕk sĕn′ trĭk) *adj-* 1 odd, peculiar, or unconventional: *Hermits are eccentric persons. His behavior was quite eccentric.* 2 not having the same center; not concentric: *two eccentric circles.* 3 turning about a point or axis not at the center: *an eccentric wheel.*

ec·cen·tric·i·ty (ĕk′ sən trĭs′ ə tē) *n-* [*pl.* **ec·cen·tric·i·ties**] 1 odd and unusual behavior, action etc.: *my aunt's little eccentricities.* 2 condition of being eccentric. 3 the amount or degree by which something is eccentric.

ec·cle·si·as·tic (ĭ klē′ zē ăs′ tĭk) *adj-* (also **ec·cle′ si·as′ ti·cal**) of or having to do with the church or with church organization and government. *n-* a clergyman.

ech·e·lon (ĕsh′ ə lŏn′) *n-* 1 part of an organization, especially of a military unit, thought of as a level from the top down or a step from the front to the rear: *a high echelon of command; the rear echelon.*

ech·o (ĕk′ ō) *n-* [*pl.* **ech·oes**] 1 repetition of a sound due to the reflection of sound waves. 2 the repeated sound.

e·clat (ā klä′) *n-* 1 striking or sensational effect; brilliance; dash: *to perform with éclat.* 2 loud applause: *The audience responded with éclat.* [from French *éclat,* from *éclater,* meaning "to burst forth."]

ec·lec·tic (ĕ klĕk′ tĭk) *adj-* choosing or making use of what one considers the best ideas in various sources or systems of thought, learning, art, etc.: *his eclectic philosophy of life.* *n-* person who so chooses and selects. —*adv-* **ec·lec′ ti·cal·ly.**

e·clipse (ĭ klĭps′) *n-* complete or partial apparent darkening of the sun by the passage of the moon between it and the earth, or of the moon by the shadow of the earth. *vt-* [**e·clipsed, e·clips·ing**] to throw into the shade; outshine: *Alan's last role eclipsed all his others.*

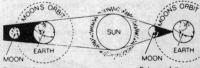

Eclipse of the moon   Eclipse of the sun

The eclipse of the sun is seen where
the moon's shadow touches the earth

e·col·o·gy (ĭ kŏl′ ə jē) *n-* branch of biology that deals with the relationships of organisms to each other and to their environment.

e·co·nom·ic (ĕk′ə nŏm′ ĭk, ē′kə-) *adj-* having to do with the production, distribution, and use of wealth, goods, and services: *the* economic *history of the country.*

e·co·nom·i·cal (ē′ə nŏm′ I kəl, ĕk′ə nŏm′-) *adj-* wise in the use of money, materials, effort, etc.; practical and thrifty: *an* economical *wife.* —*adv-* e′ co·nom′ i·cal·ly.

e·co·nom·ics (ĕk′ə nŏm′ĭks, ē′kə-) *n-* 1 (takes singular verb) science of the production, distribution, and use of wealth, goods, and services. 2 (takes plural verb) management and use of money, goods, etc.

e·con·o·mize (I kŏn′ə mĭz′) *vt-* [e·con·o·mized, e·con·o·miz·ing] to cut down on waste or expenses; be thrifty and sparing. *vt-* to use sparingly and to the best advantage: *to* economize *one's efforts.*

e·con·o·my (I kŏn′ə mē) *n-* [*pl.* e·con·o·mies] 1 thrifty use of money, goods, etc; also, an instance of this: *We must practice* economy.

ec·ru (ĕ′krōō′, ā′krōō′) *n-* a pale, yellowish brown. *adj-*: *curtains of* ecru *linen.*

ec·sta·sy (ĕk′stə sē) *n-* [*pl.* ec·sta·sies] feeling or state of deep emotion, especially of rapturous joy.

ec·stat·ic (ĕk stăt′ Ik) *adj-* feeling, producing, or expressing rapturous joy. —*adv-* ec·stat′ i·cal·ly.

ec·u·men·i·cal (ĕk′ yə mĕn′ I kəl) *adj-* 1 of or having to do with the Christian churches throughout the world: *an* ecumenical *council.* 2 worldwide in scope; universal. —*adv-* ec′ u·men′ i·cal·ly.

ec·ze·ma (ĕg zē′ mə, ĕk′sə mə) *n-* skin disease in which watery blisters and crusts form, usually accompanied by redness, itching, and burning.

ed·dy (ĕd′ē) *n-* [*pl.* ed·dies] 1 current of air, water, etc., that runs opposite to the main current, thus causing whirlwinds or whirlpools. 2 small whirlwind or whirlpool.

e·de·ma (I dē′ mə) *n-* any swelling of the body caused by an unusual accumulation of fluid in the spaces between tissues, organs, etc.

edge (ĕj) *n-* 1 extreme or outermost border; rim; margin: *the* edge *of the brook.* 2 thin, sharp, cutting part of a knife, tool, etc. 3 *Informal* margin or advantage: *to win by a slight* edge; *to have an* edge *on one's opponents.*

ed·i·ble (ĕd′ ə bəl) *adj-* fit or safe to be used for food; eatable: *Some fish are* edible. —*n-* ed′ i·bil′ i·ty.

e·dict (ē′ dĭkt′) *n-* command from an official authority that has the strength of a law; decree.

ed·i·fi·ca·tion (ĕd′ ə fə kā′ shən) *n-* mental or moral improvement: *A speech intended for our* edification.

ed·i·fice (ĕd′ ə fəs) *n-* a building, especially one that is large and impressive.

ed·i·fy (ĕd′ ə fī′) *vt-* [ed·i·fied, ed·i·fy·ing] to instruct and benefit, especially in morals, religion, etc.: *His example* edified *us.*

ed·it (ĕd′ It) *vt-* 1 to correct, revise, and prepare (manuscript) for publication. 2 to review, select, and arrange (motion-picture film, electronic tape, etc.) before offering to the public. 3 to select, arrange, and comment on (poems, essays, etc.) published as a single work or collection.

e·di·tion (I dĭsh′ ən) *n-* 1 particular published form of a literary or musical work: *a new* edition *of "Little Women"; the third* edition *of an encyclopedia.* 2 all the copies of a newspaper or magazine printed at one time.

ed·u·cate (ĕj′ə kăt′, ĕd′yōō-) *vt-* [ed·u·cat·ed, ed·u·cat·ing] to develop and improve by teaching or training; add to the knowledge or experience of: *to* educate *children; to* educate *one's mind.*

ed·u·ca·tor (ĕj′ə kā′ tər, ĕd′ yōō-) *n-* 1 teacher or other official of a school. 2 expert on education.

e·duce (ē dyōōs′, -dōōs′) *vt-* [e·duced, e·duc·ing] to draw forth; bring out; elicit: *to* educe *desired information by skillful questioning.* —*adj-* e·duc′ i·ble.

eel (ēl) *n-* any of various snakelike fishes with slippery skin. —*adj-* eel′ like′.

Eel

ee·rie or **ee·ry** (ĕr′ ē) *adj-* [ee·ri·er, ee·ri·est] 1 strange and frightening: *the* eerie *cry of an owl.* 2 uneasy; edgy: *an* eerie *feeling.* —*adv-* ee′ ri·ly. *n-* ee′ ri·ness.

ef·face (I fās′) *vt-* [ef·faced, ef·fac·ing] to erase; wipe out; destroy. —*n-* ef·face′ ment. *n-* ef·fac′ er.

efface (**oneself**) to keep (oneself) in the background.

ef·fect (I fĕkt′) *n-* 1 result of the action or influence of one thing, person, etc., on another or others; consequence: *the* effect *of a medicine; the* effect *of poverty.* 2 convincing illusion: *Sound* effects *are important in TV.*

ef·fec·tive (I fĕk′ tĭv) *adj-* 1 having the power to produce a result, especially a desired result: *an* effective *medicine; an* effective *argument.* 2 in force: *The law will be* effective *next week.* —*adv-* ef·fect′ ive·ly. *n-* ef·fect′ ive·ness.

ef·fec·tu·al (I fĕk′ chōō əl) *adj-* producing or able to produce desired results: *an* effectual *law; an* effectual *person.* —*adv-* ef·fec′ tu·al·ly. *n-* ef·fec′ tu·al·ness or ef·fec′ tu·al′ i·ty (-chōō ăl′ ə tē).

ef·fem·i·nate (I fĕm′ ə nət) *adj-* of a man or boy, having more feminine qualities than are suitable to a male; womanish; unmanly. —*n-* ef·fem′ i·na·cy or ef·fem′ i·nate·ness. *adv-* ef·fem′ i·nate·ly.

ef·fer·vesce (ĕf′ ər vĕs′) *vi-* [ef·fer·vesced, ef·fer·vesc·ing] 1 to give off gas in bubbles, as a carbonated drink does. 2 to be lively, gay, and full of enthusiasm.

ef·fer·ves·cent (ĕf′ ər vĕs′ ənt) *adj-* 1 forming or giving off bubbles of gas: *Champagne is an* effervescent *wine.* 2 full of bubbling enthusiasm: *her* effervescent *personality.* —*n-* ef′ fer·ves′ cence: *That ginger ale has lost its* effervescence. *adv-* ef′ fer·ves′ cent·ly.

ef·fete (ĕ fēt′) *adj-* no longer productive or vigorous; exhausted in power, effectiveness, etc.: *an* effete *civilization.* —*adv-* ef·fete′ly. *n-* ef·fete′ ness.

ef·fi·ca·cious (ĕf′ə kā′ shəs) *adj-* able to do what is expected or required; successful in desired function; effective: *an* efficacious *remedy; an* efficacious *person.* —*adv-* ef′ fi·ca′ cious·ly. *n-* ef′ fi·ca′ cious·ness.

ef·fi·ca·cy (ĕf′ I kə sē) *n-* [*pl.* ef·fi·ca·cies] the power to produce results, especially desired results.

ef·fi·cien·cy (I fĭsh′ ən sē) *n-* [*pl.* ef·fi·cien·cies] 1 ability to produce desired results with the least amount of time, expense, or labor; effective use of effort or energy. 2 *Physics* of an engine or other machine, the ratio of the useful work delivered by it to the amount of energy supplied to it.

ef·fi·cient (I fĭsh′ ənt) *adj-* producing the desired results with the least output of time, expense, and labor. —*adv-* ef·fi′ cient·ly.

ef·fi·gy (ĕf′ə jē) *n-* [*pl.* ef·fi·gies] portrait, statue, or other likeness of a person; especially, a crude image representing a hated person.

in **effigy** symbolically, in the form of a crude image.

ef·flo·res·cence (ĕ′ flə rĕs′ əns) *n-* 1 act, state, or season of flowering. 2 *Chemistry* loss of water of crystallization by certain crystals when exposed to air. 3 any rash, eruption, or lesion of the skin. —*adj-* ef′ flo·res′ cent.

ef·flu·vi·um (ĕ flōō′ vē əm) *n-* [*pl.* ef·flu·vi·a (-ə) or ef·flu·vi·ums] vapor or odor, especially one that is foul-smelling or poisonous.

ef·fort (ĕf′ ərt) *n-* 1 a putting forth of physical or mental power; exertion: *With great* effort, *he held back an angry reply.* 2 a try; an attempt: *The dog made an* effort *to get through the opening.* 3 something produced by work; achievement: *his latest literary* effort.

ef·fron·ter·y (I frŭn′tə rē) *n-* [*pl.* ef·fron·ter·ies] shameless boldness or impudence; insolence; audacity.

ef·ful·gence (I fŭl′ jəns) *n-* great brightness or splendor; radiance. —*adj-* ef·ful′ gent. *adv-* ef·ful′ gent·ly.

ef·fu·sion (I fyōō′ zhən) *n-* 1 a pouring or gushing forth, especially an unrestrained outpouring of ideas or feelings. 2 *Medicine* (1) escape of fluid into a part or tissue of the body. (2) such escaped fluid. 3 *Chemistry* passage of gas under pressure through small openings.

ef·fu·sive (I fyōō′ sĭv) *adj-* showing or expressing excessive enthusiasm or feeling; gushing: *his* effusive *thanks.* —*adv-* ef·fu′ sive·ly. *n-* ef·fu′ sive·ness.

¹egg (ĕg) *n-* 1 the oval or round body produced by hens and used as food; also, a similar body produced by the females of many animals, from which the young develop. Birds, insects, fish, and most reptiles hatch from eggs. 2 (also **egg cell**) reproductive cell produced by female animals and many plants. 3 *Informal* person;

fellow: *He's a good* egg. [from an Old Norse word.]

²egg (ĕg) *vt-* to urge or goad (often used with "on"): *She egged him on to mischief.* [from Old Norse eggja, originally meaning "to give an edge to."]

egg·plant (ĕg′plănt′) *n-* 1 plant that bears a large, oval, purple-skinned fruit. 2 its fruit, eaten as a vegetable.

egg·shell (ĕg′shĕl′) *n-* 1 the shell of an egg, especially a bird's egg. 2 a very light tan. *adj-* 1 very light tan. 2 having a slight gloss: *an eggshell enamel.* 3 thin and fragile: *fine eggshell china.*

e·gis (ē′jəs) aegis.

eg·lan·tine (ĕg′lən tīn′, -tēn′) *n-* wild rose with fragrant pink or white flowers; sweetbrier.

e·go (ē′gō) *n-* [*pl.* **e·gos**] 1 the self or individual personality, especially as it is aware of being distinct from other selves and other things; separate identity.

Eggplant

ei·der (ī′dər) or **eider duck** *n-* large sea duck of northern latitudes, valued for its soft breast feathers.

eight (āt) *n-* 1 amount or quantity that is one greater than 7; 8. 2 *Mathematics* (1) the cardinal number that is the sum of 7 and 1. (2) a numeral such as 8 that represents this cardinal number.

eight·een (ā′tēn′) *n-* 1 amount or quantity that is one greater than 17. 2 *Mathematics* (1) the cardinal number that is the sum of 17 and 1. (2) a numeral such as 18 that represents this cardinal number.

ei·ther (ē′thər, ī′thər) *determiner* (traditionally called adjective or pronoun) 1 one or the other of two: *You may take either seat.* *He looked at two cars, but didn't buy either.* 2 each of two: *Trees lined either side of the street.* *adv-* also (used only after a negative): *I didn't go, and he didn't go,* either. *n-* any of two: *We'll take either of them.*

e·jac·u·late (ĭ jăk′yə lāt′) *vt-* [**e·jac·u·lat·ed, e·jac·u·lat·ing**] 1 to exclaim; blurt out. 2 to eject or discharge (a stream or flow of fluid).

e·jac·u·la·tion (ĭ jăk′yə lā′shən) *n-* 1 a sudden exclamation or cry. 2 act or process of ejaculating.

e·ject (ĭ jĕkt′) *vt-* to push, throw, or force out; expel: *to eject a used cartridge.* —*n-* **e·jec′tion.**

¹eke (ēk) [**eked, ek·ing**] **eke out** 1 to just manage to make (a living): *He eked out a living by writing.* 2 to add enough to (something) to make do; supplement: *to eke out a meal of leftovers by adding rice.* [from Old English ēcan.]

¹e·lab·o·rate (ĭ lăb′ər ət) *adj-* carefully worked out in great detail; painstakingly prepared; intricate: *to make elaborate plans; elaborate costumes for a play.* —*adv-* **e·lab′o·rate·ly.** *n-* **e·lab′o·rate·ness.**

²e·lab·o·rate (ĭ lăb′ə rāt′) *vt-* [**e·lab·o·rat·ed, e·lab·o·rat·ing**] to work out with great care and detail: *The general elaborated his plan.* —*n-* **e·lab′o·ra′tion.**

elaborate on to give more details about.

e·lan (ā län′) *n-* dash and enthusiasm; vivacity; ardor. [from French.]

Eland. 3 1 2—6 ft high at shoulder

e·land (ē′lənd) *n-* large South African antelope having twisted horns on both the male and the female.

e·lapse (ĭ lăps′) *vi-* [**e·lapsed, e·laps·ing**] of time, to go by; pass: *Many days elapsed before they returned.*

e·las·tic (ĭ lăs′tĭk) *adj-* 1 able to spring back to normal size, shape, or position after being stretched or pressed together: *Rubber is an elastic substance.* 2 easily changed or adapted to fit circumstances; flexible: *an elastic foreign policy;*

e·las·tic·i·ty (ĭ lăs′tĭs′ə tē, ē′lăs′-) *n-* 1 condition or quality of being elastic: *the elasticity of a rubber band; the elasticity of his temperament.* 2 *Physics* property of

matter that causes an object or substance to return to its original form or shape after a stretching, bending, or otherwise deforming force has been removed.

e·late (ĭ lāt′) *vt-* [**e·lat·ed, e·lat·ing**] to make excited with joy or pride; raise the spirits of: *Winning first prize elated her.* —*adv-* **e·lat′ed·ly.**

e·la·tion (ĭ lā′shən) *n-* feeling of exultant joy or pride.

el·bow (ĕl′bō) *n-* 1 the joint in the arm between wrist and shoulder; also, the outer part of the arm at this point. 2 something bent at an angle, such as a curved section of pipe. *vt-* to nudge, jostle, or push with or as if with the outer part of the arm: *She elbowed the other shoppers aside.*

Pipe elbow

¹eld·er (ĕl′dər) *adj-* older: *Which is the elder sister?* *n-* 1 older or more experienced person: *Young Indians respected the elders of the tribe.* 2 an officer of certain churches. [from Old English eldra.]

e·lect (ĭ lĕkt′) *vt-* 1 to choose or select by vote: *The club elects officers in May.* 2 to decide; prefer: *Tom elected to stay at home last night.* *adj-* chosen for an office but not yet serving: *the governor-elect.*

e·lec·tion (ĭ lĕk′shən) *n-* 1 an electing or a being elected: *his election to office.* 2 the process of choosing a person or persons for office by voting: *a presidential election.*

e·lec·tive (ĭ lĕk′tĭv) *adj-* 1 chosen by election: *an elective official.* 2 filled by election: *an elective office.* 3 open to choice; not compulsory: *an elective course of study.* *n-* school course not included in a student's required subjects.

e·lec·tor (ĭ lĕk′tər) *n-* 1 voter, especially a qualified voter. 2 member of the electoral college.

e·lec·tor·ate (ĭ lĕk′tər ət) *n-* all the persons entitled to vote in an election; the qualified voters.

e·lec·tric (ĭ lĕk′trĭk) *adj-* 1 of or produced by electricity; producing, transmitting, or using electricity: *an electric generator; an electric current; an electric train.* 2 thrilling; exciting: *An electric quiver ran through the crowd.*

e·lec·tri·cian (ĭ lĕk′trĭsh′ən) *n-* person who installs, repairs, or works with electrical wiring or appliances.

e·lec·tric·i·ty (ĭ lĕk′trĭs′ə tē) *n-* 1 transfer of energy in a flow of electrons from one place to another. For example, energy in falling water drives a generator which drives electrons through a wire. The electrons in turn drive motors in homes and factories. 2 potential energy of a stationary electric charge; static electricity.

e·lec·tri·fy (ĭ lĕk′trə fī′) *vt-* [**e·lec·tri·fied, e·lec·tri·fy·ing**] 1 to charge with electricity. 2 to equip (a house, railway, etc.) for the use of electricity. 3 to thrill: *His speech electrified the audience.*

e·lec·tro·cute (ĭ lĕk′trə kyōōt′) *vt-* [**e·lec·tro·cut·ed, e·lec·tro·cut·ing**] to kill by electric shock. —*n-* **e·lec′tro·cu′tion.**

e·lec·trode (ĭ lĕk′trōd′) *n-* 1 either pole of an electric battery or any other source of electricity. 2 in an electron tube, transistor, etc., any one of the parts that give off, collect, or control the flow of electrons.

e·lec·trol·y·sis (ĭ lĕk′trŏl′ə səs) *n-* 1 process of decomposing a chemical compound by passing an electric current through its solution. 2 the destruction of hair roots by means of an electric current.

el·e·gance (ĕl′ə gəns) *n-* refinement and good taste.

el·e·gant (ĕl′ə gənt) *adj-* 1 having or showing good taste and refinement; *courtly; elegant manners.* 2 *Informal* very pleasing. —*adv-* **el′e·gant·ly.**

el·e·gi·ac (ĕl′ə jī′ăk) *adj-* of, or in the form of an elegy.

el·e·gy (ĕl′ə jē) *n-* [*pl.* **el·e·gies**] poem of a mournful or serious nature, often lamenting the dead.

el·e·ment (ĕl′ə mənt) *n-* 1 (also **chemical element**) substance that cannot be broken down into simpler substances by ordinary chemical means. Gold, iron, hydrogen, and oxygen are elements. 2 one of the main principles or steps of a subject; necessary part of a whole: *to learn the elements of arithmetic; to have all the elements of a good story.*

el·e·men·tal (ĕl′ə mĕn′təl) *adj-* of or having to do with basic principles or characteristics, especially of the physical world: *an elemental force.*

el·e·men·ta·ry (ĕl' ə mĕn' tə rē) *adj-* of or having to do with first steps or principles; introductory.

el·e·phant (ĕl' ə fənt) *n-* largest living land animal, native to Africa and Asia and having a thick, gray, wrinkled hide, two curved ivory tusks, and a trunk.

· Asian elephant 8–10 ft high

el·e·phan·ti·a·sis (ĕl' ə fən-tī' ə səs) *n-* filariasis.

el·e·phan·tine (ĕl' ə fən tēn', -tīn') *adj-* of, like, or suggestive of an elephant; slow and heavy.

el·e·vate (ĕl' ə vāt') *vt-* [el·e·vat·ed, el·e·vat·ing] 1 to raise to a higher level; lift: *to elevate a window shade.* 2 to raise to a higher rank or status: *He was elevated to the peerage.* 3 to improve the mental or moral quality of: *Great ideas elevate the mind.*

el·e·va·tion (ĕl' ə vā' shən) *n-* 1 raised place: *The house is built on a slight elevation.* 2 height, especially above sea level: *The elevation of the land at that point is 958 feet.* 3 a raising or a being raised.

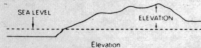

Elevation

el·e·va·tor (ĕl' ə vā' tər) *n-* 1 anything that lifts up. 2 movable platform or enclosed car that carries people, freight, etc., up and down between different levels or floors, usually inside a building. 3 in aeronautics, either of two flaps or control surfaces that are hinged to the horizontal parts of an airplane's tail and are used to make the tail go up or down. For picture, see *airplane*. 4 building equipped to store and process grain; grain elevator.

Grain elevator

e·lev·en (ĭ lĕv' ən) *n-* 1 amount or quantity that is one greater than ten; 11. 2 *Mathematics* (1) the cardinal number that is the sum of 10 and 1. (2) a numeral such as 11 that represents this cardinal number. 3 a football team. *as determiner* (traditionally called adjective or pronoun): *There are eleven ships here and eleven there.*

elf (ĕlf) *n-* [*pl.* elves (ĕlvz)] small goblin, fairy, or sprite, sometimes mischievous, sometimes helpful.

elf·in (ĕl' fĭn) *adj-* suggestive of an elf; odd and charming: *her elfin laughter.*

e·lic·it (ĭ lĭs' ĭt) *vt-* to draw out; bring forth; evoke: *to elicit a reply.* *Hom-* illicit.

e·lide (ĭ līd') *vt-* [e·lid·ed, e·lid·ing] to omit or slur (a syllable or vowel) in pronouncing a word or words.

e·li·gi·ble (ĕl' ə jə bəl) *adj-* 1 qualified or entitled to participate in or receive: *to be eligible for promotion; eligible to play; eligible for citizenship.* 2 suitable for marriage. *—n-* el'i·gi·bil'i·ty. *adv-* el'i·gi·bly.

e·lim·i·nate (ĭ lĭm' ə nāt') *vt-* [e·lim·i·nat·ed, e·lim·i·nat·ing] 1 to get rid of; dispose of; remove: *to eliminate all possibility of error; to eliminate contestants in a race.* 2 to leave out of consideration; omit.

e·li·sion (ĭ lĭzh' ən) *n-* 1 the omission or slurring over of a syllable or vowel sound in pronouncing a word or words. Example: the omission of the sound of the "i" of "is" in "What's that?", or of the "e" of "de" in French "louis d'or." 2 an omitting or dropping out of a word, paragraph, passage, etc. *Hom-* Elysian.

e·lite (ā lēt') *n-* 1 the best or most esteemed members of a society, profession, etc.: *Colonel Curtis is among the military elite.* 2 a type size for typewriters. *as modifier*: *an elite regiment; an elite typewriter.*

e·lix·ir (ĭ lĭk' sər) *n-* 1 sweet solution, usually of water and alcohol, that is used as a medium for medicine.

¹**ell** (ĕl) *n-* old measure of length, chiefly for cloth, varying from 27 to 45 inches. [from Old English **eln.**]

²**ell** (ĕl) *n-* an addition to a building, constructed at right angles to the main structure; L. [from the letter "L."]

el·lipse (ĭ lĭps') *n-* 1 closed plane curve, similar to an oval but having both ends equal in size. 2 *Mathematics* closed plane curve drawn so that, for any point P on the curve, the sum of the distances from P to two fixed points called foci is constant.

Foci of an ellipse

el·lip·sis (ĭ lĭp' səs) *n-* [*pl.* el·lip·ses (-sēz')] 1 in grammar, the omission of a word or words strictly required by grammatical rule but unnecessary for the sense of the statement. Example: "It is warmer today than yesterday" instead of "It is warmer today than it was yesterday."

el·lip·tic (ĭ lĭp' tĭk) *or* **el·lip·ti·cal** (-tĭ kəl) *adj-* 1 of, having to do with, or shaped like an ellipse or part of an ellipse. 2 in grammar, showing or using ellipsis. *—adv-* el·lip'ti·cal·ly.

elm (ĕlm) *n-* 1 tall shade tree with arching or outspread branches. 2 the hard, tough wood of this tree.

Elm

el·o·cu·tion (ĕl' ə kyōō' shən) *n-* art or style of reciting or speaking in public, especially a stilted or pompous style no longer popular.

e·lon·gate (ē lŏng' gāt') *vt-* [e·lon·gat·ed, e·lon·gat·ing] to lengthen; extend: *to elongate a line; to elongate a story.* *vi-*: *Earthworms elongate and contract at will.*

e·lope (ĭ lōp') *vi-* [e·loped, e·lop·ing] to go or run away secretly to be married. *—n-* e·lope' ment. *—n-* e·lop' er.

e·lo·quence (ĕl' ə kwəns) *n-* 1 ability to convey the intended meaning very well; power of expression: *the preacher's eloquence.* 2 good ordering and expression; expressiveness: *the eloquence of his appeal.* 3 art of effective speaking; oratory; elocution.

else (ĕls) *adv-* 1 instead; otherwise: *How else could I do it? I asked him when our club could meet.* 2 in addition; next: *What else do you want?* 3 if not; if this advice or command is ignored: *Do as I do, or else you may fall.* *adj-* different; other: *You looked like someone else.*

else·where (ĕls' hwâr) *adv-* in, at, or to some other place; somewhere else: *I'll meet you elsewhere.*

e·lu·ci·date (ĭ lōō' sə dāt') *vt-* [e·lu·ci·dat·ed, e·lu·ci·dat·ing] to make clear; clarify; explain: *to elucidate a difficult point.* *—n-* e·lu' ci·da' tion.

e·lude (ĭ lōōd', -lyōōd') *vt-* [e·lud·ed, e·lud·ing] 1 to escape by being quick or clever; evade: *to elude one's pursuers.* 2 to evade the memory or recognition of (someone): *Her name eludes me.*

▶Should not be confused with ALLUDE.

e·lu·sive (ĭ lōō' sĭv, -lyōō' sĭv) *adj-* 1 hard to catch; tending to escape or slip away: *an elusive butterfly.* 2 hard to understand, remember, or express: *an elusive idea.* *—adv-* e·lu'sive·ly. *n-* e·lu'sive·ness.

e·ma·ci·ate (ĭ mā' shē āt') *vt-* [e·ma·ci·at·ed, e·ma·ci·at·ing] to cause to waste away; make thin: *Hunger emaciated the survivors.* *—adj-* e·ma' ci·a' ted.

em·a·nate (ĕm' ə nāt') *vi-* [em·a·nat·ed, em·a·na·ting] to flow out from a source: *Light emanates from the sun.*

e·man·ci·pate (ĭ măn' sə pāt') *vt-* [e·man·ci·pat·ed, e·man·ci·pat·ing] to set free from slavery or strict control; liberate. *—n-* e·man' ci·pa' tion.

¹**e·mas·cu·late** (ĭ măs' kyə lāt') *vt-* [e·mas·cu·lat·ed, e·mas·cu·lat·ing] 1 to remove the masculinity of. 2 to deprive of strength and vigor: *Too much luxury can emasculate a nation.*

em·balm (ĕm bäm', -bälm') *vt-* to preserve (a dead body) with spices, chemicals, etc.

em·bark (ĕm bärk') *vi-* to go on board ship as a passenger: *to embark for France.* *vt-* to put on board ship: *to embark cargo.*

embark on to begin: *to embark on a law career.*

em·bar·rass (ĕm bâr' əs) *vt-* 1 to cause (a person) to feel self-conscious; fluster; disconcert: *His teacher's praise embarrassed Tom.*

em·bas·sy (ĕm′bə sē) n- [pl. **em·bas·sies**] 1 residence or office of an ambassador. 2 an ambassador and his assistants.

em·bed (ĕm bĕd′) vt- [em·bed·ded, em·bed·ding] to set (something) firmly in surrounding matter: They embedded the posts in concrete. Also **imbed**.

em·bel·lish (ĕm bĕl′ ĭsh) vt- 1 to adorn; ornament; beautify: They embellished the altar with carvings of roses. 2 to add fanciful details to, especially a story; elaborate. —n- em·bel′lish·ment.

em·ber (ĕm′bər) n- 1 a glowing piece of wood or coal in the ashes of a fire. 2 embers smoldering ashes.

em·bez·zle (ĕm bĕz′ əl) vt- [em·bez·zled, em·bez·zling] to steal (money) entrusted to one: The cashier embezzled a sum of money from the bank. —n- em·bez′zle·ment: The embezzlement was discovered. n- em·bez′zler.

em·bit·ter (ĕm bĭt′ ər) vt- to make bitter, morose, or resentful; sour: The death of her only son embittered the woman.

em·bla·zon (ĕm blā′ zən) vt- 1 to inscribe or adorn with heraldic symbols. 2 to adorn or light up with bright colors: Stars emblazoned the sky.

em·blem (ĕm′ bləm) n- something that stands for something else; also, symbol that can be seen: He wore the emblem of a famous regiment.

em·blem·at·ic (ĕm′ blə măt′ ĭk) or **em·blem·at·i·cal** (-ĭkəl) adj- symbolic; serving as an emblem: The laurel wreath is emblematic of victory.

em·bod·i·ment (ĕm bŏd′ ĭ mənt) n- 1 an embodying. 2 a perfect example of something; epitome; personification: He was the embodiment of helpfulness.

em·bod·y (ĕm bŏd′ ē) vt- [em·bod·ied, em·bod·y·ing] 1 to put into a form that can be touched or seen: to embody an idea in marble. 2 to collect into a united whole: The bylaws are embodied in this pamphlet. 3 to include or incorporate: The new law will be embodied in the present code.

em·bold·en (ĕm bōl′ dən) vt- to make bold; give courage to: The cheers emboldened the boxer.

em·bo·lism (ĕm′ bə lĭz′ əm) n- sudden blocking of a blood vessel by an embolus.

em·boss (ĕm bòs′, -bŏs′) vt- 1 to raise above a surface by pressure of a die: to emboss a border on a paper napkin. 2 to decorate with raised figures: The printer embossed the paper with my monogram.

em·brace (ĕm brās′) vt- [em·braced, em·brac·ing] 1 to grasp in the arms; hug: Mitzi ran down the path and embraced her father. 2 to take up; adopt: The class gladly embraced the museum's offer of a tour. 3 to include: Biology embraces botany and zoology. n- a hug.

em·bra·sure (ĕm brā′ zhər) n- an opening in the wall of a fortification from which to fire guns.

em·broil (ĕm broil′) vt- to involve (a person or persons) in difficulties, quarrels, etc.: His pride embroiled him in squabbles.

em·bry·o (ĕm′ brē ō) n- [pl. em·bry·os] 1 early form of an animal during development from a fertilized egg and before being hatched or born. 2 an unsprouted plant germ in a seed. 3 an early stage of growth or development: A frontier fort was the embryo of the city of Pittsburgh.

Embryo of fish

em·cee (ĕm′ sē′) Informal n- master of ceremonies. vt- to perform as master of ceremonies of: to emcee a banquet. vi-: He emceed at the banquet.

e·mend (ĭ mĕnd′) vt- to correct, usually by making changes in: to emend a text.
►For usage note see AMEND.

e·men·da·tion (ē′ mĕn dā′ shən) n- a correction, especially of written material.

em·er·ald (ĕm′ ər əld) n- 1 a precious stone of a clear, deep-green color. 2 the color of this stone. adj-: The sea was emerald and calm.

e·merge (ĭ mûrj′) vi- [e·merged, e·merg·ing] 1 to come forth into view: The sun emerged from a bank of clouds. 2 to become known; appear: The facts emerged slowly.

e·mer·gen·cy (ĭ mûr′ jən sē) n- [pl. e·mer·gen·cies]

sudden or unexpected happening that makes quick action necessary. as modifier: an emergency exit; an emergency light.

em·er·y (ĕm′ ə rē) n- very hard dark corundum used in powdered form for grinding or polishing.

e·met·ic (ĭ mĕt′ ĭk) n- a medicine that causes vomiting. as modifier: an emetic drug.

em·i·grant (ĕm′ ə grənt) n- person who leaves his country to settle in another. as modifier: an emigrant Hungarian.
►Should not be confused with IMMIGRANT.

em·i·grate (ĕm′ ə grāt′) vi- [em·i·grat·ed, em·i·grat·ing] to leave one's own country to settle in another: He emigrated to Mexico. —n- em′ i·gra′ tion.
►Should not be confused with IMMIGRATE.

em·i·nence (ĕm′ ə nəns) n- 1 high standing; great distinction: He has achieved eminence in the medical profession. 2 high ground; an elevation. 3 Eminence in the Roman Catholic Church, a title of honor given to a cardinal (preceded by "Your" or "His").

em·i·nent (ĕm′ ə nənt) adj- outstanding; distinguished: an eminent writer. —adj- em′ i·nent·ly.

em·is·sar·y (ĕm′ ə sĕr′ ē) n- [pl. em·is·sar·ies] person sent on a mission or errand, especially one of a confidential nature: the President's emissary to the new nation.

e·mis·sion (ĭ mĭsh′ ən, ē-) n- 1 act or process of emitting: the emission of light. 2 something emitted: Heat is one of the emissions from a light bulb. —adj- e·mis′ sive: an emissive source of light.

e·mit (ĭ mĭt′, ē-) vt- [e·mit·ted, e·mit·ting] to send forth; discharge: A volcano emits lava.

e·mol·li·ent (ĭ mŏl′ yənt, -ē ənt) adj- softening; soothing to the skin: an emollient oil. n- a softening substance.

e·mol·u·ment (ĭ mŏl′ yə mənt) n- pay; wages; salary.

e·mote (ē mōt′) vi- [e·mot·ed, e·mot·ing] to express emotion, especially for theatrical effect.

e·mo·tion (ĭ mō′ shən) n- 1 strong feeling: to speak with emotion. 2 any particular feeling, such as joy, fear, etc.

e·mo·tion·al (ĭ mō′ shən əl) adj- 1 having to do with the emotions; based on feeling: a silly, emotional quarrel. 2 stirring the emotion: His talk on loyalty was full of emotional appeal for the audience.

em·pa·thy (ĕm′ pə thē) n- the ability to feel with another and to see the world through his eyes; identification.

em·per·or (ĕm′ pər ər) n- ruler of an empire.

em·pha·sis (ĕm′ fə sĭs) n- [pl. em·pha·ses (-sēz′)] 1 strong attention or stress; concentration (on): an emphasis on correct spelling. 2 stress of the voice, given to one or more words or syllables.

em·pha·size (ĕm′ fə sīz′) vt- [em·pha·sized, em·pha·siz·ing] to stress; place special value or importance on.

em·phat·ic (ĕm făt′ ĭk) adj- 1 said or done with special force or emphasis: an emphatic reply. 2 striking; forceful; definite: the emphatic contrast between black and white. —adv- em·phat′ i·cal·ly.

em·pire (ĕm′ pīər′) n- 1 group of countries under the control of one ruler. 2 country of which the ruler bears the title of emperor. 3 absolute power or authority. 4 power; sovereignty: the responsibilities of empire.

em·pir·i·cal (ĕm pĭr′ ĭ kəl) adj- based on what has actually happened and been observed rather than on theory or supposed rules: an empirical opinion. Also em·pir′ ic. —adv- em·pir′ i·cal·ly.

em·pir·i·cism (ĕm pĭr′ ə sĭz′ əm) n- 1 action based entirely on knowledge of what has actually happened and been observed. 2 in philosophy, the theory that all human knowledge is of this sort. See also rationalism. —n- em·pir′ i·cist.

em·ploy (ĕm ploi′) vt- 1 to give work to (a person) for pay; hire: We hope to employ a new secretary tomorrow. 2 to make use of: He employed his spare time to good advantage. 3 to occupy; take up: Driving employs much of my time. n- service: He is in my uncle's employ.

em·ploy·ment (ĕm ploi′ mənt) n- 1 the act of hiring: He was busy with the employment of new help. 2 a being employed; having work: Full employment keeps a country prosperous.

em·po·ri·um (ĕm pôr′ ē əm) n- [pl. em·po·ri·ums or

em·por·i·a (-ē ə)] **1** store with varied merchandise (often used humorously). **2** trade center; marketplace.

em·pow·er (ĕm pou′ ər) *vt-* to give power or authority to; authorize: *The sheriff empowered the posse to act.*

em·press (ĕm′ prəs) *n-* the wife of an emperor, or a woman ruling an empire.

emp·ty (ĕmp′ tē, ĕm′ tē) *adj-* [emp·ti·er, emp·ti·est] **1** containing nothing; unoccupied; void: *an empty closet; an empty house.* **2** without meaning; barren: *an empty promise; an empty dream; his empty words.*

em·py·re·an (ĕm pīr′ē ən, ĕm′ pī′ rē′ən) *n-* **1** the heavens. **2** the highest heaven in ancient astronomy, consisting of fire or light. *adj-* heavenly; celestial. *—adj-* **em·pyr′e·al** or **em′py·re′al.**

e·mu (ē′ myōō′) *n-* large, three-toed Australian bird resembling the ostrich.

em·u·late (ĕm′ yə lāt′, -yōō lāt′) *vt-* [em·u·lat·ed, em·u·lat·ing] to strive to equal or surpass (someone): *We emulate people we admire.* *—n-* **em·u·la′tion.**

e·mul·sion (ĭ mŭl′ shən) *n-* **1** liquid mixture in which one liquid, usually a fat, is suspended throughout another in the form of very fine drops that do not dissolve or cluster together. See also *suspension.* **2** a coating applied to photographic films, plates, etc., to make them sensitive to light.

en·a·ble (ĭn ā′ bəl) *vt-* [en·a·bled, en·a·bling] to give (one or something) power or ability to do something: *The scholarship enabled her to go to college.*

en·act (ĭn ăkt′) *vt-* **1** to make into law: *Congress enacted a bill to lower tariffs.* **2** to act the part of: *He enacted the hero.* **3** to represent dramatically: *They enacted the Nativity.*

en·act·ment (ĭn ăkt′ mənt) *n-* **1** an enacting; a making into law: *the enactment of labor legislation.* **2** law or decree.

e·nam·el (ĭ năm′ əl) *n-* **1** any of various substances used to coat the surface of metal, glass, or pottery for protection and decoration. It forms a hard glossy surface. **2** paint that dries with a glossy surface. **3** hard, white outer surface of the teeth.

en·clo·sure (ĕn klō′ zhər) *n-* **1** a closing or shutting in: *The enclosure of the porch with glass was done quickly.*

en·camp (ĕn kămp′) *vi-* to settle in or make a camp: *The legion encamped across the Rhone.* *vt-* *The officer encamped his troops in the valley.*

en·camp·ment (ĕn kămp′ mənt) *n-* **1** the making of a camp; settlement in a camp. **2** a camp.

en·case (ĕn kās′) *vt-* [en·cas·ed, en·cas·ing] to enclose (something) in or as in a box or case. Also **incase.**

en·chain (ĕn chān′) *vt-* to bind with or as with chains.

en·chant (ĕn chănt′) *vt-* **1** to bewitch; overcome by magic: *Merlin enchanted the knight's sword.* **2** to delight greatly: *Her voice enchanted us.*

en·cir·cle (ĕn sûr′ kəl) *vt-* [en·cir·cled, en·cir·cling] **1** to make a circle around; surround: *The crowd encircled the winning team.* **2** to go completely around: *Satellites can encircle the earth.* *—n-* **en·cir′cle·ment.**

en·clave (ĕn′ klāv′) *n-* **1** territory enclosed by land to which it is not politically subject: *The Vatican is an enclave within Italy.* **2** district of a country or city inhabited by a minority group: *the Christian enclave in a Muslim city.*

en·co·mi·um (ĕn kō′ mē əm) *n-* [*pl.* en·co·mi·ums or en·co·mi·a (-mē ə)] a formal statement of praise; eulogy.

en·com·pass (ĕn kŭm′ pəs) *vt-* **1** to surround; encircle: *Enemy forces encompassed the camp.* **2** to include: *His education encompasses many branches of knowledge.*

en·core (äng′ kôr) *interj-* again! once more! (a cry to a performer for a repetition or for something additional). *n-* a response to such a request: *She played two encores.*

en·coun·ter (ĕn koun′ tər) *n-* **1** unexpected meeting: *Our encounter with the famous actor was exciting.* **2** a fight or battle: *a frightening encounter between two gangs.* *vt-* **1** to meet unexpectedly: *We encountered an old friend yesterday.* **2** to meet in conflict; fight.

en·cour·age (ĕn kûr′ ĭj) *vt-* [en·cour·aged, en·cour·ag·ing] **1** to give hope or courage to: *The medical report encouraged us.* **2** to urge by showing approval: *Her*

parents encouraged her to study the piano. **3** to aid; foster: *to encourage a plant's growth.*

en·croach (ĕn krōch′) *vi-* **1** to infringe or intrude upon another's domain or privileges: *The enemy encroached upon our waters.* **2** to spread or pass beyond the natural limits: *The flooding river encroached on the land.*

en·cum·ber (ĕn kŭm′ bər) or **in·cum·ber** (ĭn kŭm′ bər) *vt-* **1** to impede; hinder: *The girl's tight skirt encumbered her when she tried to hurry.* **2** to weigh down; burden: *to be encumbered with debts.*

en·cy·cli·cal (ĕn sĭ′ klĭ kəl) *n-* letter addressed by the Pope to the bishops of the Roman Catholic Church. Also **encyclical letter.**

en·cy·clo·pe·di·a (ĕn sĭ′ klə pē′ dē ə) *n-* a book or set of books containing articles, usually arranged in alphabetical order, on all branches of knowledge or on some special subject. Also **en·cy·clo·pae′di·a.** *as modifier: an encyclopedia salesman.*

end (ĕnd) *n-* **1** point or part at which something begins or leaves off: *both ends of the stick.* **2** farthest or last part of anything: *the end of the road; the end of a rope.* **3** point at which something ceases to exist; final limit: *I'm at the end of my patience.*

en·dan·ger (ĕn dān′ jər) *vt-* to put in danger; jeopardize: *He endangered his life by careless driving.*

en·dear (ĕn dēr′) *vt-* to make (someone) dear (to someone): *Her kindness endeared her to us all.*

en·dear·ment (ĕn dēr′ mənt) *n-* a spoken expression of affection, especially a phrase or single word.

en·deav·or (ĕn dĕv′ ər) *vt-* to attempt; strive; try hard: *He will endeavor to swim across the channel.* *n-* effort; attempt: *He made every endeavor to win her friendship.*

en·dem·ic (ĕn dĕm′ ĭk) *adj-* belonging or restricted to a given people or region: *a disease endemic in India.*

end·less (ĕnd′ ləs) *adj-* **1** lasting forever; having no end. **2** joined at the ends; continuous: *an endless chain.* *—adv-* **end′less·ly.** *n-* **end′less·ness.**

en·dorse (ĕn dôrs′, -dôrs′) *vt-* [en·dorsed, en·dors·ing] **1** to approve; support; sanction: *Congress endorsed the President's plan.* **2** to write one's name on the back of (a check or other document) as a legal sign that one approves or acknowledges payment of money or some other transaction. Also **indorse.** *—n-* **en·dors′er.**

en·dow (ĕn dou′) *vt-* **1** to provide with a permanent fund or source of income by gift (often followed by "with"): *Mr. Allen generously endowed his college.* **2** to equip; furnish (always followed by "with"): *He endowed his children with his keen sense of humor.*

en·dur·a·ble (ĕn dŏŏr′ ə bəl, ĕn dyŏŏr′ -) *adj-* such as can be endured; bearable. *—adv-* **en·dur′a·bly.**

en·dur·ance (ĕn dŏŏr′ əns, ĕn dyŏŏr′ -) *n-* **1** ability to bear up under strain, suffering, fatigue, or hardship: *A long-distance swimmer needs great endurance.* **2** ability to withstand hard wear or use: *to test the endurance of a car. as modifier: an endurance record.*

en·dure (ĕn dŏŏr′, -dyŏŏr′) *vt-* [en·dured, en·dur·ing] **1** to bear bravely; suffer: *The pioneers endured many hardships.* **2** to put up with; tolerate; bear: *She cannot endure the cold.*

en·e·my (ĕn′ ə mē) *n-* [*pl.* en·e·mies] **1** person who harbors hatred or works actively against another; unfriendly opponent; foe; adversary. **2** hostile military force, nation, etc. **3** anything that harms or injures: *Cancer is an enemy of humanity. as modifier: a fleet of enemy warships.*

en·er·get·ic (ĕn′ ər jĕt′ ĭk) *adj-* very active; industrious; vigorous. *—adv-* **en·er·get′i·cal·ly.**

en·er·gy (ĕn′ ər jē) *n-* [*pl.* en·er·gies] **1** material power of the universe; ability to do work: *Einstein studied the relation of energy to matter.* **2** ability to put forth muscular effort; vigor: *He needed all his energy to win.* **3** mental or physical force: *He spoke with energy.*

en·er·vate (ĕn′ ər vāt′) *vt-* [en·er·vat·ed, en·er·vat·ing] to sap the force and vitality of; weaken physically or mentally. *—n-* **en·er′va′tion.**

en·fee·ble (ĕn fē′ bəl) *vt-* [en·fee·bled, en·fee·bling] to weaken; make feeble: *Sickness enfeebled him.*

en·force (ĕn fôrs′) *vt-* [en·forced, en·forc·ing] **1** to compel obedience to: *The police enforce the law.* 2 to impose by force; compel: *to enforce silence.*

en·fran·chise (ěn frǎn'chīz') *vt-* [en·fran·chised, en·fran·chis·ing] 1 to give (a person) the right to vote: *Wyoming enfranchised women in 1890.* 2 to free, as from slavery. —*n-* en·fran'chise'ment.

en·gage (ěn gāj') *vt-* [en·gaged, en·gag·ing] 1 to be the concern or subject of; occupy: *Work engaged most of his time.* 2 to get the right to use; reserve for use: *to engage a suite of rooms.* 3 to hire; employ: *to engage a new gardener.* 4 to attract and hold: *The squabble engaged his attention.* 5 to bind or pledge (oneself): *He engaged himself to pay the debt.*

en·grave (ěn grāv') *vt-* [en·graved, en·grav·ing] 1 to cut letters or designs into the surface of (wood, metal, stone, etc.) for display or for printing: *to engrave a silver cup*; *to engrave plates for a new dollar bill.* 2 to print (cards, bills, etc.) from blocks or plates cut in this way.

en·gross (ěn grōs') *vt-* 1 to occupy wholly; fill the mind or time of: *His hobby engrosses him.* 2 to prepare the official copy of (a state document).

en·gulf (ěn gŭlf') *vt-* to swallow up; overwhelm; bury: *High waves engulfed the swimmers.*

en·hance (ěn hǎns') *vt-* [en·hanced, en·hanc·ing] to add to; increase: *Flowers enhanced her beauty.*

e·nig·ma (ĭ nĭg'mə) *n-* person or thing not easily understood; puzzle; riddle: *His intentions remained an enigma.*

en·join (ěn join') *vt-* 1 to order emphatically; direct; urge: *to enjoin someone to leave*; *to enjoin silence.* 2 to issue a legal injunction against: *The court enjoined the defendant to pay his taxes.*

en·joy (ěn joi') *vt-* 1 to take pleasure or delight in: *We enjoyed the picnic.* 2 to possess; have the use of: *I enjoy good health.*

en·large (ěn lärj') *vt-* [en·larged, en·larg·ing] to make larger; add to; increase in quantity, extent, etc.: *to enlarge a house*; *enlarge a photograph.* *vi-* to grow larger: *The population gradually enlarges.*

en·gage·ment (ěn gāj'mənt) *n-* 1 a promise to marry; betrothal. 2 appointment; promise to meet someone somewhere at a fixed time: *I have a three o'clock engagement with my lawyer.* 3 employment: *The actress had a six weeks' engagement in a summer theater.*

en·gen·der (ěn jěn'dər) *vt-* to give birth to; bring into being; create: *Truthfulness engenders confidence.*

en·gine (ěn'jən) *n-* 1 machine that changes energy into mechanical power by using the pressure of hot steam, burning gasoline, hydrazine, etc., or by electrically accelerating a stream of ions, as in one type of rocket engine. 2 any machine or instrument: *an engine of war.*

Steam and internal-combustion (gasoline) engines

en·gi·neer (ěn'jə nêr') *n-* 1 person who designs, develops, and helps to build machines, structures, electrical systems, etc. Most engineers are graduates of colleges of engineering, with degrees in mechanical engineering, civil engineering, electrical engineering,

en·light·en (ěn lī'tən) *vt-* to furnish with knowledge; free from ignorance; instruct; inform: *Let me enlighten you as to your duties.* —*n-* en·light'en·ment.

en·list (ěn lĭst') *vt-* 1 to enroll, especially for military service: *to enlist men for the army.* 2 to attract and gain (someone's help) for a cause: *We enlisted his services for the Red Cross.* *vi-* 1 to enter the armed forces without being drafted. 2 to join any cause.

en·liv·en (ěn lī'vən) *vt-* to put life into; invigorate; brighten: *Edgar's new records enlivened the party.*

en·mi·ty (ěn'mə tē) *n-* [pl. en·mi·ties] hatred; ill will; hostility: *an enmity between two nations.*

en·no·ble (ěn nō'bəl) *vt-* [en·no·bled, en·no·bling] 1

1 to make noble and dignified; exalt: *His life was ennobled by his generosity.* 2 to raise to the nobility.

en·nui (än'wē') *n-* boredom resulting from inactivity; discontent; weariness.

e·nor·mi·ty (ĭ nòr'mə tē, ĭ nôr'-) *n-* [pl. e·nor·mi·ties] hugeness in wickedness: *the enormity of his offense.* 2 a great wrong or crime: *Hitler's many enormities.*
▶Should not be confused with ENORMOUSNESS, which means great size of anything.

e·nor·mous (ĭ nòr'məs, ĭ nôr'-) *adj-* very large; huge. —*adv-* e·nor'mous·ly. *n-* e·nor'mous·ness.

e·nough (ĭ nŭf') *determiner* (traditionally called adjective or pronoun) sufficient; as much or as many as necessary or desirable: *Do we have enough food for tomorrow? Yes, we have enough.*

en·rage (ěn rāj') *vt-* [en·raged, en·rag·ing] to make very angry; infuriate: *Teasing enraged the dog.*

en·rapt (ěn răpt') *adj-* rapt; in a state of rapture.

en·rap·ture (ěn răp'chər) *vt-* [en·rap·tured, en·rap·tur·ing] to move to rapture; fill with delight.

en·rich (ěn rĭch') *vt-* 1 to make better or more effective by desirable additions: *to enrich flour*; *to enrich soil.* 2 to make (one's mind, an experience, one's life, etc.) fuller and more satisfying. 3 to make more beautiful; adorn. 4 to make wealthy: *Grandfather's investments enriched the whole family.* —*n-* en·rich'ment.

en·roll or **en·rol** (ěn rōl') *vt-* [en·rolled, en·roll·ing] 1 to put the name (of a person or persons) on a list or register: *to enroll students for a special class.* 2 to make a member: *The club enrolled him.* *vi-* to become a member; register: *He enrolled yesterday.*

en·roll·ment or **en·rol·ment** (ěn rōl'mənt) *n-* 1 number of persons admitted to a group: *The enrollment of the school is one thousand.* 2 admission to membership: *her enrollment in the Girl Scouts.*

en route (än rōōt', ěn-) *adv-* on the way: *The plane is en route to London.*

en·sconce (ěn skŏns') *vt-* [en·sconced, en·sconc·ing] 1 to place; settle comfortably: *We ensconced her in the sofa with a book.* 2 to establish in a secret place; hide: *The boys ensconced themselves in the cave.*

en·sem·ble (än sǎm'bəl) *n-* 1 all the parts of a thing viewed together as a whole; total effect. 2 things selected as a set for some purpose; outfit: *a camping ensemble including a folding table*; *an ensemble of lightweight luggage.*

en·shrine (ěn shrīn') *vt-* [en·shrined, en·shrin·ing] 1 to place or preserve on an altar or in a holy place. 2 to cherish; keep sacred: *They enshrined his memory in their hearts.* —*n-* en·shrine'ment.

en·shroud (ěn shroud') *vt-* to cover completely; conceal; wrap; envelop; shroud: *Fog enshrouds the city.*

en·sign (ěn'sīn, -sən) *n-* 1 a national flag or banner used on ships. 2 pennant showing office, rank, or authority: *the general's ensign.* 3 (ěn'sən) in the U.S. Navy, a commissioned officer next below a lieutenant (junior grade) and next above a warrant officer.

Norwegian ensign

en·slave (ěn slāv') *vt-* [en·slaved, en·slav·ing] 1 to make a slave of; place in bondage. 2 to dominate completely: *Fear of poverty enslaved him.* —*n-* en·slave'ment.

en·snare (ěn snâr') *vt-* [en·snared, en·snar·ing] to trap; snare; trick: *to ensnare birds in a net.*

en·sue (ěn sōō', -syōō') *vi-* [en·sued, en·su·ing] to follow in order; result; come afterward: *The ship ran aground and panic ensued.*

en·tail (ěn tāl') *vt-* 1 to impose; require; make necessary: *Success entails hard work.* 2 to bequeath (land, property, etc.) in such a way that the heirs cannot give or will it away. —*n-* en·tail'ment.

en·tan·gle (ěn tǎng'gəl) *vt-* [en·tan·gled, en·tan·gling] 1 to ensnare; enmesh: *I entangled my fishing line in the reeds. They entangled him in their plot.*

en·ter (ěn'tər) *vt-* (in senses 1, 3, and 5 considered intransitive when the direct object is implied but not expressed) 1 to go or come into: *He entered the house.*

en·ter·prise (ĕn' tər prīz') *n-* 1 an undertaking; project: *a difficult* enterprise; *a business* enterprise. 2 willingness or energy to start new projects; initiative: *a spirit of* enterprise; *man of* enterprise. See also *free enterprise.*

en·ter·tain (ĕn' tər tān') *vt-* 1 to receive as a guest; give food and drink to: *They will* entertain *friends at dinner tonight.* 2 to amuse; divert; interest: *That magician has* entertained *many audiences.* 3 to consider; keep in mind: *He is* entertaining *the offer of a new job.* *vi-* to receive guests: *We* entertained *in the garden.*

en·thrall or **en·thral** (ĕn thrôl') *vt-* [en·thralled, en·thral·ling] to hold under a spell; charm; captivate: *The singer* enthralled *his audience.*

en·throne (ĕn thrōn') *vt-* [en·throned, en·thron·ing] 1 to place on a throne or in a position of power: *to* enthrone *a king.* 2 to place in a position of reverence or devotion: *to* enthrone *a hero.* —*n-* en·throne'ment.

en·thu·si·asm (ĕn thōō' zē ăz' əm) *n-* strong and joyous feeling of interest or admiration (for): *Rain did not affect our* enthusiasm.

en·thu·si·as·tic (ĕn thōō' zē ăs' tĭk) *adj-* full of enthusiasm; keenly interested: *an* enthusiastic *baseball fan.* —*adv-* en·thu'si·as'ti·cal·ly.

en·tice (ĕn tīs') *vt-* [en·ticed, en·tic·ing] to lead on by arousing hope or desire; lure; tempt: *He* enticed *the dog with a bone.* —*n-* en·tice'ment. *adv-* en·tic'ing·ly.

en·tire (ĕn tīər') *adj-* 1 whole; complete: *the* entire *family; the* entire *program.* 2 unbroken: *an* entire *series.* 3 total: *his* entire *ignorance of the matter.*

en·tire·ty (ĕn tīər' tē) *n-* the whole; the total.
    in its entirety as a whole; completely.

en·ti·tle (ĕn tī' təl) *vt-* [en·ti·tled, en·ti·tling] 1 to give (someone) a right or privilege (to): *The law* entitles *every person accused of a crime to a trial.* 2 to give a title to: *Mark Twain* entitled *a book "The Adventures of Tom Sawyer."*

en·ti·ty (ĕn' tə tē) *n-* [*pl.* en·ti·ties] 1 independent being or existence: *Some Indian tribes try to preserve their* entity. 2 something real in itself or distinct in character: *The United States is an* entity *rather than a loose confederation. Love and beauty are* entities *in themselves.*

en·tomb (ĕn tōōm') *vt-* 1 to place in a grave or tomb; bury. 2 to serve as a tomb for. —*n-* en·tomb'ment.

en·to·mol·o·gy (ĕn' tə mŏl' ə jē) *n-* branch of zoology that deals with insects.

en·trails (ĕn' trəlz, -trālz') *n- pl.* the internal parts of man or animals, especially the bowels.

en·train (ĕn trān') *vi-* to board a train: *We* entrained *at noon. vt-* to put aboard a train: *to* entrain *troops.*

¹**en·trance** (ĕn' trəns) *n-* 1 door or passage through which one enters: *the* entrance *to a tunnel.* 2 an entering: *The actress makes a dramatic* entrance *wherever she goes.*

²**en·trance** (ĕn trăns') *vt-* [en·tranced, en·tranc·ing] 1 to put under a spell. 2 to fill with delight; enrapture: *The ballet* entranced *her.* [from en- meaning "in" plus **trance** meaning "a spell."] —*n-* en·trance'ment.

en·trap (ĕn trăp') *vt-* [en·trapped, en·trap·ping] to lure into a trap, especially into a bad moral or legal situation. —*n-* en·trap'ment.

en·treat (ĕn trēt') *vt-* to ask earnestly; beg; beseech: *to* entreat *a favor.* —*adv-* en·treat'ing·ly.

en·treat·y (ĕn trē' tē) *n-* [*pl.* en·treat·ies] earnest request; prayer: *He was deaf to her* entreaties.

en·tree (än' trā') *n-* 1 entrance; privilege of entering; access: *He gained* entree *to the exclusive club.* 2 the main dish of a meal. Also **entrée.**

en·try (ĕn' trē) *n-* [*pl.* en·tries] 1 a going into; entering: *Their* entry *into the country was illegal.* 2 place through which one goes or comes in, such as a vestibule. 3 item recorded in a list, diary, etc.: *an* entry *in the ship's log.* 4 person or thing entered in a contest.

en·twine (ĕn twīn') *vt-* [en·twined, en·twin·ing] 1 to wind or twine around: *Ivy* entwined *the cottage.* 2 to twist together: *They* entwined *their hands as they walked.*

e·nu·mer·ate (ĭ nōō' mə rāt', ĭ nyōō'-) *vt-* [e·nu·mer·at·ed, e·nu·mer·at·ing] 1 to list or name one by one. 2 to count; number. —*n-* e·nu'mer·a'tion.

e·nun·ci·ate (ĭ nŭn' sē āt') *vt-* [e·nun·ci·at·ed, e·nun·

ci·at·ing] 1 (considered intransitive when the direct object is implied but not expressed) to pronounce or utter (words, sounds, etc.): *to* enunciate *one's "t's" clearly.* 2 to proclaim; announce: *to* enunciate *a theory.*

e·nun·ci·a·tion (ĭ nŭn' sē ā' shən) *n-* 1 manner of pronouncing words or sounds: *her clear* enunciation. 2 statement; announcement: *an* enunciation *of policy.*

en·vel·op (ĕn vĕl' əp) *vt-* to enfold in or as in a wrapper, so as to cover or conceal: *Fog* enveloped *the city.*

en·ve·lope (ĕn' və lōp', än'-) *n-* 1 flat paper wrapper for enclosing letters. 2 any outer covering, especially that of a dirigible or balloon.

en·vi·a·ble (ĕn' vē ə bəl) *adj-* admirable or desirable enough to cause envy: *He has an* enviable *school record.*

en·vi·ous (ĕn' vē əs) *adj-* feeling or showing envy; jealous: *to be* envious *of someone's success.* —*adv-* en·vi·ous·ly. —*n-* en·vi·ous·ness.

en·vi·ron (ĕn vī' rən, -ərn) *vt-* to form a circle or ring around; encircle: *Forests* environ *the city.*

en·vi·ron·ment (ĕn vī' ərn mənt, ĕn vī' rən-) *n-* 1 all the things that are around or in the neighborhood of a person, building, etc.; physical surroundings: *the* environment *of the new school.* 2 all the influences, ideas, conditions, etc., among which a person lives: *a good family* environment.

en·vi·rons (ĕn vī' rənz, -ərnz) *n- pl.* the surroundings of a city; suburbs; outskirts.

en·voy (ĕn' voi, än'-) *n-* 1 messenger. 2 government official sent on a mission to another government. 3 a diplomat ranking next below an ambassador. 4 l'envoi, the last stanza of a ballade.

en·vy (ĕn' vē) *n-* [*pl.* en·vies] 1 feeling of discontent aroused by the advantages or possessions of another; resentful jealousy: *He was filled with* envy *at his friend's accomplishment.* 2 the object of such a feeling: *Her beauty was the* envy *of all the girls.*

en·wrap (ĕn răp') *vt-* [en·wrapped, en·wrap·ping] to enclose; envelop; enfold.

en·zyme (ĕn' zīm') *n-* protein that starts or speeds up chemical action in other substances without undergoing any permanent change itself. Enzymes are made by the cells of all living organisms.

e·on (ē' ŏn', -ən) *n-* extremely long period of time; an eternity; age: *rocks lasting through* eons. Also **aeon.**

ep·au·let or **ep·au·lette** (ĕp' ə lĕt') *n-* shoulder ornament on a uniform, usually signifying rank.

Epaulet

e·phed·rine (ĭ fĕd' rĭn) *n-* drug extracted from certain Chinese plants or made synthetically, and used to raise the blood pressure, to treat asthma and hay fever, and to dilate the pupil of the eye.

e·phem·er·al (ĭ fĕm' ər əl) *adj-* 1 lasting for only a short time; fleeting; transitory: *When compared to the age of the earth, man's life is* ephemeral.

ep·ic (ĕp' ĭk) *n-* long narrative poem in a lofty style that tells of heroes and heroic deeds. The "Iliad" is an epic. *adj-* 1 of or related to such a poem: *an* epic *hero.* 2 grand; majestic; noble: *an* epic *achievement.*

ep·i·cure (ĕp' ə kyōōr') *n-* person who is devoted to refined pleasures, especially eating and drinking.

ep·i·dem·ic (ĕp' ə dĕm' ĭk) *n-* 1 general attack of a disease in a particular area: *The town had an* epidemic *of measles.* 2 widespread occurrence of anything: *an* epidemic *of robberies.*

ep·i·gram (ĕp' ə grăm') *n-* terse, witty saying. Example: "All men are equal, but some are more equal than others."

ep·i·lep·sy (ĕp' ə lĕp' sē) *n-* disease of the nervous system marked by fits of fainting with or without convulsive jerking of the muscles.

ep·i·log or **ep·i·logue** (ĕp' ə lôg', -lŏg') *n-* 1 concluding part of a story, poem, etc., usually giving added information or comment. 2 speech recited at the end of a play.

e·pis·co·pa·cy (ĭ pĭs' kə pə sē) *n-* [*pl.* e·pis·co·pa·cies] 1 church government by bishops. 2 office, rank, or term of office of a bishop. 3 bishops as a group.

ep·i·sode (ĕp′ə sōd′) *n-* **1** section or incident in a literary work: *the episode of whitewashing the fence in "Tom Sawyer."* **2** outstanding incident in a person's life, in history, etc. **3** an installment of a story or play published or performed serially.

e·pis·tle (ĭ pĭs′əl) *n-* **1** letter, especially a formal one. **2 Epistle** one of the letters or collections of letters written by the Apostles and forming part of the New Testament.

ep·i·taph (ĕp′ ə tăf′) *n-* writing inscribed on a tomb, tombstone, etc., in memory of the person buried there.

ep·i·thet (ĕp′ə thĕt′) *n-* **1** adjective or other descriptive term used to express some characteristic quality. Examples: "fleet-footed" in "fleet-footed Achilles," or "the Fat" in "Charles the Fat." **2** insulting name: *to hurl epithets at someone.*

e·pit·o·me (ə pĭt′ə mē) *n-* **1** most typical or ideal representative of something; embodiment: *Samson is the epitome of courage.* **2** short summary of a writing; synopsis; abstract.

e·pit·o·mize (ə pĭt′ə mīz′) *vt-* [e·pit·o·mized, e·pit·o·miz·ing] **1** to be the most typical or ideal representative of; embody most perfectly: *Samson epitomizes courage.* **2** to summarize; abridge.

ep·och (ĕp′ ək) *n-* **1** period of time in which unusual or important events take place; era: *The epoch of space exploration began with the launching of the first earth satellite.*

eq·ua·ble (ĕk′wə bəl, ē′kwə-) *adj-* **1** steady and unchanging; even: *an equable climate.* **2** not readily upset; serene and tranquil: *an equable disposition.* —*n-* e′qua·bil′i·ty. *adv-* eq′ua·bly.

e·qual (ē′kwəl) *adj-* **1** having the same size, amount, value, rank, etc.; alike; identical: *I want an equal share; men equal before the law.* **2** fairly matched; even: *an equal contest.* **3** belonging to all; shared: *our equal rights; equal duties.*

e·qual·i·ty (ē kwŏl′ə tē) *n-* [*pl.* e·qual·i·ties] **1** sameness; identity. **2** treatment, rights, etc., that are the same for all persons. **3** *Mathematics* statement that two variables, quantities, etc. are equal, usually in the form of an equation.

e·qual·ize (ē′kwə līz′) *vt-* [e·qual·ized, e·qual·iz·ing] to make equal or even. —*n-* e′qual·i·za′tion.

e·qua·nim·i·ty (ĕk′ wə nĭm′ə tē, ē′kwə-) *n-* evenness of mind or temper; calmness; serenity.

e·qua·tion (ĭ kwā′zhən) *n-* **1** a statement that two quantities are equal: $3 + 3 = 6$ *is an equation.* **2** in arithmetic, any sentence with "equals" for its verb. Example: $x + 3 = 7.$

e·qua·tor (ĭ kwā′tər) *n-* **1** an imaginary circle around the earth that is equally distant from the North and South Poles and divides the earth into the northern and southern hemispheres. **2** any similar circle around another planet or the sun. **3** the celestial equator.

e·qua·to·ri·al (ĕk′wə tôr′ē əl, ē′kwə-) *adj-* **1** having to do with or located near the earth's equator. **2** like conditions near the earth's equator: *a week of equatorial heat.* —*adv-* e′qua·to′ri·al·ly.

e·ques·tri·an (ĭ kwĕs′trē ən) *n-* **1** man or boy riding a horse. **2** man or boy regarded as a rider of horses: *Tom's a good equestrian.* *adj-* **1** of or related to horses or horsemanship: *his equestrian training.* **2** performing with horses, as in a circus: *an equestrian artist.*

e·qui·dis·tant (ē′kwə dĭs′tənt) *adj-* separated by equal distances; equally distant.

e·qui·lat·er·al (ē′kwə lăt′ər əl) *adj-* in geometry, having all sides of the same length: *an equilateral triangle.* —*adv-* e′qui·lat′er·al·ly.

e·qui·lib·ri·um (ē′kwə lĭb′rē əm) *n-* **1** balance: *A tightrope walker keeps his equilibrium with a pole.* **2** evenness of mind and emotions; aplomb.

e·quine (ĕk′wīn′, ē′kwīn′) *adj-* of or like a horse.

e·qui·noc·tial (ē′kwə nŏk′təl əl, ĕk′wə-) *adj-* **1** pertaining to the equinoxes, or having day and night of equal length. **2** occurring at the time of an equinox.

e·qui·nox (ĕ′kwə nŏks′, ĕk′wə-) *n-* **1** either of the two days each year on which the sun is directly above the equator. On these days, day and night are of equal

length everywhere on earth. The **vernal equinox** occurs about March 21, and the **autumnal equinox** occurs about September 22.

e·quip (ĭ kwĭp′) *vt-* [e·quipped, e·quip·ping] to supply with something needed or useful; fit out: *to equip a polar expedition.*

e·qui·poise (ĕk′wə poiz′, ē′ kwə-) *n-* **1** equality of weight or force; equilibrium; balance. **2** weight or force that counterbalances another; counterpoise.

eq·ui·ta·ble (ĕk′wə tə bəl) *adj-* just; fair; impartial: *an equitable decision.* —*adv-* eq′ui·ta·bly.

eq·ui·ty (ĕk′ wə tē) *n-* [*pl.* eq·ui·ties] **1** fairness; justice: *No one questions the equity of this transaction.* **2** in law, a body of rules based on natural principles of justice, administered in special courts, and distinct from statutes.

e·quiv·a·lent (ĭ kwĭv′ə lənt) *adj-* **1** equal in value, amount, meaning etc.: *Cheating is equivalent to lying.* **2** *Mathematics* (1) having the same solution set: equivalent *equations.* (2) having equal areas or volumes: equivalent *figures.* (3) having the same value: equivalent *fractions.*

e·quiv·o·cal (ĭ kwĭv′ə kəl) *adj-* of doubtful or uncertain meaning, value, etc.; ambiguous: *an equivocal reply.* —*adv-* e·quiv′o·cal·ly. *n-* e·quiv′o·cal·ness.

e·quiv·o·cate (ĭ kwĭv′ə kāt′) *vi-* [e·quiv·o·cat·ed, e·quiv·o·cat·ing] to deceive by making equivocal or ambiguous statements: *He would rather equivocate than give a direct, truthful answer.* —*n-* e·quiv′o·ca′tion. *n-* e·quiv′o·ca′tor: *An equivocator makes me uneasy.*

e·rad·i·cate (ĭ răd′ə kāt′) *vt-* [e·rad·i·cat·ed, e·rad·i·cat·ing] to destroy completely; annihilate; wipe out: *Vaccination has nearly eradicated smallpox.* —*adj-* e·rad′i·ca·ble (-kə bəl). *n-* e·rad′i·ca′tion. *n-* e·rad′i·ca′tor: *I need ink eradicator to correct this error.*

e·rase (ĭ rās′) *vt-* [e·rased, e·ras·ing] **1** to remove (a mark, word, etc.); rub out: *Please erase that misspelled word.* **2** to remove markings from: *Please erase the blackboard.*

e·rect (ĭ rĕkt′) *vt-* **1** to construct or build: *They will erect a new building.* **2** to set up; establish; found: *to erect a new government.* **3** to set upright; raise: *to erect a flagpole.*

erg (ûrg) *n-* unit of work equal to the work done in lifting one gram one centimeter.

er·mine (ûr′mən) *n-* **1** any of various weasels valued for their white winter fur. **2** the winter fur of these animals.

Ermine, about 14 in long

e·rode (ĭ rōd′) *vt-* [e·rod·ed, e·rod·ing] **1** to wear away by rubbing or by the washing or blowing away of particles; eat away: *Rain and wind eroded the hillside. The wiring was eroded by acid.* **2** to form by wearing away: *Water eroded gullies in the hill.*

err (ĕr, ûr) *vi-* to make a mistake; do wrong; be incorrect: *To err is human.*

er·rand (ĕr′ ənd) *n-* **1** trip for a special purpose: *an errand of mercy.* **2** thing to be done on such a trip: *I've finished my errands.*

er·rant (ĕr′ ənt) *adj-* **1** roving in search of adventure: *an errant knight.* **2** mistaken; wrong: *his errant behavior.*

er·rat·ic (ĭ răt′ĭk) *adj-* **1** wandering; straying: *an erratic journey.* **2** odd; eccentric: *her erratic behavior.* *n-* in geology, a large boulder deposited by glacial action, whose composition is unlike that of the native bedrock. —*adv-* er·rat′i·cal·ly.

er·ro·ne·ous (ĭ rō′ nē əs) *adj-* incorrect; mistaken: *an erroneous belief.* —*adv-* er·ro′ne·ous·ly. *n-* er·ro′ne·ous·ness.

er·ror (ĕr′ ər) *n-* **1** mistake; inaccuracy: *an error in spelling; an error of 5 per cent in his total.* **2** wrongness of conduct or belief: *the error of his ways.* **3** in baseball, a misplay by a member of the team in the field that permits the batting team to gain a base, score a run, etc.

er·u·dite (ĕr′ ə dīt′ ĕr′ yə-) *adj-* learned; scholarly: *an erudite lecture.* —*adv-* er′u·dite′ly.

er·u·di·tion (ĕr′ ə dĭsh′ ən, ĕr′ yə-) *n-* scholarly knowledge; learning: *a man of great erudition.*

e·rup·tion (I rŭp'shən) *n-* 1 a bursting out or forth; outbreak: *the eruption of a volcano; an eruption of violence.* 2 rash on the skin.

es·ca·late (ĕs'kə lāt') *vt-* [es·ca·lat·ed, es·ca·lat·ing] to cause (something) to increase in scale, intensity, etc.: *to escalate a skirmish into a battle. vi-: The border clash escalated into a war.* —*n-* es'ca·la'tion.

es·ca·pade (ĕs'kə pād') *n-* brief, wild break from restraint; reckless adventure; spree.

es·cape (I skāp') *vi-* [es·caped, es·cap·ing] 1 to get away or get free; break loose: *to escape from prison.* 2 to avoid capture, harm, etc.: *He escaped by hiding in a cellar.* 3 to flow out; issue: *Gas is escaping from that pipe. vt-* 1 to get away from: *to escape prison.* 2 to avoid: *to escape capture.*

es·chew (ĕs chŏō') *vt-* to avoid; shun: *to eschew wine.*

¹es·cort (ĕs'kôrt', -kört') *n-* 1 group of persons, ships, or planes that accompanies and safeguards another: *An escort of destroyers accompanied the aircraft carrier.* 2 man or boy who attends or accompanies a woman or girl: *He will be my escort at the dance.*

²es·cort (ĕs kôrt', -kört') *vt-* to attend or accompany: *Jet fighters escorted the bombers. He escorted her home.*

Es·ki·mo (ĕs'kə mō') *n-* [*pl.* Es·ki·mos, also Es·ki·mo] a member of a Mongoloid people living on the Arctic shores of North America, Greenland, and northeastern Asia. *adj-: an Eskimo boot.*

Es·ki·mo·an (ĕs'kə mō'ən) *n-* a family of languages spoken along the shores of Greenland and Labrador, ir the Hudson Bay area, along the Arctic coast of North America, and in western and northern Alaska. Also called **Eskimo-Aleut.**

Eskimos

e·soph·a·gus (I sŏf'ə gəs) *n-* the part of the digestive tract between the throat and the stomach; gullet. For picture, see *intestine.*

es·o·ter·ic (ĕs'ə tĕr'Ik) *adj-* 1 intended for or understood by a small, select group of persons: *an esoteric philosophy.* 2 secret; confidential: *an esoteric club.* —*adv-* es'o·ter'i·cal·ly.

es·pe·cial (ə spĕsh'əl) *adj-* special. —*adv-* es·pe'cial·ly.

es·pi·o·nage (ĕs'pē ə nĭj, -ə näzh') *n-* 1 spying; the work of a government spy. 2 the systematic use of spies.

es·pous·al (ĕs pou'zəl) *n-* 1 an espousing of a cause, principle, etc.; advocacy. 2 betrothal. 3 wedding.

es·pouse (ə spouz') *vt-* [es·poused, es·pous·ing] 1 to be a follower of; advocate; support: *to espouse the cause of liberty.* 2 to give or take in marriage.

¹es·say (ĕs'ā) *n-* 1 short piece of writing on a single subject, generally giving the personal views of the author. 2 (*also* ĕ sā') an attempt; an experiment.

es·sence (ĕs'əns) *n-* 1 that which makes a thing what it is; true inward nature: *A friendly attitude is the very essence of peace.* 2 concentrated extract of a plant, food, etc.; also, such an extract dissolved in alcohol: *the essence of roses.* 3 a perfume.

es·sen·tial (ə sĕn'shəl) *adj-* necessary; not to be done without; basic: *Food is essential for life. n-* something basic and necessary. —*adv-* es·sen'tial·ly.

es·tab·lish (I stăb'lIsh) *vt-* 1 to found; set up: *to establish a school.* 2 to settle; place firmly: *He established his son in business.* 3 to cause to be accepted: *to establish a rule.* 4 to prove legally or beyond any doubt: *to establish a fact.*

es·tate (ī stāt') *n-* 1 large house and the large area of land belonging to it: *an estate in the country.* 2 everything owned by a person; property: *His estate was divided among his children.* 3 position or stage in life: *He reached man's estate at the age of 21.*

es·teem (ī stēm') *vt-* 1 to think highly of; regard as valuable: *The staff officers esteem the general.* 2 to consider; look upon as: *I shall esteem it an honor. n-* high opinion; respect: *to enjoy great esteem.*

es·ter (ĕs'tər) *n-* any of a large group of organic compounds formed when acids and alcohols react.

es·thet·ic (ĕs thĕt'Ik) *adj-* 1 of or related to beauty in art or nature: *the esthetic appeal of a magnificent sunset.* 2 deeply aware of or sensitive to beauty: *an esthetic personality.* Also **aesthetic.** —*adv-* es·thet'i·cal·ly.

es·ti·ma·ble (ĕs'tə mə bəl) *adj-* 1 worthy of respect or honor; deserving esteem: *an estimable contribution to science.* 2 such as can be estimated or reckoned; calculable: *an estimable cost.* —*adv-* es'ti·ma·bly.

¹es·ti·mate (ĕs'tə māt') *vt-* [es·ti·mat·ed, es·ti·mat·ing] to form an opinion or judgment about (value, amount, size, etc.): *to estimate a man's character; to estimate the size of a room.*

²es·ti·mate (ĕs'tə mət) *n-* 1 calculation of cost or value: *The carpenter gave an estimate of $45 for the job.* 2 written statement of such a calculation. 3 judgment; opinion: *a rough estimate of his qualifications.*

es·trange (I strānj') *vt-* [es·tranged, es·trang·ing] 1 to make (someone who has been friendly or affectionate) feel indifferent or unfriendly: *to estrange one's friends through neglect.* 2 to remove or separate (oneself) from family, friends, etc.; alienate. —*n-* es·trange'ment.

es·tro·gen (ĕs'trə jən) *n-* any of a small group of hormones that promote female secondary sex characteristics, such as the growth and development of the womb, milk glands, etc.

etch·ing (ĕch'Ing) *n-* 1 the process or art of making pictures or designs on metal plates, glass, etc., by means of acid. 2 picture or design printed from a metal plate engraved by such means; also, the plate itself.

e·ter·nal (I tûr'nəl) *adj-* 1 without beginning or end; timeless: *an eternal universe.* 2 without stopping; perpetual; unending: *her eternal chatter.* 3 always the same; unchanging; immutable: *an eternal principle.* —*adv-* e·ter'nal·ly.

e·ter·ni·ty (I tûr'nə tē) *n-* [*pl.* e·ter·ni·ties] 1 time without beginning or end; everlasting time. 2 time that seems endless: *I've waited an eternity for an answer.* 3 life after death: *He hovered between life and eternity.*

e·ther (ē'thər) *n-* 1 light, colorless, sweet-smelling, volatile, and flammable liquid compound of carbon, hydrogen, and oxygen, [$(C_2H_5)_2O$]. Ether is used as a solvent and as an anesthetic in surgery. 2 in early science, a thin invisible material believed to fill all the unoccupied space of the universe.

e·the·re·al (I thêr'ē əl) *adj-* 1 light; airy; delicate: *What ethereal music!* 2 heavenly; unearthly: *Angels are ethereal.* —*adv-* e·the're·al·ly. —*n-* e·the're·al·ness.

eth·i·cal (ĕth'I kəl) *adj-* 1 in keeping with moral principles or standards of proper action: *It is not ethical for a lawyer to reveal confidences.* 2 of or having to do with ethics. —*adv-* eth'i·cal·ly. n- eth'i·cal·ness.

eth·ics (ĕth'Iks) *n-* 1 (takes singular verb) branch of philosophy that deals with the principles of right and wrong action. 2 (takes plural verb) standards of right conduct or proper action, often within a particular profession: *His legal ethics are questionable.*

eth·nic (ĕth'nIk) *adj-* of, having to do with, or typical of a group or division of mankind with similar traits, customs, historical background, etc. —*adv-* eth'ni·cal·ly: *tribes that are ethnically similar.*

eth·nol·o·gy (ĕth nŏl'ə jē) *n-* branch of anthropology that deals with the historical background, geographical distribution, and customs of groups or divisions of mankind. —*adj-* eth'no·log'i·cal. *adv-* eth'no·log'i·cal·ly.

eth·yl (ĕth'əl) *n-* chemical radical (C_2H_5), composed of carbon and hydrogen, with a valence of one.

et·i·quette (ĕt'I kət, -kĕt') *n-* rules and customs of correct behavior, especially on social occasions.

et·y·mol·o·gy (ĕt'ə mŏl'ə jē) *n-* [*pl.* et·y·mol·o·gies] 1 the scientific study of word origins and histories. 2 origin and history of a word; especially, a statement or brief description showing the changing forms and meanings of a word.

eu·lo·gy (yōō'lə jē) *n-* [*pl.* eu·lo·gies] formal praise of a person's character, accomplishments, etc., either in a speech or in writing: *to deliver a funeral eulogy.*

eu·phe·mism (yōō'fə mIz'əm) *n-* mild or less offensive

expression used instead of one that is plainer or more accurate. Examples: "pass on" for "die"; "throw up" for "vomit." —*adj-* eu′phe·mis′tic. *adv-* eu′phe·mis′ti·cal·ly.

eu·pho·ny (yōō′fə nē) *n-* pleasantness of sound, especially in the use of words.

eu·pho·ri·a (yōō fôr′ē ə) *n-* a feeling of health and well-being.

Eu·sta·chi·an tube (yōō stā′shən) *n-* slender tube or canal that connects the middle ear and the throat, and serves to equalize the air pressure on the inner and outer surfaces of the eardrum. For picture, see *ear.*

eu·tha·na·sia (yōō′ thə nā′ zhə, -zhē ə) *n-* the causing of a painless, easy death for a person suffering from a painful, incurable disease or injury.

e·vac·u·ate (I vǎk′ yōō āt′) *vt-* [e·vac·u·at·ed, e·vac·u·at·ing] 1 to leave (a place) empty; abandon: *to evacuate a burning building.* 2 to remove or withdraw (people) from a place: *to evacuate troops from a fort.* *vi-*: to expel wastes from the bowels. —*n-* e·vac′u·a′tion.

e·vade (I vād′) *vt-* [e·vad·ed, e·vad·ing] to avoid or escape from by a trick, deceptive action, etc.; elude: *to evade pursuers; to evade responsibility.*

e·val·u·ate (I vǎl′ yōō āt′) *vt-* [e·val·u·at·ed, e·val·u·at·ing] 1 to declare or estimate the value or worth of; appraise: *A judge must carefully* evaluate *all evidence presented at a trial.*

ev·a·nes·cent (ěv′ ə něs′ ənt) *adj-* tending to disappear or fade away; fleeting: *an evanescent memory of early childhood.* —*n-* ev′a·nes′cence. *adv-* ev′a·nes′cent·ly.

e·van·gel·i·cal (ē′ văn′ jěl′ I kəl, ē′ vən-) *adj-* 1 of or according to the four Gospels of the New Testament. 2 founded on or holding the belief that faith in Jesus Christ is the only means of religious salvation: *an evangelical church.* 3 showing the fervor of an evangelist.

e·van·ge·lism (I văn′ jə lĭz′ əm) *n-* earnest efforts to win followers to the gospel of Jesus Christ, especially by an intense and emotional style of preaching.

e·van·ge·list (I văn′ jə lĭst) *n-* 1 person who preaches the gospel of Jesus Christ, especially a traveling preacher who holds revival meetings. 2 **Evangelist** any one of the four writers of the Gospels of the New Testament; Matthew, Mark, Luke, or John.

e·vap·o·rate (I văp′ ə rāt′) *vi-* [e·vap·o·rat·ed, e·vap·o·rat·ing] 1 to change from solid or liquid into vapor: *Gasoline* evaporates *faster than water.* 2 to disappear like vapor; fade: *Their hopes* evaporated. *vt-* 1 to cause to change to vapor. 2 to concentrate by heating or drying to remove moisture. —*n-* e·vap′o·ra′tion.

e·va·sion (I vā′ zhən) *n-* the act of evading; clever escape, avoidance, or putting off: *an evasion of one's pursuers.*

eve (ēv) *n-* 1 time or day just before an important or significant event: *the eve of the battle; the eve of their departure.* 2 (often **Eve**) the evening or day before a holiday, especially a religious holiday: *Christmas Eve.*

e·ven (ē′ vən) *adj-* [e·ven·er, e·ven·est] 1 level; smooth: *an even surface.* 2 on the same line; at a level: *water even with the top of the bucket.* 3 not having or showing marked differences or variation; steady; uniform: *an even pulse; an even temper; an even tone of voice.*

eve·ning (ēv′ nĭng) *n-* the close of day and early part of the night; late hours of daylight and early hours of darkness. *as modifier:* the evening *meal.*

e·vent (I věnt′) *n-* 1 a happening; occurrence: *When did the event take place?* 2 item in a program, especially in a series of sports activities: *a track event.*

e·vent·ful (I věnt′ fəl) *adj-* full of happenings or incidents, especially, interesting or important ones: *an eventful day.* —*adv-* e·vent′ful·ly. *n-* e·vent′ful·ness.

e·ven·tu·al (I věn′ chōō əl) *adj-* happening as the result of events or circumstances; ultimate: *His eventual success is certain.* —*adv-* e·ven′tu·al·ly.

e·ven·tu·al·i·ty (I věn′ chōō ǎl′ ə tē) *n-* [*pl.* e·ven·tu·al·i·ties] possible occurrence or circumstance: *I'll be there in any* eventuality.

e·ven·tu·ate (I věn′ chōō āt′) *vi-* [e·ven·tu·at·ed, e·ven·tu·at·ing] to happen in the end; result: *The quarrel* eventuated *in open warfare.*

ev·er (ěv′ ər) *adv-* 1 at any time: *Did you* ever *ride a horse? Will he* ever *come back?* 2 always; forever: *It was* ever *thus. They were happy* ever *after.* 3 (intensifier only) *How did you* ever *finish so quickly?*

ev·er·glade (ěv′ ər glād′) *n-* low, swampy area.

ev·er·green (ěv′ ər grēn′) *adj-* bearing leaves or needles throughout the year; not deciduous. *n-*: *Holly and most pines are evergreens.*

ev·er·last·ing (ěv′ ər lǎs′ tǐng) *adj-* lasting or seeming to last forever; eternal: *our everlasting gratitude; that everlasting noise.*

Evergreens

eve·ry (ěv′ rē) *determiner-* (traditionally called adjective) 1 all the individual members or parts of a group, category, kind, etc.; each: *I expect* every *man to do his duty. He comes* every *day.* 2 all or any possible: *I have* every *confidence in him. He has had* every *opportunity.*

e·vict (I vĭkt′) *vt-* to put out (a person or persons) from a place, especially by legal force; expel: *to evict a family from a house.* —*n-* e·vic′tion.

ev·i·dence (ěv′ ə dəns) *n-* 1 facts from which to judge or draw a conclusion: *What* evidence *do you have that he was here?* 2 in law, the facts, testimony, objects, etc., that are admitted according to certain rules as proper for consideration in a trial, hearing, etc.

ev·i·dent (ěv′ ə dənt) *adj-* easy to see or understand; plain; obvious: *His earnest intentions are evident to all.* —*adv-* ev′i·dent′ly: *He is evidently earnest.*

e·vil (ē′ vəl) *n-* 1 the causing of suffering, fear, death, etc.; opposite of good. 2 any cause of suffering, etc.. *e·vince* (I vĭns′) *vt-* [e·vinced, e·vinc·ing] to show; make evident: *to evince great bravery; to evince displeasure.*

e·vis·ce·rate (I vĭs′ ə rāt′) *vt-* [e·vis·ce·rat·ed, e·vis·ce·rat·ing] to remove the intestines or internal organs of. —*n-* e·vis′ce·ra′tion.

e·voke (I vōk′) *vt-* [e·voked, e·vok·ing] to call forth; call up; produce: *His letter* evoked *an angry answer.*

ev·o·lu·tion (ěv′ ə lōō′ shən) *n-* 1 growth; gradual development, especially through a series of forms or stages: *the evolution of the modern university.* 2 Biology theory that plants and animals of types now living have developed from earlier and simpler forms of life by the process of natural selection.

e·volve (I vŏlv′) *vi-* [e·volved, e·volv·ing] to grow or develop gradually: *An oak tree* evolves *from a tiny acorn.* *vt-* to work out or produce in gradual stages: *to evolve a new method.* —*n-* e·volve′ment.

ewe (yōō) *n-* female sheep. *Homs-* yew, you.

ew·er (yōō′ ər) *n-* large jug or water pitcher.

ex·ac·er·bate (ěk sǎs′ ər bāt′, ěg zǎs′-) *vt-* [ex·ac·er·bat·ed, ex·ac·er·bat·ing] to make (feelings, symptoms, ills, etc.) sharper or more severe; make worse; aggravate. —*n-* ex·ac′er·ba′tion.

▶For usage note see AGGRAVATE.

ex·act (ěg zǎkt′) *adj-* 1 accurate and correct in all parts or details: *an exact copy; exact measurements.* 2 strict and precise in regard to facts, details, etc.: *an exact mind.* *vt-* to insist upon; require: *to exact payment of a loan; to exact strict obedience.* —*n-* ex·act′ness.

ex·act·ing (ěg zǎk′ tǐng) *adj-* 1 requiring great skill, precision, or concentration: *an exacting task.* 2 making many or unreasonable demands; severe: *an exacting employer.* —*adv-* ex·act′ing·ly.

ex·ac·tion (ěg zǎk′shən) *n-* a requiring or demanding of payment, especially an unjust or difficult payment.

ex·ag·ger·ate (ěg zǎj′ə rāt′) *vt-* [ex·ag·ger·at·ed, ex·ag·ger·at·ing] to enlarge beyond truth or reason; overstate: *to exaggerate one's exploits.* *vi-*: *Herbert always* exaggerates.

ex·ag·ger·a·tion (ěg zǎj′ə rā′shən) *n-* 1 an exaggerating; misleading enlargement or overemphasis. 2 statement that exaggerates: *a story full of exaggerations.*

ex·alt (ěg zôlt′) *vt-* 1 to raise in rank and dignity: *The people* exalted *him to the office of President.* 2 to praise highly; glorify: *They* exalted *God in their hymns.*

▶Should not be confused with EXULT.

ex·am·ine (ĕg zăm'ən) *vt-* [ex·am·ined, ex·am·in·ing] 1 to look at carefully; inspect; investigate: *He examined the ameba under the microscope.* 2 to question in order to find out information, etc.: *to examine a witness.*

ex·am·ple (ĕg zăm'pəl) *n-* 1 one part of a group, category, collection, etc., that shows what the whole is like; sample; specimen: *This painting is an example of her best work.* 2 an exercise or problem that illustrates a process, method, or rule: *an example in arithmetic.*

ex·as·per·ate (ĕg zăs'pə rāt') *vt-* [ex·as·per·at·ed, ex·as·per·at·ing] to irritate greatly; annoy keenly: *Her folly exasperated him.* —*adv-* ex·as'per·at'ing·ly.

ex·ca·vate (ĕks'kə vāt') *vt-* [ex·ca·vat·ed, ex·ca·vat·ing] 1 to dig or hollow out: *to excavate a cave in a hillside.* 2 to uncover by digging: *They excavated the ruins of an ancient city. vi-* to dig.

ex·ceed (ĕk sēd') *vt-* 1 to go beyond the limit of; overdo: *to exceed one's authority.* 2 to excel; surpass: *His courage exceeds mine.*

ex·ceed·ing·ly (ĕk sē'dĭng lē) *adv-* very; remarkably.

ex·cel (ĕk sĕl') *vi-* [ex·celled, ex·cel·ling] to be superior to others in ability or quality: *Arthur excels in sports. vt-: Carlo excels Arthur in arithmetic.*

ex·cel·lence (ĕk'sə ləns) *n-* superior quality; outstanding ability or worth.

ex·cel·lent (ĕk'sə lənt) *adj-* of unusually high quality; very good: *an excellent player.* —*adv-* ex'cel·lent·ly.

ex·cept (ĕk sĕpt') *prep-* outside of; apart from; barring: *He ate everything except dessert. conj-* (also except that) apart from the fact that: *I could go except I don't want to. vt-* to leave out; exclude: *He excepted their names from his list of guests.*

¹**ex·cerpt** (ĕk'sûrpt', ĕg'zûrpt') *n-* part or passage taken from a longer work: *some excerpts from an opera.*

²**ex·cerpt** (ĕk sûrpt', ĕg zûrpt') *vt-* to take out or select (a part or passage) from a longer work.

ex·cess (ĕk'sĕs', ĕk sĕs') *n-* 1 quantity that is more than is usual or desirable; overabundance: *He has an excess of energy.* 2 amount by which one thing is more than another or more than required: *an excess of rolls over frankfurters.*

ex·change (ĕks chānj') *vt-* [ex·changed, ex·chang·ing] 1 to give (something) for something else; trade; barter: *to exchange a toy for a book.* 2 to give and receive; interchange: *to exchange ideas.* 3 to return (a purchase) and take something else: *to exchange a dress for a larger one.*

¹**ex·cise** (ĕk sīz') *vt-* [ex·cised, ex·cis·ing] to remove by or as if by cutting out: *to excise a tumor; to excise a paragraph.* [from Latin *excisus* meaning "having been cut out."] —*n-* ex·ci'sion (ĕk sĭzh'ən).

²**ex·cise** (ĕk'sīz') or **excise tax** *n-* tax imposed on certain articles within the country where they are manufactured, sold, or used. *as modifier: to collect excise duties.* [from early Dutch *excijs*, from Old French *acceis*, which goes back to Latin *ad-*, "to," plus *census* meaning "a tax; census."]

ex·cite (ĕk sīt') *vt-* [ex·cit·ed, ex·cit·ing] 1 to stir the mind or emotions of: *The President's stirring speech excited us.* 2 to call forth; arouse: *to excite pity.* 3 to cause to become active; stimulate: *The odor of food excites the salivary glands.*

ex·claim (ĕks klām') *vt-* to speak or cry out suddenly in surprise, anger, pleasure, etc.: *"Aha!" he exclaimed.*

ex·clude (ĕks klōōd') *vt-* [ex·clud·ed, ex·clud·ing] 1 to shut or keep out; prevent from entering: *to exclude someone from a club; to exclude sound.* 2 to leave out; omit: *to exclude unnecessary material from a report.*

ex·com·mu·ni·cate (ĕks'kə myōō'nə kāt') *vt-* [ex·com·mu·ni·cat·ed, ex·com·mu·ni·cat·ing] to cut off officially from the membership or communion of a church. —*n-* ex'com·mu'ni·ca'tion.

ex·co·ri·ate (ĕks skôr'ē āt') *vt-* [ex·co·ri·at·ed, ex·co·ri·at·ing] to strip or rub away the skin of; hence, to criticize or scold with harsh severity.

ex·cre·tion (ĕks krē'shən) *n-* 1 act or process of excreting. 2 something excreted.

ex·cru·ci·at·ing (ĕks krōō'shē ā'tĭng) *adj-* extremely painful; torturing: *an excruciating toothache; excruciating embarrassment.* —*adv-* ex·cru'ci·at'ing·ly.

ex·cur·sion (ĕks kûr'zhən) *n-* 1 a short trip generally made by a group of people for a special purpose or for pleasure. 2 a special round trip at a reduced fare.

¹**ex·cuse** (ĕks kyōōz') *vt-* [ex·cused, ex·cus·ing] 1 to pardon; forgive: *He excused his brother's mistake.* 2 to free from duty, obligation, attendance, etc.: *She excused him from the test.* 3 to explain or justify: *Her shyness excuses her awkwardness.*

ex·e·crate (ĕk'sə krāt') *vt-* [ex·e·crat·ed, ex·e·crat·ing] 1 to declare to be evil; denounce violently; damn. 2 to detest; abhor. *vi-* to curse; swear.

ex·e·cute (ĕk'sə kyōōt') *vt-* [ex·e·cut·ed, ex·e·cut·ing] 1 to carry out, perform, or make: *to execute a plan.* 2 to put to death according to law. 3 to make legal by signing or sealing: *to execute a lease.*

ex·ec·u·tive (ĕg zĕk'yə tĭv) *n-* 1 person who directs, manages, or supervises the affairs of a business, institution, or organization. 2 person, group, or branch of government responsible for putting laws into effect.

ex·ec·u·tor (ĕg zĕk'yə tər) *n-* in law, a person who is appointed in a will to see that its terms are carried out. —*n- fem.* ex·ec'u·trix' (-trĭks').

ex·em·pla·ry (ĕg zĕm'plə rē) *adj-* 1 worthy to serve as a model; praiseworthy: *The boy's conduct was exemplary.* 2 serving as a warning: *to administer exemplary punishment.* —*adv-* ex·em'pla·ri·ly. —*n-* ex·em'pla·ri·ness.

ex·em·pli·fy (ĕg zĕm'plə fī') *vt-* [ex·em·pli·fied, ex·em·pli·fy·ing] to show or serve as an example of; illustrate; demonstrate: *This picture exemplifies the artist's style.*

ex·empt (ĕg zĕmpt') *vt-* to free from a tax, duty, obligation, etc., to which others are subject; excuse: *to exempt a student from a test. adj-: He is exempt from the test.*

ex·er·cise (ĕk'sər sīz') *vt-* 1 [ex·er·cised, ex·er·cis·ing] 1 to put into action; use: *to exercise authority, care, or self-control.* 2 to use in order to train or develop: *to exercise the muscles or the mind. vi-* to perform some bodily activity for physical fitness: *to exercise every day.*

ex·hale (ĕks'hāl') *vt-* [ex·haled, ex·hal·ing] to breathe out or give off as if by breathing forth: *He exhaled a deep breath. The swamp exhaled an unpleasant odor. vi-: He exhaled deeply.*

ex·haust (ĕg zôst') *vt-* 1 to tire out completely: *The game exhausted him.* 2 to use up; drain: *He exhausted my patience.* 3 to discuss or treat thoroughly: *to exhaust a subject.* 4 to draw or force out: *to exhaust air from a chamber.*

ex·ert (ĕg zûrt') *vt-* to put forth; bring to bear; to put to use: *to exert one's influence.*

ex·hib·it (ĕg zĭb'ĭt) *vt-* 1 to show; display: *to exhibit the symptoms of a cold; to exhibit great courage.* 2 to show publicly; put on display: *to exhibit paintings.*

ex·hil·a·rate (ĕg zĭl'ə rāt') *vt-* [ex·hil·a·rat·ed, ex·hil·a·rat·ing] to make cheerful or joyous; enliven: *The news that he had won the contest exhilarated him.* —*adv-* ex·hil'a·rat'ing·ly: *an exhilaratingly fine day.*

ex·hort (ĕg zôrt', -zôrt') *vt-* to urge by appeal or argument; advise strongly: *He exhorted the jury to make a just decision. vi-: The lawyer exhorted earnestly.*

ex·hume (ĕg zyōōm') *vt-* 1 [ex·humed, ex·hum·ing] to dig up (a buried corpse); disinter. 2 to bring to light (something forgotten or hidden); uncover; reveal.

ex·i·gen·cy (ĕk'sə jən sē, ĕg zĭj'ən sē) *n-* [*pl.* ex·i·gen·cies] 1 situation that needs immediate attention. 2 pressing necessity; urgency. Also ex'i·gence.

ex·ile (ĕg'zīl', ĕk'sīl') *n-* 1 absence, usually compulsory, from one's home or country; banishment: *They demanded the exile of the king. The writer lived in exile.* 2 person who is banished or goes away from his country for a long time: *The exile returned after many years.*

ex·ist (ĕg zĭst') *vi-* 1 to have actual being, be: *He believes goblins really exist.* 2 to live or continue to go on living: *Plants cannot exist without water.* 3 to be found; occur: *Such conditions exist only in large cities.*

ex·it (ĕg'zĭt, ĕk'sĭt) *n-* 1 way or passage through which

ex·on·er·ate (ĕg zŏn´ə rāt´) *vt-* [ex·on·er·at·ed, ex·on·er·at·ing] to free from blame; acquit or clear of an accusation or responsibility: *The jury exonerated the accused man.* —*n-* ex·on´er·a´tion.

ex·or·bi·tant (ĕg zôr´ bə tənt, ĕg zŏr´-) *adj-* going beyond the expected limits; excessive; out of all reason: *an exorbitant price.* —*n-* ex·or´bi·tance: *The exhorbitance of his demand astounds me.* —*adv-* ex·or´bi·tant·ly.

ex·ot·ic (ĕg zŏt´ ĭk) *adj-* 1 from another part of the world; not native; strange: *an exotic plant.* 2 having the charm of strangeness: *an exotic Spanish dance.* —*adv-* ex·ot´ic·al·ly.

ex·pand (ĕk spănd´) *vi-* to increase in size or volume; grow larger; swell: *Metals expand when heated.* *vt-* 1 to make larger, wider, or broader; enlarge: *to expand one's nostrils; to expand a short story into a novel.* 2 to open or spread out: *to expand a folded bag.*

ex·panse (ĕk spăns´) *n-* 1 wide, open space or area: *the great expanse of the ocean.* 2 the extent to which a thing has been spread out: *the expanse of her skirt.*

ex·pa·ti·ate (ĕk spā´ shē āt´) *vi-* [ex·pa·ti·at·ed, ex·pa·ti·at·ing] to talk or write freely and at length: *to expatiate upon the beauty of the place.*

¹ex·pa·tri·ate (ĕk spā´ trē āt´) *vt-* [ex·pa·tri·at·ed, ex·pa·tri·at·ing] to banish (a person) from his native country; exile. *vi-* to withdraw oneself from one's native land: *He expatriated before the war.* —*n-* ex·pa´tri·a´tion.

ex·pect (ĕk spĕkt´) *vt-* 1 to look forward to as likely or certain to come or happen: *to expect to go on a trip; to expect a storm.* 2 to consider necessary or desirable; require: *I expect you to do a good job.* 3 *Informal* to think likely; suppose: *I expect he can do it.*

ex·pec·to·rate (ĕk spĕk´ tə rāt´) *vt-* [ex·pec·to·rat·ed, ex·pec·to·rat·ing] to eject (phlegm, saliva, etc.) from the throat or lungs by coughing or spitting; also, to spit. *vi-:* *to expectorate into a basin.* —*n-* ex·pec´to·ra´tion.

ex·pe·dite (ĕk´ spə dīt´) *vt-* [ex·pe·dit·ed, ex·pe·dit·ing] 1 to hasten; help forward; quicken: *to expedite progress.* 2 to carry out quickly: *He expedited the stowing of the cargo.* —*n-* ex´pe·dit´er.

ex·pe·di·tion (ĕk´ spə dĭsh´ ən) *n-* 1 trip for a special purpose: *a hunting expedition.* 2 group of people making such a trip: *The expedition departed for the South Pole.* 3 efficiency and promptness: *to do a task with expedition.*

ex·pense (ĕk spĕns´) *n-* 1 a spending of money, time, labor, etc.: *He was educated at considerable expense.* 2 cost: *the expense of an education.* 3 cause of spending: *Food, rent, and clothing are our chief expenses.* 4 loss, injury, or sacrifice: *a victory won at terrible expense.*

ex·per·i·ment (ĕk spĕr´ ə mənt) *n-* a test or trial to discover something or to confirm or disprove something: *The chemist's experiments proved his theory to be correct.* *vi-* to make a test or tests to find out something: *to experiment with electricity.* —*n-* ex·per´i·ment´er.

ex·pire (ĕk spīər´) *vi-* [ex·pired, ex·pir·ing] 1 to come to an end; cease to be in effect; terminate: *My driver's license has expired.* 2 to breathe out; exhale. 3 to die.

ex·plain (ĕk splān´) *vt-* (considered intransitive when the direct object is implied but not expressed) 1 to make plain or clear; tell the meaning of: *to explain the solution of a problem.* 2 to account for; give the reason or cause of: *to explain one's conduct.* —*adj-* ex·plain´a·ble.

ex·pli·cate (ĕk´ splə kāt´) *vt-* [ex·pli·cat·ed, ex·pli·cat·ing] to explain carefully and in detail. —*n-* ex´pli·ca´tion.

ex·plic·it (ĕk splĭs´ ĭt) *adj-* clear and unmistakable in meaning or intent: *brief but explicit instructions; to be explicit in stating one's viewpoint.* See also *implicit.* —*adv-* ex·plic´it·ly. —*n-* ex·plic´it·ness.

ex·plode (ĕk splōd´) *vi-* [ex·plod·ed, ex·plod·ing] 1 to undergo a quick and violent change, accompanied by an intense discharge of heat and usually a large volume

ex·pound (ĕk spound´) *vt-* to set forth in detail; explain or interpret: *to expound the law.* —*n-* ex·pound´er.

ex·press (ĕk sprĕs´) *vt-* 1 to make known, especially by the use of language; show; reveal: *to express an idea clearly; to express joy.* 2 to represent; symbolize: *The statue expresses the belief in freedom.* 3 to send (some-

thing) by a speedy means of transportation.

ex·punge (ĕk spŭnj´) *vt-* [ex·punged, ex·pung·ing] to blot or rub out; erase; wipe out: *to expunge a mark.*

ex·pur·gate (ĕk´ spər gāt´) *vt-* [ex·pur·gat·ed, ex·pur·gat·ing] to alter by taking out whatever seems offensive to good taste or morality: *to expurgate a book.* —*n-* ex´pur·ga´tion.

ex·qui·site (ĕk´ skwĭz ət, ĕk skwĭz´-) *adj-* 1 pleasing because of great beauty, delicacy, refinement, etc.: *an exquisite rose; exquisite cabinet work.* 2 keenly felt; intense: *an exquisite joy.*

ex·tend (ĕk stĕnd´) *vt-* 1 to lengthen: *to extend a road; to extend a visit.* 2 to stretch out: *to extend an arm.* 3 to enlarge; increase; expand: *to extend one's power.* 4 to give; offer: *to extend a warm welcome; to extend credit.*

ex·te·ri·or (ĕk stēr´ ē ər) *n-* 1 outer part; outside: *The exterior of the house is white.* 2 outward or visible appearance: *His gruff exterior is misleading.* *adj-* 1 on, for, or coming from the outside; outer: *an exterior door; a good exterior paint; exterior assistance.*

ex·ter·mi·nate (ĕk stûr´ mə nāt´) *vt-* [ex·ter·mi·nat·ed, ex·ter·mi·nat·ing] to get rid of by killing; wipe out: *to exterminate harmful insects.* —*n-* ex·ter´mi·na´tion.

ex·ter·nal (ĕk stûr´ nəl) *adj-* 1 on, of, or from the outside: *an external layer; an external force.* 2 visible or apparent to an observer: *the external appearance of success.*

ex·tinct (ĕk stĭngkt´) *adj-* 1 no longer existing as a form of life: *the dinosaur is an extinct animal.* 2 no longer active or burning: *an extinct volcano.*

ex·tin·guish (ĕk stĭng´ gwĭsh) *vt-* 1 to put out: *to extinguish a fire.* 2 to put an end to; destroy: *to extinguish hope.* —*adj-* ex·tin´guish·a·ble. *n-* ex·tin´guish·er: *a fire extinguisher.*

ex·tol (ĕk stōl´) *vt-* [ex·tolled, ex·tol·ling] to praise highly: *to extol another's virtues.* —*n-* ex·tol´ler.

ex·tort (ĕk stôrt´, -stôrt´) *vt-* to obtain by force, threats, blackmail, etc.: *to extort money; to extort a confession.*

¹ex·tract (ĕk străkt´) *vt-* 1 to pull out; draw out with effort: *to extract a tooth; to extract information.* 2 to obtain by pressing, cooking, or some other special process: *to extract oil from olives;*

ex·tra·dite (ĕk´ strə dīt´) *vt-* [ex·tra·dit·ed, ex·tra·dit·ing] 1 to surrender (someone) in one State or country to the legal agents of another State or country where the person is accused of a crime. 2 to obtain the surrender of (an accused person in another State or country).

ex·traor·di·nar·y (ĕk strôrd´ən ĕr´ ē, ĕk strôrd´-) *adj-* beyond the usual size, shape, course, etc.; unusual; very special. —*adv-* ex·traor´di·nar´i·ly.

ex·trav·a·gance (ĕk străv´ ə gəns) *n-* 1 excess or lack of moderation, especially in spending money: *His extravagance will put him in debt.* 2 something excessive, something unduly costly: *His car is an extravagance.*

ex·treme (ĕk strēm´) *adj-* 1 highest; greatest; utmost: *with extreme joy; in extreme danger.* 2 excessive: *his extreme modesty.* 3 severe; drastic: *to take extreme measures.* 4 farthest: *The extreme end of the yard.*

ex·tri·cate (ĕk´ strə kāt´) *vt-* [ex·tri·cat·ed, ex·tri·cat·ing] to release or set free from danger or difficulty: *to extricate oneself from danger.* —*n-* ex´tri·ca´tion.

ex·trin·sic (ĕk strĭn´ zĭk, -sĭk) *adj-* 1 not belonging or necessary to the nature of something; extraneous; unessential: *His questions are extrinsic to the argument.*

ex·ude (ĕg zōōd´, -zyōōd´) *vt-* [ex·ud·ed, ex·ud·ing] to give forth; send out; emit: *to exude sweat; to exude confidence.* *vi-:* *Sweat exuded from every pore.* —*n-* ex´u·da´tion.

ex·ult (ĕg zŭlt´) *vi-* to feel great joy or triumph; rejoice (at): *The team exulted at winning.* —*adv-* ex·ult´ing·ly. ▶Should not be confused with EXALT.

eye (ī) *n-* 1 the bodily organ with which a person or animal sees. 2 a gaze; look: *Archie cast a longing eye at the cake.* 3 close watch: *Keep an eye on the baby.* 4 something thought to resemble an eye, such as the hole where a needle is threaded or the bud of a potato.

F

F, f (ĕf) *n-* [*pl.* **F's, f's**] **1** the sixth letter of the English alphabet. **2 F** *Music* the fourth note of the C-major scale.
f *Music* forte.
F 1 *Mathematics* symbol for function. **2** *Chemistry* symbol for fluorine.
f. **1** female; feminine. **2** franc. **3** following.
F. 1 February. **2** Friday. **3** Fahrenheit. **4** French.
fa (fä) *Music n-* the fourth note of a musical scale.
face (fās) *n-* **1** the front of the head; visage: *The eyes, nose, and mouth are parts of the* face. **2** front, principal, or usable side of something, such as that of a playing card, a clock, or a coin. **3** look or expression: *a sour* face. **4** public reputation and dignity; personal worth: *to lose* face; *to save one's* face. **5** *Informal* impudence; nerve. **6** (1) in printing, the surface of a type or plate that makes the impression. (2) the size or style of the letters or characters; also, the letters or characters themselves. **7** *Mathematics* a plane surface of a solid figure. *as modifier:* tan face *powder.* *vt-* [**faced, fac·ing**] **1** to turn toward; be opposite to: *She* faced *me.* **2** to stand bravely against; confront: *to* face *the enemy.* **3** to be threatened with; expect to suffer: *Unless we act, we* face *ruin and defeat.* **4** to put an outer layer on: *to* face *a house with shingles.* *vi-* to stand with the front toward a certain direction: *The windows* face *east.* Face *left.*

    face to face with faces turned toward one another; in confrontation: *They stood* face *to* face. **in the face of** in the presence of; threatened by: *He showed courage* in the face of *danger.* **make a face** to twist the features to show disgust, disapproval, etc.; grimace. **put a (certain) face on** to speak or behave so as to give a (certain) impression of something: *He* put a good face on *our efforts.* **to (someone's) face** openly; in (someone's) presence: *He didn't dare say it to my* face.
    face out to withstand (a crisis) boldly until it has passed.
    face up to confront bravely: *to* face up to *danger.*
fact (făkt) *n-* **1** something true, real, and actual: *A scientist needs* facts. **2** reality; actuality: *Can you tell* fact *from fancy in this situation?* **3** thing, event, etc., that is said to be true or real: *Check the* facts *in the report.*
    as a matter of fact, in fact, in point of fact in truth; really; actually.
fac·tion (făk'shən) *n-* group of people within a political party, company, etc., who oppose another group, usually to advance their own interests. *—adj-* **fac'tion·al:** *an organization torn by* factional *strife.*
fac·tion·al·ism (făk'shən əl iz'əm) *n-* spirit or tendency of breaking up into factions: *a party split by* factionalism. *—n-* **fac'tion·al·ist.**
fac·tious (făk'shəs) *adj-* **1** given to forming factions or rival groups: *a factious* leader. **2** quarrelsome: *a* factious *spirit.* *—adv-* **fac'tious·ly.** *n-* **fac'tious·ness.**
fac·ti·tious (făk tish'əs) *adj-* not natural or spontaneous; artificial: *a* factitious *smile.* *—adv-* **fac·ti'tious·ly.** *n-* **fac·ti'tious·ness.**
fac·tor (făk'tər) *n-* **1** something that helps to bring about a result: *Diet and exercise are important* factors *in healthy living.* **2** in arithmetic, any number which can be multiplied by another number to get a given product: *The* factors *of 10 are 2 and 5.* **3** *Mathematics* to resolve or separate (a number or an expression) into factors.
fac·tor·i·za·tion (făk'tər ə zā'shən) *n-* expression which shows results of factoring. Example: 10 = 2 × 5.
fac·to·ry (făk'tə rē) *n-* [*pl.* **fac·to·ries**] place in which goods are manufactured.
fac·to·tum (făk'tō'təm) *n-* person employed to do various tasks, usually minor; handyman.
fac·tu·al (făk'chōō əl) *adj-* of, based on, or consisting of facts; real: *a* factual *report.* *—adv-* **fac'tu·al·ly.**
fac·ul·ty (făk'əl tē) *n-* [*pl.* **fac·ul·ties**] **1** special ability or skill to do something; talent: *She has a* faculty *for saying the right thing.* **2** a power of the mind or body: *the* faculty *of sight.* **3** staff of teachers.
faint (fānt) *vi-* to lose consciousness briefly. *n-* brief loss of consciousness. *adj-* [**faint·er, faint·est**] **1** weak; exhausted; dizzy or sick. **2** indistinct; dim: *a* faint *noise*; *a* faint *light.* **3** feeble; halfhearted: *a* faint *attempt at courtesy.* *—adv-* **faint'ly.** *n-* **faint'ness.** *Hom-* feint.

fair trade *n-* trade under a law or agreement which allows manufacturers to set a minimum price for their products, and forbids dealers to sell for less.
fair-trade (fâr' trād') *vt-* [**fair-trad·ed, fair-trad·ing**] to fix a price on or sell according to a law or agreement requiring fair trade. *adj-:* *a* fair-trade *law.*
fair·way (fâr' wā') *n-* in golf, the grassy space between the tee and the green and within fixed boundaries.
fair-weath·er (fâr wĕth' ər) *adj-* suitable only in good weather: *a* fair-weather *road.*
fair-weather friend *n-* friend who is dependable and helpful only when one has no trouble or grief.
fair·y (fâr'ē) *n-* [*pl.* **fair·ies**] an imaginary being of tiny, human shape, usually having magical powers. *as modifier:* *a* fairy *tale.*
fair·y·land (fâr'ē lănd') *n-* **1** the country of the fairies. **2** any beautiful, enchanting place.
fairy ring *n-* ring of mushrooms produced from the extensions of the mushroom mycelia underground.
fairy tale *n-* **1** a story about fairies, witches, or unreal beings, as "Puss-in-Boots." **2** highly fanciful lie: *He told a* fairy tale *about having been an army captain.*
fait ac·com·pli (fĕ' tə kŏⁿ plē') *French* accomplished fact; something that can no longer be changed.
faith (fāth) *n-* **1** trust; confidence: *Do you have* faith *in his word?* **2** belief in God. **3** system of religious belief: *the Christian* faith; *the Jewish* faith. **4** promise of loyalty: *to keep or break* faith.
    bad faith dishonesty; insincerity. **break faith** to fail to fulfill one's principles, a promise, etc. **in faith** indeed; really and truly. **in good faith** honestly. **keep faith** to stick to one's principles, a vow, etc.
fa·kir (fə kêr') *n-* in the Muslim religion, a begging monk. [from Arabic *faqir* meaning "a poor man."]
fal·chion (fŏl'chən) *n-* in the Middle Ages, a short sword with a wide, curved blade.
fal·con (făl' kən, fôl' -) *n-* any of several small, swift hawks that can be trained to hunt birds and small game.
fal·con·er (făl' kən ər, fôl' -) *n-* person who trains, hunts with, or breeds falcons.
fal·con·ry (făl' kən rē, fôl' -) *n-* **1** the art of training falcons to hunt. **2** the sport of hunting with falcons.
fal·de·ral (făl' də răl') *n-* folderol.
fall (fôl) *vi-* [**fell** (fĕl), **fall·en, fall·ing**] **1** to come down; drop: *He* fell *off the chair.*

Falcon, about 18 in long

Rain fell *heavily.* **2** to lessen; decrease: *The temperature* fell *to zero. Her voice* fell *to a whisper.* **3** to be wounded or killed: *to* fall *in battle.* **4** to be defeated or overthrown: *The city* fell *after a siege of three months.* **5** to yield to a moral error or fault; sin: *Adam* fell *through disobedience to God.* **6** to lose dignity, reputation, etc.: *He* fell *in her estimation.* **7** to happen; occur: *Christmas* fell *on Sunday last year.* **8** to come or happen by right or chance, or at a particular place: *The estate* fell *to the eldest son.* The accent mark falls *on the first syllable.* **9** to pass into a certain physical or mental condition: *to* fall *ill; to* fall *asleep.* **10** to be uttered: *A sigh* fell *from his lips.* **11** to be divided or classified: *His writings* fall *into three types: novels, plays, and essays.* *n-* **1** a coming down; a dropping: *a* fall *of rain.* **2** amount that comes down: *There'll be a heavy* fall *of snow.* **3** distance covered by something dropping: *It's only a short* fall. **4** a lessening; decrease: *a* fall *in prices.* **5** capture; overthrow; loss of power: *the* fall *of a city.* **6** a yielding to moral error; sin: *the* fall *of Adam.* **7** loss of dignity, reputation, etc.: *a* fall *from favor.* **8** autumn. **9** in wrestling, a victory attained by pinning an opponent's shoulders to the floor; also, one of the parts of a match that comes to an end with such a victory or a time limit. **10 falls** waterfall. **11 the Fall** the sin of Adam and Eve. *as modifier:* *a brisk* fall *day.*

fal·ter (fôl′tər) *vi-* 1 to move or act in an uncertain or unsteady way; waver; hesitate: *He faltered at the door, wondering if he should go in.* 2 to speak with hesitation; stammer: *He faltered as he tried to find the right words.* —*n-* fal′ter·er. *adv-* fal′ter·ing·ly.

fame (fām) *n-* widespread reputation, especially of a favorable kind; renown: *Edison's fame as an inventor.*

fam·i·ly (făm′lē, -ə lē) *n-* [*pl.* **fam·i·lies**] 1 parents and their children: *The Brown family lives next door.* 2 the children of a married couple: *Mr. and Mrs. Brown have a large family.* 3 persons closely related by birth; all people descended from the same ancestor: *The Nelson family has been in New York for 250 years.* 4 group of related plants, animals, languages, etc.: *Lions and tigers belong to the cat family.* *as modifier:* a family resemblance; family *Bible.*

family name *n-* last name; surname.

family skeleton *n-* something shameful or scandalous which a family keeps secret.

family tree *n-* ancestors or descendants of a family; lineage; also, a diagram or chart of this.

fam·ine (făm′ən) *n-* 1 extreme scarcity of food. 2 starvation. 3 shortage of some one thing, especially a crop.

fam·ished (făm′ĭsht) *adj-* very hungry; starving: *The famished dogs snarled over a scrap of meat.*

fa·mous (fā′məs) *adj-* widely known; renowned; famed: *Admiral Byrd was a famous explorer.*

fa·mous·ly (fā′məs lē) *Informal adv-* wonderfully.

¹fan (făn) *n-* anything used to stir or drive air, especially a motor-driven set of revolving blades, or a piece of paper or cloth moved back and forth in the hand. *vt-* [**fanned, fan·ning**] 1 to wave something to cast a breeze on: *to fan oneself; to fan a fire.* 2 to stir up; excite: *to fan enthusiasm.* 3 in baseball, to strike out (a batter). *vi-* in baseball, to strike out. [from Old English **fann,** from Latin **vannus** meaning "a fan for winnowing grain."]

Fans

fan out to spread apart while moving forward: *The hunters fanned out to cover the whole field.*

²fan (făn) *n-* enthusiastic supporter; buff: *a baseball fan; a movie fan.* [American word partly from **fanatic** and partly from **the fancy** meaning "followers of a certain hobby."] ·

fa·nat·ic (fə năt′ĭk) *n-* person having unduly strong and unreasonable beliefs about something: *a fanatic about diet.* *adj-* (also **fa·nat′ic·al**) wild and unreasonable: *a fanatic belief in witchcraft.* —*adv-* fa·nat′ic·al·ly.

fan·tas·tic (făn tăs′tĭk) *adj-* 1 (also **fan·tas′ti·cal**) imaginative; unreal: *He told some fantastic story about riding a subway in the desert.* 2 odd; queer; grotesque: *a fantastic shape.* —*adv-* fan·tas′ti·cal·ly.

fan·ta·sy (făn′tə sē, -zē) *n-* [*pl.* **fan·ta·sies**] 1 imagination; unrestrained fancy. 2 thing imagined or not real; daydream; fanciful idea: *Her wealth is sheer fantasy.* 3 poem, play, or story showing much imagination or having fanciful ideas: *"Peter Pan" is a fantasy.*

far (fär) *adj-* [**far·ther, far·thest,** or **fur·ther, fur·thest** (See note at *farther.*)] 1 not near; distant: *a far land; a far past.* 2 more distant of two: *the far side of the street.* 3 covering a long distance or time: *a far journey.* *adv-* 1 to or at a great or definite distance: *He came far before he rested. I will go only so far.* 2 beyond what is right and proper: *Don't go too far with your accusations.* 3 by a great deal; very much: *He is far wiser than I.*

as far as or **so far as** to the extent that: *You may go now, as far as I'm concerned.* **by far** or **far and away** very much: *He is by far the worst speaker I've ever heard.* **far and near** or **far and wide** everywhere: *They came from far and near to hear him.* **go far** to be successful. **how far** to what distance or extent: *How far will you go to stop him?* **so far** up to now: *We've had no danger so far.* **so far so good** up to now there has been no trouble.

fas·cist (făsh′ĭst′) *n-* believer in or supporter of fascism.

fas·ten (făs′ən) *vt-* 1 to join; attach: *to fasten a shelf to a wall.* 2 to close or cause to close securely: *to fasten the lock.* 3 to keep fixed steadily: *to fasten attention on.*

fas·ten·er (făs′ən ər) *n-* device that closes an opening, or attaches one thing to another.

fas·ten·ing (făs′ən ĭng) *n-* something that fastens or holds things together, such as a bolt, clasp, or chain.

fas·tid·i·ous (făs tĭd′ē əs) *adj-* hard to please; very critical or particular: *to be fastidious about food or clothes.* —*adv-* fas·tid′i·ous·ly. *n-* fas·ti′di·ous·ness.

fast·ness (făst′nəs) *n-* 1 fortified, secure place; stronghold: *a mountain fastness.* 2 a condition of being fast.

fat (făt) *n-* oily substance found in animals and plants. Fats are compounds of carbon, hydrogen, and oxygen. *adj-* [**fat·ter, fat·test**] 1 having much of this substance: *This meat is fat.* 2 heavy with flesh; plump. 3 well-filled. *vt-* [**fat·ted, fat·ting**] to fatten. —*n-* fat′ness.

the fat of the land the best of everything.

fa·tal (fā′təl) *adj-* 1 causing death: *a fatal accident.* 2 causing great harm or ruin: *a fatal mistake.* —*adv-* fa′tal·ly.

fa·tal·ism (fā′tə lĭz′əm) *n-* philosophic principle or belief that all events are determined in advance, and that therefore one cannot control or change what will happen. —*n-* fa′ta·list. *adj-* fa′ta·lis′tic: *a fatalistic attitude.* *adv-* fa′ta·lis′ti·cal·ly: *to think fatalistically.*

fa·tal·i·ty (fə tăl′ə tē) *n-* [*pl.* **fa·tal·i·ties**] 1 death in a disaster: *There were two fatalities in the plane crash.* 2 tendency or likeliness to be doomed: *There is a fatality in all his undertakings.* 3 deadly effect or influence: *the fatality of a disease.*

fat·back (făt′băk′) *n-* fatty, unsmoked salt pork from the back of a hog.

fate (fāt) *n-* 1 power that is believed to control and decide what will happen; destiny. 2 what happens to someone; one's lot: *We wondered about the fate of the missing pilot.* 3 **the Fates** in classical mythology, the three goddesses who controlled human destiny. *Hom-* fete. —*adj-* fat′ed: *a man fated to succeed.*

fate·ful (fāt′fəl) *adj-* 1 decisive; a fateful *day.* 2 foretelling or seeming to foretell disaster; ominous: *a fateful prophecy.* 3 deadly; bringing death: *a fateful arrow.* —*adv-* fate′ful·ly. *n-* fate′ful·ness.

fa·ther (fä′thər) *n-* 1 male parent. 2 male ancestor; forefather. 3 founder or important leader: *the Pilgrim Fathers.* 4 one of the chief writers and teachers of the early Christian church. 5 **Father** form of address for an ordained priest. 6 **the Father** (also **our Father**) God. *vt-* 1 to be the male parent of; beget. 2 to originate or invent. —*n-* fa′ther·less.

FBI Federal Bureau of Investigation.

FCC or **F.C.C.** Federal Communications Commission.

F clef *Music n-* bass clef.

Fe symbol for iron.

fe·al·ty (fē′əl tē) *n-* 1 in feudal times, the pledge of a vassal to be faithful to his lord. 2 loyalty; allegiance.

fear (fēr) *n-* 1 feeling of fright, alarm, or extreme anxiety; dread; terror: *a fear of ghosts; to tremble with fear.* 2 awe; reverence: *a fear of God.* *vt-* 1 to be afraid of; be alarmed by; be frightened by: *Cats fear water.* 2 to feel awe toward: *to fear God.* *vi-* to be afraid.

fear for to be afraid or apprehensive about (someone or something that is threatened): *to fear for one's life.*

fear·ful (fēr′fəl) *adj-* 1 causing alarm or fright; awful; terrible: *That was a fearful storm.* 2 afraid; apprehensive: *The passengers were fearful of an accident.* —*adv-* fear′ful·ly. *n-* fear′ful·ness.

fear·less (fēr′ləs) *adj-* unafraid; courageous; brave. —*adv-* fear′less·ly. *n-* fear′less·ness.

fear·some (fēr′səm) *adj-* frightening; alarming; terrifying. —*adv-* fear′some·ly. *n-* fear′some·ness.

fea·si·ble (fē′zə bəl) *adj-* 1 possible to do or accomplish: *a feasible project.* 2 such as can be used or dealt with: *a feasible route up a mountain.* 3 reasonable; possible

fed (fĕd) *p.t. & p.p.* of **feed.**

fed up *Slang* disgusted; bored; wearied.

fed·er·al (fĕd′ər əl) *adj-* of, belonging to, or making up a nation formed by the union of smaller states.

fed·er·a·tion (fed′ ə rā′ shən) n- 1 a union by agreement of states or other units, in which the units delegate part or all of their authority to the governing body of the whole. 2 act or process of forming such a union.

fee (fē) n- 1 charge or payment, as for service by a professional man, or for a right to do something: a doctor's fee. 2 fief. 3 (also **fee simple**) land estate inherited or held by a person in his own right.

fee·ble (fē′ bəl) adj- [fee·bler, fee·blest] lacking strength or vigor; very weak. —n- fee′ble·ness. adv- fee′ bly.

fee·ble-mind·ed (fē′ bəl mīn′ dəd) adj- mentally subnormal; having very little power to think or to learn. —adv- fee′ ble-mind′ ed·ly. n- fee′ ble-mind′ ed·ness.

feed (fēd) vt- [fed (fēd), feed·ing] 1 to supply food for: to feed the poor. 2 to give food to; put food into the mouth of: to feed a baby. 3 to give as food: to feed meat to a dog. 4 to add to or supply with something: to feed fuel to a fire. vi- to take food; eat: The dogs fed hungrily. n- 1 food for animals; fodder. 2 Informal a meal.

feed on (or **upon**) to draw nourishment from; eat.

feed·back (fēd′ bak′) n- in an electronic device, machine, living organism, etc., process in which a portion of the output is returned to the input in order to control or change the output.

feed·er (fē′ dər) n- 1 person or thing that feeds. 2 device that supplies material to a machine. 3 a branch stream, railway, etc., supplying a main channel or line.

feeder line n- 1 a conductor or series of conductors that supply electricity to a certain point in a system for distribution to other parts. 2 gas or water main, railway, etc., that supplies a main line.

feel (fēl) vt- [felt (fēlt), feel·ing] 1 to examine by touch: to feel someone's pulse; to feel a piece of cloth. 2 to be aware of (something) by touch: I felt the rain on my face. 3 to have a sense of; be moved or affected by: to feel pity; to feel an insult. 4 to be sure of without proof: I feel it to be so. vi- 1 to search by touch; grope: to feel for a match. 2 to be aware of being in some definite condition of mind or body: to feel faint. 3 to have sympathy: to feel deeply for someone. 4 to seem to the touch: The air feels damp. n- a quality perceived by touch.

feel like 1 Informal to have a desire for: I feel like taking a walk. 2 to seem to the touch: It feels like silk.

feel out to find out what (someone) thinks about something.

feel up to Informal to feel well enough to.

feel·er (fē′ lər) n- 1 part of an animal that gives it information by touch, such as a cat's whisker or an insect's antenna. 2 something said or done to find out the opinions or purposes of others.

fe·line (fē′ līn′) adj- 1 of or pertaining to the cat family. 2 catlike: his feline grace. n- animal of the cat family.

¹fell (fēl) p.t. of **fall**.

²fell (fēl) vt- to cause to fall; shoot, knock, or cut down: to fell a deer; to fell a tree. [from Old English fellan, "to cause to fall," from feallan "to fall."] —n- fell′ er.

³fell (fēl) adj- [fell·er, fell·est] 1 cruel and vicious; totally wicked: a fell villain. 2 Archaic deadly. [from Old French fel, from felon meaning "felon."]

⁴fell (fēl) n- 1 animal's hide. 2 thin, tough membrane between the skin and muscles of many animals. [from Old English.]

fel·lah (fēl′ ə) n- [pl. fel·la·hin (fēl′ ə hēn′), fel·la·heen] peasant or agricultural worker in Egypt and other Arab countries.

fel·loe (fēl′ ō) n- felly. Hom- fellow.

fel·low (fēl′ ō) n- 1 man or boy: a friendly fellow. 2 companion; associate: a fellow in misfortune. 3 one of a matched pair. 4 member of a learned society. 5 in the governing body of a college or university. 5 a graduate student who receives an annual sum from a college or university for a stated period of study. 6 Informal a girl's sweetheart. as modifier: a fellow worker; fellow students. Hom- felloe.

hail fellow well met having a hearty greeting for everybody.

fel·ly (fēl′ ē) n- [pl. fel·lies] wooden rim of a wheel, into which the outer ends of the spokes are fitted. Also felloe.

fe·male (fē′ māl′) n- 1 a living thing, especially a woman or girl, of the sex that bears offspring. adj- 1 of or belonging to the sex that produces young. 2 of or having to do with a plant whose flowers have only pistils; pistillate. 3 in mechanics, having to do with a hollow fitting, plug, etc., threaded or bored to receive a corresponding part within it.

fem·i·nine (fēm′ ə nīn) adj- 1 of, relating to, typical of, or suitable for females: a feminine fashion; a feminine voice. 2 having the characteristics of a woman: her feminine ways. 3 Grammar belonging to a class of words that in English name people, animals, or things that are or are considered female, and in other languages name or describe many words without regard to female characteristics. —adv- fem′ i·nine·ly.

¹fer·ment (fûr mĕnt′) vi- to go through a chemical change because of the action of tiny living plants such as yeasts, certain bacteria, etc. vt-: 1 to cause to undergo this change: The bacteria fermented the milk. 2 to stir up; agitate.

²fer·ment (fûr′ mĕnt′) n- 1 substance containing yeasts, molds, bacteria, etc., that cause fermentation. 2 state of unrest, agitation, or excitement: The whole nation was in a ferment over the election.

fer·men·ta·tion (fûr′ mĕn tā′ shən) n- 1 the chemical changing of organic substances through the action of enzymes produced by certain yeasts and bacteria, especially through the action of yeasts on fruit sugar to produce alcohol. 2 process of causing or undergoing this change.

fer·mi·um (fĕr′ mē əm) n- man-made, radioactive, metal element. Symbol Fm, At. No. 100.

Fern frond

fern (fûrn) n- any of a large group of plants that have featherlike or leafy fronds and do not produce flowers or seeds. —adj- fern′ like′. adj- fern′ y [fern·i·er, fern·i·est]: a ferny glade.

fe·ro·cious (fə rō′ shəs) adj- fierce; savage: a ferocious lion; a ferocious attack. —adv- fe·ro′ cious·ly. n- fe·ro′ cios·ness.

fer·ti·liz·er (fûr′ tə lī′ zər) n- material, such as a chemical or manure, used to make soil more productive.

fer·ule (fēr′ əl) n- a rod or flat stick, formerly used to punish children in school. Homs- feral, ferrule.

fer·vent (fûr′ vənt) adj- strong or warm in feeling; intense; earnest. —n- fer′ ven·cy. adv- fer′ vent·ly.

fer·vid (fûr′ vĭd) adj- fiery in feeling; earnest; impassioned: a fervid loyalty; fervid oratory. —adv- fer′ vid·ly. n- fer′ vid·ness.

fer·vor (fûr′ vər) n- warmth and earnestness of feeling.

-fest combining form Slang occasion when a type of activity is performed: singfest; talkfest. [probably from German Fest meaning "a feast; fete."]

fes·tal (fĕs′ təl) adj- of or relating to a feast, holiday, or festival. —adv- fes′ tal·ly.

fes·ter (fĕs′ tər) vi- 1 to form or become filled with pus: The wound festered. 2 to linger painfully; cause a sore feeling; rankle: The insult festered in his mind.

fes·ti·val (fĕs′ tə vəl) n- 1 time of rejoicing and feasting, usually in memory of some special event. 2 periodic entertainment or cultural activity: a music festival.

Festival of Lights n- Hanukkah.

fes·tive (fĕs′ tĭv) adj- of or having to do with a feast or festival; gay; joyous; merry: a festive occasion; a festive scene. —adv- fes′ tive·ly.

few (fyōō) determiner (traditionally called adjective or pronoun) a small number of; not many: There are few people here. Many are called but few are chosen. n- 1 a small number only; small minority: In that village, few of the houses are white. 2 the few the minority: He is among the few.

a few a small, indefinite number: I saw a few people today. **quite a few** more than a small number.

fic·tion (fĭk′ shən) n- 1 literary works, such as novels and short stories, which tell of imaginary events and characters. 2 anything made up or imagined; hence, not fact: His excuse was pure fiction. —adj- fic′ tion·al.

field (fēld) *n-* 1 piece of open land used for planting, pasture, etc.: *a cornfield.* 2 land yielding some product: *an oil* field. 3 piece of land which has a special use: *a football* field. 4 an open space; *a field of snow.* 5 place of military operations or battle: *headquarters in the* field; *battlefield.* 6 area or sphere of special interest or activity: *the field of medicine.* 7 background against which something is seen: *a flag with stars on a field of blue.* 8 participants in a contest or sport: *to be sixth in a field of nine.* 9 area of work away from a central office or headquarters: *We now have six salesmen in the* field. 10 area that can be seen, especially through a microscope, telescope, etc. 11 *Physics* (1) region in which a force acts on an object that is brought into the region: *an electric* field; *a magnetic* field. (2) the force itself that acts at any particular point in the region. *as modifier:* a field *hospital. vt-* 1 in baseball, to catch and properly dispose of (the ball, a fly, a grounder, etc.). 2 to enter (a team, players, etc.) in an athletic event. *vi-* in baseball, to play as an infielder or outfielder.

take the field to go on the field for a game, battle etc.

sweep the field to win in all events or contests.

fi·er·y (fī′ə rē) *adj-* [fi·er·i·er, fi er·i·est] 1 flaming; burning. 2 resembling a fire: *a hery sunset.* 3 spirited; passionate; ardent: *a fiery speech.* 4 easily aroused: *a fiery temper.* —*n-* fi′er·i·ness.

fi·es·ta (fē ĕs′tə) *n-* festival, especially a saint's day as celebrated in Spain or Latin America with parades and music.

fife (fīf) *n-* small, shrill-toned musical instrument resembling the flute. *vt-* [fifed, fif·ing] to play on a fife: *He* fifed *a tune. vi-: He* fifed *happily.* —*n-* fif′er.

fif·teen (fĭf′tēn′) *n-* 1 amount or quantity that is one greater than 14. 2 *Mathematics* (1) the cardinal number that is the sum of 14 and 1. (2) a numeral such as 15 that represents this cardinal number. *as determiner* (traditionally called adjective or pronoun): *There are* fifteen *girls here and* fifteen *there.*

Boy playing fife

fif·teenth (fĭf′tēnth′) *adj-* 1 next after fourteenth. 2 the ordinal of 15; 15th. *n-* 1 the next after the fourteenth; 15th. 2 one of fifteen equal parts of a whole or group. 3 the last term in the name of a fraction having a denominator of 15: 1/15 *is one* fifteenth. *adv-: She finished* fifteenth *in the swimming race.*

fifth (fĭfth) *adj-* 1 next after fourth. 2 the ordinal of 5; 5th. *n-* 1 the next after the fourth; 5th. 2 one of five equal parts of a whole or group. 3 the last term in the name of a common fraction having a denominator of 5: 1/5 *is one* fifth. 4 *Music* an interval of five tones on the scale counting the extremes, as from A to E in the tuning of a violin, and the harmonic combination of these tones. 5 a quantity of alcoholic liquor equal to one-fifth of a gallon or four-fifths of a quart; also the bottle holding this much. *adv-: He spoke of you* fifth.

fifth column *n-* in wartime, civilians within a country who secretly aid its enemies. —*n-* **fifth columnist.**

fifth·ly (fĭfth′lē) *adv-* as fifth in a series.

fifth wheel *n-* 1 an extra, superfluous wheel for a four-wheeled vehicle. 2 *Informal* superfluous thing or person.

fif·ti·eth (fĭf′tē əth) *adj-* 1 next after forty-ninth. 2 the ordinal of 50; 50th. *n-* 1 the next after the forty-ninth; 50th. 2 one of fifty equal parts of a whole or group. 3 the last term in the name of a fraction having a denominator of 50: 1/50 *is one* fiftieth. *adv-: He stood* fiftieth *in his class.*

fif·ty (fĭf′tē) *n-* [*pl.* fif·ties] 1 amount or quantity that is one greater than 49. 2 *Mathematics* (1) the cardinal number that is the sum of 49 and 1. (2) a numeral such as 50 that represents this cardinal number. *as determiner* (traditionally called adjective or pronoun): *There are* fifty *rabbits here and* fifty *there.*

fight·er (fī′tər) *n-* 1 person who engages in physical conflict with another. 2 person who struggles or battles for a cause: *Patrick Henry was a fighter for liberty.* 3 professional boxer. 4 (also **fighter plane**) fast, maneuverable aircraft used mainly to attack enemy planes.

fig·ment (fĭg′mənt) *n-* something merely imagined; fiction: *Ghosts are a figment of the imagination.*

fig·ur·a·tive (fĭg′yər ə tĭv) *adj-* 1 using figures of speech: *a figurative style of writing.* 2 metaphorical; not literal: *a figurative meaning of a word.* 3 showing by a recognizable figure; emblematic; representational: *Much drawing is not figurative, but abstract.* —*adv-* fig′ur·a·tive·ly. *n-* fig′ur·a·tive·ness.

fig·ure (fĭg′yər) *n-* 1 shape; outline: *a figure in the darkness; a slim figure.* 2 person as he appears to others: *a pitiful figure.* 3 a likeness of something, especially one that is molded or carved: *a figure of Lincoln on a coin.* 4 an illustrative drawing: *The note refers to Figure 6.* 5 a design or pattern, as in fabrics. 6 pattern made by movement in skating or dancing. 7 figure of speech. 8 symbol for a number: *to write letters and figures.* 9 price: *to buy at a low figure.* 10 *Mathematics* (1) flat surface bounded by lines (plane figure). (2) space bounded by lines (solid figure). 11 figures arithmetic; use of numbers: *Are you good at figures? vi-* [fig·ured, fig·ur·ing] 1 to appear or play a part (in) something: *His name figures in the news.* 2 to make calculations: *I don't just guess, I* figure. *vt- Informal* to calculate; reason: *He* figured *that it was time to leave.*

figure on to take into consideration or account.

figure out to understand by reasoning or calculating.

film (fĭlm) *n-* 1 thin layer or coating: *a film of oil on water.* 2 haze; blur: *a film of mist.* 3 thin sheet or roll of transparent and flexible material coated with an emulsion sensitive to light and used for making photographs. 4 motion picture. *vt-* 1 to cover with a thin coating: *Ice* filmed *the window.* 2 to make a motion picture of: *to* film *a play. vi-* 1 to become covered or obscured with mist or haze: *His eyes* filmed *with tears.* 2 to be suitable for use in a motion picture: *The script* films *well. His face* films *badly.* —*adj-* film′like′.

film·strip (fĭlm′strĭp′) *n-* strip of photographic film that is projected one frame or picture at a time.

film·y (fĭl′mē) *adj-* [film·i·er, film·i·est] 1 very thin; sheer. 2 covered with a thin layer of something; hazy; dim. —*adv-* film′i·ly. *n-* film′i·ness.

Fins of a fish and of a skin diver

fil·ter (fĭl′tər) *n-* material or device used to permit the passage of certain things while stopping others. Filters are made for liquids, light rays, gases, radio or sound signals, etc. *vt-* 1 to stop the passage of by use of such material or device: *to filter impurities from oil.* 2 to pass through such a device: *to* filter *oil to remove impurities. vi-* to pass or move slowly through something.

fil·ter·a·ble (fĭl′tər ə bəl) or **fil·tra·ble** (fĭl′trə bəl) *adj-* 1 such as can be held back by a filter. 2 of microorganisms, such as can pass through a filter.

filth (fĭlth) *n-* 1 offensive dirt. 2 foulness; obscenity.

filth·y (fĭl′thē) *adj-* [filth·i·er, filth·i·est] 1 covered with or containing filth; dirty; foul. 2 nasty; underhanded: *a filthy trick.* 3 offensive; obscene: *a filthy word.* —*adv-* filth′i·ly. *n-* filth′i·ness.

fil·trate (fĭl′trāt′) *n-* liquid that passes through a filter. *vt-* [fil·trat·ed, fil·trat·ing] to filter. —*n-* fil·tra′tion.

fin (fĭn) *n-* 1 any of the thin, bony, skin-covered parts of a fish's body by which it balances, steers, and drives itself.

fi·nance (fĭ năns′, fī′năns′) *n-* 1 management of money affairs: *A banker is skilled in finance.* 2 finances income; funds; revenue: *The firm's finances are in good shape. vt-* [fi·nanced, fi·nanc·ing] to provide money or credit for: *The bank financed the factory.*

find (find) *vt-* [**found** (found), **find·ing**] 1 to look for and get back: *Did you* find *your pen?* 2 to discover by chance or accident: *He* found *a dime in the street.* 3 to learn or discover: *to* find *the answer.* 4 to reach; get to: *The bullet* found *its mark.* 5 to determine; declare: *The jury* found *him guilty.* 6 to set aside: *to* find *time for play.* 7 *Archaic* to furnish or provide. *n-* valuable or pleasing discovery: *The ancient manuscript was quite a* find.

find oneself to discover one's abilities.

find out to discover.

fine art *n-* 1 one of the arts, such as painting, music, sculpture, poetry, etc., usually thought to be concerned with creating beauty. 2 any skill requiring delicacy.

fine-drawn (fīn' drôn') *adj-* drawn to extreme subtlety or fineness: *a* fine-drawn *distinction.*

fin·er·y (fī' nə rē) *n-* [*pl.* **fin·er·ies**] showy dress or ornaments: *The girls came to the party in their best* finery.

fi·nesse (fĭ nĕs') *n-* 1 skill; delicacy of execution: *to play a flute with* finesse. 2 skillful management; subtle strategy: *to handle a situation with* finesse. 3 in card games, an attempt to take a trick by playing the lower of two cards not in sequence, on the chance or knowledge that the opponent who has already played has the card in between. *vi-* [**fi·nessed, fi·nes·sing**] to make such a play in a card game. *vt-* to play (a certain card) for such a reason.

fin·ger (fĭng' ər) *n-* 1 one of the five separate parts of the end of the hand, especially one of the four besides the thumb; digit. 2 part of a glove made to hold one of these. 3 anything that resembles one of these in form or use. *vt-* to use one or more fingers to touch, press, or play on: *to* finger *cloth*; *to* finger *a guitar.*

THUMB
FOREFINGER
MIDDLE FINGER
RING FINGER
PINKIE

Fingers

put (one's) **finger on** to point out exactly: *He* put his finger on *the answer.* **twist** (someone) **around** (one's) **little finger** to manage (someone) easily; control (someone) completely.

finger bowl *n-* small bowl to hold water for rinsing the fingers during or after a meal.

fin·ger·ing (fĭng' ər ĭng) *n-* 1 a touching or feeling with the fingers. 2 the placing of the fingers on a musical instrument in playing it; also, notation on a piece of music showing this.

fin·ger·ling (fĭng' ər lĭng) *n-* small salmon or trout.

fin·ger·nail (fĭng' gər nāl') *n-* hard, protective, hornlike covering at the end of a finger. For picture, see *nail*.

finger painting *n-* 1 the making of pictures on a specially prepared paper by applying a thick paint with the fingers and palms. 2 picture created in this way.

fi·nis (fĭn' ĭs) *n-* the end; conclusion. [from Latin.]

fin·ish (fĭn' ĭsh) *vt-* 1 to bring to an end; complete; conclude: *to* finish *a piece of work.* 2 to treat the surface (of something) in some way: *to* finish *wood.* 3 to use up completely: *to* finish *a glass of milk.* *vi-*: *The mystery story* finished *abruptly.* *n-* 1 completion; end: *the* finish *of a race.* 2 surface or texture: *a glossy* finish; *a* fire-bug (flər' bŭg') *n- Informal* a pyromaniac.

fire·bug (flər' bŭg') *n- Informal* a pyromaniac.

fire control *n-* 1 the control or putting out of fires. 2 *Military* the control of gunfire, rockets, missiles, etc., especially by the use of special equipment.

fire·crack·er (flər' krăk' ər) *n-* small roll of paper which contains gunpowder and a fuse; cracker. Firecrackers explode loudly and are used at celebrations.

fire·damp (flər' dămp') *n-* dangerous, explosive gas formed in coal mines.

fire·dog (flər' dôg') *n-* andiron.

fire·eat·er (flər' ē' tər) *n-* 1 performer who pretends to eat fire. 2 someone eager to fight or quarrel.

fire engine *n-* truck equipped to fight fires.

fire escape *n-* a device, such as a ladder, metal stairway, or chute, to provide escape from a burning building.

fire extinguisher *n-* any portable apparatus, such as a small tank containing chemicals, used for smothering small fires with water or chemicals.

fire·fly (flər' flī') *n-* [*pl.* **fire·flies**] small flying beetle that periodically gives off a glowing light.

¹firm (fûrm) *adj-* [**firm·er, firm·est**] 1 solid; not yielding easily; not soft. 2 fixed in place; not easily moved: *a* firm *post; a* firm *foundation.* 3 steady; not shaking: *a* firm *voice.* 4 not easily changed; steadfast: *a* firm *belief.* 5 not varying; also, not subject to change: *a* firm *price.* *vt-* to fix; make secure or compact: *to* firm *a pole in the ground.* *vi-*: *The cheese* firmed *nicely.* [from Old French *ferme*, "steadfast."] —*adv-* firm' ly. *n-* firm' ness.

firm up 1 to become more solid or steadier: *The stock market* firmed up *tonight.* 2 to strengthen or complete.

²firm (fûrm) *n-* business concern, house, or company, especially a business partnership. [from Italian and Spanish *firma* meaning "signature; firm name," from *firmar*, "to sign," from Latin *firmare*, "to confirm."]

fir·ma·ment (fûr' mə mənt) *n-* the sky; the heavens.

first (fûrst) *adj-* 1 coming before all others in time, place, order, quality, importance, etc.: *He was* first *in his class*, 2 ordinal of 1; 1st: *He lived on* 1st *Avenue.* *adv-* 1 before all others in time, place, order, etc.: *He spoke of you* first. 2 rather than do (something); before doing (something); sooner: *I would die* first. *n-* 1 person or thing that is before all others in time, place, order, etc.: *We were the* first *to go.* 2 the slowest and most powerful forward driving gear in most motor vehicles; low. 3 in baseball, first base: *He's safe on* first!

at first in the beginning: *She didn't want to go* at first. **first and last** altogether; all in all: *He was* first and last *a scientist.* **from the first** since the beginning: *She was a nuisance* from the first. **in the first place** to start with.

first aid *n-* treatment or help given a sick or hurt person before regular medical treatment from a doctor is obtained. *as modifier* (**first-aid**): *a* first-aid *kit.*

first-born (fûrst' bôrn') *adj-* born first; oldest. *n-* the first child born to a couple.

first class *n-* 1 the highest or best type: *a mind of the* first class. 2 most expensive class of cabin, seating, service, etc., on a ship, train, or airplane. 3 mail consisting of letters, postcards, and sealed matter. —*adj-* (**first-class**): *a* first-class *cabin*; first-class *mail.* *adv-* (**first-class**): *to travel* first-class.

first fruits *n- pl.* 1 the earliest harvest of a crop. 2 the earliest results of any undertaking.

first-hand (fûrst' hănd') *adj-* direct from the original source: *a* first-hand *account.* *adv-*: *I heard it* first-hand.

first lady *n-* 1 the wife of the President of the United States or of the governor of a State. 2 the leading woman of a profession.

first lieutenant See *lieutenant*.

first·ly (fûrst' lē) *adv-* as first in a series.

first offender *n-* person who has been legally declared guilty of breaking the law for the first time.

first papers *n-* documents filed by a foreigner declaring intention to become a citizen of the United States.

first person *Grammar n-* form of a pronoun or verb used to indicate the speaker or speakers. Example: I, me, my, we, us, our, I go, we have. *as modifier* (**first-person**): *a* first-person *pronoun.*

first-rate (fûrst' rāt') *adj-* excellent; very good; of the best quality: *a* first-rate *book.*

first sergeant *n-* in the Army and Marine Corps, the highest ranking noncommissioned officer in a company.

firth (fûrth) *Scottish n-* a narrow arm of the sea; mouth of a river.

fis·cal (fĭs' kəl) *adj-* 1 relating to money matters; financial. 2 having to do with the public treasury or revenues: *U.S.* fiscal *policy.* —*adv-* fis' cal·ly.

fiscal year *n-* any twelve-month period on which the accounting of a business or government is based

fish (fĭsh) *n-* [*pl.* fish; fish·es (kinds of fish)] 1 any of a variety of cold-blooded water animals having a backbone, fins, and gills. They usually have scaly bodies. 2 the flesh of water animals, used for food. *vi-* 1 to catch, or try to catch water animals: *Dad* fishes *for recreation.* 2 to search (inside something): *He* fished *in his pocket for a dime.* 3 to seek to gain something by indirect means: *to* fish *for an invitation; to* fish *for a compliment.* *vt-* 1 to catch or try to catch. 2 to try to catch water animals in: *to* fish *a stream for rainbow trout.*

¹fit (fĭt) *adj-* [**fit·ter, fit·test**] **1** suitable; proper; appropriate; right (for): *a banquet* fit *for a king; weather* fit *for flying.* **2** in good physical condition: *to feel* fit. *vt-* [**fit·ted, fit·ting**] **1** to be suitable, proper, or right for; befit: *The music* fitted *the occasion.* **2** to be right for in size, shape, function, etc.: *Does this light bulb* fit *the socket?* **3** to make the right size, shape, etc.; adapt: *to* fit *a suit for a customer.* **4** to put carefully into place: *to* fit *a piece into a jigsaw puzzle.* **5** to supply: *to* fit *a ship for a long voyage.* *vi-* to be of the right size, shape, etc.: *Your coat* fits *well. The two parts* fit *together.* *n-* adjustment of one thing to another: *a perfect* fit; *a loose* fit. [from earlier English fyt of doubtful origin.] —*adv-* **fit'ly.** *n-* **fit'ness.**

see (or think) **fit** to to decide to; choose to.

fit in 1 to have a suitable place or position: *She doesn't* fit in *with that crowd.* **2** to agree; be in keeping.

fit out (or **up**) to supply with what is suitable for a purpose: *to* fit *oneself out for a journey.*

²fit (fĭt) *n-* **1** sudden, violent attack of disease or illness: *a* fit *of epilepsy; a* fit *of indigestion.* **2** sudden outburst: *a* fit *of laughter.* [from Old English fitt, "a struggle."] by (or in) **fits and starts** in efforts that start and stop irregularly: *He does his homework* by fits and starts.

fitch (fĭch) *n-* the European polecat; also, its fur. Also **fitch'ew** (fĭch'ōō).

fit·ful (fĭt'fəl) *adj-* not regular; stopping for a short time and then starting again; spasmodic: *a baby's* fitful *crying;* fitful *sleep.* —*adv-* **fit'ful·ly.** *n-* **fit'ful·ness.**

fit·ter (fĭt'ər) *n-* **1** person who adjusts or puts together pipes or parts of machinery. **2** person who adjusts and alters clothing to make it fit.

fit·ting (fĭt'ĭng) *adj-* suitable; proper: *a* fitting *moment for a word of praise.* *n-* **1** session with a tailor or seamstress to have a garment made or altered to fit. **2** anything used in adjusting or connecting: *a pipe* fitting. **3** fittings the equipment or necessary fixtures of a house, shop, car, etc. —*adv-* **fit'ting·ly.**

five (fīv) *n-* **1** amount or quantity that is one greater than 4. **2** *Mathematics* (1) the cardinal number that is the sum of 4 and 1. (2) a numeral such as 5 that represents this cardinal number. *as determiner* (traditionally called adjective or pronoun): *There are* five *boys here and* five *there.*

five-and-ten (fīv'ən tĕn') *n-* variety store which sells inexpensive items including many which cost only five or ten cents. Also **five-and-dime.**

five·fold (fīv'fōld') *adj-* **1** five times as many or as much. **2** having five parts: *a* fivefold *solution to the problem.* *adv-* *Mechanization increased factory output* fivefold.

Five Nations *n-* confederacy, formed about 1570, of Iroquoian Indians of the Mohawk Valley, New York, including the Mohawks, Onondagas, Cayugas, Oneidas, and Senecas. See also *Six Nations.*

fix (fĭks) *vt-* **1** to make firm; fasten: *The sailors* fixed *a new mast on the boat.* **2** to set definitely; establish: *He* fixed *a time and place for our meeting.* **3** to repair: *A plumber* fixed *the leaky pipe.* **4** to arrange; prepare: *Mother* fixed *lunch.*

fl. 1 fluid. **2** flourished.

Fla. Florida.

flab·ber·gast (flăb'ər găst') *Informal vt-* to astonish: *His ignorance will* flabbergast *you.*

fla·con (flăk'ən, flä kŏn') *n-* bottle, often ornamental, with a tight cap or stopper: *a* flacon *of perfume.*

¹flag (flăg) *n-* piece of cloth bearing marks or patterns that give it a certain meaning; banner; pennant: *a signal* flag; *a school* flag. *vt-* [**flagged, flag·ging**] **1** to signal with or as if with such a piece 'of cloth: *to* flag *a train.* **2** to place a banner or pennant on. [from an Old Norse form similar to Danish **flag,** "to flutter (as in the wind)"; part of the meaning comes from **²flag.**]

United States flag

flash·back (flăsh'băk') *n-* interruption in a story, motion picture, etc., to describe earlier events.

flash bulb *n-* electric bulb which gives a very strong light for a short time, used in photography. Also **flash' lamp'.**

flash card *n-* card with a word, phrase, arithmetic example, etc., on it, held up by a teacher in front of a class for rapid review or an aid in learning.

flash flood *n-* sudden flood caused by a heavy rainfall in the surrounding area.

flash·gun (flăsh' gŭn') *n-* device used to hold and set off a flash bulb.

flash·ing (flăsh' ĭng) *n-* sheet metal used for waterproofing, especially at roof angles, chimney bases, etc.

flash·light (flăsh' lĭt') *n-* **1** small, portable electric light that uses batteries for power. **2** flash of light, used to take a photograph.

flat·ter·y (flăt' ə rē) *n-* [*pl.* **flat·ter·ies**] excess praise.

flat·tish (flăt' ĭsh) *adj-* rather flat; somewhat flat.

flat·top (flăt' tŏp') *n- Slang* aircraft carrier.

flat·u·lent (flăch' ə lənt, flăt' yōo-) *adj-* **1** affected by or tending to cause gas in the stomach or intestines. **2** pretentious; pompous; conceited. —*n-* **flat'u·lence.**

flat·ware (flăt' wâr') *n-* tableware that is more or less flat, such as plates, knives, and forks, as distinguished from bowls, pitchers, etc.

flat·work (flăt' wûrk') *n-* laundry such as sheets, towels, napkins, etc., which can be pressed by a machine rather than by a hand iron.

flat·worm (flăt' wûrm') *n-* any of various flat-bodied worms, most of which are parasitic on vertebrate animals, including man.

flaunt (flônt) *vt-* to show off; display arrogantly: *to* flaunt *one's superior knowledge.* *vi-* **1** to go about boldly or impudently: *to* flaunt *through the streets.* **2** to wave showily: *flags* flaunting *in the breeze.* —*adv-* **flaunt'ing·ly:** *He* flauntingly *showed his contempt.*

flau·tist (flô' tĭst, flou'-) *n-* flutist.

fla·vor (flā' vər) *n-* **1** taste of something that is eaten or drunk: *stew with a spicy* flavor. **2** substance that gives

flee (flē) *vi-* [**fled** (flĕd), **flee·ing**] **1** to hurry or run away, especially from danger: *The deer* fled *as we approached.* **2** to disappear quickly; vanish: *His troubles* fled. *vt-* **1** to run away from: *to* flee *a burning house.* **2** to avoid; shun: *to* flee *evil.* **Hom-** flea.

fleece (flēs) *n-* **1** the woolly coat that covers a sheep; also, all the wool shorn or cut off a sheep at one time. **2** anything like the coat of a sheep. *vt-* [**fleeced, fleec·ing**] **1** to cut wool off a sheep. **2** to rob, cheat, or swindle (someone). —*n-* **fleec'er.**

fleec·y (flē' sē) *adj-* [**fleec·i·er, fleec·i·est**] of or like fleece; soft and light: *a* fleecy *cloud.* —*n-* **fleec'i·ness.**

flense (flĕns) *vt-* [**flensed, flens·ing**] to strip blubber or skin from: *to* flense *a whale.*

flesh (flĕsh) *n-* **1** the soft parts of the body between the skin and bones, consisting chiefly of muscle and fat. **2** the meat of animals, birds, or fish used as food. **3** soft pulp of fruits and vegetables used as food. **4** the body, as distinguished from the mind and soul: *The spirit is willing, but the* flesh *is weak.* **5** a light, pinkish tan. —*adj-* **flesh' less.**

flesh and blood kin: *Your brothers and sisters are your own* flesh and blood. **in the flesh** in the actual, living state, rather than as a picture or image.

flesh-col·ored (flĕsh' kŭl' ərd) *adj-* light pinkish tan.

flesh·ly (flĕsh' lē) *adj-* **1** of or having to do with the body: *our* fleshly *ills.* **2** worldly rather than spiritual. —*n-* **flesh' li·ness.**

flesh·pots (flĕsh' pŏts') *n- pl.* physical luxuries and comforts; high living; also, places providing them.

flesh wound *n-* wound not affecting a bone or vital organ.

flex (flĕks) *vt-* **1** to bend: *to* flex *one's knees; to* flex *a bow by tightening the bowstring.* **2** to tighten or contract (a muscle).

flex·i·ble (flĕk' sə bəl) *adj-* **1** easily bent: *a* flexible *fishing rod.* **2** capable of fitting to new conditions; adaptable: *a* flexible *person; a* flexible *form of government.* —*n-* **flex'i·bil'i·ty.** *adv-* **flex'i·bly.**

flex·ion (flĕk' shən) *n-* a bending or turning, as of an arm or muscle.

flex·or (flĕk′sər) *n-* muscle that bends or flexes a joint in an arm or a leg. See also *extensor*.

flex·ure (flĕk′shər) *n-* 1 a bending or a being bent. 2 the part bent.

flick (flĭk) *n-* light, quick stroke or motion: *to give a horse a flick with the whip; a flick of the wrist. vt-* to strike or move lightly and quickly: *He flicked the horse gently.*

¹**flick·er** (flĭk′ər) *vi-* 1 to shine or burn unsteadily; waver: *A candle flickers in the breeze.* 2 to move back and forth; tremble; quiver: *The shadows flickered on the wall. n-* unsteady light or movement; flutter: *the flicker of a candle; the flicker of an eyelid.* [from Old English *flicorian* meaning "to flutter."] —*adv-* **flick′er·ing·ly**: *The candle burned* flickeringly. *adj-* **flick′er·y.**

²**flick·er** (flĭk′ər) *n-* North American woodpecker with a bright red mark at the neck and yellow under the wings and tail. [probably an imitation of the cry.]

flied (flīd) *p.t. & p.p.* of **fly** (to hit a baseball).

fli·er (flī′ər) *n-* 1 aviator. 2 anything that flies or moves very rapidly, such as an express train. 3 daring or risky investment intended to make money quickly: *a flier in stocks.* 4 advertising leaflet.

flies (flīz) 1 plural of the noun **fly.** 2 form of the verb **fly** used with "he," "she," "it," or singular noun subjects in the present tense.

¹**flight** (flīt) *n-* 1 act, process, or manner of flying: *The bat has a zigzag flight.* 2 the passage or distance flown: *the London-New York flight; a short flight.* 3 swift passage: *the flight of time.* 4 a flying group: *a flight of geese; a flight of arrows.* 5 a group or series of steps: *He lived three flights up.* 6 a passing beyond the usual: *a flight of imagination.* [from Old English *flyht,* "a flying."]
    take flight to begin flying; rise in flight.

²**flight** (flīt) *n-* hasty departure: *his flight from the burning building.* [from earlier English *fliht,* "a fleeing," from *flēon,* related to English *flee.*]
    put to flight to cause to flee. **take flight** or **take to flight** to flee; run away.

flight·less (flīt′ləs) *adj-* unable to fly: *The ostrich is a flightless bird.*

flight path *n-* path or route taken by an aircraft, guided missile, or spacecraft in flight.

flight·y (flī′tē) *adj-* [flight·i·er, flight·i·est] shifting rapidly and aimlessly in interest and enthusiasm; giddy; frivolous: *a flighty young girl; flighty conversation.* —*adv-* **flight′i·ly.** *n-* **flight′i·ness.**

flim·flam (flĭm′flăm′) *Informal n-* a cheating by deception; trickery. *vt-* [flim·flammed, flim·flam·ming] to cheat or trick. —*n-* **flim′flam′mer.**

flim·sy (flĭm′zē) *adj-* [flim·si·er, flim·si·est] 1 fragile; not solid; poorly made: *The flimsy boat was crushed like an eggshell.* 2 weak; not convincing: *a flimsy excuse.* —*adv-* **flim′si·ly.** *n-* **flim′si·ness.**

flinch (flĭnch) *vi-* to draw back or away from pain, danger, an unpleasant duty, etc.: *He flinches at noise.*

flint (flĭnt) *n-* 1 very hard quartz, usually dull gray, that produces sparks when struck against steel. 2 a piece of this quartz; also, a piece of metal alloy used to produce sparks in cigarette lighters.

flint·lock (flĭnt′lŏk′) *n-* old-fashioned gun fired by a spark from a flint and steel attached to it.

Flintlock

flint·y (flĭn′tē) *adj-* [flint·i·er, flint·i·est] 1 made of or like flint. 2 hard; unyielding: *a flinty look.* —*adv-* **flint′i·ly.** *n-* **flint′i·ness.**

flip (flĭp) *Informal adj-* [flip·per, flip·pest] saucy; flippant: *a flip remark.* [probably from Old Norse *fleipa* or *flipa,* "to babble."]

flir·ta·tion (flûr tā′shən) *n-* 1 act of flirting. 2 brief, light romance.

flir·ta·tious (flûr tā′shəs) *adj-* playfully romantic; coquettish: *a flirtatious girl; a flirtatious glance.* —*adv-* **flir·ta′tious·ly.** *n-* **flir·ta′tious·ness.**

flit (flĭt) *vi-* [flit·ted, flit·ting] 1 to move or fly lightly and quickly; dart: *The bird* flitted *about.* 2 to pass quickly.

flitch (flĭch) *n-* side or strip of cured pork, especially bacon.

flit·ter (flĭt′ər) *vi-* to flutter.

fliv·ver (flĭv′ər) *Slang n-* a cheap or dilapidated old car.

float (flōt) *vi-* 1 to be held up by liquid or air: *Wood floats on water.* A *balloon floats in the air.* 2 to move or drift freely: *A cloud floated across the sky.*

float·er (flō′tər) *n-* 1 person or thing that floats. 2 person who moves aimlessly from place to place or job to job.

floating island *n-* soft custard pudding topped with meringue or whipped cream.

floating rib *n-* in human beings, one of the two lowest pairs of ribs, which are attached only to the vertebrae.

floc·cu·lent (flŏk′yə lənt) *adj-* having or resembling soft, fluffy tufts or shreds of wool or similar material. —*n-* **floc′cu·lence.**

¹**flock** (flŏk) *n-* 1 a group of animals or birds of one kind which travel or feed together: *a flock of sheep; a flock of geese.* 2 large number of people together, especially the members of a single church: *The minister greeted his flock. vi-* to come together or move in crowds: *People flocked to the beaches.* [from Old English **flocc.**]

²**flock** (flŏk) *n-* small tuft or mass of very short, woolly fibers. *vt-* to cover (a fabric or wallpaper) with such tufts. [from Old French **floc,** from Latin **floccus.**]

flock·ing (flŏk′ĭng) *n-* short, woolly fibers applied to wallpaper or fabric in an ornamental design.

floe (flō) *n-* large sheet or mass of ice drifting on the sea. Hom- **flow.**

flog (flŏg) *vt-* [flogged, flog·ging] to beat hard with a stick or whip. —*n-* **flog′ger.**

flood (flŭd) *n-* 1 great flow of water; especially, a body of water overflowing its banks. 2 a great outpouring or abundance resembling a deluge: *a flood of tears; a flood of letters.*

flood plain *n-* plain bordering a river and frequently flooded by it, especially such a plain formed by deposits of soil left by floods.

flood tide *n-* the incoming tide; also, the point or time of highest tide.

floor (flôr) *n-* 1 the part of a room that one walks on, or a surface resembling this: *a wooden floor; the ocean floor.* 2 all the rooms on one level in a building; story. 3 the main part of an assembly hall, where members sit and speak.

floor leader *n-* in either of the houses of Congress, a person who is chosen by his political party to direct its business and strategy on the floor.

floor show *n-* series of performances by singers, dancers, or comedians in a nightclub.

floor·walk·er (flôr′wôk′ər) *n-* person employed in a large store to supervise clerks and direct customers.

flop (flŏp) *vi-* [flopped, flop·ping] 1 to drop or fall heavily or clumsily: *She flopped into a chair.* 2 to move or flap about: *to flop like a fish out of water.* 3 *Slang* to fail. *vt-: He flopped his suitcase on the floor. n-* 1 act or sound of flopping. 2 *Slang* a failure.

flop·py (flŏp′ē) *adj-* [flop·pi·er, flop·pi·est] tending to flap or move loosely about: *a rabbit with floppy ears.* —*adv-* **flop′pi·ly.** *n-* **flop′pi·ness.**

flor·a (flôr′ə) *n-* the plants of a particular region, environment, or period of time. See also *fauna.*

flo·ral (flôr′əl) *adj-* of or like flowers: *a floral design; a floral fragrance.* —*adv-* **flor′al·ly.**

Flor·en·tine (flôr′ən tēn′, flôr′·) *n-* a native of Florence, Italy. *adj-* 1 of or relating to Florence or its inhabitants. 2 relating to a dull, brushed finish used on gold or silver jewelry.

flo·res·cence (flôr ĕs′əns, flə rĕs′·) *n-* a blossoming or period of blossoming. —*adj-* **flo·res′cent:** *a florescent rosebush.*

flo·ret (flôr′ət) *n-* small flower, especially one of many forming a dense cluster of a single flowering head.

flor·id (flôr′ĭd, flŏr′·) *adj-* 1 bright in color; flushed: *a florid complexion.* 2 full of flowery ornamentation; elaborate and showy: *a florid style of writing.*

flor·in (flôr´ ən, flŏr´ -) *n-* any of various European coins, including a British silver coin worth two shillings.

flo·rist (flôr´ ĭst, flŏr´ -) *n-* a person who grows or sells flowers as a business.

floss (flôs, flŏs) *n-* 1 soft, glossy silk or cotton thread used in embroidering, crocheting, etc. 2 soft, silky fibers in certain plant pods or husks, such as the milkweed.

floss·y (flôs´ē, flŏ´ sē) *adj-* [floss·i·er, floss·i·est] 1 of or like floss; soft and silky. 2 *Slang* showy and pretentious in an effort to be elegant.

flo·ta·tion (flō tā´ shən) *n-* 1 act or process of floating. 2 the sale of stock in a new business to get enough money to start operation. 3 in mining, a method of separating crushed or powdered ores by putting them in a special liquid which will float only certain particles. *as modifier: a flotation process.*

flo·til·la (flō tĭl´ ə) *n-* 1 fleet of small vessels; also, a small fleet. 2 in the U.S. Navy, a unit of two or more squadrons of vessels of the same type.

flot·sam (flŏt´ səm) *n-* the wreckage of a ship or its cargo found floating in the sea. See also *jetsam*.

¹flounce (flouns) *vi-* [flounced, flounc·ing] to move or go in a jerky, impatient, or angry manner: *She flounced out of the room.* *n-* jerky, impatient, motion. [of uncertain origin; perhaps from Old Norse, and related to Swedish *flunsa* meaning "to plunge."]

²flounce (flouns) *n-* strip of cloth gathered and sewn along an edge of something; ruffled border. *vt-* [flounced, flounc·ing] to add such a border to (something). [from earlier *frounce*, probably from Old French *froncer*, "to wrinkle (the brow, etc.)." from Latin *frons*, "brow."]

¹floun·der (floun´ dər) *vi-* to make awkward, blundering efforts to get through or out of something; struggle clumsily: *to flounder about in a swamp; to flounder through a speech.* [apparently from ²flounder, from the motion of the fish.]

²floun·der (floun´ dər) *n-* [*pl.* floun·der; floun·ders (kinds of flounder)] any of various flatfishes used for food. [from Old French *flondre*, from Old Norse, as in Swedish *flundra.*]

Flounder

flour (flou´ ər) *n-* fine meal of ground wheat or other grain. *vt-* to sprinkle or cover with this. *Hom-* flower.

flour·y (flou´ rē) *adj-* 1 of or resembling flour. 2 smeared or covered with flour.

flout (flout) *vt-* to mock; scoff at; treat with scorn: *to flout the authorities.* *n-* flout´ er.

flow (flō) *vi-* 1 to move or run along as fluids do: *Water flows. Blood flows in a vein.* 2 to abound; be plentiful: *Wine flowed at the feast.* 3 to move or pour forth like a stream: *Goods flowed into the stores. His words flowed.* 4 to appear to move in a pleasing, continuous motion.

flow·er (flou´ ər) *n-* 1 in seed-bearing plants, a part which contains the organs of reproduction and from which the seeds develop. Most flowers have petals and are often brightly colored, but some are tiny and inconspicuous. 2 any plant grown for, or noticeable because of, its blossoms: *tc plant flowers.* 3 the best part: *the flower of the country's youth; in the flower of life.* *vi-* to bloom. *Hom-* flour. —*adj-* flow´ er·less. *adj-* flow´ er·like´.

STAMEN · PISTIL
PETAL · SEPAL
Parts of a flower

flow·ered (flou´ ərd) *adj-* having flowers or a design resembling flowers: *a flowered dress.*

flow·er·et (flou´ ər ət) *n-* little flower; floret.

flowering plant *n-* any of a large and major group of highly evolved plants whose seeds are enclosed in a fruit; angiosperm.

flow·er·pot (flou´ ər pŏt´) *n-* container, usually of baked clay, in which to plant or keep growing plants.

flow·er·y (flou´ ə rē) *adj-* [flow·er·i·er, flow·er·i·est] 1 full of or resembling flowers: *a flowery meadow; a flowery fragrance.*

flown (flōn) *p.p.* of ¹fly.

flu (floo) *n-* influenza. *Hom-* flew, flue.

flub (flŭb) *Informal vt-* [flubbed, flub·bing] to fail clumsily at (doing something); bungle. *n-* a bungling error.

fluc·tu·ate (flŭk´ choo āt´) *vi-* [fluc·tu·at·ed, fluc·tu·at·ing] to rise and fall; also, to vary unsteadily; waver: *Prices may fluctuate.* —*n-* fluc´ tu·a´ tion.

flue (floo) *n-* 1 pipe or passage for carrying off smoke, hot air, etc., such as that in a chimney. 2 (also **flue pipe**) an organ pipe that produces a tone when a current of air strikes the lip or opening in the side of the pipe. *Hom-* flew, flu.

flu·en·cy (floo´ ən sē) *n-* ease and smoothness, especially in speaking.

flu·ent (floo´ ənt) *adj-* 1 spoken or produced with ease; smooth and flowing: *to speak fluent Spanish; the fluent motions of a dancer.* 2 using words in a smooth, flowing manner: *a fluent speaker.* —*adv-* flu´ ent·ly.

fluff (flŭf) *n-* 1 soft, light, downy material: *The kitten looked like a ball of fluff.* 2 *Informal* a mistake in making a speech, acting a part, etc. *vt-* 1 to shake or puff out into a soft mass: *The bird fluffed its feathers.* 2 *Informal* to make a mistake in speaking or saying (something).

fluff·y (flŭf´ ē) *adj-* [fluff·i·er, fluff·i·est] resembling, consisting of, or covered with fluff. —*n-* fluff´ i·ness.

flu·id (floo´ ĭd) *n-* substance that will flow; a liquid or a gas. *adj-* 1 able to flow; not solid; liquid or gaseous: *Molten steel is fluid.* 2 not fixed or settled; likely to change: *My plans are fluid.* —*adv-* flu´ id·ly.

fluid dram *n-* unit of liquid measure equal to 1/8 fluid ounce or about 3.7 cubic centimeters; about a teaspoonful.

fluid drive *n-* in an automobile transmission, a kind of clutch, consisting of two platelike turbine blades enclosed in an oil-filled case. Engine power rotates one blade, setting the oil in motion, thus causing the other blade to rotate. Also **fluid clutch.**

flu·id·i·ty (floo ĭd´ ə tē) *n-* condition of being fluid.

fluid ounce *n-* unit of liquid measure equal to 1/16 pint.

¹fluke (flook) *n-* 1 flattened, pointed end of an arm of an anchor. 2 one of the two lobes of a whale's tail. 3 barbed or pointed head of a harpoon, arrow, lance, etc. [origin uncertain; perhaps from ³fluke.]

²fluke (flook) *n-* stroke of good or bad luck: *He won by a lucky fluke.* [origin uncertain.] —*adj-* fluk´ y [flu·ki·er, flu·ki·est].

³fluke (flook) *n-* 1 any of various parasitic flatworms. 2 any of various flounders. [from Old English floc.]

flume (floom) *n-* 1 narrow gorge or ravine through which a stream flows. 2 artificial channel for water.

flum·mox (flŭm´ əks) *Informal vt-* to throw into confusion; bewilder.

flung (flŭng) *p.t. & p.p.* of fling.

flunk (flŭngk) *Informal vt-* 1 to fail (a subject, test, etc.). 2 to give a failing mark to. *vi-* : *He flunked in English.* **flunk out** to be discharged from a school because of bad marks.

flunk·y (flŭng´ kē) *n-* [*pl.* flunk·ies] 1 person who meekly serves and tries to please another; toady.

flu·o·res·cence (floo´ ə rĕs´ əns, flôr ĕs´ -) *n-* 1 the emitting of electromagnetic radiation, usually as light, by certain substances when exposed to radiation of another wavelength. See also *phosphorescence.* 2 the emitted radiation. —*adj-* flu·o·res´ cent.

fluorescent lamp *n-* tubular electric lamp in which glowing filaments produce ultraviolet light in reaction with mercury vapor, and this light in turn causes the inner coating of phosphor to fluoresce brightly.

flu·o·ri·date (floo´ ə ri dāt´, flôr´ ə-) *vt-* [flu·o·ri·dat·ed, flu·o·ri·dat·ing] to treat with fluorides; especially, to add fluorides to (drinking water) in order to prevent tooth decay. —*n-* flu·o·ri·da´ tion.

flu·o·ride (floo´ ə rīd´, flôr´ īd´) *n-* any chemical compound that consists of fluorine combined with another element or radical.

flu·o·rine (floo´ ə rēn´, flôr´ ēn´) *n-* pale yellow poisonous gas that is one of the most reactive elements. Symbol F, At. No. 9, At. Wt. 18.9984.

flu·o·rite (flõõ′ ə rīt′, flôr′ ĭt′) *n-* mineral calcium fluoride (CaF₂), found in various colors. It is used to make metals melt more easily in soldering, making steel, etc. Also **flu′ or·spar** (flõõ′ ər spär′, flôr′-).

fluor·o·scope (flõõ′ ər ə skōp′, flôr′-) *n-* device for studying the shadows cast on a fluorescent screen by an object placed between the screen and a source of X rays; especially, such a machine used to examine people.

flur·ry (flûr′ē) *n-* [*pl.* **flur·ries**] 1 confusion or bustle; commotion: *a flurry of excitement.* 2 light, brief fall of snow, or a sudden gust of wind. *vt-* [**flur·ried, flur·ry·ing**] to confuse; agitate; fluster.

flush (flŭsh) *vi-* 1 to become red; glow; blush: *Her cheeks flushed with excitement. He flushed with embarrassment.* 2 to flow and spread rapidly: *Water flushed into the room. vt-* 1 to cleanse or wash out with a strong flow of water: *to flush a clogged pipe.*

flut·ing (flõõ′ tĭng) *n-* series of decorative grooves: *to ornament the legs of a table with fluting.*

flut·ist (flõõ′ tĭst) *n-* person who plays the flute. Also **flautist**.

flut·ter (flŭt′ ər) *vi-* 1 to fly or move with an irregular flapping of the wings: *The wounded bird fluttered along the ground.* 2 to flap, wave, or beat rapidly: *The leaves fluttered in the breeze. My heart fluttered with excitement.* 3 to move about nervously and excitedly: *The anxious hostess fluttered from guest to guest. vt-* to cause to move with a flapping or rapid motion: *The bird fluttered its wings. She fluttered her eyelashes at him. n-* 1 rapid, irregular motion or change. 2 state of nervous excitement. —*n-* **flut′ ter·er.** *adj-* **flut′ ter·y.**

flu·vi·al (flõõ′ vē al) *adj-* of or produced by a stream.

flux (flŭks) *n-* 1 constant flowing; continuous change: *Conditions are in flux.* 2 any flow or discharge, especially an abnormal flow of matter from the body.

¹**fly** (flī) *vi-* [**flew** (flõõ), **flown** (flōn), **fly·ing**] 1 to move through the air with or as if with wings: *Birds fly south in the fall. The arrow flew to the target.* 2 to move or go very swiftly; speed: *He flew to her aid.*

fly·blown (flī′ blōn′) *adj-* covered with maggots or blowfly eggs; hence, rotten, dirty, or corrupt.

²**by-by-night** (flī′ bī nīt′) *n-* shifty or untrustworthy person, especially one who sets up a shaky or dishonest business for a quick profit. *adj-: a fly-by-night business.*

fly·cast·ing (flī′ kås′ tĭng) *n-* skill or practice of fishing with artificial flies. —*n-* **fly′ cast′ er.**

fly·catch·er (flī′ kăch′ ər) *n-* any of several related birds that catch insects in flight.

fly dope *n-* substance used to make artificial fishing flies waterproof.

fly·ing (flī′ ĭng) *adj-* 1 able to fly or move through the air as if with wings. 2 brief and hurried; fleeting: *a flying visit.* 3 moved by or streaming in the air: *gay, flying banners.*

flying boat *n-* seaplane having a body like a boat hull and a small float under each wing.

flying buttress *n-* arched support whose top rests against and strengthens a wall, used in Gothic architecture.

flying colors *n-* striking success or honor; triumph: *to pass a test with flying colors.*

flying field *n-* level area where airplanes land or take off; small airport.

flying fish *n-* any of several fishes found mainly in warm seas and having long winglike fins that enable them to make gliding leaps above the surface of the water.

flying fox *n-* any of various large, fruit-eating bats native to warm areas of Asia, Africa, and America.

Flying fish
8–18 in long

flying jib *n-* in a sailing ship, a small sail at the foremost part, attached to an extension of the bowsprit called the **flying jib boom.**

flying machine *n-* in earlier times, an airplane or similar flying craft.

flying saucer or **flying disk** *n-* any of various unidentified disk-shaped objects which people say they have seen flying in the sky at great speeds.

flying squirrel *n-* an American squirrel that makes long, gliding leaps by stretching out the loose folds of skin connecting its front and hind legs.

flying start *n-* in a race, a getaway from the starting position at top speed; hence, any swift beginning seemingly destined for success.

fly·leaf (flī′ lēf′) *n-* [*pl.* **fly·leaves**] blank sheet of paper at the beginning or end of a book.

fly·pa·per (flī′ pā′ pər) *n-* paper covered with a sticky or poisonous substance, hung to trap and kill flies.

fly·speck (flī′ spĕk′) *n-* small spot of dirt left by a fly; hence, any similar small spot.

fly·trap (flī′ trap′) *n-* 1 any device for catching flies. 2 any plant that traps insects; Venus's-flytrap.

fly·way (flī′ wā) *n-* route along which birds travel in their regular migrations.

fly·weight (flī′ wāt′) *n-* boxer who weighs 112 pounds or less.

fly·wheel (flī′ hwēl′) *n-* heavy wheel used in a machine to help regulate and make more uniform the speed of the working parts.

Fm symbol for fermium.

FM frequency modulation.

f-number *n-* in photography, a number obtained by dividing the focal length of a lens by its diameter as regulated by the diaphragm. The smaller the number, the larger the opening is.

foal (fōl) *n-* the young of the horse or other closely related animal, especially one less than a year old. *vi-* to bring forth such young.

foam (fōm) *n-* frothy mixture of many tiny bubbles, such as that formed on a liquid by shaking, constant movement, fermentation, etc.: *the foam formed by the breaking waves. vi-* to form or produce a mass of tiny bubbles; froth. —*adj-* **foam′ y** [**foam·i·er, foam·i·est**]. **foam at the mouth** 1 to produce a mass of frothy saliva, as a dog with rabies does. 2 *Informal* to be furious.

fog (fŏg, fôg) *n-* 1 cloud or mass of water vapor near the surface of the earth or water; thick mist. 2 any haziness or blurred condition: *the fog on a photographic film.* 3 confused or bewildered state: *Her mind is in a fog. vt-* [**fogged, fog·ging**] to cover, blur, or obscure with or as if with a thick mist. *vi-* to become foggy.

fog bank *n-* dense, low mass of fog, especially over a body of water.

fog·bound (fŏg′ bound′, fôg′-) *adj-* surrounded by fog that obscures visibility and makes traveling unsafe.

fog·gy (fŏg′ ē, fôg′-) *adj-* [**fog·gi·er, fog·gi·est**] 1 full of or obscured by fog: *a foggy day.* 2 hazy; blurred: *a foggy photograph.* 3 not clear; confused: *such foggy notions.* —*adv-* **fog′ gi·ly.** *n-* **fog′ gi·ness.**

fog·horn (fŏg′ hôrn′, fôg′ hôrn′, -hôrn′) *n-* horn or similar device that sends warning signals to ships in a fog.

fo·gy (fō′ gē) *n-* [*pl.* **fo·gies**] person having old-fashioned or stuffy ideas and habits. Also **fo′ gey.**

foi·ble (foi′ bal) *n-* minor failing or weakness.

foil (foil) *vt-* to interfere with and prevent from being successful; thwart; balk: *to foil an attempt to escape.* [from Old French **fouler,** "trample under foot," from Latin **fullāre,** from **fullō,** "a fuller (of cloth)."]

fold·er (fōl′ dər) *n-* 1 outer cover, often a sheet of heavy paper folded double, for holding papers. 2 booklet, circular, etc., made by folding a large sheet. 3 device or machine that folds, especially one used in binding books.

fo·li·age (fō′ lē lj) *n-* the leaves of a plant; also, leaves in general: *a plant with evergreen foliage; autumn foliage.*

fo·li·a·tion (fō′ lē ā′ shən) *n-* 1 of a plant, the producing of leaves, or a being in leaf. 2 the numbering of pages in a book, manuscript, etc.; pagination.

fo·li·o (fō′ lē ō′) *n-* [*pl.* **fo·li·os**] 1 book of the largest standard size, made from sheets of paper folded only once; also, the size of a book thus made. 2 in printing, the number of a page. *as modifier: a folio edition of Shakespeare's works. vt-* to number (book pages).

folk (fōk) *n-* 1 [*pl.* **folk**] a people having, or assumed to have, the same customs, traditions, historical background, etc.: *the Celtic folk; country folk.* 2 (often **folks**) *Informal* people: *Some folks are always on the go.*

fol·low (fŏl′ō) *vt-* (in sense 1 considered intransitive when the direct object is implied but not expressed) **1** to come or go after: *Please follow me. Lead, and we'll follow.* **2** go along: *to follow a path.*

fond (fŏnd) *adj-* [fond·er, fond·est] **1** loving or affectionate; sometimes, foolishly or excessively so: *a fond look; his fond parents.* **2** deeply felt; cherished: *my fondest hopes.* —*adv-* fond′ly.
fond of having a strong liking for.

fon·dant (fŏnd′dənt) *n-* sweet, creamy sugar mixture used for making candy, icings, etc.; also, a candy made from such a mixture.

fon·dle (fŏn′dəl) *vt-* [fon·dled, fon·dling] to stroke or touch lovingly; caress. —*n-* fon′ dler.

fond·ness (fŏnd′nəs, fŏn′-) *n-* liking; affection.

fon·due (fŏn dyōō′) *n-* dish made from melted cheese, usually served with pieces of toast or other food to be dipped into it.

food (fōōd) *n-* **1** any substance eaten or taken in by a plant or animal to help it live and grow; especially, solid nourishment in contrast to liquid. **2** something that provides aid, stimulation, etc., especially for the mind: *This is food for thought.*

food chain *n-* succession in which various organisms feed upon one another and thus depend upon one another.

food fish *n-* any fish commonly eaten as food by human beings, as distinguished from game fish.

food·stuff (fōōd′ stŭf′) *n-* anything used as food.

fool (fōōl) *n-* **1** person who lacks sense, insight, or judgment; silly or unwise person. **2** in former times, a jester. *vt-* to trick; deceive. *vi-* to act silly; play or joke foolishly. —*adj- Informal* silly; senseless: *That was a fool thing to do!*

foot·fall (fōōt′ fôl′) *n-* sound of a footstep.

foot·gear (fōōt′ gêr′) *n-* footwear.

foot·hill (fōōt′ hĭl′) *n-* one of the low hills at the base of a mountain or mountain range.

foot·hold (fōōt′ hōld′) *n-* **1** place on which to stand or step; footing: *a foothold on a narrow ledge.* **2** position from which to proceed in any undertaking.

foot·ing (fōōt′ ĭng) *n-* **1** firm placing of the feet: *He lost his footing and fell on the ice.* **2** foothold. **3** position or standing; basis: *to start out on an equal footing.*

foot·less (fōōt′ ləs) *adj-* **1** lacking a foot or feet. **2** pointless; ineffectual: *idle,* footless *fancies.* —*adv-* foot′ less·ly. *n-* foot′less·ness.

foot·lights (fōōt′ lĭts′) *n- pl.* row of lights along the front of the floor of the stage in a theater.

foot·loose (fōōt′ lōōs′) *adj-* free to travel about or live as one wishes.

foot·man (fōōt′ mən) *n-* [*pl.* foot·men] male servant, usually in uniform, who answers the door, waits on table, opens car doors, etc.

foot·note (fōōt′ nōt′) *n-* note of explanation at the bottom of a page, usually indicated in the body of the text by a number or symbol referring to it.

for (fôr, fŏr, fər) *prep-* **1** useful or needed in the case of; suited to: *a bag for potatoes; a knife for cutting.* **2** meant to belong to; directed to: *a gift for you; a letter for Maria.* **3** to have or to do: *It's time for tea.*

force (fôrs) *n-* **1** a push or pull that can produce a change in the motion of something; that which causes or tends to cause an object to accelerate or decelerate. **2** strength;

fore- *prefix* **1** before in time or order: *the forenoon; to foretell.* **2** situated in front: *a forepaw; the forelock.* **3** front part of: *the forearm; the foredeck.*

fore-and-aft (fôr′ ənd ăft′) *adj-* following or in a line with the direction of a ship's length: *a vessel with* fore-and-aft *sails.* *adv-* fore and aft lengthwise; from stem to stern.

fore·head (fŏr′ hĕd′, fôr′ əd) *n-* the part of the face above the eyes; brow.

for·eign (fŏr′ ən, fôr′ -) *adj-* **1** belonging to or coming from another country or nation: *She speaks a foreign language.* **2** having to do with other nations or countries: *a foreign correspondent; the President's foreign policy.* **3** not related or not belonging:

fore·short·en (fôr shôr′ tən, -shôr′ tən) *vt-* to shorten, lengthen, widen, or narrow (lines and shapes) in drawing so as to make such things as extended arms, headlong bodies, etc., appear as an observer might see them.

fore·sight (fôr′ sīt′) *n-* **1** a knowing or seeing beforehand. **2** careful planning; heedful thought for the future; prudence: *Lack of* foresight *caused a shortage.*

fore·sight·ed (fôr′ sī′ təd) *adj-* having or marked by foresight: *a* foresighted *approach to the problem.* —*adv-* fore′ sight′ ed·ly. *n-* fore′ sight′ ed·ness.

fore·skin (fôr′ skĭn′) *n-* fold of skin that covers the end of the male sex organ in human beings, part or all of which is removed in circumcision.

for·est (fôr′ əst, fŏr′-) *n-* a growth of trees covering a large tract of land; large woods. *as modifier: the* forest *animals. vt-* to cover with trees or forest. —*adj-* for′ est·ed: *a heavily* forested *region.*

fore·stall (fôr stôl′) *vt-* to prevent or thwart by action taken in advance: *His quick stop* forestalled *an accident.* —*n-* fore·stall′ er.

for·est·a·tion (fôr′ ə stā′ shən, fŏr′-) *n-* extensive planting and care of trees to make or restore a forest.

fore·stay (fôr′ stā′) *n-* strong rope or cable from the foremast to the bow of a ship, to support the foremast.

for·est·er (fôr′ ə stər, fŏr′-) *n-* **1** person whose work is taking care of a forest and the wildlife in it. **2** forest dweller.

for·est·ry (fôr′ ə strē, fŏr′-) *n-* science of planting and caring for forests, including good lumbering practice and conservation.

fore·taste (fôr′ tāst′) *n-* sample of what something will be like later: *The early frost was a* foretaste *of winter.*

fore·tell (fôr tĕl′) *vt-* [fore·told, fore·tell·ing] to tell in advance; predict: *Who can* foretell *what will happen?* —*n-* fore·tell′ er.

fore·thought (fôr′ thôt′) *n-* planning in advance; prudence; heed for the future; foresight: *His* forethought *in saving enabled him to buy a house.*

fore·top (fôr′ tŏp′) *n-* platform at the top of the lowest section of the foremast of a ship.

for·ev·er (fôr ĕv′ ər, fər-) *adv-* **1** always; eternally; without ever ending. **2** continually; most of the time: *He is* forever *watching television.*

for·ev·er·more (fôr ĕv′ ər môr′, fər-) *adv-* from now on; forever.

fore·warn (fôr wôrn′) *vt-* to caution in advance: *The weather bureau* forewarned *us of the hurricane.*

fore·went (fôr wĕnt′) *p.t.* of forego. See *forgo.*

fore·word (fôr′ wûrd′) *n-* preface; introductory matter, especially to a book.

for·feit (fôr′ fət, fôr′ -) *vt-* to lose or give up because of neglect or fault: *The team failed to show up and* forfeited *the game. n-* something lost as the result of neglect, fault, etc; forfeiture. —*n-* for′ feit·er.

for·fei·ture (fôr′ fĭ chər, fôr′-) *n-* **1** the losing of something as a punishment or because of neglect or wrongdoing: *He paid for careless driving with the* forfeiture *of his license.* **2** a forfeit.

for·fend (fôr fĕnd′, fôr-) *vt- Archaic* prevent.

for·gath·er or **fore·gath·er** (fôr găth′ ər, fôr-) *vi-* to assemble; come together.

for·gave (fôr găv′, fôr-, fər-) *p.t.* of forgive.

¹forge (fôrj) *n-* **1** hearth for heating metals, consisting of a fire fanned by a forced draft of air. **2** blacksmith shop; smithy. *vt-* [forged, forg·ing] **1** to shape (heat-softened metal) with a hammer or other tool, either by hand or by machine. **2** to write or copy (a document or another's name) with intent to deceive; counterfeit: *to* forge *a signature; to* forge *a check.* [from Old French, from Latin fabrica meaning "workshop."]

Forge

forg·er (fôr′ jər) *n-* person who counterfeits checks, signatures, documents, paintings, etc.

for·ger·y (fôr′ jə rē) *n-* [*pl.* for·ger·ies] **1** a copying or imitating of something with intent to deceive.

for·get·ful (fòr gèt' fəl, fòr-, fər-) *adj-* 1 in the habit of forgetting; having a poor memory; absent-minded: *I write things down because I'm* forgetful. 2 neglectful: *He is* forgetful *of his duties.* —*adv-* for·get' ful·ly.

for·get·ful·ness (fòr gèt' fəl nəs, fòr-, fər-) *n-* 1 habit of forgetting; absent-mindedness. 2 loss or lack of memory.

for·get-me-not (fòr gèt' mē nòt', fòr) *n-* small plant with tiny blue flowers.

for·giv·a·ble (fòr giv' ə bəl, fòr-, fər-) *adj-* of a kind that can be forgiven; not very serious: *a* forgivable *offense.* —*adv-* for·giv' a·bly.

for·give (fòr giv', fòr-, fər-) *vt-* [for·gave (-gāv'), for·giv·en, for·giv·ing] 1 to pardon; excuse: *She* forgave *his clumsiness. He* forgave *his attackers.* 2 to require no repayment of (a debt); remit. —*n-* for·giv' er.

for·give·ness (fòr giv' nəs, fòr-, fər-) *n-* 1 pardon: *He asked* forgiveness. 2 act of forgiving or pardoning.

for·giv·ing (fòr giv' ĭng, fòr-, fər-) *adj-* 1 showing forgiveness: *a* forgiving *gesture.* 2 tending to forgive: *a* forgiving *nature.* —*adv-* for·giv' ing·ly. *n-* for·giv' ing·ness.

for·go (fòr gō') *vt-* [for·went (-wènt'), for·gone (-gòn', -gōn'), for·go·ing] to give up; do without: *Ann decided to* forgo *candy to lose weight.*

for·got (fòr gòt', fòr-, fər-) *p.t.* of forget.

for·got·ten (fòr gòt' ən, fòr-, fər-) *p.p.* of forget. *adj-* no longer remembered: *a* forgotten *book.*

fork (fòrk, fôrk) *n-* 1 instrument with two or more long points, prongs, or tines, such as a table fork, a pitchfork, a tuning fork, or a trident.

for·lorn (fòr lòrn', fôr lôrn') *adj-* 1 lonely or wretched: *He felt* forlorn *at his pet's death.* 2 neglected; deserted: *a* forlorn *old house.* —*adv-* for·lorn' ly. *n-* for·lorn' ness.

forlorn hope *n-* 1 a vain hope. 2 an extremely difficult or improbable undertaking.

form (fòrm, fôrm) *n-* 1 the outward shape, structure, or contour of something: *a rounded* form; *the pointed* form *of a cone.* 2 a body, especially the human body: *the tall* form *of Mr. Brown.* 3 kind or variety: *A tree is a* form *of plant life.* 4 state or character in which a thing appears: *water in the* form *of ice.*

for·mer·ly (fòr' mər lē, fôr'-) *adv-* in past time; once: *People* formerly *traveled in carriages.*

form-fit·ting (fòrm' fĭt' ĭng, fôrm'-) *adj-* closely fitted to the body: *a* formfitting *dress.*

for·mic (fòr' mĭk, fôr'-) *adj-* 1 having to do with, or made from, formic acid. 2 of or having to do with ants.

For·mi·ca (fòr' mī' kə) *n-* trade name for a strong, synthetic resin used to make counter tops, paneling, etc. Also formica.

formic acid *n-* colorless acid (HCOOH) having a strong odor and found in plants and certain insects such as the ant. It is used for dyeing and finishing cloth.

for·mi·da·ble (fòr' mĭ də bəl, fôr'-) *adj-* 1 causing fear or cautious respect: *a* formidable *army; a* formidable *danger.* 2 hard to deal with, overcome, or accomplish: *To climb the mountain was a* formidable *task.* —*n-* for' mi·da·bil' i·ty. *adv-* for' mi·da·bly.

form·less (fòrm' ləs, fôrm'-) *adj-* lacking a regular or definite shape; amorphous. —*adv-* form' less·ly. *n-* form' less·ness.

for·mu·la (fòrm' yə lə, fôrm'-) *n-* [*pl.* for·mu·las or for·mu·lae (-lē)] 1 a set of rules; detailed instructions; recipe: *the* formula *for a cough medicine; a* formula *for international peace.* 2 a certain set of words habitually used at certain times: *the* formula *"sincerely yours" at the end of a letter.* 3 in chemistry, a statement that tells the elements that make up something: H_2O *is the* formula *for water.* 4 in mathematics, a statement of a rule or process: *A = lw is the* formula *for finding the area of a rectangle (area equals length times width).*

for·mu·late (fòr' myə lāt', fôrm'-) *vt-* [for·mu·lat·ed, for·mu·lat·ing] to put into definite form; to state in an orderly way: *to* formulate *plans.* —*n-* for' mu·la' tion.

for·ni·cate (fòr' nə kāt', fôr-) *vi-* [for·ni·cat·ed, for·ni·cat·ing] to have unlawful sexual intercourse.

for·sake (fər sāk', fòr-) *vt-* [for·sook (-sŏŏk'), for·sak·en, for·sak·ing] to give up; abandon. —*n-* for·sak' er.

for·sooth (fər sōōth') *Archaic adv-* indeed; in truth.

for·swear (fòr swàr', fòr-) *vt-* [for·swore (fòr swôr', fòr swòr'), for·sworn (fòr swôrn', fòr swòrn'), for·swear·ing] to give something up: *to* forswear *smoking.*

for·syth·i·a (fər sĭth' ē ə, fòr-) *n-* cultivated shrub that bears bright yellow flowers in early spring.

fort (fòrt) *n-* 1 an area or structure built to withstand attack. 2 a permanent military camp or station. *Hom-* ¹forte.

¹forte (fòrt) *n-* special talent; field of best effort: *My* forte *is music.* [from earlier French, from Old French fort, "strong," from Latin fortis, "strong."] *Hom-* fort.

²for·te (fòr' tā, -tē) *Music adv- & adj-* loudly; loud; with power: *Play this passage* forte. *Listen to the* forte *passage.* [from Italian, from Latin fortis, "strong."]

forth (fòrth) *adv-* 1 onward; forward (in time, place, or order): *to go* forth *to battle; from this day* forth. 2 out, as from hiding or concealment: *The plants put* forth *tender new shoots. Hom-* fourth.

and so forth and so on; and the like; et cetera: *They were singing, dancing,* and so forth.

forth·com·ing (fòrth' kŭm' ĭng) *adj-* 1 about to appear or happen; approaching: *We put notices of* forthcoming *activities on the bulletin board.* 2 available; at hand: *Money for the project will be* forthcoming *when needed.*

forth·right (fòrth' rīt') *adj-* honest and direct; straightforward; frank: *a* forthright *reply.* —*adv-* forth' right' ly. *n-* forth' right' ness.

forth·with (fòrth' wĭth', -wĭth') *adv-* at once.

for·ti·eth (fòr' tē əth, fôr'-) *adj-* 1 next after thirty-ninth. 2 the ordinal of 40; 40th. *n-* 1 the next after the thirty-ninth; 40th. 2 one of forty equal parts of a whole or group. 3 the last term in the name of a fraction having a denominator of 40: 1/40 *is one* fortieth. *adv-*: *His boat finished* fortieth *in the race.*

for·ti·fi·ca·tion (fòr' tə fə kā' shən) *n-* 1 a making strong; preparation against attack: *the* fortification *of a canal;* fortification *against sickness.* 2 a protective wall, mound of earth, or other structure, sometimes temporary, as on a battlefield. 3 a fort or system of forts.

for·ti·fy (fòr' tə fī') *vt-* [for·ti·fied, for·ti·fy·ing] 1 to strengthen against attack by building forts, walls, etc.: *to* fortify *a city.* 2 to make strong: *Vitamins help to* fortify *us against colds.* —*n-* for' ti·fi·er.

for·tis·si·mo (fòr tĭs' ə mō) *Music adv- & adj-* very loudly; very loud: *Play this passage* fortissimo. *Listen to the* fortissimo *passage.*

for·ti·tude (fòr' tə tōōd', fòr' tə tyōōd', fôr'-) *n-* courage or firmness in meeting pain, danger, or trouble.

fort·night (fòrt' nĭt') *chiefly Brit. n-* two weeks.

fort·night·ly (fòrt' nĭt' lē) *chiefly Brit. adv-* every two weeks: *to meet* fortnightly. *adj-* occurring every two weeks: *a* fortnightly *meeting.* *n-* magazine, journal, etc., that appears every two weeks.

for·tress (fòr' trəs) *n-* stronghold; fort or fortification.

for·tu·i·tous (fòr tyōō' ə təs, -tōō' ə təs) *adj-* 1 happening by chance; accidental: *our* fortuitous *meeting.* 2 lucky; fortunate: *a* fortuitous *accident.* —*adv-* for·tu' i·tous·ly. *n-* for·tu' i·tous·ness.

for·tu·nate (fòr' chə nət, fôr'-) *adj-* favored by chance; lucky. —*adv-* for' tu·nate·ly.

for·tune (fòr' chən, fôr'-) *n-* 1 what happens to a person, either for good or ill; chance; luck: *He had the bad* fortune *to lose his bicycle.* 2 destiny; fate: *It was his* fortune *to rise to fame.* 3 a large amount of money; wealth; riches: *He made a* fortune *in the steel business.*

fortune cookie *n-* crisp, thin, folded cookie containing a slip of paper with a prediction or piece of advice.

fortune hunter *n-* a seeker of wealth, especially by means of marriage.

for·tune-tell·er (fòr' chən tèl' ər, fôr'-) *n-* one who attempts or pretends to predict another's future by looking at playing cards, gazing at a crystal ball, etc. —*n-* for' tune·tell' ing.

for·ward (fòr' wərd, fôr'-) *adv-* (also for' wards) 1 to or toward the front; to the fore; onward; ahead: *to leap* forward; *to run* forward *on a ship; to pass papers* forward. 2 toward the future: *from this time* forward.

for·ward·ly (fôr′ wərd lē, fôr′-) *adv-* impudently; boldly.

for·ward·ness (fôr′ wərd nəs, fôr′-) *n-* 1 condition of being advanced or in front. 2 impudence; boldness.

forward pass *n-* in football, a throwing of the ball toward the opponent's goal line.

for·went (fôr wĕnt′, fôr-) *p.t.* of forgo.

fosse (fôs) *n-* moat; ditch surrounding a castle.

Two kinds of fossil

fos·sil (fŏs′ əl) *n-* 1 actual remains of ancient animals and plants found buried in the earth or imbedded in rock, as fossil ferns in coal, fossil shells in mountain shale, etc. 2 a preserved indication of the existence of a living organism, such as dinosaur footprints in mud that has turned to rock. 3 *Informal* person or thing which is out of date or old fashioned. *as modifier:* a fossil fern.

fos·sil·ize (fŏs′ əl īz′) *vt-* [fos·sil·ized, fos·sil·iz·ing] to change into a fossil; petrify. *vi-* to become a fossil. —*n-* **fos′ sil·i·za′ tion.**

fos·ter (fŏs′ tər, fôs′-) *vt-* 1 to advance; promote; encourage: *The children's concerts foster an appreciation of music.* 2 to nurture; nourish; bring up; care for: *to foster a child.* *adj-* belonging to a family though not related by blood: *a foster child.* —*n-* **fos′ ter·er.**

foster brother *n-* male foster child in a family having another child or children.

foster child *n-* child who is raised or cared for by parents who are not its own either by blood relation or legal adoption.

foster father *n-* man who serves as father of a foster child.

foster mother *n-* woman who serves as mother of a foster child.

foster parent *n-* a foster father or foster mother.

foster sister *n-* female foster child in a family having another child or children.

fought (fôt) *p.t. & p.p.* of fight.

foul (foul) *adj-* [foul·er, foul·est] 1 offensive; disgusting: *a foul smell.* 2 evil; wicked; vile: *a foul deed.* 3 stormy; inclement: *a foul day;* foul *weather.* 4 unfair; underhanded: *to succeed by fair means or foul.*

fou·lard (fōō lärd′) *n-* satiny fabric with a twill weave, usually of silk and either plain or printed.

foul ball *n-* in baseball, a ball hit or tipped so as to fall outside the foul lines or to roll or bounce across either base line between first or third base and home plate.

foul line *n-* in baseball, a line coinciding with a base line and extending to the wall.

foul-mouthed (foul′ moutht′, -mouthd′) *adj-* using vulgar or profane language.

foul play *n-* 1 treachery, especially a resort to violence: *The marchers met with foul play.* 2 dishonest dealing.

foul tip *n-* in baseball, a ball hit glancingly so that it continues toward the catcher or backstop, hits the plate or the ground behind the plate, etc.

¹**found** (found) *p.t. & p.p.* of find. *Archaic adj-* equipped and fitted out: *a well-found ship.* *n-* provisions; board.

²**found** (found) *vt-* to begin; establish; set up: *to found a colony; to* found *a new business.* [from Old French **fonder,** from Latin **fundāre,** "bottom."]

³**found** (found) *vt-* to form, especially metal, by melting and pouring into a mold; cast. [from Old French **fondre,** from Latin **fundere,** "to pour."]

foun·da·tion (foun dā′ shən) *n-* 1 the part of a building or other structure, often partly underground, which bears the weight; also, the surface or underground rock, soil, etc., on which something is built. 2 basis: *His religious faith has a firm foundation.* 3 believable or valid evidence.

¹**found·er** (foun′ dər) *vi-* 1 to become filled with water and sink: *Our boat leaked and began to* founder. 2 of a horse, to become lame or otherwise disabled. 3 to collapse; fail: *The business foundered.* [from Old French **fondrer,** meaning "go to the bottom," from Old French **fond,** from Latin **funda.**]

²**found·er** (foun′ dər) *n-* person who establishes or founds: *the* founders *of a colony.* [from ²found.]

³**found·er** (foun′ dər) *n-* person who makes metal castings, especially type. [from ³found.]

found·ling (found′ ling) *n-* baby or child that is found after having been deserted.

found·ry (foun′ drē) *n-* [*pl.* found·ries] 1 place where metal castings are made. 2 the process of casting metal.

fount (fount) *n-* 1 source: *a fount of wisdom; a* fount *of knowledge.* 2 *Archaic* fountain.

foun·tain (foun′ tən) *n-* 1 a spring of water. 2 a place or machine where water or other drinks may be had: *a drinking* fountain; *a soda* fountain. 3 a jet or jets of water: *The fountain rose in feathery plumes of water.* 4 the structure, often ornamental, from which these jets come: *This fountain is made of bronze.* 5 a source or reservoir: *A library is a* fountain *of knowledge.*

Fountain

four hundred *n-* the established inner social circle of a community: *My neighbors belong to the* four hundred.

four-in-hand (fôr′ in hănd′) *n-* 1 necktie tied with a slipknot and having ends that hang down over each other. 2 a team of four horses driven by a single driver.

four-leaf clover *n-* a clover having four leaflets instead of the usual three. It is thought to bring good luck to those who find it or keep it.

four-o'clock (fôr′ ə klŏk′) *n-* bushy, cultivated plant with variously colored flowers that open in cloudy weather or the late afternoon and close in the morning.

four-post·er (fôr′ pōs′ tər) *n-* bedstead with four posts, usually tall and often with a canopy and curtains.

four·score (fôr′ skôr′) *n-* four times twenty; eighty.

four·some (fôr′ səm) *n-* 1 a group of four, especially two mixed couples. 2 game or players in a game, especially golf, in which two pairs of partners play each other.

four·square (fôr′ skwâr′) *adj-* 1 honest; forthright. 2 having four equal sides; square.

Fox (fŏks) *n-* [*pl.* Fox·es, also Fox] one of a tribe of Algonquian Indians who formerly lived in Wisconsin around Lake Winnebago and the Fox River. They now live on a reservation in Iowa. *adj-:* a Fox *village.*

fractional distillation *n-* process of separation of liquids, in which the temperature of a mixture of liquids is slowly raised so that each liquid vaporizes as its boiling point is reached.

fractional numeral *n-* numeral composed of two numerals with a horizontal bar between them, such as ⅔.

frac·tious (frăk′ shəs) *adj-* 1 unruly; rebellious. 2 irritable; cross; fretful. —*adv-* **frac′ tious·ly.** *n-* **frac′ tious·ness.**

frac·ture (frăk′ chər) *n-* 1 process of breaking or cracking. 2 a break or crack, especially in a bone.

frag·ile (frăj′ əl) *adj-* frail; easily broken: *a fragile vase.* —*adv-* **frag′ ile·ly.** *n-* **fra·gil′ i·ty** (frə jĭl′ ə tē).

¹**frag·ment** (frăg′ mənt) *n-* 1 part broken off or separated from a whole; portion; piece: *the fragments of the broken jar.* 2 incomplete or unfinished part: *sentence* fragment.

²**frag·ment** (frăg mĕnt′) *vt-* to break into pieces: *to* fragment *rocks.* *vi-:* Glass fragments *easily.*

frag·men·tar·y (frăg′ mən tĕr′ ē) *adj-* broken and incomplete; disconnected: *a fragmentary report.*

frag·men·ta·tion (frăg′ mən tā′ shən) *n-* act or process of breaking, shattering, especially of rocks.

fra·grance (frā′ grəns) *n-* pleasant odor; sweet smell.

fra·grant (frā′ grənt) *adj-* pleasing in odor; sweet-smelling. —*adv-* **fra′ grant·ly.**

frail (frāl) *adj-* [frail·er, frail·est] 1 physically weak: *a* frail *child.* 2 delicate; frail *[...];* easily broken; unsubstantial. —*adv-* **frail′ ly.** *n-* **frail′ ness.**

freak (frēk) *n-* 1 abnormal animal or plant (offensive when applied to persons). 2 strange, sudden whim. *adj-* abnormal and unusual; bizarre: *a freak accident.*

freak·ish (frēk′ ĭsh) *adj-* abnormal or unnatural; odd: *a freakish event.* —*adv-* **freak′ ish·ly.** *n-* **freak′ ish·ness.**

freck·le (frĕk′ əl) *n-* small tan or brown spot on the skin. *vt-* [**freck·led, freck·ling**] to mark with such spots. *vi-* to become marked with such spots.

freck·led (frĕk′ əld) *adj-* covered with freckles: *a freckled face.* Also **freck′ ly.**

free (frē) *adj-* [**fre·er, fre·est**] 1 not controlled or dominated by others; having or showing liberty; independent: *a free people; a free country; a free choice.*

free·dom (frē′ dəm) *n-* 1 the state of being free; liberty: *to fight for freedom.* 2 free or complete use: *He was given the freedom of the city.* 3 familiarity; outspokenness: *to ask personal questions with too much freedom.*

French horn *n-* brass wind instrument with a long, coiled tube and flaring end. It has a mellow tone.

French leave *Slang n-* hasty, unceremonious departure, often in secret.

French horn

French·man (frĕnch′ mən) *n-* [*pl.* **French·men**] man who is a native or inhabitant of France. —*n- fem.* **French′ wom′ an.**

French Revolution *n-* revolution that began in France in 1789 and led to the overthrow of the French monarch and the proclamation of a republic in 1792.

French toast *n-* slices of bread dipped in egg and milk and fried quickly.

Fri·day (frī′ dā, -dē) *n-* the sixth day of the week.

fried (frīd) *p.t. & p.p.* of **fry.**

fried·cake (frīd′ kāk′) *n-* small cake, such as a doughnut or cruller, that is fried in deep fat.

friend (frĕnd) *n-* 1 person one knows and likes. 2 ally. 3 person who gives support to someone or something. **make friends with** to become friendly with.

Friend (frĕnd) *n-* member of the Society of Friends; Quaker.

friend·less (frĕnd′ ləs) *adj-* without any friends. —*n-* **friend′ less·ness.**

friend·ly (frĕnd′ lē) *adj-* [**friend·li·er, friend·li·est**] 1 like a friend; kind; amiable: *a friendly person; a friendly gesture.* 2 not hostile; amicable; peaceable: *a friendly country on the border.* 3 favorable: *a friendly wind.* —*n-* **friend′ li·ness.**

friend·ship (frĕnd′ shĭp) *n-* relationship between persons who like and respect each other; warm affection.

fright·ful (frīt′ fəl) *adj-* 1 horrible; causing fear or terror: *a frightful disaster.* 2 unpleasant; disagreeable; ugly: *a frightful noise.* —*adv-* **fright′ ful·ly.** *n-* **fright′ ful·ness.**

frig·id (frĭj′ ĭd) 1 freezing; very cold: *a frigid climate.* 2 very unfriendly; hostile; chilly: *a frigid silence.* —*n-* **fri·gid′ i·ty** or **frig′ id·ness.** *adv-* **frig′ id·ly.**

Frigid Zone *n-* former term for the north and south polar regions.

fri·jol (frē hōl′) *Spanish n-* [*pl.* **fri·jo·les** (frē hō′ lās)] bean used widely as food by Mexicans and the Spanish-speaking people of southwestern United States.

frill (frĭl) *n-* 1 narrow, gathered or pleated strip of decorative trimming; ruffle: *a frill on a dress.* 2 frills *Informal* useless or excessive ornaments, activities, etc. —*adj-* **frill′ y** [**frill·i·er, frill·i·est**].

frizz·y (frĭz′ ē) *adj-* [**frizz·i·er, frizz·i·est**] forming or having tight curls; kinky. —*adv-* **frizz′ i·ly.** *n-* **frizz′ i·ness.**

fro (frō) **to and fro** back and forth.

frock (frŏk) *n-* 1 woman's or child's dress. 2 long robe or outer garment, especially one worn by a monk or clergyman.

from (frŭm, frŏm) *prep-* 1 starting at; starting at: *to work from noon until three o'clock.* 2 at a distance measured in relation to: *a mark three inches from the end of the board.*

front (frŭnt) *n-* 1 first or foremost part of any thing or place: *The front of the bus was empty.*

front page *n-* the first page of a newspaper, usually reserved for the most important or sensational news. *as modifier* (**front-page**): *It was front-page news.*

frosh (frŏsh) *Slang n-* freshman.

frost (frŏst, frôst) *n-* 1 small, featherlike ice crystals formed on the ground and exposed objects when dew or water vapor freezes. 2 freezing weather; freezing temperature: *The first frost came in early November.*

frost·bite (frŏst′ bīt′ , frôst′ -) *n-* frozen or partially frozen condition of some part of the body.

frost·bit·ten (frŏst′ bit′ ən, frôst′ -) *adj-* suffering from or affected by frostbite.

frost·ed (frŏst′ əd, frôst′ -) *adj-* 1 having a dull, whitish surface: *a frosted glass.* 2 covered with frosting. 3 frozen.

frost·ing (frŏs′ tĭng, frôs′ -) *n-* 1 mixture of sugar, egg whites, and liquid used for covering cakes or pastry. 2 dull finish on glass or metal that looks like frost.

frost·y (frŏs′ tē, frôs′ -) *adj-* [**frost·i·er, frost·i·est**] 1 cold with frost: *a frosty morning.* 2 covered with frost: *the frosty grass.* 3 cold and unfriendly: *a frosty smile; a frosty stare.* —*adv-* **frost′ i·ly.** *n-* **frost′ i·ness.**

froth (frŏth, frôth) *n-* 1 mass of small bubbles, such as that formed on top of some liquids after they have been shaken or poured: *the foaming froth on a glass of root beer.* 2 shallow, worthless ideas, talk, etc. *vi-* to foam: *Mad dogs often froth at the mouth.*

froth·y (frŏ′ thē, -thē) *adj-* [**froth·i·er, froth·i·est**] 1 of, covered with, or resembling froth: *a frothy layer of soapsuds.* 2 without substance; frivolous; trivial. —*adv-* **froth′ i·ly.** *n-* **froth′ i·ness.**

frown (froun) *n-* a drawing together of the brows when one is displeased or in thought; stern look. *vi-* to have such an expression on one's face. —*adv-* **frown′ ing·ly.** **frown on** to disapprove of: *to frown on gambling.*

frow·zy (frou′ zē) *adj-* [**frow·zi·er, frow·zi·est**] having a sloppy appearance; slovenly; untidy. —*n-* **frow′ zi·ness.**

froze (frōz) *p.t.* of **freeze.**

fro·zen (frō′ zən) *p.p.* of **freeze.**

fruc·tose (frŭk′ tōs′ , frŏŏk′ -) *n-* very sweet, yellowish-white sugar, occurring in many fruits and in honey; fruit sugar; levulose.

fru·gal (frŏŏ′ gəl) *adj-* 1 not wasteful; thrifty; economical: *a frugal housewife.* 2 not plentiful and not expensive: *a frugal supper.* —*n-* **fru·gal′ i·ty** (frŏŏ găl′ ə tē) also **fru′ gal·ness.** *adv-* **fru′ gal·ly.**

fruit (frŏŏt) *n-* 1 the fleshy part of a plant that contains the seeds and is often good to eat. 2 the seed or seed-bearing part of a plant. Acorns, grains, and strawberries are fruits. 3 product or result: *the fruit of hard work.*

fruit cake *n-* rich cake with raisins, nuts, citron, etc.

fruit fly *n-* small, two-wing fly that lays its eggs on ripe fruit. It has been used in many studies of inheritance.

fruit·ful (frŏŏt′ fəl) *adj-* 1 producing fruit: *a fruitful tree.* 2 yielding results; productive: *a fruitful discussion.* —*adv-* **fruit′ ful·ly.** *n-* **fruit′ ful·ness.**

fru·i·tion (frŏŏ ĭsh′ ən) *n-* 1 realization or attainment; fulfillment: *the fruition of my most cherished hopes.* 2 the bearing of fruit.

fruit·less (frŏŏt′ ləs) *adj-* 1 without result; unsuccessful: *We made a fruitless search for the lost money.* 2 bearing no fruit. —*adv-* **fruit′ less·ly.** *n-* **fruit′ less·ness.**

fruit sugar *n-* fructose.

fruit·y (frŏŏ′ tē) *adj-* [**fruit·i·er, fruit·i·est**] having the taste or smell of fruit.

frump (frŭmp) *n-* dowdy, slovenly woman. —*adj-* **frump′ ish** or **frump′ y** [**frump·i·er, frump·i·est**].

frus·trate (frŭs′ trāt′) *vt-* [**frus·trat·ed, frus·trat·ing**] to foil; baffle; defeat. —*n-* **frus·tra′ tion.**

¹**full** (fŏŏl) *adj-* [**full·er, full·est**] 1 filled; able to hold no more: *a full pail.* 2 complete; whole; entire; maximum: *a full hour; full moon; full speed ahead.*

full·er (fŏŏl′ ər) *n-* one who thickens cloth by moistening, heating, and pressing.

fuller's earth *n-* soft clay used for filtering fats and oils and for cleaning woolen cloth before fulling.

full-fledged (fŏŏl′ flĕjd′) *adj-* 1 with all its feathers grown; mature: *a full-fledged bird.* 2 fully developed or qualified; having full status: *a full-fledged doctor.*

fun (fŭn) *n-* amusement; sport; pleasure.

in fun in jest. **make fun of** or **poke fun at** to ridicule.

func·tion (fŭngk′ shən) *n-* **1** proper or natural work; purpose: *The* function *of the heart is to pump blood.*

fun·da·men·tal (fŭn′ də měn′ təl) *n-* **1** an essential or basic part: *Learning to recognize letters is a* fundamental *of reading.*

fu·ner·al (fyōō′ nər əl) *n-* the final disposing of the body of a dead person; also, the rites and services connected with this. *as modifier: a* funeral *bouquet.*

funeral home *n-* an undertaker's establishment, where dead bodies are prepared for burial and where funeral services may be held; mortuary. Also **funeral parlor.**

fu·ner·ar·y (fyōō′ nə rĕr′ ē) *adj-* having to do with or used for a funeral or funerals: *a* funerary *custom.*

fu·ne·re·al (fyōō nêr′ ē əl) *adj-* **1** suitable for a burial. **2** mournful; gloomy. —*adv-* **fu·ne′ re·al·ly.**

fun·gi (fŭn′ jī, -gī) *pl.* of **fungus.**

fun·gi·cide (fŭn′ jə sīd′, fŭng′ gə-) *n-* anything that kills fungus growths. —*adj-* **fun′ gi·cid′ al.**

fun·gous (fŭng′ gəs) *adj-* **1** of, relating to, or caused by a fungus. **2** growing and spreading rapidly, as some funguses do. *Hom-* fungus.

fun·gus (fŭng′ gəs) *n-* [*pl.* **fun·gi** (fŭn′ jī, -gī) or **fun·gus·es**] one of a group of plants, without leaves or green color, which feed upon plants or animal matter. Bacteria, molds, mushrooms, toadstools, and mildews are fungi. *as modifier: a* fungus *disease. Hom-* fungous.

Fungi

fu·nic·u·lar (fyōō nĭk′ yə lər) *n-* (also **funicular railway**) railway in which the cars are pulled up and let down a slope by ropes or cables, especially one in which a car going up counterweights one going down.

fur (fŭr) *n-* **1** thick, soft hair that covers certain animals. **2** skin of an animal with the hair on it; pelt. **3** garment made of such skins: *We put our* furs *in storage for the summer.* **4** any light, furry covering, such as a coating on the tongue. *adj-: a* fur *hat. vt-* [**furred, fur·ring**]

fur·be·low (fŭr′ bə lō) *n-* **1** ruffle, flounce, or other trim on women's clothing. **2** furbelows showy ornamentation, such as spangles on a dancer's costume.

fur·bish (fŭr′ bĭsh) *vt-* to make bright by rubbing or polishing; renew. —*n-* **fur′ bish·er.** *n-* **fur′ bish·ment.**

Fu·ries (fyoor′ ēz) *n-* in Greek and Roman mythology, the three goddesses who avenge unpunished crimes.

fu·ri·ous (fyoor′ ē əs) *adj-* **1** very angry: *He was* furious *at the insult.* **2** violent: *a* furious *storm.* —*adv-* **fu′ ri·ous·ly.** *n-* **fu′ ri·ous·ness.**

furl (fŭrl) *vt-* to roll up and fasten to a spar, pole, etc. ►Should not be confused with **REEF.**

fur·long (fŭr′ lông) *n-* one eighth of a mile; 220 yards.

fur·lough (fŭr′ lō) *n-* leave of absence, especially for an enlisted man in military service. *vt-* to give leave of absence to.

fur·nace (fŭr′ nəs) *n-* an enclosed structure in which fuel is burned to produce heat for heating a building, separating metal from ore, baking pottery, etc.

fur·nish (fŭr′ nĭsh) *vt-* **1** to supply; provide: *Jane will* furnish *cookies for the party.* **2** to equip with furniture: *to* furnish *a house.* —*n-* **fur′ nish·er.**

fur·nish·ings (fŭr′ nĭsh ĭngz) *n- pl.* **1** the necessary furniture and fittings of a house. **2** articles of clothing and accessories of dress.

fur·ni·ture (fŭr′ nə chər) *n-* movable articles such as tables, desks, chairs, beds, etc.

fu·ror (fyoor′ ər, -ôr) *n-* **1** great outburst of excitement or enthusiasm spreading among many people; stir: *The news caused a* furor. **2** rage; fury.

fur·ther (fŭr′ thər) *compar.* of **far.** *adj-* **1** additional; more: *to need* further *help; to say one thing* further.

fuse (fyōōz) *vt-* [**fused, fus·ing**] **1** to melt, especially by heating. **2** to blend or combine by melting: *to* fuse *copper and tin. vi-* **1** to melt. **2** to blend and intermix as if melted together: *My ideas* fuse *with his. n-* piece of metal which fills a gap in an electric circuit.

fu·see (fyōō′ zē′) *n-* **1** kind of friction match that will burn in the wind.

fu·se·lage (fyōō′ sə läzh′, -lǐj′) *n-* the body of an airplane, to which the wings, rudder, etc., are attached.

fusel oil (fyōō′ zəl) *n-* poisonous, oily, colorless mixture of various alcohols that is used as a solvent in chemical processes. It is a by-product of fermentation.

fu·si·ble (fyōō′ zə bəl) *adj-* of a nature that allows being melted without change in chemical composition

fu·sil (fyōō′ zəl) *n-* kind of flintlock musket.

fu·sil·ier or **fu·sil·eer** (fyōō′ zə lêr′) *n-* **1** formerly, a soldier armed with a fusil. **2** member of any of several British regiments.

fu·sil·lade (fyōō′ zə lād′) *n-* **1** the firing of many guns at once or in quick succession. **2** a number of questions or comments made in rapid order. *vt-* [**fu·sil·lad·ed, fu·sil·lad·ing**]: *to* fusillade *enemy troops.*

fu·sion (fyōō′ zhən) *n-* **1** a melting as a result of heat: *the* fusion *of iron in a furnace.* **2** a mixing or blending by melting: *Bronze is made by the* fusion *of copper and tin.* **3** a blending or union of separate things into one.

fusion bomb *n-* bomb in which the nuclei of a light element fuse to form a heavier element, resulting in the release of huge amounts of energy.

fu·sion·ist (fyōō′ zhən ĭst) *n-* in politics, person who supports the merging of different parties or factions.

fuss (fŭs) *n-* **1** needless activity; unnecessary stir, especially in small matters: *to make a* fuss *about entertaining.* **2** gushing praise or attention: *a* fuss *over an important guest.* **3** complaint: *a* fuss *over the weather. vi-* to make an unnecessary stir: *to* fuss *over dinner.* —*n-* **fuss′ er.**

fuss·y (fŭs′ ē) *adj-* [**fuss·i·er, fuss·i·est**] **1** painstaking in a nervous way; fastidious; finicky: *a* fussy *housekeeper.* **2** requiring delicate and patient work; exacting: *Watch repairing is a* fussy *job.* **3** petulant; irritable: *a* fussy *baby.* —*adv-* **fuss′ i·ly.** *n-* **fuss′ i·ness.**

fus·tian (fŭs′ chən) *n-* **1** kind of coarse twilled cotton cloth, such as corduroy or velveteen. **2** napped cloth of linen and cotton or wool. **3** high-sounding speech; empty wordiness. *adj-* **1** made of such cloth. **2** pretentious; pompous.

fust·y (fŭs′ tē) *adj-* [**fust·i·er, fust·i·est**] **1** moldy; musty; stuffy. **2** antiquated. —*adv-* **fust′ i·ly.** *n-* **fust′ i·ness.**

fu·tile (fyōō′ təl, -tĭl′) *adj-* useless and hopeless; not getting anywhere: *He made a* futile *attempt to save the patient.* —*adv-* **fu′ tile·ly.** *n-* **fu·til′ i·ty** (fyōō tĭl′ ə tē).

fu·ture (fyōō′ chər) *n-* time, events, etc., that are yet to come: *The* future *looks bright. adj-* yet to happen; coming: *to predict* future *events.* —*adj-* **fu′ ture·less.**

future perfect tense *Grammar n-* verb tense, formed with the auxiliary verb "shall" or "will," and "have," indicating action to take place before a specified future time. Example: *When you come tomorrow, I shall have finished this task.* Also **future perfect.**

future tense *Grammar n-* verb tense, formed with the auxiliary verb "shall" or "will," indicating action in time to come. Example: *I shall see you soon.*

fu·tur·ism (fyōō′ chə rĭz′ əm) *n-* movement in art, literature, and music, beginning about 1910, that stressed the forceful qualities of the present age. —*n-* **fu′ tur·ist.**

fu·tur·is·tic (fyōō′ chə rĭs′ tĭk) *adj-* **1** of or relating to the future or to futurism. **2** very much advanced in design or idea; suited to the future; ahead of its time: *a* futuristic *building.* —*adv-* **fu′ tur·is′ ti·cal·ly.**

fu·tu·ri·ty (fyōō tōōr′ ə tē, fyōō tyōōr′-) *n-* [*pl.* **fu·tu·ri·ties**] **1** the future. **2** condition of being future.

fuze (fyōōz) [1]**fuse.**

fuzz (fŭz) *n-* fine, light particles of hair, down, etc.: *the* fuzz *on a peach.*

fuzz·y (fŭz′ ē) *adj-* [**fuzz·i·er, fuzz·i·est**] **1** covered with or resembling fuzz or down: *a* fuzzy *peach.* **2** vague; blurred; not clear: *the* fuzzy *outline of hills through the fog.* —*adv-* **fuzz′ i·ly.** *n-* **fuzz′ i·ness.**

-fy *suffix* (used to form verbs from adjectives) to cause to be; also, to become: to *simplify; liquefy.* **2** (used to form verbs from nouns) to make similar to or typical of: *to* citify. [from Old French *-fier*, from Latin *-ficāre*, from **facere**, "to make, do."]

G

G, g (jē) *n-* [*pl.* **G's, g's**] **1** the seventh letter of the English alphabet. **2** *Music* the fifth note of the C-major scale. **3** *Physics* (1) g symbol for the acceleration caused by gravity, about 32 feet per second per second. (2) g's expression, in multiples of the earth's gravitational force, for the inertial force a body is subjected to when accelerating or deaccelerating: *The astronauts experienced a force of 8 g's during liftoff.*

g. 1 gram or grams. **2** goalie. **3** goalkeeper. **4** guard.

Ga symbol for gallium.

Ga. Georgia.

gab (găb) *Informal vi-* [gabbed, gab·bing] to talk idly and much; chatter. *n-* idle talk; prattle.

gab·ar·dine (găb'ər dēn') *n-* twilled fabric with a hard surface and a sheen, made of wool, cotton, or rayon, and used for raincoats, suits, etc. Also **gab'er·dine'**.

gab·ble (găb'bəl) *vi-* [gab·bled, gab·bling] **1** to talk disconnectedly, or without meaning; jabber. **2** to make a clatter of meaningless sounds. *n-* rapid, meaningless sounds: *the gabble of geese.* —*n-* **gab'bler**.

gab·by (găb'ē) *Informal adj-* [gab·bi·er, gab·bi·est] talkative: *a gabby neighbor.* —*n-* **gab'bi·ness**.

ga·ble (gā'bəl) *n-* **1** the section of an outside wall in the shape of a vertical triangle between the slopes of a ridged roof. **2** any similar construction, as over a window. —*adj-* **ga'bled**: *a gabled window.*

Gable

¹gad (găd) *n-* **1** sharp rod or switch; goad for driving cattle. **2** pointed iron or steel tool for loosening ore. [from Old Norse *gaddr*, "a goad."]

²gad (găd) *vi-* [gad·ded, gad·ding] to go from place to place; ramble: *to gad about town.* [from Middle English *gadden*, of uncertain origin.] —*n-* **gad'der**.

gad·a·bout (găd'ə bout') *Informal n-* person who wanders or rushes about idly.

gad·fly (găd'flī') *n-* [*pl.* **gad·flies**] **1** kind of fly that stings horses and cattle. **2** person who annoys or goads.

gadg·et (găj'ət) *Informal n-* **1** small device or tool having a special use: *a gadget for coring apples.* **2** an object whose name and use one does not know.

gad·o·lin·i·um (găd'ə lĭn'ē əm) *n-* metallic rare-earth element. Symbol Gd, At. No. 64, At. Wt. 157.25.

Gael (gāl) *n-* **1** a Celt of Ireland, Scotland, or the Isle of Man, especially one who speaks Gaelic. **2** Scottish Highlander. *Hom-* gale.

gaf·fer (găf'ər) *n-* respectable and good old man, especially a countryman (now used humorously).

gag (găg) *n-* **1** something forcibly put into or on a person's mouth to keep him from talking or crying out; also, something put into the mouth to hold it open. **2** strategy or rule to prevent or limit freedom of discussion. **3** *Slang* a remark or act designed to get a laugh. *vt-* [gagged, gag·ging] **1** to stop up the mouth. **2** to silence by force or law. **3** to cause to retch: *The medicine gagged him.* *vi-* **1** to choke; strain as in vomiting: *to gag on a bone.* **2** *Slang* to tell a joke.

¹gage (gāj) *Archaic n-* **1** a promise; pledge. **2** challenge to combat or pledge to fight indicated by throwing down or picking up a glove; also, the object thrown down. *vt-* [gaged, gag·ing] **1** to pledge. **2** to risk or stake in combat. **3** to wager. [from Old French *gage*, of Germanic origin. It is very closely related to **wage**.]

²gage (gāj) gauge. [from Old French *gauger* meaning "to measure."]

³gage (gāj) *n-* greengage. [from Sir William **Gage**, an Englishman who first brought this fruit to his country.]

gai·e·ty (gā'ə tē) *n-* [*pl.* **gai·e·ties**] **1** merriment; cheerfulness; gay spirits: *a time of gaiety.* **2** gay, bright appearance: *the gaiety of the room.* Also **gayety**.

gai·ly (gā'lē) *adv-* **1** merrily; happily. **2** brightly; strikingly: *the gaily painted walls.*

gain·er (gā'nər) *n-* **1** person or thing that gains. **2** dive in which the person jumps forward, does a complete backward somersault, and enters the water feet first.

gain·ful (gān'fəl) *adj-* profitable; paid: *to find some gainful occupation.* —*adv-* gain'ful·ly. *n-* gain'ful·ness.

gain·say (gān'sā') *vt-* [gain·said, gain·say·ing] to deny or dispute: *I can't gainsay that.* —*n-* gain'say·er.

gainst or **'gainst** (gĕnst, gănst) against.

gait (gāt) *n-* **1** way a person or animal walks or runs. **2** any of the several foot movements of a horse, such as a walk, trot, or canter. *vt-* to train to step at a regular pace: *to gait a horse.* *Hom-* gate.

gait·ed (gā'təd) *adj-* **1** stepping in a particular way: *fast-gaited.* **2** trained to a gait or gaits: *a gaited horse.*

gai·ter (gā'tər) *n-* **1** covering of cloth or leather for the lower leg or ankle, fitting over the top of the shoe. **2** shoe with an elastic strip on each side. **3** a kind of overshoe with a cloth top.

Gaiter

gal (găl) *Slang n-* girl or young woman.

gal. gallon or gallons.

ga·la (gā'lə, găl'ə) *n-* festival; gay celebration. *adj-* festive: *Their party was a gala affair.*

ga·lac·tic (gə lăk'tĭk) *adj-* of or relating to a galaxy or galaxies.

Gal·a·had (găl'ə hăd') *n-* in Arthurian legend, the noblest and purest knight of the Round Table, who was successful in his quest of the Holy Grail.

Gal·a·te·a (găl'ə tē'ə) *n-* in Greek mythology, an ivory statue of a maiden brought to life by Aphrodite after the sculptor, Pygmalion, had fallen in love with it.

Ga·la·tians (gə lā'shənz) *n-* **1** inhabitants of ancient Galatia. **2** (takes singular verb) book of the New Testament, written by St. Paul and known as the Epistle to the Galatians.

gal·ax·y (găl'ək sē) *n-* [*pl.* **gal·ax·ies**] **1** vast separate system of stars, dust and gas clouds, distinct clusters of stars, etc. Each galaxy contains billions of stars, and millions of galaxies make up the universe. **2** any brilliant group: *a galaxy of great pianists.* **3** Galaxy the Milky Way Galaxy.

gale (gāl) *n-* **1** strong wind, especially one with a velocity between about 30 and 60 miles per hour. **2** outburst: *a gale of laughter.* *Hom-* Gael.

ga·le·na (gə lē'nə) *n-* a blueish-gray mineral lead sulfide, which is the chief ore of lead.

Gal·i·le·an (găl'ə lē'ən) *adj-* of or relating to Galilee. *n-* **1** native of Galilee. **2** contemptuous term for Christians in ancient times. **3** the Galilean Jesus Christ.

¹gall (gôl) *n-* **1** bitter fluid made by the liver and stored in the gall bladder; bile. **2** anything bitter or distasteful. **3** spite; rancor. **4** *Slang* insolence; impudence. [from Old English *galla*.] *Hom-* Gaul.

gall·fly (gôl'flī') *n-* [*pl.* **gall·flies**] any of various insects that deposit their eggs on plants and cause galls.

Gal·lic (găl'ĭk) *adj-* of or pertaining to ancient Gaul or modern France.

Gal·li·cism or **gal·li·cism** (găl'ə sĭz'əm) *n-* **1** a French word, phrase, or manner of speech used in other languages. **2** a French trait or habit.

gall·ing (gôl'ĭng) *adj-* chafing; exasperating; vexing.

gal·li·um (găl'ē əm) *n-* rare silvery-gray metal element. Symbol Ga, At. No. 31, At. Wt. 69.72.

gal·li·vant (găl'ə vănt') *Informal vi-* to gad about joyfully.

gall·nut (gôl'nŭt') *n-* ³gall.

gal·lon (găl'ən) *n-* unit of liquid measurement. The standard gallon in the United States equals four quarts or 231 cubic inches; the imperial gallon in the United Kingdom and the Commonwealth equals 277.420 cubic inches or five U.S. quarts.

ga·lore (gə lôr′) *adj-* very many; in abundance (used after the noun it modifies): *pretty girls galore.*

ga·losh (gə lŏsh′) *n-* [*pl.* ga·losh·es] high protective overshoe, usually made of rubber or plastic. —*adj-* **ga·loshed′**: *bundled up and galoshed for the snow.*

ga·lumph (gə lŭmf′, -lŭmp′) *vi-* 1 to move along with a heavy, clumsy tread; clump: *The bashful boys galumphed across the stage.* 2 originally, to ride along in triumph.

gal·van·ic (găl văn′ĭk) *adj-* 1 of or relating to electricity produced by chemical action; also, producing such electricity: *a galvanic cell.* 2 stimulating; electrifying: *a galvanic personality.* —*adv-* **gal·van′i·cal·ly.**

gal·va·nize (găl′ və nīz′) *vt-* [gal·va·nized, gal·va·niz·ing] 1 to coat (iron or steel) with zinc to prevent rusting. 2 to excite; stir up; arouse, as if by an electric shock: *He galvanized us into action.* —*n-* **gal′va·ni·za′tion.**

gal·va·nom·e·ter (găl′ və nŏm′ ə tər) *n-* instrument used to detect the presence of an electric current, measure its intensity, and determine its direction.

gam·bit (găm′ bĭt) *n-* 1 chess move, especially an opening move, in which a player sacrifices a piece in order to gain a favorable position. 2 any opening action.

gam·ble (găm′ bəl) *vi-* [gam·bled, gam·bling] 1 to play for money or a prize: *to gamble at cards.* 2 to take a risk on something uncertain, especially for gain: *They gambled on good weather for the early flight.* *vt-* to risk or squander for uncertain gain: *to gamble one's reputation.* *n-* any risk or act that does not have a sure result. *Hom-* gambol. —*n-* **gam′bler.**

gamble away to lose by the risking of stakes: *to gamble away a fortune.*

gam·bling (găm′ blĭng) *n-* betting or risking something for uncertain gain; playing at cards, roulette, etc.; gaming; wagering. *as modifier:* *a gambling debt.*

gam·bol (găm′ bəl) *n-* a dancing or skipping about for joy or sport; frolic. *vi-* [gam·boled, gam·bol·ing]: *The lambs gamboled in the meadow.* *Hom-* gamble.

gam·brel roof (găm′ brəl) *n-* ridged, two-sided roof with each side having a steeply sloped lower section and a flatter upper section.

¹game (gām) *n-* 1 form of play, especially a contest, played according to rules: *Football is a popular game.* 2 single contest played according to rules: *a game of checkers.* 3 unit or division of a match, as in tennis. 4 materials or equipment needed for such play: *The store sells toys and games.* 5 amusement; joke; playful trick; also, jest. 6 *Informal* plan; scheme: *I can see through your game.* 7 wild animals, fish, or birds that are hunted for sport; also, the flesh used for food. 8 *Slang* business; profession. *adj-* 1 having to do with wildlife hunted for sport: *to enforce game laws.* 2 plucky; courageous: *a game fighter.* *vi-* [gamed, gam·ing] to play for a stake or prize. [from Old English *gamen* meaning "sport; joy."] —*adv-* **game′ ly.** *n-* **game′ ness.**

make game of to make fun of; ridicule. **play the game** to play according to the rules; be straightforward. **the game is up** the plan, intrigue, etc., has failed.

²game (găm) *Informal adj-* lame: *a game leg.* [perhaps from dialectal French *cambi*, "bent."]

game bird *n-* any bird commonly and legally hunted for sport and food, such as partridge or pheasant.

game·cock (gām′ kŏk′) *n-* rooster trained for cockfights.

game fish *n-* any fish usually caught for sport.

game·keep·er (gām′ kē′ pər) *n-* person in charge of animals or birds that are to be bred or protected as game, especially on a private estate.

game of chance *n-* any game whose outcome depends entirely or chiefly upon chance; gambling game.

game·some (gām′ səm) *adj-* merry; gay. —*adv-* **game′ some·ly.**

game·ster (gām′ stər) *n-* person who gambles often.

gam·ete (găm′ ēt′, gə mēt′) *n-* either of the two reproductive cells (egg and sperm) that can unite to form a new individual. Most gametes have half the number of chromosomes that all other body cells have; germ cell.

ga·me·to·phyte (gə mē′ tə fīt′) *n-* in the life cycle of plants, the phase or generation that produces the sex cells. See also *sporophyte.*

game warden *n-* official responsible for the enforcement of laws that restrict hunting and fishing.

gam·in (găm′ ən) *n-* 1 child of the streets; urchin. 2 elfin child. *Hom-* gammon. —*n- fem.* **gam·ine′** (gă mēn′).

gam·ing (gā′ mĭng) *n-* gambling.

gam·ma (găm′ ə) *n-* 1 third letter of the Greek alphabet, similar to G. 2 unit of mass and weight equal to one-millionth of a gram; a microgram. 3 *Physics* unit used to express the intensity of a magnetic field. One gamma equals 1 /100,000 gauss.

gamma globulin *n-* one of the globulins extracted from human blood plasma. It contains antibodies and is used in the treatment of measles and hepatitis.

gamma rays *n-* very penetrating electromagnetic radiation of shorter wavelength than X rays.

gam·mon (găm′ ən) *n-* cured ham or strip of bacon; the lower end of a flitch. *Hom-* gamin.

gam·ut (găm′ ət) *n-* 1 the whole series of recognized musical notes. 2 the entire range of anything: *to run the gamut of emotion from joy to despair.*

gam·y (gā′ mē) *adj-* [gam·i·er, gam·i·est] 1 plucky; ready; spirited. 2 having the flavor of game, especially of nearly spoiled game. —*adv-* **gam′ i·ly.** *n-* **gam′ i·ness.**

gan·der (găn′ dər) *n-* 1 male goose. 2 simpleton.

gang (găng) *n-* 1 group of persons, especially a working crew: *a gang of laborers.* 2 neighborhood group of boys and young men often organized along racial or ethnic lines and sometimes fighting other such groups; street gang. 3 criminal organization; mob. 4 large group or set of anything: *a whole gang of troubles.* 5 a set of tools or machines arranged for use together: *a gang of snowplows.* *vt-* to put together or operate as a group: *to gang machines; to gang switches.* *vi-* to form a group: *The boys ganged around the cheerleader.* *Hom-* gangue.

gang together to go around habitually in a group.

gang up on to attack (someone) as a group.

gan·gling (găng′ glĭng) *adj-* spindling and awkward: *a gangling youth.* Also **gang′ ly.**

gan·gli·on (găng′ glē ən) *n-* [*pl.* gan·gli·a (-glē ə) or gan·gli·ons] knot of nerve-cell bodies outside of the central nervous system.

gang·plank (găng′ plăngk′) *n-* movable bridge used at a pier for entering or leaving a ship.

gang plow *n-* plow designed to make several parallel rows of furrows at once.

gan·grene (găng′ grēn′) *n-* death or decay of tissue in a living animal body because the blood supply has been cut off. —*adj-* **gan′ gre·nous** (găng′ grə nəs).

gang·ster (găng′ stər) *n-* member of a criminal gang.

gangue (găng) *n-* in mining, the worthless rock found in a vein of ore. *Hom-* gang.

gang·way (găng′ wā′) *n-* 1 gangplank; also, the opening in the side of a ship used to admit passengers or freight. 2 passageway; aisle. *interj-* Stand aside and make room!

gar·goyle (gär′ goil′) *n-* a spout jutting from a building to carry off water. Gargoyles are often in the shape of grotesque human beings or animals.

gar·ish (gâr′ ĭsh, găr′-) *adj-* unpleasantly showy; too bright or glaring; gaudy: *The beautiful road was spoiled by a string of garish billboards.* —*adv-* **gar′ ish·ly.** *n-* **gar′ ish·ness.**

gar·land (gär′ lənd) *n-* wreath or strand of intertwined leaves, flowers, etc., worn or used as decoration. *vt-* to decorate with such an ornament.

Gargoyle

gar·lic (gär′ lĭk) *n-* 1 plant related to the onion, having a bulb with a strong taste and odor. 2 the bulb of this plant, used to flavor food.

gar·ment (gär′ mənt) *n-* any article of clothing. *as modifier:* *the garment industry.* *vt-* to clothe; dress.

gar·ner (gär′ nər) *vt-* to gather in; store away: *to garner grain; to garner sayings from a book.*

gar·net (gär′ nət) *n-* 1 crystalline mineral, usually deep red in color, used as a semiprecious gem and as an abrasive. 2 a deep red color. *adj-*: *a garnet ring;* garnet *taffeta.*

garnet paper n- paper coated with crushed garnet and used as an abrasive.

gar·nish (gär′ nĭsh) vt- to decorate, adorn, or embellish, especially a dish of food: to garnish a steak with parsley. n- decoration, especially on food. —n- gar′ nish·er.

gar·nish·ee (gär′ nə shē′) vt- [gar·nish·eed, gar·nish·ee·ing] 1 in law, to claim and hold (property, money, etc.) from a person who owes money, until the settlement of the debt. 2 in law, to issue a garnishment to.

gar·nish·ment (gär′ nĭsh mənt) n- 1 in law, legal warning that a person's property is to be given to a creditor because of debt. 2 subtraction of a definite sum from someone's salary to pay a creditor.

gar·ni·ture (gär′ nə chər) n- something used as decoration, especially on food.

gar·ret (găr′ ət) n- attic.

gar·ri·son (găr′ ə sən) n- 1 group of soldiers stationed in a fort or in a town for defense. 2 fort or town where soldiers are stationed for defense. vt- to station soldiers in (a fort or town) for defense: to garrison a town.

gar·rote or **ga·rotte** (gə rŏt′) vt- [gar·rot·ed or ga·rott·ed, gar·rot·ing or ga·rott·ing] to strangle (someone) with a metal strip, rope, wire, etc. n- 1 a strangling in this manner, formerly used as a method of execution. 2 implement used for this. —n- gar·rot′ er.

gar·ru·lous (găr′ ə ləs, also găr′ yə-) adj- very talkative; chattering. —adv- gar′ ru·lous·ly. n- gar′ ru·lous·ness or gar·ru′ li·ty (gə rōō′ lə tē).

gar·ter (gär′ tər) n- 1 band or strap, often elastic and having a fastener, used to hold up a sock or stocking. 2 **Garter** Order of the Garter.

garter snake n- any of a group of harmless American snakes that are striped along the back. Garter snakes bring forth live young.

gas (găs) n- [pl. gas·es or gas·ses] 1 any substance in the gaseous state under the general conditions of temperature and pressure existing on earth. 2 vapor. 3 any mixture of gases that will burn and be used for heating and cooking. 4 Informal any of various vapors used as anesthetics. 5 a gaseous substance or mist used as a weapon: tear gas; poison gas. 6 Informal gasoline. as modifier: a gas mask. vt- [gassed, gas·sing] to injure or poison with gas.

gas chamber n- room in which people or animals are killed by poison gas.

gas jet n- nozzle or other fixture with an opening through which gas may flow.

gas·ket (găs′ kət) n- 1 thin piece of rubber, metal, etc., used to make a joint or seal through which liquids or gases will not flow. 2 rope used to tie furled sails fast.

gas·light (găs′ līt′) n- 1 light made by burning gas. 2 lamp or fixture for producing such a light. —adj- gas′ lit: The shadows flickered in the gaslit room.

gas mantle n- perforated cone or sheath of a heat-resisting material that gives light by incandescence when it is put over a gas flame.

gas mask n- covering for the face connected to an air filter and used to protect against poisonous gases.

gas·o·line or **gas·o·lene** (găs′ ə lĕn′) n- colorless liquid mixture of hydrocarbons refined from petroleum. Gasoline turns to vapor easily, and the vapor burns violently. It is used chiefly as a fuel for engines.

gasp (găsp) vi- 1 to catch one's breath in surprise, distress, or the like. 2 to struggle for breath: The fish in the boat were gasping. vt- to utter in a breathless manner: to gasp an urgent message. n- a short, sudden breath: He gave a gasp when he saw the tiger.

the (or **one's**) **last gasp** the very end; dying breath.

gas station n- filling station.

gas·sy (găs′ ē) adj- [gas·si·er, gas·si·est] 1 filled with gas. 2 of or like gas. —n- gas′ si·ness.

gas·tric (găs′ trĭk) adj- of or relating to the stomach.

gastric juice n- the acid mixture of digestive juices secreted by the cells of the stomach lining.

gastric ulcer n- ulcer on the stomach lining, usually related to an excess secretion of hydrochloric acid, often caused by anxiety.

gas·tri·tis (găs′ trī′ təs) n- inflammation of the stomach.

gate crasher Informal n- person who enters a place without being invited or without paying.

gate·house (gāt′ hous′) n- house at an entrance or gateway of an estate, park, etc.

gate·post (gāt′ pōst′) n- either of the two posts between which a gate swings.

gate·way (gāt′ wā′) n- 1 opening fitted with a gate. 2 way of entering or achieving: The Panama Canal is a gateway to the Pacific. Reading is a gateway to knowledge.

gath·er (găth′ ər) vt- 1 to bring to oneself: He gathered a crowd around him. She gathered the child in her arms. 2 to pick and collect: to gather sea shells; to gather a harvest. 3 to gain slowly; pick up: to gather speed; to gather strength. 4 to draw together in small folds: to gather a skirt at the waist. 5 to conclude; understand (usually takes a clause as object): I gather that you have trouble with grammar. vi- to come together: A crowd gathered at the gate. n- in sewing, one of a series of small folds or puckers.

be gathered to one's fathers of a person, to die.

gather up to draw together; pick up.

gath·er·er (găth′ ər ər) n- person who gathers, especially a member of a tribe of people who gather plants, grains, etc., for their needs.

gath·er·ing (găth′ ər ĭng) n- meeting or social function at which people come together.

Gat·ling gun (găt′ lĭng) n- early machine gun with a revolving cluster of barrels, fired by turning a crank.

gauche (gōsh) adj- awkward or inept, especially in social behavior. [from French gauche, "left" with the meaning "left-hand" or "awkward."] —n- gauche′ ness.

gau·che·rie (gō′ chə rē) n- gauche manner or act.

gau·cho (gou′ chō) n- [pl. gau·chos] South American cowboy, usually of Spanish and Indian ancestry.

gaud (gôd) n- cheap or showy trinket or ornament.

gaud·y (gô′ dē) adj- [gaud·i·er, gaud·i·est] bright and gay in a flashy or showy way: a gaudy orange and purple necktie. —adv- gaud′ i·ly. n- gaud′ i·ness.

gauge (gāj) n- 1 a standard measurement: Wire is available in various gauges. 2 any of various instruments for measuring size, quantity, force, etc.: a wire gauge; a wind gauge. 3 any means or standard for making a comparison, judgment, etc. vt- [gauged, gaug·ing] to measure, estimate, or judge with or as if with a measuring device: to gauge the diameter of wire; to gauge a person's character. Also gage. —adj- gauge′ a·ble. n- gaug′ er.

Wire gauge

Gaul (gôl) n- 1 ancient name of the part of Europe west of the Alps and north of the Pyrenees. 2 native or inhabitant of this region. 3 a Frenchman. Hom- gall.

gaunt (gônt) adj- [gaunt·er, gaunt·est] 1 very thin; bony; emaciated: to be weak and gaunt after a long illness. 2 barren and desolate; grim. —adv- gaunt′ ly. n- gaunt′ ness.

MODERN

¹**gaunt·let** (gônt′ lət) n- 1 in the Middle Ages, a mailed glove to protect wrists and hands from wounds. 2 glove with a flaring cuff, especially a canvas or leather working glove with a deep, stiff cuff to protect the wrist. 3 the cuff itself. [from French gantelet, from gant, "glove," from an earlier Germanic word.]

MEDIEVAL

Gauntlets

take up the gauntlet to assume a challenge; espouse a cause, especially a controversial one. **throw down the gauntlet** to challenge someone.

²**gaunt·let** (gônt′ lət) n- double line of men who strike out at a person who is forced to run between them as a punishment. Also **gantlet.** [from earlier **gantlope**, from Swedish **gatlopp**, "a running down a lane."]

run the gauntlet 1 to undergo such punishment. 2 to be exposed to severe criticism, extreme danger, etc.

Gau·ta·ma (gô′ tə mə, gou′-) *n-* Buddha.

gauze (gôz) *n-* thin, transparent, loosely woven fabric, often used for bandages. —*adj-* **gauze′ like′.**

gauz·y (gô′ zē) *adj-* [gauz·i·er, gauz·i·est] like gauze; soft, delicate, and insubstantial. —*n-* **gauz′ i·ness.**

gave (gāv) *p.t.* of **give.**

gav·el (găv′ əl) *n-* small mallet used by presiding officers, judges, etc., to call a group to order.

gav·i·al (gā′ vē əl) *n-* large, fish-eating crocodilian of India. The gavial has long, slender jaws and webbed feet.   Gavel

ga·votte (gə vŏt′) *n-* **1** dance popular in the 17th and 18th centuries somewhat resembling the minuet. **2** music for this dance.

Ga·wain (gə wăn′, gä′ wən) *n-* in Arthurian legend, a knight of the Round Table, nephew of King Arthur.

gawk (gôk) *Informal vi-* to stare stupidly or in astonishment. *n-* clumsy, stupid person.

gawk·y (gô′ kē) *adj-* [gawk·i·er, gawk·i·est] clumsy; awkward. —*adv-* **gawk′ i·ly.** *n-* **gawk′ i·ness.**

gay (gā) *adj-* [gay·er, gay·est] **1** merry; lighthearted; lively: *a gay party; the gay music.* **2** bright and cheerful: *a gay color.* —*n-* **gay′ ness.**

gay·e·ty (gā′ ə tē) gaiety.

gay·ly (gā′ lē) gaily.

gaz. gazette.

gaze (gāz) *vi-* [gazed, gaz·ing] to look long and steadily: *Janet gazed at the scenery as the train sped on. n-* a long, steady look. —*n-* **gaz′ er.**

ga·ze·bo (gə zē′ bō) *n-* [*pl.* **ga·ze·bos** or **ga·ze·boes**] small, outdoor pavilion or summerhouse.

ga·zelle (gə zĕl′) *n-* any of several small, brown to white antelopes of Africa, Arabia, and Asia, having short curving horns and large dark eyes. The gazelle is known for its speed and grace.

ga·zette (gə zĕt′) *n-* newspaper or other periodical, especially an official journal.

gaz·et·teer (găz′ ə tēr′) *n-* a list of geographical terms with explanations, appearing as a separate work or as an appendix to another.

Gazelle 20—35 in high at shoulder

gear·ing (gēr′ ing) *n-* **1** all the gears of a machine. **2** act of equipping with gears.

gear·shift (gēr′ shĭft′) *n-* **1** mechanism, usually operated by a lever, designed to connect and disconnect gears. **2** the lever itself, especially in motor vehicles.

geck·o (gĕk′ ō) *n-* [*pl.* **geck·os, geck·oes**] small, harmless house lizard, useful in destroying insects. Geckos have toe pads and can run along walls and ceilings.   Gecko. about 6 in long

gee (jē) *interj-* **1** *Informal* c .clamation of surprise, pleasure, etc. **2** command given to a horse or ox to turn right (see also ³*haw*). *vi-* [geed, gee·ing] to turn to the right: *The horses geed. vt-: He geed the team of horses.*

geese (gēs) *pl.* of **goose.**

ge·fil·te fish (gə fĭl′ tə) *n-* mixture of chopped fish, crumbs, eggs, and seasoning, formed into balls or patties, and cooked in a fish stock.

Ge·hen·na (gə hĕn′ ə) *n-* **1** in the Bible, a valley outside Jerusalem. **2** in the New Testament, hell; hence, any place of torment.

Gei·ger counter (gī′ gər koun′ tər) *n-* instrument that consists of a Geiger-Müller tube and an electronic counting device that registers one count whenever an ionization takes place in the tube. It is used to detect and measure the intensity of ionizing radiation. Also **Geiger-Müller counter.**

Gei·ger-Mül·ler tube (gī′ gər myl′ ər) *n-* sealed, thin-walled, glass tube filled with gas and containing two electrodes between which a current flows when charged particles ionize the gas.

gei·sha (gā′ shə) *n-* [*pl.* **gei·sha** or **gei·shas**] Japanese woman educated to provide entertainment and companionship for men.

gel (jĕl) *n-* mixture formed when particles of a certain size are evenly dispersed in a liquid. Gels flow like liquids, or become firm and jellylike, depending on the temperature. Raw egg white and the protoplasm of all living cells are gels. *vi-* [gelled, gel·ling] to become such a mixture. *Hom-* jell.

gel·a·tin (jĕl′ ə tən) *n-* clear, jellylike substance made from the bones, hoofs, and skin of animals or from some vegetables. It is sold in the form of a powder and used in making jellies, marshmallows, and ice cream, as well as in glue, medicine, etc. Also **gel′ a·tine.**

ge·lat·i·nous (jə lăt′ ə nəs) *adj-* of, like, or containing gelatin; jellylike.

geld (gĕld) *vt-* to castrate (a horse or other animal.)

geld·ing (gĕl′ dĭng) *n-* castrated animal, especially a horse.

gel·id (jĕl′ ĭd) *adj-* frigid; frozen.

gem (jĕm) *n-* **1** precious stone, especially one cut or set as an ornament. **2** anything of great value or beauty: *This Toscanini album is the gem of my entire record collection.* —*adj-* **gem′ like′.**

FACET   BEZEL

Gem

gen·der (jĕn′ dər) *n-* **1** sex, male or female. **2** *Grammar* (1) the distinction between words or forms of a word that corresponds roughly to that between male, female, and sexless things. (2) any of the three types of this distinction: masculine, feminine, and neuter. In English, gender is shown chiefly by the personal pronouns. "He," "his," and "him" are masculine. "She," "her," and "hers" are feminine. "It" and "its" are neuter. Some English nouns have feminine suffixes such as "-ess."

gene (jēn) *n-* the part of a chromosome that is responsible for the transmission of a particular trait from parent to child. The color of a child's eyes is determined by some of the genes of his parents. *Hom-* jean.

ge·ne·al·o·gist (jē′ nē ŏl′ ə jĭst, jĕn′ ē-) *n-* maker of genealogies; specialist in genealogy.

ge·ne·al·o·gy (jē′ nē ŏl′ ə jē, jĕn′ ē-) *n-* [*pl.* **gen·e·al·o·gies**] **1** method or system of investigating the descent of a person or family from an ancestor. **2** an account of such a descent; pedigree. —*adj-* **gen′ e·a·log′ i·cal** (-ə lŏj′ ĭ kəl). *adv-* **gen′ e·a·log′ i·cal·ly.**

gen·e·ra (jĕn′ ə rə) *pl.* of **genus.**

gen·er·al (jĕn′ rəl, jĕn′ ər əl) *adj-* **1** having to do with all or nearly all: *a general panic.* **2** widespread: *Afternoon tea is a general custom in England.* **3** not limited to one thing, class, or region: *the general public; a physician with a general practice.* **4** not definite; not in detail: *I have a general idea how rockets work.* **5** chief or head: *postmaster general. n-* **1** in the Army and Air Force, a commissioned officer who ranks next below a General of the Army or a General of the Air Force and next above a lieutenant general. **2** in the Marine Corps, a commissioned officer of the highest grade, ranking above a lieutenant general. **3** form of address for a brigadier general, major general, lieutenant general, and General of the Army or Air Force.

in general for the most part; usually.

general assembly *n-* **1** representatives of a State, organization, etc., meeting together as a legislative group. **2** school assembly attended by the entire school. **3 General Assembly** deliberative body of the United Nations, made up of delegates of all member states.

General Court *n-* the legislature of the States of Massachusetts or New Hampshire.

general delivery *n-* **1** postal department which handles mail for persons who call for it instead of having it delivered to a street address. **2** mail so delivered.

gen·er·a·lis·si·mo (jĕn′ ər ə lĭs′ ə mō′) *n-* [*pl.* **gen·er·a·lis·si·mos**] in certain countries, the supreme commander of the armed forces.

gen·er·al·i·ty (jĕn′ ə răl′ ə tē) *n-* [*pl.* **gen·er·al·i·ties**] **1** general statement that may be too broad to be useful: *to talk in generalities.* **2** the large part of; the mass: *The generality of citizens in the United States eat well.*

gen·er·al·i·za·tion (jĕn′rə lə zā′shən) *n-* 1 a generalizing. 2 generalizing statement: *to make* generalizations.

gen·er·al·ize (jĕn′rə līz′) *vi-* [**gen·er·al·ized, gen·er·al·iz·ing**] 1 to treat a subject as a whole rather than in parts; be vague, superficial, or casual by emphasizing a general aspect: *The speaker generalized on the need for better housing but neglected to offer any program.* 2 to make a general rule from facts or specific instances.

gen·er·al·ly (jĕn′rə lē) *adv-* 1 most of the time; usually: *We generally have dinner at six o'clock.* 2 in most places or by most people; widely: *The new styles have been generally accepted.* 3 without being definite about particular things or persons: *to speak generally.*

General of the Air Force *n-* in the Air Force, the highest rank; also, a commissioned officer holding this rank. A General of the Air Force ranks above a general.

General of the Army *n-* in the Army, the highest rank; also, a commissioned officer holding this rank. A General of the Army ranks above a general.

general practitioner *n-* doctor who does not limit his practice to any special field of medicine.

gen·er·al·ship (jĕn′rəl shĭp′) *n-* 1 rank or office of a general. 2 leadership and skill; especially in war.

general staff *n-* 1 group of the highest-ranking officers, who direct the military affairs of a nation: *the German general staff.* 2 group of officers who assist and advise the commander of a division or higher military unit.

general store *n-* comparatively small retail store that carries a large variety of merchandise.

gen·er·ate (jĕn′ə rāt′) *vt-* [**gen·er·at·ed, gen·er·at·ing**] to produce; bring into existence: *Water power often is used to generate electricity. A friendly smile generates good will.* —*adj-* **gen′er·a·tive** (jĕn′ ər ə tĭv).

gen·er·a·tion (jĕn′ ə rā′shən) *n-* 1 all the people who are born at about the same time: *Our generation is produc·ng many scientists.* 2 one step in the line of family descent. Grandparents, their children, and grandchildren make up three generations. 3 period of time, about 30 years, between the birth of one generation and the next. 4 act or process of producing: *the generation of power.*

gen·er·a·tor (jĕn′ə rā′tər) *n-* 1 *Physics* machine that produces electricity from mechanical energy, usually by means of a rotating armature between the poles of a magnet; dynamo. 2 *Chemistry* apparatus used to produce a gas or vapor. 3 person or thing that generates.

ge·ner·ic (jə nĕr′ĭk) *adj-* 1 of or including an entire kind or class; general, not specific. 2 of or relating to a genus: *the generic name of a plant.* —*adv-* **ge·ner′i·cal·ly.**

gen·er·os·i·ty (jĕn′ ə rŏs′ə tē) *n-* [*pl.* **gen·er·os·i·ties**] 1 willingness to share or give; unselfishness. 2 freedom from spitefulness or meanness; nobility: *He showed generosity in praising his opponent.* 3 a generous act.

gen·er·ous (jĕn′ər əs) *adj-* 1 unselfish; free in giving or sharing: *to be generous to people in need.* 2 noble; not mean or spiteful: *a generous nature.* 3 large; plentiful: *a generous supply of paper.* —*adv-* **gen′er·ous·ly.** *n-* **gen′er·ous·ness.**

gen·e·sis (jĕn′ə sĭs) *n-* [*pl.* **gen·e·ses** (-sēz)] 1 a beginning; the coming into being of anything: *We can see the genesis of this novel in an early short story of his.* **Genesis** the first book of the Bible, in which the creatio of the world is described.

ge·net·ic (jə nĕt′ĭk) *adj-* of, relating to, or resulting from heredity through genes; hereditary.

genetic code *n-* the arrangement of chemical bases in the DNA molecule that controls the traits of an organism.

ge·net·i·cist (jə nĕt′ə sĭst) *n-* one trained or skilled in genetics, and usually engaged in it as a profession.

ge·net·ics (jə nĕt′ĭks) *n-* branch of biology dealing with heredity and the genes.

Geneva Convention *n-* an international agreement, drawn up at Geneva in 1864, on the treatment and care of prisoners, the sick, and the wounded during war.

gen·ial (jēn′yəl) *adj-* 1 smilingly pleasant; warmly friendly: *a genial greeting.* 2 favorable to comfort and growth; warm or mild: *a genial climate.* —*n-* **gen·i·al′i·ty** (jĕn ē ăl′ə tē). *adv-* **gen′ial·ly.**

gen·teel (jĕn tēl′) *adj-* polite and correct in manners and behavior, especially in a self-conscious way. —*adv-* **gen·teel′ly.** *n-* **gen·teel′ness.**

gen·tian (jĕn′shən) *n-* any of several related plants with deep blue flowers, such as the fringed gentian.

gen·tile or **Gen·tile** (jĕn′tīl′) *n-* 1 person who is not a Jew. 2 among Mormons, anyone not a Mormon. *adj-* 1 not Jewish. 2 not Mormon.

gen·til·i·ty (jĕn tĭl′ə tē) *n-* [*pl.* **gen·til·i·ties**] 1 good manners or refinement of a well-bred person. 2 traditions, background, etc., of persons of distinguished family or ancestry.

Fringed gentian

gen·tle·folk (jĕn′təl fōk′) *n-* *pl.* in England, people of wealth and property ranking below the nobility; gentry.

gen·tle·man (jĕn′təl mən) *n-* [*pl.* **gen·tle·men**] 1 a well-bred, considerate man. 2 a man: *There is a gentleman to see you.* 3 **gentlemen** formal salutation in a business letter. 4 in England, a man of wealth or property ranking below a nobleman. —*n-* **gen′tle·man·like**′.

gen·tle·man·ly (jĕn′təl mən lē) *adj-* courteous and well-bred; gentlemanlike. —*n-* **gen′tle·man·li·ness**

gentleman's agreement *n-* arrangement or decision agreed to without formal contract, signature, etc.

gen·tle·wom·an (jĕn′təl wōōm′ən) *n-* [*pl.* **gen·tle·wom·en**] 1 a well-bred, considerate woman; lady. 2 in England, a woman from a family of wealth and property having a rank below that of the nobility.

gen·try (jĕn′trē) *n-* gentlefolk.

gen·u·flect (jĕn′yə flĕkt′) *vi-* to bend the knee, especially in religious worship. —*n-* **gen·u·flec′tion.**

gen·u·ine (jĕn′yōō ən) *adj-* real; not false; true: *a genuine pearl.* —*adv-* **gen′u·ine·ly.** *n-* **gen′u·ine·ness.**

ge·nus (jē′nəs) *n-* [*pl.* **gen·er·a** (jĕn′ ər ə)] one of the groupings or categories that is used in the classification of living organisms. A genus belongs to a family and is made up of one or more species.

geo- *combining form* earth; surface of the earth: *geophysics*; *geocentric*; *geomorphology.* [from Greek gê, meaning "the earth."]

ge·o·cen·tric (jē′ ō sĕn′trĭk) *adj-* 1 having to do with, measured, or apparently seen in relation to the earth's center. 2 relating to or based on the idea that the earth, not the sun, is the center of the solar system and the universe: *a geocentric theory.*

ge·ode (jē′ōd′) *n-* 1 a round rock having a cavity or hollow space lined with small crystals. 2 the cavity itself.

ge·o·des·ic (jē′ə dĕs′ĭk, -dē′sĭk) *n-* (also **geodesic line**) the shortest line on a curved surface that connects two points on that surface. A great circle is a geodesic line. *adj-* of or having to do with the geometry of such lines.

Geor·gian (jôr′jən, jōr′-) *adj-* 1 of or pertaining to any of the kings of England named George, or to the art, styles, customs, etc., of their reign. 2 of or relating to the State of Georgia or to its citizens. 3 of or relating to Georgia, a constituent republic of the Soviet Union, or to the language of its people. *n-* 1 a person living during the reign of any one of the Georges of England, or characterized by the ideas and manners current then. 2 a native of the State of Georgia in the United States. 3 a native of Georgia in the Soviet Union.

Ger. 1 German. 2 Germany.

ge·ra·ni·um (jə rā′nē əm) *n-* 1 any of several wild plants having deeply cut leaves and lavender or pinkish flowers. 2 any of several plants cultivated for their showy clusters of bright red, pink, or white blossoms.

Wild geranium

ger·fal·con (jûr' fâl' kən, -fôl' ken, -fô' kən) *gyrfalcon.*

ger·i·at·rics (jĕr' ē ə' triks) *n-* (takes singular verb) branch of medicine that studies and treats the diseases and problems of old age.

germ (jûrm) *n-* 1 tiny living organism that causes disease; microbe. Germs can be seen only with a microscope. 2 tiny mass of living matter that may develop into an animal or plant: *Wheat germ is the living part of the wheat grain.* 3 a spore. 4 something minor or undeveloped that may grow; a beginning: *the germ of war; the germ of an idea.*

ger·man (jûr' mən) *adj-* having a father and mother or grandparents the same as one's own: *my cousin-german.*

Ger·man (jûr' mən) *adj-* of or relating to Germany, its people, or their language. *n-* 1 the language of Germany, spoken also in Austria and part of Switzerland. 2 a native of Germany.

ger·mane (jər mān') *adj-* relevant; pertinent; related: *Your remarks are not germane to the subject.*

Ger·man·ic (jər măn' ĭk) *n-* branch of the Indo-European language family including German, English, Dutch, Afrikaans, Flemish, and the Scandinavian tongues. *adj-* of or pertaining to the Teutonic peoples, or to the languages spoken by them.

ger·ma·ni·um (jər mā' nē əm) *n-* metallic, grayish-white element used to make transistors. Symbol Ge, At. No. 32, At. Wt. 72.59.

German measles *n-* (takes singular verb) contagious virus disease characterized by a sore throat, fever, and a skin rash, and dangerous to the fetus during the first three months of pregnancy; rubella.

German shepherd *n-* breed of dog with a large body, pointed ears, and a smooth coat, often used in police work and for guiding blind people.

German silver *n-* nickel silver.

germ cell *n-* a reproductive cell; gamete.

ger·mi·ci·dal (jûr' mə sī' dəl) *adj-* deadly to germs.

ger·mi·cide (jûr' mə sīd') *n-* substance used to kill germs, especially germs causing disease.

ger·mi·nal (jûr' mə nəl) *adj-* 1 of or having to do with a germ cell or germ. 2 having to do with an early stage of growth or development; coming into being: *a germinal thought.*

ger·mi·nate (jûr' mə nāt') *vi-* [ger·mi·nat·ed, ger·mi·nat·ing] to sprout; start to grow. *vt-* to cause to grow: *Warmth and moisture germinate seeds.* —*n-* ger·mi·na' tion.

germ theory *n-* 1 theory that infectious diseases are caused by the activities of tiny living organisms inside the body. 2 theory that all living organisms originate only from previously existing living organisms.

germ warfare *n-* use of bacteria and other disease-causing organisms as weapons of war.

ger·ry·man·der (jĕr' ē mǎn' dər) *vt-* to divide (a state, voting district, etc.) in such a way as to give an unfair advantage to a particular political party or group. *n-* 1 the act of making such a district. 2 a district so formed.

ger·und (jĕr' ənd) *Grammar n-* English verb form ending in "-ing" and used as a noun. In the sentence "Seeing is believing," "seeing" and "believing" are gerunds. A gerund can take a direct object and can be modified by an adverb: *Believing him was easy.* ("Him" is the direct object.) *Seeing poorly is better than not seeing at all.* ("Poorly" and "at all" are adverbs.)

Ge·sta·po (gə stä' pō) *n-* the Nazi secret police, which operated especially against those opposing the regime.

get about 1 to move around. 2 to become known: *News gets about quickly.*

get across *Informal* to make understood: *He got his meaning across.*

get along 1 to be on good terms. 2 to succeed moderately: *He's not rich but he gets along.* 3 to move on.

get around *Informal* 1 to move around and observe: *We ought to listen to him because he gets around.* 2 of news, to spread about. 3 to bypass (a difficulty). 4 to win over: *I can always get around Mother.*

get at to reach: *Put it where the dog can't get at it.*

get away 1 to leave; depart. 2 to escape.

Geth·sem·a·ne (gĕth sĕm' ə nē) *n-* garden near Jerusalem, the scene of Christ's suffering and arrest; hence, any mental or spiritual agony.

get-to·geth·er (gĕt' tə gəth' ər) *Informal n-* a social gathering of any kind.

get-up (gĕt' ŭp') *Informal n-* 1 outfit o costume, especially an unusual one. 2 general appearance.

gew·gaw (gyōō' gô') *n-* decorative object or trinket of slight value: *Her house was filled with gewgaws.*

gey·ser (gī' zər) *n-* a hot spring that throws a jet of steam and hot water into the air, often at regular intervals.

ghast·ly (gǎst' lē) *adj-* [ghast·li·er, ghast·li·est] 1 horrible; shocking: *The survivors told ghastly stories of the disaster.* 2 like a ghost; deathly pale: *The sick man's face looked ghastly.* 3 *Informal* very bad or unpleasant: *a ghastly mistake.* *adv-* *His face turned ghastly pale.* —*n-* ghast' li·ness.

Geyser

ghee (gē) *n-* in India, an oil prepared from melted butter made from buffalo milk, and used in cooking and in medicine.

gher·kin (gûr' kən) *n-* small cucumber used for pickling.

ghet·to (gĕt' ō) *n-* [*pl.* ghet·tos] 1 section of a city in which Jews were formerly forced to live. 2 any section where a minority group lives together, often under crowded or undesirable conditions.

ghost (gōst) *n-* 1 the spirit of a dead person, thought of as appearing or making its presence known to the living. 2 any faint, shadowy thing or appearance: *the ghost of a smile; ghosts on a television screen.* —*adj-* ghost' like'.

give up the ghost to die.

ghost·ly (gōst' lē) *adj-* [ghost·li·er, ghost·li·est] 1 of or like a ghost; spectral. 2 *Archaic* of or having to do with spiritual or religious matters. —*n-* ghost' li·ness.

ghost town *n-* deserted town or village that was formerly busy or prosperous.

ghost writer *n-* person who writes a speech, book, etc., for someone else whose name appears as the author.

ghoul (gōōl) *n-* 1 robber of dead bodies or of graves. 2 in Muslim folklore, an evil spirit who robs graves and preys on the dead. 3 one who enjoys corrupt or loathsome things. —*adj-* ghoul' ish. *adv-* ghoul' ish·ly. *n-* ghoul' ish·ness.

G.H.Q. general headquarters.

GI (jē' ī') *Informal n-* [*pl.* GIs or GI's] enlisted man in the U.S. Army: *He was a GI all through the war.* *adj-* 1 of or relating to army enlisted men: *the GI sort of humor.* 2 issued, used, or required by the army: *a pair of GI shoes.*

gib·ber (jĭb' ər) *vi-* to chatter foolishly or without making sense; babble. *n-* 1 foolish chatter. 2 gibberish.

gib·ber·ish (jĭb' ər ĭsh) *n-* garbled speech or writing.

gib·bet (jĭb' ət) *n-* a kind of gallows. *vt-* to execute by hanging.

gib·bon (gĭb' ən) *n-* a small ape of Southeast Asia, having very long arms and no tail.

gib·bous (jĭb' əs, gĭb'-) *adj-* 1 of the moon or a planet, being more than half full but not having all the apparent disk illuminated. 2 swollen or protuberant on one side; also, humpbacked. —*adv-* gib' bous·ly. *n-* gib' bous·ness.

gibe (jīb) *n-* remark expressing scorn or contempt; taunt. *vt-* [gibed, gib·ing] to sneer at; taunt: *They gibed him for his mistakes.* *vi-* to jeer (at); scoff (at): *They gibed at his speech.* —*adv-* gib' ing·ly: *He answered the critics gibingly.*

Gibbon about 3 ft tall

gib·lets (jĭb' ləts) *n- pl.* the heart, liver, and gizzard of poultry.

gid·dy (gid' ē) *adj-* [gid·di·er, gid·di·est] 1 dizzy; light-headed; having the feeling of spinning about. 2 causing dizziness: *a giddy height.* 3 not serious; frivolous: *a giddy young girl.* —*adv-* gid'di·ly. *n-* gid'di·ness.

Gid·e·on (gid' ē ən) *n-* a hero of Israel who delivered his people from slavery and idolatry.

gift (gift) *n-* 1 a present; a thing given: *The girls exchanged Christmas gifts.* 2 natural ability; talent: *a gift for singing.*
in (one's) gift in (one's) power to give or bestow.

gift·ed (gif' təd) *adj-* having ability; talented.

¹**gig** (gig) *n-* 1 an open, two-wheeled carriage pulled by a horse. 2 a fast and light boat carried on shipboard for the captain's use. [from earlier **gig(ge)** meaning "a child's top; a whirling contrivance," of uncertain origin.]

²**gig** (gig) *n-* set of barbed hooks drawn through a school of fish to hook them through the body. *vt-* [gigged, gig·ging] to catch fish by this method. [from earlier **fizgig,** from Spanish **fisga** meaning "a harpoon."]

gi·gan·tic (jī găn' tĭk) *n-* of giant size, power, etc.; huge; enormous. —*adv-* gi·gan'ti·cal·ly.

gig·gle (gig' əl) *vi-* [gig·gled, gig·gling] 1 to laugh in a nervous, mischievous, or silly way. *n-* a light, silly, or mischievous laugh. —*n-* gig'gler. *adj-* gig'gly.

Gi·la monster (hē' lə) *n-* large, venomous orange and black lizard of southwestern United States and northern Mexico.

Gila monster. up to 20 in long

¹**gild** (gild) *vt-* [gild·ed or gilt, gild·ing] 1 to cover with gold or with any gold-colored substance: *to gild a picture frame.* 2 to make golden: *The setting sun gilded the sky.* 3 to make (something unpleasant) seem more attractive; gloss over: *It is a lie, no matter how he gilds it.* [from Old English **gyldan,** from **gold,** "golden."] *Hom-* guild.

²**gild** (gild) guild. [from Old Norse **gildi.**]

gild·ing (gil' ding) *n-* 1 thin layer of gold or similar material used to cover something. 2 surface produced in this way. 3 a deceptively pleasing appearance.

¹**gill** (gil) *n-* 1 bodily organ of young amphibians, fish, and other aquatic animals, which takes up oxygen from the surrounding water and gives up carbon dioxide to it. 2 one of the many soft, thin vertical plates on the underside of a mushroom cap. [from earlier English **gille,** perhaps from a Scandinavian word.]

²**gill** (jil) *n-* unit of liquid measure equal to one fourth of a pint. [from Old French **gelle** meaning a "wine measure," from Late Latin **gillo,** "a receptacle."]

gill slit *n-* one of the several pairs of vertical slits in the throats of young amphibians and fish through which water passes from the mouth over the gills.

gil·ly·flow·er (jil' ē flou' ər) *n-* any of various related plants, such as the wallflower or the stock.

gilt (gilt) *adj-* covered with, or of the color of, gold; gilded: *a gilt statue.* *n-* paint made from powdered gold or something resembling it. *Hom-* guilt.

gin·seng (jin' sěng´) *n-* 1 herb, native to China and North America, having a thick root that is used in Oriental medicine. 2 root of this plant; also, a preparation extracted from it.

Gip·sy (jip' sē) Gypsy.

gipsy moth Gypsy moth.

gi·raffe (jə răf´) *n-* African animal with long legs and a very long neck. It is the tallest of all mammals and feeds on the leaves of tall trees, and chews a cud.

Giraffe. about 18 ft high

gird (gûrd) *vt-* [gird·ed or girt, gird·ing] 1 to surround; encircle: *Mountains girded the valley.* 2 to make ready; prepare: *to gird oneself for battle.* *vi-* 1 to make oneself ready; prepare: *to gird for action.* 2 to fasten something (on) with a belt or cord: *to gird on a sword.*
gird up (one's) loins to prepare for action or battle.

gird·er (gûr' dər) *n-* strong, horizontal beam, often of steel, which supports the floor of a building or bridge.

Girder

gir·dle (gûr' dəl) *n-* 1 sash or belt worn about the waist. 2 light, elastic undergarment worn by women to support and slim the waist and hips. 3 anything that surrounds like a belt: *a girdle of green around a city.* *vt-* [gir·dled, gird·ling] 1 to bind with or as with a belt. 2 to encircle: *Clouds girdled the moon.* 3 to cut off a strip of bark in a complete circle around (a tree or branch).

girl (gûrl) *n-* 1 female child or young woman. 2 female servant.

girl·friend (gûrl' frĕnd´) *n-* 1 woman courted by a man; sweetheart. 2 girl or woman who is a friend.

girl·hood (gûrl' hŏŏd) *n-* the time or condition of being a girl.

girl·ish (gûr' lish) *adj-* like a girl; of a girl: *a girlish giggle.* —*adv-* girl'ish·ly. *n-* girl'ish·ness.

Girl Scouts *n-* 1 (takes singular or plural verb) organization for training girls in physical fitness, good citizenship, and helpfulness to others. 2 girl scout member of the Girl Scouts.

girt (gûrt) *p.t.* & *p.p.* of gird.

girth (gûrth) *n-* 1 distance around: *a man's girth at the waist; the girth of a tree trunk.* 2 strap fastened around an animal to hold a saddle, blanket, etc., in place. *vt-* to fasten with a strap or band.

gist (jist) *n-* the main point or idea of a matter; essence: *the gist of a story or speech.*

give (giv) *vt-* [gave (gāv), giv·en, giv·ing] 1 to hand over to another freely or as a present: *I gave him a pencil.* 2 to pay in exchange for something received: *I gave five dollars for this pin.* 3 to sacrifice; devote: *He gave his life for his country.* 4 to administer: *to give a dose of medicine.* 5 to deal; inflict (a blow, beating, etc.). 6 to deliver: *to give a speech.* 7 to state; utter: *to give an opinion; to give a shout.* 8 to perform; present: *to give a play.* 9 to provide; furnish: *to give heat; to give advice; to give joy.* 10 to furnish as entertainment: *to give a party.* 11 to transmit; communicate: *He gave me the measles. Please give her my love.* 12 to allot; assign: *to give homework.* 13 to grant: *to give permission.* 14 to entrust: *I give it into your charge.* 15 to pledge: *to give one's word.* 16 to execute (a bodily movement): *He gave a leap for joy.* *vi-* 1 to present gifts; contribute: *He gave freely to the hospital.* 2 to yield, as to force, pressure, motion, etc.: *The old floor gave under my feet.* *n-* yielding to pressure; elasticity; flexibility: *An airplane wing must have a certain amount of give.* —*n-* giv'er.

give and take to make mutual concessions.

give away 1 to give up possession of. 2 to make known; reveal: *to give away a secret.*

give back to return.

give in to yield; surrender.

give it to (someone) *Informal* to punish (someone).

give off send out; emit: *to give off an odor.*

give out 1 to send out; distribute. 2 to make known. 3 to become exhausted, worn out, or used up.

give over 1 to surrender; yield. 2 to set apart for a purpose; devote: *to give over land for a park.*

give rise to to cause or produce; result in.

give up 1 to surrender; yield. 2 to stop doing something: *to give up smoking.* 3 to stop trying; admit failure.

give way 1 to retreat; withdraw; yield the right of way. 2 to yield or submit (to): *Don't give way to despair.* 3 to collapse, as a bridge under a heavy load.

give-and-take (giv' ən tāk´) *n-* 1 compromise. 2 conflict and rivalry: *the give-and-take of daily life.*

give·a·way (giv' ə wā´) *Informal n-* 1 clear evidence of something. 2 something given away.

giv·en (giv' ən) *adj-* 1 stated; specified: *What can we judge from the given facts?* 2 granted: *a God-given talent.*
given to in the habit of: *He is given to bragging.*

given name *n-* name given at birth; first name.

giz·zard (giz' ərd) *n-* muscular second stomach of birds, in which food is crushed and ground.

Gk. Greek.

gla·cé (glä sā´) *French adj-* 1 coated with a sugar glaze; candied. 2 iced; frosted. 3 having a glossy surface.

gla·cial (glā´shəl) *adj-* 1 of, relating to, or caused by a glacier or glaciation: *a glacial stream; glacial landscape.* 2 icy; frigid: *a glacial wind.* 3 unfriendly: *a glacial look.* —*adv-* **gla´cial·ly.**

glacial period *n-* 1 any of the four times in the earth's history, beginning about 800 million years ago, during which ice sheets covered large areas of the earth's surface. The latest of the four was the Pleistocene. 2 one of the four times during the Pleistocene epoch when ice advances occurred. 3 the Pleistocene epoch. Also **glacial epoch.**

gla·ci·ate (glā´shē āt´, -sē āt´) *vt-* [gla·ci·at·ed, gla·ci·at·ing] to form glaciers or ice sheets on: *The ice glaciated half the continent.* —*n-* **gla·ci·a´tion.**

gla·ci·at·ed (glā´shē ā´təd, glā´sē-) *adj-* 1 covered with an ice sheet or glaciers. 2 scraped, scoured, filled, or otherwise changed by glaciers: *a glaciated valley.*

gla·cier (glā´shər) *n-* huge, moving mass of ice, on land, formed by the pressure of many snowfalls.

glass (glăs) *n-* 1 hard, brittle substance, usually transparent or translucent, made from sand mixed with soda, potash, and other chemicals, and shaped at high heat by pressing, blowing, extruding, etc. 2 an article made of this substance, such as a mirror, drinking vessel, etc. 3 instrument for seeing, such as a telescope or microscope. 4 glassful. 5 **glasses** eyeglasses; spectacles. *as modifier: a glass bowl; glass windows.*

glass blowing *n-* the shaping of molten glass by forcing air into it through a tube. —*n-* **glass blower.**

glass·ful (glăs´fŏŏl´) *n-* the amount held by a drinking glass.

glee (glē) *n-* 1 gaiety; joy; merriment. 2 song for male voices in three or more parts, without accompaniment.

glee club *n-* a chorus, especially a male chorus in a school or college.

glee·ful (glē´fəl) *adj-* full of glee; merry; gay. —*adv-* **glee´ful·ly.** *n-* **glee´ful·ness.**

glen (glĕn) *n-* narrow, secluded valley.

glen·gar·ry (glĕn găr´ē) *n-* [*pl.* **glen·gar·ries**] Scottish cap with creased top and straight sides.

glib (glĭb) *adj-* [glib·ber, glib·best] quick and ready; without much thought or sincerity; facile: *a glib talker; a glib excuse.* —*adv-* **glib´ ly.** *n-* **glib´ ness.**

glide (glīd) *vi-* [glid·ed, glid·ing] 1 to move smoothly and easily without apparent effort: *Skaters glided on the ice.* 2 to pass imperceptibly: *The years glide by.* 3 to fly or soar on wings while not applying driving power. *n-* 1 smooth, sliding movement. 2 movement through the air on wings while no driving power is being applied. 3 in phonetics, sound produced while the organs of speech are shifting from the position for one sound to that for another.

glid·er (glī´dər) *n-* 1 winged aircraft without an engine, designed to be towed behind an airplane or launched into flight. 2 outdoor seat that swings backward and forward on chains within a low supporting framework.

Glider

glo·ry (glôr´ē) *n-* [*pl.* **glo·ries**] 1 fame and honor: *Scientific achievements bring glory to a nation.* 2 praise; credit: *the glory of a distinguished career.* 3 reason for pride: *The Colosseum was the glory of ancient Rome.* 4 highest state of magnificence or prosperity: *Greece in her glory.* 5 radiant beauty; splendor: *the glory of a sunset.* 6 halo. *vi-* [glor·ied, glor·y·ing] to rejoice in; be proud of (usually followed by "in" or "at").

go to glory to die. in one's glory at one's happiest or most successful.

¹**gloss** (glŏs) *n-* 1 smooth shining surface; luster: *the gloss of satin.* 2 a deceptive appearance: *the gloss of respectability.* *vt-* to make smooth and lustrous. [from Old Norse glossi, "a blaze," or glys, "luster."]

gloss over to cover up or excuse a mistake or wrong act.

glove (glŭv) *n-* 1 covering for the hand with a separate sheath for each finger and the thumb. 2 padded covering to protect the hand: *a baseball glove.* —*adj-* **gloved:** *a gloved hand.*

hand in glove with in close agreement or cooperation with. handle with kid gloves to treat gently.

glov·er (glŭv´ər) *n-* person who makes gloves.

glow (glō) *vi-* 1 to give off intense light and heat without flame: *Embers glowed after the fire died.* 2 to give off light but not heat: *The face of the clock glows in the dark.* 3 to shine with brilliant color: *The trees glow with autumn splendor.* 4 to be warm or flushed, as from exercise. 5 to have the appearance, color, etc., of good health. 6 to radiate; be suffused (with): *to glow with pride.* *n-* 1 a giving off of light from something that is red-hot or white-hot. 2 brightness; light: *the glow of a firefly; a red glow at sunset.* 3 special appearance or tone: *a glow of happiness; a glow of health.*

glue (glōō) *n-* 1 substance used to join and bond things together, made from animal hides, hooves and horns, sinews, etc. 2 any of various substances made from rubber, casein, blood, synthetic resin, etc., and used for the same purpose; cement; adhesive. *as modifier: a glue pot; a glue joint.* *vt-* [glued, glu·ing] to join or bond together with such a substance.

glu·ey (glōō´ē) *adj-* [glu·i·er, glu·i·est] 1 like glue; sticky. 2 smeared with glue.

glum (glŭm) *adj-* [glum·mer, glum·mest] silent and gloomy; sullen. —*adv-* **glum´ ly.** *n-* **glum´ ness.**

glut (glŭt) *n-* an oversupply: *a glut of wheat on the market.* *vt-* [glut·ted, glut·ting] 1 to more than satisfy; overstuff: *He glutted his appetite with rich food.* 2 to oversupply with goods in excess of the demand: *to glut the market.*

glu·ten (glōō´tən) *n-* a sticky protein substance found in the flour of certain grains, especially wheat.

glu·ti·nous (glōō´tən əs) *adj-* like glue; sticky. —*adv-* **glu´ tin·ous·ly.**

glut·ton (glŭt´ən) *n-* 1 person who eats too much; pig. 2 person who is very greedy (for something): *a glutton for reading.* [from Old French **glutun,** from Latin **glut(t)ōn-,** from **glutire,** "to swallow; gulp."]

goal (gōl) *n-* 1 place at either end of a field or other playing area where the score is made in football, basketball, hockey, lacrosse, etc. 2 a score: *Our team made a goal.* 3 line or mark at the end of a race: *The winner will be the first person to cross the goal.* 4 aim; purpose. *What is your goal in life?* 5 planned destination: *His goal was Paris.*

goal·ie (gō´lē) *Informal n-* goalkeeper.

goal·keep·er (gōl´kē´pər) *n-* player who protects the goal for his team.

goal line *n-* line marking the goal in a game.

goal post *n-* one of a pair of posts with a crossbar, forming the goal in football, soccer, etc.

goat (gōt) *n-* 1 cud-chewing animal about the size of, and related to, the sheep, usually having short horns and a beard. It is valued for its milk, skin, meat, and, in some varieties, for its hair. 2 *Informal* innocent person made to take blame or punishment, or to seem a fool; butt; scapegoat. —*adj-* **goat´ like´.**

get (someone's) goat *Slang* to anger; annoy.

Goat about 3 ft long

goat·ee (gō tē´) *n-* small, pointed beard on the chin or on the lower lip.

goat·herd (gōt´hûrd´) *n-* one who tends goats, especially while at pasture.

goat·skin (gōt´skĭn´) *n-* 1 the skin of a goat. 2 leather made from this. 3 container for wine or water made of this leather. *as modifier: a goatskin cloak.*

goat·suck·er (gŏt´sŭk´ər) *n-* any of various insect-eating birds that fly by night, such as the whippoorwill or nighthawk.

¹**gob** (gŏb) *Slang n-* sailor in the United States navy. [an American word of uncertain origin.]

God (gŏd) *n-* the Creator and Ruler of the universe; the Lord; the Supreme Being; the Almighty; Jehovah.

god (gŏd) *n-* 1 a male being who is thought of and worshiped as having greater than human powers over nature and human affairs. 2 image, object, etc., worshipped as having divine powers. 3 something that takes all of a person's interest or devotion: *Money is his god.*

god·child (gŏd′ chīld′) *n-* [*pl.* **god·chil·dren**] child for whose religious training a godfather or godmother promises to assume responsibility.

god·daugh·ter (gŏd′ dô′ tər) *n-* female godchild.

god·dess (gŏd′ əs) *n-* 1 female deity. 2 woman greatly admired for her charm, beauty, etc.

god·fa·ther (gŏd′ fä′ thər) *n-* man who promises at the baptism or confirmation of someone else's child to assume responsibility for the child's religious training.

god·head (gŏd′ hĕd′) *n-* 1 divine nature; divinity. 2 **Godhead** God; Supreme Being.

god·hood (gŏd′ hŏŏd′) *n-* the state or quality of being a god; divinity.

god·less (gŏd′ ləs) *adj-* 1 not believing in or worshiping God. 2 wicked. —*n-* **god′ less·ness.**

god·like (gŏd′ līk′) *adj-* like or suitable to a god; divine.

god·ly (gŏd′ lē) *adj-* [**god·li·er, god·li·est**] obeying and loving God; pious: *a godly man.* —*n-* **god′ li·ness.**

god·moth·er (gŏd′ mŭth′ ər) *n-* woman who promises at the baptism or confirmation of someone else's child to assume responsibility for the child's religious training.

god·par·ent (gŏd′ pâr′ ənt, -pâr′ ənt) *n-* godfather or godmother.

God's acre *n-* churchyard or cemetery.

god·send (gŏd′ sĕnd′) *n-* something unexpected and very welcome, as if sent by God.

god·son (gŏd′ sŭn′) *n-* male godchild.

God·speed (gŏd′ spēd′) *n-* a wish for good luck and success, especially on a journey.

god·wit (gŏd′ wĭt′) *n-* bird with a long bill and long legs, related to the snipes and curlews.

goes (gōz) 1 form of the verb **go** used with "he," "she," "it," or singular noun subjects, in the present tense. 2 plural of the noun **go.**

gold (gōld) *n-* 1 heavy, precious, metal element, of a yellow color in its pure state, used for making coins and jewelry and kept in reserve by governments to give value to their currencies. Symbol Au, At. No. 79, At. Wt. 196.967. 2 color of this metal. 3 money; wealth: *He has lots of gold.* 4 that which is the highest or best in quality: *a heart of gold.* *adj-*: *a gold watch.*

go·nad (gō′ năd′) *n-* male or female reproductive gland, testis or ovary.

gon·do·la (gŏn′ də lə) *n-* 1 narrow, sharp-pointed boat, with high, ornamental ends, rowed with a single oar by a standing boatman. It is used for transportation in Venice. 2 freight car with low sides and no top. 3 the cabin of a dirigible.

Gondola

good (gŏŏd) *adj-* [**bet·ter** (bĕt′ ər), **best** (bĕst)] 1 above average in quality: *some good food; a good book.* 2 suited to the purpose; producing favorable results: *a good day for swimming; drugs good for a fever.* 3 well-behaved: *a good child.* 4 morally excellent: *He tried to live a good life.* 5 kind; friendly: *God is good.* 6 enjoyable; pleasant: *a good time.* 7 fresh; not spoiled: *two good eggs.* 8 proper; becoming: *to show good manners.* 9 thorough; complete: *a good scolding.* 10 fairly great; more than a little: *a good supply.* 11 able; skilled: *a good surgeon.* 12 valid; sound: *a good excuse.* 13 real; not counterfeit: *a good five-dollar bill.* *n-* 1 whatever is desirable, beneficial, etc.: *He did more harm than good.* 2 merit; worth: *There is some good in everyone.* 3 profit; advantage; benefit: *I tell you for your own good.* *interj-* exclamation of pleasure, satisfaction, etc.

good·y-good·y (gŏŏd′ ē gŏŏd′ ē) *Informal n-* [*pl.* **good·y-good·ies**] person who is, or pretends to be, more virtuous than others. *adj-*: *his goody-goody attitude.*

goo·ey (gŏŏ′ ē) *Slang adj-* [**goo·i·er, goo·i·est**] 1 sticky; gluey: *a gooey paint.* 2 chewy and rich: *a gooey candy.*

goon (gōōn) *Slang n-* 1 stupid person. 2 hoodlum, especially one hired to attack workers on strike.

goose (gōōs) *n-* [*pl.* **geese** (gēs)] 1 any of several water birds, larger than a duck, with webbed feet, stout bodies, and a long neck. See also **gander, gosling.** 2 the female of this bird, as distinguished from the male, or gander. 3 flesh of this bird, used as food. 4 silly person. —*adj-* **goose′ like′.**

Wild goose 2-3 ft long

cook (someone's) goose *Informal* to ruin someone's chances, plans, hopes, etc.

goose·ber·ry (gōōs′ bĕr′ ē, gōōz′ bə rē) *n-* [*pl.* **goose·ber·ries**] 1 round, juicy berry, usually picked while it is still green. 2 the prickly bush it grows on.

Gor·gon (gôr′ gən, gôr′-) *n-* 1 in Greek mythology, any one of three sisters, of whom Medusa is best known, whose appearance was so terrifying that any person who looked at them was turned to stone. 2 **gorgon** a hideous or terrifying woman.

go·ril·la (gə rĭl′ ə) *n-* the largest of the manlike apes, native to Africa. *Hom-* **guerrilla.**

gor·mand·ize (gôr′ mən dīz′, gôr′-) *vi-* [**gor·mand·ized, gor·mand·iz·ing**] to stuff oneself with food; eat greedily. —*n-* **gor′ mand·iz′ er.**

gorse (gôrs, gôrs) *n-* spiny shrub bearing yellow flowers and found on wasteland in Europe; furze.

gor·y (gôr′ ē) *adj-* [**gor·i·er, gor·i·est**] bloody. —*adv-* **gor′ i·ly.** *n-* **gor′ i·ness.**

gosh (gŏsh) *Informal interj-* exclamation of surprise, distress, etc.

Gorilla about 6 ft tall

gos·hawk (gŏs′ hôk′) *n-* any of several powerful, short-winged hawks. For picture, see **hawk.**

Go·shen (gō′ shən) *n-* 1 region in Egypt allotted to the Israelites. 2 any place of peace and plenty.

gos·ling (gŏz′ lĭng) *n-* young goose. .

gos·pel (gŏs′ pəl) *n-* 1 the teachings of Jesus and the Apostles. 2 **Gospel** (1) any of the first four books of the New Testament, by Matthew, Mark, Luke, and John. (2) part of one of these books read at a religious service. 3 anything believed as absolutely true.

gos·sa·mer (gŏs′ ə mər) *n-* 1 fine, silky thread or web made by a spider. 2 any thin, light, delicate fabric: *a scarf of gossamer.* *adj-* (also **gos′ sa·mer·y**) light and thin: *a gossamer cloud.*

gos·sip (gŏs′ əp) *n-* 1 idle talk, often unfriendly, about people and their affairs. 2 person fond of such talk. *vi-*:

grab bag *n-* bag or box containing small concealed or wrapped articles, from which a person is permitted to draw one, as at a fair, party, etc.

grace (grās) *n-* 1 easy, flowing manner; beauty of movement: *the grace of a dancer.* 2 charming quality; pleasing manner: *a young lady with many graces.* 3 sense of right: *He had the grace to say he was sorry.* 4 divine help or favor. 5 kindness or leniency, especially extra time given to pay a debt: *You have five days' grace to settle this note.* 6 short prayer of thanks before or after a meal. 7 **Grace** title of an archbishop, duke, or duchess, preceded by "Your," "His," or "Her." 8 **Graces** in Greek mythology, three sister goddesses who had control over all beauty and charm in people and in nature. *vt-* [**graced, grac·ing**] to favor or honor: *The queen graced the table with her presence.*

in (one's) good (or bad) graces in (one's) favor (or disfavor): *He is in her good graces.*

grace·ful (grās′ fəl) *adj-* showing or having charm and elegance of movement, posture, form, or expression: *a graceful dancer; a graceful letter of thanks.* —*adv-* **grace′ ful·ly.** *n-* **grace′ ful·ness.**

²grad·u·ate (grăj′ ōō ət) *n-* **1** person who has finished a course of study in a school and has received a diploma. **2** tube, flask, or other container marked with lines or numbers for measuring liquids or solids. *as modifier*: *a graduate school*; *to take graduate courses*; *a club for graduate students*; *a graduate nurse.*

grad·u·a·tion (grăj′ ōō ā′ shən) *n-* **1** ceremony at which diplomas are given to students of a school; commencement exercises. **2** a mark showing spaces, degrees, amounts, etc., on an instrument or container used for measuring; also, a series of such marks. **3** gradual change or shift: *the graduation from light to dark.*

¹graft (grăft) *n-* **1** twig or branch of one plant set into another of which it will become a living part. **2** plant or tree resulting from such an operation. **3** piece of skin, bone, etc., transplanted from one part of the body to another, or from one body to another. *vt-* (also **engraft**, **ingraft**) to transfer or implant (a living branch, piece of tissue, etc.) into another living organism: *to graft a branch of white rose into a red rose bush.* [from earlier **graff**, from Old French *graffe* meaning "a writing tool," from Latin and Greek *graphion*, "stylus," because a twig inserted in a tree trunk was thought to resemble a writing instrument held in the hand.] —*n-* **graft′er.**

Graft

²graft (grăft) *n-* the gaining of money or advantages through dishonest use of one's position, especially by a public official; also, the money or advantages thus gained. *vi-* to use one's position to gain money or advantages dishonestly. [of uncertain origin.] —*n-* **graft′er.**

gra·ham (grā′ əm) *adj-* made from coarsely ground whole-wheat: *a box of graham crackers*; *graham flour.*

Grail (grāl) *n-* in medieval legend, the cup used by Christ at the Last Supper. Also **Holy Grail.**

grain (grān) *n-* **1** seed of wheat, rice, oats, corn, and other cereal plants. **2** plant or plants bearing such seeds: *a field of grain.* **3** tiny, hard particle of sugar, salt, sand, etc. **4** a tiny bit: *There isn't a grain of truth in her story.* **5** very small unit of weight. One pound is equal to 7,000 grains. **6** lines and patterns in wood or stone caused by the way the fibers or layers are arranged.
go against the grain to be contrary to one's nature.

grand (grănd) *adj-* [**grand·er**, **grand·est**] **1** great in size or general effect; impressive: *a grand spectacle*; *a grand palace.* **2** full of dignity, pride, or authority: *a grand lady*; *grand manners.* **3** including everything; complete: *the grand total.* **4** most important; main: *the grand ballroom.* **5** *Informal* very good or satisfying: *We had a grand time.* *n- Slang* a thousand dollars. —*adv-* **grand′ly.** *n-* **grand′ness.**

graph (grăf) *n-* **1** diagram that shows by lines, bars, etc., the relationship between two or more things. **2** *Mathematics* representation of a given equation as a set of points in relation to coordinates.

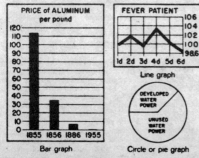

PRICE of ALUMINUM
per pound

Bar graph

FEVER PATIENT

Line graph

DEVELOPED WATER POWER

UNUSED WATER POWER

Circle or pie graph

grass (grăs) *n-* **1** any of a large family of plants having jointed stems and narrow leaves called blades. Wheat, corn, bamboo, and sugar cane are all grasses. **2** lawn or turf. **3** green herbage eaten by grazing animals. —*adj-* **grass′less.** *adj-* **grass′like′.**

grass·hop·per (grăs′ hŏp′ ər) *n-* leaping insect with wings and long, powerful hind legs, related to the locust and katydid.

Grasshopper, about 1 1/4 in long

grass·land (grăs′ lănd′) *n-* land, usually without trees, on which grass grows abundantly.

grass roots *n- pl.* voters who speak for themselves rather than through a political organization.

grass snake *n-* **1** any of various small, harmless European snakes that live in marshes. **2** garter snake.

grass widow *n-* woman who is divorced or otherwise separated from her husband. —*n- masc.* **grass widower.**

grass·y (grăs′ ē) *adj-* [**grass·i·er**, **grass·i·est**] **1** covered with grass. **2** of or like grass. —*n-* **grass′i·ness.**

grate (grāt) *vt-* [**grat·ed**, **grat·ing**] **1** to make into bits or powder by rubbing on a rough surface: *to grate cheese.* **2** to irritate: *to grate someone's feelings.* *vi-* (often followed by "on," "upon," or "against") **1** to rub or scrape so as to produce a harsh, irritating sound: *The chalk grated on the blackboard.* **2** to cause an irritating effect, as if by scraping: *Her shrill voice grates on my nerves.* [from Old French *grater*, meaning "to scratch; scrape," from an earlier Germanic word.] *Hom-* **great.**

grat·i·tude (grăt′ ə tōōd′, -tyōōd′) *n-* thankfulness for help, kindness, or good fortune.

gra·tu·i·tous (grə tōō′ ə təs, grə tyōō′-) *adj-* **1** without cost: *to give gratuitous advice to a client.* **2** without cause; unwarranted: *a gratuitous insult.* —*adv-* **gra·tu′i·tous·ly.** *n-* **gra·tu′i·tous·ness.**

gra·tu·i·ty (grə tōō′ ə tē, grə tyōō′-) *n-* [*pl.* **gra·tu·i·ties**] extra money given for services; tip.

Gr. Br. or **Gr. Brit.** Great Britain.

grave (grāv) *n-* **1** hole in the ground in which a dead body is placed for burial. **2** any place of burial: *The sea was his grave.* **3** death. [from Old English *græf*, "a place dug out; a grave," and related to ³**grave.**]

²grave (grāv) *adj-* [**grav·er**, **grav·est**] **1** serious; solemn; thoughtful: *Everyone was grave at the inauguration.* **2** needing serious thought; important: *The President has grave responsibilities.* *n-* grave accent. [from French, from Latin *gravis* meaning "heavy."] —*adv-* **grave′ly.** *n-* **grave′ness.**

³grave (grāv) *vt-* [**graved**, **grav·en**, **grav·ing**] to shape, carve, or engrave with or as if with a chisel or other pointed tool. [from Old English *grafan*, and related to ¹**grave** and **engrave.**]

grave accent (grăv, grāv) *n-* accent mark [`] placed over certain vowels to indicate a particular sound of the vowel, as in the French "mère." In English it is sometimes used to show that the ending -ed is pronounced as a separate syllable, as in "agèd."

grave·dig·ger (grāv′ dĭg′ ər) *n-* person who digs graves for a living.

grav·i·tate (grăv′ ə tāt′) *vi-* [**grav·i·tat·ed**, **grav·i·tat·ing**] **1** to move, or tend to move, in response to a gravitational force. **2** to move as if drawn by such a force. *vt-* in mining, to cause to move by the force of gravity.

grav·i·ta·tion (grăv′ ə tā′ shən) *n-* **1** *Physics* the force of attraction between any two objects in the universe. The larger the product of the masses of the two objects, the greater the force, and the further apart the objects are, the weaker the force. **2** a gravitating. —*adj-* **grav′i·ta′tion·al.**

grav·i·ty (grăv′ ə tē) *n-* [*pl.* **grav·i·ties**] **1** the attractive force that draws all objects at or near the surface of the earth toward its center; also, the similar force of any other heavenly body. **2** seriousness; solemnity; importance: *The child quickly sensed the gravity of the occasion.*

gra·vy (grā′ vē) *n-* [*pl.* **gra·vies**] fat and juices that come from cooking meat, or a sauce made from these.

grease (grēs, grēz) *n-* 1 melted or softened animal fat. 2 any thick, oily substance, especially one used as a lubricant. *vt-* [greased, greas·ing] 1 to cover with fat: *to grease a baking dish.* 2 to lubricate. *Hom-* Greece.
grease the hand (or **palm**) **of** *Informal* to bribe or tip.
grease·paint (grēs' pānt') *n-* any of the various creams or pastes of different colors, used as theatrical makeup.
grease·wood (grēs' wood') *n-* any of several spiny shrubs that grow on the dry plains of western United States. The wood contains some oil and is sometimes used locally for fuel.
greas·y (grē' sē, -zē) *adj-* [greas·i·er, greas·i·est] 1 covered with or containing grease: *His hands were greasy. The food was greasy.* 2 feeling or looking like grease; smooth and slippery. —*adv-* **greas' i·ly.** *n-* **greas' i·ness.**
great (grāt) *adj-* [great·er, great·est] 1 large in size; vast: *a great forest.* 2 large in number: *a great crowd.* 3 more than usual in degree, intensity, etc.: *a great clap of thunder; to be in great pain.* 4 long in time or extent
green (grēn) *n-* 1 the color of growing grass and leaves. Green is between blue and yellow on the spectrum. 2 a grassy area. 3 in golf, smooth grass around a hole. 4 **greens** (1) leaves, wreaths, etc., used as decoration. (2) leafy vegetables used for food: *beet greens; dandelion greens.* *adj-* [green·er, green·est] 1 having the color of growing grass and leaves: *a green felt.* 2 unripe: *The fruit is still green.* 3 untrained; inexperienced: *He is still green at his job.* 4 not dried; unseasoned: *The lumber is still green.* 5 having a sickly color: *Her face turned green, and she fainted.* —*n-* **green' ness.**
green with envy extremely envious.
gren·a·dier (grĕn' ə dēr') *n-* 1 in former times, a foot soldier who threw grenades. 2 member of a special British army regiment called the **Grenadier Guards.**
gren·a·dine (grĕn' ə dēn') *n-* syrup made from pomegranates, used as a flavoring.
grew (grōō) *p.t.* of **grow.**
grey (grā) *chiefly Brit.* gray.
grey·beard (grā' bērd') graybeard.
grey·hound (grā' hound') *n-* a slender, sharp-faced, long-legged dog, famous for its grace and speed, used in racing and sometimes in hunting.

Greyhound, about 2 ft. high at shoulder

grid (grĭd) *n-* 1 a grating of parallel iron bars; gridiron. 2 in electronics, an electrode that controls the flow of electrons from cathode to anode in a vacuum tube.
grid·dle (grĭd' əl) *n-* flat, heavy pan or similar utensil, used for cooking pancakes.
grid·dle·cake (grĭd' əl kāk') *n-* pancake baked on a griddle.
grid·i·ron (grĭd' ī' ərn) *n-* 1 rack of parallel bars on which to broil meat, etc. 2 something that looks like this, especially a football field.
Gridiron
grief (grēf) *n-* 1 deep sorrow; great sadness. 2 cause or source of sorrow.
come to grief to meet with disaster; fail.
griev·ance (grē' vəns) *n-* real or imagined wrong considered as a source of annoyance or resentment; cause for complaint.
grieve (grēv) *vt-* [grieved, griev·ing] to feel sorrow: *I grieve over your misfortune.* *vt-* to cause sorrow to; distress: *Your misfortune grieves me.*
grim (grĭm) *adj-* [grim·mer, grim·mest] 1 cruel; fierce: *a grim battle.* 2 unyielding: *a grim determination.* 3 forbidding; threatening: *a grim cliff.* 4 frightening; horrible: *a grim tale.* —*adv-* **grim' ly.** *n-* **grim' ness.**
gri·mace (grĭ mās', grĭm' əs) *n-* a twisting or distortion of the face especially to show pain, disgust, or disapproval: *to make a grimace.* *vi-* [gri·maced, gri·mac·ing]: *He grimaced when I said I'd be late.*
grime (grīm) *n-* dirt that is rubbed or ground into the skin or other surface.

grind (grīnd) *vt-* [ground (ground), grind·ing] 1 to crush into small pieces or a powder: *to grind wheat; to grind coffee beans.* 2 to make or produce by this process: *to grind flour.* 3 to grate; rub harshly: *to grind one's teeth.* 4 to smooth or sharpen by rubbing against a rough surface: *to grind an ax.* 5 to oppress; crush: *The tyrant ground the people under his heel.* 6 to operate by turning a crank: *to grind a pepper mill.* *n-* 1 something produced by crushing or powdering: *a coarse grind of coffee.* 2 *Informal* long, continuous, monotonous activity: *the daily grind at the office.* 3 *Informal* student who works hard, taking little time for recreation.
grind out to produce or make by long, strenuous effort: *to grind out a living.*
grind·er (grīn' dər) *n-* 1 person who sharpens tools, utensils, etc. 2 machine for grinding.
grind·stone (grīnd' stōn') *n-* disk of fine-grained stone, turned by a crank or treadle, and used for sharpening tools.
Grindstone
have (or **keep**) **one's nose to the grindstone** to work long and hard at something.
grip (grĭp) *vt-* [gripped, grip·ping] 1 to grasp tightly: *If you grip the side of the cart, you won't fall out.* 2 to appeal strongly to; interest very much: *this story grips the imagination.* *n-* 1 tight grasp; strong hold or handclasp. 2 manner in which something is grasped: *the proper grip for a fencing foil.* 3 handle or other part of a tool, racket, golf club, firearm, etc., meant to be grasped. 4 valise; suitcase. *Hom-* grippe. —*adj-* **grip' less.** *n-* **grip' per.** *adv-* **grip' ping·ly.**
come to grips 1 to fight; enter into combat: *The two armies finally came to grips.* 2 to confront; become involved (with): *We must come to grips with this problem.*
gripe (grīp) *vt-* [griped, grip·ing] 1 *Informal* to irritate; annoy: *Your antics gripe me.* 2 to cause pain in the bowels of (someone). *vi-* 1 *Informal* to complain. *n-* 1 *Informal* complaint. 2 gripes pain in the bowels.
gris·tly (grĭs' lē) *adj-* [grist·li·er, grist·li·est] partly or wholly made up of gristle: *A gristly bear makes tough chewing.*
grist·mill (grĭst' mĭl') *n-* mill for grinding grain.
grit (grĭt) *n-* 1 small, hard particles of sand, stone, etc. 2 ability to endure hardships; firm spirit: *It took grit to start a farm in Alaska.* *vt-* [grit·ted, grit·ting] to press or grind together: *to grit one's teeth.*
grits (grĭts) *n- pl.* coarsely ground grain or meal; especially, coarsely ground hominy.
grit·ty (grĭt' ē) *adj-* [grit·ti·er, grit·ti·est] 1 like, containing, or made of grit. 2 brave and determined; plucky. —*n-* **grit' ti·ness.**
griz·zled (grĭz' əld) *adj-* 1 streaked with gray: *a grizzled beard.* 2 gray-haired: *a grizzled old man.*
griz·zly (grĭz' lē) *adj-* [griz·zli·er, griz·zli·est] grayish; grizzled. *n-* [*pl.* griz·zlies] grizzly bear. *Hom-* grisly.
grizzly bear *n-* large bear of the mountains of northwestern North America, having brown, white-tipped hair.
Grizzly bear, 8-10 ft. long
gros·beak (grōs' bēk) *n-* any of several birds related to the finches, such as the **rose-breasted grosbeak**, the male of which is black and white, with a rose-colored breast.
gros·grain (grō' grān') *n-* fabric of heavily corded silk or rayon. *as modif-: a grosgrain hatband.*
gross (grōs) *adj-* 1 including everything; total: *the gross profits of a business.* 2 thick; heavy: *the gross body of a hippopotamus.* 3 very bad and easily seen; glaring: *a gross mistake.* 4 coarse; vulgar: *Her gross manners offended her companions.* *n-* [*pl.* gross] 12 dozen; 144. *vt-* to earn as a total sum, without deductions: *He grosses $500,000 a year.* —*adv-* **gross' ly.** *n-* **gross' ness.**

ground (ground) *n-* 1 surface of the earth; land; soil: *to touch* ground; *fertile* ground; *frozen* ground 2 land for a particular use: *hunting* grounds. 3 land beneath a body of water: *The ship hit* ground. 4 in electricity, a conductor or connection that leads an electric current into the earth. 5 **grounds** (1) land around a building or house. (2) basis; reasons: *the grounds for his defense.* (3) sediment or dregs, especially of coffee, left over after brewing. *vt-* 1 to establish; found: *to ground a government on democratic principles.* 2 to run (a ship) aground. 3 to teach (someone) the fundamentals of a subject: *to ground someone in algebra.* 4 to connect (an electrical conductor) with the earth. 5 to force (an airplane or pilot) to stay on land. *vi-* 1 to fall to or reach the earth; land: *The astronauts have grounded safely.* 2 to run aground: *The ship* grounded. 3 in electricity, to become connected with or lead into the earth. 4 in baseball, to hit a grounder. [from Old English **grūnd**.]

group (groop) *n-* 1 number of persons or things clustered together or considered as a whole: *a group of people on the street corner; the science group.* 2 *Biology* any number of plants or animals considered to have common qualities. 3 *Chemistry* two or more atoms, forming a part of a molecule, that react as a single unit: *the hydroxyl group* (OH^-) 4 *Mathematics* a set of elements that satisfy the conditions of closure, identity, inverse, and the associative law, when a given operation is performed. *as modifier:* a group activity. *vi-* to gather together: *The people* grouped *slowly.* *vt-* to arrange or place together: *to group chairs in circles.*

group·er (groo′ pər) *n-* [*pl.* **group·er**; **group·ers** (kinds of grouper)] any of various large fishes of warm seas, related to the sea basses.

group·ing (groo′ ping) *n-* arrangement in a group: *the grouping of people in a photo.*

¹**grouse** (grous) *n-* [*pl.* **grouse**] any of several wild birds related to and resembling the domestic chicken and the pheasant. [probably from Old French *griesche* or *greoches* meaning "gray."]

²**grouse** (grous) *Informal vi-* [groused, grous·ing] to complain; grouch. *n-* complaint. *—n-* grous′ er. [of uncertain origin.]

Ruffed grouse about 18 in long

grove (grōv) *n-* group of trees growing together: *a grove of birches: an orange* grove; *a pine* grove.

grov·el (grŏv′ əl, grŭv′-) *vi-* 1 to lie flat or crawl on the ground, as if begging for mercy: *to grovel in the dust.* 2 to act in a cringing, servile manner. *—n-* grov′ el·er.

grow (grō) *vi-* [grew (groo), grown (grōn), grow·ing] 1 of a living organism, to become bigger by natural development; increase in size by the multiplication of cells. 2 to spring up naturally; come from seed: *Daisies grow in meadows.* 3 to increase: *The volume of their shouts grew to a roar.* 4 to become: *The sky began to grow dark.* *vt-* 1 to plant and care for; cultivate: *He grows tomatoes ≀ his garden.* 2 to develop: *to grow a mustache.*

grow on (or **upon**) to become gradually more attractive to: *This painting grows on me.*

grow out of 1 to be a result of: *Most prejudices grow out of ignorance.* 2 to get too big or mature for: *to grow out of one's clothes; to grow out of bad habits.*

grow up to become an adult.

grow·er (grō′ ər) *n-* 1 something that grows in a certain way: *That plant is a fast grower.* 2 person who cultivates a particular kind of plant: *a grower of tomatoes.*

growl (groul) *n-* low, threatening sound, such as that made by an angry dog, or a surly or irritated person. *vi-:* *The bear* growled *at the crowd. vt-:* *Jack* growled *an answer to his roommate. —n-* growl′ er.

grown (grōn) *p.p.* of **grow**. *adj-* fully developed; mature. *Hom-* groan.

grown·up (grōn′ ŭp′) *Informal n-* an adult; mature person.

grown-up (grōn′ ŭp′) *adj-* of or suitable for an adult

guard (gärd) *vt-* 1 to protect or defend from harm, theft, etc.: *to guard a city; to guard a collection of gems.* 2 to watch over: *to guard a prisoner; to guard one's speech.* 3 in some games, to protect (a card or piece); also, to prevent (an opponent) from scoring. *n-* 1 protection; defense: *Vaccination is our best* guard *against smallpox.* 2 man or body of men employed to control or protect: *a prison* guard; *the President's* guard. 3 a device for protection: mudguard; *shoulder* guard. 4 in fencing, a position of defense. 5 either of two football players on each side of the center of a forward line. 6 one of the defensive players in basketball.

keep guard to watch over. **off guard** unprepared to defend oneself or respond: *The teacher caught him* off guard *with a question.* **on guard** wary; in position to defend oneself. **on (one's) guard** prepared against danger or surprise: *Be* on your guard *against hitchhikers.* **stand guard** to act as a sentry.

guard against to prevent by being careful and watchful: *to guard against colds; to guard against mistakes.*

guard cell *n-* one of the two crescent-shaped cells that control the flow of gases into and out of the stomata of plants by regulating the size of the opening.

guard·ed (gär′ dəd) *adj-* 1 protected: *a heavily guarded fort.* 2 careful; cautious: *a guarded answer.*

guard·i·an (gär′ dē ən) *n-* 1 person or thing that protects: *The Bill of Rights is the* guardian *of our liberties.* 2 person who, by law, has the care of another person or his property or both.

guard·i·an·ship (gär′ dē ən ship′) *n-* position, duties, and rights of a guardian.

guard·rail (gärd′ rāl′) *n-* 1 handrail or bar placed alongside some dangerous area or valuable object to prevent accidents or damage. 2 safety rail or beam laid parallel to railway tracks to help keep the wheels in position at dangerous points.

guard·room (gärd′ room′) *n-* 1 the room occupied by a military guard on duty. 2 place of temporary imprisonment for soldiers.

gua·va (gwä′ və) *n-* tree or shrub of tropical America, yielding a pear-shaped fruit from which various preserves are made; also, the fruit.

gua·yu·le (gwī ōō′ lě) *n-* shrub of Mexico and southwestern United States· that yields a rubber; also, the rubber produced from this plant.

gu·ber·na·to·ri·al (goo′ bər nə tôr′ ē əl) *adj-* of or relating to a governor or to his office: *a gubernatorial election.*

gudg·eon (gŭj′ ən) *n-* [*pl.* **gudg·eon**; **gudg·eons** (kinds of gudgeon)] 1 any of several small European fishes related to the carp and used for bait. 2 any of various other fishes, including some minnows.

guer·don (gûr′ dən) *n-* a reward for courage.

guer·ril·la or **gue·ril·la** (gə ril′ə) *n-* person who carries on irregular warfare; especially, one of an independent band engaged in harassing an enemy in wartime; partisan. *as modifier:* in guerrilla *warfare.* *Hom-* gorilla.

guess (gĕs) *vt-* 1 to form an opinion of without certain knowledge: *Historians* guess *that the Gypsies originated in India.* 2 to estimate; surmise: *to guess one's weight.* 3 to solve correctly by surmising: *He* guessed *it!* 4 to think; suppose: *I* guess *we should hurry.* *vi-:* *He doesn't know; he is only* guessing. *n-:* *His* guess *about the weather was wrong. —n-* guess′ er.

guess·work (gĕs′ wûrk′) *n-* result obtained by guessing; conjecture.

guest (gĕst) *n-* 1 person who is entertained by a host. 2 person who stays temporarily at a hotel, inn, etc.

guff (gŭf) *Slang n-* stuff and nonsense; baloney.

guf·faw (gə fô′) *n-* coarse or loud burst of laughter. *vi-:* *He* guffawed *over the crude joke.*

guid·ance (gī′ dəns) *n-* 1 a guiding: *the policeman's* guidance *of traffic.* 2 advice given to a person about what studies or job he should choose, or about personal problems; also, the profession and study of such counseling. 3 the controlling of a guided missile's route. *as modifier:* a guidance *counselor; a* guidance *system.*

guide (gīd) *n-* 1 person who shows the way or directs; especially, a person hired or paid to conduct hunting or fishing trips, visits through museums, etc. 2 thing that shows the way: *A compass was our guide.* 3 device that regulates or directs the position or motion of something: *a paper guide on a typewriter.* 4 person or thing taken as a model. 5 a guidebook. *vt-* [guid·ed, guid·ing] 1 to lead; steer: *Tugs guided the ship into the dock. The President guided us to peace.* 2 to direct; instruct: *The book guided us in the repair of the car.*

guide·book (gīd' bŏŏk') *n-* book of directions, information, etc., about a museum, travel. etc.

guided missile *n-* missile whose course may be changed during flight either by radio, by a preset program, or by its response to surrounding forces.

guide·post (gīd' pōst') *n-* post or marker to direct travelers.

guide word *n-* in a reference work, one of the two words at the top of a page, over the columns of text, which show the first and last entries on that page.

gui·don (gī' dən) *n-* 1 small standard or flag for a single company of troops. 2 the person who carries it.

guild (gĭld) *n-* 1 in the Middle Ages, an organization of men in the same trade or craft whose aim was to keep their standards high and protect their interests. 2 organization of people for a common purpose. *Hom-* gild.

guild·er (gĭl' dər) *n-* Dutch silver coin; also, the monetary unit of the Netherlands; gulden.

guild·hall (gĭld' hôl') *n-* meeting place of a guild.

guile (gīl) *n-* sly trickery; deceit; cunning: *He used guile to get his way.* —*adj-* guile'ful. *adv-* guile'ful·ly. *n-* guile'ful·ness.

guile·less (gīl' ləs) *adj-* free from guile; innocent; frank; open. —*adv-* guile'less·ly. *n-* guile'less·ness.

guil·le·mot (gĭl' ə mŏt') *n-* any of several narrow-billed auks found in northern seas.

guil·lo·tine (gĭl' ə tēn') *n-* apparatus for beheading a person by means of a heavy, slanted knife dropping between two upright guides. *vt-* [guil·lo·tined, guil·lo·tin·ing] to behead with this instrument.

Guillotine

guilt (gĭlt) *n-* 1 the fact of having done something wrong, especially of having broken a law: *to establish the guilt of the accused man.* 2 the feeling of having done wrong, whether real or imaginary. *Hom-* gilt. —*adj-* guilt'less. *adv-* guilt'less·ly.

guilt·y (gĭl' tē) *adj-* [guilt·i·er, guilt·i·est] 1 deserving of blame: *Who was guilty of singing off key?* 2 responsible for a crime; convicted: *The jury declared him guilty of robbery.* 3 showing guilt; having to do with guilt: *a guilty look; a guilty conscience.* —*adv-* guilt'i·ly. *n-* guilt'i·ness.

guin·ea (gĭn' ē) *n-* 1 formerly, a British gold coin worth 21 shillings. 2 now, a British monetary unit equal to 21 shillings.

guinea fowl *n-* 1 gray-and-white speckled domestic fowl having a small featherless head with a bright-red comb. 2 flesh of this fowl, as food. Also **guinea hen.**

Guinea fowl
about 18 in long

guinea pig *n-* small, plump, gentle animal of the rat family, with short legs and short ears. The guinea pig is kept for a pet or for experiments.

Guin·e·vere (gwĭn' ə vēr', -vər) *n-* in Arthurian legend, wife of King Arthur. She was in love with Lancelot.

guise (gīz) *n-* 1 external appearance; likeness: *Henry arrived in the guise of a sailor.* 2 cloak; pretense: *to cheat a man under the guise of friendship.*

Guinea pig
about 9 in long

gui·tar (gĭ tär') *n-* musical instrument having six strings and a hollow wooden body. It is played by plucking the strings with the fingers or a pick.

Guitar

gulch (gŭlch) *n-* ravine; gorge.

gul·den (gŏŏl' dən) *n-* guilder.

gulf (gŭlf) *n-* 1 large area or arm of a sea or ocean, partly enclosed by land. 2 deep hollow in the earth; abyss. 3 wide separation: *The quarrel left a gulf between them.*

gulf·weed (gŭlf' wēd') *n-* sargasso.

¹**gull** (gŭl) *n-* large, light-colored, web-footed sea bird of graceful, often hovering, flight, found everywhere near coasts. It is a valuable scavenger and is protected by law in many places. [perhaps from Welsh gwylan or Cornish gullan.]

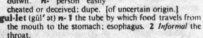

Herring gull
about 2 ft long

²**gull** (gŭl) *vt-* to cheat; deceive; outwit. *n-* person easily cheated or deceived; dupe. [of uncertain origin.]

gul·let (gŭl' ət) *n-* 1 the tube by which food travels from the mouth to the stomach; esophagus. 2 *Informal* the throat.

gul·li·ble (gŭl' ə bəl) *adj-* easily fooled or deceived. —*n-* gul'li·bil'i·ty. *adv-* gul'li·bly.

gul·ly (gŭl' ē) *n-* [*pl.* gul·lies] ditch or channel worn by water. *vt-* [gul·lied, gul·ly·ing]: *Heavy rains gullied the hillside.*

gulp (gŭlp) *vt-* 1 to swallow quickly or greedily: *The horse gulped the water.* 2 to hold back as if by swallowing; stifle: *to gulp back a sob. vi-* to catch one's breath as if swallowing: *He gulped with relief. n-* big swallow: *to empty a glass in one gulp.* —*n-* gulp'er.

¹**gum** (gŭm) *n-* 1 sticky substance obtained from trees. It dissolves in water but hardens in the air. It is used in making glue, drugs, and other products. 2 this or a similar substance prepared for some industrial use, as in drugs. 3 chewing gum. 4 natural rubber. 5 gum tree. 6 gums rubber overshoes. *vt-* [gummed, gum·ming] to smear or stick with mucilage or glue: *to gum a stamp. vi-* to become stiff or sticky. [from Old French gomme, from Latin gummi, from Greek kommi.]

²**gum** (gŭm) *n-* firm, pink flesh around the roots of the teeth. [from Old English gōma meaning "palate."]

gum tree *n-* any of various trees which exude gum.

gum·wood (gŭm' wŏŏd') *n-* wood of a gum tree.

gun (gŭn) *n-* 1 weapon that shoots a projectile by the force of exploding gunpowder or compressed air; firearm. Rifles, pistols, and cannons are guns. 2 tool that shoots something out: *a grease gun; a spray gun.* 3 a shooting of a gun as a salute or signal: *a salute of twenty-one guns; a starting gun.* 4 *Slang* a throttle. *vi-* [gunned, gun·ning] to shoot or hunt with a firearm. *vt-* 1 to shoot (a person). 2 to open up the throttle of.

give (something) the gun Slang to speed something up.
go great guns Slang to go along or perform at a top level of speed and efficiency. *spike (someone's) guns* to spoil another's plans. *stick to one's guns* to be firm; not yield or retreat.

gun down to shoot and destroy.
gun for 1 to pursue in order to harm or kill. 2 to aim for (a favor, position, etc.); seek for.

gun·boat (gŭn' bōt') *n-* small warship for use on rivers and coastal waters.

gun carriage *n-* the structure, often with wheels, upon which a cannon is mounted.

gun·cot·ton (gŭn' kŏt' ən) nitrocellulose.

gun·fire (gŭn' fīr') *n-* the shooting off of guns; firing.

gun·lock (gŭn′lŏk′) *n-* mechanism of a gun that controls the hammer or firing pin to fire the charge, especially in old types of guns such as the flintlock.

gun·man (gŭn′mən) *n-* [*pl.* **gun·men**] man armed with a gun, usually for criminal purposes.

gun metal *n-* 1 variety of bronze, formerly used in making cannon, etc. 2 metal alloy treated to look like this bronze. 3 the color of this bronze, dark gray with a blue or purple tinge. *adj-* (**gun-metal**): *a gun-metal plate; a gun-metal sky.*

gun moll *Slang n-* armed female gangster.

gun·nel (gŭn′əl) *n-* gunwale.

gun·ner (gŭn′ər) *n-* 1 man whose duty is firing a gun, especially on a military ship or airplane. 2 in the Navy and Marine Corps, a warrant officer in charge of guns and gunnery supplies. 3 person who hunts with a gun.

gun·ner·y (gŭn′ə rē) *n-* science of artillery; the knowledge and use of guns.

gun·ning (gŭn′ĭng) *n-* the hunting of game, especially small game, with a gun.

gun·ny (gŭn′ē) *n-* [*pl.* **gun·nies**] 1 strong, coarse material made of jute or hemp fiber, used in baling. 2 (also **gunny sack**) bag or sack made of this material: *The gunny of flour split open.*

gun·pit *n-* an excavation in which artillery is placed for concealment.

gun·shot (gŭn′shŏt′) *n-* 1 shot fired from a gun. 2 range of a gun: *The bear was within gunshot.*

gun·shy (gŭn′shī′) *adj-* afraid of a gun or the sound of gunfire: *a gun-shy horse.*

gun·smith (gŭn′smĭth′) *n-* person who makes or repairs firearms.

gun·stock (gŭn′stŏk′) *n-* shaped or molded part of a gun, usually of wood, by which it is held.

gun·wale (gŭn′əl) *n-* upper edge of the side of a boat.

gup·py (gŭp′ē) *n-* [*pl.* **gup·pies**] tiny fresh-water fish often kept in aquariums because of its bright coloring.

gur·gle (gûr′gəl) *vi-* [**gur·gled, gur·gling**] 1 to flow with a bubbling sound: *The brook gurgled.* 2 to make this sound: *The baby gurgled.* *n-: the gurgle of milk poured from a bottle.*

gush (gŭsh) *vi-* 1 to burst out violently; pour forth suddenly: *Oil gushed from the well.* 2 *Informal* to speak with too much enthusiasm, admiration, etc.: *The caller gushed over the baby.* *vt-: The volcano gushed lava.* *n-* 1 sudden bursting out: *a gush of blood; a gush of anger.* 2 *Informal* silly, sentimental talk or display of affection.

gush·er (gŭsh′ər) *n-* 1 oil well with a strong, natural flow that makes pumping unnecessary. 2 *Informal* person who speaks sentimentally and effusively.

gush·ing (gŭsh′ĭng) *adj-* 1 pouring out. 2 *Informal* sentimental; effusive: *a gushing manner.* —*adv-* **gush·ing·ly.**

gush·y (gŭsh′ē) *Informal adj-* [**gush·i·er, gush·i·est**] given to being effusive or sentimental: *a gushy person.* —*adv-* **gush′i·ly.** *n-* **gush′i·ness.**

gus·set (gŭs′ət) *n-* 1 small, triangular or diamond-shaped piece of cloth inserted in a garment to ease or widen a part, or strengthen a seam. 2 metal bracket for strengthening an angle.

gust (gŭst) *n-* 1 sudden rush or strong puff of wind. 2 outburst of feeling, as of laughter or rage.

gus·ta·to·ry (gŭs′tə tôr′ē) *adj-* having to do with the sense of taste: *Dinner was a gustatory joy.*

gus·to (gŭs′tō) *n-* zest; relish; enjoyment.

gust·y (gŭs′tē) *adj-* [**gust·i·er, gust·i·est**] 1 marked by bursts of wind: *a gusty day.* 2 given to sudden outbursts: *his gusty laughter.* —*adv-* **gust′i·ly.** *n-* **gust′i·ness.**

gut (gŭt) *n-* 1 alimentary canal; especially, the intestine. 2 catgut. 3 narrow channel or passage. 4 **guts** (1) bowels; entrails. (2) *Slang* courage; grit; also, impudence. *vt-* [**gut·ted, gut·ting**] 1 to extract the entrails from.

gut·ter·snipe (gŭt′ər snīp′) *n-* poor and tattered person, especially a child, who spends much time in the streets.

gut·tur·al (gŭt′ər əl) *adj-* 1 having to do with the throat. 2 harsh and grating, as when formed in the throat: *his guttural speech.* *n-* a sound formed or modified in the throat. Example: (g) as in "go." —*adv-* **gut′tur·al·ly.**

gut·ty (gŭt′ē) *Slang adj-* [**gut·ti·er, gut·ti·est**] showing or having vitality or impudence.

[1]**guy** (gī) *n-* wire or rope used to keep something steady: *the guys of a tent pole.* *vt-* to steady with such a wire or rope. [from Old French **guie,** from **guier,** "to guide."]

[2]**guy** (gī) *Informal n-* man; fellow. *vt-* to ridicule: *His friends guyed him good-naturedly.* [from an effigy (called a **guy**) which is burned in England every year on November 5 to commemorate the failure of **Guy Fawkes** to blow up the Houses of Parliament in 1605.]

guz·zle (gŭz′əl) *Informal vt-* [**guz·zled, guz·zling**] to drink greedily: *to guzzle a lemonade.* *vi-: He guzzled all evening.* —*n-* **guz′zler.**

gym (jĭm) *n-* gymnasium.

gym·na·si·um (jĭm nā′zē əm) *n-* 1 large room or building for athletic practice or indoor sports. 2 **Gymnasium** in some European countries, a secondary school equivalent to high school and the first two years of college in the United States. *as modifier: the gymnasium floor.*

gym·nast (jĭm′nǎst′) *n-* person skilled in gymnastics.

gym·nas·tics (jĭm nǎs′tĭks) *n- pl.* 1 (takes singular verb) special physical exercises such as tumbling, rope climbing, etc., for developing the body. 2 vigorous exercise or twistings of the body. —*adj-* **gym·nas′tic.**

gym·no·sperm (jĭm′nō spûrm′) *n-* any of a group of plants, (**Gymnospermae**), producing seeds without a seed case or true fruit. See also **angiosperm.**

gy·ne·col·o·gist (jīn′ə kŏl′ə jĭst, gī′nə-) *n-* doctor who specializes in the treatment of women's diseases and disorders. —*n-* **gy′ne·col′o·gy.**

gyp (jĭp) *Slang vt-* [**gypped, gyp·ping**] to cheat or defraud. *n-* 1 fraud; swindle. 2 (also **gypper**) a cheat; swindler.

gyp·sum (jĭp′səm) *n-* mineral calcium sulfate ($CaSO_4·2H_2O$), used in making plaster of Paris.

Gyp·sy (jĭp′sē) *n-* [*pl.* **Gyp·sies**] 1 member of a wandering Caucasian people with dark skin and black hair, who probably migrated from India to Europe around 1500. 2 the language of these people; Romany. *adj-: a Gypsy violinist; a Gypsy fortuneteller.* Also **Gip′sy.**

gy·ro (jī′rō) *n-* 1 gyroscope. 2 gyrocompass.

gyro- *combining form* functioning by means of a gyroscope: *a gyrostabilizer.* [from Greek **gyros** meaning "a ring; circle."]

gy·ro·com·pass (jī′rō kŭm′pəs) *n-* a compass that is kept pointing north by a gyroscope.

gy·ro·ho·ri·zon (jī′rō hə rī′zən) *n-* gyroscopic instrument in an airplane that shows whether the plane is pointing up or down or tilting left or right.

gy·ro·pi·lot (jī′rō pī′lət) *n-* mechanism in an airplane or boat, controlled by a gyroscope, and which automatically holds the craft on a preset line of travel.

gy·ro·scope (jī′rə skōp′) *n-* device consisting of a heavy wheel mounted on gimbals. When the wheel is spinning rapidly, its axis tends to point in the same direction, no matter how the mounting is titled. Gyroscopes are used in navigational instruments, rocket guidance systems, and as toys, etc.

Gyroscope

gy·ro·scop·ic (jī′rə skŏp′ĭk) *adj-* 1 of or relating to a gyroscope or its action. 2 controlled by a gyroscope.

gy·ro·sta·bi·liz·er (jī′rō stā′bə līz′ər) *n-* gyroscopic mechanism designed to reduce the rolling motion of a ship or airplane.

gyve (jīv) *Archaic n-* fetter for the leg. *vt-* [**gyved, gyv·ing**] to fetter or shackle. **Hom-** jive.

H

H, h (āch) *n-* [*pl.* **H's, h's**] eighth letter of the English alphabet.

H 1 symbol for hydrogen. 2 symbol for henry.

ha (hä) *interj-* exclamation expressing wonder, suspicion, doubt, mirth, joy, etc.

hab·it (hăb′ ĭt) *n-* 1 action repeated so often that one does it automatically: *the* habit *of nail biting.* 2 usual practice; custom: *the habit of a daily walk.* 3 addiction: *the tobacco habit.* 4 usual mental or moral pattern or make-up: *the scientist's* habit *of mind.* 5 type of dress worn for a certain activity or by members of a religious group, or the like. *vt-* to dress (oneself): *They* habited *themselves in black.*

Habits

NUNS   RIDING

hab·it·a·ble (hăb′ ə tə bəl) *adj-* fit or suitable for living in: *a* habitable *house.*

¹**hack** (hăk) *vt-* to cut unevenly or irregularly: *He* hacked *the loaf of bread into chunks.* *vi-* 1 to make rough cuts: *He* hacked *at the tree.* 2 to give short dry coughs. *n-* 1 a cut or gash. 2 short, dry cough. [from Old English *haccian.*]

²**hack** (hăk) *n-* 1 coach, carriage, or taxi for hire. 2 horse for hire. 3 all-purpose horse. 4 one who does dull work for hire: *a literary* hack. *adj-* 1 of or for a taxi or hired carriage, etc.: *a* hack *stand.* 2 done, or working, merely for money; hired: *to do* hack *work; a* hack *writer.* [short for **hackney**, from **Hackney**, England, a town where people would hire horses for a journey outbound from London. Some horses were worn-out nags.]

hack·a·more (hăk′ ə môr′) *n-* rawhide or rope halter used chiefly for breaking horses. [American word, probably from Spanish *jáquima* meaning "halter."]

hack·ber·ry (hăk′ bĕr′ ē) *n-* [*pl.* **hack·ber·ries**] 1 any of several U.S. trees or coarse shrubs related to the elm. 2 the sweet, red or dark-purple edible berry of these.

hack·le (hăk′ əl) *n-* neck plumage of a domestic fowl.

hack·man (hăk′ mən) *n-* [*pl.* **hack·men**] driver of a carriage or cab.

hack·ney (hăk′ nē) *n-* [*pl.* **hack·neys**] 1 horse used chiefly for riding or driving. 2 carriage or hack kept for hire. *vt-* to wear out by common use; hence, to make trite. *adj-* let out for hire: *a* hackney *coach.*

¹**hail** (hāl) *n-* 1 rounded bits of ice, usually small, that fall in showers like rain; hailstones. 2 anything that falls like hailstones: *a* hail *of rocks; a* hail *of curses.* *vi-* to rain hailstones. *vt-* to shower; pour down: *to* hail *blows upon someone.* [from Old English *hægel* with the same meaning.] *Hom-* hale.

²**hail** (hāl) *vt-* 1 to call out to in greeting: *to* hail *a friend.* 2 to signal: *to* hail *a taxi.* *n-* 1 a greeting. 2 a shout. [from an ancient greeting *be* heil(l) meaning "be hale; be of good health." **Heill** is an Old Norse word related to ¹hale.] *Hom-* hale. —*n-* **hail′ er.**

within hail within shouting distance.

hail from to come from: *He* hails from *Omaha.*

hail-fel·low (hāl′ fĕl′ ō) *adj-* comradely; friendly and informal: *The convention was a* hail-fellow *affair.* Also **hail-fel′ low-well-met.**

hail·stone (hāl′ stōn′) *n-* ball or pellet of ice that is formed in thunder clouds.

hail·storm (hāl′ storm′, -storm′) *n-* storm of hail.

hair (hâr) *n-* 1 mass of threadlike growths forming the coat or fur of an animal, or such natural growth on a person's skin. 2 any one of these threadlike growths. 3 something resembling these growths, such as the fibers on some plants. 4 very small distance, space, or degree: *The bullet missed him by a* hair. *Hom-* hare. —*adj-* **haired:** *a long-haired dog.* *adj-* **hair′ like′.**

not turn a hair to remain absolutely calm. **split hairs** to make tiny distinctions in an argument.

hair·ball (hâr′ bôl′) *n-* ball of fur which forms in the stomach of animals that lick their fur.

hair·pin (hâr′ pĭn′) *n-* metal or plastic pin with two prongs, used to hold the hair in place. *adj-* U-shaped; doubling back on itself like such a pin: *a* hairpin *turn.*

hair-rais·ing (hâr′ rā′ zĭng) *adj-* terrifying.

hair·split·ter (hâr′ splĭt′ ər) *n-* person who insists upon petty and unimportant distinctions in reasoning; quibbler. —*n-* **hair′ split′ ting.**

hair·spring (hâr′ sprĭng′) *n-* delicate, hairlike spring which regulates the balance wheel in a watch.

hair-trig·ger (hâr′ trĭg′ ər) or **hair-trig·gered** (-ərd) *adj-* 1 reacting quickly to the slightest pressure or stimulus: *a* hair-trigger *temper.* 2 very quick; split-second: *He swerved in a* hair-trigger *response to danger.*

hair trigger *n-* gun trigger so adjusted that a mere touch discharges the weapon.

hair·y (hâr′ ē) *adj-* [**hair·i·er, hair·i·est**] 1 covered with hair: *a* hairy *animal.* 2 of or like hair: *the* hairy *husk of coconuts.* —*n-* **hair′ i·ness.**

Hai·tian (hā′ shən) *n-* 1 a native or inhabitant of Haiti. 2 the French dialect spoken by most of the people of Haiti. *adj-:* *a* Haitian *official.*

Haj or **Hadj** (hăj) *n-* pilgrimage to Mecca required of every Muslim at least once in his lifetime, after which he is called **Haj**i or **Hadj**i (hăj′ ē), and can use that title.

hake (hāk) *n-* [*pl.* **hake; hakes** (kinds of hake)] any of several ocean food fishes related to the cod.

hal·berd (hăl′ bərd) *n-* weapon of the 15th and 16th centuries combining spear and battle-ax. Also **hal′ bert** (hăl′ bərt).

hal·ber·dier (hăl′ bər dêr′) *n-* soldier armed with a halberd.

hal·cy·on (hăl′ sē ən) *n-* a fabled bird identified with the kingfisher and supposedly able to bring calm weather so that it might nest at sea. *adj-* peaceful; happy; calm: *summer's* halcyon *days.*

¹**hale** (hāl) *adj-* strong; healthy; robust. [from Old English *hāl,* related to **whole.**] *Hom-* hail.

²**hale** (hāl) *vt-* [**haled, hal·ing**] to pull or drag by, or as by, force: *to* hale *a man into court.* [from Old French *haler,* from a early Germanic word. It is related to **haul.**] *Hom-* hail.

half (hăf) *n-* [*pl.* **halves** (hăvz)] 1 either one of the two equal parts or groups into which an object or collection of objects can be divided: *He bought* half *of a cake. He sold* half *of his stamp collection.* 2 number that represents such a part. 3 thirty minutes: *It is* half *past nine.* 4 in football, basketball, etc., either of the two equal periods of a game, usually separated by an interval. 5 *Informal* a halfback. *adj-* 1 being either of the two equal, or roughly equal, parts: *a* half *pound; a* half *share in the company.* 2 partial; incomplete: *a* half *truth.* *adv-* partly; partially: *He was* half *asleep.*

do (something) by halves to do something badly or in an incomplete way. **go halves** *Informal* to share equally. **in half** into halves. **not by half** almost not at all; hardly at all. **not half bad** rather good.

half dollar *n-* silver coin of the United States and Canada, worth fifty cents.

half eagle *n-* former gold coin of the United States, worth five dollars.

half gainer *n-* dive made by leaping forward while doing half of a backward somersault and plunging into the water headfirst, facing the board.

half-heart·ed (hăf′ här′ təd) *adj-* lacking enthusiasm or interest: *a* halfhearted *attempt.* —*adv-* **half′ heart′ ed·ly.** *n-* **half′ heart′ ed·ness.**

half-hour (hăf′ our′) *n-* 1 a period of thirty minutes. 2 the point thirty minutes after the beginning of an hour: *The clock strikes on the* half-hour. *as modifier: a* half-hour *program.*

half-hour·ly (hăf′ our′ lə) *adj-* occurring once every thirty minutes, or at intervals of a half-hour: *a* half-hourly *signal.* *adv-: The clock struck* half-hourly.

half-life (hăf′ līf′) *Physics n-* amount of time during which half of the atoms in a given sample of a radioactive element disintegrate.

hal·ter (hôl´ tər) *n-* 1 rope or strap by which an animal is
is led or tied. 2 noose for hanging
criminals. 3 backless blouse that
ties around the neck.

halve (hăv) *vt-* [halved, halv·ing]
1 to divide something into two
equal parts: *to halve the melon.*
2 to lessen something by half: *This
machine halves the work.* **Hom-**
have.

halves (hăvz) *pl.* of **half.**

Halter

hal·yard (hăl´ yərd) *n-* rope or tackle on a ship, for
hoisting or lowering a sail, yard, or flag.

ham (hăm) *n-* 1 thigh of a hog, especially this part
smoked and salted, used as food. 2 the back of the thigh
and the buttock. 3 *Slang* actor or performer who
overacts. 4 *Informal* amateur radio operator. *vi-*
[hammed, ham·ming] *Slang* to perform in a showy,
exaggerated manner; overact.

Ham (hăm) *n-* in the Bible, the youngest son of Noah.

ham·a·dry·ad (hăm´ ə drī´ ăd´) *n-* 1 in Greek mythology,
a wood nymph. 2 king cobra. 3 baboon of northern
Africa.

Ha·man (hā´ mən) *n-* in the Old Testament, a Persian
high official who plotted to destroy the Jews, and was
hanged when his plot was disclosed to the king.

ham·burg·er (hăm´ bûr´ gər) *n-* 1 finely ground beef.
2 small part of such meat, especially one served on a
sliced roll or bun. Also **ham´ burg.** [American word, a
special use of German **Hamburger** meaning "coming
from (the city of) Hamburg."]

hame (hăm) *n-* one of the two curved bars on the collar
of a horse's harness, to which the traces are fastened.

ham·let (hăm´ lət) *n-* small village.

Ham·let (hăm´ lət) *n-* in Shakespeare's play of this name,
the hero, a prince of Denmark, who seeks to avenge his
father's murder.

ham·mer (hăm´ ər) *n-* 1 tool having a head of metal,
wood, etc., attached crosswise at the end of a handle,
and used for driving nails,
beating metals, etc. 2 anything resembling this in action or use, such as a part of
a gun that strikes to detonate
the ammunition, or one of
the parts that strikes the

Hammers

strings of a piano. 3 the outer one of the three tiny,
sound-transmitting bones in the middle ear (for picture,
see *¹ear*). *vt-* 1 to pound or beat with or as if with a
heavy tool: *to hammer iron into horseshoes*; *to hammer
the table with one's fist.* 2 to drive, force, etc., by or as if
by pounding: *to hammer nails*; *to hammer a lesson into
someone's mind.* *vi-* to strike with heavy blows; pound;
bang: *to hammer against the door.* **—n-** **ham´ mer·er.**
adj- **ham´ mer·less.** *adj-* **ham´ mer·like´.**

hammer and tongs *Informal* with all one's strength or
energy: *to go at a task hammer and tongs.*

hammer away to work hard and persistently.

hammer out to work out by thought or effort: *to hammer
out one's difficulties.*

hammer and sickle *n-* emblem consisting of a crossed
hammer and sickle, shown on the flag of the Soviet
Union, and symbolizing the worker and the peasant.

ham·mer·head (hăm´ ər hĕd´) *n-* fierce shark having a
long head at right angles to its body, and eyes at the
ends of the head. For picture, see *shark.*

hal·i·but (hăl´ ə bət) *n-* [*pl.* **hal·i·but**; **hal·i·buts** (kinds
of halibut)] the largest of the flatfish, used as food.

hal·ite (hăl´ līt, hăl´ īt) *n-* rock salt; sodium chloride
(NaCl) as it is found in rocky deposits in the earth.

hal·i·to·sis (hăl´ ə tō´ səs) *n-* bad or unpleasant breath.

hall (hôl) *n-* 1 passageway leading to rooms in a building.
2 room, vestibule, etc., at the entrance of a building.
3 large room, especially one used for public gatherings.
4 public building: *the town hall.* 5 one of the buildings
of a college, university, etc. 6 *chiefly Brit.* large, impressive home; manor house. **Hom-** haul.

hal·lah (кнä´ lə) chalah.

hal·le·lu·jah or **hal·le·lu·iah** (hăl´ ə lōō´ yə) *n-* cry or
song of praise to God. *interj-* "Praise be to God."

hall·mark (hôl´ märk´) *n-* mark stamped on gold or
silver articles to testify to their purity; hence, any
distinguishing characteristic or mark of genuineness.
vt- to stamp with such a mark.

hal·loo (hə lōō´) *n-* a shout to attract attention, to urge
on hounds in a hunt, etc.: *loud halloos for help.* *interj-*:
He shouted "Halloo!" to his hounds. *vi-*: *The hunter
hallooed to his hounds.*

hal·low (hăl´ ō) *vt-* to make sacred; set apart or honor as
holy; consecrate.

hal·lowed (hăl´ ōd´) *adj-* 1 made holy; consecrated:
Parts of Jerusalem are hallowed ground. 2 honored or
regarded as sacred: *our hallowed traditions.*

Hal·low·een (hăl´ ō ēn´) *n-* evening of October 31;
eve of All Saints' Day. Also **Hal·low·e'en.**

hal·lu·ci·na·tion (hə lōō´ sə nā´ shən) *n-* a seeming to
see, hear, or experience something which is not there,
especially as a result of illness, stimulation by a drug,
etc.; also, something seen or experienced thus.

hall·way (hôl´ wā´) *n-* entrance hall or passageway in a
building; corridor.

ha·lo (hā´ lō) *n-* [*pl.* **ha·los** or **ha·loes**] 1 circle of light
around a shining body, such as the sun or moon. 2 in
pictures, a ring, disk, or burst of light, surrounding or
above the heads of holy persons; also, anything resembling this. 3 glory or splendor with which one en-
dows a person or an object highly prized. *vt-* to surround
with, or as if with, a circle of light.

ham·mock (hăm´ ək) *n-* swinging bed made of heavy
cloth or a network of cords, and suspended by cords at
both ends.

¹ham·per (hăm´ pər) *n-* large
basket or similar container,
having a cover and often
made of wicker: *a picnic
hamper; a clothes hamper.*
[from Old French **hanapier,**
"a case to hold a cup," from
early Germanic **knap(p),** "a
beaker."]

Hammock

²ham·per (hăm´ pər) *vt-* to obstruct or hinder the motion
of; impede: *His heavy equipment hampered his progress.*
[from Middle English **hampren** of the same meaning.]

ham·ster (hăm´ stər) *n-* small rodent with a short tail
and cheek pouches.

ham·string (hăm´ strĭng´) *n-* 1 in man, either of two
groups of tendons at the back of the knee. 2 in animals,
the large tendon above and behind the hock. *vt-*
[ham·strung (hăm´ strŭng´), ham·string·ing] 1 to lame
or cripple by cutting this tendon. 2 to hamper; frustrate:
His rivals hamstrung him.

hand (hănd) *n-* 1 the part of the arm below the wrist,
including the fingers. 2 a pointer on a dial. 3 skill;
deftness: *Try your hand at this game.* 4 handwriting:
I recognized his hand on the envelope. 5 workman;
assistant: *a hired hand; a farm hand.* 6 side: *to meet
trouble on every hand; to stand at the king's right hand.*
7 (often **hands**) control; power: *The matter is in your
hands.* 8 assistance: *Give me a hand in moving this desk.*
9 active part: *He had a hand in making this decision.*
10 in card playing, (1) a round of a game. (2) the cards
held by a player. (3) an individual player. 11 *Informal*
applause: *Give him a big hand.* 12 way of handling or
doing something; touch: *a light hand on the reins; the
hand of an artist.* 13 source: *knowledge at first hand.*
14 pledge of assurance; promise: *He gave me his hand
on the bargain.* 15 promise to marry or permit marriage
with. 16 measure of about four inches, used chiefly in
determining the height of horses. *vt-* to pass, give, etc.,
by, or as if by, holding with the fingers: *to hand someone
a book.* as *modifier:* a hand drill. **—adj-** **hand´ like´.**

at hand near; within reach in distance or time. **by hand**
using the hands rather than machines. **change hands** to pass
from one person to another. **clean hands** freedom from
blame or turpitude; innocence.

hand·craft (hănd′ krăft′) *n-* skilled use of the hands in making useful objects; also, an art or process requiring such skill; handicraft. —*adj-* hand′ craft ed: *a hand-crafted cabinet.*

hand·cuff (hănd′ kŭf′) *n-* one of a pair of hinged metal bracelets joined by a short chain and locked about a prisoner's wrist or wrists. *vt-: He handcuffed the prisoner.*

Handcuffs

hand·ed (hăn′ dəd) *adj-* 1 having or using a certain hand: *a left-handed pitcher.* 2 using hands in a certain way: *He was heavy-handed at the piano.* 3 requiring or using a certain number of hands: *a one-handed operation.*

hand·ful (hănd′ fŏŏl′) *n-* 1 amount one hand can hold: *a handful of clay; several handfuls of nails.* 2 very small number or amount: *Only a handful of people came.*

hand·grip (hănd′ grĭp′) *n-* 1 grip or clasp of the hand. 2 handle.

hand·i·cap (hăn′ dĭ kăp′) *n-* 1 something that hinders or prevents activities that are normal for others in the group; defect; disability; disadvantage; hindrance.

hang (hăng) *vt-* [**hung** (hŭng), **hang·ing**] 1 to suspend from a nail, hook, or the like: *to hang curtains; to hang a picture.* 2 to attach by hinges so that the object can swing to and fro: *to hang a door.* 3 [*p.p. & p.t.* **hanged**] to execute on the gallows. 4 to cause to droop: *He hung his head in shame.* 5 to decorate or cover with suspended things: *to hang a wall with pictures.* *vi-* 1 to dangle; be suspended: *a lamp hung from the ceiling.* 2 to loom (over) something threateningly: *The danger of a flood hung over the village.* 3 to depend (on or upon): *My decision hangs on your answer.* 4 to float: *Clouds hang over the city.* 5 to die by execution on the gallows. 6 to fall or drape in a certain way: *This curtain hangs well.* 7 to hold (on or onto) something for support: *to hang on to the banister.* *n-* 1 manner in which a thing falls or drapes: *the hang of a skirt.* 2 *Informal* right manner of doing or using; knack: *to get the hang of a new dance.*

hang around *Informal* to loiter or linger about.

hang back to be unwilling or reluctant.

hang fire to delay or be delayed, usually temporarily.

hang on 1 to keep trying, struggling, etc.; persist; not give up: *to hang on in spite of troubles.* 2 to listen very carefully to: *He hung on her words.*

hang out at *Slang* to frequent; hang around in.

hang over to be about to happen; threaten.

hang together to stick together; be of a piece.

hang up to put a telephone receiver back in place, and so end a telephone conversation.

▶HANG has two past tense forms. HANGED is used only to refer to executions. *He was hanged this morning at dawn.* For all other meanings use HUNG.

hang·ar (hăng′ ər) *n-* shed for housing airplanes and other aircraft. *Hom-* hanger.

hang·dog (hăng′ dôg′) *adj-* having an ashamed, cringing appearance: *a hangdog look.*

hang·er (hăng′ ər) *n-* 1 device such as a hook, peg, or wire frame upon which something may be hung: *a coat hanger.* 2 person who hangs something. *Hom-* hangar.

hang·er-on (hăng′ ər ŏn′) *n-* [*pl.* **hang·ers-on**] follower chiefly interested in his own profit; parasite.

hap·haz·ard (hăp′ hăz′ ərd) *adj-* happening by chance; not planned; aimless: *a haphazard conversation.* —*adv-* hap′ haz′ ard·ly. *n-* hap′ haz′ ard·ness.

hap·less (hăp′ ləs) *adj-* unlucky. —*adv-* hap′ less·ly. *n-* hap′ less·ness.

hap·ly (hăp′ lē) *Archaic adv-* perhaps; by chance.

hap·pen (hăp′ ən) *vi-* 1 to take place; occur: *How did the accident happen?* 2 to act by chance so as; chance: *We happened to meet on the street.*

happen on (or **onto**) to find by chance; meet with: *We happened on a house in the woods.*

happen to 1 to be the experience of: *What happened to John to make him so happy?* 2 to be the fate or disposition of; become of: *What happened to Jane?*

hap·py (hăp′ ē) *adj-* [**hap·pi·er, hap·pi·est**] 1 having or showing joy, pleasure, contentment, etc.: *a happy person; a happy smile.* 2 lucky; fortunate: *a happy turn of events.* 3 very apt; good: *a happy selection of colors.*

hap·py-go-luck·y (hăp′ ē gō lŭk′ ē) *adj-* gay; light-hearted; trusting to luck.

ha·ra·ki·ri (hăr′ ə kĭ′ rē) *n-* suicide by cutting open the abdomen with a dagger.

ha·rangue (hə răng′) *n-* long, noisy speech; tirade. *vt-* [**ha·rangued, ha·rangu·ing**] to address in this manner: *He harangued me about my poor showing.* *vi-: The speaker harangued for hours on the Senate floor.*

har·ass (hăr′ əs, hə răs′) *vt-* 1 to annoy or worry constantly: *The daily complaints harassed her.* 2 to trouble by raids or pillage. —*n-* har′ ass·ment or har·ass′ ment.

har·bin·ger (här′ bĭn jər) *n-* person or thing that announces what is coming: *a harbinger of doom.*

har·bor (här′ bər) *n-* 1 protected part of a sea, lake, or river which can serve as a shelter for ships. 2 any place of shelter or safety. *vt-* 1 to shelter or lodge: *He was forced to harbor an escaped convict.* 2 to keep in one's mind: *to harbor a grudge.* —*adj-* har′ bor·less.

hard (härd) *adj-* 1 solid; firm; rigid: *a hard bone.* 2 not easy; difficult: *a hard problem.* 3 strong; forceful; vigorous: *a hard blow on the chin.* 4 industrious; hard-working: *a hard worker.* 5 harsh; unsympathetic: *a hard face.* 6 heavy; severe: *a hard winter.* 7 containing a high percentage of alcohol: *Rum is hard liquor.* 8 of the letters "c" and "g," pronounced as in "cat" and "go." 9 of money, metal rather than currency; also, exchangeable for gold. *adv-* 1 with effort and energy: *He studied hard. He was breathing hard.* 2 with strength or violence: *to hit hard.* 3 in a painful manner: *He was hit hard by her deceit.* 4 so as to be solid: *to freeze hard.*

  hard and fast fixed; unchangeable. **hard by** close; near. **hard of hearing** deaf or partially deaf. **hard put** to it to have great difficulty. **hard up** *Informal* to be in great need of money.

hard-bit·ten (härd′ bĭt′ ən) *adj-* tough; unyielding: *a hard-bitten negotiator.*

hard-boiled (härd′ boild′) *adj-* 1 of an egg, boiled until white and yolk become solid. 2 *Informal* unfeeling; hardened by experience; tough: *a hard-boiled judge.*

hard coal *n-* anthracite.

hard·en (här′ dən) *vi-* 1 to become hard: *The mixture hardened as it dried.* 2 to become firm; steady: *The market hardened toward the end of the day.* 3 to become rigid, unbending, or unyielding: *Their courage hardened as the battle went against them.* 4 to become cruel and forbidding: *His heart hardened toward his nephews. Her face hardened in scorn.* *vt-: He hardened his muscles. The good news hardened the stock market.*

hard·head·ed (härd′ hĕd′ əd) *adj-* 1 not easily swayed by feeling; practical; shrewd: *a hardheaded businessman.* 2 stubborn; obstinate. —*adv-* hard′ head′ ed·ly. *n-* hard′ head′ ed·ness.

hard·heart·ed (härd′ här′ təd) *adj-* not showing pity or sympathy. —*adv-* hard′ heart′ ed·ly. *n-* hard′ heart′ ed·ness.

har·di·hood (här′ dĭ hŏŏd′) *n-* boldness; daring.

har·di·ness (här′ dĭ nəs) *n-* 1 strength; robustness. 2 hardihood; boldness.

hard·ly (härd′ lē) *adv-* 1 barely; scarcely: *There is hardly enough food.* 2 not likely: *That is hardly the case.*

hard-mouthed (härd′ moutht′) *adj-* of a horse, not sensitive to a bit in the mouth.

hard·ness (härd′ nəs) *n-* condition of being unyielding or hard; resistance to being dented, penetrated, or scratched: *The hardness of the diamond is such that it can cut glass.* See also *Moh's scale.*

hard palate *n-* bony part of the palate; the front part of the roof of the mouth. For picture, see *palate.*

hard·pan (härd′ păn′) *n-* 1 compact layer in soil, often clayey, that roots cannot penetrate. 2 solid foundation.

hard sauce *n-* creamed mixture of butter, powdered sugar, and flavoring, used on puddings.

hard sell *Informal n-* high-pressure advertising or salesmanship, often loud and fast-talking.

hard·ware (härd′wâr′) *n*- 1 tools, nails and screws, kitchen utensils, electrical fittings, etc., usually made of metal. 2 equipment that is solid and durable: *military hardware*. 3 side arms.

hard water *n*- water containing dissolved salts of calcium and magnesium, especially magnesium carbonate. Unless removed, these salts react with soap to form an insoluble scum in water.

hard·wood (härd′wŏŏd′) *n*- 1 strong, heavy wood from certain broadleaf trees such as the maple or oak. 2 tree that yields such wood. *adj*-: *a hardwood floor*.

har·dy (här′dē) *adj*- [har·di·er, har·di·est] 1 strong; robust; able to bear suffering or hardship: *A hardy soldier can march all night.* 2 daring; bold: *a hardy adventurer.* 3 of plants, able to endure extremes of temperature, moisture, etc. —*adv*- hard′i·ly.

hare (hâr) *n*- member of the rabbit family that jumps rather than runs. It has longer ears and more powerful legs than the rabbit and does not burrow. Some hares, such as the jackrabbit, are called rabbits. Hom- hair.

Varying hare. about 18 in. long

hare·bell (hâr′bĕl′) *n*- plant with a slender stalk and blue flowers shaped like bells.

hare-brained (hâr′brānd′) *adj*- silly; rash.

hare·lip (hâr′lĭp′) *n*- divided condition of the upper lip, existing from birth. —*adj*- hare′lipped′.

ha·rem (hâr′əm, här′-) *n*- 1 part of a Muslim house where the women live. 2 women who live in this area.

hark (härk) *vi*- to listen; listen closely (used especially as an exclamation).

hark back to go back or refer to: *This superstition harks back to the Middle Ages. He is always harking back to his war service.*

hark·en (här′kən) *vi*- to listen closely; pay attention to.

har·mo·ni·za·tion (här′mə nə zā′shən) *n*- a putting or bringing into harmony: *the harmonization of ideas.*

har·mo·nize (här′mə nīz′) *vt*- [har·mo·nized, har·mo·niz·ing] 1 to bring into agreement or accord: *to harmonize colors.* 2 to cause to agree; reconcile: *to harmonize conflicting opinions.* 3 to arrange in musical harmony, as a melody. *vi*- 1 to play or sing in parts. 2 to be in agreement; blend: *The two styles of furniture harmonized.* —*n*- har′mo·niz′er.

har·mo·ny (här′mə nē) *n*- [*pl.* har·mo·nies] 1 pleasing combination or arrangement of parts, things, etc.: *the harmony of a color scheme.* 2 agreement in feelings, opinions, etc.: *the harmony between the two parties.* 3 pleasing combination of musical sounds. 4 *Music* combination of musical tones to form chords; also, the study of this.

Harness

har·ness (här′nəs) *n*- 1 arrangement of straps and metal pieces by which an animal is hitched to a vehicle or, sometimes, controlled for riding. 2 any such arrangement of straps. *vt*- 1 to put such an arrangement on (a horse, dog, etc.). 2 to make useful in a controlled way: *to harness a waterfall; to harness one's strength.*

harp (härp) *n*- large triangular musical instrument with many strings, played by plucking the strings with the fingers. *vi*- to play on such an instrument. —*n*- harp′er.

harp on (or **about**) to repeat or talk about at great length.

Woman playing harp

harp·ist (här′pĭst) *n*- person who plays a harp.

har·poon (här pōōn′) *n*- barbed spear with a rope attached, either shot from a gun or thrown, and used to catch whales, large fish, etc. *vt*- to strike or kill with a harpoon: *He harpooned a seal.* —*n*- har·poon′er.

Harpoons

harpoon gun *n*- gun that fires a harpoon.

harp·si·chord (härp′sə kôrd′, -kôrd′) *n*- keyboard instrument, developed before the piano, having wire strings that are plucked by quill or leather points.

Har·py (här′pē) *n*- [*pl.* Har·pies] 1 in Greek mythology, one of several filthy, winged monsters who are part woman and part bird. 2 **harpy** shrewish woman.

har·que·bus (här′kwə bəs) *n*- portable gun of the 15th and 16th centuries, later replaced by the musket.

Harquebus

har·ri·dan (här′ə dən) *n*- vicious, nasty old woman.

[1]**har·ri·er** (hă′ē ər) *n*- 1 cross-country runner. 2 small dog used to hunt hares. [from hare.]

[2]**har·ri·er** (här′ē ər) *n*- 1 person who harries. 2 any of various long-legged hawks. [from harry.]

har·row (här′ō) *n*- farm implement with sharp iron teeth or sharp steel disks. It is drawn by a horse or tractor over plowed land to break up the soil or cover up seed. *vt*- 1 to cultivate (land, a field, etc.) with such an implement. 2 to distress; trouble; disturb painfully: *Fear of failure harrowed him.* —*n*- har′row·er.

Disk harrow

har·row·ing (här′ō ĭng) *adj*- causing pain, fear, or torment: *The crash was a harrowing experience.*

har·ry (här′ē) *vt*- [har·ried, har·ry·ing] 1 to torment; vex: *He harried the speaker with many questions.* 2 to keep raiding; plunder: *Pirates harried the galleons.*

harsh (härsh) *adj*- [harsh·er, harsh·est] 1 unkind; hard; severe: *a harsh command.* 2 rough; coarse: *a harsh wool.* 3 unpleasant; disagreeable: *a harsh sound.* —*adv*- harsh′ly. *n*- harsh′ness.

hart (härt) *n*- male red deer over five years old; stag. Hom- heart.

harte·beest (här′tə bēst′) *n*- any of several large African antelopes with ringed horns.

harts·horn (härts′hôrn′, -hôrn′) *n*- 1 antler of a hart, formerly the chief source of ammonia. 2 preparation of ammonia, used mainly for smelling salts.

har·um-scar·um (hâr′əm skâr′əm, hăr′əm skär′-) *Informal adj*- reckless; rash; irresponsible. *adv*- in a reckless manner; rashly: *He ran harum-scarum into the fight. n*- person who behaves recklessly.

har·vest (här′vəst) *n*- 1 a ripe crop of grain, fruit, etc.: *a large harvest of apples.* 2 the gathering of a crop: *The farmer hired men for the wheat harvest.* 3 the season when crops are gathered, usually late summer or early fall. 4 result or reward: *His grades are the harvest of hard work. vt*- to gather in; reap: *to harvest corn. vi*-: *They harvested last week.*

har·vest·er (här′vəs tər) *n*- 1 person who gathers a crop; reaper. 2 machine for gathering crops, especially grain.

har·vest·man (här′vəst mən) *n*- [*pl.* har·vest·men] 1 daddy-longlegs. 2 man who harvests; harvester.

ha·ven (hā′ vən) *n-* 1 a sheltered harbor or port for ships. 2 any place of shelter or safety; refuge: *The weary travelers found haven at the inn.*

have-not (hăv′ nŏt′) *n-* person, group, or country with very little wealth or few resources. *as modifier: a* have-not *nation.*

have·n't (hăv′ ənt) have not.

hav·er·sack (hăv′ ər săk′) *n-* soldier's or hiker's canvas bag for carrying provisions, worn over the shoulders or hung by a strap from a shoulder.

hav·oc (hăv′ ək) *n-* wide and general destruction; ruin; devastation: *The hurricane caused havoc in the town.*

cry havoc to give the signal to an army for pillage and destruction. **play havoc** to destroy; ruin; devastate.

¹**haw** (hò) *n-* 1 the small, red, berrylike fruit of a hawthorn. 2 hawthorn. [from Old English **haga** meaning "a hawthorn fruit; a hedge."]

²**haw** (hò) *n-* sound made by a speaker who is unsure of himself or is searching for words. See also ²*hem.* [perhaps an imitation of the sound.]

³**haw** (hò) *interj-* command given to a horse, oxen, etc., to turn left. See also *gee. vi-: The horses hawed. vt-: He hawed the team of horses.* [of unknown origin.]

Ha·wai·ian (hə wî′ ən) *n-* 1 a native or naturalized citizen of Hawaii. 2 the Polynesian language of the Hawaiian Islands. *adj-: the Hawaiian guitar.*

¹**hawk** (hòk, hŏk) *n-* any of several swift, powerful birds of prey having a curved beak and sharp talons. Some kinds of hawks are trained to hunt other birds and small game. *vi-* to hunt with a hawk or falcon. [an alteration of Old English **hafuc.**] *Hom-* hock. *—adj-* **hawk′ like′.**

hay (hā) *n-* grass, clover, alfalfa, etc., cut and dried for food for cattle or horses. *vi-* to cut and dry grass, alfalfa, etc., for hay. *Hom-* hey.

hit the hay *Slang* to go to bed. **make hay** to take advantage of one's opportunities.

hay·cock (hā′ kŏk′) *n-* small, dome-shaped pile of hay stacked in a field.

hay fever *n-* sneezing, watery eyes, running nose, headache, etc., caused by an allergic reaction to the pollen of certain plants, especially ragweed.

hay·fork (hā′ fork′, -fôrk′) *n-* 1 long-handled pitchfork. 2 motor-driven mechanical fork for turning and moving hay.

hay·loft (hā′ lòft′, -lôft′) *n-* the upper part of a barn or stable, where hay is stored; haymow.

hay·mak·er (hā′ mā′ kər) *Slang n-* hard, swinging punch with the fist intended as a knockout blow.

hay·mow (hā′ mou′) *n-* 1 hayloft. 2 a pile of hay in a barn or stable.

hay·rack (hā′ răk′) *n-* 1 rack mounted on a wagon body for hauling hay. 2 rack for holding hay so that animals can eat it (for picture, see **rack**).

hay·rick (hā′ rĭk′) *n-* haystack.

hay·ride (hā′ rīd′) *n-* pleasure ride by a group in a wagon partly filled with hay.

hay·seed (hā′ sēd′) *n-* 1 grass seed that falls from hay when it is shaken. 2 *Slang* country person; yokel.

hay·stack (hā′ stăk′) *n-* large pile of hay stacked in the open air.

hay·wire (hā′ wîər′) *n-* wire for tying up bales of hay or straw. *adj- Informal* 1 poorly made, improvised, or repaired, as if hastily wired together: *a haywire contraption.* 2 not working properly; also, crazy: *The clock is haywire. He is haywire.*

haz·ard (hăz′ ərd) *n-* 1 the chance of harm, damage, or loss; danger; risk: *Arctic exploration is full of hazards.* 2 person, thing, or condition that can cause damage or destruction: *Reckless drivers and speeding cars are hazards to other motorists.* 3 on a golf course, a sand pit, pond, or other obstacle in which a ball may be trapped. 4 an old game played with dice, from which craps developed. *vt-* 1 to leave to chance; expose to danger; risk: *People who are careless with fire hazard their lives.* 2 to offer; venture: *He hazarded a guess.*

head (hěd) *n-* 1 the part of the body of man and most animals that contains the brain, mouth, eyes, ears, etc., and is located at the top of an upright body or the front of a four-legged or crawling body in ordinary motion. 2 the enlarged top part of something resembling this: *the head of a nail; the head of a hammer.* 3 top or upper part: *the head of a staircase; the head of a river; the head of a sail.* 4 front end: *the head of a parade; the train's head.* 5 the round, firm, top part of a plant: *a head of lettuce.* 6 of a bed, cot, bunk, etc., the end at which the upper part of the body lies. 7 top or highest position of rank, authority, etc.: *at the head of the government; at the head of the table.* 8 person of highest rank; chief; ruler: *the head of a company.* 9 picture or sculpture of the face and top part of a person; portrait: *a marble head of Caesar.* 10 topic or title: *He arranged his report under three heads.* 11 headline. 12 [*pl.* head] a single animal or person: *ten head of cattle; seats at ten dollars a head.* 13 (often **heads**) the main side of a coin, often stamped with the image of the face and top part of a person: *If it's heads I win, tails you win.* 14 mental ability; mind: *to have a good head for figures.* 15 foam or froth on top of a glass of beer, ale, etc. 16 the raised, middle, and sorest part of a pimple, boil, etc. 17 pressure or amount of pressure: *a good head of steam.* 18 the tight membrane of a drum, tambourine, etc., that one strikes to produce sound. *as modifier: the head man of a firm; the head car of the motorcade.* *vt-* 1 to be in charge of; lead; direct (often with "up"): *Our teacher heads the history department.* 2 to be at the front or top of; precede: *The honored guests headed the parade. Her name heads the honor roll.* 3 to cause to go in a certain direction: *The pilot headed his plane toward the sea.* 4 in soccer, to hit (the ball) with the head. *vi-* to go or move in a certain direction: *to head west; to head for danger. —adj-* **head′ less.**

bring to a head to bring to a climax or crisis: *The committee's new petition brought the entire matter to a head.* **come to a head** 1 to come to a climax or crisis. 2 to fill with pus, as a boil does. **give (someone) his head** to let someone go or do as he chooses. **go to (one's) head** 1 to make one conceited: *His quick success went to his head.* 2 to make one intoxicated. **hang (one's) head** to show that one is ashamed by or as if by lowering the head: *Bill is head and shoulders above Tom in tennis.* **head and shoulders above** much better than: *Bill is head and shoulders above Tom in tennis.* **head over heels** 1 in a somersault: *He stumbled and fell head over heels.* 2 completely; thoroughly: *They were head over heels in love.* **hide (one's) head** to show that one is ashamed by or as if by lowering the head or concealing the face. **keep (one's) head** to remain calm and self-controlled; not get excited: *He kept his head during the riot.* **keep (one's) head above water** to survive; avoid disaster: *Some poor families can barely keep their heads above water.* **lose (one's) head** to lose self-control; become excited: *The fans lost their heads and threw things at the umpire.* **make head or tail of** to make sense of; understand (usually expressed negatively): *He couldn't make head or tail of that poem.* **off** (or **out of**) one's **head** crazy; insane; irrational. **on** (or **upon**) one's **head** as one's total responsibility: *Let success or failure be on my head.* **(one's) head off** very much; excessively: *to laugh your head off; to talk his head off.* **over (one's) head** 1 too hard or strange to understand: *Nuclear physics is over my head.* 2 over the authority of another without consulting him: *He went over the supervisor's head and brought the matter to the president.* **put** (or **lay**) **heads together** to discuss or plan together; scheme. **take it into (one's) head** to get the idea or notion: *He took it into his head that he should be the manager.* **turn (one's) head** to cause to become conceited.

head off 1 to get in front of and turn aside: *The posse headed off the rustlers at the pass.* 2 to prevent; avert: *Quick thinking headed off a collision.*

head·ache (hěd′ āk′) *n-* 1 a continuous pain in the head. 2 *Informal* a cause of trouble or bother; annoyance.

head·board (hěd′ bôrd′) *n-* board or frame at or forming the head of a bed.

health (hĕlth) *n-* 1 freedom from sickness, deformity, etc.: Health *is a blessing.* 2 condition of the parts and the functioning of something, especially of the body or mind: *good* health; *failing* health; *the* health *of the steel industry.* 3 a toast to (a person's) happiness and good bodily condition: *to drink his* health. *as modifier: a* health *problem;* health *education; a* health *commissioner.*

health·ful (hĕlth′ fəl) *adj-* good for the health; giving health; wholesome: *a* healthful *food; a* healthful *climate.* —*adv-* **health′ ful·ly.** *n-* **health′ ful·ness.**
►Should not be confused with HEALTHY.

health insurance *n-* insurance coverage or policy that entitles one to medical care, hospitalization, etc., for the payment of a fixed periodic fee.

health·y (hĕl′ thē) *adj-* [health·i·er, health·i·est] 1 having good health: *a* healthy *child.* 2 showing good health or welfare: *a* healthy *appetite; a* healthy *glow in one's cheeks.* 3 contributing to safety or welfare: *a* healthy *respect for tigers.* —*adv-* **health′ i·ly.** *n-* **health′ i·ness.**
►Should not be confused with HEALTHFUL.

heap (hēp) *n-* 1 many things lying one on another; pile: *a* heap *of rocks.* 2 *Informal* a large amount; a lot: *a* heap *of money; a* heap *of trouble. vt-* 1 to put into a pile: *He* heaped *the baggage in one corner.* 2 to fill up; load: *The cook* heaped *each plate with meat and potatoes.* 3 to give in large amounts: *He* heaped *gifts on his grandchildren. They* heaped *insults on the enemy. vi-* to become piled: *Drifting snow* heaps *up quickly.*

hear (hēr) *vt-* [heard (hûrd), hear·ing] 1 to become aware of (sound waves or their source) through the ears: *I* hear *the crying of a baby. I* heard *the coyotes last night.* 2 to become informed of: *He* heard *the news on the radio.* 3 to pay attention to; listen to: *Please* hear *what I have to say.* 4 to give a chance to be heard, especially in a formal situation: *The king* heard *the petitioners. The judge* heard *three cases today.* 5 to grant: *Lord,* hear *our plea. vi-* 1 to be aware of sound through the ears: *A deaf person can't* hear. 2 to be told; get news; learn: *I never* heard *of it. Hom-* here. —*n-* **hear′ er.**

hear from 1 to get a message from. 2 to be dealt with or punished by: *Don't do it or you'll* hear *from me.*
hear out to listen to (someone) until he has finished.
will not hear of will not permit or agree to.

hear·ing (hēr′ ing) *n-* 1 the sense by which sound is perceived; ability to hear: *His* hearing *was impaired by the explosion.* 2 the distance over which sound can be heard: *In the park they kept the children within* hearing. 3 chance to be heard: *The mayor gave him a* hearing. 4 a formal meeting to discuss or investigate something.

hearing aid *n-* small battery-operated sound amplifier and speaker, worn in or near the ear to improve hearing.

heark·en (här′ kən) harken.

hear·say (hēr′ sā) *n-* something heard about from the talk of other persons; rumor; gossip. *adj-* based on what is heard from someone else, and not on personal knowledge: *a* hearsay *account;* hearsay *evidence.*

hearse (hûrs) *n-* vehicle for carrying a coffin at a funeral.

heart (härt) *n-* 1 the hollow, muscular organ in the chest that pumps blood through the body. 2 the innermost part; center; core: *the* heart *of the jungle;* hearts *of lettuce.* 3 one's deepest being or beliefs; true nature: *I knew in my* heart *that I was wrong. His* heart *was not in his work.* 4 state of mind; mood: *a heavy* heart. 5 tender feelings; sympathy; compassion: *His loneliness touched our* hearts. 6 courage: *the* heart *of a lion.* 7 energy; spirit; enthusiasm: *Put more* heart *into your work.* 8 a design [♥] pointed at the bottom and divided at the top into two equal lobes. 9 any one of a suit of playing cards marked with this design in red. 10 **hearts** (1) a suit of cards marked in this way. (2) a card game whose object is to win all or none of the cards so marked. *Hom-* hart.

heart·ache (härt′ āk′) *n-* sorrow; grief.

AORTA
PULMC IARY ARTERY
AURICLES
VENTRICLES
Human heart

hearth·stone (härth′ stōn′) *n-* 1 flat stone forming a hearth. 2 the center of a home; fireside.

heart·i·ly (här′ tə lē) *adv-* 1 in a warm, friendly way; cordially: *She greeted us* heartily. 2 enthusiastically: *They laughed* heartily. 3 with a good appetite. 4 completely; thoroughly: *I* heartily *agree with you.*

heart·i·ness (här′ tĭ nəs) *n-* 1 warmth; cordiality. 2 strength; vigor. 3 enthusiasm; zest. 4 abundance of appetite or food.

heart·land (härt′ lănd′) *n-* 1 most important region or center of some activity: *The Midwest is the* heartland *of American farming.* 2 in geopolitics, a region that gives its possessor control over surrounding regions and a position of great military strength.

heart·less (härt′ ləs) *adj-* without sympathy or pity; cruel; callous: *It is* heartless *to mistreat animals.* —*adv-* **heart′ less·ly.** *n-* **heart′ less·ness.**

heart-rend·ing (härt′ rĕn′ dĭng) *adj-* causing extreme grief; very distressing: *a* heart-rending *bit of news;* heart-rending *cries for help.* —*adv-* **heart′ rend′ ing·ly.**

hearts·ease or **heart's-ease** (härts′ ēz′) *n-* 1 any of various violets. 2 ease of mind; tranquility.

heart·sick (härt′ sĭk′) *adj-* very unhappy; despondent.

heart·strings (härt′ stringz′) *n- pl.* the deepest feelings; strongest emotions: *Sick babies tug at my* heartstrings.

heart-to-heart (härt′ tōō härt′) *adj-* frank and direct; intimate; sincere: *a* heart-to-heart *talk.*

heart·wood (härt′ wōōd′) *n-* the hard, tough, inner wood of a tree.

heart·y (här′ tē) *adj-* [heart·i·er, heart·i·est] 1 warm and sincere; friendly; cordial: *a* hearty *welcome.* 2 in excellent health; strong; vigorous: *a* hearty *old man.* 3 full of enthusiasm; not restrained: *a* hearty *laugh.* 4 abundant and nourishing; satisfying: *a* hearty *meal.* 5 needing much food to be satisfied: *a* hearty *appetite. n-* [*pl.* **heart·ies**] good fellow; comrade; mate: *Keep a lookout for whales, my* hearties.

heat (hēt) *n-* 1 warmth, especially great warmth: *the* heat *of a fire; the* heat *of the sun.* 2 high temperature: *He doesn't mind the* heat. 3 *Physics* form of energy associated with the rapid, random motion of molecules. Heat is transferred from one substance to another by conduction, convection, or radiation and usually produces a rise in temperature. 4 the cost of warming a house, building, or apartment: *We include* heat *in the tenant's rent.* 5 intense feeling; excitement: *He says rash things in the* heat *of an argument.* 6 in sports, a single race or contest in a series, especially to eliminate the poorest competitors from the finals. 7 periodic condition of a female animal when she is ready for mating. *vt-* to make hot or warm: *A furnace* heats *the house. vi-: The soup is* heating *on the stove.*

heat up 1 to make or become hot or warm: *Please* heat *up the baby's bottle.* 2 to become warmer than is proper or desired: *This engine* heats *up quickly.*

heat·ed (hē′ təd) *adj-* hot; inflamed; hence, angry; vehement: *a* heated *argument.* —*adv-* **heat′ ed·ly.**

heat·er (hē′ tər) *n-* a stove, furnace, or radiator for warming a room or automobile.

heat exchanger *n-* device that transfers heat from a liquid or gas on one side of a wall or barrier to another fluid on the other side, thereby increasing the temperature of one fluid while cooling the other.

heath (hēth) *n-* 1 in Great Britain, flat wasteland, often overgrown with shrubs; moor. 2 any one of several low-growing shrubs found on wasteland. Heather belongs to this family of plants.

hea·then (hē′ thən) *n-* 1 person who does not believe in the Christian, Jewish, or Muslim God. 2 person who worships many gods or has no god; pagan. 3 uncivilized person; barbarian; savage. 4 **the heathen** such persons collectively. *adj-: a* heathen *idol;* heathen *customs.* —*adj-* **hea′ then·ish.**

hea·then·dom (hē′ thən dəm) *n-* heathen peoples, countries, beliefs, or practices.

heath·er (hĕth′ ər) *n-* tiny-leaved shrub with stalks of small, pale-purple blossoms, common in Scotland and England. —*adj-* **heath′ er·y.**

heav·en (hĕv′ən) *n-* 1 in some religions, the dwelling place of God and the angels and of the souls of good people after death. 2 any place or period of great happiness; state of bliss: *Our vacation in the Rockies was heaven.* 3 the **heavens** the sky; place where the sun, moon, and stars appear. 4 **Heaven** the Deity; God; Providence: *We pray Heaven grant us lasting peace.*

move heaven and earth to do everything within one's power: *I moved heaven and earth to get you here.*

heav·en·ly (hĕv′ən lē) *adj-* 1 of or relating to the dwelling place of God; divine: *the heavenly choirs.* 2 fit for heaven; beyond compare; very beautiful: *a heavenly day.* 3 of the sky; celestial: *The sun, moon, and stars are heavenly bodies.* —*n-* **heav′en·li·ness.**

heav·en·ward (hĕv′ən wərd) *adj-* directed or going toward heaven: *a heavenward gaze.* *adv-* (also **heav′en·wards**) toward heaven.

Heav·i·side layer (hĕv′ĭ sīd′) *n-* layer of the ionosphere closest to the earth; E layer.

heav·y (hĕv′ē) *adj-* [**heav·i·er, heav·i·est**] 1 having much weight; hard to lift, carry, or move: *a heavy man; a heavy bag of groceries; a heavy trunk.* 2 of greater than average weight, thickness, or density for its kind: *a heavy winter jacket; heavy socks; heavy legs; heavy cream; heavy oil for summer driving; a heavy fog.* 3 of great amount or force: *a heavy rain; heavy traffic; a heavy blow to the head.* 4 using or dealing in large quantities: *a heavy buyer; a heavy smoker.* 5 weighed down; loaded; full: *trees heavy with apples; sleepy children with heavy eyes.* 6 weighed down with sorrow; very sad: *Her heart was heavy at leaving home.* 7 hard to bear; harsh; oppressive: *a heavy fine; heavy taxes.* 8 hard to digest; rich; fatty: *to eat heavy foods.* 9 very cloudy and dark; overcast; gloomy: *a heavy sky.* 10 hard to travel over; full of obstacles; rough: *a heavy road; heavy going; heavy seas.* 11 hard to read or understand; not clear and flowing: *a heavy book; a heavy style of writing.* 12 loud and deep; powerful: *a heavy bass voice.* 13 of large size or capacity compared with others of its general type: *a heavy cruiser; heavy artillery.* —*adv-* **heav′i·ly.** —*n-* **heav′i·ness.**

He·brew (hē′brōō) *n-* 1 member or descendant of the Semitic group who were the chief inhabitants of ancient Palestine; Israelite; Jew. 2 the Semitic language of the ancient Hebrews. 3 the official language of modern Israel. *adj-:* *a book of Hebrew songs.*

Hebrews, Epistle to the (hē′brōōz′) *n-* book of the New Testament addressed to Hebrew Christians.

Hec·a·te (hĕk′ə tē, also hĕk′ət) *n-* in Greek mythology, the goddess of the underworld. She was later associated with sorcery.

hec·a·tomb (hĕk′ə tōm′) *n-* in ancient Greece, public sacrifice of 100 oxen to the gods; hence, any great slaughter.

heck·le (hĕk′əl) *vt-* [**heck·led, heck·ling**] to interrupt and try to confuse (a public speaker) with annoying questions or remarks. —*n-* **heck′ler.**

hect·are (hĕk′târ′) *n-* in the metric system, a unit of land measure equal to 100 ares (10,000 square meters or 2.471 acres.)

hec·tic (hĕk′tĭk) *adj-* 1 very exciting; full of activity or commotion: *a hectic day at the fair.* 2 flushed and hot;

hedge·hop (hĕj′hŏp′) *vi-* [**hedge·hopped, hedge·hop·ping**] to fly an airplane close to the ground, especially for dusting crops, trees, etc. —*n-* **hedge′hop′per.**

hedge·row (hĕj′rō′) *n-* tall, heavily entangled row of trees and thick bushes, growing on a low mound, that borders fields and pastures in some parts of Europe.

he·don·ism (hē′də nĭz′əm) *n-* 1 in philosophy, the idea that pleasure or happiness is the chief good and the proper goal of all human activity. 2 a living for pleasure; self-indulgence. —*n-* **he′don·ist.** *adj-* **he·don·ist′ic.**

heed (hēd) *vt-* to pay careful attention to; mind; observe: *to heed advice; to heed traffic regulations.* *vi-:* *Some boys just won't heed.* *n-* careful attention; notice: *He gave no heed to the warning.* *Hom-* he'd.

heed·ful (hēd′fəl) *adj-* careful; attentive; watchful;

height (hīt) *n-* 1 measurement from the head to the foot; stature: *a man of average height.* 2 distance from the ground or bottom to the top: *the height of a figure or building.* 3 the distance something rises above the earth or above sea level; altitude; elevation: *the height of an airplane; the height of a mountain.* 4 the state of being high: *Some people are afraid of height.* 5 a high place; hill: *a house on the height overlooking the river; to be afraid of heights.* 6 the highest point; top; summit: *The writer reached the height of his career at thirty.* 7 the extreme; utmost degree: *the height of popularity or of ignorance. Hom-* hight.

height·en (hī′tən) *vt-* 1 to make higher; raise; elevate: *They heightened the fence around the backyard.* 2 to increase in strength, degree, or effect: *His sarcastic tone only heightened her anger.* *vi-* to become higher, stronger, or greater: *The suspense heightened.*

hei·nous (hā′nəs) *adj-* very wicked; hateful; atrocious. —*adv-* **hei′nous·ly.** *n-* **hei′nous·ness.**

heir (âr) *n-* 1 person who receives or has the right to receive money, property, or title at the death of the owner. In law, an **heir apparent** [*pl.* **heirs apparent**] is one who will become an heir if he outlives the person from whom the inheritance will pass; an **heir presumptive** [*pl.* **heirs presumptive**] is one who will become an heir if his right is not canceled by the birth of another more closely related. 2 a person or group that inherits qualities from others who have lived before: *We are the heirs of Greek and Roman civilization. Hom-* air, ²are, e'er, ere.

fall heir to to inherit: *He fell heir to his uncle's farm.*

heir·ess (âr′əs) *n-* a woman or girl who inherits, or is in line to inherit, money, property, or a title.

heir·loom (âr′lōōm′) *n-* piece of personal property handed down in a family from generation to generation.

He·ji·ra (hə jī′rə) Hegira.

held (hĕld) *p.t.* & *p.p.* of **hold.**

Hel·en of Troy (hĕl′ən əv troi′) *n-* in Greek mythology, the beautiful wife of Menelaus, king of Sparta. Her elopement with Paris caused the Trojan War.

hel·i·cal (hĕl′ĭ kəl, hē′lĭ-) *adj-* of, relating to, or in the form of a helix; spiral.

hel·i·con (hĕl′ĭ kŏn′) *n-* large, coiled brass instrument similar to a tuba, used by marching bands.

hel·i·cop·ter (hĕl′ə kŏp′tər) *n-* aircraft with rotary wings mounted on a vertical drive shaft and turned by an engine or by jets in the wing-tips.

he·lio- *combining form* sun: **heliograph.** [from Greek

Helicopter

²**helm** (hĕlm) *Archaic n-* helmet. [from Old English helm meaning "helmet; any protection or cover."]

hel·met (hĕl′mət) *n-* protective head covering of metal, plastic, or other tough, resistant material: *a soldier's helmet; a fireman's helmet.*

helms·man (hĕlmz′mən) *n-* [*pl.* **helms·men**] person who steers or guides a ship or boat; pilot.

Hel·ot (hĕl′ət) *n-* 1 member of the lowest social class of ancient Sparta. 2 helot a serf or slave.

ROMAN

MODERN INDUSTRIAL

Helmets

help (hĕlp) *vt-* 1 to aid; assist: *to help a friend in trouble.* 2 to keep from; avoid: *He could not help dropping the glass.* 3 to be a remedy or cure for: *Nothing helps my headache.* *vi-* to give aid or support; be helpful: *They offered to help. It didn't make him completely happy, but it helped. Tom helped start the car.* *n-* 1 support; aid; assistance: *to give help in time of disaster.* 2 person or people who work for one: *the hired help.* 3 person or thing that aids or assists: *You were a big help at the party.* 4 remedy or solution: *There is no help for her illness.* —*n-* **help′er.**

hem·i·sphere (hĕm′ ə sfēr′) *n-* 1 half of the globe of the earth. 2 half of any sphere. 3 either the right or the left half of the cerebrum.

hem·i·spher·ic (hĕm′ə sfēr′ ĭk, -sfĕr′ ĭk) or **hem·i·spher·i·cal** (-ĭ kəl) *adj-* 1 of, or relating to a hemisphere: *a hemispheric alliance.* 2 (usually **hemispherical**) having the shape of a hemisphere.

hem·line (hĕm′ līn′) *n-* lower edge of a skirt.

hem·lock (hĕm′ lŏk′) *n-* 1 any of several evergreen trees related to the pines. 2 the wood of such a tree. 3 any of several poisonous plants related to the carrot and parsley.

hemo- *combining form* blood: *a hemophiliac; hemoglobin.* Also **haemo-.** [from Greek *haima,* "blood."]

he·mo·glo·bin (hē′mə glō′bən) *n-* protein and iron pigment contained in the red blood cells. Hemoglobin transfers oxygen from the lungs to the body tissues and brings carbon dioxide from the tissues to the lungs.

he·mol·y·sis (hē mŏl′ ə səs) *n-* destruction of red blood cells, resulting in the release of hemoglobin into the plasma. —*adj-* **hem·o·lyt·ic.** (hē′ mə līt′ ĭk)

he·mo·phil·i·a (hē′ mə fĭl′ yə) *n-* hereditary blood disorder of males, marked by the failure of the blood to coagulate normally, and by prolonged bleeding from even a very small wound.

he·mo·phil·i·ac (hē′ mə fĭl′ē ăk′) *n-* person with hemophilia; bleeder.

hem·or·rhage (hĕm′ ər ĭj) *n-* bleeding from a damaged artery, vein, etc., especially a great or continuous flow of blood. *vi-* [**hem·or·rhaged, hem·or·rhag·ing.**] to bleed profusely.

hem·or·rhoids (hĕm′ ə roidz′) *n- pl.* painful swellings of the veins in the anal region; piles.

hemp (hĕmp) *n-* 1 tall Asiatic plant having tough fibers used for making rope and coarse cloth. 2 hashish.

hemp·en (hĕm′ pən) *adj-* made of or resembling hemp.

hem·stitch (hĕm′ stĭch′) *n-* ornamental stitch often used to trim hems. It is made by pulling out several parallel threads from the cloth and gathering the cross threads into small, uniform bundles to form an open design. *vt-:* *to* hemstitch *a cloth.* —*n-* **hem′ stitch′ er.**

hen (hĕn) *n-* 1 adult female of the domestic fowl. See also *rooster, cock, chicken, chick.* 2 female of other birds. 3 female of various other animals, such as the lobster and certain fishes. 4 *Slang* a woman, especially a fussy old woman.

Hen

hen·bane (hĕn′ bān′) *n-* poisonous plant related to the nightshade. It has sticky, hairy leaves and yellowish-brown flowers.

hence (hĕns) *adv-* 1 from this time: *School starts two weeks hence.* 2 from this place: *a mile hence.*

herb (ûrb, *also* hûrb) *n-* 1 any plant that has a soft, juicy stem rather than a woody one. Most herbs wither to the ground or die completely after flowering. 2 any such plant used as a medicine or for seasoning.

her·ba·ceous (hûr′ bā′ shəs, ûr′-) *adj-* 1 having the characteristics of herbs: *a herbaceous plant.* 2 consisting of herbs: *a herbaceous border in a garden.*

herb·age (ûr bĭj, *also* hûr′-) *n-* growing grass and herbs, especially when used for pasturage.

herb·al (ûr′ bəl, hûr′-) *adj-* of or having to do with herbs. *n-* book about herbs or plants.

herb·al·ist (ûr′ bə līst, hûr′-) *n-* person who grows, collects, or deals in herbs, especially medicinal plants.

her·bar·i·um (hûr′ bâr′ē əm, ûr′-) *n-* [*pl.* **her·bar·i·ums** or **her·bar·i·a** (-ē ə)] 1 collection of dried plants, usually scientifically classified. 2 room or building where such a collection is kept.

herb·i·cide (hûr′ bə sīd, ûr′-) *n-* chemical used to kill plants or inhibit their growth. —*adj-* **herb′ i·ci′ dal:** *a herbicidal compound.*

herb·i·vore (hûr′ bə vôr′, ûr′-) *n-* a herbivorous animal.

her·biv·or·ous (hər blv′ ər əs) *adj-* feeding on vegetable matter; plant-eating.

here (hēr) *adv-* 1 to or toward this place: *Please come here.* 2 in or at this place or spot: *The vase is here on the table. Is it here that we turn?* 3 at this point: *I disagree with you here. The audience interrupted him here.* *pron-* this place or point: *Where do we go from here? interj-* exclamation to indicate that one is present in a roll call, to attract attention, etc. *Hom-* hear.

here and there scattered about; in various places. **neither here nor there** unrelated to the point; irrelevant. ►HERE and THERE are often used unnecessarily, as in *"Read* this *here book. Sharpen* that *there pencil." "Read this book"* is sufficient. However, if you wish to emphasize a particular object, you may use these words after the noun or pronoun. *Read that book* there; *don't read this one* here.

hex (hĕks) *Informal n-* evil spell; jinx. *vt-* to cast an evil spell on. [American word from Pennsylvania German, from German **hexe.**]

hexa- *combining form* six: *a hexagon; hexapod.* [from Greek **hexa-,** from **hex,** "six."]

hex·a·gon (hĕk′ sə gŏn′) *n-* polygon with six sides and six angles.

hex·ag·o·nal (hĕk săg′ ə nəl) *adj-* having six sides. —*adv-* **hex·ag′ o·nal·ly.**

hex·am·e·ter (hĕk săm′ ə tər) *n-* verse consisting of lines having six poetic feet or measures; also, a line in such meter. *as modifier: lines of* hexameter *verse.*

hex·a·pod (hĕk′ sə pŏd′) *n-* insect; member of the class of insects (**Insecta**) which includes all the true or six-legged insects, such as bees, flies, etc.

hey (hā) *interj-* exclamation to attract someone's attention, express surprise, etc. *Hom-* hay.

hey·day (hā′ dā′) *n-* time of greatest power, glory, vigor, etc.: *He was greatly admired in his heyday.*

Hf symbol for hafnium.

Hg symbol for mercury.

H.H. 1 His Highness. 2 Her Highness. 3 His Holiness.

hhd. hogshead.

hi (hī) *interj-* 1 *Informal* exclamation of greeting. 2 shout to attract attention. *Hom-* hie, high.

H.I. Hawaiian Islands (unofficial).

hi·a·tus (hī ā′ təs) *n-* gap, blank space, or break, especially in a manuscript.

hi·ba·chi (hē bä′ chē) *Japanese n-* portable pot-shaped container covered with a heavy wire grill in which charcoal is burned to warm a room, broil foods, etc.

hi·ber·nate (hī′ bər nāt′) *vi-* [**hi·ber·nat·ed, hi·ber·nat·ing**] to spend the winter in a state resembling sleep, as do bears, raccoons, etc. See also *estivate.*

hi·ber·na·tion (hī′ bər nā′ shən) *n-* 1 the act of hibernating. 2 sleeplike state of an animal that hibernates.

¹hid·ing (hī′ dĭng) *n-* state of being concealed; concealment: *to remain in hiding.* [from ¹**hide.**]

²hid·ing (hī′ dĭng) *Informal n-* a beating; thrashing. [from ²**hide.**]

hie (hī) *Archaic vt-* [**hied, hy·ing** or **hie·ing**] to betake; hurry (followed by "me," "him," "myself," "himself," etc.): *He hied himself to the castle. Hom-* hi, high.

hi·er·ar·chy (hī′ ə rär′ kē) *n-* [*pl.* **hi·er·ar·chies**] 1 organization or system in which standing is based on rank, grade, etc.: *a business hierarchy; the church hierarchy.* 2 governing body or group of officials, clergymen, etc., organized in this way.

hi·er·o·glyph (hī′ ər ə glĭf′) *n-* one of the characters making up a system of hieroglyphic writing, usually a more or less recognizable image of an animal, a man, the sun, a stalk of grain, etc.

hi·er·o·glyph·ic (hī′ ər ə glĭf′ ĭk) *n-* 1 a hieroglyph. 2 system of writing using hieroglyphs; especially, that used by the ancient Egyptians. 3 writing that resembles this in being hard to read or decipher: *It was written in George's hieroglyphic. adj-: a hieroglyphic inscription.* —*adv-* **hi′ er·o·glyph′ i·cal·ly.**

Hieroglyphics

hi·fi (hī′ fī′) *n-* 1 high fidelity. 2 *Informal* phonograph using high-fidelity equipment. *adj-: a hi-fi set.*

hill (hil) *n-* 1 elevation of the earth that is not as high as a mountain. 2 heap or mound of earth: *an ant* hill. 3 a heap of earth around a plant, or the heap and the plant: *a hill of beans.*

hill·bil·ly (hil' bil' ē) *n-* [*pl.* **hill·bil·lies**] person from the mountain regions of southern United States (often used to show disfavor).

hill·ock (hil' ak) *n-* small hill.

hill·side (hil' sid') *n-* side or slope of a hill.

hill·top (hil' tŏp') *n-* the top part of a hill.

hill·y (hil' ē) *adj-* [**hill·i·er**, **hill·i·est**] having many hills; not level: *through* hilly *country.*

hilt (hilt) *n-* handle of a dagger or sword.
to the hilt completely; entirely: *It pleased me to the hilt.*

Hilt

hi·lum (hi' lam) *n-* [*pl.* **hi·la** (-la)] 1 in botany, scar left on a seed at the point where it was attached to the ovule. 2 in anatomy, notch or opening where ducts, nerves, etc., enter or leave an organ.

him (him) *pron-* objective case of **he:** *I see* him. *Pass* him *the bread. I did it for* him. *Hom-* hymn.

him·self (him sĕlf') *pron-* 1 reflexive form of **him;** his own self: *He hid* himself *under the table. He is proud of* himself. 2 his normal or true self: *After a moment of dizziness, he came to* himself. 3 intensive form of **he:** *He* himself *will come.* 4 *Irish* he: *I am sure* himself *will not deny it.*
by himself 1 alone: *He came* by himself. 2 without any help: *He built the shed* by himself.

¹hind (hind) *adj-* [**hind·er**, **hind·most** or **hind·er·most**] at the back; rear: *the* hind *legs of a dog.* [from earlier **hinder,** from Old English *hindan,* "from behind."]

²hind (hind) *n-* female of the deer, especially the red deer. See also **hart.** [from Old English.]

³hind (hind) *n-* 1 in Scotland and northern England, a farm worker. 2 *Archaic* peasant. [alteration of earlier **hine,** short for Old English *hine man* meaning "member of a household; household servant."]

¹hin·der (hin' dar) *vt-* to get in the way of; put obstacles in the way of; impede; prevent: *The sand* hindered *our walking.* [from Old English *hindrian,* from ²**hinder.**]

²hind·er (hin' dar) *compar.* of ¹**hind.** [from Old English, meaning "backwards."]

Hin·di (hin' dē) *n-* the principal language of northern India, belonging to the Indo-European family of languages.

hind·most (hind' mōst') or **hind·er·most** (hin' dar-), *superl.* of ¹**hind.**

hind·quar·ter (hind' kwôr' tar) *n-* 1 either side of the hind part of a carcass of beef, veal, lamb, etc. 2 **hind·quarters** haunches.

hin·drance (hin' drans) *n-* 1 person or thing that hinders; obstacle. 2 a hindering: *the* hindrance *of one's plans.*

hind·sight (hind' sit') *n-* 1 ability to look back and see what should have been done. 2 rear sight of a gun.

Hin·du (hin' dōō) *n-* native or inhabitant of India whose religion is Hinduism. *adj-* of or relating to such persons or to Hinduism: *a* Hindu *festival;* a Hindu *god.*

Hip·po·crat·ic oath (hip' a krăt' ĭk) *n-* the ethical guide for the medical profession, based on an oath attributed to Hippocrates.

hip·po·drome (hip' a drōm') *n-* 1 in ancient Greece or Rome, a race course for horses and chariots. 2 arena for circuses, sports events, etc.

hip·po·pot·a·mus (hip' a pŏt' a mas) *n-* [*pl.* **hip·po·pot·a·mus·es** or **hip·po·pot·a·mi** (-mī, -mē)] large African plant-eating river animal with a tough hide, a huge mouth, and short legs.

Hippopotamus. about 14 ft long

hire (hiar) *vt-* [**hired, hir·ing**] 1 to employ for pay: *The manager* hired *a secretary.* 2 to pay for the use of: *to* hire *a truck.* *n-* money paid as wages or as rent: *That man is not worth his* hire.
for hire available in return for payment.

his·tor·i·cal (hi stŏr' ĭ kal) *adj-* 1 of or relating to history: *a* historical *event;* a historical *study.* 2 based on history: *a* historical *novel.* 3 historic. *—adv-* **his·tor'i·cal·ly.**

his·to·ry (his' ta rē, his' trē) *n-* [*pl.* **his·to·ries**] 1 record of past facts and events: *We shall read a* history *of the United States.* 2 past events or facts connected with a thing, person, nation, etc.: *the weird* history *of that family.* 3 branch of learning which deals with past events: *a class in* history.

his·tri·on·ic (his' trē ŏn' ĭk) *adj-* 1 overly dramatic or emotional in one's speech or manner; artificial; affected. 2 of or relating to actors or acting.

his·tri·on·ics (his' trē ŏn' ĭks) *n-* 1 (takes plural verb) display of dramatic and affected behavior: *Her* histrionics *offend me.* 2 (takes singular verb) the art of stage performance.

hit (hit) *vt-* [**hit, hit·ting**] (in senses 1, 3, and 4 considered intransitive when the direct object is implied but not expressed) 1 to give a blow to; strike: *to* hit *someone on the chin; to* hit *a ball.* 2 to bump or crash forcibly: *He* hit *his head on the door.* 3 to fly into or dash against forcibly: *The arrow* hit *the target. The car* hit *the railing.* 4 to become suddenly clear or known to: *The answer just now* hit *me.* 5 in baseball, to make (a specified base hit): *to* hit *a double.* 6 to reach; come up to: *He* hit *his stride. We* hit *eighty miles an hour.* *vi-* 1 to crash (against something). 2 in baseball, to make a base hit. *n-* 1 stroke, blow, etc., that reaches its mark: *I have three* hits *and two misses.* 2 successful or popular song, play, etc. 3 in baseball, a base hit. *—n-* **hit' ter.**
hard hit affected deeply: *He was* hard hit *by his father's death.* **hit or miss** without worrying about the outcome; in an aimless or haphazard manner.
hit and run in baseball, to make a hit-and-run play.
hit it off to get along well with one another.
hit on (or **upon**) to come or light on; happen on: *He finally* hit on *the right answer.*
hit out at to attack violently with blows or harsh words.

hit-and-run (hit' an rŭn') *adj-* 1 done by or involving someone who immediately drives or runs away: *a* hit-and-run *accident; a* hit-and-run *driver; a* hit-and-run *attack.* 2 in baseball, having to do with a play in which a base-runner starts his throw to the batter, and the batter tries to hit the ball, preferably behind the runner.

hitch (hĭch) *vt-* to attach; tie; fasten: *Please* hitch *the horse to the wagon.* *vi-* to pull (up) with a short jerk: *Tom* hitched *up his trousers.* *n-* 1 short jerk: *Tom gave his trousers a* hitch. 2 obstacle; delay; halt: *There was a sudden* hitch *in the program.* 3 kind of knot; especially, a temporary knot.

TIMBER HITCH
HALF HITCH
Hitches

hitch·hike (hĭch' hik') *vi-* [**hitch·hiked, hitch·hik·ing**] to travel by asking for rides along the way: *He* hitchhiked *across the United States.* *—n-* **hitch' hik' er.**

hitching post *n-* post for hitching horses.

hith·er (hith' ar) *adv-* here: *Come* hither!

hith·er·to (hith' ar tōō') *adv-* up to this time.

hith·er·ward (hith' ar ward) or **hith·er·wards** (-wardz) *adv-* hither.

Hit·tite (hit' tit') *n-* member of an ancient people whose powerful empire lasted from 2000-1200 B.C. in Asia

hive (hiv) *n-* 1 box or house for honeybees. For picture, see *beehive.* 2 swarm of bees living in this place. 3 place where there are crowds of busy people: *The big store was a* hive *of activity.* *vt-* [**hived, hiv·ing**] to put (bees) into a hive. *vi-* to live together in or as in a hive.

hives (hivz) *n- pl.* (takes singular or plural verb) an itching skin rash, often caused by an allergy.

H.M.S. 1 His (or Her) Majesty's Ship. 2 His (or Her) Majesty's Service.

ho (hō) *interj-* exclamation used to attract attention, express delight, surprise, etc. *Hom-* hoe.

Ho symbol for holmium.

hoar (hôr) *adj-* hoary. *Hom-* whore.

hoard (hôrd) *n-* supply of things that is stored up or hidden away: *a hoard of gold. vt-:* to hoard *valuable coins. Hom-* horde. **—n- hoard' er.**

hoar·frost (hôr' frôst', -frŏst') *n-* tiny drops of dew frozen on plants, trees, the ground, etc.; rime.

hoar·hound (hôr' hound') horehound.

hoarse (hôrs) *adj-* [hoars' er, hoars' est] 1 rough, harsh, or gruff in sound: *A cold had made Jane's voice hoarse.* 2 having a rough, harsh voice: *Jane was hoarse from a cold. Hom-* horse. **—adv- hoarse' ly. n- hoarse' ness.**

hoar·y (hôr' ē) *adj-* [hoar·i·er, hoar·i·est] 1 white or gray. 2 old; venerable. **—n- hoar' i·ness.**

hoax (hōks) *n-* mischievous trick or fraud; especially, a practical joke to deceive the public. **—n- hoax' er.**

1hob (hŏb) *n-* ledge at the back or sides of the inside of a fireplace on which food is kept warm. [a form of **hub**, originally meaning "a projection."]

2hob (hŏb) *n-* elf or goblin. [probably from **Hob**, an old nickname for Robin (Goodfellow) or Robert.]

  play (or raise) hob *Informal* to make mischief.

hob·ble (hŏb' əl) *vi-* [hob·bled, hob·bling] to limp or walk with difficulty: *The old man hobbled along on his cane. vt-* 1 to tie two legs of (an animal) loosely together to hinder its movements. 2 to hinder; hamper: *to hobble our progress. n-* 1 limping or halting walk. 2 rope, strap, etc., used to hobble an animal.

Hobble

hob·ble·de·hoy (hŏb' əl dē hoi') *n-* 1 adolescent boy. 2 awkward, gawky boy.

hob·by (hŏb' ē) *n-* [*pl.* hob·bies] subject or interest pursued mainly for pleasure in one's spare time; avocation: *His hobby is boating.*

hob·by·horse (hŏb' ē hôrs', -hôrs') *n-* 1 toy made of a stick with a horse's head, on which children pretend to ride. 2 wooden horse on rockers or on a merry-go-round. 3 favorite or pet idea; subject, etc.

hob·gob·lin (hŏb' gŏb' lĭn) *n-* 1 troublesome elf. 2 imaginary thing that causes fear; bogey.

hob·nail (hŏb' nāl') *n-* 1 large-headed nail on the sole of a heavy shoe to lessen wear or prevent slipping. 2 pattern of closely spaced tufts or bosses on glass, fabrics, etc. **—adj- hob' nailed'.**

Hobnails

hob·nob (hŏb' nŏb') *vi-* [hob·nob·bed, hob·nob·bing] to be on close or friendly terms (with): *He hobnobs with the rich.*

hock·ey (hŏk' ē) *n-* 1 (also **ice hockey**) game played on ice between two teams of six players each wearing skates and carrying curved sticks which are used to drive a hard rubber disk called a "puck" into the opponent's goal. 2 (also **field hockey**) similar game played on an outdoor field between teams of eleven players each, with a ball instead of a puck.

ho·cus-po·cus (hō' kəs pō' kəs) *n-* 1 meaningless words and phrases used in magic. 2 trickery of a magician or juggler; sleight of hand; also, any trickery used to cover up deception. *vt- Informal* to trick.

MASON'S

COAL

Hods

hod (hŏd) *n-* 1 bucket for carrying coal. 2 V-shaped trough on a long handle, for carrying bricks or mortar.

hodge·podge (hŏj' pŏj') *n-* jumble; confused mixture: *a hodgepodge of toys.*

hoe (hō) *n-* tool with a flat blade on a long handle, used for digging up weeds, loosening soil, etc. *vt-* [hoed, hoe·ing]: *Early in the morning Barney hoed his garden. vi-:* Barney hoed *all afternoon. Hom-* ho. **—n- ho' er.**

hoist (hoist) *vt-* to lift up; raise, especially by means of tackle, cranes, etc.: *to hoist the sails of a ship. n-* 1 apparatus for raising things: *The elevator is a hoist.* 2 a lifting; push upward; boost: *a hoist over the wall.*

hoist with (one's) own petard to be caught or hurt by a scheme one has made against someone else.

hoi·ty-toi·ty (hoi' tē toi' tē) *interj-* exclamation of surprise and contempt. *adj-* haughty; arrogant.

ho·kum (hō' kəm) *Slang n-* meaningless talk or writing; claptrap; bunk.

1hold (hōld) *vt-* [held, hold·ing] 1 to have or keep in the hand; grasp; grip; clasp: *to hold a bouquet.* 2 to keep in a certain pose or manner: *She held her head erect.* 3 to contain: *This jug holds one gallon.* 4 to keep by force; protect; defend: *to hold a fort.* 5 to control; keep back; check: *It is better to hold your temper before you speak out angrily.* 6 to believe; accept: *Most Americans hold the opinion that democracy is desirable.* 7 to carry on; conduct: *to hold a meeting; to hold a church service.* 8 to occupy; keep: *He held the office of secretary. vi-* 1 to grasp or grip; clasp: *You must hold tightly to the rope.* 2 to remain or continue: *Please hold still. Our ranks held despite the withering fire. My promise still holds. The wind held from the south.* 3 to be faithful or loyal (to): *to hold to one's promise.* 4 to be true or in force: *The same rule holds for everyone. n-* 1 a grasp; grip: *Take a good hold on the handle.* 2 something that may be grasped for support. 3 influence; control: *She has some sort of hold over him.* 4 Music symbol placed over [⌢] or under [⌣] a note or rest to show that it is to be prolonged; pause. [from Old English h(e)aldan.]

  get (or take) hold of 1 to get a grip on; take or seize. 2 to get control of: *You ought to get hold of yourself.*

  hold forth to speak at length; lecture or preach: *He held forth for two hours.*

  hold good to be accepted as true or valid: *Will his statements hold good in court?*

  hold in to check; keep back; restrain.

  hold off 1 to keep at a distance. 2 to keep from capturing, advancing, etc.: *We held off the enemy for days.* 3 to put off; delay: *He held off calling me.*

  hold on 1 to retain a grip or grasp on something. 2 to continue or persist: *They held on until help came.* 3 *Informal* wait! stop!

  hold (one's) own to retain one's present position; not fall behind.

  hold (one's) peace to refrain from speaking or interfering.

  hold out to last; remain firm; stand: *The pioneers held out against hunger and cold all winter.*

  hold over 1 to postpone for later consideration: *We will hold over the new business.* 2 to keep for an additional period: *The movie is being held over another week.*

  hold up 1 to delay; hinder: *He held up our departure.* 2 to rob by force, usually with a gun.

  hold water *Informal* to be true or valid.

  hold with to approve of; agree with: *Grandma does not hold with all the new cooking methods.*

2hold (hōld) *n-* space below the main deck of a ship, in which cargo is stored. [from **hole** and Dutch **hol**, "ship's cavity."]

hold·back (hōld' băk') *n-* 1 something that restrains or hinders; check. 2 on a horse-drawn vehicle, the strap or iron on the shaft attached to the harness that permits the horse to stop or push back the vehicle.

hold·up (hōld' ŭp) *n-* 1 armed robbery or attempt to rob. 2 a delay: *a traffic holdup due to an accident.*

hole (hōl) *n-* 1 opening in or through something: *a hole in the tablecloth.* 2 cavity in a solid body or mass: *a hole in a tooth.* 3 place hollowed in the ground by an animal; burrow: *A woodchuck lives in a hole.* 4 on a golf course, a sunken cup into which a ball is driven. *vt-* [holed, hol·ing] 1 to drive or dig an opening, excavation, etc., into: *They holed the mountain for a tunnel. The rock holed the ship.* 2 in golf, to hit into the cup: *He holed the ball in four strokes. Hom-* whole.

  burn a hole in one's pocket of money, to make one anxious to spend it. **pick holes in**, to pick out mistakes

hol·low (hŏl′ō) **adj-** [**hol·low·er**, **hol·low·est**] 1 empty inside; not solid. 2 having a cuplike shape; concave. 3 sunken: *She had hollow cheeks after her illness.* 4 deep, muffled, and echoing: *We heard hollow sounds from the cave.* 5 unreal; insincere; false: *He spoke hollow words of praise.* **n-** 1 empty space; cavity. 2 valley. **vt-** to scoop (out): *The children hollowed out the pumpkin.* —**adv-** hol′ low·ly. **n-** hol′ low·ness.

hol·ly (hŏl′ē) **n-** [*pl.* **hol·lies**] 1 shrub or small tree with stiff, prickly, glossy evergreen leaves and bright-red berries. 2 branches of this shrub used as a decoration: *Decorate the halls with holly.*

hol·ly·hock (hŏl′ē hŏk′) **n-** tall plant with hairy leaves and large flowers of various colors growing from the main stem.

Holly

holm (hōm, hōlm) **n-** 1 evergreen oak with tough, hard wood and glossy leaves, found in Southern Europe. 2 wood of this tree. Also **holm oak**.

Holmes, Sherlock (hōlmz, shûr′ lŏk′) See *Sherlock Holmes.*

home (hōm) **n-** 1 place where a person lives; residence; house; domicile. 2 family group: *He kept his home together though his business kept him moving.* 3 country, State, town, etc., where one was born or raised, or where one lives. 4 place where an animal is commonly found; habitat: *The polar bear's home is the Arctic.* 5 institution for care or relief: *an orphan home*; *home for the aged.* 6 the goal in some games; especially, home plate in baseball. *as* **modifier**: *a happy home life*; *his home town.* **adv-** 1 to or at one's residence, native place, etc.: *to go home.* 2 to the point aimed at; to the heart: *to drive a nail home*; *to say something that strikes home.* **vi-** [**homed**, **hom·ing**] 1 to move or aim toward a certain point from which signals radiate: *The planes home on the radio beacon near the airport.* 2 to return to base, residence, house, etc., from a distance, as some pigeons do. **vt-** to cause (an airplane, guided missile, etc.) to seek a certain point or target that radiates waves or signals: *We can home a rocket on the heat from engine exhausts.* —**adj- home′** less.

at home 1 at ease; comfortable: *They feel at home with each other.* 2 willing to see or entertain: *The Allens are at home to all their neighbors.* **bring home** to convey or teach forcibly: *The sight of wounds and death brings home the horror of war.*

home base **n-** home plate.

home·bred (hōm′ brĕd′) **adj-** bred at home; native; domestic: *a homebred strain of wheat.*

home economics **n-** the study of home management, including cooking, clothing, child care, etc.

home·land (hōm′ lănd′) **n-** nation of one's birth or allegiance.

home·like (hōm′ līk′) **adj-** comfortable, friendly, etc., like a home.

home·ly (hōm′ lē) **adj-** [**home·li·er**, **home·li·est**] 1 homelike; plain; simple: *The speaker used homely everyday words.* 2 having plain features; not handsome or beautiful: *Lincoln had a homely but noble face.* 3 not polished or refined: *the homely but hospitable manners of this part of the country.* —**n-** home′ li·ness.

home·made (hōm′ mād′) **adj-** made, or as if made, at home: *to like homemade food.*

home·mak·er (hōm′ mā′ kər) **n-** woman in a home who cooks the food, takes care of the children, etc.; housewife. —**n-** home′ mak′ ing.

home plate **n-** in baseball, the five-sided slab at which a player stands while batting and which marks the last of the four bases a player must touch to score a run; home base.

ho·mer (hō′ mər) **n-** in baseball, a home run.

Ho·mer·ic (hō mĕr′ ĭk) **adj-** of or pertaining to Homer, his poems, his style, or the civilization and times about which he wrote.

hon·ey·bee (hŭn′ ē bē′) **n-** bee that makes honey. Large colonies are kept in hives to produce honey.

hon·ey·comb (hŭn′ ē kōm′) **n-** framework of six-sided cells with walls of wax, built by bees to hold honey and eggs. **vt-** to pierce with many holes or tunnels: *The beam was honeycombed with ant tunnels.*

Honeybee, about 3/4 in. long

hon·ey·dew (hŭn′ ē dōō′, -dyōō′) **n-** 1 sweet, sticky substance found on the stems and leaves of certain trees and plants in hot weather. 2 sweet substance secreted on the leaves of plants by certain insects, such as aphids, scale insects, etc.

honeydew melon **n-** smooth-skinned white melon with a sweet, light-green flesh.

hon·eyed (hŭn′ ĕd) **adj-** 1 covered, filled with, or made of honey. 2 sweet or flattering; soothing; coaxing: *her honeyed words.* Also **hon′ ied.**

Honeycomb

honey locust **n-** large, thorny North American tree bearing long, flat pods.

hon·ey·moon (hŭn′ ē mōōn′) **n-** holiday taken by a man and woman just after their wedding. **vi-**: *They will honeymoon in Canada.* —**n-** hon′ ey·moon′ er.

hon·ey·suck·le (hŭn′ ē sŭk′ əl) **n-** vine or bush with dark green leaves and sweet-smelling, tubular flowers that are usually white, yellow, or pink.

honk (hŏngk) **n-** 1 call of a wild goose. 2 any sound like this call: *the honk of a horn.* **vi-** to make such a sound: *We heard the geese honk.* **vt-** to sound or blow (a horn). —**n-** honk′ er.

Honeysuckle

hon·ky·tonk (hŏng′ kē tŏngk′) *Slang* **n-** cheap, noisy saloon, nightclub, etc. *as* **modifier**: *a honkytonk neighborhood*; honkytonk *music.*

hon·or (ŏn′ ər) **n-** 1 high esteem; great respect: *to show honor to one's parents.* 2 high rank; distinction; dignity: *the honor of being president*; *the honor of knighthood.* 3 excellent reputation; good name: *to defend one's honor.* 4 strong feeling for right or justice; uprightness; integrity: *a man of honor.* 5 glory; fame; renown: *to seek honor by engaging in daring adventures.* 6 cause of respect or esteem; source of credit: *Sheila is an honor to her family.* 7 act of respect or social courtesy: *It is an honor to be invited to this ceremony. He did her the honor of attending her party.* 8 virtue or chastity, especially of women. 9 in card games such as bridge, an ace, king, queen, jack, or ten. 10 **Honor** title for a high official such as a judge or mayor, preceded by "Your," "His," or "Her." 11 **honors** (1) public acts or ceremonies of respect: *funeral honors.* (2) distinguished standing in school or college. (3) recognition of merit; award: *He won first honors in the exhibition.* **vt-** 1 to treat with respect or deference: *to honor one's parents.* 2 to show respect or esteem to: *They honored him by making him captain of the team.* 3 to accept and pay when due: *The bank will honor my check.* Also, *chiefly Brit.,* honour.

hood·wink (hood′ wĭngk′) **vt-** to mislead by a trick, deceive; cheat. —**n-** hood′ wink′ er.

hoof (hoof, hōof) **n-** [*pl.* **hoofs** or **hooves** (hoovz, hōovz)] the horny covering of the toes of some animals, such as the horse or cow. It is the part of the foot that rests on the ground and supports the weight of the animal in walking or running. **vi-** *Informal* to go on foot; walk; dance, etc. (often followed by "it"). —**adj- hoof′** less. **adj-** hoof′ like′.

HORSE'S

DEER'S

Hooves

on the hoof alive; not butchered: *The price of steers was 12 cents a pound on the hoof.*

hope (hōp) *n-* 1 desire for something with a feeling that the desire may be fulfilled; desire accompanied by expectation: *He has hopes of making money.* 2 the thing desired: *Success in business was his constant hope.* 3 feeling of trust and confidence that the future will turn out well: *Never lose hope.* 4 cause or source of such a feeling: *He is the hope of the family. vt-* [hoped, hop·ing] to wish and expect; desire confidently or expectantly (takes only a clause or an infinitive as object): *I hope that you can come. I hope to come. vi-* 1 to have a strong wish (for) something one expects may occur: *We hope for the best.* 2 to wish and expect that things will turn out well: *He continued to hope.* **hope against hope** to go on having hope although fulfillment seems unlikely.

hope chest *n-* chest or box in which a young woman collects articles to use when she is married.

hope·ful (hōp′ fəl) *adj-* 1 full of hope; full of confident expectation: *He is hopeful that he will be able to go.* 2 expressing hope: *a few hopeful words.* 3 giving hope; promising success or a good outcome: *a hopeful sign. n-* person who expects or is expected to succeed. —*adv-* **hope′ ful·ly.** *n-* **hope′ ful·ness.**

hope·less (hōp′ ləs) *adj-* 1 without hope. 2 having or showing little likelihood of success: *a hopeless task.* —*adv-* **hope′ less·ly.** *n-* **hope′ less·ness.**

Ho·pi (hō′ pē) *n-* [*pl.* **Ho·pis,** also **Ho·pi**] one of a group of American Pueblo Indians who now live in northeastern Arizona. *adj-:* a Hopi *rug.*

hop·per (hōp′ ər) *n-* 1 person or thing that hops. 2 any of various hopping insects, such as the leaf hopper. 3 container or chute from which something is fed to a machine, mill, bin, process, etc.

Hopper

hop·scotch (hōp′ skŏch′) *n-* children's game, in which the players toss a small object into a series of numbered spaces of a diagram drawn on the ground, and then hop from space to space to pick it up.

horde (hôrd) *n-* 1 crowd; swarm; multitude. 2 a wandering tribe of people. *Hom-* hoard.

hore·hound (hôr′ hound′) *n-* 1 plant related to the mints, with small white flowers and aromatic leaves from which an extract is taken. 2 candy or cough medicine flavored with this extract. **Also hoarhound.**

ho·ri·zon (hə rī′ zən) *n-* 1 the line where the earth and sky seem to meet. 2 the limit of one's knowledge, interest, experience, etc.

Horizontal

hor·i·zon·tal (hôr′ ə zŏn′ təl) *adj-* parallel to the plane of the horizon; at right angles to a vertical line; flat; level. *n-* line, surface, plane, etc., that is parallel to the horizon. —*adv-* **hor′ i·zon′ tal·ly.**

hor·mone (hôr′ mŏn′, hôr′-) *n-* 1 secretion produced by a gland, such as the pituitary gland, and carried by the blood to other parts of the body, where it may regulate growth, other glands, etc. 2 a similar substance in plants.

horn (hôrn, hŏrn) *n-* 1 hard, bony, often pointed and curved growth or projection on the heads of certain animals, such as the cow or goat. 2 the substance or material of which such growths are made. 3 anything pointed and curved like such projections, such as the points of the crescent moon. 4 container or wind instrument made by hollowing out such growths: *a powder horn.* 5 *Music* any of a group of brass wind instruments: *a French horn.* 6 something that sticks up on the head of an animal, such as the eyestalk of a snail. 7 device that makes a loud sound as a warning signal: *an automobile horn. as modifier:* a horn *spoon;* the horn *rims of eyeglasses.* —*adj-* **horn′ less.** *adj-* **horn′ like′.**

Horns

draw (or **pull**) **in** one's **horns** to hold oneself back.
horn in *Slang* to intrude or meddle.

horse (hôrs, hŏrs) *n-* 1 large, plant-eating animal with four legs, solid hoofs, and a long mane and tail, used for drawing vehicles and for riding. 2 the full-grown male of this animal. See also **colt, filly, gelding, mare, stallion.** 3 movable frame, usually consisting of two pairs of legs joined by a crossbar, used as a support. 4 in gymnastics, a padded or wooden block used for vaulting. 5 mounted soldiers; cavalry: *a regiment of horse. as modifier: a* horse *race. vt-* [horsed, hors·ing] to mount on or supply with a steed. *Hom-* hoarse.
horse of another color *Informal* an entirely different matter, situation, action.
horse around *Slang* to engage in horseplay.

hos·pi·tal (hŏs′ pĭ təl) *n-* place, usually having a trained staff and special equipment, for the care and treatment of the sick and injured. *as modifier:* a hospital *ward;* hospital *patient;* hospital *building.*

hos·pi·tal·i·ty (hŏs′ pə tăl′ ə tē) *n-* [*pl.* hos·pi·tal·i·ties] warm, generous reception of guests and strangers.

hos·pi·tal·i·za·tion (hŏs′ pĭ tə lə zā′ shən) *n-* 1 a hospitalizing or being hospitalized. 2 period of stay in a hospital. 3 form of insurance that provides complete or partial coverage against hospital expenses.

hour (our) *n-* 1 amount of time equal to 1/24 of the length of time from one noon to the next; sixty minutes. 2 time of day indicated by a clock, watch, etc.: *The hour is three o'clock.* 3 one of the twelve numbers on a clock: *This clock chimes the hours.* 4 loosely reckoned period of time: *the children's hour.* 5 any particular time: *in the hour of danger.* 6 a class session, 60 minutes or less; also, a unit of college or university credit covering one such session per week. 7 unit of distance reckoned by the time taken to travel it: *three hours distant.* 8 **hours** fixed or stated times for work, school, etc.: *office hours; school hours.* 9 **Hours** (1) a time for daily liturgical devotion; canonical hours. (2) the book containing the prayers for these daily periods. *Hom-* our.
after hours after the regular hours for business, work, school, etc. **of the hour** of the present; of the day: *man of the hour.*

hour·glass (our′ glăs′) *n-* device for measuring the passage of one hour, consisting of two rounded glass sections connected by a narrow neck through which sand trickles. The passage of sand from one section to the other takes one hour.

hou·ri (hŏŏr′ ē) *n-* one of the beautiful maidens of the Muslim paradise.

hour·ly (our′ lē) *adj-* 1 occurring every hour, or at intervals of an hour: *an hourly time signal;* hourly *bus service.* 2 computed in terms of an hour's work, operation, etc.: *his hourly wages. adv-: The chimes ring* hourly.

Hourglass

house (hous) *n-* [*pl.* hous·es (hou′ zĭz)] 1 building or other structure made to live in; dwelling. 2 building made for a particular purpose: *a house of worship; a* fraternity *house; the opera* house. 3 **House** division of a lawmaking body or group: *the House of Representatives.* 4 family, especially a ruling family: *a prince of the ruling*

how (hou) *adv-* 1 in what way or manner: *Tell me how you did that trick. How are we to interpret his remarks?* 2 by what means: *Just how do you plan to get here?* 3 to what extent, degree, or amount: *We don't know how serious his injuries are. How much paper do you need?* 4 in what state or condition: *Find out how he is today.* 5 for what reason; why: *I wonder how he could laugh at such a time.* 6 at what price: *Mr. Danton, how do you sell those oranges? n-* manner, means, method, etc.: *I don't understand the how or why of it.*
how about *Informal* 1 what do you say to or think of: *She asked, "How about going to the theater?"* 2 would you like to have: *Our hostess said, "How about some more ice cream?"* **how come** *Informal* why is it that.

HP, H.P., hp., or **h.p.** 1 horsepower. 2 high pressure.
H.Q. or **h.q.** headquarters.

huge (hyōōj) *adj-* [**hug·er, hug·est**] **1** very large; enormous: *The elephant is a huge animal.* **2** very great: *The party was a huge success.* —*adv-* **huge′ly**: *We enjoyed ourselves hugely.* *n-* **huge′ness.**

Hu·gue·not (hyōō′gə nòt′) *n-* a French Protestant of the sixteenth or seventeenth century.

hu·la (hōō′lə) *n-* Hawaiian dance which tells a story. The dancers move their arms and hands to describe different things and events, and sway their hips in time to the music. Also **hu′la-hu′la.**

hulk (hŭlk) *n-* **1** wreck of an old ship; dismantled hull. **2** heavy, clumsy ship. **3** overgrown, awkward person or thing: *a hulk of a man.*

hulk·ing (hŭl′kĭng) *adj-* big and clumsy: *The giant's hulking form filled the doorway.*

¹**hull** (hŭl) *n-* body or framework of a ship, seaplane, etc., without rigging or upper structures. [from Dutch **hul,** from **hol,** "the hold of a ship," and influenced by ²**hull.**] **hull down** of a ship, so far away that only the part above the hull is visible.

hum·din·ger (hŭm′dĭng′ər) *Slang n-* person or thing of remarkable excellence.

hum·drum (hŭm′drŭm′) *adj-* dull; monotonous: *a humdrum life.* *n-* dull routine; monotony.

hu·mer·us (hyōō′mər əs) *n-* **1** in man, bone of the upper arm, from the shoulder to the elbow. **2** corresponding bone in the forelimb of other animals. *Hom-* **humorous.**

hu·mid (hyōō′mĭd) *adj-* damp; moist: *The air is humid before a rain.* —*n-* **hu′mid·ness.**

hu·mid·i·fy (hyōō mĭd′ə fī′) *vt-* [**hu·mi·di·fied, hu·mi·di·fy·ing**] to give dampness to: *The vaporizer humidifies the air.* —*n-* **hu·mid′i·fi′er.**

hu·mid·i·ty (hyōō mĭd′ə tē) *n-* **1** dampness; moisture. **2** amount of moisture or water vapor in the air: *a day of high humidity.* **3** relative humidity.

hu·mi·dor (hyōō′mə dòr′, -dôr′) *n-* container which keeps cigars or tobacco fresh and moist.

hu·mil·i·ate (hyōō mĭl′ē āt′) *vt-* [**hu·mil·i·at·ed, hu·mil·i·at·ing**] to put to shame; cause to lose dignity and pride: *Jack was humiliated when his little sister outran him.* —*adv-* **hu·mil′i·a·ting·ly.**

hu·mil·i·a·tion (hyōō mĭl′ē ā′shən) *n-* a lowering or injuring of pride; a putting or being put to shame: *The child's tantrum caused the mother great humiliation.*

hu·mil·i·ty (hyōō mĭl′ə tē) *n-* modest sense of one's own importance; meekness: *to accept with humility.*

hum·ming·bird (hŭm′ĭng bûrd′) *n-* any of various tiny, bright-colored, long-billed birds that feed upon the nectar of flowers. The rapid movement of their wings in flight makes a hum.

hum·mock (hŭm′ək) *n-* small hill or rounded mound. —*adj-* **hum′mock·y.**

Ruby throated hummingbird about 3 1 2 in long

hu·mor (hyōō′mər) *n-* **1** cause of laughter or amusement; funniness: *the humor in a good joke; the humor of the incident.* **2** ability to be amusing; wit; also, writings, lectures, etc., showing this: *Mark Twain's humor.* **3** mood; state of mind: *Don't bother him when he is in a bad humor.* *vt-* to yield to the whims of; indulge. —*adj-* **hu′mor·less.**
out of humor not in a good mood; cross or irritable.

hu·mor·ist (hyōō′mər ĭst) *n-* person who writes or says amusing things.

hu·mor·ous (hyōō′mər əs) *adj-* funny; amusing; comical: *a humorous story; a humorous situation.* *Hom-* **humerus.** —*adv-* **hu′mor·ous·ly.** *n-* **hu′mor·ous·ness.**

hu·man (hyōō′mən) *adj-* **1** of, belonging to, or having the qualities of man or mankind: *the human species; human nature; human kindness.* **2** having to do with mankind: *the study of human affairs.* *n-* *Informal* a person. —*n-* **hu′man·ness.**

human being *n-* member of the human species; person.

Hun (hŭn) *n-* member of a barbarous nomadic people who invaded Europe in the fifth century under Attila, their powerful king and general.

hunch (hŭnch) *n-* **1** a feeling or suspicion; premonition: *to have a hunch; to follow a hunch.* **2** a hump. *vt-* to bend (the back or shoulders) to form a hump. *vi-* **1** to bend (over): *He hunched over his desk. He hunched over to avoid the blow.* **2** to pull one's arms, shoulders, and legs tightly against one's body: *He hunched into a ball to keep warm.*

hur·dle (hûr′dəl) *n-* **1** kind of fence in movable sections. **2** frame or other barrier over which runners or horses jump in a kind of race. **3** obstacle. **4** hurdles race in which runners must jump over frames. *vt-* [**hur·dled, hur·dling**] **1** to surmount an obstacle. **2** to leap over with a running stride. —*n-* **hur′dler.**

Hurdle

hur·dy-gur·dy (hûr′dē gûr′dē) *n-* [*pl.* **hur·dy-gur·dies**] mechanical musical instrument played by turning a handle, often in the streets.

hurl (hûrl) *vt-* **1** to throw with force; fling violently: *to hurl a rock through a window.* **2** to utter or speak with violence: *They hurled insults.* —*n-* **hurl′er.**

hurl·y-burl·y (hûr′lē bûr′lē) *n-* confusion.

Hu·ron (hyōōr′ŏn) *n-* [*pl.* **Hu·rons,** also **Hu·ron**] one of a group of Iroquoian Indians who lived in Ontario and the St. Lawrence River valley. *adj-* : *a Huron canoe.*

hur·rah (hə rä′) *interj-* shout expressing joy, applause, or triumph. *vi-* to utter such a shout. Also **hur·ray′** (hə rä′).

hur·ri·cane (hûr′ə kān′) *n-* vast and destructive tropical storm with very heavy rains and violent winds, exceeding 73 miles per hour, that spiral around a calm center of low atmospheric pressure.

hur·ried (hûr′ēd) *adj-* showing haste; hasty; done in a hurry: *It was a hurried trip.* —*adv-* **hur′ried·ly.**

hur·ry (hûr′ē) *vi-* [**hur·ried, hur·ry·ing**] to move or act quickly: *I have to hurry or I shall be late.* *vt-* to cause to move or act quickly; rush: *Please don't hurry me. Let's hurry this job.* *n-* [*pl.* **hur·ries**] impatient or needless haste: *No need for hurry, we have all day.*

hurt (hûrt) *vt-* [**hurt, hurt·ing**] **1** to cause pain to: *That hangnail hurts my finger.* **2** to grieve or offend: *She was hurt by those spiteful remarks.* **3** to damage; harm: *It won't hurt this watch to wear it in water.* *vi-* to cause pain: *That bruise hurts. Not being accepted for the team hurts.* *n-* injury; wound; harm: *a hurt to one's pride.*

hurt·ful (hûrt′fəl) *adj-* harmful; causing pain or injury. —*adv-* **hurt′ful·ly.**

hur·tle (hûr′təl) *vi-* [**hur·tled, hur·tling**] **1** to rush, speed, shoot, or fly wildly or at great speed: *The jet hurtled through the air.* **2** to dash; throw oneself; rush recklessly: *The boys hurtled out of the door.*

hus·band (hŭz′bənd) *n-* man who has a wife. *vt-* to use carefully; save: *to husband one's supplies.*

hus·band·man (hŭz′bənd mən) *n-* [*pl.* **hus·band·men**] farmer.

hus·band·ry (hŭz′bən drē) *n-* **1** farming; agriculture; especially, the raising of farm animals. **2** careful management: *By good husbandry Mr. White amassed a considerable fortune.*

hush (hŭsh) *vt-* to make quiet: *to hush a crying child.* *vi-* : *We were asked to hush during the music.* *n-* silence; stillness: *Not a sound broke the hush of the evening.*

hush money *Informal n-* bribe offered to persuade someone not to talk.

hush puppy *n-* fried ball of cornmeal dough.

husk (hŭsk) *n-* outermost covering of certain nuts and grains, such as corn and coconuts; also, any worthless outer covering. *vt-* to remove such a covering from: *to husk corn.* —*n-* **husk′er.**

Butternut husks

husking bee *n-* gathering of friends and neighbors to help a farmer husk his corn. Also **husking.**

¹**husk·y** (hŭs′kē) *adj-* [husk·i·er, husk·i·est] somewhat hoarse; almost like a whisper: *a husky voice.* [perhaps from husk, with reference to the dry, rough qualities of husks.] —*adv-* husk′i·ly. *n-* husk′i·ness.

²**husk·y** (hŭs′kē) *adj-* [husk·i·er, husk·i·est] big and strong: *a husky boy.* —*n-* husk′i·ness. [of uncertain origin, perhaps from the toughness of husks.]

³**husk·y** (hŭs′kē) *n-* [*pl.* husk·ies] Eskimo dog. Also **Husky.** [American word of uncertain origin.]

hus·sar (hə zär′) *n-* soldier of the light cavalry.

hus·sy (hŭz′ē, *also* hŭs′-) *n-* [*pl.* hus·sies] 1 an indecent or forward woman. 2 pert, mischievous girl.

hus·tings (hŭs′tǐngz) *chiefly Brit. n-* platform for making election speeches; stump.

hydraulic brakes *n-* brakes operated by the pressure of fluid in cylinders.

hydraulic mining *n-* mining by the direct use of a powerful stream of water.

hy·drau·lics (hī′drô′lǐks) *n-* (takes singular verb) branch of science that deals with the principles and practical engineering applications of water and other liquids in motion.

hy·dra·zine (hī′drə zēn′) *n-* liquid compound of hydrogen and nitrogen (N_2H_4) that is a rocket fuel.

hy·dride (hī′drīd′) *n-* compound of hydrogen and an element or radical.

hydro- *combining form* 1 water: hydro*graphy*; hydro*phone.* 2 *Chemistry* indicating a compound of hydrogen: hydro*fluoric acid.* [from Greek *hydro-*, from *hydor*, "water."]

hy·dro·bro·mic acid (hī′drō brō′mǐk) *n-* strong, colorless acid which is a solution of hydrogen bromide gas (HBr) in water.

hy·dro·car·bon (hī′drə kär′bən) *n-* any of a vast number of organic compounds, such as butane and benzene, that contains only hydrogen and carbon.

hy·dro·chlo·ric acid (hī′drə klôr′ǐk) *n-* strong, colorless acid (HCl) that is a water solution of hydrogen chloride gas. It is the acid in gastric juice.

hy·dro·cy·an·ic acid (hī′drō sī ăn′ǐk) *n-* very poisonous, colorless, volatile, liquid compound (HCN) having the odor of almonds; prussic acid.

hy·dro·dy·nam·ics (hī′drō dī năm′ǐks) *n-* (takes singular verb) branch of science that studies the motion of liquids, and the forces interacting between a liquid and a solid object that moves through it or is immersed in it. —*adj-* hy′dro·dy·nam′ic. *adv-* hy′dro·dy·nam′i·cal·ly.

hy·dro·e·lec·tric (hī′drō ə lěk′ trǐk) *adj-* of or having to do with electricity produced from water power.

hy·dro·fluor·ic acid (hī′drə flôr′ǐk, -flōō′ər ǐk) *n-* corrosive water solution of hydrogen fluoride (HF) used in the etching and frosting of glass.

hy·dro·foil (hī′drə foil′) *n-*
1 vane mounted on struts beneath the hull of a boat and designed to raise the boat above water when it reaches a certain speed. 2 boat having such vanes.

One type of hydrofoil

hy·dro·gen (hī′drə jən) *n-* odorless, colorless, flammable gas that is the lightest of the elements. It combines with oxygen to form water and with many other elements to form acids and most organic compounds. Symbol H, At. No. 1, At. Wt. 1.00797. —*adj-* hy·drog′e·nous (hī drŏj′ə nəs).

hy·dro·gen·ate (hī drŏj′ə nāt′) *vt-* [hy·dro·gen·at·ed, hy·dro·gen·at·ing] 1 to treat with hydrogen in a chemical reaction. 2 to combine with hydrogen. —*n-* hy′dro·gen·a′tion.

hydrogen bomb *n-* thermonuclear bomb of tremendous explosive power resulting from the fusion of hydrogen atoms; H-bomb.

hydrogen peroxide or **peroxide** *n-* colorless, unstable liquid (H_2O_2) used especially in water solutions of varying strengths as a bleaching or disinfecting agent and as a rocket propellant.

hydrogen sulfide *n-* poisonous, colorless, flammable gas (H_2S), having an odor of rotten eggs.

hy·dro·sphere (hī′drə sfēr′) *n-* all of the water and ice on earth and in the atmosphere.

hy·dro·stat·ics (hī′drō stăt′ǐks) *n-* (takes singular verb) branch of science that deals with the study of liquids at rest and their pressures on objects in them. —*adj-* hy′dro·stat′ic.

hy·dro·ther·a·py (hī′drō ther′ə pē) *Medicine n-* the use of water in the treatment of various diseases.

hy·dro·trop·ism (hī drŏt′rə pǐz′əm) *n-* tendency of a

hy·gien·ist (hī jē′nǐst, hī jěn′ ǐst) *n-* person who is a student of or expert in hygiene.

hy·gro·graph (hī′grə grăf′) *n-* a hygrometer that automatically records its readings on a chart.

hy·grom·e·ter (hī grŏm′ə tər) *n-* instrument that measures the humidity or amount of moisture in the air. —*adj-* hy′gro·met′ric.

hy·gro·scop·ic (hī′grə skŏp′ǐk) *adj-* 1 having the property of taking up and holding moisture from the air, as salt does in damp weather. 2 of or relating to this property or process.

hy·men (hī′mən) *n-* membrane partly closing the vagina.

Hy·men (hī′mən) *n-* in Greek mythology, the god of marriage.

hy·me·ne·al (hī′mə nē′əl) *adj-* of or relating to marriage; nuptial: *a hymeneal celebration.*

hy·men·op·ter·ous (hī′mə nŏp′tər əs) *adj-* of, having to do with, or belonging to the large group of insects (**Hymenoptera**), including the ants, bees, and wasps, that have four wings and usually live in colonies.

hymn (hǐm) *n-* 1 song of praise to God. 2 any song of praise, thanksgiving, or the like. *Hom-* him. —*adj-* hymn′like.

hym·nal (hǐm′nəl) *n-* book of hymns.

hymn·book (hǐm′bŏŏk′) *n-* hymnal.

hyper- *prefix* 1 abnormally great; excessive: hyper*acidity.* 2 excessively: hyper*critical.* [from Greek *hyper-*, meaning "over; above; exceedingly."]

hy·per·a·cid·i·ty (hī′pər ə sǐd′ə tē) *n-* excess acid, especially in the stomach.

hy·per·bo·la (hī pûr′bə lə) *n-*
1 a curve formed by the intersection of a double right-circular cone with a plane that cuts both parts of the cone and is parallel to the axis of the cone but does not contain it. A hyperbola thus has two branches. —*adj-* hy·per·bol′ic.

Hyperbola

hy·per·bo·le (hī pûr′bə lē) *n-* figure of speech that states much more than the truth; exaggeration for effect. Examples: The day was endless. The driver was about ten feet tall.

hy·per·bol·ic (hī′pər bŏl′ǐk) *adj-* 1 extreme or inordinate: *a really* hyperbolic *exaggeration.* 2 greatly exaggerated or overstated: *his* hyperbolic *praise of the book.* 3 of, related to, or having the form of a hyperbola: *a* hyperbolic *surface.*

hy·per·crit·i·cal (hī′pər krǐt′ǐ kəl) *adj-* tending to complain about trivial things; overly sensitive to the faults of others. —*adv-* hy′per·crit′ti·cal·ly.

Hy·per·i·on (hī pēr′ē ən) *n-* 1 in Greek mythology, the son of Uranus and the father of Helios. 2 in Homer's "Iliad," Helios himself. 3 in later times, Apollo.

hy·per·o·pi·a (hī′pə rō′ pē ə) *n-* farsightedness.

hy·per·sen·si·tive (hī′pər sěn′sə tĭv) *adj-* very sensitive; especially, having very tender feelings that are easily wounded or offended. —*n-* hy·per·sen′si·tive·ness. *n-* hy·per·sen′si·tiv′i·ty.

hy·per·son·ic (hī′pər sŏn′ǐk) *adj-* of, having to do with, or characterized by speeds that are at least 5 times the speed of sound.

hy·per·ten·sion (hī′pər těn′shən) *n-* abnormally high blood pressure.

hy·per·thy·roid·ism (hī′pər thī′roid ǐz′əm) *n-* condition resulting from excessive activity of the thyroid gland. It is marked by an increased metabolic rate, weight loss, increased heart rate, and nervousness.

hy·per·tro·phy (hī pûr′trə fē) *n-* increased size of a part or organ, due to growth instead of a tumor.

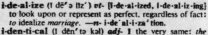

I

I, i (ī) *n*- [*pl.* **I's, i's**] **1** the ninth letter of the English alphabet. **2** Roman numeral for the number one.

¹I (ī) *pron*- (used as a singular subject in the first person) the person who is speaking or writing. [a reduced form of Old English *ic* of the same meaning.] *Homs*- ²ay or aye, eye.

²I symbol for iodine.

I. 1 Island. **2** Islands. **3** Isle; Isles.

Ia. Iowa.

i·amb (ī′ămb′) *n*- **1** a measure or foot in poetry made up of one unaccented syllable followed by one accented syllable. **2** a line in poetry made up of such measures. Example: "Was this′/the face′/that launched′/a thou′/ sand ships′?" —*adj*- **i·am′bic.**

Ian *suffix* See -an.

ice age *n*- **1** a time when large areas of the earth were covered by sheets of ice and glaciers. **2 Ice Age** the Pleistocene epoch in geology, noted for its glaciation.

ice bag *n*- rubberized cloth container designed to hold ice and to be applied to the body as a cold pack.

ice·berg (īs′bûrg′) *n*- **1** mass of floating ice, often of great size, detached from the base of a glacier. Only about one ninth of its mass shows above water. **2** person with a cold disposition.

PART
BELOW
WATER

Iceberg

ice·boat (īs′bōt′) *n*- sailing vehicle for use on ice. It is shaped like a cross, with runners at each end of the crosspiece and one at the stern for steering.

ice·bound (īs′bound′) *adj*- **1** surrounded by ice so as to be unable to move: *an icebound ship.* **2** unusable because of ice: *an icebound harbor.*

ice·box (īs′bŏks′) *n*- refrigerator, especially one that uses ice but does not make it.

ice·break·er (īs′brāk′ər) *n*- a ship with strong engines and prow that cuts channels in frozen rivers, lakes, or harbors to permit the passage of ships.

ice·cap (īs′kăp′) *n*- ice sheet.

ice cream *n*- frozen dessert made with milk, cream, sugar, flavoring, and sometimes gelatin and eggs.

ice field *n*- very large sheet of floating sea ice.

ice·house (īs′hous′) *n*- building where ice is stored.

Ice·land·ic (īs lăn′dĭk) *adj*- of or relating to Iceland, its people, or their language. *n*- the North Germanic language of the people of Iceland. The older forms of this language are known as **Old Icelandic** or **Old Norse.**

Iceland spar *n*- calcite.

ice·man (īs′măn′) *n*- [*pl.* **ice·men**] person who supplies and delivers ice.

ice pack *n*- **1** floating ice mass consisting of separate pieces jammed together and frozen solid. **2** ice bag.

ice pick *n*- hand tool with a needlelike spike, used for chipping blocks of ice into smaller pieces.

ice sheet *n*- **1** either of the two immense, permanent masses of ice, thousands of feet deep, that cover most of Greenland and Antarctica. The ice in an ice sheet moves slowly outward in all directions from the regions of greatest thickness; ice cap. **2** any flat mass of covering ice, such as the large ice floes in the Arctic.

ice·skate (īs′skāt′) *vi*- [**ice·skat·ed, ice·skat·ing**] to skate with ice skates. —*n*- **ice skater.**

i·ci·cle (ī′sĭk′əl, -sə kəl) *n*- hanging spike of ice.

Icicles

ic·i·ly (ī′sə lē) *adv*- in a cold or icy manner.

ic·i·ness (ī′sē nəs) *n*- condition of being frozen, icy, or chilly.

ic·ing (ī′sĭng) *n*- **1** coating for cakes and cookies made usually with sugar, butter, milk or water, and flavoring, etc.; frosting. **2** formation of layers of ice on airplane wings, ship decks, etc.

i·con (ī′kŏn′) *n*- **1** in the Eastern Orthodox Church, a sacred picture of Christ, the Virgin, etc., usually brightly painted on a wooden panel. **2** any image, especially a picture. Also **ikon.**

i·de·al·ize (ī dē′ə līz′) *vt*- [**i·de·al·ized, i·de·al·iz·ing**] to look upon or represent as perfect, regardless of fact: *to idealize marriage.* —*n*- **i·de′al·i·za′tion.**

i·den·ti·cal (ī děn′tə kəl) *adj*- **1** the very same: *the identical spot.* **2** exactly alike: *No two faces are identical.* —*adv*- **i·den′ti·cal·ly.** *n*- **i·den′ti·cal·ness.**

identical twins *n*- human twins of the same sex, developed from a single fertilized ovum and, as a result, having identical hereditary characteristics. See also *fraternal twins.*

i·den·ti·fi·ca·tion (ī děn′tə fə kā′shən) *n*- **1** an identifying or being identified: *the identification of criminals.* **2** proof that someone or something is what is claimed: *He showed his driver's license as identification.*

i·den·ti·fy (ī děn′tə fī′) *vt*- [**i·den·ti·fied, i·den·ti·fy·ing**] **1** to discover or state the identity of; recognize; name: *He identified the bridge in the snapshot.* **2** to make, consider, or treat as identical: *to identify wealth with success.* **3** to associate: *He refused to identify himself with their scheme.* *vi*- to feel a kinship or oneness with another person: *The girl identified with the heroine of the story.* —*adj*- **i·den′ti·fi′a·ble**: *The ship was not identifiable.* *adv*- **i·den′ti·fi′a·bly.** *n*- **i·den′ti·fi·er.**

i·den·ti·ty (ī děn′tə tē) *n*- [*pl.* **i·den·ti·ties**] **1** who a person is; what a thing is: *The identity of the author is unknown.* **2** sameness; oneness: *She noticed the identity of their papers.* **3** particular personality; individuality: *to assert one's identity.* **4** *Mathematics* (1) element in a set that, when combined in an operation with any other element, does not change that element. For addition, the identity element is 0, and for multiplication, it is 1: $7 + 0 = 7$; $9 \times 1 = 9$. (2) expression stating the equivalence of two terms: $6 = 6$.

i·de·o·graph (ĭd′ē ə grăf′) *n*- picture or symbol used in a writing system to represent an idea or thing rather than the particular word or phrase for it. For example, a picture of a lion might be used to suggest power. Also **i′de·o·gram** (ĭd′ē ə grăm′). —*adj*- **i′de·o·graph′ic.** *adv*- **i′de·o·graph′i·cal·ly.**

i·de·ol·o·gy (ĭd′ē ŏl′ə jē, ī′dē-) *n*- [*pl.* **i·de·ol·o·gies**] system of ideas and theories about human life, especially that of some political party, nation, etc. —*adj*- **i′de·o·log′i·cal** (ĭd′ē ə lŏj′ĭ kəl). *adv*- **i′de·o·log′i·cal·ly.**

ides (īdz) *n*- *pl.* (takes singular or plural verb) in the ancient Roman calendar, the 15th of March, May, July, and October; the 13th of the other months.

id·i·o·cy (ĭd′ē ə sē) *n*- [*pl.* **id·i·o·cies**] **1** almost total lack of intelligence; extreme mental deficiency. **2** very foolish act; extreme foolishness.

id·i·om (ĭd′ē əm) *n*- **1** a group of words whose meaning must be known as a whole because it cannot be learned from the meanings of the same words used separately. "To go back on" doesn't only mean "to move backward onto," but also "to betray or fail." **2** the language used by the people of a certain region, group, class, etc.: *the American idiom; the idiom of sailors.* **3** a particular person's way of using words: *Shakespeare's idiom.*

id·i·o·mat·ic (ĭd′ē ə măt′ĭk) *adj*- **1** given to, or marked by, the use of idiom: *to speak idiomatic French.* **2** peculiar to the language of a country or region; colloquial. **3** having the nature of an idiom: *an idiomatic*

ig·nite (ĭg nīt′) *vt*- [**ig·nit·ed, ig·nit·ing**] to set fire to; set on fire: *to ignite twigs.* *vi*- to catch fire; take fire: *The dry leaves ignited from a spark.* —*n*- **ig·nit′er.**

ig·ni·tion (ĭg nĭsh′ən) *n*- **1** act of catching fire or lighting a fire. **2** system in an internal-combustion engine that ignites the fuel. *as modifier: an ignition engine.*

ig·no·ble (ĭg nō′bəl) *adj*- **1** of low character; mean; base: *A cheat is an ignoble man.* **2** shameful; disgraceful: *an ignoble defeat.* —*n*- **ig·no′ble·ness.** *adv*- **ig·no′bly.**

ig·no·min·i·ous (ĭg′nə mĭn′ē əs) *adj*- **1** disgraceful; shameful; dishonorable: *an ignominious act.* **2** humiliating: *an ignominious punishment.* —*adv*- **ig′no·min′i·ous·ly.** *n*- **ig′no·min′i·ous·ness.**

ig·no·min·y (ĭg′nə mĭn′ē, ĭg nŏm′ə nē) *n*- [*pl.* **ig·no·min·ies**] disgrace or dishonor; also, a cause of this.

ig·no·ra·mus (ĭg nə răm′əs, -rā′məs) *n*- [*pl.* **ig·no·ra·mus·es**] ignorant person.

ig·no·rant (Ig′ nə rənt) *adj-* 1 lacking in knowledge or education: *He is ignorant of the customs in other countries.* 2 unaware: *He was ignorant of the facts.* 3 based on ignorance: *an ignorant answer.* —*adv-* ig′no·rant·ly.

ig·nore (Ig nôr′) *vt-* [ig·nored, ig·nor·ing] to pay no attention to; refuse to notice.

i·gua·na (I gwä′ nə) *n-* any of several long-tailed lizards, especially a tropical American lizard with a crest of scales along its back and a puffed out throat.

IGY (I′ jē′ wī′) International Geophysical Year.

i·kon (I′ kŏn′) icon.

il·e·um (Il′ē əm) *n-* lowest division of the small intestine. *Hom-* ilium.

Iguana different kinds vary from a few inches to 6 ft long

Il·i·ad (Il′ē əd) *n-* ancient Greek epic poem, by Homer, telling some of the events of the siege of Ilium (Troy).

il·i·um (Il′ē əm) *n-* the large upper portion of either of the hipbones. For picture, see *pelvis. Hom-* ileum.

ilk (Ilk) *n-* breed; sort; kind: *thieves and others of that ilk.*

ill (Il) *adj-* [worse, worst] 1 sick; not well; diseased: *The child is ill.* 2 disagreeable; hostile: *his ill humor; ill will.* 3 harmful: *an ill turn.*

ill-fat·ed (Il′ fā′ təd) *adj-* 1 destined to misfortune; doomed: *an ill-fated marriage.* 2 bringing, or resulting in, misfortune: *an ill-fated meeting.*

ill-fa·vored (Il′ fā′ vərd) *adj-* unattractive; ugly.

ill-got·ten (Il′ gŏt′ ən) *adj-* obtained by evil or unlawful methods: *an ill-gotten fortune.*

ill-hu·mored (Il′ hyŏō′ mərd) *adj-* bad-tempered; disagreeable: *an ill-humored man.* —*adv-* ill′-hu′ mored·ly.

il·lib·er·al (I lĭb′ ər əl) *adj-* 1 narrow-minded. 2 stingy; close; ungenerous: *an illiberal allowance.* —*n-* il·lib′er·al′i·ty (-ăl′ ə tē).

il·lic·it (I lĭs′ It) *adj-* illegal; forbidden: *an illicit trade. Hom-* elicit. —*adv-* il·lic′ it·ly. *n-* il·lic′ it·ness.

il·lim·it·a·ble (I lĭm′ ə tə bəl) *adj-* without limits; boundless; vast: *his illimitable ambition.* —*adv-* il·lim′ it·a·bly.

Il·li·nois (Il′ ə noi′, -noiz′) *n-* [*pl.* Il·li·nois] a member of a confederacy of Algonquian Indians who lived in Illinois, Iowa, and Wisconsin.

il·lit·er·a·cy (I lĭt′ ər ə sē) *n-* [*pl.* il·lit·er·a·cies] inability to read and write.

il·lit·er·ate (I lĭt′ ər ət) *adj-* 1 unable to read and write. 2 showing lack of education: *an illiterate letter. n-* person unable to read and write. —*adv-* il·lit′er·ate·ly.

ill-man·nered (Il′ măn′ ərd) *adj-* impolite; rude. —*adv-* ill-man′ nered·ly.

ill-na·tured (Il′ nā′ chərd) *adj-* cross; disagreeable; surly. —*adv-* ill′ na′tured·ly.

ill·ness (Il′ nəs) *n-* 1 condition of being sick: *She stayed home because of illness.* 2 disease; malady.

il·log·i·cal (I lŏj′ I kəl) *adj-* not logical; contrary to reason. —*adv-* il·log′ i·cal·ly. *n-* il·log′ i·cal·ness.

ill-spent (Il′ spĕnt′) *adj-* badly spent; wasted: *an ill-spent hour.*

im·age·ry (Im′ Ij rē) *n-* [*pl.* im·age·ries] 1 mental pictures collectively, especially those formed in the imagination of an artist, poet, etc. 2 language which causes the mind to form pictures.

im·ag·i·na·ble (I măj′ ə nə bəl) *adj-* such as can be imagined or pictured in the mind; conceivable: *the greatest joy imaginable.* —*adv-* im·ag′ i·na·bly.

im·ag·i·nar·y (I măj′ ə nĕr′ ē) *adj-* existing only in the mind or imagination; not real.

im·ag·i·na·tion (I măj′ ə nā′ shən) *n-* 1 the power of the mind to form pictures; ability to form mental pictures of things not actually present or seen:

im·be·cile (Im′ bə səl) *n-* 1 person with a weak mind, having less intelligence than a moron but more than an idiot. 2 *Informal* silly or stupid person. *adj-* 1 weak-minded. 2 stupid; foolish: *an imbecile remark.*

im·be·cil·ic (Im′ bə sĭl′ Ik) *adj-* imbecile.

im·be·cil·i·ty (Im′ bə sĭl′ ə tē) *n-* [*pl.* im·be·cil·i·ties] 1 weakness of mind. 2 folly; absurdity.

im·ma·ture (Im′ ə chŏōr′, -tyŏōr′) *adj-* 1 not ripe; not fully grown or developed; not finished or perfected: *an immature ear of corn; immature plans.* 2 behaving in a childish way: *an immature man.* —*adv-* im′ ma·ture′ly.

im·ma·tu·ri·ty (Im′ ə chŏōr′ ə tē, -tyŏōr′ ə tē) *n-* condition of being immature; unripeness; childishness.

im·meas·ur·a·ble (I mĕzh′ ər ə bəl) *adj-* boundless; impossible to measure. —*adv-* im·meas′ur·a·bly.

im·me·di·a·cy (I mē′ dē ə sē) *n-* [*pl.* im·me·di·a·cies] 1 condition of being free from anything coming in between; direct relationship; closeness: *the immediacy of the school to his house; the immediacy of danger at the front.* 2 present necessity: *the immediacy of their needs.*

im·me·di·ate (I mē′ dē ət) *adj-* 1 happening or coming at once; instant: *an immediate reply; our immediate needs.* 2 having to do with the present: *the immediate question;*

im·me·mo·ri·al (Im′ ə môr′ ē əl) *adj-* beyond reach of memory or record. —*adv-* im′ me·mo′ri·al·ly.

im·mense (I mĕns′) *adj-* enormous; huge; great: *an immense building; an immense success.* —*adv-* im·mense′ ly. *n-* im·mense′ ness or im·men′ si·ty.

im·merse (I mûrs′) *vt-* [im·mersed, im·mers·ing] 1 to plunge or dip into a liquid: *to immerse a dress in dye.* 2 to baptize by plunging (a person) entirely under water. 3 to engage deeply; absorb: *He was immersed in his work.*

im·mer·sion (I mûr′ zhən) *n-* 1 an immersing or being immersed; especially, a baptism by immersing. 2 *Astronomy* disappearance of a heavenly body behind another, or into its shadow.

im·mi·grant (Im′ ə grənt) *n-* person who comes into a country to make it his permanent home.

▶Should not be confused with EMIGRANT.

im·mi·grate (Im′ ə grāt′) *vi-* [im·mi·grat·ed, im·mi·grat·ing] to enter a foreign country intending to settle there permanently. —*n-* im′ mi·gra′ tion.

▶Should not be confused with EMIGRATE.

im·mi·nent (Im′ ə nənt) *adj-* about to happen; threatening: *an imminent storm; imminent death. Hom-* immanent. —*n-* im′ mi·nence. —*adv-* im′ mi·nent·ly.

im·mo·bile (I mō′ bəl) *adj-* immovable; also, motionless: *his immobile features.* —*n-* im′ mo·bil′ i·ty.

im·mo·bi·lize (I mō′ bə lĭz′) *vt-* [im·mo·bi·lized, im·mo·bi·liz·ing] to make unable or difficult to move or use: *Illness immobilized him.* —*n-* im·mo′ bi·li·za′ tion.

im·mod·er·ate (I mŏd′ ər ət) *adj-* not moderate; extreme; excessive: *an immoderate appetite for sweets.* —*adv-* im·mod′ er·ate·ly. *n-* im·mod′ er·ate·ness or im·mod′ er·a·cy or im·mod′ er·a′ tion.

im·mod·est (I mŏd′ əst) *adj-* not modest; especially, not decent or proper: *an immodest dress; immodest behavior.* —*adv-* im·mod′ est·ly. *n-* im·mod′ est·y.

im·mo·late (Im′ ō lāt′) *vt-* [im·mo·lat·ed, im·mo·lat·ing] to offer in sacrifice; especially, to kill as a victim for sacrifice. —*n-* im′ mo·la′ tion.

im·mor·al (I môr′ əl, I môr′-) *adj-* 1 contrary to conscience or what is considered right: *their immoral conduct.* 2 wicked; unscrupulous. —*adj-* im·mor′al·ly.

im·mo·ral·i·ty (Im′ ô răl′ ə tē, Im′ ə-) *n-* [*pl.* im·mo·ral·i·ties] 1 reverse of morality; immoral nature or condition. 2 immoral behavior; wickedness.

im·mor·tal (I môr′ təl, I môr′-) *adj-* 1 living forever; freed from death: *the immortal soul.* 2 never to be forgotten; of everlasting fame. 3 having to do with something more than human; divine; heavenly: *an immortal vision. n-* 1 person who never dies. 2 person whose fame is undying. 3 the immortals in mythology, the gods. —*adv-* im·mor′ tal·ly.

im·mor·tal·i·ty (Im′ ôr tăl′ ə tē, im′ ər tăl′ ə tē) *n-* 1 individual life that never ends. 2 everlasting fame.

im·mor·tal·ize (I môr′ tə lĭz′, I môr′-) *vt-* [im·mor·tal·ized, im·mor·tal·iz·ing] 1 to give everlasting fame to; cause to be remembered. 2 to give unending life to. —*n-* im·mor′ tal·i·za′ tion.

im·mov·able (I mŏō′ və bəl) *adj-* 1 not movable; firmly fixed: *an immovable object.* 2 firm; unchanging or unyielding: *an immovable stubborness. n-* **immovables** in law, property such as land or buildings. —*n-* im·mov′ a·bil′ i·ty. *adv-* im·mov′ a·bly.

im·mure (I myŏŏr') *vt-* [im·mured, im·mur·ing] to confine or seal within walls; shut up in. —*n-* im·mure'ment.

im·mu·ta·ble (I myōō'tə bəl) *adj-* unchangeable; unalterable. —*n-* im·mu'ta·bil'i·ty or im·mu'ta·ble·ness. *adv-* im·mu'ta·bly.

imp (Imp) *n-* 1 young or small devil; little demon. 2 mischievous child.

imp. 1 imperial. 2 imperative. 3 imported. 4 importer. 5 imperfect.

im·pact (Im'păkt') *n-* 1 the blow of one thing hitting another; collision: *the impact of baseball and bat.* 2 startling or impressive effect: *the impact of the news.*

Imp

im·pact·ed (Im păk'təd) *adj-* 1 of a tooth, so deeply wedged in the jawbone that it will not come through the gum. 2 wedged firmly.

im·pair (Im pâr') *vt-* to lessen the quantity, excellence, value, or strength of; weaken; damage; harm: *Dim light impairs the eyesight.* —*n-* im·pair'ment.

im·pale (Im pāl') *vt-* [im·paled, im·pal·ing] to pierce through with something pointed; especially, to kill by piercing with a sharp stake. —*n-* im·pale'ment.

im·pal·pa·ble (Im pāl'pə bəl) *adj-* 1 impossible to feel by touch: *the still, impalpable air; the impalpable shadows.* 2 not easily grasped by the mind: *to make impalpable distinctions.* —*n-* im·pal'pa·bil'i·ty. *adv-* im·pal'pa·bly.

im·pan·el (Im păn'əl) *vt-* 1 to enter upon a list for jury duty. 2 to select (a jury) from such a list. —*n-* im·pan'el·ment.

im·part (Im pärt') *vt-* 1 to give; bestow: *Flowers impart beauty to a room.* 2 to disclose: *to impart a secret.*

im·par·tial (Im pär'shəl) *adj-* not favoring either side; not biased; fair; just; disinterested: *an impartial referee.* —*adv-* im·par'tial·ly.

im·par·ti·al·i·ty (Im pär'shē ăl'ə tē) *n-* freedom from partiality or favoritism; fairness.

im·pass·a·ble (Im păs'ə bəl) *adj-* such as cannot be crossed or passed over, through, or along; not passable: *an impassable swamp.* —*n-* im·pass'a·bil'i·ty: *the impassability of the swamp.* *adv-* im·pass'a·bly.

im·passe (Im'pās') *n-* position or situation from which there is no obvious or logical way out; deadlock.

im·pas·sioned (im păsh'ənd) *adj-* showing strong emotion: *an impassioned speaker.*

im·pas·sive (Im păs'Iv) *adj-* showing or feeling no emotion; unmoved; calm: *an impassive audience.* —*adv-* im·pas'sive·ly. —*n-* im·pas'sive·ness or im'pas·siv'i·ty (Im'pə slv'ə tē).

im·pa·tience (Im pā'shəns) *n-* 1 lack of patience; inability to tolerate or endure delay, restraint, etc.: *to feel impatience toward carelessness.* 2 restless eagerness: *her impatience to be off on the trip.* 3 a cultivated flowering plant related to the jewelweed.

im·pa·tient (Im pā'shənt) *adj-* 1 not patient; feeling or showing annoyance with delay, opposition, etc.: *an impatient reply.* 2 restlessly eager: *She is impatient to grow up.* —*adv-* im·pa'tient·ly.

im·peach (Im pēch') *vt-* 1 to charge (a person in public office) before a court, with misconduct in office. 2 to question or challenge (a person's honor, motives, etc.). —*adj-* im·peach'a·ble.

im·peach·ment (Im pēch'mənt) *n-* an impeaching; especially, the calling to trial of a public official for misconduct.

im·pec·ca·ble (Im pĕk'ə bəl) *adj-* not capable of sin or error. 2 free from fault or flaw: *a suit of impeccable cut.* —*n-* im·pec'ca·bil'i·ty: *the impeccability of his manners.* *adv-* im·pec'ca·bly.

im·pe·cu·ni·ous (Im'pə kyōō'nē əs) *adj-* lacking money; poor. —*adv-* im'pe·cu'ni·ous·ly.

im·pede (Im pēd') *vt-* [im·ped·ed, im·ped·ing] to hold back; obstruct; hinder: *Fog impeded our progress.*

im·ped·i·ment (Im pĕd'ə mənt) *n-* 1 something that holds back or obstructs; a hindrance. 2 a speech defect.

im·pen·i·tent (Im pĕn'ə tənt) *adj-* not sorry for one's sin or wrongdoing; unrepentant. *n-* person who is not repentant; hardened sinner. —*n-* im·pen'i·tence: *his strong-willed impenitence.* *adv-* im·pen'i·tent·ly.

im·per·son·al (Im pûr'sən əl) *adj-* 1 not aimed at or referring to any particular person: *an impersonal discussion of student problems.* 2 not prejudiced; not influenced by personal feeling: *an impersonal approach to a subject.* 3 not existing as a person: *the impersonal forces of nature.* —*n-* im·per'son·al'i·ty (-Ǎl'ə tē): *the impersonality of a court.* *adv-* im·per'son·al·ly.

im·per·son·ate (Im pûr'sə nāt') *vt-* [im·per·son·at·ed, im·per·son·at·ing] 1 to act the character of; mimic; play the part of, especially on the stage. 2 to pretend to be (another person) in order to deceive: *The spy impersonated an officer.* —*n-* im·per'son·a'tion.

im·per·son·a·tor (Im pûr'sə nā'tər) *n-* person who mimicks or pretends to be another person; especially, an entertainer who mimicks: *a clever impersonator.*

im·per·ti·nence (Im pûr'tə nəns) *n-* 1 insolence; impudence. 2 impudent act or remark: *his rude impertinences.* 3 lack of relevance or pertinence.

im·per·ti·nent (Im pûr'tə nənt) *adj-* 1 insolent; disrespectful: *an impertinent retort.* 2 not pertinent; irrelevant. —*adv-* im·per'ti·nent·ly.

im·per·turb·a·ble (Im'pər tûr'bə bəl) *adj-* not excitable; calm; unshaken. —*n-* im'per·turb'a·bil'i·ty. *adv-* im'per·turb'a·bly.

im·per·vi·ous (Im pûr'vē əs) *adj-* 1 not permitting entrance or passage (to): *a tent impervious to rain.* 2 closed (to); not receptive (to): *She is impervious to criticism.* —*adv-* im·per'vi·ous·ly. —*n-* im·per'vi·ous·ness.

im·pe·ti·go (Im'pə tī'gō) *n-* contagious skin disease marked by pus spots which later become crusted.

im·pet·u·os·i·ty (Im pĕch'ōō ŏs'ə tē) *n-* [*pl.* im·pet·u·os·i·ties] 1 impetuous nature or behavior: *the impetuosity of youth.* 2 impetuous act.

im·pet·u·ous (Im pĕch'ōō əs) *adj-* 1 given to or marked by sudden, unthinking actions; impulsive; headlong; rash: *an impetuous person; an impetuous decision to quit.* 2 moving fast or with violent force: *an impetuous*

im·pe·tus (Im'pə təs) *n-* 1 forward push; stimulus: *The tax decrease gave an impetus to industry.* 2 force or momentum by which a moving body tends to overcome resistance.

im·pi·e·ty (Im pī'ə tē) *n-* [*pl.* im·pi·e·ties] 1 lack of religious reverence. 2 irreverent or profane act.

im·pinge (Im pĭnj') *vi-* [im·pinged, im·ping·ing] 1 to strike or press (on, upon, or against): *Light rays impinge on the retina.* 2 to encroach; infringe (on): *to impinge upon our liberties.* —*n-* im·pinge'ment.

im·pi·ous (Im'pē əs, *also* Im'pī') *adj-* not pious; irreverent toward God and sacred things; profane. —*adv-* im'pi·ous·ly or Im'pī'ous·ly. *n-* im'pi·ous·ness or im'pī'ous·ness.

imp·ish (Im'plsh) *adj-* like, or suitable to, an imp; mischievous. —*adv-* imp'ish·ly. *n-* imp'ish·ness.

im·pla·ca·ble (Im plăk'ə bəl, im plā'kə-) *adj-* such as cannot be pacified, appeased, or reconciled; relentless: *an implacable hatred.* —*n-* im·pla'ca·bil'i·ty. *adv-* im·pla'ca·bly.

im·plant (Im plănt') *vt-* to plant or set in deeply; hence, to fix firmly in the consciousness: *to implant an idea.* —*n-* im'plan·ta'tion.

¹im·ple·ment (Im'plə mənt) *n-* tool or instrument with which work is done: *Hoes are garden implements.*

²im·ple·ment (Im'plə mĕnt') *vt-* to carry out by concrete means and action; put into practical effect: *to implement a plan.*

im·pli·cate (Im'plə kăt') *vt-* [im·pli·ca·ted, im·pli·ca·ting] to show or say that (someone or something) has caused or aided in something harmful: *The thief implicated two helpers.*

im·pli·ca·tion (Im'plə kā'shən) *n-* 1 something that is implied: *The implications are more important than the direct statements.* 2 an implicating in something harmful: *the thief's implication of his two helpers.*

im·post (Im'pōst') *n-* tax or duty, especially one levied by the government on goods brought into a country.

im·pos·tor (Im pŏs'tər) *n-* person who tries to deceive others by pretending to be someone or something else.

im·pos·ture (Im pŏs'chər) *n-* a fraud or deception:

im·preg·na·ble (Im prĕg′nə bəl) *adj-* secure against attack; not to be overcome or taken by force; unconquerable; invincible: *an impregnable fortress in the hills.* —*n-* im·preg′na·bil′i·ty. *adv-* im·preg′na·bly.

im·preg·nate (Im prĕg′nāt′) *vt-* [im·preg·nat·ed, im·preg·nat·ing] 1 to make pregnant; fertilize. 2 to cause to be saturated with. —*n-* im′preg·na′tion.

im·pre·sa·ri·o (Im′prə sär′ē ō, -sär′ē ō) *n-* [*pl.* im·pre·sa·ri·os] person who arranges or directs concerts, operas, etc.

¹im·press (Im′prĕs′) *n-* mark made by, or as by, a stamp; impression. [from Latin **impressum**, from **imprimere**, "to seal; press into or upon."]

²im·press (Im prĕs′) *vt-* 1 to strike (someone) as remarkable and memorable, especially in a favorable way: *His wit impressed me. The candidate does not impress me.* 2 to mark by, or as if by, pressing with a stamp or die; stamp: *to impress a seal in wax; to impress an idea on one's audience.* [from **¹impress.**] —*n-* im·press′er.

³im·press (Im prĕs′) *vt-* to force into military or naval service by seizing and holding, once a customary practice: *to impress a new crew for the frigate.* [from **²in-,** plus **²press.**] —*n-* im·press′ment.

im·pres·sion (Im prĕsh′ən) *n-* 1 an effect or impact on the mind or feelings: *Her first airplane ride made a strong impression on her.* 2 idea that is not clear or certain; especially, a judgment made quickly without strong factual basis: *I had the impression that he was in a hurry. It's only an impression, but I think this is a very good car.* 3 mark made by pressing: *the impression of a seal on wax.* 4 a mimicking; imitation: *Tom gave his impression of Winston Churchill.*

im·pres·sion·a·ble (Im prĕsh′ən ə bəl) *adj-* easily influenced; very sensitive to impressions. —*n-* im·pres′sion·a·bil′i·ty. *adv-* im·pres′sion·a·bly.

im·pres·sion·ism (Im prĕsh′ən Iz′əm) *n-* 1 style of painting that tries to capture impressions of light on surfaces with short strokes of varied colors and no clear outlines. 2 in music and literature, a style based on this, in which the total impression of a moment, scene, etc., is built by a series of sounds or words that suggest it. —*n-* im·pres′sion·ist. *adj-* im·pres′sion·is′tic.

im·pres·sive (Im prĕs′Iv) *adj-* strongly affecting the mind, feelings, or actions, especially in a favorable way: *The new government buildings are impressive.* —*adv-* im·pres′sive·ly. *n-* im·pres′sive·ness.

im·pri·ma·tur (Im′prə mā′tər) *n-* consent of an authority, especially a bishop of the Roman Catholic Church, for the publication of printed matter.

¹im·print (Im print′) *vt-* to print; impress: *They imprinted the birth certificate with an official seal.*

²im·print (Im′print′) *n-* 1 a mark; impression: *the imprint of a foot in the sand.* 2 printer's or publisher's name, and the place and date of publication, printed on the title page or at the end of a book.

im·pris·on (Im priz′ən) *vt-* 1 to put or keep in prison. 2 to keep shut up; confine: *to imprison a tiger in a cage.* —*n-* im·pris′on·ment.

im·prob·a·ble (Im prŏb′ə bəl) *adj-* not probable; not likely to happen, exist, or be true: *an improbable result; an improbable story.* —*adv-* im·prob′a·bly. *n-* im·prob′a·bil′i·ty.

im·promp·tu (Im prŏmp′tōō) *adj-* without preparation; offhand: *an impromptu picnic. adv-: to speak impromptu. n-* something, such as a musical composition, that is made, done, or performed without preparation.

im·prove (Im prōōv′) *vt-* [im·proved, im·prov·ing] to make better: *Exercise improves the posture. vi-* to become better: *Her health improved in the milder climate.* —*adj-* im·prov′a·ble. *n-* im·prov′er.
improve on to make or do something better than.

im·prove·ment (Im prōōv′mənt) *n-* 1 a making or becoming better: *Much improvement of roads is necessary.* 2 a change or addition that makes something better or more valuable: *a household improvement.*

im·prov·i·dent (Im prŏv′ə dĕnt′, -dənt) *adj-* 1 lacking in thrift or foresight. 2 not providing for the future. —*n-* im·prov′i·dence. *adv-* im·prov′i·dent·ly.

³in- *prefix* 1 into: in*ject.* 2 toward: in*cline.* 3 within: in*door.* [from Old English **in-,** from **in,** "in; into; toward."]

in. 1 inch. 2 inches.

in·a·bil·i·ty (In′ə bĭl′ə tē) *n-* [*pl.* in·a·bil·i·ties] lack of power or means: *an inability to sleep; inability to pay.*

in ab·sen·tia (ăb sĕn′chə) *Latin* when the person concerned is absent: *to convict him in absentia.*

in·ac·ces·si·ble (In′ək sĕs′ə bəl) *adj-* impossible or difficult to reach or get to: *a place inaccessible by car.* —*n-* in′ac·ces′si·bil′i·ty. *adv-* in′ac·ces′si·bly.

in·ac·cu·ra·cy (In ăk′yər ə sē) *n-* [*pl.* in·ac·cu·ra·cies] 1 lack of accuracy or exactness: *the inaccuracy of a statement.* 2 an error: *a page full of* inaccuracies.

in·ac·cu·rate (In ăk′yər ət) *adj-* not correct; not accurate; not exact. —*adv-* in·ac′cu·rate·ly.

in·ac·tion (In ăk′shən) *n-* lack of motion, especially of effort; idleness: *His inaction was his undoing.*

in·ac·tive (In ăk′tIv) *adj-* 1 not moving about; not active: *Sickness made the patient inactive.* 2 not in use or action: *an inactive bank account; an inactive volcano.* —*adv-* in·ac′tive·ly. *n-* in′ac·tiv′i·ty.

in·ad·e·qua·cy (In ăd′ə kwə sē) *n-* [*pl.* in·ad·e·qua·cies] 1 lack of what is needed or the amount needed: *an inadequacy of funds.* 2 defect; fault.

in·ad·e·quate (In ăd′ə kwət) *adj-* not sufficient; not enough to meet some need: *The dining space is inadequate for our large group.* —*adv-* in·ad′e·quate·ly.

in·ad·mis·si·ble (In′əd mis′ə bəl) *adj-* such as cannot be admitted or allowed, especially as evidence: *Hearsay evidence is inadmissible.* —*n-* in′ad·mis′si·bil′i·ty.

in·ad·vert·ence (In′əd vûr′təns) *n-* 1 lack of proper care or attention: *The mistake was due to inadvertence.* 2 error caused by such a lack: *It was an inadvertence.*

in·ap·pli·ca·ble (In ăp′ lI kə bəl) *adj-* such as cannot be suited or applied to a definite purpose; not to be used or applied: *This answer is inapplicable to the problem.* —*n-* in·ap′pli·ca·bil′i·ty. *adv-* in·ap′pli·ca·bly.

in·ap·pre·ci·a·ble (In′ə prē′shə bəl) *adj-* too small to be important; negligible: *an inappreciable difference in tone.* —*adv-* in·ap·pre′ci·a·bly.

in·ap·pro·pri·ate (In′ə prō′prē ət) *adj-* not correct or suitable: *A party dress is inappropriate for a hike.* —*adv-* in·ap·pro′pri·ate·ly. *n-* in·ap·pro′pri·ate·ness.

in·apt (In ăpt′) *adj-* 1 not suitable: *an inapt remark.* 2 inept. —*adv-* in·apt′ly. *n-* in·apt′ness.
►For usage note see INEPT.

in·apt·i·tude (In ăp′tə tōōd′, -tyōōd′) *n-* lack of special fitness or skill; unfitness: *an inaptitude for mathematics.*

in·ar·tic·u·late (In′är tIk′yə lət) *adj-* 1 incapable of speaking; dumb: *the inarticulate animals; almost inarticulate with surprise.* 2 not speaking easily or fluently: *a flustered and inarticulate man.* 3 not expressed in words: *an inarticulate rage.* 4 not jointed. —*adv-* in·ar′tic·u·late·ly. *n-* in·ar′tic′u·late·ness.

in·ar·tis·tic (In′är tIs′tIk) *adj-* not artistic. —*adv-* in′ar·tis′ti·cal·ly.

in·as·much as (In′əz mŭch′) *conj-* since; because: *You may leave now, inasmuch as you wish to.*

in·at·ten·tion (In′ə tĕn′shən) *n-* failure to put one's mind on something; heedlessness: *A moment's inattention caused the accident.*

in·at·ten·tive (In′ə tĕn′tIv) *adj-* not paying attention. —*adv-* in′at·ten′tive·ly. *n-* in′at·ten′tive·ness.

in·au·di·ble (In ŏd′ə bəl) *adj-* such as cannot be heard; not audible: *an inaudible remark.* —*adv-* in·aud′i·bly. *n-* in·aud′i·bil′i·ty.

in·au·gu·ral (In ŏg′yŏŏr əl, Ir. ŏ′gər-) *adj-* 1 having to do with an inauguration: *an inaugural parade.* 2 opening; initial; first: *His inaugural remark. n-* speech made at the beginning of a term of office.

in·au·gu·rate (In ŏ′gə rāt′, -gyə rāt′) *vt-* [in·au·gu·rat·ed, in·au·gu·rat·ing] 1 to place in office with formal ceremony; install: *to inaugurate a president.* 2 to make a formal beginning of; commence: *to inaugurate a policy.* 3 to open formally for use: *to inaugurate a park.*

in·au·gu·ra·tion (in ŏ′gə rā′shən, -gyə rā′shən) *n-* an inaugurating, especially a placing in office with formal ceremony: *the impressive Presidential inauguration.*

in·aus·pi·cious (ĭn´ ô spĭsh´ əs) *adj-* unlucky; unfavorable: *an inauspicious beginning.* **—adv-** **in·aus·pi´cious·ly.** *n-* **in·aus·pi´cious·ness.**

in·board (ĭn´ bôrd´) *adj-* **1** inside the hull of a ship or boat: *They heaved the net inboard.* **2** toward the center line of the fuselage of an aircraft. *adj-* **1** located inside the hull: *an inboard engine.* **2** on an aircraft, nearest the center line of the fuselage: *the inboard port engine.* **3** of boats, powered by an inboard engine. *n-* a small boat powered by an inboard engine: *a 20-foot inboard.*

in·born (ĭn´ bôrn´) *n-* present in a person at birth; natural: *Musicianship is often an inborn talent.*

in·bound (ĭn´ bound´) *adj-* approaching a destination: *That is the inbound plane.*

in·bred (ĭn´ brĕd´) *adj-* **1** descended from closely related ancestors: *Many royal families are inbred.* **2** natural; innate: *an inbred kindness.*

in·breed (ĭn´ brēd´) *vt-* [**in·bred, in·breed·ing**] to mate (closely related animals). *vi-* to mate or breed within a closely related group.

in·breed·ing (ĭn´ brē´ dĭng) *n-* **1** the systematic mating of successive generations of plants or animals in order to improve the breed. Inbreeding can also damage the breed if any of the original stock is defective. **2** marriage between people who are closely related.

inc. **1** incorporated. **2** inclosure. **3** inclusive. **4** including.

In·ca (ĭng´ kə) *n-* **1** the ruler or a member of the ruling family of the great Andean Indian empire destroyed by Pizarro in 1532. **2** [*pl.* **In·cas,** also **In·ca**] a member of the leading people of this Indian empire. **—adj-** **In´can** or **In·ca´ic** (ĭng kä´ ĭk).

in·cal·cu·la·ble (ĭn kăl´ kyə lə bəl) *adj-* **1** beyond estimate; very great: *His mistake did incalculable harm.* **2** not dependable; unpredictable: *a person of incalculable moods.* **—n-** **in·cal´cu·la·bil´i·ty.** *adv-* **in·cal´cu·la·bly.**

in·cen·tive (ĭn sĕn´ tĭv) *n-* a motive for action, effort, etc.: *Love of country was his incentive.*

in·cep·tion (ĭn sĕp´ shən) *n-* beginning; first stage: *The movement was successful from its inception.*

in·ces·sant (ĭn sĕs´ ənt) *adj-* constant; not stopping: *an incessant chirping of insects.* **—adv-** **in·ces´sant·ly.**

in·cest (ĭn´ sĕst´) *n-* sexual relationship between persons so closely related that their marriage is forbidden by law.

in·ces·tu·ous (ĭn sĕs´ chŏŏ əs) *adj-* between persons too closely related for lawful marriage. **—adv-** **in·ces´tu·ous·ly.** *n-* **in·ces´tu·ous·ness.**

inch (ĭnch) *n-* measure of length, twelve of which make a foot. *Abbr.* in. *vi-* to move little by little.
by inches by a slender margin: *That car missed me by inches.* **every inch** in all ways; entirely: *She was every inch a lady.* **inch by inch** little by little; bit by bit: *I climbed inch by inch.* **not yield an inch** not surrender the slightest bit. **within an inch of** extremely close to.

in·cho·ate (ĭn kō´ ət) *adj-* just beginning; not yet fully formed or in order; incipient: *to have a vague, inchoate idea.* **—adv-** **in·cho´ate·ly.** *n-* **in·cho´ate·ness.**

inch·worm (ĭnch´ wûrm´) *n-* measuring worm.

in·ci·dence (ĭn´ sə dəns) *n-* **1** the rate of separate cases or events of something; occurrence: *A high incidence of crime.* **2** the meeting of a ray of light, a bullet, line, etc., with a surface. **3** angle of incidence.

in·ci·dent (ĭn´ sə dənt) *n-* a happening; event; episode: *He told us incidents from his childhood.* *adj-* **1** coming along with something else; accompanying: *skiing and its incident risks.* **2** hitting against something, especially at an angle: *an incident light ray.*
incident to likely to happen in connection with (something else): *Risks are incident to a soldier's life.*

in·ci·den·tal (ĭn´ sə dĕn´ təl) *adj-* **1** happening in connection with something more important: *the incidental expenses of a trip;* incidental *music for a play.* **2** made or added casually; thrown in: *an incidental expense.*

in·cin·er·a·tor (ĭn sĭn´ ə rā´ tər) *n-* person or thing that incinerates, especially a furnace for burning trash.

in·cip·i·ent (ĭn sĭp´ ē ənt) *adj-* beginning to be or appear: *an incipient revolution.* **—n-** **in·cip´i·ence** or **in·cip´i·en·cy:** *the incipience of war.* *adv-* **in·cip´i·ent·ly.**

in·cised (ĭn sīzd´) *adj-* engraved; carved.

in·clined (ĭn klīnd´) **1** (*often* ĭn´ klīnd´) slanting; sloping: *an inclined surface.* **2** leaning. **3** disposed by feeling or wish: *Come see us when you are so inclined.*

inclined plane *n-* **1** a plane that makes an angle other than 90° with a horizontal plane. **2** *Physics* one of the basic "simple machines."

FORCE (EFFORT)

RESISTANCE

Inclined plane

in·cli·nom·e·ter (ĭn´ klə nŏm´ ə tər) *n-* **1** instrument used to show the direction of the earth's magnetic field at a given point by the amount of deviation from the horizontal. **2** device to measure angles of elevation or slope. **3** instrument that measures the amount by which an airplane or ship tilts from the horizontal.

in·come (ĭn´ kŭm´) *n-* amount of money one gets from labor, business, property, etc.; wages; salary.

income tax *n-* tax on net personal or business income.

in·com·ing (ĭn´ kŭm´ ĭng) *adj-* **1** coming in: *the incoming tide.* **2** coming into office: *the incoming mayor.*

in·com·men·su·ra·ble (ĭn´ kə mĕn´ shər ə bəl) *adj-* not commensurable; lacking a common unit or basis for comparison: *Love and money are incommensurable.* **—n-** **in·com·men´su·ra·bil´i·ty.** *adv-* **in·com·men´su·ra·bly.**

in·com·men·su·rate (ĭn´ kə mĕn´ shər ət) *adj-* **1** unequal; inadequate: *His strength is incommensurate to his duties.* **2** incommensurable. **—adv-** **in·com·men´su·rate·ly.**

in·com·mode (ĭn´ kə mōd´) *vt-* [**in·com·mod·ed, in·com·mod·ing**] to inconvenience; disturb; put out: *The lack of a room seriously incommoded me.*

in·com·mo·di·ous (ĭn´ kə mō´ dē əs) *adj-* **1** inconvenient; uncomfortable. **2** uncomfortably small or cramped.

in·com·mu·ni·ca·ble (ĭn´ kə myŏŏ´ nĭ kə bəl) *adj-* such as cannot be communicated.

in·com·mu·ni·ca·do (ĭn´ kə myŏŏ´ nə kä´ dō) *adj-* not allowed or unable to communicate with others: *The prisoner was held incommunicado.*

in·com·mu·ni·ca·tive (ĭn´ kə myŏŏ´ nĭ kə tĭv´) *adj-* not given to speaking freely; reserved; reticent.

in·com·pa·ra·ble (ĭn kŏm´ pə rə bəl) *adj-* **1** such as cannot be equaled or surpassed; matchless: *an incomparable beauty.* **2** such as cannot be compared; not comparable. **—adv-** **in·com´pa·ra·bly.**

in·com·pat·i·ble (ĭn´ kəm păt´ə bəl) *adj-* not compatible: *an incompatible couple; desires incompatible with one's income.* **—n-** **in·com·pat´i·bil´i·ty.** *adv-* **in·com·pat´i·bly.**

in·com·pe·tence (ĭn kŏm´ pə təns) *n-* **1** lack of ability or fitness: *the incompetence of a worker.* **2** in law, lack of qualification.

in·con·gru·ous (ĭn kŏng´ grŏŏ əs) *adj-* unsuitable; not appropriate; out of place: *His solemn face was incongruous with the gaiety of the party.* **2** lacking in agreement or harmony: *two incongruous colors.* **—adv-** **in·con´gru·ous·ly.** *n-* **in·con´gru·ous·ness.**

in·con·se·quen·tial (ĭn kŏn´ sə kwĕn´ shəl) *adj-* **1** unrelated to the subject; irrelevant. **2** trivial; unimportant. **—adv-** **in·con·se·quen´tial·ly.**

in·con·sid·er·a·ble (ĭn´ kən sĭd´ ər ə bəl) *adj-* not deserving consideration; slight; trivial. **—adv-** **in·con·sid´er·a·bly.**

in·con·sid·er·ate (ĭn´ kən sĭd´ ər ət) *adj-* thoughtless; without proper regard for others: *an inconsiderate remark.* **—adv-** **in·con·sid´er·ate·ly.** *n-* **in·con·sid´er·ate·ness.**

in·con·sist·en·cy (ĭn´ kən sĭs´ tən sē) *n-* [*pl.* **in·con·sist·en·cies**] **1** lack of sameness or agreement: *the inconsistency of two stories.* **2** contradiction: *a testimony full of inconsistencies.*

in·con·sist·ent (ĭn´ kən sĭs´ tənt) *adj-* **1** not in keeping or agreement; at variance: *His actions are inconsistent with his words.* **2** having contradictions within itself; not logical: *an inconsistent argument.* **3** not holding to the same principles, practices, etc.; changeable; fickle; *an inconsistent person.* **—adv-** **in·con·sist´ent·ly.**

in·cor·po·re·al (ĭn′kôr pôr′ē əl) *adj-* not made of matter. —*adv-* in·cor′po′re·al·ly.

in·cor·rect (ĭn′kə rěkt′) *adj-* 1 not according to fact; not true or accurate: *an incorrect report.* 2 not according to model or rule; faulty; wrong: *an incorrect approach to a problem.* 3 not in keeping with good usage or standards; improper: *very incorrect behavior.* —*adv-* in′cor·rect′ly. *n-* in′cor·rect′ness.

in·cor·ri·gi·ble (ĭn kôr′ĭj ə bəl, ĭn kŏr′-) *adj-* beyond reform or correction: *an incorrigible liar;* incorrigible *lying.* —*n-* in·cor′ri·gi·bil′i·ty. *adv-* in·cor′ri·gi·bly.

in·cor·rupt·i·ble (ĭn′kə rŭp′tə bəl) *adj-* not corruptible; honest: *an incorruptible witness.* —*n-* in′cor·rupt′i·bil′i·ty. *adv-* in′cor·rupt′i·bly.

¹in·crease (ĭn krēs′) *vt-* [in·creased, in·creas·ing] to make greater; augment; add to: *Trade increased the country's wealth. vi-: His sales increased last week.* —*adv-* in·creas′ing·ly.

²in·crease (ĭn′krēs′) *n-* 1 growth or enlargement: *an increase in business.* 2 amount that is added: *an increase of ten dollars in the price.*
    on the increase increasing; rising.

in·cred·i·ble (ĭn krěd′ə bəl) *adj-* hard to believe; beyond belief: *an incredible adventure.* —*n-* in·cred′i·bil′i·ty. *adv-* in·cred′i·bly.
    ►Should not be confused with INCREDULOUS.

in·cre·du·li·ty (ĭn′krə dyōō′lə tē, -dōō′lə tē) *n-* unwillingness to believe; lack of belief; skepticism; doubt.

in·cred·u·lous (ĭn krěj′ə ləs) *adj-* 1 doubting; skeptical; questioning as to truth and accuracy; not willing or able to believe: *to be incredulous of the statement.* 2 showing doubt: *an incredulous smile.* —*adv-* in·cred′u·lous·ly.
    ►Should not be confused with INCREDIBLE.

in·cre·ment (ĭng′krə mənt) *n-* 1 increase; enlargement. 2 amount that is added; especially, one of a series of small or regular additions: *an increment of $5 a year.*

in·crim·i·nate (ĭn krĭm′ə nāt′) *vt-* [in·crim·i·nat·ed, in·crim·i·nat·ing] to charge with, or involve in, a crime; show to be guilty: *His words incriminated him.* —*n-* in·crim′i·na′tion. *adj-* in·crim′i·na·to′ry.

in·crust (ĭn krŭst′) encrust.

in·crus·ta·tion (ĭn′krŭs tā′shən) *n-* 1 an encrusting or being encrusted. 2 crust or hard coating. 3 ornamental layer, inlay, etc.: *a diadem with incrustations of diamonds.*

in·cu·bate (ĭng′kyə bāt′) *vt-* [in·cu·bat·ed, in·cu·bat·ing] 1 to sit upon (eggs) in order to hatch them. 2 to keep (eggs, bacteria, etc.) under conditions favorable for hatching, development, etc.: *to incubate a bacterial culture.* 3 to give form to or develop gradually: *He*

in·dec·o·rous (ĭn děk′ər əs) *adj-* in bad taste; not suitable; improper: *her indecorous behavior;* indecorous *speech.* —*adv-* in·dec′o·rous·ly. *n-* in·dec′o·rous·ness.

in·deed (ĭn dēd′) *adv-* in fact; really: *We were indeed pleased by his success.*

indef. indefinite.

in·de·fat·i·ga·ble (ĭn′dĭ făt′ĭ gə bəl) *adj-* not giving in easily to fatigue; untiring: *an indefatigable worker.* —*n-* in′de·fat′i·ga·bil′i·ty. *adv-* in′de·fat′i·ga·bly.

in·de·fen·si·ble (ĭn′dĭ fěn′sə bəl) *adj-* not defensible: *an indefensible beachhead;* indefensible *point of view.* —*n-* in′de·fen′si·bil′i·ty. *adv-* in′de·fen′si·bly.

in·de·fin·a·ble (ĭn′dĭ fī′nə bəl) *adj-* such as cannot be described or explained clearly; subtle; vague: *an indefinable charm.* —*n-* in′de·fin′a·bil′i·ty. *adv-* in′de·fin′a·bly.

in·def·i·nite (ĭn děf′ə nət) *adj-* 1 having no fixed or exact limit: *an indefinite period of time.* 2 not clear or certain; vague: *his indefinite plans.*

in·den·ture (ĭn děn′chər) *n-* 1 written agreement, especially one binding a servant or an apprentice to a master. 2 a dent; indentation. *vt-* [in·den·tured, in·den·tur·ing] to bind (a servant, apprentice, etc.) by a written agreement.

in·den·tured (ĭn děn′chərd) *adj-* bound by a written contract to work for the same master for a certain length of time: *an indentured servant.*

in·de·pend·ence (ĭn′dĭ pěn′dəns) *n-* 1 freedom from influence, support, control, or government by others. 2 income or a sum of money sufficient for one's needs.

index finger *n-* finger next to the thumb; forefinger.

index of refraction *n-* number that represents the relationship between the speed of light in a vacuum and its speed in a given transparent substance. Light travels in water about three-fourths as fast as it does in a vacuum. Water's index of refraction is 4/3.

india ink *n-* black, heavy-bodied, drawing ink.

In·di·an (ĭn′dē ən) *adj-* 1 of or pertaining to the original inhabitants of the Americas at the time of its discovery, or their descendants: *an Indian peace council.* 2 pertaining to India, its people, or their language. 3 made by or used by the American Indians, or made in India. *n-* 1 one of the original inhabitants of the Americas or their descendants. 2 native or citizen of the Republic of India or a person of Indian descent. 3 any of the languages of the American Indians.

Indian club *n-* club shaped like a bottle, swung by the hands in gymnastic exercises.

Indian corn *n-* corn; maize.

Indian file *n-* single file.

Indian giver *Informal n-* person who takes back a gift he has given.

Indian meal *n-* cornmeal.

Indian paintbrush *n-* one of a group of plants with showy flowers, growing in western United States. It is the state flower of Wyoming.

Indian paintbrush

Indian pipe *n-* leafless, waxy-white plant with a single nodding, bell-shaped, flower, growing chiefly in dense woods.

Indian pudding *n-* pudding made of cornmeal, milk, and molasses.

Indian summer *n-* period of mild weather following autumn frosts.

Indian Territory *n-* formerly, a territory of the United States set aside for the Indians; now, a part of Oklahoma.

Indian pipe

in·di·ces (ĭn′də sēz′) *pl.* of **index.**

in·dict (ĭn dīt′) *vt-* 1 to charge with an offense; accuse. 2 in law, to charge formally with a crime after a grand jury has considered the evidence: *to indict a person for theft. Hom-* indite. —*n-* in·dict′er or in·dict′or.

in·dict·a·ble (ĭn dī′tə bəl) *adj-* 1 liable to be indicted, or charged with a crime in due form of law. 2 of an offense, giving cause for indictment.

in·dict·ment (ĭn dīt′mənt) *n-* 1 an indicting or being indicted. 2 written accusation of a crime, presented to the court by a grand jury after it has considered the evidence.

In·dies (ĭn′dēz) *n- pl.* the East Indies; also, formerly, the West Indies.

in·dif·fer·ence (ĭn dĭf′rəns, -ər əns) *n-* 1 lack of interest or feeling: *to regard suffering with indifference.* 2 lack of importance: *a matter of complete indifference to us.*

in·dif·fer·ent (ĭn dĭf′rənt, -ər ənt) *adj-* 1 not caring or concerned about something; without any strong feeling one way or the other: *an indifferent audience;* indifferent *to the suffering of others.* 2 neither good nor bad; mediocre: *an indifferent book.* —*adv-* in·dif′fer·ent·ly.

in·dig·e·nous (ĭn dĭj′ə nəs) *adj-* native; born, growing, or produced naturally in certain locations, regions, or climates: *Tobacco is indigenous to America.* —*adv-* in·dig′e·nous·ly.

in·di·gent (ĭn′də jənt) *adj-* very poor; needy: *an indigent widow.* —*n-* in·di·gence. *adv-* in·di·gent·ly.

in·di·gest·i·ble (ĭn′də jěs′tə bəl, ĭn′dī-) *adj-* impossible to digest or not easily digested. —*n-* in·di·gest′i·bil′i·ty. *adv-* in·di·gest′i·bly.

in·dis·cre·tion (ĭn′dĭ skrěsh′ən) *n-* 1 imprudent act or step: *His free and easy behavior with the judge was an indiscretion.* 2 condition or habit of being indiscreet.

in·dis·crim·i·nate (ĭn′dĭ skrĭm′ə nət) *adj-* 1 not discriminating; not choosing carefully: *an indiscriminate reader.* 2 confused; jumbled: *an indiscriminate mixture of several styles.* —*adv-* in·dis·crim′i·nate·ly.

in·di·vid·u·al (ĭn′də vĭj′ ōō əl) *adj-* 1 belonging to or intended for a single person or thing: *an individual locker; an individual plate.* 2 particular; separate: *to give individual help; an individual report.* 3 having features that belong to it alone: *an individual hair style.* *n-* 1 person: *He is a kind individual.* 2 single person, animal, or thing: *the freedom of the individual.*

in·di·vid·u·al·ism (ĭn′ də vĭj′ ōō ə lĭz′ əm) *n-* 1 personal independence or freedom in thought or action; also, self-reliance. 2 economic or political belief that the interest of the individual is higher than that of the group.

in·di·vid·u·al·ist (ĭn′ də vĭj′ ə ə list) *n-* 1 person who acts and thinks on his own without relying on the thoughts or actions of others. 2 one who believes in or supports individualism. —*adj-* **in′ di·vid′ u·al·is′ tic.**

in·di·vid·u·al·i·ty (ĭn′də vĭj′ ōō ăl′ ə tē) *n-* [*pl.* **in·di·vid·u·al·i·ties**] 1 all the characteristics that make a person different from other persons: *a man of marked individuality.* 2 condition of being different from all others; personality: *Keep your individuality.* 3 condition or quality of existing separately; separate existence.

in·di·vid·u·al·ize (ĭn′də vĭj′ ōō ə lĭz′) *vt-* [**in·di·vid·u·al·ized, in·di·vid·u·al·iz·ing**] 1 to give a distinct or individual character to: *to individualize one's performance.* 2 to adapt or relate to the specific needs, abilities, etc., of the individual: *to individualize language instruction.*

in·di·vid·u·al·ly (ĭn′də vĭj′ ōō ə lē) *adv-* one by one; separately; personally: *to see them individually.*

in·di·vis·i·ble (ĭn′də vĭz′ ə bəl) *adj-* 1 such as cannot be divided; not divisible 2 *Mathematics* admitting of no further division; leaving a remainder other than zero. —*n-* **in′ di·vis′ i·bil′ i·ty.** *adv-* **in′ di·vis′ i·bly.**

in·doc·tri·nate (ĭn dŏk′ trə nāt′) *vt-* [**in·doc·tri·nat·ed, in·doc·tri·nat·ing**] 1 to instruct in principles or doctrines. 2 to teach (someone) partisan or sectarian ideas, principles, etc.: *He wants to indoctrinate young people, not to teach them to think.* —*n-* **in·doc′ tri·na′ tion.**

In·do-Eu·ro·pe·an (ĭn′dō yoor′ ə pē′ən) *adj-* of or relating to the world's largest family of languages, those spoken in most of Europe and the countries colonized by Europeans, as well as in southwestern Asia and India.

in·do·lent (ĭn′də lənt) *adj-* avoiding or disliking work or exertion; lazy. —*n-* **in′ do·lence.** *adv-* **in′ do·lent·ly.**

in·dom·i·ta·ble (ĭn dŏm′ ə tə bəl) *adj-* unconquerable; unyielding; steadfast: *an indomitable will.* —*n-* **in·dom′ i·ta·bil′ i·ty.** *adv-* **in·dom′ i·ta·bly.**

in·door (ĭn′ dôr′) *adj-* belonging to or done inside a house or building: *Chess is an indoor sport.*

in·doors (ĭn′ dôrz′) *adv-* inside or into a building: *When it rains, we play indoors. Please take them indoors.*

in·dorse (ĭn dôrs′) endorse. —*n-* **in·dorse′ ment.** *n-* **in·dors′ er.**

in·du·bi·ta·ble (ĭn dōō′ bə tə bəl, ĭn dyōō′-) *adj-* too clear or certain to be doubted; unquestionable: *an indubitable triumph.* —*n-* **in·du′ bi·ta·ble·ness.** *adv-* **in·du′ bi·ta·bly.**

in·duce (ĭn dōōs′, -dyōōs′) *vt-* [**in·duced, in·duc·ing**] 1 to persuade; prevail upon: *Money will induce him to go.* 2 to produce; bring on or about: *to induce sleep by drugs.* 3 to arrive at (a conclusion or principle) from the observation or study of particular cases. 4 to produce (an electric current or magnetic effect) by induction.

in·duce·ment (ĭn dōōs′mənt, ĭn dyōōs′-) *n-* something that persuades or influences; incentive: *The prize was an inducement to study.*

in·dulge (ĭn dŭlj′) *vt-* [**in·dulged, in·dulg·ing**] 1 to humor by giving in to: *to indulge a child.* 2 to yield to; gratify: *to indulge a liking for candy.* **indulge in** to do, take part in, or treat oneself to: *He indulges in friendly bridge parties.*

in·dul·gence (ĭn dŭl′ jəns) *n-* 1 the humoring or satisfying of another: *I request your indulgence in this matter.* 2 a giving way to one's own likings: *Too much indulgence in sweets is bad for us.* 3 something in which a person indulges: *Smoking was his only indulgence.* 4 indulgent act; favor. 5 in the Roman Catholic Church, the remission of punishment still due for sins, the guilt of which is already forgiven.

in·dul·gent (ĭn dŭl′ jənt) *adj-* yielding easily to whims or desires of others; lenient; not very strict: *an indulgent parent.* —*adv-* **in·dul′ gent·ly.**

in·dus·tri·al (ĭn dŭs′ trē əl) *adj-* 1 relating to or engaged in industry, especially manufacturing: *an industrial worker; a small industrial output.* 2 not agricultural or commercial; having highly developed industries: *an industrial nation.* 3 used in industry: *an industrial diamond; industrial alcohol.* —*adv-* **in·dus′ tri·al·ly.**

in·dus·tri·al·ist (ĭn dŭs′ trē ə lĭst′) *n-* manager or owner of a manufacturing enterprise.

in·dus·tri·al·ize (ĭn dŭs′ trē ə lĭz′) *vt-* [**in·dus·tri·al·ized, in·dus·tri·al·iz·ing**] to make industrial; to develop industries in: *to industrialize a country.* —*n-* **in·dus′ tri·al·i·za′ tion.**

Industrial Revolution *n-* the social and economic change from an agricultural to an industrial civilization that took place in England from the mid-eighteenth to mid-nineteenth century and is still continuing.

in·ef·fi·cient (ĭn′ ĭ fĭsh′ənt) *adj-* 1 requiring unnecessary time, energy, or work: *an inefficient process.* 2 wasteful of time and energy: *an inefficient worker.* —*n-* **in′ ef·fi′ cien·cy:** *He was finally discharged for inefficiency.* *adv-* **in′ ef·fi′ cient·ly.**

in·e·las·tic (ĭn′ ə lăs′ tĭk) *adj-* 1 not elastic: *Ice is an inelastic substance.* 2 not easily changed or adapted to fit circumstances; inflexible: *an inelastic supply of steel.* —*n-* **in′ e·las·tic′ i·ty.**

in·el·e·gant (ĭn ĕl′ ə gənt) *adj-* lacking in elegance, refinement, or good taste; coarse; crude: *an inelegant style.* —*n-* **in·el′ e·gance.** *adv-* **in·el′ e·gant·ly.**

in·el·i·gi·ble (ĭn ĕl′ ə jə bəl) *adj-* not eligible; unqualified for a certain position, activity, etc. *n-* person who is not eligible. —*n-* **in·el′ i·gi·bil′ i·ty.**

in·ept (ĭn ĕpt′) *adj-* 1 not fit or suited; out of place; inappropriate: *an inept remark.* 2 awkward; clumsy: *an inept carpenter.* —*adv-* **in·ept′ ly.** *n-* **in·ept′ ness.**

▶**INEPT** means clumsy or unfit: *He is an inept doctor.* **INAPT** refers to suitability: *His words were inapt.*

in·ept·i·tude (ĭn ĕp′ tə tōōd′, -tyōōd′) *n-* 1 lack of suitability; inappropriateness. 2 awkwardness; incompetence. 3 foolish or inappropriate act or remark: *a book full of ineptitudes.*

in·e·qual·i·ty (ĭn′ ĭ kwŏl′ ə tē) *n-* [*pl.* **in·e·qual·i·ties**] 1 lack of equality; difference in quality, standing, etc.: *an inequality of opportunity for education.* 2 lack of evenness or uniformity, or an instance of this: *marked inequalities in temperature.* 3 *Mathematics* statement that one quantity is either less than or more than another quantity.

in·eq·ui·ta·ble (ĭn ĕk′ wə tə bəl) *adj-* not equitable; unfair or unjust. —*adv-* **in·eq′ ui·ta·bly.**

infantile paralysis *n-* poliomyelitis.

in·fan·til·ism (ĭn′ fən tə lĭz′ əm, -tĭ lĭz′ əm) *n-* abnormal continuation or appearance of childlike traits in adults.

in·fan·try (ĭn′ fən trē) *n-* [*pl.* **in·fan·tries**] soldiers who are armed, equipped, and trained to fight on foot; foot soldiers. —*n-* **in′ fan·try·man.**

in·fat·u·ate (ĭn făch′ ōō āt′) *vt-* [**in·fat·u·at·ed, in·fat·u·at·ing**] to arouse an unreasonable passion in (someone). **infatuated with** foolishly or unreasonably in love with or devoted to (someone or something): *She is infatuated with her own beauty.*

in·fat·u·a·tion (ĭn făch′ ōō ā′ shən) *n-* state of being infatuated; foolish or unreasonable love for or devotion to someone or something.

in·fect (ĭn fĕkt′) *vt-* to cause disease, unhealthiness, or pollution in by the introduction of germs, viruses, etc.: *Escaping sewage may infect drinking water. Janet's cold infected the entire family.*

in·fec·tion (ĭn fĕk′ shən) *n-* 1 an infecting or becoming infected; especially, a causing of disease by contact with germs or viruses: *to protect a cut against infection.* 2 disease caused by germs or viruses: *a chronic infection.*

in·fec·tious (ĭn fĕk′ shəs) *adj-* 1 caused or spread by germs, viruses, etc.: *an infectious disease.* 2 tending to spread to others: *Enthusiasm is infectious.* —*adv-* **in·fec′ tious·ly:** *She giggled infectiously.* *n-* **in·fec′ tious·ness.**

in·firm (ĭn fûrm′) *adj-* weak, unsteady, or feeble, especially from old age or sickness. —*adv-* **in·firm′ ly.**

in·fir·ma·ry (ĭn fûr′ mə rē) *n-* [*pl.* **in·fir·ma·ries**] building or room in a school, factory, etc., for medical care.

in·fir·mi·ty (ĭn fûr′ mə tē) *n-* [*pl.* **in·fir·mi·ties**] 1 state of being infirm; weakness; feebleness: *the infirmity of old age.* 2 a personal flaw: *He tolerates my infirmities.*

in·flame (ĭn flām′) *vt-* [**in·flamed, in·flam·ing**] 1 to stir up; arouse: *His fiery speech inflamed the people.* 2 to make red, swollen, and painful: *The smoke from the bonfire inflamed her eyes.*

in·flam·ma·ble (ĭn flăm′ ə bəl) *adj-* 1 flammable. 2 easily excited or aroused: *an inflammable temper.* —*n-* **in·flam′ ma·bil′ i·ty.** *adv-* **in·flam′ ma·bly.**
► For usage note see FLAMMABLE.

in·flam·ma·tion (ĭn′ flə mā′ shən) *n-* 1 condition of being inflamed; redness, swelling, etc., of some part of the body. 2 act of stirring up, or the condition of being stirred up: *the inflammation of public feeling.*

in·flam·ma·to·ry (ĭn flăm′ ə tôr′ ē) *adj-* 1 tending to excite or arouse anger, violence, revolt, etc.: *an inflammatory speech.* 2 related to or causing inflammation: *an inflammatory infection.*

in·flate (ĭn flāt′) *vt-* [**in·flat·ed, in·flat·ing**] 1 to swell by filling with air or gas; distend: *to inflate a balloon.* 2 to puff up with pride or self-satisfaction: *David's new honors helped to inflate his already high opinion of himself.* 3 to increase (prices, values, etc.) beyond the usual degree. *vi-* to become blown up or puffed up. —*adj-* **in·flat′ a·ble.** *n-* **in·flat′ er** or **in·fla′ tor.**

in·fla·tion (ĭn flā′ shən) *n-* 1 process of inflating, or the condition of being inflated. 2 a rise in prices and a fall in the value of money, caused by an increase in the amount of money available to buy goods and services, or by a scarcity of goods and services.

in·flu·en·tial (ĭn′ flōō ĕn′ shəl) *adj-* having influence; exerting power: *an influential man.* —*adv-* **in′ flu·en′ tial·ly.**

in·flu·en·za (ĭn′ flōō ĕn′ zə) *n-* contagious virus disease marked by an inflamed nose and throat, headache, fever, muscular pains, etc.; flu.

in·flux (ĭn′ flŭks′) *n-* a flowing or steady moving in; inflow: *an influx of water; an influx of tourists.*

in·fold (ĭn fōld′) enfold.

in·form (ĭn fôrm′, -fôrm′) *vt-* to tell; make known to; give information to: *Please inform me when she arrives.* *vi-* to give information that causes another to be accused or suspected (usually followed by "against" or "on"): *The thief informed on his accomplices.*

in·gen·u·ous (ĭn jĕn′ yōō əs) *adj-* simple and natural; without guile: *the ingenuous questions of a child.* —*adv-* **in·gen′ u·ous·ly.** *n-* **in·gen′ u·ous·ness.**
►Should not be confused with INGENIOUS.

in·gest (ĭn jĕst′) *vt-* to take food into the body for digestion. —*n-* **in·ges′ tion.**

in·gle·nook (ĭng′ gəl nōōk′) *n-* corner beside a fireplace.

in·glor·i·ous (ĭn glôr′ ē əs) *adj-* dishonorable or disgraceful; shameful: *an inglorious defeat.* —*adv-* **in·glor′ i·ous·ly.** *n-* **in·glor′ i·ous·ness.**

in·got (ĭng′ gət) *n-* bar or other mass of cast metal produced at a refinery, smelting plant, etc.

in·graft (ĭn grăft′) engraft.

in·grain (ĭn grān′, ĭn′-) *vt-* to fix deeply, especially in the mind or spirit: *to ingrain a belief in someone's mind.*

in·hab·it·a·ble (ĭn hăb′ ə tə bəl) *adj-* such as can be inhabited; suitable for living in or occupying: *an inhabitable island.*

in·hab·it·ant (ĭn hăb′ ə tənt) *n-* permanent or habitual dweller in a place: *The town has 6,000 inhabitants.*

in·hab·it·ed (ĭn hăb′ ə təd) *adj-* lived in, having dwellers or residents: *This island is inhabited.*

in·hal·ant (ĭn hā′ lənt) *n-* medicine to be inhaled.

in·ha·la·tor (ĭn′ hə lā′ tər) *n-* device from which one can inhale air, medicine, etc.

in·hale (ĭn hāl′) *vt-* [**in·haled, in·hal·ing**] to draw into the lungs; breathe in: *to inhale fresh air.*

in·i·ti·a·tive (ĭ nĭsh′ ə tĭv) *n-* 1 first or introductory step in an undertaking: *He took the* initiative *in producing the play.* 2 ability to see and readiness to undertake what must be done, without detailed instructions, urging, etc.; enterprise: *He has plenty of* initiative *and would do well in this job.* 3 the right of citizens to introduce new laws, or the method of doing so.

in·i·ti·a·tor (ĭ nĭsh′ ē ā′ tər) *n-* person who initiates, especially one who starts or introduces something new.

in·lay (ĭn′ lā′) *n-* 1 pieces of ivory, wood, metal, etc., set into the surface of something to form a design; also, a design made with such materials. 2 filling of gold, porcelain, etc., shaped and cast to fit snugly into a cavity in a tooth. *vt-* (*also* ĭn′ lā′) [**in·laid, in·lay·ing**] 1 to set (pieces of ivory, wood, etc.) into a surface to form a design. 2 to decorate with such designs.

in·let (ĭn′ lĕt′) *n-* 1 small bay, cove, or arm of the sea. 2 entrance: *the inlet of a water main.*

in·mate (ĭn′ māt′) *n-* one of a group living in the same place, especially in a prison or other institution.

in me·mo·ri·am (ĭn mə môr′ ē əm) *Latin* in or to the memory of a particular person.

Inlets on Maine coast

in·most (ĭn′ mōst′) *adj-* 1 most personal, private, or intimate; deepest: *a person's* inmost *thoughts; a person's* inmost *longings.* 2 farthest in; innermost.

inn (ĭn) *n-* 1 small hotel, usually in the country. 2 restaurant or tavern. *Hom-* in.

in·nate (ĭ nāt′) *adj-* arising from or belonging to the inner nature of a person or thing; not acquired; intrinsic: *an innate love of freedom.* —*adv-* **in·nate′ ly.**

in·no·va·tion (ĭn′ ə vā′ shən) *n-* 1 something new or different, such as a change in customs or ways of doing things: *The automobile was a great innovation in transportation.* 2 an introducing or bringing in something new: *the innovation of plastics into industry.*

in·nu·en·do (ĭn′ yōō ĕn′ dō) *n-* [*pl.* **in·nu·en·does**] suggestion or hint, usually unfavorable; insinuation: *His conversation is full of sly innuendoes.*

in·nu·mer·a·ble (ĭ nōō′ mər ə bəl, ĭ nyōō′-) *adj-* too many to be counted; countless: *the innumerable stars.* —*n-* **in·nu′ mer·a·ble·ness.** *adv-* **in·nu′ mer·a·bly.**

in·oc·u·late (ĭ nŏk′ yə lāt′) *vt-* [**in·oc·u·lat·ed, in·oc·u·lat·ing**] 1 to produce a mild case of disease in (a person or animal) by injecting or swallowing its bacteria or virus, usually in order to prevent future attacks: *to* inoculate *a child against typhoid.* 2 to introduce germs, molds. etc., into, usually for a scientific purpose. 3 to implant or instill (ideas, opinions, etc.) in the mind of.

in·oc·u·la·tion (ĭ nŏk′ yə lā′ shən) *n-* 1 an inoculating. 2 something injected or put in by inoculating.

in·of·fen·sive (ĭn′ ə fĕn′ sĭv) *adj-* 1 not offensive or unpleasant. 2 not harmful; innocuous. 3 not warlike, threatening, or dangerous; peaceable. —*adv-* **in′ of· fen′ sive·ly.** *n-* **in′ of·fen′ sive·ness.**

in·op·er·a·ble (ĭn ŏp′ ər ə bəl) *adj-* such as cannot be corrected or treated by surgery.

in·op·er·a·tive (ĭn ŏp′ ər ə tĭv′) *adj-* not in working condition: *The radio was inoperative.*

in·op·por·tune (ĭn ŏp′ ər tōōn′, -tyōōn′) *adj-* 1 happening at the wrong time: *an inopportune remark.* 2 inconvenient.

in·rush (ĭn′ rŭsh′) *n-* a pouring in; sudden invasion: *an inrush of waters; an inrush of campers.*

in·sane (ĭn sān′) *adj-* 1 not sane; seriously ill mentally; crazy; psychotic. 2 used by or for persons who are not sane: *an insane ward in a hospital.* —*adv-* **in·sane′ ly.**

in·san·i·tar·y (ĭn săn′ ə tĕr′ ē) *adj-* so unclean as to be a risk to health; contaminated: *the insanitary drinking water; insanitary living conditions.*
►Should not be confused with UNSANITARY.

in·san·i·ty (ĭn săn′ ə tē) *n-* [*pl.* **in·san·i·ties**] 1 severe mental illness; madness; psychosis. 2 in law, mental condition that prevents one from knowing the difference between right and wrong. 3 extreme folly or senselessness: *Climbing an icy cliff alone is sheer insanity.*

Amebic
ingestion

in·sid·er (!n sī′ dər) *n*- person in the ruling group of some organization, or one who can get information not available to most people.

in·sid·i·ous (In sĭd′ ē əs) *adj*- doing harm secretly or in a hidden manner: *an insidious disease; insidious gossip.* —*adv*- in·sid′i·ous·ly. *n*- in·sid′i·ous·ness.

in·sight (ĭn′ sīt′) *n*- 1 ability to see (into) and to understand: *a good teacher's insight into the problems of the students.* 2 an instance of this.

in·sig·ni·a (in sĭg′ nē ə) *n*- 1 *pl.* [*sing.* in·sig·ne (ĭn sĭg′ nē)] emblems of rank or honor: *A colonel with all his insignia.* 2 [*pl.* in·sig·ni·as] one such emblem: *the insignia of a commander.*

Insignia

in·sig·nif·i·cant (ĭn′ sĭg nĭf′ ə kənt) *adj*- of small or no importance; having little meaning or value: *an insignificant sum; an insignificant person.* —*n*- in′ sig·nif′ i·cance. *adv*- in·sig·nif′ i·cant·ly.

in·sin·cere (ĭn′ sĭn sêr′) *adj*- not sincere; not truly meant or felt. —*adv*- in′ sin·cere′ ly. *n*- in′ sin·cer′ i·ty (ĭn′ sĭn sêr′ ə tē).

in·sin·u·ate (in sĭn′ yōō āt′) *vt*- [in·sin·u·a·ted, in·sin·u·a·ting] 1 to hint slyly; imply: *The lawyer insinuated that the witness was lying.* 2 to put in by clever, indirect means: *As he spoke he insinuated his critical comments.*

in·sin·u·a·tion (in sĭn′ yōō ā′ shən) *n*- indirect or sly hint; implied meaning; innuendo: *to be slandered by insinuations; to resent insinuations.*

in·sip·id (in sĭp′ ĭd) *adj*- 1 without flavor; tasteless: *the insipid food.* 2 uninteresting; dull: *an insipid novel.* —*n*- in′ sip·id′ i·ty or in·sip′ id·ness. *adv*- in·sip′ id·ly.

in·sist (ĭn sĭst′) *vt*- 1 to make an urgent demand: *I insist that you go.* 2 to state firmly and immovably: *He insists that he is right.*

insist on to demand or require: *I insist on the best.*

in·sol·vent (ĭn sŏl′ vənt) *adj*- unable to pay all debts; bankrupt. *n*- person who cannot pay all his debts. —*n*- in·sol′ ven·cy.

in·som·ni·a (ĭn sŏm′ nē ə) *n*- inability to sleep.

in·so·much (ĭn′ sō mŭch′) *adv*- to such a degree or extent: *If a man lies often, he is* insomuch *untrustworthy.* **insomuch as** inasmuch as.

in·sou·ci·ance (ĭn sōō′ sē əns) *n*- lack of concern or caring; indifference; lightheartedness.

in·spect (ĭn spĕkt′) *vt*- 1 to examine carefully, especially to check for faults, errors, etc.: *Each morning the foreman inspected our work.* 2 to examine or review (troops, military equipment, etc.) officially.

in·spec·tion (ĭn spĕk′ shən) *n*- 1 an inspecting; careful examination for faults, errors, etc.: *In some States, inspection of automobiles must be made twice a year.* 2 official review or examination of troops, military equipment, etc.

in·spec·tor (ĭn spĕk′ tər) *n*- 1 person who inspects. 2 high-ranking officer in a police department.

in·spi·ra·tion (ĭn′ spə rā′ shən) *n*- 1 a stirring of mind, feelings, or imagination that leads to action or creation: *The artist's inspiration came from his everyday surroundings.* 2 person or thing that inspires: *The music of the band was an inspiration to the marchers.* 3 bright idea; impulse or sudden thought that leads to action or creation: *Your suggesting that we take an extra canteen was an inspiration.* 4 a drawing of air into the lungs. —*adj*- in′ spir·a′ tion·al. *adv*- in′ spi·ra′ tion·al·ly.

in·spire (ĭn spīər′) *vt*- [in·spired, in·spir·ing] 1 to stir deeply; breathe life into; arouse to action. 2 to be the cause of; arouse; call forth: *Honesty inspires respect. Her beauty inspired the poem.* *vi*- to draw air into the lungs. —*adv*- in·spired′ ly. *n*- in·spir′ er. *adv*- in·spir′ ing·ly.

1in·stall·ment (ĭn stôl′ mənt) *n*- an establishing in position or office; installation. [from Medieval Latin *installāre*, from Latin *in-*, "in; into," plus *stallum*, "a position; seat; 1stall," from a Germanic word.]

2in·stall·ment (ĭn stôl′ mənt) *n*- 1 any one of several parts that follow in a series: *The second installment of the story will appear next month.*

in·stead (ĭn stĕd′) *adv*- as a substitute or alternative: *They didn't come to our house, so we went to theirs* instead. **instead of** in place of: *I will go instead of you.*

in·step (ĭn′ stĕp′) *n*- 1 arched upper side of the foot between the toes and the ankle. 2 part of a shoe, slipper, stocking, etc., that covers this part of the foot.

Instep

in·sti·gate (ĭn′ stə gāt′) *vt*- [in·sti·gat·ed, in·sti·gat·ing] to cause by prompting, urging, or incitement: *to instigate a revolt.* —*n*- in′ sti·ga′ tion.

in·sti·ga·tor (ĭn′ stə gā′ tər) *n*- person who instigates.

in·still or **in·stil** (ĭn stĭl′) *vt*- [in·stilled, in·still·ing] to add little by little; put in gradually; impart; implant; infuse: *to instill respect for the rights of others.*

1in·stinct (ĭn′ stĭngkt′) *n*- 1 inborn urge to do things in a certain way; natural untaught way of acting: *Squirrels gather food for winter by instinct.* 2 talent; natural ability: *He has a happy instinct for saying the right thing.*

2in·stinct (ĭn stĭngkt′) *adj*- filled or infused (with): *to be instinct with love; to be instinct with joy.*

in·stinc·tive (ĭn stĭngk′ tĭv) *adj*- not gained through learning or experience; inborn; natural: *an instinctive fear of loud noises.* —*adv*- in·stinc′ tive·ly.

in·sti·tute (ĭn′ stə tōōt′, -tyōōt′) *n*- 1 school, museum, or other such institution: *an art institute; California Institute of Technology.* 2 building or group of buildings that houses one of these. *vt*- [in·sti·tut·ed, in·sti·tut·ing] 1 to begin; start; originate: *We instituted a search for him.* 2 to establish: *The club instituted new laws.*

in·struct (ĭn strŭkt′) *vt*- 1 to teach: *He instructs two classes.* 2 to direct; order: *We instructed him to report.*

in·struc·tion (ĭn strŭk′ shən) *n*- 1 an instructing; education: *Ann got her early instruction at home, but Ralph went to school.* 2 lessons: *Some grade schools give instruction in foreign languages.* 3 **instructions** directions or orders: *We couldn't understand the instructions.* —*adj*- in·struc′ tion·al: *an instructional manual.*

in·struc·tive (ĭn strŭk′ tĭv) *adj*- informative; giving knowledge: *an instructive talk on art.* —*adv*- in·struc′ tive·ly. *n*- in·struc′ tive·ness.

in·struc·tor (ĭn strŭk′ tər) *n*- teacher, especially a college teacher holding the lowest rank of full-time appointment. —*n- fem.* in·struc′ tress.

1in·stru·ment (ĭn′ strə mənt) *n*- 1 tool used for some particular kind of work: *a surgeon's instruments.* 2 means by which something is accomplished: *The army was the dictator's instrument for controlling the country.* 3 person who is someone else's tool: *Jones was merely an instrument of the criminal gang.* 4 device used to measure, control, or examine: *Airplanes carry many instruments. A thermostat is an instrument to control a furnace. The telescope and microscope are scientific instruments.* 5 device by which musical sounds are made, such as the harp, flute, etc. 6 legal or financial document such as a deed, writ, check, mortgage, etc. *as modifier*: *an instrument panel; an instrument case.*

2in·stru·ment (ĭn′ strə mənt′) *vt*- 1 to provide with devices for measuring and controlling: *to instrument a guided missile.* 2 *Music* to orchestrate.

in·stru·men·tal (ĭn′ strə mĕn′ təl) *adj*- 1 helping to bring about; serving as a means: *He was instrumental in our finding a new home.* 2 performed on or written for a musical instrument. —*adv*- in′ stru·men′ tal·ly.

in·stru·men·tal·ist (ĭn′ strə mĕn′ tə lĭst) *n*- person who plays a musical instrument, especially as a professional.

in·stru·men·ta·tion (ĭn′ strə mən tā′ shən) *n*- 1 the instrumenting of some vehicle, device, apparatus, etc.; also, the field of science and engineering specializing in this. 2 all the instruments of a particular vehicle, apparatus, etc.

instrument landing *n*- landing of an aircraft by means of its instruments and with the help of ground radio and radar devices, usually made in a fog or storm.

in·su·lar (ĭn′ sə lər, -syə lər) *adj*- 1 of or relating to an island or its people: *an insular custom.* 2 living or situated on an island: *an insular city.* 3 forming an island: *an insular reef.* 4 detached; isolated: *an insular location.*

in·su·late (ĭn′sə lāt′) *vt-* [**in·su·lat·ed, in·su·lat·ing**] 1 to cover, line, or surround with a material or device that will not conduct electricity, heat, sound, etc.: *to insulate a wire; to insulate a roof.* 2 to set apart; isolate: *to insulate one's mind from disturbing ideas.*

in·su·la·tion (ĭn′sə lā′shən) *n-* 1 material used to prevent the passage of heat, sound, electricity, etc. 2 an insulating: *Let's start the insulation of the attic.* 3 condition of being insulated: *The rock wool in the walls provides heat insulation.*

in·su·la·tor (ĭn′sə lā′tər) *n-* something that prevents the passage of heat, electricity, sound or other influences.

in·su·lin (ĭn′sə lĭn) *n-* hormone given off by certain cells in the pancreas, which helps the body to use sugar and protein.

Electric insulators

¹in·sult (ĭn sŭlt′) *vt-* to treat a person or thing rudely or scornfully; affront: *to insult with vile names.*

²in·sult (ĭn′sŭlt′) *n-* a rude or scornful action or speech; an affront: *To question a man's honesty is an insult.*

in·sult·ing (ĭn sŭl′tĭng) *adj-* 1 showing rudeness, scorn, or contempt: *an insulting manner.* 2 giving offense to another: *an insulting question.* —*adv-* **in·sul′ting·ly.**

in·su·per·a·ble (ĭn sōō′pər ə bəl) *adj-* not to be surmounted or overcome: *These are insuperable difficulties.* —*adv-* **in·su′per·a·bly.**

in·sup·port·a·ble (ĭn′sə pôr′tə bəl) *adj-* unbearable; intolerable: *an insupportable grief.* —*adv-* **in′sup·port′a·bly.**

in·sur·a·ble (ĭn shōōr′ə bəl) *adj-* able, proper, or suitable to be insured: *The man was not insurable because of his dangerous occupation.*

in·take (ĭn′tāk′) *n-* 1 a taking in: *an intake of money; an intake of water.* 2 the amount taken in: *The intake of each boiler is 3,000 gallons an hour.* 3 pipe or channel through which a fluid is brought in, or the opening where a fluid enters.

in·tan·gi·ble (ĭn tăn′jə bəl) *adj-* 1 such as cannot be touched: *Time, hope, and darkness are intangible.* 2 difficult to grasp with the mind; vague; hazy: *an intangible fear; intangible suspicions.* —*n-* **in·tan′gi·bil′i·ty:** *I recognize the intangibility of my suspicions.* —*adv-* **in·tan′gi·bly.**

in·te·ger (ĭn′tə jər) *n-* any positive or negative whole number, or zero.

in·te·gral (ĭn′tə grəl) *adj-* 1 helping to make up something whole: *Sincerity is an integral part of friendship.* 2 making a unit; whole; complete: *an integral arrangement.* —*adv-* **in′te·gral·ly.**

in·te·grate (ĭn′tə grāt′) *vt-* [**in·te·gra·ted, in·te·gra·ting**] 1 to bring parts together to make a whole: *to integrate studies with athletics in the school day.* 2 to make schools, housing, transportation, etc., open to all races on an equal basis. *vi-* to become open or accessible to all races on an equal basis.

in·te·gra·tion (ĭn′tə grā′shən) *n-* an integrating or being integrated: *the integration of parts of an automobile; the integration of races in a school.*

in·teg·ri·ty (ĭn tĕg′rə tē) *n-* 1 honesty; uprightness; moral soundness: *The integrity of the mayor was not questioned during the scandal.* 2 wholeness; completeness.

in·tem·per·ate (ĭn tĕm′pər ət) *adj-* 1 not moderate; not restrained; excessive: *his intemperate language.* 2 given to excessive use of alcoholic liquors. —*adv-* **in·tem′per·ate·ly.** *n-* **in·tem′per·ate·ness:** *The intemperateness of his speech startled the audience.*

in·tend (ĭn tĕnd′) *vt-* 1 to have as a purpose; mean: *He did not intend to go away.* 2 to design for a purpose or group: *The author intended this book for adults.*

in·tend·ed (ĭn tĕn′dəd) *adj-* meant; planned; had in mind as a purpose or a meaning: *the intended meaning of a remark. n-* Archaic person to whom one is engaged to be married.

in·tense (ĭn tĕns′) *adj-* 1 extreme; very great: *an intense pain.*

in·ter·cept (ĭn′tər sĕpt′) *vt-* 1 to seize, catch, or stop on the way: *to intercept a message; to intercept a forward pass.* 2 *Mathematics* to bound or delimit (a line, surface, etc.) by marking off. *n-* *Mathematics* 1 the distance from the origin to the point where a given curve cuts a co-ordinate axis; also, the point of interception. 2 an intercepted segment or part. —*n-* **in′ter·cep′tion.**

in·ter·cep·tor (ĭn′tər sĕp′tər) *n-* 1 person or thing that intercepts: *the interceptor of the message.* 2 kind of fighter plane used to attack bombers.

in·ter·ces·sion (ĭn′tər sĕsh′ən) *n-* an interceding. *Hom-* intersession.

in·ter·ces·sor (ĭn′tər sĕs′ər) *n-* person who intercedes.

¹in·ter·change (ĭn′tər chānj′) *vt-* [**in·ter·changed, in·ter·chang·ing**] 1 to put persons or things in the place of each other: *You can interchange the parts of these machines.* 2 to exchange. *vi-* to exchange partners or positions: *The dancers continually interchanged.*

²in·ter·change (ĭn′tər chānj′) *n-* 1 a putting of persons or things in the other's place: *an interchange of notes or goods.* 2 an exchanging: *an interchange of ambassadors.* 3 place where one may enter or leave a superhighway.

in·ter·change·a·ble (ĭn′tər chān′jə bəl) *adj-* designed so as to be put in place of one another: *Tires on an automobile are interchangeable.* —*n-* **in′ter·change·a·bil′i·ty.** *adv-* **in′ter·change′a·bly.**

in·ter·con·ti·nen·tal (ĭn′tər kŏn′tə nĕn′təl) *adj-* 1 traveling or capable of traveling from one continent to another: *an intercontinental flight.* 2 of or relating to things existing between continents.

in·ter·cos·tal (ĭn′tər kŏs′təl) *adj-* between the ribs: *an intercostal muscle.*

in·ter·course (ĭn′tər kôrs′) *n-* 1 dealings, relations, and communications: *The intercourse between the two countries has been peaceful.* 2 sexual relations.

in·ter·de·nom·i·na·tion·al (ĭn′tər dĭ nŏm′ə nā′shən əl) *adj-* of or relating to mutual action among several religious denominations.

in·ter·de·part·men·tal (ĭn′tər dĭ pärt′mĕn′təl) *adj-* existing or carried on between departments.

in·ter·de·pen·dence (ĭn′tər dĭ pĕn′dəns) *n-* dependence on each other or one another.

in·ter·de·pend·ent (ĭn′tər dĭ pĕn′dənt) *adj-* dependent on each other or one another: *an interdependent group; interdependent nations.* —*adv-* **in′ter·de·pen′dent·ly.**

¹in·ter·dict (ĭn′tər dĭkt′) *vt-* 1 to prohibit or forbid; restrain; prevent: *to interdict the use of drugs; to interdict an enemy attack.* 2 to cut off from the spiritual services of a church. —*n-* **in′ter·dict′ion.**

²in·ter·dict (ĭn′tər dĭkt′) *n-* a formal prohibition.

in·ter·est (ĭn′trəst, ĭn′tər ĭst) *n-* 1 desire to take part in, work at, or hear about: *Omar shows an interest in sports.*

in·ter·lace (ĭn′tər lās′) *vt-* [**in·ter·laced, in·ter·lac·ing**] to lace or weave together; intertwine: *to interlace strips of cloth.* *vi-*: *The brown threads and the green interlaced.*

in·ter·lard (ĭn′tər lärd′) *vt-* to mix or vary with something different or irrelevant, often in order to give variety; intersperse: *to interlard a speech with jokes.*

in·ter·line (ĭn′tər līn′) *vt-* [**in·ter·lined, in·ter·lin·ing**] to fit (a garment) with an extra inner lining. [from inter- plus ²line.]

in·ter·lin·ing (ĭn′tər lī′nĭng) *n-* extra inner lining placed between the lining and the outer fabric.

in·ter·link (ĭn′tər lĭngk′) *vt-* to link together.

in·ter·lock (ĭn′tər lŏk′) *vt-* 1 to fit (pieces, parts, etc.) closely together. 2 to lock together or interlace tightly with something else: *The two deer interlocked horns.* 3 to arrange (switches, signals, etc.) in such a way that they must be operated in a certain order or together, to prevent accidents. *vi-*: *The branches of the tree interlocked in a dense hedge. The pieces of the puzzle interlocked.*

in·ter·loc·u·tor (ĭn′tər lŏk′yə tər) *n-* 1 person who asks questions or takes part in a conversation with another. 2 in a minstrel show, a performer who puts questions to other performers.

in·ter·loc·u·to·ry (ĭn′tər lŏk′yə tôr′ē) *adj-* 1 in law, not final; pronounced during the course of an action: *an interlocutory divorce.*

in·ter·me·di·ate (In′ tər mē′ dē ət) *adj-* being or coming between two points, stages, things, or persons: *The tadpole is an intermediate stage of a frog's growth.* *n-* go-between; mediator. —*adv-* in′ ter·me′ di·ate·ly.

in·ter·ment (In tûr′ mənt) *n-* burial.

in·ter·mez·zo (In′ tər mĕt′ sō) *n-* [*pl.* in·ter·mez·zos or in·ter·mez·zi (-sĕ)] short piece of music played between the acts or scenes of an opera or drama.

in·ter·mi·na·ble (In tûr′ mə nə bəl) *adj-* lasting or seeming to last forever; endless: *an interminable speech.* —*adv-* in·ter′ mi·na·bly.

in·ter·min·gle (In′ tər mIng′ gəl) *vi-* [in·ter·min·gled, in·ter·min·gling] to mix together; join together; mingle: *The visitors soon intermingled with the crowd.* *vt-: The author intermingled tragedy and comedy in his play.*

in·ter·mis·sion (In′ tər mIsh′ ən) *n-* 1 interval of time between two parts of a performance or other proceeding. 2 pause; interruption: *He worked without intermission.*

in·ter·mit·tent (In′ tər mIt′ ənt) *adj-* alternately starting and stopping; repeated at intervals; coming and going: *an intermittent rain.* —*adv-* in·ter·mit′ tent·ly.

in·ter·mix (In′ tər mIks′) *vi-* to mix or blend together: *Joy and sorrow intermixed in his life.* *vt-: He intermixes humor and pathos in his writing.* —*n-* in′ ter·mix′ ture.

¹in·tern (In tûrn′) *vt-* to confine or detain (enemy or belligerent persons, ships, etc.), especially during a war

²in·tern (In′ tûrn′) *n-* recently graduated physician who is getting final training in a hospital. *vi-: Tom interned at the county hospital.* Also **interne.**

in·ter·nal (In tûr′ nəl) *adj-* 1 existing or situated within the surface or boundary of something; inner: *The heart is an internal organ.* 2 within a country; domestic: *the internal affairs of a country.* —*adv-* in·ter′ nal·ly.

internal-combustion engine *n-* engine in which the fuel burns inside the engine itself, most often in a cylinder. Gasoline engines and jet engines are examples.

in·ter·na·tion·al (In′ tər nàsh ən əl) *adj-* having to do with, or going on between, two or more nations or their people: *an international organization;* international trade. —*adv-* in·ter·na′ tion·al·ly.

in·tern·ment (In tûrn′ mənt) *n-* an interning of a belligerent ship, person, etc.; also, the period of this.

in·tern·ship (In′ tûrn ship′) *n-* period during which one is a medical intern; also, the training received.

in·ter·pen·e·trate (In′ tər pĕn′ ə trāt′) *vt-* to penetrate thoroughly or between. —*n-* in′ ter·pen′ e·tra′ tion.

in·ter·phase (In′ tər fāz′) *n-* stage in mitosis between successive cell divisions, in which the DNA molecules of the nucleus replicate themselves in preparation for the next division. During interphase, the cell grows and matures. Interphase is the usual stage of body cells.

in·ter·plan·e·tar·y (In′ tər plăn′ ə tĕr′ ē) *adj-* between the planets of the solar system: *an interplanetary rocket.*

in·ter·play (In′ tər plā′) *n-* action of things, ideas, etc, on each other; interaction: *the interplay of minds.*

in·ter·re·late (In′ tər rē lāt′) *vt-* [in·ter·re·lat·ed, in·ter·re·lat·ing] to bring (something) into a mutual relationship: *to interrelate two plans.* *vi-: Their ideas do not interrelate well.* —*n-* in′ ter·re·la′ tion.

in·ter·re·lat·ed (In′ tər rē lā′ təd) *adj-* having a connection between each other; mutually related.

in·ter·re·la·tion·ship (In′ tər rē lā′shən ship′) *n-* mutual relationship.

in·ter·ro·gate (In tĕr′ ə gāt′) *vt-* [in·ter·ro·gated, in·ter·ro·gat·ing] to question, especially question closely or systematically; examine: *to interrogate a spy.* —*n-* in·ter′ ro·ga′ tor.

in·ter·stel·lar (In′ tər stĕl′ ər) *adj-* among the stars.

in·ter·stice (In tûr′ stəs) *n-* [*pl.* in·ter·stic·es (-stə sēz′)] narrow space or crevice; chink.

in·ter·sti·tial (In′ tər stIsh′ əl) *adj-* 1 of or having to do with an interstice. 2 *Biology* situated between the cells of a tissue: *Lymph is an interstitial fluid.*

in·ter·trib·al (In′ tər trī′ bəl) *adj-* taking place or existing between tribes: *an intertribal war.*

in·ter·twine (In′ tər twIn′) *vi-* [in·ter·twined, in·ter·twin·ing] to twine and twist together; interlace: *Ivy and wisteria vines intertwined above the door.*

in·ter·vene (In′ tər vĕn′) *vi-* [in·ter·vened, in·ter·ven·ing] 1 to come or be (between): *The years that intervene between grade school and college bring many changes.* 2 to get in the way; interfere: *If nothing unexpected intervenes, we shall go as planned.* 3 to step in to settle: *to intervene in a quarrel.* —*n-* in′ ter·ven′ er.

in·ter·ven·tion (In′ tər vĕn′ shən) *n-* 1 an interfering: *an intervention in the affairs of another.* 2 a coming between: *A friend's intervention prevented a fight.*

in·ter·view (In′ tər vyōō′) *n-* 1 personal meeting to discuss something: *the foreman's interviews with job seekers.* 2 account or record of such a discussion: *Smith's interview with the governor was published in the papers.* *vt-: The reporter interviewed the visiting diplomat.* —*n-* in′ ter·view′ er.

in·ter·weave (In′ tər wĕv′) *vt-* [in·ter·wove, in·ter·wov·en or in·ter·wove, in·ter·weav·ing] to twist or weave together; intertwine: *to interweave silk with cotton.* *vi-: Yarn interweaves easily.*

in·tes·tate (In tĕs′ tāt′) *adj-* 1 not having made a will: *to die intestate.* 2 not disposed of by a will.

in·tes·ti·nal (In tĕs′ tIn əl) *adj-* having to do with the intestines: *an intestinal tract.* —*adv-* in·tes′ ti·nal·ly.

in·ti·ma·tion (In′ tə mā′ shən) *n-* a hint; indirect suggestion: *He gave no intimation of leaving.*

in·tim·i·date (In tIm′ ə dāt′) *vt-* [in·tim·i·dat·ed, in·tim·i·dat·ing] to make afraid by threats; frighten; cow. —*n-* in·tim′ i·da′ tion.

in·tim·i·da·tor (In tIm′ ə dā′ tər) *n-* one who intimidates.

in·to (In′ tōō) *prep-* 1 to the inside of: *to fall into a pond; to walk into a building.* 2 to a time in: *He worked all night and into the next day.* 3 to the form or state of: *The water changed into steam.* 4 against: *He crashed into the wall. He walked into the wind.*

in·tol·er·a·ble (In tŏl′ ər ə bəl) *adj-* very hard to endure; unbearable: *the intolerable heat.* —*adv-* in·tol′er·a·bly.

in·tol·er·ance (In tŏl′ ər əns) *n-* 1 unwillingness to allow customs, behavior, opinions, beliefs, etc., not like one's own.

in·tox·i·cant (In tŏk′ sə kənt) *n-* 1 that which intoxicates, especially alcohol. 2 anything that excites or elates.

in·tox·i·cate (In tŏk′ sə kāt′) *vt-* [in·tox·i·cat·ed, in·tox·i·cat·ing] 1 to make drunk. 2 to fill with wild excitement; elate: *The warm spring air intoxicated the colt.* —*adv-* in·tox′ i·cat′ ing·ly. *n-* in·tox′ i·ca′ tion.

intra- *prefix* within: intramural; intrastate. [from Latin intrā, "within; inside; inside of."]

►For usage note see INTER-.

in·trac·ta·ble (In trăk′ tə bəl) *adj-* unmanageable; not easily controlled: *an intractable temper; an intractable metal.* —*n-* in·trac′ ta·bil′ i·ty. *adv-* in·trac′ta·bly.

in·tra·mu·ral (In′ trə myōōr′ əl) *adj-* 1 entirely within the walls or limits of a city, university, etc. 2 limited to the members of a school, college, or other organization.

in·tran·si·gent (In trăn′ sĭ jənt) *adj-* uncompromising; not reconcilable: *an intransigent rebel.* *n-* one who is uncompromising. —*n-* in·tran′ si·gence. *adv-* in·tran′ si·gent·ly.

in·tran·si·tive (In trăn′ sə tIv) *Grammar adj-* of verbs, not having an object. Examples: *He sits. He laughed. John rode down the street.* *n-: That verb is an intransitive.* —*adv-* in·tran′ si·tive·ly.

in·tra·state (In′ trə stāt′) *adj-* within a State.

in·tra·ve·nous (In′ trə vē′ nəs) *adj-* within or into a vein: *an intravenous drug.* —*adv-* in·tra·ve′ nous·ly.

in·tro·duc·tion (in′ trə dŭk′ shən) *n-* 1 an introducing or being introduced. 2 beginning section of a book, speech, etc., meant to prepare the audience for what is to follow. 3 book that introduces beginners to a subject.

in·tro·duc·to·ry (In′ trə dŭk′ tə rē) *adj-* serving to introduce; prefatory: *an introductory paragraph.*

in·tro·spec·tion (in′ trə spĕk′shən) *n-* examination of one's own thoughts and feelings.

in·tro·spec·tive (In′ trə spĕk′ tIv) *n-* examining or inclined to examine one's own thoughts and feelings; subjective. —*adv-* in′ tro·spec′ tive·ly.

in·tro·ver·sion (In′ trə vûr′ zhən) *n-* 1 act of looking inward or within. 2 tendency to be chiefly occupied with one's own mental or emotional processes.

in·va·lid·i·ty (In′ və lĭd′ ə tē) *n-* lack of validity.

in·val·u·a·ble (In văl′ yŏŏ ə bəl) *adj-* having a worth or value beyond measure; priceless: *an invaluable friend; an invaluable jewel.* —*adv-* **in·val′u·a·bly.**

in·var·i·a·ble (In vâr′ē ə bəl, In vâr′-) *adj-* never changing; constant; not variable: *a man of invariable habits.* —*n-* **in·var′i·a·bil′i·ty.** *adv-* **in·var′i·a·bly.**

in·va·sion (In vā′ zhən) *n-* an invading or being invaded.

in·vec·tive (In věk′ tĭv) *n-* violent, bitter accusation or attack in words; abusive language.

in·veigh (In vā′) *vi-* to speak violently and bitterly (against): *The lawyer inveighed bitterly against the accused criminal.* *n-* **in·veigh′er.**

in·vei·gle (In vā′gəl) *vt-* [**in·vei·gled, in·vei·gling**] to persuade by deception or flattery; lure: *to inveigle him into going.* —*n-* **in·vei′gle·ment.** *n-* **in·vei′gler.**

in·vent (In věnt′) *vt-* 1 to make or devise (something new): *James Watt invented the steam engine.* 2 to make up; fabricate: *to invent an excuse.*

in·ves·ti·ga·tion (In věs′ tə gā′shən) *n-* thorough inquiry: *an investigation of the fire.*

in·ves·ti·ga·tor (In věs′ tə gāt′) *n-* person who investigates; especially, one whose job is to investigate.

in·ves·ti·ture (In věs′ tə chər) *n-* 1 ceremony of installing a person in office. 2 garment or covering.

in·vest·ment (In věst′ mənt) *n-* 1 an investing: *an investment in oil stocks; an investment of one's time.* 2 amount invested: *The original investment doubled in value.* 3 something in which money is invested: *The new house was a valuable investment.*

in·ves·tor (In věs′ tər) *n-* person who invests money in hope of profit.

in·vet·er·ate (In vět′ ər ət) *adj-* 1 of long standing; deep-rooted: *an inveterate hatred.* 2 habitual: *an inveterate liar.* —*adv-* **in·vet′er·ate·ly.**

in·vid·i·ous (In vĭd′ ē əs) *adj-* 1 likely to provoke ill will or envy; offensive: *an invidious remark.* 2 unfairly partial or biased: *an invidious criticism.* —*adv-* **in·vid′i·ous·ly.** —*n-* **in·vid′i·ous·ness.**

in·vig·or·ate (In vĭg′ə rāt′) *vt-* [**in·vig·or·at·ed, in·vig·or·at·ing**] to give strength and energy to; animate. —*adv-* **in·vig′or·at·ing·ly.** —*n-* **in·vig′or·a′tion.**

in·vin·ci·ble (In vĭn′ sə bəl) *adj-* such as cannot be conquered or overcome; unconquerable: *an invincible army.* —*n-* **in·vin′ci·bil′i·ty.** —*adv-* **in·vin′ci·bly.**

in·vi·o·la·ble (In vī′ ə lə bəl) *adj-* 1 such as must not be violated; sacred: *an inviolable vow; inviolable laws.* 2 such as cannot be destroyed: *an inviolable spirit.* —*n-*

in·ward (In′ wərd) *adj-* 1 toward the inside or center: *an inward push.* 2 at or near the center; inner. *adv-* (also **in′ wards**) 1 into or toward the inner self: *His thoughts turned inward.* 2 toward the inside or center.

in·ward·ly (In′ wərd lē) *adv-* internally; especially, in the mind or feelings: *He was inwardly ashamed.*

in·ward·ness (In′ wərd nəs) *n-* tendency to be inward in one's thinking and feeling; introspective behavior.

i·o·dide (I′ ə dīd′) *n-* compound of iodine and another element or radical.

i·o·dine (I′ ə dīn′) *n-* grayish-black, solid element that gives off a purple vapor when heated. It is used with alcohol as a general antiseptic, and its compounds are used in medicine, photography, and many industries. Symbol I, At. No. 53, At. Wt. 126.9044.

i·o·dize (I′ ə dīz′) *vt-* [**i·o·dized, i·o·diz·ing**] to treat or saturate with iodine or an iodide.

I·on·ic (I ŏn′ Ik) *adj-* 1 of or relating to ancient Ionia or its people. 2 of or relating to an order of classical architecture distinguished by scroll-like decorations on the capitals of pillars. *n-* dialect of ancient Ionia or Attica; classic Greek.

Ionic capital and column

i·on·i·za·tion (I′ ə na zā′ shən) *n-* 1 *Chemistry* the dissociation of certain compounds into ions when they are dissolved. 2 *Physics* process in which ions are formed when atoms lose their outer electrons under the impact of radiation or when an electrical current passes through a gas.

i·rid·i·um (I rĭd′ ē əm) *n-* silvery, hard, brittle metal element found in platinum ores. Iridium is used in the manufacture of bearings. Symbol, Ir, At. No. 77, At. Wt. 192.2.

i·ris (I′ rəs) *n-* [*pl.* **i·ris·es**] 1 the circular, colored part of the eye located between the cornea and the lens. For picture, see *eye.* 2 plant with large flowers and sword-shaped leaves; also, its flower; flag.

I·ris (I′ rəs) *n-* in Greek mythology, the goddess of the rainbow, and in the "Iliad," the messenger of the gods.

I·rish (I′ rĭsh) *n-* 1 a native or citizen of Ireland. 2 the ancient or modern language of the people of Ireland; also, the dialect of English spoken there. 3 **the Irish** the people of Ireland and their ancestors and descendants, collectively. *adj-: a table-cloth of Irish linen.*

Iris

i·ron·stone (I′ ərn stōn′) *n-* 1 (also **ironstone china**) hard, usually white pottery with a glassy surface. 2 iron ore.

i·ron·ware (I′ ərn wâr′) *n-* articles made of iron.

i·ron·wood (I′ ərn wŏŏd′) *n-* any of various trees with very, hard, heavy wood, such as acacias, ebonies, etc.

i·ron·work (I′ ərn wûrk′) *n-* 1 iron articles; also, work in iron. 2 **ironworks** place where iron is smelted or articles are made from it.

i·ron·work·er (I′ ərn wûr′ kər) *n-* person who works in iron or on steel construction jobs.

i·ro·ny (I′ rə nē) *n-* [*pl.* **i·ro·nies**] 1 humorous or sarcastic way of expressing the direct opposite of what is really meant. To say "That's good!" when someone makes a mistake is irony. 2 situation or happening that is the direct opposite of what was intended or expected.

Ir·o·quois (Ir′ ə kwoi′) *n-* [*pl.* **I·ro·quois**] 1 member of the American Indian confederacy including the Cayugas, Mohawks, Oneidas, Onondagas, and Senecas, and later the Tuscaroras, and others. 2 any of the languages of these people. *adj-: an Iroquois legend.*

ir·ra·di·ate (I rā′ dē āt′) *vt-* [**ir·ra·di·at·ed, ir·ra·di·at·ing**] 1 to direct light upon or through; illuminate. 2 to treat with or expose to electromagnetic radiation, etc.: *to irradiate milk with ultraviolet rays.* —*n-* **ir·ra′di·a′tion.**

ir·ra·tion·al (I rāsh′ ən əl) *adj-* 1 not rational; lacking or not using reasoning powers. 2 contrary to reason; absurd: *an irrational fear.* —*adv-* **ir·ra′tion·al·ly.**

ir·ra·tion·al·i·ty (I răsh′ ən ăl′ ə tē) *n-* [*pl.* **ir·ra·tion·al·i·ties**] 1 irrational behavior or condition. 2 something which shows lack of reason.

irrational number *n-* a real number that cannot be expressed in the form a/b, where "a" and "b" are integers. For example, $\sqrt{2}$ and π are irrational numbers.

ir·re·claim·a·ble (I′ rĭ klā′ mə bəl) *adj-* such as cannot be reclaimed: *miles of irreclaimable land.* —*n-* **ir′re·claim′a·ble·ness.** *adv-* **ir′re·claim′a·bly.**

ir·re·con·cil·a·ble (I răk′ ən sī′ lə bəl) *adj-* such as cannot be reconciled: *two irreconcilable foes.* *n-* person who refuses to yield or accept compromises. —*n-* **ir·rec′on·cil′a·bil′i·ty** or **ir·rec′on·cil′a·ble·ness.** *adv-* **ir·rec′on·cil′a·bly.**

ir·re·cov·er·a·ble (I′ rĭ kŭv′ ər ə bəl) *adj-* such as cannot be recovered: *an irrecoverable opportunity.* —*n-* **ir′re·cov′er·a·ble·ness.** *adv-* **ir′re·cov′er·a·bly.**

ir·re·deem·a·ble (I′ rĭ dē′ mə bəl) *adj-* such as cannot be redeemed: *an irredeemable loss.* —*n-* **ir′re·deem′a·ble·ness.** *adv-* **ir′re·deem′a·bly.**

ir·re·duc·i·ble (I′ rĭ dōō′ sə bəl, -dyōō′ sə bəl) *adj-* 1 such as cannot be reduced: *their irreducible expenses.* 2 such as cannot be simplified: *an irreducible fraction.* —*n-* **ir′re·duc′i·bil′i·ty** or **ir′re·duc′i·ble·ness.** *adv-* **ir′re·duc′i·bly.**

ir·re·spon·si·ble (I′ rĭ spŏn′ sə bəl) *adj-* not responsible; not to be depended upon: *an irresponsible laundry.* —*n-* **ir′re·spon′si·bil′i·ty,** *adv-* **ir′re·spon′si·bly.**

ir·re·triev·a·ble (I′ rĭ trē′ və bəl) *adj-* such as cannot be retrieved: *The posted letter was irretrievable.* —*n-* **ir′re·triev′a·ble·ness.** *adv-* **ir′re·triev′a·bly.**

ir·ri·ta·bil·i·ty (Ir′ə tə bĭl′ə tē) *n-* 1 ease of being irritated or angered. 2 *Biology* a fundamental characteristic of living organisms and their cells that enables them to respond to changes in the environment.

ir·ri·ta·ble (Ir′ə tə bəl) *adj-* 1 easily annoyed or angered; cranky. 2 extremely sensitive: *an irritable skin condition.* —*n-* ir′ri·ta·ble·ness. *adv-* ir′ri·ta·bly.

ir·ri·tant (Ir′ə tənt) *n-* something that irritates; especially, that which causes sensitiveness or inflammation. *adj-* causing physical irritation.

ir·ri·tate (Ir′ə tāt′) *vt-* [ir·ri·tat·ed, ir·ri·tat·ing] 1 to make sore; cause to become inflamed: *Strong soap can irritate a baby's skin.* 2 to make impatient or angry; annoy: *He irritates me.* —*adv-* ir′ri·tat′ing·ly. ►For usage note see AGGRAVATE.

ir·ri·ta·tion (Ir′ə tā′shən) *n-* 1 an irritating or being irritated: *He showed his irritation when we came late.* 2 something that irritates: *His lateness is a constant irritation.* 3 soreness; inflammation: *a small skin irritation.*

ir·rupt (I rŭpt′) *vi-* 1 to rush in with force: appear suddenly: *The water irrupted through the dike.* 2 of an animal population, to increase suddenly in numbers. ►Should not be confused with ERUPT.

ir·rup·tion (I rŭp′shən) *n-* 1 a bursting or rushing in. 2 sudden increase in numbers. —*adv-* ir·rup′tive.

is (Iz) form of be used with "he," "she," "it," or singular noun subjects, in the present tense. as is in the condition found in, whether damaged, soiled, etc.: *The chair sells for $30 as is.*

I·sa·iah (I zā′ə) *n-* 1 in the Bible, a great Hebrew prophet of the eighth century B.C. 2 a book of the Bible attributed to him. In the CCD Bible, I·sa′ia.

is·chi·um (Ĭs′kē əm) *n-* the lowest portion of either of the hipbones. For picture, see *pelvis*.

I·seult (ē sōōlt′) *n-* in Arthurian legend, wife of King Mark of Cornwall. She was beloved by Tristram.

-ish *suffix* (used to form adjectives) 1 somewhat; rather: *black*ish; *sweet*ish. 2 resembling; having the characteristics of: *hogg*ish; *boy*ish. 3 having to do with (a national group): *English*; *Swed*ish. 4 *Informal & chiefly Brit.* approximately; about: *fifty*ish.

Ish·ma·el (Ish′mā əl) *n-* in the Bible, the exiled son of Abraham; hence, an outcast.

Ish·tar (Ish′tär′) *n-* in Assyrian and Babylonian mythology, the goddess of love and fertility. She was identified with the Phoenician Astarte.

i·sin·glass (I′zən glǎs′) *n-* 1 a gelatin made from the dried air bladders of fish and used in glues, printing inks, etc. 2 mica, especially when used as a window in stoves.

I·sis (I′sǝs) *n-* in Egyptian mythology, the goddess of love and fertility; sister and wife of Osiris.

Is·lam (Ĭs lăm′) *n-* 1 the religion of the Muslims, first taught by the prophet Mohammed in the 7th century A.D. The Muslims worship one God, Allah, and consider Mohammed as the last of the true prophets. 2 the Muslims as a group, their culture, and their lands. —*adj-* Is·lam′ic (-lăm′Ik, -lăm′Ik): *an Islamic prophet.*

is·land (I′lǝnd) *n-* 1 piece of land completely surrounded by water. 2 something like such a piece of land: *a safety island in the street.*

ITA Initial Teaching Alphabet.

ital. 1 italic. 2 italics.

I·tal·i·an (I tǎl′yǝn) *n-* 1 a native or inhabitant of Italy, or one of his descendants. 2 the Romance language of Italy. *adj-*: *unforgettable* Italian *landscapes.*

i·tal·ic (I tǎl′Ik, I-) *adj-* having to do with a type in which the letters slant to the right. *n-* 1 type of this style. 2 italics letters in slanting type.

i·tal·i·cize (I tǎl′ə sIz′) *vt-* [i·tal·i·cized, i·tal·i·ciz·ing] 1 to print with letters that slant toward the right. 2 to underline (a letter or word) in writing.

itch (Ich) *n-* 1 sensation of tingling and irritation in the skin. 2 contagious skin disease characterized by this sensation.

i·tem·ize (I′tə mIz′) *vt-* [i·tem·ized, i·tem·iz·ing] to list the separate items of: *to itemize a milk bill.*

it·er·ate (It′ər āt′) *vt-* [it·er·at·ed, it·er·at·ing] to repeat: *to iterate a threat.* —*n-* it′er·a′tion. *adj-* it′er·a·tive: *an iterative appeal for help.*

i·tin·er·ant (I tĭn′ər ǝnt, I tĭn′-) *adj-* 1 wandering from place to place: *a troupe of itinerant musicians.* 2 traveling a circuit in one's duties: *an itinerant preacher.* *n-* wandering person. —*adv-* i·tin′er·ant·ly.

i·tin·er·ar·y (I tĭn′ə rĕr′ē, I tĭn′-) *n-* [*pl.* i·tin·er·ar·ies] 1 proposed route for a journey, or a route actually taken. 2 record of a journey. 3 traveler's guidebook.

-ition *suffix* (used to form nouns) 1 act or process of: *defin*ition (act of defining); *oppos*ition; *compet*ition. 2 the condition or state of: *malnutr*ition; *amb*ition. 3 that which performs the action of: *prohib*ition; *pet*ition. 4 the result of: *compos*ition. (Many words ending in "-ition" can have two or all three of these meanings. Examples: *defin*ition; *compos*ition; *inhib*ition.)

-itious *suffix* (used to form adjectives) marked by; relating to; having the quality of: *factit*ious (not genuine; artificial); *fictit*ious (invented or imagined).

-itis *suffix* (used to form nouns) 1 inflammation of: *bron*chitis; *appendic*itis; *mening*itis. 2 *Informal* excessive fondness for; weakness for: *telephon*itis; *television*itis.

it'll (It ǝl) 1 it will. 2 it shall.

its (Its) *determiner* (possessive case of the pronoun "it," now usually called possessive adjective) 1 of or belonging to it: *The tree lost its leaves.* 2 inhabited by it: *The turtle returned to its pond.*

it's (Its) 1 it is. 2 it has (auxiliary verb only).

it·self (It′sĕlf′) *pron-* 1 its own self: *The cat was licking itself.* 2 word used for emphasis: *The frame itself is worth more than the picture.* by itself 1 alone: *The owl perched by itself.* 2 without any help: *The door opened by itself.*

-ity *suffix* (used to form nouns) 1 state, condition, or quality: *inferior*ity; *superior*ity; *atroc*ity; *fratern*ity; *patern*ity (condition of being a father); *mortal*ity. 2 property of a substance: *dens*ity; *conduct*ivity.

-ive *suffix* (used to form adjectives) 1 relating to; having the nature, character, or quality of: *fest*ive (relating to a feast or festival); *attract*ive; *mass*ive. 2 having a tendency to; given to: *destruct*ive; *disrupt*ive; *explos*ive. (Many adjectives ending in "-ive" are also used as nouns. Examples: *explos*ive; *sedat*ive; *incent*ive.)

J

J, j (jā) *n-* [*pl.* J's, j's] the tenth letter of the English alphabet.

jab (jăb) *vt-* [jabbed, jab·bing] to stab or poke: *He jabbed me with his elbow. n-* quick stab; sharp poke.

jab·ber (jăb'ər) *vi-* to talk rapidly and indistinctly; chatter; babble. *n-: the* jabber *of monkeys.* —*n-* jab'ber·er.

Jab·ber·wock (jă'bər wŏk') *n-* imaginary monster in the nonsense poem "Jabberwocky," included in Lewis Carroll's "Through the Looking Glass."

ja·bot (zhă bō') *n-* ruffle of lace or cloth down the front of a blouse, bodice, or shirt.

jack (jăk) *n-* 1 any of various portable mechanical or hydraulic devices that exert a powerful force and are used chiefly to raise cars or other heavy loads. 2 playing card with a picture of a young man; knave. It comes between the ten and the queen. 3 small flag flown on a ship to show its nationality. 4 electrical device in which a long, slim plug is inserted to make a connection. 5 male animal, especially a donkey. 6 man or boy, especially one employed in manual labor or as a sailor: *jack-of-all-trades*; Jack Tar. 7 *Slang* money. 8 bootjack. 9 small metal piece with six projections, used in a children's game. 10 jacks children's game using such metal pieces and a rubber ball, in which the pieces are picked up in various ways as the ball bounces. *vt-* (often used with "up") 1 to raise or lift with or as if with a mechanical or hydraulic device: *to jack the car up; to jack up prices.* 2 to spur on; exhort: *to jack up a lazy student.*

Raising car with jack

jack·al (jăk'əl) *n-* 1 wild dog of Asia and Africa, about the size of a fox. It feeds on carrion and small game. 2 person who does base or menial work for another; lackey.

Jackal, about 15 in high at shoulder

jack·a·napes (jăk'ə nāps') *n-* saucy or conceited fellow; also, a pert child.

jack·ass (jăk'ăs') *n-* 1 male donkey. 2 stupid person; blockhead.

jack boot or **jack·boot** (jăk'bōōt') *n-* military boot reaching above the knee.

jack·daw (jăk'dô') *n-* dusky, black, mischievous, European crow. It can learn to imitate human speech.

jack·et (jăk'ət) *n-* 1 short, coatlike garment. 2 life jacket. 3 any covering meant to insulate, protect, or toughen. —*adj-* jack'et·ed.

Jack Frost *n-* frost or wintry weather thought of as a person.

Jackdaw, about 14 in long

jack·ham·mer (jăk'hăm'ər) *n-* rock drill powered by compressed air.

jack-in-the-box (jăk'ĭn thə bŏks') *n-* doll on a spring attached to the bottom of a box so that the doll pops up when the lid is released.

SPATHE

jack-in-the-pul·pit (jăk'ĭn thə pōōl'pĭt) *n-* North American plant, growing in damp woods, with a spike of tiny yellow flowers arched over by a hoodlike spathe.

jack-knife (jăk'nīf') *n-* [*pl.* jack·knives] 1 large pocketknife with blades that can be folded back into the handle. 2 fancy dive in which the diver bends double, then straightens out.

SPADIX

jack-of-all-trades (jăk'əv ôl'trădz') *n-* man who can do all kinds of jobs; handyman.

Jack-in-the-pulpit

jack-o'-lan·tern (jăk'ə lăn'tərn) *n-* hollowed-out pumpkin having a face cut in it, and a light inside.

jack·pot (jăk'pŏt') *n-* 1 everything gambled for, in one large prize or pot; especially, the whole contents of a gambling slot machine. 2 in poker, a deal in which all players enter, and in which a pair of jacks or better is needed to open the betting.

hit the jackpot 1 to win a jackpot. **2** to have a sweeping and important success.

jack rabbit *n-* long-eared western hare able to make 20-foot jumps.

jack·screw (jăk'skrōō') *n-* jack that increases or decreases its pressing force as a screw is turned.

Jack·so·ni·an (jăk sō'nē ən) *adj-* having to do with Andrew Jackson, his policies, or his era.

jack·straw (jăk'strô') *n-* one of the light strips of wood or metal used in the child's game, jackstraws, in which a player tries to lift a strip out of a pile with a hook or magnet without moving other strips.

Ja·cob (jā'kəb) *n-* a Hebrew patriarch, son of Isaac, and ancestor of the twelve tribes of Israel.

Jac·o·bite (jăk'ə bīt') *n-* in English history, a follower of James II after his dethronement in 1688, or a supporter of one of his descendants.

Jacob's ladder (jā'kəbz lăd'ər) *n-* 1 in the Bible, a ladder reaching from earth to heaven, seen by Jacob in a dream. 2 a rope ladder with wooden rungs.

jac·quard (jə kärd') *n-* 1 fabric such as brocade or damask with an intricate figured weave. 2 loom equipped to weave such fabric.

¹jade (jād) *n-* 1 hard stone, in a range of green, bluish-green, and greenish-white shades, used for jewelry and ornaments. 2 (also jade green) light bluish green. *adj-: a* jade *silk.* [a shortened form of earlier French ejade, from a Spanish phrase piedra de ljada meaning "stone for (curing pain) of the side."]

²jade (jād) *n-* 1 worthless or worn-out horse. 2 a worthless woman. *vt-* [jad·ed, jad·ing] to wear out or tire, as with overwork. [from Middle English iade, from Scottish yawd or yald, perhaps from Old Norse jalda meaning "a mare."]

jad·ed (jā'dəd) *adj-* 1 exhausted. 2 dulled by having too much of something; satiated: *a jaded appetite.*

jag (jăg) *n-* sharp, projecting point; a notch. *vt-* [jagged, jag·ging] to cut or tear making a ragged edge.

jail·bird (jāl'bûrd') *Informal n-* prisoner or habitual criminal.

jail·break (jāl'brāk') *n-* an escape from jail.

jail·er or **jail·or** (jā'lər) *n-* person in charge of a jail.

ja·lop·y (jə lŏp'ē) *Slang n-* old, dilapidated automobile.

jal·ou·sie (jăl'ə sē) *n-* 1 blind made of overlapping horizontal slats that may be adjusted to let in light and air while keeping out sun or rain; venetian blind. 2 window made of glass louvers that may be adjusted to admit air and keep out rain. *as modifier: a* jalousie *door.*

¹jam (jăm) *vt-* [jammed, jam·ming] 1 to pack tightly; cram: *He jammed all his clothes into one suitcase.* 2 to put or place forcibly; crush down: *He jammed his hat on his head.* 3 to make unworkable or unmovable by sticking or blocking some part: *Threads* jammed *the sewing machine. An accident* jammed *traffic. vi-* to become unworkable or unmovable because of a sticking or blocking: *The rifle* jammed. *The window* jammed. *n-: a log jam; a traffic jam.* [perhaps a changed form of champ, "to chew noisily."]

²jam (jăm) *n-* preserve made by boiling fruit with sugar until thick. [probably a special use of ¹jam, since in making jam, much fruit is packed tightly together.]

jamb (jăm) *n-* one of the upright sides of a doorway, window opening, or fireplace.

jam·bo·ree (jăm bə rē') *n-* 1 noisy, lively party or spree. 2 large gathering of the Boy Scouts.

James (jāmz) *n-* in the Bible, either of two apostles, St. James the Greater, or St. James the Less. A book of the New Testament is attributed to James the Less.

jam session *n-* gathering of jazz musicians to improvise freely on various numbers for the fun of it.

Jan. January.

jan·gle (jăng′ gəl) *vi-* [**jan·gled, jan·gling**] 1 to make a noise that is harsh or discordant: *The alarm clock jangled.* *vt-* 1 to cause to make such a sound: *He jangled the bunch of keys.* 2 to set on edge; irritate: *That banging door jangles my nerves.* *n-*: *the jangle of an alarm clock.* *—n-* jan′ gler.

jan·i·tor (jăn′ ə tər) *n-* man whose job it is to clean and take care of a building. *—adj-* jan′ i·tor′ i·al.

Jan·u·ar·y (jăn′ yo͞o ĕr′ ē) *n-* the first month of the year, having 31 days.

Ja·nus (jā′ nəs) *n-* in Roman mythology, the god of portals, able to look into the past and the future. He is usually represented with two faces.

ja·pan (jə păn′) *n-* 1 Japanese lacquer, a hard, brilliant varnish for wood or metal; also, any coating resembling it. 2 lacquered articles decorated in a Japanese style. *vt-* [**ja·panned, ja·pan·ning**]: *to japan a tray.*

Jap·a·nese (jăp′ ə nēz′) *n-* [*pl.* **Jap·a·nese**] 1 a native or inhabitant of Japan or his descendants. 2 the language of Japan. 3 the **Japanese** the people of Japan and their ancestors and descendants, collectively. *adj-*: *a Japanese garden; a Japanese camera.*

Japanese beetle *n-* small, bronze-green beetle that was accidentally introduced into the United States from Japan and is very destructive to vegetation.

¹**jar** (jär) *vt-* [**jarred, jar·ring**] 1 to cause to shake: *The blast jarred the house.* 2 to cause a shock to: *The news jarred him.* *vi-* 1 to produce a harsh sound or jolting motion: *The brakes jarred as the car stopped.* 2 to come into or be in conflict: *His ideas jarred with mine.* *n-* 1 sudden shake; jolt; shock. 2 harsh sound. [of uncertain origin.]

jar on to have an unpleasant effect on.

²**jar** (jär) *n-* 1 wide-mouthed container of pottery or glass. 2 contents of a jar; jarful. [from French **jarre,** from Arabic **jarrah,** "earthenware water vessel."]

Jar

jar·di·niere (zhär′ də nyĕr′, jär′ də nêr′) *n-* container or stand for holding plants or flowers.

jar·ful (jär′ fo͝ol′) *n-* the amount held by a jar.

jar·gon (jär′ gən) *n-* 1 specialized language of a group, trade, or profession; cant: *the jargon of space scientists.* 2 confused or meaningless speech or writing; gibberish. 3 mixed language, such as pidgin English, that simplifies communication between different peoples.

jas·mine or **jas·min** (jăz′ mən) *n-* any of several climbing shrubs with very fragrant white, red, or yellow flowers.

Ja·son (jā′ sən) *n-* in Greek legend, the hero who led the Argonauts in search of the Golden Fleece.

jas·per (jăs′ pər) *n-* cloudy quartz, usually red, brown, or yellow, used for ornamental objects.

ja·to unit (jā′ tō′) *n-* one or more small rocket motors attached to an aircraft to give extra power for takeoff.

jaun·dice (jŏn′ dəs, jôn′-) *n-* 1 disease in which the skin and eyeballs turn yellow, caused by the abnormal presence of bile in the blood and body fluids. 2 mental condition, such as jealousy, which distorts the judgment. *vt-* [**jaun·diced, jaun·dic·ing**] to affect or prejudice (the mind of) by envy, jealousy, etc.

jaunt (jônt) *vi-* short pleasure trip. *vi-* to make such a trip.

jaun·ty (jŏn′ tē) *adj-* [**jaun·ti·er, jaun·ti·est**] gay and carefree in manner, appearance, etc.; dashing: *his jaunty stride; a jaunty hat.* *—adv-* jaun′ ti·ly. *n-* jaun′ ti·ness.

Ja·va (jăv′ ə) *n-* 1 a kind of coffee obtained from Java and other Indonesian islands. 2 a breed of black-and-white domestic fowl. 3 *Slang* any coffee.

Java man *n-* species of apelike men of the Pleistocene epoch, known from the fossil remains found in Java; Pithecanthropus.

Jav·a·nese (jăv′ ə nēz′) *adj-* of or pertaining to Java or its people, language or culture.

jave·lin (jăv′ lən) *n-* short, light spear thrown by hand, now chiefly thrown for distance in sports contests.

jaw (jô) *n-* 1 one of the two bones that frame the mouth and in which the teeth are set; also, the part of the face in the region of these bones. 2 (often **jaws**) anything suggesting the action or form of these two bones: *the jaws of a vise.* *vi- Slang* to talk idly. *—adj-* jaw′ less.

jaw·bone (jô′ bōn′) *n-* one of the two bones in which the teeth are set; jaw.

jaw·break·er (jô′ brā′ kər) *Informal n-* 1 word that is difficult to pronounce. 2 round, very hard candy.

jay (jā) *n-* any of several noisy, often brightly colored birds related to the crows, such as the bluejay.

jay·walk (jā′ wôk′) *Informal vi-* to cross a street without obeying traffic rules and signals. *—n-* jay′ walk′ er.

jazz (jăz) *n-* 1 kind of American popular music that uses odd combinations of rhythm. Jazz musicians like to make up their own treatment of tunes and harmonies as they go along. 2 *Slang* nonsense; foolishness. *as modifier: a jazz musician; a jazz band.* *vt-* to play or sing (music) in a jazzy manner. *—n-* jazz′ man.

jazz up *Slang* to make more lively or exciting.

jazz·y (jăz′ ē) *adj-* [**jazz·i·er, jazz·i·est**] 1 resembling or typical of jazz. 2 *Slang* showy; flashy. *—adv-* jazz′ i·ly. *n-* jazz′ i·ness.

jeal·ous (jĕl′ əs) *adj-* 1 afraid of losing someone's affection or love: *a jealous suitor.* 2 feeling ill will and envy: *She is jealous because she didn't win the prize.* 3 anxiously careful and watchful: *He is jealous of his good name.* *—adv-* jeal′ ous·ly. *n-* jeal′ ous·ness.

jeal·ous·y (jĕl′ ə sē) *n-* [*pl.* **jeal·ous·ies**] 1 the feeling, attitude, etc., of someone who is jealous: *He could not conceal his jealousy from his rival.* 2 an instance of jealous feeling: *their petty jealousies.*

jean (jēn) *n-* 1 closely woven, heavy cotton cloth used for making work clothes, children's play clothes, etc. 2 **jeans** trousers, usually dark blue, made from this cloth. *Hom-* gene.

jeep (jēp) *n-* small, powerful motorcar originally made for military use. It is now used where power and ruggedness are required.

Jeep

jeer (jēr) *vt-* to shout or rail mockingly at; taunt; deride: *The crowd jeered the losing team.* *vi-*: *The crowd jeered at the players.* *n-* derisive cry or remark; taunt. *—n-* jeer′ er. *adv-* jeer′ ing·ly.

Jeep

Jehovah's Witnesses *n-* (takes plural verb) sect of Christians who are pacifists and who do not acknowledge the authority of the state in matters of conscience.

je·june (jə jo͞on′) *adj-* lacking interest or point; dull; empty: *a jejune tale; jejune ideas.*

je·ju·num (jə jo͞o′ nəm) *n-* the portion of the small intestine that extends from the duodenum to the ileum.

jell (jĕl) *vi-* 1 to turn to jelly. 2 *Informal* to take shape; assume definite form: *His plans haven't jelled.* *Hom-* gel.

jel·ly (jĕl′ ē) *n-* [*pl.* **jel·lies**] 1 food consisting of fruit juice cooked with sugar and thickened by cooling to a soft, clear, substance that holds its shape when removed from a mold; also, any similar food made from meat juice, gelatin, etc. 2 any of various substances resembling this: *petroleum jelly.* *vi-* [**jel·lied, jel·ly·ing**] to thicken into a substance of this kind: *The soup jellied as it cooled.* *vt-* to cover with or cause to become such a substance: *to jelly fruits in a salad; to jelly soup by cooling it.* *—adj-* jel′ ly·like′.

jel·ly·fish (jĕl′ ē fish′) *n-* [*pl.* **jel·ly·fish; jel·ly·fishes** (kinds of jellyfish)] any of several boneless sea creatures with an umbrella-shaped, partly transparent body that looks like jelly. Some kinds have slender, stinging threads on the underside.

Jellyfish, 1 in. to 12 ft across

jen·net (jĕn′ ət) *n-* 1 small Spanish horse. 2 female donkey.

jen·ny (jĕn′ ē) *n-* [*pl.* **jen·nies**] 1 spinning jenny. 2 the female of some animals. *as modifier: the jenny wren.*

jeop·ard·ize (jĕp′ ər dīz′) *vt-* [**jeop·ard·ized, jeop·ard·iz·ing**] to put in danger; risk: *to jeopardize one's life.*

jeop·ard·y (jĕp′ ər dē) *n-* 1 danger; peril: *His safety is in jeopardy.* 2 in law, the risk to which a defendant is exposed when he is on trial for a crime.

jer·bo·a (jər bō′ə) *n-* any of various small, nocturnal animals of Asia and Africa, related to the rats, and having very long hind legs used for leaping.

jer·e·mi·ad (jĕr′ə mī′əd) *n-* long, mournful complaint or lamentation; sorrowful story.

Jer·e·mi·ah (jĕr′ə mī′ə) *n-* 1 in the Old Testament, a Hebrew prophet during the seventh century B.C. 2 a book of the Bible containing his prophecies. In the CCD Bible, **Jer′ e·mi′ a.**

¹jerk (jûrk) *vt-* 1 to give a quick pull, twist, toss, or push to: *to jerk a coat off; to jerk a fish out of water.* 2 *Informal* to prepare (ice cream sodas) at a soda fountain. *vi-* to move abruptly, or with sudden starts and stops: *The train jerked along. n-* 1 quick, sudden pull, twist, or similar motion. 2 *Slang* stupid or annoying person. [of uncertain origin.] **—n- jerk′er.**

²jerk (jûrk) *vt-* to convert (meat) into jerky. [from ²jerky.]

jer·kin (jûr′kĭn) *n-* close-fitting, waist-length jacket without sleeves, often made of leather, and worn chiefly by men in former times.

jerk·wa·ter (jûrk′wô′tər, -wŏt′ər) *Informal adj-* small and unimportant: *a jerkwater town.*

¹jerk·y (jûr′kē) *adj-* [jerk·i·er, jerk·i·est] moving abruptly, or with sudden starts and stops; not smooth: *a jerky motion.* [from ¹jerk.] **—adv- jerk′i·ly. n- jerk′i·ness.**

²jerk·y (jûr′kē) *n-* meat, especially beef, that has been cut into thin strips and dried in the sun. Also **jerked beef.** [from Spanish **charqui,** from Peruvian Indian **ccharqui.**]

Jerkin

Jer·o·bo·am (jĕr′ə bō′əm) *n-* 1 king who founded the kingdom of Israel. 2 **jeroboam** large champagne bottle holding about four quarts.

jer·ry-built (jĕr′ē bĭlt′) *adj-* built quickly and poorly.

jer·sey (jûr′zē) *n-* [*pl.* **jer·seys**] 1 close-textured knitted fabric of wool, cotton, nylon, etc. 2 shirt, sweater, or similar garment made of this material. 3 **Jersey** one of a breed of small dairy cattle that originated in the island of Jersey and is noted for the richness of its milk.

jes·sa·mine (jĕs′ə mĭn) *n-* jasmine. The yellow jessamine is the State flower of South Carolina.

Jes·se (jĕs′ē) *n-* in the Bible, the father of David.

jest (jĕst) *n-* 1 funny remark intended to make people laugh. 2 an object of fun or joking. *vi-* to speak in a teasing or humorous way; joke.

in jest in a joking way; not seriously.

jest·er (jĕs′tər) *n-* person who makes jokes; especially, in former times, a man who was expected to entertain a king or nobleman by jokes and odd actions.

Jes·u·it (jĕz′ŏŏ ĭt, jĕzh′-) *n-* member of the Society of Jesus, an order of Roman Catholic priests.

Je·sus (jē′zəs) *n-* Jesus of Nazareth, on whose life, death, and teachings the Christian religion is based; Christ. Also **Jesus Christ.**

¹jet (jĕt) *n-* 1 stream of gas, liquid, etc., gushing or squirting from an opening: *A jet of water spurted from the fountain.* 2 spout or nozzle out of which such a stream comes: *a gas jet.* 3 jet engine or jet plane. *as modifier: a jet airport. vi-* [**jet·ted, jet·ting**] 1 to shoot, gush or spout out: *Steam jetted from the punctured pipe.* 2 to travel by jet plane. *vt-* to squirt or pour (liquid or gas) in a stream. [from Old French *jeter* meaning "to throw or fling out or about; push forward," from Latin *jactāre.*]

²jet (jĕt) *n-* 1 hard, black mineral similar to coal, which can be highly polished and is used for making ornaments, buttons, etc. 2 (usually **jet-black**) a deep, glossy black. *adj-: a string of jet beads.* [from Old French *jaiet,* from a Greek word *gagatēs,* that comes from *gagai,* a town in Asia near Greece where the mineral was mined.]

jet engine *n-* engine in which continuous burning of fuel forces a stream of compressed gas from the rear. The escaping gases push the craft forward in the same way that air escaping from an inflated balloon causes it to dart forward when it is released.

jet plane *n-* airplane driven by a jet engine. Also **jet airplane.**

jet-pro·pelled (jĕt′ prə pĕld′) *adj-* driven by a jet engine.

jet propulsion *n-* the propelling of an aircraft, boat, car, etc., by jet engine.

jet·sam (jĕt′səm) *n-* cargo thrown overboard to lighten a ship in danger, especially such cargo that has been washed ashore. See also *flotsam.*

jet stream *n-* 1 in meteorology, a high-altitude, high-velocity wind that generally travels from west to east. 2 powerful stream of gas shot from a jet or rocket engine.

jet·ti·son (jĕt′ə sən) *vt-* 1 to throw (cargo) overboard to lighten a ship in danger. 2 to throw away; get rid of. *n-* the throwing overboard of cargo, especially to lighten a ship in danger.

jet·ty (jĕt′ē) *n-* [*pl.* **jet·ties**] 1 structure built out into the water to break the force of the waves. 2 landing pier.

Jew (jōō) *n-* 1 a descendant of the Hebrew people. 2 anyone whose religion is Judaism. 3 originally, a member of the tribe of Judah.

jew·el (jōō′əl) *n-* 1 precious stone; gem. 2 valuable ornament set with gems. 3 piece of precious stone or other hard material used as a bearing in the works of a watch. 4 person or thing that is highly valued: *His new secretary is a jewel. This is the jewel of my collection.* **—adj- jew′eled:** *a jeweled pin. adj- jew′el·like.*

jew·el·er (jōō′lər, jōō′ə lər) *n-* person who makes, repairs, or deals in jewelry.

jew·el·ry (jōō′əl rē, jōō′əl′-) *n-* ornaments of silver, gold, etc., set with gems; jewels.

jew·el·weed (jōō′əl wēd′, jōō′əl-) *n-* tall plant with dangling orange or yellow flowers, and seed cases that burst open at a touch when they are ripe; touch-me-not.

Jew·ess (jōō′əs) *n-* Jewish woman or girl (term often considered offensive).

jew·fish (jōō′fĭsh′) *n-* [*pl.* **jew·fish;** **jew·fishes** (kinds of jewfish)] one of various large fish related to the sea basses and found in warm seas.

Jew·ish (jōō′ĭsh) *adj-* of, relating to, or characteristic of the Jews, their religion, or their customs. *n- Informal* Yiddish.

Jew·ry (jōō′rē) *n-* 1 the Jewish people. 2 *Archaic* [*pl.* **Jew·ries**] district inhabited by Jews; ghetto.

jew's-harp or **jews'-harp** (jōōz′ härp′) *n-* small musical instrument which is held between the teeth. It has a thin, flexible metal strip that produces twanging tones when it is struck with the fingers.

Jew's harp

Jez·e·bel (jĕz′ə bĕl′) *n-* in the Bible, the wicked wife of a king of Israel; hence, any bold, vicious woman.

¹jib (jĭb) *n-* small three-cornered sail in front of the foremast. [of uncertain origin.]

cut of (someone's) jib *Informal* a person's outward appearance or manner.

²jib (jĭb) *vi-* & *vt-* [**jibbed, jib·bing**] ¹jibe.

³jib (jĭb) *n-* projecting arm of a crane, derrick, etc. [probably from **gibbet,** from Old French *gibet,* from an earlier Germanic word meaning "forked stick."]

jib boom *n-* a spar that serves to lengthen the bowsprit of a vessel, and to which a jib is attached.

Jib

¹jibe (jīb) *vi-* [**jibed, jib·ing**] 1 to cause or permit a fore-and-aft rigged sail and its boom to swing suddenly from one side of a boat to the other when sailing before the wind. 2 to change the course of a boat by thus maneuvering the sail. *vt-* to maneuver (a sail or boat) in this manner. [from Dutch *gijben* or *gijpen.*] *Hom-* gibe.

²jibe (jīb) *vt-* gibe. [a variation of **gibe,** perhaps from Old French *giber* meaning "to handle roughly."]

³jibe (jīb) *Informal vi-* [**jibed, jib·ing**] to be in agreement; coincide. [of uncertain origin.] *Hom-* gibe.

jig·ger (jĭg′ər) *n-* chigger. [a variation of **chigger,** from **chigoe,** from a West Indian word.]

jig·gle (jĭg′əl) *vt-* [**jig·gled, jig·gling**] to move with short, quick jerks: *His feet jiggled in time to the music. vt-: He jiggled his feet. n-* slight, jerky motion; slight shake.

jif·fy (jĭf′ē) *Informal n-* [*pl.* **jif·fies**] moment; instant.

jig (jĭg) *n-* 1 quick, lively dance; also, the music for this dance: *an Irish jig.* 2 any of several kinds of fishhook that are drawn through the water with a jerky or twitching motion. 3 device used to guide, control, or hold a tool or piece of work in place during a mechanical operation. *vi-* [**jigged, jig·ging**] 1 to dance a quick, lively dance. 2 to move with a jerky or bobbing motion. 3 to fish by jerking a hook through the water.

¹**jig·ger** (jĭg′ər) *n-* 1 person who jigs. 2 small glass or cup used to measure liquor. 3 quantity of liquor it holds, usually 1½ oz. 4 *Informal* any thing, device, or part whose name is unknown or cannot be remembered. 5 a jig for fishing. 6 any of various mechanical devices that operate with a jerky motion. [of uncertain origin.]

jilt (jĭlt) *vt-* to discard or desert (a lover, sweetheart, etc.): *She jilted her fiancé.* *n-* person who discards a lover, sweetheart, etc. —*n-* **jilt′er.**

Jim Crow *Slang n-* discrimination against Negroes, especially by law or illegally enforced customs.

jim·my (jĭm′ē) *n-* [*pl.* **jim·mies**] short crowbar used by burglars to open doors, windows, etc. *vt-* [**jim·mied, jim·my·ing**] to force open with such a crowbar.

jim·son weed (jĭm′sən) *n-* tall, coarse, very poisonous plant related to the nightshades, having trumpet-shaped white flowers and leaves with an unpleasant smell.

jin·gle (jĭng′gəl) *n-* 1 light tinkling or ringing sound: *the jingle of sleigh bells.* 2 pleasing or catchy succession of sounds in a poem, often with little sense. 3 simple poem or song, often using nonsense words, marked by catchy, repeated sounds. "Hickory, dickory, dock" is a jingle. *vi-* [**jin·gled, jin·gling**] to make a light tinkling or ringing sound: *The bells jingled.* *vt-* He jingled *the bells.*

jin·gly (jĭng′glē) *adj-* [**jin·gli·er, jin·gli·est**] having or producing a tinkling, repeated sound.

jin·go (jĭng′gō) *n-* [*pl.* **jin·goes**] person who favors a warlike policy in foreign affairs.

jin·go·ism (jĭng′gō iz′əm) *n-* attitude, belief, etc., supporting a warlike policy in foreign affairs. —*n-* **jin′go·ist.** *adj-* **jin′go·is′tic.**

jinn (jĭn) *n-* [*pl.* **jinns** or **jinn**] in Muslim legend, a spirit appearing in both human and animal forms, and having a supernatural influence over mankind for good and evil; genie. Also **jin′ni** (jĭn′ē) or **jin′nee.**

jin·rik·i·sha or **jin·rick·sha** (jĭn rĭk′shô, -shä) *n-* light two-wheeled vehicle drawn by a man, originally used in Japan. Also **ricksha** or **rickshaw.**

Jinrikisha

jinx (jĭngks) *Slang n-* person or thing that brings bad luck. *vt-* to bring bad luck to.

jit·ney (jĭt′nē) *Slang n-* 1 a nickel. 2 bus or car that carries passengers for a small fare.

jit·ter·bug (jĭt′ər bŭg′) *Slang n-* 1 a dance in which couples move rhythmically to swing music, twirling and using improvised acrobatic movements. 2 person who dances this dance. *vi-* [**jit·ter·bugged, jit·ter·bug·ging**] to dance in such a manner.

jit·ters (jĭt′ərz) *Slang n-* (takes singular verb) extreme nervousness. —*adj-* **jit′ter·y.**

jiu·jit·su or **jiu·ju·tsu** (jōō jĭt′sōō) jujitsu.

Ji·va·ro (hē′vä′rō) *n-* [*pl.* **Ji·va·ro** or **Ji·va·ros**] one of a group of South American Indians who live in Ecuador and eastern Peru, and are famous for head-hunting.

jive (jīv) *Slang n-* 1 swing music. 2 special vocabulary of jazz musicians or jazz fans. *vi-* [**jived, jiv·ing**] to dance or play swing music. *Hom-* **gyve.**

job (jŏb) *n-* 1 something a person has to do; duty; responsibility: *It is his job to empty the trash.* 2 paid position; employment; work: *He has a job as a teacher.* 3 piece of work: *Do a better job.* 4 *Informal* difficult task: *It is quite a job to clean the cellar.* *vt-* [**jobbed, job·bing**] 1 to buy up (goods) for resale in smaller quantities. 2 to sublet (work) to different contractors, workmen, etc. *vi-* to do an occasional piece of work for pay.

Job (jŏb) *n-* 1 in an Old Testament book, a man who patiently suffered great adversity. 2 the book itself.

job·ber (jŏb′ər) *n-* 1 person who buys a large amount of goods from manufacturers and sells it in smaller quantities to retail dealers. 2 person who does piecework.

job·hold·er (jŏb′ hōl′dər) *n-* person with a regular job.

job·less (jŏb′ləs) *adj-* without a job; unemployed.

job lot *n-* miscellaneous collection of goods, often of inferior quality, bought and sold together.

jock·ey (jŏk′ē) *n-* man whose profession is riding race horses. *vt-* to move or shift (something) about to gain a good position: *The drivers jockeyed their cars.* *vi-* 1 to move or maneuver in this way: *to jockey for position.* 2 to ride a horse in a race.

jo·cose (jō kōs′) *adj-* humorous; playful; joking: *a jocose manner.* —*adv-* **jo·cose′ly.** *n-* **jo·cose′ness** or **jo·cos′i·ty** (jō kŏs′ə tē).

joc·u·lar (jŏk′yə lər) *adj-* 1 given to joking: *a jocular person.* 2 humorous; funny; jesting: *a jocular reply.* —*n-* **joc′u·lar′i·ty** (-yə lär′ə tē). *adv-* **joc′u·lar·ly.**

joc·und (jŏk′ənd) *adj-* merry; pleasant; cheerful. —*n-* **jo·cun′di·ty** (jō kŭn′də tē). *adv-* **joc′und·ly.**

jodh·purs (jŏd′pərz) *n- pl.* riding breeches that fit loosely above the knee and closely between the knee and ankle.

Jo·el (jō′əl) *n-* 1 in the Bible, a Hebrew prophet. 2 a book of the Old Testament attributed to him.

¹**jog** (jŏg) *vt-* [**jogged, jog·ging**] 1 to push or shake slightly; jar; nudge: *to jog someone's elbow.* 2 to stir up; revive: *to jog someone's memory.* *vi-* to move at a slow, jolting pace or trot; *The old horse jogged along.* *n-* 1 slight shake; nudge. 2 (also **jog trot**) slow, steady gait that is faster than a walk. [of uncertain origin.] —*n-* **jog′ger.**

²**jog** (jŏg) *n-* sharp, sudden bend, turn, or change of direction: *a jog in the road; a jog in a wall.* *vi-* [**jogged, jog·ging**] to make or have such a bend: *The road jogs to the left.* [a variation of **jag,** from Middle English **jagge,** from Old English *sceaga,* meaning "notch; uneven tear."]

jog·gle (jŏg′əl) *vt-* [**jog·gled, jog·gling**] to give (something) a slight shake; nudge; jolt. *n-* slight shake; jolt.

John (jŏn) *n-* one of the twelve apostles, reputed to be the author of the fourth Gospel. Also **St. John the Divine.**

John Bull *n-* imaginary man thought to personify the English people; hence, a typical Englishman.

John Doe *n-* in legal papers, a made-up name for an unknown person; also, name for any unspecified person.

John Han·cock (jŏn hăn′kŏk′) *Informal n-* a person's signature. [from John Hancock, whose signature on the Declaration of Independence is bold and legible.]

John Henry *n-* 1 in American Negro folklore, a railroad worker of unusually great strength. 2 *Informal* a person's signature; John Hancock.

john·ny·cake (jŏn′ē kāk′) *n-* bread made of cornmeal mixed with milk or water, eggs, etc.

John·ny·jump·up (jŏn′ē jŭmp′ ŭp′) *n-* garden plant related to the violets, and resembling a small pansy.

John·ny·on·the·spot (jŏn′ē ŏn′ tho spŏt′) *n- Informal* person who is always on hand at the right time.

John the Baptist *n-* the forerunner and baptizer of Jesus. John was beheaded by Herod.

join (join) *vt-* 1 to put together; fasten; connect: *to join hands; to join a hose to a faucet.* 2 to come together with; meet and unite with: *The brook joins the river.* 3 to become a member of; become associated with: *to join a club.* 4 to make into one; unite: *to join a couple in marriage.* 5 to take into the company of: *He joined us for a swim.* *vi-* 1 to become associated or united: *The two roads join at this point.* 2 to take part with others; participate: *to join in a conversation.* *n-* joint.

join·er (join′ər) *n-* 1 person or thing that joins. 2 skilled carpenter who finishes the inside woodwork for houses. 3 jointer. 4 *Informal* person who joins many clubs, organizations, etc.

join·er·y (joi′nə rē) *n-* 1 skill or trade of a joiner; skilled work in wood. 2 things made by a joiner.

joint·er (join′tər) *n-* 1 person who joints. 2 a plane or a power-driven tool used to smooth and straighten the parts of wood that will make a joint. Also **joiner.**

joint·ly (joint′lē) *adv-* together; in combination.

joint resolution *n-* resolution passed by both houses of Congress, which has the force of law when signed by the President.

jok·er (jō'kər) *n-* 1 person who jokes. 2 extra playing card in a deck of cards, used in some games as a card of the highest value. 3 clause which seems unimportant but actually changes the meaning of a document.

jol·li·fi·ca·tion (jŏl'ə fə kā'shən) *Informal n-* festivity; rejoicing; merrymaking.

jol·li·ty (jŏl'ə tē) *n-* [*pl.* **jol·li·ties**] merriment; gaiety.

jol·ly (jŏl'ē) *adj-* [jol·li·er, jol·li·est] merry; gay; full of fun or laughter. *vt-* [jol·lied, jol·ly·ing] *Informal* to tease, humor, or flatter with good-humored joking.

Jolly Roger *n-* the pirate flag, usually having a white skull and crossbones on a black field; the black flag.

jolt (jōlt) *vt-* to shake with jerky movements; jar: *The rough ride jolted us.* *vi-* to move along in a jerky manner: *The carriage jolted down the hill.* *n-* a sudden jerk, bump, shake, or shock: *The train stopped with a jolt.*

Jo·nah (jō'nə) *n-* 1 Hebrew prophet who was thrown overboard, swallowed by a great fish, and cast up alive after three days. 2 book of the Old Testament telling this story. In the CCD Bible, **Jo'na.** 3 anyone bringing bad luck.

Jon·a·than (jŏn'ə thən) *n-* in the Bible, a son of Saul and close friend of David.

jon·quil (jŏng'kwĭl, jŏn'kwĭl) *n-* plant related to the narcissus and daffodil, with fragrant, trumpet-shaped, yellow or white flowers; also, the flower itself.

Jo·seph (jō'zəf, -səf) *n-* 1 in the Bible, a son of Jacob sold into slavery in Egypt by his brothers. 2 (also **Saint Joseph**) foster parent of Jesus and husband of Mary. 3 **Joseph of Arimathea** a wealthy disciple of Jesus who buried Him in his own tomb.

josh (jŏsh) *Informal vt-* to make fun of in a good-humored way; tease playfully. *vi-* to joke playfully.

Josh·u·a (jŏsh'ə wə) *n-* 1 in the Bible, the successor of Moses and leader of the Israelites. 2 book of the Old Testament. In the CCD Bible, **Jo'su·e** (jŏs'ōō ē).

Joshua tree *n-* a yucca of southwestern United States, with short leaves and clusters of greenish-white flowers.

Jo·si·ah (jō sī'ə) *n-* in the Bible, a king of Judah around the seventh century B.C. In the CCD Bible, **Jo·si'a.**

joss stick (jŏs) *n-* thin stick of incense.

jos·tle (jŏs'əl) *vt-* [jos·tled, jos·tling] to push roughly; elbow. *n-* a shove; push. —*n-* **jos'tler.**

jot (jŏt) *vt-* [jot·ted, jot·ting] to write down briefly and quickly: *to jot down an address.* *n-* tiny bit; iota.

joule (jōōl) *n-* unit of work in the mks system defined as the work done when a force of one newton acts through a distance of one meter. A joule is equal to 10⁷ ergs or 0.7375 foot-pounds.

jounce (jouns) *vt-* [jounced, jounc·ing] to shake up and down; jolt; bounce: *The old car jounced the passengers.* *vi-*: *The car jounced.* *n-* sudden jerk; jolt.

jour·nal (jûr'nəl) *n-* 1 daily record of news or events; diary. 2 daily record of acts of a legislature or transactions of a business. 3 newspaper or periodical appearing at regular intervals. 4 in machines, the part of a shaft or axle that turns in a bearing.

jour·nal·ese (jûr'nə lēz') *n-* careless style of writing supposed to be characteristic of newspapers.

jour·nal·ism (jûr'nə lĭz'əm) *n-* the work of publishing, editing, or writing for a newspaper or magazine.

jour·nal·ist (jûr'nə lĭst') *n-* person who writes for or edits a newspaper or magazine.

jour·nal·is·tic (jûr'nə lĭs'tĭk) *adj-* of or having to do with journalism or journalists. —*adv-* **jour'nal·is'ti·cal·ly:** *He writes journalistically.*

jour·ney (jûr'nē) *n-* 1 trip, especially a long one, or one taking considerable time. 2 distance traveled in a certain time: *a day's journey.* *vi-* to make a trip; travel.

jour·ney·man (jûr'nē mən) *n-* [*pl.* **jour·ney·men**] person who has finished his apprenticeship in a trade or skill and works for another.

joust (joust, *also* jŭst) *n-* a combat, often in sport, between two mounted knights with lances. *vi-* to take part in such a contest. —*n-* **joust'er.**

joy·ful (joi'fəl) *adj-* full of gladness; showing or causing joy; happy; joyous. —*adv-* **joy'ful·ly.** *n-* **joy'ful·ness.**

joy·less (joi'ləs) *adj-* without joy; not causing joy; cheerless; dismal; dull: *a joyless home; a joyless future.*

joy·ride (joi'rīd') *n-* automobile ride for pleasure, especially a reckless ride. —*n-* **joy'rid'er.**

J.P. justice of the peace.

Jr. or **jr.** junior.

ju·bi·lant (jōō'bə lənt) *adj-* showing great joy; triumphantly joyful; exultant: *The crowd was jubilant.* —*n-* **ju'bi·lance:** *the jubilance of the crowd.* —*adv-* **ju'bi·lant·ly.**

ju·bi·la·tion (jōō'bə lā'shən) *n-* triumphant rejoicing.

ju·bi·lee (jōō'bə lē') *n-* 1 anniversary, especially the 50th or 25th. 2 any time of great and general rejoicing.

Ju·dah (jōō'də) *n-* 1 in the Old Testament, a son of Jacob. 2 the tribe descended from him. 3 the ancient Hebrew kingdom which included the tribe of Benjamin as well as Judah. In the CCD Bible, **Ju·da.**

Ju·da·ic (jōō dā'ĭk) *adj-* of or relating to the Jews or Judaism.

Ju·da·ism (jōō'dē ĭz'əm, jōō'dĭz'əm) *n-* 1 one of the world's great religions; the religion of the Jews. Judaism was among the first religions that taught a belief in one God, and was the ancestor of Christianity. 2 the traditions of thought, morality, and culture associated with this religion.

Ju·das (jōō'dəs) *n-* 1 the disciple who betrayed Jesus. 2 any betrayer. Also **Judas Is·car'i·ot** (ĭs kâr'ē ət).

Judas tree *n-* tree bearing stemless, rose-pink flowers early in the spring, before the leaves appear.

Jude (jōōd) *n-* disciple of Jesus who wrote the New Testament book called the Epistle of Jude. Also **St. Jude.**

Ju·de·o-Chris·tian (jōō dā'ō krĭs'chən) *adj-* of or relating to the ethical and cultural traditions common to Judaism and Christianity.

judge (jŭj) *n-* 1 official who presides in a court of law and hears cases, passes sentences, etc. 2 person who decides the winner in a contest: *a judge in a dog show.* 3 person who has enough experience or knowledge to decide on the quality, value, or extent of something: *a judge of cattle; a good judge of distance.* *vt-* [judged, judg·ing] (considered intransitive when the direct object is implied but not expressed) 1 to hear cases, pass sentences, etc., in a court of law. 2 to decide (a contest, argument, dispute, etc.). 3 to think; consider: *I judged this to be true.* 4 to form an opinion about: *to judge the merits of a play.* 5 to criticize and blame. —*n-* **judg'er.**

Judg·es (jŭj'əz) *n-* (takes singular verb) the seventh book of the Old Testament.

judge·ship (jŭj'shĭp') *n-* position, duties, or term of office of a judge.

judg·ment or **judge·ment** (jŭj'mənt) *n-* 1 a judging; making a decision after careful consideration: *the judgment of a criminal.* 2 decision made after careful consideration: *The judgment of the court was in his favor.* 3 opinion; estimation: *In his judgment this car is the best buy.* 4 good sense: *a man of excellent judgment.* 5 misfortune considered as a punishment from God.

Judgment Day *n-* the day of the Last Judgment.

ju·di·ca·to·ry (jōō'dĭ kə tôr'ē) *adj-* of or relating to legal justice and courts of justice.

ju·di·ca·ture (jōō'dĭ kə chər) *n-* system of courts of justice in a country; judiciary.

ju·di·cial (jōō dĭsh'əl) *adj-* 1 having to do with a judge or court of law: *the judicial proceedings.* 2 ordered, enforced, or allowed by a judge or court of law: *a judicial decision.* 3 suited for judging or tending to judge: *a judicial mind.* —*adv-* **ju·di'cial·ly.**

ju·di·ci·ar·y (jōō dĭsh'ē er ē, -dĭsh'ə rē) *n-* [*pl.* **ju·di·ci·ar·ies**] 1 system of courts of justice in a country. 2 judges of these courts. 3 branch of government that administers justice. *adj-* having to do with judges, courts of law, or the procedures of a court; judicial.

ju·di·cious (jōō dĭsh'əs) *adj-* showing good judgment; sensible. —*adv-* **ju·di'cious·ly.** *n-* **ju·di'cious·ness.**

ju·jit·su (jōō jĭt'sōō) *n-* Japanese style of wrestling and self-defense that uses the strength and weight of an opponent in order to defeat him. Also **jiujitsu, jiujutsu.**

juke box (jōōk) *Informal n-* large automatic phonograph operated by dropping a coin in a slot and pushing a button to make the record selection.

ju·lep (jōō'ləp) *n-* drink made of bourbon, sugar, fresh mint, and crushed ice.

Ju·li·an calendar (jōō′ lē ən) *n-* calendar introduced by Julius Caesar in 46 B.C., giving most years 365 days but every fourth year, 366 days. It has been superseded by the Gregorian calendar.

ju·li·enne (jōō′ lē ĕn′) *n-* clear soup containing vegetables cut into thin strips. *adj-* cut into thin strips: *served with julienne potatoes.*

Ju·li·et (jōō′ lē ĕt′) *n-* the young heroine of Shakespeare's "Romeo and Juliet."

Ju·ly (jōō lī′, jə-) *n-* the seventh month of the year, having 31 days.

jum·ble (jŭm′ bəl) *vt-* [jum·bled, jum·bling] to mix in a confused way; put together without order: *to* jumble *things together.* *n-* confused mass; disorder.

jum·bo (jŭm′ bō) *Informal adj-* large; huge: *a* jumbo *ice-cream cone.* *n-* [*pl.* jum·bos] large person, animal, or thing. [from *Jumbo,* a very large circus elephant.]

jump (jŭmp) *n-* 1 a leap, spring, or bound: *a* jump *off a diving board.* 2 distance covered by a leap: *a* jump *of six feet.* 3 something to be leaped or hurdled: *The third* jump *was a low hedge.* 4 in sports, a contest featuring a leap: *the 'high* jump. 5 sudden start or jerk: *a startled* jump. 6 sudden rise: *a* jump *in temperature.* *vi-* 1 to spring from the ground; leap; bound: *to* jump *over a puddle.* 2 to give a sudden start: *to* jump *in fright.* 3 to rise suddenly: *Prices* jumped. 4 to pass or change abruptly (from one thing to another): *to* jump *from one subject to another.* 5 to spring down from or out of a window, plane, etc.: *to* jump *from a plane.* *vt-* 1 to cause to leap, spring, or bound: *to* jump *a horse over a hurdle.* 2 to leap over; pass over; skip: *to* jump *a brook; to* jump *ten pages.* 3 *Informal* to leap upon: *to* jump *a train.* 4 *Informal* to leave or quit suddenly: *to* jump *town.*

  get the jump on *Slang* to get an advantage over.

  jump a claim to seize mining rights or a piece of land claimed by another.

  jump at to accept eagerly and quickly.

  jump off to begin; go into action.

  jump the gun *Slang* to begin a race before the signal.

  jump the track to leave the rails suddenly.

junk (jŭngk) *n-* kind of Chinese sailing vessel with a flat bottom, high stern, and lugsails. [from Portuguese *junco,* originally from Malay *jong.*]

jun·ket (jŭng′ kət) *n-* 1 food made of curdled milk that has been sweetened and flavored. 2 feast or picnic. 3 pleasure trip or excursion, especially one made by a government official or committee at public expense and announced as a necessary business trip. *vi-: The senator* junketed *to Europe last summer.* *—n-* jun′ ket·er.

Chinese junk

junk·ie (jŭng′ kē) *Slang n-* 1 junkman. 2 narcotic addict, especially a heroin addict. Also junk′ y.

junk·man (jŭngk′ măn′) *n-* [*pl.* junk·men] person who earns a living by buying and selling junk.

Ju·no (jōō′ nō′) *n-* in Roman mythology, the goddess of marriage, wife of Jupiter, and queen of the gods, identified with the Greek Hera.

Ju·no·esque (jōō′ nō ĕsk′) *adj-* of or having the stately beauty of Juno.

jun·ta (hŏŏn′ tə, jŭn′ tə) *n-* 1 administrative or legislative council, especially in Spain or Latin America. 2 small group of persons in control of a government, especially after a revolution: *a country ruled by a military* junta. 3 (also jun′ to) conspiratorial group; cabal.

Ju·pi·ter (jōō′ pə tər) *n-* 1 in Roman mythology, the ruler of gods and men, identified with the Greek Zeus; Jove. 2 the largest planet in the solar system, fifth in order of distance from the sun.

Ju·ras·sic (jə răs′ ĭk) *n-* the second of the three periods of the Mesozoic era, marked by the existence of dinosaurs and many other reptiles. *adj-: a* Jurassic *reptile.*

ju·rid·i·cal (jŏŏr ĭd′ I kəl) *adj-* of or related to law or legal proceedings; legal. *—adv-* ju·rid′ i·cal·ly.

ju·ris·dic·tion (jŏŏr′ əs dĭk′ shən) *n-* 1 lawful right to govern, make laws, or, especially, to administer justice: *the jurisdiction of Congress; the jurisdiction of Michigan; the jurisdiction of the county courts.* 2 the limits within which such a right may be exercised; range of authority or control: *This is not in my* jurisdiction. 3 right to represent certain workers in a labor union.

ju·ris·pru·dence (jŏŏr′ əs prōō′ dəns) *n-* 1 science or philosophy of law. 2 any system or branch of law: *medical* jurisprudence; *English* jurisprudence.

ju·rist (jŏŏr′ Ist) *n-* 1 expert in jurisprudence. 2 any attorney or judge.

ju·ror (jŏŏr′ ər) *n-* member of a jury.

ju·ry (jŏŏr′ ē) *n-* [*pl.* ju·ries] 1 group of citizens sworn under oath to listen to testimony in a legal case and reach a verdict according to such testimony. A **grand jury** is a group of 12 to 23 persons selected to examine the evidence against supposed offenders and decide whether or not to indict or send them for trial. A **petty, or trial jury,** which is composed of 12 persons, hears the evidence in an actual trial and, if possible, gives a verdict. 2 any group of persons selected to judge a contest.

ju·ry·man (jŏŏr′ ē mən) *n-* [*pl.* ju·ry·men] male juror. *—n- fem.* ju′ ry·wom′ an [*pl.* ju·ry·wom·en].

just (jŭst) *adj-* 1 not showing favor; fair; honest: *The judge handed down a* just *decision.* 2 having a sound or reasonable basis: *Ellen had a* just *dislike for the people who had mistreated her.* 3 rightly given; deserved; earned: *He received a* just *reward for his work. adv-* 1 exactly: *That is* just *what I wanted.* 2 a moment ago; very recently: *We* just *finished dinner.* 3 barely: *The*

jus·tice (jŭs′ təs) *n-* 1 fairness; right action: *We should use* justice *even in dealing with our enemies.* 2 legal administration: *a court of* justice. 3 judge; judicial officer.

  bring (someone) to justice to cause (someone) to be tried or otherwise legally punished for wrongdoing.

  do justice 1 to show or represent truly or well: *That photo does not do her* justice. *I can't do* justice *to the story.* 2 to administer legal justice.

justice of the peace *n-* local magistrate having limited jurisdiction, such as trying minor offenses, administering oaths, performing marriages, etc.

jus·ti·fi·a·ble (jŭs′ tə fī′ ə bəl) *adj-* such as can be justified or defended; defensible: *Is it* justifiable *for a starving man to steal bread?* *—n-* jus′ ti·fi′ a·bil′ i·ty: *the* justifiability *of his complaint. adv-* jus′ ti·fi′ a·bly.

jus·ti·fi·ca·tion (jŭs′ tə fə kā′ shən) *n-* 1 a justifying or being justified. 2 something that justifies: *Poverty is no* justification *for stealing.*

jus·ti·fy (jŭs′ tə fī′) *vt-* [jus·ti·fied, jus·ti·fy·ing] 1 to show to be right or just; defend with good reason: *How do you* justify *your absence?* 2 to declare free from blame: *The verdict* justified *him in the eyes of the law.* 3 in printing, to give (lines) the proper length by spacing; also, to make the right-hand margin (of a page) straight and even.

jut (jŭt) *vi-* [jut·ted, jut·ting] to stick (out); thrust itself (out); project: *The peninsula* juts *out into the bay.*

jute (jōōt) *n-* 1 fiber of a tropical plant, used to make burlap and rope. 2 the plant itself.

Jute (jōōt) *n-* member of a Germanic tribe living in Jutland, some of whom, with the Angles and Saxons, invaded and settled in Britain during the fifth century.

ju·ve·nile (jōō′ və nĭl, -nīl′) *adj-* 1 young; youthful; childish; immature: *Pouting is a* juvenile *manner of getting your own way.* 2 of or for young people: *a* juvenile *book.* *n-* 1 young person. 2 book for young people. 3 actor who plays youthful parts.

juvenile court *n-* law court having jurisdiction in cases involving children under a certain age, usually 18.

juvenile delinquency *n-* criminal offenses or antisocial acts committed by children under a certain age, usually 18. *—n-* juvenile delinquent.

jux·ta·pose (jŭks′ tə pōz′) *vt-* [jux·ta·posed, jux·ta·pos·ing] to place close together or side by side: *to* juxtapose *light and dark paper.*

jux·ta·po·si·tion (jŭks′ tə pə zĭsh′ ən) *n-* a juxtaposing or a being juxtaposed: *the* juxtaposition *of two colors.*

K

K, k (kā) *n-* [*pl.* **K's, k's**] the eleventh letter of the English alphabet.

K symbol for potassium.

K. 1 kilogram. 2 king. 3 knight.

Kaa·ba (kä′ bə) *n-* sacred black stone in the courtyard of the great mosque at Mecca, thought to have been given to Abraham by the archangel Gabriel.

ka·bob (kə bòb′) *n-* 1 shish kebab. 2 in India, roast meat.

ka·chi·na (kə chē′ nə) *n-* one of various mythical ancestral spirits worshipped by the Hopi and other Pueblo Indians; also, a carved and painted wooden doll representing one of these spirits.

Kad·dish (kä′ dǐsh) *n-* in Judaism, a prayer recited by mourners.

Kaf·fir (kǎf′ ər) *n-* a Negro (used as a term of contempt by southern African white people). Also **Kaf′ ir.**

Kai·ser (kī′ zər) *n-* title applied to the emperors of the Holy Roman Empire and to the former emperors of Austria-Hungary and Germany.

kale (kāl) *n-* 1 vegetable similar to cabbage, having loose, curly leaves instead of a head. 2 leaves of this plant, eaten as a cooked vegetable or as a salad.

ka·lei·do·scope (kə lī′ də skōp′) *n-* tube-shaped optical toy lined with mirrors and containing loose bits of colored glass, which are reflected as changing geometrical patterns when the tube is rotated.

ka·lei·do·scop·ic (kə lī′ də skòp′ ĭk) *adj-* like a kaleidoscope; continually and rapidly changing: *the kaleidoscopic events of our time.* —*adv-* **ka·lei′ do·scop′ i·cal·ly.**

kal·so·mine (kǎl′ sə mǐn′) calcimine.

ka·mi·ka·ze (kǎm′ ə kä′z ē) *n-* in World World II, a Japanese suicide attack in which planes loaded with high explosives dive into a target: also, the plane or

kan·ga·roo (kǎng′ gə rōō′) *n-* [*pl.* **kan·ga·roos**] any of various plant-eating mammals of Australia having short forelegs, powerful hind legs with which it leaps, and a long, strong tail. The female Kangaroo has a pouch for carrying her young. Adults of some types reach a height of over six feet. —*adj-* **kan′ ga·roo′ like′.**

kangaroo rat *n-* any of various gnawing animals of Mexico and southwestern United States, having strong, well-developed hind legs, and a long tail.

Kans. Kansas.

ka·o·lin or **ka·o·line** (kā′ ə lǐn) *n-* a fine, usually white clay that is a pure natural form of aluminum sulfate. It is used to make porcelain.

ka·pok (kā′ pòk′) *n-* mass of silky fibers in the seed pods of a tropical tree called the **kapok tree,** used for stuffing cushions, mattresses, life preservers, etc.

ka·put (kə pōōt′, kä-) *Informal adj-* defeated or destroyed.

ka·ra·kul (kär′ ə kəl) *n-* 1 valuable pelt of the newborn lambs of the astrakhan, or curly-haired sheep of Russia and Asia. 2 this breed of sheep. Also **caracul.**

kar·at (kär′ ət) *n-* unit of measure for stating the purity of gold. In commercial use, 24 karats is pure gold. *Homs-* carat, caret, carrot.

ka·ra·te (kə rä′ tē) *n-* method of self-defense, originating in Japan, in which sudden, sharp blows are given with the side of the hand and fingertips.

kar·ma (kär′ mə) *n-* 1 in Hinduism and Buddhism, the total of good and evil in one's previous life or incarnation, which determines one's next life or incarnation. 2 less correctly, one's fate or destiny.

kar·roo or **ka·roo** (kə rōō′) *n-* [*pl.* **kar·roos**] in South Africa, a dry tableland or plateau.

ka·ty·did (kā′ tē dǐd′) *n-* any of several green insects that resemble and are closely related to grasshoppers. The males produce shrill sounds with their front wings.

kau·ri (kou′ rē) *n-* 1 any of several large, resinous New Zealand timber trees related to the pines. 2 wood of this tree. 3 resin distilled from such a tree, used in varnishes for linoleum, etc.

Katydid, 1 1/2—2 in long

kea (kē′ ə) *n-* large, greenish New Zealand parrot which normally feeds on insects

keep·er (kē′ pər) *n-* 1 person who guards, watches, or takes care of something: *a keeper at the zoo; a storekeeper.* 2 *Informal* fish large enough to be legally kept when caught.

keep·ing (kē′ pǐng) *n-* care; charge: *in his keeping.*

in keeping with in agreement with; in harmony with.

keep·sake (kēp′ sāk′) *n-* something kept in memory of the giver or of an occasion; memento.

keg (kĕg) *n-* 1 small cask or barrel. 2 amount one of these holds when full: *four kegs of water.* 3 unit of weight for nails, equal to 100 pounds.

Keg

kelp (kĕlp) *n-* 1 kind of large brown seaweed. 2 ashes of such seaweed, a source of iodine.

kel·pie or **kel·py** (kĕl′ pē) *Scottish n-* water spirit, usually in the shape of a horse, that is supposed to cause or warn of death by drowning.

Kel·vin (kĕl′ vən) *adj-* naming or relating to a temperature scale on which absolute zero (—273.16°C) is the zero point. The temperature intervals on the Kelvin scale are the same as on the centigrade thermometer.

ken (kĕn) *n-* range of sight or understanding; comprehension; perception: *That's beyond my ken.*

ken·nel (kĕn′ əl) *n-* 1 place where dogs are bred, raised for sale, or looked after. 2 doghouse.

ke·no (kē′ nō) *n-* game similar to bingo or lotto.

ke·pi (kā′ pē, kĕp′ ē) *n-* military cap having a round, flat top and a visor, worn by French soldiers and policemen.

kept (kĕpt) *p.t. & p.p. of* **keep.**

ker·a·tin (kĕr′ ə tən) *n-* tough, insoluble protein that forms the outer layers or substance of skin, hair, nails, feathers, horns, and scales of vertebrate animals.

ker·chief (kûr′ chǐf) *n-* 1 piece of cloth used to cover the head or tie around the neck. 2 handkerchief.

kerf (kûrf) *n-* 1 cut made by a saw or torch; also, the width of such a cut. 2 place where a felled tree is cut.

kern (kûrn) *Archaic n-* Irish foot soldier or peasant.

ker·nel (kûr′ nəl) *n-* 1 soft, inner part of a nut or fruit, often used for food. 2 seed or grain of such plants as corn, wheat, and rye. 3 central or important part of a structure, plan, argument, etc.; core; nucleus. *Hom-* colonel.

ker·o·sene (kĕr′ ə sēn′) *n-* thin, oily hydrocarbon that is distilled from petroleum or coal and used as a heating and jet fuel.

Walnut kernel

Ker·ry blue terrier (kĕr′ ē) *n-* breed of terriers originating in Ireland, having a soft, bluish-gray coat and a long head.

kes·trel (kĕs′ trəl) *n-* small European falcon noted for hovering in the air with its head always to the wind.

ketch (kĕch) *n-* small fore-and-aft rigged sailboat having two masts, of which the shorter is nearest the stern.

ketch·up (kĕch′ əp) *n-* sauce made of tomatoes and spices. Also **catchup, catsup.**

ket·tle (kĕt′ əl) *n-* metal pot used to heat liquids; especially, a teakettle.

kettle of fish *Informal* situation; predicament.

ket·tle·drum (kĕt′ əl drŭm′) *n-* large, bowl-shaped brass or copper drum with parchment stretched over the top; one of the tympani. For picture, see **drum.**

¹**key** (kē) *n-* 1 piece of shaped metal used for turning the bolt in a lock to fasten or open something. 2 anything like this in shape or use: *a key to wind a toy; a key to open a can.* 3 place or position controlling entrance: *New Orleans is the key to the Mississippi.* 4 main clue; means of finding a solution or explanation: *This letter is the key to the whole mystery.* 5 list or table that explains a map, chart, etc.: *a color key to a map; a key to a test.* 6 any of a set of levers, buttons, etc., pressed down by the finger on a piano, typewriter, etc., to make it work. 7 series of musical tones related to one tone (keynote): *the key of F.* 8 tone or pitch: *She sang off key.* *adj-* important; necessary; vital: *Steel is a key industry.* *vt-* to make appropriate to; adjust: *to key a TV program to the interests of children.* [from Old English cæg(e), meaning "a key; a solution."] *Hom-* quay. —*adj-* **key′ less.**

key up to stimulate; excite: *The players were all keyed up.*

²**key** (kē) *n-* in southeastern United States, a low island or reef. [from Spanish *cayo*, from a native West Indian word, influenced by ¹key and **quay**.] *Hom-* quay.

key·board (kē' bôrd') *n-* complete series of keys by means of which a piano, organ, etc., is played, or a typewriter, adding machine, etc., is operated.

Keyboard of a piano

keyed (kēd) *adj-* 1 of musical instruments or certain machines, having keys. 2 *Music* set in a certain key. 3 of an arch, secured with a keystone. 4 of a map, test, etc., provided with an explanation or answers.

key·hole (kē' hōl') *n-* small hole in a door or lock for inserting a key.

key·note (kē' nōt') *n-* 1 first note of a musical scale. 2 main idea; chief theme.

keynote speech *n-* political speech, especially at a nominating convention, that outlines the basic policy of a party.

key·stone (kē' stōn') *n-* 1 stone in the middle of an arch that holds the other stones in place. 2 essential thing upon which other things depend: *Freedom is the keystone of democracy.*

key word *n-* the main or essential word in a sentence, passage, puzzle, etc.

Keystone

kg. 1 kilogram. 2 keg.

khak·i (kăk' ē, kä' kē) *n-* 1 yellowish-brown color. 2 cloth of a dull yellow-brown color. *adj-* 1 having this color. 2 made of this cloth: *a khaki uniform.*

¹**khan** (kän) *n-* 1 in the Middle Ages, the title of Genghis Khan or any of his imperial successors who ruled most of Asia. 2 in Iran, Afghanistan, etc., a title of respect given to certain dignitaries. [from Turkish **khān**.]

²**khan** (kän) *n-* in the Orient, an inn. [from Persian **khān**, from Arabic.]

khe·dive (kə dēv') *n-* title of any of the Turkish viceroys who ruled Egypt from 1867 to 1914.

kib·butz (kĭ bŏŏts') *n-* [*pl.* **kib·butz·es** or **kib·but·zim** (kĭ bŏŏt sēm')] Israeli farm settlement in which the property and labor are shared in common; collective farm.

kib·itz (kĭb' əts) *Informal vt-* to look on and give unwanted advice at a card game. *—n- kib' itz·er.*

kick (kĭk) *vt-* 1 to hit or strike with the foot: *to kick a rock.* 2 to move or drive by doing this: *to kick a ball across a field.* 3 in football, to make or score (an extra point or field goal) by kicking. *vi-* 1 to thrust out with the foot: *to kick and prance in a dance.* 2 to spring back; recoil: *The shotgun kicks when it's fired.* 3 *Informal* to complain; grouse. 4 in football, to punt. *n-* 1 blow or thrust with the foot: *He gave the can a swift kick.* 2 a recoil: *That gun has some kick to it.* 3 *Slang* a thrill.

kick back 1 to recoil. 2 *Slang* to return a part of (one's salary, fee, etc.).

kick in *Informal* to contribute one's share of (money).

kick off 1 in football, to kick the ball toward the opposing team to begin play at the beginning of each half or after a touchdown or field goal. 2 *Slang* to die.

kick out *Informal* to eject forcibly from a place.

kick the bucket *Slang* to die.

kick upstairs *Informal* to promote (someone) in order to remove him from a job of real responsibility.

kick over the traces to defy authority; have a fling.

kick·back (kĭk' băk') *n-* 1 *Informal* sudden, strong reaction or recoil. 2 *Slang* a returning of a part of one's salary or fee; also, the amount returned.

kick·er (kĭk' ər) *n-* 1 person who kicks, especially a football player who specializes in kicking. 2 small marine engine, especially an outboard motor.

kick·off (kĭk' ôf') *n-* in football, a place kick toward the opposing team, which begins the play at the beginning of each half or after a touchdown or field goal.

kid (kĭd) *n-* 1 young goat. 2 leather made from the skin of a young goat. 3 *Informal* child; youth. *adj-* 1 made of the skin of a young goat: *white kid gloves.* 2 *Informal* younger or youngest: *my kid sister.* *vt- Slang* [kid·ded, kid·ding] 1 to deceive; fool. 2 to play or fool with; tease: *I didn't mean it; I was just kidding you.* *vi- Slang* to make jokes and quips; be frivolous and amusing: *Please stop kidding.*

kid·dush (kĭd' əsh, kĭ dōōsh') *n-* in Judaism, a prayer said over wine, especially to commence the Sabbath.

kid·nap (kĭd' năp') *vt-* [kid·naped or kid·napped, kid·nap·ing or kid·nap·ping] to carry off and hold (some-

kid·ney (kĭd' nē) *n-* 1 either of the two glandular organs of the animal body located in the lower back near the spine. The kidney regulates the composition of the blood and eliminates waste products in the form of urine. 2 sort or kind: *a man of his kidney.*

Kidneys showing position from back

kidney bean *n-* 1 edible, reddish-brown seed of a common garden plant that is a member of the bean family. 2 the plant itself.

kidney stone *n-* small hard mass formed in the kidney by the crystallization of urinary salts.

kid·skin (kĭd' skĭn') *n-* leather made from the skin of a young goat, used especially for gloves and shoes.

¹**kill** (kĭl) *vt-* 1 to deprive of life; slay. 2 to destroy: *Frost kills crops.* 3 to defeat; reject; discard: *The senators killed the tax bill.* 4 spend (time) idly: *We killed an hour looking out the window.* *vi-* to cause death; slay: *He killed without conscience.* *n-* act of causing death, especially in hunting; also, the dead prey. [from Middle English **kyllen**, probably related to **quell**.] *—n- kill' er.*

²**kill** (kĭl) *n-* stream, creek, or channel (found in place names). [American word from Dutch **kil**.]

kill·deer (kĭl' dēr') *n-* kind of plover with brown back and wings, orange-brown tail, and white breast crossed by two brown bands. For picture, see *plover.*

killer whale *n-* large, flesh-eating sea mammal.

kill·ing (kĭl' ĭng) *n- Informal* sudden gain or profit.

kill·joy (kĭl' joi') *n-* person who ruins the joy of others.

kiln (kĭl, also kĭln) *n-* oven for baking pottery.

ki·lo (kĭl' ō, kē' lō) *n-* [*pl.* **ki·los**] 1 kilogram. 2 kilometer.

kilo- *combining form* thousand: *a kilogram.*

kil·o·cy·cle (kĭl' ə sī' kəl) *n-* 1 unit of frequency equal to 1000 cycles per second. 2 1000 cycles.

kil·o·gram (kĭl' ə grăm') *n-* unit of mass and weight in the metric system equal to 1000 grams or about 2.2 pounds. Also **kil' o·gramme.**

kil·o·gram-me·ter (kĭl' ə grăm' mē' tər) *n-* unit of work equal to the work done in raising a mass of one kilogram through a distance of one meter against the force of gravity. One kilogram-meter equals about 9.8×10^7 ergs or about 7.2 foot-pounds.

kil·o·li·ter (kĭl' ə lē' tər) *n-* unit of volume or capacity equal to 1000 liters. Also **kil' o·li' tre.**

kil·o·me·ter (kə lŏm' ə tər, also kĭl' ə mē'-) *n-* unit of distance equal to 1000 meters or about 3,281 feet. Also **kil' o·me' tre.**

kil·o·ton (kĭl' ə tŭn') *n-* 1 unit of weight equal to 1000 tons. 2 unit of explosive force or power, equal to that produced by 1000 tons of TNT.

kil·o·watt (kĭl' ə wŏt') *n-* unit of electrical power equal to 1000 watts.

kil·o·watt-hour (kĭl' ə wŏt' our') *n-* unit of energy equal to the energy expended by 1000 watts of electrical power during a time period of one hour.

kilt (kĭlt) *n-* short, pleated skirt worn by men of Celtic lands, especially by Scottish Highlanders.

kil·ter (kĭl' tər) **out of kilter** *Informal* not in working condition; out of order.

ki·mo·no (kə mō' nə) *n-* [*pl.* **ki·mo·nos**] 1 loose outer garment bound with a broad sash, worn by men and women in Japan. 2 woman's dressing gown.

Kimono

kin (kĭn) *n-* person's family; relatives. *adj-* 1 related: *John is kin to me.* 2 similar; alike: *This book is kin to that one in subject.*

next to kin person or persons most closely related; immediate family.

-kin *suffix* (used to form nouns) little; small: *lambkin.*

¹kind (kīnd) *adj-* [**kind·er, kind·est**] 1 gentle and loving. 2 thoughtful; considerate: *It was kind of you to send flowers.* [from Old English (ge)cynde, "fitting; natural; inborn," related to ²**kind.**]

²kind (kīnd) *n-* sort; class; variety: *What kind of apple is that? It takes all kinds of people.* [from English cynd meaning "natural character; class." It is related to **kin.**]

in kind 1 with something of the same sort: *to return an evil deed in kind.* 2 with goods rather than money: *to pay a debt in kind.* **kind of** *Informal* somewhat; rather: *This is kind of stupid.*

kin·der·gar·ten (kĭn′ dər gär′ tən, -gär′ dən) *n-* school or class for children, usually between four and six years of age, in which children learn to work and play together and begin to develop their individual abilities.

kind·heart·ed (kīnd′ här′ təd) *adj-* generous and sympathetic; thoughtful of others. —*adv-* **kind′ heart′ ed·ly.** *n-* **kind′ heart′ ed·ness.**

kin·dle (kĭn′ dəl) *vt-* [**kin·dled, kin·dling**] 1 to set fire to; light: *to kindle a fire.* 2 to make bright or shining: *Excitement kindled her face.* 3 to arouse; stir up: *The insult kindled his anger.* *vi-* 1 to catch fire: *The dry wood kindled immediately.* 2 to become aroused or stirred up: *to kindle with enthusiasm.* 3 to become bright and glowing: *Her eyes kindled with excitement.*

kin·dling (kĭnd′ lĭng) *n-* material for starting a fire, such as small pieces of wood.

kind·ly (kīnd′ lē) *adj-* [**kind·li·er, kind·li·est**] gentle and thoughtful of others; kind: *He is a kindly man who will help anyone.* *adv-* 1 in a kind, friendly way: *He treated me kindly and took care of me.* 2 please be good enough to: *Will you kindly explain?* —*n-* **kind′ li·ness.**

take kindly to to be pleasant or agreeable to.

kind·ness (kīnd′ nəs) *n-* 1 gentleness to and thoughtfulness of others; a being kind: *He showed kindness by helping us.* 2 helpful or thoughtful act; kind act.

kin·dred (kĭn′ drəd) *n-* relatives. *adj-* of the same kind; related: *Writing and spelling are kindred studies.*

kine (kīn) *Archaic n- pl.* cows; cattle.

kine·scope (kĭn′ ə skōp′) *n-* 1 picture tube. 2 a movie of a television program.

ki·net·ic (kĭ nĕt′ ĭk) *adj-* of, having to do with, or due to motion.

kinetic energy *n-* energy that an object or particle has as a result of its motion. *See also potential energy.*

kin·folk (kĭn′ fōk′) *n- pl.* one's relatives; kin. Also **kinsfolk.**

king (kĭng) *n-* 1 male sovereign of a country; monarch. 2 person or thing that is thought of as being very important or powerful: *The lion is the king of the jungle.* 3 playing card with the picture of a crowned male monarch. 4 in checkers, a piece which has been moved over to the opponent's last row on the board and can now move backwards or forwards. 5 in chess, the principal piece, whose imminent capture ends the game.

king·bird (kĭng′ bûrd′) *n-* any of various quarrelsome birds related to the flycatchers.

king·bolt (kĭng′ bōlt′) *n-* vertical bolt that connects the axle of the front wheels of a vehicle to its body, and serves as a pivot in turning; kingpin.

king cobra *n-* large, very poisonous cobra of India and southeastern Asia; hamadryad. It is the world's largest venomous snake.

king crab *n-* 1 horseshoe crab. For picture, see *horseshoe crab.* 2 any of various large edible crabs of the northern Pacific, with a small body and very long legs.

king·dom (kĭng′ dəm) *n-* 1 country that has a king or queen; monarchy. 2 one of the three groups into which all natural things are divided: *the animal kingdom.* 3 domain; realm: *the kingdom of the mind.*

king·fish (kĭng′ fĭsh′) *n-* [*pl.* **king·fish;** king·fishes (kinds of kingfish)] any of various sea fishes, especially a large food fish of the North American Atlantic coast.

king·fish·er (kĭng′ fĭsh′ ər) *n-* a crested bird with a blue back and white breast and neckband. It catches fish with its long, black beak as it flies over the surface of the water.

Kingfisher about 1 ft long

king·ly (kĭng′ lē) *adj-* [**king·li·er, king·li·est**] of or suitable for a king: *a kingly treasure; his kingly rights.* —*n-* **king′ li·ness.**

king·mak·er (kĭng′ mā′ kər) *n-* one who is influential in the selection of a king or other powerful person.

king·pin (kĭng′ pĭn′) *n-* 1 in bowling, the foremost or center pin. 2 *Informal* the most important or influential person. 3 kingbolt.

Kings (kĭngz) *n-* (takes singular verb) 1 either of two historical books in the Old Testament, "I and II Kings." 2 in the CCD Bible, the four "King" books, corresponding to "I and II Samuel" and "I and II Kings."

king·ship (kĭng′ shĭp′) *n-* 1 power, office, or dignity of a king. 2 art or manner of ruling a kingdom.

king·size (kĭng′ sīz′) *adj-* larger than the usual: *a king-size sheet.*

king snake *n-* any of various large, nonpoisonous snakes of southern and central United States, which often feed on other snakes.

kink (kĭngk) *n-* 1 twist, curl, or sharp bend in a rope, wire, hair, etc. 2 stiffness in some part of the body; cramp: *a kink in the neck.* 3 odd twist of mind or character; strange notion. *vt-* to cause to form twists, curls, or bends: *to kink a hose.* *vi-* 1 *Don't let that cord kink.*

kin·ka·jou (kĭngk′ ə jōō′) *n-* flesh-eating, tree-dwelling mammal of Central and South America related to the raccoons and having large eyes, soft, brownish fur, and a long tail capable of grasping.

kink·y (kĭng′ kē) *adj-* [**kink·i·er, kink·i·est**] full of curls or twists; frizzy.

kin·ni·ki·nic (kĭn′ ĭ kə nĭk′) *n-* mixture of dried leaves and bark of certain plants, formerly smoked by certain North American Indians.

kins·folk (kĭnz′ fōk′) *n- pl.* kinfolk.

kin·ship (kĭn′ shĭp′) *n-* 1 family relationship. 2 relatedness; connection; similarity.

kins·man (kĭnz′ mən) *n-* [*pl.* **kins·men**] male relative. —*n- fem.* **kins′ wom′ an.**

ki·osk (kē′ ŏsk′-, kĭ′-) *n-* 1 in Turkey and Iran, an open summerhouse or pavilion. 2 small, similar structure, used as a newsstand, refreshment booth, etc.

Ki·o·wa (kī′ ə wə) *n-* [*pl.* **Ki·o·was,** also **Ki·o·wa**] member of a small tribe of American Plains Indians who now live in southwestern Oklahoma.

kip (kĭp) *n-* untanned hide of a young or small animal.

kip·per (kĭp′ ər) *vt-* to cure (fish) by salting and drying or smoking. *n-* fish that has been thus cured.

kirk (kûrk) *Scottish n-* church.

kir·tle (kûr′ təl) *Archaic n-* 1 woman's dress, skirt, or petticoat. 2 man's coat or tunic.

kis·met (kĭz′ mət) *n-* destiny; fate.

kiss (kĭs) *n-* 1 to touch or press with the lips as a caress, greeting, or sign of respect. 2 to touch gently; caress: *The waves kissed the shore.* *n-* *a kiss on one's cheek; the kiss of the waves on the shore.* —*adj-* **kiss′ a·ble.**

kiss·er (kĭs′ ər) *n-* person who kisses.

kit (kĭt) *n-* 1 set or collection of tools, materials, etc., for a particular job or purpose: *a kit for building a model boat; a soldier's kit.* 2 case, box, or bag for holding these.

kite (kīt) *n-* frame of light wood over which is stretched a silk or paper covering, flown at the end of a long string. [¹**kite** in a later, special use, from the fact that a kite looks like a bird in the sky.]

kith and kin (kĭth) *n- pl.* friends and relatives.

kith·a·ra (kĭth′ ə rə) *n-* cithara.

kit·ten (kĭt′ ən) *n-* young cat.

kit·ten·ish (kĭt′ ən ĭsh) *adj-* 1 lively and playful; frisky. 2 coy; coquettish. —*adv-* **kit′ ten·ish·ly.** *n-* **kit′ ten·ish·ness.**

Box kite and common kite

km. or **km** kilometer; kilometers.

knack (nǎk) *n-* 1 right or best way of doing something: *I want to dance well, but I can't get the knack of it.* 2 special skill; talent; aptitude: *a knack for carpentry.*

knap·sack (nǎp′sak′) *n-* sturdy canvas bag for clothing, food, etc., carried on the back by straps fitting over the shoulders or attached to a carrying frame; rucksack.

knave (nāv) *n-* 1 in earlier times, a male servant or man of humble birth. 2 dishonest or deceitful person; scoundrel. 3 in card games, a jack. *Hom-* nave.

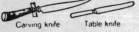
Knapsack

knav·er·y (nā′ və rē) *n- [pl.* **knav·er·ies**] dishonesty; treachery.

knav·ish (nā′vish) *adj-* deceitful; cunning in a dishonest way. *—adv-* **knav′ish·ly.** *n-* **kna′vish·ness.**

knead (nēd) *vt-* 1 to mix and work into a mass, usually with the hands: *to knead clay.* 2 to work over or treat with the hands or fingers; massage. *Hom-* need.

knee (nē) *n-* 1 joint of a human leg between the thigh and the lower leg; also, the corresponding part of a four-footed animal. 2 anything resembling this part, such as a sharply curved brace. 3 part of a pair of trousers or other garment covering this joint.

    bring (someone) **to** (his) **knees** to conquer or cow (someone); make (someone) surrender.

knee·cap (nē′ kǎp′) *n-* small, flat, movable bone that covers the front of the knee; patella. Also **knee′pan.**

kneel (nēl) *vi- [* **knelt** (nēlt) or **kneeled, kneel·ing**] to go down on one or both knees, usually as a sign of reverence or earnest pleading: *to kneel in prayer.*

knell (nēl) *n-* the slow sounding of a bell to announce a death or a funeral. *vt-* to ring (a bell) slowly or solemnly. *vi-:* *The church bells knelled all morning.*

knew (nōō, nyōō) *p.t.* of **know.** *Hom-* gnu, new.

Knick·er·bock·er (nĭk′ər bŏk′ ər) *n-* 1 a descendant of the early Dutch settlers of New York State. 2 a New Yorker.

knick·er·bock·ers (nĭk′ər bŏk′ ərz) *n-* (takes plural verb) knickers, especially those worn by men in the 17th and 18th centuries.

Knicker-bockers

knick·ers (nĭk′ ərz) *n-* (takes plural verb) full-cut breeches that gather and reach just below the knee.

knick·knack (nĭk′nǎk′) *n-* any small decorative ornament. Also **nicknack.**

knife (nīf) *n- [pl.* **knives**] 1 cutting tool of many forms with a keen, usually single-edged blade. 2 sharp cutting blade in a machine. *vt- [knifed, knif·ing]* to cut or stab with such an implement: *to knife an enemy in a fight.* *vi-* to cut or slice (through). *—adj-* **knife′ like′.**

Carving knife   Table knife   Pocket knife

knight (nīt) *n-* 1 during the Middle Ages, a mounted warrior in the service of his feudal superior; especially, such a man who has served as a squire and been ceremonially inducted into the order of chivalry. 2 today, a man honored by the British sovereign. He ranks below a baronet and is addressed with his given name preceded by "Sir." 3 in chess, the piece shaped like a horse's head. *vt-* to raise to the rank of knight. *Hom-* night.

knight-er·rant (nīt′ĕr′ ənt) *n- [pl.* **knights-er·rant**] medieval knight who roamed in search of adventure.

knight-er·rant·ry (nīt ĕr′ən trē) *n- [pl.* **knight-er·ran·tries**] 1 life and experience of a knight-errant. 2 exaggerated romantic adventure or scheme.

knight·hood (nīt′ hŏŏd′) *n-* 1 character, rank, or dignity of a knight; chivalry. 2 whole body or class of knights.

knight·ly (nīt′ lē) *adj- [knight·li·er, knight·li·est]* like a knight; chivalric. *Hom-* nightly. *—n-* **knight′li·ness.**

knish (knĭsh) *n-* rich crust folded over seasoned meat, cheese, or potato filling and baked or fried.

knit (nĭt) *vt- [knit or knit·ted, knit·ting]* 1 to make (a fabric or garment) by looping a single thread or yarn on needles either by hand or by machine: *to knit a sweater.* 2 to make a stitch in knitting of the type usually found on the right side of a garment. See also *purl.* 3 to unite closely; lock or draw together: *to knit one's fingers; to be knit together by common interests.* 4 to frown: *to knit one's brows.* *vi-* 1 to weave thread or yarn in loops by the use of needles: *Grandmother knits.* 2 to become closely joined or united: *The broken bone knit well.* *—n-* **knit′ ter.**

knit·ting (nĭt′ ĭng) *n-* garment, fabric, etc., being knitted by hand.

knitting needle *n-* straight, slender, pointed rod, used in knitting by hand. For picture, see *needle.*

Knitting

knit·wear (nĭt′ wâr′) *n-* knitted clothing.

knives (nīvz) *pl.* of **knife.**

knob (nŏb) *n-* 1 rounded handle of a door, drawer, umbrella, etc. 2 rounded swelling, lump, or mass on a surface. 3 knoll. *—adj-* **knob′ like′.**

knob·by (nŏb′ē) *adj- [knob·bi·er, knob·bi·est]* 1 bumpy; having protuberances: *a knobby hand.* 2 like a knob. *—n-* **knob′ bi·ness.**

knock (nŏk) *vi-* 1 to give a sharp blow; rap (on): *to knock with one's fist; to knock on the wall.* 2 to collide; bump: *He knocked into many people as he ran.* 3 to rap on a door in order to show one's presence outside. 4 of internal-combustion engines, to jar or pound noisily: *The engine knocks.* *vt-* 1 to strike or beat; give a blow to: *to knock a lamp down.* 2 to strike (something) against something else: *to knock one's head against a wall.* 3 *Slang* to criticize unfavorably; disparage. *n-* 1 sharp, quick blow; rap: *a knock at the door.* 2 a noisy banging: *a knock in the pipes.* 3 the pounding, pinging noise and vibration made by an internal-combustion engine when fuel burns faster than the pistons can move.

    knock about (or **around**) 1 to toss (someone or something) here and there with blows: *The waves knocked the boat about.* 2 to wander about in search of adventure or pleasure: *He knocked about quite a lot in his youth.*

    knock down 1 to sell to the highest bidder at an auction: *He knocked the antique vase down to a dealer.* 2 to take apart; disassemble.

    knock off *Informal* 1 to stop what one is doing: *We'll knock off at 3 o'clock. Please knock off the noise.* 2 to do quickly: *We'll knock this job off.* 3 to kill or otherwise dispose of: *They knocked off their rivals.*

    knock out 1 to cause (someone) to lose consciousness, especially by a blow. 2 to make quickly.

    knock together to build or put together hastily.

knock·a·bout (nŏk′ ə bout′) *n-* small sloop. *adj-* 1 noisy and rough; boisterous: *a knockabout game.* 2 suitable for rough use: *an old knockabout car.*

knock·down (nŏk′ doun′) *adj-* 1 hard enough to knock someone or something down; rough; fierce: *a knock-down blow; a knockdown battle.* 2 made so as to be easily put together and taken apart: *a knockdown book-case.* *n-* 1 a knocking down: *a knockdown in a boxing match.* 2 something easily put together or taken apart.

knock·er (nŏk′ ər) *n-* 1 person who knocks. 2 ring, knob, or the like, hinged to a metal plate on a door.

knock-kneed (nŏk′ nēd′) *adj-* having the legs bent inward so that the knees touch.

knock·out (nŏk′ out′) *n-* 1 in boxing, the knocking of a fighter to the floor so that he does not get up before the referee counts ten; also, a victory scored in this way. 2 *Slang* something very attractive or spectacular. *as modifier: a knockout blow; a knockout dress.*

Knocker

knoll (nōl) *n-* small, round hill.

knot (nŏt) *n-* 1 any of many forms of interweaving or tying together a cord or cords. 2 enlargement of a muscle, gland, etc.; lump. 3 hard lump in wood, different in color and grain from surrounding wood, where a branch has grown. 4 group; gathering: *There was a knot of people on the street.* 5 complication or entanglement: *a problem full of knots.* 6 unit of speed used by ships and airplanes, equal to a rate of one nautical mile per hour. *vt-* [knot·ted, knot·ting] 1 to tie or fasten together: *to knot a tie; to knot a rope.* 2 to entangle. *vi-* to become tangled: *Wet rope knots.* [from Old English *cnotta.*] *Homs-* naught, not. —*adj-* knot′·less.

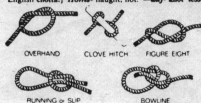

OVERHAND   CLOVE HITCH   FIGURE EIGHT

RUNNING or SLIP   BOWLINE

CARRICK BEND   SQUARE

Knots

²knot (nŏt) *n-* sandpiper of northern regions that migrates south in winter. *Homs-* naught, not. (of uncertain origin.)

knot·hole (nŏt′ hōl′) *n-* round hole in a board where a knot has fallen out.

knot·ty (nŏt′ ē) *adj-* [knot·ti·er, knot·ti·est] 1 full of knots: *a knotty cord.* 2 hard to solve or explain; difficult: *a knotty problem.*

know (nō) *vt-* [knew (nōō, nyōō), known (nōn), know·ing] 1 to perceive with the mind; understand clearly: *He knows his subject.* 2 to have a grasp of through study or practice: *to know music; to know French.* 3 to recognize: *I knew him instantly.* 4 to be familiar with: *to know the road.* 5 to have information about; be aware of: *I know his reasons.* 6 to have in the memory: *to know a song.* 7 to be certain of: *to know the truth.* 8 to distinguish: *to know right from wrong.* 9 to experience: *to know hardship. Hom-* no. —*adj-* know′·a·ble.

be in the know to have inside or secret information.

know-how (nō′ hou′) *Informal n-* special ability to do something well; technical skill. *Hom-* nohow.

know·ing (nō′ ĭng) *adj-* astute: *a knowing smile.*

know·ing·ly (nō′ ĭng lē) *adv-* 1 fully aware of the facts, results, etc.; deliberately: *He would never insult you knowingly.* 2 in a knowing manner: *to smile knowingly.*

knowl·edge (nŏl′ ĭj) *n-* 1 what has been learned by study or observation; learning. 2 familiarity from study or experience: *a knowledge of the area; a knowledge of painting.*

to (or to the best of) one's knowledge as far as one knows; on the best information one has.

know·ledge·a·ble (nŏl′ ĭ jə bəl) *adj-* well informed; knowing a great deal. —*adv-* know′ledge·a·bly.

known (nōn) *p.p.* of know.

knuck·le (nŭk′ əl) *n-* 1 finger joint, especially one of the joints connecting the fingers to the hand. 2 a cut of meat from a joint of an animal. 3 knuckles (also brass knuckles) set of metal finger rings or guards worn over the doubled fist for use as a weapon. *vi-* [knuck·led, knuck·ling] to keep the joints of the fingers close to the ground in shooting a marble.

knuckle down to apply oneself earnestly.

knuckle under to give in; submit.

knurl (nûrl) *n-* 1 knot; knob; lump. 2 small ridge such as on the edge of a thumbscrew or coin. —*adj-* knurled.

k.o. or K.O. (kā′ ō′) in boxing, a knockout.

ko·al·a (kō ä′lə) *n-* Australian animal that looks like a small bear. It has soft gray fur and large ears and lives in trees, and the female carries her young in a pouch.

kohl (kōl) *n-* preparation used by Muslim and Hindu women to darken the edges of the eyelids.

kohl·ra·bi (kōl răb′ ē) *n-* type of cabbage that forms no head but has a fleshy, edible stem.

kola (kō′ lə) *n-* small tropical tree bearing a brownish, bitter nut that yields caffeine and is used in beverages as a stimulant.

Kol Ni·dre (kōl nĭd′ rā′, kōl nĭd′ rē′, -rə) *n-* in Judaism, a prayer chanted in the service on the eve of Yom Kippur; also, the music to which the prayer is set.

koo·doo (kōō′ dōō′) kudu.

kook·a·bur·ra (kōōk′ ə bûr′ ə) *n-* Australian bird of the kingfisher type, noted for its raucous call, which resembles loud laughter.

ko·peck or ko·pek (kō′ pĕk′) *n-* Russian coin, the hundredth part of a ruble.

Ko·ran (kôr′ än′, kə rän′, -rän′) *n-* the sacred writings of the Muslims, recording the revelations of Allah (God) to Mohammed. It is written in Arabic.

Ko·re·an (kə rē′ ən) *adj-* of or pertaining to Korea, its people, or their language. *n-* 1 a native of Korea, or his descendants. 2 the language of these people.

Korean War *n-* war between North and South Korea (1950-1953) in which the United Nations supported South Korea. It was the first time that the United Nations took police action in a conflict. Many United States soldiers were involved.

ko·sher (kō′ shər) *adj-* 1 sanctioned by Jewish law, especially by those laws pertaining to food and its preparation. 2 serving or dealing in such food.

kow·tow (kou′ tou′) *n-* traditional Chinese greeting of respect and worship, made by kneeling and touching the forehead to the ground. *vi-* to show deference by such an act; hence, to be humble, obsequious, servile.

KP (kā′ pē′) *Informal n-* [*pl.* KP's or KPs] enlisted man assigned to kitchen police: *to be a KP two days in a row.*

K.P. 1 (also KP) kitchen police. 2 Knights of Pythias. 3 Knights of St. Patrick.

Kr symbol for krypton.

kraal (kräl) *n-* 1 South African village consisting of a group of huts surrounded by a stockade for protection against enemies. 2 pen for livestock in South Africa.

K ration *n-* in the U.S. Army during World War II, a small package of food meant to be a full day's emergency ration for one man.

Krem·lin (krĕm′ lən) *n-* 1 the citadel of Moscow, housing many of the Soviet Union's government offices. 2 the government of the Soviet Union. 3 kremlin the citadel of any Russian city.

kris (krēs) *n-* Malay or Indonesian dagger or short sword with a ridged and twisting blade.

Kriss Krin·gle (krĭs′ krĭng′ gəl) *n-* Santa Claus.

kryp·ton (krĭp′ tŏn′) *n-* rare inert gaseous element present in the atmosphere. The spectral wavelength of a krypton isotope is used to define the meter's length. Symbol Kr, At. No. 36, At. Wt. 83.80.

ku·dos (kōō′ dŏs′, kyōō′ dŏs′) *n-* praise; credit; glory.

ku·du (kōō′ dōō′) *n-* large grayish-brown African antelope with large, spirally twisted horns. Also koodoo.

kud·zu (kōōd′ zōō′) *n-* trailing Asiatic vine used for fodder and soil improvement, with edible roots and stems which yield fiber.

ku·lak (kōō′ lăk′) *n-* Russian peasant or farmer who opposed the Soviet collectivization of farms.

kum·quat (kŭm′ kwŏt′) *n-* small citrus fruit with sour pulp and sweet, edible rind, used for making preserves. 2 tree or shrub bearing this fruit. Also cumquat.

Kurd (kûrd, kōōrd) *n-* a member of nomadic people living mainly in Kurdistan.

Kur·dish (kûr′ dĭsh, kōōr′-) *n-* the Iranian language of the Kurds. *adj-* of or pertaining to the people of Kurdistan or their language: *valuable Kurdish rugs.*

Ku·te·nai (kōō′ tə nā′) *n-* [*pl.* Ku·te·nais, also Ku·te·nai] 1 one of a North American Indian people living on both sides of the United States-Canada border near the Pacific coast. 2 the language of these people.

kw. or **kw** kilowatt; kilowatts.

Kwa·ki·utl (kwä′kē ōō′təl) *n-* [*pl.* **Kwa·ki·utls,** also **Kwa·ki·utl**] 1 one of a tribe of North American Indians living on the northwest coast of British Columbia and on Vancouver Island. 2 the language of these people. *adj-:* *a* Kwakiutl *fish dish.*

K.W.H. or **kwh** kilowatt-hour; kilowatt-hours.

Ky. Kentucky.

kym·o·graph (kī′mə grăf′) *n-* instrument for recording waves or periodic variations, such as of muscular contractions, pulse beats, etc., on a continuous graph. It often consists of a movable pen that traces a line on a moving paper scroll or cylinder.

Kyr·i·e e·le·i·son (kĭr′ē ā′ē lā′ə sŏn′) *n-* 1 "Lord have mercy on us," the first words of an ancient song and prayer

L

L, l (ĕl) [pl. **L's, l's**] 1 the twelfth letter of the English alphabet. 2 Roman numeral for 50.

l. or **l** 1 left. 2 liter or liters.

L. or **£** pound sterling.

la (lä) Music n- the sixth note of a musical scale.

La symbol for lanthanum.

La. Louisiana.

lab (lăb) Informal n- laboratory.

la·bel (lā' bəl) n- 1 tag, sticker, words, etc., attached to or printed on an article and giving information about it: a label in a dress; a label on a can. 2 an identifying or descriptive phrase, word, or symbol: "Adj-," "n-," are labels used to identify parts of speech. vt- [la·beled, la·bel·ing] 1 to give an identifying mark to. 2 to call; describe: to label someone a liar. —n- la' bel·er.

la·bi·al (lā' bē əl) adj- 1 of or relating to the lips. 2 formed by the lips in speaking, as the consonants /p/ and /b/ are. n- sound, or a letter representing a sound, formed by the lips.

la·bor (lā' bər) n- 1 physical or mental toil; work. 2 difficult task: the labors of Hercules. 3 workers, especially when considered as a class or as members of labor unions: a law to benefit labor. 4 process of giving birth to a child; especially, the contractions of the womb preceding the birth. vi- 1 to exert mental or physical effort; toil. 2 to be burdened or distressed: to labor under a handicap. 3 to move slowly and heavily. 4 of a ship, to pitch and roll. vt- to work out in detail: to labor a topic. Also Brit. **labour.**

lab·o·ra·to·ry (lăb' rə tôr' ē) n- [pl. **lab·o·ra·to·ries**] room, building, or buildings where scientific research and experiments are carried on.

Labor Day n- holiday to honor labor, celebrated on the first Monday of September in most States of the United States.

la·bored (lā' bərd) adj- produced with effort; forced; not natural: a labored speech.

la·bor·er (lā' bər ər) n- worker, especially one who does heavy physical work that does not require much training.

la·bo·ri·ous (lə bôr' ē əs) adj- requiring great effort or hard work: a laborious task. —adv- la·bor' i·ous·ly. n- la·bor' i·ous·ness.

la·bor·ite (lā' bə rīt') n- person who supports the interests of the working class or the labor unions. adj-: a laborite point of view; a laborite tendency.

labor party n- political party that supports the interests of labor or the labor unions.

la·bor·sav·ing (lā' bər sā' vĭng) adj- designed to replace or diminish human labor, especially manual labor: a labor-saving device.

labor union n- organization of workers joined to protect and further their mutual interests.

La·bour·ite (lā' bər īt') n- member of the **Labour Party**, the major left wing party of Great Britain.

la·bur·num (lə bûr' nəm) n- poisonous tree or shrub, with clusters of yellow flowers.

lab·y·rinth (lăb' ə rĭnth') n- 1 confusing network of passages winding into and about one another, so it is

Labyrinth

lac·er·ate (lăs' ə rāt') vt- [lac·er·at·ed, lac·er·at·ing] 1 to tear badly; mangle: The shattered glass lacerated his hand. 2 to distress; cause mental anguish to: Sharp criticism lacerated his pride.

lac·er·a·tion (lăs' ə rā' shən) n- 1 a lacerating; tearing. 2 the jagged wound resulting from this.

lace·wing (lās' wĭng') n- any of various insects with four lacelike wings and brilliant eyes.

lach·ry·mal (lā' krə məl) adj- of or relating to the glands that secrete tears: the lachrymal ducts. n- pl. **lachrymals** glands that produce tears. Also **lacrimal.**

lach·ry·mose (lā' krə mōs') adj- 1 tearful; weeping. 2 tending to cause tears; sad; mournful: a lachrymose tale of woe. —adv- lach' ry·mose·ly.

la·crosse (lə krôs') n- field game played by two teams of ten players each (boys or men) or twelve players each (girls or women), in which the object is to send the ball into the opponents' goal by means of a long-handled racket. [American word from Canadian French **la crosse** meaning literally "the crosier; hooked stick."]

lac-, lacti-, or **lacto-** combining form milk. [from Latin lac, lactis meaning "milk."]

lac·tase (lăk' tās') n- enzyme of the intestinal juice that accelerates the reaction in which lactose is split into two simpler sugars, including glucose. It also occurs in certain bacteria.

lac·tate (lăk' tāt') n- any salt of lactic acid. vi- [lac·tat·ed, lac·tat·ing] to secrete milk. —n- lac' ta' tion.

lac·te·al (lăk' tē əl) adj- 1 of or like milk; milky. 2 conveying or containing chyle. n- any of the tiny vessels that carry chyle.

lac·tic (lăk' tĭk) adj- of milk; derived from milk.

lactic acid n- an organic acid ($C_3H_6O_3$) found in cells and muscle tissue. It is produced from carbohydrate fermentation and is present in sour milk, fermented vegetable juices, etc.

lac·tose (lăk' tōs') n- hard, white, crystalline sugar ($C_{12}H_{22}O_{11}$) that occurs in the milk of all mammals; milk sugar.

la·cu·na (lə kyōō' nə, -kōō' nə) n- [pl. **la·cu·nae** (-ē) or **la·cu·nas**] 1 an empty space; blank; gap: a lacuna in the manuscript. 2 a tiny pit or hollow in bones or tissues.

lac·y (lā' sē) adj- [lac·i·er, lac·i·est] of or like lace; having a delicate, open pattern. —n- lac' i·ness.

lad (lăd) n- boy or young man.

lad·der (lăd' ər) n- 1 device of parallel bars or ropes with evenly spaced crosspieces between them, used for climbing. 2 upward path: the ladder of social success.

ladder truck n- fire truck carrying ladders of various lengths; especially, an aerial ladder truck equipped with a hydraulically operated extension ladder.

lade (lād) vt- [lad·ed, lad·ed or lad·en, lad·ing] 1 to load, especially with cargo. 2 to dip (liquid) with a ladle. vi- to take on cargo. Hom- laid.

lad·en (lā' dən) adj- 1 loaded: a heavily laden ship. 2 weighed down; burdened: a man laden with grief.

lad·ing (lā' dĭng) n- 1 the loading of cargo or freight. 2 cargo or freight loaded.

la·dle (lā' dəl) n- long-handled bowl-shaped spoon or dipper. vt- [la·dled, la·dling] to use such a spoon; dip. —n- la' dler.

Ladle

la·dy (lā' dē) n- [pl. **la·dies**] 1 a woman: the lady next door; the lady in the second row. 2 woman who is especially polite, well-bred, etc.: Mrs. Allen is a real lady. 3 the wife of a man of high standing: the colonel's lady. 4 Lady (1) in Great Britain, title and form of address for a woman of high social rank, either by birth or by marriage to a knight or nobleman. (2) Our Lady.

la·dy·bug (lā' dē bŭg') or **la·dy·bird** (lā' dē bûrd') n- round-backed beetle, usually reddish-brown with large black spots. It is valuable as an enemy of harmful insects.

la·dy·fin·ger (lā' dē fĭng' gər) n- small sponge cake of long, thin shape.

lady in waiting n- woman who attends a queen or princess.

Ladybug

la·dy·like (lā' dē līk') adj- courteous and neat in a feminine way; well-bred; refined: a ladylike appearance.

la·dy·love (lā' dē lŭv') n- sweetheart.

La·dy·ship (lā' dē shĭp') n- title for Ladies (used with "Her" or "Your"): Her Ladyship is not at home.

la·dy's-slip·per or **la·dy·slip·per** (lā' dē slĭp' ər) n- any of a group of wild orchids with a flower that resembles a slipper.

lag (lăg) vi- [lagged, lag·ging] 1 to fail to keep pace; fall back: The slow runner lagged behind the others in the race. 2 to fall off; slacken: Interest lagged towards the end of the performance. vt- to pitch or shoot (a marble) at a mark. n- a falling behind in movement or progress; also, the amount of such falling behind. —n- lag' gard.

la·ma (lä′mə) *n-* Buddhist priest or monk of Tibet or Mongolia.

la·ma·ser·y (lä′mə sĕr′ē) *n-* [*pl.* **la·ma·ser·ies**] in Tibet and Mongolia, a monastery of lamas.

lamb (lăm) *n-* 1 young sheep. 2 flesh of this animal, used as food. 3 skin or hide of this animal. 4 gentle, innocent, or helpless person, especially a child. 5 **the Lamb** Christ. *vi-* to give birth to lambs. —*adj-* **lamb′ like′.**

Lamb

lam·baste (lăm băst′) *Slang* *vt-* [lam·bast·ed, lam·bast·ing] 1 to beat; assault violently. 2 to scold; chastise severely.

lam·bent (lăm′bənt) *adj-* 1 playing lightly over a surface; flickering: *a lambent flame.* 2 softly radiant: *the lambent light of stars.* 3 having lightness or brilliance: *a lambent sense of humor.* —*n-* **lam′ben·cy:** *The lambency of a full moon.* *adv-* **lam′bent·ly.**

lamb·kin (lăm′kĭn) *n-* 1 little lamb. 2 cherished child.

lance (lăns) *n-* 1 weapon consisting of a long pole or shaft with a sharp metal point. 2 soldier equipped with this weapon. 3 any sharp-pointed instrument resembling this, such as a fish spear, a surgeon's knife, etc. *vt-* [lanced, lanc·ing] 1 to stab or pierce with a long, sharp spear. 2 to cut open (a boil, cyst, etc.).

lan·guage (lăng′gwĭj) *n-* 1 all of the systems by which human beings combine sounds into meaningful units, such as words, and these into larger patterns to convey ideas and feelings. 2 any of the several thousand such systems that are or have been used by people belonging to different groups: *the French language; the Cherokee language; the Hittite language.* (Most of these show family relationships with others.) 3 words and expressions chiefly used within a certain field of knowledge or activity; terminology: *the language of science; the language of baseball; the language of poetry.* 4 any way or means of communicating: *the language of the animals.* 5 the particular words, phrases, and sentences chosen or constructed by a person or group; diction: *to use simple language; to admire Shakespeare's language.* *as modifier: a language instructor.*

lan·guid (lăng′gwĭd) *adj-* 1 weak or drooping, as if from exhaustion; lacking energy or strength: *Hot weather makes people languid.* 2 lacking briskness, or quickness of movement; slow: *a languid walk.* —*adv-* **lan′guid·ly.**

lan·guish (lăng′gwĭsh) *vi-* 1 to lose health, strength, or animation; become weak; droop; fade: *The roses languished in the summer heat.* 2 to waste away or suffer under unfavorable conditions: *to languish in prison; to languish in poverty.* 3 to pine (for); long: *The exiles languished for their native land.* —*n-* **lan′guish·er.**

lan·guish·ing (lăng′gwĭsh′ĭng) *adj-* 1 becoming languid; drooping; lacking strength, energy, or alertness. 2 sentimentally dreamy; melancholy: *a languishing look.* —*adv-* **lan′guish·ing·ly.**

lan·guor (lang′gər) *n-* 1 weakness; fatigue; listlessness; weariness of body or mind: *The intense heat filled the travelers with languor.* 2 sentimental dreaminess; a soft, tender mood: *a pleasant languor.* —*adj-* **lan′guor·ous.** *adv-* **lan′guor·ous·ly.**

lan·gur (läng gŏor′) *n-* any of various large, slender, long-tailed Asiatic monkeys.

lank (lăngk) *adj-* 1 tall and lean: *a lank figure.* 2 of hair, straight and limp. —*n-* **lank′ness.**

lank·y (lăng′kē) *adj-* [lank·i·er, lank·i·est] awkwardly tall and thin. —*adv-* **lank′i·ly.** *n-* **lank′i·ness.**

lan·o·lin or **lan·o·line** (lăn′ə lĭn) *n-* natural fatty coating of sheep's wool. It is used in cosmetics, ointments, soaps, etc.

lar·i·at (lăr′ē ət) *n-* long rope with a sliding noose, used to catch horses or cattle or to tether them; lasso. [American word from Spanish **la reata**, "the rope."]

¹lark (lärk) *n-* 1 any of a group of small, European songbirds, especially the skylark. 2 a similar North American bird, the meadowlark. [from Old English **lewerce, läferce.** In Scotland "laverock" is still used for "lark."]

lar·yn·gi·tis (lăr′ən jī′təs) *n-* inflammation of the larynx, marked by hoarseness or loss of voice.

lar·ynx (lăr′ĭngks) *n-* [*pl.* **la·ryn·ges** (lə rĭn′jēz′) or **lar·ynx·es**] enlargement of the upper part of the windpipe that in man and most mammals contains the vocal cords. —*adj-* **la·ryn′ge·al** (lə rĭn′jəl): *a laryngeal inflammation.*

las·car (lăs′kər) *n-* sailor, artilleryman, or army servant of India.

las·civ·i·ous (lə sĭv′ē əs) *adj-* sensual; lewd; lustful. —*adv-* **las·civ′i·ous·ly.** *n-* **las·civ′i·ous·ness.**

la·ser (lā′zər) *n-* device that generates a single frequency of intense, polarized light, all of whose waves are in phase with each other. [shortened from *light amplification by stimulated emission radiation.*] *Hom-* lazar.

¹lash (lăsh) *n-* 1 the flexible part of a whip; thong. 2 stroke given with a whip. 3 one of the small hairs along the edge of the eyelid; eyelash. *vt-* 1 to strike with a whip: *It used to be common punishment to lash criminals.* 2 to switch to and fro: *The caged lion lashed its tail.* 3 to beat; strike violently: *The wind lashed the trees.* 4 to rebuke or scold severely; castigate: *He lashed me with a torrent of angry words.* 5 to stir up; arouse: *The speaker lashed the crowd into a frenzy.* [of uncertain origin.] **lash out** to attack, especially with words; strike out.

²lash (lăsh) *vt-* to fasten with a cord or rope: *The Indians lashed poles together to make the framework for a tepee.* *n-* the cord or rope itself. [perhaps from Old French *lace* meaning "a lace; a tie."]

¹lash·ing (lăsh′ĭng) *n-* a whipping. [from ¹lash.]

²lash·ing (lăsh′ĭng) *n-* 1 act of binding. 2 cord, rope, etc., used for binding. 3 **lashings** bindings. [from ²lash.]

lass (lăs) *n-* girl; young woman.

lass·ie (lăs′ē) *n-* girl; young woman; lass.

las·si·tude (lăs′ə tōōd′, -tyōōd′) *n-* weariness of mind or body; lack of energy; listlessness.

las·so (lăs′ō) *n-* [*pl.* **las·sos** or **las·soes**] noosed rope used by cowboys to catch cattle, etc.; lariat. *vt-* to catch with such a rope.

Cowboy twirling lasso

¹last (lăst) *adj-* 1 coming after all others in time, place, order, etc. final: *The last letter of the alphabet is z.* 2 directly before the present: *the dance last night.* 3 most recent: *The last time I saw him was yesterday.* 4 being only one remaining: *the last cookie in the jar.* 5 least likely; least fitted: *He is the last man for such a job.* *adv-* 1 after all others: *The slowest runner comes in last in the race.* 2 most recently: *When did you last go to the dentist?* *n-* 1 person, thing, or part that is at the end: *the last of his family; the last of the story.* 2 end: *to be loyal to the last.* [from Old English *latost,* "latest."]

at last finally. **breathe one's last** to die. **see the last of** to see for the last time.

²last (lăst) *vi-* 1 to go on; continue: *The rain lasted three days.* 2 to be enough; hold out: *This much bread ought to last for two days.* 3 to hold up; endure: *Stone buildings last longer than wooden ones.* [from Old English *læstan,* "follow in the track of; continue," from Old English *läst,* "footstep; track." It is related to ³last.]

³last (lăst) *n-* model or form in the shape of the foot, on which shoes are made or repaired. [from Old English *læst,* "a boot," from Old English *läst,* "a footstep."]

stick to (one's) last to stay within (one's) own field of knowledge and skill; mind (one's) own business.

last·ing (lăs′tĭng) *adj-* keeping up or continuing a long time; enduring; permanent: *a lasting friendship.* —*adv-* **last′ing·ly.** *n-* **las′ting·ness.**

Last Judgment *n-* in some religions, the final judging of every person at the end of the world.

last·ly (lăst′lē) *adv-* finally; in conclusion; at the end: *And lastly, we shall sum up what we learned.*

last quarter *n-* the third phase of the moon, between the full moon and the new moon. For picture, see *moon.*

last straw *n-* the last of a series of irritations, which provokes a reaction from the sufferer.

Last Supper *n-* Christ's last meal with his disciples.

last word *n-* 1 final expression in an exchange of words. 2 final decision. 3 authoritative treatment or statement: *This book is the last word on politics.* 4 *Informal* the most up-to-date thing of its kind.

lat. latitude.

latch (lăch) *n-* 1 locking device consisting of a bar pivoted at one end, the free end of which may be raised from or lowered into a notch to fasten a door, etc. 2 any of several devices used for a similar purpose: *a window* latch. *vt-* to fasten; lock: *Please latch the screen door.*

Latch on door

on the latch fastened only with a latch; not locked.

latch·key (lăch′ kē′) *n-* key that unlocks a latch, especially at the main entrance of a dwelling.

latch·string (lăch′ strĭng′) *n-* string that, passed through a hole in a door, releases the inside latch from outside.

late (lāt) *adj-* [lat·er, lat·est] 1 after the usual or expected time: *Spring is late this year.* 2 tardy: *He was late for work today.* 3 during the final or latter part; toward the end: *The leaves began to fall in late autumn.* 4 of recent time or date; happening not long ago: *the late floods; his late illness.* 5 no longer living: *the late Mr. Barnes.* *adv-* 1 after the usual or expected time; tardily: *She arrived late.* 2 at or toward an advanced time: *Spring came late.* —*n-* late′ ness.

of late lately: *He has been rather absent-minded of late.*

late·com·er (lāt′ kŭm′ ər) *n-* person or thing that arrives late, or after most others.

la·teen sail (lə tēn′) *n-* three-cornered sail attached to a yard that slants across a low mast.

Late Latin *n-* a form of Latin used by writers from the third to the sixth centuries A.D.

Lateen sails

late·ly (lāt′ lē) *adv-* not long ago; recently: *His work has improved lately.*

la·tent (lā′ tənt) *adj-* hidden; present but not active: *his latent strength; a latent talent for the theater; a latent disease.* —*n-* la′ ten·cy: *The disease remained undetected during the period of latency.* *adv-* la′ tent·ly.

lat·er·al (lăt′ ər əl) *adj-* of, at, or coming from the side: *a lateral pass.* —*adv-* lat′ er·al·ly.

la·tex (lā′ tĕks′) *n-* any of several milky juices found in various plants and trees, from which various products are made. Natural rubber is made from the latex of one kind of tropical tree.

lath (lăth) *n-* one of the thin, narrow strips of wood fastened to the frame of a building and used to support the plaster of walls and ceilings.

lath·ing (lăth′ ĭng, lă**th**′-) *n-* 1 framework of laths, used to support plaster on walls. 2 act of putting such a framework in place.

Lat·in (lăt′ ən) *adj-* 1 of or relating to ancient Rome (Latium), its people, their culture, or their language. 2 of or relating to people whose language is that of France, Italy, Portugal, and Spain. 3 of or belonging to the Roman Catholic Church, as distinguished from the Eastern Christian churches. *n-* 1 the language of ancient Rome, and until recently the principal language of the Catholic Church. 2 member of a people whose language is derived from Latin or who live in Latin America. 3 inhabitant of ancient Latium.

Latin American *n-* native or inhabitant of Latin America. *adj-* (**Latin-American**): *in current* Latin-American *literature.*

Latin cross *n-* right-angle cross with the horizontal bar crossing a longer vertical bar near the top. For picture, see ¹*cross.*

Lat·in·ist (lăt′ ən ĭst) *n-* someone well versed or specializing in the Latin language; Latin scholar.

Latin Quarter *n-* section of Paris, south of the Seine, frequented by students and artists.

laud (lôd) *vt-* to praise; extol: *We lauded the writer for his excellent book.* *n-* **lauds** (or **Lauds**) prayers of praise, which, together with Matins, form the first of the canonical hours.

laud·a·ble (lôd′ ə bəl) *adj-* praiseworthy; deserving of esteem: *a laudable achievement.* —*adv-* laud′ a·bly.

lau·da·num (lo′ də nəm) *n-* solution of opium in alcohol.

laud·a·to·ry (lo′ də tôr′ ē) *adj-* containing or giving praise; commendatory: *a laudatory remark.*

laugh (lăf) *vi-* 1 to make sounds and facial movements to express joy, amusement, scorn, etc. (at or over): *Everybody laughed at the joke.* *vt-* to move or affect (someone) by laughing; cause (something to happen) as a result of laughing: *We laughed him out of his bad mood. Just laugh your troubles away.* *n-* series of sounds and facial movements expressing joy, amusement, etc.

laugh off to disregard as unimportant; shrug off.

laugh on the other side of the mouth (or **face**) to regret one's amusement later.

laugh up one's sleeve to laugh secretly or privately, especially at someone's mistake.

laugh·a·ble (lăf′ ə bəl) *adj-* provoking laughter; amusing; comical (often used to show disfavor): *Her efforts to be sophisticated were laughable.* —*adv-* laugh′ a·bly.

laugh·ing (lăf′ ĭng) *adj-* 1 uttering laughter. 2 full of or calling forth laughter: *This is no laughing matter.*

laughing gas *n-* nitrous oxide.

laughing stock *n-* an object of laughter or scorn.

laugh·ter (lăf′ tər) *n-* act or sound of laughing.

launch (lônch) *n-* 1 formerly, the largest boat carried by a warship. 2 motor-driven pleasure boat, usually without a deck or partly decked. [from Spanish *lancha* of the same meaning.]

Launch

¹**launch** (lônch) *vt-* 1 to lower or cause (a vessel) to be lowered into the water, especially for the first time; set afloat. 2 to start off; begin: *to launch a new business; to launch an attack.* 3 to hurl; cause to go forth with force: *to launch a glider; to launch a rocket.* [from Old French *lancier* meaning "to throw a lance," from Latin *lancea,* "a lance."] —*n-* launch′ er.

launch into to begin with vigor.

launch out to begin something uncertain or hazardous.

launching pad *n-* platform from which a rocket or missile is launched.

laun·der (lôn′ dər, lŏn′-) *vt-* to wash and iron: *to launder a dress.* *vi-*: *This linen launders well.* —*n-* laun′ der·er.

laun·dress (lôn′ drəs, lŏn′-) *n-* woman who makes a living by washing and ironing clothes.

laun·dro·mat (lôn′ drə măt′) *n-* commercial laundry, usually self-service, with coin-operated washing and drying machines. [from Laundromat, trademark.]

laun·dry (lôn′ drē, lŏn′-) *n-* [*pl.* laun·dries] 1 clothes and linens to be washed. 2 place where clothes and linens are washed; also, a business engaged in such work.

laun·dry·man (lôn′ drē mən, lŏn′-) *n-* [*pl.* laun·dry·men] man who works for a laundry, especially to collect and deliver laundry.

laun·dry·wo·man (lôn′ drē wŏŏm′ ən) *n-* [*pl.* laun·dry·wo·men] laundress.

lau·re·ate (lôr′ ē ət) *n-* person to whom an award or other honor has been given for achievement in arts or science; especially, a poet laureate.

law·less (lo′ ləs) *adj-* 1 without laws: *a lawless country.* 2 not obeying the laws: *a lawless bandit.* —*adv-* law′ less·ly. *n-* law′ less·ness.

law·mak·er (lo′ mā′ kər) *n-* person who has a part in enacting laws; legislator.

law·mak·ing (lo′ mā′ kĭng) *n-* the enacting of laws; legislation. *as modifier: a* lawmaking *assembly.*

law·man (lo′ mən) *n-* [*pl.* law·men] sheriff or other peace officer.

¹**lawn** (lôn) *n-* stretch of ground covered with grass that is kept closely cut, especially such ground near or around a house. [from earlier **laund,** from Old French **launde** meaning "wooded ground."]

²lawn (lôn) *n-* thin, fine cloth, usually of cotton or linen. [from an earlier English phrase, **laune lynen**, meaning "linen from Laon."] Laon is the French town where it was first woven.]

lawn mower *n-* machine used to cut grass.

lawn tennis See *tennis.*

law·ren·ci·um (lô rĕn´ sē əm) *n-* radioactive, metal, man-made element. Symbol Lw, At. No. 103.

law·suit (lô´ sōōt´) *n-* question or claim to be decided in a court of law.

law·yer (lô´ yər) *n-* person trained in the law and engaged in it as a profession; attorney.

lax (lăks) *adj-* 1 careless; negligent; not strict: *to have* lax *morals*; lax *behavior*; lax *discipline.* 2 not tight or firm; loose; slack: *a* lax *rope.* —*adv-* **lax´ly.** *n-* **lax´ ness.**

lax·a·tive (lăk´ sə tĭv) *n-* medicine or remedy used to make the bowels move. *adj-: a* laxative *food.*

lax·i·ty (lăk´ sə tē) *n-* [*pl.* **lax·i·ties**] lack of strictness or carefulness: *a* laxity *of discipline.*

¹lay (lā) *vt-* [**laid** (lād), **lay·ing**] 1 to put or place: *to* lay *a book on the table; to* lay *one's hand on someone's shoulder; to* lay *great stress on education.* 2 to put down in a certain position or place: *to* lay *linoleum; to* lay *bricks; to* lay *a submarine cable.* 3 to bring or beat down: *One blow* laid *him on the floor.* 4 to put down or quiet; settle: *to* lay *the dust by sprinkling.* 5 to impose: *to* lay *a tax.* 6 to charge: *to* lay *an accusation; to* lay *the blame for an accident.* 7 to assert; put forward; to give for examination: *to* lay *claim to the fortune; to* lay *one's case before the authorities.* 8 to prepare: *to* lay *careful plans.* 9 to bring into a particular state: *The wind* laid *the branches bare.* 10 to produce (eggs): *Ants* lay *eggs.* 11 to bet: *to* lay *a wager.* 12 to set in time or place: *to* lay *a scene in colonial times.* *vi-* to produce eggs. [from Old English *lecgan* meaning literally "to make lie," from *licgan* meaning **²lie.**] *Hom-* lei.

lay of the land layout of the land or general situation.

lay about to strike out in all directions.

lay aside 1 to put down or away: *to* lay *one's work aside.* 2 to save for future needs: *to* lay *money aside.*

lay away 1 to save: *to* lay *money away.* 2 to set something aside until paid for.

lay by to save: *to* lay *by money for a vacation.*

lay down 1 to proclaim forcefully; assert: *to* lay *down the rules.* 2 to give up or sacrifice (one's life). 3 to bet: *He* laid *down $5 on number 7.* 4 to give as partial payment: *Mr. Jones* laid *down $500 toward the purchase of a car.*

lay for *Slang* to wait for.

lay hold on to get a grip on.

lay in to store: *Squirrels* lay *in food for the winter.*

lay into *Slang* to attack (a person) verbally or physically.

lay off 1 to put out of work temporarily; discharge: *He* laid *off the workers while the factory was being rebuilt.* 2 to mark off. 3 *Slang* to refrain from.

lay low 1 to knock down. 2 to defeat or kill. 3 *Informal* lie low.

lay on 1 to apply; spread: *to* lay *the paint on in a thin coat.* 2 to strike; hit: *to* lay *on with blows.*

lay (oneself) out to take pains; make an effort.

lay open to cut open.

lay out 1 to mark off; plot: *to* lay *out a garden.* 2 to spend: *to* lay *out money.*

lay to to go at something; apply oneself with vigor.

lay up 1 to put aside; store: *to* lay *up a supply of groceries.* 2 to cause to stay in bed, or be inactive because of illness or injury.

³lay (lā) *adj-* 1 having to do with a person who is not a clergyman: *a* lay *assistant to the minister.* 2 of a person, outside any profession: *In legal matters it is better to have expert advice than a* lay *opinion.* [from Old French *lai*, from Latin *lāicus*, from Greek *lāïkos*, from *lāos* meaning "people."] *Hom-* lei.

⁴lay (lā) *n-* short poem or song. [probably from Old French *lai*, of Celtic origin.] *Hom-* lei.

lay·er (lā´ ər) *n-* 1 one thickness of a material spread over a surface: *the outer layer of skin; the layers of the earth.* 2 someone or something that lays: *a hen that's a good layer; a bricklayer.* —*adj-* **lay´ ered.** *n-* **lay´ er·ing.**

²lead (lĕd) *n-* 1 soft, gray, heavy metal element. Its chief ore is galena, and it is used in piping, solder, and radiation shielding. Symbol Pb, At. No. 82, At. Wt. 207.19. 2 the baked mixture of powdered graphite and clay used in the form of rods in pencils. 3 in printing, one of the thin strips of metal used for spacing between lines. 4 small mass of metal used on the end of a line for finding the depth of water. 5 **leads** metal framework of windows with small panes of clear or stained glass. [from Old English **lēad.**] *Hom-* led.

lead·en (lĕd´ ən) *adj-* 1 made of lead. 2 hard to move; heavy: *His legs were* leaden *from fatigue.* 3 sluggish; dull; depressed: *the team's* leaden *spirits after defeat.* 4 dull gray: *a* leaden *sky.* —*adv-* **lead´ en·ly.**

lead·er (lē´ dər) *n-* 1 person who guides, conducts, or directs: *an orchestra* leader. 2 person who holds the first place or is fitted to do so: *a born* leader. 3 length of gut, plastic, or wire used between a fishing line and the hook or lure. —*adj-* **lead´ er·less.**

lead·er·ship (lē´ dər shĭp´) *n-* 1 ability to lead. 2 guidance. 3 position of a leader.

lead·ing (lē´ dĭng) *n-* a guiding or conducting; guidance; direction. *adj-* 1 guiding; directing. 2 first or among the first in achievement, quality, sales, etc.; foremost.

leading question *n-* question so expressed as to draw forth or suggest the answer desired by the asker.

leak (lēk) *n-* 1 hole, crack, or other opening which lets something pass in or out accidentally: *The roof had a bad* leak. 2 a passing in or out accidentally: *The gas* leak *is serious.* *vi-* 1 to pass in or out accidentally: *Water is leaking from this bucket.* 2 to let something pass in or out accidentally: *The boat* leaks *like a sieve.* 3 to be revealed accidentally or deliberately: *Plans for a surprise attack* leaked *out.* *vt-: This pipe* leaks *gas. He* leaked *important information to the press.* *Hom-* leek.

leak·age (lē´ kĭj) *n-* 1 the process of leaking in or out: *the* leakage *of gas; the* leakage *of military information.* 2 that which leaks in or out: *Gas* leakage *into the refrigerator spoiled the food.* 3 the quantity that leaks: *The broken faucet had a* leakage *of two gallons an hour.*

leak·y (lē´ kē) *adj-* [**leak·i·er, leak·i·est**] permitting the accidental entrance or escape of a gas or liquid: *a* leaky *faucet; a* leaky *boat.* —*n-* **leak´ i·ness.**

¹lean (lēn) *vi-* 1 to slant, slope, or incline from a straight position: *There is a famous tower in Italy that* leans. 2 to bend the upper part of the body: *He* leaned *over the table.* 3 to rest on or against something for support: *Don't* lean *on your desk.* 4 to depend; rely on: *She still* leans *on her mother.* 5 to be inclined; show a preference: *Her interests* lean *toward sports.* *vt-* to place (something) in a slanting position: *The painter* leaned *the ladder against the wall.* [from a blend of Old English **hlēonian** meaning "to lean," and **hlænan** meaning "to cause to lean."] *Hom-* lien.

²lean (lēn) *adj-* [**lean·er, lean·est**] 1 thin; without fat: *the* lean *meat.* 2 not productive; scant: *a* lean *year.* [from Old English **hlæ̆ne,** "thin."] *Hom-* lien. —*n-* **lean´ ness.**

Le·an·der (lē ăn´ dər) *n-* in Greek legend, Hero's lover.

lean·ing (lē´ nĭng) *n-* inclination; tendency; bent.

lean-to (lēn´ tōō´) *n-* [*pl.* **lean-tos**] 1 temporary shelter of sloping branches, thatch, etc., built by campers, hunters, etc. 2 small building with a roof sloping toward its free side, built against another building.

Camper's lean-to

leap (lēp) *vi-* [**leaped** or **leapt** (lĕpt, lēpt) **leap·ing**] 1 to jump or spring: *He* leaped *from the rock. The salmon* leaped *up the falls.* 2 to move quickly, as if with a jump: *He* leaped *to his feet.* *vt-* 1 to pass over with a jump or bound: *The runner* leaped *the ditch.* 2 to cause to jump: *to* leap *a horse.* *n-* jump; bound. —*n-* **leap´ er.**

leap at to seize at (something): *to* leap *at an opportunity.*

leap·frog (lēp´ frŏg´, -frôg´) *n-* game in which each player takes turns running and jumping over the bent back of the player in front of him, and then bends over in his turn for the next runner.

learn (lûrn) *vt-* [**learned** or **learnt** (lûrnt), **learn·ing**] 1 to gain knowledge of or skill in: *She is learning French. The baby has learned how to walk.* 2 to memorize: *to learn a poem and recite it.* 3 to become informed of; find out: *I regret to learn the sad news.* 4 to become skillful, able, or informed: *She has never cooked, but she can learn.* 2 to find out: *He learned of her whereabouts from a friend.* —*n-* **learn′er.**
►For usage note see TEACH.

learn·ed (lûr′nəd) *adj-* having or showing much knowledge; scholarly: *a learned man.* —*adv-* **learn′ed·ly.**

learn·ing (lûr′nĭng) *n-* knowledge gained by study.

lease (lēs) *n-* 1 written agreement for the renting of land or buildings for a certain time: *We signed a two-year lease for this house.* 2 the period of time agreed upon in such an agreement: *How long is your lease on that land?* *vt-* [**leased, leas·ing**] to rent (something) according to the terms of an agreement: *He leased the land for a year.*

new lease on life new chance to enjoy oneself, make use of an opportunity, etc.

lease·hold (lēs′hōld′) *n-* 1 a holding of land or other property by lease. 2 the land or other property so held.

leash (lēsh) *n-* a strap, chain, or cord for holding or leading a dog or other animal. *vt-* to fasten or hold with such a tether: *to leash a dog.*

hold in leash to keep in check; to hold back or under control. **on leash** held and controlled by a leash.

least (lēst) *adj-* (*superl.* of **little**) smallest in amount, size, degree, importance, etc.: *Who did the least work? He argues over the least thing.* *adv-* (*superl.* of **little**) to the smallest extent or degree: *to like something least.* *n-* the smallest: *the least of my worries.*

at least or **at the least** at any rate; as a minimum concession: *You could at least talk to him.* **not in the least** not at all: *"Do you mind doing this?" "Not in the least!"*

leav·en·ing (lĕv′ən ĭng) *n-* leaven.

leaves (lēvz) *pl.* of **leaf.**

leave-tak·ing (lēv′tā′kĭng) *n-* act or ceremony of departing; good-by; farewell: *a formal leave-taking.*

leav·ings (lē′vĭngz) *n- pl.* remains; things left over.

lech·er·ous (lĕch′ər əs) *adj-* excessively pursuing sexual activity. —*adv-* **lech′er·ous·ly.** *n-* **lech′er·ous·ness.**

lech·er·y (lĕch′ə rē) *n-* excessive sexual indulgence.

lec·i·thin (lĕs′ə thĭn′) *n-* one of a group of waxlike organic compounds found in all living organisms, especially in nervous tissue.

lec·tern (lĕk′tərn) *n-* tall desk from which a minister, teacher, etc., reads or consults his notes while addressing an audience.

lec·ture (lĕk′chər) *n-* 1 talk or address before an audience or class: *a series of lectures on art.* 2 lengthy reproof; also, a scolding: *She gave them a lecture on their bad manners.* *vi-* [**lec·tured, lec·tur·ing**] to give an address: *He lectured on modern literature.* *vt-* to reprove at length; also, to scold: *I had to lecture the children on their behavior.* —*n-* **lec′tu·rer.**

led (lĕd) *p.t. & p.p.* of ¹**lead.** *Hom-* ²**lead.**

Le·da (lē′də) *n-* in Greek mythology, the beloved of Zeus and mother of Helen of Troy.

ledge (lĕj) *n-* 1 narrow shelf along a wall: *a window ledge.* 2 shelflike ridge of rock: *a ledge on the cliff.*

ledg·er (lĕj′ər) *n-* the main account book of a business firm, in which the final summaries of receipts and payments are recorded.

lee (lē) *n-* side away from the wind; sheltered side: *the lee of a ship.* *adj-:* *the lee side of an island.* *Hom-* **lea.**

leech (lēch) *n-* 1 any of a group of segmented worms which fasten themselves to the skin and suck blood. Formerly, leeches were much used in medicine to draw blood from patients. 2 person who gets all he can out of another; parasite. 3 *Archaic* doctor. *Hom-* **leach.**

lee·chee (lē′chē) litchi.

leek (lēk) *n-* plant of the onion family, used in seasoning. *Hom-* **leak.**

leer (lēr) *n-* a sly or nasty sidelong look which expresses a feeling of malice, lust, etc. *vi-:* *He leered at his helpless victim.* *Hom-* **Lear.**

leg (lĕg) *n-* 1 one of the limbs of the body that give it support and by which men and animals walk and run. 2 part of a garment which covers one of these limbs: *a trouser leg.* 3 something like such a limb in use or appearance: *a table leg.* 4 stage of a journey or other undertaking: *the last leg of a trip.* 5 *Mathematics* one of two sides of a triangle, the third being the base. *vi-* [**legged, leg·ging**] to walk or run (usually followed by "it"). —*adj-* **leg′less.**

not have a leg to stand on to have no support or proof whatever for one's opinion or action. **on (one's) last legs** *Informal* near exhaustion, death, etc. **pull (one's) leg** *Informal* tease; deceive jokingly.

leg·a·cy (lĕg′ə sē) *n-* [*pl.* **leg·a·cies**] 1 property or money left to someone by a will. 2 something handed down.

leg work *n-* 1 work of a legman. 2 any errands, small tasks, etc., involving much walking.

le·hu·a (lā hōō′ə) *n-* tree of the Pacific islands, with brilliant red flowers and hard wood.

lei (lā, lā′ē) *n-* Hawaiian wreath of flowers. *Hom-* **lay.**

lei·sure (lē′zhər, lĕzh′ər) *n-* 1 freedom from work or duties. 2 time available for or devoted to recreation, relaxation, etc. *as modifier:* *Her leisure time was spent in reading. The habits of the leisure classes have changed.* —*adj-* **lei′sured:** *a leisured man.*

at leisure 1 having spare time. 2 not occupied. 3 with no hurry. **at (one's) leisure** at one's convenience; when one has free time.

lei·sure·ly (lē′zhər lē, lĕzh′ər lē) *adj-* 1 slow; not hurried: *a leisurely walk.* 2 free and restful: *a leisurely afternoon at the beach.* *adv-* slowly and without hurrying: *to stroll leisurely.* —*n-* **lei′sure·li·ness.**

lem·ming (lĕm′ĭng) *n-* small rodent of the arctic regions resembling a mouse. Periodically, millions of lemmings move in a mass into the sea and drown.

lem·on (lĕm′ən) *n-* 1 small, oval, yellow fruit with a sour juice used to flavor foods and drinks. 2 the tree which bears this fruit. 3 a pale yellow. 4 *Slang* something or someone disappointing, undesirable, inadequate, etc. *adj-:* *a lemon dress; lemon sherbet.*

lem·on·ade (lĕm′ə nād′) *n-* a drink made of lemon juice, sugar, and water.

lend-lease (lĕnd′ lēs′) *n-* as authorized by the Congress, the furnishing of such articles as aircraft, ships, munitions, food, etc., to a friendly nation whose defense is vital to the safety of the United States. *as modifier:* *a lend-lease program.* *vt-* [**lend-leased, lend-leas·ing**] to furnish (such articles): *to lend-lease food.*

length (lĕngkth) *n-* 1 the measure of a thing from end to end; the longer or longest measure of a thing, as distinguished from its width and thickness: *the length of a boat; the length of a board.* 2 extent in space or time: *the length of a race course; the length of an interview.* 3 a specified distance considered as a unit of measure: *an arm's length.* 4 piece of something, usually of a certain size, cut from a larger piece: *a length of rope.*

at full length stretched out. **at length** 1 in full; in detail: *to describe a trip at length.* 2 finally; at last. **go to any length** (or **lengths**) to do whatever is necessary; stop at nothing. **keep at arm's length** to avoid being friendly with; treat with coldness.

length·en (lĕngth′ən) *vt-* to make longer: *to lengthen a skirt.* *vi-:* *The days lengthen in spring.*

Len·i-Len·a·pe or **Len·ni-Len·a·pe** (lĕn′ē lĕn′ə pē′) See *Delaware.*

len·i·ty (lĕn′ə tē) *n-* mildness; leniency; gentleness.

lens (lĕnz) *n-* 1 piece of transparent material curved on one or both sides. It spreads or focuses the light rays passing through it. 2 unit consisting of two or more such glass pieces cemented together, used in high-quality cameras, microscopes, etc. 3 crystalline lens of the eye. For picture, see *eye.* 4 any device that focuses radiation other than light, as in an electron microscope.

Lens as a burning glass

Lent (lĕnt) *n-* period of penitence and self-denial observed in the Roman Catholic and other Christian churches from Ash Wednesday to Easter, excluding the Sundays.

Lent·en (lĕn´tən) *adj-* **1** pertaining to or suitable for Lent. **2** lenten meager; spare.

len·til (lĕn´tĭl) *n-* **1** a pod-bearing plant. **2** the seeds of this plant, cooked and eaten like peas and beans.

len·to (lĕn´tō) *Music adj- & adv-* slow; slower than adagio but faster than largo.

l'en·voi or **l'en·voy** (lĕn´voi´, län´voi´) *Fr.* lä[n] vwä´) *n-* **1** a postscript to a poem or prose work, often as a dedication. **2** the concluding stanza of a ballade.

Le·o (lē´ō) *n-* northern constellation thought to outline the figure of a lion.

le·o·nine (lē´ə nīn´) *adj-* of or like a lion.

leop·ard (lĕp´ərd) *n-* large tawny cat with black spots, or sometimes all black, found in Asia and Africa. *adj-* made of the skin of this animal. —*n- fem.* **leop´ard·ess.** *adj-* **leop´ard·like´.**

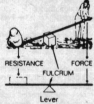

Leopard, 7—8 ft long

lep·er (lĕp´ər) *n-* person suffering from leprosy.

lep·i·dop·ter·an (lĕp´ə dŏp´tər ən) *n-* any member of an order of insects (**Lepidoptera**), which includes moths, butterflies, etc.

lep·i·dop·ter·ous (lĕp´ə dŏp´tər əs) *adj-* belonging to or characteristic of the lepidopterans.

lep·re·chaun (lĕp´rə kôn´, -kŏn´) *n-* in Irish folklore, an elf resembling a little old man, who knows of hidden treasure.

lep·ro·sy (lĕp´rə sē) *n-* a germ disease causing gradual loss of feeling, swellings and sores on the skin, wasting away of the flesh, and deformities; Hansen's disease. —*adj-* **lep´rous.**

lese majesty (lēz) *n-* in law, a crime against the sovereign or ruling power; treason.

le·sion (lē´zhən) *n-* **1** any abnormal condition of tissue or disability of an organ in any part of the body, caused by injury or disease. **2** injury; damage.

les·pe·de·za (lĕs´pə dē´zə) *n-* any of various shrubby leguminous plants used for forage.

less (lĕs) *determiner* (traditionally called adjective or pronoun) **1** smaller in quantity: *Mexico has less area than the United States.* **2** not so much: *Make less noise, please!* **3** *Informal* fewer. **4** shorter: *We'll get home in less time if we fly.* **5** lower in rank, degree, or importance: *no less a person than the king.* *n-* a smaller quantity: *He bought less of the fabric than I did.* *adv-* (*compar.* of **little**) to a smaller degree or extent; not so: *He was less scared than surprised. You should walk less and sleep more.* *prep-* minus: *four months less five days.* See also *lesser.*

  none the less nevertheless. **the less** even less.

  ►Use LESS with things you do not count by units, such as water or color, and use FEWER with things you can count, such as gallons of water or shades of color: *This tank holds less water than that one. This tank holds a hundred gallons fewer than that one. This picture has less color than the other one. This picture has fewer shades of red than the other one.*

-less *suffix* (used to form adjectives) **1** without; lacking: *treeless; endless; valueless.* **2** unable to do something specified: *sleepless; restless.* **3** beyond any power or ability to: *countless, resistless.*

le·thal (lē´thəl) *adj-* causing death; deadly: *a lethal gas.*

le·thar·gic (lə thär´jĭk) *adj-* **1** feeling or overcome by lethargy; sleepy; dull; sluggish. **2** having to do with or causing lethargy. —*adv-* **le·thar´gi·cal·ly.**

leth·ar·gy (lĕth´ər jē) *n-* [*pl.* **leth·ar·gies**] **1** unnatural drowsiness. **2** lack of interest; apathy; indifference.

Le·the (lē´thē) *n-* in Greek mythology, a river in Hades, a drink of whose water produced loss of memory; hence, oblivion. —*adj-* **Le´the´an.**

let's (lĕts) let us: *Turn off the TV and let's go.*

Lett (lĕt) *n-* one of a people living in Latvia and closely related to the Lithuanians. *Hom-* let.

let·tuce (lĕt´əs) *n-* leafy garden vegetable used mainly in salads and as a garnish.

let·up (lĕt´ ŭp´) *Informal n-* **1** a lessening or slackening, such as of effort or intensity: *The wind blew without letup.* **2** a pause; stop: *A brief letup in our work.*

leu·co·cyte or **leu·ko·cyte** (lōō´kə sīt´) *n-* white blood cell.

leu·ke·mi·a (lōō kē´mē ə) *Medicine n-* disease marked by an excessive multiplication of the white blood cells; cancer of the blood.

Lev. Leviticus.

¹lev·ee (lĕv´ē) *n-* **1** high bank built along a river to prevent floods. **2** landing place or quay. [American word from Louisiana French **levée** meaning "something raised," and related to ²**levee**.] *Hom-* levy.

²lev·ee (lĕv´ē) *n-* **1** morning reception once held by a king or other person of high rank on awakening from sleep. It was considered a great honor to be invited to a levee. **2** in England, an afternoon court assembly at which the king or queen receives only men. **3** any social reception. [from French **levé**, from Old French **lever**, from Latin **levare** meaning "to raise."] *Hom-* levy.

lev·el (lĕv´əl) *n-* **1** spirit level. **2** a specified height above some reference point: *The water rose to a level of 29 feet.* **3** place from which altitude is measured: *18 feet above sea level; three stories above ground level.* **4** relative place, degree, position, etc.; plane; rank: *to sink to the level of a common thief; a high level of intelligence; a formal level of usage in English.* **5** floor or story of a structure: *The refreshment stand is on the upper level. adj-* **1** horizontal; parallel to the surface of still water; smooth; flat: *a level floor; a level pasture.* **2** at the same height or plane: *a bracket level with my chin.* **3** steady; consistent; not wavering: *a level head; a level tone. vt-* **1** to smooth; make even; make horizontal: *to level a road; to level a floor.* **2** to tear down; raze: *to level a whole city.* **3** to knock down: *He leveled his opponent in two rounds.* **4** to make equal or the same; equalize: *Death levels us all.* **5** to aim: *to level a gun at a deer; to level criticism at the government.* —*n-* **lev´el·er.** *adv-* **lev´el·ly.** *n-* **lev´el·ness.**

  (one's) level best *Informal* the best one can do; one's very best: **on a level** at the same height, plane, rank, etc.: *His work is on a level with the best.* **on the level** *Slang* **1** honest; fair. **2** honestly and fairly.

level off **1** to make flat or even. **2** to come or bring into a level position: *The plane leveled off at 8,000 feet.*

lev·el·head·ed (lĕv´əl hĕd´əd) *adj-* **1** having good common sense and sound judgment; sensible. **2** cool in stress and danger; unruffled.

lev·er (lĕv´ər, *also* lē´vər) *n-* **1** bar used to pry up or lift a heavy object. **2** a simple machine based on the fact that when light pressure is applied on the long end of a bar resting on a fixed point, it will lift a heavy weight on the short end. **3** projecting piece used to operate or adjust a mechanism: *a gearshift lever.*

RESISTANCE   FORCE

FULCRUM

Lever

lev·er·age (lĕv´ər ĭj) *n-* **1** the action or use of a lever. **2** mechanical power gained by using a lever.

Le·vi (lē´vī´) *n-* in the Old Testament, the third son of Jacob and the founder of one of the tribes of Israel.

Le·vi·a·than (lə vī´ə thən) *n-* **1** in the Bible, a sea monster of enormous size. **2** anything huge, such as a whale or a large ship. Also **le·vi´a·than.**

lev·y (lĕv´ē) *vt-* [**lev·ied, lev·y·ing**] **1** to impose, raise, or collect (a tax, fine, etc.) by force or authority: *to levy a tax.* **2** to draft or enlist for military service: *to levy an army.* **3** to wage (war). *n-* [*pl.* **lev·ies**] **1** the imposing or collection of taxes, fines, etc. **2** forced enlistment of men for military service: *the greatest levy of troops in history.* **3** money, troops, etc. collected by force or authority. *Hom-* levee.

levy on to seize by law in order to collect money.

lewd (lōōd, lyōōd) *adj-* [**lewd·er, lewd·est**] obscene; indecent: *a lewd song.* —*adv-* **lewd′ly, n-** **lewd′ness.**

lex (lĕks) *Latin n-* [*pl.* **le·ges** (lē′jĕz)] law.

lex·i·cal (lĕk′sĭ kəl) *adj-* 1 of or having to do with words, especially with their meaning; semantic. 2 of or having to do with a lexicon or dictionary. —*adv-* **lex′i·cal·ly.**

lex·i·cog·ra·pher (lĕk′sə kŏ′grə fər) *n-* person who makes or helps to make a dictionary.

lex·i·co·graph·ic (lĕk′sĭ kə grăf′ĭk) *or* **lex·i·co·graph·i·cal** (-i kəl) *adj-* of or having to do with lexicography or with dictionaries. —*adv-* **lex′i·co·graph′i·cal·ly.**

lex·i·cog·ra·phy (lĕk′sə kŏ′grə fē) *n-* the art or occupation of making dictionaries.

lex·i·con (lĕk′sə kŏn′) *n-* dictionary, especially one of an ancient language.

Ley·den jar (lī′dən) *n-* early kind of capacitor consisting of a glass jar coated with a conducting material on its inner and outer sides. The jar has an insulated, one-hole stopper containing a metal rod that is connected to the inner coating by a metal chain.

SEAL
BRASS BALL
BRASS ROD
GLASS
METAL FOIL
BRASS CHAIN
Leyden jar

Li symbol for lithium.

li·a·bil·i·ty (lī′ə bĭl′ə tē) *n-* [*pl.* **li·a·bil·i·ties**] 1 legal responsibility. 2 tendency toward; susceptibility: *a person's liability to disease.* 3 something that handicaps; disadvantage; hindrance: *Poor eyesight is a liability.* 4 something owed; debt. 5 **liabilities** sum of what a person or company owes.

li·a·ble (lī′ə bəl) *adj-* legally responsible: *If the car is damaged, I will consider you* liable.

be liable to 1 *Informal* to have the tendency to: *He is liable to* goof. 2 to be subject to (a tax, punishment, etc.): *to* be liable *to* arrest. **be liable for** to be legally responsible for: *to* be liable *for one's debts.*

►LIABLE is sometimes used in conversation in the sense of "likely" or "probable." In careful writing and speaking, reserve LIABLE for the legal sense. *I am* liable *for damage done by my dog.* But: *It is* likely *to rain.*

li·ai·son (lē′ə zŏn′, lē ă′zŏn′) *n-* 1 a linking up of parts or groups; especially, communication and cooperation

lib·er·ate (lĭb′ə rāt′) *vt-* [**lib·er·at·ed, lib·er·at·ing**] 1 to set free: *to liberate a slave.* 2 to free (a gas, radical, etc.) from chemical combination. —*n-* **lib′er·a′tion.**

lib·er·a·tor (lĭb′ə rā′tər) *n-* person who liberates, especially one who brings freedom to a people or nation.

lib·er·tar·i·an (lĭb′ər târ′ē ən) *n-* 1 supporter of the doctrine of free will. 2 person who advocates liberty, especially of thought and conduct.

lib·er·tine (lĭb′ər tēn′) *n-* person who gives free rein to his lewd impulses and desires; rake. *adj-* loose in morals; lascivious; lewd.

lib·er·ty (lĭb′ər tē) *n-* [*pl.* **lib·er·ties**] 1 freedom from foreign rule or harsh, unreasonable government: *The colonies fought to gain their* liberty. 2 freedom from captivity, prison, slavery, etc.: *The prisoner pleaded for his* liberty. 3 freedom from control: *Freedom of speech is a precious* liberty. 4 freedom of choice; right or power

li·cense (lī′səns) *n-* 1 legal permission to do something; also, the document showing this permission: *a driver's* license; *a fishing* license. 2 freedom or right to ignore rules for the sake of effect: *poetic* license. 3 abuse of freedom; unrestrained liberty. 4 loose and lawless behavior; immoral action: *the unbelievable* license *of the invading soldiers. vt-* [**li·censed, li·cens·ing**] to give legal written permission (to do something): *to license a doctor to practice.* Also, *chiefly Brit.,* **li′cence.** —*n-* **li′cens·er** *or* **li′cen·sor.**

li·cen·see (lī′sən sē′) *n-* person who receives a license.

li·cen·tious (lī sĕn′chəs) *adj-* 1 unrestrained by law or morality; lawless; immoral. 2 lewd; dissolute; libertine. —*adv-* **li·cen′tious·ly. n-** **li·cen′tious·ness.**

li·chee (lē′chē) *n-* 1 edible fruit of an Asiatic tree related to the soapberries, having a thin, brittle shell and a single hard seed surrounded by a sweet pulp. 2 the tree itself. Also **litchi.**

life belt *n-* life preserver made like a belt.

life·blood (līf′blŭd′) *n-* 1 blood essential to life. 2 anything essential to life; source of vital strength and energy: *Research is the lifeblood of our society.*

life·boat (līf′bōt′) *n-* boat for saving people at sea.

life buoy *n-* a float, usually a ring filled with light material or air, for keeping a person afloat in the water.

life cycle *n-* the entire series of changes in form and function that an organism undergoes from a specified stage to the same stage in the next generation.

life expectancy *n-* probable number of years of life of an individual, especially as determined statistically in terms of age, sex, environment, etc.

life·guard (līf′gärd′) *n-* expert swimmer trained in rescue work, who looks after the safety of bathers.

life insurance *n-* 1 agreement by which a company insures a person's life in return for certain payments. The company agrees to pay a certain sum of money, at the purchaser's death, to a person he names. 2 amount of money to be received stated in such an agreement.

life jacket *n-* life preserver made like a jacket or vest.

life·less (līf′ləs) *adj-* 1 dead: *a lifeless body.* 2 never having been alive; without life: *a lifeless statue.* 3 without living things: *a lifeless planet.* 4 not lively; dull. —*adv-* **life′less·ly. n-** **life′less·ness.**

life·like (līf′līk′) *adj-* seeming to be or closely imitating a living thing or real life. —*n-* **life′like′ness.**

life·line (līf′līn′) *n-* 1 any rope used for lifesaving, especially one shot by rocket to a ship in distress. 2 line attached to a lifeboat or life buoy for saving life. 3 signal rope used by a diver by which he is lowered or raised from the water. 4 route by which supplies can be sent to a place which cannot otherwise be reached.

life·long (līf′lòng′) *adj-* lasting throughout life.

life net *n-* strong net or sheet of canvas used by firemen to catch persons jumping from high places without injuring them.

life preserver *n-* a ring, belt, or jacket, either inflatable or filled with material that floats, used to keep a person afloat in the water.

life raft *n-* raft, often inflatable, used for saving people at sea.

life·sav·er (līf′sā′vər) *n-* 1 person or thing that saves people from drowning. 2 *Informal* person or thing that saves someone from a serious difficulty.

Life-preserver

like (līk) *vt-* [**liked, lik·ing**] 1 to find agreeable or pleasant; enjoy: *All his classmates* like *him. Do you* like *sports?* 2 to approve of or admire: *I* like *his spirit. vi-* to prefer; choose: *I will go when I* like. *n-* **likes** preferences: *What are your likes and dislikes?* [from Old English **lícian**, "be pleasing to (someone)." Originally **lícian** meant "be like or equal," thus "fitting and proper" and "pleasing."]

-like *suffix* meaning "resembling" or "similar to": *childlike.*

like·li·hood (līk′lē hŏŏd′) *n-* probability; chance.

like·ly (līk′lē) *adj-* [**like·li·er, like·li·est**] 1 reasonably expected (to); apt (to): *He is* likely *to make the All-Star team.* 2 suitable; promising: *a likely place to stop; a likely lad for the job.* 3 probable: *a likely consequence.* 4 hardly believable (used sarcastically): *a likely tale. adv-* probably: *They will* likely *be late.*

►For usage note see LIABLE.

lik·en (līk′kən) *vt-* to say (anything) is like another; compare: *She* likened *me to a cat.* **Hom-** lichen.

like·ness (līk′nəs) *n-* 1 picture; representation; portrait: *That photograph is a good* likeness *of you.* 2 appearance; form: *an enemy in the* likeness *of a friend.* 3 resemblance; similarity: *the* likeness *between the two sisters.*

like·wise (līk′wīz′) *adv-* 1 in the same manner: *Go and do* likewise. 2 also; too: *He is tall and* likewise *strong.*

lik·ing (līk′kĭng) *n-* 1 fondness: *I have a* liking *for books.* 2 taste: *This food is not to my* liking.

li·lac (līk′lək, -lăk′) *n-* 1 shrub with clusters of fragrant white or pinkish-purple blossoms; also, the blossoms of this shrub. 2 the color of its blossom; a light, pinkish purple. *adj-:* *a lilac and orange dress.*

lily pad *n-* one of the large, rounded, floating leaves of the water lily.

lil·y-white (lĭl′ē hwīt′) *adj-* 1 white as a lily. 2 *Informal* excluding, or discriminating against, Negroes.

li·ma bean (lī′mə) *n-* any of several varieties of bean grown for their broad, flat, edible seeds; also, the green or greenish-white seed.

limb (lĭm) *n-* 1 arm or leg of a man or animal or the wing of a bird. 2 one of the main branches of a tree. 3 *Astronomy* the edge of a heavenly body, as seen from earth; also, the earth's edge, as seen from a spacecraft. —*adj-* **limb′less.**

lim·ber (lĭm′bər) *adj-* able to bend and move easily; supple; flexible: *a limber tree branch; a limber body.* *vt-* to make supple or nimble: *Exercise limbers the body.* [from **limb.**] —*n-* **lim′ber·ness.**
limber up to make or become supple and nimble through exercise, etc.: *The dancers limbered up.*

lim·ber (lĭm′bər) *n-* detachable front part of a gun carriage. [apparently from French **limoniere**, meaning literally "belonging to the shafts."]

lim·bo (lĭm′bō) *n-* 1 a place of confinement or oblivion. 2 in some Christian theologies, an abode of the souls of just people born before Christ, and of unbaptized infants.

Lim·burg·er (lĭm′bûr′gər) *n-* a soft, white, and strong-smelling cheese. Also **Limburger cheese, Lim′burg cheese.**

lime (lĭm) *n-* chemical compound of calcium and oxygen, prepared by burning limestone, bones, or shells; calcium oxide (CaO_2). It is used for making cement, for improving acid soil, etc. [from Old English **lim.**]

lime (lĭm) *n-* 1 yellowish-green citrus fruit, somewhat like a lemon. 2 the tree bearing this fruit. 3 a yellowish-green color. *adj-*: *a lime pie; a lime silk.* [from French, from Spanish **lima**, from Persian **līmu(n)**, "lemon."]

lime (lĭm) *n-* linden [from earlier English **line**, from Old English **lind**, meaning "linden."]

lime·kiln (lĭm′kĭl′ *also* -kĭln′) *n-* furnace in which limestone, shells, etc., are burned to obtain lime.

lime·light (lĭm′lĭt′) *n-* 1 brilliant light produced by playing an intensely hot flame upon lime, formerly used as a spotlight in the theater. 2 prominent position before the public; glare of publicity.

lim·er·ick (lĭm′ər ĭk) *n-* humorous poem of five lines. The first, second, and fifth lines rhyme, as do the third and fourth:
There once was an old man of Lyme
Who married three wives at a time.
When asked why a third,
He replied, "One's absurd,
And bigamy, sir, is a crime."

lime·stone (lĭm′stōn′) *n-* rock used for building, road making, etc. It yields lime when burned.

lime·wa·ter (lĭm′wŏt′ər, -wôt′ər) *n-* solution of lime and water, used in medicine.

lim·it (lĭm′ət) *n-* 1 that which confines, ends, or checks: *a speed limit.* 2 point not to be passed; furthest point: *to reach the limit of one's endurance.* 3 (usually **limits**) border or boundary: *the city limits.* 4 maximum or minimum allowed: *a limit of two chances per person.* 5 something nearly intolerable: *That is the limit!* *vt-* to restrict or confine: *to limit the amount of candy one eats.* —*adj-* **lim′it·a·ble:** *his limitable authority.* *n-* **lim′i·ter.** *adj-* **lim′it·less:** *It has limitless possibilities.*
go the limit to go as far, or do as much, as one can.

lim·ou·sine (lĭm′ə zēn′) *n-* large, usually luxurious automobile, especially one in which the driver's seat is separated by a glass partition from the back seat.

limp (lĭmp) *n-* lame, halting walk. *vi-* He limped *off the tennis court.* [possibly from Old English **lemphealt**, meaning "lame."]

limp (lĭmp) *adj-* 1 lacking stiffness, firmness, or strength: *a limp shirt; to be limp with relief.* 2 weak in character. [of uncertain origin.] —*adv-* **limp′ly.** *n-* **limp′ness.**

lim·pet (lĭm′pət) *n-* shellfish with a flat, cone-shaped shell, found clinging tightly to rocks or piling.

lim·pid (lĭm′pĭd′) *adj-* transparent; sparklingly clear: *a limpid pool.* —*adv-* **lim′pid·ly.** *n-* **lim·pid′i·ty** or **lim′pid·ness.**

line (lĭn) *vt-* [**lined, lin·ing**] to cover the inner surface of: *to line curtains; to line a box.* [from earlier **line** meaning "piece of linen cloth; flax," partly from ¹**line** and partly from Old English **lin**, "flax."]

lin·e·age (lĭn′ē ĭj) *n-* line of ancestors; also, all the descendants of one ancestor.

lin·e·al (lĭn′ē əl) *adj-* 1 pertaining to or in the direct descent from an ancestor: *his lineal heirs.* 2 linear. —*adv-* **lin′e·al·ly.**

lin·e·a·ment (lĭn′ē ə mənt) *n-* (usually **lineaments**) outline or feature, especially of the face.

lin·e·ar (lĭn′ē ər) *adj-* 1 consisting of lines: *a linear drawing.* 2 having length only: *a straight line is a linear curve.* 3 along a line: *Light waves exhibit linear motion.* 4 of or having to do with straight-line equations.

linear equation *n-* equation whose graph is a straight line. Example: $3x - 2 = 24$.

linear measure *n-* 1 measurement of length or distance. 2 system of measures for length; also, one such measure: *The mile and the inch are linear measures.*

line·back·er (lĭn′băk′ər) *n-* in football, a defensive player stationed just behind the line of scrimmage.

line drive *n-* in baseball, a batted ball that travels in a nearly straight line, usually not far from the ground.

line graph *n-* graph in which the values represented by points are connected by straight lines.

line·man (lĭn′mən) *n-* [*pl.* **line·men**] 1 man who puts up and repairs telephone or telegraph wires. 2 inspector of railroad tracks. 3 in surveying, person who carries the tape, line, or chain. 4 in football, player, such as a guard or tackle, whose main position is in the line.

lin·en (lĭn′ən) *n-* 1 the thread spun from flax fibers. 2 the strong, loosely .woven cloth made of this thread. 3 **linens** articles once made of linen, but now made of cotton and other materials as well. They include sheets, tablecloths, towels, and sometimes shirts and underwear. *as modifier:* *a linen dress.*

line of fire *n-* course within which gunfire is directed.

line of force or **line of flux** *n-* one of a group of imaginary lines drawn to illustrate the field around a magnet.

line of scrimmage *n-* in football, a line across the field and parallel with the goal lines, established at each point where the ball is placed.

line of sight *n-* 1 line between a person's eye and the object or point at which he is looking. 2 line, unbroken by the horizon, between transmitting and receiving antennas.

lin·er (lī′nər) *n-* 1 large, fast commercial ship belonging to a shipping line. 2 in baseball, a ball hit straight and low; line drive. 3 person who makes lines: *a road liner.* [from ¹**line.**]

lin·er (lī′nər) *n-* 1 person who makes, fits, or attaches linings. 2 lining: *a helmet liner.* [from ²**line.**]

line segment *Mathematics n-* set of points made up of two given points and all the points between them.

lines·man (līnz′mən) *n-* [*pl.* **lines·men**] 1 in football, an official who has charge of marking the progress of the ball in play and the distance to be gained.

line-up or **line·up** (līn′ŭp′) *n-* 1 persons arranged in a line, as for identification: *a police line-up.* 2 in team sports, the arrangement of a team's players before a game or play; also, the players themselves: *Dick is in today's line-up.* 3 *Informal* any grouping.

-ling *suffix* (used to form nouns) 1 one connected or related to: *nurseling; hireling.* 2 small; diminutive (often used contemptuously): *duckling; princeling.*

lin·ger (lĭng′gər) *vi-* 1 to remain long or be reluctant to go; tarry: *They lingered at the beach.* 2 to delay; procrastinate: *to linger over a decision.* —*n-* **lin′ger·er.**

lin·ge·rie (län′jə rā′, län′jə rē′, *French* län zhə rē′) *n-* women's undergarments and sleeping clothes.

lin·go (lĭng′gō) *Informal n-* [*pl.* **lin·goes**] 1 language; dialect, used humorously or contemptuously of an unfamiliar speech. 2 special vocabulary of a profession or other field of interest; jargon: *baseball lingo.*

lin·gua fran·ca (lĭng′gwə frăng′kə) *n-* 1 mixture of Italian, French, Spanish, Greek, and Arabic, spoken in the Mediterranean area.

liquid measure *n-* 1 system of measuring liquids. 2 any unit of such a system: *The pint and the liter are liquid measures.*

liquid oxygen *n-* oxygen liquefied by extremely low temperatures and high pressures, used in steel making, rocket propellants, etc.

liquid state *n-* one of the three physical states of matter in which a substance has a definite volume but not definite shape. A liquid takes the shape of a container with equal or greater volume. See also *gaseous state* and *solid state.*

liq·uor (lĭk′ ər) *n-* 1 any strong alcoholic drink, such as gin, whiskey, or brandy. 2 any liquid, such as broth, syrup, or brine.

li·ra (lēr′ ə) *n-* [*pl.* lī·re (lē′ rā′) or lī·ras] 1 monetary unit of Italy. 2 in Turkey and Syria, a pound.

lisle (līl) *n-* fine, hard-twisted cotton thread, or a fabric knitted from it, used especially for stockings.

lisp (lĭsp) *vi-* to pronounce (s) or (z) incorrectly as (th). A person who lisps would pronounce "sunspot" as "thŭnthpŏt," and "zip" as "thĭp." *vt-: to lisp a poem. n-: She spoke with a lisp.* —*n-* lisp′ er.

lis·some or **lis·som** (lĭs′ əm) *adj-* 1 lithe; supple: *a lissome young girl.* 2 nimble; swift and light in motion. —*adv-* lis′ some·ly.

list (lĭst) *n-* series of names, items, titles, etc.; catalog; roll; register. *vt-* to name or write down, usually in some order: *to list the items one has held.* [from Old French liste meaning "list; border; strip," from an early Germanic lista of the same meaning.]

list (lĭst) *vi-* to tilt or lean to one side in the water: *The ship listed to starboard. n-: The ship developed a bad list.* [special use of ³list in the sense of "inclination to."]

list (lĭst) *Archaic vi-* to please; choose. [from Old English lystan meaning "to be pleasing (to someone); to incline (someone) toward."]

list (lĭst) *n-* 1 edge or selvage of cloth. 2 band of cloth. 3 ridge alongside a plowed furrow. 4 slender strip of wood. *vt-* 1 to cover with strips of cloth. 2 to trim away a strip from the edge of (a board). 3 to plow with a lister. [from Old English lĭst, related to ¹list.]

list (lĭst) *Archaic vi-* to listen. [from Middle English listen, from Old English hlystan, "to hear."]

lis·ten (lĭs′ ən) *vi-* 1 to pay attention in order to hear; make an effort to hear: *to listen carefully for a footfall.* 2 to heed advice or instruction: *You'll never do that job right if you don't listen.* 3 to hear purposely for pleasure, instruction, etc.: *to listen to music.* —*n-* lis′ ten·er.

listen in 1 to tune in a radio station to hear a broadcast. 2 to eavesdrop, as on the telephone.

list·er (lĭs′ tər) *n-* 1 kind of plow that digs furrows for planting seeds. 2 (also **lister planter**) such a plow equipped with attachments for dropping seeds in the furrow and then covering the seeds.

list·less (lĭst′ ləs) *adj-* lacking energy or desire to move or act; indifferent; languid; lethargic: *Hot, humid weather made him listless.* —*adv-* list′ less·ly. *n-* list′ less·ness.

list price *n-* retail price for merchandise as quoted by a store or catalog.

lists (lĭsts) *n- p.* 1 in medieval days, the enclosure or the field in which tournaments were fought by knights in shining armor. 2 any place of contest.

lit (lĭt) *p.t. & p.p.* of ¹light and ³light.

lit·er·al·ly (lĭt′ ər ə lē) *adv-* 1 in a literal manner: *to translate literally; to speak literally.* 2 *Informal* (intensifier only): *I literally broke my back getting the job done.*

lit·er·ar·y (lĭt′ ə rĕr′ ē) *adj-* 1 of or relating to literature or to authors: *a literary masterpiece; literary studies.* 2 especially fit for writing: *a literary talent.*

lit·er·ate (lĭt′ ər ət) *adj-* 1 able to read and write. 2 marked by learning and culture, especially in literature. *n-* person who can read and write. —*adv-* lit′ er·ate·ly.

lit·er·a·ture (lĭt′ ər ə chər, -tyo͝or′) *n-* 1 written works, especially such imaginative works as poems, plays, essays, and stories considered valuable for their style, form, and subject matter. 2 any collection or body of such works from a particular country, period of time, etc.: *American literature; modern literature.* 3 everyday writing.

lit·i·gant (lĭt′ ə gənt) *n-* either party in a lawsuit.

living room *n-* room where a family spends most of its indoor leisure; sitting room.

living wage *n-* wage large enough to support a person and his family with modest comfort and security.

liz·ard (lĭz′ ərd) *n-* reptile usually having a slender body tapering into a long tail, four legs with five-toed feet, a scaly skin, ear holes, and movable eyelids. There are some 2,500 kinds. —*adj-* liz′ ard·like′.

Collared lizard about 1 ft long

ll. lines.

lla·ma (lä′ mə) *n-* South American cud-chewing mammal related to the camel but having no hump. It is often used as a beast of burden, and its long, light-brown or white hair is valued as a fiber for making cloth.

lla·no (lä′ nō) *n-* [*pl.* lla·nos] in Spanish American countries, a treeless, grassy plain.

LL.D. (ĕl′ ĕl′ dē′) Doctor of Laws.

lo (lō) *interj-* look! see! behold!: *and, lo! he was turned into a frog.* *Hom-* low.

load (lōd) *vt-* 1 to put into or upon: *to load a car; to load a donkey.* 2 to put (cargo) into or upon a vehicle, ship, etc.: *to load bananas.* 3 to burden; weigh down; also, to supply lavishly; heap: *to load a man with work; to load a person with gifts.*

Llama 4–5 ft high at shoulder

lob (lŏb) *vt-* [lobbed, lob·bing] to throw, strike, or send (a ball or other object) in a high arc: *to lob a tennis ball.* *vi-: She lobbed into the back court.* *n-* 1 in tennis and other sports, a ball sent in a high arc. 2 in cricket, a ball sent underhand.

lo·bate (lō′ bāt′) *adj-* 1 having lobes. 2 resembling a lobe.

lob·by (lŏb′ ē) *n-* [*pl.* lob·bies] 1 hall, corridor, or room which is an entrance or a waiting room: *a hotel lobby.* 2 person or group that tries to influence members of a legislature for or against a measure. *vt-* [lob·bied, lob·by·ing] to try to influence members of a legislature for or against a measure: *to lobby for a law.*

lob·by·ist (lŏb′ ē ĭst) *n-* person who lobbies.

lobe (lōb) *n-* a rounded, projecting part of something, especially of a leaf or animal organ: *the lobe of the ear.* —*adj-* lobed.

Lobe of leaf   Ear lobe

lo·be·lia (lō bĕl′ yə) *n-* any of several herbaceous plants with red or blue, or occasionally white, flowers.

lob·lol·ly pine (lŏb′ lŏl′ ē) *n-* 1 a pine of southern United States, having coarse bark. 2 the wood of this tree, valued as lumber.

lob·ster (lŏb′ stər) *n-* large sea crustacean with five pairs of legs, the first developed into powerful pincers; also, its flesh, used as food.

lobster pot *n-* cage with a funnel-shaped net inside, used as a trap for catching lobsters.

lo·cal (lō′ kəl) *adj-* 1 having to do with a particular place: *the local news.* 2 limited to a single part of the body: *a local irritation; a local injury.* 3 stopping at all stations: *a local train.* *n-* train, bus, etc., that stops at all stations.

local anesthetic *n-* anesthetic that acts only on the part of the body immediately around the point of application.

Lobster, about 1 ft long

local color *n-* tone or feeling given to writing, news reporting, etc., by describing the appearance of a locality, and the customs, speech, dress, and life of its population.

lo·cale (lō kăl′) *n-* place or setting of some event, development, work, etc.: *The tale's locale is Moose Jaw.*

lo·cal·ism (lō′ kəl ĭz′ əm) *n-* 1 attachment to, or interest in, one's own locality. 2 word, expression, or custom used in a particular region.

lo·cal·i·ty (lō kăl′ ə tē) *n-* [*pl.* **lo·cal·i·ties**] general region, place, or district; neighborhood.

lo·cal·ize (lō′ kə līz′) *vt-* [**lo·cal·ized, lo·cal·iz·ing**] to restrict to a particular place: *to localize an epidemic.* *vi-* to become local: *The pain* localized *after a time.* —*n-* **lo′ cal·i·za′ tion.**

lo·cal·ly (lō′ kə lē) *adv-* with respect to a particular place or region, especially to the place at hand.

local option *n-* power granted to a county, town, etc., to decide whether certain laws shall be carried out.

lo·cate (lō′ kāt′) *vt-* [**lo·cat·ed, lo·cat·ing**] 1 to seek out and fix the position of; find: *to locate a friend's house*; *to locate an oil leak.* 2 to determine the position, site, or limits of and mark: *to locate a gold mine*; *to locate a boundary.* 3 to place or establish in a particular spot; station: *He* located *his store on a busy corner.* *vi-* to settle: *The family* located *in Arizona finally.*

be located to have a special location or situation.

lo·ca·tion (lō kā′ shən) *n-* 1 a locating or being located: *the location of a missing person.* 2 position or place: *The bank is in a central location.* 3 piece of land marked out for a particular use; site: *a good location for a new school.* 4 place, outside a studio, where a motion picture is filmed.

loch (lŏкн) *Scottish n-* lake.

lock (lŏk) *n-* 1 any device for fastening a door, window, lid, drawer, or the like, especially one operated by a key. 2 section of a canal or other waterway, with watertight gates at each end, for raising or lowering boats to another water level. 3 firing mechanism of a gun. *vt-* 1 to fasten or secure with, or as if with, a device: *to lock a safe.* 2 to shut up or in; confine or secure: *to lock in a criminal*; *to lock papers in a drawer.* 3 to make fast or rigid by the linking or jamming of parts: *to lock the wheels of a car*; *to lock the gears*; *to lock together pieces of a picture puzzle.* *vi-* 1 to become fastened by a device: *The door* locks *automatically.* 2 to become securely joined or linked; also, to jam: *The wheels* locked. [from Old English *loc*, "a fastening; bolt; bar; lock."]

Locks in the Panama Canal

lock, stock, and barrel in its entirety; completely.

under lock and key put securely away as in a safe.

lock on to the guidance systems of rockets, torpedoes, etc., to detect and remain fixed on a target, by means of radio, heat, or sound waves.

lock out 1 to keep out by fastening a door on the inside. 2 to prevent (employees) from entering their place of work except on the employer's terms.

lock (lŏk) *n-* 1 portion of hair that hangs together; tress or curl. 2 **locks** all the hair of the head. [from Old English *locc*, of the same meaning.]

lock·er (lŏk′ ər) *n-* 1 drawer, chest, small trunk, or compartment with a lock; especially, one of a number of cupboards for individual use in a public building such as a gymnasium. 2 in a ship, a compartment or chest for clothes, ammunition, etc.

lodg·er (lŏj′ ər) *n-* person who rents one or more rooms in another person's house.

lodg·ing (lŏj′ ĭng) *n-* 1 temporary place to live or to sleep. 2 **lodgings** room or rooms rented to live in.

lodg·ment or **lodge·ment** (lŏj′ mənt) *n-* 1 a lodging or being lodged; also, an instance of this: *the lodgment of a complaint*; *the lodgment of a bone in the throat.* 2 firm or safe place for something. 3 something deposited or accumulated: *a lodgment of grime.*

loess (lŭs) *n-* yellowish, fine-grained sediment forming deposits in many places throughout the world. It is thought to be eroded soil that is carried by the wind.

loft (lŏft, lôft) *n-* 1 attic; garret. 2 storage place just below the roof of a barn; hayloft. 3 gallery; balcony: *a choir loft.* 4 upper floor in a warehouse, factory building, etc. 5 large open floor used to lay out full-scale plans, such as those for boats or sails.

loft·y (lŏf′ tē, lôf′-) *adj-* [**loft·i·er, loft·i·est**] 1 very high: *the lofty mountain peaks.* 2 noble and dignified; elevated: *his lofty ambitions.* 3 proud; haughty: *a lofty manner.* —*adv-* **loft′ i·ly.** *n-* **loft′ i·ness.**

log (lŏg, lôg) *n-* 1 length of wood cut from the trunk or a branch of a felled tree. 2 any of various devices for measuring the speed of a ship; especially, the **patent log,** which records the rotations of a small propeller towed on a long line behind the ship. 3 (also **log′ book**′) book in which a regular and frequent record of operation is kept in a ship, airplane, radio station, etc. *vt-* [**logged, log·ging**] 1 to fell and remove timber from (land); lumber. 2 to enter (facts) in the record book of a ship, airplane, etc. 3 to cover (a certain distance) in a ship or airplane: *They* logged *90 miles the second day.* 4 to travel at (a certain speed): *to log five knots for six hours.* *vi-* to cut and remove timber.

lo·gan·ber·ry (lō′ gən bĕr′ ē) *n-* [*pl.* **lo·gan·ber·ries**] 1 large, dark-red berry of a plant that is a cross between the raspberry and the blackberry. 2 the plant itself.

log·a·rithm (lŏg′ ə rĭth′ əm, lôg′-) *Mathematics n-* of a given number, another number that indicates the power to which a fixed number called the base must be raised in order to obtain the given number. If the base is 10, the logarithm of 1000 is 3, since $10^3 = 1000$.

loge (lōzh) *n-* box or f... nt of the mezzanine in a theater.

log·ger (lŏg′ ər, lôg′-) *n-* 1 person whose work is logging; lumberjack. 2 machine for handling logs.

log·ger·head (lŏg′ ər hĕd′, lôg′-) *n-* large sea turtle.

at loggerheads unable to agree; at odds.

log·ging (lŏg′ ĭng, lôg′-) *n-* the work or business of cutting trees, sawing the trunks and branches into logs, and moving the logs to a sawmill.

log·ic (lŏj′ ĭk) *n-* 1 sound reasoning; clear thinking: *Be guided by logic, not by feelings.* 2 way or method of reasoning: *His logic is faulty.* 3 branch of philosophy that deals with reasoning; science of reason. 4 system or method of reasoning: *Aristotle's logic; deductive logic.*

log·i·cal (lŏj′ ĭ kəl) *adj-* 1 in agreement with sound reasoning; sensible: *It is logical to look for a fire if you smell smoke.* 2 of or related to the science or study of logic. —*adv-* **log′ i·cal·ly.**

lo·gi·cian (lə jĭsh′ ən) *n-* person skilled in logic; especially, a philosopher who specializes in logic.

lo·gis·tics (lə jĭs′ tĭks) *n-* (takes singular verb) the movement, supply, and maintenance of troops and military equipment.

log·jam (lŏg′ jăm′, lôg′-) *n-* tangled mass of floating logs that have blocked up a river.

loin (loin) *n-* 1 the lower part of the back of the body between the ribs and the hip bones. 2 cut of meat from this part of an animal.

loi·ter (loi′ tər) *vi-* 1 to go slowly and stop frequently on the way; linger: *Don't loiter on your way home from school.* 2 to sit or stand idly; spend time idly; loaf: *No loitering is allowed in the courthouse.* —*n-* **loi′ ter·er.**

loll (lŏl) *vi-* 1 to sit, lie, or stand in a lazy, very relaxed way: *He was so tired that he just* lolled *on the sofa.* 2 to hang or droop loosely: *The sick dog lay with his tongue* lolling *out of his mouth.*

lol·li·pop (lŏl′ ē pŏp′) *n-* hard sugar candy on the end of a small stick; sucker. Also **lol′ ly·pop′.**

lone (lōn) *adj-* 1 alone; isolated; solitary: *one lone tree.* 2 single; sole; only: *the lone survivor.* *Hom-* loan.

lone·ly (lōn′ lē) *adj-* [**lone·li·er, lone·li·est**] 1 unhappy from lack of companionship: *He was lonely on his first long trip by himself.* 2 remote; isolated; seldom visited: *a lonely mountain village.* —*n-* **lone′ li·ness.**

lone·some (lōn′ səm) *adj-* 1 sad because alone; lonely: *a lonesome widow.* 2 not often visited; desolate: *a lonesome road.* —*adv-* **lone′ some·ly.** *n-* **lone′ some·ness.**

long (lŏng) *adj-* [**long·er, long·est**] 1 great or greater than usual in distance or time from beginning to end; not short or brief: *Get a long string for the kite.*

lon·gev·i·ty (lŏn jĕv′ ə tē) *n-* very long life.

long face *n-* sad or disappointed facial expression.

long·hand (lông′ hănd′) *n-* ordinary handwriting: *We sign our names in* longhand. See also *shorthand*.

long·horn (lông′ hôrn′, -hŏrn′) *n-* breed of cattle with long horns, formerly common in Mexico and south-western United States.

long·ing (lông′ ĭng) *n-* strong desire: *a* longing *for candy.* *adj-*: *The children cast* longing *looks at the cake.* —*adv-* **long′ing·ly.**

lon·gi·tude (lŏn′ jə tōōd′, lŏn′-, -tyōōd′) *n-* distance east or west of the prime meridian, measured in de-grees, and represented on maps and globes by great circles that run between the North and South Poles.

lon·gi·tu·di·nal (lŏn′ jə tōō′ də nəl, lŏn′-, -tyōō′ də nəl) *adj-* 1 of or having to do with length or longitude.
2 running lengthwise: *The planks of a boat are* longi-tudinal. —*adv-* **lon·gi·tu′di·nal·ly.**

long-lived (lông′ līvd′, -lĭvd′) *adj-* living or existing a long time: *a* long-lived *tree.*

long-play·ing (lông′ plā′ ĭng) *adj-* of phonograph records, made to be played at 33⅓ revolutions per minute.

long-range (lông′ rānj′) *adj-* 1 designed to cover a long distance: *a* long-range *missile.* 2 covering a long period of time in the future: *He has made* long-range *plans.*

long·shore·man (lông′ shôr′ mən) *n-* [*pl.* **long·shore·men**] man who is employed to load and unload ships at a seaport; stevedore.

long shot *Informal n-* something that has only a small chance of turning out well; anything that has heavy odds against it: *That bet is a* long shot.
by a long shot *Informal* by very much; by a great deal: *He missed* by a long shot. **not by a long shot** *Informal* emphatically not; certainly not.

long-stand·ing (lông′ stăn′ dĭng) *adj-* happening or lasting for a long time: *a* long-standing *dispute.*

long-suf·fer·ing (lông′ sŭf′ ər ĭng) *adj-* patiently bear-ing injury, insult, etc., for a long time: *a* long-suffering *victim of practical jokes.*

long suit *n-* 1 in card games, the suit in which a player holds the most cards. 2 something in which one is strongest; strong point; forte.

long ton *n-* gross ton.

long-wind·ed (lông′ wĭn′ dəd) *adj-* 1 long and tiresome; tedious: *a* long-winded *lecture.* 2 capable of continued exertion without becoming short of breath: *a* long-winded *runner.* 3 capable of holding the breath for a long time: *a* long-winded *diver.* —*adv-* **long′-wind′ ed·ly.** *n-* **long′-wind′ ed·ness.**

look (lŏŏk) *vi-* 1 to direct the eyes: *Please* look *at the blackboard.* 2 to search: *I've been* looking *everywhere for you.* 3 to appear; seem: *She* looks *happy.* 4 to face: *My window* looks *out on the road.* 5 *Informal* to expect: *I* look *to hear from you soon.* *vt-* 1 to appear to be or to fit: *He* looks *his age. She* looks *the part.* 2 *Informal* to pay attention to; watch: *You should* look *what you're doing.* *n-* 1 glance: *Take a* look *at this.*
look to 1 to see to; be sure of: *You must* look to *it that you are on time.* 2 to count on: *I* look to *him for help.*
look up to search for; try to find: *We'll* look up *the time of the show in the newspaper.*
look up to to respect highly.

look·er-on (lŏŏk′ ər ŏn′, -ŏn′) *n-* [*pl.* **look·ers-on**] person who watches or looks on; onlooker.

looking glass *n-* mirror.

look·out (lŏŏk′ out′) *n-* 1 person who watches to guard against attack or to see what is happening: *The bandits posted a* lookout *on the hill.* 2 careful watch: *Keep a good* lookout *and let me know when you see the train coming.* 3 place from which to watch or look out.
4 *Informal* care; concern; business: *If he gets into trouble, it's his* lookout, *not mine.*

loop (lōōp) *n-* 1 the shape of a noose, tied, or fastened in this shape: *a button* loop. 2 anything bent, or curve in a stream, road, etc., suggesting this shape. 4 airplane stunt of flying a vertical circle. *vt-:* *to* loop *a thread; to* loop *an airplane.* *vi-:* *The airplane* looped *high in the air. The road* loops *near the monument.*

loop·hole (lōōp′ hōl′) *n-* 1 small opening in the wall of a fortifica-tion through which a gun may be fired. 2 omission or lack of clear-ness in a law, contract, etc., which permits it to be broken or gotten around; basis for an evasion.

Decorative loops on a uniform

loose (lōōs) *adj-* [**loos·er**, **loos·est**]
1 not firmly fixed, tied or bound: *a* loose *board;* loose *papers in a box.* 2 not tied up; not confined; free: *The dog got* loose *and ran away.* 3 not tightly or closely packed; not compact: *a* loose *weave; the* loose *sand.* 4 not tight or close-fitting:

Loophole

a loose *collar.* 5 not sufficiently controlled: *his* loose *talk;* loose *conduct.* 6 not exact or strict: *A* loose *count showed there were more than 50 people.* *vt-* [**loosed, loos·ing**] 1 to set free; release: *to* loose *one from any obligation.* 2 to make less tight; relax; loosen: *to* loose *one's grip.* 3 to untie; unfasten: *to* loose *one's hair.* 4 to shoot: *to* loose *an arrow.* —*adv-* **loose′ ly.** *n-* **loose′ ness.**
break loose to get away or escape suddenly: *He broke* loose *from his captors.* **cut loose 1** to disconnect or separate; unfasten. 2 *Informal* to have fun in a wild, uncontrolled manner; go on a spree. **let** (or **set** or **turn**) **loose** to free; release. **on the loose** not confined or restrained; free.

loose end *n-* something that remains to be taken care of; unfinished or undecided matter. Also **loose thread.**
at loose ends confused or uncertain; unsettled.

loose-joint·ed (lōōs′ join′ təd) *adj-* 1 having loose joints. 2 having free and easy movements; limber: *a* loose-jointed *runner.* —*adv-* **loose′-joint′ ed·ly.** *n-* **loose′-joint′ ed·ness.**

loose-leaf (lōōs′ lēf′) *adj-* having, or designed to have, pages that can be easily inserted or taken out.

loos·en (lōō′ sən) *vt-* 1 to make loose or less tight: *to* loosen *a screw;* loosen *one's belt.* 2 to unfasten; undo: *Just* loosen *the halter and let the horse graze.* 3 to make less dense or compact: *One should* loosen *the soil before planting.* *vi-: The jar lid may* loosen *if you heat it.*

loot (lōōt) *n-* things stolen or taken by force; plunder; booty: *The pirates buried their* loot *on an island.* *vt-* to rob by force; plunder: *The outlaws attacked and* looted *the train.* *vi-: The thief* looted *as he went.* **Hom-** lute.

lop (lŏp) *vt-* [**lopped, lop·ping**] to cut; chop (often followed by "off" or "from"): *to* lop *the branches from a tree; to* lop *off a large piece.* [from Old English **loppede** meaning "cut off."]

lop (lŏp) *vi-* [**lopped, lop·ping**] to hang limply; flop. [probably a form of ¹**lap.**]

lope (lōp) *n-* easy swinging stride or gait; slow canter: *The horse went into a* lope. *vi-* [**loped, lop·ing**] to move with such a stride or gait: *We* loped *through the forest. We* loped *after the ball.* *vt-: to* lope *one's horse.*

lop-eared (lŏp′ ērd′) *adj-* having ears that droop.

lop·sid·ed (lŏp′ sīd′ əd) *adj-* having one side lower than the other; heavier or larger on one side than on the other. —*adv-* **lop′ sid′ ed·ly.** *n-* **lop′ sid′ ed·ness.**

Lord's Prayer *n-* prayer taught by Christ, beginning with the words "Our Father"; Paternoster.

Lord's Supper *n-* 1 the Last Supper. 2 the Eucharist; Holy Communion.

lore (lôr) *n-* 1 traditions, legends, tales, etc., of or about a special group: *Indian* lore; *Gypsy* lore. 2 learning or knowledge about a special subject: *bird* lore.

lor·gnette (lôr nyĕt′, lôr-) *n-* 1 eyeglasses fastened to a long handle. 2 long-handled opera glasses.

lot (lŏt) *n-* 1 piece or plot of ground: *an empty lot.* 2 *Informal* great deal; quite a bit: *We have a lot of work to do.* 3 group of things taken together: *A new lot of shoes just arrived in the store.* 4 piece, of wood, straw, etc., used to decide something by chance: *We will draw lots for the prize.* 5 use of this method to decide something by chance: *The class chose their representative by lot.* 6 luck; fate: *Poverty is his lot.*

cast (or throw) in (one's) lot with to join and share the good or bad fortunes of.

▶Either LOT or LOTS may be used in conversation. *He has lots (a lot) of money.* In writing, a more specific phrase is usually desirable. *He has a half million dollars.*

loth (lŏth) loath.

lo·tion (lŏ′ shən) *n-* liquid preparation used to soothe, treat, or beautify the skin.

lots (lŏts) *adv-* considerably: *He is lots better.*

lot·ter·y (lŏt′ ə rē) *n-* [*pl.* lot·ter·ies] scheme of distributing prizes in which people buy numbered tickets, the winning ticket or tickets being selected by lot.

lo·tus (lŏ′ təs) *n-* 1 plant related to the water lily, found in Egypt and India. The lotus is a sacred and symbolic flower in the Buddhist and Hindu religions. 2 plant of the pea family, with red, pink, or white flowers. 3 in Greek legend, a fruit supposed to cause a dreamy languor in those who ate it.

Indian lotus

loud (loud) *adj-* [loud·er, loud·est] 1 having a strong and powerful sound: *a loud voice; a loud knocking.* 2 noisy: *a loud party.* 3 too bright; too colorful; gaudy: *a loud necktie. adv-: He spoke loud and clear.* —*adv-* loud′ ly. *n-* loud′ ness.

loud·speak·er (loud′ spē′ kər) *n-* part of a radio, phonograph, television set, etc., which changes electrical signals into sound waves.

lou·is d'or (lōō′ ē dôr′, -dôr′) *n-* French coin used in the 17th and 18th centuries. Also **lou′ is.**

Louisiana French *n-* French spoken in Louisiana since the seventeenth century and including words borrowed from the Spanish and Indian languages.

Louisiana Purchase *n-* French territory in the New World, extending from the Mississippi to the Rocky Mountains, and from Canada to the Gulf of Mexico, which the United States bought in 1803.

lounge (lounj) *vi-* [lounged, loung·ing] to move, act, or rest in a relaxed, lazy manner. *n-* 1 comfortable room to relax in; especially, a room for eating, drinking, or smoking in a hotel, on a train, etc.: *He watched TV in the airport lounge.* 2 couch or sofa. —*n-* loung′ er.

lour (lou′ ər) [2]lower.

Body louse

louse (lous) *n-* [*pl.* lice (līs)] 1 small, wingless insect that lives in the hair and on the bodies of men and animals. 2 insect that sucks the sap of plants; aphid. 3 *Slang* [*pl.* lous·es] mean, contemptible person.

lous·y (lou′ zē) *adj-* [lous·i·er, lous·i·est] 1 infested with lice. 2 *Slang* mean or worthless. —*n-* lous′ i·ness.

love (lŭv) *n-* 1 strong feeling of affection for another: *a mother's love; the love between husband and wife; love for a friend.* 2 strong liking for something; fondness: *a love for music.* 3 sweetheart; someone dear: *She is my love.* 4 in tennis, no score. 5 Love Cupid; Eros. *vt-* [loved, lov·ing] 1 to have a deep affection for. 2 to have a fondness for: *I love going to a baseball game. vi-* to feel deep affection: *He loves with all his heart.*

fall in love to begin to feel love for a person or thing. for the love of for the sake of. in love having or experiencing the feeling of love, especially for one of the opposite sex. make love to kiss, hug, etc., as lovers do.

love affair *n-* romantic attachment or union, especially between a man and woman not married to each other.

love apple *Archaic n-* tomato.

love·bird (lŭv′ bûrd′) *n-* 1 small parrot that appears to show great affection for its mate. Lovebirds are often kept as cage birds. 2 lovebirds very affectionate couple.

low (lō) *vi-* to make the sound that a cow makes; moo. *n-: He heard the low of a hungry cow.* [from Old English hlōwan meaning "bellow."] Hom- lo.

low·boy (lō′ boi′) *n-* low chest of drawers on legs.

low·bred (lō′ brĕd′) *adj-* 1 crude and vulgar in behavior; ill-bred. 2 coming from parents or ancestors in the lower ranks of society.

low·brow (lō′ brou′) *Informal n-* person who lacks culture or refinement; uncultivated person. *adj-: one's lowbrow taste in art.*

Low Church *n-* group in the Anglican Communion that emphasizes evangelical principles and favors simple ceremony. *adj-* (Low-Church): *a Low-Church service.* See also *High Church.* —*n-* Low′ -Church′ man.

low-down (lō′ doun′) *Slang n-* the truth; especially, facts that are not known to most people.

low-down (lō′ doun′) *Informal adj-* low and mean; contemptible: *He's a low-down, dirty rat.*

low·er (lō′ ər) *compar.* of [1]low. *vt-* 1 to make less; reduce: *to lower the price of milk.* 2 to make less loud: *Please lower your voice.* 3 to reduce the height or level of: *to lower the water in a canal.* [from [1]low.]

low·er (lou′ ər) *vi-* 1 to look sullen; scowl; frown. 2 to appear gloomy and threatening: *The sky lowered in the east. n-* scowl; frown. Also **lour.** [from Middle English louren, luren, from early Dutch lüren, "leer; frown."]

low·er·case (lō′ ər kās′) *n-* in printing, the small letters as distinct from the capital letters. —*adj-: a lowercase letter.*

low·er·most (lō′ ər mōst′) *adj-* lowest.

lowest terms *n-* of fractions, the form in which the numerator and the denominator have no common factor other than 1.

low frequency *n-* any radio frequency from 30 to 300 kilocycles, used to send radio and television signals. *adj-* (low-frequency): *a low-frequency receiver.*

low-keyed (lō′ kēd′) or **low-key** (lō′ kē′) *adj-* restrained; subdued: *a low-keyed novel.*

low·land (lō′ lənd) *n-* low, level country.

low·land·er (lō′ lən dər, lō′ lăn′-) *n-* person who was born or lives in a lowland.

low·ly (lō′ lē) *adj-* [low·li·er, low·li·est] low in rank, position, standard, etc.; humble: *The king was kind even to his lowly servants.* —*n-* low′ li·ness.

low-mind·ed (lō′ mīn′ dəd) *adj-* having low and vulgar feelings, thoughts, etc.; coarse. —*adv-* low′-mind′ ed·ly. *n-* low′-mind′ ed·ness.

low-pitched (lō′ pĭcht′) *adj-* 1 having a low tone or range of tone. 2 slightly sloped: *a low-pitched roof.*

low-pressure (lō′ prĕsh′ ər) *adj-* 1 having or operating at the lower range of efficient pressure: *a low-pressure boiler.* 2 of atmospheric pressure, having a barometric reading lower than that of surrounding areas or lower than the average: *a low-pressure area.* 3 *Informal* easy and casual; not insistent: *a low-pressure salesman.*

low-spir·it·ed (lō′ spĭr′ ə təd) *adj-* sad and melancholy; downhearted. —*adv-* low′-spir′ it·ed·ly. *n-* low′-spir′ it·ed·ness.

low tide *n-* the tide at its lowest point at a particular place, occurring twice a day; also, the time at which this low point is reached.

lu·bri·ca·tor (lōō′ brə kā′ tər) *n-* 1 person or device that applies a lubricant. 2 a lubricant.

lu·cent (lōō′ sənt) *adj-* 1 shining; luminous. 2 transparent.

lu·cerne (lōō sûrn′, *also* lōō′ sərn) *chiefly Brit. n-* alfalfa.

lu·cid (lōō′ sĭd) *adj-* 1 clear; easy to understand: *a lucid explanation.* 2 sane; mentally sound: *An insane person often has lucid moments.* 3 bright or transparent: *the lucid lake.* —*adv-* lu′ cid·ly. *n-* lu′ cid·ness.

lu·cid·i·ty (lōō sĭd′ ə tē) *n-* clarity; also, ease of understanding: *I like the lucidity of his writing.*

Lu·ci·fer (lōō′ sə fər) *n-* 1 rebellious archangel who was cast out of heaven. He is identified with Satan. 2 the planet Venus as morning star.

luck (lŭk) *n-* 1 fortune; chance: *That's his hard luck.* 2 good fortune: *My luck seems to have run out.*

down on (one's) luck having bad luck; unlucky. in luck lucky; fortunate. out of luck unlucky.

lug (lŭg) *vt-* [**lug·ged, lug·ging**] to carry or drag by putting forth great effort: *He lugged the television set into the room.* [from Old Norse *lugga*, "to pull by the hair."]

lug (lŭg) *n-* 1 something that sticks out more or less like an ear and is used as a handle or support. 2 *Informal* stupid fellow; lout; blockhead. [from an early English word perhaps related to Old Norse *lugg* meaning "forelock; hair of the head."]

lug·gage (lŭg′ ĭj) *n-* bags, suitcases, trunks, and boxes a person takes on a trip; baggage.

lug·ger (lŭg′ ər) *n-* sailboat with one or more lugsails.

lug·sail (lŭg′ sāl′, -səl) *n-* four-sided sail that is tied to a spar crossing the mast at an angle, and has no boom.

Lugger with lugsails

lu·gu·bri·ous (lə gōō′ brē əs) *adj-* mournful or sad in an affected or exaggerated manner; woeful. —*adv-* lu·gu′bri·ous·ly. *n-* lu·gu′bri·ous·ness.

lug·worm (lŭg′ wûrm′) *n-* any of various segmented worms found in sandy seashores and used for bait.

Luke (lōōk) *n-* disciple of Christ, physician and companion of St. Paul, reputed to be the author of the third Gospel and of the Acts of the Apostles in the New Testament. Also **St. Luke**.

luke·warm (lōōk′ wôrm′) *adj-* 1 fairly warm; not hot or cold; tepid: *a lukewarm bath.* 2 showing no enthusiasm; indifferent: *the lukewarm applause.* —*adv-* luke′ warm′ ly. *n-* luke′ warm′ ness.

lull (lŭl) *vt-* to quiet; calm: *The sound of the waves lulled me to sleep. n-* a quiet period; a temporary lessening of noise, activity, etc: *a lull in a storm; a lull in the talk.*

lul·la·by (lŭl′ ə bī′) *n-* [*pl.* **lul·la·bies**] song to lull a baby to sleep.

lum·ba·go (lŭm bā′ gō) *n-* pain in the lower part of the back, caused by injury, disease, etc.

lum·bar (lŭm′ bər, -bär′) *adj-* of or having to do with the back and sides of the body between the ribs and hips. *Hom-* lumber.

lum·ber (lŭm′ bər) *n-* wood that has been cut into planks, boards, shingles, etc.: *I need some lumber to build a shelf. vt-* to cut down the trees of (an area) and saw them into planks, boards, etc.: *My grandfather lumbered that mountainside. vi-* to cut down and saw trees as a business or occupation. [from earlier **lumber-room** meaning "room for storing furniture, etc."] *Hom-* lumbar.

lum·ber (lŭm′ bər) *vi-* to move in a clumsy, heavy way: *The bear lumbered up to our car.* [from Middle English *lomeren,* from Old Norse *hlymar* meaning "a loud noise; rumbling."] *Hom-* lumbar. —*adv-* lum′ ber·ing·ly.

lum·ber·ing (lŭm′ bər ĭng) *n-* business or occupation of cutting down trees, sawing them into lumber, etc.

lum·ber·jack (lŭm′ bər jăk′) *n-* man who cuts down trees for lumber and moves them to a sawmill; logger.

lum·ber·man (lŭm′ bər mən) *n-* [*pl.* **lum·ber·men**] 1 man who cuts trees and prepares and ships lumber. 2 man who buys and sells lumber.

lum·ber·yard (lŭm′ bər yärd′) *n-* place where lumber is stored and sold.

lu·men (lōō′ mən) *n-* 1 space or inside diameter of any tubular body structure, including an artery, vein, etc.

lu·na·cy (lōō′ nə sē) *n-* [*pl.* **lu·na·cies**] 1 mental illness; madness. 2 wild, extreme folly or foolhardiness: *That stunt was pure lunacy.*

lu·na moth (lōō′ nə) *n-* North American moth that has a whitish body and light-green wings which may have a spread of 3½ inches.

lu·nar (lōō′ nər) *adj-* of or relating to the moon: *a lunar landscape.*

lunar eclipse *n-* the partial or total obstruction of the moon's reflected light when the moon passes through the earth's shadow. For picture, see *eclipse.*

Luna moth

lunar month *n-* the 28 days from one new moon to the next new moon.

lung (lŭng) *n-* either of two spongelike organs in the chest of man and other air-breathing animals, used for breathing.

lunge (lŭnj) *n-* [**lunged, lunging**] sudden forward movement; jump or leap forward, usually in order to strike or seize. *vi-* to make such a movement.

BRONCHUS

TRACHEA

lung·fish (lŭng′ fĭsh′) *n-* [*pl.* **lung·fish; lung·fishes** (kinds of lungfish)] any of a group of fishes with gills plus an air bladder used like a lung. It can breathe in the air as well as in the water.

Lungs

lu·pine (lōō′ pən) *n-* 1 any of various garden plants related to the peas, with blue, white, or purple flowers; also, the flower of this plant. 2 the edible seeds of the white lupine. [from French *lupin,* from Latin *lupinum* or *lupinus,* ultimately of same origin as ²lupine.]

lu·pine (lōō′ pĭn′) *adj-* 1 of or relating to a wolf. 2 ravenous; fierce. [from Latin *lupinus,* "wolflike," from *lupus,* "wolf."]

lurch (lûrch) *n-* a sudden leaning or swaying motion to one side: *The bus gave a lurch as one wheel went into a ditch. vi-* to make a lurch or lurches; stagger or sway: *As the boat pitched, the passengers lurched against the rail.* [apparently from the sense of "stoop" of a dialectal variant of **lurk**.]

lurch (lûrch) **in the lurch** in a difficult or embarrassing situation. [from earlier French *lourche,* the name of a table game and a move in that game.]

lure (lŏŏr, lyŏŏr) *vt-* [**lured, lur·ing**] to attract or draw by promising profit or pleasure; tempt with promises; entice: *The sound of the circus parade lured the children away from their studies. n-* 1 thing that attracts by offering pleasure or profit; attraction; allurement: *Gold was the lure that started a rush to California in 1849.* 2 artificial minnow, piece of shiny metal, or other device used to attract and catch fish. —*n-* lur′ er.

lu·rid (lŏŏr′ ĭd, lyŏŏr′-) *adj-* 1 sensational; striking or shocking: *the lurid career of a criminal.* 2 glaring in color; gaudy: *The lurid posters attracted attention.* 3 shining with a fiery glow: *a lurid shape seen through the smoke.* —*adv-* lu′ rid·ly. *n-* lur′ rid·ness.

lurk (lûrk) *vi-* 1 to hide or remain secretly in or near a place: *The burglar lurked in the bushes until the watchman had passed.* 2 to sneak or slink; move furtively: *I saw a man lurking around the building.* —*n-* lurk′ er.

lus·cious (lŭsh′ əs) *adj-* 1 very pleasant and sweet to taste or smell; delicious: *a luscious ripe peach.* 2 pleasing to any of the senses: *the luscious music.* —*adv-* lus′ cious·ly. *n-* lus′ cious·ness.

lush (lŭsh) *adj-* 1 juicy and luxuriant in growth: *the lush grass.* 2 covered with rich growth: *a lush meadow. n-* *Slang* an alcoholic. —*adv-* lush′ ly. *n-* lush′ ness.

lust (lŭst) *n-* 1 intense sexual desire. 2 very strong craving or desire: *a lust for power; a lust for gold. vi-* 1 to have intense sexual desire. 2 to have a very strong craving or desire: *The dictator lusted for conquest.*

lus·ter or **lus·tre** (lŭs′ tər) *n-* 1 a shine or brilliance of a surface that reflects light; gloss: *New cars have a high luster.* 2 brightness; radiance: *Tinsel and colorful balls gave luster to the Christmas tree.* 3 glory; splendor: *The runner's victory added new luster to his fame.* 4 In ceramics, an iridescent, glossy, metallic glaze.

lus·ter·ware (lŭs′ tər wâr′) *n-* pottery having a lustrous, iridescent glaze.

lust·ful (lŭst′ fəl) *adj-* driven by, or full of, lust. —*adv-* lust′ ful·ly. *n-* lust′ ful·ness.

lus·trous (lŭs′ trəs) *adj-* shiny; glossy; gleaming: *a lustrous silk gown.* —*adv-* lus′ trous·ly.

lust·y (lŭs′ tē) *adj-* [**lust·i·er, lust·i·est**] strong and healthy; vigorous: *a lusty boxer; a lusty shout.*

lu·te·ti·um or **lu·te·ci·um** (lōō tē′ shē əm) *n-* metallic rare-earth element. Symbol Lu, At. No. 71, At. Wt. 174.97.

Lu·ther·an (lōō′ thər ən) *adj-* of or relating to Martin

Luther or to the church he founded. **n-** member of a Protestant church adhering to Luther's doctrines and principles.

Lu·ther·an·ism (lōō′ thər ə niz′ əm) **n-** the religious doctrines and system of worship of the Lutherans.

lux·u·ri·ance (lug zhŏŏr′ ē əns, lŭk shŏŏr′-) **n-** richness and abundance, especially in growth.

lux·u·ri·ant (lŭg zhŏŏr′ ē ənt, lŭk shŏŏr′-) **adj-** abundant, rich, or vigorous in growth: *the luxuriant vegetation of the tropics.* —**adv- lux·u′ ri·ant·ly.**

▶Should not be confused with LUXURIOUS.

lux·u·ri·ate (lŭg zhŏŏr′ ē āt′, lŭk shŏŏr′-) **vi-** 1 to enjoy or express oneself indulgently, especially in feeling or circumstance: *to luxuriate in grief; to luxuriate in a bubble bath.* 2 to grow richly and abundantly.

lux·u·ri·ous (lŭg zhŏŏr′ ē əs, lŭk shŏŏr′-) **adj-** marked by or providing luxury: *the luxurious new theater.* —**adv- lux·u′ ri·ous·ly. n- lux·u′ ri·ous·ness.**

▶Should not be confused with LUXURIANT.

lux·u·ry (lŭg′ zhə rē, lŭk′ shə-) **n-** [*pl.* **lux·u·ries**] 1 something that is not necessary for life but can make it more enjoyable or comfortable. Luxuries are often things that are expensive or difficult to get. 2 way or condition of life in which a person enjoys great comfort and many fine things: *Most Americans live in luxury compared to people of very poor countries.* 3 great comfort or pleasure: *the luxury of a soft easy chair.*

-ly *suffix* (forming adjectives) 1 like; having the nature of; characteristic of: *brotherly; soldierly.* 2 happening at particular intervals: *weekly; daily; hourly.* [from Old English -lic.]

-ly *suffix* (forming adverbs) 1 in a given manner: *weakly; quietly.* 2 at every (particular interval): *weekly; hourly.* [from Old English -lice, from -lic, ¹-ly.]

ly·ce·um (lī sē′ əm) **n-** 1 an association for literary study, popular lectures, debate, etc. 2 building where it meets.

ly·co·po·di·um (lī′ kə pō′ dē əm) **n-** 1 one of the two groups of club mosses, often used in Christmas decorations. 2 a fine, yellow, flammable powder, consisting of the spores of one club moss, which is used in the making of pills and fireworks.

lye (lī) **n-** 1 sodium hydroxide. 2 formerly, a strong alkali obtained by soaking wood ashes and used in soap making. *Hom-* lie.

ly·ing (lī′ ing) *pres. p.* of ¹lie.

ly·ing (lī′ ing) *pres. p.* of ²lie.

lymph (lĭmf) **n-** the usually clear, yellowish fluid that circulates in the lymph vessels (lymphatics), contains lymphocytes, and bathes all the body cells.

lym·phat·ic (lĭm făt′ ĭk) **adj-** 1 of or having to do with lymph, lymph vessels, or lymph nodes. 2 lacking energy; sluggish; indifferent. **n-** thin-walled vessel transporting lymph.

lymph node or **lymph gland** **n-** one of the many, bean-shaped enlargements of the lymph vessels that contain and produce lymphocytes.

lym·pho·cyte (lĭm′ fə sīt′) **n-** white blood cell, especially one of the phagocytes made in the lymph glands.

lynch (lĭnch) **vt-** to kidnap and kill (an accused or suspected wrongdoer), thus denying the right to legal trial. —**n- lynch′ er.**

lynch law **n-** practice of lynching instead of respecting the legal rights of those suspected of crime.

lynx (lĭngks) **n-** short-tailed wildcat with tufted ears and a light gray or brown speckled coat; especially, the larger gray variety called the **Canada lynx.** *Hom-* links.

Lynx, about 3 ft long

ly·on·naise (lī′ ə nāz′) **adj-** prepared with finely sliced onions: *We ate lyonnaise potatoes.*

Ly·ra (lī′ rə) **n-** constellation of stars thought to outline the figure of a lyre.

lyre (līər) **n-** musical instrument like a small harp with three to ten strings. Lyres were used by the ancient Greeks to accompany singing and poetry. *Hom-* liar.

lyre·bird (līər′ bûrd′) **n-** an Australian bird, the male of which has a very long tail that resembles the shape of a lyre when spread.

Lyre

lyr·ic (lĭr′ ĭk) **adj-** 1 like a song; musical. 2 of or having to do with a kind of short poem that usually expresses very personal feelings. **n-** 1 a short poem expressing such feelings. 2 lyrics words for a song.

lyr·i·cal (lĭr′ ĭ kəl) **adj-** 1 like a song; musical; lyric: *the lyrical call of a bird.* 2 showing great emotion; poetical.

M

M, m (ĕm) *n-* [*pl.* **M's, m's**] 1 the thirteenth letter of the English alphabet. 2 Roman numeral for 1,000.

m. or **m** 1 meter or meters. 2 mile or miles. 3 minute or minutes. 4 male; masculine.

M 1 Medieval. 2 Middle.

M. monsieur.

ma (mä) *Informal n-* mother.

M.A. Master of Arts.

ma'am (măm) madam.

ma·ca·bre (mə kä' brə, -bər) *adj-* 1 gruesome; ghastly; horrible: *The battlefield was a macabre sight.* 2 unduly interested in death; morbid: *a macabre love of funerals.*

mac·ad·am (mə kăd' əm) *n-* 1 pavement of crushed stone, closely packed and rolled. 2 the stone so used.

mac·ad·am·ize (mə kăd' ə mīz') *vt-* [**mac·ad·am·ized, mac·ad·am·iz·ing**] to cover (a road) with macadam.

ma·caque (mə kăk', -kăk') *n-* any of various short-tailed monkeys of Asia and North Africa.

mac·a·ro·ni (măk' ə rō' nē) *n-* food made of wheat-flour paste, shaped into hollow tubes and dried.

mac·a·roon (măk' ə rōōn') *n-* cookie made of sugar, egg whites, and almonds or coconut.

ma·caw (mə kö') *n-* any of various large tropical American parrots with a strong, hooked bill, brilliant plumage, and a harsh voice.

Mac·beth (mək bĕth') *n-* Scottish king; hero of Shakespeare's play "Macbeth."

Macaw, about 3 ft long

Mac·ca·bees (măk' ə bēz') *n- pl.* 1 family of Jewish patriots who led a successful religious revolt against the Syrians (175-164 B.C.) 2 four books of the Old Testament Apocrypha. The first two are accepted as canonical by Roman Catholics. —*adj-* **Mac'ca·be'an.**

¹mace (mās) *n-* 1 club with a spiked head, used as a weapon in medieval times. 2 ornamental club or staff carried by or before an official as a symbol of power. [from Old French *mace,* from Late Latin **mattea,** "a hacking or digging tool," and related to **mattock.**]

Mace

²mace (mās) *n-* a spice ground from the dried covering of the nutmeg occurring between the husk and the seed. [from Old French **mac(e)is,** from Greek **maker** meaning "the reddish rind of an Indian tree."]

mac·e·rate (măs' ə rāt') *vt-* [**mac·er·at·ed, mac·er·at·ing**] 1 to soften or separate the parts of (a solid substance) by soaking or digestion. 2 to weaken by, or as if by, fasting. —*n-* **ma'cer·a'tion.**

ma·che·te (mə shĕt' ē, -chĕt' ē) *n-* long, heavy blade used for cutting vegetation by hand. [from Spanish, from **macho,** "hammer; ax."]

Machete

Mach·i·a·vel·li·an (măk' ē ə vĕl' ē ən) *adj-* of or resembling the crafty, unscrupulous practices recommended by Niccolò Machiavelli for governing a principality. *n-* anyone using crafty or unscrupulous methods.

mach·i·nate (măk' ə nāt', măsh'-) *vt-* [**mach·i·nat·ed, mach·i·nat·ing**] to form harmful plots; scheme.

mach·i·na·tion (măk' ə nā' shən, măsh'-) *n-* scheme or plot; sly intriguing: *the lawyer's machinations.*

mach·i·na·tor (măk' ə nā' tər, măsh'-) *n-* person who machinates.

ma·chine (mə shēn') *n-* 1 device using applied energy to do work. Machines convert energy from one form to another, transfer energy from place to place, multiply force or speed, or change the direction of a force. The wheel and axle, pulley, lever, screw, wedge, and inclined plane are simple machines. 2 apparatus with moving parts, made up of simple machines: *a sewing machine.* 3 person who acts mechanically, without intelligence, or with unfailing regularity. 4 person very highly trained in

mackerel sky *n-* pattern of clouds made up of rows of small clouds resembling the markings on a mackerel's back; cirrocumulus.

mack·i·naw (măk' ə nö') *n-* 1 heavy jacket, often plaid. 2 heavy, napped, often plaid, woolen cloth.

mack·in·tosh (măk' ən tŏsh') *n-* 1 raincoat. 2 lightweight, waterproof fabric.

mac·ro·cosm (măk' rə kŏz' əm) *n-* 1 the whole world; universe. 2 large thing or system when compared with a small thing or system that resembles or represents it in miniature: *American society as a* macrocosm *can be better understood by studying a typical American small town.* See also **microcosm.**

ma·cron (mā' krŏn', măk' rŏn') *n-* mark [-] written or printed over a vowel to show that it is long when pronounced.

mad (măd) *adj-* [**mad·der, mad·dest**] 1 out of one's mind; insane. 2 *Informal* angry: *He was so mad that his face was red.* 3 foolish; rash: *It was mad of him to try to swim in the icy water.* 4 *Informal* very enthusiastic: *to be* mad *about baseball.* 5 wild; excited; frantic: *a mad rush toward the exit.* 6 having rabies: *a mad dog.*

mad·am (măd' əm) *n-* [*pl.* **mes·dames** (mā däm')] polite word used in speaking or writing to a woman.

mad·ame (mă däm') *n-* [*pl.* **mes·dames** (mā däm')] French title or form of address for a married woman, equivalent to "Mrs."

mad·cap (măd' căp') *n-* lively, spirited person who acts on impulse: *You never know what that* madcap *will do next! adj-* lively or rash: *the children's* madcap *tricks.*

mad·den (măd' ən) *vt-* 1 to cause to become insane; craze. 2 to cause to become very angry; enrage; infuriate.

mad·den·ing (măd' ən ing) *adj-* 1 such as to drive one crazy or frantic with irritation. 2 infuriating; enraging. —*adv-* **mad'den·ing·ly:** *a* maddeningly *long wait.*

mad·der (măd' ər) *n-* 1 European plant with clusters of small, yellowish flowers, and roots from which a red dye is obtained; also, any of various related plants.

Ma·dei·ra (mə dèr' ə) *n-* sweet, amber-colored, fortified wine made on the island of Madeira.

mad·e·moi·selle (măd' mwə zĕl', măd' mə-) *n-* [*pl.* **mes·de·moi·selles** (măd' mwə zĕl', măd' mə-)] French title or form of address equal to "Miss."

made-to-order (mād' tōō òr' dər, -òr' dər) *adj-* made at a person's request; custom-made; tailor-made.

made-up (măd' ŭp') *adj-* invented; fabricated, such as a story: *That is a* made-up *tale.*

mad·house (măd' hous') *n-* 1 *Informal* hospital or other institution for insane people. 2 noisy, disorderly place: *The children's room was a* madhouse.

mad·ly (măd' lē) *adv-* in a wild and frenzied manner: *The crowd swarmed* madly *over the playing field.*

mad·man (măd' măn') *n-* [*pl.* **mad·men**] insane man; lunatic. —*fem.* **mad'wom'an.**

mad·ness (măd' nəs) *n-* 1 illness of the mind; insanity. 2 wild or foolish behavior: *It's* madness *to go so fast.*

Ma·don·na (mə dŏn' ə) *n-* 1 statue or painting representing Mary and the infant Jesus. 2 **the Madonna** the Virgin Mary.

ma·dras (măd' rəs, mə drăs') *n-* cotton fabric originally made in India and usually having a plaid or striped pattern. *as modifier: a* madras *jacket.*

mad·ri·gal (măd' rə gəl) *n-* unaccompanied song having parts for several voices in which the theme and its variations are interwoven.

Mae·ce·nas (mī sē' nəs) *n-* 1 wealthy Roman statesman who gave financial support to Horace and Virgil. 2 any wealthy and generous supporter of literature or art.

mael·strom (māl' strəm, -strōm') *n-* 1 wild and dangerous force or place: *The battle was a* maelstrom *of flying steel.* 3 **Maelstrom** whirlpool near the northwestern coast of Norway.

ma·es·tro (mī' strō') *n-* [*pl.* **maes·tros**] recognized master in music, such as a composer or conductor.

Mae West (mā' wĕst') *n-* inflatable life jacket for aviators, named after a famous actress.

mag. 1 magazine. 2 magnet. 3 magnetism. 4 *Astronomy* magnitude.

Ma·gi (mā' jī') *n- pl.* [*sing.* **Ma·gus** (mā' gəs)] 1 in the Bible, the three "wise men of the east" who brought gifts to the infant Jesus. 2 the priestly caste in Media and Persia.

mag·nil·o·quent (måg nĭl′ ə kwənt) *adj-* pompously eloquent in speaking or writing; boastful. **—n· mag′ nil′ o·quence. adv-** **mag·nil′ o·quent·ly.**

mag·ni·tude (måg′ nə tōōd′, -tyōōd′) *n-* 1 size; largeness: *the magnitude of the universe; the magnitude of a task.* 2 *Astronomy* brightness of a star or other heavenly body as expressed by a number on an accepted scale. Apparent magnitude refers to brightness as actually observed from the earth, and absolute magnitude to brightness as it would appear if the body were at a certain fixed distance from the observer.

mag·no·li·a (måg nō′ lē ə, -nól′ yə) *n-* 1 ornamental tree with shiny leaves, and large white or pink, fragrant flowers. 2 the flower. It is the State flower of Louisiana and Mississippi.

Magnolia

mag·num o·pus (måg′ nəm ō′ pəs) *Latin* chief work; masterpiece: *"Paradise Lost" is Milton's magnum opus.*

mag·pie (måg′ pī′) *n-* 1 a large black-and-white bird of the crow family. Magpies gather in chattering flocks. 2 person who chatters.

ma·guey (mə gā′) *n-* [*pl.* **ma·gueys**] 1 any of several Mexican agaves yielding fiber; especially, the century plant. 2 any of several hard fibers obtained from these plants and used for making rope, coarse cloth, etc.

Mag·yar (mŏ′ dyŏr, *also* måg′ yär) *n-* 1 a member of the main ethnic group of people living in Hungary. 2 the Hungarian language.

Magpie, about 20 in long

ma·ha·ra·ja or **ma·ha·ra·jah** (mä′ hə rä′ jə, -zhə) *n-* Hindu prince above a raja in rank.

ma·ha·ra·ni or **ma·ha·ra·nee** (mä′ hə rä′ nē) *n-* 1 wife of a maharaja. 2 ruling princess of India.

ma·hat·ma (mə hät′ mə, -hät′ mə) *n-* 1 title of respect, meaning "great soul," given to a wise and holy man in Asian religions. 2 such a person.

Ma·hi·can (mə hē′ kən) *n-* [*pl.* **Ma·hi·cans**, also **Ma·hi·can**] one of a tribe of Algonquian Indians who formerly lived near the Hudson River and eastward. Also **Mohican.**
►Should not be confused with MOHEGAN.

mah·jongg or **mah·jong** (mä′ zhŏng′, -jŏng′) *n-* American version of a Chinese game of skill and chance, played with small tiles somewhat resembling dominoes.

ma·hog·a·ny (mə hŏg′ ə nē) *n-* [*pl.* **ma·hog·a·nies**] 1 any of several tropical trees having a hard wood, often used for making furniture. 2 the wood of this tree. 3 a reddish-brown color. *adj-: a* mahogany *stain.*

ma·hout (mə hout′) *n-* elephant driver and keeper.

maid (mād) *n-* 1 female servant. 2 *Archaic* unmarried woman; maiden. *Hom-* made.

maid·en (mā′ dən) *n-* girl; unmarried woman; maid. *adj-* 1 unmarried: *my* maiden *aunt.* 2 of or like a young girl. 3 first: *a* maiden *voyage; a* maiden *effort.*

maid·en·hair (mā′ dən hâr′) *n-* delicate fern found in deep and shady woods.

maid·en·hood (mā′ dən hŏŏd′) *n-* time when a girl is a maiden; also, the condition of being a maiden.

maid·en·ly (mā′ dən lē′) *adj-* like or suitable to a young girl; modest; gentle. *—n- mai′ den·li·ness.*

maiden name *n-* last name of a woman before marriage.

maid-in-wait·ing (mād′ ən wā′ tĭng) *n-* [*pl.* **maids-in-wait·ing**] girl or young woman who attends a queen or other great lady as part of her household.

maid of honor *n-* unmarried woman who acts as chief companion to the bride at a wedding.

Maid of Or·léans (mād′ əv ôr′ lēnz′) *n-* Joan of Arc.

maid·serv·ant (mād′ sûr′ vənt) *Archaic* *n-* female servant.

Mai·du (mī′ dōō) *n-* [*pl.* **Maidus**, also **Maidu**] member of a tribe of American Indians who lived in California between the Feather and American rivers. *adj-: a* Maidu *custom.*

¹mail (māl) *n-* 1 letters, packages, magazines, etc., sent through the post office: *There was no* mail *today.* 2 government system of carrying and delivering letters, magazines, etc.: *Send that parcel by* mail. *vt-* to put into the mail: *to* mail *a package to a friend. as modifier: a* mail *train; a* mail *bag.* [from Middle English **male** meaning "a wallet; bag," from Old French, from Old High German **ma(s)ha**. Wallets and traveling bags were once used to carry mail.] *Hom-* male.

CHAIN

²mail (māl) *n-* armor, especially garments made of or covered with interlocking metal links, metal rings, or overlapping metal scales. [from Old French **maille**, from Latin **macula** meaning "a spot; mesh of a net."] *Hom-* male. *—adj-* **mailed.**

SCALE

mail·a·ble (mā′ lə bəl) *adj-* such as can conveniently be mailed or may legally be mailed: *a* mailable *package.*

Mail

mail·box (māl′ bŏks′) *n-* 1 box in which mail is placed when delivered. 2 box in which mail is placed to be collected by the post office.

mail drop *n-* slot or chute where mail can be inserted.

mail·er (mā′ lər) *n-* 1 person who mails. 2 an addressing or postage-stamping machine. 3 mailing container.

mail·man (māl′ măn′, -mən) *n-* [*pl.* **mail·men**] person who collects and delivers mail; postman.

mail order *n-* an order sent by mail for merchandise to be delivered and paid for by mail. A company set up to fill such orders is a **mail-order house.** *as modifier* **(mail-order):** *a* mail-order *electronics firm.*

maim (mām) *vt-* to deprive (someone) of the use of a part of the body; mutilate; cripple: *A leg wound* maimed *the soldier for life.*

main (mān) *adj-* most important; central; master; principal: *a* main *street; the* main *idea. n-* 1 pipe, line, cable, etc., from which lesser ones branch off: *Water and gas* mains *usually run under the streets.* 2 wide stretch of sea; the open sea: *Treasure ships sailed across the Spanish* Main *from South America to Spain.* *Homs-* Maine, mane.

by main force with sheer, unaided strength: *The boy lifted the weight by* main force. **in the main** for the most part: *I agree with you* in the main. **with might and main** with strength and application.

Maine (mān) *n-* U.S. battleship that blew up and sank in the harbor of Havana, Cuba, February 15, 1898.

main·land (mān′ lənd) *n-* continent or broad stretch of land, as distinct from the islands off its coast. *—n-* **main′ land·er.**

main·ly (mān′ lē) *adv-* chiefly; principally; for the most part.

main·mast (mān′ măst′, -məst) *n-* a ship's chief mast.

main·sail (mān′ səl, *also* -sāl′) *n-* the largest sail on the mainmast of a ship.

main·sheet (mān′ shēt′) *n-* rope used to flatten the mainsail and set it at the proper angle to the wind.

main·spring (mān′ spring′) *n-* 1 spring that makes a watch or clock go. 2 chief driving force: *Personal ambition was the* mainspring *of his career.*

main·stay (mān′ stā′) *n-* 1 strong rope or cable holding in place the mainmast of a sailing ship. 2 main support: *Bread is a* mainstay *of one's daily diet.*

main stem *n-* 1 *Informal* main street. 2 main railroad line.

main·stream (mān′ strēm′) *n-* chief current or tendency; most meaningful tradition or line of development: *the* mainstream *of American thought.*

Main Street *n-* the chief business street of a town or city; hence, a group or locality in which money and business are the only interests.

main·top (mān′ tŏp′) *n-* platform at the head of the mainmast of a ship.

main yard *n-* on a ship, the spar from which the mainsail is hung.

Maltese cat *n-* a short-haired domestic cat with bluish-gray fur.

Maltese cross *n-* a cross having four arms which are equal and have wide, notched ends.

mal·tose (mòl' tōs') or **malt sugar** *n-* crystalline sugar (C₁₂H₂₂O₁₁) consisting of two molecules of glucose and formed when starch is digested.

mal·treat (màl trēt') *vt-* to treat cruelly or roughly; misuse: *He maltreated his horse.* —*n-* **mal·treat·ment.**

ma·ma (mä' mə, *also Brit.* mə mä') *n-* mother (used chiefly when speaking to or about one's own mother).

mam·bo (mäm' bō') *n-* [*pl.* **mam·bos**] fast dance of Haitian origin, similar to a rumba; also, the music for this dance. *vi-* to perform this dance.

¹**mam·ma** (mä' mə) *n-* [*pl.* **mam·mae** (-mē)] mammary gland. [from Latin *mamma* with the same meaning.]

²**mam·ma** (mä' mə) mama.

mam·mal (mäm' əl) *n-* animal that has a backbone and, in the female, milk glands for feeding its young. Most mammals are four-footed furry or hairy animals. Human beings, bats, and whales are also mammals. —*adj-* **mam·mal'ian** (mə mäl' ē ən).

mam·ma·ry gland (mäm' ə rē) *n-* gland that secretes milk, and from which female mammals suckle their young.

mam·mon (mäm' ən) *n-* 1 material wealth considered as a bad influence or unworthy goal. 2 **Mammon** the personification of greed and worldly gain.

mam·moth (mäm' əth) *n-* large, hairy elephant with curved tusks. Mammoths became extinct several thousand years ago. *adj-* gigantic; huge.

Mammoth up to 13 ft high at shoulder

mam·my (mäm' ē) *n-* [*pl.* **mam·mies**] 1 mama. 2 formerly, especially in the South, a Negro woman servant entrusted with the care of children.

man (män) *n-* [*pl.* **men** (mèn)] 1 adult male of the human species. 2 mankind; the human race: *the progress of man.* 3 person; human being: *Every man to his own taste.* 4 person having qualities considered very manly, such as strength and bravery: *to act like a man.* 5 male employee; worker; hand: *The contractor has ten men on the job.* 6 playing piece in chess, checkers, or similar games. 7 husband or lover. *vt-* [**manned, man·ning**] 1 to furnish or staff with workers or helpers: *to man a ship.* 2 to take one's place for work or duty at: *He was ordered to man the gun.* 3 to brace or nerve (oneself): *He manned himself for the task.*

man and boy *Informal* during much of a person's life: *I've known him thirty years, man and boy.* **man and wife** husband and wife. **to a man** without exception.

Man. Manitoba.

man about town *n-* man who leads a very active social life, and is often seen at night clubs, the theater, etc.

man·a·cle (män' i kəl) *n-* handcuff; fetter. *vt-* [**man·a·cled, man·a·cling**] to place handcuffs or fetters on.

man·age (män' ij) *vt-* [**man·aged, man·ag·ing**] 1 to be in charge of: *to manage a store; to manage a baseball team.* 2 to control: *to manage a wild horse.* 3 to contrive; succeed somehow: *I managed to get away.*

man·age·a·ble (män' ə jə bəl) *adj-* such as can be managed or controlled: *a manageable horse; a manageable task.* —*n-* **man·age·a·bil'i·ty.**

man·a·tee (män' ə tē') *n-* large, plant-eating mammal that lives in rivers and bays; sea cow.

Man·chu (män' chōō') *n-* 1 one of a Mongolian people from Manchuria, who conquered China in 1643 and established a dynasty that lasted until 1912. 2 the language of these people. *adj-: the Manchu armies.*

man·da·mus (män dā' məs) *n-* in law, a writ or document from a superior court, directing a person, corporation, or lower court to perform some public duty or act.

Man·dan (män' dän') *n-* [*pl.* **Man·dans,** *also* **Man·dan**] one of an almost extinct tribe of American Indians who lived in North Dakota.

man·da·rin (män' də rīn', -rən) *n-* 1 member of one of the nine grades of highly educated public officials under the Chinese Empire. 2 (*also* **mandarin orange**) Chinese variety of orange with a sweet pulp and a rind that peels easily. 3 **Mandarin** northern dialect of Chinese; also, formerly, the court language of the Chinese Empire.

man·da·tar·y (män' də tèr' ē) *n-* [*pl.* **man·da·tar·ies**] nation, person, etc., to which a mandate has been issued.

man·date (män' dāt') *n-* 1 official order; command; decree. 2 political instructions from voters to their representatives in a legislature, as expressed by the results of an election. 3 formerly, a charge from the League of Nations to a member nation, authorizing it to govern conquered territory. 4 a territory so governed (see also *trust territory*). *vt-* [**man·dat·ed, man·dat·ing**] to put (a territory) under supervisory control.

man·da·tor·y (män' də tôr' ē) *adj-* 1 containing or required by an official command; compulsory; obligatory. 2 of or relating to a League of Nations mandate. *n-* [*pl.* **man·da·tor·ies**] mandatary.

man·di·ble (män' də bəl) *n-* 1 bone of the lower jaw. 2 jawlike part, such as the upper or lower part of a bird's beak, or biting part of an insect's mouth.

man·do·lin (män' də lin') *n-* musical instrument with a rounded, tapering sound box and eight wire strings, played by plucking.

Mandolin

man·drake (män' drāk') *n-* 1 Old World plant with a very large, forked root, formerly believed to have magic powers. 2 the May apple.

man·drel (män' drəl) *n-* 1 snug-fitting cylindrical or conical piece of metal on which something can be held for shaping on a lathe or similar machine. 2 similar device around which metal, glass, etc., may be shaped or cast. *Hom-* mandrill.

man·drill (män' drəl) *n-* large, fierce western African monkey related to the baboons. It has conspicuous blue and red markings on its face. *Hom-* mandrel.

mane (mān) *n-* the long hair on the top of the head and on the neck of a horse, lion, zebra, and some other animals. *Homs-* main, Maine. —*adj-* **maned.**

man-eat·ing (män' ē' tīng) *adj-* likely to attack and eat human beings: *a man-eating shark.* —*n-* **man'-eat'er.**

ma·neu·ver (mə nōō' vər) *n-* 1 planned and supervised movement of troops or ships. 2 skillful action, move, etc.: *a clever maneuver.* 3 **maneuvers** practice exercises carried out by military forces: *to send new recruits out on maneuvers.* *vi-* 1 to perform planned military movements: *Battleships maneuvered off the coast.* 2 to plan with art and skill; scheme: *He maneuvered for a seat next to the celebrity.* *vt-* 1 to move (troops, ships, etc.) according to a plan: *The admiral maneuvered his fleet into attack position.* 2 to move, manage, or manipulate in a clever, skillful way: *He maneuvered his car into a small space.* Also **manoeuvre.**

ma·neu·ver·a·ble (mə nōō' vər ə bəl) *adj-* such as can be maneuvered; moved, operated, or managed with ease: *a fast, maneuverable airplane.* —*n-* **ma·neu'ver·a·bil'i·ty:** *This device gives greater maneuverability.*

man Friday *n-* devoted and helpful assistant; right-hand man. [from the name of the servant and constant companion of Robinson Crusoe.]

man·ful (män' fəl) *adj-* manly; determined; brave. —*adv-* **man'ful·ly.** *n-* **man'ful·ness.**

man·ga·nese (mäng' gə nēz', -nēs') *n-* hard, brittle, grayish-white metal element, used in glass, paint, and hard steel. Symbol Mn, At. No. 25, At. Wt. 54.938.

mange (mänj) *n-* contagious skin disease of domestic animals, caused by parasites.

man·ger (män' jər) *n-* box or trough in which food for horses or cattle is placed.

man·grove (mäng' grōv', män'-) *n-* tropical tree or shrub that grows in swampy ground. Its wide-spreading branches send down roots that look like tree trunks and form thickets.

ma·nip·u·la·tion (mə nĭp′ yə lā′ shən) *n-* 1 a manipulating or a being manipulated. 2 in the treatment of certain diseases or injuries, the moving of a joint or limb with the hands in order to improve its condition.

man·i·tou (măn′ ə tōō′) *n-* in the religion of the Algonquian Indians, the power or spirit that rules nature. [American word from Algonquian **manitto** meaning "he is a god."] Also **man′i·to′** or **man′i·tu′**.

man·kind (măn′ kīnd′) *n-* the human species.

man·like (măn′ līk′) *adj-* 1 like or typical of a man. 2 resembling a human being: *a manlike ape.*

man·ly (măn′ lē) *adj-* [man·li·er, man·li·est] having the qualities befitting a man; courageous, honorable, resolute, etc. —*n-* man′li·ness.

man-made (măn′ măd′) *adj-* made by man, rather than by the processes of nature: *Rayon is a man-made material.*

man·na (măn′ə) *n-* 1 in the Bible, food miraculously supplied to the children of Israel during their wandering in the wilderness. 2 any much-needed thing that is unexpectedly supplied: *The praise was manna to him.*

man·ne·quin (măn′ə kən, -kĭn′) *n-* 1 person, usually a woman, employed as a model to display clothes. 2 jointed model of the human figure, used especially to display clothes. *Hom-* manikin.

man·ner (măn′ər) *n-* 1 habitual personal behavior; individual style: *a kind manner; a rapid manner of speaking.* 2 any way or style in which a thing is done: *a painting in the Chinese manner; the usual manner of handling a problem.* 3 sort; type; also, kinds or species: *What manner of man is he? We catch all manner of fish in the bay.* 4 **manners** (1) social behavior: *He has good manners.* (2) habits and customs: *the manners of the ancient Romans. Hom-* manor.

man·nered (măn′ərd) *adj-* 1 having a particular kind of manner or manners: *a well-mannered girl.* 2 having or marked by mannerisms: *a mannered style of writing.*

man·ner·ism (măn′ə rĭz′əm) *n-* distinctive or peculiar action, gesture, style, etc., especially if habitual or affected.

man·ner·less (măn′ər lĭs) *adj-* lacking good manners.

man·ner·ly (măn′ər lē) *adj-* polite. *adv-* politely; respectfully. —*n-* man′ner·li·ness.

man·ni·kin (măn′ə kən, -kĭn′) manikin.

man·nish (măn′ĭsh) *adj-* characteristic of or suitable for a man; masculine: *his mannish stride; her gruff, mannish voice.* —*adv-* man′nish·ly. *n-* man′nish·ness.

ma·noeu·vre (mə nōō′ vər) maneuver.

man-of-war (măn′ əv wôr′, -ə wôr′) *n-* [*pl.* **men-of-war**] warship used in former times.

man·nom·e·ter (mə nŏm′ə tər) *n-* instrument for measuring the pressure of gases.

man·or (măn′ər) *n-* 1 under the feudal system, a piece of land granted to a nobleman, part of which he occupied while the rest was occupied and farmed by serfs. 2 in later times, a piece of land similarly granted, but farmed by tenants. 3 mansion, especially one on a large farm or country estate. *Hom-* manner.

ma·nor·i·al (mə nôr′ē əl) *adj-* of or belonging to a manor.

man·pow·er (măn′ pou′ər) *n-* 1 total number of people working or available for work in an industry, nation, etc.; especially, the number of men available for military service. 2 (often **man power**) power supplied by the physical effort of a human being.

man·tel·piece (măn′ təl pēs′) *n-* shelf above a fireplace; mantel.

man·til·la (măn tē′yə) *n-* scarf, usually of lace or a sheer silk, worn over the head and shoulders by Spanish and Latin American women.

man·tis (măn′təs) *n-* [*pl.* **man·tis·es** or **man·tes** (-tēz′)] (often **praying mantis**) any of several long, slender insects related to the grasshoppers, which prey on other insects. Mantises often take a position with the front legs bent as if in prayer.

Praying mantis,
2–5 in. long

man·tle (măn′ təl) *n-* 1 long, loose cloak. 2 anything that covers or conceals: *night's mantle of darkness.* 3 layer of the earth located between the crust and core. The mantle is considered to be about 1800 miles thick. 4 protective membrane covering the body of a mollusk, which secretes the shell. 5 a gas mantle. 6 the back and upper part of the wings of a bird. *vt-* [man·tled, man·tling] to cover with or as if with a cloak. *Hom-* mantel.

Mantle

man·u·al (măn′ yōō əl, măn′ yəl) *adj-* of or with the hands; done or operated by the hands: *a manual skill; manual work.* *n-* 1 small guidebook or instruction book. 2 drill in the handling of a rifle, saber, or other weapon.

manual alphabet *n-* alphabet used by deaf-mutes, consisting of signs made with the fingers, each sign representing a letter.

man·u·al·ly (măn′ yōō ə lē, măn′ yə lē) *adv-* by hand or with the hands: *This machine is manually controlled.*

manual training *n-* training in work that is done with the hands, such as woodworking, metalwork, etc.

manuf. manufacture; manufacturer; manufacturing.

man·u·fac·ture (măn′ yə făk′ chər) *vt-* [man·u·fac·tured, man·u·fac·tur·ing] 1 to make by hand or by machinery, usually in large numbers: *to manufacture shoes in a large factory.* 2 to make or make up: *to manufacture an excuse.* *n-* 1 a making; production, especially by machinery and in large numbers: *the manufacture of household appliances.* 2 something produced by industrial means; product.

man·u·fac·tur·er (măn yə făk′ chər ər) *n-* person or company whose business is manufacturing.

man·u·mis·sion (măn′ yə mĭsh′ ən) *n-* a freeing or being freed from slavery; emancipation.

mark (märk) *n-* the unit of money and a coin of Germany. See also **deutsche mark, ostmark.** [from German]. *Hom-* marque.

Mark (märk) *n-* the evangelist who is said to have written the second Gospel of the New Testament. Also St. Mark.

mark·down (märk′ doun′) *n-* a lowering of price, especially of retail price; also, amount it is reduced.

marked (märkt) *adj-* 1 clear; plain; noticeable: *a marked improvement in health.* 2 having a mark or marks.

mark·ed·ly (mär′ kəd lē) *adv-* in a clear and obvious manner; noticeably: *He has markedly improved.*

marked man *n-* person singled out as an object of another's hatred, vengeance, etc.

mark·er (mär′ kər) *n-* 1 something used as a sign or indicator: *a marker for the exact spot.* 2 person or device used to keep score in a game or to grade exams.

mar·ket (mär′ kət) *n-* 1 place where goods are sold: *a food market.* 2 buying and selling; trade, especially in specific goods or services: *The used-car market is very active when new models come out.* 3 area or country where goods may be sold: *a foreign market for cars.* 4 demand: *There is a big market for warm clothing during the winter.* 5 stock market. *vi-* to buy food and other household items: *I marketed this morning. vt-* to sell; offer for sale: *We market tires.* —*n-* mar′ket·er.
in the market for wanting to buy. **on the market** up for sale. **play the market** to buy and sell in, or speculate in, the stock market.

mar·ket·a·ble (mär′ kə tə bəl) *adj-* such as can be sold; suitable for sale: *His invention is not marketable.* —*n-* mar′ket·a·bil′i·ty.

mar·ket·ing (mär′ kə tĭng) *n-* branch of business study and practice that deals with all the processes involved in selling goods. Marketing includes advertising, transporting and storing, selling, getting information about possible products and sales, etc.

market·place (mär′ kət plās′) *n-* 1 place where goods, especially food and household things, are sold. 2 the world of trade; commerce.

market value *n-* the current or prevailing price.

mark·ing (mär′ kĭng) *n-* mark or pattern of marks.

marks·man (märks′ mən) *n-* [*pl.* **marks·men**] person who is skilled in shooting.

marks·man·ship (märks′ mən ship′) *n-* ability as a marksman.

mark·up (märk′ ŭp′) *n-* amount or percentage of the cost of an article, added to the cost to determine the selling price.

marl (märl) *n-* a crumbly soil consisting of clay, sand, and calcium carbonate in the form of shell fragments; also, any crumbly earth layer.

mar·lin (mär′ lən) *n-* [*pl.* **mar·lin;** **mar·lins** (kinds of marlin)] any of various large deep-sea fishes with bills, related to the sailfish. *Hom-* marline.

mar·line (mär′ lən) *n-* small, two-stranded cord used aboard sailing ships for binding the end of a rope to prevent fraying. *Hom-* marlin.

Marmoset 18 in long

mar·line·spike or **mar·lin·spike** (mär′ lən splk′) *n-* pointed iron tool used to separate the strands of rope or wire cable for splicing.

mar·ma·lade (mär′ mə lād′) *n-* jellylike preserve made of the pulp and peel of fruits, especially oranges.

mar·mo·set (mär′ mə sĕt′, -zĕt′) *n-* South American monkey about the size of a squirrel, with long silky fur.

mar·mot (mär′ mət) *n-* 1 any of various stout-bodied, gnawing animals with coarse fur and a short bushy tail, related to the squirrels. 2 woodchuck.

¹**ma·roon** (mə rōōn′) *n-* dark-red or reddish-brown color. *adj-:* *a maroon cloak.* [from French **marron**, "chestnut," from Greek **máraon.**]

²**ma·roon** (mə rōōn′) *vt-* to leave helpless and alone, especially on a desolate island or coast: *The loss of our boat marooned us for two nights.* [from French **marron**, "(escaped) slave of the West Indies", from Spanish **cimarron**, "wild."]

Marmot, about 27 in long

marque (märk) *Archaic n-* seizure by a country of things, especially ships, belonging to its enemy; reprisal. *Hom-* mark.

mar·quee (mär kē′) *n-* 1 large, projecting canopy or shelter, often used as a signboard, over the entrance of a theater, hotel, etc. 2 *chiefly Brit.* large, open-sided tent, often used for an outdoor entertainment or party.

mar·quis (mär′ kwĭs, *Fr.* mär kē′) *n-* nobleman ranking next below a duke. Also, *Brit.,* **mar′ quess** (mär′ kwĭs).

mar·quise (mär kēz′) *n-* 1 wife or widow of a French marquis. 2 pointed oval shape of some cut gems; also, a ring or jewel having gems set in such a shape. *as modifier:* *a marquise diamond.*

mar·qui·sette (mär′ kwə sĕt′) *n-* very sheer fabric of cotton, silk, or synthetic, having a fine mesh weave.

mar·riage (mår′ lj) *n-* 1 the relationship between a husband and wife; married life. 2 a marrying; wedding. *as modifier:* *the marriage vows.*

mar·riage·a·ble (mår′ lj ə bəl) *adj-* suitable for marrying; unmarried, and above the legal age for marriage.

mar·ried (mår′ ĕd) *adj-* 1 of or related to marriage: *a married life.* 2 joined in marriage; wedded: *a married couple; a married woman.*

¹**mar·ry** (mår′ ĕ) *vt-* [**mar·ried, mar·ry·ing**] 1 to take for a husband or wife; wed: *John asked Ann to marry him.* 2 to join as husband and wife; perform the wedding ceremony for: *A minister married them.* 3 to give in marriage: *He married his youngest daughter to a writer.* *vi-* to enter into a marriage: *He married young.* [from Old French **marier**, from Latin **marītāre**, from **marīta** "woman having a husband," from **mas, maris,** "man."]

²**mar·ry** (mår′ ĕ) *Archaic interj-* exclamation of anger, surprise, etc. [oath on the name of the Virgin Mary.]

Mars (märz) *n-* 1 in Roman mythology, the god of war. He is identified with the Greek Ares. 2 seventh largest planet in the solar system, and the fourth in order from the sun.

Mar·seil·laise (mär′ sə lĕz′, *Fr.* mär sä yĕz′) *n-* the national anthem of France, composed during the French Revolution.

marsh (märsh) *n-* low wet land; swamp.

mar·shal (mär′ shəl) *n-* 1 federal officer having duties like those of a sheriff. 2 fire or police chief. 3 official in charge of ceremonies: *the marshal of a parade.* 4 in some armies and air forces, an officer higher than or equivalent to a general. *vt-* to put in order; organize: *to marshal ideas for a debate. Hom-* martial.

marsh gas *n-* methane.

marsh·mal·low (märsh′ mĕl′ ō, -măl′ ō) *n-* soft, spongy, white candy with a vanilla flavor.

marsh mallow *n-* tall mallow that grows in marshes and has large pink flowers.

marsh marigold *n-* plant that grows in wet places and has bright yellow flowers; cowslip.

marsh·y (mär′ shē) *adj-* [**marsh·i·er, marsh·i·est**] of or like a marsh or swamp. —*n-* **marsh′ i·ness.**

mar·su·pi·al (mär sōō′ pē əl) *n-* any of an order of mammals (**Marsupialia**), the females of which have an abdominal pouch in which the very immature young finish developing. Except for the oppossum, all marsupials are native to Australia.

mart (märt) *n-* market.

mar·ten (mär′ tən) *n-* 1 slender-bodied animal of the weasel family, valued for its dark-brown fur. 2 the fur of this animal. *Hom-* martin.

American marten, about 2 ft long

Mar·tha (mär′ thə) *n-* in the New Testament, a sister of Lazarus and Mary.

mar·tial (mär′ shəl) *adj-* of, like, or suited to war or military life: *a martial spirit; martial music.* —*adv-* **mar′ tial·ly.** *Hom-* marshal.

martial law *n-* military rule or authority imposed on a country or region in place of civil law, during a war or other emergency.

Mar·tian (mär′ shən) *adj-* of or relating to the planet Mars. *n-* a supposed inhabitant of Mars.

mar·tin (mär′ tən) *n-* any of several birds related to the swallows. One of the most common is the purple martin. *Hom-* marten.

Purple martin, about 8 in long

mar·ti·net (mär′ tə nĕt′) *n-* person who requires strict obedience to rules; rigid disciplinarian: *The sergeant was too much of a martinet.*

mar·tin·gale or **mar·tin·gal** (mär′ tən gǎl′) *n-* 1 in a horse's harness, a forked strap which passes from the girth between the forelegs up to the headgear, for holding the head down. 2 in sailing ships, a spar extending downward from the point where the bowsprit and jib boom are joined, for holding the stays that brace the jib boom against upward stress.

mar·tyr (mär′ tər) *n-* 1 person who suffers torture or death for the sake of his religion or principles. 2 one who endures great suffering, especially for a long time and without complaint. *vt-* 1 to torture or put to death for loyalty to a belief. 2 to persecute; torture.

a martyr to a sufferer from: *For a long time he has been a martyr to her tantrums.*

mar·tyr·dom (mär′ tər dəm) *n-* 1 a suffering of torture or death for the sake of one's principles or religion. 2 any long, intense suffering: *the martyrdom of arthritis.*

mar·vel (mär′ vəl) *n-* extraordinary thing; amazing example; a wonder: *A large dam is a marvel of modern engineering. vi-* to be struck with wonder (at): *We marveled at the Grand Canyon.*

mar·vel·ous (mär′ vəl əs) *adj-* astonishing; wonderful. —*adv-* **mar′ vel·ous·ly.** —*n-* **mar′ vel·ous·ness.**

Marx·ism (märk′ slz′ əm) *n-* the social, political, and economic teachings of Karl Marx and Friedrich Engels.

Mas·sa·chu·set (măs′ ə chōō′ sŏt) n- [pl. **Mas·sa·chu·sets**, also **Más·sa·chu·set**] one of a tribe of Algonquian Indians who formerly lived around Massachusetts Bay.

mas·sa·cre (măs′ ə kər) n- a brutal, wholesale killing of a large number of people; slaughter. vt- [mas·sa·cred, mas·sa·cring]: to massacre settlers.

mas·sage (mə säzh′, -säj′) n- a rubbing, kneading, or vibrating of some part of the body to increase blood circulation, relieve stiffness or soreness, etc. vt- [mas·saged, mas·sag·ing]: to massage the scalp.

mass-energy equation n- an equation, developed by Albert Einstein, expressing the interchangeability of matter and energy. In the equation, $E = mc^2$, E is the energy in joules, m is the mass in kilograms, and c is the velocity of light, 3×10^8 meters per second.

mas·seur (mă sûr′) n- man whose job is giving massages. —n- fem. **mas·seuse** (mă sōōz′).

mas·sive (măs′ ĭv) adj- 1 solid and heavy; bulky: He was blocked by a massive door. 2 strong and imposing: his massive features; massive evidence. —adv- **mas′ sive·ly.** n- **mas′ sive·ness.**

mass medium n- [pl. **mass media**] medium of communication, such as newspapers, radio, television, and motion pictures, that reaches and influences great numbers of peoples.

mass meeting n- meeting of a large number of people to learn about or act on some issue.

mass number n- atomic mass number.

mass-pro·duce (măs′ prə dōōs′, -dyōōs′) vt- [mass-pro·duced, mass-pro·duc·ing] to manufacture in large quantities: They mass-produced costume jewelry.

mass production n- manufacture of goods in large quantities, especially by the use of assembly lines. as modifier (mass-production): a mass-production process.

¹**mast** (măst) n- 1 on boats and ships, an upright pole for supporting sails, crow's-nest, radio antenna, hoisting tackle, etc. 2 any upright pole, such as a flagpole, a tall radio antenna, or the main post of a derrick. [from Old English mæst meaning originally "bough or trunk of a tree."] —adj- **mast′less.**
before the mast 1 formerly, the quarters of common sailors, situated forward of the foremast. 2 as a common sailor: to sail before the mast.

²**mast** (măst) n- chestnuts, beechnuts, etc., especially when used as feed for pigs. [from Old English mæst meaning "fattening material."]

mas·ter (măs′ tər) n- 1 person who rules, directs, or controls a person or thing: a dog's master; a slave's master. 2 person of great skill or ability; expert: a master at storytelling. 3 captain of a ship. 4 chiefly Brit. male teacher. 5 Master (1) title used before a young boy's name, instead of Mr. (2) Master of Arts or Master of Science. vt- 1 to get control over; dominate: to master one's temper. 2 to become skillful or expert in: to master a foreign language. adj- 1 chief; main: the master bedroom. 2 controlling or operating everything: a master switch; a master key. 3 fully skilled and experienced; able to teach the occupation to and judge the ability of others: a master carpenter.

mas·ter-at-arms (măs′ tər ət ärmz′) n- [pl. **mas·ters-at-arms**] in the Navy, a petty officer whose duty aboard ship is enforcing law and order.

mas·ter·ful (măs′ tər fəl) adj- 1 expert; showing mastery: The tennis champion had a masterful serve. 2 domineering; authoritative: his masterful tone. —adv- **mas′ ter·ful·ly.** n- **mas′ter·ful·ness.**

mas·ter·mind (măs′ tər mīnd′) n- person of great ability and knowledge, who is the chief planner or director of large or complex projects: the mastermind behind the revolt. vt-: to mastermind a revolt.

Master of Arts n- 1 degree given by a college or university to a person who has completed a prescribed course of graduate work in literature, philosophy, history, etc. 2 person who has received this degree. Abbr. M.A. or A.M.

master of ceremonies n- 1 person, usually an entertainer, who presides over the activities and introduces performers or speakers in a show or at a formal dinner. 2 person who determines and supervises the formal procedures followed in a ceremony.

Master of Science n- 1 degree given by a college or university to a person who has completed a prescribed course of graduate work in one of the sciences. 2 person who has received this degree. Abbr. M.S. or M.Sc.

mas·ter·piece (măs′ tər pēs′) n- 1 something, especially a work of art, showing great skill or genius: an artistic masterpiece. 2 the best thing that a person has written, made, painted, etc.: "Huckleberry Finn" is said to be Mark Twain's masterpiece. Also **mas′ter·work′.**

master sergeant n- 1 in the Army and Marine Corps, a noncommissioned officer who ranks next below a sergeant major and above all other sergeants. 2 in the Air Force, a noncommissioned officer ranking below warrant officers but above other sergeants and all airmen.

mas·ter·stroke (măs′ tər strŏk′) n- masterly or ingenious act, decision, etc.; feat.

mas·ter·y (măs′ tə rē) n- 1 control or domination; rule: to have mastery over one's own temper. 2 skill and knowledge; command: a mastery of arithmetic.

mast·head (măst′ hĕd′) n- 1 top of a ship's mast, especially of the lower mast, used as a lookout. 2 the block of printing in a newspaper or magazine that gives the names of the publisher and editors, the address of the editorial offices, etc.

mas·tic (măs′ tĭk) n- 1 small evergreen tree of the Mediterranean region related to the cashews. 2 yellowish or greenish gum or resin that oozes from the bark of this tree and is used in making varnishes. 3 pasty, quick-drying cement.

mas·ti·cate (măs′ tə kāt′) vt- [mas·ti·cat·ed, mas·ti·cat·ing] 1 to chew (food). 2 to grind or knead (rubber, wood, etc.) to a pulp. —n- **mas′ ti·ca′ tion.**

mas·tiff (măs′ tĭf) n- large, short-haired dog with heavy jowls, usually light-brown in color.

mas·to·don (măs′ tə dŏn′, -dən) n- any of various large, extinct mammals related to present-day elephants but sometimes having tusks in the lower jaw.

Mastiff, about 3 1 2 ft high at shoulder

mas·toid (măs′ toid′) adj- of or having to do with either of knobs of the skull that can be felt behind the ears.

¹**mat** (măt) n- 1 flat piece of cloth, plastic, woven straw, etc., used mainly as covering for a floor or table: a door mat; a place mat on the table. 2 pad covering the floor for gymnasium exercises or wrestling. 3 anything entangled in a thick mass: a mat of hair. vt- [mat·ted, mat·ting] to tangle together in a thick mass: The sea

ma·tri·cide (mă′ trə sīd′, mă′-) n- 1 murder of one's own mother. 2 one who murders his own mother.

ma·tric·u·late (mə trĭk′ yə lāt′) vi- [ma·tric·u·lat·ed, ma·tric·u·lat·ing] to register in a college or university as a candidate for a degree; enroll. vt-: The college refused to matriculate him. —n- **ma·tric′ u·la′ tion**

mat·ri·mo·ny (mă′ trə mō′ nē) n- [pl. **mat·ri·mon·ies**] marriage. —adj- **mat·ri·mo′ ni·al:** a matrimonial vow. adv- **mat′ ri·mo′ ni·al·ly.**

ma·trix (mă′ trĭks) n- [pl. **ma·tri·ces** (-trĭ sēz′) or **ma·trix·es**] 1 substance, object, organ, etc., within which anything begins, forms, develops, or is contained: Soil is the matrix in which seeds sprout. 2 Biology (1) the substance between the cells of a tissue. (2) the cells that form a tooth or nail. 3 the womb. 4 any mold in which something is cast; especially, in printing, the mold in which type characters are cast. 5 in geology, rock in which fossils, crystals, etc., are imbedded.

ma·tron (mă′ trən) n- 1 married woman or widow, especially an older one. 2 woman attendant or guard in an institution: the matron in a prison.

Matt. Matthew.

May apple *n-* plant of North America with large leaves, a large, white flower, and a small, yellow fruit.

may·be (mā′ bē) *adv-* perhaps; possibly.

May·day (mā′ dā′) *n-* the international radiotelephone distress signal used by ships or aircraft. [from French **m'aidez** meaning "Help me."]

May Day *n-* the first day of May, long celebrated as a spring festival with outdoor dances, games, and other activities, and now often marked by parades or other demonstrations of labor organizations. *as modifier* (**May-Day**): *this year's May-Day celebration.*

may·flow·er (mā′ flou′ ər) *n-* 1 any of several plants, such as the trailing arbutus, that flower in May or early spring. 2 **Mayflower** the sailing ship that brought the Pilgrims from England to the New World in 1620.

may·fly (mā′ flī′) *n-* [*pl.* **may·flies**] any of various delicate, short-lived insects, with large, transparent front wings.

may·hap (mā′ hăp′) *Archaic adv-* perhaps.

may·hem (mā′ hěm′) *n-* in law, the offense of injuring a person, violently and unlawfully, so as to mutilate.

May·ing (mā′ ĭng) *n-* the celebration of May Day.

mayn't (mānt) may not.

may·on·naise (mā′ ə nāz′) *n-* thick sauce or dressing of egg yolks, oil, lemon juice or vinegar, and seasoning.

may·or (mā′ ər) *n-* chief elected official of a city or town. —*adj-* **may′or·al**.

may·or·al·ty (mā′ ər əl tē) *n-* [*pl.* **may·or·al·ties**] the office or term of office of a mayor.

may·pole (mā′ pōl′) *n-* tall pole, decorated with ribbons and flowers, around which people dance on May Day.

May queen *n-* girl chosen to be the queen of a May-Day celebration.

maze (māz) *n-* 1 confusing network of passageways, tunnels, etc. 2 confusion or indecision; bewilderment: *I was in such a maze I couldn't answer.* *Hom-* maize.

ma·zur·ka (mə zûr′ kə) *n-* lively Polish dance; also, the music for such a dance. Also **ma·zour′ka**.

ma·zy (mā′ zē) *adj-* [**ma·zi·er**, **ma·zi·est**] like a maze; winding and confusing.

mb millibar.

mc or **m.c.** 1 megacycle. 2 millicurie.

M.C. or **MC** (ěm′ sē′) *n-* master of ceremonies.

Md. Maryland.

M.D. or **MD** Doctor of Medicine.

me (mē) *pron-* objective case of I: *He saw me. Pass me the bread. He did it for me.* *Hom-* mi.

Me. Maine (unofficial).

M.E. 1 Methodist Episcopal. 2 mechanical engineer. 3 mining engineer. 4 Middle English.

me·a cul·pa (mā′ ə kŭl′ pə) *Latin* [*pl.* **me·a cul·pas**] It is my fault.

¹**mead** (mēd) *n-* grassy field; meadow. [from Old English **mǣd**.] *Homs-* Mede, meed.

²**mead** (mēd) *n-* intoxicating drink made of fermented honey, water, and spices. [from Old English **meodu** of the same meaning.] *Homs-* Mede, meed.

mead·ow (měd′ ō) *n-* grassy field used for grazing animals or growing hay.

mead·ow·lark (měd′ ō lärk′) *n-* North American songbird having a yellow breast with a black, V-shaped mark.

mea·ger (mē′ gər) *adj-* 1 scanty; insufficient; unsatisfactory: *a meager diet.* 2 lean; thin: *a meager face.* Also **mea′gre**. —*adv-* **mea′ger·ly**. *n-* **mea′ger·ness**.

¹**meal** (mēl) *n-* 1 breakfast, lunch, dinner, or supper; regular occasion when food is served: *to eat candy between meals.* '2 food eaten or served at a regular time: *three meals a day.* [from Old English **mel** meaning "mark; fixed time; time when food is taken; the food itself."]

²**meal** (mēl) *n-* 1 coarsely ground grain, especially corn meal. 2 any ground material resembling this: *fish meal.* [from Old English **me(o)lu, mealu** meaning "that which is ground."]

meal·ie (mē′ lē) *n-* 1 in Africa, an ear of Indian corn. 2 **mealies** in Africa, corn; maize. *Hom-* mealy.

meal·time (mēl′ tīm′) *n-* time fixed for a meal.

meal·y (mē′ lē) *adj-* [**meal·i·er**, **meal·i·est**] 1 dry and powdery; like meal: *a dish of mealy potatoes.* 2 of or containing meal: *a mealy dough.* 3 covered with meal. 4 mealy-mouthed. *Hom-* mealie. —*n-* **meal′ i·ness**.

meal·y-mouthed (mē′ lē moutht′, -mouthd′) *adj-* afraid or unwilling to use plain language; not outspoken; not sincere.

¹**mean** (mēn) *vt-* [**meant** (měnt), **mean·ing**] 1 to express or indicate the idea of; have the sense of: *One word often means several things.* 2 to have in mind; intend: *He means to go. He means harm.* 3 to be a sign of: *Those black clouds mean rain.* 4 to design for or direct toward: *He meant those words for all of us.* *vi-* to have a specified value or importance: *His good name means everything to him.* [from Old English **mǣnan**, "tell; communicate by telling; moan," related to **moan**.] *Hom-* mien.

mean harm to to be unkindly disposed toward.

mean well to have good intentions: *He means well, although he sometimes behaves badly.*

mean well by to be kindly disposed toward.

²**mean** (mēn) *adj-* [**mean·er**, **mean·est**] 1 humble; low: *of mean birth.* 2 not generous: *as mean as a miser.* 3 shabby: *a mean slum area.* 4 inferior; poor: *clothes of mean quality.* 5 dishonorable; base; petty: *a mean motive.* 6 *Informal* spiteful; unkind: *a mean remark.* 7 dangerous; vicious: *a mean animal.* 8 *Informal* difficult: *a mean problem to solve.* 9 *Slang* excellent; first-rate: *to play a mean game of bridge.* [from Old English (**ge**)**mǣne** meaning "common; general."] *Hom-* mien. —*adv-* **mean′ ly.** *n-* **mean′ ness.**

no mean not insignificant; not inferior; not ordinary: *He is an actor of no mean talent.*

³**mean** (mēn) *n-* 1 something that is midway between two things that are opposite: *Gray is the mean between black and white.* 2 *Mathematics* average. 3 in logic, middle term of a syllogism. 4 **means** (1) way by which something is accomplished: *A boat was the means of rescue.* (2) wealth: *a man of means.* (3) *Mathematics* the second and third terms of a proportion. In the proportion a : b = c : d, b and c are the means (see also *extremes*). *adj-* 1 halfway between two extremes: *a mean height; a mean course.* 2 average; medium: *today's mean temperature.* [from Old French **mien**, from Latin **mediānus** meaning "in the middle," from **medius**, "middle."] *Hom-* mien.

by all means 1 at any cost; without fail: *You should by all means see the show.* 2 of course; certainly. **by means of** by the use of; through: *He won by means of clever tricks.* **by no means** in no way; not at all. **not by any means** not at all; in no way.

me·an·der (mē ăn′ dər) *vi-* 1 to follow a winding course: *The brook meanders across the meadow.* 2 to wander along in an aimless way. *n-* 1 a winding or turn of a stream. 2 (often **meanders**) a winding course; a rambling movement. 3 an ornamental, geometric pattern of winding lines. 4 **Meander** winding river flowing past Troy to the Aegean Sea; the Menderes.

mean distance *Astronomy n-* the average of the minimum and maximum distances of a planet or satellite from the body around which it revolves.

mean·ing·ful (mē′ nĭng fəl) *adj-* 1 having meaning: *A word is a meaningful unit of language.* 2 full of meaning; significant; important. —*adv-* **mean′ ing·ful·ly.**

mean·ing·less (mē′ nĭng ləs) *adj-* having no meaning or significance; making no sense: *a meaningless remark.* —*adv-* **mean′ ing·less·ly.**

meant (měnt) *p.t. & p.p.* of **mean**.

mean·time (mēn′ tīm′) *n-* 1 time between occasions: *He called yesterday and today, and in the meantime I thought it over.* 2 present time or time remaining: *I'll do as I've always done, for the meantime.* *adv-* meanwhile.

mean time *n-* time based on the average length of the day from midnight to midnight throughout the year. The exact length of the day varies because the earth's orbit is not a perfect circle; universal time.

mean·while (mēn′ hwīl′) *adv-* 1 in the time between two occasions; between now and then: *The test is tomorrow; meanwhile, we must study.* 2 during the same time: *The girls prepared lunch; meanwhile, the boys built a fire.*

med·al (mĕd′əl) *n*- flat metal badge, often coin-shaped, honoring an important event or given as a reward for a heroic or important act or service; decoration. *Hom*- meddle.

med·a·list (mĕd′əl ist) *n*- 1 designer or maker of medals. 2 person to whom a medal has been awarded. 3 in golf, winner of a kind of contest scored on the basis of total strokes rather than holes won or lost.

me·dal·lion (mə dăl′yən) *n*- 1 large medal. 2 an ornament, usually set in a round frame, consisting of a raised design or figures and used in decorating walls, fabrics, leather goods, etc.

Medal

Medallion

Medal of Honor *n*- highest U.S. military decoration, awarded to persons who have shown extraordinary gallantry in action, at the risk of their lives and beyond the call of duty. It is given in the name of Congress, and is often called the **Congressional Medal of Honor.**

med·dle (mĕd′əl) *vi*- [**med·dled, med·dling**] 1 to interfere in other people's affairs. 2 to touch, handle, or tamper with other people's possessions without permission. *Hom*- medal. —*n*- med′dler.

med·dle·some (mĕd′əl səm) *adj*- in the habit of meddling. —*n*- med′dle·some·ness.

Mede (mēd) *n*- a native or inhabitant of ancient Media in Persia. *Homs*- mead, meed.

Me·de·a (mĭ dē′ə) *n*- in Greek legend, Jason's wife, who helped him obtain the Golden Fleece.

me·di·a (mē′dē ə) *n*- [*pl.* of **medium**] newspapers, magazines, radio, television, and other means of communication and advertising, collectively.

►Careful writers and speakers do not use MEDIA as a singular noun. *Radio is a medium of communication, and one of the mass media.*

me·di·ae·val (mē′dē ē′vəl, mə dē′vəl) medieval.

me·di·al (mē′dē əl) *adj*- 1 of or having to do with the middle; situated in the middle. 2 having to do with the mean; average. 3 in phonetics, neither beginning nor ending a word, as the syllable "di" in "medial." —*adv*- me′di·al·ly.

me·di·an (mē′dē ən) *adj*- of, having to do with, or located in the middle; central. *n*- 1 the middle number in a series of numbers. The median in a series that has an even number of terms is the average of the two middle terms. 2 in geometry, the line drawn from any vertex of a triangle to the midpoint of the side opposite the vertex; also, the line joining the midpoints of the legs of a trapezoid.

¹**me·di·ate** (mē′dē āt′) *vt*- [**me·di·at·ed, me·di·at·ing**] 1 to bring about by acting as a mediator: *to mediate a settlement.* 2 to settle (a dispute, differences, etc.) by friendly intervention. *vi*- to act as a mediator to bring about peace or agreement. —*n*- me′di·a′tion.

²**me·di·ate** (mē′dē ət) *adj*- acting through or involving an intermediate agency or agent; indirect: *A disease transmitted by mediate contact.*

me·di·a·tor (mē′dē ā′tər) *n*- person or group that mediates to bring about peace or agreement.

med·i·cal (mĕd′ĭ kəl) *n*- of or relating to the study and practice of medicine or the treatment of disease by the use of medicine. —*adv*- med′i·cal·ly.

med·ic·a·ment (mə dĭk′ə mənt) *n*- drug or other substance used for healing or curing; remedy; medicine.

med·i·cate (mĕd′ə kāt′) *vt*- [**med·i·cat·ed, med·i·cat·ing**] 1 to treat with any curative or healing substance. 2 to put medicine into: *to medicate an ointment.*

med·i·ca·tion (mĕd′ə kā′shən) *n*- 1 a medicating; treatment with medicine. 2 medicament.

me·dic·i·nal (mə dĭs′ə nəl) *adj*- 1 having the power to prevent or cure disease, relieve pain, etc.: *a medicinal preparation.* 2 of or like a medicine: *a medicinal taste.*

med·i·cine (mĕd′ə sən) *n*- 1 drug or other substance to prevent or cure disease, relieve pain, etc. 2 the scientific study that deals with the prevention, treatment, and cure of disease; the art of healing, especially the practices which are not chiefly surgical. 3 medical profession. 4 among North American Indians, any object thought to have magical powers of healing, protection, or the like; also, magical power.

take one's medicine to endure suffering, fatigue, punishment, etc.

medicine ball *n*- heavy, stuffed, leather-covered ball thrown from one person to another for physical exercise.

medicine man *n*- among North American Indians, a person supposed to have magic power over evil spirits, diseases, etc.; shaman.

medicine show *n*- traveling show at which remedies and nostrums are advertised and sold.

me·di·e·val (mē′dē ē′vəl, mə dē′vəl) *adj*- of or relating to the Middle Ages, the period in European history from about 500 A.D. to about 1400 A.D. Also **medi-aeval.** —*adv*- me′di·e′val·ly.

Medieval Latin *n*- a form of Latin used by the literary writers and churchmen of the Middle Ages.

me·di·o·cre (mē′dē ō′kər) *adj*- not outstanding; neither very good nor very bad.

me·di·oc·ri·ty (mē′dē ŏk′rə tē) *n*- [*pl.* **me·di·oc·ri·ties**] 1 lack of either goodness or badness in skill or value. 2 mediocre person; person of average ability.

med·i·tate (mĕd′ə tāt′) *vi*- [**med·i·tat·ed, med·i·tat·ing**] to think deeply, especially about morals and spiritual matters; contemplate; reflect: *to meditate upon morals.* *vt*- to consider; plan: *to meditate revenge.*

med·i·ta·tion (mĕd′ə tā′shən) *n*- deep thought; quiet, serious reflection and contemplation.

med·i·ta·tive (mĕd′ə tā′tĭv) *adj*- given to long and serious thought; pensive. —*n*- med′i·ta′tive·ness.

Med·i·ter·ra·ne·an (mĕd′ə tə rā′nē ən) *adj*- of or relating to the sea which separates Europe from Africa, or to the people and culture of the countries bordering it.

me·di·um (mē′dē əm) *n*- [*pl.* **me·di·ums** or **me·di·a** (-dē ə)] 1 (*pl.* **me·di·ums**) middle position: *a happy medium between extremes.* 2 means or agent through which something is accomplished: *an advertising medium.* 3 substance in which a thing exists: *pigment in an oil medium.* 4 substance through which something acts or is carried: *Air is a medium for sound.* 5 (*pl.* **me·di·ums**) person assumed to be a messenger between spirits and living persons. *adj*- occupying a middle position, condition, or state.

medium frequency *n*- radio frequency ranging between 300 and 3000 kilocycles.

med·lar (mĕd′lər) *n*- 1 small, European tree related to the roses and quinces. 2 its hard, bitter fruit.

med·ley (mĕd′lē) *n*- [*pl.* **med·leys**] 1 a mixture or confused mass; jumble: *a medley of sounds.* 2 musical piece made up of several different songs or pieces.

me·dul·la (mə dŭl′ə) *n*- [*pl.* **me·dul·las** or **me·dul·lae** (-ē)] 1 the soft, centrally located part of any organ or body structure, such as a bone, hair, etc.; also, in botany, the pith. 2 medulla oblongata.

medulla ob·lon·ga·ta (ŏb′ lŏng gŏt′ə) *n*- the cylindrical extension of the spinal cord into the brain, containing centers that regulate respiration and the heart rate.

med·ul·lar·y (mĕd′ə lĕr′ē, mə dŭl′ə rē) *adj*- of or relating to marrow or to a medulla.

me·du·sa (mə dōō′sə, -dyōō′sə) *n*- [*pl.* **me·du·sas** or **me·du·sae** (-sē, -zē)] 1 jellyfish. 2 **Medusa** in Greek mythology, one of the Gorgons slain by Perseus.

meed (mēd) *Archaic n*- something well-deserved; reward; fit recompense. *Homs*- mead, Mede.

meek (mēk) *adj*- [**meek·er, meek·est**] 1 very patient, gentle, and mild; humble. 2 not inclined to assert oneself. —*adv*- meek′ly. *n*- meek′ness.

meer·schaum (mēr′shŏm′, -shəm) *n*- 1 white, soft, clayey mineral found chiefly in Asia Minor. 2 tobacco pipe having a bowl of this substance.

meet (mēt) *Archaic adj*- proper; fitting; right: *It is meet to give thanks unto the Lord.* [from Old English *gemǣte, gemēte.*] *Homs*- meat, mete. —*adv*- meet′ly.

mel·o·dy (mĕl' ə dē) *n-* [*pl.* **mel·o·dies**] 1 an arrangement of musical sounds making up a tune: *a familiar melody.* 2 chief part in a piece of music; air: *The sopranos carry the melody.* 3 any sound considered to be like the sound of music: *the melody of poetry.*

mel·on (mĕl' ən) *n-* the fleshy, juicy, round or oval fruit of any of several vines, such as the watermelon, muskmelon, or cantaloupe.

Melons

Mel·pom·e·ne (mĕl pŏm' ə nē) *n-* in Greek mythology, the Muse of tragedy.

melt (mĕlt) *vt-* 1 to change from a solid to a liquid state by heating: *to melt butter.* 2 to dissolve: *This detergent melts grease.* 3 to soften; make tender or gentle: *The baby's smile* melted *her heart.* *vi-:* *The snow* melted *quickly in the sun.* *I* melted *when she smiled.* *n-* something changed from a solid to a liquid state; also, the amount so changed: *a* melt *of steel.* —*n-* **melt'** er.

melt away to disappear: *The fog melted away.*

melt into to pass or shade gradually into each other; blend; merge: *The blue sea seems to melt into the sky.*

melting point *n-* temperature at which a solid becomes liquid. Crystalline solids have specific melting points, while amorphous solids, like glass, do not.

melting pot *n-* 1 crucible. 2 place where differences of custom, nationality, etc., are fused into a common pattern: *New York has been a great melting pot.*

mem·ber (mĕm' bər) *n-* 1 one of a group or set: *a club member*; *a member of the United Nations*; *a member of a rare species of plant.* 2 a limb or other projecting part of the body. 3 *Mathematics* either of the sides of an algebraic equation. *as modifier:* *a member nation.*

mem·ber·ship (mĕm' bər shĭp') *n-* 1 enrollment or participation: *a membership in a club.* 2 number of people who belong: *The membership in the art class is limited to 30.* *as modifier:* *a membership committee.*

mem·brane (mĕm' brān') *n-* thin, flexible sheet or layer of animal or vegetable tissue that serves as a cover or a lining of an organ: *mucous membrane.*

mem·bra·nous (mĕm' brə nəs, mĕm brā'-) *adj-* 1 of, like, or relating to a membrane: *a membranous tissue.* 2 forming a membrane: *a membranous throat disease.*

me·men·to (mə mĕn' tō) *n-* [*pl.* **me·men·tos** or **me·men·toes**] anything that serves as a reminder; souvenir.

mem·o (mĕm' ō) *Informal n-* [*pl.* **mem·os**] memorandum.

mem·oir (mĕm' wär') *n-* 1 record or account of events, written from the author's personal knowledge or experience. 2 biography; biographical sketch or notice. 3 **memoirs** (1) autobiography. (2) record of the activities of a club or society.

mem·o·ra·bil·ia (mĕm' ər ə bĭl' ē ə) *n-* 1 things worthy of remembrance or record. 2 the record of such things.

mem·o·ra·ble (mĕm' ə rə bəl) *adj-* worth being remembered; unforgettable: *a memorable day.* —*n-* **mem' o·ra·ble·ness.** *adv-* **mem' o·ra·bly.**

mem·o·ran·dum (mĕm' ə răn' dəm) *n-* [*pl.* **mem·o·ran·dums** or **mem·o·ran·da** (-də)] 1 brief note written to remind one of something. 2 a brief written report or communication, especially one of a business nature. 3 in law, informal document stating the terms of a contract or transaction. 4 in diplomacy, informal statement or summary regarding some subject of discussion between two governments.

me·mo·ri·al (mə môr' ĭ əl) *n-* 1 something that serves to commemorate: *the Lincoln Memorial.* 2 written statement of facts addressed to a public body, official, etc., usually accompanied by a request or protest. 3 (usually **memorials**) historical records; memoirs.

Memorial Day *n-* day set aside to honor soldiers and sailors killed in war. It is May 30 in most States.

me·mo·ri·al·ize (mə môr' ē ə līz') *vt-* [**me·mo·ri·al·ized, me·mo·ri·al·iz·ing**] 1 to address a petition or memorial to. 2 to commemorate.

mem·o·rize (mĕm' ə rīz') *vt-* [**mem·o·rized, mem·o·riz·ing**] to learn by heart; fix in the memory: *to memorize a speech.* —*n-* **mem' o·ri·za' tion.** *n-* **mem' o·riz' er.**

mé·nage (mā näzh') *n-* 1 household; domestic establishment. 2 household management.

me·nag·er·ie (mə nǎj' ə rē) *n-* 1 collection of wild animals in cages, kept for exhibition. 2 place where they are kept.

mend (mĕnd) *vt-* 1 to repair: *to mend a coat*; *to mend a harness.* 2 to reform; make right: *The thief promised to mend his ways.* *vi-* to return to good health; also, of a bone, to knit: *The child* mended *quickly.* —*n-* **mend' er.**

on the mend getting better.

men·da·cious (mĕn dā' shəs) *adj-* 1 given to lying; not truthful: *a mendacious person.* 2 false; not true: *a mendacious statement.* —*adv-* **men·da' cious·ly.** *n-* **men·da' cious·ness.**

men·dac·i·ty (mĕn dǎs' ə tē) *n-* 1 untruthfulness; habitual lying. 2 a lie.

men·de·le·vi·um (mĕn' də lē' vē əm) *n-* short-lived, artificially produced, radioactive element. Symbol Md, At. No. 101.

men·di·cant (mĕn' dĭ kənt) *n-* beggar. *adj-* practicing begging; living on alms: *a mendicant religious order.*

Men·e·la·us (mĕn' ə lā' əs) *n-* in Greek legend, a king of Sparta, brother of Agamemnon and husband of Helen.

men·folk (mĕn' fōk') *n- pl.* 1 men. 2 the men of a group.

men·ha·den (mĕn hā' dən) *n-* [*pl.* **men·ha·den; men·ha·dens** (kinds of menhaden)] any of several fishes related to the herrings, used for fertilizer and oil. [American word from the Algonquian name.]

me·ni·al (mē' nē əl, mĕn' yəl) *adj-* 1 of, relating to, or suitable for servants: *a menial occupation.* 2 lowly; degrading: *a menial task.* *n-* 1 servant who performs lowly tasks. 2 servile person. —*adv-* **me' ni·al·ly.**

me·nin·ges (mə nĭn' jēz) *n- pl.* [*sing.* **me·ninx** (mē' nĭngks', mĕn' ĭngks')] the three membranes that envelop the brain and the spinal cord. —*adj-* **me·nin' ge·al.**

men·in·gi·tis (mĕn' ən jī' təs) *n-* inflammation of the membranes enveloping the spinal cord and brain.

me·nis·cus (mə nĭs' kəs) *n-* [*pl.* **me·nis·cus·es** or **me·nis·ci** (-sī', -kī', -sē)] 1 crescent or crescent-shaped body. 2 curved surface of a liquid in a tube or other vessel. The surface curves up along the walls when the liquid wets them, and down when it does not. 3 a lens concave on one side and convex on the other.

Me·nom·i·nee (mə nŏm' ə nē) *n-* [*pl.* **Me·nom·i·nees,** also **Me·nom·i·nee**] member of a tribe of Algonquian Indians who are still living in north-central Wisconsin. *adj-: a Menominee chief.*

Men·non·ite (mĕn' ə nīt') *n-* a member of a Protestant sect that was established in Friesland in the sixteenth century and is still active in parts of Europe and the United States. They oppose military service, the taking of oaths, and the holding of public office.

me·no·rah (mə nôr' ə) *n-* candlestick used in Jewish religious services and rituals, such as the seven-branched type used in temples or a Hanukkah candle-holder.

Menorah

menses (mĕn' sēz') *n- pl.* menstruation.

men·stru·al (mĕn' strōō əl) *adj-* of or relating to menstruation.

men·stru·ate (mĕn' strōō āt', mĕn' strāt') *vi-* [**men·stru·at·ed, men·stru·at·ing**] to discharge the menstrual flow.

men·stru·a·tion (mĕn strōō' ā' shən, mĕn strā' shən) *n-* periodic flow of bloody fluid from the uterus, discharged through the female genital tract; period. It is associated with ovulation and normally occurs in women about every 28 days.

men·su·ra·tion (mĕn' sə rā' shən) *n-* 1 the act or process of measuring. 2 the branch of mathematics dealing with the measurement of lengths, areas, and volumes.

-ment *suffix* (used to form nouns from verbs) 1 the act of: *enforcement*; *infringement.* 2 the condition or state of being: *contentment*; *disappointment.* 3 the means or instrument of: *adornment*; *argument.* 4 the thing produced by or the result of: *pavement*; *attachment.*

men·tal (mĕn' təl) *adj-* 1 of, in, or relating to the mind: *a mental process.* 2 of or relating to diseases of the mind: *a mental patient.* —*adv-* **men' tal·ly.**

men·tor (mĕn' tôr', -tər) *n-* wise and trusted teacher.

mes·sage (měs′ĭj) *n-* 1 communication directed to another or others, especially in the form of spoken or written words: *to telephone a message to a friend; a message in Morse code; the President's message to Congress.* 2 subject or idea intended to teach or influence: *a novel with a message.*

mes·sen·ger (měs′ən jər) *n-* person who carries messages or does errands: *a telegraph messenger; a diplomatic messenger.* as *modifier: a messenger boy.*

mess hall *n-* room or building where a large group of people, especially soldiers or sailors, eat together.

Mes·si·ah (mə sī′ə) *n-* 1 in the Old Testament, the expected king and deliverer of the Jews; the Christ. 2 in the New Testament, Jesus, regarded as the savior of mankind. 3 **messiah** any expected leader or savior of a people, nation, etc.

Mes·si·an·ic (měs′ē ăn′ĭk) *adj-* of or relating to the Messiah.

mes·sieurs (mə syûr′) *pl.* of **monsieur.**

mess kit *n-* compact set of eating utensils, used by soldiers in the field, campers, etc.

mess·mate (měs′ māt′) *n-* one of a group of persons who eat together regularly, as in the army or navy.

Messrs. (měs′ərz) Messieurs. (used as plural of **Mr.**).

mess·y (měs′ē) *adj-* [**mess·i·er**, **mess·i·est**] dirty or untidy; sloppy; unpleasant: *a messy kitchen; a messy job of cleaning up.* —*adv-* **mess′i·ly.** *n-* **mess′i·ness.**

mes·ti·zo (měs tē′zō) *n-* [*pl.* **mes·ti·zos**] person of mixed racial ancestry; especially, in Latin America, a descendant of American Indians and of Europeans. [from Spanish, ultimately from Latin **misctere** meaning "to mix."] —*n- fem.* **mes·ti′za** (-zə).

met (mět) *p.t. & p.p.* of ¹**meet.**

met·a·bol·ic (mět′ə bŏl′ĭk) *adj-* of or having to do with metabolism; caused or produced by metabolism. —*adv-* **met′a·bol′i·cal·ly.**

me·tab·o·lism (mə tăb′ə lĭz′ əm) *n-* 1 the sum of all the chemical processes that occur in living organisms. See also *anabolism* and *catabolism.* 2 *Informal* rate at which the body consumes energy: basal metabolism. A person with **high metabolism** consumes energy at a faster rate than one with **low metabolism.**

met·a·car·pal (mět′ə kär′pəl) *n-* any of the five slender bones of the palm of the hand. as *modifier: a* metacarpal *fracture.*

met·al (mět′əl) *n-* 1 chemical element that is usually solid and shiny when pure or polished, that can be melted by heat, and that can conduct electricity. Gold, silver, copper, tin, iron, and aluminum are metals. 2 mixture of such elements, such as brass or bronze; alloy. 3 basic or essential quality; spirit: *a man of fine metal.* 4 *Chemistry* any element that can replace the hydrogen of an acid to form a base. as *modifier: a* metal *tip on an arrow.* *Hom-* mettle.

me·tal·lic (mə tăl′ĭk) *adj-* 1 consisting of or containing metal: *a metallic compound; a metallic thread.* 2 resembling metal.

met·al·loid (mět′ə loid′) *n-* chemical element having some of the properties of both a metal and a nonmetal. One metalloid is arsenic, which is both silvery gray and a poor conductor. as *modifier: a* metalloid *element.*

met·al·lur·gy (mět′ə lûr′jē) *n-* science of separating metals from their ores and preparing them for use. —*adj-* **met′al·lur′gi·cal.**

met·al·lur·gist (mět′ə lûr′jĭst) *n-* person skilled in and usually occupied in metallurgy.

met·al·work (mět′əl wûrk′) *n-* 1 articles or decorations made of metal. 2 the making of such articles. —*n-* **met′al·work′er.**

met·al·work·ing (mět′əl wûr′kĭng) *n-* art or process of making things out of metal. as *modifier: the* metalworking *trade.*

met·a·mor·phic (mět′ə môr′fĭk, -môr′fĭk) *adj-* 1 produced by or showing a change of form, shape, or structure. 2 in geology, of, relating to, or formed by metamorphism: *a* metamorphic *rock.*

met·a·mor·phism (mět′ə môr′fĭz′əm, -môr′fĭz′əm) *n-* the change in the composition, texture, and internal structure of rock by heat, pressure, the introduction of new materials, or the action of water.

met·a·mor·phose (mět′ə môr′fōz′, -môr′fōz′) *vt-* [**met·a·mor·phosed**, **met·a·mor·phos·ing**] 1 to change into a different form or nature: *The wicked witch* metamorphosed *the princess into a bird.* 2 in geology, to cause to undergo metamorphosis. *vi-* to undergo change of form, shape, or structure.

met·a·mor·pho·sis (mět′ə môr′fə səs, -môr′fə səs) *n-* [*pl.* **met·a·mor·pho·ses** (-sēz′)] 1 a change in form or structure. 2 *Biology* changes in form, structure, or function as a result of development, especially the change of an insect larva into a pupa and then into the adult form. 3 transformation, especially by sorcery.

met·a·phase (mět′ə fāz′) *n-* the stage in mitosis during which the chromosomes first move to the equatorial plane, located midway between the poles of the spindle fibers, and then split lengthwise.

met·a·phor (mět′ə fôr′, -fôr′) *n-* figure of speech in which a name, action, or descriptive word ordinarily applied to a certain object is applied to another in order to suggest a likeness between them. A metaphor is distinguished from a simile by not having "as" or "like" to introduce it. Example: His fist is a hammer. —*adj-* **met′a·phor′i·cal.** *adv-* **met′a·phor′i·cal·ly.**

met·a·phys·i·cal (mět′ə fĭz′ĭ kəl) *adj-* 1 of or having to do with metaphysics. 2 hard to understand; abstract. —*adv-* **met′a·phys′i·cal·ly.**

met·a·phy·si·cian (mět′ə fə zĭsh′ən) *n-* person skilled in metaphysics; abstract philosopher.

met·a·phys·ics (mět′ə fĭz′ĭks) *n-* (takes singular verb) branch of philosophy that deals with such subjects as the basic or absolute nature, character, and causes of being and knowing.

me·tas·ta·sis (mə tă′stə səs) *Medicine n-* [*pl.* **me·tas·ta·ses** (-sēz′)] 1 the spread of a disease from one part or organ to another not directly connected with it. This may occur in certain types of cancer. 2 the disease in its new site.

me·tas·ta·size (mə tă′stə sīz′) *Medicine vi-* [**me·tas·ta·sized, me·tas·ta·siz·ing**] to spread through the body from one part or organ to another not directly connected with it, as certain malignancies do.

met·a·tar·sal (mět′ə tär′sal) *n-* any one of the five long bones of the foot between the ankle and the toes. as *modifier: a* metatarsal *fracture; the* metatarsal *region.*

met·a·zo·an (mět′ə zō′ən) *n-* any of the group of animals (**Metazoa**) whose cells are differentiated into tissues, organs, etc. All multicellular animals are metazoans. See also *protozoan.*

mete (mēt) *vt-* [**met·ed, met·ing**] to give a share of, by or as if by measuring out; distribute; allot: *The judge* meted *out punishment to each criminal.* *Homs-* meat, meet.

me·tem·psy·cho·sis (mět′ əm sī′ kō′ səs) *n-* [*pl.* **me·tem·psy·cho·ses** (-sēz′)] passage of the soul after death into the body of another person or animal.

me·te·or (mē′tē ər) *n-* piece of matter that falls toward the earth at great speed from outer space; shooting star. Meteors burn with a bright glow when they hit the air around the earth, and are usually burned up before they reach the ground. See also *meteorite.*

me·te·or·ic (mē′ tē ôr′ĭk, -ôr′ĭk) *adj-* 1 of meteors or a meteor: *a dazzling* meteoric *display.* 2 like a meteor; brilliant or dazzling for a short time: *the* meteoric *careers of some popular singers.*

me·te·or·ite (mē′tē ə rīt′) *n-* mass of metal or stone that has fallen to earth from outer space. See also *meteor.*

me·te·o·ro·log·i·cal (mē′tē ər ə lŏj′ĭ kəl) *or* **me·te·or·o·log·ic** (-lŏj′ĭk) *adj-* of or having to do with weather and climate or with meteorology. —*adv-* **me′te·or·o·log′i·cal·ly.**

me·te·o·rol·o·gist (mē′tē ə rŏl′ə jĭst) *n-* person skilled in and usually occupied in meteorology.

me·te·o·rol·o·gy (mē′tē ə rŏl′ə jē) *n-* the science of weather and climate.

-meter *combining form* instrument for measuring: *altimeter.* [from French **-metre** from **mètre** from Greek **metron** meaning "measure; measuring instrument."]

meth·ane (měth′ ān′) *n-* colorless, odorless gas (CH_4) found in nature as natural gas and as marsh gas. It is highly flammable, and is used as fuel.

mi·cro·scop·ic (mī' krə skŏp' ĭk) *adj-* **1** seen or perceived only through a microscope: *a microscopic animal.* **2** of or having to do with a microscope; made or done with a microscope: *a microscopic lens*; *a microscopic examination of a blood sample.* **3** like a microscope; able to see the smallest detail: *a microscopic eye.*
—*adv-* **mi' cro·scop' i·cal·ly.**

mi·cros·co·py (mī krŏs' kə pē) *n-* process or technique of using the microscope as a means of scientific study.

mi·cro·sec·ond (mī' krō sĕk' ənd) *n-* one millionth of a second in time.

mi·cro·wave (mī' krō wāv') *n-* any electromagnetic wave whose wavelength is less than 1 meter. Microwaves are used in radar and television.

¹**mid** (mĭd) *adj-* **1** in phonetics, pronounced with the tongue between high and low positions, as it is for vowels such as (ā), (ĕ), and (ə): *the mid vowels.* **2** middle: *the mid part of June.* [from Old English midd, "middle."]

²**mid** or '**mid** (mĭd) amid. [shortened from **amid.**]

mid- *prefix* **1** in the middle part of what is indicated: *a* mid-*Victorian style.* **2** occurring in the center among others; central: *the* midpoint; midiron.

mid·af·ter·noon (mĭd' ăf' tər nōōn') *n-* middle part of the afternoon; time around 3 and 4 p.m. *as modifier: a* midafternoon *swimming party.*

mid·air (mĭd' âr') *n-* in the air above the earth: *The bomb exploded in* midair.

Mi·das (mī' dəs) *n-* in Greek legend, a king of Phrygia who had the power to turn anything he touched into gold.

mid-channel (mĭd' chăn' əl) *n-* middle part of a channel, measured from side to side.

mid-course (mĭd' kôrs') *in* mid-course *at a point part way through a continuous motion, journey, etc.: The rocket changed direction in* mid-course.

mid·day (mĭd' dā') *n-* middle of the day; noon. *as modifier: the* midday *meal; in the* midday *sun.*

mid·den (mĭd' ən) *n-* See *kitchen midden.*

mid·dle (mĭd' əl) *n-* **1** approximate center of anything: *the* middle *of the room.* **2** point halfway between the beginning and the end: *the* middle *of the movie; the* middle *of the week.* **3** point halfway between two sides of something long and continuous, such as a road, river, etc. **4** part of the body between the chest and the hips: *The ball hit him square in the* middle. *adj-* **1** halfway between two points, ends, sides, etc.; central: *the* middle *room.* **2** not at either extreme of a range; intermediate: *people of* middle *income.*

middle age *n-* time of a person's life between youth and old age, usually considered to include the years between 40 and 60. —*adj-* (**middle-aged**): *a* middle-aged *man.*

Middle Ages *n-* the medieval period of European history, from about 500 A.D. to about 1400 A.D.

middle C *Music n-* note written on the first line below the staff in the treble clef, or on the first line above the staff in the bass clef; also, the tone this represents.

middle class *n-* **1** in the United States, the economic class between the rich and the poor. It has usually been taken to include small businessmen, professional people, office workers, etc. **2** especially in countries having a hereditary nobility, the social class between the aristocracy and the laborers. —*adj-* (**middle-class**): *a* middle-class *family; a* middle-class *neighborhood.*

middle ear *n-* the cavity behind the eardrum; tympanum. It contains three tiny bones (anvil, hammer, and stirrup) that transmit sound waves from the eardrum to the inner ear. For picture, see ¹*ear.*

midge (mĭj) *n-* very small fly, gnat, or similar flying insect; hence, a very small person.

midg·et (mĭj' ət) *n-* **1** very small person, not deformed but much below the normal size. **2** any thing very small of its kind. *as modifier: a* midget *racing car.*

mid·i·ron (mĭd' ī' ərn) *n-* golf club having an iron or steel head with a slightly slanted face. It is used for hitting the ball moderate distances.

mid·land (mĭd' lənd) *n-* middle or central part of a country; the interior. *as modifier: the* midland *plains of the United States.*

mid-length (mĭd' lĕngth') *adj-* neither long nor short; of medium length: *a* mid-length *skirt.*

mid·mor·ning (mĭd' môr' nĭng, mĭd' môr'-) *n-* middle part of the morning; time around 10 a.m. *as modifier: a* midmorning *conference.*

mid·most (mĭd' mōst') *adj-* exactly in the middle or nearest the middle.

mid·night (mĭd' nīt') *n-* the middle of the night; 12 o'clock at night. *adj-* **1** of or at 12 o'clock at night: *a* midnight *supper.* **2** very dark: *a* midnight *blue.*
burn the midnight oil to study or work far into the night.

midnight sun *n-* the sun seen continuously for several months during the summer in arctic and antarctic regions. It is visible even at midnight.

mid-ocean ridge *n-* a series of interconnected, underwater mountain ranges that occur in the Atlantic Ocean, Indian Ocean, and the southern and eastern Pacific Ocean.

mid·point (mĭd' point') *n-* point or place exactly in the middle: *the* midpoint *of a line; the* midpoint *of his career.*

mid·rib (mĭd' rĭb') *n-* the vein along the center of a leaf.

mid·riff (mĭd' rĭf') *n-* **1** the muscular partition separating the cavity of the chest from that of the abdomen; diaphragm. **2** part of the body between the chest and the waist: *a fatty bulge at the* midriff.

mid·sec·tion (mĭd' sĕk' shən) *n-* **1** *Informal* part of the body between the chest and the hips; belly; midriff. **2** part of an airplane between the nose and the tail.

mid·se·mes·ter (mĭd' sə mĕs' tər) *n-* **1** examination given near the middle of a semester. **2** time around the middle of a semester. *as modifier: a* midsemester *grade.*

mid·ship·man (mĭd' shĭp' mən) *n-* [*pl.* **mid·ship·men**] **1** man in training to become an officer in the U.S. Navy or Coast Guard, especially at a naval academy. **2** junior officer in the British navy.

mid·ships (mĭd' shĭps') amidships.

¹**midst** (mĭdst) *n-* middle place or part; middle; center. [from Middle English **middest**, based on ¹**mid**.]
in our (or **their** or **your**) **midst** among us, them, or you: *There is a stranger* in our midst. **in the midst of** **1** in the middle of: *He stood* in the midst of *the crowd.* **2** existing together with: *poverty* in the midst of *plenty.*

²**midst** or '**midst** (mĭdst) amidst. [from **amidst.**]

mid·stream (mĭd' strēm') *n-* the middle of a stream.

mid·sum·mer (mĭd' sŭm' ər) *n-* **1** the middle of the summer, halfway between spring and fall. **2** the day, occurring about June 21, that has the longest period of daylight in the year. *as modifier: the* midsummer *heat.*

mid·term (mĭd' tûrm') *adj-* taking place in the middle of a term: *a* midterm *examination. n-* (often **midterms**) examination in the middle of a school or college term; also, period in which these examinations are given.

mid·town (mĭd' toun') *n-* central part of a town or city. *as modifier: the* midtown *office of the bank.*

mid-Vic·to·ri·an (mĭd' vĭk tôr' ē ən) *adj-* **1** of or having to do with the middle portion of the reign of Queen Victoria, about 1850 to 1880. **2** relating to or characteristic of the art, fashions, ideas, or standards of morality and taste of this period; hence, prudish, conventional, or old-fashioned. *n-* **1** person who lived during this period. **2** person of prudishly old-fashioned tastes, ideas, or attitudes.

mi·graine (mī' grān') *n-* severe headache, often concentrated on one side of the head and accompanied by dizziness and nausea.

mi·grant (mī' grənt) *adj-* moving from place to place, especially with the changes of season; migratory: *He hired* migrant *workers to harvest his peaches. n-* person, animal, or bird that migrates.

mi·grate (mī' grāt') *vi-* [**mi·grat·ed, mi·grat·ing**] **1** to travel from one region to another as the seasons change: *Ducks and geese* migrate *southward in the fall.* **2** to move to a new home in a different region: *The pioneers* migrated *to the West.*

mi·gra·tion (mī grā' shən) *n-* **1** act of migrating: *the* migration *of birds.* **2** number of people, birds, or animals that migrate: *a large* migration *of ducks.*

mi·gra·tor·y (mī' grə tôr' ē) *adj-* moving from place to place; wandering; roving: *a* migratory *worker;* migratory *birds; the* migratory *life of a tramp.*

mile (mīl) *n-* a measure of length or distance. On land, a **statute mile** is equal to 5,280 feet. In the United States, a **geographical mile** (or **nautical mile** or **air mile**) is equal to 6,080.20 feet.

mile·age (mī′lĭj) *n-* 1 distance or number of miles covered in traveling. 2 use one gets from something, according to miles traveled: *high mileage from a gallon of gasoline.* 3 money allowed for traveling expenses, estimated at a certain rate per mile.

mile·post (mīl′ pōst′) *n-* signpost along a road, stating the distance in miles to a certain point.

mil·er (mī′ lər) *n-* runner or horse trained to compete in races of one mile.

mile·stone (mīl′ stōn′) *n-* 1 roadside stone used to mark distance. 2 important event: *a milestone in history.*

mi·lieu (mēl yōō′) *n-* surroundings; environment: *the familiar milieu of one's own home.*

mil·i·tant (mīl′ ə tənt) *adj-* 1 ready to fight; warlike: *a militant nation.* 2 aggressive and prepared to fight in support of a cause: *a militant defender of freedom. n-* person who is aggressive in support of a cause. —*adv-* **mil′ i·tant·ly.** *n-* **mil′ i·tan·cy.**

mil·i·ta·rism (mīl′ ə tə rĭz′ əm) *n-* 1 tendency to uphold a nation's power by means of a strong army and navy. 2 policy of being ready to fight on the slightest provocation. 3 government or rule by military interests; military ideals or spirit. —*n-* **mil′ i·ta·rist.**

mil·i·ta·ris·tic (mīl′ ə rĭs′ tĭk) *adj-* of or having to do with militarism; having military ideals or spirit: *a militaristic government.* —*adv-* **mil′ i·ta·rist′ i·cal·ly.**

mil·i·ta·rize (mīl′ ə tə rīz′) *vt-* [mil·i·ta·rized, mil·i·ta·riz·ing] 1 to prepare or equip for war; convert (a nation) to a military power: *Hitler militarized Germany after 1933.* 2 to fill with military ideals or spirit. —*n-* **mil′ i·ta·ri·za′ tion.**

mil·i·tar·y (mīl′ ə tĕr′ ē) *adj-* 1 of or having to do with war, arms, or the armed forces: *to receive military training; military history.* 2 of, for, or by soldiers: *a military band; a military uniform. n-* **the military** the armed forces. —*adv-* **mil′ i·tar′ i·ly.**

military police *n-* (takes plural verb) soldiers whose duties are to keep order, arrest soldiers guilty of misconduct, protect civilians of an occupied area, guard prisoners of war, etc. See also *shore patrol.*

mil·i·tate (mīl′ ə tāt′) *vi-* [mil·i·tat·ed, mil·i·tat·ing] to act, work, or operate (against) someone or something: *His obvious rashness militated against him.*

mi·li·tia (mə lĭsh′ ə) *n-* body of citizens who are trained for defense of their country in emergencies. In the United States the militia is called the National Guard.

mi·li·tia·man (mə lĭsh′ ə mən) *n-* [*pl.* **mi·li·tia·men**] member of the militia.

milk (mĭlk) *n-* 1 white fluid produced by female mammals for feeding their young. The milk of several domestic animals, such as cows and goats, is used for human food. 2 liquid resembling this, especially the juice of certain plants or fruits: *Coconut milk makes a refreshing drink. as modifier: a milk carton; an old milk truck. vt-* 1 to draw milk from: *to milk a cow.* 2 to cheat; take unfair advantage of; exploit: *The swindler milked his unsuspecting victims. vi-* to draw milk from a cow, goat, etc.: *He likes to milk.* —*adj-* **milk′ like′.**

milk·er (mĭl′ kər) *n-* 1 person or machine that milks. 2 cow or goat that gives milk: *She's a good milker.*

milk·maid (mĭlk′ mād′) *n-* woman or girl who milks cows or works in a dairy.

milk·man (mĭlk′ măn′) *n-* [*pl.* **milk·men**] man who sells or delivers milk.

milk of magnesia *n-* chalky white liquid, chiefly magnesia, used as a laxative and an antacid.

milk shake or **milk·shake** (mĭlk′ shāk′) *n-* a drink of beaten milk, flavoring, and often ice cream.

milk snake *n-* small, gray or reddish-brown king snake with black markings, that feeds on mice, frogs, etc. It is harmless to people and easily tamed. Milk snakes were once thought to get their food by milking cows.

milk·sop (mĭlk′ sŏp′) *n-* weak, timid man or boy.

milk sugar *n-* lactose.

Milky Way *n-* the glowing, cloudlike band of light stretching across the night sky in a great circle, and consisting of gas, vast dust clouds, and about 100 billion (1 x 10¹¹) stars.

Milky Way galaxy *n-* the flattened, spiral galaxy to which the sun, solar system, and Milky Way belong; the Galaxy.

¹**mill** (mĭl) *n-* 1 machine or implement for grinding or pulverizing: *a pepper mill.* 2 building containing such machinery, especially for grinding grain. 3 any factory: *a paper mill; a cotton mill; a steel mill. vt-* 1 to grind: *to mill flour.* 2 to cut or stamp ridges across the edge of (a coin). 3 to shape with a milling machine. *vi-* to surge around, as a restless crowd does. [from Old English myl(e)n, from Late Latin molina, from Latin mola meaning "millstone."] *Hom-* mil.

Mill

through the mill *Informal* through a hard and trying experience or period of training.

²**mill** (mĭl) *n-* the thousandth part of a dollar; one tenth of a cent. [from Latin **millesimus** meaning "thousandth," from **mille**, "one thousand."] *Hom-* mil.

mill·dam (mĭl′ dăm′) *n-* barrier built across a stream to form a mill pond.

mil·len·ni·um (mə lĕn′ ē əm) *n-* [*pl.* **mil·len·ni·ums** or **mil·len·ni·a** (-nē ə)] 1 a period of a thousand years. 2 according to the Bible, the time when Christ will return and reign on earth for a thousand years; hence, a period of perfection. —*adj-* **mil·len′ ni·al.**

mill·er (mĭl′ ər) *n-* 1 man who owns or runs a mill for grinding grain into flour or meal. 2 milling machine. 3 any moth with wings that seem dusted with flour.

mil·li·am·pere (mĭl′ ē ăm′ pēr′) *n-* electrical unit equal to one thousandth of an ampere.

mil·li·bar (mĭl′ ə bär′) *n-* unit for measuring atmospheric pressure, equal to a force of 1,000 dynes per square centimeter. Standard pressure at sea level is 1,013 millibars. *Abbr.* mb

mil·li·gram (mĭl′ ə grăm′) *n-* unit of weight in the metric system, equal to one thousandth of a gram. Also, *chiefly Brit.,* **mil′ li·gramme′.** *Abbr.* mg. or mg

mil·li·li·ter (mĭl′ ə lē′ tər) *n-* unit of capacity in the metric system, equal to one thousandth of a liter. Also *chiefly Brit.,* **mil′ li·li′ tre.** *Abbr.* ml. or ml

mil·li·me·ter (mĭl′ ə mē′ tər) *n-* unit of length in the metric system equal to one thousandth of a meter. Also, *chiefly Brit.,* **mil′ li·me′ tre.** *Abbr.* mm. or mm

mil·li·ner (mĭl′ ə nər) *n-* trimmer, maker, or seller of women's hats.

mil·li·ner·y (mĭl′ ə nĕr′ ē) *n-* 1 articles sold by a milliner, especially women's hats, but including laces, ribbons, and other trimmings. 2 the business of a milliner.

mill·ing (mĭl′ ĭng) *n-* 1 work in or of a mill, especially the making of flour and other cereal foods. 2 the ridges around a milled coin. 3 work of a milling machine.

milling machine *n-* machine tool for cutting and shaping metal by moving it against rotating cutters.

mil·lion (mĭl′ yən) *n-* 1 one thousand thousands; 1,000,000. 2 an indefinitely large number: *They asked millions of questions. as modifier* (always preceded by another determiner): *a million dollars here and a million there.*

mil·lion·aire (mĭl′ yə nâr′) *n-* a person having a million dollars or more, or property worth such an amount. —*n- fem.* **mil′ lion·air′ ess.**

mil·lion·fold (mĭl′ yən fōld′) *n-* million times: *This is larger by a millionfold. adj-* amounting to a million times: *a millionfold increase in production.*

mil·lionth (mĭl′ yənth) *adj-* 1 last in a series of a million. 2 the ordinal of 1,000,000. *n-* 1 the last in a series of a million. 2 one of a million equal parts of a whole or group. 3 the last term in the name of a common fraction having a denominator of 1,000,000, or of the corresponding decimal fraction .000001.

mind·ed (mīn′dəd) *adj-* 1 having a mind of a certain kind or with a particular interest: *mathematics*-minded; *strong*-minded. 2 disposed or inclined; intending: *to be* minded *to swim*.

mind·ful (mīnd′fəl) *adj-* aware (of); conscious (of); thoughtful: *Father was always mindful of the needs of the family*. —*adv-* mind′ful·ly. *n-* mind′ful·ness.

mind·less (mīnd′ləs) *adj-* 1 showing no intelligence; dull-witted; stupid: *a mindless oaf*. 2 careless; heedless. —*adv-* mind′less·ly. *n-* mind′less·ness.

mind reader *n-* person who claims or is thought to be able to know another's thoughts. —*n-* mind reading.

mine (mīn) *pron-* (possessive pronoun) thing or things belonging to me: *This hat is mine. Mine is green. adj- Archaic* my (used before words beginning with a vowel): *I will raise mine eyes unto the hills*. [from Old English **min** meaning "my; of me."]

²**mine** (mīn) *n-* 1 pit or excavation from which minerals, precious stones, etc., are dug; also, a deposit of ore or coal. 2 rich supply or source: *He is a mine of information*. 3 explosives placed underground or in the water to delay or destroy enemy troops, vehicles, or ships. *vt-* [mined, min·ing] 1 to get by digging underground: *to* mine *coal*. 2 to dig into, as for ore or metals: *The company mined the entire hillside*. 3 to bury or place explosives in (a place where they will harm the enemy): *They mined the field. vi-* to work at digging up minerals. [from Old French **mine**, of Celtic origin.]

mine·field (mīn′fēld′) *n-* an area, either on land or in water, in which explosive mines have been laid.

mine·layer (mīn′lā′ər) *n-* naval vessel that plants explosive mines in the water.

min·er (mī′nər) *n-* person who works in or owns a mineral deposit. *Hom-* minor.

min·er·al (mīn′ər əl) *n-* substance that is neither animal nor vegetable; especially, a substance taken from the earth by mining: *Salt is a common mineral. adj-: our mineral resources*; mineral oil.

min·er·al·o·gy (mīn′ə rŏl′ə jē) *n-* science of minerals that deals with their origin, structure, classification, etc. —*adj-* min′er·a·log′i·cal (mīn′ər ə lŏj′ i kəl).

min·er·al·o·gist (mīn′ə rŏl′ə jĭst) *n-* person who is expert in and usually works in mineralogy.

mineral oil *n-* oil from a mineral source; especially, a clear oil used as a laxative.

mineral water *n-* water having a high mineral content; especially, water from springs and wells that is drunk and otherwise used for its supposed healthful effects.

Mi·ner·va (mĭ nûr′və) *n-* in Roman mythology, the goddess of wisdom who presided over useful and ornamental arts. She is identified with the Greek Athena.

min·e·stro·ne (mĭn′ə strōn′, -strō′nē) *n-* thick vegetable soup of Italian type, having a meat stock as base.

mine·sweep·er (mīn′swē′pər) *n-* naval vessel that removes explosive mines from the water, or explodes them

Ming (mĭng) *n-* the Chinese dynasty that ruled from 1368 to 1644, a period noted for the skill of its artists and artisans, especially in porcelains. *adj-: a* Ming *vase*.

min·gle (mĭng′gəl) *vi-* [min·gled, min·gling] 1 to mix: *The waters of the Missouri and Mississippi rivers mingle near St. Louis*. 2 to associate: *The soldiers were forbidden to mingle with their prisoners. vt-* to mix; intermingle: *One should not mingle sheep with tigers*.

ming tree *n-* 1 potted evergreen tree that has been artificially stunted. 2 an imitation dwarf tree made by combining various plant materials.

min·i·a·ture (mĭn′ē ə chər, mĭn′ə chər) *adj-* very small in scale; minute; tiny: *a miniature train; a miniature camera; a miniature Doberman pinscher. n-* 1 small model or reproduction: *a miniature of the Liberty Bell*. 2 a tiny portrait: *She wears a miniature in a brooch.* **in miniature** in a tiny size or scale: *Rex is his father in miniature*.

min·i·a·tur·ize (mĭn′ə chər īz′, mĭn′ē ə-) *vt-* [min·i·a·tur·ized, min·i·a·tur·iz·ing] to make (something) in small scale or size; especially, to design or make (radios, electron tubes, mechanisms, etc.) in very small size: *to* miniaturize *the guidance system of a rocket*.

min·im (mĭn′əm) *n-* 1 smallest liquid measure, equal to one sixtieth of a fluid dram; about one drop. 2 in penmanship, a down stroke. 3 in music, a half note.

min·i·mal (mĭn′ə məl) *adj-* pertaining to or being a minimum.

min·i·mize (mĭn′ə mīz′) *vt-* [min·i·mized, min·i·miz·ing] 1 to reduce to the smallest degree, part, or proportion: *These devices minimize the danger of the flight.* 2 to make little of; deny the seriousness of: *He minimized the importance of what he had done.* —*n-* min′i·mi·za′tion. *n-* min′i·miz′er.

min·i·mum (mĭn′ə məm) *n-* [*pl.* min·i·mums or min·i·ma (-mə)] 1 smallest amount possible or allowable: *Practice your music a minimum of an hour a day*. 2 lowest point or degree reached: *a minimum of 28° on the thermometer. adj-* 1 least possible or allowable; lowest possible: *the minimum mark for passing.* 2 lowest known or recorded: *a minimum rainfall of an inch a year*.

minimum wage *n-* wage fixed by law or contract as the lowest an employer may pay an employee

min·ing (mī′nĭng) *n-* 1 the work or business of taking ores, coal, etc., from the earth: *Coal mining is the chief industry of several states.* 2 the burying or planting of explosive mines. *as modifier: a* mining *engineer*.

min·ion (mĭn′yən) *n-* a flattering servant or follower: *He became the prince's minion. Hom-* minyan.

min·is·ter (mĭn′ə stər) *n-* 1 clergyman, especially in a Protestant church. 2 diplomat sent to a foreign country to represent his government. 3 in some countries, the head of a major government department. *vi-* to give help, attention, or service: *Doctors minister to the sick.*

min·is·te·ri·al (mĭn′ə stêr′ē əl) *adj-* of or relating to a minister or to his office or duties.

min·is·trant (mĭn′ə strənt) *adj-* serving; giving aid. *n-* one who serves or aids.

min·is·tra·tion (mĭn′ə strā′shən) *n-* 1 act of serving or aiding: *the ministration of a priest*. 2 service or aid given.

min·is·try (mĭn′ə strē) *n-* [*pl.* min·is·tries] 1 the work, profession, or office of a clergyman: *He is studying for the ministry*. 2 in some countries, a major government department; also, the building this occupies. 3 service or

misc. 1 miscellaneous. 2 miscellany.

mis·cal·cu·late (mĭs kăl′kyə lāt′) *vt-* [mis·cal·cu·lat·ed, mis·cal·cu·lat·ing] to make a mistake in; misjudge: *He miscalculated the amount. vi-* to make an error in judgment or foresight. —*n-* mis′cal′cu·la′tion.

mis·called (mĭs′ kōld′) *adj-* called by a wrong or unsuitable name.

mis·car·riage (mĭs′ kăr′ ĭj) *n-* 1 a failing or going wrong: *a miscarriage of justice*. 2 premature delivery of an embryo or a fetus that cannot survive.

mis·car·ry (mĭs′ kăr′ē) *vi-* [mis·car·ried, mis·car·ry·ing] 1 to go astray. 2 of plans, intentions, etc., to be unsuccessful. 3 of a woman, to deliver an embryo or a fetus that cannot survive.

mis·cast (mĭs′ kăst′) *vt-* [mis·cast, mis·cast·ing] 1 to give an unsuitable role to (a performer). 2 to choose an unsuitable performer, or performers for.

mis·ce·ge·na·tion (mĭs′ə jə nā′shən) *n-* mating between persons of different races. [from Latin *miscere* meaning "to mix," plus Latin *genus*, "race."]

mis·cel·la·ne·ous (mĭs′ə lā′nē əs) *adj-* made up of more than one kind; mixed; heterogeneous: *a miscellaneous group; a miscellaneous catch of fish.* —*adv-* mis′cel·la′ne·ous·ly. *n-* mis′cel·la′ne·ous·ness.

mis·cel·la·ny (mĭs′ə lā′nē) *n-* [*pl.* mis·cel·la·nies] 1 group of things of different kinds: *a miscellany of goods in the shop window*. 2 book, periodical, or the like, containing a variety of literary compositions.

mis·chance (mĭs chăns′, mĭs′-) *n-* 1 bad luck; misfortune: *By mischance, he slipped and fell.* 2 piece of bad luck; mishap.

mis·chief (mĭs′chəf) *n-* 1 foolish or thoughtless behavior that can harm or injure. 2 harm; injury: *People who carry tales about others can do great mischief.* 3 teasing; merry pranks: *She is full of mischief and is the life of every party.* 4 person who causes mischief, plays tricks, etc.: *That child is a little mischief.*

mis·cue (mis'kyōō') *n-* 1 in billiards, a stroke in which the cue slips. 2 mistake or error; slip-up. *vi-* [mis·cued, mis·cu·ing] 1 to make a billiards shot in which the cue slips. 2 to make a mistake. 3 in a play or other performance, to give or respond to the wrong cue. *vt-* to give (a performer) a wrong cue.

mis·date (mis'dāt') *vt-* [mis·dat·ed, mis·dat·ing] to give an incorrect date to.

mis·deal (mis'dēl') *vi-* [mis·dealt, mis·deal·ing] to deal cards wrongly. *n-* (*also* mis'dēl') a wrong dealing of a card or cards.

mis·deed (mis'dēd') *n-* wrong act; crime.

mis·de·mean·or (mis'di mē'nǝr) *n-* 1 in law, any crime not punishable by death, by a term in a State prison, or by a prison term exceeding one year. See also *felony* 2 any misbehavior.

mis·di·rect (mis'dǝ rĕkt', -dī rĕkt') *vt-* 1 to give false or incorrect instructions to: *He misdirected the tourist.* 2 to use or apply wrongly or foolishly: *to misdirect one's energies.* 3 to place a wrong address on (a letter, parcel, etc.). —*n-* mis'di·rec'tion.

mis·do·ing (mis'dōō'ing) *n-* wrongdoing.

mi·ser (mī'zǝr) *n-* greedy and stingy person who loves money for its own sake; especially, one who hoards wealth and lives as though he were poor.

mis·er·a·ble (miz'ǝr ǝ bǝl) *adj-* 1 unhappy; wretched: *The dog gave a miserable howl when we left him alone.* 2 bad; worthless: *a miserable meal of stale bread and burnt meat.* 3 causing unhappiness, trouble, or annoyance: *a miserable headache.* —*n-* mis'er·a·ble·ness. *adv-* mis'er·a·bly.

Mi·se·re·re (miz'ǝ rĕr'ĕ, -rĕr'ĕ) *n-* 1 in the Bible, Psalm 51 (in the Vulgate and CCD version, Psalm 50). 2 musical setting for this psalm.

mi·ser·ly (mī'zǝr lē) *adj-* greedy and tight-fisted; stingy; grasping. —*n-* mis'er·li·ness.

mis·er·y (miz'ǝ rē) *n-* [*pl.* mis·er·ies] 1 great unhappiness, wretchedness, pain, etc.: *He is in misery with a bad toothache.* 2 wretched conditions: *Some people rise from misery to fortune.* 3 cause of distress or suffering: *toothaches and other miseries.*

mis·fire (mis'fīǝr') *vi-* [mis·fired, mis·fir·ing] 1 of firearms, explosives, internal-combustion engines, etc., to fail to fire, explode, or ignite at the proper time. 2 of plans, endeavors, etc., to fail in reaching desired effects or results. *n-* a misfire in an engine.

mis·fit (mis'fit') *n-* 1 something that does not fit properly: *His coat was a misfit and his trousers baggy.* 2 person who is out of place among his associates or not properly adjusted to his environment: *Ned felt like a misfit in the new school.*

mis·for·tune (mis'fôr'chǝn, -fôr'chǝn) *n-* 1 bad luck; adversity: *In spite of all his misfortune he had a cheerful spirit.* 2 stroke of bad luck; unlucky accident: *The hailstorm was a misfortune for the farmers.*

mis·give (mis'giv') *Archaic vt-* & *vi-* [mis·gave, mis·giv·en, mis·giv·ing] to fail in confidence or courage.

mis·giv·ing (mis'giv'ing) *n-* feeling of doubt, distrust, or worry: *He had no misgivings about his ability.*

mis·gov·ern (mis'gŭv'ǝrn) *vt-* to rule badly; mismanage. —*n-* mis'gov'ern·ment.

mis·guide (mis'gīd') *vt-* [mis·guid·ed, mis·guid·ing] to mislead; influence to wrong conduct or thought. —*n-* mis'guid'ance.

mis·guid·ed (mis'gī'dǝd) *adj-* 1 incorrect; wrong; erroneous: *a misguided belief.* 2 under an improper influence: *a misguided boy.* —*adv-* mis'guid'ed·ly.

mis·han·dle (mis'hăn'dǝl) *vt-* [mis·han·dled, mis·han·dling] to handle or treat badly; also, mismanage.

mis·hap (mis'hăp') *n-* minor accident or stroke of bad luck: *The spilling of the gravy was his only mishap.*

mish·mash (mish'măsh') *n-* confused mixture; jumble; medley; hodgepodge.

mis·in·form (mis'in fôrm', -fôrm') *vt-* to give incorrect or false information to: *The clerk misinformed me.* —*n-* mis'in·for·ma'tion.

mis·in·ter·pret (mis'in tûr'prǝt) *vt-* to form a wrong or false impression of; misconstrue; misconceive; misunderstand: *He misinterpreted the article.* —*n-*

mis·judge (mis'jŭj') *vt-* [mis·judged, mis·judg·ing] to make an error in judgment; make a wrong estimate of: *The baseball player misjudged the ball and dropped it.* *vi-*: *Everyone misjudges at some time or another.* —*n-* mis'judg'ment *or* mis'judge'ment.

mis·lay (mis'lā') *vt-* [mis·laid, mis·lay·ing] 1 to lose temporarily; put in a wrong place or place later forgotten: *Dad mislaid the key and can't unlock the door.* 2 to lay or set down incorrectly: *to mislay a carpet.*

mis·lead (mis'lēd') *vt-* [mis·led, mis·lead·ing] 1 to deceive; give a false impression: *Her glowing account of the movie misled me.* 2 to lead astray: *Bad companions misled Joe and got him into trouble.*

mis·like (mis'līk') *Archaic vt-* [mis·liked, mis·lik·ing] to have an aversion to; dislike.

mis·man·age (mis'măn'ij) *vt-* [mis·man·aged, mis·man·ag·ing] to direct or administer (an organization, business, etc.) poorly. —*n-* mis'man·age·ment.

mis·match (mis'măch') *vt-* 1 to match (opponents in sports) unfairly or unsuitably: *to mismatch an amateur with a professional.* 2 to put together (things that do not belong together or go together well): *to mismatch a striped blouse with a plaid skirt.* *n-* a wrong or unsuitable matching or bringing together: *Their marriage was a mismatch.*

mis·name (mis'nām') *vt-* [mis·named, mis·nam·ing] to name wrongly or inappropriately; miscall.

mis·no·mer (mis'nō'mǝr) *n-* wrong name or term; incorrect use of a name: *It would be a misnomer to call a "hat" a "bird."*

mi·sog·a·mist (mǝ sŏg'ǝ mist') *n-* person who hates marriage.

mi·sog·y·nist (mǝ sŏj'ǝ nist') *n-* person who hates women.

mis·place (mis'plās') *vt-* [mis·placed, mis·plac·ing] 1 to put somewhere and then forget where; mislay: *I have misplaced the letter with his new address.* 2 to put in the wrong place: *to misplace a comma.* 3 to give (trust, love, etc.) where it is not deserved. —*n-* mis'place'ment.

¹mis·play (mis'plā') *n-* in sports, a faulty play; error: *The misplay cost us the game.*

²mis·play (mis'plā') *vt-* in sports, to handle in a faulty manner: *He misplayed the ball.*

¹mis·print (mis'print') *vt-* to print (a letter, word, etc.) incorrectly.

²mis·print (mis'print') *n-* a mistake in printing.

mis·pro·nounce (mis'prǝ nouns') *vt-* [mis·pro·nounced, mis·pro·nounc·ing] to utter with a wrong sound or to accent a wrong syllable: *Clarence mispronounces "granted" as "granite."* —*n-* mis'pro·nun'ci·a'tion (prǝ nŭn'sē ā'shǝn).

mis·quote (mis'kwōt') *vt-* [mis·quot·ed, mis·quot·ing] to quote the words of (a person, book, etc.) incorrectly. —*n-* mis'quo·ta'tion.

mis·read (mis'rēd') *vt-* [mis·read, mis·read·ing] 1 to read incorrectly: *to misread directions.* 2 to misunderstand; interpret wrongly: *She sometimes misreads my expression and thinks I am angry.*

mis·rep·re·sent (mis'rĕp'rǝ zĕnt') *vt-* to give a wrong impression of; report incorrectly, either willfully or through carelessness. —*n-* mis'rep're·sen·ta'tion.

mis·rule (mis'rōōl') *vt-* [mis·ruled, mis·rul·ing] to govern badly or unjustly. *n-* 1 disorder; unjust control; bad government. 2 confusion or tumult; disorder

miss (mis) *n-* 1 young unmarried woman; girl: *She's a pretty little miss.* 2 **Miss** title used before the name of a girl or unmarried woman: *She was Miss Cole before she married.* [a shortened form of *mistress.*]

Miss. Mississippi.

mis·sal (mis'ǝl) *n-* in the Roman Catholic Church, a book containing the prayers read or sung during the Mass throughout the year. *Hom-* missile.

mis·shap·en (mis'shā'pǝn) *adj-* poorly shaped; deformed. —*adv-* mis'shap'en·ly.

mis·sile (mis'ǝl) *n-* 1 guided missile. 2 any projectile, such as a bullet, mortar shell, spear, stone, etc. *as modifier:* *a missile launcher. Hom-* missal.

mis·sile·man (mis'ǝl mǝn) *n-* [*pl.* mis·sile·men] person who designs, builds, or operates guided missiles.

Mö·bi·us strip (mō′bē əs, mφ′-) *n-* a surface studied in topology that, despite its apparent form, has only a single side and edge. It is made by half twisting one end of a paper strip and then fastening it to the other end.

mob·ster (mōb′stər) *Slang n-* gangster.

moc·ca·sin (mōk′ə sən) *n-* 1 soft, flat-soled leather shoe originally worn by American Indians. 2 water moccasin.

Moccasin

moccasin flower *n-* any of several lady's-slippers common in the United States, usually with a pink flower.

mo·cha (mō′kə) *n-* fine coffee originally grown in Mocha, Arabia. *adj-* flavored with coffee or with coffee and chocolate: *a cake with mocha icing.*

mock (mōk) *vt-* 1 to ridicule; make fun of: *He mocked his opponent's ideas.* 2 to mimic scornfully or teasingly: *to mock someone's way of speaking.* 3 to defy or scorn: *to mock the law.* *vi-* to express contempt or derision: *He mocked at the idea of a peaceful settlement.* *adj-* not real or genuine; make-believe: *a mock wedding; a mock battle.* *n-* something ridiculous or contemptible: *to make a mock of justice.* —*n-* **mock′er.** *adv-* **mock′ing·ly.**

mock·er·y (mōk′ə rē) *n-* [*pl.* **mock·er·ies**] 1 scornful contempt; derision; ridicule: *The mockery in his voice was obvious.* 2 person or thing made fun of. 3 poor or disrespectful imitation: *The trial was a mockery of justice.*

mock-he·ro·ic (mōk′ hī rō′ ĭk) *adj-* ridiculing or satirizing heroic action, character, or style: *a mock-heroic poem.* —*adv-* **mock′-he·ro′i·cal·ly.**

mock·ing·bird (mōk′ ĭng bûrd′) *n-* bird of southern United States, about the size of a robin, noted for imitating the calls of other birds.

mock orange *n-* ornamental shrub with fragrant white flowers, related to the lilac; syringa.

Mockingbird
10 1 2 in long

mock turtle soup *n-* soup made of meat, seasoned to taste like soup made from the green turtle.

mock-up (mōk′ ŭp′) *n-* model of an airplane, machine, etc., usually full-sized, for teaching, testing, or display.

mod·al (mō′dəl) *Grammar n-* the term used for those auxiliary verbs such as "can," "do," "may," "will," etc., which combine with infinitives to form finite verb phrases. Examples: *Henry and James may arrive tonight. I should leave in half an hour.*

mode (mōd) *n-* 1 way, method, or manner of doing something: *a mode of speaking; a mode of travel.* 2 style or fashion in the manner of dress: *Top hats were the mode.*

mod·er·a·tion (mōd′ə rā′shən) *n-* 1 a moderating; becoming milder or less extreme: *a gradual moderation of the climate.* 2 a limiting or restraining, especially of personal behavior; avoidance of overdoing or over-indulging: *to eat with moderation.*

in moderation within reasonable bounds; not to excess.

mod·e·ra·to (mōd′ə rä′tō) *Music adj- & adv-* in moderate tempo; slower than allegretto but faster than andante.

mod·er·a·tor (mōd′ə rā′tər) *n-* 1 person or thing that restrains: *Courtesy is a moderator of conduct.* 2 presiding officer, especially at a panel discussion.

mod·ern (mōd′ərn) *adj-* of or having to do with the present or the recent past: *a modern painting.* *n-* 1 person of recent or present times. 2 person with up-to-date views, manners, habits, etc. —*n-* **mod′ern·ness.**

modern history *n-* history of events since about 1500 A.D.

mod·ern·ism (mōd′ər nĭz′ əm) *n-* 1 way of thinking or acting characteristic of modern times; any present-day practice, usage, taste, style, or idea. 2 style or theory of modern art, especially of painting, architecture, etc., that breaks with past traditions. —*n-* **mod′ern·ist:** *In architecture he is a modernist.* *adj-* **mod′ern·is′tic.**

mod·ern·i·ty (mə dûr′nə tē) *n-* condition of being modern.

mod·est (mōd′əst) *adj-* 1 not boastful or vain of one's own worth; unassuming. 2 not grand or showy; simple: *a modest house; the modest violet.* 3 not excessive or extreme; moderate: *a modest ambition; a modest price.* 4 having or showing a sense of what is proper or suitable; decent. —*adv-* **mod′est·ly.**

mod·es·ty (mōd′ə stē) *n-* 1 lack of conceit; freedom from vanity. 2 decency in behavior, dress, etc. 3 simplicity; moderation: *the modesty of his needs.*

mod·i·cum (mōd′I kəm) *n-* small amount: *a modicum of success.*

mod·i·fi·ca·tion (mōd′ə fə kā′shən) *n-* 1 a modifying; changing. 2 a change; alteration: *Your plans need some modifications.* 3 something that has been modified: *This plan is a modification of his first one.*

mod·i·fi·er (mōd′ə fī′ ər) *n-* 1 someone or something that modifies. 2 *Grammar* word or group of words that modifies another word or word group. A one-word modifier may be an adjective, an adverb, or a noun. Examples:

I like the *red* chair. (adjective limiting a noun)
The house is just *over the hill*. (adverb clarifying a prepositional phrase)
He drove *slowly*. (adverb limiting a verb)
The train is *very* fast. (adverb strengthening an adjective)
He had a *business* conference. (noun modifier limiting another noun)

mod·i·fy (mōd′ə fī′) *vt-* [mod·i·fied, mod·i·fy·ing] 1 to change; alter: *Having learned the facts, he modified his opinion.* 2 *Grammar* to limit the meaning of, or describe, a word or group of words in the same part of the sentence. In the following sentences, "red" is a modifier (adjective) modifying "kite": *We had a red kite. The red kite won the prize.* —*adj-* **mod′i·fi′a·ble.**

mod·ish (mō′dĭsh) *adj-* fashionable; stylish: *a modish hat.* —*adv-* **mod′ish·ly.** —*n-* **mod′ish·ness.**

mo·diste (mō dēst′) *n-* woman who makes fashionable clothes as a business.

Mo·doc (mō′dŏk′) *n-* [*pl.* **Mo·docs**, also **Mo·doc**] member of a tribe of American Indians who lived in California and Oregon and are now in Oklahoma.

mod·u·lar arithmetic (mōj′ ə lər) *n-* any of a group of numeration systems in which numbers are arranged as on a clock's face, so that addition proceeds in a clockwise direction, and subtraction in a counterclockwise direction. In modular arithmetic, starting at the noon position, $3 + 11 = 2$.

mod·u·late (mōj′ə lāt′) *vt-* [mod·u·lat·ed, mod·u·lat·ing] 1 to vary the tone, volume, or pitch of: *to modulate the voice.* 2 to adjust; regulate. 3 to vary the amplitude, frequency, etc., of (a carrier wave) according to the sound or picture being broadcast. *vi-* *Music* to pass from one key to another in a composition or passage.

mod·u·la·tion (mōj′ə lā′shən) *n-* 1 a modulating or a being modulated. 2 *Music* a passing from one key to a related key. 3 in electronics, the process in which the amplitude, frequency, or phase of a carrier wave is made to vary in accordance with the signal, sound, etc., being broadcast; also, the result of this process. See also *amplitude modulation* and *frequency modulation.*

mod·u·la·tor (mōj′ə lā′tər, mōd′yə-) *n-* electronic device for producing modulation.

mod·ule (mōj′ōol′, mōd′yōol′) *n-* 1 any standardized unit of measurement. 2 an assembly of parts used as a unit in house construction, furniture, missiles, etc.

mod·u·lus (mōj′ə ləs) *n-* [*pl.* **mod·u·li** (-lē, -lī)] 1 number that shows the extent to which a substance has a certain property; coefficient. 2 *Mathematics* in a modular arithmetic, the number of numbers.

mo·dus o·pe·ran·di (mō′dəs ŏp′ə rän′dē, -dī′) *Latin* manner in which a person or thing works or operates.

mo·dus vi·ven·di (mō′dəs və vĕn′dē) *Latin* manner of living; especially, a practical, often temporary method of getting along.

Mo·gul (mō′gəl) *n-* 1 one of the Mongolian Muslims who conquered India in the 16th century. Each emperor was called the **Great Mogul.** 2 a descendant of these people. 3 **mogul** any important or powerful person. *adj-:* *the Mogul empire.*

mold·board (mōld′ bôrd′) *n-* the curved metal plate of a plow that lifts and turns the soil.

¹**mold·er** (mōl′ dər) *vi-* to crumble to dust by natural decay: *The old walls* moldered. [probably from ¹**mold.**]

²**mold·er** (mōl′ dər) *n-* person or thing that molds, shapes, or influences: *a molder of public opinion.* [from ¹**mold.**]

mold·ing (mōl′ dĭng) *n-* 1 act of shaping by or as if by a mold. 2 a thing so shaped. 3 strip of wood or plaster placed along the wall or ceiling of a room for hanging pictures or for decoration.

mold·y (mōl′ dē) *adj-* [**mold·i·er, mold·i·est**] 1 covered with mold: *the moldy* bread. 2 damp; musty: *a moldy cellar.* —*n-* **mold′ i·ness.**

¹**mole** (mōl) *n-* dark-colored spot or growth on the skin. [from Old English **māl** of the same meaning.]

²**mole** (mōl) *n-* small animal with brownish or grayish velvety fur and tiny, almost sightless eyes. Its large front feet are suited to digging, and it spends most of its life underground. [from Middle English **molle.**]

³**mole** (mōl) *n-* 1 solid stone wall or pier built out into the sea to break the force of the waves. 2 harbor formed by such a breakwater. [from French, from Latin **mōlēs,** "mass: heap."]

Mole about 6 in long

⁴**mole** (mōl) *Chemistry n-* gram molecule. Also **mol.** [from German **mol,** shortened from **molekulargewicht,** "molecular weight."]

mo·le·cu·lar (mə lĕk′ yə lər) *adj-* of, having to do with, or produced by molecules.

molecular weight *n-* of a molecule, the sum of the atomic weights of its atoms.

mol·e·cule (mŏl′ ə kyōōl′) *n-* 1 *Chemistry* the smallest particle of an element or compound that can exist independently and still retain the chemical properties of a larger amount of the element or compound. He, O₂, and H₂O are molecules. 2 any tiny part or thing.

mole·hill (mōl′ hĭl′) *n-* mound made by a mole.

mo·lest (mə lĕst′) *vt-* 1 to interfere with; annoy; disturb. 2 to annoy in an indecent way. —*n-* **mo′ les·ta′ tion.** *n-* **mo·lest′ er.**

moll (mŏl) *Slang n-* female gangster or female companion of a gangster.

mol·li·fy (mŏl′ ə fī′) *vt-* [**mol·li·fied, mol·li·fy·ing**] to soothe; calm; make less violent: *to mollify an angry person.* —*n-* **mol′ li·fi·ca′ tion.**

mol·lusk (mŏl′ əsk) *n-* any of a large phylum (**Mollusca**) of animals having soft bodies usually enclosed in a hard shell. Snails, oysters, clams, and octopuses are mollusks. Also **mol′ lusc.**

mol·ly·cod·dle (mŏl′ ē kŏd′ əl) *n-* coddled or pampered person, especially a man or boy. *vt-* [**mol·ly·cod·dled, mol·ly·cod·dling**]: *Don't* mollycoddle *him.*

Mo·loch (mō′ lŏk′, also mŏl′ ək) *n-* ancient Semitic deity to whom human sacrifices were offered; hence, anything demanding frightening sacrifices. Also **Mo′ lech.**

molt (mōlt) *vi-* to shed a shell, feathers, skin, horns, etc., which are replaced by a new growth. *vt-*: *The snake* molted *its skin.* *n-* the act or process of thus shedding. Also **moult.**

molt·en (mōl′ tən) *adj-* made fluid by heat; melted: *a drop of* molten *lead.*

mol·to (mōl′ tō′) *Music adv-* much; very.

mo·ment (mō′ mənt) *n-* 1 instant; certain point in time: *I waved the* moment *I saw you.* 2 present time: *the hero of the* moment. 3 importance: *news of great* moment.

mo·men·tar·i·ly (mō′ mən tĕr′ ə lē) *adv-* 1 at or for the moment; for a short time: *I am* momentarily *out of cash.* 2 in a moment; very soon: *He will be here* momentarily. 3 moment by moment: *He is growing* momentarily *worse.*

mo·men·tar·y (mō′ mən tĕr′ ē) *adj-* 1 lasting for a moment: *a momentary* silence. 2 happening at any moment: *A spy must expect* momentary *capture.* —*n-* **mo′ men·tar′ i·ness.**

mo·men·tous (mō mĕn′ təs) *adj-* very important; of great consequence: *a* momentous *decision.* —*adv-*

mo·men·tum (mō mĕn′ təm) *n-* 1 *Physics* a measure of the amount of force required to stop a moving body within a given time, defined as the product of its mass and velocity. 2 forward motion; impetus.

Mon. Monday.

mo·nad·nock (mə năd′ nŏk′) *n-* hill or mass of resistant rock which stands well above the surface of a surrounding plain. Monadnocks are remnants of highlands.

mon·arch (mŏn′ ərk) *n-* 1 hereditary ruler of a constitutional monarchy, such as a king or queen; also, the supreme ruler of a kingdom or empire, such as an emperor. 2 the chief of its class or kind: *The lion is the* monarch *of all beasts.* 3 large, orange and black American butterfly. —*adj-* **mon·ar′ chal** (mə när′ kəl): *the king's* monarchal *bearing.*

mo·nar·chic (mə när′ kĭk) or **mo·nar·chi·cal** (-kĭ kəl) *adj-* having to do with or characteristic of a monarch or monarchy. —*adv-* **mo·nar′ chi·cal·ly.**

mo·nar·chism (mŏn′ ər kĭz′ əm) *n-* 1 belief in or support of monarchy as a form of government. 2 principles or system of government by a monarch.

mon·ar·chist (mŏn′ ər kĭst) *n-* person who believes in or supports monarchy as a form of government.

mon·ar·chy (mŏn′ ər kē) *n-* [*pl.* **mon·ar·chies**] nation or system of government headed by a monarch. In an **absolute monarchy** the ruler has unlimited power, but in a **constitutional monarchy** his power is limited by law.

mon·as·ter·y (mŏn′ ə stĕr′ ē) *n-* [*pl.* **mon·as·ter·ies**] house for persons, especially monks, bound by religious vows, and living and working in seclusion; also, the people living there. —*adj-* **mon′ as·te′ ri·al:** *the* monasterial *quiet of the corridor.*

mo·nas·tic (mə năs′ tĭk) *adj-* having to do with or characteristic of monasteries or monks and their manner of life: *a room of* monastic *simplicity;* monastic *discipline.* —*adv-* **mo·nas′ ti·cal·ly.**

mo·nas·ti·cism (mə năs′ tə sĭz′ əm) *n-* the system, rules, or conditions of life in monasteries.

mon·a·tom·ic (mŏn′ ə tŏn′ ĭk) *Chemistry adj-* having a single atom in the molecule: *Helium is* monatomic.

mon·au·ral (mŏn′ ôr′ əl) *adj-* 1 of or having to do with a single ear: *a* monaural *hearing aid.* 2 monophonic. —*adv-* **mon·au′ ral·ly.**

Mon·day (mŭn′ dē, -dā) *n-* the second day of the week.

mo·ne·cious (mə nē′ shəs) monoecious.

Mo·nel metal (mō nĕl′) *n-* trademark name of a nickel alloy containing copper, iron, and manganese, used in machine parts because of its high resistance to corrosion.

mon·e·tar·y (mŏn′ ə tĕr′ ē) *adj-* 1 of or having to do with coinage or currency: *The dollar is the* monetary *unit of the United States.* 2 of or having to do with money: *a* monetary *gift;* monetary *theory.*

mon·ey (mŭn′ ē) *n-* [*pl.* **mon·eys** or **mon·ies**] 1 coins or paper currency issued by a government as a medium of exchange, a means of payment, or a measure of value. 2 anything else used this way, such as bank notes, checks, wampum, etc. 3 wealth. 4 **monies** or **moneys** sums of money. —*adj-* **mon′ ey·less.**

in the money *Informal* finishing first, second, or third in a race. **make money** to make a profit or earn a salary or payment.

mon·ey·bag (mŭn′ ē băg′) *n-* 1 bag for holding money. 2 **moneybags** *Slang* (takes singular verb) very rich person.

mon·ey·chang·er (mŭn′ ē chān′ jər) *n-* 1 person whose business is exchanging the money of one country for that of another at an established rate. 2 device that holds and dispenses coins of various denominations.

mon·eyed (mŭn′ ēd) *adj-* 1 having much money; rich. 2 resulting from great wealth: *a* moneyed *elegance.*

mon·ey·lend·er (mŭn′ ē lĕn′ dər) *n-* person whose business is lending money at some rate of interest.

money order *n-* an order for the payment of a stated sum of money; especially, such an order sold by the government at a post office.

Mon·gol (mŏng′ gol) *n-* 1 a member of any of the native peoples of Mongolia or nearby regions. 2 the language of these people; Mongolian. 3 member of the Mongoloid division of the human species.

mon·o·logue or **mon·o·log** (mŏn′ə lôg′, -lŏg′) *n*- a long speech by a single person, especially in a play.

mon·o·ma·ni·a (mŏn′ə mā′nē ə) *n*- 1 insanity in regard to one single subject or class of subjects. 2 preoccupation with one idea; craze. —*n*- **mon·o·ma′ni·ac**.

mo·no·mi·al (mō nō′mē əl, mə-) *n*- 1 *Mathematics* an expression consisting of a single term. 2 *Biology* a scientific name consisting of a single word. *adj*-: *a monomial term*.

mon·o·phon·ic (mŏn′ə fŏn′ ĭk) *adj*- 1 *Music* having a single melodic line, or one part that predominates over the accompanying parts. See also *polyphonic*. 2 of or having to do with recordings or broadcasts using a single channel, not stereophonic; monaural.

mon·o·plane (mŏn′ə plān′) *n*- airplane with one pair of wings. Most modern airplanes are monoplanes.

mo·nop·o·list (mə nŏp′ə lĭst′) *n*- person, organization, etc., having a monopoly or promoting monopolies. —*adj*- **mo·nop′o·lis′tic**.

mo·nop·o·lize (mə nŏp′ə līz′) *vt*- [**mo·nop·o·lized**, **mo·nop·o·liz·ing**] 1 to gain a monopoly of (a product, service, industry, etc.). 2 to take the whole of: *to monopolize the attention of another*. —*n*- **mo·nop′o·liz′er**.

mo·nop·o·ly (mə nŏp′ə lē) *n*- [*pl.* **mo·nop·o·lies**] 1 exclusive control of the use, sale, or distribution of a commodity or service by one person or one group of persons: *One bus company has a monopoly of our city's transportation*. 2 a thing controlled in this way: *Coinage is a government monopoly*. 3 organization exercising such control. 4 a monopolizing; exclusive possession.

mon·o·pro·pel·lant (mŏn′ō prə pĕl′ənt) *n*- a single, usually liquid substance for propelling a rocket.

mon·o·rail (mŏn′ə rāl′) *n*- 1 single rail along which railway cars run, or from which they are suspended. 2 a railway using a single track.

mon·o·syl·lab·ic (mŏn′ə sə lăb′ ĭk) *adj*- 1 having only one syllable. 2 consisting of words of one syllable.

mon·o·syl·la·ble (mŏn′ə sĭl′ə bəl) *n*- word or other utterance of one syllable.

mon·o·the·ism (mŏn′ə thē′ ĭz′ əm) *n*- belief in only one God. —*n*- **mon′o·the′ist**. *adj*- **mon′o·the·is′tic**.

mon·o·tone (mŏn′ə tōn′) *n*- 1 utterance of one syllable after another without change of pitch or key: *to speak in a monotone*. 2 a single color: *illustrations in monotone*. 3 unvarying and tedious style or manner.

mo·not·o·nous (mə nŏt′ə nəs) *adj*- always the same; tiresome because of sameness: *a monotonous voice*. —*adv*- **mo·not′o·nous·ly**. *n*- **mo·not′o·nous·ness**.

mo·not·o·ny (mə nŏt′ə nē) *n*- dull sameness; lack of variety; tedious uniformity: *the monotony of his stories*.

Mon·o·type (mŏn′ə tīp′) *n*- 1 trademark name for a typesetting machine that casts and sets separate metal pieces of type for each character. See also *Linotype*. 2 **monotype** the type produced by such a machine.

mon·o·va·lent (mŏn′ə vā′ lənt) *adj*- having a valence of one.

mo·nox·ide (mə nŏk′ sīd′) *Chemistry n*- oxide containing only one atom of oxygen in each molecule.

Mon·roe Doctrine (mən rō′) *n*- statement of policy made by President Monroe in 1823, expressing the idea that the United States would look with disfavor on any attempt of a European nation to extend its control or influence in the Western Hemisphere.

Mon·sei·gneur or **mon·sei·gneur** (mŏn′ sĕ′ nyŭr′) *n*- [*pl.* **Mes·sei·gneurs** (mā′ sĕ′ nyŭr′)] *French* title equivalent to "my lord," given to clergymen of high rank.

mon·sieur (mə syŭr′) *n*- [*pl.* **mes·sieurs** (mā′ syŭr′)] *French* title of courtesy equivalent to "Mr." or "Sir."

Mon·si·gnor or **mon·si·gnor** (mŏn sēn′ yər) *n*- [*pl.* **Mon·si·gnors** or **Mon·si·gno·ri** (-yôr′ē)] a title of honor given by the Pope to deserving clergymen of the Roman Catholic Church.

mon·soon (mŏn sōōn′) *n*- 1 wind in the Indian Ocean and Southern Asia which blows from the southwest from April to October, and from the northeast from October to April. 2 rainy season that comes with this wind when it blows from the southwest.

moo (mōō) *n*- [*pl.* **moos**] the sound made by a cow. *vi*- to make the sound of a cow.

moral victory *n*- a defeat felt to be a victory because of spiritual satisfactions or hopes gained from it.

mo·rass (mə răs′) *n*- soft, swampy ground; bog.

mor·a·to·ri·um (môr′ə tôr′ ē əm, mŏr′-) *n*- [*pl.* **mor·a·to·ri·ums** or **mor·a·to·ri·a** (-ē ə)] 1 period of time over which payment of a debt may be legally delayed; also, the legal authorization granted in an emergency to make use of such a delay. 2 any temporary ban, suspension, or deferment of action.

mo·ray (môr′ā′) *n*- any of various brightly colored, voracious, eellike, marine fishes with sharp, knifelike teeth, found in all warm seas. Also **moray eel**.

mor·bid (môr′ bĭd′, môr′-) *adj*- 1 having too much to do with unpleasant and gloomy things; not healthy: *Reading a great many horror stories may show a morbid taste*. 2 caused by or having to do with disease: *A cancer is a morbid growth in the body*. —*adv*- **mor′ bid·ly**. *n*- **mor′ bid·ness**.

mor·bid·i·ty (môr bĭd′ə tē) *n*- [*pl.* **mor·bid·i·ties**] 1 morbid or gloomy outlook or state of mind. 2 amount of sickness or proportion of sick people in a place.

mor·dant (môr′ dənt, môr′-) *adj*- 1 biting; keen; sarcastic: *a mordant wit*. *n*- 1 substance that serves to fix certain colors in dyeing. 2 acid that eats into a metal surface, used in etching. —*n*- **mor′ dan·cy**.

Mor·de·cai (môr′ də kī′, môr′-) *n*- in the Old Testament, the cousin of Esther, who helped her save the Jews from destruction.

more (môr) *determiner* (traditionally called adjective or pronoun) a greater amount, degree, or number of: *You have more energy and more time than I*. *He wants more money and more help*. *He got more for his car than he expected*. *n*- an additional amount or number of: *Please buy more of that cake*. *adv*- 1 (used often to form the comparative of adjectives and adverbs) to a greater extent or degree: *This sofa is more comfortable than a bench. This sofa seats five men more comfortably than that bench*. 2 again: *We shall see her once more*. 3 in addition: *one word more*.

　more or less about: *The hat will cost you $15 more or less*. *the more* or *all the more* (used adverbially) even more: *That made me like him the more*.

mo·rel (mə rĕl′) *n*- any of various small edible mushrooms resembling a sponge.

more·o·ver (môr ō′ vər) *adv*- and in addition; besides; also; furthermore: *He is fast; moreover, he is tall*.

mo·res (môr′ āz′) *n*- *pl.* 1 in anthropology, the customs and the rules for right or wrong behavior that form the basis of a social group: *The mores of the tribe forbid marriage between cousins*. 2 customs or special rules or any group or place: *the mores of a newspaper office*.

mor·ga·nat·ic (môr′ gə nắt′ ĭk, môr′-) *adj*- relating to the marriage of a man of royal birth or high rank with a woman of lower station. Neither the wife nor children may share the man's rank or inherit his property.

Mor·gan le Fay (môr′ gən lə fā′, môr′-) *n*- in Arthurian legend, King Arthur's half sister, an enchantress.

morgue (môrg, môrg) *n*- 1 building or room where dead bodies are temporarily kept until identified or claimed for burial. 2 reference library of a newspaper, where early issues, clippings, etc., are filed.

mor·i·bund (môr′ə bŭnd′, môr′-) *adj*- dying: *a moribund man; a moribund civilization*.

Mor·mon (môr′ mən, môr′-) *n*- a member of the Church of Jesus Christ of Latter-day Saints. *adj*-: *a Mormon doctrine*.

morn·ing (môr′ nĭng, môr′-) *n*- the first part of the day, from midnight until noon, or from dawn until noon. *as modifier*: *a morning walk*. *Hom*- mourning.

morning coat *n*- a cutaway.

morn·ing-glor·y (môr′ nĭng glôr′ ē, môr′-) *n*- any of various climbing vines bearing heart-shaped leaves and trumpet-shaped, variously colored blossoms that open in early morning and close in bright sunlight, or in the evening.

mor·on (môr' ŏn) n- 1 person whose mental ability does not develop beyond that of a child between 8 and 12 years old. 2 *Informal* very stupid or foolish person. —*adj-* **mo·ron'ic.** *adv-* **mo·ron'i·cal·ly.**

mo·rose (mə rōs', môr' ōs') *adj-* gloomy; sullen. —*adv-* **mo·rose'ly.** n- **mo·rose'ness.**

mor·pheme (môr' fēm', môr'-) n- in linguistics, a unit of meaning that cannot be divided into smaller units of meaning. Morphemes can be words, or parts of words such as stems, prefixes, suffixes, etc. Examples: "green," "rock," and "has" are morphemes. "Rider" is made up of two morphemes, "ride" and "(e)r," and "cupfuls" is made up of three, "cup," "ful" and "s."

Mor·phe·us (môr' fē əs, môr'-) n- in Greek mythology, the god of sleep and dreams.

mor·phine (môr' fēn', môr'-) n- narcotic drug from opium, used medically to deaden pain or to produce sleep.

mor·phol·o·gy (môr fŏl' ə jē, môr'-) n- 1 branch of biology which deals with the form and structure of plants and animals, without regard to functions or life processes. 2 form and structure of an organism considered as a whole. 3 branch of linguistics which deals with the formation of words, their internal structure, inflections, derivations, etc. —*adj-* **mor'pho·log'ic** (-fə lŏj'ĭk) or **mor'pho·log'i·cal** (-ĭ kəl).

mor·ris (môr' əs, môr'-) n- old English folk dance.

morris chair n- large wooden easy chair with an adjustable back and removable cushions.

mor·row (môr' ō, môr'-) n- 1 the day after any particular day. 2 morning: *Good* morrow.

Morse code (môrs, môrs) n- 1 alphabet devised by S. F. B. Morse for sending messages by telegraph and also used for radio telegraphy and signaling by flashing light. Letters are represented by long and short spacing between clicks, or long and short sounds or flashes. 2 a modified form of this alphabet now in prevalent use, the **International Morse Code.**

mor·sel (môr' səl, môr'-) n- small piece; bit; scrap.

mor·tal·i·ty (môr tăl' ə tē) n- [*pl.* **mor·tal·i·ties**] 1 condition of being mortal or subject to death. 2 loss of life, especially on a large scale: *the mortality from war or disease.* 3 number of deaths in a given period in a given area; death rate. 4 human race; mankind. *as modifier: a high mortality rate;* mortality *figures.*

mor·tal·ly (môr' tə lē, môr'-) *adv-* 1 in such a manner as to cause death; fatally: *to be mortally wounded.* 2 deeply; bitterly; extremely: *to be mortally grieved.*

¹**mor·tar** (môr' tər, môr'-) n- building material made of lime, cement, sand, and water, used to hold stones or bricks together. [from Middle English **morter,** from Old French **mortier,** from Latin **mortārium** meaning "material pounded in a mixing trough."]

²**mor·tar** (môr' tər, môr'-) n- heavy bowl of glass, earthenware or other material in which drugs, spices, and the like are pounded or ground to powder with a pestle. [from Old English **mortere,** from Latin **mortārium** meaning "a mixing trough."]

³**mor·tar** (môr' tər, môr'-) n- kind of cannon for firing shells in a high curve. [from French **mortier** meaning "a short muzzle-loading cannon"; ²**mortar.**]

Mortar and pestle

mor·tar·board (môr' tər bôrd', môr'-) n- 1 square board with a handle on the underside, for holding mortar. 2 academic cap, with a square, flat, wide top.

mort·gage (môr' gĭj, môr'-) n- 1 legal assignment of property, especially real estate, to a creditor as security for the repayment of a loan. 2 contract by which such a transfer is made. 3 title or claim created by such a contract. *vt-* [**mort'gaged, mort'gag·ing**] 1 to make over (property) as security for a loan. 2 to pledge: *to* mortgage *one's future for a present advantage.*

mort·ga·gee (môr' gə jē', môr'-) n- person, bank, etc., that loans money in return for a mortgage.

mort·gag·or or **mort·gag·er** (môr' gə jər, môr'-) n- person who mortgages his property as security.

mor·ti·cian (môr tish' ən) n- undertaker.

mor·tu·ar·y (môr' chōō ĕr' ē, môr'-) n- [*pl.* **mor·tu·ar·ies**] funeral home. *adj-* connected with burial of the dead: *solemn* mortuary *rites.*

mos. months.

mo·sa·ic (mō zā' ĭk) n- 1 picture or design made by fitting together bits of colored glass, stone, or tile. 2 (also **mosaic disease**) any of several virus diseases of plants, marked by wrinkling and mottling of the leaves. *as modifier: a* mosaic *floor.*

Mosaic

Mo·sa·ic (mō zā' ĭk) *adj-* of or pertaining to Moses, the Hebrew leader and lawgiver, or to laws and writings attributed to him.

Mosaic Law n- the code of laws contained in the first five books of the Bible and attributed to Moses.

Mo·ses (mō' zəs) n- in the Old Testament, the Hebrew prophet and lawgiver who led the Israelites out of Egypt to the Promised Land.

mo·sey (mō' zē) *Slang vi-* 1 to go away. 2 to stroll.

Mos·lem (mŏz' ləm) Muslim.

mosque (mŏsk) n- a Muslim house of worship.

Mosque

mos·qui·to (mə skē' tō) n- [*pl.* **mos·qui·toes** or **mos·qui·tos**] any of various long-legged, two-winged insects, the female of which punctures the skin of men and animals, and feeds on the blood it sucks out. Some mosquitoes carry diseases, including malaria and yellow fever.

mosquito boat n- PT boat.

mosquito net n- screen, curtain, or canopy of fine net or gauze placed over windows, beds, etc., for keeping out mosquitoes.

Mosquito

moss (môs) n- 1 a small plant with tiny leaves. Moss grows in thick clusters which form a mat on damp ground, rocks, trees, etc. 2 any of various lichens and other plants resembling this, such as **Iceland moss,** an arctic lichen sometimes used for food and medicine. —*adj-* **moss' like'.**

moss agate n- agate with markings resembling moss.

moss·back (môs' băk') n- 1 old turtle having a growth of moss or seaweed on its back. 2 *Slang* fogy.

moss·y (mô' sē) *adj-* [**moss·i·er, moss·i·est**] 1 covered with moss: *a mossy stone.* 2 like moss: *a mossy coating.*

most (mōst) *determiner* (traditionally called adjective or pronoun) greatest in amount, degree, or number: *That is the car with* most *speed and gadgets. The pocketbook with the* most *money is hers.* n- 1 the majority (of); the larger part or number (of): *I have read* most *of the book. Most of his suits were at the cleaner's.* 2 the greatest quantity, amount, or degree; utmost: *This is the* most *I can do for you.* *adv-* 1 to the greatest extent or degree: *I like plums* most. 2 very: *a most diligent student.* 3 used often to form the superlative of adjectives and adverbs: *He was* most *wise. He replied* most *wisely to all their questions.*

at (or **at the**) **most** not more than; at the very limit: *She will pay only $20 at most.* **for the most part** usually.

Mother's Day n- a holiday to honor all mothers, celebrated on the second Sunday in May.

Mother Superior n- nun who is at the head of a convent of religious women.

mother tongue n- 1 one's native language. 2 language from which another language originates.

mother wit n- natural intelligence or common sense.

moth·y (mô' thē) *adj-* [**moth·i·er, moth·i·est**] 1 motheaten. 2 infested with moths.

motor coach *n-* bus powered by a motor, usually a gasoline engine. Also **mo'tor·bus'.**

mo·tor·cy·cle (mō' tər sī'kəl) *n-* motor-driven, two-wheeled vehicle, larger and heavier than a bicycle, with one or two riding seats and sometimes with a sidecar attached. *vi-* [mo·tor·cy·cled, mo·tor·cy·cling]: *We motorcycled to New York.*

Motorcycle

mo·tor·cy·clist (mō' tər sī'klist) *n-* person driving or riding on a motorcycle.

motor generator *n-* an electric motor and a generator with their shafts coupled, used for converting AC to DC or vice-versa, or for transforming voltage.

mo·tor·ist (mō' tər ĭst) *n-* person who drives or travels in an automobile.

mo·tor·ize (mō' tə rīz') *vt-* [mo·tor·i·zed, mo·tor·iz·ing] 1 to equip with a motor. 2 to supply with motor vehicles: *We have motorized our entire army since World War I.* *—n- mo'tor·i·za'tion.*

mo·tor·man (mō' tər mən) *n-* [*pl.* mo·tor·men] 1 operator of a streetcar or an electric train. 2 the operator of a motor.

motor nerve *n-* nerve that carries impulses from the central nervous system to a muscle, thus stimulating it to contract.

motor pool *n-* group of government or military vehicles dispatched by a central agency and available for use by authorized personnel.

motor scooter *n-* motor-driven, two-wheeled vehicle similar to a child's scooter but with one or two seats.

mo·tor·ship (mō' tər shĭp') *n-* ship propelled by internal-combustion engines, especially Diesel engines.

mot·tle (mŏt' əl) *vt-* [mot·tled, mot·tling] to mark with spots of various colors; dapple; blotch. *n-* 1 a spot; blotch. 2 arrangement of colored spots or blotches, such as those in marble.

mot·tled (mŏt' əld) *n-* spotted or streaked with different colors: *a mottled wallpaper.*

mot·to (mŏt' ō) *n-* [*pl.* mot·toes or mot·tos] 1 sentence, phrase, or word used as a guiding rule or principle: *"Early to bed and early to rise" was his* motto. 2 sentence or phrase expressing a principle, slogan, or the like, inscribed on a coin, seal, flag, etc.: *In the United States, the coins all bear the* motto *"In God We Trust."*

mould (mōld) mold.

mould·er (mōl' dər) molder.

mould·ing (mōl' dĭng) molding.

mould·y (mōl' dē) moldy.

moult (mōlt) molt.

mound (mound) *n-* 1 heap or bank of earth, stones, or sand. 2 small hill or knoll. 3 heap or mass of anything: *His foot rested on a mound of pillows.* 4 in baseball, a small, raised area from which the pitcher throws.

¹**mount** (mount) *n-* mountain. [partly from Old English *munt* and partly from Old French *mont*, both of which come from Latin *mons, montis*, "mountain."]

²**mount** (mount) *vt-* 1 to climb; ascend: *to mount stairs.* 2 to get up on: *to mount a horse; to mount a platform.* 3 to put on, or furnish with, a horse. 4 to set or place on something raised: *to mount a house on stilts.* 5 to put in position or set up for use: *to mount cannon on a hilltop; to mount an engine.* 6 to provide a setting, frame, or support for: *to mount a jewel; to mount a picture; to mount stamps in an album.* 7 to prepare (a specimen, insect, etc.) for examination or display: *to*

mountain chain *n-* connected row of mountains.

moun·tain·eer (moun' tə nêr') *n-* 1 person who lives in a mountain region. 2 person who climbs mountains as a sport or occupation.

moun·tain·eer·ing (moun' tə nêr' ĭng) *n-* the sport or occupation of climbing mountains, especially above the timber line with the aid of ropes and other gear.

mountain goat *n-* goatlike antelope of the Rocky Mountains, having shaggy white hair and black horns and hoofs.

mountain laurel *n-* low, gnarled evergreen shrub of eastern North America with white or pink flowers.

mountain lion *n-* a large, tawny cat of western America; catamount; cougar; panther; puma.

moun·tain·ous (moun' tə nəs) *adj-* 1 having many mountains: *a* mountainous *country.* 2 like a mountain; huge; enormous: *The waves were mountainous during the gale.* *—adv-* **moun'tain·ous·ly.** *n-* **moun' tain·ous·ness.**

Mountain lion. about 8 ft long

mountain range *n-* group of mountains forming a distinct geological or geographical unit.

mountain sheep *n-* any of various wild sheep inhabiting mountains, especially the Rocky Mountain bighorn.

moun·tain·side (moun' tən sīd') *n-* slope of a mountain: *We camped on a mountainside during our vacation.*

Mountain Standard Time See *standard time.*

moun·tain·top (moun' tən tŏp') *n-* top or summit of a mountain.

moun·te·bank (moun' tĭ băngk') *n-* person who sells quack medicines, especially from a public platform; hence, any charlatan.

mount·ed (moun' tĭd) *adj-* 1 seated or riding on a horse. 2 serving on horseback: *a detachment of* mounted *police.* 3 placed on or in a suitable support, setting, etc.: *a* mounted *photograph.*

mount·ing (moun' tĭng) *n-* 1 a rising or climbing; also, a getting on horseback. 2 a placing on a suitable support; a preparing for use, study, or observation: *the* mounting *of butterflies in a case.* 3 a support, fixture, or setting: *the* mounting *of a jewel; the* mounting *of a gun.*

mourn (môrn) *vi-* to feel or show sorrow or grief; lament; especially, to grieve or be sorrowful for the dead: *The people* mourned *over the death of the king.* *vt-* *Tommy* mourned *the loss of his pet dog.* **Hom-** morn.

mourn·er (môr' nər) *n-* 1 person who grieves or is sorrowful; especially, person who attends a funeral. 2 at religious revival meetings, person who professes penitence for sin.

mourn·ful (môrn' fəl) *adj-* sorrowful; sad: *the* mournful *cry of a dove.* *—adv-* **mourn'ful·ly.** *n-* **mourn'ful·ness.**

mouse (mous) *n-* [*pl.* mice (mīs)] 1 any of several small gnawing animals with soft gray or brown fur. The common house mouse is gray, has small beady eyes and a long tail, and is most active at night. 2 *Informal* timid or cowardly person. 3 *Slang* a black eye; bruise caused by a blow. *vi-* [moused, mous·ing] 1 to hunt or catch mice. 2 to prowl and pry.

House mouse about 7 in long

mous·er (mouz' ər) *n-* cat that catches mice.

mouse·trap (mous' trăp') *n-* trap for catching mice; also, stratagem or plot to defeat or destroy someone.

mousse (mōōs) *n-* delicate dessert made of whipped cream, whites of eggs, sugar, etc., flavored and frozen.

mous·tache (mŭs' tăsh', mə stăsh') mustache.

mous·y (mou' sē) *adj-* [mous·i·er, mous·i·est] 1 of, relating to, or resembling a mouse: *a* mousy *color.* 2 infested with, or smelling of, mice. 3 quiet; timid; shy: *a* mousy *person.* *—n-* **mous' i·ness.**

¹**mouth** (mouth) *n-* [*pl.* mouths (mouthz, mouths)] 1 opening in the head of a person or animal through which he takes in food and drink. This opening is also used to form sounds. 2 something resembling such an opening in shape or function: *the* mouth *of a cave.* 3 person or animal who needs food: *to have four* mouths *to feed.* 4 place where a river flows into another body of water: *The* mouth *of the Mississippi is near New Orleans.*

down at the mouth downhearted; sad. **with open mouth** amazed; dumbfounded.

²**mouth** (mouth) *vt-* 1 to utter or speak, especially in an affected or pompous way: *to* mouth *big phrases.* 2 to speak indistinctly; mumble: *The speaker* mouthed *his words.* *—n-* **mouth' er.**

musk (mŭsk) *n*- oily substance with a strong odor, obtained from a gland of the male musk deer and used in making perfumes; also, the odor of this substance.

musk deer *n*- small, hornless deer, found in the high parts of central Asia.

mus·keg (mŭs' kĕg) *n*- bog or marsh of the colder regions of North America, especially one in which sphagnum moss grows.

mus·kel·lunge (mŭs' kə lŭnj') *n*- [*pl.* **mus·kel·lunge**] large pike of North America, a prized game fish.

mus·ket (mŭs' kət) *n*- old-fashioned gun, replaced by the rifle.

Flintlock musket

mus·ket·eer (mŭs' kə tēr') *n*- foot soldier armed with a musket; especially, one of the royal bodyguard in France during the 17th and 18th centuries.

mus·ket·ry (mŭs' kə trē) *n*- 1 skill of firing guns such as muskets; also, the fire from such guns. 2 muskets collectively.

musk·mel·on (mŭsk' mĕl'- ən) *n*- 1 any of various round melons with sweet flesh and a tough rind, such as the cantaloupe. 2 the vine it grows on.

Musk ox, about 5 ft high at shoulder

musk ox *n*- long-haired animal of Greenland and arctic North America, related to both sheep and cattle.

musk·rat (mŭsk' rat') *n*- 1 North American water rodent with webbed hind feet and glossy, brown fur. 2 the fur of this animal. *as modifier*: *a muskrat coat.*

musk·y (mŭs' kē) *adj*- [**musk·i·er, musk·i·est**] having an odor like that of musk. —*n*- **musk' i·ness.**

Mus·lim (mŭz' ləm) *n*- a believer in Islam, the religion founded by Mohammed. *adj*- of or relating to the followers of Islam or to their customs: *a Muslim country.* Also **Moslem.**

Muskrat, about 2 ft long including tail

mus·lin (mŭz' lən) *n*- any of various sheer or heavy cotton fabrics of plain weave. *as modifier*: *a muslin sheet.*

muss (mŭs) *Informal vt*- to make untidy; rumple or soil. *n*- state of disorder; mess.

mus·sel (mŭs' əl) *n*- any of several mollusks found in fresh or salt water, especially an edible marine kind with a bluish-black shell. *Hom*- **muscle.**

Mus·sul·man (mŭs' əl mən) *Archaic n*- a Muslim.

Mussel, 2·3 in. long

muss·y (mŭs' ē) *Informal adj*- [**muss·i·er, muss·i·est**] disarranged; messy. —*adv*- **muss' i·ly.** —*n*- **muss' i·ness.**

must (mŭst) *auxiliary verb* 1 am, are, òr is required or obliged to; have to: *Citizens must obey the laws.* I must *go now.* 2 ought to; should: *I must try to see her more often.* 3 am, are, or is almost certain to: *This must be what he means. Her coat isn't here, so she* must *have gone. n*- *Informal* something that is necessary, required, or essential: *In winter, warm clothes are a must.*

mus·tache (mŭs' tăsh', mə stäsh') *n*- hair that grows on a man's upper lip, especially when left unshaven, but trimmed and groomed. Also **moustache.**

mus·ta·chi·o (mə stăsh' ē ō) *n*- [*pl.* **mus·ta·chi·os**] (usually **mustachios**) mustache, especially a large one.

mus·tang (mŭs' tăng') *n*- small, sturdy, wild or half-wild horse of western North America plains.

mu·tant (myōō' tənt) *n*- plant or animal produced as a result of mutation. *adj*- of or resulting from mutation.

my·col·o·gy (mī kŏl' ə jē) *n*- science or study of fungi.

my·na or **my·nah** (mī' nə) *n*- any of several starlings of Asia, such as the hill myna of India, which may be taught to say a few words.

Myn·heer (min' hēr') *Dutch n*- 1 title of courtesy equivalent to "Mr." 2 **mynheer** form of address equivalent to "sir."

my·o·pi·a (mī ō' pē ə) *n*- condition affecting the eyesight so that only objects at close range are seen clearly; nearsightedness.

my·op·ic (mī ŏp' ĭk) *adj*- 1 affected by or characteristic of myopia; nearsighted: *a myopic stare.* 2 showing lack of foresight; shortsighted. —*adv*- **my·op' i·cal·ly.**

myr·i·ad (mĭr' ē əd) *n*- a vast number. *adj*- countless; innumerable: *the myriad stars.*

myr·i·a·pod (mĭr' ē ə pŏd') *n*- a centipede or millipede, formerly classified together as **Myriapoda.**

Myr·mi·don (mûr' mə dŏn', -dən) *n*- 1 in Greek legend, one of a band of warriors who followed Achilles in the Trojan War. 2 **myrmidon** any follower who carries out orders without question.

myrrh (mûr) *n*- fragrant, gummy resin with a bitter taste, obtained from several shrubs of Arabia and eastern Africa. It is used in medicines, perfumes, and incense.

myr·tle (mûr' təl) *n*- 1 any of various sweet-smelling evergreen shrubs with shiny leaves, white or pink flowers, and black berries. 2 trailing plant with dark, shining, evergreen leaves and blue or violet flowers; periwinkle.

my·self (mī sĕlf') *pron*- 1 reflexive form of **me**; my own self: *I let myself into the house. I am pleased with myself.* 2 my normal or true self: *I don't feel quite myself today.* 3 intensive form of **I**: *I myself saw it.* 4 *Irish* I: *Indeed, myself will do it.*

by myself 1 alone: *I sat by myself in the garden.* 2 without any help: *I cooked this meal by myself.*

mys·te·ri·ous (mī stêr' ē əs) *adj*- not understood or explained; of unknown cause or origin; puzzling: *a mysterious light in the sky; her mysterious smile.* —*adv*- **mys·te' ri·ous·ly.** —*n*- **mys·te' ri·ous·ness.**

mys·ter·y (mĭs' tə rē) *n*- [*pl.* **mys·ter·ies**] 1 something that is secret, hidden, or unexplained: *The name of the thief is a* mystery. 2 something not known or not understandable: *the mystery of the creation of life.* 3 secrecy; obscurity: *a stranger shrouded in* mystery. 4 a religious ritual or sacrament.

mystery play *n*- in medieval times, a religious drama based on incidents from the Bible.

mys·tic (mĭs' tĭk) *adj*- 1 of or relating to beliefs, practices, etc., that have hidden or secret meaning: *the mystic rites of ancient religions.* 2 of or relating to mysticism. 3 magical or mysterious: *the mystic beauty of the night. n*- person who believes that he can have direct spiritual communication with God.

mys·ti·cal (mĭs' tĭ kəl) *adj*- 1 having a spiritual meaning not explained by reason or logic. 2 of or relating to direct communication with God or absolute truth. —*adv*- **mys' ti·cal·ly.**

mys·ti·cism (mĭs' tə sĭz' əm) *n*- 1 belief that direct spiritual knowledge of God or absolute truth comes through meditation, inspiration, etc. 2 spiritual qualities of a mystic. 3 vague or illogical thinking.

mys·ti·fy (mĭs' tə fī') *vt*- [**mys·ti·fied, mys·ti·fy·ing**] to bewilder; baffle; perplex: *His actions mystify me.* —*n*- **mys' ti·fi·ca' tion.**

myth (mĭth) *n*- 1 traditional story, often founded on some fact of nature or an event in the early history of a people, and embodying some religious belief of that people. 2 any imaginary person, thing, or event. 3 belief having no sound or logical basis.

myth·i·cal (mĭth' ĭ kəl) *adj*- 1 existing in myths: *Hercules was a* mythical *hero.* 2 imaginary; made-up: *a mythical kingdom.* —*adv*- **myth' i·cal·ly.**

myth·o·log·i·cal (mĭth' ə lŏj' ĭ kəl) *adj*- of, relating to, or existing in mythology: *a mythological monster.* —*adv*- **myth' o·log' i·cal·ly.**

my·thol·o·gy (mī thŏl' ə jē) *n*- [*pl.* **my·thol·o·gies**] 1 body of myths in which are recorded a people's beliefs concerning their origin, gods, heroes, etc. 2 study of these stories and beliefs.

N

N, n (ĕn) *n-* [*pl.* **N's, n's**] the fourteenth letter of the English alphabet.

n (ĕn) *Mathematics n-* an indefinite number.

n. 1 noun. 2 noon.

N symbol for nitrogen.

N. 1 north. 2 northern.

Na symbol for sodium.

N.A. North America.

NAACP or **N.A.A.C.P.** National Association for the Advancement of Colored People.

nab (năb) *Informal vt-* [**nabbed, nab·bing**] 1 to seize and arrest: *to nab a thief.* 2 to seize suddenly; grab.

na·bob (nā′ bŏb′) *n-* 1 governor of a province in India under the Mogul Empire. 2 any rich and powerful man.

na·celle (nə sĕl′) *n-* enclosure on an aircraft for an engine, or for the crew.

na·cre (nā′ kər) *n-* mother-of-pearl.

na·dir (nā′ dīr′, -dər) *n-* 1 that part of the celestial sphere directly beneath the place where one stands, and opposite to the zenith. 2 the lowest point: *the nadir of his career.*

¹nag (năg) *vi-* [**nagged, nag·ging**] to scold or find fault continually, often about little things. *vt-* to torment with tiresome insistence: *He nagged his father for a car. n-* person, especially a woman, who constantly scolds or finds fault. [probably from Old Norse *nagga* meaning "nibble; peck; gnaw."]

²nag (năg) *n-* horse, especially one that is old and worn out. [from Middle English *nagge,* of uncertain origin.]

nag·ging (năg′ ĭng) *adj-* 1 always scolding or finding fault: *a nagging husband.* 2 causing constant annoyance or discomfort: *a nagging backache.* —*adv-* **nag′ ging·ly.**

Na·hau·tl (nä′ wä′ təl) *n-* the language of the Aztecs and some Indian peoples of southern Mexico and Central America. *adj-: a Nahuatl word.*

nai·ad (nā′ ăd′, nī′ ăd′, -əd) *n-* [*pl.* **nai·ads** or **nai·a·des** (-ə dēz)] in classical mythology, one of the nymphs who dwelled in fountains, rivers, lakes, etc.

nail (nāl) *n-* 1 slender, sharp-pointed, metal spike or pin made to fasten together pieces of wood, leather, etc., by being driven through or into them. 2 horny growth on the upper side of the end of a finger or toe; also, a similar part, such as a claw, on a bird or animal. *vt-* 1 to fasten, fix, or secure with or as if with a metal spike or pin: *He nailed a shelf to a wall. Panic nailed him to his chair.* 2 *Slang* to get or catch: *to nail a contract; nail a thief.* 3 *Slang* to hit.

FINISHING
WIRE
HORSESHOE
FINGER
Nails

hit the nail on the head to be exactly to the point, especially in making an observation or criticism.
on the nail with exact accuracy, promptness, etc.

nail down *Informal* to settle finally and in all details.

nail file *n-* small metal file for shaping the fingernails.

nail polish *n-* lacquer for the fingernails.

nail set *n-* punch with a very small tip, used in driving nails flush with, or below, the surface.

nain·sook (nān′ sŏŏk′) *n-* fine, soft muslin with a plain, striped, or checked weave.

na·ive or **na·ïve** (nä ēv′) *adj-* 1 simple, childlike, and unaffected; artless; unsophisticated: *a naive young*

na·po·le·on (nə pō′ lē ən) *n-* 1 rich dessert made of several layers of flaky pastry filled with custard or whipped cream. 2 former gold coin of France.

nar·cis·sism (när′ sə sĭz′ əm) *n-* excessive or abnormal admiration for oneself; self-love.

nar·cis·sus (när′ sĭs′ əs) *n-* [*pl.* **nar·cis·sus·es** or **nar·cis·si** (-ī′, -ē′)] 1 any of various spring-blooming plants that grow from bulbs, with white, cream-colored, or yellow flowers; also, the flower itself. The jonquil and the daffodil are kinds of narcissus. 2 **Narcissus** in Greek legend, a beautiful young man who fell in love with his own reflection in the water and was changed into the flower that bears his name.

Narcissus

na·tion (nā′ shən) *n-* 1 the people of an independent country, considered as a unified group: *The entire nation celebrates Independence Day.* 2 an independent country: *to travel from one end of the nation to the other.* 3 a people united by the same customs, history, beliefs, etc., but not necessarily living together in one country. 4 tribe or federation, especially of American Indians.

na·tion·al (năsh′ ən əl) *adj-* 1 of, relating to, or characteristic of a nation: *the national government; our national customs; national pride.* 2 of, affecting, or throughout a nation as a whole: *a national problem; a national election; national advertising. n-* citizen or subject: *He is a British national.* —*adv-* **na′ tion·al·ly.**

national bank *n-* commercial bank chartered and supervised by the national government.

National Guard *n-* the military forces of a State, supported in part by the Federal government, which become part of the Army or Air Force when called into active service during national emergencies.

na·tion·al·ism (năsh′ ən ə lĭz′ əm) *n-* ardent belief in the importance of one's nation, its people, customs, and language, and its right to independence. This belief sometimes disregards the rights of other countries. —*n-* **na′ tion·al·ist.** *adj-* **na′ tion·al·is′ tic.**

na·tion·al·i·ty (năsh′ ə năl′ ə tē) *n-* [*pl.* **na·tion·al·i·ties**] 1 legal status as a citizen of a nation; citizenship: *a man of Russian birth and French nationality.* 2 national background or origin: *My grandparents were of Swedish nationality.* 3 group of people united by language, customs, etc., and part of a larger group or nation: *The Kurds are one of the nationalities of Iran.*

na·tion·al·ize (năsh′ ən ə līz′) *vt-* [**na·tion·al·ized, na·tion·al·iz·ing**] 1 to place (an industry, public service,

nau·sea (nô′ sē ə, -zē ə, nô′ shə, -zhə) *n-* 1 sickness of the stomach, with an urge to vomit; queasy feeling. 2 great disgust; loathing.

nau·se·ate (nô′ sē āt′, -zē āt′) *vt-* [**nau·se·at·ed, nau·se·at·ing**] to affect with nausea or with a feeling of strong disgust; sicken. —*adv-* **nau′ se·at′ ing·ly.**

nau·seous (nô′ shəs, nô′ sē əs) *adj-* 1 causing nausea; nauseating; sickening: *a nauseous odor.* 2 feeling nausea; nauseated.

▶Many people still insist that NAUSEOUS is correct only in sense 1. Unless you are sure you won't be misunderstood, avoid the word in favor of NAUSEATING or NAUSEATED, whichever you mean.

nau·ti·cal (nô′ tĭ kəl) *adj-* having to do with ships, sailors, and navigation. —*adv-* **nau′ ti·cal·ly.**

nautical mile See **mile.**

nau·ti·lus (nô′tə ləs) *n-* [*pl.* **nau·ti·lus·es** or **nau·ti·li** (-lī′,-lē′)] 1 (also **pearly nautilus** or **chambered nautilus**) mollusk having a pearly, spiral shell divided into narrow compartments. 2 (also **paper nautilus**) related mollusk with a very thin, delicate shell. 3 **Nautilus** name of the first atomic submarine.

Shell of pearly nautilus

Nav·a·ho (năv′ə hō) *n-* [*pl.* **Nav·a·hos** or **Nav·a·hoes**, also **Nav·a·ho**] one of a tribe of American Indians of southwestern United States, now on reservations in Arizona, New Mexico, and Utah. Also **Nav′ a·jo.**

na·val (nā′ vəl) *adj-* of or having to do with a navy or warships. *Hom-* navel. —*adv-* **na′ val·ly.**

nave (nāv) *n-* main, central part of a church, between the side aisles. *Hom-* knave.

na·vel (nā′ vəl) *n-* depression or mark in the center of the abdomen, where the umbilical cord was attached at birth. *Hom-* naval.

nav·i·ga·tor (năv′ ə gā′ tər) *n-* person skilled in navigation; especially, a person who determines or plots the course of a ship, airplane, or spaceship.

na·vy (nā′ vē) *n-* [*pl.* **na·vies**] 1 the branch of a nation's military force responsible for warfare at sea. 2 all of the warships belonging to such a force. 3 navy blue. 4 **Navy** (1) the naval force of the United States. (2) *Informal* the U.S. Naval Academy at Annapolis, Maryland. *adj-: a Navy depot; a navy sweater.*

navy bean *n-* small, oval, white bean.

near·ly (nēr′ lē) *adv-* 1 almost: *I tripped and* nearly *fell.* 2 closely: *First cousins are* nearly *related.*

near·sight·ed (nēr′ sī′ tǝd) *adj-* of, related to, or having the condition of eyesight in which only objects at close range are seen clearly; myopic. *—adv-* **near′ sight′ ed·ly.** *n-* **near′ sight′ ed·ness.**

neat (nēt) *adj-* [**neat·er, neat·est**] 1 clean and orderly; tidy: *a* neat *desk.* 2 simple and pleasing in appearance: *a* neat *dress.* 3 skillful; clever: *a* neat *job of carpentry.* 4 *Informal* very good. *—adv-* **neat′ ly.** *n-* **neat′ ness.**

′neath or **neath** (nēth) *prep-* beneath.

neat′s-foot oil *n-* light-yellow oil obtained from the feet and shinbones of cattle, used to condition leather.

Nebr. Nebraska.

Neb·u·chad·nez·zar (nĕb′ yǝ kǝd nĕz′ ǝr, nĕb′ ǝ-) *n-* king of Babylon (605-562 B.C.) who conquered Jerusalem and enslaved the Jews.

neb·u·la (nĕb′ yǝ lǝ) *n-* [*pl.* **neb·u·lae** (-lē, -lī) or **neb·u·las**] 1 one of the billions of cloudlike masses of gas and dust, often luminous, in the universe. 2 galaxy.

neb·u·lar (nĕb′ yǝ lǝr) *adj-* of or relating to a nebula or nebulas: *a* nebular *shape.*
▶Should not be confused with NEBULOUS.

nebular hypothesis *Astronomy n-* hypothesis that the solar system was formed from a rotating mass of gas at high temperature.

neb·u·lous (nĕb′ yǝ lǝs) *adj-* vague; unclear; cloudy; indistinct. *—adv-* **neb′ u·lous·ly.** *n-* **neb′ u·lous·ness.**
▶Should not be confused with NEBULAR.

nec·es·sar·i·ly (nĕs′ ǝ sĕr′ ǝ lē) *adv-* as a matter of course: *A forecast of rain does not* necessarily *mean rain.*

nec·es·sar·y (nĕs′ ǝ sĕr′ ē) *adj-* 1 needed; required; essential: *He made the* necessary *adjustments in the controls.* 2 following by necessity; inescapable; unavoidable: *the* necessary *result of his foolishness.* *n-* **necessaries** things that cannot be done without; necessities.

nec·es·si·tate (nǝ sĕs′ ǝ tāt′) *vt-* [**nec·es·si·tat·ed, nec·es·si·tat·ing**] to make necessary; require; demand: *The threat of riot* necessitates *prompt action by the police.*

nec·es·si·ty (nǝ sĕs′ ǝ tē) *n-* [*pl.* **nec·es·si·ties**] 1 something needed; something one cannot get along without: *Water is a* necessity *of life.* 2 situation or occasion that calls for help: *In case of* necessity, *you can call on me.* 3 extreme poverty; lack of things needed for life: *Cruel* necessity *forced him to beg.* 4 a compelling force or need: *the* necessity *of sleep.*

neck·er·chief (nĕk′ ǝr chĭf) *n-* handkerchief or scarf worn around the neck.

neck·lace (nĕk′ lǝs) *n-* string of beads or jewels, or an ornament of metalwork, worn about the neck.

neck·line (nĕk′ lĭn′) *n-* the border of a garment, especially a woman's garment, at the neck or chest.

neck·piece (nĕk′ pēs′) *n-* article of clothing like a scarf, usually of fur, worn around the neck.

neck·tie (nĕk′ tī′) *n-* narrow band of cloth worn around the neck under the collar and tied in front in a knot or bow; cravat.

neck·wear (nĕk′ wâr′) *n-* articles of clothing, such as scarves or ties, to be worn around the neck.

Necklace

nec·ro·man·cy (nĕk′ rǝ măn′ sē) *n-* 1 pretended art of foretelling the future by calling up the spirits of the dead. 2 magic; sorcery. *—n-* **nec′ ro·man′ cer.**

nec·tar (nĕk′ tǝr) *n-* 1 sweet liquid found in some flowers: *Bees use* nectar *to make honey.* 2 in Greek mythology, a drink of the gods. 3 any delicious or pleasant drink.

nec·tar·ine (nĕk′ tǝ rēn′) *n-* kind of peach having a smooth skin; also, the tree bearing this fruit.

née or **nee** (nā) *adj-* born (used only before the maiden name of a married woman to show her maiden name): *Mrs. John Miller,* nee *Brown.* *Homs-* nay, neigh.

ne·glect (nǝ glĕkt′) *n-* failure to do what should be done; lack of care: *The garden, overgrown with weeds, showed* neglect. *vt-* 1 to fail to do (what should be done) through carelessness or on purpose: *Don't* neglect *your homework.*

neg·li·gi·ble (nĕg′ lǝ jǝ bǝl) *adj-* not worth much attention; of little account or value: *a* negligible *loss; a* negligible *contribution.* *—adv-* **neg′ li·gi·bly.**

ne·go·ti·a·ble (nǝ gō′ shǝ bǝl, -shē ǝ bǝl) *adj-* 1 in business, such as can be passed from one person to another by endorsement or delivery and serves the purpose of cash: *a* negotiable *bond; a* negotiable *promissory note.* 2 such as can be settled by negotiation: *Their quarrel did not prove to be* negotiable. *—n-* **ne·go′ ti·a·bil′ i·ty** to negotiate.

ne·go·ti·ate (nǝ gō′ shē āt′) *vt-* [**ne·go·ti·at·ed, ne·go·ti·at·ing**] 1 to discuss and make the arrangements for (a business deal, treaty, loan, etc.): *to* negotiate *a treaty.* 2 to sell or make a fair exchange: *to* negotiate *a sale of property.* 3 to clear, pass, or surmount (something): *The old car could hardly* negotiate *the hill.* *vi-* to discuss or exchange terms, proposals, etc.; parley: *The two sides agreed to* negotiate.

ne·go·ti·a·tion (nǝ gō′ shē ā′ shǝn) *n-* act of negotiating; the talking over and settling the terms of a treaty, business agreement, etc.

ne·go·ti·a·tor (nǝ gō′ shē ā′ tǝr) *n-* person who negotiates.

Ne·gress (nē′ grǝs) *n-* Negro woman or girl (term often considered offensive).

Ne·gri·to (nǝ grē′ tō) *n-* [*pl.* **Ne·gri·tos** or **Ne·gri·toes**] one of a group of small, dark-skinned people living in the Philippines and other parts of southeastern Asia.

Ne·gro (nē′ grō′) *n-* [*pl.* **Ne·groes**] member of the Negroid division of the human species, especially of the peoples of Africa south of the Sahara or their descendants. *adj-: a* Negro *community; a* Negro *spiritual.*

Ne·groid (nē′ groid′) *adj-* of or relating to a major division of the human species, considered to include native peoples of Africa south of the Sahara and of numerous islands in the western Pacific. Negroid peoples are characterized by brown eyes, black, often tightly curled hair, and usually brown to black skin.

Ne·he·mi·ah (nē′ hǝ mī′ ǝ) *n-* 1 a Jewish leader of the 5th century B.C. 2 a book of the Old Testament describing the rebuilding of Jerusalem. In the CCD Bible it is called Esdra II.

neigh (nā) *n-* the sound that a horse makes; a whinny. *vi-* to make this sound. *Homs-* nay, née.

neigh·bor (nā′ bǝr) *n-* 1 person who lives nearby. 2 person, country, or thing that is near another: *Canada is our* neighbor *to the north.* 3 fellow man: *"Love thy* neighbor *as thyself."*

neigh·bor·hood (nā′ bǝr hŏŏd′) *n-* 1 area or district where a person lives: *Our* neighborhood *has a new shopping center.* 2 the people living nearby or near one another: *The* neighborhood *held a barbecue.*
   in the neighborhood of near; not far from: *The town is* in the neighborhood of *the Great Lakes.*

neigh·bor·ing (nā′ bǝr ĭng) *adj-* near; nearby: *in a* neighboring *village.* 2 adjoining: *Henry and Edward just bought two* neighboring *lots of land.*

neigh·bor·ly (nā′ bǝr lē) *adj-* friendly; kindly; proper or suitable for neighbors: *The people here are very* neighborly. *—n-* **neigh′ bor·li·ness.**

nei·ther (nē′ thǝr, nī′-) *determiner* (traditionally called adjective or pronoun) not one and not the other: *Neither car is here.* Neither *is here.* *n-* not one or the other (of two): *I want* neither *of them.* *conj-* 1 (used with "nor" to introduce two negative alternatives):

ne·o·phyte (nē′ ǝ fīt′) *n-* beginner; novice.

ne·o·prene (nē′ ǝ prēn′) *n-* a synthetic rubber having high resistance to heat, light, oxidation, and oils.

neph·ew (nĕf′ yōō′) *n-* son of one's brother or brother-in-law, or of one's sister or sister-in-law.

ne·phri·tis (nǝ frī′ tǝs) *n-* inflammation of one or both kidneys. *—adj-* **ne·phrit′ ic** (nǝ frĭt′ ĭk).

nep·o·tism (nĕp′ ǝ tĭz′ ǝm) *n-* too great official favor and preferment shown by a person in power to members of his family.

Nep·tune (nĕp′ tōōn′,-tyōōn′) *n-* 1 in Roman mythology, the god of the sea. He is identified with the Greek Poseidon. 2 the fourth largest planet in the solar system, eighth in order of distance from the sun

nerve fiber *n-* a single axon or dendrite.

nerve impulse *n-* the "message" passing along a nerve fiber. It consists of a traveling wave of electrochemical changes associated with the migration of ions across the membrane of a nerve cell.

nerve·less (nûrv′ləs) *adj-* 1 lacking nerves. 2 *Archaic* weak; paralyzed. —*adv-* **nerve′less·ly.**

nerve-rack·ing or **nerve-wrack·ing** (nûrv′ răk′ ĭng) *adj-* very upsetting or shocking to the nerves and senses; destroying one's ease and poise: *a nerve-racking two hours*; *a nerve-racking noise.*

ner·vous (nûr′ vəs) *adj-* 1 of or relating to the nerves: *the nervous system.* 2 easily excited; highstrung: *A nervous person gets upset often.* 3 fearful; tense; uneasy; restless. —*adv-* **ner′vous·ly.** —*n-* **ner′vous·ness.**

nervous system *n-* the total system of nerve cells, nerves, brain, spinal cord, and receptors with which an animal responds to external and internal stimuli.

nerv·y (nûr′ vē) *Slang adj-* [**nerv·i·er, nerv·i·est**] audacious; impudent; brash.

-ness *suffix* (used to form nouns from adjectives) condition or quality of being: *hardness; rashness; loveliness.*

Robin's nest

Oriole's nest   Wasp's nest

nest (nĕst) *n-* 1 place where a bird lays eggs and cares for its young. 2 place for the same use made by wasps and some other insects. 3 den or burrow, especially the part of it used for sleeping and caring for young: *We found a squirrel's nest in the hollow tree.* 4 any warm and cozy place. 5 a group of things fitting neatly into one another: *This nest of boxes came from Japan.* *vi-* to build or use a place for laying eggs and caring for young: *Birds nested in the maple tree.* *vt-* 1 to place in or as if in such a place: *to nest one's head in the pillows.* 2 to fit into one another: *The boys nested the cartons to save space.*

nest egg *n-* 1 real or false egg left in a nest to encourage the hen to lay eggs there. 2 money put aside; savings.

nest·er (nĕs′ tər) *n-* formerly, in western United States, a homesteader who settled on open range land (chiefly a contemptuous term used by cattlemen). *Hom-* Nestor.

nes·tle (nĕs′ əl) *vi-* [**nes·tled, nes·tling**] to lie close and snug; snuggle; settle comfortably: *A child nestles in its mother's arms.* *vt-* to press closely; cuddle: *The little girl nestled her doll in her arms.* —*n-* **nes′ tler.**

nest·ling (nĕst′ lĭng, nĕs′-) *n-* bird too young to fly.

Nes·tor (nĕs′ tər, -tôr′) *n-* 1 in the "Iliad," a wise old Greek king. 2 **nestor** any wise old man. *Hom-* nester.

net·ting (nĕt′ ĭng) *n-* 1 a making of nets. 2 a fabric made of meshes. 3 a texture made from crossed wires, such as a fence. 4 network.

net·tle (nĕt′ əl) *n-* any of several plants which have stems and leaves with hairs or spines that irritate the skin on contact. *vt-* [**net·tled, net·tling**] to vex or annoy: *Joe's questions nettled the chairman.*

net·work (nĕt′ wûrk′) *n-* 1 a net. 2 system or arrangement of lines that cross: *a network of wires.* 3 a chain of radio or television stations which carry the same programs.

Nettle

neur- or **neuro-** *combining form* nerve: *a neuritis*; *neurology.* [from Greek **neuron** meaning "sinew."]

new·ly·wed (nōo′ lē wĕd′, nyōo′-) *n-* person recently married.

new moon *n-* the moon just before or shortly after it enters its first quarter and is barely visible or seen as a slender, growing crescent. For picture, see *moon.*

news (nōoz, nyōoz) *n-* (takes singular verb) 1 recent or fresh information: *Have you had any news from our old friend Tom?* 2 recent events or fresh information reported in the newspaper or over the radio or television.

news·boy (nōoz′ boi′, nyōoz′-) *n-* newspaper seller.

news·cast (nōoz′ kåst′, nyōoz′-) *n-* radio or television news report.

news·cast·er (nōoz′ kås′ tər, nyōoz′-) *n-* radio or television news reporter. —*n-* **news′ cast′ ing.**

news·deal·er (nōoz′ dē′ lər, nyōoz′-) *n-* businessman dealing in newspapers, especially one with a shop or stand where they are for sale.

news·let·ter (nōoz′ lĕt′ ər, nyōoz′-) *n-* news report and comment, printed in the form of a letter and usually mailed out periodically to subscribers.

news·pa·per (nōoz′ pā′ pər, nyōoz′-) *n-* daily or weekly publication containing current news, editorials, articles, pictures, advertisements, etc., and consisting of unattached sheets of printed paper folded together.

news·pa·per·man (nōoz′ pā′ pər mən, nyōoz′-) *n-* [*pl.* **news·pa·per·men**] reporter, editor, or other journalist employed by a newspaper. Also **news′ man′.**

news·print (nōoz′ print′, nyōoz′-) *n-* cheap paper made mainly of wood pulp and used for newspapers.

news·reel (nōoz′ rēl′, nyōoz′-) *n-* motion picture of current news events.

news·room (nōoz′ rōom′, nyōoz′-) *n-* room where news is received, edited, sent out, etc., such as one in a radio or television studio.

news·stand (nōoz′ stånd′, nyōoz′-) *n-* stand or store where newspapers and periodicals are sold.

news·wor·thy (nōoz′ wûr′ thē, nyōoz′-) *adj-* interesting enough to be printed as news.

news·y (nōo′ zē, nyōo′-) *adj-* [**news·i·er, news·i·est**] *Informal* full of news.

newt (nōot, nyōot) *n-* one of several kinds of small, harmless, insect-eating salamanders that remain amphibious throughout their adult life; eft.

Newt, about 4 in. long

New Testament *n-* one of the two main divisions of the Bible, containing accounts of the life and teachings of Jesus, and writings of some of the early Christians.

new·ton (nōo′ tən, nyōo′-) *n-* unit of force in the mks system, defined as the amount of force required to give a

nick (nĭk) *n-* a notch; small cut or chip: *a nick in the rim of a glass.* *vt-* to make a notch, a small cut, or a chip in: *The bullet nicked the tree trunk.*

in the nick of time at the last, crucial moment.

nick·el (nĭk′ əl) *n-* 1 hard, silver-white metal element, used chiefly in alloys and for plating. Symbol Ni, At. No. 28, At. Wt. 58.71. 2 in the United States and Canada, a coin of nickel and copper, worth five cents.

nick·el·o·de·on (nĭk′ ə lō′ dē ən) *n-* 1 an early type of coin-operated music machine; jukebox. 2 formerly, a motion picture theater charging five cents for admission.

nickel silver *n-* lustrous, white alloy of nickel, zinc, and copper; German silver.

nick·nack (nĭk′ năk′) knickknack.

nick·name (nĭk′ nām′) *n-* 1 shortened or familiar form of a person's name, such as "Ed" for "Edward" or "Johnny" for "John." 2 substitute for a person's real name, sometimes given in fun, such as "Red" for someone with red hair. *vt-* [**nick·named, nick·nam·ing**] to give such a name to.

nic·o·tine (nĭk′ ə tēn′) *n-* poisonous, oily alkaloid from tobacco, used as an insecticide and tanning agent.

nic·o·tin·ic acid (nĭk′ ə tĭn′ ĭk, -tē′ nĭk) *n-* vitamin of the vitamin B complex, important in metabolism and found in many foods; niacin. Lack of it causes pellagra.

nic·ti·ta·ting membrane (nĭk′ tə tā′ tĭng) *n-* thin, translucent tissue found in the eyes of birds and some other vertebrates and functioning as a third eyelid.

niece (nēs) *n-* daughter of one's brother or brother-in-law, or of one's sister or sister-in-law.

nif·ty (nĭf′ tē) *Slang adj-* [**nif·ti·er, nif·ti·est**] excellent; very good.

nig·gard (nĭg′ ərd) *n-* miser; stingy person.

nig·gard·ly (nĭg′ ərd lē) *adj-* 1 stingy; frugal to excess. 2 very small; scant: *to give niggardly aid.* *adv-* stingily. —*n-* **nig′ gard·li·ness.**

night latch *n-* latch with a spring-loaded bolt opened from outside by a key and from inside by a knob.

night letter *n-* telegram sent at night at a reduced rate and delivered the following morning.

night·long (nīt' lông') *adj-* lasting all the night.

night·ly (nīt' lē) *adv-* every night: *The wolf howls nightly from the hill. adj-* happening every night: *the nightly howl of the wolf.* Hom- knightly.

night·mare (nīt' mâr') *n-* 1 a very bad and frightening dream. 2 terrifying experience: *The train crash was a nightmare I shall never forget.*

night owl *n-* person who works at night or enjoys staying up late at night.

night rider *n-* horseman who rides at night to frighten or punish.

night·shade (nīt' shād') *n-* any of several plants related to the tomato and potato, including deadly nightshade; especially, a vine with purple flowers and clusters of bright red berries.

night·shirt (nīt' shûrt') *n-* loose-fitting men's garment like a lengthened shirt, worn in bed.

night·time (nīt' tīm') *n-* the period between dusk and dawn; night. - *as modifier:* the nighttime hours.

Nightshade

night watch *n-* 1 guard kept for protection at night. 2 person or persons on guard at night. 3 period of time during which a night guard is on duty.

ni·hil·ism (nī' ə lĭz' əm, nī' hĭl' ĭz' əm) *n-* 1 doctrine holding that all present forms of social organization are so evil that they must be destroyed before anything better can be built. 2 violent revolution; anarchism; terrorism. —*n-* nī' hĭl·ist. *adj-* nī' hil·is' tic.

Nike (nī' kē) *n-* in Greek mythology, the goddess of victory, usually represented as a winged figure bearing a wreath and palm branch.

nim·ble (nĭm' bəl) *adj-* [nim·bler, nim·blest] 1 quick and active; agile: *Squirrels are nimble in climbing trees.* 2 quick in thought or reply; clever and alert: *a nimble mind.* —*n-* nim' ble·ness. *adj-* nim' bly.

nim·bo·stra·tus (nĭm' bō strā' təs, -strāt' əs) *n-* in meteorology, a thick, shapeless cloud occurring in dark gray layers at low altitudes and usually accompanied by rain or snow; nimbus.

nim·bus (nĭm' bəs) *n-* [*pl.* nim·bus·es or nim·bi (-bī, -bē)] 1 the halo or cloud of light represented in pictures as surrounding the heads of divinities, saints, and sovereigns. 2 a feeling or atmosphere of splendor surrounding a person or thing. 3 nimbostratus (for picture, see cloud).

Nim·rod (nĭm' rŏd') *n-* in the Bible, a great grandson of Noah famed as a mighty hunter.

nin·com·poop (nĭn' kəm poōp') *Informal n-* silly or stupid person; fool.

nine (nīn) *n-* 1 amount or quantity that is one greater than 8; 9. 2 *Mathematics* (1) the cardinal number that is the sum of 8 and 1. (2) a numeral such as 9 that represents this cardinal number. 3 *Informal* baseball team. *as determiner* (traditionally called adjective or pronoun): *There are nine players here and nine there.*

nine·fold (nīn' fōld') *adj-* 1 nine times as many or as much. 2 having nine parts: *a ninefold flower. adv-:* *They increased their output ninefold.*

nine·pins (nīn' pĭnz') *n-* (takes singular verb) game in which one rolls a ball at nine wooden pins set up at one end of a bowling alley.

ninth (nīnth) *adj-* 1 next after eighth. 2 the ordinal of 9; 9th. *n-* 1 the next after the eighth; 9th. 2 one of nine equal parts of a whole or group. 3 the last term in the name of a fraction having a denominator of 9: *1/9 is one* ninth. 4 *Music* (1) an interval of nine tones on the scale counting the extremes, as from C to D in the octave above. (2) The harmonic combination of these tones. *adv-:* *She finished ninth in her class.*

ni·o·bi·um (nī ō' bē əm) *n-* gray or silver-white, hard metal element used in stainless steel and other alloys.

No symbol for nobelium.

No. 1 north; northern. 2 number.

No·ah (nō' ə) *n-* in the Old Testament, a patriarch who built an ark in which he, his family, and every kind of animal survived the Flood. In the CCD Bible, No' e.

no·be·li·um (nō bē' lē əm) *n-* man-made, radioactive element produced by bombarding curium with carbon nuclei. Symbol No, At. No. 102.

No·bel Prize (nō' bĕl', nō bĕl') *n-* one of five cash prizes established by Alfred E. Nobel (1833-96) a Swedish inventor, to be awarded annually in the fields of physics, chemistry, physiology or medicine, literature, and the furtherance of peace.

no·bil·i·ty (nō bĭl' ə tē) *n-* 1 greatness of character: *We did not agree with his methods, but admired the* nobility *of his aims.* 2 in some countries, high social position by reason of birth or of title conferred by the ruler. 3 the nobility persons of noble rank, collectively.

no·ble (nō' bəl) *adj-* [no·bler, no·blest] 1 having or showing very high character and great ideals: *a noble person; a noble life; a noble sacrifice.* 2 in some countries, having a high social position by birth or by title conferred by the ruler: *a noble family.* 3 handsome and impressive: *a noble building; a noble brow. n-* nobleman or noblewoman. —*n-* no' ble·ness. *adv-* no' bly.

no·ble·man (nō' bəl mən) *n-* [*pl.* no·ble·men] man of noble birth or rank; peer. —*n- fem.* no' ble·wom' an [*pl.* no·ble·wom·en].

no·blesse o·blige (nō' blĕs' ō blēzh') *French* nobility obligates; persons of hereditary wealth and power must be generous and protective towards their inferiors.

no·bod·y (nō' bŏd' ē, -bə dē) *pron-* no one; no person. *n-* [*pl.* no·bod·ies] person of no importance or influence: *He felt like a nobody in their presence.*

nock (nŏk) *n-* notch at the end of an arrow or bow for holding the bowstring. *vt-* 1 to put a notch in (an arrow or a bow). 2 to fit (an arrow) to a bowstring. 3 to fit (a bowstring) into the notches at the end of a bow.

noc·tur·nal (nŏk tûr' nəl) *adj-* 1 of the night; happening or done at night: *a nocturnal sound;* nocturnal *activity.* 2 active at night: *a nocturnal animal.* 3 of plants, having flowers that are open at night and closed in the daytime. —*adv-* noc·tur' nal·ly.

noc·turne (nŏk' tûrn') *n-* 1 picture of a night scene. 2 quiet, melancholy musical piece, especially when written for the piano.

nod (nŏd) *vt-* [nod·ded, nod·ding] (in senses 1 and 2 considered intransitive when the direct object is implied but not expressed). 1 to bow (the head) and raise it quickly as a greeting or as a sign of assent or agreement: *The boy* nodded *his head when asked if he had lost something.* 2 to express or indicate (agreement, recognition, etc.) by such a motion: *to nod a greeting to a friend. vi-* 1 to let the head droop forward as one drowses. 2 to sway or bend near the top: *Flowers nod in the breeze. n-* quick bending of the head, used as a sign of greeting assent, approval, etc.: *a friendly nod.* —*n- nod' der.*

node (nōd) *n-* 1 knot, knob, or swelling. 2 the part of a plant stem from which leaves arise. 3 *Astronomy* one of the two points at which the orbit of a celestial body crosses the ecliptic; also, one of two points on the earth's equator where the orbit of an artificial satellite crosses. —*adj-* nod' al.

nod·ule (nŏj' oōl', nŏd' yoōl') *n-* 1 small lump: *a nodule of tin ore.* 2 small knot or swelling, especially on the root of a plant or on some part of the body; tubercle. —*adj-* nod' u·lar: *a nodular growth.*

No·el (nō ĕl') *n-* 1 Christmas. 2 noel a Christmas carol.

nog·gin (nŏg' ən) *n-* 1 *Informal* head. 2 small mug or cup. 3 small amount of drink, usually a gill.

no·how (nō' hou') *Slang adv-* not in any manner or way; not at all. Hom- know-how.

noise (noiz) *n-* sound, especially if loud, harsh, or confused. *vt-* [noised, nois·ing] to spread by rumor (followed by "about" or "around"): *He* noised *the story about.*

noise·less (noiz' ləs) *adj-* producing no noise, or much less noise than is usual; quiet; silent: *a noiseless machine.* —*adv-* noise' less·ly. *n-* noise' less·ness.

non·com·pli·ance (nŏn′ kəm plī′ əns) *n-* refusal or failure to comply.

non com·pos men·tis (nŏn′ kŏm′ pəs mĕn′ təs) *Latin* not of sound mind; mentally unfit.

non·con·duc·tor (nŏn′ kən dŭk′ tər) *n-* material that has the property of preventing the passage of sound, heat, or electricity; insulator: *Glass is a nonconductor of electricity.* —*adj-* **non′ con·duct′ ing.**

non·con·form·ist (nŏn′ kən fôr′ mĭst, -fôr′ mĭst) *n-* 1 person who does not conform to established beliefs or customs. 2 **Nonconformist** one of a group of English Protestants who dissented from the Church of England in the seventeenth century.

non·con·form·i·ty (nŏn′ kən fôr′ mə tē, fôr′ mə tē) *n-* failure or refusal to conform.

non·con·sum·a·ble (nŏn′ kən sōō′ mə bəl, -syōō′ mə bəl) *adj-* of natural resources, such as cannot be used up: *Sunshine and air are nonconsumable natural resources.*

non·con·ta·gious (nŏn′ kən tā′ jəs) *adj-* not contagious: *a noncontagious disease.*

non·de·script (nŏn′ də skrĭpt′) *adj-* not remarkable in any way; having no special character.

none (nŭn) *n-* (takes singular or plural verb) 1 not any; no part or quantity: *He has done none of his work.* 2 no one; not one: *I see none of them here.* *Hom-* nun.
►Since NONE is usually used in a plural compound, the plural verb is generally the most natural: *It is true that none of the boys were good. None of the people are coming.* It is artificial to use the singular verb: *I know none of the boys is there.*

non·en·ti·ty (nŏn ĕn′ tə tē) *n-* [*pl.* **non·en·ti·ties**] 1 something that does not exist or exists only in the imagination. 2 person of no importance or influence; a nobody.

non·es·sen·tial (nŏn′ ə sĕn′ chəl) *adj-* not essential; of little importance. *n-: We left* nonessentials *behind.*

none·the·less (nŭn′ thə lĕs′) *adv-* nevertheless. Also **none the less.**

non·ex·ist·ent (nŏn′ ĭg zĭs′ tənt) *adj-* not existing; unreal: *a nonexistent place.* —*n-* **non′ ex·ist′ ence.**

non·fer·rous (nŏn′ fĕr′ əs) *adj-* not containing or composed of iron; especially, relating to metals other than iron, such as gold, silver, or copper: *a nonferrous ore.*

non·fic·tion (nŏn′ fĭk′ shən) *n-* essays, biographies, travel books, and other literature that is not fiction.

non·fil·ter·a·ble virus (nŏn′ fĭl′ tər ə bəl) *n-* virus that is too big to pass through a porcelain or other filter.

non·fi·nite (nŏn′ fī′ nīt′) *adj-* not finite, especially in grammatical function: *a nonfinite verb.* See also *finite.*

non·flam·ma·ble (nŏn′ flăm′ ə bəl) *adj-* not flammable.
►For usage note see FLAMMABLE.

non·flow·er·ing (nŏn′ flou′ ər ĭng) *adj-* of plants, having no flowering stage during their life cycle.

non·in·flam·ma·to·ry (nŏn′ ĭn flăm′ ə tôr′ ē) *adj-* not inflammatory, usually as a result of purpose.

non·in·ter·fer·ence (nŏn′ ĭn tər fêr′ əns) *n-* policy or habit of not interfering; also, an instance of this.

non·in·ter·ven·tion (nŏn′ ĭn tər vĕn′ shən) *n-* refusal to intervene in the affairs of another country; especially, a policy of such refusal.

non·liv·ing (nŏn′ lĭv′ ĭng) *adj-* not having life; inanimate.

non·met·al (nŏn′ mĕt′ əl) *n-* any of the group of elements lacking the properties of a metal, such as the ability to conduct heat and electricity. —*adj-* **non′ met·al′ lic.**

non·pa·reil (nŏn′ pə rĕl′) *n-* 1 person or thing that has no equal in excellence; paragon.

non·par·ti·san (nŏn′ pär′ tə zən) *adj-* not partisan; especially, not swayed by or representing any political party.

non·pay·ment (nŏn′ pā′ mənt) *n-* failure to pay.

non·per·form·ance (nŏn′ pər fôr′ məns, -fôr′ məns) *n-* failure or refusal to carry out responsibilities.

non·plus (nŏn plŭs′, nŏn′-) *vt-* [**non·plused** or **non·plussed, non·plus·ing** or **non·plus·sing**] to bewilder; throw into confusion; bring to a standstill: *Her refusal to decide nonplused Hal.*

non·poi·son·ous (nŏn′ poi′ zə nəs) *adj-* not poisonous; not toxic.

non·ver·bal (nŏn′ vûr′ bəl) *adj-* not using or expressed in words.

non·vi·o·lence (nŏn′ vī′ ə ləns) *n-* belief that only peaceful means should be used to solve problems and defend one's principles. —*adj-* **non′ vi′ o·lent:** *a nonviolent revolution.*

non·vot·er (nŏn′ vō′ tər) *n-* person who is not entitled to vote or does not bother to.

¹**noo·dle** (nōō′ dəl) *n-* narrow strip of dried dough, usually made with egg and eaten in soup or cooked as a casserole. [from German Nudel.]

²**noo·dle** (nōō′ dəl) *n-* 1 silly or stupid person; blockhead. 2 *Informal* the head. [of uncertain origin.]

nook (nŏŏk) *n-* 1 small, out-of-the-way place: *I tried to find a quiet nook for studying.* 2 corner: *a chimney nook.*

noon (nōōn) *n-* midday; 12 o'clock in the middle of the day: *He went home at noon.* *as modifier: the noon whistle.*

noon·day (nōōn′ dā′) *adj-* at noon; occurring at midday: *a noonday meal; the noonday sun.*

no one (nō′ wŭn′) *pron-* nobody: *I saw no one.*

noon·time (nōōn′ tīm′) *n-* noon. Also, *Archaic,* **noon′ tide** (nōōn′ tīd′).

noose (nōōs) *n-* 1 loop made with a slipknot, which binds tighter as the cord is drawn through the knot. 2 the noose execution by hanging.

Noot·ka (nōōt′ kə) *n-* [*pl.* **Noot·kas,** also **Noot·ka**] 1 one of a tribe of North American Indians living in northwestern Washington and on Vancouver Island. 2 the language of these people. *adj-: some* Nootka *weapons.*

Noose

nor (nôr, nôr) *conj-* 1 (used with "neither" to introduce two negative alternatives or with "not" to introduce more than two): *I want neither the gray suit nor the brown. He chose not the first nor the second nor the third, but the fourth.* 2 (used in place of "and . . . not" to introduce a second negative statement): *He hasn't gone, nor do I think he will go.*

Nor·dic (nôr′ dĭk, nôr′-) *adj-* of, relating to, or belonging to the Germanic peoples of northern Europe, especially of Scandinavia. *n-* member of one of these peoples.

norm (nôrm, nôrm) *n-* 1 average or mean: *The norm for daily production is about eight units.* 2 standard or pattern of growth, work, conduct, etc.; especially one based on what is normal in experience and observation.

nor·mal (nôr′ məl, nôr′-) *adj-* 1 giving no cause for special concern or alarm; usual; regular; standard: *a normal condition; a normal temperature.* 2 of average physical or mental development: *a normal child of 12 years. n-* 1 usual condition: *During the flood the river rose five feet above normal.* 2 *Mathematics* a perpendicular. —*n-* **nor·mal′ i·ty** (nôr măl′ ə tē, nôr-). *adv-* **nor′ mal·ly.**

nor·mal·cy (nôr′ məl sē, nôr′-) *n-* ordinary condition of things; normality: *Business returned to normalcy.*

nor·mal·ize (nôr′ mə līz′, nôr′-) *vt-* [**nor·mal·ized, nor·mal·iz·ing**] to make normal; to bring to a usual regular or standard condition: *a plan to normalize prices.* —*n-* **nor′ mal·i·za′ tion:** *a normalization of diplomatic relations. n-* **nor′ mal·iz′ er.**

northeast by east *n-* the direction halfway between east-northeast and northeast.

northeast by north *n-* the direction halfway between northeast and north-northeast.

north·east·er (nôr′ ēs′ tər, nôrth′-, nôrth′-) *n-* storm or gale from the northeast.

north·east·er·ly (nôrth′ ēs′ tər lē, nôrth′-) *adj-* 1 generally toward the northeast: *a northeasterly route.* 2 of winds, generally from the northeast: *a northeasterly breeze.* *adv-* generally northeastward: *We sailed northeasterly for three days.*

north·east·ern (nôrth′ ēs′ tərn, nôrth′-) *adj-* located in or to the northeast: *the northeastern part of the state.*

north·east·ward (nôrth′ ēst′ wərd, nôrth′-) *adj-* toward the northeast: *a northeastward route.* *adv-* (also **north′ east′ wards**): *We walked* northeastward.

north·er (nôr′ thər, nôr′-) *n-* storm or gale from the north.

north-north-west (nôrth´nôrth´wêst´, nôrth´nôrth´-) *n-* the direction halfway between north and northwest.

North Pole *n-* 1 northern end of the earth's axis. 2 **north pole** the pole of a magnet that points north when a magnet swings freely about a vertical axis.

North Star *n-* Polaris.

north-ward (nôrth´wərd, nôrth´-) *adv-* (also **north´ wards**) toward the north: *He traveled northward. adj-: a northward journey. n-: mountains to the northward.*

north-west (nôrth´wêst´, nôrth´-) *n-* 1 the direction halfway between north and west; also, the point of the compass indicating this direction. 2 the part of any area lying in this direction as seen from the center of the area. 3 **the Northwest** (1) the northwestern part of the United States, especially Washington, Oregon, and Idaho, and adjacent Canada. (2) formerly, the territory of the United States lying north of the Ohio River. *adj-* 1 in or to the northwest: *a northwest current.* 2 of winds, from the northwest. *adv-* toward the northwest: *The wagons moved northwest.*

northwest by north *n-* the direction halfway between north-northwest and northwest.

northwest by west *n-* the direction halfway between northwest and west-northwest.

north-west-er (nôr wês´tər, nôrth´-, nôrth´-) *n-* storm or gale from the northwest.

north-west-er-ly (nôrth´wês´tər lē, nôrth´-) *adj-* 1 generally toward the northwest: *a northwesterly route.* 2 of winds, generally from the northwest: *a northwesterly breeze. adv-* generally northwestward: *The plane flew northwesterly.*

north-west-ern (nôrth´wês´tərn, nôrth´-) *adj-* located in or to the northwest: *the northwestern part of the state.*

Northwest Passage *n-* supposed water route between the Atlantic and Pacific oceans north of Canada. It was the goal of early explorers.

north-west-ward (nôrth´wêst´wərd, nôrth´-) *adj-* toward the northwest: *a northwestward airplane flight. adv-* (also **north´ west´ wards**): *We drove northwestward.*

Nor-we-gian (nôr wē´jən) *n-* 1 a native or inhabitant of Norway, or one of his descendants. 2 the Germanic language of the Norwegian people. *adj-: We wore Norwegian costumes.*

nose (nōz) *n-* 1 the part of the face containing the nostrils, through which people and animals breathe and usually smell.

nos-tal-gia (nō stäl´jə) *n-* wistful yearning for things and events of the past: *She had a nostalgia for the 1930's.*

nos-tril (nôs´trəl) *n-* either of the two outer openings of the nose.

nos-trum (nôs´trəm) *n-* 1 a patent or quack medicine. 2 a favorite remedy or pet scheme for curing.

nos-y or **nos-ey** (nō´zē) *Informal adj-* [nos-i-er, nos-i-est] prying; inquisitive. *—adv-* nos´i-ly. *n-* nos´i-ness.

not (nôt) *adv-* word used to make negative statements: *He is not here at the moment.* *Homs-* knot, naught.

no-ta-ble (nō´tə bəl) *adj-* worthy of notice or attention; memorable: *a notable event in the history of our country. n-* important or distinguished person. *—adv-* no´ ta-bly: *We met some charming people, notably Joe's cousin Sally.*

no-ta-rize (nō´tə rīz´) *vt-* [no-ta-rized, no-ta-riz-ing] to witness (a document) legally and stamp as legally witnessed, in the capacity of a notary.

no-ta-ry (nō´tə rē) *n-* [*pl.* no-ta-ries] public official empowered to witness documents and, by his seal and signature, guarantee that the maker has sworn that they are true and correct. Also **notary public.** *—adj-* no-tar´i-al: *a notarial signature.*

note-book (nōt´book´) *n-* 1 book with blank pages in which to write notes, reminders, school assignments, observations, etc.

not-ed (nō´təd) *adj-* well-known; famous; celebrated: *He is a noted musician.*
▶Should not be confused with NOTORIOUS.

note-worthy (nōt´wûr´thē) *adj-* worthy of attention or notice; outstanding; remarkable: *His discovery is a noteworthy contribution to science. —adv-* note´ worth´i-ly. *n-* note´ worth´i-ness.

no-tion (nō´shən) *n-* 1 general idea; conception; understanding: *They didn't have the slightest notion of what he was saving.* 2 belief; opinion; view: *He has a strange notion that the earth is flat.* 3 a desire; impulse; whim: *She had a notion to buy a new hat.* 4 **notions** small, useful articles such as pins, thread, buttons, etc.

no-to-chord (nō´tə kôrd´, -kôrd´) *n-* the elastic, rodlike structure in the adult stage of some primitive vertebrates that serves as the internal skeleton; also, a similar structure occurring in all embryos, which is the forerunner of the spinal cord.

no-to-ri-e-ty (nō´tə rī´ə tē) *n-* condition of being notorious; unfavorable publicity or reputation: *his notoriety as a gambler; to gain notoriety.*

no-to-ri-ous (nō tôr´ē əs) *adj-* widely known and disapproved of; famous for some undesirable trait, act, etc.: *a notorious pirate; his notorious greed. —adv-* no-to´ ri-ous-ly. *n-* no-to´ ri-ous-ness.
▶Should not be confused with NOTED.

no-trump (nō´trump´) *n-* in card games, a bid calling for or establishing play without any suit as trump. *adj-: a* no-trump *bid; a* no-trump *hand.*

not-with-stand-ing (nôt´with stän´ding, nôt´with-) *prep-* in spite of: *The property was finally sold, notwithstanding its high price. adv-* still; nevertheless; yet: *Tired as we were, we struggled on notwithstanding.*

nou-gat (nōō´gət) *n-* chewy, sweet candy containing almonds or other nuts, and sometimes candied fruit.

nought (nôt, nôt) naught.

noun (noun) *Grammar n-* word, usually a name, that can fill the subject position in a sentence and also be the chief word of a phrase in the subject position. Most English nouns have a plural formed by adding "-s" or "-es," and many have possessive forms ending in "-'s" or "-s." A **proper noun** is the name of a particular person or thing and is always capitalized when written. Any other noun is called a **common noun** and is usually not capitalized when written.

noun phrase *Grammar n-* group of words having a noun as its chief word (nucleus). Examples: the dog; a large dog; sad weeping; a proud Spaniard. See also *phrase.*

nour-ish (nûr´ĭsh) *vt-* 1 to provide (an animal or plant) with food necessary for health and growth: *Water and sunlight nourish plants.* 2 to promote the development of; encourage; foster: *Good books nourish people's minds.*

nour-ish-ing (nûr´ĭsh ĭng) *adj-* providing excellent nourishment; nutritious: *Milk is a nourishing food.*

nour-ish-ment (nûr´ĭsh mənt) *n-* 1 food, or something like food, that helps to keep up or strengthen the body or mind, promote growth, or improve well-being. 2 act or process of nourishing or of being nourished.

Nov. November.

no-va (nō´və) *n-* [*pl.* no-vae (-vē) or no-vas] star that suddenly explodes, becoming many times brighter and then gradually fading away in a few weeks or months.

¹nov-el (nôv´əl) *adj-* new and unusual: *a novel invention; a novel experience.* [from Old French **novel** meaning "new," from Latin **novellus**, from **novus**, "new."]

²nov-el (nôv´əl) *n-* 1 long, narrative story, usually of book length, written about imaginary characters treated as if they were real: *"Treasure Island" is a famous novel about pirates and hidden treasure.* [from Italian **novella**, from Latin **novella** meaning literally "new things," and related to **¹novel.**]

nov-el-ette (nôv´əl ĕt´) *n-* short novel.

nov-el-ist (nôv´əl ĭst) *n-* person who writes novels.

no-ve-na (nō vē´nə) *n-* in the Roman Catholic Church, a devotion consisting of a prayer or service for a special intention, repeated on nine consecutive days.

nov-ice (nôv´əs) *n-* 1 person without experience in a business, occupation, or activity; beginner. 2 person who is in training to enter a religious order but has not yet taken the vows.

no-vi-ti-ate (nō vĭsh´ē ət) *n-* 1 state or period of being a novice or beginner. 2 period of training and testing for admission to a religious order. 3 part of a religious house where novices live during their training.

No-vo-cain (nō´və kān´) *n-* trademark name of a local anesthetic; procain.

nub (nŭb) *n-* 1 small piece, knob, or lump. 2 *Informal* central idea or meaning; gist: *the nub of a story.*

nub·bin (nŭb′ən) *n-* 1 imperfectly developed fruit or ear of corn. 2 small knob, bump, or growth.

nub·ble (nŭb′əl) *n-* small lump or knob.

nub·bly (nŭb′lē) *adj-* [nub·bli·er, nub·bli·est] having a rough, lumpy surface or texture: *a nubbly fabric.*

nub·by (nŭb′ē) *adj-* [nub·bi·er, nub·bi·est] nubbly.

nu·bile (nōō′bĭl′, nyōō′bĭl′, -bəl) *adj-* of a girl, old enough or mature enough to be married. —*n-* **nu·bil′i·ty** (-bĭl′ə tē).

nu·cle·ar (nōō′klē ər, nyōō′-) *adj-* 1 of, having to do with, or resembling the nucleus of a cell, atom, etc. 2 of, having to do with, or using atomic power; *the nuclear age; a nuclear war.*

nuclear energy *n-* atomic energy.

nuclear fission *n-* the breakdown or disintegration of the nucleus of an atom, with the release of large quantities of energy; atomic fission.

nuclear fusion *n-* the combining of the nuclei of two or more atoms to form the nucleus of a heavier atom, resulting in the release of huge amounts of energy; atomic fusion.

nuclear physics *n-* branch of physics dealing with the nucleus of the atom.

nuclear reactor *n-* structure in which a continuing nuclear fission reaction (chain reaction) takes place and is kept under control; atomic pile; atomic furnace; atomic reactor.

nu·cle·i (nōō′klē ī, nyōō′) *pl.* of **nucleus.**

nu·cle·ic acid (nōō klē′ ĭk, nyōō-) *n-* any of the group of organic acids that direct and control a living organism's metabolism.

nu·cle·o·lus (nōō klē′ə ləs, nyōō-) *n-* [*pl.* **nu·cle·o·li** (-lī)] small, usually rounded structure, rich in RNA, found in the nucleus of a cell.

nu·cle·on (nōō′ klē ŏn′, nyōō′-) *n-* proton or neutron in the nucleus of an atom.

nu·cle·on·ics (nōō′ klē ŏn′ ĭks, nyōō′-) *n-* (takes singular verb) the study of the practical applications of nuclear physics.

nu·cle·o·plasm (nōō′ klē ō plăz′ əm, nyōō′-) *n-* the protoplasm of the nucleus of a cell.

nu·cle·o·pro·tein (nōō′ klē ō prō′ tēn, nyōō′-) *n-* any of the large group of compounds consisting of one or more proteins and a nucleic acid.

nu·cle·us (nōō′ klē əs, nyōō′-) *n-* [*pl.* **nu·cle·i** (-klē ī) or **nu·cle·us·es**] 1 core or center around which something develops or grows: *Bob, Mary, and Dorothy formed the nucleus of the drama group.* The nucleus *of the city consisted of only five square blocks.* 2 *Physics* the positively charged, dense, central part of an atom, which contains almost all its mass. 3 *Biology* the dense round or oval body present in living cells and controlling all chemical functions of the cell. For picture, see *cell.* 4 a nerve center. 5 the main part of a comet that glows when near the sun. 6 *Grammar* the chief or central word in a phrase. In the noun phrase "the big brown bear," the nucleus is "bear." In the verb phrase "should have gone," the nucleus is "gone." See also *phrase.*

nude (nōōd, nyōōd) *adj-* without clothes; naked; bare. *n-* painting, sculpture, or photograph of an unclothed human figure. —*adv-* **nude′ ly.** *n-* **nude′ ness** or **nu′di·ty.**
in the nude without clothes; naked.

nudge (nŭj) *vt-* [nudged, nudg·ing] to push or touch gently: *Henry nudged me to get my attention.* *n-* gentle push or poke.

nud·ism (nōō′ dĭz əm, nyōō′-) *n-* belief in, or practice of, going regularly without clothes. —*n-* **nud′ ist.**

nui·sance (nōō′ səns, nyōō′-) *n-* 1 person, thing, or action that annoys or is troublesome. 2 in law, anything that offends or does injury to an individual or the public.

null (nŭl) *adj-* 1 having no force, effect, value etc. 2 equal to nothing; nonexistent.
null and void without legal force or effect; not binding.

nul·li·fi·ca·tion (nŭl′ ə fə kā′shən) *n-* 1 the act of nullifying, or the condition of being nullified. 2 doctrine that a State has the right to refuse to obey or enforce an act of Congress or a Federal court decision.

nul·li·fy (nŭl′ ə fī′) *vt-* [nul·li·fied, nul·li·fy·ing] 1 to make of no value; destroy: *to nullify the pleasure of going by complaining.* 2 to deprive of effect or legal force; invalidate: *to nullify a decision.* —*n-* **nul′ li·fi′ er.**

nul·li·ty (nŭl′ ə tē) *n-* [*pl.* **nul·li·ties**] 1 complete absence of value, effect, or importance. 2 law or legal document that is no longer valid.

null set *Mathematics* *n-* a set containing no elements; empty set.

Num. Numbers.

numb (nŭm) *adj-* [numb·er, numb·est] lacking or having lost the power to feel or move: *to be numb with cold; to be numb with grief.* *vt-* to cause to be without feeling; deaden: *The icy wind numbed our fingers.* —*adv-* **numb′ ly.** *n-* **numb′ ness.**

num·ber (nŭm′ bər) *n-* 1 *Mathematics* an idea that can answer the questions of how many and how much, in regard to a collection of units. A numeral or its equivalent is used to indicate the value of a number, and numbers are categorized according to their kind and function. See also *cardinal number, even number, natural number, odd number, ordinal number, prime number,* and *real number.* 2 a total of persons, things, or units taken together; sum: *the number of students in a class; the number of eggs in a carton.* 3 word, figure, or numeral that stands for this total: *the number 12.* 4 figure or numeral that identifies a person or thing: *a locker number; a license number; a house or apartment number.* 5 one of a series, especially of publications: *the January number of a magazine.* 6 musical piece played or sung as part of a performance: *For her next number, she will sing a folk song.* 7 *Informal* person or thing picked out for special attention: *That dress is a cute number.* 8 *Grammar* form of a word which shows whether it refers to one or more than one: *"Man" is singular and "men" is plural in number.* 9 **numbers** (1) power or force based on size or amount of members, units, etc.: *They were beaten by superior numbers.* (2) arithmetic. (3) poetic meter or form. (4) (also **numbers pool**) kind of lottery in which bets are made that a given number will appear. *vt-* 1 to count: *I number the people in the group to be 26.* 2 to amount to: *The school's library numbers about 5,000 books.* 3 to give a numeral to: *We numbered the tickets 1 to 500.* 4 to limit in sum or total: *The days of his life are numbered.* 5 to include: *We number him among our closest friends.* —*n-* **num′ ber·er.**
a number of many; several: *The sale attracted a number of shoppers.* **beyond (or without) number** too many to be counted: *Stars beyond number appeared.*

num·ber·less (nŭm′ bər ləs) *adj-* 1 too many to be counted. 2 not having a number: *a numberless page.*

number line *Mathematics* *n-* a line on which points are marked off and assigned numbers.

Numbers (nŭm′ bərz) *n-* (takes singular verb) the fourth book of the Old Testament, in which the census of Israel is recorded.

numb·skull (nŭm′ skŭl′) numskull.

nu·mer·a·ble (nōō′ mər ə bəl, nyōō′-) *adj-* such as can be counted or numbered.

num·er·al (nōō′ mər əl, nyōō′-) *n-* 1 figure or other symbol that stands for a number. See also *Arabic numerals, Roman numerals.* 2 word that names such a symbol. 3 **numerals** number composed of the last two digits of a student's year of graduation. Official numerals are awarded to and worn by students, usually freshmen, who have participated in intermural competitive sports.

nu·mer·ate (nōō′ mə rāt′, nyōō′-) *vt-* [nu·mer·at·ed, nu·mer·at·ing] to count or number; enumerate.

nu·mer·a·tion (nōō′ mə rā′ shən, nyōō′-) *n-* 1 the act or process of numbering or counting. 2 the writing or representing of numbers by symbols.

nu·mer·a·tor (nōō′ mə rā′ tər, nyōō′-) *n-* 1 the numeral above the line in a fraction. In the fraction ³₄, 3 is the numerator. 2 the first of two numbers in a ratio. 3 person or device that counts or numbers.

nu·mer·i·cal (nōō mèr′ ĭ kəl, nyōō-) *adj-* expressed in, consisting of, or having to do with numbers: *Arithmetic uses numerical values. Arrange the numbered sheets in numerical order.* —*adv-* **nu·mer′ i·cal·ly.**

nu·mer·ous (nōō′ mər əs, nyōō′-) *adj-* 1 more than a few; many: *I had numerous telephone calls this morning.* 2 many in number: *a numerous collection of butterflies.* —*adv-* nu′ mer·ous·ly. *n-* nu′ mer·ous·ness.

nu·mis·mat·ics (nōō′ məz măt′ lks, nyōō′-) *n-* (takes singular verb) science of coins or medals; also, the collecting of coins or medals as a hobby or occupation. —*adj-* nu′ mis·mat′ ic.

nu·mis·mat·ist (nōō mlz′ mə tĭst′, nyōō-) *n-* person who collects coins or medals, or is an expert on them.

num·skull (nŭm′ skŭl′) *n-* stupid person; blockhead.

nun (nŭn) *n-* woman who has taken religious vows and lives in a convent. Many nuns do teaching, nursing, charitable work, etc. *Hom-* none.

nun·ci·o (nŭn′ sē ō′, nōōn′-) *n-* [*pl.* nun·ci·os] permanent representative or ambassador of the Pope to a foreign government.

nup·tial (nŭp′ shəl) *adj-* of or having to do with marriage or a wedding: *the nuptial day; a nuptial ceremony.* *n-* (usually nuptials) a marriage or wedding.

nurse (nûrs) *n-* 1 person, usually a woman, trained to take care of people who are sick or cannot care for themselves, and to assist physicians in their work. 2 one who takes care of a young child or children not her own. *vt-* [nursed, nurs·ing] 1 to care for or wait on in sickness: *She nursed her husband back to health.* 2 to feed (a baby) milk at the breast. 3 to give special care to; tend carefully: *to nurse a young plant; to nurse a flickering fire.* 4 to keep up; cherish; harbor: *to nurse a grudge.* *vi-* 1 to care for the sick or infirm. 2 to take milk at the breast; suckle.

nurse·maid (nûrs′ mād′) *n-* girl or woman who takes care of a child or children.

nurs·er·y (nûrs′ə rē) *n-* [*pl.* nurs·er·ies] 1 baby's or child's room. 2 a place where babies or young children are cared for and tended. 3 a place where garden plants, trees, or shrubs are raised, usually for sale.

nursery rhyme *n-* short poem in rhyme for young children. "Little Miss Muffet" is a nursery rhyme.

nursery school *n-* school for young children, usually between the ages of three and five.

nurs·ing (nûr′ sĭng) *n-* profession or work of a nurse. *as modifier:* a nursing school.

nursing bottle *n-* bottle fitted with a rubber nipple and used for feeding babies.

nursing home *n-* residence or private hospital where aged, chronically ill, or helpless people are cared for.

nurs·ling (nûrs′ lĭng) *n-* 1 baby; infant. 2 person or thing that is lovingly and tenderly cared for.

nur·ture (nûr′ chər) *vt-* [nur·tured, nur·tur·ing] 1 to feed and care for; promote the growth of; rear. 2 to train; educate; develop: *The music teacher carefully nurtured the girl's voice.* *n-* 1 food and care; nourishment. 2 training; education; development. —*n-* nur′ tur·er.

nut (nŭt) *n-* 1 a fruit of certain trees, such as the walnut, pecan, almond, or chestnut, consisting of a kernel or seed enclosed in a hard, woody, or leathery shell. 2 the seed or kernel when removed from the shell.

bolt fits. 4 *Slang* person who behaves in an odd or irrational manner; crazy person. —*adj-* nut′ llke′.
     hard nut to crack 1 problem that is hard to solve. 2 person who is difficult to deal with.

nut·hatch (nŭt′ hăch′) *n-* any of several small, gray and white birds that creep down the trunks of trees headfirst.

nut·meg (nŭt′ mĕg′) *n-* 1 hard, nutlike kernel of the seed of an East Indian tree. It is grated and used as a spice. 2 the tree itself.

nut·pick (nŭt′ pĭk′) *n-* sharp tool for removing the kernels from cracked nuts.

nu·tri·ent (nōō′ trē ənt, nyōō′-) *n-* substance, especially a food, that promotes growth and nourishes. *adj-* promoting growth; nourishing: *a nutrient substance.*

nu·tri·ment (nōō′ trə mənt, nyōō′-) *n-* anything that provides nourishment; food.

nu·tri·tion (nōō trĭsh′ ən, nyōō-) *n-* 1 a nourishing or being nourished with food; especially, the process by which an animal or plant uses food to promote growth. 2 nourishment; food. —*adj-* nu·tri′ tion·al (-ən əl): *a nutritional deficiency.* *adv-* nu·tri′ tion·al·ly.

nu·tri·tious (nōō trĭsh′ əs, nyōō-) *adj-* promoting growth and good health; nourishing: *a nutritious diet.* —*adv-* nu·tri′ tious·ly. *n-* nu·tri′ tious·ness.

nu·tri·tive (nōō′ trə tĭv′, nyōō′-) *adj-* of or having to do with nutrition. —*adv-* nu′ tri·tive·ly.

nuts (nŭts) *Slang adj-* 1 crazy. 2 very enthusiastic (about).

nut·shell (nŭt′ shĕl′) *n-* hard covering around a nut.
     in a nutshell in a few words; briefly.

nut·ting (nŭt′ ĭng) *n-* the gathering of nuts.

nut·ty (nŭt′ ē) *adj-* [nut·ti·er, nut·ti·est] 1 full of nuts; flavored with nuts: *a nutty cake.* 2 reminding one of nuts: *a nutty flavor.* 3 *Slang* foolish; queer; crazy. —*n-* nut′ ti·ness.

nux vom·i·ca (nŭks vŏm′ I kə) *n-* 1 poisonous seed of an East Indian tree, from which strychnine and other substances used in medicine are obtained. 2 the tree bearing these seeds.

nuz·zle (nŭz′ əl) *vt-* [nuz·zled, nuz·zling] to rub or press with the nose: *The puppy nuzzled its mother.* *vi-* to press or nestle close; snuggle.

NW or **N.W.** 1 northwest. 2 northwestern.

N.W.T. Northwest Territories (Canada).

N.Y. New York.

N.Y.C. New York City.

ny·lon (nī′ lŏn′) *n-* 1 any of several synthetic plastic substances from which fibers, cloth, machine parts, etc., are manufactured. 2 nylons stockings made with fibers of this substance. *as modifier:* a nylon jacket.

nymph (nĭmf) *n-* 1 in Greek and Roman mythology, a minor goddess of nature, living in the mountains, woods, streams, etc.; hence, any beautiful maiden. 2 immature insect, such as a dragonfly or mayfly, in a stage of development that resembles the adult form. —*adj-* nymph′ like.

O

O, o (ō) *n-* [*pl.* **O's, o's**] 1 the fifteenth letter of the English alphabet. 2 zero; naught. 3 anything shaped like the letter O.

o ohm.

¹O (ō) *interj-* exclamation used in speaking formally to someone: *Hear us, O Lord.* **Homs-** oh, owe.

²O symbol for oxygen.

WHITE OAK

LIVE OAK

Oaks

o' (ō, ǝ) *prep-* (now used chiefly in compound words). 1 of the: *four o'clock.* 2 of: *will-o'-the wisp.*

oaf (ōf) *n-* stupid, clumsy fellow.

oaf·ish (ō'fĭsh) *adj-* of or like an oaf; stupid and clumsy. **—adv- oaf'ish·ly. n- oaf'ish·ness.**

oak (ōk) *n-* 1 any of various trees that bear acorns. 2 the hard, durable wood of these trees. *as modifier:* an oak *cabinet; sturdy oak floors.*

oak apple *n-* rounded swelling produced on the leaves and twigs of oak trees by certain wasps. Also **oak gall.** For picture, see ³gall.

oak·en (ō'kǝn) *adj-* made of oak: *an oaken bucket.*

oa·kum (ō'kǝm) *n-* hemp fiber in loosely twisted strands, treated with tar and used for caulking seams and joints.

oar (ôr) *n-* 1 implement with a flat or somewhat curved blade and a long handle, used to row or steer a boat. 2 a rower. *vt-* to row. **Homs-** o'er, or, ore.

OARLOCK

Oar

put (one's) oar in to interfere; be meddlesome.

oar·lock (ôr'lŏk') *n-* device consisting of a U-shaped notch mounted on a metal pin, used for holding an oar in place while in use; rowlock. For picture, see **oar.**

oars·man (ôrz'mǝn) *n-* [*pl.* **oars·men**] person who rows a boat.

O.A.S. Organization of American States.

o·a·sis (ō ā'sǝs) *n-* [*pl.* **o·a·ses** (-sēz)] the irrigated land near a desert waterhole or river; hence, any place providing refreshment, relief, etc.

Caravan leaving an oasis

oat (ōt) *n-* 1 a cereal plant, the seeds of which are used as food or as fodder for horses. 2 **oats** the seed or grain of this plant.

feel (one's) oats *Informal* 1 to be lively and frisky, often in a boisterous manner. 2 to feel or act important. **sow (one's) wild oats** of a young man; to live a wild or dissipated life.

oat·en (ō'tǝn) *adj-* made of oats, oatmeal, or oat straw.

oath (ōth; *pl.* ōths, ōthz) *n-* 1 solemn statement, usually accompanied by an appeal to God as a witness, that one will tell the truth or keep a promise: *He gave his oath to tell the whole story.* 2 careless or profane use of the name of God or of anything sacred. 3 curse word: *to shout oaths in anger.*

take oath to make a solemn promise or declaration, especially on being installed in office. **under oath** bound by an oath to tell the truth.

oat·meal (ōt'mēl') *n-* 1 rolled or ground oats. 2 porridge made from this. *as modifier:* an oatmeal *cookie.*

O·ba·di·ah (ō'bǝ dī'ǝ) *n-* 1 minor Hebrew prophet of the 6th century B.C. 2 book of the Old Testament containing his prophecies. In the CCD Bible, **Ab'di·a.**

ob·du·ra·cy (ŏb'dǝr ǝ sē, ŏb'dyǝr-) *n-* 1 hardness of heart; callousness. 2 stubbornness.

Oats

ob·du·rate (ŏb'dǝr ǝt, ŏb'dyǝr-) *adj-* 1 not to be moved by appeals to the feelings; hardhearted; callous: *an obdurate kidnapper.* 2 stubborn; unyielding; obstinate: *an obdurate insistence on being heard.* **—adv- ob'du·rate·ly. n- ob'du·rate·ness.**

o·be·di·ence (ō bē'dē ǝns) *n-* a doing what one is told to do; willingness to obey: *If you are kind and patient, you can teach most dogs obedience.*

o·be·di·ent (ō bē'dē ǝnt) *adj-* obeying orders, rules, etc.; submitting to the command or will of others: *an obedient child.* **—adv- o·be'di·ent·ly.**

o·bei·sance (ō bā'sǝns, -bē'sǝns) *n-* 1 a movement or bending of the body that shows obedience or respect: bow or curtsy. 2 respect; homage; deference.

ob·e·lisk (ŏb'ǝ lĭsk') *n-* tapering, four-sided column with a tip shaped like a pyramid. Many examples may be found among the monuments of ancient Egypt.

Obelisk

o·bese (ō bēs') *adj-* very fat; corpulent. **—n- o·bes'i·ty** or **o·bese' ness.**

o·bey (ō bā') *vt-* (considered intransitive when the direct object is implied but not expressed) 1 to yield to the authority or commands of: *to obey one's parents.* 2 to carry out; comply with: *to obey a command.* 3 to act in accordance with; be guided by; follow: *to obey one's conscience.*

ob·fus·cate (ŏb'fǝs kāt') *vt-* [ob·fus·cat·ed, ob·fus·cat·ing] to make less clear; prevent from being easily understood; confuse. **—n- ob'fus·ca'tion.**

o·bi (ō'bē) *n-* broad sash worn with kimono.

o·bit (ō bĭt') *Informal n-* obituary.

o·bit·u·ar·y (ǝ bĭch' ŏŏ ĕr'ē, ō-) *n-* [*pl.* **o·bit·u·ar·ies**] printed announcement of a person's death, often with a brief account of his life. *as modifier:* the obituary *page of a newspaper;* an obituary *notice.*

obj. 1 object. 2 objection. 3 objective.

¹ob·ject (ǝb jĕkt') *vi-* 1 to protest; show disapproval: *Mother always objects when we leave the turtles in the bathtub.* 2 to be opposed: *The girls objected to our plans.* *vt-* to offer as an argument, criticism, or opposing reason: *He objected that nobody would have time for so much extra work.* **—n- ob·jec'tor.**

²ob·ject (ŏb'jĭkt) *n-* 1 thing that has shape and can be touched or seen: *The only object rescued from the fire was an old chair.* 2 purpose; goal; ambition: *the object of the meeting; one's object in life.* 3 person or thing that arouses feeling or action: *an object of pity; an object of praise.* 4 *Grammar* a noun, pronoun; noun phrase, or noun clause which follows a transitive verb or a preposition. Most transitive verbs take only one object, called the **direct object;** but there are a few which take two objects, the first of which is an **indirect object,** and the second the direct object. An object which follows a preposition is called an **object of a preposition.** Examples:

The cat ate the mouse (direct object).

The old woman gave her poor doggie a bone (indirect object).

I lent him my grammar book (indirect object).

I lent it to the new boy (object of preposition).

ob·jec·tion (ǝb jĕk'shǝn) *n-* 1 feeling or expression of opposition, dislike, or disapproval: *The cat showed his objection to the stray dog by arching his back.* 2 reason for opposing something: *My only objection to the trip is that it will cost too much.*

ob·jec·tion·a·ble (ǝb jĕk'shǝn ǝ bǝl) *adj-* likely to be objected to; undesirable; unpleasant: *He uses objectionable language.* **—adv- ob·jec'tion·a·bly.**

ob·jec·tive (ǝb jĕk' tǐv) *adj-* 1 not influenced by emotions, prejudices, etc.; unbiased: *an objective description of an accident; an objective point of view.* 2 having actual existence; real; not imaginary: *Space travel is now an objective fact.* *n-* 1 something one strives to reach or gain; aim; goal: *Our objective is to reach the top of the hill.* 2 (also **object glass** or **objective lens**) in a microscope or telescope, the lens or combination of lenses nearest the thing being examined. 3 *Grammar* the objective case; also, a word in the objective case. **—adv- ob·jec'tive·ly.**

ob·jet d'art (ôb′ zhā där′) *French* n- [*pl.* **ob·jets d'art** (-zhā där′)] thing having artistic merit or value.

ob·late (ôb′ lāt′, ō′ blāt′) *adj-* generally circular or spherical but flattened at both ends of a diameter (the two poles). **—n- ob′ late′ness.**

ob·la·tion (ə blā′ shən, ō-) n- 1 the act of making a religious offering or sacrifice; especially, the offering of the bread and wine of the Communion. 2 anything presented as a religious offering or sacrifice.

ob·li·gate (ôb′ lə gāt′) vt- [ob·li·gat·ed, ob·li·gat·ing] to bind by a promise, contract, or sense of duty: *The law* obligates *a father to support his children.*

ob·li·ga·tion (ôb′ lə gā′shən) n- 1 the binding power of a promise, contract, or sense of duty: *The builder was under* obligation *to complete the house by spring.* 2 any duty imposed by law, by social relations, or by good will: *the* obligations *of good citizenship.* 3 debt of gratitude, loyalty, affection, etc.: *I feel an* obligation *to those who help me.* 4 legal debt: *He is careful to meet his* obligations *promptly.*

ob·li·ga·to (ôb′ lə gä′ tō) obbligato.

ob·lig·a·to·ry (ə blĭg′ ə tôr′ ē) *adj-* required or imposed by duty, rule, law, etc.; compulsory: *Attendance in classes is* obligatory.

o·blige (ə blīj′) vt- [o·bliged, o·blig·ing] 1 to place under a duty or obligation; compel: *The law* obliges *us to pay taxes.* 2 (considered intransitive when the direct object is implied but not expressed) to do (someone) a favor: *Will you* oblige *me by lending me your skates? He's always willing to* oblige. **—n- o·blig′ er.**

be obliged to be grateful to.

o·blig·ing (ə blī′jĭng) *adj-* helpful; willing to help; kindly: *The police in your city are most* obliging *to travelers.* **—adv- o·blig′ing·ly. n- o·blig′ing·ness.**

o·blique (ō blēk′, ə-, *also* ō blīk′) *adj-* 1 neither vertical nor horizontal; slanting; diagonal: *The wind drove the rain in* oblique *lines.* 2 neither parallel nor perpendicular to a reference line. 3 not direct or straightforward: *an* oblique *answer.* n-: *The line is an* oblique. **—adv- o·blique′ly. n- o·blique′ ness.**

Oblique lines

oblique angle n- any acute or obtuse angle.

o·bliq·ui·ty (ə blĭk′ wə tē) n- [*pl.* o·bliq·ui·ties] 1 condition of being oblique; also, the amount by which something is oblique; obliqueness; slant: *The* obliquity *of the flagpole is 10° from the vertical.* 2 deviation from accepted principles of conduct or ways of thinking.

o·blit·er·ate (ə blĭt′ə rāt′) vt- [o·blit·er·at·ed, o·blit·er·at·ing] 1 to destroy completely; wipe out; erase: *The earthquake* obliterated *an entire city.* 2 to cover or hide from view; cause to become invisible: *A cloud* obliterated *the sun.* **—n- o·blit′ er·a′ tion.**

o·bliv·i·on (ə blĭv′ē ən) n- 1 condition of being forgotten: *A single great work has saved many a writer from* oblivion. 2 unawareness of what is going on; obliviousness; also, unconsciousness.

o·bliv·i·ous (ə blĭv′ē əs) *adj-* unaware; inattentive: *He roared down Main Street in his car,* oblivious *of traffic lights.* **—adv- o·bliv′ i·ous·ly. n- o·bliv′ i·ous·ness.**

ob·long (ôb′ lông′) n- a right-angled figure that is longer than it is wide. *adj-* having parallel sides and greater length than width: *an* oblong *shoe box.*

Oblongs

ob·lo·quy (ôb′ lə kwē′) n- [*pl.* ob·lo·quies] 1 words spoken in abuse of another or others; violent reproach, accusation, etc. 2 disgrace.

ob·scu·ri·ty (əb skyōōr′ə tē) n- [*pl.* ob·scur·i·ties] 1 lack of clear meaning: *The* obscurity *of the speaker's remarks confused his audience.* 2 condition of being unknown: *Many once famous names have now passed into* obscurity. 3 dimness; indistinctness: *the* obscurity *of the carving on the old monument.*

ob·se·quies (ôb′ sə kwēz′) n- *pl.* funeral ceremonies.

ob·se·qui·ous (əb sē′ kwē əs) *adj-* too ready or eager to please or obey; fawning: *the* obsequious *courtiers.* **—adv- ob·se′ qui·ous·ly. n- ob·se′ qui·ous·ness.**

ob·serv·a·ble (əb zûr′ və bəl) *adj-* such as can be observed; noticeable: *There is an* observable *improvement in his batting average.* **—adv- ob·serv′ a·bly.**

ob·serv·ance (əb zûr′ vəns) n- 1 a customary or commemorative celebration: *Passover and Easter are annual* observances. 2 the following or keeping of prescribed rules: *strict* observance *of the Sabbath.* 3 observation.

ob·serv·ant (əb zûr′ vənt) *adj-* 1 quick to notice; watchful: *The baby is very* observant *of everything that goes on.* 2 mindful of duties or authority; attentive: *an* observant *nurse.* **—adv- ob·serv′ ant·ly.**

ob·ser·va·tion (ôb′ sər vā′ shən, ôb′ zər-) n- 1 act of watching or seeing: *A half-hour's* observation *taught me the game.* 2 ability to see clearly and examine with exactness: *Try to develop your powers of* observation. 3 thing noted by observing: *Write your* observations *of the experiment in your notebooks.* 4 a being seen; notice: *Certain birds often escape* observation *because of protective coloring.* 5 a remark or comment that results from observing: *an* observation *about the weather.*

ob·ser·va·tion·al (ôb′ sər vā′ shən əl, ôb′ zər-) *adj-* of or resulting from observation.

ob·ser·va·to·ry (əb zûr′ və tôr′ ē) n- [*pl.* ob·ser·va·tor·ies] 1 building or group of buildings fitted with telescopes and other equipment for studying the heavens. 2 tower or place from which there is an extensive view.

ob·serve (əb zûrv′) vt- [ob·served, ob·serv·ing] 1 to see; notice; watch carefully: *to* observe *a flash of lightning; to* observe *the growth of a flower.* 2 to say; remark: **—ob·serv·er** (əb zûr′ vər) n- 1 one who watches: *He stood apart as an* observer *of the fight.* 2 person who follows or conforms to rules and customs: *a strict* observer *of the Sabbath.* 3 an official delegate at a meeting who takes note of the proceedings but has no part in them.

ob·sess (əb sĕs′, ōb-) vt- to rule or trouble the mind of, especially as a fixed idea: *The dream of great riches* obsessed *him.*

ob·ses·sion (əb sĕsh′ ən) n- fixed idea not easily driven from the mind: *Tidiness is an* obsession *with her.*

ob·ses·sive (əb sĕs′ ĭv) *adj-* resulting from or resembling an obsession: *an* obsessive *desire for fame and fortune.* **—adv- ob·ses′ sive·ly.**

ob·sid·i·an (əb sĭd′ ē ən) n- dark, glassy rock formed from magma that has been pushed out by volcanic action and has cooled very quickly.

ob·so·les·cent (ôb′ sə lĕs′ənt) *adj-* passing out of use: *an* obsolescent *word.* **—n- ob′ so·les′ cence.**

ob·so·lete (ôb′ sə lēt′) *adj-* no longer used or practiced: *an* obsolete *firearm; an* obsolete *custom.*

ob·sta·cle (ôb′ stə kəl) n- thing that blocks or stands in the way; obstruction; hindrance; impediment.

ob·stet·ric (əb stĕt′ trĭk) *adj-* of or having to do with obstetrics; *an* obstetric *instrument.* Also **ob·stet′ ri·cal.** **—adv- ob·stet′ ri·cal·ly.**

ob·ste·tri·cian (ôb′ stə trĭsh′ ən) n- doctor specializing in obstetrics.

ob·stet·rics (əb stĕt′ rĭks) n- (takes singular verb) the branch of medicine dealing with the birth of children.

ob·sti·na·cy (ôb′ stə nə sē) n- stubbornness; determination not to yield: *the* obstinacy *of mules.*

ob·sti·nate (ôb′ stə nət) *adj-* unyielding; not giving in to pressure or reasoning; stubborn: *Once John got an idea, he was so* obstinate *that nobody could argue him out of it.* **—adv- ob′ sti·nate·ly. n- ob′ sti·nate·ness.**

ob·strep·er·ous (əb strĕp′ ər əs) *adj-* clamorous; turbulently noisy; boisterous, especially in resistance to control, advice, etc. **—adv- ob·strep′ er·ous·ly. n- ob·strep′ er·ous·ness.**

ob·struct (əb strŭkt′) vt- 1 to block; close: *A fallen tree* obstructed *the road.* 2 to be or get in the way of: *Frost on the windshield* obstructed *the driver's view.* 3 to prevent or slow down the progress of; hinder; impede: *Late snows* obstructed *the progress of the tennis court.*

ob·struc·tion (əb strŭk′ shən) n- 1 something that blocks: *an* obstruction *in the drain.* 2 a blocking: *Heavy snows caused* obstruction *of railroads and highways.*

ob·struc·tion·ism (əb strŭk′ shə nĭz′ əm) n- act or policy of deliberately hindering work or progress, especially in a legislative body. **—n- ob·struc′ tion·ist.**

oc·clude (ə klōōd′) vt- [oc·clud·ed, oc·clud·ing] 1 to shut up or out. 2 to close. 3 Chemistry to adsorb: Carbon occludes nitrogen. 4 in meteorology, of an advancing cold front, to force (warm air) upwards, and so cut it off from the ground. vi- of the grinding surfaces of the upper and lower teeth, to meet evenly.

occluded front n- weather front formed when an advancing mass of cold air forces a warm air mass upwards.

oc·clu·sion (ə klōō′ zhən) n- an occluding; especially, the fitting together of the upper and lower teeth.

oc·cult (ə kult′, ŏk′ ŭlt′) adj- 1 hidden and mysterious; secret. 2 relating to supernatural forces.

oc·cul·ta·tion (ŏk′ əl tā′ shən) n- 1 a hiding or disappearance from view. 2 Astronomy the abrupt cutting off of a star's or planet's light when another heavenly body, especially the moon, passes in front of it.

oc·cult·ism (ŏk′ ŭl tĭz′ əm, ə kŭl′-) n- belief in or investigation of the mysterious, the supernatural, or the magical; also, any practices based on such beliefs.

oc·cu·pan·cy (ŏk′ yə pən sē) n- [pl. oc·cu·pan·cies] 1 a taking possession of or holding space in. 2 period during which anything is occupied.

oc·cu·pant (ŏk′ yə pənt) n- 1 person who lives in or makes use of a building, house, room, etc. 2 person who holds a position.

oc·cu·pa·tion (ŏk′ yə pā′ shən) n- 1 business, trade, or job: Selling automobiles is his occupation. 2 an occupying or being occupied: Quick occupation of these new houses is expected. 3 seizure and holding: the occupation of an enemy stronghold. as modifier: the occupation troops; occupation currency.

oc·cu·pa·tion·al (ŏk′ yə pā′ shən əl) adj- having to do with or resulting from one's work, business, or profession: an occupational disease; occupational hazards.

oc·cu·py (ŏk′ yə pī′) vt- [oc·cu·pied, oc·cu·py·ing] 1 to take up; fill up: The dinner and entertainment occupied two hours. 2 to settle in or live in: My friend is waiting to occupy the new house he just bought. 3 to take and keep possession of: The army advanced and occupied ten square miles of enemy territory. 4 to hold; have: A student council occupies an important place in school affairs. 5 to keep busy. —n- oc′ cu·pi′ er.

oc·cur (ə kûr′) vi- [oc·curred, oc·cur·ring] 1 to take place; happen: Several accidents have occurred at that corner. 2 to be found; appear; exist: How many times does the word "the" occur in the sentence you are reading? occur to to come into the mind of; suggest itself to.

oc·cur·rence (ə kûr′ əns) n- 1 something that happens; event: An eclipse of the sun is a rare occurrence. 2 a taking place; an occurring.

o·cean (ō′ shən) n- 1 the vast body of salt water covering three-fourths of the earth's surface. 2 any of the four main divisions of this body: the Atlantic Ocean, the Pacific Ocean, the Indian Ocean, and the Arctic Ocean. as modifier: an ocean voyage; ocean currents.

o·ce·an·ic (ō′ shē ăn′ ĭk) adj- of, appearing in, or produced by the ocean: the oceanic plant life.

o·cean·og·ra·phy (ō′ shən ŏg′ rə fē) n- science that deals with the study of oceans and seas, including their currents, chemical make-up, topography, etc. —n- o′ cean·og′ ra·pher.

Ocelot about 4 ft long

o·ce·lot (ō′ sə lŏt′, ŏs′ ə-) n- large cat with a spotted yellow or gray coat, of Central and South America.

o·cher or **o·chre** (ō′ kər) n- 1 variety of clay containing iron ore and ranging in color from yellow to red, used as a pigment in paints. 2 dark-yellow color. adj-: an ocher carpet.

o'clock (ə klŏk′) adv- 1 according to the clock: Let's meet at three o'clock. 2 in air warfare, position of an attacker, target, etc. as thought of on an imaginary clock face.

Oct. October.

octa- or **octo-** combining form eight: an octagon; octopus (eight-footed). [from Greek okto and okta, "eight."]

oc·ta·gon (ŏk′ tə gŏn′) n- 1 polygon with eight sides and eight angles. 2 (also regular octagon) polygon having eight equal sides and eight equal angles.

oc·tag·o·nal (ŏk tăg′ ə nəl) adj- having eight sides. —adv- oc·tag′ o·nal·ly.

oc·ta·he·dron (ŏk′ tə hē′ drən) n- geometric solid with eight plane sides.

Octagon

oc·tane (ŏk′ tān′) n- any of a small group of oily, liquid hydrocarbons, all having the formula C_8H_{18}, which occur in petroleum.

octane number n- a number that shows how much a fuel knocks as compared with a specified fuel mixture burned under standard test conditions. A gasoline with an octane number of 75 will knock as much as a mixture of 75 parts of a certain octane and 25 parts of another hydrocarbon. A higher octane number produces less knocking. Also octane rating.

oc·tant (ŏk′ tənt) n- 1 one-eighth of a circle, or an angle of 45°. 2 navigational instrument used to determine the height above the horizon of heavenly bodies. It is similar to the sextant but has an arc of 45°.

oc·tave (ŏk′ təv, also -tāv′) n- 1 Music (1) the difference in pitch between a tone and another tone having twice as many vibrations per second or half as many vibrations per second. (2) either of two tones so related in frequency and having the same name. In the drawing, the middle C is an octave of either the lower C or the higher C. (3) two such tones sounded together; also, all the tones between them. 2 any unit of eight parts; especially, an eight-day festival or observance in religion. 3 in poetry, a stanza of eight lines; especially, the first eight lines of a sonnet.

OCTAVE OCTAVE
Octaves on piano

oc·ta·vo (ŏk tā′ vō, -tā′ vō) n- [pl. oc·ta·vos] 1 in printing, a sheet of paper folded into eight leaves or sixteen pages. 2 book made of such sheets. as modifier: an octavo volume. Abbr. 8vo.

oc·tet (ŏk tĕt′) n- 1 Music (1) composition for eight voices or instruments. (2) the eight performers of such a composition. 2 any group of eight.

Oc·to·ber n- the tenth month of the year, having 31 days.

oc·to·ge·nar·i·an (ŏk′ tə jə nâr′ ē ən) n- person who is eighty to eighty-nine years old. as modifier: my octogenarian grandpa.

oc·to·pus (ŏk′ tə pəs) n- [pl. oc·to·pus·es] sea animal living mostly on the sea floor and having a bulb-shaped body from which extend eight long tentacles with sucking disks on the underside for grasping prey.

TENTACLES
Octopus a few inches to 20 ft spread

ode (ōd) n- lofty and dignified lyric poem, usually in honor of a person or thing.

O·din (ō′ dən) n- in Germanic mythology, the supreme god and the ruler of all the other gods.

o·di·ous (ō′ dē əs) adj- hateful or offensive; repulsive; disgusting: Torture is odious to civilized people. —adv- o′ di·ous·ly. n- o′ di·ous·ness.

o·di·um (ō′ dē əm) n- 1 hatred; contempt: the odium we feel for a deliberate liar. 2 disgrace; stigma: the odium of having been a traitor in wartime.

o·dom·e·ter (ō dŏm′ ə tər) n- device for measuring distance traveled, especially of a vehicle.

o·dor (ō′ dər) n- scent; smell: a musty odor; a pleasant odor. —adj- o′ dor·less.

o·dor·if·er·ous (ō′ də rĭf′ ər əs) adj- having or giving off an odor, especially a pleasant one: an odoriferous blossom. —adv- o′ dor·if′ er·ous·ly. n- o′ dor·if′ er·ous·ness.

o·dor·ous (ō′ dər əs) adj- having or giving off an odor, especially an unpleasant one. —adv- o′ dor·ous·ly.

of·fen·sive (ə fĕn' sĭv) *adj-* 1 causing offense or resentme⁻t; annoying; disagreeable: *Helen's loud laughter was offensive to her quiet friend.* 2 unpleasant to the senses: *Some people think that onions have a very offensive smell.* 3 having to do with attack: *to forbid the use of offensive weapons*; *the* offensive *team*. *n-* attack: *the enemy's offensive.* —*adv-* of·fen'sive·ly. *n-* of·fen'sive·ness.

of·fer (ŏ' fər, ŏf' ər) *n-* 1 voluntary proposal: *We appreciate your kind* offer *of assistance.* 2 a price bid: *an offer of $500 for the old car.* 3 attempt or endeavor: *an* offer *at resistance.* *vt-* 1 to volunteer; proffer: *Many strangers* offered *help.* 2 to suggest for acceptance or refusal; propose: *The committee* offered *a plan to the club.* 3 to present as a part of religious worship or sacrifice: *to offer a prayer in thanksgiving.* 4 to put up for sale: *We* offered *the house at a fair price.* 5 to attempt: *Will the rebels* offer *any resistance?* *vi-* to present itself; arise: *She will travel any time the opportunity* offers.

of·fer·ing (ŏ' far ing, ŏf' ər-) *n-* something offered or given; especially, a religious gift, contribution, or sacrifice: *She placed her* offering *in the collection plate.*

of·fer·to·ry (ŏ' far tôr' ē, ŏf' ər-) *n-* [*pl.* of·fer·tor·ies] 1 musical composition performed in church when the collection is made. 2 the collection itself. 3 the part of a Mass or Holy Communion in which the sacramental bread and wine are offered to God before consecration.

off·hand (ŏf' hănd', ŏf'-) *adv-* without giving much thought or preparation: *Tell me* offhand, *how many beans are in this jar.* *adj-* 1 said or done without preparation: *He made a few* offhand *remarks.* 2 informal; casual: *an* offhand *manner.*

off·hand·ed (ŏf' hăn' dəd, ŏf'-) *adj-* offhand. —*adv-* off'hand'ed·ly. *n-* off'hand'ed·ness.

of·fice (ŏ' fəs, ŏf' əs) *n-* 1 place where business or professional services are carried on or clerical work is done: *a doctor's* office. 2 position; post: *the* office *of mayor.* 3 duty, charge, or service: *She performs the* office *of hostess very graciously.* 4 branch or department of government: *U.S. Post* Office; *the British Foreign* Office. 5 offices something done for a person; service: *Through his kind* offices *I received immediate aid.* *as modifier: an* office *boy;* office *problems.*

office holder *n-* person holding a public office.

of·fi·cer (ŏf' ə sər, ŏf' ə-) *n-* 1 person elected or appointed to a position of authority, trust, or responsibility: *class* officers; *company* officers; *police* officer. 2 person who has rank or authority to command in the armed services, especially one who holds a commission or warrant. 3 captain or mates on a commercial ship.

officer of the day *n-* officer at a military post who is responsible for security, maintenance of order, performance of the guard, etc., on a given day.

of·fi·cial (ə fĭsh' əl) *n-* person who holds a position of authority: *All the company's* officials *are in a meeting.* *adj-* 1 having to do with a position of trust or authority: *The President has many* official *duties to perform.* 2 coming from the proper authority; approved: *The report is considered* official. —*adv-* of·fi'cial·ly.
►Should not be confused with OFFICIOUS.

of·fi·cial·dom (ə fĭsh' əl dəm) *n-* officials taken as a class, especially in respect to presumed rigidity, adherence to rules, lack of individual initiative, etc.

of·fi·ci·ate (ə fĭsh' ē āt') *vi-* [of·fi·ci·at·ed, of·fi·ci·at·ing] to perform an official duty or ceremony: *The mayor* officiated *at the Memorial Day Ceremony.*

of·fi·cious (ə fĭsh' əs) *adj-* too forward in offering advice or unwanted services; meddlesome: *an* officious *manner.* —*adv-* of·fi'cious·ly. *n-* of·fi'cious·ness.
►Should not be confused with OFFICIAL.

off·ing (ŏ' fĭng, ŏf' ĭng) *n-* the open sea, visible from shore but beyond anchoring ground; hence, immediate distance or near future.

off·ish (ŏ' fĭsh, ŏf' ĭsh) *Informal adj-* cool and reserved; distant; aloof.

off·key (ŏf' kē', ŏf'-) *adj-* 1 not on pitch: *Her singing was* off-key. 2 not suitable, harmonious, or proper: *an* off-key *chair; an* off-key *joke.* *adv-: She sang* off-key.

¹**off·set** (ŏf' sĕt', ŏf' sĕt') *vt-* [off·set, off·set·ting] to make up for; take the place of: *Skill may* offset *weakness.*

²**off·set** (ŏf' sĕt') *n-* 1 something that makes up for something else; compensation: *Success is an* offset *for failure.* 2 printing process in which a rubber cylinder transfers an inked impression from a plate to a sheet of paper.

off·shoot (ŏf' shŏŏt', ŏf'-) *n-* branch from the main stem of a plant, family, etc.: *French is an* offshoot *of Latin.*

off·shore (ŏf' shôr', ŏf'-) *adj-* 1 in a seaward position away from the shore: *an* offshore *light.* 2 of winds, coming from the shore and moving seaward. *adv-: The ship anchored* offshore. *The wind blew* offshore.

off·side (ŏf' sīd', ŏf'-) *adj-* 1 in football, illegally ahead of the ball before it is played. 2 in ice hockey, ahead of the puck in the attacking zone. *adv-: The tackle* jumped offside.

off·spring (ŏf' sprĭng', ŏf'-) *n-* [*pl.* off·spring *or* off·springs] 1 child or children; descendant or descendants of a person or animal. 2 something created: *the* offspring *of a vivid imagination.*

off·stage (ŏf' stāj', ŏf'-) *adj-* out of the view of the audience: *The play required many* offstage *sound effects.* *adv-: The actor went* offstage.

oft (ŏft, ôft) *Archaic* often.

of·ten (ŏf' ən, ôf'-) *adv-* frequently; many times.

of·ten·times (ŏf' ən tīmz', ôf'-) *adv-* often. Also **oft' times'.**

o·gle (ō' gəl, ŏ'-) *vt-* [o·gled, o·gling] to look at with desire; eye amorously. *n-* amorous or flirtatious look. —*n-* o'gler.

o·gre (ō' gər) *n-* 1 imaginary, man-eating giant. 2 person or thing that is viewed with dread: *the* ogre *of war.*

oh *or* **Oh** (ō) *interj-* exclamation of surprise, wonder, sorrow, etc.: Oh! *how awful! Homs-* ¹O, owe.

ohm (ōm) *n-* unit of electrical resistance in the mks system, equal to the resistance of a conductor through which an electromotive force of 1 volt produces a current of 1 ampere.

ohm·me·ter (ōm' mē' tər) *n-* instrument for measuring electrical resistance in ohms.

Ohm's law (ōmz) *n-* a law first stated by Georg Ohm: in an electrical circuit, the current in amperes is equal to the electromotive force in volts divided by the resistance in ohms.

-oid *suffix* (used to form nouns) that which resembles or has the quality of: *a spheroid.*

oil (oil) *n-* 1 any one of many greasy or fatty substances, usually liquid, obtained from animals, plants, or minerals: *whale* oil; *olive* oil. 2 petroleum. 3 oil color. 4 oil painting. *as modifier: an* oil *derrick.* *vt-* to lubricate: *to* oil *a squeaky hinge.*
   burn the midnight oil to study or work until late at night.

oil burner *n-* heating element burning oil, such as one in a furnace, stove, etc.

oil·cloth (oil' klŏth') *n-* cloth waterproofed by a coating of oil paint and used for table coverings, shelf linings, etc.

oil color *n-* 1 coloring matter used for oil paint. 2 artist's oil paint.

oil field *n-* region that is rich in petroleum deposits, especially deposits under development.

oil pan *n-* the lower section of the crankcase of an internal combustion engine, used as a reservoir for lubricating oil.

oil shale *n-* black or brownish-black, compact shale containing petroleum.

oil·skin (oil' skĭn') *n-* 1 oiled, waterproof fabric used for clothing and coverings. 2 garment of this cloth.

oil slick *n-* patch of oil floating on water.

oil·stone (oil' stōn') *n-* flat block of stone, emery, or other abrasive, used with oil for sharpening blades.

oil well *n-* well from which petroleum is taken.

oil·y (oi' lē) *adj-* [oil·i·er, oil·i·est] 1 like, containing, or covered with oil: *the* oily *feeling of waxed paper; a box of* oily *rags.* 2 too smooth in speech or manner; unctuous. —*adv-* oil'i·ly. *n-* oil'i·ness.

oint·ment (oint' mənt) *n-* salve, often perfumed or medicated, used to soften the skin or to soothe rashes, burns, etc.

O·jib·wa (ō jĭb' wä) *n-* [*pl.* O·jib·was, also O·jib·wa] Chippewa. *adj-: the puckered* Ojibwa *moccasin.*

ol·i·gar·chy (ŏl′ ə gär′ kē) *n-* [*pl.* **ol·i·gar·chies**] 1 government in which the supreme power is in the hands of a few. 2 state so governed. 3 the few who rule such a state; oligarchs. —*adj-* **ol′i·gar′chic** or **ol′i·gar′chi·cal.**

Ol·i·go·cene (ŏl′ ĭ gō sēn′) *n-* the middle epoch of the Tertiary period of geological time, between the Eocene and Miocene; also, a rock from this epoch. In the Oligocene, mammals evolved rapidly and the great apes appeared. *adj-: an Oligocene fossil.*

ol·ive (ŏl′ ĭv) *n-* 1 the small, oval fruit of an evergreen tree which grows in warm regions. Olives are pickled in brine when either green or ripe, or pressed for their fine oil. 2 the tree itself. 3 the fine wood of this tree, used in making cabinets and ornaments. 4 a greenish-yellow color, like that of unripe olives. *adj-: an olive cabinet; an olive dress.*

Olives

olive branch *n-* branch from an olive tree, used as a symbol of peace.

olive drab *n-* 1 greenish-brown color. 2 cloth of this color, much used by the military for camouflage and uniforms. 3 uniform made of this cloth.

olive oil *n-* oil pressed from ripe olives, used in cooking, for salads, in making soap, etc.

Ol·mec (ŏl′ měk′) *n-* [*pl.* **Ol·mecs,** also **Ol·mec**] one of a tribe of Indians who lived in southern Mexico between 800 B.C. and 200 A.D. *adj-: an Olmec sculpture.*

O·lym·pi·ad (ə lĭm′ pē ăd′, ō-) *n-* 1 in ancient Greece, the period of four years between two successive celebrations of the Olympic games, used as a system of reckoning time. 2 the ancient or modern Olympic games.

O·lym·pi·an (ə lĭm′ pē ən, ō-) *adj-* 1 of or relating to the gods of Mount Olympus. 2 godlike; majestic. 3 (also **O·lym′ pic**) of or relating to the city of Olympia or the Olympic games. *n-* 1 one of the gods dwelling on Mount Olympus. 2 participant in the Olympic games. 3 native of Olympia.

O·lym·pic games (ə lĭm′ pĭk, ō-) *n-* 1 festival of ancient Greece, with contests in athletics, music, and poetry. 2 modern international sports competition held every four years in a different country. Amateur athletes from many countries compete. Also **O·lym′ pics.**

O·lym·pus (ə lĭm′ pəs, ō-) *n-* in Greek legend, a mountain in Thessaly, held to be the home of the gods; hence, any place or condition of serene and remote authority.

o·ma·sum (ō mä′ səm) *n-* [*pl.* **o·ma·sa** (-sə)] third of the four chambers of the stomach of a cud-chewing animal, in which true digestion begins.

o·me·ga (ō mē′ gə, -mĕg′ ə) *n-* 1 last letter of the Greek alphabet. Omega is equivalent to the long o (ō) in English. 2 the end.

om·e·let or **om·e·lette** (ŏm′ ə lət) *n-* eggs beaten with milk, cooked, and folded over, often with chopped ham, cheese, jelly, etc., as a filler.

o·men (ō′ mən) *n-* sign or happening supposed to foretell good or bad luck; augury; portent.

om·i·nous (ŏm′ ə nəs) *adj-* like an omen of bad luck; threatening: *Dark, ominous clouds foretold a storm.* —*adv-* **om′ i·nous·ly.** *n-* **om′ i·nous·ness.**

o·mis·sion (ō mĭsh′ ən) *n-* 1 an omitting; a leaving out: *the omission of a signature.* 2 thing omitted or left out.

o·mit (ō mĭt′) *vt-* [**o·mit·ted, o·mit·ting**] 1 to leave out; fail to include: *Copy the names of the group but omit your own.* 2 to fail to do; neglect; leave undone: *Jack omitted packing his toothbrush.*

om·nip·o·tence (ŏm nĭp′ ə təns) *n-* 1 infinite or unlimited power. 2 **Omnipotence** God, the all-powerful.

om·nip·o·tent (ŏm nĭp′ ə tənt) *adj-* 1 all-powerful: *The emperor thought himself omnipotent.* 2 **the Omnipotent** God; the Almighty. —*adv-* **om·nip′ o·tent·ly.**

om·ni·pres·ent (ŏm′ nĭ prĕz′ ənt) *adj-* 1 present everywhere. 2 *Informal* seeming to be present all the time: *the omnipresent hecklers.* —*n-* **om′ ni·pres′ ence.**

om·nis·cient (ŏm nĭsh′ ənt) *adj-* knowing everything; having unlimited knowledge. —*n-* **om·nis′ cience.**

om·niv·o·rous (ŏm nĭv′ ər əs) *adj-* eating both meat and vegetables. —*adv-* **om·niv′ o·rous·ly.** *n-* **om·niv′ o·rous·ness.**

on (ŏn, ôn, *also* ən *when unstressed*) *prep-* 1 so as to be supported by: *Sit on this chair. I'll hang a picture on the wall.* 2 located upon: *spots on the rug; blisters on my feet.* 3 situated at or along: *a house on the river; a town on the border.* 4 against: *to hit one's head on the floor; to trip on a loose board.* 5 covering: *gloves on her hands; new paint on the ceiling.* 6 in the process or condition of: *a book on order; a house on sale; a union on strike.* 7 for the purpose of: *to go on vacation; to travel on business.* 8 subject to the effect and limits of: *to buy on credit; to live on borrowed time; to base one's beliefs on the evidence.* 9 available by: *water on tap; a doctor on call.* 10 following; keeping to: *to be on the trail; to stay on course.* 11 toward; unto: *Have pity on him.* 12 onto; into: *A door opening on the garden.* 13 meant for; directed or applied to: *Blessings on you.* 14 a member of: *He is on the board of directors.* 15 about; concerning: *a talk on Alaska; to agree on a plan.* 16 in the course of; during: *to leave on Tuesday.* 17 while or after: *They discovered, on opening the box, that it was empty.* 18 at the exact moment or point of: *to arrive on time; to hit it on the right spot.* 19 justified or supported by: *I did it on principle. I heard it on good authority.* 20 with the aid or use of: *to live on fish.* 21 added to: error on error. 22 *Informal* in the possession of: *I don't have a cent on me.* 23 *Informal* pointed toward: *He had a gun on me.* 24 *Informal* at the expense of: *The beer is on me.* 25 *Informal* taking as medicine, drink, etc.: *The doctor has him on penicillin.* *adv-* 1 further; more: *Please go on. The governor spoke on.* 2 additionally: *to add on six; to pile it on.* 3 forward; onward: *The army pushed on.* 4 in or at the present place: *to hold on; to stay on; to hang on.* 5 in operation: *The radio is on.* 6 set to start or permit operation: *The switch is on.* 7 *Informal* scheduled: *There is a party on tonight. What's on at the movies?* 8 *Informal* in progress.

be on to *Informal* to be aware of or alerted to. **on and off** occasionally; not regularly: *I go bowling on and off.* **on and on** for a long time without stopping: *to talk on and on.* **have something on (someone)** *Informal* to have damaging information, evidence, etc., against (someone).

once (wŭns) *adv-* 1 at one time; formerly: *We once lived in Ohio.* 2 single time: *Sing the song through just once.* 3 at any time; ever: *If she once starts talking, she is hard to stop.* *conj-* if ever; whenever: *I don't wake easily, once I get to sleep.* *n-* one time: *I say once is enough.*

all at once 1 all at the same time. 2 suddenly. **at once** 1 at the same time. 2 immediately. **once and for all** for the last time; finally. **once in a while** from time to time; occasionally. **once upon a time** a long time ago.

on·slaught (ŏn′ slôt′, ôn′ slôt′) *n-* violent attack or onset: *the onslaught of troops; the onslaught of a storm.*

Ont. Ontario.

on·to (ŏn′ tōō′, ôn′-) *prep-* 1 to a position on: *Let's get onto the boat.* 2 *Informal* aware of: *I'm onto your game.*

o·nus (ō′ nəs) *n-* burden; obligation.

on·ward (ŏn′ wərd, ôn′-) *adv-* (also **on′ wards**) forward; toward a farther point in time or distance: *to move onward into new territory.* *adj-: the onward march.*

on·yx (ŏn′ ĭks) *n-* kind of quartz in layers of various colors, used as a semiprecious gem.

oo·dles (ōō′ dəlz) *Informal n- pl.* a great plenty.

¹ooze (ōōz) *vi-* [**oozed, ooz·ing**] to flow out; seep: *The mud oozed between the child's squeezing fingers.* *vt-* to give out little by little through a small opening or openings: *His pores oozed perspiration.* *n-* 1 slow flow or leak: *an ooze of cream.* 2 something that flows or leaks out slowly. [from Middle English **wosen, wos,** from Old English **wōs** meaning "sap; juice."]

²ooze (ōōz) *n-* soft, slimy mud, especially at the bottom of a body of water. [from Middle English **wose,** from Old English **wāse** meaning "mud; slime."]

¹oo·zy (ōō′ zē) *adj-* [**oo·zi·er, oo·zi·est**] flowing or exuding slowly. [from ¹**ooze.**]

²oo·zy (ōō′ zē) *adj-* [**oo·zi·er, oo·zi·est**] slimy; muddy; mucky. [from ²**ooze.**] —*n-* **oo′ zi·ness.**

o·paque (ō pāk′) *adj-* 1 not permitting light to pass through; not transparent: *An opaque window shade shuts out the sunlight.* 2 very hard to understand, especially because of poor thought; obscure: *an opaque essay.* —*adv-* o·paque′ly. *n-* o·paque′ness.

op. cit. in the book, article, etc., cited or referred to [from Latin *opere citato.*]

ope (ōp) *Archaic vt-* & *vi-* [oped, op·ing] to open.

o·pen (ō′ pən) *adj-* 1 not closed, covered, sealed, or blocked: *an open window; an open boat; an open book; an open drain; an open mind; a road open to traffic.* 2 not yet filled or taken; available: *The job is still open. I have an evening open next week.* 3 free or accessible to all; public: *an open market; an open meeting.* 4 undecided or unsettled; pending: *That murder case is still open.* 5 not hidden or concealed; overt: *a case of open hostility; open lawlessness.* 6 frank and sincere; straightforward: *an open face.* 7 generous: *to give with an open hand.* 8 having openings or holes: *an open fabric.* 9 exposed; unprotected: *The city is open to attack. He is open to temptation.* 10 *Music* not stopped or not produced by stopping with the finger, a slide, key, etc.: *an open string; an open tone.* 11 of a syllable, ending in a vowel, as "de-" in "de·pend." *vt-* 1 to cause to be no longer closed, covered, etc.: *to open a door; to open a map; to open a road to traffic.* 2 to make an opening in: *to open a boil.* 3 to make accessible or available: *Railroads helped open the West.* 4 to make receptive to new and different ideas, suggestions, etc.; enlighten: *Traveling to foreign places helps to open your mind.* 5 to disclose; lay bare: *to open one's heart to a friend.* 6 to begin: *He opened the meeting with a reading of the minutes.* 7 to start operating: *to open a business; to open the new thruway. vi-* 1 to move or part so as to uncover or create an opening: *The door opened quietly. The curtains opened.* 2 to begin: *Services opened with a hymn.* 3 to start operating: *The bridge opened last Saturday.* 4 to appear as a gap or other opening: *A huge crack opened in the earth.* —*n-* o′ pen·er.

the open any wide, clear space, especially the outdoors: *We lived in the open all summer.* **open to 1** exposed to: *One side of the shed is open to the weather.* **2** subject or liable to: *He is open to criticism.* **3** ready to consider: *I am open to any interesting offers.*

open (one's) eyes to reveal surprising or unexpected things to (one): *His angry outbursts really opened my eyes to his true personality.*

open into (or onto) to give access to or a view of: *The kitchen has a door that opens into the dining room.*

open up to speak in an honest and straightforward manner, especially after a prolonged silence.

open air *n-* outdoors: *We spent the morning in the open air. as modifier* (open-air): *an open-air concert.*

open door *n-* 1 policy of giving all nations equal opportunity to trade in a certain area, as China did in the early twentieth century. 2 free admission to all. *as modifier* (open-door): *the open-door policy in China.*

o·pen-eyed (ō′ pən īd′) *adj-* 1 watchful; observant; vigilant. 2 shown by a wide stare of disbelief: *a look of open-eyed amazement.*

o·pen-faced (ō′ pən fāst′) *adj-* having an honest, frank face.

o·pen-hand·ed (ō′ pən hăn′ dəd) *adj-* generous. —*adv-* o′ pen-hand′ ed·ly. *n-* o′ pen-hand′ ed·ness.

o·pen-heart·ed (ō′ pən här′ təd) *adj-* 1 frank and honest; candid. 2 generous. —*adv-* o′ pen-heart′ ed·ly. *n-* o′ pen-heart′ ed·ness.

o·pen-hearth (ō′ pən härth′) *adj-* 1 of or relating to a process of making steel, in which pig iron and other materials are melted in a furnace with a saucer-shaped hearth, by the heat of burning gases reflected from the roof. 2 of or having to do with the steel so made.

open house *n-* 1 party or other social event for all who wish to come. 2 period or occasion during which a school, institution, etc., is open to interested observers.

o·pen·ly (ō′ pən lē) *adv-* without secrecy; without trying to hide or conceal: *He openly rebelled against the king.*

open market *n-* market in which any buyer or seller may trade and compete; free market.

o·pen-mind·ed (ō′ pən mīn′ dəd) *adj-* able to consider new facts, ideas, and opinions; unprejudiced; impartial. —*adv-* o′ pen-mind′ ed·ly. *n-* o′ pen-mind′ ed·ness.

o·pen-mouthed (ō′ pən moutht′, -mouthd′) *adj-* 1 gaping in wonder or amazement. 2 greedy.

o·pen·ness (ō′ pən nəs) *n-* 1 lack of secrecy. 2 open-mindedness. 3 frankness; straightforwardness.

open season *n-* period of the year during which hunting or fishing of specified game is not prohibited.

open sesame *interj-* in the "Arabian Nights," a magic saying used to open a secret, locked door. *n-* something that gives a person entrance to. closed or restricted places: *His talent was an open sesame to success.*

open shop *n-* factory or business where nonunion employes may be hired. See also *closed shop, union shop.*

open syllable *n-* spoken syllable that consists of or ends with a vowel or diphthong.

o·pen·work (ō′ pən wŭrk′) *n-* carving, embroidery, etc., having many small cutouts or openings.

¹op·er·a (ŏp′ ər ə) *n-* musical drama in which all or most of the lines are sung to the accompaniment of an orchestra. Operas are usually more serious in theme and more difficult to sing than operettas and musicals. See also *grand opera, comic opera. as modifier: an opera singer.* [from Italian, from **opera in musica,** "an effort in music," from Latin **opera,** "effort."]

²op·er·a (ō′ pə rə) *pl.* of **opus.**

op·er·a·ble (ŏp′ ər ə bəl) *adj-* 1 such as can be treated by surgery. 2 possible to do or carry out; practicable: *Is the plan operable?*

opera glasses *n- pl.* small binoculars for use in watching stage performances.

opera hat *n-* top hat with a collapsible crown.

opera house *n-* theater for operas.

op·er·ate (ŏp′ ə rāt′) *vi-* [op·er·at·ed, op·er·at·ing] 1 to go, work, or run; function: *A jet engine should operate smoothly.* 2 to have a certain effect or influence: *Some drugs operate harmfully on the body.* 3 to perform surgery: *Is Dr. Thomas operating today?* 4 to carry on military activity: *The unit will operate behind enemy lines. vt-* 1 to cause to work or run: *Can he operate that car?* 2 to be in charge of or manage (a business).

op·er·at·ic (ŏp′ ə răt′ ĭk) *adj-* of, in, related to, or suitable for opera: *an operatic tenor; operatic dialogue.* —*adv-* op·er′at′i·cal·ly.

op·er·a·tion (ŏp′ ə rā′ shən) *n-* 1 act or process of working or running; also, the way something works or operates.

op·er·a·tive (ŏp′ ər ə tĭv′) *adj-* 1 actively used, enforced, etc.; operating; in force and effect: *That law is no longer operative.* 2 related to physical or practical work: *a man's operative skills.* 3 in medicine, related to operations: *postoperative care. n-* 1 secret agent or private investigator. 2 *Archaic* worker, especially in a factory.

op·er·a·tor (ŏp′ ə rā′ tər) *n-* 1 someone who works or runs a machine, mechanism, etc.: *an X-ray operator; a telephone switchboard operator.* 2 person who manages a business or other enterprise: *He is a big mine operator.* 3 *Informal* person who gets what he wants by shrewd, vigorous, and somewhat irregular means.

op·er·et·ta (ŏp′ ə rĕt′ ə) *n-* light and humorous musical play with much spoken dialogue, usually having a romantic theme and a dancing chorus.

o·phid·i·an (ō fĭd′ē ən) *n-* member of the group of reptiles (**Ophidia**) to which all snakes belong; snake. —*adj-: an ophidian reptile; an ophidian head.*

oph·thal·mi·a (ŏf thăl′ mē ə, also ŏp-) *n-* inflamation of the eye or its membranes or lids.

oph·thal·mol·o·gist (ŏf′ thăl mŏl′ ə jĭst′, also ŏp′-) *n-* doctor who specializes in ophthalmology.

oph·thal·mol·o·gy (ŏf′ thăl mŏl′ ə jē, also ŏp′-) *n-* the branch of medicine dealing with the structure, functions, and diseases of the eye.

o·pi·ate (ō′ pē ət, -āt′) *n-* 1 medicine that contains opium and is used to induce sleep, kill pain, etc. 2 anything that induces sleep, soothes, or relaxes. *adj-: an opiate drug.*

o·pine (ō pīn′) *Archaic vt-* [o·pined, o·pin·ing] to have or express as an opinion; suppose (takes only a clause as an object): *He opined that it was too late*

op·pro·bri·um (ə prō′ brē əm) *n-* disgrace or severe reproach resulting from shameful or infamous conduct; scorn; infamy: *There is great opprobrium attached to the name of Benedict Arnold.*

op·tic (ŏp′ tĭk) *adj-* relating to the eye or to sight: *the optic nerve.* *n-* **optics** (takes singular verb) the science which treats of light, the laws of vision, and the construction of optical instruments.

op·ti·cal (ŏp′ tĭ kəl) *adj-* 1 relating to optics. 2 of or having to do with the eyesight: *an optical illusion.* 3 made to assist sight: *an optical instrument.* —*adv-* **op′ ti·cal·ly.**

optical illusion *n-* an error in judging the size, shape, distance, etc., of visually perceived objects. Example: the moon appears to be much bigger near the horizon than high in the sky. For picture, see *illusion.*

op·ti·cian (ŏp tĭsh′ ən) *n-* one who makes or sells eyeglasses and other optical instruments.

optic nerve *n-* nerve connecting the retina of the eye with the part of the brain associated with seeing.

op·ti·mal (ŏp′ tə məl) *adj-* best or most favorable for a particular purpose: *the optimal conditions for take-off.*

op·ti·mism (ŏp′ tə mĭz′ əm) *n-* 1 tendency to see only the brighter side of things, or to expect or hope for the best. 2 the belief that everything happens for the best, or that the world is constantly getting better. —*n-* **op′ ti·mist.** *adj-* **op′ ti·mis′ tic.** *adv-* **op′ ti·mis′ ti·cal·ly.**

op·ti·mum (ŏp′ tə məm) *n-* [*pl.* **op·ti·mums** or **op·ti·ma** (-mə)] the best or most favorable condition, amount, degree, etc.: *Conditions for growth are at an optimum.* *adj-* optimal: *an optimum temperature for hatching.*

op·tion (ŏp′ shən) *n-* 1 right or power of choosing; choice; discretion: *You have the option to take it or leave it.* 2 the act of choosing: *You can make your decision after his option.* 3 something that is or can be chosen: *I have the option of giving an oral report or taking a written exam.* 4 purchased right to buy or sell something at a specified price within a specified time.

op·tion·al (ŏp′ shən əl) *adj-* left to one's choice or preference; elective: *an optional course of study.* —*adv-* **op′ tion·al·ly.**

op·tom·e·trist (ŏp tŏm′ ə trĭst′) *n-* specialist in examining the eyes for visual defects, and in fitting a person with eyeglasses to correct such defects. —*n-* **op·tom′ e·try.**

op·u·lent (ŏp′ yə lənt) *adj-* 1 very rich; wealthy; affluent: *an opulent rajah.* 2 plentiful; abundant; ample: *a full, opulent figure.* —*n-* **op′ u·lence.**

o·pus (ō′ pəs) *n-* [*pl.* **op·er·a** (ō′ pə rə)] a literary or musical work; especially, one of the works of a composer numbered in the order in which they were published.

or (ôr) *conj-* 1 (used with "either," and often with "whether," to introduce two, and only two, alternatives): *I want either peach pie or chocolate ice cream. Whether you go or stay is of no concern to me.* 2 (used after a statement to introduce any number of additional alternatives): *I want chocolate or strawberry, or possibly butter pecan.* 3 else; otherwise: *You'd better go, or you'll be sorry.* 4 in other words; namely: *The puma, or cougar, is found in the Americas.* *Homs-* oar, o'er, ore.

-or *suffix* (used to form nouns) person who or a thing that: *inheritor; possessor.*

or·a·cle (ôr′ ə kəl, ŏr′-) *n-* 1 in ancient Greece and Rome, a priest, a priestess, or other agency believed to receive messages from a god and give them as prophecies to human beings. 2 message so given. 3 place where such messages were given. 4 person whose wisdom and

Or·ange·man (ôr′ ĭnj mən, ŏr′-) *n-* [*pl.* **Or·ange·men**] member of a secret society organized in Northern Ireland in 1795 to support Protestantism.

orange pekoe *n-* choice black tea of India, Ceylon, and Java, made from the youngest leaves at the tip of the stem. See also *pekoe.*

o·rang·u·tan (ə răng′ ə tăng′) *n-* long-armed, tree-dwelling ape of Borneo and Sumatra having reddish-brown hair. Also **o·rang′-u·tang′.**

o·rate (ôr ăt′) *vi-* [**o·rat·ed, o·rat·ing**] to speak in a grand manner; declaim.

o·ra·tion (ôr ā′ shən) *n-* formal public speech, usually given on a special occasion: *a funeral oration.*

or·a·tor (ôr′ ə tər, ŏr′-) *n-* public speaker, especially a skillful one.

or·a·tor·i·cal (ôr′ ə tôr′ ĭ kəl, ŏr′ ə tôr′-) *adj-* of or suitable to orators or oratory: *an oratorical style.* —*adv-* **or′ a·tor′ i·cal·ly.**

or·a·tor·i·o (ôr′ ə tôr′ ē ō, ŏr′-) *n-* [*pl.* **or·a·tor·i·os**] large, dramatic musical work, usually on a sacred theme, sung by solo voices and chorus to orchestral accompaniment, without action, scenery, or costumes.

¹**or·a·to·ry** (ôr′ ə tôr′ ē, ŏr′-) *n-* 1 the art of speaking in public. 2 skill and eloquence in public speaking: *Abraham Lincoln's Gettysburg Address is an example of great oratory.* [from Latin **ars ōrātōria** meaning "the oratorical art," from **ōrāre,** "to plead (a case); speak eloquently."]

²**or·a·to·ry** (ôr′ ə tôr′ ē, ŏr′-) *n-* [*pl.* **or·a·to·ries**] chapel for private prayer. [from Latin **ōrātōrium** meaning "of or for prayer," from **ōrāre,** "to pray; plead."]

orb (ôrb, ŏrb) *n-* 1 globe; sphere. 2 the sun, moon, or any other heavenly body. 3 the eye. 4 a sphere having an upright cross on top of it, used as a symbol of royal power and justice.

or·bit (ôr′ bĭt, ŏr′-) *n-* 1 path followed by one heavenly body around another; also, path in which a man-made satellite or spacecraft moves about a heavenly body. 2 circle or range of influence: *Poland is within the Communist orbit.* 3 the bony cavity which contains the eye. *vt-* 1 to place (a man-

Orbit of a satellite

or·der·ly (ôr′ dər lē, ŏr′-) *adj-* 1 well arranged and tidy: *Mother kept the house clean and orderly.* 2 having regard for order or system; systematic: *An orderly person plans his work.* 3 free from trouble or disorder; well managed or behaved; peaceable: *an orderly crowd.* *n-* [*pl.* **or·der·lies**] 1 soldier assigned to an officer to carry messages and otherwise assist him. 2 attendant in a hospital. —*n-* **or′ der·li·ness.**

Order of the Garter *n-* the highest order of knighthood in Great Britain.

or·di·nal or **ordinal number** (ôr′ də nəl, ŏr′-) *n-* kind of number that shows the position of an object in a series. "First," "1st," "third," "3rd," "tenth," and "10th" are ordinals. See also *cardinal number.*

or·di·nance (ôr′ də nəns, ŏr′-) *n-* official law, rule, or decree, especially one made by the authorities of a town or city: *Please observe the no smoking ordinance.* ▶Should not be confused with ORDNANCE.

or·di·nar·i·ly (ôr′ də nêr′ ə lē, ŏr′-) *adv-* usually; normally; customarily: *Our dog ordinarily sleeps quietly.*

or·di·nar·y (ôr′ də nêr′ ē, ŏr′-) *adj-* 1 usual; customary; normal: *to follow one's ordinary routine.* 2 commonplace; mediocre: *It's just an ordinary dress.*

in ordinary 1 in regular service: *a painter in ordinary to a king.* 2 of a ship, out of commission. out of the ordinary unusual; extraordinary.

ordinary seaman *n-* seaman who works as a deckhand on a ship, and is subordinate to an able-bodied seaman.

or·di·nate (ôr′ də nət, ŏr′-) *n-* in plane geometry, the second of two co-ordinates used to locate a point with regard to two axes. The ordinate is customarily the vertical distance of a point from the x axis, measured along a line parallel to the y axis. For picture, see *abscissa.*

or·di·na·tion (ôr′ də nā′ shən, ŏr′-) *n-* admission to the ministry of a church by means of an official ceremony; also, the ceremony itself.

ord·nance (ôrd′ nəns, ŏrd′-) *n-* all types of military weapons and ammunition, especially artillery. ▶Should not be confused with ORDINANCE.

Or·do·vi·ci·an (ôr′ də vĭsh′ ən) *n-* the second of the six periods of the Paleozoic era. Primitive fish first appeared during the Ordovician. *adj-: the Ordovician period.*

ore (ôr) *n-* rock or mineral containing enough of one or more elements, usually metals, to make the mining of it profitable. *Homs-* oar, o'er, or.

Oreg. Oregon.

organ grinder *n-* street musician who plays a hand organ or hurdy-gurdy.

or·gan·ic (ôr găn′ ĭk) *adj-* 1 having to do with the organs of an animal or plant: *an organic disease.* 2 relating to or derived from living matter: *Fossils are remains of organic bodies.* 3 designating or related to a chemical compound containing carbon: *the study of organic chemistry.* 4 made up of related parts: *an organic whole.* 5 belonging to, or inherent in, the constitution or organization of something; fundamental: *an organic fault.* —*adv-* **or·gan′i·cal·ly.**

organic chemistry *n-* branch of chemistry that studies the compounds of carbon.

or·gan·ism (ôr′ gə nĭz′ əm, ôr′-) *n-* 1 living plant or animal: *a microscopic organism.* 2 something similar to this; complex, organized whole: *the social organism.*

or·gan·ist (ôr′ gə nĭst′, ôr′-) *n-* person who plays the organ.

or·gan·i·za·tion (ôr′ gə nə zā′ shən) *n-* 1 a uniting or being united, so that people or things work well together; an organizing or being organized: *the organization of a campaign; the* organization *of a club.* 2 way in which parts of a whole are arranged: *the* organization *of our government.* 3 group of people united to do certain work: *the Red Cross* organization.

Organization of American States *n-* association of twenty Latin American republics and the United States. It is a regional organization within the framework of the United Nations and provides for inter-American co-operation and the peaceful settlement of controversies.

or·ga·nize (ôr′ gə nīz′, ôr′-) *vt-* [or·ga·nized, or·ga·niz·ing] 1 to put together in working order; unite or group so that things or persons work well together: *The coach* organized *a good football team by much drilling and hard work.* 2 to plan and arrange: *A scientist must* organize *his work carefully.* 3 to cause (workers) to join or form a labor union; also, to cause the workers of (a factory, industry, etc.) to join or form a labor union. *vi-* to form, or join in, an organization: *The workers* organized *for higher wages and shorter hours.* —*n-* **or′ gan·iz′ er.**

or·gan·za (ôr găn′ zə) *n-* fine, sheer, crisp fabric used mainly as a stiffening under dresses.

or·gy (ôr′ jē, ôr′-) *n-* [*pl.* **or·gies**] 1 orgies among the ancient Greeks and Romans, secret rites performed as part of the worship of certain gods, especially the god of wine, and accompanied by wild, ecstatic songs and dances, drinking, etc. 2 wild, drunken, or lustful revel; debauch. 3 any spell of uncontrolled or excessive activity: *an orgy of eating.*

or·i·el (ôr′ ē əl) *n-* large bay window projecting from the outside wall of a building and often supported by a bracket.

o·ri·ent (ôr′ ē ĕnt) *vt-* 1 to place facing the east. 2 to place in the right relation to the points of the compass: *At night I can* orient *myself if I find the North Star.* 3 to adjust or adapt to new or unfamiliar surroundings, ideas, etc.: *It doesn't take very long to* orient *yourself when you move to a new city. I need some time to* orient *my thinking.* *n-* the east.

Oriel

O·ri·ent (ôr′ ē ĕnt) *n-* the countries of Asia, especially the Far East and the islands off the coat of Asia; opposite of Occident.

o·ri·en·tal (ôr′ ē ĕn′ təl) *adj-* 1 eastern. 2 of or pertaining to the countries in the Orient or their people: *strange* oriental *music.* *n-* Oriental 1 person belonging to or descended from one of the native peoples of the Orient. 2 a Mongolian.

o·ri·en·tate (ôr′ ē ən tāt′) *vi-* [or·i·en·tat·ed, or·i·en·tat·ing] to face a specified direction, especially the east. *vt-* to orient.

or·i·fice (ôr′ ə fĭs, ôr′-) *n-* outlet or opening; vent: *The nostril is the nasal* orifice.

orig. 1 original. 2 originally.

or·i·gin (ôr′ ə jĭn, ôr′-) *n-* 1 beginning; start; source: *Nobody knows the* origin *of that rumor.* 2 family background; ancestry: *After he grew famous, he never concealed his humble* origin.

o·rig·i·nal (ə rĭj′ ə nəl) *adj-* 1 first; earliest: *The Indians were the* original *inhabitants of America.* 2 imaginative; producing new ideas; creative: *Your story shows you have an* original *mind.* 3 not copied; new; done for the first time: *Our teacher wrote an* original *Thanksgiving pageant.* *n-* 1 the first model from which something is copied: *This is a copy of our Constitution but the* original *is in Washington, D.C.* 2 language in which something is first written: *to read French books in the* original.

o·rig·i·nal·i·ty (ə rĭj′ ə nǎl′ ə tē) *n-* [o·rig·i·nal·i·ties] 1 novelty; freshness: *That idea has great* originality. 2 ability to create or invent: *Fred's* originality *is seen best in his posters.* 3 any novel or original thing; innovation.

o·rig·i·nal·ly (ə rĭj′ ə nə lē) *adv-* 1 at first; in the beginning: *The capital of the United States was* originally *Philadelphia.* 2 in a new and fresh way: *The stage decorations were designed very* originally.

o·rig·i·nate (ə rĭj′ ə nāt′) *vi-* [o·rig·i·nat·ed, o·rig·i·nat·ing] to start; begin: *The fire* originated *in the engine room.* *vt-* to invent; make up: *The Chinese* originated *fireworks.* —*n-* **o·rig′ i·na′ tion.** *n-* **o·rig′ i·na′ tor:** *the* originator *of a new product.*

os·cil·lo·scope (ə sĭl′ ə skōp′) *n-* instrument that makes visible the fluctuations of an electric current on the fluorescent screen of a cathode-ray tube similar to a television picture tube.

os·cu·late (ŏs′ kyə lāt′) *vi-* [os·cu·lat·ed, os·cu·lat·ing] to kiss. —*n-* **os′ cu·la′ tion.**

¹-ose *suffix* (used to form adjectives) 1 full of: *verbose.* 2 like; having the nature of: *grandiose; jocose.* [from Latin *-osus.*]

²-ose *Chemistry suffix* (used to form nouns) sugar or other carbohydrate: *lactose; fructose; levulose.* [from *glucose.*]

O·see (ō′ sē, ō sē′) Hosea.

o·sier (ō′ zhər) *n-* 1 any of various willows with flexible twigs used in baskets, furniture, etc. 2 twig of this willow. 3 any of various dogwoods, especially the **red-osier dogwood.** *as modifier:* *an* osier *chair;* osier *furniture.*

O·si·ris (ō sī′ rəs) *n-* in Egyptian mythology, the god of the underworld; husband and brother of Isis.

-osity *suffix* (used to form nouns from adjectives ending in "-ose"): *jocosity; verbosity; grandiosity.*

os·mi·um (ŏz′ mē əm) *n-* bluish-white metal element that occurs and is used with platinum and iridium in alloys. Symbol Os, At. No. 76, At. Wt. 190.2.

os·mo·sis (ŏs mō′ səs, ŏz-) *n-* the migration of a liquid solvent, especially water, through a semipermeable membrane separating solutions of different concentration. In the living cell, water passes through the membrane from the region of higher concentration of water to the region of lesser concentration. —*adj-* **os·mot′ ic** (-mŏt′ ĭk): *the* osmotic *pressure.*

os·mot·ic (ŏs′ mŏt′ ĭk, ŏz′-) *adj-* relating to or resulting from osmosis: *an* osmotic *flow;* osmotic *pressure.*

os·prey (ŏs′ prē) *n-* [*pl.* **os·preys**] a large fish-eating hawk; fish hawk.

os·si·fi·ca·tion (ŏs′ ĭ fə kā′ shən) *n-* 1 process of bone formation, in which the flexible cartilage of the skeleton is replaced by bony tissue. 2 something that has become hardened or changed into bone.

Osprey about 2 ft long

os·si·fy (ŏs′ ə fī′) *vt-* [os·si·fied, os·si·fy·ing] 1 to change into bone or bony tissue. 2 to harden; make rigid or unprogressive; *Prejudice* ossifies *the mind.* *vi-* 1 to be transformed into bone: *His knee cartilages* ossified *with age.* 2 to become rigid or set in a conventional pattern.

os·te·op·a·thy (ŏs′ tē ŏp′ ə thē′) *n-* a method of treatment which, while recognizing the value of ordinary medical and surgical treatment, holds that many diseases are due chiefly to displacement of body parts, especially the bones, and in healing lays stress on manipulating the displaced parts into place with the hands. —*adj-* **os′ te·o·path′ ic** (-tē ə păth′ ĭk): *an* osteopathic *physician.*

ot·ter (ŏt′ər) *n-* **1** any of various fish-eating water mammals related to the weasel, valued for their brown fur. **2** the fur of this animal.
as modifier: an otter *hat; an* otter *paw.*

River otter about 3 1 2 ft long

Ot·to·man (ŏt′ə mən) *n-* [*pl.* **Ot·to·mans**] **1** a Turk. **2 ottoman** (1) a low, cushioned seat. (2) a footstool. (3) a heavy fabric with a plain weave made of wool, silk, or synthetic fiber. *adj- the* Ottoman *Empire; an* Ottoman *cloth.*

ouch (ouch) *interj-* exclamation of sudden pain.

¹ought (ôt) *auxiliary verb* **1** am, is, or are morally bound or obliged (to): *You* ought *to be kind to your pets. We* ought *to pay the workmen.* **2** am, is, or are almost certain or expected (to): *The piano* ought *to sound better when it is tuned. This top* ought *to fit the jar.* **3** am, is, or are almost obliged (to): *We* ought *to leave now if we are not going to be late.* [from Old English **āhte,** from **āgan** meaning "to owe."] *Hom-* aught.

Ottoman

▶For the negative of OUGHT TO, use "ought not to": *He* ought not (to) *go.* Good speakers avoid the expressions "hadn't ought to" or "oughtn't to."

²ought (ôt) **²**aught.

ought·n't (ôt′ ənt) ought not.

▶For usage note see OUGHT.

¹ounce (ouns) *n-* **1** in ordinary weight, 1/16 of a pound. **2** in troy weight, for weighing drugs and precious metals, 1/12 of a pound. **3** in liquid measure, 1/16 of a pint or 1/8 of a standard half-pint kitchen measuring cup. [from Old French **unce,** from Latin **uncia** meaning literally "a twelfth part," and very closely related to **inch.**]

²ounce (ouns) *n-* snow leopard. [from Old French **once,** from earlier **lonce,** from Latin and Greek **lynx** meaning "lynx."]

our (our, är) *determiner* (possessive case of the pronoun "we," now usually called possessive adjective) of, belonging to, done, or made by us: *This is* our *house. We wrote* our *play in three days. Hom-* hour or are.

Our Father *n-* the Lord's Prayer.

Our Lady *n-* the Virgin Mary.

ours (ourz, ärz) *pron-* (possessive pronoun) thing or things belonging to us: *Those books are* ours.

our·selves (our sĕlv′z, är-) *pron-* **1** reflexive form of **us;** our own selves: *We dressed* ourselves. **2** our normal or true selves: *We weren't quite* ourselves *yesterday.* **3** intensive form of **we:** *We* ourselves *saw it.*
by ourselves 1 alone: *We sat by* ourselves *in the garden.* **2** without any help: *We painted the house by* ourselves.

-ous *suffix* (used to form adjectives from nouns) **1** full of; of the nature of; like: *poison*ous; *glamor*ous. **2** *Chemistry* with a valence relatively lower than compounds or ions having an adjective ending in "-ic": *chlor*ous; *sulfur*ous.

oust (oust) *vt-* to drive or force out: *The umpire* ousted *him from the game.*

oust·er (ous′ tər) *n-* an ousting; also, an instance of this: *The* ouster *of the dictator failed to pacify the country.*

out- *prefix* **1** at a distance away from: *an* outbuilding, outpost; outlying. **2** forth; away: *an* outcry; outburst; outcast. **3** greater than; better than: *to* outdo; outdistance; outrun. **4** more than; longer than: *to* outlive, outlast.

out-and-out (out′ ənd out′) *adj-* outright; thoroughgoing; unqualified; complete: *That's an* out-and-out *lie!*

out·bid (out′ bĭd′) *vt-* [out·bid, out·bid·ding] to offer to pay more for something than someone else: *He* outbid *all the others at the auction.*

out·board (out′ bôrd′) *adv-* **1** outside the hull of a ship. **2** away from the center line of the fuselage of an aircraft. *adj-* **1** located on or attached to the outside of a boat: *the* outboard *motor.* **2** located farthest away from the center line of the fuselage of an aircraft: *the* outboard *starboard engine.* **3** of boats, powered by an outboard motor. *n-* a boat powered by an outboard motor.

outboard motor *n-* gasoline engine complete with shaft and propeller, attached to the outside of the stern of a small boat.

Outboard motor

out·bound (out′ bound′) *adj-* outward bound; leaving a port, terminal, airfield, etc.: *An* outbound *plane flew by.*

out·brave (out′ brāv′) *vt-* [out·braved, out·brav·ing] to face and withstand with courage and defiance; brave out.

out·break (out′ brāk′) *n-* **1** an appearance of a disease, riot, or other harmful condition: *an* outbreak *of influenza.* **2** outburst: *The bad news resulted in an* outbreak *of temper.*

out·build·ing (out′ bĭl′ dĭng) *n-* small building like a shed, separate from a main building.

out·burst (out′ bûrst′) *n-* sudden, violent gush; a bursting forth: *an* outburst *of anger; an* outburst *of lava from a volcano.*

out·cast (out′ kăst′) *n-* person or animal driven out or rejected by others. *adj-* driven out; exiled: *an* outcast *wolf, driven from the pack.*

out·class (out′ klăs′, out′-) *vt-* to surpass or excel in quality, skill, etc.: *This model* outclasses *all the competition.*

out·come (out′ kŭm′) *n-* result: *His speed made the* outcome *of the race certain.*

out·dat·ed (out′ dā′ tǝd) *adj-* old-fashioned; out-of-date; obsolete or obsolescent: *The plant was using* outdated *machinery.*

out·dis·tance (out′ dĭs′ tǝns) *vt-* [out·dis·tanced, out·dis·tanc·ing] to leave (something or someone) behind by traveling faster: *The rabbit* outdistanced *the hunting dog.*

out·do (out′ dōō′) *vt-* [out·did, out·done, out·do·ing] to do better than; surpass: *He can* outdo *me in every subject but science.*

out·door (out′ dôr′) *adj-* **1** in the open air: *Football is an* outdoor *game.* **2** fond of the open air: *an* outdoor *man.*

out·doors (out′ dôrz′) *n-* (takes singular verb) world outside of buildings; the open air, especially in the country: *Campers can enjoy the* outdoors. *adv-* in the open: *It's too nice a day not to go* outdoors.

out·er (ou′ tǝr) *adj-* **1** having to do with the outside: *the* outer *layer of skin.* **2** among the farthest from the center or inside: *Uranus is one of the* outer *planets of our solar system.* **3** among the farthest from the mainland: *the* outer *islands.*

outer ear See **¹ear.**

out·er·most (ou′ tǝr mōst′) *adj-* farthest out from the center or other place of reference: *the* outermost *planet; the* outermost *island of the Hawaiian group.*

outer space *n-* **1** the space immediately beyond the earth's atmosphere. **2** interplanetary or interstellar space.

out·face (out′ fās′, out′-) *vt-* [out·faced, out·fac·ing] to cause (someone) to back down by facing him boldly and defiantly; stare down: *He* outfaced *his accusers.*

out·field (out′ fēld′) *n-* **1** part of a baseball field beyond the infield. **2** baseball players who play in the outfield; the outfielders. *as modifier: the* outfield *grass.*

out·field·er (out′ fēl′ dǝr) *n-* in baseball, any of the three players, the right fielder, the center fielder, and the left fielder, who play in the outfield.

out·fight (out′ fīt′, out′-) *vt-* [out·fought, out·fight·ing] to defeat by fighting harder, better, or longer than: *to* outfight *the enemy.*

out·fit (out′ fĭt′) *n-* **1** set of equipment used for a special purpose: *a fishing* outfit; *a camping* outfit. **2** complete costume: *She wore a tweed* outfit. **3** *Informal* group of persons taken as a unit, such as a business firm, army corps, etc.: *This is an excellent* outfit *to work for. vt-* [out·fit·ted, out·fit·ting] to equip for a special purpose: *The Geographic Society will* outfit *an expedition to Antarctica.* *—n-* out′ fit′ ter.

out·flank (out′ flăngk′, out′-) *vt-* to place (an enemy) in a dangerous or untenable position by passing around his side or wing.

o·ver·work (ō′vər wûrk′) *vt-* 1 to cause to work too hard; demand too much work from: *The foreman overworked his men.* 2 to use (an idea, phrase, joke, etc.) so much that it becomes tiresome. *vi-* to work harder or longer than is good for one: *He has overworked for months. n-: He is sick from overwork.*

o·ver·wrought (ō′vər rôt′) *adj-* 1 too excited; very nervous and tense: *an overwrought spectator.* 2 too elaborate: *an overwrought style; overwrought designs.*

ovi- *combining form* egg: *an oviduct; oviform.* Also **ovo-** [from Latin *ov-*, from *ovum* meaning "egg."]

o·vi·duct (ō′və dŭkt′) *n-* tube in a female animal through which eggs travel from an ovary to the outside of the body, or to an organ having a connection with the outside of the body.

o·vi·form (ō′və fôrm′, -fôrm′) *adj-* shaped like an egg.

o·vip·a·rous (ō vĭp′ər əs) *adj-* producing offspring from eggs that hatch outside the body. Birds and most fish are oviparous. See also *ovoviviparous, viviparous.*

o·vi·pos·i·tor (ō′və pŏz′ə tər) *n-* organ in the female of certain insects, such as the cricket and the grasshopper, for depositing eggs outside the body. It is located at the extreme end of the abdomen.

o·void (ō′void′) *adj-* having the shape of an egg; egg-shaped. *n-* anything shaped like an egg.

o·vo·vi·vip·a·rous (ō′vō vī′vĭp′ər əs) *adj-* bringing forth living offspring that develop in eggs or egglike sacs within but not attached to the mother. Certain fishes and snakes, such as the guppy and the copperhead, are ovoviviparous. See also *oviparous, viviparous.*

o·vu·lar (ō′vyə lər) *adj-* of, relating to, or like an ovule.

o·vu·late (ō′vyə lāt′, *also* ŏv′yə-) *vi-* [o·vu·lat·ed, o·vu·lat·ing] to produce eggs or ovules, or to discharge them from an ovary. —*n-* o′vu·la′tion.

o·vule (ō′vyōōl′) *n-* 1 small part within the ovary of a plant, which develops into a seed when fertilized. 2 small egg, especially one in an early stage of development.

o·vum (ō′vəm) *n-* [*pl.* o·va (ō′və)] female germ cell; egg cell.

owe (ō) *vt-* [owed, ow·ing] 1 to be under obligation to pay or give: *He owes two dollars to his brother. We owe loyalty to our country. I owe you an apology.* 2 to be indebted for: *He owes his life to the fireman who saved him. vi-* to be in debt: *She still owes for the groceries.* Hom*s-* ¹O, oh.

ow·ing (ō′ĭng) *adj-* not paid; due: *bills that are owing.*
owing to because of; as a result of: *The crops are poor, owing to the drought.*
▶See usage note at DUE TO.

owl (oul) *n-* any of a group of birds of prey with flat faces, large eyes, and a short, hooked beak. Owls have a hooting call and a noiseless flight. They usually hunt at night.

owl·et (ou′lət) *n-* young owl.

owl·ish (ou′lĭsh) *adj-* having the appearance or characteristics of an owl; especially, solemn and seemingly wise: *an owlish look.*

own (ōn) *adj-* (always preceded by a possessive adjective) 1 of or belonging particularly to someone or something: *I have my own bicycle. This room is his own.* 2 (intensifier only): *She is my own sister. I cooked my own dinner. vt-* 1 to possess; have ownership of: *We used to rent this house but now own it.* 2 to admit; acknowledge: *I own that I was at fault.*
come into (one's) own to obtain the success or recognition that one deserves. **hold (one's) own** to survive or defend oneself with one's own resources. **of (one's) own** belonging to oneself alone: *He has a room of his own.* 2 of that or those belonging to one: *She needed a dress and I gave her one of my own.* **on (one's) own** responsible for one's own work, support, actions, etc. **own up** to admit one's guilt, error, etc.; confess: *He owned up to his part in the scheme.*

own·er (ō′nər) *n-* person who owns something; proprietor. —*adj-* own′er·less.

Horned owl.
18-25 in long

own·er·ship (ō′nər shĭp′) *n-* condition of being an owner; right of possession: *The ownership of land carries responsibilities. A deed indicates ownership of property.*

ox (ŏks) *n-* [*pl.* ox·en (ŏk′sən)] 1 full-grown male of domestic cattle, especially one that has been castrated and trained for hauling, farm work, etc. 2 any of various animals related to domestic cattle, especially the buffaloes and bisons.

ox·al·ic acid (ŏk săl′ĭk) *n-* colorless, poisonous organic acid found in some plants and produced synthetically. It is used in dyeing and bleaching.

ox·a·lis (ŏk săl′əs) *n-* any of several plants with small white, rose-colored, or yellow flowers, and leaves divided into three parts; wood sorrel.

ox·blood (ŏks′blŭd′) *n-* a deep, brownish-red color. *adj-: an oxblood vase.*

ox·bow (ŏks′bō′) *n-* 1 U-shaped wooden collar placed under and around the neck of one of a team of oxen. Two oxbows and a crosspiece form a yoke. 2 U-shaped bend in a river.

ox·cart (ŏks′kärt′) *n-* cart drawn by oxen.

ox-eye daisy (ŏk′sī′) See *daisy.*

ox·ford (ŏks′fərd) *n-* 1 low shoe that laces over the instep. 2 (also **oxford cloth**) cotton fabric with a plain weave, used chiefly for making men's shirts. *as modifier: an oxford shirt.*

oxford gray *n-* a very dark gray.

ox·i·da·tion (ŏk′sə dā′shən) *n-* a combining with oxygen, as in all combustion.

ox·ide (ŏk′sīd′) *n-* a compound of oxygen and, usually, one other element.

ox·i·dize (ŏk′sə dīz′) *vi-* [ox·i·dized, ox·i·diz·ing] to combine with oxygen; change into oxide: *Iron oxidizes quickly in damp weather. vt-* to cause to combine with oxygen; convert into an oxide.

ox·i·diz·er (ŏk′sə dī′zər) *Space n-* a liquid or solid that chemically combines with fuel to produce the gases that propel a rocket. An oxidizer does not necessarily contain oxygen.

oxidizing agent *n-* the atom or ion that takes up electrons during a chemical reaction.

Ox·o·ni·an (ŏk sō′nē ən) *adj-* of or having to do with Oxford University or the town of Oxford, England. *n-* student or graduate of Oxford University.

oxy- *combining form* oxygen; containing or combined with oxygen: *an oxyacetylene torch; oxyhemoglobin.* [from oxygen.].

ox·y·acet·y·lene torch (ŏk′sē ə sĕt′ə lēn) *n-* blowtorch using a mixture of oxygen and acetylene to produce a very hot flame. It is used in cutting and welding metals.

ox·y·gen (ŏk′sə jən) *n-* colorless, gaseous element that makes up one-fifth of the atmosphere. Free oxygen is absorbed in respiration, and is essential to almost all living organisms. Symbol O, At. No. 8, At. Wt. 15.9994.

ox·y·gen·ate (ŏk′sə jə nāt′) *vt-* [ox·y·gen·at·ed, ox·y·gen·at·ing] to combine or treat with oxygen. —*ox′y·gen·a′tion.*

oxygen mask *n-* device that is connected to a supply of pure oxygen and fits closely over the mouth and nose.

oxygen tent *n-* tentlike or boxlike enclosure connected to a steady supply of oxygen. It is placed over the head and shoulders of patients who need help in breathing.

ox·y·hem·o·glo·bin (ŏk′sī hē′mə glō′bən, -hĕm′ə glō′bən) *n-* scarlet compound of oxygen and hemoglobin formed in the red blood cells when the blood passes through the lungs.

o·yez (ō′yā′, -yĕz′) *interj-* cry meaning "hear ye," usually called three times to demand attention in a courtroom. Also *o′yes′.*

Oyster

oys·ter (ois′tər) *n-* shellfish with a rough, hinged, double shell, found in shallow sea water and valued as food. Some kinds produce pearls. —*adj-* oy′ster·like′.

oys·ter·man (ois′tər mən) *n-* [*pl.* oy·ster·men (ois′tər men)] man who gathers, raises, or sells oysters.

oyster plant *n-* salsify.

P

P, p (pē) *n-* [*pl.* **P's, p's**] the sixteenth letter of the English alphabet.

p. 1 page. 2 participle. 3 ¹piano.

P 1 *Music* ²piano (softly). 2 (also **p.**) baseball pitcher.

P symbol for phosphorus.

pa (pä, pò) *Informal n-* father.

Pa symbol for protactinium.

PA public-address system.

Pa. Pennsylvania.

pace (pās) *n-* 1 a single step: *Walk ten paces to the north.* 2 length of a single step, especially when established as a unit of measurement. 3 speed, in walking, running, working, etc.; rate of progress: *He kept a steady pace.* 4 way of walking or running; especially, a horse's gait in which the legs on the same side are lifted and put down together. *vt-* [**paced, pac·ing**] 1 to walk back and forth over in anxiety, anger, etc.: *The expectant father paced the floor.* 2 to match (a runner) step for step, usually to train him. 3 to cause to act in a desired rhythm. *vi-* 1 to walk with long, even steps. 2 of a horse, to move at a gait called a pace.

keep pace with to run or go as fast as; keep up with: *He tried to keep pace with us.* **put (someone) through his paces** to have someone demonstrate his special skills or accomplishments: *The coach put the rookie through his paces.* **set the pace** (1) to set a speed for others to keep up with. (2) to be an example or model for others to follow: *The foreman's work set the pace for us.* **pace off** to measure by even steps: *to pace off 50 feet.*

pace·mak·er (pās' mā' kər) *n-* one who sets the pace in a race or other competition.

pac·er (pā' sər) *n-* one who paces; especially, a horse whose gait is a pace.

pach·y·derm (pắk' I dûrm') *n-* one of a group of thick-skinned animals, such as the elephant, rhinoceros, or hippopotamus.

pa·cif·ic (pə sĭf' Ik) *adj-* 1 not quarrelsome; peaceable: *the pacific words at an international conference; a pacific people who are not inclined to make war.* 2 calm; tranquil: *rowing on pacific waters.* —*adv-* **pa·cif'i·cal·ly.**

Pa·cif·ic (pə sĭf' Ik) *adj-* of or pertaining to the Pacific Ocean. *n-* the Pacific Ocean.

pac·i·fi·ca·tion (pās' I fə kā' shən) *n-* a pacifying or being pacified.

Pacific Standard Time See *standard time.*

package deal *n-* offer or arrangement to sell a number of things as a single unit or as part of a single transaction.

package store *n-* a store that sells alcoholic beverages only in bottles to be taken away from the premises.

pack·ag·ing (pắk' əj Ing) *n-* 1 process or method of putting goods in containers sold as single units. 2 art of designing and using such containers.

pack animal *n-* any animal that carries goods upon its back, such as a mule, horse, or camel.

pack·er (pắk' ər) *n-* 1 person or machine that packs articles or goods into bags or other containers: *He works as a packer at the warehouse. She is a very tidy packer.* 2 person or company whose business is preparing and packaging food: *a meat packer.*

pack·et (pắk' ət) *n-* 1 small bundle or package: *a packet of seeds; a packet of tea.* 2 a small ship that sails regularly on a fixed route, carrying passengers, mail, and merchandise.

pack·ing (pắk' Ing) *n-* 1 the work or business of preparing and packaging food for shipment to wholesalers. 2 soft material used to insulate articles from breakage in shipping containers, to fill cracks and joints in pipes, to stop bleeding in a wound, etc.

packing house or **packing plant** *n-* factory where meats, fruits, or vegetables are prepared and packed for shipment to wholesalers.

pack rat *n-* North American rat that collects small articles and packs them in its nest; wood rat.

pack·sack (pắk' săk') *n-* traveling bag of sturdy cloth or other material, usually carried strapped across the back.

pack·sad·dle (pắk' săd' əl) *n-* saddle shaped for carrying loads and worn by a pack animal.

pag·eant (pặj' ənt) *n-* colorful play, procession, or similar display to celebrate a legend or historical event.

pag·eant·ry (pặj' ən trē) *n-* [*pl.* **pag·eant·ries**] 1 brilliant show or display; pomp. 2 pageants collectively. 3 art of creating and staging pageants.

pag·i·na·tion (pặj' ə nā' shən) *n-* the numbering or arrangement of the pages in a book, manuscript, etc.

pa·go·da (pə gō' də) *n-* in some Asian countries, a temple or memorial building, often richly decorated, having several stories, each with an overhanging projection.

Pagoda

paid (pād) *p.t. & p.p.* of **pay.**

pail (pāl) *n-* 1 open container with a handle over the top, used for holding or carrying liquids; bucket. 2 pailful. *Hom-* pale.

pail·ful (pāl' fŏŏl') *n-* amount held by a pail.

pain (pān) *n-* 1 severe soreness or distress of body; ache: *a sharp pain in the knee.* 2 distress of mind; sorrow: *to suffer the pain of defeat.*

pal (pǎl) *Informal n-* close friend; chum. *vi-* [**palled, pal·ling**] to have a friendly companionship.

pal·ace (pǎl' əs) *n-* 1 official home of a ruler or, in some countries, of a bishop. 2 large, splendid house or other building. *as modifier:* *the palace wall.*

pal·a·din (pǎl' ə din) *n-* any of the knights of Charlemagne; hence, any champion of a cause.

pal·an·quin (pǎl' ən kēn') *n-* in the Orient, a covered litter for one person, carried on men's shoulders.

pal·at·a·ble (pǎl' ət ə bəl) *adj-* 1 having a pleasant taste; enjoyable to eat. 2 agreeable; pleasant to the feelings. —*n-* **pal'at·a·bil'i·ty.** *adv-* **pal'at·a·bly.**

pal·ate (pǎl' ət) *n-* 1 the roof of the mouth. The bony front part is the hard palate, and the fleshy back part is the soft palate. 2 sense of taste: *These grapes please my palate.* *Hom-* palette, pallet.

Palate

pa·la·tial (pə lā' shəl) *adj-* of, resembling, or characteristic of a palace; magnificent: *a palatial hotel.* —*adv-* **pa·la'tial·ly.**

pal·a·tine (pǎl' ə tīn') *n-* in former times, a count, earl, or other nobleman who was given royal privileges within his own domain.

pa·la·ver (pə lǎv' ər) *n-* 1 conference or parley, originally between people of primitive culture and Europeans. 2 idle talk. *vi-* to talk idly, especially at great length.

pale (pāl) *adj-* [**pal·er, pal·est**] 1 lacking normal color; wan: *Sick people often have pale faces.* 2 light in color: *a pale pink.* 3 not bright; dim; faint: *the pale light of the new moon.* *vi-* [**paled, pal·ing**] to lose normal color; turn white: *She paled when she heard the bad news.* *vt-* to cause to lose color. [from Old French, from Latin *pallidus,* and related to **pallid.**] *Hom-* pail. —*adv-* **pale'ly.** *n-* **pale'ness.**

pale (pāl) *n-* 1 pointed stake or picket in a fence. 2 fence or boundary; limits; bounds: *His acts placed him beyond the pale of decent society.* *vt-* [**paled, pal·ing**] to enclose or fence with pointed stakes or pickets. [from Old French *pal,* from Latin *palus,* "stake."] *Hom-* pail.

Pales

pale·face (pāl' fās') *n-* light-skinned person; name supposedly given to those of European ancestry by North American Indians.

Pa·le·o·cene (pā' lē ə sēn') *n-* the earliest of the five epochs of the Tertiary period of geologic time. *adj-*: *the Paleocene epoch.*

Pa·le·o·lith·ic (pā' lē ə lĭth' ik) *adj-* in anthropology, of or relating to a period of early human culture in which chipped or flaked stone tools were made.

pa·le·on·tol·o·gist (pā' lē ən tŏl' ə jĭst) *n-* person who is expert in, and usually occupied in, paleontology.

pa·le·on·tol·o·gy (pā' lē ən tŏl' ə jē) *n-* science dealing with fossils and prehistoric forms of life.

pal·met·to (păl mĕt′ō, păl-) *n-* [*pl.* **pal·met·tos** or **pal·met·toes**] any of several kinds of palm trees with fan-shaped leaves, some of which grow in southern United States and the West Indies.

palm·is·try (pä′ mĭs′ trē, päl′-) *n-* art of supposedly reading character or foretelling the future from the lines and marks of a person's hand. —*n-* **palm′ ist.**

palm oil *n-* fatty, buttery substance obtained from the fruits of certain palm trees and used in making soaps, candles, margarine, etc.

Palm Sunday *n-* the Sunday before Easter, commemorating Christ's triumphal entry into Jerusalem, when branches of palm leaves were strewn before him.

palm·y (pä′ mē, päl′-) *adj-* [**palm·i·er, palm·i·est**] 1 full of palm trees. 2 prosperous; flourishing: *the palmy days of his youth.*

pal·o·min·o (păl′ ə mē′ nō) *n-* [*pl.* **pal·o·min·os**] tan or cream-colored horse with a white mane and tail, bred chiefly in southwestern United States. [from American Spanish meaning "like a dove; dove-colored," from *paloma,* "dove."]

pal·pa·ble (păl′ pə bəl) *adj-* 1 such as can be touched or felt. 2 easily seen; plain; obvious: *a palpable error.* —*n-* **pal′ pa·bil′ i·ty.** *adv-* **pal′ pa·bly.**

pal·pate (păl′ pāt′) *vt-* [**pal·pat·ed, pal·pat·ing**] to examine by touch, especially for medical diagnosis. —*n-* **pal′ pa′ tion.**

pal·pi·tate (păl′ pə tāt′) *vt-* [**pal·pi·tat·ed, pal·pi·tat·ing**] to beat or throb rapidly; flutter; tremble: *The boy's heart palpitated with terror.* —*n-* **pal′ pi·ta′ tion.**

pal·pus (păl′ pəs) *n-* [*pl.* **pal·pi** (păl′ pī′)] one of the jointed feelers attached to the mouth parts of insects, crustaceans, etc. Also **palp.**

pal·sied (păl′ zēd′) *adj-* affected by palsy; trembling.

pal·sy (pôl′ zē) *n-* [*pl.* **pal·sies**] abnormal condition in which there is a loss of ability to control the movement of part of the body, characterized by paralysis or uncontrollable trembling.

pal·ter (pôl′ tər) *vi-* 1 to deal carelessly or slightingly; trifle: *to palter with the truth.* 2 to act deceitfully, especially in bargaining or arguing.

pal·try (pôl′ trē) *adj-* [**pal·tri·er, pal·tri·est**] almost worthless; trifling; petty: *Two dollars is a paltry donation for a millionaire to make.* —*n-* **pal′ tri·ness.**

pam·pa (păm′ pə) *n-* (often **pampas**) vast, grassy, treeless plains of South America.

pam·per (păm′ pər) *vt-* to give way to the wishes or desires of; humor; indulge: *to pamper a sick child.* —*n-* **pam′ per·er.**

pam·phlet (păm′ flət) *n-* small book with comparatively few pages and a paper cover.

pam·phlet·eer (păm′ flə tēr′) *n-* writer of pamphlets, especially on controversial subjects.

pan (păn) *n-* 1 broad, usually shallow container of metal or glass, used for cooking, baking, and other household uses. 2 any similar container, such as either of the dishes for holding things weighed on scales, or the shallow receptacle for washing out gold from dirt or gravel. *vt-* [**panned, pan·ning**] 1 to cook in a frying pan: *to pan fish.* 2 to wash (gravel or dirt) in a vessel to separate out the gold. 3 *Informal* to criticize severely: *The critics panned the new play.* [from Old English **panne,** from Medieval Latin **panna.**] **pan out** to turn out; result: *The venture panned out well.*

Pans

pan (păn) *vt-* [**panned, pan·ning**] to move (a motion picture or television camera) from one side to another.

pan·go·lin (păng gō′ lən) *n-* heavily armored ant-eating mammal of Asia, the Malay Archipelago, and Africa.

pan·han·dle (păn′ hăn′ dəl) *n-* 1 the handle of a pan. 2 piece of land shaped like this. *vi- Informal* [**pan·han·dled, pan·han·dling**] to approach a person and beg; ask for a handout of money. —*n-* **pan′ han′ dler.**

pan·ic (păn′ Ik) *n-* fear so great as to cause loss of self-control: *The sound of shooting put the crowd into a panic.* *vi-* [**pan·icked, pan·ick·ing**] to have such a fear: *The crowd panicked. vt-: The shooting panicked the crowd.*

pan·to·mime (păn′ tə mīm′) *n-* 1 actions, gestures, and facial expressions that show meaning without words: *We acted out the story in pantomime.* 2 play acted out without any talking. —*n-* **pan′ to·mim′ ist.**

pan·to·the·nic acid (păn′ tə thē′ nĭk) *n-* vitamin of the B-complex, necessary for many metabolic processes. Lack of this vitamin causes disturbances of the nervous system, fatigue, etc.

pan·try (păn′ trē) *n-* [*pl.* **pan·tries**] room or closet where food, dishes, etc., are stored.

pants (pănts) *n-* (takes plural verb) 1 trousers. 2 panties.

pap (păp) *n-* 1 soft food for infants. 2 *Slang* fees or favors from official patronage. 3 *Slang* worthless, insipid, and insubstantial matter: *comic books and other pap.*

pa·pa (pä′ pə, *also Brit.,* pə·pä′) *n-* father (used chiefly when referring to or addressing one's own father).

pa·pa·cy (pä′ pə sē) *n-* [*pl.* **pa·pa·cies**] 1 office, authority, or dignity of the Pope. 2 all the popes since Peter. 3 Roman Catholic system of church government.

pa·pal (pä′ pəl) *adj-* of or having to do with the popes or the papacy: *the papal crown.*

pa·paw (pò′ pò′, pə pò′) pawpaw.

pa·pa·ya (pə pī′ ə) *n-* 1 yellow fruit of a tropical American evergreen tree. 2 the tree itself. *as modifier: a can of papaya juice.* [American word from Spanish **papaya** meaning "fruit," from **papayo,** "tree."]

pa·per (pä′ pər) *n-* 1 material made from wood pulp, rags, straw, etc., usually in the form of a thin sheet: *wrapping paper.* 2 sheet of this material: *Write your address on this paper.* 3 newspaper. 4 written assignment; essay or report: *My history paper is due tomorrow.* 5 (usually **papers**) written matter; document: *legal papers; official papers.* 6 **papers** record that gives information about the person carrying it; identification. 7 small package made of paper: *a paper of pins. as modifier: a paper lantern. vt-* to cover with wallpaper: *He is papering the dining room.* —*adj-* **pa′ per·y:** *a papery texture.*

Papayas

on paper in writing; in a written form: *Let's have that contract on paper.*

pa·per·back (pä′ pər băk′) *n-* book having a paper binding, and usually sold more cheaply than the same book bound in leather, cardboard, etc. *as modifier: a paperback volume.*

paper boy *n-* boy who delivers or sells newspapers.

pa·per·hang·er (pä′ pər hăng′ ər) *n-* person whose job is to put up wallpaper.

paper knife *n-* knife to open envelopes or uncut pages.

paper money *n-* notes issued by a government, a bank, etc., and used as currency.

paper profits *n-* in finance, a profit that would be realized if a stock were sold.

pa·per·weight (pä′ pər wāt′) *n-* any heavy thing, often ornamental, used to hold down loose papers.

paper work *n-* work involving the handling of forms, filing, attending to correspondence, etc.

pa·pier-mâché (pä′ pər mə shā′) *n-* hard, strong material made of paper pulp mixed with glue, rosin, or other substances, and molded into various shapes. *as modifier: a papier-mâché mask.*

pa·pil·la (pə pĭl′ ə) *n-* [*pl.* **pa·pil·lae** (-ē′)] a minute projection, such as those found on the tongue. —*adj-* **pa′ pil·la′ ry** (păp′ ə lĕr′ ē).

pa·pist (pä′ pĭst) *n-* follower of the papacy; Roman Catholic (chiefly used to show disfavor). *adj-: the papist faction; having papist sympathies.*

par·a·dise (păr′ ə dīs′, pĕr′-) *n-* 1 heaven. 2 place or condition of beauty or happiness: *Hawaii has been called an island paradise.* 3 **Paradise** the Garden of Eden.

par·a·dox (păr′ ə dŏks′, pĕr′-) *n-* 1 statement that seems to contradict itself but expresses an element of truth: *"Make haste slowly" is a paradox.* 2 person or thing which seems to show contradictions: *It is a paradox that the germ which causes a disease may be used to prevent it.*

par·a·dox·i·cal (păr′ ə dŏk′ sĭ kəl) *adj-* seemingly contradictory, but possibly true. —*adv-* **par′ a·dox′ i·cal·ly.**

par·a·mount (pår′ ə mount′) *adj-* above all others; supreme: *The family was her* paramount *concern.*

par·a·mour (pår′ ə mŏŏr′) *n-* person who takes the place of husband or wife in an unlawful relationship.

par·a·noi·a (pår′ ə noi′ ə, pèr′-) *n-* 1 mental disorder in which a person has delusions of persecution or grandeur, without showing any other sign of disorder. 2 tendency for individuals, groups, or nations to distrust others without real cause.

par·a·pet (pår′ ə pət, -pèt′) *n-* 1 low wall around a roof or terrace or along a stairway or bridge to keep people from falling off. 2 protective wall on a fortification.

Parapet

par·a·pher·na·li·a (pår′ ə fə nál′ yə, pèr′-) *n-* (takes plural verb) assorted pieces of equipment.

par·a·phrase (pår′ ə fråz′, pèr′-) *vt-* [par·a·phrased, par·a·phras·ing] to express the meaning (of a writing or speech) in one's own words. *n-:* a paraphrase *of a poem.*

par·a·ple·gic (pår′ ə plē′jĭk, pèr′-) *n-* person who is paralyzed below the waist.

par·a·site (pår′ ə sīt′, pèr′-) *n-* 1 plant or animal that lives in or on another of a different species and gains nourishment from it. See also *epiphyte.* 2 person who associates with another to gain some advantage for himself.

par·a·sit·ic (pår′ ə sĭt′ĭk, pèr′-) *adj-* of or having to do with a parasite. —*adv-* **par′ a·sit′ i·cal·ly.**

par·a·sol (pår′ ə sòl′, pèr′-) *n-* small, light umbrella used by women to protect them from the sun.

par·a·thy·roid glands (pår′ ə thī′ roid′, pèr′-) *n-* either of usually two pairs of small endocrine glands located on or within the thyroid gland. They produce a hormone that regulates the level of calcium in the blood.

par·a·troop·er (på′ ə trōō′ pər, pèr′-) *n-* soldier trained to land from the air by parachute.

par·a·troops (pår′ ə trōōps′, pèr′-) *n- pl.* soldiers trained to parachute from airplanes.

par·a·ty·phoid (pår′ ə tī′foid′, pèr′-) *adj-* of or having to do with paratyphoid fever. *n-* paratyphoid fever.

paratyphoid fever *n-* an infectious disease similar to typhoid but less severe, caused by a related bacterium.

par·boil (pår′ boil′) *vt-* to cook partially by boiling.

par·cel (pår′səl) *n-* 1 package; bundle. 2 group of persons or things of one kind: *a parcel of thieves; a parcel of lies.* 3 piece or section: *a parcel of land. vt-* to divide and distribute (often followed by "out"): *The captain* parceled *out the food.*

parcel post *n-* division of the postal service that carries packages. *adv-:* We sent it parcel post. *adj-:* a parcel post *package.*

parch (pårch) *vt-* 1 to dry up: *The desert sun* parched *his throat.* 2 to roast slightly by heating: *to* parch *corn over a fire. vi-:* The land parched *under the hot sun.*

parch·ment (pårch′ mənt) *n-* 1 writing material prepared from the skin of sheep or goats. 2 manuscript written on this material. 3 heavy paper resembling this material as *modifier:* a parchment *scroll.*

par·don (pår′ dən) *vt-* 1 to release from penalty: *to* pardon *an offender.* 2 to forgive: *to* pardon *an offense.* 3 to overlook; excuse: *Please* pardon *my mistake. n-* 1 forgiveness. 2 release from punishment. 3 polite indulgence: *I beg your* pardon. —*adj-* **par′ don·a·ble:** *a* pardonable *offense. adv-* **par′ don·a·bly.** *n-* **par′ do·ner.**

par ex·cel·lence (pår′ ĕk′ sə lä⁴s′) *French* in the highest degree; preeminently: *scientist* par excellence.

par·fait (pår fā′) *n-* 1 dessert served cold and made of syrup, fruit, whipped cream, and ice cream in layers. 2 frozen custard made with whipped cream and syrup.

pa·ri·ah (pə rī′ ə) *n-* 1 member of one of the lowest castes in southern India. 2 person shunned by others; outcast.

par·ing (pår′ ĭng) *n-* something that has been pared off: *an apple* paring; *a* paring *of cheese.*

Par·is (pår′əs) *n-* in Greek mythology, the son of Priam and Hecuba. He carried Helen off to Troy, thereby causing the Trojan War.

par·ka (pår′ kə) *n-* short coat with a hood.

par·ri·cide (pår′ə sĭd′) *n-* 1 the murder of a close relative, especially a parent. 2 one who commits such a crime. —*adj-* **par′ ri·ci′ dal.**

par·rot (pår′ ət) *n-* 1 tropical bird with a hooked beak and bright feathers, often kept as a pet. It may learn to repeat words and phrases. 2 one who repeats ideas rather than originates. *vt-* to repeat from memory rather than understanding: *He* parroted *my opinions. —adj-* **par′ rot·like′.**

Green parrot, about 17 in. long

parrot fever *n-* psittacosis.

par·ry (pår′ ē) *vt-* [par·ried, par·ry·ing] to turn aside or deflect: *to* parry *a question; to* parry *a blow. n-* [*pl.* **par·ries**] 1 in fencing, a defensive move made to ward off or deflect a thrust. 2 any quick turning aside (of a blow, question, etc.).

parse (pårs) *vt-* [parsed, pars·ing] 1 in grammar, to analyze or describe (a sentence) by stating the parts of speech and their relation to each other. 2 to name the part of speech of (a word) and its position in a sentence. *vi-:* This sentence doesn't parse *easily.*

Par·see (pår′ sē′) *n-* one of a Zoroastrian sect in India, descendants of the Persians who settled there in the 8th century. Also **Par′ si.**

par·si·mo·ni·ous (pår′ sə mŏ′ nē əs) *adj-* extremely and unnecessarily careful in the handling of money; stingy: *a parsimonious old miser.* —*adv-* **par′ si·mo′ ni·ous·ly.** *n-* **par′ si·mo′ ni·ous·ness.**

par·si·mo·ny (pår′ sə mŏ′ nē) *n-* extreme and unnecessary economy; stinginess.

pars·ley (pår′ slē) *n-* plant related to the carrot. Its leaves are used as a garnish and for flavoring.

par·take (pår tāk′) *vi-* [par·took, par·tak·en, par·tak·ing] to take part; participate: *to* partake *in the activities of the school.* —*n-* **par·tak′ er.**
partake of 1 to take some of or share in: *to* partake of *a meal.* 2 to be like; resemble: *Your impatience* partakes of *rudeness.*

Par·the·non (pår′ thə nŏn′) *n-* the temple of Athena built on the Acropolis in Athens in the 5th century B.C.

Par·thi·an shot (pår′ thē ən) *n-* sharp parting remark. [from the ancient Parthian custom of discharging arrows while seemingly retreating.]

par·tial (pår′ shəl) *adj-* 1 incomplete; in part: *I made a partial payment on a new radio.* 2 biased: *I can't make a fair judgment because I'm* partial. —*adv-* **par′ tial·ly.**
partial to fond of: *She is very* partial *to apple cake.*

par·ti·al·i·ty (pår′ shē ål′ ə tē) *n-* [*pl.* **par·ti·al·i·ties**] 1 fondness or inclination for a person or thing: *John shows a strong* partiality *for mystery books.* 2 favoritism; bias.

par·tic·i·pant (pår tĭs′ ə pənt) *n-* person who takes part in some activity: *He was a* participant *in the decision.*

par·tic·i·pate (pår tĭs′ ə pāt′) *vi-* [par·tic·i·pat·ed, par·tic·i·pat·ing] to take part (in); share (in): *He is sick, or he would* participate *in the game.* —*n-* **par·tic′ i·pa′ tion.** *n-* **par·tic′ i·pa′ tor:** *a* participator *in sports.*

par·ti·cip·i·al (pår′ tə sĭp′ē əl) *Grammar adj-* of or having to do with a participle: *a* participial *phrase.* —*adv-* **par′ ti·cip′ i·al·ly.**

par·ti·ci·ple (pår′ tə sĭp′ əl) *Grammar n-* either of two verb forms that are used with the auxiliaries "be" and "have" to form tenses.

par·tic·u·lar·ly (pər tĭk′ yə lər lē) *adv-* unusually; especially: *to be* particularly *careful.*

part·ing (pår′ tĭng) *n-* a taking leave; departure; separation: *the* parting *of friends. adj-* farewell; done on leaving: *The thieves fired a* parting *shot at us.*

par·ti·san (pår′ tə zən) *n-* 1 supporter of a person or idea: *He was a partisan of the king against the parliament.* 2 (also **par′ ti·zan**) resistance fighter; guerrilla. *adj-* one-sided: *She takes a very* partisan *view of that quarrel.*

par·ti·san·ship (pår′ tə zən shĭp′) *n-* loyalty, especially unreasonable loyalty to a person or cause.

pass·a·ble (pás′ ə bəl) *adj-* 1 fair; fairly good; not open to great objection: *a book in* passable *condition.* 2 such as can be traveled: *a* passable *road.* —*adv-* **pass′ a·bly.**

pas·sage (pás′ ij) *n-* 1 a passing or moving from one place to another. 2 corridor, aisle, hallway, etc. 3 trip; journey, especially a voyage: *a calm* passage *across the Atlantic.* 4 permission or right to pass through, over, or into: *The government granted the consul* passage *across the country.* 5 verse, sentence, etc., from a writing or speech: *a* passage *from a poem.* 6 approval of a bill, law, etc.: *The* passage *of the bill was certain.* 7 course or progress: *the* passage *of time.* 8 *Archaic* conflict.

pas·sage·way (pás′ ij wā′) *n-* any way affording passage for persons or things; especially, a hall or corridor.

passbook (pás′ bŏŏk′) *n-* book issued by a bank, showing the deposits, withdrawals, and balance in a depositor's account.

pas·sé (pá sā′) *adj-* out of date; outmoded.

passed ball *n-* in baseball, an error charged against a catcher when he fails to stop a pitch that is within his reach, and thus permits a base runner to advance.

pas·sen·ger (pás′ ən jər) *n-* person, not the driver, who rides in a vehicle, ship, plane, etc.

passenger pigeon *n-* extinct North American pigeon.

pass·er·by (pás′ ər bī′) *n-* [*pl.* **pass·ers·by**] one who goes past or by, especially along a street.

pas·ser·ine (pás′ ə rīn′) *adj-* 1 of or having to do with an order of birds that includes all those that sing, as well as many others, ranging widely in size. 2 of or having to do with a sparrow. *n-: a migrating* passerine.

pas·sim (pás′ ĭm) *adv-* here and there; in different passages (used as a reference note).

pass·ing (pás′ ĭng) *adj-* 1 going by: *the* passing *years.* 2 brief; not lasting: *a* passing *glance, a* passing *fashion.* 3 equal to or better than a required standard: *a* passing *grade.* *n-* 1 a going by. 2 enactment; the making into law: *the* passing *of an amendment.* 3 death; ending.

in passing incidentally; parenthetically: *Let us say,* in passing, *that. . . .*

pas·sion (pásh′ ən) *n-* 1 any strong feeling, such as love, hate, etc. 2 enthusiasm; intense desire: *a* passion *for learning.* 3 object of intense feeling or interest: *Antiques are Mrs. Oldham's* passion. 4 outburst of violent wrath; great rage: *Philip flew into a* passion *when Bob broke his bat.* 5 **Passion** the suffering and death of Christ on the cross; also, the last part of the Gospels relating this.

pas·sion·ate (pásh′ ən ət) *adj-* 1 filled with strong feeling or eager desire. 2 hot-tempered; wrathful. 3 intense; overwhelming. —*adv-* **pas′ sion·ate·ly.** *n-* **pas′ sion·ate·ness.**

passion flower *n-* any of several tropical American shrubs or vines with berries and showy flowers.

pas·sion·less (pásh′ ən ləs) *adj-* 1 without, or apparently without, anger, intense love, ardor, etc.; tranquil; unmoved. 2 objective; detached.

Passion Play or **passion play** *n-* drama dealing with the suffering and death of Christ.

Passion flower

paste·board (pāst′ bôrd′) *n-* stiff material made of pressed pulp or of layers of paper pasted together. *as modifier: a* pasteboard *box.*

pas·tel (pás tĕl′) *n-* 1 chalklike crayon used in drawing. 2 picture made with such crayons. 3 any light, soft color. *as modifier: a* pastel *portrait;* pastel *blue.*

pas·tern (pás′ tərn) *n-* the part of the foot of a horse and related animals that is between the fetlock and hoof.

pas·teur·ize (pás′ chə rīz′) *vt-* [pas·teur·ized, pas·teur·iz·ing] to destroy certain harmful bacteria in (milk or other foods) by heating followed by rapid cooling. —*n-* **pas′ teur·i·za′ tion.**

pas·tille (pá stēl′) *n-* 1 lozenge; troche. 2 small, usually cone-shaped mass of aromatic substances, used to fumigate or scent a room.

pas·time (pás′ tīm′) *n-* any game, sport, amusement, or hobby which makes time pass happily.

patch pocket *n-* flat pocket sewn to the outside of a garment.

patch test *n-* test for allergy, in which a small pad of paper or cloth is soaked in a solution of a suspected substance and applied to the skin.

patch·work (pách′ wûrk′) *n-* 1 work consisting of a collection of odds and ends roughly put together; jumble. 2 fabric made of irregular pieces of material sewn together at the edges often used to make quilts. 3 act of making such fabric: *Mother enjoys doing* patchwork. *as modifier: The* patchwork *treaty satisfied nobody.*

patch·y (pách′ ē) *adj-* [patch·i·er, patch·i·est] like patchwork; uneven; irregular: *a picture filled with* patchy *color; a* patchy *report.* —*n-* **patch′ i·ness.**

pate (pāt) *n-* the top of the head.

pâté (pä tā′) *n-* paste made of ground meat.

pa·tel·la (pə tĕl′ ə) *n-* kneecap. —*adj-* **pa·tel′ lar:** *a patellar bruise.*

pat·en (pát′ ən) *n-* plate of precious metal for the eucharistic bread. *Hom-* patten.

pat·ent (pát′ ənt) *n-* 1 right granted by the federal government to an inventor, which gives him exclusive control of the manufacture, use, and sale of his invention for a certain length of time; also, the document granting such a right. 2 transfer to a person of title to federal land; also, the official document transferring such title, or the land itself. *as modifier: a* patent *attorney. vt-* to obtain a patent on. —*adj-* **pat′ ent·a·ble.**

pat·ent (pát′ tənt, pát′ ənt) *adj-* clear to all; obvious; evident: *That is a* patent *lie.* —*adv-* **pat′ ent·ly.**

pat·en·tee (pát′ ən tē′) *n-* person who holds a patent.

patent leather *n-* leather, usually black, with a smooth, shiny surface.

patent medicine *n-* medicine that is sold directly to the public without prescription.

Patent Office *n-* bureau of the U.S. Department of Commerce where patent claims are examined and patents granted.

pa·ter (pā′ tər, pä′-) *Brit. Informal n-* father.

pa·ter·nal (pə tûr′ nəl) *adj-* 1 of or like a father: *our* paternal *home;* paternal *advice.* 2 related through the father: *a* paternal *grandmother.* —*adv-* **pa·ter′ nal·ly.**

pa·ter·nal·ism (pə tûr′ nə lĭz′ əm) *n-* system or doctrine of government or business management that combines strong, centralized authority with concern for the welfare of the employees. —*adj-* **pa·ter′ nal·ist′ ic.**

pa·ter·ni·ty (pə tûr′ nə tē) *n-* 1 fatherhood. 2 male parentage: *to trace the* paternity *of a child.*

pa·ter·nos·ter (pát′ ər nŏs′ tər) *n-* 1 *Latin* our father. 2 the Lord's Prayer, which in Latin begins with "Pater Noster . . .". Also **Pa′ ter Nos′ ter.**

path (páth) *n-* 1 narrow track worn by human or animal footsteps: *an Indian* path *through the forest.* 2 way made for walking: *a garden* path. 3 course of travel: *the earth's* path *around the sun.* 4 way of conduct: *the* path *of goodness.* —*adj-* **path′ less.**

path- or **patho-** combining form disease: *a* patho*logy laboratory; a* patho*genic germ.* [from Greek **páthos** meaning "suffering; feeling."]

pa·thet·ic (pə thĕt′ ĭk) *adj-* arousing feelings of pity or sympathy; pitiful: *the* pathetic *cries of the wounded.* —*adv-* **pa·thet′ i·cal·ly.**

path·find·er (páth′ fīn′ dər) *n-* person who finds or leads the way through strange or unknown areas; trailblazer: *a* pathfinder *in the wilderness; a* pathfinder *in science.*

path·o·gen·ic (páth′ ə jĕn′ ĭk) *adj-* causing disease: *a* pathogenic *organism.*

path·o·log·i·cal (páth′ ə lŏj′ ĭ kəl) *adj-* 1 of or related to pathology: *a* pathological *medical report.*

pa·trol·man (pə trōl′ mən) *n-* [*pl.* **pa·trol·men**] *n-* uniformed policeman of the lowest rank, especially one assigned to patrol a certain area.

patrol wagon *n-* closed truck used by police to take prisoners to and from a jail.

pa·tron (pā′ trən) *n-* 1 person who supports or aids a special cause, person, etc.: *Most of the orchestra's expenses are paid by* patrons. 2 regular customer, especially of a restaurant. —*n- fem.* **pa′ tron·ess.**

Paul (pòl) *n-* Roman soldier, originally named Saul, who was converted to Christianity and became a missionary. He was the author of several New Testament epistles. Also **Saint Paul.** *Homs-* pall, pawl.

Paul Bun·yan (bùn′ yən) *n-* lumberjack hero of American folklore, noted for his superhuman strength.

paunch (pònch) *n-* 1 abdomen or belly, especially a large belly. 2 first stomach of a cud-chewing animal; rumen.

paunch·y (pòn′chē) *adj-* [paunch·i·er, paunch·i·est] having a large belly. *—n-* paunch′ i ·ness.

pau·per (pó′pər) *n-* very poor person, especially, one living on charity.

pau·per·ize (pó′pə rīz′) *vt-* [pau·per·ized, pau·per·iz·ing] to bring to extreme poverty; make very poor: *Bad investments* pauperized *us.* *—n-* pau′ per·i·za′ tion.

pause (pòz) *n-* 1 brief stop or rest: *Everyone welcomed the* pause *during the long test.* 2 brief stop in speaking, shown in writing by a comma, period, etc. 3 *Music* hold. *vi-* [paused, paus·ing] to stop or rest for a short time: *Dan* paused *to consult his notes.*

pa·vane (pə văn′, -vān′) *n-* slow, stately dance of the 16th and 17th centuries; also the music for this dance.

pave (pàv) *vt-* [paved, pav·ing] to cover with concrete, asphalt, etc.

pave the way to make the way easier, smoother, etc.; prepare the way.

pave·ment (pàv′ mənt) *n-* hard surface covering a road, sidewalk, or court.

pa·vil·ion (pə vĭl′yən) *n-* 1 ornamental shelter in a park, garden, etc., open at the sides and used for dancing, or entertainments. 2 large tent, often with a peaked roof. 3 any of the related buildings making up a hospital or sanitarium: *a maternity* pavilion. 4 any of the buildings that house exhibitions or entertainments at a fair or exposition.

Pavilion

pav·ing (pā′vĭng) *n-* 1 concrete, asphalt, or other material used for pavement. 2 pavement.

paw (pò) *n-* foot of a four-footed animal with claws, especially of a mammal. *vt-* 1 to scrape or beat with the front foot: *The horse* pawed *the ground.* 2 to handle or touch roughly or clumsily: *During the sale hundreds of women* pawed *the reduced coats.*

pawl (pòl) *n-* a curved, pivoted device that engages the teeth of a ratchet wheel, and either drives or prevents it from rotating in an undesired direction. For picture, see *ratchet.* *Homs-* pall, Paul.

¹pawn (pòn) *vt-* to leave (something of value) with the lender as security for a loan: *He* pawned *his watch for $20.* *n-* thing left to be security for a loan. [from Old French *pan* meaning "pledge; surety," from early Germanic pand.]

in pawn in a lender's possession as security for a loan.

²pawn (pòn) *n-* 1 the least valuable and the smallest piece in the game of chess. 2 person deliberately used by another; tool: *I was just a* pawn *for his ambitions.* [from Old French paon, peon, from Late Latin pedōn meaning "foot soldier; flatfoot," from the stem of inflected forms of Latin pes, "foot."]

pawn·bro·ker (pòn′ brō′ kər) *n-* person whose business is lending money at interest on goods left with him as security for the loan.

Paw·nee (pó′ nē′) *n-* [*pl.* Paw·nees, *also* Paw·nee] 1 a member of a tribe of American Indians who formerly lived between the Platte and Arkansas rivers, and now are in Oklahoma. 2 the language of these people. *adj-*: *the* Pawnee *scalp lock.*

peace·ful (pēs′ fəl) *adj-* 1 calm; serene; undisturbed: *a* peaceful *country snow scene.* 2 not given to quarrels or violence; liking peace: *a* peaceful *tribe of Indians.* *—adv-* peace′ful·ly. *n-* peace′ ful·ness.

peace·mak·er (pēs′ mā′ kər) *n-* one who restores, or tries to restore, peaceful relations between foes.

peace offering *n-* offering, such as a gift or promise, that is made to keep or bring about peace.

peace officer *n-* officer, such as a policeman or sheriff, whose duty is to preserve law and order.

pe·cul·iar (pə kyōōl′ yər) *adj-* 1 odd; queer; strange: *a* peculiar *idea.* 2 special; particular: *This rare orchid will be of* peculiar *interest to a botanist.* *—adv-* pe·cul′ iar·ly. **peculiar to** possessed exclusively by; characteristic of: *Each person's fingerprints are* peculiar *to himself.*

pe·cu·li·ar·i·ty (pə kyōō′ lē ăr′ ə tē) *n-* [*pl.* pe·cu·li·ar·i·ties] 1 odd or queer trait or characteristic. 2 distinctive feature or quality: *A keen sense of smell is a* peculiarity *of the bloodhound.* 3 oddness; strangeness: *In New York* peculiarity *attracts less notice than in most places.*

pe·cu·ni·ar·y (pə kyōō′ nē ēr′ ē) *adj-* of or related to money; financial.

ped·a·go·gic (pĕd′ ə gŏj′ ĭk) *or* ped·a·go·gi·cal (-ĭ kəl) *adj-* of or related to teaching: *modern* pedagogic *methods.* *—adv-* ped′ a·go′ gi·cal·ly.

ped·a·gogue (pĕd′ ə gŏg′) *n-* teacher; especially, a narrow-minded or pedantic teacher.

ped·a·go·gy (pĕd′ ə gŏj′ ē, -gŏ′ jē) *n-* art or science of teaching.

ped·al (pĕd′ əl) *n-* foot-controlled lever used to operate a mechanism: *a brake* pedal; *a bicycle* pedal; *a piano* pedal. *as modifier:* *a* pedal *rod.* *vt-* to move or operate by using pedals: *to* pedal *a bicycle.* *vi-:* *He jumped on his bicycle and* pedaled *off.* *Hom-* peddle.

Pedal

ped·ant (pĕd′ ənt) *n-* learned person, especially a teacher or scholar, who shows a lack of common sense and imagination, a concern with trivial detail, and a rigid adherence to formal rules.

pe·dan·tic (pə dăn′ tĭk) *adj-* of or like a pedant or pedantry: *a* pedantic *scholar; a* pedantic *book.* *—adv-* pe·dan′ ti·cal·ly.

ped·ant·ry (pĕd′ ən trē) *n-* the practices, attitudes, or character of a pedant; strict following of rules, concern with trivial detail, etc., in learning.

ped·dle (pĕd′ əl) *vt-* [ped·dled, ped·dling] 1 to sell (goods carried with one) on the street or from house to house: *He* peddles *fruit in our neighborhood.* 2 to distribute from place to place: *He* peddles *handbills. She loves to* peddle *gossip.* *vi-:* *He* peddles *for a living.* *Hom-* pedal.

ped·dler (pĕd′ lər) *n-* 1 (*also* ped′ lar) merchant who sells small articles which he carries from place to place. 2 someone who peddles.

ped·es·tal (pĕd′ əs təl) *n-* 1 base or shaft for holding or displaying something: *The bust stood on a* pedestal. 2 the attached base of a tall lamp or vase. 3 place of high regard or admiration: *Mary set her movie hero on a* pedestal.

Pedestal

pe·des·tri·an (pə dĕs′ trē ən) *n-* person who goes on foot, especially where vehicles are present. *adj-* 1 of or for people on foot: *crowded* pedestrian *traffic; a* pedestrian *bridge.* 2 not inspired; dull; plodding: *a* pedestrian *lecture; a* pedestrian *performance.*

ped·i·greed (pĕd′ ə grēd′) *adj-* having a known pedigree or family tree: *a* pedigreed *wolfhound.*

ped·i·ment (pĕd′ ə mənt) *n-* 1 in Greek architecture, a triangular gable over the front of some buildings. 2 any similarly shaped decorative piece over a door, fireplace, bookcase, etc.

Pediment

ped·lar (pĕd′ lər) *See* peddler.

pe·dom·e·ter (pə dŏm′ ə tər) *n-* instrument that counts the number of steps taken by the person carrying it and thus measures the distance covered in walking.

pe·dun·cle (pĭ dŭng′ kəl) *n-* the stalk of a solitary flower or flower cluster.

peek (pēk) *vi-* to look in a cautious or sly way, often through a small or hidden opening; peep: *The hunter* peeked *through the bushes and saw a deer approaching.* *n-* cautious or sly look; peep. *Homs-* peak, pique.

peel (pēl) *vt-* to remove the skin or outer covering from: *to* peel *an orange.* 2 to remove in a layer or strips: *to* peel *the bark from a twig.*

peer (pēr) *vi-* **1** to look closely, especially out of curiosity: *Please stop peering over my shoulder to see what I'm doing.* **2** to peep out; come into sight: *The sun peered from behind a cloud.* [from a Germanic language, probably from early Dutch **pieren.**]

peer·age (pēr' ĭj) *n-* **1** peers or noblemen as a group; the aristocracy. **2** the rank or dignity of a nobleman. **3** book or list containing the genealogies of peers.

peer·ess (pēr' əs) *n-* woman who is a member of the peerage or nobility, especially in Great Britain.

peer·less (pēr' ləs) *adj-* without equal; matchless: *a princess of peerless beauty.*

peeve (pēv) *Informal vt-* **[peeved, peev·ing]** to vex or irritate. *n-* gripe; grudge: *He had several peeves.*

pee·vish (pē' vĭsh) *adj-* annoyed and fretful. —*adv-* **pee'vish·ly.** *n-* **pee'vish·ness.**

pee·wee (pē' wē') *n-* **1** pewee. **2** *Informal* someone or something extremely small. *as modifier: a peewee shortstop.*

peg (pĕg) *n-* **1** short piece of wood, metal, or plastic used to fasten something or to hang something on: *a tent peg; a clothes peg.* **2** step, degree, or level, especially of a person's worth, ability, etc.: *His reputation was lowered a peg by the rumors.* **3** *Informal* a quick throw: *the shortstop's peg to the plate.* *vt-* **[pegged, peg·ging]** *Informal* to throw quickly: *The catcher pegged the ball to second.*

peg away to work steadily: *to peg away at one's work.*

peg out to mark with pegs; stake out.

take down a peg to humble.

Peg·a·sus (pĕg' ə səs) *n-* **1** in Greek mythology, a winged horse, the steed of the Muses. **2** a northern constellation.

peg leg *Informal n-* **1** artificial leg, usually attached to the knee. **2** person who wears such a leg.

P.E.I. Prince Edward Island.

Pe·king·ese (pē' kĭn ēz', pē' kĭng·) *n-* [*pl.* **Pe·king·ese**] **1** native or inhabitant of Peking. **2** the dialect spoken in Peking. **3** any breed of small, long-haired, flat-faced dogs, first raised in China. Also **Pe'kin·ese'.**

Pekingese, about 15 in long

Pe·king man (pē' kĭng') *n-* genus of apelike man, known from the fossil remains found in the Pleistocene deposits of limestone caves near Peking, China.

pe·koe (pē' kō) *n-* choice black tea of India, Ceylon, and Java, made from leaves near the tip of the stem but older than those used for orange pekoe. *Hom-* picot.

pe·lag·ic (pə lăj' ĭk) *adj-* pertaining to or living in the ocean, especially near the surface and far from land.

pelf (pĕlf) *n-* money; wealth, especially if improperly acquired.

pel·i·can (pĕl' ə kən) *n-* large water bird with a long bill, the lower part of which has a pouch for storing freshly caught fish.

Pelican, about 5 ft long

pel·lag·ra (pə lăg' rə, -lā' grə) *n-* in pathology, a skin **pen.** peninsula.

pe·nal (pē' nəl) *adj-* **1** of or pertaining to punishment or to punished persons: *our penal laws; penal labor; penal colony.* **2** warranting punishment: *a penal offense.*

pe·nal·ize (pē' nə līz', pĕn' nə·) *vt-* **[pe·nal·ized, pe·nal·iz·ing]** to impose a punishment, penalty, or disadvantage on: *The referee penalized the team for unnecessary roughness.*

pen·al·ty (pĕn' əl tē) *n-* [*pl.* **pen·al·ties**] **1** punishment for a crime or offense: *The penalty for treason is death.* **2** fine, forfeit, or handicap imposed for breaking a law or rule: *Our football team lost five yards as a penalty for being offside.*

pen·guin (pĕng' gwĭn) *n-* any of various related seabirds found near the South Pole. Penguins cannot fly but use their wings to swim.

pen·i·cil·lin (pĕn' ə sĭl' ən) *n-* any of a group of powerful germ-killing drugs, made from molds and used in treating infectious diseases.

pen·i·cil·li·um (pĕn' ə sĭl' ē əm) *n-* any of a genus of molds (**Penicillium**) that grow on fruits, cheese, etc. At least two species produce penicillins.

Emperor penguin, about 3 1/2 ft long

pen·in·su·la (pə nĭn' sə lə, -syə lə) *n-* area of land almost entirely surrounded by water: *Italy is a peninsula shaped like a boot.*

pen·in·su·lar (pə nĭn' sə lər, -syə lər) *adj-* of, like, or on a peninsula: *a peninsular war.*

pe·nis (pē' nəs) *n-* external genitourinary organ of a male animal.

pen·i·tence (pĕn' ə təns) *n-* repentance; remorse; sorrow for wrongdoing.

pen·i·tent (pĕn' ə tənt) *adj-* sorrowful over one's wrong ways and willing to correct them; repentant. *n-* person who is sorry for wrongdoing and is willing to make amends. —*adv-* **pen'i·tent·ly.**

Peninsula (Florida)

pen·i·ten·tial (pĕn' ə tĕn' shəl) *adj-* of or pertaining to penitence or to penance: *Lent is a penitential season.*

pen·i·ten·tia·ry (pĕn' ə tĕn' chə rē) *n-* [*pl.* **pen·i·ten·tia·ries**] prison, especially a state or federal prison, for persons convicted of serious crimes. *as modifier: a penitentiary offense.*

pen·knife (pĕn' nīf') *n-* [*pl.* **pen·knives**] small pocketknife.

pen·man (pĕn' mən) *n-* [*pl.* **pen·men**] **1** person skilled in handwriting. **2** writer; author.

pen·man·ship (pĕn' mən shĭp') *n-* art or style of handwriting.

pen name *n-* fictitious name used by an author; pseudonym; nom de plume.

pen·nant (pĕn' ənt) *n-* **1** long, narrow flag or streamer used on ships. **2** triangular flag used as a decoration or as a school or club flag. **3** flag awarded to a championship team; also, the championship it signifies.

Navy commission pennant

pen·ni·less (pĕn' ĭ ləs) *adj-* without any money; impoverished; very poor.

pen·non (pĕn' ən) *n-* **1** swallow-tailed or triangular flag or streamer, formerly borne on a lance. **2** any flag.

Pennsylvania Dutch *n-* **1** descendants of German and Swiss immigrants who settled in Pennsylvania during the eighteenth century. **2** the German dialect spoken by these people. Also **Pennsylvania German.**

pen·ny (pĕn' ē) *n-* [*pl.* **pen·nies**] **1** cent. **2** [*pl.* **pence**] British coin equal to one twelfth of a shilling.

a pretty penny *Informal* large sum of money. **turn an honest penny** to acquire money by proper means.

penny arcade *n-* low-cost amusement center made up largely of coin-operated devices.

pen·ny-pinch (pĕn' ē pĭnch') *vi-* to give or spend money very reluctantly. —*n-* **penny pincher.**

pen·ny·weight (pĕn' ē wāt') *n-* troy weight equal to 24 grains, or 1/20 of an ounce. *Abbr.* dwt.

pen·ny-wise (pĕn' ē wīz') *adj-* saving small sums; niggardly; also, wise about trivial matters.

penny-wise and pound-foolish thrifty with small amounts but wasteful with large ones.

pep·per-and-salt (pĕp′ər ən sôlt′) *adj-* having small flecks of black and white mixed together: *a pepper-and-salt tweed*; pepper-and-salt *hair.*

pep·per·corn (pĕp′ər kôrn′, -kôrn′) *n-* small, dried berry of the pepper plant.

pepper mill *n-* small grinder, often used at table, in which peppercorns are ground.

pep·per·mint (pĕp′ər mĭnt′) *n-* 1 strong-smelling, cool-tasting plant of the mint family. 2 oil from this plant, used in flavoring. 3 candy flavored with this oil.

pep·per·y (pĕp′ə rē) *adj-* 1 containing or suggestive of pepper: *a peppery meal.* 2 hot-tempered; spirited or fiery: *a peppery quarterback.* —*n-* pep′per·i·ness.

pep·py (pĕp′ē) *Informal adj-* [pep·pi·er, pep·pi·est] lively; energetic; full of pep. —*n-* pep′pi·ness.

pep·sin (pĕp′sən) *n-* 1 enzyme formed by the gastric glands of animals as a natural aid to digestion. 2 preparation from this substance used in medicine.

pep·tic (pĕp′tĭk) *adj-* 1 relating to, producing, or containing pepsin. 2 pertaining to digestion.

peptic ulcer *n-* an ulcer of the lower end of the esophagus, stomach, or duodenum.

pep·tone (pĕp′tōn′) *n-* any of a number of soluble substances into which proteins are changed by the gastric and pancreatic juices.

Pe·quot (pē′kwŏt′) *n-* [*pl.* Pe·quots, *also* Pe·quot] one of a tribe of American Indians who formerly lived in Connecticut and parts of Rhode Island.

per (pər) *prep-* 1 for each: *Melissa earns $10 per day.* 2 by means of; through: *You will receive a note* per *special delivery.* 3 according to: *We have 300 filters in stock per inventory.*

per·ad·ven·ture (pûr′ əd vĕn′chər) *Archaic adv-* perhaps.

per·am·bu·late (pə răm′byə lāt′) *vt-* [per·am·bu·lat·ed, per·am·bu·lat·ing] to walk through or over, especially in order to inspect or oversee. *vi-* to walk or stroll around. —*n-* per·am′bu·la′tion.

per·am·bu·la·tor (pə răm′byə lā′tər) *n-* 1 person who perambulates. 2 *chiefly Brit.* small baby carriage.

per an·num (pər ăn′əm) *Latin* each year; annually: *He gets a pension of $1,000 per annum.*

per·cale (pər kāl′) *n-* fine, closely woven cotton fabric.

per cap·i·ta (pər kăp′ə tə) *Latin* to, for, or by each person: *a per capita tax; per capita output.*

per·ceive (pər sēv′) *vt-* [per·ceived, per·ceiv·ing] 1 to become aware of through the senses: *to perceive a sound; to perceive a dim light.* 2 to understand: *I perceived that he was about to refuse.*

per·cent or **per cent** (pər sĕnt′) *n-* 1 one of a hundred parts; hundredth: *Six percent of a hundred apples is six apples.* 2 proportion of an original quantity, expressed as a specified number of hundredths: *An increase in speed of five percent.* 3 percentage. *as modifier: a six* percent *interest on a loan.* Also **per cen′tum.**

per·cent·age (pər sĕn′tĭj) *n-* 1 portion that can be stated in percent: *A certain percentage of his wages is taken in taxes.* 2 *Informal* favorable odds; advantage: *He was a gambler who looked for the percentage.*

►In sense 1, PERCENT is now more common than PERCENTAGE: *Taxes take a large percent (percentage) of the profit.*

per·cen·tile (pər sĕn′tīl′) *n-* number that indicates a person's relative performance on a test as compared with others. Someone with a percentile of 89 has equaled or exceeded the performance of 89% of the others taking the same test.

per·func·to·ry (pər fŭngk′tə rē) *adj-* half-hearted or careless; with the minimum necessary attention: *a perfunctory thanks; perfunctory work.* —*adv-* per·func′to·ri·ly. *n-* per·func′to·ri·ness.

per·go·la (pûr′gə lə, pər gō′-) *n-* latticework over a walk or veranda, used as a trellis for climbing plants; arbor.

per·haps (pər hăps′) *adv-* maybe; possibly: *If you go,* perhaps *I'll join you.*

pe·ri (pĕr′ē) *n-* in Persian mythology, a fairy or elf descended from disobedient angels and barred from paradise until the completion of their penance.

peri- *prefix* 1 around; about; surrounding: *a perimeter.* 2 near: *the perigee (near the earth).* [from Greek **peri-,** from **perí** meaning "around."]

per·i·anth (pĕr′ē ănth′) *n-* the sepals and petals considered together, especially when indistinguishable or nearly so, as in lilies and tulips.

per·i·car·di·um (pĕr′ə kär′dē əm) *n-* [*pl.* per·i·car·di·a (-də ə)] membrane that encloses and protects the heart.

per·i·carp (pĕr′ə kärp′) *n-* ripened layers that form the wall of a plant ovary and enclose the seeds; seed vessel.

per·i·gee (pĕr′ə jē′) *n-* closest point to the earth in the orbit of the moon or another satellite. See also *apogee.*

per·i·he·lion (pĕr′ə hēl′yən) *n-* [*pl.* per·i·he·lia (-yə)] closest point to the sun in the orbit of a planet or comet.

per·il (pĕr′əl) *n-* 1 very great danger; exposure to loss of life or to great injury; risk: *The sailor adrift at sea was in great peril.* 2 something dangerous; hazard: *Icebergs are a peril to ships. vt-* to expose to danger or risk: *He* periled *his job by lack of attention.*

periodic table *Chemistry n-* table in which the elements are arranged according to the periodic law.

per·i·os·te·um (pĕr′ē ŏs′tē əm) *n-* [*pl.* per·i·os·te·a (tē ə)] tough, fibrous membrane that covers the bones except at the joints. It contains blood vessels that nourish the bone.

per·i·pa·tet·ic (pĕr′ə pə tĕt′ĭk) *adj-* walking around; also, done or performed while walking around: *a peripatetic discussion.*

pe·riph·e·ral (pə rĭf′ər əl) *adj-* of or pertaining to the periphery or outer bounds of anything: *the peripheral parts of a city.* —*adv-* pe·riph′e·ral·ly.

pe·riph·e·ry (pə rĭf′ə rē) *n-* [*pl.* pe·riph·er·ies] outer bounds or limits of anything: *an airport located outside the periphery of a city.*

per·i·scope (pĕr′ə skōp′) *n-* tube fitted with mirrors and lenses by which a person in a submarine or trench can see what is going on above the surface without exposing himself.

per·ish (pĕr′ĭsh) *vi-* 1 to die. 2 to spoil; decay: *Some fruits* perish *quickly if not properly packed.* 3 to disappear; vanish; become extinct: *Dinosaurs perished long ago.*

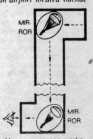

How a periscope works

per·ish·a·ble (pĕr′ish ə bəl) *adj-* likely to spoil quickly: *Fresh fruits and vegetables are* perishable *foods. n-* (usually **perishables**) things that are likely to spoil quickly. —*n-* per′ish·a·bil′i·ty.

per·lite (pûr′līt′) *n-* glassy rock with a concentric, shell-like structure, occurring as small globules and used as an insulating material.

per·ma·nence (pûr′mə nəns) *n-* quality or state of being permanent; continued existence: *the permanence of the universe.* Also **per′ma·nen·cy.**

per·ma·nent (pûr′mə nənt) *adj-* lasting forever or for a long time: *the permanent ice at the poles; a permanent job. n-* permanent wave. —*adv-* per′ma·nent·ly.

permanent wave *n-* artificially induced wave in the hair that lasts for several months.

per·man·ga·nate (pər măng′gə nāt′) *n-* 1 potassium permanganate. 2 the negative radical (MnO_4^-).

per·me·a·ble (pûr′mē ə bəl) *adj-* having tiny pores that allow the passage of fluids or gases; porous: *a permeable membrane.* —*n-* per′me·a·bil′i·ty.

per·me·ate (pûr′mē āt′) *vt-* [per·me·at·ed, per·me·at·ing] 1 to pass through the pores or crevices of: *Water* permeates *sand.* 2 to spread itself through; pervade: *The scent permeated the house.* —*n-* per′me·a′tion.

Per·mi·an (pûr′mē ən) *n-* the last of the six periods of the Paleozoic era. In the Permian, reptiles became the dominant animal life. *adj-* a Permian *fossil.*

per·mis·si·ble (pər mĭs′ə bəl) *adj-* such as can be permitted; allowable: *Stealing bases is permissible in a baseball game.* —*adv-* per·mis′si·bly.

per·pen·dic·u·lar (pûr′ pən dĭk′ yə lər) *adj-* 1 straight up and down; vertical: *Two* perpendicular *posts supported the roof.* 2 at a right angle to a line or plane: *The flagpole is perpendicular to the ground.* *n- Mathematics* line or plane at right angles to another line or plane. —*adv-* per′ pen·dic′ u·lar·ly.

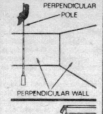

PERPENDICULAR POLE

PERPENDICULAR WALL

per·pe·trate (pûr′ pə trāt′) *vt-* [per·pe·trat·ed, per·pe·trat·ing] to perform (a wrongful act); commit (a crime, error, etc.); be guilty of: *Clive* perpetrated *a cruel joke on his little brother.* —*n-* per′ pe·tra′ tion. *n-* per′ pe·tra′ tor.

per·pet·u·al (pər pěch′ ᴏᴏ əl) *adj-* 1 lasting forever; unfailing; constant: *A* perpetual *fire burns at the Tomb of the Unknown Soldier.* 2 continuous; unceasing: *to indulge in* perpetual *chatter.* —*adv-* per·pet′ u·al·ly.

The flagpole is perpendicular to the wall of the building

per·pet·u·ate (pər pěch′ ᴏᴏ āt′) *vt-* [per·pet·u·at·ed, per·pet·u·at·ing] to cause to continue forever or for an indefinitely long time, especially in people's memories: *to* perpetuate *a myth; to* perpetuate *the memory of a great man.* —*n-* per′ pet′ u·a′ tion.

per·pe·tu·i·ty (pûr pə tōō′ ə tē) *n-* indefinitely long period of time; eternity.

in perpetuity for a limitless period of time: *He willed his paintings to the museum* in perpetuity.

per·plex (pər plěks′) *vt-* to fill with confusion or uncertainty; puzzle: *His strange silence* perplexes *me.* —*adv-* per·plex′ ing·ly: *a* perplexingly *difficult problem.*

per·plex·i·ty (pər plěk′ sə tē) *n-* [*pl.* per·plex·i·ties] 1 condition of being perplexed; confusion; bewilderment: *I'm in* perplexity *over the meaning of the question.* 2 something that puzzles or confuses.

per·qui·site (pûr′ kwə zət) *n-* gain or profit made from one's employment in addition to regular wages or salary. ►Should not be confused with PREREQUISITE.

per se (pər sā′) *Latin* of itself; as such; intrinsically: *Diamonds* per se *are valuable.*

per·se·cute (pûr′ sə kyōōt′) *vt-* [per·se·cut·ed, per·se·cut·ing] 1 to harass or abuse repeatedly or continuously: *He* persecutes *people with continuous faultfinding.* 2 to oppress or put to death on account of religion, politics, or race: *The Roman emperors* persecuted *the early Christians.* —*n-* per′ se·cu′ tor. ►Should not be confused with PROSECUTE.

per·se·cu·tion (pûr′ sə kyōō′ shən) *n-* 1 a persecuting or a being persecuted; especially, treatment with injustice or abuse: *He suffered* persecution *for his religion.*

Per·seph·o·ne (pər sěf′ ə nē) *n-* in Greek mythology, a daughter of Zeus and Demeter, who was abducted by Pluto and became queen of the Underworld. She is identified with the Roman Proserpina.

Per·se·us (pûr′ sē əs, pûr′ sōōs′) *n-* 1 in Greek mythology, a son of Zeus and a mortal, who slew Medusa and saved Andromeda from a sea monster. 2 a northern constellation.

per·se·ver·ance (pûr′ sə vēr′ əns) *n-* continued effort in spite of difficulties; steadfastness: *He made his discoveries after years of study and* perseverance.

per·spi·ca·cious (pûr′ spə kā′ shəs) *adj-* having or showing the ability to perceive, understand, or judge clearly; discerning; perceptive: *a* perspicacious *mind.* —*adv-* per′ spi·ca′ cious·ly. *n-* per′ spi·ca′ cious·ness. ►Should not be confused with PERSPICUOUS.

per·spi·cac·i·ty (pûr′ spə kǎs′ ə tē) *n-* clearness and accuracy of understanding; discernment; perspicaciousness.

per·spi·cu·i·ty (pûr′ spə kyōō′ ə tē) *n-* clearness of thought, expression, or style; lucidity; perspicuousness.

Pe·sach (pä′ säкн′) *n-* Passover.

pes·ky (pěs′ kē) *Informal adj-* [pes·ki·er, pes·ki·est] annoying; bothersome.

pe·so (pā′ sō) *n-* [*pl.* pe·sos] 1 the basic unit of money in certain Spanish-American countries and the Philippines. Its value varies in different countries. 2 formerly, a silver coin of Spain; piece of eight.

pes·si·mism (pěs′ ə mǐz′ əm) *n-* 1 tendency to emphasize the dark and gloomy aspects of a situation, especially in a cynical way, or to predict the worst possible outcome for something. 2 belief that the world is essentially evil or that evil is more powerful than good. —*n-* pes′ si·mist. *adj-* pes′ si·mis′ tic. *adv-* pes′ si·mis′ ti·cal·ly.

pest (pěst) *n-* 1 someone or something that annoys or causes trouble; nuisance. 2 something, such as a weed or insect, that causes serious damage. 3 widespread, deadly, contagious disease; plague; pestilence.

pes·ter (pěs′ tər) *vt-* to be a nuisance to; annoy; bother.

pest·hole (pěst′ hōl′) *n-* place in which dangerous contagious diseases are likely to occur and to spread.

pest·house (pěst′ hous′) *n-* a hospital or wing of a hospital for people having contagious diseases.

pes·ti·cide (pěs′ tə sīd′) *n-* substance used to destroy harmful or destructive insects, plants, etc.

pes·tif·er·ous (pěs tǐf′ ər əs) *adj-* 1 *Informal* annoying; bothersome. 2 having a harmful effect; especially, carrying an infectious disease. —*adv-* pes·tif′ er·ous·ly.

pes·ti·lence (pěs′ tə ləns) *n-* deadly, widespread, contagious disease; plague, especially bubonic plague.

pes·ti·lent (pěs′ tə lənt) *adj-* 1 deadly: *a* pestilent *disease; a* pestilent *drug.* 2 very bad for health, morals, or society: *the* pestilent *traffic in narcotics.* 3 making mischief; irritable; vexatious: *the* pestilent *barking of a dog.* —*adv-* pes′ ti·lent·ly.

pes·ti·len·tial (pěs′ tə lěn′shəl) *adj-* 1 resembling, caused by, or resulting in pestilence. 2 very harmful.

pes·tle (pěs′ əl, pěs′ təl) *n-* implement with a blunt, often rounded end, used for pounding and crushing substances, especially in a mortar. For picture, see ²*mortar.*

pet (pět) *n-* 1 animal of any kind kept for companionship, amusement, etc., rather than for a practical purpose. 2 favorite or especially beloved person or thing. *as modifier: a* pet *turtle; a* pet *idea.* *vt-* [pet·ted, pet·ting] 1 to stroke or smooth as one would a favorite animal; caress. 2 to treat with special kindness and consideration; pamper: *to* pet *a sick child.* *vi-* to kiss, embrace, etc., as lovers do. [of uncertain origin, perhaps related to French petit meaning "little."]

pet (pět) *n-* peevish state of mind; fit of ill-humor. [of unknown origin.]

pet·al (pět′ əl) *n-* one of the divisions, often brightly colored, forming the corolla of a flower. —*adv-* pet′ aled: *a many-petaled flower.* *adj-* pet′ al·like′.

Petals

pe·tard (pə tärd′) *n-* case filled with explosives, used in former times to knock down a wall or gate.

hoist with (or by) one's own petard harmed or defeated as a result of one's own actions, scheming, etc.

pet·cock (pět′ kŏk′) *n-* small faucet or valve, used for releasing steam, air, liquid, etc., from a pipe.

Pe·ter (pē′ tər) *n-* 1 one of the twelve apostles; also St. Peter or Simon Peter. 2 either one of two epistles of the New Testament attributed to him.

pe·ter out (pē′ tər) *Informal vi-* to grow gradually less and then disappear: *My energy* petered out.

Peter Pan *n-* boy who remained a child forever, the hero of a play of the same name by James M. Barrie.

Peter Pan collar *n-* turned-down, rounded collar.

pet·rol (pě′ trəl) *Brit. n-* gasoline. *Hom-* petrel.

pet·ro·la·tum (pě′ trə lā′ təm) *n-* greasy, jellylike substance obtained from petroleum. Also **petroleum jelly.**

pe·tro·le·um (pə trō′ lē əm) *n-* an oily mixture of numerous hydrocarbons found in the earth's crust. Gasoline and motor oils are made from petroleum.

pe·trol·o·gist (pə trŏl′ ə jĭst) *n-* person who is expert in, and usually occupied in, petrology.

pe·trol·o·gy (pə trŏl′ ə jē) *n-* science that deals with the origin, formation, composition, and structure of rocks.

pe·wee (pē′ wē′) *n-* any of several small, insect-eating birds that look somewhat like the phoebe. The bird's call suggests its name. Also **peewee**.

pe·wit (pē′ wĭt′) *n-* any of several birds having a high, shrill cry, especially the lapwing.

pew·ter (pyōō′ tər) *n-* **1** alloy of tin and other metals, used for dishes, candlesticks, and other utensils. **2** articles made of this alloy. *as modifier: a pewter mug.*

Pfc. private first class.

pfd. preferred.

pH (pē′ āch′) *Chemistry n-* a number assigned to a solution that indicates its relative acidity. Pure water has a pH of 7.0, which is regarded as neutral.

Pha·ë·thon (fā′ ə thŏn′) *n-* in Greek mythology, a son of Helios, the sun god. He endangered the safety of the world by trying to drive his father's chariot across the sky, and was slain by a thunderbolt thrown by Zeus.

pha·e·ton (fā′ ə tən) *n-* **1** light, four-wheeled, horse-drawn carriage, completely open or open at the sides. **2** automobile having a similar construction.

phag·o·cyte (făg′ ə sīt′) *n-* any of the white blood cells that engulf and destroy bacteria and damaged red blood cells.

pha·lanx (fā′ lăngks′) *n-* **1** [*pl.* **pha·lanx·es**] in ancient Greece, a company of heavily armed soldiers drawn in close ranks; hence, any similarly massed group of people or things. **2** [*pl.* **pha·lan·ges** (fə lăn′ jēz′,)] one of the bones of the fingers or toes.

phan·tasm (făn′ tăz′ əm) *n-* **1** imaginary being, such as a ghost or specter; phantom. **2** any deceptive or ghostly image, illusion, etc. —*adj-* **phan·tas′ mal:** *a phantasmal hallucination.*

phan·ta·sy (făn′ tə zē) fantasy.

phan·tom (făn′ təm) *n-* **1** ghost; specter; apparition. **2** anything ghostly or unreal in appearance or effect. *as modifier: We saw phantom horses in the night.*

Phar·aoh (fâr′ ō) *n-* any of the rulers of ancient Egypt.

Phar·i·see (făr′ ə sē, fâr′-) *n-* **1** one of a former religious sect of Jews who laid strict emphasis on the literal observance of the Law. **2** **pharisee** anyone who observes the form rather than the spirit in religion.

phar·ma·ceu·ti·cal (fär′ mə sōō′ tĭ kəl) *adj-* of or having to do with pharmacy or prescription drugs. *n-* a medicinal product.

phar·ma·cist (fär′ mə sĭst′) *n-* person trained in the preparation of medicines; druggist.

phar·ma·col·o·gy (fär′ mə kŏl′ ə jē) *n-* the science of the preparation, use, and effects of drugs.

phar·ma·co·poe·ia (fär′ mə kə pē′ ə) *n-* **1** book, especially one serving as an official authority, that gives ingredients and formulas for the preparation of drugs and other medicines. **2** collection of drugs.

phar·ma·cy (fär′ mə sē) *n-* [*pl.* **phar·ma·cies**] **1** art or profession of preparing medicines. **2** drugstore.

pha·ryn·ge·al (fə rĭn′ jē əl, făr′ ən jē′ əl) *adj-* of, having to do with, or produced in the pharynx.

phar·ynx (fâr′ ĭngks) *n-* [*pl.* **pha·ryn·ges** (fə rĭn′ jēz′) or **phar·ynx·es**] expanded, upper part of the digestive tube, situated between the mouth and nasal cavities and the esophagus.

phase (fāz) *n-* **1** stage in the progress or development of a thing: *an early phase of airplane flight; a phase of mitosis.* **2** one side or view of a subject: *The admiral wrote about the naval phase of the invasion.*

phon·ics (fŏn′ ĭks) *n-* (takes singular verb) method of teaching reading that uses as a base the pronunciation of groups of letters.

phono- *combining form* sound: *a phonograph* (instrument for reproducing sound). Also **phon-:** *phonic.*

pho·no·graph (fō′ nə grăf′) *n-* machine for reproducing sound from a disk with grooves in it; record player. *as modifier: a phonograph needle.*

pho·no·graph·ic (fō′ nə grăf′ ĭk) *adj-* of or having to do with a phonograph or the reproduction of sounds by means of a phonograph. —*adv-* **pho′ no·graph′ i·cal·ly.**

pho·nol·o·gy (fə nŏl′ ə jē) *n-* the analysis of the sound patterns used in particular languages, and in languages in general, focusing on the smallest units which distinguish one word from another.

physical science *n-* any science that deals with the properties, structure, etc., of matter that is not living.

physical therapy *n-* treatment of diseases and injuries by physical or external means, rather than by drugs.

phy·si·cian (fə zĭsh′ ən) *n-* person licensed to practice medicine; doctor.

phys·i·cist (fĭz′ ə sĭst) *n-* person who is a specialist in the science of physics and engaged in it as a profession.

phys·ics (fĭz′ ĭks) *n-* (takes singular verb) the science that deals with motion, matter, and energy, and their precise relationships. *as modifier: a physics course.*

phys·i·og·no·my (fĭz′ ē ŏg′ nə mē) *n-* [*pl.* **phys·i·og·no·mies**] **1** the special features or expression of one's face; facial appearance: *a stern physiognomy.* **2** outward appearance or form of anything; contour.

phys·i·og·ra·phy (fĭz′ ē ŏg′ rə fē) *n-* physical geography. —*n-* **phys′ i·og′ ra·pher.** *adj-* **phys′ i·o·graph′ ic** (-ē ə-grăf′ ĭk).

phys·i·o·log·i·cal (fĭz′ ē ə lŏg′ ĭ kəl) *adj-* of, or having to do with physiology. —*adv-* **phys′ i·o·log′ i·cal·ly.**

phys·i·ol·o·gist (fĭz′ ē ŏl′ ə jĭst′) *n-* person trained in the science of physiology and engaged in it as a profession.

phys·i·ol·o·gy (fĭz′ ē ŏl′ ə jē) *n-* branch of biology that deals with the processes and functions in living things.

phys·i·o·ther·a·py (fĭz′ ē ō thĕr′ ə pē) *n-* physical therapy.

phy·sique (fĭ zēk′) *n-* structure or appearance of the body: *That football player has a powerful physique.*

pi (pī) *n-* **1** the sixteenth letter of the Greek alphabet. **2** *Mathematics* Greek letter π used to symbolize the ratio of the circumference of a circle to its diameter. Pi is approximately 3.1416 or 3 1/7. *Hom-* **pie.**

P.I. Philippine Islands.

pi·a ma·ter (pī′ ə mă′ tər) *n-* a delicate membrane resembling a cobweb, which is the innermost of three membranes covering the brain and spinal cord.

pi·a·nis·si·mo (pē′ ə nĭs′ ə mō) *Music adj- & adv-* very soft: *Listen to the pianissimo passage. Play the passage pianissimo. Abbr.* pp

GRAND

UPRIGHT

Pianos

pi·an·ist (pē ăn′ ĭst, pē′ ə nĭst) *n-* person who plays the piano, especially as a professional musician.

pi·an·o (pē ăn′ ō) *n-* [*pl.* **pi·an·os**] large musical instrument with tuned steel strings that are struck by felt-covered hammers operated by a keyboard. Also **pi·an′ o·for′ te** (-fôr′ tā, -fôr′ tē, -fôrt′). [shortened from Italian **pianoforte**, from [2]**piano** plus **forte**, meaning "strong."]

pi·an·o (pē ăn′ ō) *Music adj- & adv-* soft; softly: *to play a piano passage; to play a passage piano. Abbr.* p [from Italian **piano**, from Latin **plānus** meaning "smooth."]

pi·az·za (pē ăz′ ə) *n-* **1** in Italy, a public square. **2** large porch; veranda.

pi·ca (pī′ kə) *n-* **1** in printing, a unit of measure equal to about 1/6 inch; also, a size of type (12-point) equal to this. **2** similar type size for typewriters. *as modifier: a pica typewriter.*

Piazzas

pi·ca·dor (pĭk′ ə dôr′) *n-* in a bullfight, a horseman who tires and weakens the bull by pricking it with a lance.

phos·phor·ic acid (fŏs fôr′ ĭk, -fŏr′ ĭk) *n-* colorless acid or crystalline solid (H_3PO_4), used in fertilizers.

phos·pho·rus (fŏs′ fə rəs) *n-* a nonmetallic solid element found in nature only in the combined state. Three forms of phosphorus exist, but under ordinary conditions it is a white or yellow waxy solid that is poisonous and phosphorescent. Symbol P, At. No 15, At. Wt. 30.9738.

pho·to (fō′ tō) *n-* [*pl.* **pho·tos**] *Informal* photograph.

photo- *combining form* **1** light: *a photosensitive film; photosynthesis.*

pho·to·gen·ic (fō′ tə jĕn′ Ik) *adj-* 1 having such good form or color as to make an effective subject for a photograph: *a photogenic face.* 2 *Biology* producing or giving off light, as a firefly does; phosphorescent.

pho·to·graph (fō′ tə grăf′) *n-* picture made with a camera containing a film or glass plate which is sensitive to light. *vt-* to take a picture of with a camera. *vi-* to look or appear a certain way as the subject of such pictures: *Her baby photographs well.*

pho·tog·ra·pher (fə tŏg′ rə fər) *n-* person who takes photographs, especially as an occupation.

pho·to·graph·ic (fō′ tə grăf′ Ik) *adj-* 1 having to do with photography: *a photographic lens.* 2 able to remember accurately: *a photographic mind.* 3 sharp; clear; distinct: *in photographic detail.* —*adv-* pho′to·graph′i·cal·ly.

pho·tog·ra·phy (fə tŏg′ rə fē) *n-* the art or process of taking pictures with a camera.

pho·tom·e·ter (fō tŏm′ ə tər) *n-* any instrument that measures the intensity of light.

pho·to·mi·cro·graph (fō′ tō mī′ krə grăf′) *n-* photograph of what is seen through a microscope.

pho·ton (fō′ tŏn′) *n-* a quantum of radiant energy, especially of light.

pho·to·sen·si·tive (fō′ tō sĕn′ sə tĭv′) *adj-* sensitive or receptive to light or other radiant energy.

pho·to·sphere (fō′ tō sfēr′) *n-* the shining surface of the sun, as ordinarily seen from the earth.

pho·to·stat (fō′ tə stăt′) *n-* 1 Photostat *Trademark* type of camera used for photographing documents, maps, etc., directly on the surface of prepared paper. 2 photograph made with such a camera. *vt-* [pho·to·stat·ed, pho·to·stat·ing] to photograph with such a camera.

pi·èce de ré·sis·tance (pyès′ də rā′ zǐs täns′) *French* 1 most important item in a group. 2 main dish.

piece·meal (pēs′ mēl′) *adv-* in portions or parts; by degrees; bit by bit: *to do a job piecemeal.* *adj-: a piecemeal task.*

piece of eight *n-* old Spanish and Spanish-American silver coin, worth eight reals, or one peso.

piece·work (pēs′ wûrk′) *n-* work paid for by the piece or job, not by the hour. —*n-* piece′work′er.

pied (pīd) *adj-* 1 having two or more colors in patches; piebald: *Our black and white cat has a pied coat.* 2 wearing many-colored clothing: *the Pied Piper of Hamelin.*

pied·mont (pēd′ mŏnt′) *n-* area at the base of a mountain. *as modifier: a piedmont valley.*

pie graph *n-* a circular graph divided into wedges, each of which is proportional in size to the fraction it represents. Also **pie chart.** For picture, see *graph.*

pie·plant (pī′ plănt′) *n-* rhubarb.

pier (pēr) *n-* 1 landing place for ships that extends over the water; wharf. See also ¹dock. 2 supporting pillar, such as one at an end of an arch. 3 the part of a wall between openings. 4 buttress. *Hom-* peer.

Piers of arch

piggy bank *n-* child's bank for saving coins, made in the shape of a pig.

pig·head·ed (pǐg′ hĕd′ əd) *adj-* stubborn; obstinate.

pig iron *n-* crude iron as it comes from the blast furnace. It is usually cast into pigs for later refining.

pig·ment (pǐg′ mənt) *n-* 1 any substance used to give color to something, especially paints. 2 material that gives color to living things: *the pigment in the skin; the pigment in plants.* —*adj-* pig′men·tar′y (-mən tĕr′ ē): *a pigmentary layer of cells.*

pig·men·ta·tion (pǐg′ mən tā′ shən) *n-* the coloring in a plant, animal, or person due to the presence of a pigment in the tissues.

pig·ment·ed (pǐg mĕn′ təd) *adj-* colored by a pigment.

pig·my (pǐg′ mē) pygmy.

pig·nut (pǐg′ nŭt′) *n-* 1 thin-shelled nut of a certain kind of hickory tree. 2 the tree itself.

pig·pen (pǐg′ pĕn′) *n-* 1 place for keeping pigs. 2 very dirty and sloppy place.

pig·skin (pǐg′ skǐn′) *n-* 1 the hide of a pig, or the leather made from it.

pile·driv·er (pīl′ drī′ vər) *n-* machine for hammering piles into the ground.

piles (pīlz) *n- pl.* hemorrhoids.

pil·fer (pǐl′ fər) *vi-* to steal in small amounts: *A rat had pilfered from the pantry.* *vt-: The thief pilfered coins.*

pil·grim (pǐl′ grǐm) *n-* 1 traveler to a holy place: *Many pilgrims still journey to the Holy Land every year.* 2 traveler; wanderer. 3 Pilgrim or Pilgrim Father one of the Englishmen who landed from the ship "Mayflower" and founded the colony of Plymouth, Massachusetts, in 1620.

pil·grim·age (pǐl′ grə mǐj) *n-* journey made because of reverence or affection, especially to a sacred place.

pil·ing (pī′ lǐng) *n-* a number of piles driven into position as part of a structure.

pill (pǐl) *n-* 1 medicine in the form of a small disk or ball. 2 *Informal* unpleasant or disagreeable person.

a bitter pill to swallow anything hard or unpleasant to bear: *The loss was a bitter pill to swallow.*

pil·lage (pǐl′ ĭj) *vt-* [pil·laged, pil·lag·ing] to rob or plunder: *The bandits pillaged two villages in the west.* *vi-: They pillaged through the countryside.* *n-* 1 a robbing or plundering. 2 whatever is taken as plunder: *A lot of pillage was recovered from the outlaws.* —*n-* pil′lag·er.

pil·lar (pǐl′ ər) *n-* 1 column used to hold up a floor, or the like, or as a monument or high pedestal. 2 a firm supporter; mainstay: *a pillar of society; a pillar of the church.* *vt-* to brace or support with columns (often followed by "up"): *to pillar up a floor or roof.* —*adj-* pil′lared.

from pillar to post from one place or situation to another, as if driven by circumstances.

Pillar

pill·box (pǐl′ bŏks′) *n-* 1 small box for holding or carrying pills. 2 small concrete fort protecting a border, beach, etc. 3 a woman's small round hat.

pil·lion (pǐl′ yən) *n-* pad put behind the saddle of a horse, motorcycle, or motor scooter as a second seat.

ride pillion to ride as the second and rear person on a horse, motorcycle, or motor scooter.

pil·lo·ry (pǐl′ ə rē) *n-* [*pl.* pil·lo·ries] framework with openings for the neck and wrists of a person held up to public shame, used in olden times to punish minor lawbreakers. *vt-* [pil·lo·ried, pil·lo·ry·ing] 1 to punish by this instrument. 2 to expose to public shame: *The newspapers pillory dishonest politicians.*

Pillory

pil·low (pǐl′ ō) *n-* support for the head in resting or sleeping; cushion. *vt-* to rest on or as if on such a support; cushion: *He pillowed his head on the sofa.*

pil·low·case (pǐl′ ō kās′) *n-* removable cloth cover, open at one end, to hold a pillow. Also **pil′low·slip**′.

pi·lot (pī′ lət) *n-* 1 person who flies a plane or other aircraft: *a bomber pilot.* 2 man who guides a large ship, usually into or out of a harbor. 3 any leader or guide. *vt-* 1 to fly (a plane) or guide (a ship). 2 to lead or guide. —*adj-* pi′lot·less.

pi·lot·age (pī′ lə tǐj) *n-* 1 the guiding of ships in or out of a port, channel, etc. 2 fee paid for such service.

pilot balloon *n-* small balloon launched to show the direction and force of the wind.

pi·lot·house (pī′ lət hous′) *n-* enclosed space on the bridge of a ship that contains the steering wheel, compass, and other navigational equipment; wheelhouse.

pilot light *n-* 1 small flame in a gas stove or hot-water heater that burns continuously and is used to light the main burners. 2 light, usually red, that shows when a machine or appliance is turned on.

pilot project *n-* limited organization set up to find the best methods and practices for some full-scale effort. When the project is a factory, it is called a **pilot plant.**

Pilt·down man (pǐlt′ doun′) *n-* a type of primitive man supposed to have lived in Europe during the ice age. It was proved to be a hoax.

pin·hole (pĭn′hōl′) *n-* 1 small hole made by a pin or as if by a pin. 2 hole into which a pin or peg fits.

¹pin·ion (pĭn′yən) *n-* the wing, or any of the stiff flying feathers, of a bird. *vt-* 1 to bind the wings or clip the wing tips of (a bird). 2 to tie or fasten firmly: *to pinion a person's arms to his sides.* [from Old French *pignon*, from Latin **penna** meaning "feather."] *Hom-* piñon.

²pin·ion (pĭn′yən) *n-* 1 a wheel with cogs that engage those of a larger toothed wheel or rack, so that motion is imparted from one to the other. 2 small gear wheel in a set of gears. For picture, see *gear.* [from French **pignon**, which in Old French meant "battlement" as well as "feather," and related to ¹**pinion.**] *Hom-* piñon.

¹pink (pĭngk) *n-* 1 very pale red color: *the pink and gold of the morning sky.* 2 highest degree; peak: *the pink of health; the pink of perfection.* 3 any of various plants with narrow, pointed leaves and pink, red, or white flowers; especially, a garden plant related to the carnation, with fringed petals and a spicy fragrance; also, the flower of any of these plants. 4 *Informal* person with moderate leftist views in politics. *adj-* 1 very pale red in color: *Sunrise turned the sky pink in the east.* 2 *Informal* moderately leftist in politics. [from **pink** meaning originally "a flower with pinked (fringed) edges," from ²**pink.**] *—adj-* pink′ish.
in the pink in the best of health.

²pink (pĭngk) *vt-* 1 to cut or scallop the edge of (cloth, leather, paper, etc.) in a notched pattern. 2 to prick or pierce with a pointed weapon or instrument. [from Middle English **pynken.**]

pink·eye (pĭngk′ī′) *n-* conjunctivitis.

pin·kie (pĭng′kē) *Informal n-* fourth and smallest finger, not counting the thumb. For picture, see *finger.*

pin money *n-* 1 money allowed to a wife by her husband for her private expenses. 2 any small sum of money to be used for incidental personal expenses.

pin·nace (pĭn′əs) *n-* 1 formerly, a small boat that attended a larger vessel and was used to transport messages, supplies, etc. 2 any boat carried by a ship.

pin·na·cle (pĭn′ə kəl) *n-* 1 peak or highest point: *the pinnacle of a mountain; the pinnacle of fame.* 2 high point like a spire: *a pinnacle of rock.* 3 small tower or turret above the rest of a building.

pin·nate (pĭn′āt′) *adj-* having parts arranged symmetrically along two sides of an axis, as in a feather: *a pinnate leaf. —adv-* pin′nate·ly.

pi·noch·le or **pi·noc·le** (pē′nŏk′əl, -nŭk′əl) *n-* any of several card games for two to six players, using a pack of 48 cards having two each of the ace, king, jack, ten, and nine of each suit; also, one of the scoring combinations in these games.

pi·ñon (pĭn′yən) *n-* pine tree of western United States, having edible seeds; also, the seed itself. *Hom-* pinion.

pin·point (pĭn′point′) *vt-* 1 to show the exact location of, by or as if by sticking a pin into a map: *The detectives pinpointed the criminal's hideout.* 2 to mark, determine, or define precisely: *to pinpoint a target; to pinpoint a cause or influence; to pinpoint the meaning of a word. n-* 1 point of a pin. 2 something very small or unimportant. 3 exact or precise location. *as modifier: the pinpoint bombing of a target.*

pin·prick (pĭn′prĭk′) *n-* 1 tiny puncture made by a pin or other fine point. 2 trivial annoyance or irritation.

pin·stripe (pĭn′strīp′) *n-* very thin stripe, as in certain fabrics used for suits.

pint (pīnt) *n-* liquid or dry measure equal to half a quart.

pin·to (pĭn′tō) *adj-* marked with spots of more than one color; pied; mottled. *n-* [*pl.* **pin·tos**] horse or pony with such spots.

pin-up (pĭn′ŭp′) *Informal n-* picture of a pretty girl.

pin·wheel (pĭn′hwēl′) *n-* 1 toy wheel of different-colored pieces of paper, plastic, etc., pinned to an end of a stick so as to revolve in the wind. 2 kind of firework that revolves when lighted.

pin·worm (pĭn′wûrm′) *n-* small, threadlike, parasitic worm that infests the colon and rectum.

pin·y (pī′nē) *adj-* [**pin·i·er, pin·i·est**] of or relating to pine trees, especially to their scent or resin.

pip·ing (pī′pĭng) *n-* 1 the pipes of a building, machine, system, etc.: *new piping for the engine.* 2 music of the bagpipe, fife, etc. 3 shrill sound, such as the song of a bird. 4 strip of material along a seam or fold, used as a trimming. *adj-* 1 shrill: *a piping voice.* 2 (also **piping hot**) very hot: *a piping bowl of soup.*

pip·it (pĭp′ət) *n-* any of several small birds resembling sparrows, noted for wagging their tails as they walk.

pip·pin (pĭp′ən) *n-* any of several kinds of apples, especially a sweet, yellow or greenish-yellow eating apple.

pip·squeak (pĭp′skwēk′) *n- Slang* person or thing that is very small or insignificant.

pi·quant (pē′kənt) *adj-* 1 agreeably sharp to the taste: *a piquant sauce.* 2 arousing interest; clever; stimulating: *the piquant comments of a good critic.* 3 having a lively and attractive charm: *a piquant face or manner. —adv-* pi′quant·ly. *n-* pi′quan·cy.

pique (pēk) *n-* slight anger or resentment. *vt-* [**piqued, pi·quing**] 1 to wound the pride of; displease: *Their rudeness piqued her.* 2 to stir up; arouse; excite: *to pique one's curiosity.* 3 to pride (oneself): *The actor piqued himself on his good looks. Homs-* peak, peek.

pi·qué (pē kā′, pĭ-) *n-* firm-textured fabric, usually of cotton, woven with a ribbed effect or with a small, indented diamond or honeycomb pattern.

pi·ra·cy (pī′rə sē) *n-* [*pl.* **pi·ra·cies**] 1 armed robbery on the high seas. 2 the use of another's invention, literary work, or the like, without permission.

pi·rate (pī′rət) *n-* 1 robber on the high seas. 2 person who uses another's invention or creation without permission. *vt-* [**pi·rat·ed, pi·rat·ing**] 1 to rob at sea. 2 to use (another's invention or creation) without permission: *The company is being sued for pirating an invention.*

pi·rat·i·cal (pī răt′ĭ kəl) *adj-* of or like piracy or pirates: *to engage in piratical practices. —adv-* pi·rat′i·cal·ly.

pi·rogue (pə rōg′, pē-) *n-* 1 canoe made of a hollowed-out log. 2 any boat shaped like a canoe.

pir·ou·ette (pĭr′ŏŏ ĕt′) *n-* a whirling or turning about on the toes. *vi-* [**pir·ou·et·ted, pir·ou·et·ting**] to turn on the toes rapidly in one spot.

pis·ca·to·ry (pĭs′kə tôr′ē) *adj-* 1 having to do with fishes or with fishing: *articles on piscatory subjects.* 2 making a living by fishing: *a piscatory people.* Also **pis′ca·to·ri·al.**

Pis·ces (pĭs′ēz, pĭs′ēz) *n-* constellation south of Andromeda, supposed to resemble a pair of fish in outline.

Pistil

pis·ta·chi·o (pĭs tăsh′ē ō) *n-* [*pl.* **pis·ta·chi·os**] 1 small tree of southern Europe and Asia, having a greenish, almond-flavored nut, the kernel of which is used for flavoring. 2 the nut itself. 3 a very pale green color. *—adj-* a dish of pistachio *ice cream; a pistachio scarf.*

pis·til (pĭs′təl) *n-* the part in the center of a flower that produces the seed. *Hom-* pistol.

pitch·out (pĭch′out′) *n-* 1 in baseball, a pitch deliberately wide of the plate so that the batter cannot hit it, usually made to enable the catcher to check or put out a base runner trying to steal a base. 2 in football, a lateral pass made behind the line of scrimmage.

pitch·o·ver (pĭch′ō′vər) *Space n-* point in the flight of a rocket when it departs from a vertical flight path.

pitch pipe *n-* small metal pipe that sounds a single tone. It is used to set the pitch for a singer or instrument.

pitch·y (pĭch′ē) *adj-* [**pitch·i·er, pitch·i·est**] 1 full of, or smeared with, pitch or tar. 2 black; extremely dark; pitch-black: *thick pitchy smoke. —n-* pitch′i·ness.

pit·e·ous (pĭt′ē əs) *adj-* arousing sorrow or pity; pitiful: *An injured animal is a piteous sight. —adv-* pit′e·ous·ly. *n-* pit′e·ous·ness.

pit·fall (pĭt′fôl′) *n-* 1 hidden pit used as a trap for animals. 2 hidden danger, trap, or unexpected difficulty.

pith (pĭth) *n-* 1 soft, spongy tissue forming a central core, especially in the stem of certain plants. 2 important or essential part: *the pith of a lecture.*

pit·head (pĭt′hĕd′) *n-* top of a mining shaft; also, grounds or buildings next to a mining shaft.

Pith·e·can·thro·pus (pĭth′ə kăn′thrə pəs, -kăn′thrō′ pəs) *n-* Java man.

pla·ce·bo (plə sē′ bō) *n-* [*pl.* **pla·ce·bos** or **pla·ce·boes**] useless but harmless preparation given to a patient to humor him, especially when his illness is thought to be due to emotional disturbances.

place kick *n-* in football, a kick for a field goal after the ball has been placed on the ground in front of the kicker by another player.

place mat *n-* small table mat serving as an individual table cover.

place·ment (plàs′ mənt) *n-* **1** act of placing; especially, the finding of employment for a person or the assignment of a student to a class or course. **2** location or arrangement: *the placement of the furniture in a room.* **3** in football, the placing of the ball on the ground for a place kick; also, the kick itself.

pla·cen·ta (plə sĕn′ tə) *n-* thé rounded, spongy organ that connects the uterus and the developing embryo and provides the embryo with its nourishment.

plac·er (plàs′ ər) *n-* deposit of loose surface soil or gravel that contains gold or other valuable minerals.

placer mining *n-* mining by washing loose surface deposits so that the lighter matter is carried away and the heavier particles of valuable metal remain. —*n-* **placer miner.**

plac·id (plàs′ ĭd) *adj-* calm; tranquil: *a placid lake;* placid *behavior.* —*adv-* **plac′ id·ly.** *n-* **plac′ id·ness.**

pla·cid·i·ty (plə sĭd′ ə tē) *n-* calmness; tranquillity.

plack·et (plàk′ ət) *n-* **1** the finished opening or slit, with or without a zipper, in the upper part of a skirt, dress, or blouse, to make it easy to put on. **2** hidden pocket in a woman's skirt.

pla·gia·rism (plā′ jə rĭz′ əm) *n-* **1** a stealing and using, as one's own, of another's ideas, words, etc.; literary theft. **2** the material stolen. —*n-* **pla′ gia·rist.**

pla·gia·rize (plā′ jə rīz′) *vt-* [pla·gia·rized, pla·gia·riz·ing] to steal and use (another's ideas, words, etc.) as one's own. *vi-: He deliberately* plagiarized *from earlier novels.* —*n-* **pla′ gia·riz′ er.**

plague (plāg) *n-* **1** any dangerous disease that spreads quickly; an epidemic, especially of bubonic plague. **2** thing causing misery or great trouble; affliction: *A* plague *of locusts devoured the crops.* **3** *Informal* a nuisance. *vt-* [plagued, pla·guing] **1** to afflict with disease, evil, or disaster: *A severe unemployment problem* plagued *the nation.* **2** to pester or annoy: *The child* plagued *his uncle with questions.*

plagu·y or **plagu·ey** (plā′ gē) *Informal adj-* annoying; irritating; vexatious.

plaice (plàs) *n-* [*pl.* **plaice;** **plaices** (kinds of plaice)] **1** large European flatfish or flounder. **2** any of various American flatfishes or flounders. *Hom-* place.

plaid (plàd) *n-* **1** pattern of weaving made by crossing bands of different colors at right angles; tartan.

plain·clothes·man (plān′ klōz′ mən) *n-* [*pl.* **plain·clothes·men**] police officer wearing ordinary clothes when on duty; especially, a detective.

Plains Indian *n-* member of any of the tribes of North American Indians who formerly inhabited the Great Plains of the United States extending from the Mississippi and Missouri rivers to the Rocky Mountains.

plain sailing *Informal n-* easy progress or an easy part of a task.

plains·man (plānz′ mən) *n-* [*pl.* **plains·men**] person who lives on the plains.

plain·song (plān′ sóng′) *n-* medieval church music having a single line of vocal melody that is not divided into regular bars and is sung without accompaniment.

plain·spo·ken (plān′ spō′ kən) *adj-* frank and direct in speech.

plaint (plānt) *n-* **1** *Archaic* lamentation; lament; moaning. **2** a complaint.

plain·tiff (plān′ tĭf) *n-* person who brings suit in a court of law; complainant.

plain·tive (plān′ tĭv) *adj-* sad; melancholy: *a* plaintive *song.* —*adv-* **plain′ tive·ly.** *n-* **plain′ tive·ness.**

plait (plāt) *n-* **1** flat fold; pleat. **2** a braid. *vt-* **1** to pleat: *Mother* plaited *paper on the edge of the shelf.* **2** to braid: *to* plait *one's hair.* *Hom-* plate.

plan·tain (plăn′ tən) *n-* **1** tropical plant bearing a kind of banana. **2** edible fruit of this plant. [from West Indian **prattana,** influenced by Spanish **plátano.**]

plan·tain (plăn′ tən) *n-* common weed with large leaves that lie on or near the ground. Each plant has slender stalks that become solid spikes of tiny, greenish flowers. [from Old French word that comes from a Latin word **plantāgō,** from **planta,** "sole of the foot."]

Plantain

plan·ta·tion (plăn tā′ shən) *n-* **1** farm that is usually large and located in a warm region, and is devoted to the cultivation of a single commercial crop: *a cotton* plantation; *a rubber* plantation. **2** group of plants or trees under cultivation; also, the land on which such plants and trees are planted: *a* plantation *of maple trees.*

plant·er (plăn′ tər) *n-* **1** person, machine, or implement that sows or plants. **2** person who owns or manages a plantation. **3** an ornamental container in which plants and flowers are grown.

plant louse *n-* aphid.

plan view *n-* drawing or photograph picturing something as if seen from directly above it.

plaque (plăk) *n-* **1** flat, thin piece of metal, porcelain, or earthenware upon which a picture or design has been enameled or carved, and which is used chiefly as a wall ornament. **2** brooch or similar ornament worn as a badge of an honorary order.

plash (plăsh) *n-* splash or splashing sound: *the plash of a fountain.* *vi-* to splash lightly (against).

-plasm *combining form* the more fluid substance of a cell; cytoplasm; protoplasm.

plas·ma (plăz′ mə) *n-* **1** straw-colored liquid that remains after the blood cells have been removed from whole blood. Plasma contains proteins, salts, water, etc. **2** *Physics* the gaseous mixture of neutral particles, ionized particles, and free electrons that is the form in which most of the matter of the universe occurs. Plasmas occur in fluorescent light bulbs, jet exhausts, and the ionosphere, and in suns, galaxies, etc.

plasma sheath *n-* layer of ionized gas enveloping a body moving through an atmosphere at hypersonic speeds. The plasma sheath interrupts radio communication during the reentry of a spacecraft.

plas·ter (plăs′ tər) *n-* **1** mixture of lime, sand, and water which hardens as it dries and is used to coat walls. **2** substance spread on a cloth and applied to the body as a remedy: *a mustard* plaster. **3** plaster of Paris. *vt-* **1** to cover or repair with building plaster: *to* plaster *a wall; to* plaster *up a hole.*

plas·ter·board (plăs′ tər bōrd′) *n-* thin board composed of plaster and paper or felt in alternate layers and covered on both sides with heavy paper, used in building walls, partitions, etc.

plaster cast *n-* **1** a copy or cast of a statue or other object made by molding plaster of Paris. **2** hard, molded covering used to keep a broken bone motionless while healing.

plas·ter·ing (plăs′ tər ĭng) *n-* **1** a putting on of plaster. **2** a covering of plaster on a wall, ceiling, etc.

plaster of Paris *n-* a white powdery substance which, when mixed with water, forms a quick-setting paste. It is used for making casts, moldings, statuettes, etc.

plas·tic (plăs′ tĭk) *n-* any of a large group of materials manufactured from organic compounds and other chemicals and made into useful shapes by heat, pressure, etc. Rayon and cellophane are two types of plastics. *adj-* **1** made of one or more of these materials: *a* plastic *toy.* **2** having to do with or made by molding or modeling: *We made pottery and clay figures in* plastic *arts class.* **3** such as can be molded: *a* plastic *material.* —*n-* **plas·ti′ ci·ty** (plăs tĭs′ ə tē): *This clay has good* plasticity.

plat·en (plăt′ ən) *n-* 1 in some printing presses, the flat part that presses the paper against the type. 2 the roller of a typewriter.

plat·form (plăt′ fôrm) *n-* 1 flat, horizontal surface, usually raised above the surrounding ground or floor: *a railroad platform; a speaker's platform.* 2 statement of a group's beliefs and policies: *a political platform.*

plat·ing (plā′ tĭng) *n-* 1 a coating of a metal over another metal to add beauty, hardness, corrosion resistance, etc.

plat·i·num (plăt′ ə nəm) *n-* 1 heavy, silver-white precious metal element. It is very resistant to heat and acids, and is used in scientific apparatus and jewelry and as a catalyst. Symbol Pt, At. No. 78, At. Wt. 195.09. 2 a silvery-white color. *adj-: a platinum ring.*

plat·i·tude (plăt′ ə tōōd′, -tyōōd′) *n-* trite and commonplace remark, usually moralistic; truism.

plat·i·tu·di·nous (plăt′ ə tōō′ də nəs, -tyōō′ də nəs) *adj-* 1 having the nature of a platitude; commonplace; trite: *a platitudinous remark.* 2 full of or given to platitudes: *a platitudinous speaker.*

Pla·ton·ic (plə tŏn′ ĭk) *adj-* 1 of or relating to the Greek philosopher Plato or to his ideas, doctrines, and maxims. 2 **platonic** referring to purely mental or spiritual relationships between two persons: *their platonic friendship.*

pla·toon (plə tōōn′) *n-* 1 in the Army and Marines, one of the units of a company, usually consisting of four squads and commanded by a lieutenant. 2 in football, a group of players trained specially for offense or defense, who periodically enter and leave the game as a unit. *vi-* in sports, to alternate with other players: *One squad platoons with the others. vt-: The coach platoons Joe and Tom at quarterback.*

plat·ter (plăt′ ər) *n-* 1 large, usually oval, flat dish for serving a main course. 2 *Slang* phonograph record.

Platter

plat·y·pus (plăt′ ə pəs) *n-* Australian, egg-laying, water-loving, furry mammal with webbed feet and a bill like that of a duck; duckbill; duckbilled platypus.

plau·dit (plô′ dĭt) *n-* enthusiastic applause or other expression of praise.

Platypus, about 20 in. long

plau·si·ble (plô′ zə bəl) *n-* 1 seemingly true or reasonable: *a plausible excuse.* 2 apparently believable or worthy of confidence: *a plausible salesman.* —*n- plau′ si·bil′ i·ty. adv- plau′ si·bly.*

play (plā) *vi-* 1 to have fun; amuse oneself; take part in recreation. 2 to take part in a game; also, to gamble. 3 to act or behave in a certain way: *to play false with a friend.* 4 to act in a drama; perform: *He plays in summer theater.* 5 to be performed: *"Cleopatra" is playing tonight at the movies.*

pla·ya (plī′ ə) *n-* shallow lake bed of a desert basin, in which water gathers during the rainy season.

play·a·ble (plā′ ə bəl) *adj-* such as can be played; suitable for being played or played on: *The actor complained that his part was not playable. The old violin is still playable.*

play·act·ing (plā′ ăk′ tĭng) *n-* 1 the acting in plays; dramatic performance. 2 insincere or affected behavior.

play·back (plā′ băk′) *n-* 1 the playing over or reproducing of a new record or tape for critical examination. 2 part of a recording machine that reproduces sound recordings.

play·bill (plā′ bĭl′) *n-* 1 poster advertising a play. 2 theater program.

play·let (plā′ lət) *n-* a short play.

play·mate (plā′ māt′) *n-* one who plays with another person; playfellow.

play·off (plā′ of′, -ôf′) *n-* game or match played to break a tie.

play·pen (plā′ pĕn′) *n-* small, usually portable, enclosure in which a small child may play safely by himself.

play·thing (plā′ thĭng′) *n-* thing to play with; toy.

play·wright (plā′ rīt′) *n-* person who writes plays; dramatist.

pla·za (plăz′ ə, plä′ zə) *n-* public square or open place in a city or town.

plume (plōōm) *n-* 1 fluffy, curly feather or tuft of feathers. 2 fluffy decoration, like a tuft of ostrich feathers: *The horses had plumes in their bridles. vt-* [**plumed, plum·ing**] 1 to smooth (feathers) with the beak. 2 to adorn with or as if with feathers.

Plume

plume (oneself) on to show pride in.

plum·met (plŭm′ ət) *n-* 1 lead weight attached to the end of a line for measuring depths; plumb. 2 plumb bob. *vi-* to fall or plunge straight downward.

plump (plŭmp) *adj-* [**plump·er, plump·est**] well filled out; well rounded: *a plump chicken. vt-* to cause to become round (often followed by "up" or "out"): *The maid plumped up the cushions. vi-: Her cheeks plumped out.* [of uncertain origin.] —*n- plump′ ness.*

plump (plŭmp) *vi-* to fall, sit, or drop heavily or suddenly: *She plumped into a chair. vt-: She plumped the bundles on the table. adv-* heavily and suddenly; also, straight down: *He fell plump into the water. n-* sudden heavy fall; also, sound made by such a fall. [from Middle English **plumpen**, possibly an imitation of a sound.]

plum pudding *n-* rich steamed pudding made of flour, suet, raisins, currants, and spices.

plum·y (plōō′ mē) *adj-* [**plum·i·er, plum·i·est**] 1 covered or adorned with plumes. 2 like a plume; feathery.

plun·der (plŭn′ dər) *vt-* to loot, rob, or pillage: *Bandits plundered the wagon train. n-* a pillaging or taking by force; also, that which is taken; loot: *The retreating army left its plunder behind.* —*n- plun′ der·er.*

plunge (plŭnj) *vt-* [**plunged, plung·ing**] 1 to thrust suddenly into a liquid, hole, or any substance that can be penetrated: *He plunged his foot into the water. The hunter plunged his spear into the boar's neck.* 2 to place suddenly (into): *to plunge a country into war. vi-* 1 to fall or rush headlong; drive or leap (into) some place or situation: *Ed plunged into the pool.* 2 to pitch or move sharply forward or downward: *The ship plunged through the waves.* 3 *Informal* to speculate or gamble heavily. *n-* 1 sudden dive, leap, or rush: *He took a plunge into the cool water.* 2 a swim. 3 *Informal* reckless bet or investment; hazardous speculation.

plung·er (plŭn′ jər) *n-* 1 person or thing that plunges. 2 *Informal* person who speculates or gambles extravagantly or rashly. 3 any device, such as the piston of a pump, that acts with a plunging motion. 4 suction cup made of rubber and attached to a handle, used to free clogged drains of obstructions.

plunk (plŭngk) *vt-* to pluck quickly the (strings of a banjo, guitar, etc.). *vi-* 1 to sound with a sharp, vibrating noise; twang. 2 to fall heavily or abruptly. *n-* 1 twanging sound. 2 a direct blow, whack; also, its sound.

plunk down to put or fall down quickly and abruptly: *He plunked his book down on the desk. He plunked down on the sofa.*

plu·per·fect (plōō′ pûr′ fĭkt) *Grammar n-* past perfect tense.

plur. 1 plural. 2 plurality.

plu·ral (plŏōr′ əl) *adj-* 1 consisting of or indicating more than one. 2 *Grammar* of or relating to the form of the word that names more than one: *a plural noun. n- Grammar* form of a word that shows that more than one is meant. The plural of "cat" is "cats," of "child," "children." —*adv- plu′ ral·ly.*

po·di·um (pō′ dē əm) *n-* raised platform from which a conductor leads an orchestra.

po·em (pō′ əm) *n-* 1 any composition written in poetry. A poem may be from two lines to several volumes in length. 2 any work of art or thing of beauty having the effect of poetry.

po·e·sy (pō′ ə sē) *Archaic n-* 1 poems collectively; poetry. 2 the art of writing poetry.

po·et (pō′ ət) *n-* 1 person who writes poetry. 2 any artist having the ability to move others by the beauty of his work.

po·et·ess (pō′ ət əs) *n-* female poet (often used to show disfavor).

point-blank (point' blăngk') *adj-* 1 aimed directly at a target: *a point-blank shot.* 2 so close that missing a target is unlikely or impossible: *to shoot at point-blank range.* 3 blunt and direct; forthright: *a point-blank question. adv-* directly: *I asked him point-blank.*

point-ed (poin' tǝd) *adj-* 1 having a sharp end or apex. 2 directed toward a particular person or thing: *her pointed remarks; his pointed curiosity.* —*adv-* point' ed·ly. *n-* point' ed·ness.

point-er (poin' tǝr) *n-* 1 thing that points to or toward something. 2 slender stick used to point with, used by teachers, lecturers, etc. 3 short-haired hunting dog trained to stand and point with its nose toward game. 4 *Informal* piece of advice.

Pointer, about 4 ft long

point-less (point' lǝs) *adj-* 1 without a point; blunt: *a pointless pencil.* 2 having no purpose, sense, or worthwhile result: *a pointless anecdote; a pointless attempt.*

point of honor *n-* something which closely touches one's honor, reputation, principles, ethical standards, etc.

point of order *n-* in parliamentary procedure, a query as to whether business or debate in progress is being properly conducted according to rule.

point of view *n-* 1 personal outlook; attitude: *his conservative point of view.* 2 position from which one looks at or considers something.

poise (poiz) *n-* 1 calmness and coolness of manner; self-possession: *his poise in addressing the audience.* 2 balance; equilibrium: *the poise of a tightrope walker.* 3 manner of carrying the head and body; carriage: *the poise of a ballet dancer. vt-* [poised, pois·ing] to balance: *The diver poised on the edge of the pool. vt-:* The seal poised the ball on its nose.

poi-son (poi' zǝn) *n-* 1 substance that can injure or kill when it is taken in or absorbed by a living thing. 2 anything that can corrupt or injure a person's character: *the poison of envy. vt-* 1 to injure or kill with a harmful or deadly substance. 2 to cause to become deadly or harmful by the addition of something: *Sewage poisoned the drinking water.* 3 to corrupt; ruin: *Envy poisoned their friendship.* —*n-* poi' son·er.

poison ivy *n-* bushy or climbing plant having leaves composed of three leaflets, and small, greenish flowers and berries. Touching the plant usually causes a painful rash.

poison oak *n-* shrubby plant closely related to and resembling poison ivy.

poi-son-ous (poi' zǝn ǝs) *adj-* 1 having properties that may injure or kill; venomous: *a poisonous snake.* 2 like a poison; harmful: *a poisonous rumor.* —*adv-* poi' son·ous·ly. *n-* poi' son·ous·ness.

Poison ivy

poke (pōk) *n-* pokeweed. *as modifier: a poke salad.* [American word from earlier puccoon, from the Algonquian name.]

poke (pōk) *n-* a bag; sack. [probably from Old Norse poki or earlier Dutch poke meaning "bag."]

poke-ber-ry (pōk' běr' ē) *n-* [*pl.* poke·ber·ries] 1 berry of the pokeweed. 2 the plant itself.

poke bonnet *n-* bonnet with a deep, projecting brim that shades the face.

¹**pok-er** (pō' kǝr) *n-* someone or something that pokes; especially, a metal rod used to stir a fire. [from ¹poke.]

²**pok-er** (pō' kǝr) *n-* card game played with money or chips, in which the players bet against each other on the value of their cards. [American word of uncertain origin.]

poker face *n-* face held expressionless.

poke-weed (pōk' wēd') *n-* tall, shrubby plant with pointed clusters of small, greenish-white flowers and dark purple berries; poke; pokeberry. The root and seeds of the plant are poisonous, but the young shoots are eaten as greens.

pop-lar (pŏp' lǝr) *n-* 1 any of various fast-growing trees related to the willows, some of which have slender, upturned branches. The aspen and the cottonwood are poplars. 2 the soft wood of these trees. *as modifier: the poplar leaves.*

pop-lin (pŏp' lĭn) *n-* strong, durable cloth of cotton, rayon, silk, or wool, having a fine, crosswise rib.

pop-o-ver (pŏp' ō' vǝr) *n-* light, air-filled muffin which rises over the edge of the muffin pan when baking.

Poplar leaves and catkins

pop-per (pŏp' ǝr) *n-* 1 covered metal basket or container for heating popcorn. 2 person or thing that pops.

pop-py (pŏp' ē) *n-* [*pl.* pop·pies] any of several plants with deeply notched leaves, hairy stems, and large-petaled, often scarlet flowers; also, the flower itself. Some kinds of poppy are a source of opium.

pop-py-cock (pŏp' ē kŏk') *Informal n-* foolish talk; nonsense.

pop-py-seed (pŏp' ē sěd') *n-* the small, black seeds of the poppy, used in cooking and baking.

Poppy

pop-u-lace (pŏp' yǝ lǝs) *n-* the common people, especially of a particular locality; the masses.

pop-u-lar (pŏp' yǝ lǝr) *adj-* 1 well liked generally or by a group: *a popular man.* 2 widespread; common; prevalent; general: *a popular myth; a popular remedy.* 3 of, for, or representing the people: *Democracy is popular government.* 4 suited to the average understanding and taste: *a popular explanation; popular music.* 5 within the means of average persons: *goods at popular prices.* 6 springing from or created by the common people: *Folk tales are of popular origin.*

popular front *n-* coalition of political parties, usually leftist, labor, and liberal.

pop-u-lar-i-ty (pŏp' yǝ lăr' ǝ tē, -lěr' ǝ tē) *n-* a being well liked by many people.

pop-u-lar-ize (pŏp' yǝ lǝ rīz') *vt-* [pop·u·lar·ized, pop·u·lar·iz·ing] to make popular. —*n-* pop' u·lar·i· za' tion. *n-* pop' u·lar·i' zer.

pop-u-lar-ly (pŏp' yǝ lǝr lē) *adv-* generally; familiarly: *Louis is popularly known as "Slim."*

popular vote *n-* total number of votes cast in a national election, as distinguished from the electoral vote.

pop-u-late (pŏp' yǝ lāt') *vt-* [pop·u·lat·ed, pop·u·lat·ing] 1 to fill or supply with inhabitants; to people: *to populate a frontier region.* 2 to inhabit: *Bands of Gypsies once populated this area.*

pop-u-la-tion (pŏp' yǝ lā' shǝn) *n-* 1 the total number of people living in a city, country, or region. 2 the people themselves or any one group of the people: *the adult population.* 3 the act or process of populating.

Pop-u-list (pŏp' yǝ lĭst) *n-* member of a U.S. political party that was formed in 1891 and that advocated government control of utilities, an income tax, and the free coinage of gold and silver.

pop-u-lous (pŏp' yǝ lǝs) *adj-* having many people; thickly populated: *a populous community.* —*n-* pop' u·lous·ness.

pore (pôr) *vi-* [pored, por·ing] to study with close attention; ponder; concentrate: *to pore over books.* [from Middle English po(u)ren, perhaps from Scandinavian pora, "to move or work slowly."] *Homs-* poor, pour.

por-gy (pôr' gē, pôr'-) *n-* [*pl.* porgy or porgies (kinds of porgy)] any of several salt-water food fishes of Atlantic and Mediterranean waters.

por-i-fer-an (pôr ĭf' ǝ rǝn, pǝ rĭf'-) *n-* a sponge.

pork (pôrk) *n-* the flesh of pigs, used for food.

pork-er (pôr' kǝr) *n-* a pig, especially when fattened for use as food.

por-nog-ra-phy (pôr nŏg' rǝ fē) *n-* grossly obscene writing, pictures, etc.

port (pòrt) *n*- sweet, usually dark-red wine, originally from Portugal. [from **Oporto**, a city in Portugal.]

port·a·ble (pòr′ tə bəl) *adj*- such as can be carried conveniently: *a portable typewriter.*

por·tage (pòr′ tĭj) *n*- 1 the carrying of boats and goods overland from one river or lake to another. 2 the route taken. *vt*- [por·taged, por·tag·ing] to carry (boats and goods) overland from one river or lake to another: *to portage a canoe. vi-: We portaged from the river to the lake.*

por·tal (pòr′ təl) *n*- gate; door; entrance: *the portal of the castle.*

portal-to-portal based on or including the whole time one is on the employer's property on a workday, rather than the time one actually works.

port·cul·lis (pòrt kŭl′ əs) *n*- heavy grating that can be lowered to close the entrance of a castle or fort.

Portcullis

porte-co·chere (pòrt′ kō shēr′) *n*- 1 large gateway through which a carriage may drive into a courtyard. 2 extension of a porch roof over a driveway to permit carriages to stop under cover.

por·tend (pòr tĕnd′) *n*- to give warning or sign of; foreshadow: *Ancient sailors believed that a certain bird following their ship would portend danger.*

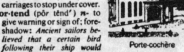
Porte-cochère

por·tent (pòr′ tĕnt) *n*- something that foretells or hints at a coming event; a warning, especially of trouble; omen: *The witchdoctor told of signs and portents.*

por·ten·tous (pòr tĕn′ təs) *adj*- 1 foreshadowing evil; threatening: *a portentous dream.* 2 remarkable; extraordinary: *a portentous event.* —*adv*- **por·ten′ tous·ly.** *n*- **por·ten′ tous·ness.**

por·ter (pòr′ tər) *n*- 1 person hired to carry baggage at a depot, airport, or hotel. 2 attendant in the parlor car or sleeping car of a train. [from Old French port(e)our, from Latin **portātor**, from **portāre** meaning "to carry."]

por·ter (pòr′ tər) *n*- doorkeeper. [from Old French **portier**, from Latin **porta** meaning "gate; door."]

por·ter (pòr′ tər) *Brit. n*- heavy, dark-brown beer. [shortened from **porter's** ale, from ²**porter**. It was once drunk mostly by porters.]

por·ter·house (pòr′ tər hous′) *n*- choice cut of beefsteak having considerable tenderloin and a T-shaped bone. Also **porterhouse steak.**

port·fo·li·o (pòrt fō′ lē ō) *n*- [*pl.* **port·fo·li·os**] 1 case for carrying loose papers, drawings, etc.; briefcase. 2 office of a minister of the government: *Mr. Allen accepted a portfolio in the new administration.* 3 all the stocks, bonds, etc., held by one person or investing institution.

Por·tia (pòr′ shə) *n*- in Shakespeare's "Merchant of Venice," the heroine who impersonates a lawyer and contests Shylock's claim.

por·ti·co (pòr′ tə kō) *n*- [*pl.* **por·ti·coes** or **por·ti·cos**] entrance porch having its roof supported by columns.

por·tiere (pòr tē ēr′) *n*- curtain or drapery hung across a doorway.

Portico

pol·len (pŏl′ ən) *n*- grains which are the male cells produced by a flower to fertilize egg cells of the same or other flowers.

pol·li·nate (pŏl′ ə nāt′) *vt*- [pol·li·nat·ed, pol·li·nat·ing] to transfer (pollen) from the anther of a flower to the stigma of the same flower or another flower. —*n*- **pol′ li·na′ tor:** *Bees are pollinators of some flowers.*

pol·li·na·tion (pŏl′ ə nā′ shən) *n*- the transfer of pollen from the anthers to the stigmas of flowers, which results in the start of the process by which seeds are formed.

pol·li·wog or **pol·ly·wog** (pŏl′ ĭ wŏg′) *n*- tadpole.

pol·y·gon (pŏl′ ĭ gŏn′) *n*- a closed plane figure having three or more sides.

po·lyg·y·ny (pə lĭj′ ə nē) *n*- custom or practice of having more than one wife at a time. —*adj*- **po·lyg′ y·nous:** *Muslims are polygynous by tradition.*

PARALLELOGRAM
PENTAGON NONAGON

pol·y·he·dron (pŏl′ ĭ hē′ drən) *n*- [*pl.* **pol·y·he·drons** or **pol·y·he·dra** (-drə)] in geometry, a solid figure bounded by plane faces.

Some polygons

pol·y·mer (pŏl′ ə mər) *n*- any of a very large number of complex chemical compounds that are the result of the stringing together of molecules of simpler compounds. Nylon and cellulose are polymers. —*adj*- **pol′ y·mer′ ic** (pŏl′ ə mĕr′ ĭk).

pol·y·mer·ize (pə lĭm′ ə rīz′, pŏl′ ə mə rīz′) *vi*- [pol·y·mer·ized, pol·y·mer·iz·ing] to combine into a polymer. *vt*- to make (something) into a polymer. —*n*- **pol·y′ mer·i·za′ tion** or **pol′ y·mer·i·za′ tion.**

Pol·y·ne·sian (pŏl′ ə nē′ zhən) *n*- 1 one of any of the peoples of Polynesia. 2 the languages of these people. *adj-: a Polynesian island.*

pol·y·no·mi·al (pŏl′ ĭ nō′ mē əl) *n*- in mathematics, an expression containing two or more terms. The expression $a(b + c^2)$ is a polynomial. —*adj-: a polynomial expression.*

pol·yp (pŏl′ əp) *n*- 1 small water animal without a backbone, shaped like a flower. Most polyps build skeletons of lime around themselves. For picture, see **coral.** 2 a tumor; especially, a benign tumor.

pol·y·sty·rene (pŏl′ ĭ stī′ rēn′) *n*- a polymer of styrene used to make many plastics.

pol·y·syl·lab·ic (pŏl′ ĭ sə lăb′ ĭk) *adj*- consisting of several syllables; especially, consisting of more than three syllables: *a polysyllabic word.*

pol·y·tech·nic (pŏl′ ĭ tĕk′ nĭk) *adj*- of or having to do with many arts or sciences, especially in their practical application: *a polytechnic institute.*

pol·y·the·ism (pŏl′ ĭ thē′ ĭz′ əm) *n*- belief in the existence of more than one god; also, the worship of such gods. —*n*- **pol′ y·the′ ist.** *adj*- **pol′ y·the·is′ tic.**

po·made (pō măd′) *n*- perfumed ointment for the hair. *vt*- [po·mad·ed, po·mad·ing]: *She pomaded her hair.*

pome (pōm) *n*- a kind of fruit, consisting of a ripened, fleshy calyx surrounding the ripened ovary. The pear and apple are pomes.

pome·gran·ate (pŭm′ grăn′ ət, pŏm′-) *n*- 1 fruit with a thick red skin and many seeds, each surrounded by red, juicy pulp that has a pleasant, acid taste. 2 the tree that bears this fruit. *as modifier: a pomegranate syrup.*

Pomegranate

Pom·e·ra·ni·an (pŏm′ ə rā′ nē ən) *n*- small dog having long, silky hair, a curled-up tail, and a pointed muzzle.

pom·mel (pŭm′ əl, pŏm′-) *n*- 1 the raised front of a saddle. 2 knob on the handle of a sword. *vt*- to pummel.

pomp (pŏmp) *n*- solemn or showy display, ceremony, etc.

pom·pa·dour (pŏm′ pə dôr′) *n*- hair style in which the hair is combed up from the forehead, often over a pad, or straight back from the forehead.

po·lice (pə lēs′) *n*- 1 a department of government set up to keep order, enforce law, and deal with criminals. 2 (takes plural verb) the persons in such a force. *vt*- [po·liced, po·lic·ing] 1 to patrol or keep in order as a policeman: *Soldiers policed the occupied territory.* 2 to clean up (a military camp, quarters, etc.). *as modifier: a police escort; a police record.*

police court *n*- a city court having jurisdiction over minor criminal cases and empowered to hold for trial all persons charged with more serious crimes.

police dog *n*- 1 German shepherd. 2 any dog trained to help the police in their work.

po·lice·man (pə lēs′ mən) *n*- [*pl.* **po·lice·men**] member of a police force. —*n- fem.* **po·lice′ wom′ an.**

pos·i·tive·ly (pŏs′ ə tĭv′ lē) *adv-* 1 in a positive manner. 2 (*often* pŏs′ ə tĭv′ lē),utterly and undoubtedly.

pos·i·tron (pŏz′ ə trŏn′) *Physics n-* the positively charged antiparticle corresponding to the electron.

poss. 1 possessive. 2 possession.

pos·se (pŏs′ ē) *n-* 1 group of men authorized by a sheriff to assist in carrying out the law. 2 group of people temporarily organized to carry out a search.

pos·sess (pə zĕs′) *vt-* 1 to have; own: *King Midas possessed much gold.* 2 to occupy; control: *At one time the Spanish possessed Florida.* 3 to influence strongly: *I don't know what possesses him to act like that!* —*n-* **pos·ses′ sor:** *She is the possessor of many jewels.*

pos·sessed (pə zĕst′) *adj-* in the complete control of some emotion, desire, or force, especially of a supernatural power: *They screamed as if possessed.*

pos·ses·sion (pə zĕsh′ ən) *n-* 1 ownership; control and custody: *The pirate tried to get possession of the treasure.* 2 something owned or possessed: *There were few possessions she prized as much as the old locket.* 3 control; occupancy: *The new cook took full possession of our kitchen.* 4 land under control of a government, but not officially part of that government's national territory: *Guam is a possession of the United States.* 5 a controlling by some force, especially a supernatural power.

pos·ses·sive (pə zĕs′ ĭv) *adj-* 1 having or relating to a strong desire to own or keep: *a possessive man; a possessive interest in jewelry.* 2 *Grammar* showing possession: *the possessive case; a possessive pronoun.* *n- Grammar* the possessive case or a word in the possessive case. See ¹case. —*adv-* **pos·ses′ sive·ly.** *n-* **pos·ses′ sive·ness.**

possessive adjective *Grammar n-* term usually applied to a personal or relative pronoun in the possessive case when the thing possessed is expressed. Examples: *John gave me his book. The boy whose hat fell off won the race.*

possessive pronoun *Grammar n-* any of the pronouns that show possession and can be used in place of noun phrases. They are "mine," "ours," "yours," "his," "hers," "its," "theirs," "whose." Example: *This dog is yours; that one is mine.*

pos·si·bil·i·ty (pŏs′ ə bĭl′ ə tē) *n-* [*pl.* **pos·si·bil·i·ties**] 1 chance; likelihood: *There's no possibility of his coming now.* 2 something that might happen: *Failure is a possibility.* 3 condition of being possible: *Let's not confuse possibility with probability.* 4 **possibilities** good or desirable results: *Your plan has good possibilities.*

post (pōst) *n-* 1 place where a person is stationed or assigned for duty. 2 military camp or station: *Most of the officers live off the post.* 3 position of trust: *His grandfather held a post in a large bank.* 4 local unit or chapter of a military veteran's organization. 5 trading post. *vt-* to station or assign: *The commander posted him to duty in Japan.* [from French *poste* meaning "a (military) station or stage in a road," from Latin **pos(i)tum,** meaning literally "placed."]

post- *prefix* after; coming after: *to postdate; postwar.*

post·age (pōs′ tĭj) *n-* cost of sending something by mail, usually paid by buying an official **postage stamp** and affixing it to the card, letter, or package.

postage meter *n-* office machine that prints the amount of postage required on pieces of outgoing mail. It can print only as much postage as has been previously paid for at the post office.

post·al (pōs′ təl) *adj-* relating to mail or the mail system.

post·card (pōst′ kärd′) *n-* mailing card, often with a picture on one side. Also **postal card.**

post chaise (shāz) *n-* in earlier times, a carriage with fast horses, in which mail and passengers were carried along regular routes more quickly than by coach.

post·date (pōst′ dāt′) *vt-* [**post·dat·ed, post·dat·ing**] to mark on or assign to (a check, document, etc.,) a date later than the actual date.

post·ed (pōs′ təd) *adj-* informed: *Keep us posted.*

post·er (pōs′ tər) *n-* 1 placard, sign, etc., by which something is advertised or announced. 2 billposter.

pos·te·ri·or (pŏs tēr′ ē ər) *adj-* 1 later in time; subsequent (to). 2 towards the rear; hinder. *n-* buttocks.

pos·tu·late (pŏs′ chə lāt′) *vt-* [**pos·tu·lat·ed, pos·tu·lat·ing**] to state or infer (something that is not or cannot be proven); to claim the truth of: *To tell someone to do a thing postulates that it can be done.* *n-* (*usually* pŏs′ chə lət) something assumed in order to account for or lead to something else; axiom; premise.

pos·ture (pŏs′ chər) *n-* 1 way a person holds his body; carriage: *Poor posture is unhealthy and unsightly.* 2 position or pose of the body: *to assume an awkward posture.* *vi-* [**pos·tured, pos·tur·ing**] to take a certain bodily position, especially a ridiculous or affected one. —*adj-* **pos′ tur·al:** *a postural defect.*

post·voc·al·ic (pōst′ vō kăl′ ĭk) *adj-* coming immediately after a vowel.

post·war (pōst′ wôr′) *adj-* coming after a war.

po·sy (pō′ zē) *n-* [*pl.* **po·sies**] flower or bunch of flowers.

pot (pŏt) *n-* 1 china or earthenware container: *a flower pot.* 2 metal or earthenware cooking vessel; kettle: *She put the bean pot in the oven.* 3 (also **pot′ ful′**) the amount a pot will hold: *Belle made a pot of soup.* 4 in poker and other games, the money at stake in any given hand: *to win a large pot.* *vt-* [**pot·ted, pot·ting**] 1 to transplant into a flowerpot. 2 to preserve (meat) in a china or earthenware container or jar. 3 to shoot (a bird or animal) with a potshot.

keep the pot boiling to meet living expenses. **go to pot** to go to ruin: *The store went to pot.*

po·ta·ble (pō′ tə bəl) *adj-* drinkable.

po·ta·bles (pō′ tə balz) *n- pl.* beverages; drinks.

pot·ash (pŏt′ ăsh′) *n-* white, alkaline compound of potassium and oxygen, used in making soap, glass, fertilizers, etc.

po·tas·si·um (pə tăs′ ē əm) *n-* a soft, silver-white metal element used in making explosives, soap, fertilizer, etc. Symbol K, At. No. 19, At. Wt. 39.102.

potassium nitrate *n-* white, crystalline compound (KNO_3) used in fertilizers, gunpowder, and in medicine; saltpeter.

potassium permanganate *n-* a dark-purple compound ($KMnO_4$) that is a strong oxidizing agent and is used as a bleach, germicide, etc.

po·ta·to (pə tā′ tō) *n-* [*pl.* **po·ta·toes**] 1 (also *Irish* **potato**) rounded tuber growing underground from the roots of a plant native to tropical America, widely used as a vegetable and a source of flour and starch. 2 the plant itself. 3 sweet potato. *as modifier: a potato pancake.*

potato beetle *or* **potato bug** *n-* beetle with black and yellow stripes, that eats the leaves of potatoes and other plants.

potato chip *n-* thin slice of potato that has been immersed in very hot fat or oil and fried crisp.

Pot·a·wot·o·mi (pŏt′ ə wŏt′ ə mē) *n-* [*pl.* **Pot·a·wot·o·mis**, *also* **Pot·a·wot·o·mi**] 1 one of a tribe of American Indians who formerly lived along the lower shores of Lake Michigan. 2 the Algonquian language of these Indians. *adj-: the* Potawotomi *cone-shaped lodges.*

Potato leaf. tuber. and flower

pot·bel·ly (pŏt′ bĕl′ ē) *n-* 1 a protruding belly. 2 person who has such a belly. —*adj-* **pot′ bel′ lied.**

potbelly stove *or* **potbellied stove** *n-* upright wood- or coal-burning stove with bulging sides.

pot·boil·er (pŏt′ boi′ lər) *n-* a literary or artistic work, often inferior, done merely to earn money.

po·tent (pō′ tənt) *adj-* 1 strong; very effective: *a potent medicine.* 2 having authority or power: *a potent ruler.* —*n-* **po′ ten·cy:** *the potency of their political organization.* *adv-* **po′ tent·ly.**

po·ten·tate (pō′ tən tāt′) *n-* powerful monarch or ruler.

po·ten·tial (pə tĕn′ shəl) *adj-* capable of coming into existence or being developed; possible but not actual: *Our mineral deposits are a great source of potential wealth.*

pound·al (poun′ dəl) *n-* unit of force equal to the force that will cause an acceleration of 1 foot per second per second in a mass of 1 pound.

pound cake *n-* rich, plain cake, originally made from a pound each of flour, sugar, and butter, and many eggs.

pound-foolish (pound′ fōō′ lĭsh) *adj-* spending large amounts of money foolishly.

pour (pôr) *vt-* to cause to flow in a stream: *to pour milk from a pitcher.* *vi-* 1 to stream: *Water poured from the broken pipe.* 2 to go in or out in large numbers: *The pupils poured out onto the playground.* 3 to rain heavily. 4 to preside at serving tea, cakes, etc., at a reception or other social occasion. *Homs-* poor, pore. —*n-* pour′ er. **pour out** to tell in detail freely: *to pour out a story.*

pour·boire (pōōr′ bwär′) *French* a tip; gratuity.

pout (pout) *vi-* to push out or pucker the lips in sullenness, displeasure, etc. *n-* sullen or sulky expression made in such a way. —*adj-* pout′ y [pout·i·er, pout·i·est]: *a pouty expression.*

pout·er (pou′ tər) *n-* 1 person who pouts. 2 pigeon that puffs out its crop and stands and walks erectly.

pov·er·ty (pŏv′ ər tē) *n-* 1 lack of money or the necessities of life. 2 lack of something needed or wanted; poorness: *the poverty of the soil.*

pov·er·ty-strick·en (pŏv′ ər tē strĭk′ ən) *adj-* extremely poor; destitute.

pow·der (pou′ dər) *n-* 1 any dry material in fine particles; especially, a medicine or beauty preparation in such form: *talcum powder*; *tooth powder.* 2 gunpowder or another finely divided explosive. *vt-* 1 to make into fine particles: *to powder sugar.* 2 to cover and sprinkle with or as with fine particles: *to powder toast with cinnamon.* 3 to use fine particles on (the face and body). *vi-* to be reduced to very small particles: *Talc powders easily.*

take a powder *Slang* to run away; to make a quick getaway.

P.O.W. or **POW** prisoner of war.

powder horn *n-* horn of a cow or other animal, fashioned to carry and funnel gunpowder.

powder puff *n-* soft pad used for applying powder to the skin.

Powder horn

powder room *n-* rest room for women.

pow·der·y (pou′ də rē) *adj-* 1 like powder; in the form of powder: *A powdery snow is good to ski on.* 2 covered or sprinkled with any kind of powder: *The bee's legs were powdery with pollen.* 3 easily crumbled or reduced to powder: *a powdery stone.*

pow·er (pou′ ər) *n-* 1 strength; vigor: *The pitcher had plenty of power but little control. The power of his argument won many to his side.* 2 ability to act or do something: *They did everything in their power to win the game.*

pot·herb (pŏt′ ûrb′) *n-* 1 any leafy green vegetable, such as spinach, that is cooked and used as food. 2 any herb, such as thyme, that is used to season cooked food.

pot·hole (pŏt′ hōl′) *n-* 1 deep, round depression in the rock bed of a stream. 2 any deep, round hole or pit, especially one in the surface of a street or road.

pot·hook (pŏt′ hŏŏk′) *n-* 1 S-shaped iron hook for hanging or carrying pots over an open fire. 2 hooked stroke in handwriting.

po·tion (pō′ shən) *n-* a drink, especially one with magical powers.

pot·latch (pŏt′ lăch′) *n-* among various Indian tribes of the Northwest, a ceremony in which property is given away, or sometimes ostentatiously destroyed, as a display of wealth. [American word from Chinook Indian *potshatl* meaning "gift."]

pot·luck (pŏt′ lŭk′) *n-* whatever meal or food is available for a family or guest without special preparation.

pot·pie (pŏt′ pī′) *n-* pie made in a deep dish, usually containing meat or fish and vegetables, and having a crust only on the top.

pot·pour·ri (pō pŏŏ rē′) *n-* 1 mixture; medley: *a potpourri of songs from musical comedies.* 2 mixture of dried flowers and spices used to perfume a room.

pot roast *n-* meat, usually beef, browned in a pot and simmered in a small amount of water until tender.

power brakes *n- pl.* brakes on a motor vehicle that use engine power to increase the force of the driver's pressure on the brake pedal.

power dive *n-* airplane dive that is accelerated by the power of the engine or engines.

power-driv·en (pou′ ər drĭv′ ən) *adj-* run by an engine or a motor: *a power-driven saw.*

pow·er·ful (pou′ ər fəl) *adj-* having great power, strength, or influence: *a powerful engine.* —*adv-* pow′ er·ful·ly.

pow·er·house (pou′ ər hous′) *n-* 1 place where power is generated, especially electrical power. 2 *Slang* powerful person.

pow·er·less (pou′ ər ləs) *adj-* not having power or ability to act, resist, or help; weak; helpless. —*adv-* pow′ er·less·ly. *n-* pow′ er·less·ness.

power of attorney *n-* in law, a written statement authorizing a person to act as the attorney or business agent of someone else.

power pack *n-* compact unit used to provide power for an electrical or electronic device, often by converting one type of electrical energy into another.

power plant *n-* 1 engine or other source of power, along with its installation and accessories. 2 powerhouse.

power politics *n-* international politics based on the threat of military or economic force.

power shovel *n-* excavating machine having a toothed, box-shaped or bucket-shaped digging device at the end of a movable beam.

power steering *n-* steering system of a car, truck, etc., that lessens the driver's effort by taking power from the engine.

power take-off *n-* device on the engine or gear box of a truck, tractor, boat, etc., that permits engine power to be used for driving other machines.

power tool *n-* saw, drill, hammer, or other tool driven by a motor, especially by an electric motor.

Pow·ha·tan (pou hăt′ ən) *n-* [*pl.* Pow·ha·tans, also Pow·ha·tan] 1 a member of a tribe of Algonquian Indians who lived in the tidewater section of Virginia and were led by Chief Powhatan, the father of Pocohontas. 2 a confederacy of thirty tribes of these Indians. *adj-* the Powhatan *village.*

pow·wow (pou′ wou′) *n-* 1 ceremonial feast or dance held by North American Indians to gain religious or magical aid for a hunt, war, etc. 2 North American Indian priest or medicine man. 3 *Informal* any meeting or gathering held in order to confer or discuss, especially a noisy one: *The big shots had a powwow.* *vi-* to hold such a ceremony or discussion.

pox (pŏks) *n-* 1 disease marked by an eruption, or breaking out on the skin. 2 syphilis.

pp pianissimo.

pp. pages.

p.p. past participle.

P.P. 1 parcel post. 2 postpaid.

pr. 1 pair. 2 price.

Pr symbol for praseodymium.

P.R. 1 Puerto Rico. 2 proportional representation.

prac·ti·ca·ble (prăk′ tĭ kə bəl) *adj-* such as can be done, practiced, or used: *a practicable plan.* —*n-* prac′ ti·ca·bil′ i·ty: *The practicability of Jack's plan was questionable.* *adv-* prac′ ti·ca·bly.

▶PRACTICABLE usually refers to plans and procedures and the possibility of carrying them out successfully. PRACTICAL refers to persons who are sensible and realistic, or things, actions, etc. that are sensible and continuously useful: *It is practical to put money aside for a rainy day, but many persons do not find this plan to be a practicable one.*

prac·ticed or **prac·tised** (prăk′ tĭst) *adj-* highly experienced: *a practiced carpenter.*

prac·tise (prăk′ tĭs) *vt-* & *vi-* [prac·tised, prac·tis·ing] to practice.

prac·ti·tion·er (prăk tĭsh′ ə nər) *n-* person engaged in a profession, especially medicine.

prae·tor (prē′ tər) *n-* in ancient Rome, a magistrate who acted as judge, general, and administrator.

prae·tor·i·an (prē tôr′ ē ən) *adj-* 1 of or relating to a praetor.

preach·y (prē′chē) *adj-* [**preach·i·er, preach·i·est**] 1 characterized by long and tiresome moralizing: *a preachy lecture*. 2 given to preaching: *a preachy person*. —*n-* **preach′i·ness**.

pre·am·ble (prē′ăm′bəl) *n-* 1 introduction to a statute or law, giving the reason for passing the law: *the preamble to the Constitution*. 2 introductory statement or event, especially when it explains what is to follow.

pre·ar·range (prē′ə rānj′) *vt-* [**pre·ar·ranged, pre·ar·rang·ing**] to arrange previously or beforehand: *They prearranged our meeting*. —*n-* **pre′ar·range′ment**.

Pre·cam·bri·an (prē′kăm′brē ən) *adj-* of or having to do with any period of geological time preceding the Cambrian.

pre·car·i·ous (prĭ kâr′ē əs) *adj-* uncertain; risky or perilous: *a precarious perch in a tree*. —*adv-* **pre·car′i·ous·ly**. *n-* **pre·car′i·ous·ness**.

pre·cau·tion (prĭ kô′shən) *n-* care taken beforehand to prevent harm, loss, etc.: *the precautions against fire*. —*adj-* **pre·cau′tion·ar′y**: *a precautionary measure*.

pre·cede (prē sēd′) *vt-* [**pre·ced·ed, pre·ced·ing**] to go or happen before in time, place, rank, importance, etc.: *He preceded me in line*. *vi-* to take precedence.

pre·ced·ence (prĕs′ə dəns) *n-* 1 a coming or being before in time, order, rank, or importance. 2 superiority in rank; especially, the right of going before others in ceremonies and formal occasions.

take precedence to be of the greater importance or higher rank; have priority.

prec·e·dent (prĕs′ə dənt) *n-* an act or event of the past that can serve as a guide or justification for later actions, decisions, etc.: *a law without precedent*.

pre·cept (prē′sĕpt′) *n-* a rule of conduct or moral behavior intended as a guide or example; maxim.

pre·cep·tor (prē sĕp′tər) *n-* person who guides or instructs; teacher. —*n- fem.* **pre·cep′tress**.

pre·ces·sion (prē sĕsh′ən) *n-* 1 a going before others; a going forward. 2 the wobbling motion exhibited by any spinning body, such as a gyroscope or the earth, when an external force acts to shift the axis of rotation of the body.

pre·cinct (prē′sĭngkt′) *n-* 1 area in a town or city marked off as a police or voting district. 2 space enclosed by walls or boundaries, especially within a church: *the precinct of a cathedral*. 3 precincts surrounding regions; environs: *the town and its immediate precincts*.

pre·cious (prĕsh′əs) *adj-* 1 of great price; costly: *The crown was studded with precious stones*. 2 highly valued; much loved: *Freedom is a precious right*. 3 affectedly elegant or refined: *a precious style of writing*; precious manners. 4 (intensifier only): *a precious nuisance*. *adv-* very; extremely: *He has precious little to say for himself*. —*adv-* **pre′cious·ly**. *n-* **pre′cious·ness**.

precious stone *n-* rare, valuable gem, such as the diamond, emerald, or ruby.

prec·i·pice (prĕs′ə pəs) *n-* steep, nearly vertical or overhanging cliff; hence, any potentially disastrous situation.

pre·cip·i·tant (prĭ sĭp′ə tənt) *adj-* headlong; abrupt; precipitate. —*n-* **pre·cip′i·tance** or **pre·cip′i·tan·cy**.

¹**pre·cip·i·tate** (prĭ sĭp′ə tāt′) *vt-* [**pre·cip·i·tat·ed, pre·cip·i·tat·ing**] 1 to bring about; hasten the happening of, especially before wanted, needed, or expected: *to precipitate a strike*. 2 to cast or hurl down from a height. 3 to condense (water vapor) into moisture that falls as rain, dew, sleet, etc. 4 to separate (a solid) from a liquid solution or suspension: *As the river moves more slowly, it precipitates silt*. *vi-* to fall in a headlong manner.

²**pre·cip·i·tate** (prĭ sĭp′ə tət) *adj-* 1 headlong; hasty; rash, especially in violence of motion.

pred·a·tor (prĕd′ə tər, -tôr) *n-* person or animal that preys or plunders.

pred·a·tor·y (prĕd′ə tôr′ē) *adj-* 1 living by preying on others: *a predatory animal*. 2 characterized by plundering or looting: *a predatory attack*. —*adv-* **pred′a·tor′i·ly**. *n-* **pred′a·tor′i·ness**.

pre·de·cease (prē′dĭ sēs′) *vt-* [**pre·de·ceased, pre·de·ceas·ing**] to die before (someone else).

pred·e·ces·sor (prĕd′ə sĕs′ər) *n-* person or thing that comes before another, especially in a job or office.

pred·i·cate (prĕd′ĭ kət) *Grammar n-* the part of a sentence which remains after the subject and all sentence modifiers have been removed. The predicate consists of a finite verb or verb phrase, which may be accompanied by an object, a complement, or both, and modifiers. Examples:

Marian coughed.
He quickly sketched a horse.
They made Joe president.
She is a good singer.
As a last resort, they jumped in and swam to shore.

pre·di·cate (prĕd′ə kāt′) *vt-* [**pre·di·cat·ed, pre·di·cat·ing**] 1 to base or found (a conclusion, argument, proposal, etc.): *He predicates his theory on these facts*. 2 to declare (something) to be a property or characteristic of something else: *to predicate wetness of water*.

predicate adjective *Grammar n-* adjective that follows a linking verb and describes the subject of the verb. Examples: *That house is old*. *The grass looks greener*.

predicate nominative *Grammar n-* 1 subjective complement that is a pronoun. 2 subjective complement that is a noun.

predicate noun *Grammar n-* a noun that is a subjective complement.

pre·dict (prĭ dĭkt′) *vt-* to announce or know about in advance; foresee; prophesy: *I predict good weather for the picnic. Who can predict the future?* —*adj-* **pre·dict′a·ble**. *adv-* **pre·dict′a·bly**. *n-* **pre·dic′tor**.

pre·dic·tion (prĭ dĭk′shən) *n-* 1 a predicting or foretelling. 2 something predicted; prophecy; forecast.

pre·di·gest (prē′dĭ jĕst′, -dī jĕst′) *vt-* to cause (food) to become partly digested, either by a natural or artificial process, before it is eaten. —*n-* **pre′di·ges′tion**.

pre·di·lec·tion (prĕd′ə lĕk′shən, prēd′ə-) *n-* preference; partiality: *a predilection for rich food*.

pre·dis·pose (prē′dĭ spōz′) *vt-* [**pre·dis·pos·ed, pre·dis·pos·ing**] 1 to make susceptible, liable, or subject: *Poor nourishment predisposes people to illness*. 2 to incline beforehand; influence: *His good manners predisposed me to like him*.

pre·dis·po·si·tion (prē′dĭs′pə zĭsh′ən) *n-* inclination or tendency toward a person or thing, which is prior to knowledge or personal contact or experience.

pre·dom·i·nant (prĭ dŏm′ə nənt) *adj-* greater in strength, power, number, amount, etc.; prevailing: *a predominant influence*; *a predominant color*. —*n-* **pre·dom′i·nance**. *adv-* **pre·dom′i·nant·ly**.

pre·dom·i·nate (prĭ dŏm′ə nāt′) *vi-* [**pre·dom·i·nat·ed, pre·dom·i·nat·ing**] 1 to be greater in numbers, power, influence, etc.: *Roses predominate in our garden*. 2 to exert control; prevail: *He predominated over his weaker comrades*. —*n-* **pre·dom′i·na′tion**.

pre·em·i·nent or **pre·em·i·nent** (prē ĕm′ə nənt) *adj-* outstanding or distinguished among others: *a preeminent statesman*. —*n-* **pre·em′i·nence** or **pre·em′i·nence**. *adv-* **pre·em′i·nently** or **pre·em′i·nent·ly**.

pre·empt or **pre·empt** (prē ĕmpt′) *vt-* 1 to take possession of before others can: *to pre-empt a parking space*. 2 to establish the first claim to (public land). —*n-* **pre·emp′tion** or **pre·emp′tion**.

preen (prēn) *vt-* 1 to clean and smooth (feathers) with the beak, as a bird does. 2 to dress or adorn (oneself) with care. 3 to express pride or satisfaction in (oneself): *He preens himself on his perfect spelling*. *vi-* to fuss or take pains over one's appearance; primp: *to preen before the mirror*.

pre·ex·is·tent or **pre·ex·is·tent** (prē′ĭg zĭs′tənt) *adj-* 1 existing before something else: *a pre-existent condition*. 2 having existence before the present life. —*n-* **pre′ex·is′tence** or **pre′ex·is′tence**.

pref. 1 preface. 2 prefix. 3 preferred.

pre·fab (prē′făb′) *n-* prefabricated thing, especially a house.

pre·fab·ri·cate (prē′făb′rə kāt′) *vt-* [**pre·fab·ri·cat·ed, pre·fab·ri·cat·ing**] 1 to construct or produce standardized parts of (a house, furniture, etc.) at a factory, so that only the assembling of the units is necessary where they are used. 2 to produce or make up in advance: *to prefabricate an excuse*. —*n-* **pre′fab′ri·ca′tion**.

preg·nan·cy (prĕg′nən sē) *n-* [*pl.* **preg·nan·cies**] 1 condition of a female carrying unborn young. 2 significance; weightiness: *the* pregnancy *of his remarks.*

preg·nant (prĕg′nənt) *adj-* 1 of a woman or a female animal, carrying unborn young. 2 full of significance or importance: *a* pregnant *statement.* 3 inventive; fruitful; fertile: *his* pregnant *imagination.*

pre·heat (prē′ hēt′) *vt-* to heat in advance.

pre·hen·sile (prē hĕn′səl, -sīl′) *adj-* adapted for grasping or seizing things: *A monkey has a* prehensile *tail.*

pre·his·tor·ic (prē′ hĭs tôr′ ĭk) *adj-* of or relating to the time before the existence of written records: *Dinosaurs were* prehistoric *animals.* Also **pre′his·tor′i·cal.** —*adv-* **pre′his·tor′i·cal·ly.**

pre·judge (prē′ jŭj′) *vt-* [**pre·judged, pre·judg·ing**] to judge in advance or without waiting to learn all the facts of a case. —*n-* **pre′ judg′ment** or **pre′ judge′ment.**

prej·u·dice (prĕj′ə dəs) *n-* 1 strong feeling for or against something, formed without any knowledge or logical reason; especially, a general antagonism toward members of other races, religions, etc. 2 injury or harm resulting from hasty or unfair judgment: *to judge a case without* prejudice *to the accused. vt-* [**pre·ju·diced, prej·u·dic·ing**] 1 to influence or fill with a strong feeling for or against someone or something. 2 to harm by an opinion or act: *to* prejudice *someone's reputation.*

prej·u·di·cial (prĕj′ə dĭsh′əl) *adj-* tending to cause disfavor; injurious; damaging: *His bad record was* prejudicial. —*adv-* **prej′u·di′cial·ly.**

prel·ate (prĕl′ə sē) *n-* [*pl.* **prel·a·cies**] 1 the position of a clergyman of high rank, such as a bishop. 2 prelates considered as a group. 3 church government by the higher orders of the clergy.

prel·ate (prĕl′ət) *n-* clergyman of high rank, such as a bishop or an archbishop.

pre·lim·i·nar·y (prĭ lĭm′ə nĕr′ ē) *adj-* coming before or preparing for an event or action: *the* preliminary *arrangements. n-* [*pl.* **pre·lim·i·nar·ies**] something that introduces or prepares for an event or action: *a* preliminary *to the talks.* —*adv-* **pre·lim′i·nar′i·ly.**

pre·lude (prĕl′yōōd, prē′lōōd′) *n-* 1 something that goes before or introduces a larger or more significant thing: *The thunder was a* prelude *to the storm.* 2 piece of music that introduces a larger work or is performed before a church service. *vt-* [**pre·lud·ed, pre·lud·ing**] to serve as an introduction to; precede.

pre·ma·ture (prē′mə chŏŏr′, -tyŏŏr′, -tŏŏr′) *adj-* happening or coming before the usual time; too early; untimely: *a* premature *arrival.* —*adv-* **pre′ma·ture′ly.**

pre·med (prē′mĕd′) *Informal adj-* premedical. *n-* a premedical student.

pre·med·i·cal (prē′mĕd′ĭ kəl) *adj-* preparing for studies leading to a medical degree: *a* premedical *student.*

pre·med·i·tate (prĭ mĕd′ə tāt′) *vt-* [**pre·med·i·tat·ed, pre·med·i·tat·ing**] to think over and plan beforehand: *to* premeditate *a crime.* —*n-* **pre·med′i·ta′tion.**

pre·mier (prĕm′yər, prĭ mêr′, prēm′ē ər) *adj-* principal; chief; first: *of* premier *importance. n-* prime minister; chief minister of government.

pre·mière (prĭ myêr′, -mêr′) *n-* first presentation of a movie, play, opera, etc.

prem·ise (prĕm′əs) *n-* 1 statement accepted as true, from which a conclusion is to be drawn; especially, in logic, one of the first two statements of a syllogism. 2 **premises** (1) property, such as land or a house, especially when mentioned in a legal document. (2) facts previously stated, especially in a legal document. *vt-* [**pre·mised, pre·mis·ing**] to state beforehand as an explanation or as a basis from which to proceed to a conclusion.

pre·pos·sess·ing (prē′ pə zĕs′ ĭng) *adj-* making a good impression; pleasing: *his* prepossessing *manner.*

pre·pos·ses·sion (prē′ pə zĕsh′ ən) *n-* 1 opinion formed in advance of actual knowledge. 2 preoccupation.

pre·pos·ter·ous (prĭ pŏs′ tər əs) *adj-* contrary to what is reasonable; very foolish: *a* preposterous *notion.* —*adv-* **pre·pos′ter·ous·ly.** *n-* **pre·pos′ter·ous·ness.**

prep school *n-* preparatory school.

present participle See *participle.*

present perfect tense *Grammar n-* verb tense formed with the auxiliary verb "have" or "has," and indicating an action or condition that began at an unstated time in the past and in some cases is still continuing. Examples: *I have waited an hour. He has taken my notebook. It has just begun to rain. I have gone there many times.* Also **present perfect.**

present tense *Grammar n-* verb tense indicating an action or condition now going on or occurring regularly. Examples: *I feel uncomfortable. He walks three miles to school every day.*

pres·er·va·tion (prĕz′ ər vā′ shən) *n-* 1 a rescuing or keeping safe from death, injury, or decay: *the* preservation *of lives in an epidemic; the* preservation *of a forest.* 2 a being preserved: *He owes his* preservation *to luck.* 3 freedom from decay or other injury; soundness: *That old house is in an excellent state of* preservation.

pre·serv·a·tive (prĭ zûr′ və tĭv′) *n-* substance which tends to prevent deterioration or decay in foods, building materials, etc. *adj-:* *a* preservative *effect.*

pre·serve (prĭ zûrv′) *vt-* [**pre·served, pre·serv·ing**] 1 to keep from injury or harm; save: *Heaven* preserve *us!* 2 to maintain; keep up: *He* preserves *a youthful appearance.* 3 to keep from spoiling or decay by canning, pickling, or some other process: *to* preserve *peaches; to* preserve *laboratory specimens. n-* 1 tract of land where animals, trees, etc., are protected. 2 (usually **preserves**) fruit that has been cooked with sugar and stored in sealed containers. —*n-* **pre·serv′ er.**

pre·set (prē′ sĕt′) *vt-* [**pre·set, pre·set·ting**] to set in advance: *He* preset *the bomb to explode at 3:00 A.M.*

pre·side (prĭ zīd′) *vi-* [**pre·sid·ed, pre·sid·ing**] 1 to act as chairman at a meeting. 2 to have direction or control (over): *to* preside *over the affairs of a house.* 3 to have an important or featured position, function, etc.: *Father* presided *at the head of the table.*

pres·i·den·cy (prĕz′ə dən sē, -dĕn′sē) *n-* [*pl.* **pres·i·den·cies**] 1 office of president. 2 length of time a president holds office.

pres·i·dent (prĕz′ə dənt, -dĕnt′) *n-* 1 the highest officer of a company, bank, college, club, etc. 2 (often **President**) the highest executive officer of a modern republic.

pres·i·dent-e·lect (prĕz′ ə dənt ē′ lĕkt′, prĕz′ ə dĕnt′-) *n-* person who has been elected to be president, but who has not yet taken office.

pres·i·den·tial (prĕz′ ə dĕn′ shəl) *adj-* of or having to do with a president or his work: *his* presidential *duties.*

pre·sid·i·um (prĭ sĭd′ ē əm, prĭ zĭd′-) *n-* 1 in Communist countries, any permanent executive committee selected to act for a larger body. 2 **Presidium** formerly, the policy-making committee of the Communist Party of the U.S.S.R., headed by the Party secretary.

¹**press** (prĕs) *vt-* 1 to thrust; push against: *to* press *a button.* 2 to squeeze; crush: *The meat packer pressed the ham into tin cans.* 3 to smooth; iron: *to* press *a shirt.*

press agent *n-* person hired to obtain publicity for a client in newspapers and other publications.

press box *n-* group of seats reserved for reporters.

press conference *n-* scheduled interview given to news reporters by a public figure.

press·ing (prĕs′ ĭng) *adj-* 1 needing immediate attention; urgent: *a* pressing *need.* 2 demanding; insistent: *his* pressing *requests for money.* —*adv-* **press′ ing·ly.**

press·man (prĕs′ mən) *n-* [*pl.* **press·men**] 1 person who operates a press, especially a printing press. 2 *Brit.* newspaper reporter.

press release *n-* information, usually in written form, given out for publication in a newspaper.

press·room (prĕs′ rōōm′) *n-* in a printing plant, the room containing the printing presses.

pres·sure (prĕsh′ ər) *n-* 1 a pressing force or weight: *the* pressure *of a clamp; the* pressure *of a roller on the road.*

pres·ti·dig·i·ta·tion (prĕs′ tə dĭj′ ə tā′ shən) *n-* the skill or actions of a juggler, magician, etc.; sleight of hand. —*n-* **pres′ ti·dig′i·ta′ tor:** *the* prestidigitator's *tricks.*

pres·tige (prĕs tēzh′, tēj′) *n-* influence or reputation gained by achievement, position, etc.: *The old scientist enjoyed great* prestige.

pres·to (prĕs′ tō) *adv-* 1 suddenly; in a trice: *The magician waved his hand, and* presto, *the coin vanished!* 2 *Music* very rapidly. *adj- Music* very rapid: *a presto passage. n-* [*pl.* **pres·tos**] *Music* piece, passage, etc., to be performed very rapidly.

pre·sum·a·ble (prĭ zōō′ ma bəl, prĭ zyōō′-) *adj-* such as may be expected or taken for granted; probable: *a presumable outcome.* —*adv-* **pre·sum′ a·bly.**

pre·sume (prĭ zōōm′, -zyōōm′) *vt-* [**pre·sumed, pre·sum·ing**] 1 to take for granted, especially without proof; suppose; assume: *Don't presume that he is guilty until he is proven so.* 2 to venture boldly, especially against someone having authority, superior knowledge, etc.; dare: *The young lawyer presumed to tell the judge he was wrong. vi-* to act with improper familiarity or unwarranted boldness; take liberties.

presume on (or **upon**) to make selfish use of; take advantage of: *to presume on a friend's hospitality.*

pre·sum·ed·ly (prĭ zōō′ mad lē, prĭ zyōō′-) *adv-* supposedly: *He is presumedly innocent of the crime.*

pre·sum·ing (prĭ zōō′ mĭng, prĭ zyōō′-) *adj-* unwarrantedly bold or self-assured; presumptuous.

pre·sump·tion (prĭ zŭmp′ shən) *n-* 1 a belief taken for granted, especially when based on something not fully proved; assumption; supposition: *a presumption of guilt, based on circumstantial evidence.* 2 unseemly self-assurance or boldness; effrontery; arrogance: *She had the presumption to ask for favors after insulting me.*

pre·sump·tive (prĭ zŭmp′ tĭv) *adj-* 1 affording reasonable grounds for belief: *the presumptive evidence.* 2 based on presumption or likelihood: *the heir presumptive.* —*adv-* **pre·sump′ tive·ly.**

►Should not be confused with PRESUMPTUOUS.

pre·sump·tu·ous (prĭ zŭmp′ chōō əs) *adj-* unwarrantedly bold or self-assured; impertinent: *a presumptuous question; presumptuous behavior.* —*adv-* **pre·sump′ tu·ous·ly.** *n-* **pre·sump′ tu·ous·ness.**

►Should not be confused with PRESUMPTIVE.

pre·sup·pose (prē′ sə pōz′) *vt-* [**pre·sup·posed, pre·sup·pos·ing**] 1 to take for granted in advance; assume beforehand. 2 to require as a foregoing condition: *Our plans* presuppose *our having the same vacation.*

pre·sup·po·si·tion (prē′ sŭp′ ə zĭsh′ ən) *n-* 1 the forming of a belief in advance of actual knowledge. 2 a belief so formed.

pre·tend (prĭ tĕnd′) *vt-* 1 to make believe: *The children pretended they were grownups.* 2 to put on an act or false show of; feign: *The acrobat pretended to lose his balance. He pretends friendship. She pretended illness.* 3 to claim falsely or without basis: *He pretends to know all the facts. vi-* 1 to put forward a claim: *to pretend to the throne.* 2 to play at make-believe.

pre·tend·ed (prĭ tĕn′ dəd) *adj-* not sincere or genuine; feigned; false: *his pretended friendship; pretended tears.* —*adv-* **pre·tend′ ed·ly.**

pre·tend·er (prĭ tĕn′ dər) *n-* 1 person who puts forward a claim to something, especially a royal title, right, etc. 2 person who pretends or feigns.

pre·tense (prĭ tĕns′, prē′ tĕns′) *n-* 1 a false appearance or action made to deceive: *a pretense of innocence.* 2 false reason; excuse; pretext: *to use any pretense to avoid work.* 3 false show or display; sham; affectation: *A sincere person is free from pretense.* 4 something imagined or pretended: *His story is all pretense.* Also **pretence.**

pre·ten·sion (prĭ tĕn′ shən) *n-* 1 a claim made on either a true or a false basis: *his pretension to a royal title.*

priest (prēst) *n-* man ordained to perform religious rites; clergyman. —*n- fem.* **priest′ ess.**

priest·hood (prēst′ hŏŏd′) *n-* 1 the office or duties of a priest. 2 priests collectively.

priest·ly (prēst′ lē) *adj-* of, like, or befitting a priest: *to carry out priestly duties.* —*n-* **priest′ li·ness.**

prig (prĭg) *n-* smug, self-righteous person who is highly critical of the morals of others; narrow-minded prude.

prig·gish (prĭg′ ĭsh) *adj-* of or like a prig; smug; censorious. —*adv-* **prig′ gish·ly.** *n-* **prig′ gish·ness.**

prim (prĭm) *adj-* [**prim·mer, prim·mest**] very proper and stiff in appearance and conduct; very neat or precise:

prime factor *Mathematics n-* factor having only itself and 1 as factors; factor that is a prime number.

prime meridian *n-* meridian designated as 0° longitude, in reference to which all other longitude is numbered; especially, the meridian passing through Greenwich, England. For picture, see *longitude.*

prime minister *n-* head of an elected government in some countries; chief minister of state; premier.

prime mover *n-* 1 original or principal force in any activity or process: *Mr. Allen was the prime mover in this campaign.* 2 engine or other machine that provides basic power for a factory, process, train of vehicles, etc.

prime number *n-* a natural number that can be divided only by 1 or itself with a zero remainder.

prim·er (prĭm′ ər) *n-* 1 book used in giving the first lessons in reading. 2 the first instruction book in any subject: *a primer in chemistry.* [from a Medieval Latin use of Latin **primārius,** "first in rank or time."]

prim·er (prī′ mər) *n-* 1 small amount of explosive in a cartridge, bomb, etc., used to set off the main charge; detonator. 2 any of various coatings used on wood, steel, plaster, etc., to form a base for the final coat or coats of paint. [from ²**prime.**]

pri·me·val (prī mē′ vəl) *adj-* belonging to the earliest times: *the primeval forests.* —*adv-* **pri·me′ val·ly.**

prim·ing (prī′ mĭng) *n-* 1 primer of an explosive charge. 2 paint or size, applied to a surface before painting.

prim·i·tive (prĭm′ ə tĭv) *adj-* 1 original; earliest; of the earliest times: *many relics of* primitive man. 2 simple and crude, as in early times: *primitive straw huts.* —*adv-* **prim′ i·tive·ly.** *n-* **prim′ i·tive·ness.**

pri·mo·gen·i·ture (prī′ mō jĕn′ ə chər) *n-* 1 the law or custom by which the eldest child, especially the eldest son, inherits all his father's property or titles; also, the right of such inheritance. 2 the condition of being the first-born child in a family.

pri·mor·di·al (prī môr′ dē əl, -môr′ dē əl) *adj-* of the earliest times; original; primeval: *the primordial matter of our solar system.* —*adv-* **pri·mor′ di·al·ly.**

primp (prĭmp) *vt-* to arrange or adorn oneself with great attention to detail and often in a vain manner; prink: *Meg primped for an hour. vt-: Meg was primping her hair.*

prim·rose (prĭm′ rōz′) *n-* 1 any of several wild or cultivated plants. Most American kinds spring from a rosette of leaves with a tall flower stalk, and bloom in summer or fall. 2 the blossom of this plant, usually yellow. 3 pale-yellow color. *adj-: a primrose dress.*

Evening primrose

primrose path *n-* the life or way of pleasure, especially the pleasures of the senses.

Pri·mus stove (prī′ məs) *n-* trademark name for a type of stove, especially a portable, kerosene-burning model, used by campers and explorers. Also **primus stove.**

prince consort *n-* husband of a reigning queen.

prince·ly (prĭns′ lē) *adj-* 1 worthy of a prince; generous; lavish: *a princely gift.* 2 of or related to a prince; royal; noble: *his princely powers.* —*n-* **prince′ li·ness.**

Prince of Peace *n-* Jesus Christ.

Prince of Wales *n-* title given to the oldest male heir to the British throne.

prin·cess (prĭn′ səs, -sĕs′) *n-* 1 in Great Britain, the daughter of a reigning monarch, or of a monarch's son. 2 wife or widow of a prince. 3 female member of a royal family.

princess royal *n-* eldest daughter of a reigning monarch.

prin·ci·pal (prĭn′ sə pəl) *adj-* main; chief; leading; most important: *our principal concern; the principal cause. n-* 1 the chief person; leader; head, especially of a school. 2 person who takes a leading part in some action: *Betty and Bob are* principals *in the play.* 3 sum of money used to earn income or interest. 4 original amount of a loan; also, the amount not yet paid. *Hom-principle.* —*adv-* **prin′ ci·pal·ly.**

prob·i·ty (prō′ bə tē) *n-* honesty and integrity; uprightness: *a man of unquestioned probity.*

prob·lem (prŏb′ ləm) *n-* 1 difficult question, issue, set of circumstances, etc., that requires an answer or solution: *the problems of our foreign policy; the problem of housing.* 2 something that causes difficulty or perplexity: *Otto is a problem to me. What's your problem?* 3 *Mathematics* statement containing or implying a question that can be answered by mathematical means: *He assigned six algebra problems. as modifier: a problem child.*

prob·le·mat·ic (prŏb′ lə măt′ ĭk) or **prob·le·mat·i·cal** (-ĭ′ kəl) *adj-* like a problem; questionable; uncertain. —*adv-* **prob′ le·mat′ i·cal·ly.**

pro·bos·cis (prə bŏs′ əs) *n-* 1 trunk of an elephant. 2 insect mouth parts adapted for piercing and sucking or just sucking, such as those of the butterfly.

pro·caine (prō′ kān′) *n-* chemical name of Novocain.

pro·ce·dure (prə sē′ jər, prō-) *n-* 1 way or system of proceeding to get something done; method: *What procedure should I follow in applying for a driver's license?* 2 Informal process. —*adj-* **pro·ce′ dur·al:** *a procedural change. adv-* **pro·ce′ dur·al·ly.**

pro·ceed (prə sēd′) *vi-* 1 to go on or forward, especially after stopping: *to proceed on a journey.*
proceed from to result or issue from.

pro·ceed·ing (prə sē′ dĭng) *n-* 1 action or course of action: *a strange proceeding.* 2 **proceedings** (1) formal actions of a court, legislature, society, etc. (2) record of such actions; minutes.

pro·ceeds (prō′ sēdz′) *n- pl.* money received from a business transaction, especially from selling something.

proc·ess (prŏs′ ĕs, -əs, prō′ sĕs′) *n-* 1 action or series of actions that bring about a particular result or product: *Training to become a doctor is a lengthy process. The company tried out a new process for making steel.* 2 in law, (1) the proceedings in a case; action or suit. (2) summons to appear in court. 3 *Biology* (1) projecting or outgrowing part of an organism or any of its structures: *a bony process.* (2) an axon or dendrite. *vt-* 1 to make or treat by a special method: *to process cheese.* 2 to examine, classify, or attend to, especially by some routine procedure: *to process recruits; process a loan.*
in process under way; being done or carried out.

pro·ces·sion (prə sĕsh′ ən) *n-* 1 formal parade; also, the persons taking part in it: *A military procession escorted the President.* 2 movement along a particular course; progression: *the procession of the choir.*

pro·ces·sion·al (prə sĕsh′ ən əl) *n-* music that accompanies a procession, especially that of a choir entering church. *as modifier: a processional hymn.*

pro·claim (prō klām′) *vt-* 1 to announce publicly or officially; declare: *to proclaim a holiday; to proclaim one's ideas to anyone who will listen.* 2 to show plainly; reveal: *His kind acts proclaimed a generous heart.*

proc·la·ma·tion (prŏk′ lə mā′ shən) *n-* 1 formal or public announcement: *The mayor read the proclamation.* 2 act of proclaiming: *the proclamation of a holiday.*

pro·cliv·i·ty (prō klĭv′ ə tē) *n-* [*pl.* **pro·cliv·i·ties**] tendency or inclination (to or toward); weakness (for): *a proclivity to gossip; a proclivity for fine wines.*

pro·con·sul (prō′ kŏn′ səl) *n-* 1 in ancient Rome, the governor and military commander of a province. 2 chief administrator of a colony or occupied area.

pro·fan·i·ty (prō făn′ ə tē, prə-) *n-* [*pl.* **pro·fan·i·ties**] use of irreverent or vulgar speech; also, an irreverent or vulgar remark: *He uttered a stream of profanities.*

pro·fess (prə fĕs′) *vt-* 1 to declare openly and freely; affirm: *to profess a dislike for playing cards.* 2 to follow or practice as a religion: *to profess Buddhism.* 3 to claim; pretend to: *He professes a knowledge of music.*

pro·fess·ed·ly (prə fĕs′ əd lē) *adv-* 1 by open declaration; avowedly: *He is professedly in disagreement.* 2 allegedly; ostensibly: *It is professedly his own idea.*

pro·fes·sion (prə fĕsh′ ən) *n-* 1 occupation, such as medicine or law, that requires special education. 2 the group of persons engaged in such an occupation: *the medical profession.* 3 open and free declaration: *a profession of faith.*

pris·on (prĭz′ ən) *n-* 1 place where convicted criminals serve their sentences of confinement; penitentiary. 2 any place where a person is held against his will: *His office was a prison to him on fine spring days.*

pris·on·er (prĭz′ ə nər) *n-* 1 person who is held in prison. 2 one who is under arrest, or held for a crime: *The prisoner pleaded guilty to a charge of reckless driving.* 3 (also **prisoner of war**) soldier captured by the enemy. 4 any person or thing held captive: *He kept his dog a prisoner in his garage.*

pris·sy (prĭs′ ē) *Informal adj-* [**pris·si·er, pris·si·est**] overly precise or fussy about matters of dress, conduct, etc.; prim; finicky. —*adv-* **pris′ si·ly.** *n-* **pris′ si·ness.**

pris·tine (prĭs′ tēn′) *adj-* 1 pure and unspoiled; uncorrupted: *the pristine beauty of a sunset.* 2 of earliest times; original: *the pristine state of society.*

prith·ee (prĭth′ ē) *Archaic interj-* I pray thee; please.

pri·va·cy (prī′ və sē) *n-* [*pl.* **pri·va·cies**] 1 physical separateness from other people; seclusion: *Hard study usually requires privacy.* 2 secrecy: *Jim and his friends studied the treasure map in privacy.* 3 the right to freedom from interference by others: *the privacy of citizens.*

pri·vate (prī′ vət) *adj-* 1 belonging to or intended for a particular person or group; not public or governmental: *a private lake; a private performance;* private *school.* 2 personal; individual: *I have private reasons for wanting to stay home.* 3 not official: *in private life; a private citizen.* 4 secret; confidential: *We made private arrangements for the surprise party. n-* 1 in the Army, an enlisted man ranking next below a private first class and next above a recruit. 2 in the Marine Corps, an enlisted man of the lowest rank. —*adv-* **pri′ vate·ly.** *n-* **pri′ vate·ness.**
in private secretly: *The thieves met in private.*

private detective *n-* person employed by a private citizen or group to investigate crimes, gather evidence, or maintain law and order.

pri·va·teer (prī′ və tēr′) *n-* 1 formerly, a privately owned and operated ship given permission by a government to attack and capture enemy ships. 2 commander or one of the crew members of such a ship. *vi-: During the War of 1812, Decatur privateered for the United States.*

private first class *n-* 1 in the Army, an enlisted man who ranks next below a corporal and next above a private. 2 in the Marine Corps, an enlisted man who ranks next below a lance corporal and next above a private.

private school *n-* school that is owned and operated by a private citizen or group.

pri·va·tion (prī vā′ shən) *n-* hardship and suffering due to a lack of the necessities of life, especially food, clothing, and shelter.

priv·et (prĭv′ ət) *n-* shrub of the olive family, having dark leaves and small white flowers, and used for hedges.

priv·i·lege (prĭv′ ə lĭj) *n-* special right or advantage granted to or enjoyed by a person or group of persons: *the privilege of a college education; the privileges that come with rank and wealth.* —*adj-* **priv′ i·leged:** *I am privileged to know him. A few privileged visitors met him.*

priv·i·ly (prĭv′ ə lē) *Archaic adv-* privately; secretly.

priv·y (prĭv′ ē) *adj- Archaic* for private, not public, use; personal. *n-* [*pl.* **priv·ies**] enclosed outdoor toilet.
privy to secretly sharing in the knowledge of: *There were only six privy to the conspiracy.*

prize (prīz) *n-* 1 reward offered or won in a contest; award: *to win first prize.* 2 something very valuable or desirable: *This puppy is the prize of the litter. as modifier: the prize painting in the show; a prize horse. vt-* [**prized, priz·ing**] to value highly; think highly of.

pro·fes·sion·al (prə fĕsh′ ən əl) *adj-* 1 having to do with a profession or career: *the professional duties of a lawyer.* 2 for pay; not amateur or temporary. *n-* 1 person who uses his skill in a sport to make money: *She took her ski lessons from a professional.* 2 *Informal* person who is highly skilled and experienced in anything. —*adv-* **pro·fes′ sion·al·ly.**

pro·fes·sor (prə fĕs′ ər) *n-* in a college or university, a teacher of the highest rank. This title is also used informally when referring to two lower academic ranks,

prof·it (prŏf'ət) *n-* 1 amount gained from a sale or business after deducting all costs or expenses; income minus expenditures. 2 benefit; advantage: *Having such an excellent teacher is to your profit.* *vt-* to be of service to; improve; benefit: *It would profit you to read better books.* *vi-*: *He profited greatly from his travels abroad.* Hom- prophet. **—adj-** prof'it·less.

prof·it·a·ble (prŏf'ĭt ə bəl) *adj-* 1 yielding financial gain or profit: *a profitable business.* 2 rewarding; beneficial; useful: *It is profitable to read good books.* **—n-** prof'it·a·ble·ness. **adv-** prof'it·a·bly.

prof·it·eer (prŏf'ə tēr') *n-* person who makes or seeks to make excessive profit during a war or other time of shortage. *vi-*: *He profiteered in coffee.*

prof·li·gate (prŏf'lə gət) *adj-* 1 wholly given up to vice; immoral; dissolute. 2 recklessly extravagant; wasteful. *n-* immoral or extravagant person. **—n-** prof'li·ga·cy: *The minister scolded him for the profligacy of his life.* *adv-* prof'li·gate·ly.

pro·found (prə found') *adj-* 1 having deep meaning or feeling; penetrating: *the profound sayings of the Bible; a* profound *scholar.* 2 complete; thorough; very great: *a* profound *silence;* profound *knowledge of science;* profound *sorrow.* 3 situated or carried very far down: *a* profound *bow.* **—adv-** pro·found'ly. *n-* pro·found'ness.

pro·fun·di·ty (prə fŭn'də tē) *n-* [*pl.* pro·fun·di·ties] 1 great depth of meaning or feeling: *the profundity of the doctor's theory.* 2 idea, theory, or subject that is deep and complex: *the profundities of philosophy.*

pro·fuse (prə fyōōs') *adj-* 1 plentiful; abundant: *a* profuse *display of flowers.* 2 generous; extravagant; lavish: *a* profuse *apology;* profuse *kindness.* **—adv-** pro·fuse'ly. *n-* pro·fuse'ness.

pro·fu·sion (prə fyōō'zhən) *n-* 1 generous quantity or amount; abundance: *a* profusion *of flowers.* 2 lavishness; extravagance: *She spent money in great* profusion.

pro·gen·i·tor (prə jĕn'ə tər) *n-* 1 direct ancestor; forefather. 2 originator: *Pasteur is one of the progenitors of modern germ theory.*

prog·e·ny (prŏj'ə nē) *n-* [*pl.* prog·e·nies] children; descendants; offspring.

prog·no·sis (prŏg nō'səs) *n-* 1 *Medicine* the probable course and outcome of a disease. 2 any prediction or forecast of events: *a weather prognosis.*

prog·nos·tic (prŏg nŏs'tĭk) *adj-* of or related to a prognosis; foretelling; predictive: *a prognostic report.* *n-* 1 omen, token, or other sign of some future happening. 2 prediction or forecast; prophecy.

prog·nos·ti·cate (prŏg nŏs'tə kāt') *vt-* [prog·nos·ti·cat·ed, prog·nos·ti·cat·ing] 1 to foretell; predict; forecast: *The fortuneteller prognosticated doom.* 2 to indicate in advance; foreshadow; presage: *The dark clouds prognosticate a storm.* **—n-** prog·nos'ti·ca'tion. *n-* prog·nos'ti·ca'tor: *a prognosticator of doom.*

pro·gram (prō'grăm') *n-* 1 list of the features and participants of an entertainment or ceremony: *a theater program; a graduation program.* 2 the entertainment or ceremony itself. 3 radio or television broadcast.

pro·lif·er·ate (prə lĭf'ə rāt') *vi-* [pro·lif·er·at·ed, pro·lif·er·at·ing] to grow or reproduce rapidly; multiply in quick succession: *Cells proliferate during cancer. Rumors proliferated within the mob.* *vt-*: *to proliferate buds; to proliferate new ideas.* **—n-** pro·lif'er·a'tion.

pro·lif·ic (prə lĭf'ĭk) *adj-* producing much; fertile: *a* prolific *author; a* prolific *animal.* **—adv-** pro·lif'i·cal·ly.

pro·lix (prō lĭks') *adj-* tediously wordy; verbose; long-winded: *a* prolix *speech.* **—n-** pro·lix'i·ty.

pro·logue or **pro·log** (prō'lŏg', -lŏg') *n-* 1 introduction to a literary work or dramatic performance; prelude. 2 any act or event that serves as an introduction or prelude to something else: *a prologue to great events.*

pro·long (prə lông') *vt-* to lengthen, especially the time of; draw out; extend: *to prolong a visit.*

pro·lon·ga·tion (prō'lông'gā'shən) *n-* 1 act of prolonging; extension: *the prolongation of one's life.* 2 added part that makes something longer: *the prolongations of a table.*

prom (prŏm) *Informal n-* formal school dance.

pro·noun (prō'noun') *n-* any of a class of words that regularly replace nouns or noun phrases. *Abbr.* pron or pron. See also *demonstrative, indefinite pronoun, interrogative pronoun, personal pronoun, possessive pronoun, reciprocal pronoun, reflexive pronoun, relative.*

pro·nounce (prə nouns') *vt-* [pro·nounced, pro·nounc·ing] 1 to utter or make the sounds of: *to pronounce a name correctly.* 2 to declare or announce, especially formally or with authority: *The minister pronounced them man and wife.* *vi-* 1 to give a decision or judgment; make a pronouncement: *to pronounce on a vital issue.* 2 to utter the sounds of speech; enunciate: *You should pronounce carefully.* **—adj-** pro·nounce'a·ble.

pro·nounced (prə nounst') *adj-* marked; decided: *a* pronounced *change of mood.* **—adv-** pro·nounc'ed·ly.

pro·nounce·ment (prə nouns'mənt) *n-* 1 official declaration; proclamation: *a pronouncement on government policy.* 2 formal statement, judgment, or opinion: *the pronouncements of hostile critics.*

pron·to (prŏn'tō) *Informal adv-* quickly; promptly. [from Spanish.]

pro·nun·ci·a·men·to (prō nŭn'sē ə mĕn'tō) *n-* [*pl.* pro·nun·ci·a·men·tos] official and public declaration.

pro·nun·ci·a·tion (prə nŭn'sē ā'shən) *n-* 1 act or manner of uttering the sounds that form words: *American pronunciation differs in several ways from British pronunciation.* 2 accepted or standard way of pronouncing a word: *"Rodeo" has two pronunciations.*

proof (prōōf) *n-* 1 a proving that something is true: *The burden of proof is on him.* 2 something by which another thing is shown to be true or correct: *Give me proof of your innocence.* 3 in photography, a trial print from a negative. 4 in printing, a trial impression taken from set type for correction: *page proofs.* 5 *Mathematics* (1) demonstration of the logical steps involved in establishing the truth or validity of an argument or statement. (2) process in which new truths are established by reasoning from already accepted principles, such as assumptions, postulates, or axioms.

proof *against* immune to: *Vaccination made him proof against smallpox.* to the proof to the test; on trial.

-proof *suffix* resistant to; safe from; protected against: *waterproof; bulletproof; fireproof.*

proof·read (prōōf' rēd') *vt-* [proof·read, proof·read·ing] to read and correct errors in (a printer's proof). **—n-** proof'read·er.

prop (prŏp) *vt-* [propped, prop·ping] (often followed by "up") 1 to hold up by placing something under or against: *They propped the roof with steel columns.* 2 to support; sustain: *We propped up his low spirits with a bit of good news.* *n-* support: *a prop for a roof.* [from Middle English* proppe, *perhaps from earlier Dutch* prop(p)e.]

prop (prŏp) *Informal n-* in the theater, a property. [shortened from (stage) property.]

prop (prŏp) *Informal n-* propeller.

prop·a·gan·da (prŏp'ə găn'də) *n-* statements, printed material, etc., designed to win the audience over to some official point of view; especially, such statements when they are based on lies and deceit. *as modifier: a* propaganda *expert;* propaganda *minister.*

prop·a·gan·dist (prŏp'ə găn'dĭst) *n-* person who spreads propaganda. *adj-: a* propagandist *campaign.*

prop·a·gan·dize (prŏp'ə găn'dīz') *vt-* [prop·a·gan·dized, prop·a·gan·diz·ing] to subject to propaganda: *to* propagandize *an aera.* *vi-* to spread propaganda: *Joe often propagandizes among the unemployed.*

prop·er (prŏp'ər) *adj-* 1 suitable; appropriate: *We wore the* proper *clothes for the sleigh ride and didn't feel the cold.* 2 naturally belonging or peculiar (to): *a climate proper to central Africa.* 3 in a narrow or exact sense: *The suburbs are not part of the city proper.* 4 measuring up to standards of good conduct or manners.

proper fraction *n-* See *fraction.*

prop·er·ly (prŏp'ər lē) *adv-* 1 appropriately; suitably: *to be properly dressed for skiing.* 2 justifiably; with reason: *quite properly afraid of fire.* 3 with accuracy; strictly: *Well,* properly *speaking, you were in the wrong.*

proper noun See *noun.*

pro·pin·qui·ty (prə pǐng′kwə tē) *n-* nearness in time, place, or blood relationship; proximity.

pro·pi·ti·ate (prə pǐsh′ē āt′) *vt-* [pro·pi·ti·at·ed, pro·pi·ti·at·ing] to win over (someone who is angry, opposed, etc.); conciliate. —*n-* **pro·pi′ti·a′tion.** *n-* **pro·pi′ti·a′tor:** *a propitiator of opposing factions.*

pro·pi·tious (prə pǐsh′əs) *adj-* 1 favorable; suitable or appropriate: *to have propitious weather; a propitious time to ask for a raise.* 2 favorably inclined; gracious. —*adv-* **pro·pi′tious·ly.** *n-* **pro·pi′tious·ness.**

pro·po·nent (prə pō′nənt) *n-* 1 person who supports or favors something specified; advocate: *a proponent of the immigration bill.* 2 person who proposes or propounds something: *the first proponent of a policy.*

pro·por·tion (prə pôr′shən) *n-* 1 number, size, degree, or amount of a thing or group as compared with another thing or group; ratio: *the proportion of men to women in a country; the proportion of sugar to flour in a cake.* 2 share; part: *a proportion of the profits.* 3 *Mathematics* a statement of equality between two ratios: *4/8 = 6/12 is a proportion.* 4 **proportions** (1) size; dimensions: *a desert of vast proportions.* (2) dimensions in relation to one another: *the harmonious proportions of a room. vt-* to put (one thing) in proper relation to another: *He proportions his rent to his salary.*

in proportion (to or with) in proper or pleasing relation: *This building is* in proportion with *its neighbor. These two rooms are* in proportion. **out of proportion (to or with)** not in proper or pleasing relation: *Her anger was* out of proportion to *the offense.*

pro·por·tion·al (prə pôr′shən əl) *adj-* 1 having or being in proper relation; proportionate: *All the parts are proportional.* 2 according to proportions: *a proportional assignment of duties.* 3 *Mathematics* of terms, varying such that corresponding values make a proportion. —*adv-* **pro·por′tion·al·ly.**

proportional representation *n-* method of election in which legislators are seated in very close proportion to the voting strength of their various parties or groups. The system makes possible the representation of relatively small parties and of many parties at once.

pro·por·tion·ate (prə pôr′shən ət) *adj-* having or being in proper relation; commensurate: *success proportionate to effort.* —*adv-* **pro·por′tion·ate·ly.**

pro·pos·al (prə pō′zəl) *n-* 1 a presenting or suggesting of a plan: *I was given the task of proposal.* 2 plan or scheme proposed: *a new proposal.* 3 offer of marriage.

pro·pose (prə pōz′) *vt-* [pro·posed, pro·pos·ing] 1 to offer for consideration or discussion; suggest: *to propose a plan.* 2 to suggest or present (someone's) name for office; nominate. 3 to intend; plan: *I propose to be the first. vi-* to make an offer of marriage.

prop·o·si·tion (prŏp′ə zǐsh′ən) *n-* 1 statement offered or taken for discussion, debate, etc.: *Let us examine the mayor's first proposition.* 2 plan; proposal: *His proposition was impractical.* 3 *Informal* matter; undertaking: *Blackmail is a dangerous proposition.* 4 *Mathematics* statement of a theorem to be demonstrated or of a problem to be solved. *vt- Slang* to make a proposal to, often of an improper nature.

pro·pound (prə pound′) *vt-* to offer for consideration, discussion, or debate; set forth (a question, problem, etc.). —*n-* **pro·pound′er.**

pro·pri·e·tar·y (prə prī′ə tĕr′ē) *adj-* 1 of, relating to, or appropriate to ownership or owners: *a proprietary interest; a proprietary attitude; proprietary rights.* 2 made and sold by exclusive legal right: *a proprietary drug. n-* [*pl.* **pro·pri·e·tar·ies**] 1 proprietor. 2 person or group to whom the English king granted a colony.

pro·pri·e·tor (prə prī′ə tər) *n-* person who has a legal title to property; owner: *the proprietor of a ranch.* —*n- fem.* **pro·pri′e·tress.**

pro·pri·e·tor·ship (prə prī′ə tər shǐp′) *n-* legal title to property; ownership.

pro·pri·e·ty (prə prī′ə tē) *n-* [*pl.* **pro·pri·e·ties**] 1 fitness; suitability; correctness: *We question the propriety of children's staying out alone after dark.* 2 **the proprieties** socially approved manners, conduct, etc., of society.

pro·te·an (prō′tē ən) *adj-* readily taking different shapes or forms: *an unstable and protean personality.*

pro·tect (prə tĕkt′) *vt-* 1 to keep safe; guard; defend against danger or injury: *to protect one's family; an overcoat to protect oneself against the cold.* 2 to foster or assist (an industry) by means of protective tariffs. —*adv-* **pro·tect′ing·ly.**

pro·tec·tion (prə tĕk′shən) *n-* 1 a protecting or being protected. 2 person or thing that protects: *New tires are a protection against blowouts.* 3 use of protective tariffs and other restrictions to protect an industry against foreign competition.

pro·tec·tion·ism (prə tĕk′shən ǐz′əm) *n-* economic doctrine that advocates protection of a country's industry by protective tariffs and other means. —*n-* **pro·tec′tion·ist.**

pro·tec·tive (prə tĕk′tǐv) *adj-* giving protection or shelter: *a protective coating over a drawing; a protective cover.* —*adv-* **pro·tec′tive·ly.** *n-* **pro·tec′tive·ness.**

protective coloring *n-* coloring that enables certain animals to blend into their environment or to seem very menacing, and thus protects them from other animals. Also **protective coloration.**

protective tariff *n-* tariff intended to protect a domestic industry from foreign competition rather than produce revenue; especially, a tax or duty placed on imported goods so that they cannot be sold more cheaply than domestic products.

pro·tec·tor (prə tĕk′tər) *n-* 1 guardian; defender: *He has chosen me as his protector.* 2 something that gives protection: *The umpire wears a chest protector.*

pro·tec·tor·ate (prə tĕk′tər ət) *n-* 1 weak country under the control or protection of a strong country. 2 relationship between two such countries.

pro·té·gé (prō′tə zhā′) *n-* person who is under the care and guidance of someone who is prominent. —*n- fem.* **pro′té·gée′.**

pro·te·in (prō′tēn′, -tē ǐn) *n-* any of a very large group of complex organic compounds consisting of amino acids bonded together in a chainlike molecule. Plants synthesize proteins directly from the basic chemicals during photosynthesis, but animals can build proteins only from amino acids derived from protein in foods. *as modifier: a protein food.* Also **pro·te·id** (prō′tē əd, prō′tēd′).

pro tem (prō′tĕm′) *adv-* for now but not permanently; temporarily: *He is president pro tem of the club.*

Prot·er·o·zo·ic (prō′tər ə zō′ǐk) *n-* era of geological time between the Paleozoic and Archeozoic in which the basic shape of the continents probably first developed. *adj-: a Proterozoic rock.*

¹**pro·test** (prō′tĕst′) *n-* 1 formal complaint or objection: *The President sent a protest to the Russian ambassador.* 2 objection; resistance: *The burglar went to jail without protest.*

under protest only after expressing objection.

²**pro·test** (prə tĕst′, prō-) *vi-* to express opposition or dissatisfaction: *We protested loudly when he shut us out. vt-* 1 to object to; express disapproval of: *We protested the extra homework.* 2 to assert or maintain strongly in the face of accusation or contradiction: *He protested his innocence.*

Prot·es·tant (prŏt′əs tənt) *n-* member of one of the branches of the Christian church that separated from the Roman Catholic Church during the Reformation. *adj-: a Protestant minister:* Protestant *beliefs.*

Prot·es·tan·tism (prŏt′əs tən tǐz′əm) *n-* beliefs, practices, etc., of Protestant Christians; also, Protestant churches collectively.

prot·es·ta·tion (prŏt′əs tā′shən, prō′təs-) *n-* a declaring or claiming: *the protestation of one's innocence.*

Pro·te·us (prō′tē əs) *n-* in Greek mythology, a sea god with prophetic powers who could change his shape.

pro·ti·um (prō′tē əm) *n-* ordinary hydrogen, the nucleus of which contains a single proton.

proto- *combining form* first in time; original; typical: *a* proto*zoan* (first animal); proto*plasm* (first or original life); proto*type.* [from Greek prōtó-, from protos meaning "first in time or rank."]

prud·ish (prōō′ dĭsh) *adj-* excessively proper in speech or behavior; priggish: *a prudish disapproval of certain books.* —*adv-* prud′ish·ly. *n-* prud′ish·ness.
►Should not be confused with PRUDENT.

prune (prōōn) *n-* 1 kind of plum that dries without spoiling. 2 dried plum. [from French, from Latin *prūnum* meaning "a plum," from Greek *prounon.*]

prune (prōōn) *vt-* [**pruned, prun·ing**] (considered intransitive when the direct object is implied but not expressed) 1 to cut branches, roots, etc., from (a plant) in order to improve it. 2 to cut away unnecessary parts from (anything) in order to improve its quality, appearance, shape, or force: *The author pruned his novel.* [from Old French *proignier,* from Late Latin *prōpāgināre,* "to propagate by using grafts," from *prōpāgo,* "a scion; graft."]

pru·ri·ent (prŏŏr′ ē ənt) *adj-* lewd in thought or desire; libidinous; lascivious; lustful. —*n-* pru′ri·ence. *adv-* pru′ri·ent·ly.

Prus·sian blue (prŭsh′ ən) *n-* any of several deep, vivid blue compounds of iron used as pigments.

prus·sic acid (prŭs′ ĭk) *n-* hydrocyanic acid.

pry (prī) *vi-* [**pried, pry·ing**] to look or inquire closely (into) something, especially in a sly manner: *to pry into other people's affairs.* [of unknown origin.] —*adv-* pry′ing·ly.

pry (prī) *vt-* [**pried, pry·ing**] 1 to raise or open (something) with or as if with a lever: *to pry the top off the jar.* 2 to move (someone or something) with great difficulty: *to pry him from his chair.* *n-* lever. [from 2*prize.*]

P.S. 1 postscript. 2 public school.

psalm (säm, sälm) *n-* sacred poem or song.

psalm·ist (sä′ mĭst, säl′-) *n-* 1 composer of sacred poems or songs. 2 the Psalmist David.

Psalms (sämz, sälmz) *n-* (takes singular verb) book in the Old Testament, containing 150 sacred songs. Also **Book of Psalms.**

Psal·ter (sòl′ tər) *n-* 1 Psalms. 2 selection or version of Psalms used in church services.

psal·ter·y (sòl′ tə rē) *n-* [*pl.* psal·ter·ies] stringed musical instrument resembling the zither.

pseu·do (sōō′ dō) *adj-* false; pretended; not real.

pseudo- *combining form* 1 false; pretended: *a pseudonym* (fictitious name). 2 closely resembling: *a pseudopod* (organic part resembling a foot). Also **pseud-** before vowels. [from Greek *pseudes* meaning "false."]

pseu·do·nym (sōō′ də nĭm′) *n-* fictitious name, especially a pen name; nom de plume.

pseu·do·pod (sōō′ dō pŏd′) or **pseu·do·po·di·um** (-pō′ dē əm) *n-* a temporary extension of the protoplasm of a living cell.

pshaw (shò) *interj-* expression showing contempt, scorn, or impatience.

p.s.i. or **psi** pounds per square inch.

psit·ta·co·sis (sĭt′ ə kō′ səs) *n-* an infectious virus disease of parrots, transmittable to man, in whom it causes a form of pneumonia; parrot fever.

pso·ri·a·sis (sə rī′ ə səs) *n-* a usually chronic, but not contagious, skin disease, in which scaly red patches form on the skin.

P.S.T. or **PST** Pacific Standard Time.

psy·che (sī′ kē) *n-* 1 human soul; mind; intelligence. 2 in psychoanalysis, the sum total of the attributes of the personality. 3 Psyche in classical mythology, a beautiful maiden, beloved by Cupid.

psy·chi·at·ric (sī′ kē ă′ trĭk) *adj-* having to do with psychiatry. —*adv-* psy′chi·at′ri·cal·ly.

psy·cho·a·nal·y·sis (sī′ kō ə nál′ ə səs) *n-* system of psychotherapy that treats mental and emotional disorders by revealing the repressed desires that persist in a patient's mind and affect his behavior, thought, etc.

psy·cho·an·a·lyst (sī′ kō ăn′ ə lĭst) *n-* person who practices psychoanalysis.

psy·cho·an·a·lyze (sī′ kō ăn′ ə līz′) *vt-* [**psy·cho·an·a·lyzed, psy·cho·an·a·lyz·ing**] to treat (someone) by psychoanalysis.

psy·cho·chem·i·cal (sī′ kō kĕm′ ĭ kəl) *n-* compound or drug, such as LSD, that acts directly on the mind and influences consciousness and behavior.

ptar·mi·gan (tär′ mĭ gən) *n-* any of several northern or alpine grouses that change their brown summer plumage to white in winter.

PT boat *n-* patrol torpedo boat, a small, high-speed vessel armed with torpedoes; mosquito boat.

pter·i·do·phyte (tə rĭd′ ə fīt′) *n-* any of many flowerless and seedless plants such as ferns or club mosses, formerly classified in a single phylum (**Peridophyta**).

Willow ptarmigan

pter·o·dac·tyl (tĕr′ ə dăk′ təl) *n-* extinct flying reptile having featherless wing membranes between the body, arm, and the greatly elongated fourth finger.

Ptol·e·ma·ic system (tŏl′ ə mā′ ĭk) *n-* theory named for the 2nd-century A.D. astronomer Ptolemy, but dating from long before his time, which held that the earth was the center of the universe around which the moon, planets, stars, etc., revolved.

Pterodactyl

pto·maine or **pto·main** (tō′ mān′) *n-* any of a group of chemicals, often poisonous, produced by the actions of certain bacteria on proteins.

pty·a·lin (tī′ ə lən) *n-* the enzyme in saliva that digests starch.

Pu symbol for plutonium.

pub (pŭb) *Brit. Informal n-* public house.

pu·ber·ty (pyōō′ bər tē) *n-* age, about fourteen for boys and twelve for girls, at which a person is physiologically capable of begetting or bearing a child.

pu·bis (pyōō′ bəs) *n-* [*pl.* pu·bes (-bēz′)] either of the bones that make up the forward arch of the pelvis. For picture, see *pelvis.* —*adj-* pu′bic.

pub·lic (pŭb′ lĭk) *adj-* 1 of, for, or having to do with the people as a whole: *in the* public *interest;* public *needs.* 2 open to everyone; not private: *a* public *library; a* public *pool.* 3 serving the people: *a* public *utility;* public *office.* 4 generally known: *He made his opinions* public. *n-* 1 group of persons having a certain interest, especially an admiration for a certain person: *the literary* public; *the young violinist's* public. 2 the public the people as a whole.

in public openly and visibly rather than privately.

public address system *n-* apparatus having one or more microphones, amplifiers, and loudspeakers, used to amplify sound in auditoriums or outdoors; PA.

pub·li·can (pŭb′ lĭ kən) *n-* 1 in England, person who keeps a public house. 2 in ancient Rome, and especially in the Bible, person who collected taxes in return for a part of what he collected.

pub·li·ca·tion (pŭb′ lə kā′ shən) *n-* 1 act or business of publishing. 2 printed and published work, such as a newspaper, magazine, book, etc. 3 a making known to the public: *This fact is not for* publication.

public defender *n-* lawyer appointed by a court to defend an accused person who cannot pay a legal fee.

public domain *n-* 1 government-owned land; land that is open to the public. 2 area of property rights not assigned to any person by copyright, patent, or other means, and hence open to anyone.

public enemy *n-* notorious criminal.

public house *Brit-* licensed saloon or tavern.

pub·li·cist (pŭb′ lə sĭst′) *n-* 1 person who writes or comments on international law or on public affairs. 2 press agent.

pug·mark (pŭg′ märk′) *n-* footprint of a wild animal.

pug·na·cious (pŭg nā′ shəs) *adj-* quick to fight; quarrelsome. —*adv-* pug·na′cious·ly. *n-* pug·na′cious·ness or pug·nac′i·ty (-năs′ ə tē).

pug nose *n-* turned-up nose, broad at the tip. —*adj-* pug′-nosed′: *a pug-nosed boy.*

pu·is·sance (pwĭs′ əns, pyōō′ ə səns) *n-* strength to do or achieve; power.

pu·is·sant (pwĭs′ ənt, pyōō′ ə sənt) *adj-* extremely powerful; mighty: *a puissant monarch.*

pul·pit (pool' pit) *n-* 1 in some churches, a small elevated balcony from which the priest or minister speaks. 2 the clergy as a group.

pulp·wood (pulp' wood') *n-* wood used for making paper.

pulp·y (pul' pe) *adj-* [pulp·i·er, pulp·i·est] consisting of or like a soft, moist mass of matter; soft; fleshy. —*n-* pulp' i·ness.

pul·que (pool' ka) *n-* Mexican fermented drink, made from the sweet sap of a century plant.

pul·sate (pul' sat') *vi-* [pul·sat·ed, pul·sat·ing] 1 to throb or beat with a regular rhythm, as the heart does. 2 to quiver; vibrate: *His voice pulsated with emotion.*

Pulpit

pul·sa·tion (pəl sa' shən) *n-* 1 a regular beating or throbbing, as of the heart. 2 a single throb or beat.

pulse (puls) *n-* 1 the throbbing or beating in an artery as blood is pumped through it by the heart. 2 any regular stroke or beat: *the pulse of the music.* *vi-* [pulsed, puls·ing] to beat; throb; vibrate. [from French pou(l)s, from Latin pulsus, from Latin pulsus (the beating (of the veins).]

pulse (puls) *n-* the seeds of such plants as peas, beans, and lentils, which are cooked and used as food; also, the plants themselves. [from Old French pols, from Latin puls meaning "a pottage of beans and meal."]

pulse jet *n-* type of jet engine that produces a pulsating thrust by the opening and closing of air valves.

pul·ver·ize (pul' və rīz') *vt-* [pul·ver·ized, pul·ver·iz·ing] 1 to grind or pound into a powder or dust. 2 to destroy completely; annihilate: *The air raid pulverized the enemy's fortifications.* *vi-* to become powder or dust.

pu·ma (pyoo' mə) *n-* mountain lion.

pum·ice (pum' əs) *n-* light, spongy, volcanic rock, used in polishing and cleaning.

pum·mel (pum' əl) *vt-* to beat with the fists; pommel.

pump (pump) *n-* machine or natural organ for moving liquids or gases by applied pressure or suction. *vt-* 1 to move (liquids or gases) by suction or applied pressure: *The heart pumps blood.* 2 to raise, draw, or force with a pump: *He pumped water from the well.* 3 to use a pump to move a liquid or gas from, into, or through: *We pumped the boat dry. He pumped up the tire.* 4 to question closely: *The woman pumped the child about his father's business.* *vi-* 1 to work a pump: *He pumped faster.* 2 to function as a pump: *Your heart pumps too fast.* [from early German pumpe.]

Pump

pump (pump) *n-* low-cut shoe without a lace, strap, or other fastening. [from Dutch pampoesje, from Javanese pampoes meaning "slipper," from Persian pāpīrsh.]

pump·er (pum' pər) *n-* 1 person or thing that pumps. 2 fire truck equipped with hoses, a powerful pump, and often a large water tank.

pum·per·nick·el (pum' pər nĭk' əl) *n-* kind of dark bread made of coarse rye flour.

pump·kin (pump' kĭn, pŭng'-) *n-* 1 a large, golden-yellow, usually round fruit of a vine. It is used for pies and as cattle food. 2 the large-leafed vine which bears this fruit.

Pumpkin

punch line *n-* last sentence or phrase of a joke, story, or speech that drives home the point.

punc·til·i·o (pŭngk tĭl' ē ō) *n-* [*pl.* punc·til·i·os] a small point of etiquette in conduct, manners, or dress; also, formal correctness; formality.

punc·til·i·ous (pŭngk tĭl' ē əs) *adj-* 1 very precise in conduct; paying careful attention to details of dress, speech, or manners. 2 very careful and exact. —*adv-* punc·til' i·ous·ly. *n-* punc·til' i·ous·ness.

punc·tu·a·tion (pŭngk' choo ā' shən) *n-* the use of periods, commas, and other marks between written words to make the meaning clear.

punctuation mark *n-* any of the marks used in punctuation. The chief punctuation marks are: the comma [,], semi-colon [;], colon [:], period [.], interrogation mark [?], exclamation mark [!], dash [—], hyphen [-], parentheses [( )], brackets [ ], quotation marks [" ....."], and single quotation marks [' . . . . .'].

punc·ture (pŭngk' chər) *n-* 1 small hole or wound made by something pointed: *The nail made a puncture in our tire.* 2 a puncturing or perforating. *vt-* [punc·tured, punc·tur·ing] to make a hole in; pierce; prick: *A nail punctured the tire.* 2 to put an end to; deflate.

pun·dit (pŭn' dĭt) *n-* 1 a learned Brahman, especially one versed in the Sanskrit language, the laws of India, the Hindu religion, etc. 2 any man of great learning.

pun·gent (pŭn' jənt) *adj-* 1 sharp or biting: *Mustard has a pungent taste.* 2 stinging; piercing; sarcastic: *a pungent remark.* —*n-* pun' gen·cy. *adv-* pun' gent·ly.

pun·ish (pŭn' ĭsh) *vt-* 1 to cause (a person) to pay a penalty for a fault or crime; chastise: *He was punished for stealing.* 2 to impose a penalty for (an offense against the law): *to punish manslaughter.* 3 to treat or handle roughly. —*n-* pun' ish·er.

pun·ish·a·ble (pŭn' ĭsh ə bəl) *adj-* liable to or deserving punishment: *In wartime, treason is punishable by death.*

pun·ish·ment (pŭn' ĭsh mənt) *n-* 1 penalty imposed for a crime or fault. 2 a punishing or being punished: *harsh punishment.* 3 *Informal* rough treatment.

pu·ni·tive (pyoo' nə tĭv') *adj-* having to do with, or inflicting, punishment: *a punitive expedition*; punitive laws. —*adv-* pu' ni·tive·ly. *n-* pu' ni·tive·ness.

punk (pŭngk) *n-* 1 a preparation that burns slowly without flame, often used in sticks to light fireworks. 2 decayed wood used as tinder. [American word from Algonquian Indian.]

punk (pŭngk) *Slang adj-* poor; worthless; trashy; also not well. *n-* a young and inexperienced man; especially, a young hoodlum. [of uncertain origin.]

pun·ster (pŭn' stər) *n-* person who habitually makes puns.

punt (pŭnt) *n-* shallow, flat-bottomed boat with square ends. *vt-* to drive (a boat) forward by pushing with a pole against a river or lake bottom: *He punted the boat along the shallow river.* 2 to transport in such a boat. [from Old English, from Latin ponto meaning "a punt; pontoon."] —*n-* punt' er.

punt (pŭnt) *n-* 1 in football, a maneuver in which a player on the team having the ball kicks the ball into the territory of the opposing team. The kicker drops the ball from his hands and kicks it before it touches the ground. 2 the kick itself; also, the distance the ball travels: *Green Bay punted on fourth down.* *vt-*: *He punted that ball sixty yards.* [probably from ¹punt, from the sense of "propelling."] —*n-* punt' er.

pu·ny (pyoo' nē) *adj-* [pu·ni·er, pu·ni·est] 1 undersized; weak: *a puny baby.* 2 half-hearted; feeble: *a puny effort.* —*n-* pu' ni·ness.

pup (pŭp) *n-* 1 young dog; puppy. 2 the young of foxes, wolves, seals, and several other mammals.

pu·pa (pyoo' pə) *n-* [*pl.* pu·pae (-pē) or pu·pas] stage in the life cycle of insects with a complete metamorphosis, coming between the larva and adult

Pupa

pu·rée (pyoo rā') *n-* 1 boiled or strained pulp of vegetables or fruit. 2 thick soup of such materials.

pure·ly (pyoor' lē) *adv-* 1 merely; only: *I am doing this work purely to please you.* 2 completely; entirely: *I have a purely unselfish interest in it.* 3 in a pure manner.

pur·ga·tive (pûr' gə tĭv') *adj-* having the power of cleansing; also, causing bowel movement. *n-* medicine for the purpose of causing bowel movement; cathartic.

pur·ga·to·ry (pûr' gə tôr' ē) *n-* 1 in Roman Catholic belief, an intermediate state or place where the souls of those who die penitent may make full satisfaction for their failings before entering heaven.

put·out (pŏŏt′ out′) *n-* in baseball, a play causing a batter or a runner to be out.

pu·tre·fac·tion (pyōō′ trə făk′ shən) *n-* 1 decomposition of organic matter by certain bacteria and fungi, resulting in foul-smelling compounds. 2 rottenness.

pu·tre·fy (pyōō′ trə fī′) *vt-* [pu·tre·fied, pu·tre·fy·ing] to cause to rot or decay with a foul odor. *vi-* to decay or become rotten.

pu·tres·cent (pyōō trĕs′ ənt) *adj-* becoming rotten; decaying. *—n-* **pu·tres′ cence.**

pu·trid (pyōō′ trĭd) *adj-* 1 rotten; decayed or decaying: *The garbage had become* putrid. 2 foul or fetid as if from rottenness: *a* putrid *odor.* *—n-* **pu·trid′ ·i·ty** or **pu·trid· ness.** *adv-* **pu′ trid·ly.**

putt (pŭt) *n-* careful stroke on the putting green to play a ball toward or into the hole. *vi-* to make such a stroke: *He* putted *badly today.* *vt-:* *He* putted *the ball too far.*

put·tee (pə tē′, pŭt′ ē) *n-* leg covering made of cloth wrapped spirally from knee to ankle, worn by soldiers or sportsmen; also, a stiff leather legging. *Hom-* putty.

put·ter (pŭt′ ər) *n-* 1 in golf, a short club with a flat metal head, used on the putting green. 2 person who putts with such a club. [from putt.]

put·ter (pŭt′ ər) *vi-* to work lazily or without much purpose; potter: *He* puttered *around the garden all day.* [a variant of potter.] *—n-* **put′ ter·er.**

putting green *n-* in golf, the plot of smooth grass around a hole.

pyr- or **pyro-** *combining form* fire; heat: *a* pyro*meter;* pyro*technic;* pyro*mania.* [from Greek **pyr-**, **pyro-**, from Greek **pŷr**, **pyrós** meaning "fire."]

pyr·a·mid (pĭr′ ə mĭd′) *n-* 1 a solid with triangular sides meeting at a point, and a flat base. 2 anything of similar shape. 3 **Pyramids** a group of Egyptian monuments having square bases and triangular sides sloping to an apex, built by the early kings to serve as their tombs. *vt-* to build up layer by layer to a peak: *to* pyramid *stock holdings.* *—adj-* **py·ram′ i·dal** (pə răm′ ə dəl): *the* pyramidal *structures of ancient Egypt.*

Pyramids

pyre (pīər) *n-* pile of wood for burning a corpse.

py·ret·ic (pī rĕt′ ĭk) *adj-* of, relating to, or affected with fever; feverish; also, causing fever.

py·re·thrum (pī rē′ thrəm, -rĕth′ rəm) *n-* 1 any of various chrysanthemums with long stems and finely cut, often fragrant leaves. Its flowers, when dried and ground into a powder, are used in medicine and as an insecticide. 2 insecticide made of the dried flowers of these plants.

Q

Q, q (kyōō) *n-* [*pl.* **Q's, q's**] the seventeenth letter of the English alphabet.

q. 1 quarter or quarterly. 2 quarto. 3 quetzal. 4 quintal.

Q.E.D. which was to be demonstrated [from Latin *quod erat demonstrandum*].

qt. 1 quantity. 2 [*pl.* **qt.** or **qts.**] quart.

¹quack (kwăk) *n-* the sound made by a duck. *vi-* to make a sound like a duck. [perhaps from early Dutch *quacken*, probably an imitation of the sound.]

²quack (kwăk) *n-* person who dishonestly, or through ignorance, pretends to be skilled in medicine or other science. *as modifier:* a quack *doctor*; a quack *medicine.* [shortened from *quacksalver*, from Dutch *kwakzalver*, "one who quacks or boasts of his salves or remedies."]

quack·er·y (kwăk' ə rē) *n-* [*pl.* **quack·er·ies**] practices, methods, claims, or remedies of a quack.

¹quad (kwŏd) *Informal n-* quadrangle of a college, prison, or similar group of buildings. [from *quadrangle.*]

²quad (kwŏd) *n-* in printing, blank type used for spacing a line. [shortened form of earlier *quadrat* (kwäd' răt').]

³quad (kwŏd) *n-* fire truck equipped with hoses, pump, ladders, and water tank, and thus able to function both as a pumper and a ladder truck. Also **pumper-ladder.** [from *quadruple.*]

quad·ran·gle (kwŏ' drăn' gəl) *n-* 1 in geometry, a plane figure with four angles and four sides. 2 four-sided court or lawn surrounded by buildings, especially on a college campus; also, buildings that surround such a court. —*adj-* **quad·ran'gu·lar.**

quad·rant (kwŏd' rənt) *n-* 1 one-fourth of the circumference of a circle; also, the plane area bounded by two perpendicular radii of a circle and the arc subtended by the radii. 2 instrument for measuring the elevation of an object above the horizon. 3 *Mathematics* in a Cartesian coordinate system, any one of the four areas into which a plane is divided by the intersection of the x and y axes. Beginning at the upper right-hand quadrant, the four areas are called, in counterclockwise order, the **first, second, third,** and **fourth quadrants.** 4 any object shaped like one quarter of a circular area.

quad·rat·ic (kwə drăt' ĭk) *adj-* 1 having to do with or resembling a square. 2 having to do with an equation, curve, etc., in which one or more terms is squared. *n-* such an equation.

quad·ren·ni·al (kwə drĕn' ē əl) *adj-* 1 lasting four years. 2 happening once in four years: *a quadrennial election.* —*adj-* **quad·ren'ni·al·ly.**

quadri- or **quadru-** *combining form* four: quadri*lateral*; quadru*ped.* Also **quadr-** before vowels: quadr*angular.* [from Latin **quadri-** or **quadru-**, from **quattuor,** "four."]

quad·ri·ceps (kwŏd' rə sĕps') *n-* big extensor muscle of the leg that forms the large, fleshy mass covering the front and sides of the thigh bone.

quad·ri·lat·er·al (kwŏd' rə lăt' ər əl) *adj-* having four sides. *n-* a four-sided polygon.

qua·drille (kwə drĭl') *n-* old-fashioned square dance for four couples; also, the music for this dance.

quad·ril·lion (kwə drĭl' yən) *n-* 1 in the United States, a thousand trillions, or 1×10^{15}. 2 in Great Britain, a million British trillions, or 1×10^{24}.

quad·ri·no·mi·al (kwŏd' rə nŏ' mē əl) *Mathematics n-* algebraic expression with four terms.

quad·ru·ped (kwŏd' rə pĕd') *n-* animal with four feet.

quad·ru·ple (kwŏ drŏŏ' pəl, -drŏŏ' pəl) *adj-* fourfold; multiplied by four; arranged in fours. *vt-* [**quad·ru·pled, quad·ru·pling**] to increase fourfold; to multiply (something) by four: *to quadruple one's income.* *vi-*: *The population quadrupled in ten years. n-* number four times as great as another.

quad·ru·plet (kwə drŭp' lət, -drŏŏ' plət) *n-* 1 any one of four children born at one birth. 2 group or combination of four things.

quaff (kwăf) *vt-* to drink in long, large swallows or gulps: *to quaff lemonade.* *vi-*: *He quaffed deeply.*

quag·mire (kwăg' mīər', kwŏg'-) *n-* 1 soft, miry ground that yields under the feet; bog. 2 difficult situation.

Quak·er (kwā' kər) *n-* member of a religious sect, the Society of Friends (originally a term of derision).

—*n- fem.* **Quak'er·ess.**

qual·i·fi·ca·tion (kwŏl' ə fə kā' shən) *n-* 1 a qualifying or being qualified; also, an instance of this. 2 limitation; modification; reservation: *to praise a performance without any* qualification. 3 (usually **qualifications**) any knowledge, strength, skill, or experience needed for a task or position: *excellent* qualifications *for the job.*

qual·i·fied (kwŏl' ə fīd') *adj-* 1 having done what is required: *a man* qualified *to vote.* 2 having the skills, experience, etc., that are required: *a man* qualified *for a job.* 3 limited; with some reservations: *a qualified statement;* qualified *praise.*

qual·i·fi·er (kwŏl' ə fī' ər) *n-* 1 person or thing that qualifies. 2 *Grammar* (1) traditionally, an adjective or adverb. (2) a word such as "very," "quite," or "rather" that comes before and modifies an adjective or adverb, and has no inflected forms. In this dictionary, these words are called adverbs.

qual·i·fy (kwŏl' ə fī') *vt-* [**qual·i·fied, qual·i·fy·ing**] 1 to make fit for any office, occupation, sport, etc.: *His work* qualifies *him for promotion.* 2 to make less strong or positive; moderate; soften; also, to alter slightly; limit in meaning: *to* qualify *a rebuke; to* qualify *a statement.* 3 to give legal authorization to: *The state has qualified him to practice medicine.* *vi-* to be or become competent or fit for an office, employment, position, etc.: *He* qualified *for the football team.*

qual·i·ta·tive (kwŏl' ə tā' tĭv) *adj-* of or relating to quality or kind. —*adv-* **qual'i·ta'tive·ly.**

qualitative analysis *n-* determination of the chemical components, elements, or radicals of a substance or mixture of substances.

qual·i·ty (kwŏl' ə tē) *n-* [*pl.* **qual·i·ties**] 1 that which makes a person or thing different from another; characteristic: *Ability to think is man's outstanding* quality. 2 a certain taste, color, tone, feeling, or other property of anything: *the sad* quality *of a song; the acid* quality *of lemons.* 3 degree of excellence; worth; value: *The shop sold goods of both high and low* quality. 4 excellence; high merit: *The restaurant was famous for the* quality *of its food.* 5 *Music* timbre; tone color. 6 *Archaic* high social position; superior rank: *persons of* quality.

qualm (kwäm, *also* kwälm; kwôm) *n-* 1 pang of doubt about one's behavior; twinge of conscience: *She felt* qualms *about repeating the gossip.* 2 sudden fear or uneasy feeling; misgiving: *He had* qualms *about climbing the cliff.* 3 sudden feeling of faintness or nausea.

qualm·ish (kwä' mĭsh, *also* kwäl'-) *adj-* 1 feeling qualms; nauseated; also, having doubts or misgivings. 2 likely to cause qualms. —*adv-* **qualm'ish·ly.** *n-* **qualm'ish·ness.**

quan·da·ry (kwŏn' də rē) *n-* [*pl.* **quan·da·ries**] condition of hesitation or doubt; dilemma.

quan·ti·ta·tive (kwŏn' tə tā' tĭv) *adj-* of or relating to total quantity or value, or to proportionate quantities or values. —*adv-* **quan'ti·ta'tive·ly.**

quan·ti·ty (kwŏn' tə tē) *n-* [*pl.* **quan·ti·ties**] 1 amount: *What* quantity *of flour was used in this cake?* 2 any indefinite, usually considerable, amount: *to buy ice in quantity.*

quar·an·tine (kwŏr' ən tēn', kwŏr'-) *n-* 1 legal restrictions on the movement of persons, goods, plants, or animals in or out of a place because of contagious disease.

quar·rel (kwŏr' əl, kwŏr'-) *n-* 1 an angry dispute, argument, or disagreement: *He has no* quarrel *with us.* *vi-* 1 to have a dispute; fight: *The brothers quarreled over the use of the car.* 2 to find fault: *to* quarrel *with a proposal.*

quar·rel·some (kwŏr' əl səm, kwŏr'-) *adj-* inclined to quarrel. —*adv-* **quar'rel·some·ly.** *n-* **quar'rel·some·ness.**

¹quar·ry (kwŏr' ē, kwôr'-) *n-* [*pl.* **quar·ries**] open pit from which marble, slate, or other stone is obtained by cutting or blasting. *vt-* [**quar·ried, quar·ry·ing**] to dig or cut from such a pit.

quart (kwôrt) *n-* 1 a measure, liquid or dry, of two pints or one quarter of a gallon. *as modifier:* a quart *bottle.*

quar·tet (kwôr′ tĕt′) *n-* 1 group of four persons or things. 2 musical composition for four singers or instruments. 3 four singers or players who perform together. Also **quar·tette′**.

quar·to (kwôr′ tō) *n-* [*pl.* **quar·tos**] 1 in printing, a sheet of paper folded into four leaves or eight pages. 2 book made of such sheets. *adj-:* a quarto *volume. Abbr.* 4vo.

quartz (kwôrts) *n-* silicon dioxide, occurring naturally in separate crystals or large masses. Pure quartz is transparent and colorless unless tinted by other minerals. Brightly colored varieties are agates and amethysts. For picture, see *crystal. as modifier:* a quartz *deposit.*

quartz glass *n-* sheet of glass made from pure quartz. Quartz glass transmits ultraviolet radiation.

quartz·ite (kwôrt′ sīt′) *n-* metamorphic rock consisting of compressed sandstone.

qua·sar (kwä′ sär′) *Astronomy n-* one of a small group of recently discovered, pointlike celestial objects. Quasars emit tremendous quantities of visible light and radio waves, and they are among the most distant objects ever detected. [shortened from *quasi-*stellar radio source.]

¹quash (kwŏsh, kwôsh) *vt-* to subdue or crush: *The troops* quashed *the rebellion.* [from Old English *cwæscan* meaning "crush out," from Old French *quasser,* from Latin *quassāre* meaning "to shatter; break."]

²quash (kwŏsh, kwôsh) *vt-* in law, to cancel or annul (an indictment, lawsuit, etc.). [from Old French *quasser,* from Latin *cassāre,* "to destroy."]

qua·si (kwä′ zē, kwä′ sī′, -zī′) *adj-* similar to but not the same as in every respect: *a quasi corporation. adv-* (used only with adjectives and adverbs to form hyphenated compounds, and sometimes called a prefix) nearly but not quite; almost: *a quasi-historical tale.*

Qua·ter·nar·y (kwŏt′ ər nĕr′ ē) *n-* the last of the two periods of the Cenozoic era. *adj-: the* Quaternary *period.*

queen mother *n-* king's widow who is also mother of a reigning sovereign.

queen post *n-* one of two upright posts placed at equal distances on either side of the center of a roof truss or other truss to tie and support the framework.

queen regent *n-* queen reigning during the childhood, absence, or incapacity of the actual sovereign.

queer (kwêr) *adj-* 1 different from what is normal; odd; peculiar: *He has a queer sense of humor.* 2 giddy; dizzy: *I sat down for a moment because I felt queer.* 3 suggestive of deceit and wrongdoing; irregular; dubious: *a* queer *transaction.* —*adv-* **queer′ ly.** *n-* **queer′ ness.**

quell (kwĕl) *vt-* to subdue; put down: *to quell a riot.*

quench (kwĕnch) *vt-* 1 to put an end to; slake: *He* quenched *his thirst at the fountain.* 2 to put out: *to* quench *a fire with a bucket of water.* —*adj-* **quench′ a·ble:** a quenchable *flame. n-* **quench′ er.** *adj-* **quench′less.**

quern (kwûrn) *n-* 1 hand mill used for grinding grain, usually made of two discs of stone. 2 small hand mill for grinding spices.

quer·u·lous (kwĕr′ ə ləs) *adj-* faultfinding; complaining; peevish: *a* querulous *answer.* —*adv-* **quer′ u·lous·ly.** *n-* **quer′ u·lous·ness.**

ques·tion (kwĕs′ chən) *n-* 1 something asked; a request for information: *Please repeat your* question. 2 objection; doubt: *The new facts raise several* questions. 3 matter to be considered or discussed.

quick (kwĭk) *adj-* [**quick·er, quick·est**] 1 done or moving with speed; fast; rapid: *a quick decision;* quick *hands.* 2 fast to notice or understand; alert; lively: *a quick mind.* 3 easily excited or aroused: *her quick temper.* *adv-* *Informal* quickly. *n-* sensitive flesh, especially under the fingernail. —*adv-* **quick′ ly.** *n-* **quick′ ness.**

to the quick very deeply. **the quick and the dead** the living and the dead.

quick·lime (kwĭk′ līm′) *n-* ¹lime.

quick·sand (kwĭk′ sănd′) *n-* very fine, wet sand which will not hold up a heavy weight and can engulf a person or animal stepping into it.

quick·sil·ver (kwĭk′ sĭl′ vər) *n-* mercury.

quick·step (kwĭk′ stĕp′) *n-* rapid marching step; also, a marching tune with a rapid tempo.

quick-tem·pered (kwĭk′ tĕm′ pərd) *adj-* easily aroused to anger: *a* quick-tempered *disposition.*

quick time *n-* marching pace of 120 thirty-inch steps per minute, the normal pace for military drill.

quick-wit·ted (kwĭk′ wĭt′ əd) *adj-* keen; alert; clever: *a* quick-witted *debater.* —*adv-* **quick′ wit′ ted·ly.**

¹quid (kwĭd) *n-* piece of chewing tobacco being chewed or taken for chewing. [a variant of **cud.**]

²quid (kwĭd) *Brit. Slang n-* [*pl.* **quid**] a pound sterling or a sovereign. [origin uncertain.]

quid pro quo (kwĭd′ prō kwō′) *n-* something given or received in return; compensation.

quién sa·be? (kē ĕn′ sä′ bā′) *Spanish* Who knows?

qui·es·cent (kwī ĕs′ ənt, kwē-) *adj-* 1 calm; still; tranquil: *a* quiescent *mood.* 2 inactive; not dangerous: *a* quiescent *volcano.* —*n-* **qui·es′ cence.** *adv-* **qui·es′ cent·ly.**

qui·et (kwī′ ət) *adj-* [**qui·et·er, qui·et·est**] 1 making little or no sound or disturbance; noiseless; silent: *The baby was quiet all night.*

qui·e·tus (kwī ē′ təs) *Archaic n-* anything which puts an end to action; especially, death.

quill (kwĭl) *n-* 1 long, stiff feather. 2 stiff, hollow shaft of a feather. 3 pen made of a feather. 4 a spinelike hair of a porcupine or hedgehog.

Quill

quilt (kwĭlt) *n-* bed cover made of two layers of cloth with a layer of wool, down, etc., between them. The layers are held together and the filling kept in place by stitching or by tufting. *vt-* to sew or otherwise work on such a bed cover: *The ladies* quilted *as they chatted. vt-* to sew (a vest, jacket, etc.) with padding between layers of cloth.

quilt·ing (kwĭl′ tĭng) *n-* 1 the making of a quilt or of quilted work. 2 the material for such work. 3 the finished work.

qui·nine (kwī′ nīn′) *n-* bitter, white alkaloid extracted from the bark of the cinchona tree. It is used in the treatment of malaria.

quin·quen·ni·al (kwĭn kwĕn′ē əl) *adj-* 1 happening every five years or once in five years. 2 lasting five years. *n-* fifth anniversary.

quin·sy (kwĭn′ zē) *n-* severe inflammation of the tonsils and throat, accompanied by swelling.

quint (kwĭnt) *Informal n-* quintuplet.

quin·tal (kwĭn′ təl) *n-* 1 hundredweight. 2 in the metric system, 100 kilograms.

quin·tes·sence (kwĭn tĕs′ əns) *n-* 1 perfect example of some quality: *He is the* quintessence *of good manners.* 2 pure essence or most refined extract of a substance.

quin·tet (kwĭn tĕt′) *n-* 1 any group of five; especially, a group of five musicians. 2 music written for five musical instruments. Also **quin·tette′.**

quin·til·lion (kwĭn tĭl′ yən) *n-* 1 in the United States, a thousand quadrillions, or 1 × 10¹⁸. 2 in Great Britain, a million British quadrillions, or 1 × 10³⁰.

quin·tup·let (kwĭn tŭp′ lət, -tōō′ plət) *n-* 1 any one of five children born at one birth. 2 group or combination of five things; quintet.

quip (kwĭp) *n-* 1 sharp or sarcastic remark, joke, or gibe. 2 witty retort. *vt-* [**quip·ped, quip·ping**] to make such remarks or retorts.

qui·pu (kē′ pōō) *n-* device made of a main cord and smaller cords, knotted and colored, used by the ancient Peruvians for recording and calculating.

quire (kwī′ ər, kwīər) *n-* one twentieth of a ream of paper; 24 or 25 sheets of uniform size and quality. *Hom-* choir.

quirk (kwûrk) *n-* 1 eccentric personal trait, usually a strange or unpleasant one; idiosyncrasy. 2 vagary; twist; turn: *by a strange* quirk *of fate.*

quirt (kwûrt) *n-* short-handled riding whip with a lash of braided rawhide.

quis·ling (kwĭz′ lĭng) *n-* citizen of a conquered nation who collaborates with the enemy, especially by taking part in a puppet government; traitor.

quit (kwĭt) *vt-* [**quit, quit·ting**] 1 to stop; discontinue; cease: *The child* quit *crying.* 2 to leave; depart from:

He quit *the army.* **3** to give up; relinquish; renounce: *He* quit *his old beliefs.* **vi-** **1** to come to a stop: *Let's quit and go home.* **2** to depart. **3** *Informal* to resign from a position. **adj-** finally free: *I'm* quit *of that debt.*

quit·claim (kwĭt′ klăm′) *n-* in law, legal paper by which a person gives up claim to, or right in, something. **vt-** to give up claim to.

quite (kwĭt) **adv-** **1** completely; entirely; wholly: *You are* quite right. **2** *Informal* to a considerable degree; rather: *It is* quite cold *today.*

quite a (or **an**) *Informal* a remarkable; an outstanding: *He's* quite a *soldier. She's doing* quite a job. **quite a few** a large number; many: *to have* quite a few *children.*

quit·rent (kwĭt′ rĕnt′) *n-* in law, in feudal times, a rent paid by a freeholder or tenant as a substitute for certain feudal services.

quits (kwĭts) **adj-** equal or even with someone, especially after returning or repaying something: *We each did the other a favor, and we're* quits.

be quits with to be even with; neither owing nor being owed by. **call it quits** to give up; have enough of something. **cry quits** to admit that one is ready to cease competing.

quit·tance (kwĭt′ əns) *n-* **1** release from a debt or obligation. **2** repayment of a favor or wrong; recompense.

quit·ter (kwĭt′ ər) *n-* person who gives up too easily, especially from laziness or cowardice.

¹quiv·er (kwĭv′ ər) **vi-** to shake or tremble rapidly: *He* quivered *in the cold. Her voice* quivers *when she sings.* **n-** a trembling motion or sound: *I see a* quiver *in the leaves.* [from Old English *cwifer* meaning "moving rapidly or briskly," and probably related to **quaver**.]

²quiv·er (kwĭv′ ər) **n-** case for holding and carrying arrows. [from Old French *cuivre,* perhaps from Old High German *kochar* or Old English *cocer.*]

qui vive (kē vēv′) *n-* **1** call of a French sentry, corresponding to "Who goes there?" **2** challenge. **3** lookout; alert. **on the qui vive,** on the alert.

Qui·xo·te (kē hō′ tě, kwĭk′ sət) See *Don Quixote.*

quix·ot·ic (kwĭk sŏt′ ĭk) **adj-** rashly and foolishly romantic, idealistic, or chivalrous. **adv- quix·ot′ i·cal·ly.**

Quiver

quiz (kwĭz) *n-* [*pl.* **quiz·zes**] informal and usually brief examination: *She did very well on the history* quiz. **vt-** [**quizzed, quiz·zing**] to question or examine informally: *I* quizzed *him on his studies.* **—n- quiz′ zer.**

quiz show or **quiz program** *n-* television show or program in which the participants or contestants answer questions, often for a prize in cash or merchandise.

quiz·zi·cal (kwĭz′ ĭ kəl) **adj-** **1** puzzled or questioning: *a* quizzical *expression.*

quoin (koin, *also* kwoin) *n-* **1** an outside corner of a building. **2** stone forming such a corner. **3** a wedge-shaped stone in an arch. **4** in printing, a wedge used for locking type into a galley or ′other frame or holder. **vt-** to supply with such wedges.

Printer's quoins

Hom- coin.

quoit (kwoit) *n-* iron or rope ring that is tossed over an upright peg in playing the game called **quoits.**

quon·dam (kwŏn′ dăm′, -dəm) **adj-** erstwhile; former.

Quon·set hut (kwŏn′ sət) *n-* trademark name for a pre-fabricated metal shelter resembling a half cylinder cut lengthwise.

quo·rum (kwôr′ əm) *n-* the number of members of any body, especially legislative, that must be present at its meeting if business is to be transacted legally or officially.

quo·ta (kwō′ tə) *n-* portion of something that is due from or allotted to a person, group, or district; share; proportion: *He met the daily* quota *of work.*

quot·a·ble (kwō′ tə bəl) **adj-** **1** such as may be repeated: *These remarks are not* quotable. **2** suitable for, or worthy of, quoting: *Mark Twain's very* quotable *remarks.*

quo·ta·tion (kwō tā′ shən) *n-* **1** a quoting of someone else's words. **2** the words thus quoted; especially, a

quotation marks *n-* pair of punctuation marks ("...") placed at the beginning and end of a word or passage to show that it is quoted. Example: "I can't find my hat," he said. A quotation within a quotation is usually enclosed in single quotation marks ('...'). Example: He asked, "Did Mary say 'Don't go'?"

quote (kwōt) **vt-** [**quot′ ed, quot′ ing**] **1** to repeat the words of another person or a passage from a book, poem, etc. **2** to enclose in quotation marks: *You should* quote *this passage in your composition.* **3** to state (a market price). **4** to refer to as evidence or illustration: *to* quote a *theory; to* quote *an incident.* **n-** *Informal* **1** the words or passage repeated. **2** quotation mark. **interj-** the quotation begins here: *In Churchill's words,* quote, *It was their finest hour,* unquote. **—n- quot′ er.**

quoth (kwōth) *Archaic* **vt-** said; spoke.

quo·tient (kwō′ shənt) *n-* an answer to a problem in division; result obtained when one number is divided by another: *If 12 is divided by 2, the* quotient *is 6.*

q.v. see this; look this up [from Latin *quod vide*].

R

R, r (är) *n-* [*pl.* **R's, r's**] the eighteenth letter of the English alphabet.

the three R's reading, writing, and arithmetic as though written "reading, 'riting, and 'rithmetic"; hence, the first essentials of education.

r 1 radius. 2 roentgen.

r. 1 ruble. 2 rupee.

R 1 ratio. 2 in chess, rook.

R. 1 rabbi. 2 Republican. 3 river. 4 road.

¹Ra (rä) *n-* in Egyptian mythology, the god of the sun; the supreme deity. Also **Re.**

²Ra symbol for radium.

rab·bet (răb′ ĭt) *n-* 1 groove or slot made in the edge or face of one piece of wood to receive the edge of another piece. 2 joint made this way. *vt-* 1 to cut such a groove in. 2 to join this way. *vi-* to be joined this way. *Hom-* rabbit.

Rabbet joints

rab·bi (răb′ ī′) *n-* [*pl.* **rab·bis** or **rab·bies**] 1 in the Jewish religion, a man authorized to teach and interpret law and ritual. 2 minister of a Jewish congregation.

rab·bin·i·cal (rə bĭn′ ĭk əl) *adj-* 1 of or relating to rabbis: *a rabbinical association; rabbinical duties.* 2 of or relating to the traditions, writings, theology, etc., of the rabbis in Judaism.

rab·bit (răb′ ĭt) *n-* 1 small burrowing animal related to the hare but having shorter ears and less powerful hind legs. Some hares, such as the jackrabbit, are called rabbits. 2 the fur of this animal. *as modifier:* rabbit *earmuffs. Hom-* rabbet.
—*adj-* rab′ bit·like′.

Rabbit (eastern cottontail)
11—17 in long

rabbit fever *n-* tularemia.

rab·ble (răb′ əl) *n-* 1 an unruly crowd; mob. 2 **the rabble** the common people (a term of contempt).

rab·id (răb′ ĭd) *adj-* 1 of, related to, or infected with rabies. 2 fanatical; excessively zealous; extremely unreasonable: *a rabid reformer.* 3 furious; raging. —*adv-* rab′ id·ly. *n-* rab′ id·ness.

ra·bies (rā′ bēz) *n-* virus disease, especially of dogs, foxes, etc., marked by fear of water, inability to swallow, frenzy, and convulsions; hydrophobia. It may be transmitted to man or other animals by a bite.

Raccoon, about 2 ft long

rac·coon (ră kōōn′) *n-* 1 grayish-brown, flesh-eating animal with a bushy, ringed tail and face markings like a black mask. 2 fur of this animal. *as modifier:* a raccoon *coat.* Also **racoon.** [American word from the Algonquian **ärähkunem,** "he scratches with the hands."]

¹race (rās) *n-* 1 contest of speed: *a boat race.* 2 contest for a prize, office, etc.: *a race for the governorship.* 3 a swift, rushing current: *a race of water in a stream. vi-* [raced, rac·ing] 1 to participate in a contest of speed. 2 to move with speed; hurry; dash: *to race for a bus; to race after a ball.* 3 of machinery, to turn or run faster than normal or too fast. *vt-* 1 to try to outdo in speed: *I'll race you to the corner.* 2 to enter or use in a contest of speed: *Will he race all three of his cars tomorrow?* 3 to cause (a motor, machinery, etc.) to run or spin faster than usual. [from Old Norse **räs** meaning "a course that is run; a rush."]

²race (rās) *n-* 1 in anthropology, any of several large divisions of the human species having similar physical characteristics and a common ancestry. 2 group of people with similar ancestry or geographical and cultural backgrounds: *the English* race. 3 large division of living creatures: *the cat* race. [from French, from Italian **razza** of the same meaning.]

race course *n-* area marked out for contests of speed.

race·horse (rās′ hòrs′, -hôrs′) *n-* horse bred and trained for competing in races, especially those in which a jockey rides the horse.

race runner *n-* swift-moving lizard of North America.

race track *n-* a field or course laid out for races.

Ra·chel (rā′ chəl) *n-* in the Old Testament, the wife of Jacob and mother of Joseph and Benjamin.

ra·chit·ic (rə kĭt′ ĭk) *adj-* of, related to, or afflicted with rickets. *n-* person afflicted with rickets.

ra·cial (rā′ shəl) *adj-* of or related to race in the human species. —*adv-* ra′ cial·ly.

racing form *n-* publication giving information about particular racehorses and horse races.

rac·ism (rā′ sĭz′ əm) *n-* 1 belief in the inborn superiority of one race, especially a person's own race, over another race of humanity. 2 behavior, politics, etc., based on such a belief. Also **ra′ cial·ism** (rā′ shə lĭz′ əm). —*n-* ra′ cist or ra′ cial·ist.

rack (răk) *n-* 1 framework of shelves, bars, or hooks on or in which articles may be hung, stored, or displayed. 2 an old instrument of torture, which stretched and dislocated a victim's joints. 3 in mechanics, a bar having teeth on one side that engage the teeth of a gear, pinion, etc. *vt-* 1 to place on a rack: *to rack billiard balls.* 2 to torment severely, as if on an instrument of torture: *The disease racked the man with pain.*

Towel rack   Hay rack   Storage rack

[probably from early German or early Dutch **rek,** "a bar; grating of bars."] *Hom-* wrack.

on the rack under severe stress.

rack (one's) brains to search intensively in one's mind for a solution.

²rack (răk) **rack and ruin** widespread and complete destruction. [variant of **wrack,** from Old English **wræc,** "a wreck; that which is driven (ashore)."] *Hom-* wrack.

³rack (răk) *n-* rapid gait of a horse in which each foot strikes the ground separately; single-foot. *vi-* to move in this gait. [origin uncertain, perhaps a variant of **²rock.**] *Hom-* wrack.

¹rack·et (răk′ ət) *n-* 1 disturbing noise; din; uproar: *The children were causing a* racket. 2 *Informal* dishonest or irregular way of earning a living or making money, often involving extortion, intimidation, or the sale of something forbidden by law. [probably an imitation of a sound.]

²rack·et (răk′ ət) *n-* net-covered oval frame ending in a straight handle, used to bat a light ball in certain games. Also **rac′ quet.**

Tennis racket

[from Old French **raquette,** from an Arabic word **rähät** meaning "the palms of the hands; a game, like tennis, in which the ball was hit with the palm."]

rack·et·eer (răk′ ə tēr′) *n-* person engaged in a criminal racket; gangster.

rack·et·y (răk′ ə tē) *adj-* causing or making a racket.

rac·on·teur (răk′ ŏn tûr′) *n-* teller of stories.

ra·coon (ră kōōn′) raccoon.

rac·quets (răk′ əts) *n-* game resembling squash racquets, but played in a larger court. Also **rack′ ets.**

rac·y (rā′ sē) *adj-* [rac·i·er, rac·i·est] 1 rapid and colorful; vivid: *a racy manner of talking.* 2 slightly improper; spicy: *a racy story.* —*adv-* rac′ i·ly. *n-* rac′ i·ness.

ra·dar (rā′ där′) *n-* device that sends out radio waves in a beam that, when reflected back from a distant object, indicates the position, distance, and direction of movement of the object. *as modifier: a radar signal.* [shortened from *radio detecting and ranging.*]

ra·di·al (rā′ dē əl) *adj-* 1 branching out from a central point; radiating like the spokes of a wheel. 2 of or having to do with a radius. —*adv-* ra′ di·al·ly.

ra·di·ant (rā′ dē ənt) *adj-* 1 giving out rays of heat or light. 2 glowing with brightness, kindness, love, etc.: *a radiant expression.* 3 made up of or sent out by radiation: *the sun's radiant heat.* —*adj-* ra′ di·ant·ly.

radiant energy *n-* energy that is transmitted from a source in electromagnetic waves. Various forms are X rays, light, and radio waves.

ra·di·ate (rā′ dē āt′) *vi-* [ra·di·at·ed, ra·di·at·ing] 1 to give out radiant energy. 2 to reach outward from a center: *Spokes radiate from the center of a wheel.* *vt-* 1 to emit energy in waves: *The walls radiated heat.* 2 to have or show (some feeling) so strongly as to affect others; communicate: *He radiates confidence.*

ra·di·a·tion (rā′ dē ā′ shən) *n-* 1 the giving off of radiant energy, such as light, and radiant heat. 2 radiant energy emitted by a radioactive substance, which is harmful to living tissues; also, X rays.

radiation pressure *n-* force exerted on a surface by radiant energy. The radiation pressure of the sun makes a comet's tail point away from the sun.

radiation shield *n-* any device used to protect living tissues or instruments from radiation.

radiation sickness *n-* disease caused by overexposure to nuclear radiation and marked by nausea, dizziness, the breakdown of tissues, and often death.

ra·di·a·tor (rā′ dē ā′ tər) *n-*
1 system of pipes through which hot water or steam is forced to heat a room or building. 2 a honeycomb tank in an automobile where water from the cooling system is cooled by the air. 3 *Physics* any source of radiant energy.

AUTOMOBILE HOUSE
Radiators

rad·i·cal (răd′ ĭ kəl) *adj-* 1 basic or fundamental; going to the roots: *a radical change of policy.* 2 extreme, especially in the support of political positions: *the radical wing of a political party.* *n-* 1 person holding such extreme opinions. 2 *Chemistry* group of atoms that acts as a unit in chemical reactions. 3 *Mathematics* (1) the indicated root of a number. Example: √9. (2) radical sign. *Hom-* radicle. *—adv-* rad′ i·cal·ly. *n-* rad′ i·cal·ness.

rad·i·cal·ism (răd′ ĭ kə lĭz′ əm) *n-* the suggesting and supporting of radical ideas; also, one or more of these ideas.

radical sign *Mathematics n-* symbol (√ ‾) that indicates which root of a radicand is to be taken. The index specifies the root, although it is usually omitted for the square root. Example: ³√

rad·i·cand (răd′ ə kănd′) *Mathematics n-* expression written under the radical sign. In √9, 9 is the radicand.

rad·i·cle (răd′ ĭ kəl) *n-* part of the embryo of a seed plant that becomes the main root of the mature plant. *Hom-* radical.

ra·di·i (rā′ dē ī′) *pl.* of **radius.**

ra·di·o (rā′ dē ō′) *n-* [*pl.* **ra·di·os**] 1 the sending and receiving of communication signals, especially sound but also television, by means of electromagnetic waves without the use of wires between sender and receiver. 2 instrument for receiving such signals; also, an instrument for sending such signals. 3 system of wireless communication; also, the business of operating it. *as modifier: a radio program.* *vt-* [ra·di·oed, ra·di·o·ing] to send messages to by means of electromagnetic waves: *We must radio the ship that help is coming.* *vi- The ship radioed for help.*

radio- *combining form* 1 radial; radially: *a radiolarian* (minute sea animal with radial extensions). 2 radio: *a radiogram; radiotelephone.* 3 radioactive: *radiocarbon;*

ra·di·o·ac·tive (rā′ dē ō ăk′ tĭv) *adj-* having to do with, caused by, or showing radioactivity.

ra·di·o·ac·tiv·i·ty (rā′ dē ō ăk tĭv′ ə tē) *n-* spontaneous disintegration of an atomic nucleus, accompanied by the emission of a nuclear particle, or of alpha, beta, or gamma rays; also, the radiation so emitted.

radio astronomy *n-* branch of science that deals with the detection and study of radio waves given off by stars and other celestial objects.

radio beacon *n-* a stationary radio transmitting station continually sending radio signals that help ships and airplanes to determine their location.

radio frequency *n-* any electromagnetic wave frequency in the range from 10 kilocycles to 30,000 megacycles, used in the transmission of radio signals.

ra·di·o·gram (rā′ dē ō grăm′) *n-* message sent by radiotelegraph.

ra·di·o·graph (rā′ dē ō grăf′) *n-* photograph made by radiation other than light, especially one made by X rays. *vt-* to produce such a photograph of.

ra·di·o·i·so·tope (rā′ dē ō ī′ sə tōp′) *n-* isotope of an element that has been made radioactive, usually by artificial means.

ra·di·o·lar·i·an (rā′ dē ō lêr′ ē ən, -lăr′ ē ən) *n-* any of an order (**Radiolaria**) of spherical, marine protozoans that resemble the ameba but have a hard, mineral skeleton with projecting, radiating spines.

ra·di·ol·o·gist (rā′ dē ŏl′ ə jĭst) *n-* doctor specializing in radiology.

ra·di·ol·o·gy (rā′ dē ŏl′ ə jē) *n-* branch of science dealing with radiant energy, especially its medical applications, such as the use of X rays to diagnose or treat disease.

ra·di·om·e·ter (rā′ dē ŏm′ ə tər) *n-* instrument that measures intensity of radiant energy.

ra·di·o·phone (rā′ dē ō fōn′) *n-* 1 any device for producing or transmitting sound by radiant energy. 2 radiotelephone.

ra·di·o·sonde (rā′ dē ō sŏnd′) *n-* instrument that is carried by a balloon and collects and transmits weather data.

ra·di·o·tel·e·graph (rā′ dē ō tĕl′ ə grăf′) *n-* telegraph using radio waves rather than cables to transmit and receive impulses.

Radiometer

ra·di·o·tel·e·phone (rā′ dē ō tĕl′ ə fōn′) *n-* transmitter used for radio communication by voice rather than by Morse code; radiophone.

radio telescope *Astronomy n-* a radio receiver and antenna system that detects and collects radio waves emitted from sources in outer space.

ra·di·o·ther·a·py (rā′ dē ō thĕr′ ə pē) *Medicine n-* treatment of disease by means of X rays or similar radiation from radioactive elements.

radio wave *n-* an electromagnetic wave of radio frequency.

rad·ish (răd′ ĭsh) *n-* 1 garden plant related to the mustard and having a pungent root. 2 its red or white root.

ra·di·um (rā′ dē əm) *n-* radioactive metal element that emits several kinds of very powerful rays, including X rays. It is used in the treatment of cancer and to make materials luminous. Symbol Ra, At. No. 88, At. Wt. 226.

ra·di·us (rā′ dē əs) *n-* [*pl.* **ra·di·i** (-ē ī′) or **ra·di·us·es**] 1 distance from the center of a circle to its circumference. For picture, see *circle.* 2 a straight line segment showing this distance. 3 area enclosed by a circle of a given radius. 4 the shorter of the two bones of the forearm, on the same side of the arm as the thumb.

ra·dix (rā′ dĭks) *n-* [*pl.* **ra·di·ces** (răd′ ə sēz′, rā′ də-) or **ra·dix·es**] 1 in botany, the root of a plant. 2 *Mathematics* base of a number system: *The radix of the decimal system is 10.*

ra·don (rā′ dŏn′) *n-* radioactive, gaseous element produced by the disintegration of radium. Symbol Rn, At. No. 86, At. Wt. 222.

raf·fi·a (răf′ ē ə) *n-* long, stringy, leaf fiber from the **raffia palm,** a cultivated tree of Madagascar. It is woven into hats, baskets, etc.

raf·fle (răf′ əl) *n-* lottery in which people buy chances for a small sum to win a prize. *vt-* [raf·fled, raf·fling]: *to raffle a television set.*

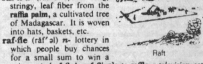
Raft

rag (răg) *n-* 1 bit of cloth, as an old, torn, worn, or useless piece, or one torn or cut from a larger piece; remnant. 2 rags torn, frayed, worn-out clothing; shreds of clothing: *a beggar's rags. as modifier: a rag doll; a rag rug.* [probably from Old Norse rogg, "shaggy piece."] *—adj-* rag′ like′.

²rag (răg) *Slang vt-* [ragged, rag·ging] 1 to scold. 2 to tease or torment. [of uncertain origin.]

³rag (răg) *n-* a tune in ragtime. [from **ragtime.**]

rag·a·muf·fin (răg′ ə mŭf′ ən) *n-* ragged, dirty child.

raid (rād) *n-* 1 *Military* sudden surprise thrust or attack, usually by a relatively small and specially trained force that withdraws immediately. 2 in police work, a sudden surprise entering of a place where criminal activity is suspected, for the purpose of confiscating equipment and making arrests. *vt-* to make such an attack or surprise entry: *to raid the enemy's beach defenses; to raid a gambling den.*

¹**rail** (rāl) *n-* 1 horizontal bar used in a fence, banister, along the deck of a ship, etc., for separating areas or holding onto. 2 metal or wooden member upon which something runs, usually on wheels: *the rails of the railroad.* 3 railroad: *to carry freight by rail.* 4 **the rail** fence surrounding a race track. [from Old French **reille**, from Latin **regula** meaning "a straight piece of wood; a ruler."]

Rail fence

²**rail** (rāl) *vi-* to scold violently; use bitter or angry language at someone (usually followed by "at" or "against"): *It does little good to rail at destiny.* [from French **railler** of uncertain origin, perhaps related to ²**rally**.]

³**rail** (rāl) *n-* any of several kinds of marsh-dwelling birds having short wings, narrow bodies, and usually long beaks and moderately long legs. [from Old French **raale** or **raale** of uncertain origin.]

¹**rail·ing** (rā'lĭng) *n-* a rail and its supports, used either as a fence or as a protective barrier near a dangerous place: *a railing around a monument.* [from ¹**rail**.]

²**rail·ing** (rā'lĭng) *n-* scolding; loud and long complaining. [from ²**rail**.]

Railing

rail·ler·y (rā'lə rē) *n-* [*pl.* **rail·ler·ies**] good-natured ridicule or banter.

rail·road (rāl'rōd') *n-* 1 permanent road with tracks for trains, locomotives, etc. 2 an entire system of transportation, including tracks, trains, buildings, etc. *vt-* 1 to ship by rail. 2 to push through rapidly so as to prevent full consideration: *to railroad a bill through Congress.* 3 *Slang* to convict or imprison on false charges or flimsy evidence.

rail·way (rāl'wā') *n-* 1 railroad. 2 any system of tracks on which cars run.

rai·ment (rā'mənt) *Archaic n-* clothing.

rain (rān) *n-* 1 moisture condensed from the air and falling in drops. 2 a fall or shower of moisture in drops: *The heavy rains flooded the land.* 3 shower of anything: *a rain of blessings.* 4 **rains** rainy season. *vi-* to fall in drops of condensed moisture from the air. *vt-* to shower; give or offer abundantly: *Friends rained presents on them.* **Hom-** reign, rein. —*adj-* **rain'less**. **rained out** canceled because of rain: *The baseball game was rained out.*

rain·bow (rān'bō') *n-* 1 arch of colored light that appears when raindrops, mist, or spray refract, reflect, and disperse the sun's rays. A rainbow shows the colors red, orange, yellow, green, blue, indigo, and violet. 2 any similar display of colors.

rainbow trout *n-* kind of trout, common in western North America, that has a red stripe on the side.

rain check *n-* 1 stub on the ticket to some outdoor event, entitling the bearer to admission at a future time in case the event is rained out. 2 renewed invitation at a later time: *May I have a rain check? I can't come today.*

rain·drop (rān'drŏp') *n-* drop of rain.

rain·fall (rān'fol') *n-* 1 shower of rain. 2 quantity of water from rain, snow, etc., falling within a given time and area. Rainfall is measured by the height of a column collected in a rain gauge.

rain forest *n-* heavy tropical forest receiving an annual rainfall of at least 100 inches, and made up of tall, broadleaf evergreens whose leaves form a continuous roof.

rain gauge *n-* device which measures rainfall by catching, and measuring the depth of, the rain that falls in a certain spot in a certain time.

rain·hat (rān'hăt') *n-* waterproof or water-resistant hat.

rain·mak·er (rān'mā'kər) *n-* person who is supposed to be able to bring on a rain. —*n-* **rain'mak'ing**.

rain shadow *n-* in meteorology, a region of lowered precipitation on the side of a mountain away from the prevailing winds.

rain·spout (rān'spout') *n-* 1 vertical pipe that drains a roof gutter. 2 waterspout.

rain squall *n-* violent windstorm accompanied by rain.

rain·storm (rān'storm', -storm') *n-* storm consisting of or accompanied by rain.

rain·wear (rān'wâr') *n-* garments worn as protection against rain, such as raincoats and overshoes.

rain·y (rā'nē) *adj-* [**rain·i·er, rain·i·est**] 1 showery: *a rainy afternoon.* 2 having much rain: *a rainy climate.* —*n-* **rain'i·ness**.

rainy day *n-* hard times; time when one is in need: *to save money for a rainy day.*

raise (rāz) *vt-* [**raised, rais·ing**] 1 to lift up: *to raise a window.* 2 to stir up; bring about: *to raise dust; to raise trouble.* 3 to build; construct: *to raise a house.* 4 to cause to develop or gather; collect: *to raise an army; to raise money.* 5 to grow; breed; rear: *to raise wheat; to raise horses; to raise a family.* 6 to present for consideration; mention: *to raise an objection.* 7 to lift up in rank, or position; promote: *They raised him to corporal.* 8 to make higher; increase: *to raise prices; to raise the bet.* 9 to reach in order to communicate with: *I can't raise him by telephone.* 10 to make rise (with yeast): *to raise dough.* 11 to end; abandon: *to raise a siege.* 12 to sight on the horizon. 13 to rouse; bring back to life: *That noise is enough to raise the dead.* *n-* an increase in amount: *a raise in pay.* —*n-* **rais'er**.

raise one's voice against to express opposition to; oppose: *He raised his voice against corruption.*

raise the roof to explode with anger.

rai·sin (rā'zən) *n-* dried sweet grape. *adj-* made of or containing raisins: *a raisin pie.*

rai·son d'ê·tre (rē zōⁿ dĕt' rə) *French* reason for being; excuse for existing.

ra·jah (rā'jə) *n-* king, prince, or chief in some parts of Asia, especially in some states of India.

¹**rake** (rāk) *n-* any of several tools like a large comb with wide spaces between the teeth, joined to a long handle. Rakes are used to collect leaves, sticks, and stones without hurting the grass, to smooth spaded ground, to dig clams, etc. *vt-* [**raked, rak·ing**] 1 to use a rake on: *Kenneth raked the lawn.* 2 to collect; gather (followed by "up" or "together"): *The reporter raked up new evidence of fraud.* 3 to search carefully and tirelessly: *Bud raked the library for material for his story.* 4 to sweep with the eye, with gunfire, etc.: *The young lookout's eyes raked the ocean for whales.* [from Old English **raca** of the same meaning.] —*adj-* **rake'like'**.

Garden rake

Leaf rake

rake over the coals to scold vigorously.

rake in *Slang* to take in (money, especially in large amounts).

²**rake** (rāk) *n-* man who promiscuously pursues women. [from Middle English **rakel**, a shortened form of **rakehell**, from Old Norse **reikal** meaning "a vagabond," and from **raka**, "to run about."]

³**rake** (rāk) *n-* slant or tilt from the horizontal or perpendicular: *the rake of a hat; the rake of a mast.* [from earlier verb **rake**, "to reach; extend," from Scandinavian **raka**, "reach; project"; related to ¹**rake**.]

rake-off (rāk'of', -of') *Informal n-* commission; share of receipts, especially in an improper transaction.

¹**rak·ish** (rā'kĭsh) *adj-* jaunty; dashing: *a rakish costume.* [from ³**rake**.] —*adv-* **rak'ish·ly**. *n-* **rak'ish·ness**.

²**rak·ish** (rā'kĭsh) *adj-* dissolute; like a rake; having loose morals: *a rakish life.* [from ²**rake**.]

ram·ble (rām'bəl) *vi-* [**ram·bled, ram·bling**] 1 to stroll without purpose or direction. 2 to flow or meander with many twists and turns: *The river rambled along.* 3 to talk or write without thought or sequence. *n-* a stroll.

ram·bler (răm′blər) *n-* 1 person or thing that rambles. 2 a climbing rose bearing small flowers in clusters.

ram·bling (răm′blǐng) *adj-* 1 wandering; walking aimlessly. 2 spread out in an irregular way: *a rambling castle.* 3 lacking plan or unity: *a rambling talk.*

ram·bunc·tious (răm bŭngk′shəs) *Informal adj-* unruly and boisterous.

ra·mie (răm′ē) *n-* 1 shrub of the East Indies, China, and Japan, yielding a soft, woody fiber. 2 the fiber of this plant, used for weaving textiles and making cord.

ram·i·fy (răm′ə fī′) *vt-* [ram·i·fied, ram·i·fying] 1 to divide into branches or divisions; branch out: *Veins ramify into many capillaries.* 2 to develop, or prove to have, many connected parts: *The more we examine the problem, the more it ramifies.* —*n-* ram′i·fi·ca′tion (-fə kā′shən): *the ramification of a river into streams.*

ram·jet (răm′jět′) *n-* jet engine in which the air for burning is compressed by the force of forward motion rather than by a compressor. See also *turbojet.*

ram·mer (răm′ər) *n-* person or thing that rams; especially, a tool used in building construction for driving stones or piles, or for packing concrete.

¹ramp (rămp) *n-* sloping walk or roadway leading from one level to another. [from Old French *ramper*, "²ramp," perhaps from an earlier Germanic word.]

Ramp

²ramp (rămp) *vi-* 1 to rush about wildly; storm about; rage. 2 to rear up on the hind legs in a threatening manner: *The bear ramped and roared.* [from Old French *ramper* meaning "to clamber; run."]

¹ram·page (răm′pāj′) *n-* fit or period of wild, destructive rage: *The horse went on a rampage.*

²ram·page (răm pāj′) *vi-* [ram·paged, ram·pag·ing] to run wildly or in a violent manner; storm; rage: *The flooded river rampaged through the countryside.*

ramp·ant (răm′pənt) *adj-* 1 spreading without control; wild; raging. 2 climbing or growing unchecked: *The weeds grew rampant in the garden.* 3 in heraldry, standing erect on the hind legs with one foreleg raised above the other, as a lion in a coat of arms. —*adv-* ram′pant·ly.

ram·part (răm′pärt, -pərt) *n-* 1 protective wall or bank of earth around a fort. 2 any protection from danger.

Rampart

ram·rod (răm′rŏd′) *n-* 1 rod used to load a gun through the muzzle, or to clean the barrel of a gun. 2 *Informal* foreman, especially of a ranch. *vt-* [ram·rod·ded, ram·rod·ding] *Informal* 1 to push through vigorously: *to ramrod a bill through a legislature.* 2 *Informal* to act as foreman of.

ram·shack·le (răm′shăk′əl) *adj-* shaky; rickety.

ran (răn) *p.t.* of *run.*

ranch (rănch) *n-* 1 in western United States and Canada, a farm with extensive grazing lands where livestock such as cattle, sheep, and horses are raised. 2 in western United States, any large farm raising a specific crop: *a fruit ranch.* *vi-* to own or manage such a farm. [American word from Spanish *rancho*, "a group that eats together; a mess," from Old French *reng*, "¹rank."]

ranch·er (răn′chər) *n-* person who owns or manages a ranch. Also **ranch′man** [*pl.* **ranch·men**].

ran·che·ro (răn chěr′ō, rän-) *n-* [*pl.* **ran·che·ros**] in southwestern United States and Mexico, person who owns, or works on, a cattle ranch.

ranch house *n-* 1 main house of a ranch. 2 one-story house with a low-pitched roof and an open floor plan.

ran·cho (răn′chō, rän′-) *n-* [*pl.* **ran·chos**] 1 in Latin America, a hut or group of huts for ranch workers. 2 in southwestern United States, a ranch.

ran·cid (răn′sĭd) *adj-* having the strong smell and taste of spoiled fat or oil: *Butter turns rancid when left out in hot weather.* —*n-* ran′cid·ness or ran·cid′i·ty.

ran·cor·ous (răng′kər əs) *adj-* full of rancor; showing or marked by rancor: *a rancorous tone; a rancorous attack.* —*adv-* ran′cor·ous·ly. *n-* ran′cor·ous·ness.

ran·dom (răn′dəm) *adj-* based entirely on chance; without plan or pattern: *a random choice; a random sampling.* —*adv-* ran′dom·ly. *n-* ran′dom·ness.

at random without plan or pattern; by chance; haphazardly: *to wander* at random *through the streets.*

ra·nee (răn′ē) *n-* rani.

rang (răng) *p.t.* of *ring.*

range (rānj) *n-* 1 limits within which someone can do something or something can be done; extent; scope: *beyond the range of his vision; within the range of possibility.* 2 limits within which something varies: *a wide range of prices; a voice with a range of two octaves.* 3 line or row; chain; series: *a range of hills or mountains.* 4 tract of land over which cattle graze. 5 large cooking stove. 6 place for target practice: *a rifle range; a missile range.* 7 distance to which a gun, cannon, etc., can shoot; also, distance of the target from the gun. 8 maximum distance a ship, plane, etc., can travel without refueling: *a bomber with a range of 3000 miles.* 9 area over which a plant or animal may be found in the wild state: *The range of the leopard is decreasing.* *vt-* [ranged, rang·ing] 1 to put in a row or in regular order: *to range cups on a shelf; to range books according to height.* 2 to put (oneself) in a certain position with reference to others: *He ranged himself with the rebels.* 3 to travel or wander over: *Cattle ranged the open prairie.* *vi-* 1 to vary within certain limits: *These motors range from 50 to 100 horsepower.* 2 to wander; roam. 3 to be found over a certain area: *The magnolia ranges northward to Ohio.*

range finder *n-* instrument for finding the distance between a target or point and the instrument itself.

rang·er (rān′jər) *n-* 1 (also **forest ranger**) officer who patrols a wilderness area, guarding the forest and its wildlife. 2 wanderer. 3 Ranger (1) Texas Ranger. (2) in the Army, a member of a special commando force.

rang·y (rān′jē) *adj-* [rang·i·er, rang·i·est] 1 long-legged, lean, and muscular: *a rangy racehorse; a rangy football player.* 2 able to wander far and wide; having a tendency to roam. —*n-* rang′i·ness.

ra·ni (răn′ē) *n-* 1 wife of a rajah. 2 Hindu queen or princess. Also **ranee.**

¹rank (răngk) *n-* 1 line; row: *a rank of soldiers.* 2 position in society or in some official group; grade. 3 high position or station: *a man of rank in his state.* 4 merit; degree of worth: *a poet of the first rank.* 5 ranks (1) an army as a whole. (2) enlisted men as distinguished from officers. *vt-* 1 to place in rows; draw up (soldiers) in line. 2 to place in a special order, especially in the order of worth: *He ranked the magazines by their story interest.* 3 to be of a higher grade or class than: *A major ranks a captain.* *vi-* to hold a certain position or grade: *She ranks high in her class.* [from Old French *reng* meaning "a row; range," from Germanic *hring*.]

²rank (răngk) *adj-* 1 growing rapidly and unchecked: *Vegetation is rank in the tropics.* 2 bad smelling or tasting: *Old bacon becomes rank.* 3 absolute; outright; arrant: *a piece of rank nonsense; a rank insult.* [from Old English *ranc* meaning "strong; bold," from an earlier Germanic word meaning "erect; long and thin."] —*adv-* rank′ly. *n-* rank′ness.

rank and file *n-* (takes singular or plural verb) 1 the ordinary members who form the bulk of an organization or group, as distinguished from the leaders or officers; especially, the ordinary members of a labor union. 2 the common soldiers of an army, including corporals and all ranks below.

rank·ing (răng′kǐng) *adj-* having first, top, or superior rank or standing: *a ranking congressman.*

ran·kle (răng′kəl) *vi-* [ran·kled, ran·kling] 1 to continue to be sore and painful: *His wound rankled.* 2 to be the source of persistent mental pain and irritation: *The insult rankled for years.* *vt-:* *The insult rankled him.*

¹rape (rāp) *vt-* [raped, rap·ing] to force (a woman) to submit to sex acts against her will. *n-* 1 act and crime of such forcing. 2 *Archaic* forcible kidnapping or carrying away of a woman or women. [from Old French *rape* or *rapt*, from Latin *raptus*, a form of *rapere* meaning "to seize and take away."]

²rape (rāp) *n-* herb related to mustard and used as food for sheep and hogs. It yields **rape seed**, from which **rape oil** is extracted to be used as a lubricant. [from Latin *rāpa* meaning "a turnip."]

Ra·pha·el (răf′ē əl, rā′ fē-) *n-* one of the seven archangels in Jewish and Christian tradition.

rap·id (răp′ ĭd) *adj-* fast; quick; swift: *We walked at a rapid pace. There was a rapid decline in stock prices.* *n-* (usually **rapids**) place in a river or stream where the water flows especially fast because of a steeper slope or narrowing of the channel. —*adv-* **rap′ id·ly.**

rap·id-fire (răp′ ĭd fīər′) *adj-* 1 able to fire in rapid succession: *a rapid-fire rifle.* 2 as quick and insistent as the quick firing of a gun; staccato: *The lawyer directed rapid-fire questions at the witness.*

rap·id·i·ty (rə pĭd′ ə tē) *n-* speed; swiftness.

ra·pi·er (rā′ pē ər) *n-* sword with a light hand guard and a straight, slender, double-edged blade, used for thrusting.

Rapier

rap·ine (răp′ ĭn) *n-* the taking and carrying off of property by force; plunder; pillage.

rap·port (ră pôr′) *n-* sympathetic relationship; agreement; harmony: *In a good class there is rapport between teacher and students.* [from French.]

rap·proche·ment (ră prôsh mäⁿ′) *French n-* a coming together in agreement or understanding, after a period of separation; new or renewed harmony: *The United Nations seeks rapprochement between East and West.*

rap·scal·lion (răp skăl′ yən) *n-* worthless person; rascal; rogue.

rapt (răpt) *adj-* carried away with pleasure or delight; enchanted; absorbed: *We listened to the organ in rapt silence. Hom-* wrapt. —*adv-* **rapt′ ly.** *n-* **rapt′ ness.**

rap·ture (răp′ chər) *n-* extreme delight or pleasure; great joy; bliss; ecstasy.

rap·tur·ous (răp′ chə rəs) *adj-* feeling, showing, or marked by great joy or delight: *a rapturous expression.* —*adv-* **rap′ tur·ous·ly.** *n-* **rap′ tur·ous·ness.**

¹rare (râr) *adj-* [**rar·er, rar·est**] 1 not common or usual; distinctive; precious: *a rare book; a rare old lace.* 2 not frequent; seldom occurring: *a rare visit to the city.* 3 not thick or dense; thin: *the rare atmosphere of high mountains.* [from French, from Latin *rārus* meaning "thin; scattered."] —*n-* **rare′ ness.**

²rare (râr) *adj-* [**rar·er, rar·est**] lightly cooked; underdone: *a rare steak.* [from earlier *rear* meaning "lightly boiled"; from Old English *hrēr* meaning "not thoroughly cooked."] —*n-* **rare′ ness.**

rare·bit (râr′ bĭt′) *n-* Welsh rabbit.

rare-earth element (râr′ ûrth′) *n-* any of a group of highly reactive metal elements from atomic number 57 (lanthenum) through 71 (lutetium), which have nearly identical chemical and physical properties.

rar·e·fac·tion (râr′ ə făk′ shən, râr′-) *n-* a making or being less dense: *the rarefaction of a gas.*

rar·e·fy (râr′ ə fī′, râr′-) *vt-* [**rar·e·fied, rar·e·fy·ing**] to cause to become less dense: *Release of pressure rarefied the gas in the chamber. vi-: The air rarefies as one climbs.*

rare·ly (râr′ lē) *adv-* 1 seldom; infrequently: *a rarely seen bat.* 2 unusually; exceptionally: *a rarely beautiful gem.*

rar·i·ty (râr′ ə tē, râr′-) *n-* [*pl.* **rar·i·ties**] 1 anything rare and unique: *First editions of Shakespeare are rarities.* 2 infrequency; scarcity; uncommonness: *the rarity of true genius.* 3 thinness; lack of density: *the rarity of the atmosphere in high altitudes.*

ras·cal (răs′ kəl) *n-* 1 bad or mean person; scoundrel. 2 mischievous person, especially a playful child. —*n-* **ras·cal′ i·ty** (răs kăl′ ə tē).

ras·cal·ly (răs′ kə lē) *adj-* dishonest; mean; base: *a rascally scheme.*

rash (răsh) *adj-* [**rash·er, rash·est**] hasty; reckless: *She regretted her rash decision.* [from earlier English *rasch,* probably of Dutch or German origin.] —*adv-* **rash′ ly.** *n-* **rash′ ness.**

rasp (răsp) *n-* 1 coarse file with raised teeth instead of ridges. 2 act of scraping with, or as if with, such a file. 3 rough, harsh sound: *Her voice had an annoying* rasp. *vt-* 1 to rub or scrape with such a file: *The blacksmith rasped the horse's hoof.* 2 to irritate: *The squeaky door rasps my nerves. vi-* to scrape roughly with a harsh sound. —*adj-* **rasp′ like′.**

Rasp

rasp·ber·ry (răz′ bĕr′ ē) *n-* [*pl.* **rasp·ber·ries**] 1 round, juicy fruit made up of small, closely set globes, usually red, but some types black, purple, or yellow. 2 bush having leaves in groups of three, and long, prickly stems, which bears this fruit. 3 *Slang* rude, splattering sound made with the tongue and lips and used to show contempt or disfavor.

Raspberry

rasp·y (răs′ pē) *adj-* [**rasp·i·er, rasp·i·est**] 1 of sounds, harsh or grating; gravelly: *a raspy voice.* 2 rough in texture; irritated or sore; also, crotchety or cranky: *a raspy throat; a raspy mood.*

rat (răt) *n-* 1 gnawing animal, usually gray, black, or brown, with small, beady eyes and a long, hairless tail. Rats look somewhat like large mice. 2 small pad used by women to roll hair over. 3 *Slang* low, worthless, or mean person; especially, an informer or deserter. *vi-* [**rat·ted, rat·ting**] 1 to hunt rats. 2 *Slang* to desert. 3 *Slang* to inform (on).

smell a rat to suspect a trick; have a feeling that something is wrong.

Brown rat, about 1 1/2 ft long

ra·tan (rā tăn′) rattan.

ratch·et (răch′ ət) *n-* mechanism consisting of a toothed wheel or bar and one or more fingers (pawls) that pivot so as to fit between two of the teeth and permit motion of the wheel or bar in only one direction. Ratchets are used on the winding stems of clocks, on jacks for hoisting cars, on winches, on wrenches, and on other devices.

PAWLS

Ratchet

¹rate (rāt) *n-* 1 amount or degree of something measured in relation to something else; especially, the number of times something occurs in a given amount of time: *a rate of increase; rate of consumption.* 2 a speed; pace: *traveling at a fast rate.* 3 set price or charge for goods, service, work, etc.: *a fair rate of pay; interest rates.* *vt-* [**rat·ed, rat·ing**] 1 to put a value on: *He rated her low in reading ability.* 2 to consider; regard: *Many people rate baseball as dull to watch.* 3 *Informal* to deserve; merit: *He rates a promotion. vi-* to be ranked or valued: *He rates high among the hitters.* [from Old French, from Medieval Latin *rāta,* "fixed; reckoned up."]

at any rate in any case; anyway. **at that** (or **this**) **rate** in that or this case; under such circumstances.

²rate (rāt) *vt-* [**rat·ed, rat·ing**] to scold sharply; chide; berate. [from Old French *reter* meaning "to impute; blame," from Late Latin *reputāre,* "to account to one's credit," from earlier meaning "to compute; reckon."]

rath·er (răth′ ər) *adv-* 1 to some extent; somewhat: *I'm rather tired after our trip.* 2 preferably: *I would rather go home now than later.* 3 more correctly; also, on the contrary; instead: *Her dress is red, or rather, it's orange-red. interj-* Brit. I should say so!

rat·ing (rā′ tĭng) *n-* 1 a placing or classifying according to relative value, merit, or standing: *a rating of the year's best novels.* 2 standing; rank; class: *a high scholastic rating; a low credit rating.* 3 *Military* title showing special training or capability: *He has the rating of machinist.* 4 power, limit of operation, etc., of some device: *a fuse with the rating of 15 amperes.*

ra·tio (rā′ shō′, rā′ shē ō′) *n-* [*pl.* **ra·tios**] 1 a relationship in quantity, amount, or size between two things, expressed as the quotient of two numbers: *There is a ratio of 3 to 1 between the volumes of the two containers.* 2 the indicated quotient of two numbers, expressions, etc., which is written as 3:1, 3/1, 3 ÷ 1, or ³⁄₁.

ra·ti·o·ci·na·tion (răt′ ē ō′ sə nā′ shən) *n-* careful and logical thinking; reasoning.

ra·tion (răsh′ ən, rā′ shən) *n-* 1 fixed share or portion; allowance: *He ate his daily* ration *of chocolate after lunch.* 2 *Military* food for one man for one day. 3 **rations** food or supplies, especially when given out in fixed amounts. *vt-* to give out in fixed amounts or otherwise limit the use of (something in short supply): *The ship-wrecked crew* rationed *their water.*

ra·tion·al (răsh′ ən əl) *adj-* 1 able to reason: *Man is a* rational *being.* 2 guided by or based on reason; logical. 3 *Mathematics* of or having to do with a rational number. —*adv-* **ra′ tion·al·ly.** *n-* **ra′ tion·al·ness.**

ra·tion·ale (răsh′ ən ăl′) *n-* basic principles that justify or explain a theory, belief, policy, line of action. etc.

ra·tion·al·ism (răsh′ ən ə lĭz′ əm) *n-* 1 habit of being reasonable and logical: *His* rationalism *sometimes broke down under the stress of emotion.* 2 in philosophy, the theory that essential knowledge can be gained by the use of reasoning alone, without experience of the senses, and that such knowledge is superior to any gained by experience. See also *empiricism.* 3 in religion, the tendency to place a high value on reason as compared with divine revelation. —*n-* **ra′ tion·al·ist.** *adj-* **ra′ tion·al·is′ ti.** *adv-* **ra′ tion·al·is′ ti·cal·ly.**

ra·tion·al·i·ty (răsh′ ə năl′ ə tē) *n-* [*pl.* **ra·tion·al·i·ties**] the ability or power to reason; the possession or use of the power of reasoning: *John's* rationality *is in doubt.*

ra·tion·al·ize (răsh′ ə nə lĭz′) *vt-* [**ra·tion·al·ized, ra·tion·al·iz·ing**] 1 to give a reasonable explanation for (actions, attitudes, etc.) that in fact arise from emotion, selfishness, or prejudice: *They said I merely* rationalized *when I explained my refusal to enter the race.* 2 to explain according to the rules of reason and nature: *to* rationalize *a miracle.* 3 to cause to conform to reason: *to* rationalize *a process.* —*n-* **ra′ tion·al·i·za′ tion.**

rational number *n-* any number that can be expressed as an integer or as a quotient of two integers. Any integer or common fraction is a rational number.

rat·line or **rat·lin** (răt′ lən) *n-* one of a series of small ropes tied between the shrouds of a ship to form a ladder.

DEADEYE

Ratlines

rat mite *n-* mite that sometimes attacks man and is a carrier of epidemic typhus.

rat race *n- Informal* life, work, or any activity thought of as frantic, pointless, and endless.

rat·tan or **ra·tan** (ră tăn′) *n-* 1 climbing palm of tropical regions, with long, smooth, reedlike stems. 2 these stems, used especially in making wicker furniture. 3 walking stick or cane made of such stems.

rat·ter (răt′ ər) *n-* 1 person or animal that hunts or catches rats. 2 *Informal* person who deserts, betrays, or informs on his associates or friends.

rat·tle (răt′ əl) *vi-* [**rat·tled, rat·tling**] 1 to make short, sharp sounds in quick succession: *Hail* rattled *on the roof. The windows* rattled *during the storm.* 2 to move with a clatter: *The wagon* rattled *along the bumpy road.* 3 to talk in a noisy, rapid manner: *She* rattled *on for an hour. vt-* 1 to cause to make rapid, sharp sounds: *The wind* rattles *the shutters.* 2 to cause to be nervous; confuse; upset: *Interruptions* rattled *the speaker. n-* 1 series of short, sharp sounds: *the* rattle *of a window.* 2 child's toy that makes a clattering sound when it is shaken. 3 series of horny rings on a rattlesnake's tail that buzz sharply when vibrated. —*adj-* **rat′ tly:** *a* rattly *car.*

rattle off to say or do quickly: *He* rattled off *the poem.*

rat·tle·brain (răt′ əl brān′) *Informal n-* stupid, flighty, and prattling person. —*adj-* **rat′ tle·brained′.**

rat·tler (răt′ əl ər, răt′ lər) *n-* 1 person or thing that makes a clattering noise, such as a freight train. 2 rattlesnake.

rat·tle·snake (răt′ əl snāk′) *n-* any of various American poisonous snakes with horny, knoblike rings at the end of the tail. The rings make a rattling sound as the snake vibrates its tail when disturbed.

Diamondback rattlesnake
4–8 ft long

rat·tle·trap (răt′ əl trăp′) *n-* anything very old or worn-out, especially an automobile or railroad car.

rat·tling (răt′ lĭng, răt′ əl ĭng) *n-* noise made by the clattering together of small hard objects. *adj-* 1 making a rapid succession of sharp, noisy sounds. 2 *Informal* quick: *to walk at a* rattling *pace.* 3 *Informal* very good; superior: *They played a* rattling *game. adv- Informal* (intensifier only): *They saw a* rattling *good movie.*

rat·trap (răt′ trăp′) *n-* 1 trap for catching rats. 2 hopeless or desperate situation.

rat·ty (răt′ ē) *adj-* [**rat·ti·er, rat·ti·est**] 1 like a rat. 2 full of rats. 3 *Informal* broken-down; shabby; run-down.

rau·cous (rò′ kəs) *adj-* 1 hoarse; harsh; raspy: *the* raucous *cry of the crow.* 2 mocking and unruly; boisterous: *the* raucous *laughter of the opposition.* —*adv-* **rau′ cous·ly.** *n-* **rau′ cous·ness.**

rav·age (răv′ ĭj) *vt-* [**rav·aged, rav·ag·ing**] 1 to lay waste; devastate; plunder; sack: *Enemy troops* ravaged *the countryside.* 2 to rob of health and vitality: *Poverty and disease* ravaged *half the population. n-* destructive action, or its result; ruin: *free from* ravage *by flood; the* ravages *of disease.* —*n-* **rav′ ag·er.**

rave (rāv) *vi-* [**raved, rav·ing**] 1 to talk in a wild and disconnected manner: *The mental patient* raved *about his imaginary business.* 2 to talk with great enthusiasm: *She* raved *about her trip to Europe. n-* 1 wild or irrational talk or action. 2 *Slang* person or thing that is the object of enthusiastic approval. 3 *Informal* extravagantly

rav·el (răv′ əl) *vt-* to separate the threads of (woven or knitted material). *vi-* 1 to come apart or unwoven; fray: *The shirt began to* ravel *at the sleeves.* 2 to entangle or confuse (now rarely used). *n-* a thread loosened from woven or knitten material. —*n-* **rav′ el·er.**

rav·el·ing (răv′ əl ĭng) *n-* thread that has raveled from woven or knitted material. Also **rav′ el·ling.**

¹**ra·ven** (rā′ vən) *n-* large bird related to the crow, having glossy black feathers that are long at the throat. *adj-* shiny black: *a girl with* raven *hair.* [from Old English **hræfn**].

²**rav·en** (răv′ ən) *vt-* 1 to devour greedily. 2 to seize with force. *vi-* to seek and devour prey. [from Middle English **ravine** meaning "booty; robbery," from Old French, from Latin **rapina** meaning "robbery," from Latin **rapere**, "to seize."]

Raven about 2 ft long

rav·en·ing (răv′ ən ĭng) *adj-* greedily or hungrily searching for prey: *Wolves are* ravening *animals.*

rav·en·ous (răv′ ə nəs) *adj-* very eager for food or other satisfaction; wanting much before one is satisfied: *a* ravenous *appetite; to be* ravenous *for riches or fame.* —*adv-* **rav′ en·ous·ly.** *n-* **rav′ en·ous·ness.**

ra·vine (rə vēn′) *n-* long, deep gully or valley, usually worn by water.

rav·ing (rā′ vĭng) *n-* wild or furious talk: *the* raving *of a crazy man. adj-* 1 talking wildly; delirious: *the* raving *speech of a person with a high fever.* 2 *Informal* very attractive or winning: *a* raving *beauty. adv- Informal* wildly; furiously: *He's* raving *mad.* —*adv-* **rav′ ing·ly.**

ra·vi·o·li (răv′ ē ō′ lē) *n-* food dish consisting of small, thin pieces of dough filled with chopped meat, cheese, etc., boiled, and usually served with a seasoned tomato sauce; also, one of the pieces.

rav·ish (răv′ Ish) *vt-* 1 to seize and carry away by force. 2 to rape. 3 to overcome with delight; enchant: *The music ravished him.* —*n-* rav′ish·er. —*n-* rav′ish·ment.

rav·ish·ing (răv′ Ish Ing) *adj-* causing great admiration; very charming; enchanting; captivating: *a ravishing beauty.* —*adv-* rav′ish·ing·ly.

raw (rò) *adj-* [raw·er, raw·est.] 1 in a natural state; unrefined; unprocessed: *One seldom uses raw lumber for building.* 2 uncooked. 3 painfully open or exposed: *a raw wound.* 4 harsh; crude: *His manners are raw.* 5 not experienced; not trained: *a raw beginner.* 6 cold; damp; chilly: *a raw wind.* —*adv-* raw′ly. *n-* raw′ness.

raw-boned (rò′ bònd′) *adj-* with little flesh on the bones; thin; gaunt: *the raw-boned face of a cowboy.*

raw·hide (rò′ hīd′) *n-* 1 hide of cattle or other animals before it is tanned. 2 whip or cord made of this hide.

raw material *n-* 1 petroleum, metal ores, coal, wood, and other materials in their natural state, needed to manufacture finished products. 2 person or persons having promising natural ability or talent which needs training: *good raw material for the football team.*

¹**ray** (rā) *n-* 1 beam of light, heat, electrons, etc.: *The sun's rays warm the earth.* 2 one of several parts sticking out from a center: *the rays of a starfish*; rays *of a daisy.* 3 *Mathematics* a set of points consisting of any given point on a line and all other points of the line on one side of the given point. 4 slight amount; trace; glimmer; gleam: *The news brought a ray of hope.* 5 *Astronomy* one of the many bright streaks seen radiating from craters on the moon's surface, especially when the moon is full. [from Old French rai, from Latin rādius, "a beam."] Homs- re, ¹Re. —*adj-* ray′less.

²**ray** (rā) *n-* any of several fishes related to the sharks and having a flat, fan-shaped body and a whiplike tail. [from Old French raie, from Latin rāia.] Homs- re, ¹Re.

Rays of starfish

Manta ray, often 20 ft across

ray·on (rā′ ŏn′) *n-* 1 smooth fiber made from cellulose, obtained from wood pulp and cotton, which is chemically treated and forced through tiny holes. 2 silklike cloth made from such fiber.

raze (rāz) *vt-* [razed, raz·ing] to tear down; level to the ground; destroy completely: *The fire razed the building.* Also **rase.** Hom- raise.

ra·zor (rā′ zər) 1 sharp-edged instrument for shaving off hair, especially mens' beards. 2 close-cutting electric clipper used for the same purpose.

ra·zor·back (rā′ zər băk′) *n-* lean, sharp-backed hog with long legs, common in southern United States. *adj-* (often **ra′ zor-backed**′) having a long, sharp back: *a small, razorbacked dog.*

SAFETY
ELECTRIC
STRAIGHT
Razors

razz (răz) *Slang vt-* to make fun of in an annoying way; tease; ridicule; heckle.

Rb symbol for rubidium.

R.C. 1 Red Cross. 2 Roman Catholic.

rd. 1 (also **Rd.**) road. 2 rod or rods. 3 round.

R.D. rural (free) delivery.

¹**re** (rā) *n-* the second note of a musical scale. [from Italian *re,* the first syllable of Latin *resōnare.*] Homs- ray, ¹Re.

²**re** (rā, rē) *prep-* in the matter of or in the case of (used in business letter writing, law, etc.). [from Latin rē, from rēs "thing; affair."] Homs- ray, ¹Re.

Re symbol for rhenium.

re- *prefix* 1 again; once more: *to rebuild; rejoin; rewrite.* 2 back again: *to repay; rebound; reclaim.* [from Latin **re-** meaning "again; over (again); back."]

reach (rēch) *vt-* 1 to come to; arrive at: *They reached home before the rain. The jury finally reached a verdict.* 2 to stretch to; extend to: *This road reaches the river.* 3 to stretch an arm or hand to touch or grasp: *He is tall and can reach the top shelf.* 4 to pass or deliver to another; hand: *Please reach me my coat.* 5 to get to; communicate with: *You can reach us by calling this phone number.* 6 to affect; influence: *The speaker just couldn't reach his audience. vi-* 1 to extend the hand to touch or grasp something: *He reached out to greet us.* 2 to try to get something: *to reach for approval or sympathy.* 3 to extend in time, space, amount, etc.: *The damage reaches into thousands of dollars. There was sand as far as the eye could reach.* 4 to extend over a desired distance: *This new cord just barely reaches. n-* 1 distance a person can stretch an arm so as to grasp or touch something: *That boxer has a long reach. The ball was out of his reach.* 2 a stretching out to touch something: *a short reach from the desk to the telephone.* 3 what one is able to understand, imagine, or do: *Advanced physics is beyond my reach.* 4 (often **reaches**) great distance or expanse: *the far reaches of Asia.*

re·act (rē ăkt′) *vi-* 1 to respond: *The ear reacts to sound. The patient reacted favorably to the treatment.* 2 to have an effect upon the person who is acting: *John's bad manners react against him.* 3 *Chemistry* to change by the action of two or more substances on each other.

re·ac·tance (rē ăk′ tans) *n-* in electricity, the opposition to the flow of an alternating or pulsating current offered either by an induction coil (**inductive reactance**) or by a capacitor (**capacitive reactance**), measured in ohms.

re·ac·tion (rē ăk′ shən) *n-* 1 response to an influence: *the ear's reaction to sound; a patient's reaction to a new medicine; the reaction of an audience to a speaker.* 2 tendency or wish to return to a former, or opposite, state of affairs: *a reaction against new ideas.* 3 *Chemistry* action of two or more substances on each other to form new substances.

re·ac·tion·ar·y (rē ăk′ shən ĕr′ ē) *n-* [*pl.* **re·ac·tion·ar·ies**] 1 person who favors a return to former conditions. 2 person who seeks to block social or political progress. *adj-: a reactionary politician; a reactionary idea.*

reaction engine *n-* any engine that expels a stream of matter to the rear at very high speed, thus generating a powerful forward thrust.

re·ac·ti·vate (rē ăk′ tə văt′, rē′-) *vt-* [re·ac·ti·vat·ed, re·ac·ti·vat·ing] to make active again; return to active duty or service: *to reactivate an army division; to reactivate a naval vessel.* —*n-* re·ac′ti·va′tion.

re·ac·tive (rē ăk′ tĭv′) *adj-* 1 of or relating to reaction or reactance. 2 tending to react: *a readily reactive substance.* 3 consisting of reaction: *his reactive behavior.* —*n-* re·ac′tiv′i·ty.

re·ac·tor (rē ăk′ tər) *n-* large tank in which controlled nuclear fission takes place. Reactors are used for producing new nuclear fuel, steam for electric power, etc.

read (rēd) *vt-* [read (rĕd), read·ing] 1 to look at and understand the meaning of (written or printed words or symbols): *to read a book; to read a thermometer; to read music.* 2 to say aloud (written or printed words): *He will read the report to the class.* 3 to understand; get the meaning of: *The radio signals were faint, but we read them. The riddle was hard to read.* 4 to show; register: *The speedometer reads 45 miles an hour.* 5 *chiefly Brit.* to study, especially at a university: *He read history at Oxford. vi-* 1 to be able to understand the meaning of written and printed matter: *Half the population cannot read.* 2 to look through and interpret the meaning of written and printed matter: *He reads constantly. They seldom read.* 3 to speak aloud something that is written or printed: *He reads to the children every day.* 4 of a text, to be as one reads it: *It reads thus.* 5 to sound, or impress someone, in a certain way: *This report reads well.* Hom- reed.

read between the lines to find a special meaning in something not actually written or said.

read into to interpret a certain way; to find more in something written or spoken than was intended.

read·a·ble (rē′də bəl) *adj-* 1 easy to read. 2 pleasant to read; interesting. 3 plainly written; legible. —*n-* read′a·bil′i·ty or read′a·ble·ness.

read·er (rē′dər) *n-* 1 person who reads or can read: *a slow* reader; *an avid* reader. 2 schoolbook with exercises for learning how to read. 3 person who reads manuscripts for a publisher to determine their merit. 4 professor's assistant who reads students' papers. 5 in some British universities, lecturer or instructor.

read·er·ship (rē′dər ship′) *n-* the persons, collectively, who read a certain magazine, newspaper, writer, etc.; literary audience: *a magazine with a small readership.*

read·i·ly (rĕd′ə lē) *adv-* 1 willingly and quickly: *He readily came to my aid when I needed him.* 2 without difficulty; easily: *The toy is readily assembled.*

read·i·ness (rĕd′ē nəs) *n-* 1 condition of being prepared: *Everything is in readiness for the arrival of guests.* 2 willingness; favorable desire: *He shows a readiness to co-operate.* 3 lack of difficulty; ease: *The readiness with which the two substances mix.* 4 the knowledge or experience needed to progress in a learning program: *reading readiness.*

read·ing (rē′dĭng) *n-* 1 a getting of information or amusement from written or printed words. 2 public recital where something is read to the audience: *Our class gave a reading of Dickens' "A Christmas Carol."* 3 written or printed words to be read: *There is little reading in this picture magazine.* 4 interpretation or manner of interpretation: *various readings of the Bible; an actor's reading of Hamlet.* 5 record shown by an instrument: *The monthly reading on the electric meter. as modifier:* a reading *textbook; a reading expert; a reading room.*

reading glass *n-* large magnifying glass, often having a handle, used for reading fine print.

re·ad·just (rē′ə jŭst′) *vt-* to adjust again; set in order again: *The jeweler readjusted my watch. vi-* to become adjusted again. —*n-* re·ad·just′ment.

read·out (rēd′out′) *n-* the transmitting of data from a transmitter in a spacecraft upon command from a ground station.

read·y (rĕd′ē) *adj-* [read·i·er, read·i·est] 1 prepared, fit, or equipped to do something: *We're packed and ready to go on the trip.* 2 prepared for immediate use; finished; complete: *Your dress is ready.* Dinner is ready. 3 willing; inclined: *always ready to obey; ready to criticize.* 4 in the proper condition; also, available: *The peaches are ready to be picked.* 5 quick; prompt: *The students gave ready answers.* 6 on hand for immediate use; available: *Storekeepers must have ready cash. vt-* [read·ied, read·y·ing] to prepare: *The sailors readied the ship for the storm.*

make ready to put in order; prepare.

read·y-made (rĕd′ē mād′) *adj-* 1 already prepared; ready for immediate use: *a ready-made chicken dinner.* 2 made in quantity from patterns; made in large numbers and many sizes: *Most shirts are ready-made.* 3 commonplace; not original; trite: *full of ready-made ideas.*

read·y-to-wear (rĕd′ē tə wâr′) *adj-* of clothing, having been made from standard patterns and available in retail stores as finished garments; ready-made.

re·a·gent (rē ā′jənt) *Chemistry n-* substance known to have a particular reaction under certain conditions, used in the analysis of chemical compounds.

¹re·al (rē′əl, rēl) *adj-* 1 true; genuine: *a real friend; real diamonds.* 2 actual; not imagined: *Was the figure you saw last night real or imaginary?* 3 in law, having to do with land or buildings: *one's real property. adv- Informal* really; very: *a real good book.* [from Middle English real, from Medieval Latin realis, "of or relating to things (in law)."] *Hom-* reel.

²re·al (rā äl′) *n-* [*pl.* re·als or re·a·les (rä äl′ās)] old Spanish and Spanish-American coin, worth 1/8 of a peso (piece of eight). The real was the "bit" on the basis of which the U.S. dollar is said to have eight bits. [from Spanish real, "royal," from Latin regalis.]

real estate *n-* land and anything on it, including buildings, fences, trees, minerals, etc. *as modifier* (real-estate): *a real-estate business.*

real image *n-* in optics, the inverted image formed by the converging or focusing of light rays. Such an image can be projected on a screen. See also *virtual image.*

re·al·ism (rē′ə lĭz′əm) *n-* 1 tendency to concern oneself chiefly with facts and practical matters, rather than with ideals. 2 in art and literature, the use of subjects and characters from ordinary life and society, without the adornment of romance. —*n-* re′al·ist.

re·al·is·tic (rē ə lĭs′tĭk) *adj-* 1 tending to be concerned chiefly with facts and practical matters: *He is a realistic man, not a dreamer.* 2 of, relating to, or representing realism in literature or art. —*adv-* re′al·is′ti·cal·ly.

re·al·i·ty (rē ăl′ə tē) *n-* [*pl.* re·al·i·ties] 1 existence in fact, as contrasted to existence in imagination, illusion, or mistaken opinion: *the reality of nuclear weapons.* 2 something or someone real: *When the boat left the dock, the trip finally became a reality.* 3 the sum total of real things; the actual state of things.

in reality actually; in fact.

re·al·i·za·tion (rē′əl ə zā′shən) *n-* 1 awareness; understanding: *Full realization of what had happened came years later.* 2 the coming or bringing of a hope, dream, fear, etc., into actual existence: *He spent years in the realization of his hope for a new hospital.* 3 something that comes or is brought into actual existence: *The new hospital was the realization of his hopes.*

re·al·ize (rē′ə līz′) *vt-* [re·al·ized, re·al·iz·ing] 1 to become fully aware of; understand fully; grasp: *She didn't realize that her actions were rude. He realized he was making a mistake.* 2 to make real; attain: *He realized his ambition.* 3 to get as profit: *Henry realized $50 on the sale of the ring.* —*adj-* re′al·iz′a·ble.

re·al·ly (rē′ə lē, rē′lē) *adv-* actually; truly; in fact.

realm (rĕlm) *n-* 1 kingdom; empire. 2 region or sphere: *the realm of fancy.* 3 special field or province: *the realm of science.*

real number *n-* one of the set of numbers comprising the rational numbers, such as 2, 3, and $-1/2$, and the irrational numbers, such as pi.

re·al·tor (rē′əl tər) *n-* person whose occupation is buying and selling real estate; especially, a member of the National Association of Real Estate Boards.

re·al·ty (rē′əl tē) *n-* [*pl.* re·al·ties] land and buildings; real estate. *as modifier:* a realty *office.*

¹ream (rēm) *n-* 1 amount of paper equal to 20 quires. The ream has been counted as 480, 500, or 516 sheets, and is now usually counted as 500 sheets. 2 reams *Informal* a large amount: *He wrote reams of bad poetry.* [from Old French raime, from Spanish resma, from Arabic rismah meaning "a bundle."]

²ream (rēm) *vt-* 1 to shape, enlarge, or taper (a hole) with a reamer. 2 to clean out by scraping: *to ream the bowl of a pipe.* [from Old English ryman meaning "to enlarge," from rum, "room."]

ream·er (rē′mər) *n-* 1 rotating metal tool, often tapered, for shaping, enlarging, or tapering holes. 2 tool for cleaning a pipe bowl. 3 person who reams. 4 utensil for pressing juice from citrus fruits.

Reamers

re·an·i·mate (rē ăn′ə māt′, rē′-) *vt-* [re·an·i·mat·ed, re·an·i·mat·ing] to bring back to life; give new strength to; encourage: *Cheers reanimated the losing player.*

reap (rēp) *vt-* 1 to cut down and gather in: *to reap grain.* 2 to cut a crop from: *to reap a field.* 3 to receive the benefit from: *He reaped the rewards of hard work. vi-* to cut and gather grain.

reap·er (rē′pər) *n-* 1 person who cuts grain; mower. 2 machine for mowing grain. 3 the Reaper (also the Grim Reaper) death.

re·ap·pear (rē′ə pêr′) *vi-* to come in sight again: *The moon reappeared from behind the clouds.* —*n-* re·ap·pear′ance.

¹rear (rēr) *n-* **1** the back part (of anything): *the rear of the bus.* **2** the space or position behind: *He was at the rear of the building.* **3** back part of an army or fleet: *the enemy in the rear.* *adj-* at, in, or near the back: *The rear entrance is for deliveries.* [from a shortened form of English **arrear** meaning "that in which one has fallen behind," from Old French **ariere**, from Latin **ad**-meaning "to" and **retrō**, "backward."]

    at (or **in**) **the rear of** behind. **bring up the rear to** come last or at the end.

²rear (rēr) *vt-* **1** to bring up and educate, raise: *to rear a child.* **2** to grow; breed: *to rear animals or plants.* **3** to build; erect: *to rear a castle.* **4** to lift; raise up: *He reared his head.* *vi-* to rise on hind legs: *The horse reared.* [from Old English **ræran**, "to raise."]

rear admiral *n-* in the Navy and Coast Guard, a commissioned officer ranking next below a vice admiral and next above a captain.

rear guard *n-* the part of a military or naval force that guards the rear.

re·arm (rē ärm′, rē′-) *vt-* to supply again with military arms, especially with newer or improved kinds: *The United States helped rearm Britain after Dunkirk.* *vi-*: *Germany rearmed in the 1930's.* —*n-* **re·arm′a·ment** (rē är′mə mənt): *the rearmament of a nation.*

rear·most (rēr′mōst′) *adj-* nearest to or farthest in the rear; last in position: *a ship's rearmost mast.*

re·ar·range (rē′ə rānj′) *vt-* [re·ar·ranged, re·ar·rang·ing] to arrange again, usually in a different order: *They rearranged the seating.* —*n-* **re′ar·range′ment.**

rear·view mirror (rēr′vyōō′) *n-* small mirror that enables a driver or pilot to see behind him.

rear·ward (rēr′wərd) *adv-* (also **rear′wards**) at or toward the rear: *A car mirror helps the driver to see rearward.* *adj-*: *He had a rearward position.*

re·as·cend (rē′ə sĕnd′) *vt-* to climb, mount, or rise again: *The firemen reascended the ladders to rescue other people.* *vi-*: *The plane reascended through the clouds.*

rea·son (rē′zən) *n-* **1** motive; purpose (for an action). **2** fact or assumption leading someone to a belief, thought, or conclusion: *We have reasons for believing that he is still in Mexico.* **3** ability to think; logical and rational faculty. **4** sanity: *He lost his reason.* **5** the realm of common sense or appropriateness: *anything within reason.* *vi-* **1** to think or argue logically: *Dr. Brown reasons so clearly that anyone can follow him.* **2** to try to use persuasion (with): *It's hard to reason with a stubborn child.* *vt-* **1** to think or believe on the basis of logic (takes only a clause as object): *He reasoned that only John could have done it.* **2** to think over carefully and completely (followed by "through"): *to reason through the possible results.* **3** to find or arrive at by means of logic (followed by "out"): *He reasoned out a good solution to the problem.* —*n-* **rea′son·er.**

    by reason of because of. **in reason** reasonable; sensible. **stand to reason** to seem reasonable or logical: *It stands to reason that plants need water and sunshine.* **without rhyme or reason** making no sense at all; having no sensible explanation.

rea·son·a·ble (rē′zən ə bəl) *adj-* **1** in keeping with reason or logic; just; fair; sensible: *a reasonable decision.* **2** using or able to use reason; sensible; rational: *He is a reasonable man.* **3** within the limits of what is probable: *a reasonable guess or conclusion.* **4** not expensive: *Chicken is reasonable this week.* —*adv-* **rea′son·a·bly.** *n-* **rea′son·a·ble·ness.**

rea·son·ing (rē′zən ĭng) *n-* **1** act or process of using thought to reach an answer, form judgments, or come to conclusions; careful and systematic thought; logic: *Jack solved the problem after long reasoning.* **2** presentation of reasons; line of argument: *It was hard to follow the speaker's reasoning.*

re·as·sem·ble (rē′ə sĕm′bəl) *vt-* [re·as·sem·bled, re·as·sem·bling] to put together or bring together again: *to reassemble a motor.* *vi-* to come together again: *The class reassembled after recess.*

re·as·sert (rē′ə sûrt′) *vt-* to state or declare again: *to reassert a claim.*

re·as·sume (rē′ə sōōm′, -syōōm′) *vt-* [re·as·sumed, re·as·sum·ing] **1** to take on again as a duty, task, responsibility, etc.; undertake again. **2** to take or adopt again: *to reassume a position; to reassume a belligerent attitude.*

re·as·sur·ance (rē′ə shōōr′əns) *n-* **1** a giving of assurance, confidence, or courage: *With the doctor's reassurance, he felt he could walk again.* **2** new assurance, confidence, or courage: *He could face the future with reassurance that he was well.*

re·as·sure (rē′ə shōōr′) *vt-* [re·as·sured, re·as·sur·ing] to give new confidence or courage to comfort: *He reassured his mother that he would be careful.*

re·a·wak·en (rē′ə wā′kən) *vt-* to cause (someone or something) to awaken again: *A fire alarm reawakened him after he dozed off. He reawakened my interest in skiing.* *vi-* *He rewakened with a start.*

re·bate (rē′ bāt′) *n-* money paid back; discount; refund: *He received a rebate from the store for paying cash.* *vt-* (*also* rĭ bāt′) [re·bat·ed, re·bat·ing] **1** to give back (part of a sum paid). **2** to make a reduction in: *to rebate a bill.*

Re·bec·ca (rə bĕk′ə) *n-* in the Old Testament, the wife of Isaac and the mother of Esau and Jacob.

¹re·bel (rĭ bĕl′) *vi-* [re·belled, re·bel·ling] **1** to oppose or take up arms against the law or government. **2** to oppose or resist any authority: *He rebels as a matter of habit.* **3** to react with anger, aversion, disgust, etc. (usually followed by "at" or "against").

²reb·el (rĕb′əl) *n-* **1** one who opposes or seeks to overthrow the government. **2** one who resists any authority. *as modifier:* *the rebel army; his rebel spirit.*

re·bel·lion (rĭ bĕl′yən) *n-* **1** a taking up of arms against the government; revolt. **2** defiance of or resistance to any form of authority: *a period of youthful rebellion.*

re·bel·lious (rĭ bĕl′yəs) *adj-* **1** opposing or defying law, government, or lawful authority: *the rebellious officers.* **2** resisting control; unruly: *a rebellious child.* —*adv-* **re·bel′lious·ly.** *n-* **re·bel′lious·ness.**

re·bind (rē′ bĭnd′) *vt-* [re·bound, re·bind·ing] to bind or cover again: *to rebind a library book.*

re·birth (rē bûrth′, rē′-) *n-* return of activity, growth, or life; revival: *a rebirth of learning; a spiritual rebirth; the rebirth of flowers after a long winter.*

re·born (rē′bôrn′) *adj-* born again; taking on new life; renewed: *a reborn delight in music.*

¹re·bound (rē′ bound′) *n-* **1** a springing or bouncing back: *The sharp rebound of the ball took him by surprise.* **2** a ball or puck that has bounced or sprung back: *Bill grabbed the rebound and passed.*

    on the rebound 1 as it bounces, up or back after hitting: *Try to catch the ball on the rebound.* **2** *Informal* recovering from a bad experience in love, work, etc.: *He was on the rebound from a hard first year at college.*

²re·bound (rĭ bound′) *vi-* to spring or bounce back: *The ball rebounded off the wall.*

re·broad·cast (rē′ brôd′kăst′) *vt-* [re·broad·cast or re·broad·cast·ed, re·broad·cast·ing] **1** to broadcast (a radio or television program) again from the same station. **2** to broadcast (a program received from another station). *n-* program that is broadcast again.

re·buff (rĭ bŭf′) *n-* **1** sudden or unexpected denial, refusal, or snub: *I met with a rebuff when I asked for the car.* **2** a driving back; sudden check; defeat. *vt-* to refuse curtly; repulse; snub: *He rebuffed my offer.*

re·build (rē bĭld′, rē′-) *vt-* [re·built, re·build·ing] to make again; build anew; reconstruct: *Please rebuild the broken steps.* *vi-* to restore oneself or one's possessions to a former, normal, or improved condition: *The town rebuilt after the earthquake.*

re·buke (rĭ byōōk′) *vt-* [re·buked, re·buk·ing] to speak to in sharp disapproval; scold; reprimand: *The judge rebuked the driver for his carelessness.* *n-* sharp criticism of one's behavior: *He listened to the rebuke in silence.*

re·bus (rē′ bəs) *n-* [*pl.* **re·bus·es**] puzzle in which words, phrases, or sentences are represented by signs and pictures of objects. Example: "2 Y's" is a rebus for "too wise."

re·but (rĭ bŭt') *vt-* [re·but·ted, re·but·ting] to oppose or contradict with argument, evidence, or proof, as in a debate. —*n-* re·but'tal: *The affirmative will now begin its rebuttal.*

rec. 1 receipt. 2 received. 3 recipe. 4 record. 5 recorded. 6 recorder. 7 recording.

re·cal·ci·trant (rĭ kăl'sə trant) *adj-* refusing to obey or submit; very stubborn or obstinate; unyielding: *a recalcitrant horse; a recalcitrant child.* *n-* person or animal that refuses to obey or submit. —*n-* re·cal'ci·trance: *The recalcitrance of that horse is maddening.*

re·call (rĭ kôl') *vt-* 1 to summon or call (somebody) back: *The President recalled Senator Baines to Washington.* 2 to bring back to mind: *That chair recalls something that I did years ago.* 3 to recreate; restore: *One cannot recall the past.* *n-* 1 a calling back; summoning: *the recall of a foreign delegate.* 2 right or procedure by which citizens may petition for a vote to remove an unsatisfactory public official from office. 3 ability to bring back to mind things once known or experienced.
beyond recall with no chance of ever being restored.

re·cant (rĭ kănt') *vi-* to deny, and acknowledge as error, one's previous statement or belief: *He recanted and was forgiven.* *vt-: He publicly recanted his unorthodox views.* —*n-* re·can·ta'tion.

¹**re·cap** (rē' kăp', *also* rē kăp') *vt-* [re·capped, re·cap·ping] to cement, mold, and vulcanize a strip of rubber on the outer surface of (a worn pneumatic tire). *n-* tire that has been so treated. [from re-, "again" and cap.]

²**re·cap** (rē kăp') *Informal* *vt-* [re·capped, re·cap·ping] to recapitulate: *The reporter recapped the news.* *n-* a recapitulation: *a recap of the news.* [from **recapitulate**.]

re·ca·pit·u·late (rē'kə pĭch'ə lāt') *vt-* [re·ca·pit·u·lat·ed, re·ca·pit·u·lat·ing] to say again briefly; to sum up the chief points of: *After listening to the speakers, he recapitulated their main arguments.* *vi-* to repeat briefly what had been said at length. —*n-* re·ca·pit'u·la'tion.

re·cap·ture (rē kăp'chər) *vt-* [re·cap·tured, re·cap·tur·ing] 1 to take back (something lost) by force; capture again: *The Marines recaptured the island yesterday.* 2 to find again (something from one's past): *to recapture one's youth.* *n-: the recapture of the island.*

re·cast (rē kăst', rē'·) *vt-* 1 to mold or cast again: *to recast a medal.* 2 to plan again or to lay out in a new fashion: *I must recast the first chapter.* 3 to provide a new cast for (a play, opera, ballet, etc.).

recd. or **rec'd.** received.

re·cede (rĭ sēd') *vi-* [re·ced·ed, re·ced·ing] 1 to withdraw; move off or away: *The airplane recedes in the distance. The waves recede from the rocks.* 2 to slope gradually away from: *The beach receded from the base of the cliff.*

re·ceipt (rĭ sēt') *n-* 1 a receiving: *the receipt of a letter.* 2 written statement stating that money or goods have been received. 3 a recipe. 4 **receipts** money taken in: *the receipts of the game.* *vt-* to sign (a statement or invoice) to indicate that something has been received.

re·ceiv·a·ble (rĭ sē'və bəl) *adj-* in business, to be collected or received: *the receivable bills; accounts receivable.*

re·ceive (rĭ sēv') *vt-* [re·ceived, re·ceiv·ing] 1 to get or be given (something): *to receive a letter; to receive a good education.* 2 to take and hold: *a barrel to receive rain water.* 3 to take up; support; sustain: *These pillars receive the full weight of the roof.* 4 to greet or accept: *The audience received the speech with wild applause.* 5 to admit into one's presence; accept; welcome: *The President received the new ambassador.* 6 to take (radio and other wave signals) from some medium and change them into sound, speech, pictures, etc. *vi-* to be at home to visitors.

re·ceiv·er (rĭ sē'vər) *n-* 1 someone who holds, takes, or is given something: *John was the receiver of the football award.* 2 receptacle; container: *an ash receiver.* 3 the part of a telephone instrument through which one speaks or listens. 4 radio, television set, or similar device that receives broadcasted signals. 5 person appointed by a court to hold and manage the property and money of a person or firm in receivership. 6 in football, a player who catches a forward pass, kickoff, etc.

re·ceiv·er·ship (rĭ sē'vər shĭp') *n-* 1 the office or duty of a receiver appointed by a court. 2 legal and financial condition of a person or company whose assets have been assigned to a receiver.

re·cent (rē'sənt) *adj-* happening not long ago; occurring lately: *The recent storm caused all that damage.* —*adv-* re'cent·ly. *n-* re'cent·ness.

Re·cent (rē'sənt) *n-* the second of the two epochs of the Quaternary period. The Recent includes the present geological period. *adj-: the Recent epoch.*

re·cep·ta·cle (rĭ sěp'tĭ kəl) *n-* 1 container; holder. 2 base of a flower where the petals, and sometimes the fruit and seeds, are attached. 3 electrical outlet in a wall or floor of a building.

re·cep·tion (rĭ sěp'shən) *n-* 1 a receiving: *Everything is ready for the reception of the first shipment.* 2 greeting or welcome: *The team was given a warm reception.* 3 formal entertainment held to greet or introduce someone: *a reception for the new club president.* 4 strength and clarity of radio or other broadcast signals received: *poor television reception.*

re·cep·tion·ist (rĭ sěp'shən ĭst) *n-* an employee in an office, usually a woman, who receives callers and directs them to the proper person or place.

re·cep·tive (rĭ sěp'tĭv) *adj-* willing or eager to receive new ideas, suggestions, etc.: *a receptive mind.* —*adv-* re·cep'tive·ly. *n-* re'cep'tiv'i·ty.

re·cep·tor (rĭ sěp'tər) *n-* in anatomy, one of the nerve endings involved in receiving stimuli.

re·cess (rĭ sěs', rē'sěs') *n-* 1 brief ceasing or adjournment of normal activity: *Congress will be in recess until January. The class took a ten-minute recess.* 2 a notch or hollow space between cliffs or in a cliff: *a pool in a rocky recess.* 3 space set back in a wall; a niche: *a bookcase built into the recess of a wall.* *vi-* to cease or rest from normal activity for a time: *Congress recessed till January.* *vt-* 1 to put (something) into an alcove or niche: *We recessed the statue into the wall.* 2 to make a hollow or niche in. 3 to declare a brief pause in the official activity of: *The judge recessed the court at noon.*

re·ces·sion (rĭ sěsh'ən) *n-* 1 a going back or retiring; withdrawal. 2 mild business depression; moderate but noticeable decline in general economic activity.

re·ces·sion·al (rĭ sěsh'ən əl) *n-* 1 hymn sung, or music played, at the close of a church service as the clergy and choir leave the chancel. 2 music played when a service, performance, etc., is over and the audience is leaving.

re·ces·sive (rĭ sěs'ĭv) *adj-* 1 receding; tending to recede or go back. 2 *Biology* of a pair of inherited factors (genes), relating to the one which is suppressed or dominated by the other and therefore appears less often in the offspring (see also *dominant*). *n-* *Biology* gene that is suppressed or dominated by another.

re·charge (rē'chärj') *vt-* [re·charged, re·charg·ing] to renew the charge of: *to recharge a battery.*

rec·i·pe (rěs'ə pē') *n-* 1 directions or formula for preparing a food: *a good recipe for a cake.* 2 plan for doing anything: *He offered a recipe for world peace.*

re·cip·i·ent (rĭ sĭp'ē ənt) *n-* person or thing that receives something: *He was the recipient of the award.* *adj-* receiving or ready to receive: *a recipient nation.*

re·cip·ro·cal (rĭ sĭp'rə kəl) *adj-* 1 done, given, or offered by each to the other; mutual: *a reciprocal promise.* 2 corresponding; equivalent: *a reciprocal privilege.* 3 working or operating together: *the reciprocal parts of a machine.* 4 *Mathematics* of or having to do with two numbers or expressions whose product is 1. *n-* 1 something given or done by each to the other; an equivalent. 2 *Mathematics* number or expression that gives a product of 1 when multiplied by a given number. The reciprocal of 3 is 1/3. The reciprocal of 3/5 is 5/3 since $3/5 \times 5/3 = 1$ —*adv-* re·cip'ro·cal·ly.

re·cite (rĭ sīt') *vt-* [re·cit·ed, re·cit·ing] 1 to repeat from memory: *He recited the poem with fine expression.* 2 to repeat in detail, especially in school: *Mary recited the lesson with great ease.* *vi-: Mary recited twice last week.* —*n-* re·cit'er.

reck (rěk) *Archaic* *vt-* to reckon; heed. *Hom-* wreck.

reck·less (rĕk′ləs) *adj-* careless; rash; heedless: *John's reckless driving.* —*adv-* reck′less·ly. *n-* reck′less·ness.

reck·on (rĕk′ən) *vt-* 1 to count; add up: *The cashier reckoned my bill.* 2 to judge; consider: *The critics reckoned the play a masterpiece.* 3 *Informal* to think; suppose: *I reckon that it will rain.* *vi-* to make calculations; compute; figure. —*n-* reck′on·er.

  reckon on (or **upon**) 1 to allow for; consider: *He didn't reckon on our strength.* 2 to count on; rely on.

  reckon with 1 to take into account: *He's a person to reckon with.* 2 to settle accounts with.

reck·on·ing (rĕk′ən ĭng) *n-* 1 a settling of an account: *a day of reckoning.* 2 a counting or computing: *the reckoning of a ship's position.* 3 thinking or planning: *I left that possibility out of my reckoning.* 4 bill for goods or services, especially at a hotel or restaurant.

re·claim (rĭ klām′) *vt-* 1 to ask for and get back: *He reclaimed his pen at the lost-and-found office.* 2 to bring into use; obtain from waste: *to reclaim desert land by irrigation.* —*adj-* re·claim′able. *n-* re·claim′er.

rec·la·ma·tion (rĕk′lə mā′shən) *n-* a restoring to useful purpose; especially, the restoring or conversion of wasteland to productive use.

re·cline (rĭ klīn′) *vi-* [re·clined, re·clin·ing] to lie down; lean back in a restful manner: *She reclined on the sofa.* *vt-*: *He reclined his tired body on the cot.*

re·cluse (rĕk′loōs′, -loōz′, rĭ kloōs′) *n-* person who lives alone and shuns the company of others. *adj-* (usually rĭ kloōs′) shut off from the world; solitary; secluded: *a recluse monastery.*

rec·og·ni·tion (rĕk′əg nĭsh′ən) *n-* 1 a recognizing. 2 approval; applause; praise.

re·cog·ni·zance (rĭ kŏg′nə zəns) *n-* 1 legal agreement to do, or keep from doing, some particular act. 2 sum of money to be paid or forfeited if an agreement is not kept.

rec·og·nize (rĕk′əg nīz′) *vt-* [rec·og·nized, rec·og·niz·ing] 1 to become aware of or perceive something known before; to identify: *He recognized his old friend's voice.* 2 to perceive; realize: *I at once recognized the conductor's ability.* 3 to accept; admit; acknowledge: *He recognized the man's right to argue his point of view.* 4 to greet in an informal way: *She recognized him with a wave of the hand.* 5 in a meeting, to acknowledge (someone) as the person entitled to be heard at the time. 6 to set up formal relations with (a foreign government): *The United States recognized the new African states.* —*adj-* rec′og·niz′a·ble. *adv-* rec′og·niz′a·bly.

¹re·coil (rĭ koil′) *vi-* 1 to shrink back; show distaste or horror: *She recoiled at the sight of the accident.* 2 to spring back or rebound: *The rifle recoiled powerfully on firing.* 3 to retreat or fall back: *The enemy recoiled.* 4 to injure the doer as if by rebounding or backfiring against him (often followed by "on" or "upon"): *His careful plan recoiled and he was caught.*

²re·coil (rē′koil′) *n-* 1 a shrinking back. 2 a springing back or rebound, especially of a gun when it is fired.

rec·ol·lect (rĕk′ə lĕkt′) *vt-* to recall; call back to mind; remember: *He recollected the days of his childhood.*

re·col·lect (rē′kə lĕkt′) *vt-* 1 to collect, or gather together again. 2 to compose (one's thoughts) again. 3 rally or summon (one's forces, courage, etc.) again.

rec·ol·lec·tion (rĕk′ə lĕk′shən) *n-* 1 the act of calling back to the mind or remembering. 2 person's memory or the period of time over which it extends: *The day you describe is not within my recollection.* 3 memory of something: *It is one of my happiest recollections.*

re·com·bine (rē′kəm bīn′) *vt-* [re·com·bined, re·com·bin·ing] to put together again; to cause to combine anew. *vi-* to combine again or anew. —*n-* re′com′bi·na′tion.

rec·om·mend (rĕk′ə mĕnd′) *vt-* 1 to speak or write favorably of; to recommend *a new book.* 2 to advise; counsel: *The doctor recommended a long rest.* 3 to make pleasing or worthy of acceptance: *His careful workmanship recommends him.* 4 to entrust to someone's care: *My doctor recommended me to a bone specialist.*

re·com·mit (rē′kə mĭt′) *vt-* [re·com·mit·ted, re·com·mit·ting] 1 to send or order back: *The judge recommitted the man to prison.* 2 to send (a bill or other measure) back to a committee.

rec·om·pense (rĕk′əm pĕns′) *vt-* [rec·om·pensed, rec·om·pens·ing] 1 to reward; repay: *She recompensed him for his devotion.* 2 to make amends for; atone for: *We will recompense your loss.* *n-* something given as reward or amends.

re·com·pose (rē′kəm pōz′) *vt-* [re·com·posed, re·com·pos·ing] 1 to compose again. 2 to put into another pattern; rearrange.

rec·on·cile (rĕk′ən sīl′) *vt-* [rec·on·ciled, rec·on·cil·ing] 1 to bring together after a quarrel; make peace between: *We reconciled the young couple.* 2 to bring into harmony; settle: *They reconciled their differences of opinion.* 3 to bring into agreement (with); make seem consistent: *It is difficult to reconcile his promises with what he actually did.* 4 to make (oneself) content with; resign (oneself) to: *He reconciled himself to his recent bad luck.* —*n-* rec′on·cil′a·bil′i·ty. *adj-* rec′on·cil′a·ble: *I don't think their differences are reconcilable.* *n-* rec′on·cile′ment. *n-* rec′on·cil′er.

rec·on·cil·i·a·tion (rĕk′ən sĭl′ē ā′shən) *n-* 1 a coming or bringing together on a friendly basis after a quarrel. 2 an adjustment of differences of opinion.

re·con·dense (rē′kən dĕns′) *vt-* [re·con·densed, re·con·dens·ing] 1 to condense again. 2 in distillation, to condense and collect (the evaporated liquid) in a separate container. *vi-* to become condensed again.

rec·on·dite (rĕk′ən dīt′, rĭ kŏn′-) *adj-* 1 very hard for the ordinary mind to understand; abstruse: *his recondite studies in higher mathematics.* 2 of or having to do with little known matters: *his recondite research in the writing of ancient Egypt.* —*adv-* re′con·dite′ly or re·con′dite·ly. *n-* re′con·dite′ness or re·con′dite′ness.

re·con·di·tion (rē′kən dĭsh′ən) *vt-* to restore (something) to good condition; overhaul: *He reconditions used cars.*

re·con·nais·sance (rĭ kŏn′ə səns) *n-* a careful exploring or probing into new territory in order to get information on which to base an expedition, attack, or other effort. *as modifier:* a reconnaissance *vehicle.*

rec·on·noi·ter or **rec·on·noi·tre** (rē′kə noi′tər, rĕk′-) *vt-* to make a reconnaissance of or into: *to reconnoiter an enemy position.* *vi-*: *The commander decided to reconnoiter again before attacking.*

re·con·quer (rē′kŏng′kər) *vt-* to conquer again; also, to regain by force (a territory that has been lost).

re·con·sid·er (rē′kən sĭd′ər) *vt-* to consider again; to think or talk about again: *to reconsider a decision.* —*n-* re′con·sid′er·a′tion.

re·con·sign (rē′kən sīn′) *vt-* to consign again; especially, to consign (articles in transit) to another person or place.

re·con·sti·tute (rē′kŏn′stə toōt′, -tyoōt′) *vt-* [re·con·sti·tut·ed, re·con·sti·tut·ing] to form or put together again; to reconstitute *a defeated political party.*

re·con·struct (rē′kən strŭkt′) *vt-* 1 to build again: *to reconstruct a steeple struck by lightning.* 2 to construct again in exactly the same way; restore to the original form: *Our historical society reconstructed a colonial town.* 3 to trace from clues or suggestions.

re·con·struc·tion (rē′kən strŭk′shən) *n-* 1 a rebuilding. 2 something restored or rebuilt: *Some of the buildings are original, but most are reconstructions.* 3 **Reconstruction** restoration of the former Confederate States to membership in the United States under the Reconstruction Acts of 1867.

¹re·cord (rĭ kôrd′, -kôrd′) *vt-* (in senses 2 and 3 considered intransitive when the direct object is implied but not expressed) 1 to set down officially for the purpose of evidence or historical data: *to record the events as they occurred.* 2 to make a tape recording or phonograph record of: *to record the operetta.* 3 to register; tell: *Clocks record time.*

²rec·ord (rĕk′ərd) *n-* 1 body of facts comprising what is known about a person or thing, especially about achievement or failure: *The student had an excellent record.* 2 official document telling of facts or events for future reference: *a congressional record; a court record.* 3 disk, cylinder, etc., for reproducing sound on a phonograph.

re·cord·er (rĭ kôr′ dər, -kōr′ dər) *n-*
1 device for recording sound on
phonograph records or magnetic
tape. 2 any of various devices for
making a permanent visual record
of something changeable, often by
tracing a line on a movable paper
tape. 3 a secretary, town clerk, or
other person who makes and keeps
written records. 4 woodwind musical instrument of the flute type,
made in several tonal ranges.

Boy playing
a recorder

re·cord·ing (rĭ kôr′ dĭng, -kōr′ dĭng) *n-* phonograph
record or magnetic tape upon which music, speech, or
other sound has been recorded; also, the music, speech,
etc., so recorded: *a new recording of an old song.*

record player *n-* phonograph.

¹re·count (rĭ kount′) *vt-* to tell or repeat in detail: *He
recounted his adventures.* [from Old French **reconter**
meaning "relate."]

²re·count (rē kount′) *vt-* to count again: *He recounted
his money.* *n- (also* rē′ kount′*)* a counting again: *a re-
count of the votes.* [from re-, "again" plus ¹count.]

re·coup (rĭ kōōp′) *vi-* to make up for a loss, either by
getting back what was lost or by getting something
equal to it: *How will he recoup after such a disaster?
Having lost six straight games, the team swore to recoup.*
vt- 1 to regain or recover (something lost): *to recoup
one's money.* 2 to give or restore something of value to
(someone) after a loss; reimburse: *The company will
recoup you for what you spent.*

re·course (rē′ kôrs′) *n-* 1 an applying to someone, or a
use of something, for aid in difficulties; resort; appeal:
a recourse to the law. 2 person or thing so applied to or
used: *Bankruptcy was my only recourse.*

re·cov·er (rĭ kŭv′ ər) *vt-* 1 to get back; regain: *He recovered his health. She recovered her lost purse.* 2 to
make up: *to recover lost time.* 3 to obtain by legal
judgment: *to recover damages for an injury or wrong.*
vi- 1 to return to a healthy or normal state: *Jack quickly
recovered from his cold.* 2 to win a legal award of
damages, compensation, etc. **—adj- re·cov′er·a·ble.
n- re·cov′er·er.**

re·cov·er (rē′ kŭv′ ər) *vt-* to put a new cover on.

re·cov·er·y (rĭ kŭv′ ə rē) *n- [pl.* **re·cov·er·ies]** 1 a return
to a healthy or normal state: *a rapid recovery from
illness.* 2 act of getting back: *the recovery of a lost coat.*

recovery room *n-* special room in a hospital, for
persons who have just undergone surgery or childbirth.

rec·re·ant (rĕk′ rē ənt) *n-* 1 faithless person; traitor.
2 coward. *adj-* cowardly; unfaithful to one's duty or a
cause: *a recreant knight.* **—n- rec′re·an·cy.**

re·cre·ate (rē′ krē āt′) *vt-* [re·cre·at·ed, re·cre·at·ing]
to make or create again. **—n- re′-cre·a′tion.**

rec·re·a·tion (rĕk′ rē ā′ shən) *n-* any form of amusement,
relaxation, or sport: *Baseball was his favorite recreation.
as modifier: a recreation hall.* **—adj- rec′re·a′tion·al.**

re·crim·i·nate (rĭ krĭm′ ə nāt′) *vi-* [re·crim·i·na·ted,
re·crim·i·na·ting] to answer one accusation or charge
with another. **—n- re·crim′i·na′tion.** *adj-* **re·crim′i·
na·to′ry:** *a recriminatory letter.*

re·cruit (rĭ krōōt′) *n-* 1 in the Army, Air Force, Navy
and Coast Guard, an enlisted man of the lowest rank.
2 new member of any organization or group. *vt-* 1 to
enlist (soldiers, sailors, etc.). 2 to make or build up by
getting new members: *We recruited a new party in six
months.* 3 to build up; restore: *to recruit one's strength.*
vi- 1 to obtain fresh supplies of something needed. 2 to
recover health and strength. **—n- re·cruit′er:** *the
recruiter for the Air Force held interviews at college
yesterday. n- re·cruit′ment: the recruitment of soldiers.*

rec·tal (rĕk′ təl) *adj-* of, having to do with, or near the
rectum.

rec·tan·gle (rĕk′ tăng′ gəl) *n-* parallelogram of which all angles are right
angles.

rec·tan·gu·lar (rĕk tăng′ gyə lər) *adj-*
shaped like a rectangle. **—adv- rec·
tan′gu·lar·ly.**

Rectangle

rectangular prism *n-* six-sided prism of which opposite sides are parallel and congruent. An ordinary
box is a rectangular prism.

rec·ti·fi·er (rĕk′ tə fī′ ər) *n-* something or someone that
rectifies; especially, a device that changes alternating
current into direct current.

rec·ti·fy (rĕk′ tə fī′) *vt-* [rec·ti·fied, rec·ti·fy·ing] 1 to
correct; amend: *to rectify a mistake.* 2 to change (an
electric current) from alternating to direct. 3 to refine or
purify (liquids) by distillation. **—n- rec′ti·fi·ca′tion.**

rec·ti·lin·e·ar (rĕk′ tə lĭn′ ē ər) *adj-* 1 in a straight line;
straight: *a rectilinear motion.* 2 made of or bounded by
straight lines: *a rectilinear pattern;* rectilinear *space.*

rec·ti·tude (rĕk′ tə tōōd′, -tyōōd′) *n-* uprightness of
moral character; goodness; integrity.

rec·tor (rĕk′ tər) *n-* 1 clergyman ·in the Protestant
Episcopal Church who has charge of a parish. 2 priest
in the Roman Catholic Church who is head of a religious
house for men. 3 head of certain universities, colleges,
and schools.

rec·to·ry (rĕk′ tə rē) *n- [pl.* **rec·to·ries]** rector's house.

rec·tum (rĕk′ təm) *n-* lower end of the large intestine that
links the colon with the anus. For picture, see *intestine.*

re·cum·bent (rĭ kŭm′ bənt) *adj-* lying down; reclining;
leaning: *a recumbent figure.*

re·cu·per·ate (rĭ kōō′ pə rāt′) *vi-* [re·cu·per·at·ed,
re·cu·per·at·ing] to recover from illness, losses, etc.:
Joe recuperated quickly after the accident. *vt-* to regain
(one's health). **—n- re·cu′per·a′tion.** *adj-* **re·cu′per·
a′tive:** *a recuperative diet.*

re·cur (rĭ kûr′) *vi-* [re·curred, re·cur·ring] 1 to occur
again: *His hay fever recurs each autumn.* 2 to return in
thought or memory: *One memory often recurred to her.*
3 to go back to an earlier subject: *After dinner, we
recurred to plans for our summer vacation.*

re·cur·rence (rĭ kûr′ əns) *n-* 1 a recurring; a return;
repetition: *the recurrence of a disease.*

re·cur·rent (rĭ kûr′ ənt) *adj-* 1 returning or happening at
intervals: *a recurrent fever.* 2 turning back in a reverse
direction: *a recurrent blood vein.* **—adv- re·cur′rent·ly.**

re·cy·cle (rē′ sī′ kəl) *vt-* [re·cy·cled, re·cy·cling] 1 to set
or establish a different cycle in (a machine, engine, or
process). 2 to reset or reestablish a cycle in (a machine,
engine, or process).

red (rĕd) *n-* 1 the color of the outermost stripes on the
American flag, of the male cardinal bird, and of blood.
Red is the lower edge of the rainbow and has the longest
wavelength of all visible light. 2 (often **Red**) a Communist. *adj-* [red·der, red·dest]: *a red flower; the* Red
army; *a red doctrine.* **—n- red′ness.**
in the red showing a net loss; losing money. **see red**
to grow very angry or unreasonably angry.

red alert *n-* final warning given to indicate that an
attack, especially an air attack, is going to take place
immediately.

red·bird (rĕd′ bûrd′) *n-* any of several birds having a
red plumage, such as the cardinal, or the scarlet tanager.

red blood cell *n-* microscopic solid, occurring naturally
in the blood, that contains the red compound hemoglobin. Also **red corpuscle.**

red-blood·ed (rĕd′ blŭd′ əd) *adj-* vigorous: *a fine, red-
blooded boy.*

red·breast (rĕd′ brĕst′) *n-* bird, especially the mature
robin, having a reddish breast.

red carpet *n-* red, plush carpeting rolled out for a distinguished person to walk on; hence, any elaborate and
costly treatment of an arriving guest. *adj-* (**red-carpet**):
They gave the astronaut the red-carpet treatment.

red·coat (rĕd′ kōt′) *n-* soldier of the British army,
especially during the Revolutionary War.

Red Cross *n-* international organization devoted ·to
caring for the sick and wounded in war and to giving
relief in times of calamities such as floods, earthquakes,
etc. **The American National Red Cross** is one of more
than a hundred affiliates.

red deer *n-* the common deer of Europe and Asia,
related to the European elk.

red·den (rĕd′ ən) *vi-* 1 to become red. 2 to blush. *vt-* to
make red.

re·deem·er the Redeemer Jesus Christ as the savior of mankind.
redeems.

re·demp·tion (ri děmp′ shən) *n-* **1** act of redeeming or buying back. **2** deliverance from sin; salvation. **3** salvation of mankind by Jesus Christ.

re·demp·tive (ri děmp′ tĭv) *adj-* redeeming, or having the power to redeem: *a redemptive act.*

re·de·vel·op (rē′ də vĕl′ əp) *vt-* **1** to develop (something) again; rebuild; renew: *to redevelop a slum area.* **2** to make the tones of (a photographic image) stronger by treating it a second time with chemicals. *vi-* to develop again. *—n- re′ de·vel′ op·ment.*

red flag *n-* anything extremely irritating, as a red cloth is thought to be to a fighting bull.

red-hand·ed (rĕd′ hăn′ dəd) *adj-* in the very act of committing or doing something, especially something wrong: *The thief was caught red-handed.*

red·head (rĕd′ hĕd′) *n-* person who has hair of a reddish color. *—adj- red′ head′ ed: a beautiful, redheaded girl.*

red heat *n-* **1** condition of being red-hot. **2** temperature at which metal turns red-hot.

red herring *n-* **1** dried, reddish-brown, smoked herring. **2** something intended to distract attention from an important topic or issue, usually as a defensive maneuver.

red-hot (rĕd′ hŏt′) *adj-* **1** red with heat; very hot. **2** inflamed with anger, enthusiasm, hatred, etc. **3** fresh from the source; up-to-the-minute: *a bit of red-hot news.*

re·di·rect (rē′ də rĕkt′) *vt-* to give a new direction or course to: *to redirect one's efforts.*

re·dis·cov·er (rē′ dĭs kŭv′ ər) *vt-* to find again; discover again.

re·dis·trib·ute (rē′ dĭs trĭb′ yət′) *vt-* [re·dis·trib·u·ted, re·dis·trib·u·ting] to reassign; distribute again. *—n- re·dis′ tri·bu′ tion.*

re·dis·trict (rē′ dĭs′ trĭkt) *vt-* to rearrange the district boundaries of (a city, state, etc.): *The legislature redistricted the state. vi-: The town redistricted.*

red lead *n-* bright scarlet powder, an oxide of lead, used as a pigment in glass and as an oxidizing agent.

red-let·ter (rĕd′ lĕt′ ər) *adj-* memorable; lucky or happy: *a red-letter day.*

red man *n-* an American Indian.

re·do (rē′ dōō′) *vt-* [re·did, re·done, re·do·ing] to do again; especially, to redecorate.

red·o·lent (rĕd′ ə lənt) *adj-* **1** giving off a pleasing odor; fragrant: *The redolent air of the garden.* **2** suggestive: *a scene redolent of romance. —n- red′ o·lence.*

re·dou·ble (rē dŭb′ əl, rē′-) *vt-* [re·dou·bled, re·doubling] **1** to increase greatly. **2** to double again.

re·doubt (ri dout′) *n-* **1** small enclosed fortification, especially a temporary one. **2** stronghold; citadel.

re·doubt·a·ble (ri dou′ tə bəl) *adj-* arousing fear or respect; valiant; brave: *He is redoubtable in the face of danger or hardship. —adv- re·doubt′ a·bly.*

re·dound (ri dound′) *vi-* to be reflected back, especially in such a way as to add or contribute: *His actions redounded to his glory.*

re·draft (rē drăft′, rē′-) *vt-* to draft again; to make a new draft or copy of.

re·dress (ri drĕs′) *vt-* to set right; remedy; *to redress a wrong. n- (also rē drĕs′)* **1** compensation: *no redress for a loss of honor.* **2** a redressing: *a redress of a wrong.*

re·dress (rē′ drĕs′) *vt-* to dress (someone or oneself) again. *vi-* to dress again.

red shift *n-* a Doppler effect shown by the spectral lines of light from distant stars, galaxies, etc., which is proportional to the rate of increase in the distance of the light source.

red·skin (rĕd′ skĭn′) *Slang n-* a North American Indian (often used to show disfavor).

red·start (rĕd′ stärt′) *n-* **1** in America, a black warbler that has bright orange patches on the wings and tail and is notable for its nervous, flitting flight. **2** in Europe, any of several thrushes notable for the constant twitching motion of their tails.

red tape *n-* excessive attention to details, rules, or forms when carrying on business, especially when this causes delay or inaction.

re·duce (ri dōōs′, -dyōōs′) *vt-* [re·duced, re·duc·ing] **1** to make less; decrease: *to reduce the price.* **2** to bring from a higher position to a lower position; degrade: *to reduce an officer to the ranks. The fire reduced the family to poverty.* **3** to conquer; subdue: *The enemy reduced the town.* **4** to bring into some particular form or condition, especially a different physical state: *We reduced the rocks to pebbles.* **5** *Chemistry* to subject (a compound) to reduction. **6** *Mathematics* to change (an expression) to an equivalent but more elementary or fundamental expression: *It is easy to reduce 15/25 to 3/5. vi-* to lose weight. *—n- re·duc′ er. adj- re·duc′ ible.*

reducing agent *Chemistry n-* substance that brings about the reduction of a compound.

re·duc·tion (ri dŭk′ shən) *n-* **1** a reducing or being reduced. **2** amount by which something is reduced: *a reduction of ten dollars.* **3** a copy (of something) that is smaller than the original. **4** *Biology* the stage in meiosis in which the number of chromosomes is reduced to one half of the original number. **5** *Chemistry* the removal of oxygen from a compound. **6** *Mathematics* process of changing an equation or an expression into its lowest terms.

re·dun·dan·cy (ri dŭn′ dən sē) *n-* [*pl.* re·dun·dan·cies] **1** use of more words than are strictly necessary to convey an idea; also, an instance of this. Example: I mean the exact same thing you do. **2** excessive amount; quantity greater than needed. Also *re·dun′ dance.*

re·dun·dant (ri dŭn′ dənt) *adj-* **1** using more words than are necessary; wordy; verbose; tautological. **2** exceeding what is needed or useful. *—adv- re·dun′ dant·ly.*

re·du·pli·cate (ri dōō′ plə kāt′, ri dyōō′-) *vt-* [re·du·pli·cated, re·du·pli·cat·ing] to make again; redouble; multiply. *—n- re·du′ pli·ca′ tion.*

red·wing (rĕd′ wĭng′) *n-* **1** (also **red-winged blackbird**) in America, a blackbird with red patches on the wings of the male. **2** in Europe, a thrush with bright-orange feathers on its sides and underwings.

red·wood (rĕd′ wŏod′) *n-* **1** kind of cone-bearing evergreen tree of the Pacific coast. Although these trees grow to giant size, their cones are small. **2** the wood of this tree.

re·ech·o or **re-ech·o** (rē ĕk′ ō) *vt-* to echo or repeat the sounds of: *The large room* reechoed *our voices. vi-* to echo or repeat again: *My shouts* reechoed *through the cave.*

reed (rēd) *n-* **1** any of various firmstemmed, jointed grasses growing in or near the water; also, one of their jointed hollow stems. **2** musical pipe made of the hollow stem of a plant. **3** thin, elastic piece of wood, metal, or plastic attached to the mouthpiece of certain musical instruments, such as the clarinet, producing a certain tone when air is blown over it. **4** reed instrument. **5** arrow. **6** part of a loom resembling a comb, that keeps the yarn evenly separated. *as modifier: a reed hut; a reed ensemble. Hom-* read. *—adj-* reed′ like′.

Redwood
cone and twig

reed instrument *n-* musical wind instrument, such as the clarinet, in which sound is produced by the vibration of one or more reeds.

reed organ *n-* harmonium.

reed·y (rē′ dē) *adj-* [reed·i·er, reed·i·est] **1** covered with or full of reeds: *a reedy swamp.* **2** resembling a reed; especially, having the thinness and fragility of reeds: *the reedy legs of a bird;* reedy *arms.* **3** resembling a reed instrument in tone; especially, like certain high, sharp, quavering tones of the clarinet: *piping,* reedy *voices. —n- reed′ i·ness.*

reef·er (rē′ fər) *n-* short, tight-fitting, usually doublebreasted jacket.

reef knot *n-* square knot.

re·en·force or **re-en·force** (rē′ ən fôrs′) reinforce.

re·en·list or **re-en·list** (rē′ ən lĭst′) *vi-* to enlist again: *The soldier* reenlisted. *vt-* to enlist (someone or something) again. *—n- re′ en·list′ ment* or *re′-en·list′ ment.*

re·en·ter or **re-en·ter** (rē ĕn′ tər) *vi-* to enter again. *vt-* to enter (someone or something) again.

re·en·trance or **re-en·trance** (rē ĕn′ trəns) *n-* a reentering; second or new entry: *an actor's* reentrance.

re·en·try or **re-en·try** (rē ĕn′ trē) *n-* 1 reentrance. 2 *Space* the return of a spacecraft to the earth's atmosphere after travel in space. 3 in law, the retaking possession of a property under a right reserved in a previous transfer of that property, such as when the landlord reclaims an apartment because the tenant has not paid the rent.

re·es·tab·lish or **re-es·tab·lish** (rē′ ə stăb′ lĭsh) *vt-* to establish again; restore: *They* reestablished *their theater group after years of inactivity.* —*n-* re′ es·tab′ lish·ment or re′·es·tab′ lish·ment.

re·ex·am·ine or **re-ex·am·ine** (rē′ ĭg zăm′ ən) *vt-* [re·ex·am·ined or re·ex·am·ined, re·ex·am·in·ing or re·ex·am·in·ing] 1 to examine again; to scrutinize again. 2 to question (a witness in a legal procedure) again after the cross-examination. —*n-* re′ ex·am′ i·na′ tion or re′·ex·am′ i·na′ tion.

re·ex·port (rē′ ĕks′ pôrt′) *n-* the shipping of goods out of a country, port, etc., into which they had been brought for such shipping and not for use. *vt-: The shipment was* reexported *to South America.*

re·fash·ion (rē′ făsh′ ən) *vt-* to make over, especially in a new or different way: *She* refashioned *the coat.*

re·fec·to·ry (rĭ fĕk′ tə rē) *n-* [*pl.* re·fec·to·ries] dining hall, especially in a monastery or convent.

re·fer (rĭ fûr′) *vt-* [re·ferred, re·fer·ring] 1 to direct (someone) to a certain place for information or aid: *I* refer *you to the dictionary for correct spelling.* 2 to turn over (to) for settlement or decision: *to refer a dispute to a referee.* 3 to explain as due to a certain cause: *The coach* referred *his failure to the sickness of the team.*

refer to 1 to seek information, advice, aid, etc., in: *to* refer *to a dictionary.* 2 to call or direct attention to; cite: *I am* referring *to the talk we had yesterday.*

ref·er·ee (rĕf′ ə rē′) *n-* 1 person who settles disputes and whose decision is final. 2 a judge in certain games such as basketball and football; umpire. 3 in law, a person before whom a question in a case is sent by a court to be investigated and decided, or reported to the court. *vt-* [ref·er·eed, ref·er·ee·ing] to act as an umpire in (a settlement or contest): *to* referee *a football game.* *vi-: Jack* refereed *yesterday.*

ref·er·ence (rĕf′ or əns) *n-* 1 a referring to an authority for information or confirmation: *a reference to a dictionary for the spelling of a word.* 2 (also **reference book** or **reference work**) a dictionary, encyclopedia, or other printed work intended chiefly as a source of information. 3 allusion; a mention: *This history contains many* references *to George Washington.* 4 person who may be asked about one's character or ability: *I gave Mr. Lawford as my* reference *when I applied for the job.* 5 written statement answering for someone's character or ability. 6 a passage or note in a book calling attention to some other book or passage. *as modifier: a* reference *book.* **in** (or **with**) **reference to** in regard to; concerning.

ref·er·en·dum (rĕf′ ə rĕn′ dəm) *n-* [*pl.* ref·er·en·dums or ref·er·en·da (-də)] 1 the submitting of a legislative act to popular vote for approval or rejection. 2 right of the people to vote upon a legislative act. 3 direct popular vote on a proposed measure.

¹**re·fill** (rē fĭl′, rē′-) *vt-* to make full again; fill again.

²**re·fill** (rē′ fĭl′) *n-* replacement; a new duplicate of something used up: *a* refill *for a ball-point pen.*

re·fill·a·ble (rē fĭl′ ə bəl) *adj-* such as can be filled again; especially, designed so as to be refilled or reloaded when something is used up: *a* refillable *pencil.*

re·fi·nance (rē′ fī′ nāns′, rē′ fə nāns′) *vt-* [re·fi·nanced, re·fi·nanc·ing] 1 to rearrange the terms of (a debt): *to* refinance *a loan.* 2 to alter the financial structure of (a company, stock or bond issue, etc.).

re·fine (rĭ fīn′) *vt-* [re·fined, re·fin·ing] 1 to make pure; rid of all unwanted matter: *to* refine *a metal; to* refine *oil.* 2 to free from coarseness, clumsiness, etc.; improve; polish: *She* refined *her table manners.* —*n-* re·fin′ er.

refine on (or **upon**) to add refinements to.

re·fined (rĭ fīnd′) *adj-* 1 freed from impurities or unwanted matter: *We use* refined *sugar.* 2 having good manners and taste; cultured; free from coarseness: *a* refined *person; a* refined *manner.* 3 having or carried out with exactness; subtle: *He took* refined *measurements.*

re·fine·ment (rĭ fīn′ mənt) *n-* 1 good manners and taste; freedom from coarseness: *a lady of great* refinement. 2 a change or addition that helps to perfect something; small but important improvement: *My invention needs a few* refinements *before we market it.* 3 a freeing from impurities or unwanted matter: *the* refinement *of sugar.*

re·fin·er·y (rĭ fīn′ ə rē) *n-* [*pl.* re·fin·er·ies] factory where sugar, ore, oil, etc., is made pure or more usable, or is made into products of several grades and types.

re·fin·ish (rē fĭn′ ĭsh) *vt-* to give (a car, a piece of furniture, etc.) new coats of paint, varnish, etc.

¹**re·fit** (rē fĭt′, rē′-) *vt-* [re·fit·ted, re·fit·ting] to make ready for use again; repair or equip with supplies again: *to* refit *a ship.* *vi-: We'll* refit *in Singapore.*

²**re·fit** (rē′ fĭt′) *n-* a making ready for renewed use.

re·flect (rĭ flĕkt′) *vt-* 1 to throw back (rays of light, heat, sound, etc.). 2 to give back an image of, as does a mirror or clear water. 3 to give back as a result: *His act* reflects *honor upon him.* *vi-* 1 to think about someone or something carefully; meditate: *The old man* reflected *about his youthful days.* 2 to think aloud.

reflect on to cast discredit on; cast doubt on: *Much of what he said* reflected on *his truthfulness.*

re·flec·tion (rĭ flĕk′ shən) *n-* 1 image of anything in a mirror or in still water: *the* reflection *of the mountains in the lake.* 2 a throwing back: *An echo is caused by the* reflection *of a sound.* 3 serious thought; meditation: *A week's* reflection *led to a new plan.* 4 statement or observation resulting from serious thought: *Einstein's* reflections *on the universe.* 5 *Physics* the turning or bouncing back of radiant energy, such as light or heat, from a surface.

Reflection in water

reflection on a casting of discredit or reproach on: *Your remarks are a* reflection on *my truthfulness.*

re·flec·tive (rĭ flĕk′ tĭv) *adj-* 1 reflecting sound or images: *the* reflective *surface of a pond.* 2 thoughtful; meditative: *a* reflective *mind.* —*adv-* re·flec′ tive·ly.

re·flec·tiv·i·ty (rē′ flĕk′ tĭv′ ə tē) *n-* [*pl.* re·flec·tiv·i·ties] 1 property or ability to throw back rays of light or other forms of radiant energy. 2 *Physics* ratio of the radiant energy reflected from a surface to the total radiant energy falling on the surface.

re·flec·tor (rĭ flĕk′ tər) *n-* 1 surface, often polished, that reflects light, heat, nuclear radiation, or other radiation. 2 any object, surface, or device that reflects or redirects radio frequency waves or sound waves. 3 telescope that uses a large mirror to reflect and focus light rays. 4 in photography, an adjustable movable screen used to reflect and control the lighting on an object.

re·flex (rē′ flĕks′) *n-* 1 in physiology, an involuntary movement or function, such as the contraction of a muscle or secretion by a gland. 2 reflection of radiant energy or sound. 3 light reflected to a shaded surface.

re·flex·ive (rĭ flĕk′ sĭv) *Grammar adj-* referring back to the subject of the construction. —*adv-* re·flex′ ive·ly.

reflexive pronoun *n-* pronoun which, although used as the object of a verb, invariably refers back to the subject. Example: *He hurt* himself *accidentally.*

re·for·est (rē fôr′ əst, -fŏr′ əst) *vt-* to replant (deforested land) with trees. —*n-* re′ for·es·ta′ tion: *the* reforestation *of land by the lumber company.*

re·form (rĭ fôrm′, -fôrm′) *vt-* to correct what is wrong with, especially by removing some evil or abuse: *The judge promised to* reform *the courts if elected.* *vi-* to give up evil ways, *n-* a change for the better; improvement: *The* reform *in the school system was long overdue.* *adj-*

re·form (rē′ fôrm′, -fôrm′) *vt-* to reshape or reorganize: *They* re-formed *the club under a new name.*

ref·or·ma·tion (rĕf′ ər mā′ shən) *n-* 1 a changing for the better; improvement in social, political, or religious affairs. 2 **Reformation** religious movement in the 16th century begun by Martin Luther, which resulted in the establishment of various Protestant churches.

re·form·a·to·ry (rĭ fôr′ mə tôr′ ē, rĭ fôr′-) *n-* [*pl.* **re·form·a·to·ries**] school or institution for the special training of young offenders against the law and for the betterment of their character and conduct.

re·form·er (rĭ fôr′ mər, rĭ fôr′-) *n-* person who speaks for, or attempts to carry out, improvements or reforms.

reform school *n-* reformatory.

re·fract (rĭ frăkt′) *vt-* to cause (light or other radiation) to undergo refraction.

re·frac·tion (rĭ frăk′ shən) *Physics n-* the bending of, or change of direction in, a ray of light or other radiation as it passes from one medium to another that has a different density, or through a medium whose density is not uniform.

re·frac·tor (rĭ frăk′ tər) *n-* telescope whose main optical elements are a converging objective lens and an eyepiece.

Refraction

re·frac·to·ry (rĭ frăk′ tə rē) *adj-* 1 disobedient; stubborn; unmanageable: *a refractory boy.* 2 not yielding to treatment: *a refractory disease.* 3 resisting heat; hard to fuse: *a refractory ore.* *n-* [*pl.* **re·frac·to·ries**] substance that resists heat or is hard to fuse, especially brick or clay that is resistant to heat.

¹**re·frain** (rĭ frān′) *n-* phrase or verse repeated at regular intervals in a poem or song; chorus; also, the musical setting for these words. [from French of the same spelling, from Latin **refringere**, "to refract," literally, "to break back."]

²**re·frain** (rĭ frān′) *vi-* to hold oneself back; restrain oneself: *Please refrain from interrupting me.* [from Old French **refrener** meaning "to bridle," from Latin **frēnum**, "a bridle" and **refrēnāre**, "to bridle."]

re·fresh (rĭ frĕsh′) *vt-* 1 to make fresh again; restore; renew after fatigue, usually with food or rest: *A nap will refresh you.* 2 to quicken; stimulate: *His words refreshed my memory.* 3 to make fresh, by wetting, cooling, etc.: *The rain refreshed the scorched lawn.* 4 to fill again or replenish with or as if with new supplies.

re·fresh·er (rĭ frĕsh′ ər) *n-* 1 something that refreshes; also, a reminder. 2 a review of material previously studied; especially, additional instruction designed to update one's professional background: *He is taking a refresher in physics.* *as modifier:* *a refresher course.*

re·fresh·ing (rĭ frĕsh′ ĭng) *adj-* 1 reviving; invigorating; restoring; renewing: *a refreshing rain.* 2 unexpectedly pleasing; pleasingly new, unusual, fresh, etc.: *her refreshing frankness.* —*adv-* **re·fresh′ ing·ly.**

re·fresh·ment (rĭ frĕsh′ mənt) *n-* 1 a refreshing or being refreshed: *the refreshment of a shower bath.* 2 something that refreshes or revives. 3 **refreshments** food, drink, or both, served at a party, meeting, etc.

re·frig·er·ant (rĭ frĭj′ ər ənt) *n-* 1 any substance, such as ice, Dry Ice, or various gases, used for refrigeration. 2 *Medicine* a drink, evaporating lotion, or other remedy used to relieve fever and thirst. *adj-:* *a refrigerant gas.*

re·frig·er·ate (rĭ frĭj′ ə rāt′) *vt-* [**re·frig·er·at·ed, re·frig·er·at·ing**] to make or keep cold; especially, to chill or freeze (food) for the purpose of preserving. —*n-* **re·frig′ er·a′ tion.**

re·frig·er·a·tor (rĭ frĭj′ ə rā′ tər) *n-* a box, cabinet, or room where food or other perishables are kept at a low temperature by means of ice or a cooling system.

reft (rĕft) *adj-* taken away by force.

re·fu·el (rē fyōō′ əl, rē′-) *vt-* to put in a fresh supply of fuel: *The attendant refueled the buses.* *vi-:* *The truck refueled at the gas station.*

ref·uge (rĕf′ yōōj′) *n-* 1 safety or shelter: *He sought refuge from the storm in a nearby barn.* 2 a place of safety or shelter: *The barn was a refuge.* 3 anyone or anything offering peace or rest: *Music was his refuge from his many cares.*

re·fund (rē′ fŭnd′) *n-* a repayment; also, money paid back or to be paid back.

re·fur·bish (rē fûr′ bĭsh) *vt-* to furbish again; renovate or improve; brighten up: *to refurbish a room.*

re·fus·al (rĭ fyōō′ zəl) *n-* 1 a refusing or denying; rejection or denial of anything offered or asked: *His plans met with a refusal.* 2 the right to accept or reject something before others have the opportunity: *She was to have first refusal if the property was offered for sale.*

¹**re·fuse** (rĭ fyōōz′) *vt-* [**re·fused, re·fus·ing**] 1 to decline to accept; reject: *to refuse an invitation; to refuse an offer; to refuse a bribe.* 2 to decline to give; deny: *to refuse permission; to refuse food.* *vi-* to decline to do something: *I asked him to leave but he refused.*

²**ref·use** (rĕf′ yōōs, -yōōz′) *n-* waste matter; garbage.

re·fute (rĭ fyōōt′) *vt-* [**re·fut·ed, re·fut·ing**] to prove false: *It was easy to refute his argument.* —*adj-* **re·fut′ a·ble:** *His argument is easily refutable.* *n-* **ref′ u·ta′ tion:** *the refutation of a statement.* *n-* **re·fut′ er.**

re·gain (rĭ gān′) *vt-* 1 to get back; recover: *to regain leadership.* 2 to reach again; return to: *The driver regained the main road after a detour.*

re·gal (rē′ gəl) *adj-* 1 of or having to do with a king; royal: *the regal power; regal descent.* 2 fit for a king; splendid: *a regal feast.* —*n-* **re·gal′ i·ty** (rĭ găl′ ə tē). *adv-* **re′ gal·ly.**

re·gale (rĭ gāl′) *vt-* [**re·galed, re·gal·ing**] 1 to entertain or amuse; delight: *They regaled their friends with music and a banquet.* 2 to feed sumptuously: *The girls regaled themselves on wild strawberries.* *vi-* to feast: *The boys regaled on apples.* —*n-* **re·gale′ ment.**

re·ga·li·a (rĭ gāl′ yə) *n- pl.* 1 signs or emblems of royalty, such as the crown and scepter. 2 insignia of a special group such as a fraternal order. 3 clothes for a special occasion: finery.

re·gard (rĭ gärd′) *vt-* 1 to look at closely; scrutinize: *Peter regarded the beggar suspiciously.* 2 to consider: *Do you regard him as fit for the job?* 3 to pay attention to; heed: *Now regard what I have to say.* 4 to concern: *My decision regards your happiness.* 5 to admire or esteem: *She regards scholarship highly.* *n-* 1 consideration; care: *to feel regard for one's safety.* 2 esteem; respect: *a high regard for truth.* 3 a look; gaze. 4 **regards** best wishes: *Please give them my regards.*

in (or with) regard to in reference to; with respect to: *John spoke in regard to the meeting.* **in this (or that) regard** regarding a particular point or matter.

re·gard·ful (rĭ gärd′ fəl) *adj-* 1 taking notice; heedful; attentive. 2 respectful. —*adv-* **re·gard′ ful·ly.** *n-* **re·gard′ ful·ness.**

re·gard·ing (rĭ gär′ dĭng) *prep-* concerning; about; in respect to.

re·gard·less (rĭ gärd′ ləs) *adj-* heedless; showing no consideration for; unmindful: *He continued to nag, regardless of her feelings.* *adv-* *Informal* anyway: *I am going out tonight, regardless.* —*adv-* **re·gard′ less·ly.**

re·gat·ta (rĭ gä′ tə, -gāt′ ə) *n-* boat race or races.

re·gen·cy (rē′ jən sē) *n-* [*pl.* **re·gen·cies**] 1 office, powers, or government of a regent or body of regents. 2 body of regents ruling a country. 3 period of government of, or territory governed by, a regent or body of regents. 4 **Regency** in English history, the period from 1811-1820 during the rule of George, Prince of Wales, later George IV. *adj-* **Regency** of or having to do with the furniture and dress of the period in English history from 1811-1820.

¹**re·gen·er·ate** (rĭ jĕn′ ə rāt′) *vt-* [**re·gen·er·at·ed, re·gen·er·at·ing**] 1 to cause to be spiritually reborn or morally improved. 2 to put new vitality and energy into; vitalize again; revive: *His discovery regenerated a whole field of study.* 3 *Biology* to grow (new tissue, a new limb or organ, etc.) in place of something lost or damaged. 4 in certain radio circuits, to amplify (a current, output, signal, etc.) by feeding a part of the output back into the input. *vi-* 1 to form again: *The lizard's tail regenerated.* 2 to become healthy and vital again: *The tissue regenerated in six days.* 3 to be spiritually reborn or morally improved. —*n-* **re·gen′ er·a′ tion.** *adj-* **re·gen′ er·a′ tive.**

²**re·gen·er·ate** (rĭ jĕn′ ər ət) *adj-* 1 completely renewed and improved, as if born anew: *a regenerate city.* 2 undergoing regeneration: *a regenerate corporation.*

re·gent (rē′ jənt) *n-* 1 person appointed to govern when a ruler is under age or incapable. 2 member of the governing board in some state universities.

reg·i·cide (rĕj′ ə sīd′) *n-* 1 the killing of a king. 2 person who kills or assists in killing a king.

re·gime or **ré·gime** (rĭ zhēm′, rā-′) *n-* 1 a system of government; method of ruling; also, period of rule of a system of government: *a communist regime; during the regime of Napoleon.* 2 orderly way of living to improve health, treat an illness, etc.; regimen.

reg·i·men (rĕj′ ə mən) *n-* 1 a system of diet, exercise, sleep, and daily routine, prescribed for some special purpose. 2 government; control.

reg·i·ment (rĕj′ ə mənt) *n-* 1 group of battalions under the command of a colonel. 2 any large number of persons; multitude. [from Old French **regiment** meaning a military division, from the same Latin sources as **²regiment**.]

²reg·i·ment (rĕj′ ə mĕnt′) *vt-* 1 to organize into a rigid pattern or system for the sake of discipline and control: *The dictator regimented even the children.* 2 to require the same rigid pattern of behavior from all: *That school is very strict and regiments the boys.* [from Late Latin **regimentum,** from Latin **regere,** "to rule; govern."]

reg·i·men·tal (rĕj′ ə mĕn′ təl) *adj-* of or having to do with a regiment: *a regimental uniform.*

reg·i·men·tals (rĕj′ ə mĕn′ təlz) *n- pl.* 1 uniform of a regiment. 2 any military uniform.

reg·i·men·ta·tion (rĕj′ ə mən tā′ shən) *n-* a regimenting or bringing into line with a plan or system; an organizing into uniform groups: *the regimentation of workers.*

re·gion (rē′ jən) *n-* 1 a part of the earth having at least one unifying trait throughout its area, which sets it apart from surrounding areas: *an industrial region; the Rocky Mountain region; tropical regions.* 2 any part of the land, sea, air, or space: *the upper regions of the atmosphere.* 3 area or sphere of thought or action: *the region of politics; in the region of science.* 4 division or part of the body: *the region of the liver.*

re·gion·al (rē′ jə nəl) *adj-* 1 of or relating to a whole region, especially a geographical one: *the regional distribution of rainfall.* 2 of or having to do with a particular region; sectional; local: *a regional election.* —*adv-* re′ gion·al·ly.

re·gion·al·ism (rē′ jə nə lĭz′ əm) *n-* 1 special attention or devotion to a particular region. 2 expression, manner of dress, custom, or other characteristic of a particular region. —*adj-* re′gion·al·ist′ic.

reg·is·ter (rĕj′ ĭs tər) *n-* 1 official written record; also, a book for keeping such records, or an entry in it: *a register of births and deaths.* 2 mechanical device that records: *a cash register.* 3 person who keeps a record; registrar: *He is register of deeds.* 4 registration; registry. 5 in a heating system, device that regulates the passage of air. 6 *Music* (1) set of organ pipes controlled by one stop. (2) range or a specific part of the range of a human voice or instrument: *the alto register.* 7 in printing, (1) exact alignment or correspondence of the lines, margins, columns, etc., on both sides of a sheet. (2) correct or exact placing of one color upon another. *vt-* 1 to enter in a record; record officially: *to register a birth; to register securities.* 2 to enroll: *to register students.* 3 to show on an instrument or scale: *Yesterday the thermometer registered 97°.* 4 to show (a response or reaction) through movement of the face or body: *He registered surprise.* 5 to protect (mail) from possible loss by paying a fee at the post office to have it specially recorded. 6 in printing, to adjust so as to obtain correct alignment. *vi-* 1 to enter one's name in a record or list: *They registered for voting.* 2 *Informal* to make an impression. 3 in printing, to be in correct alignment.

registered nurse *n-* nurse who has successfully completed two to four years of formal training and has been licensed by a state authority to administer but not prescribe medicines or treatment, to assist surgeons, etc.

¹re·gress (rĭ grĕs′) *vi-* to go back; return, especially to an earlier condition: *The project regressed to the level of six months ago.* —*adj-* re·gres′ sive: *a regressive fashion.*

²re·gress (rē′ grĕs′) *n-* 1 passage back; way of return: *A place which offers no regress.* 2 power or privilege of returning: *the right of free egress and regress.* 3 retrogression.

re·gres·sion (rĭ grĕsh′ ən) *n-* 1 a going back in movement or development. 2 *Biology* the return to an earlier, more primitive or more general form. 3 *Medicine* a lessening of the symptoms of a disease. 4 in psychiatry, a partial return to earlier and immature patterns of thought and behavior, usually as a means of escaping stress and responsibility. *vi-*: *To send one's regrets.*

re·gret (rĭ grĕt′) *vt-* [re·gret·ted, re·gret·ting] 1 to be sorry about: *to regret a mistake.* 2 to remember with a sense of loss: *to regret the years gone by.* *n-* 1 distress of mind over some past event, with the wish that it had been otherwise: *He expressed regret for his harsh words.* 2 sadness; disappointment: *I hear with regret that you will not come.* 3 regrets courteous reply declining an invitation: *to send one's regrets.*

re·gret·ful (rĭ grĕt′ fəl) *adj-* feeling or showing regret; remembering with sorrow. —*adv-* re·gret′ ful·ly. *n-* re·gret′ ful·ness.

re·gret·ta·ble (rĭ grĕt′ə bəl) *adj-* to be regretted; lamentable; deplorable. —*adv-* re·gret′ ta·bly.

re·group (rē grōop′, rē′-) *vt-* to form into new groups: *The coach regrouped the players into teams of equal ability. vi-: The troops fell back and regrouped.*

Regt. 1 regent. 2 regiment.

reg·u·lar (rĕg′ yə lər) *adj-* 1 usual; habitual; customary: *a regular seat in school.* 2 habitual or consistent in action; orderly: *a regular routine; a regular life.* 3 happening at even intervals of time: *the regular tick of a clock; the regular beating of the heart.* 4 happening again and again at fixed times: *the regular holiday of Thanksgiving; regular meals.* 5 even in form, arrangement, etc.; symmetrical: *Ann's features are very regular.* 6 *Informal* thorough; complete: *a regular rascal.* 7 conforming to established rules, customs, party platform, etc.; orthodox: *a regular Republican.* 8 belonging to a religious order; bound by religious rule: *the regular clergy.* 9 *Military* belonging to or making up a permanent armed force: *a regular Navy officer; regular Army.* 10 *Grammar* following the usual rules of declension, conjugation, or comparison: *a regular verb.* 11 *Mathematics* (1) of a polygon, having all sides and all angles equal. (2) of a polyhedron, having faces all of which are congruent regular polygons, and having all the angles congruent where these faces join. —*adv-* reg′ u·lar·ly.

regular army *n-* permanent army kept up in peace as well as in war; standing army.

reg·u·lar·i·ty (rĕg′ yə lĕr′ ə tē, -lăr′ ə tē) *n-* the condition of being regular; evenness; balance.

reg·u·late (rĕg′ yə lāt′) *vt-* [reg·u·lat·ed, reg·u·lat·ing] 1 to govern or correct according to rule or custom: *to regulate a person's own habits.* 2 to put into working order; adjust: *He regulated the furnace.* 3 to make regular or even; control: *to regulate the temperature of a room.* 4 to put or keep in proper order: *to regulate a household.* —*adj-* reg′ u·la′ tive or reg′ u·la·to′ ry (-yə lə tôr′ ē): *a regulative device on a furnace; a regulatory agency of the government.*

reg·u·la·tion (rĕg′ yə lā′ shən) *n-* 1 a regulating or being regulated: *the regulation of temperatures; foreign trade dwindling from too much regulation.* 2 a rule, direction, or law: *hospital regulations. adj-* conforming to a regular style, method, or rule: *a regulation uniform.*

reg·u·la·tor (rĕg′ yə lā′ tər) *n-* person or thing that regulates; especially, any of various devices that automatically control all or part of a machine or process.

re·gur·gi·tate (rĭ gûr′ jə tāt′) *vt-* [re·gur·gi·tat·ed, re·gur·gi·tat·ing] to cause to surge or rush back; especially, to cast out again from the stomach. *vi-* to vomit. —*n-* re·gur′ gi·ta′ tion.

re·hash (rē′ hăsh′) *vt-* to use or go over again; work into a new form, especially without real change or improvement: *The writer rehashed an old plot. n-* 1 a going over again: *a rehash of the argument.* 2 something made over into a new form: *Her book is a rehash of old stories.*

re·hear·ing (rē′hēr′ĭng) *n-* in law, a new hearing or consideration of a case by the court in which the case was originally tried.

re·hears·al (rĭ hûr′səl) *n-* **1** a practice performance, especially of a play, opera, etc., in preparation for a public performance. **2** a telling over: *a rehearsal of his summer experiences in Europe.*

re·hearse (rĭ hûrs′) *vt-* [re·hearsed, re·hears·ing] **1** to practice in preparation for a public performance; also, to train by rehearsal: *They rehearsed the play. The conductor rehearsed the soprano.* **2** to give an account of; tell: *He rehearsed the story of his life.* **3** to repeat; tell over; recite from beginning to end: *She rehearsed in detail the old story. vi-* to practice or take part in a private performance: *The actors rehearsed daily.*

re·house (rē′houz′) *vt-* [re·housed, re·hous·ing] to provide with, or place in, other housing.

reign (rān) *n-* **1** supreme rule; royal power. **2** period of rule, as of a king: *in the reign of George III. vi-* **1** to rule as a monarch. **2** to hold sway; prevail: *Terror reigned in the village.* **Homs-** rain, rein.

re·im·burse (rē′ĭm bûrs′) *vt-* [re·im·bursed, re·im·burs·ing] to pay back; repay (a person): *The company reimbursed the man for his expenses on the trip.* —*n- re′im·burse′ment.*

rein (rān) *n-* **1** one of the two long straps attached to the bit of a horse to guide and control it. **2** (often **reins**) any means of restraint or control: *a tight rein on one's temper; the reins of government. vt-* **1** to hold in, direct, or stop by means of control straps: *to rein a horse.* **2** to control; check: *to rein one's anger.* **Homs-** rain, reign.

Reins

draw rein to stop. **give free rein to** to give complete freedom to.

rein in (or **up**) to stop a horse by means of reins.

re·in·car·na·tion (rē′ĭn kär′ nā′ shən) *n-* new embodiment or incarnation; especially, in certain cults and religions, the rebirth of the soul in another body.

rein·deer (rān′dēr′) *n-* [*pl.* **rein·deer** or **rein·deers**] a northern deer with large, branching antlers, related to the caribou. It is easily tamed, and is valued as a draft animal and for its milk, meat, and hide.

Reindeer, about 6 ft long

re·in·force (rē′ĭn fôrs′) *vt-* [re·in·forced, re·in·forc·ing] to add to for strength: *to reinforce an army platoon; to reinforce a sleeve.*

reinforced concrete *n-* concrete containing metal bars or mesh for strength.

re·in·force·ment (rē′ĭn fôrs′ mənt) *n-* **1** a strengthening or a being strengthened by addition of something. **2** person or thing added in order to strengthen. **3** reinforcements fresh troops, supplies, ships, etc., sent to an area of combat.

re·in·vest (rē′ĭn vĕst′) *vt-* to invest (money) again; especially, to invest (income from other investments).

re·in·vig·o·rate (rē′ĭn vĭg′ə rāt′) *vt-* [re·in·vig·o·rat·ed, re·in·vig·o·rat·ing] to impart new vigor to.

re·is·sue (rē ĭsh′ōō) *n-* a publishing again of something previously published and allowed to go out of print; also, a copy of the thing published: *This book is a reissue. vt-* [re·is·sued, re·is·su·ing] to issue again.

re·it·er·ate (rē ĭt′ə rāt′) *vt-* [re·it·er·at·ed, re·it·er·at·ing] to say or do again or several times: *to reiterate a complaint.* —*n- re·it′er·a′tion. adj- re·it′er·a′tive.*

¹**re·ject** (rĭ jĕkt′) *vt-* **1** to turn down; refuse to take, believe, use, etc.: *He rejected my offer of assistance.* **2** to throw away as worthless; discard: *They rejected all imperfect specimens.* —*n- re·jec′tion.*

²**re·ject** (rē′jĕkt′) *n-* rejected person or thing.

re·joice (rĭ jois′) *vi-* [re·joiced, re·joic·ing] to feel or express joy or happiness: *I rejoice to hear of your good*

luck. *vt-* to gladden; delight: *The sight of her gifts rejoiced Mary greatly.*

¹**re·join** (rĭ join′) *vi-* to answer; reply to: *"I don't need any help, thank you," Mary rejoined to her brother's offer*

²**re·join** (rē′join′) *vt-* **1** to join together again. **2** to return to after separation: *Frank will rejoin us soon.*

re·join·der (rĭ join′dər) *n-* a reply or retort, especially an answer to a reply.

re·ju·ve·nate (rĭ jōō′və nāt′) *vt-* [re·ju·ve·nat·ed, re·ju·ve·nat·ing] to make young again; to cause to feel young again. —*n- re·ju′ve·na′tion.*

re·kin·dle (rē kĭn′dəl, rē′-) *vt-* [re·kin·dled, re·kin·dling] to set fire to again; also, to arouse (hope, enthusiasm, etc.) again: *to rekindle hope. vi-: His hopes rekindled.*

re·lapse (rĭ lăps′) *vi-* [re·lapsed, re·laps·ing] **1** to fall back into a former state, practice, habit, etc.; especially, to fall back into wrongdoing; backslide: *He relapsed into silence. The tribe relapsed into paganism.* **2** to fall back into illness after a state of partial recovery. *n- (also rē′lăps′)* a return to a former condition or habit; especially, a setback in recovery from a disease.

re·late (rĭ lāt′) *vt-* [re·lat·ed, re·lat·ing] **1** to tell; narrate. **2** to connect; associate: *The detective tried to relate the two clues. vi-* to be connected or associated; refer or allude (to): *The letter relates to his success.*

re·lat·ed (rĭ lā′təd) *adj-* **1** connected by blood or marriage. **2** connected in some way. —*n- re·lat′ed·ness*

re·la·tion (rĭ lā′shən) *n-* **1** a telling or narrating: *We heard his relation of what had happened.* **2** a connection between two or more things; relevance of one to another; position with respect to each other; relationship: *the relation of poverty to crime; the relation of climate to agriculture.* **3** family connection, especially by birth: *She's of no relation to me.* **4** *Informal* a relative: *He's one of my relations.* **5** *Mathematics* a set of ordered pairs. **6** **relations** dealings; affairs: *business relations.*

in (or **with**) **relation to** in regard to; concerning.

re·la·tion·ship (rĭ lā′shən shĭp′) *n-* **1** connection. **2** tie of blood, marriage, or affection between people.

rel·a·tive (rĕl′ə tĭv) *adj-* **1** measured by comparison; comparative: *the relative speeds of a car and a bicycle.* **2** having meaning only as related to something else: *More, less, small, and large are relative words. n-* **1** person connected by blood or marriage. **2** *Grammar* (traditionally called **relative pronoun**) word that introduces a subordinate clause that modifies a preceding noun, pronoun, noun phrase, or noun clause, called the antecedent of the relative. The relatives are "who," "whose," "whom," "that," "which," "when," and "where." Examples:

The boy who just entered is class president. (relative as subject)

Where is the gyroscope that was on the table? (relative as subject)

There's the man whom I met last night. (relative as object of a verb)

There's the girl of whom I was speaking. (relative as object of a preposition.)

There's the boy whose wallet I found. (relative as determiner)

This is the place where he was shot. (relative as adverb)

This is the time when he should arrive. (relative as adverb)

relative clause *n-* subordinate clause introduced by one of the relatives.

relative humidity *n-* the ratio, in percent, of the actual amount of water vapor in the air to the amount that would be present if the air were saturated at the same temperature and pressure.

rel·a·tive·ly (rĕl′ə tĭv lē) *adv-* in comparison with other persons or things: *In his town, Mr. Jackson was considered relatively rich.*

rel·a·tiv·ism (rĕl′ə tə vĭz′ əm) *n-* the assigning of worth and importance to things on the basis of their relation to other things, and therefore giving nothing a fixed and absolute value. —*n- rel′a·tiv·ist′.*

re·lay (rē′lā′) *vt-* [re·laid, re·lay·ing] to lay again: *We re-laid the tiles on the kitchen floor.*

relay race *n-* running race between teams, in which each member of a team runs part of the course.

re·lease (rĭ lēs′) *vt-* [re·leased, re·leas·ing] 1 to let go; unlock: *He released the brakes of the car.* 2 to set free: *to release a prisoner.* 3 to free from obligation or penalty: *to release a person from a promise.* 4 in law, to give up title to; surrender: *Mr. Right released his summer home* number left over after one number has been subtracted from another: *5 subtracted from 8 leaves a remainder of 3.* 3 *Mathematics* number left over after a number has been divided by another: *5 divided by 2 gives 2 and a remainder of 1. 4 divided by 2 gives 2 and a remainder of 0.*

re·mains (rĭ mānz′) *n- pl.* 1 part or parts left; remnants: *the remains of a meal.* 2 ruins, especially of ancient times: *the remains of ancient Rome.* 3 a dead body.

¹**re·make** (rē māk′, rē′-) *vt-* [re·made, re·mak·ing] to make again: *After her nap, she remade the bed.*

²**re·make** (rē′ māk′) *n-* something remade: *a remake of an old motion picture.*

re·mand (rĭ mănd′) *vt-* 1 to send or order back; especially, to send a prisoner to jail to await trial, or to send back a case to a lower court for reconsideration. *n-: The judge ordered the remand of the prisoner to jail.*

re·mark (rĭ märk′) *n-* 1 a brief comment or observation: *Did he make a remark about my lateness?* 2 notice or comment: *an object of* remark. 3 **remarks** conversation in general: *His remarks were interesting. vt-* 1 to say or write briefly and casually as a comment; mention: *He remarked that he would be in New York today.* 2 to take note of; notice; observe: *We remarked his worried look. vi-* to comment (often followed by "on" or "upon"): *He remarked upon the subject.*

re·mark·a·ble (rĭ mär′ kə bəl) *adj-* worthy of notice; extraordinary: *He has a remarkable memory.* —*n- re·mark′a·ble·ness. adv- re·mark′a·bly.*

re·mar·ry (rē mär′ ē, rē′-) *vt-* [re·mar·ried, re·mar·ry·ing] to marry (a former spouse) again. *vi-:* to marry again after being widowed or divorced: *Two years later she remarried.* —*n- re·mar′riage.*

re·me·di·a·ble (rĭ mē′ dē ə bəl) *adj-* such as can be corrected or cured; curable: *a remediable disease; a remediable fault.* —*adv- re·me′di·a·bly.*

re·me·di·al (rĭ mē′ dē əl) *adj-* for the purpose of correcting; providing a remedy: *After her accident, remedial exercises helped her walk.* —*adv- re·med′i·al·ly.*

rem·e·dy (rĕm′ ə dē) *n-* [*pl.* rem·e·dies] 1 anything to cure or relieve illness: *a headache remedy.* 2 action or method to right wrongs: *Your only remedy is to go to court. vt-* [rem·e·died, rem·e·dy·ing] 1 to cure, or cause to improve, with medicine: *to remedy a cough.* 2 to repair; make right; correct (evils, defects, faults, etc.).

re·mem·ber (rĭ mĕm′ bər) *vt-* 1 to bring back to the mind; think again of; recall: *She suddenly remembered an unpleasant experience. He can't remember her name.* 2 to retain or keep in the mind: *I remember the poem very well.* 3 to give a present to; tip: *Will you remember the elevator man at Christmas?* 4 to carry greetings for: *Please remember me to your family. vi-* to have or use the faculty of memory: *He learned to remember.*

re·mem·brance (rĭ mĕm′ brəns) *n-* 1 a remembering; a recalling to mind: *The remembrance of that day gave Jean pleasure.* 2 object or objects that call to mind persons or events: *The blue ribbon was a remembrance of Paul's first horse show.* 3 gift or token: *The pin was a remembrance from her father.* 4 the length of time over which one's memories extend; total memory: *the most remarkable event in my remembrance.* 6 **remembrances** greetings: *Give her my remembrances.*

re·mind·er (rĭ mīn′ dər) *n-* anything that helps a person to remember.

rem·i·nisce (rĕm′ ə nĭs′) *vi-* [rem·i·nisced, rem·i·nisc·ing] to think or talk about past experiences.

rem·i·nis·cence (rĕm′ ə nĭs′ əns) *n-* 1 the recollection of past experiences; remembrance. 2 **reminiscences** written or spoken account of one's past experiences.

rem·i·nis·cent (rĕm′ ə nĭs′ ənt) *adj-* 1 given to recalling the past; dwelling on the past: *a reminiscent letter.* 2 reminding or suggestive (of): *a poem reminiscent of the style of Burns.* —*adv- rem′i·nis′cent·ly.*

re·miss (rĭ mĭs′) *adj-* 1 careless in matters of duty, business, etc.; neglectful; lax: *He is remiss in keeping appointments.* 2 marked by carelessness or negligence: *The service in this restaurant is very remiss.* —*adv- re·miss′ ly. n- re·miss′ ness.*

re·mis·sion (rĭ mĭsh′ ən) *n-* 1 a canceling, discharging, or annulling: *the remission of a debt.* 2 forgiveness; pardon: *the remission of a sin.* 3 temporary lessening: *a remission of pain.*

re·mit (rĭ mĭt′) *vt-* [re·mit·ted, re·mit·ting] 1 to submit in payment: *Please remit the money you owe.* 2 to forgive or pardon: *to remit sins.* 3 to refrain from demanding or insisting upon: *He remitted the fine.* 4 to make less; relax: *He remitted his efforts.* 5 to submit (a matter) for consideration, action, etc.: *He remitted the question to the advisory committee.* 6 in law, to send back (a case) to a lower court. *vi-* 1 to become less severe; lessen in force: *Her fever remitted.* 2 to send money: *Please remit by return mail.* —*n- re·mit′ ter.*

re·mit·tance (rĭ mĭt′ əns) *n-* 1 a sending of money, especially to someone far away. 2 the money sent.

rem·nant (rĕm′ nənt) *n-* 1 small piece or part left over; fragment; scrap: *the scattered remnants of an army.* 2 piece of fabric left from a large piece and sold cheap.

re·mod·el (rē mŏd′ əl, rē′-) *vt-* to make over in a new pattern: *The tailor remodeled the suit.*

re·mon·strance (rĭ mŏn′ strəns) *n-* strong protest: *a remonstrance against prejudice.*

re·mon·strate (rĭ mŏn′ strāt′) *vi-* [re·mon·strat·ed, re·mon·strat·ing] to plead strongly in protest: *They remonstrated against higher taxes.*

re·morse (rĭ môrs′, -môrs′) *n-* painful regret or anguish caused by a feeling of guilt: *The driver felt remorse when he hit the puppy.* —*adj- re·morse′ ful. adv- re·morse′ ful·ly. n- re·morse′ ful·ness.*

re·morse·less (rĭ môrs′ ləs, -môrs′ ləs) *adj-* merciless; pitiless: *a remorseless person.* —*adv- re·morse′ less·ly. n- re·morse′ less·ness.*

re·mote (rĭ mōt′) *adj-* [re·mot·er, re·mot·est] 1 far-off; distant in time: *the remote past.* 2 far away; distant in space: *a remote land.* 3 set apart; secluded: *a house remote from the village.* 4 only distantly related or connected: *a remote relative; a remote bearing on a question.* 5 slight: *I haven't a remote idea of what you mean.* —*adv- re·mote′ ly. n- re·mote′ ness.*

remote control *n-* the control of a machine or device from a distance, especially by radio signals. *as modifier* (**remote-control**): *a remote-control system.*

¹**re·mount** (rē mount′) *vt-* 1 to go up on again: *The fireman remounted the ladder.* 2 to put (a photograph, jewel, etc.) on a new mount. *vi-* to mount a horse again.

²**re·mount** (rē′ mount′) *n-* fresh horse to replace one killed, disabled, or fatigued.

re·mov·al (rĭ mōō′ vəl) *n-* 1 a removing or being removed: *The removal of the junkyard pleased us.* 2 a moving to a new place: *the removal of furniture to a new house.* 3 a dismissing from an official position.

re·move (rĭ mōōv′) *vt-* [re·moved, re·mov·ing] 1 to take away, or off, or out: *He removed the dishes from the table. She removed her hat.* 2 to get rid of; put an end to: *I removed a cause of worry by paying the debt.* 3 to dismiss from an official position. *vi-* to move from one place to another; change residence. *n-* interval of distance; step: *many removes from his former way of life.* —*adj- re·mov′ a·ble: a removable filter. n- re·mov′ er.*

re·moved (rĭ mōōvd′) *adj-* 1 existing apart; distant: *Their house was far removed from the village.* 2 separated by a degree in relationship: *A first cousin once removed is the child of that first cousin.*

re·mu·ner·ate (rĭ myōō′ nə rāt′) *vt-* [re·mu·ner·at·ed, re·mu·ner·at·ing] 1 to make an equivalent payment to (a person) in return for a service, loss, expense, etc.; compensate; repay: *They remunerated him for his trouble.* 2 to pay for. —*n- re·mu′ner·a′tion.*

re·mu·ner·a·tive (rĭ myōō′ nə rā′ tĭv) *adj-* profitable.

Re·mus (rē′ məs) *n-* in Roman legend, the twin brother of Romulus, by whom he was slain.

re·nas·cent (rĭ năs′ ənt, rĭ nā′ sənt) *adj-* being born again; rising again into vigor: *a renascent interest.*

rheum (rōōm) *n-* 1 a watery discharge from mucous membranes of the eyes or nose. 2 a cold, or inflammation of the nasal tissues. *Hom-* room.

rheu·mat·ic (rōō măt′ ĭk) *adj-* relating to, having, or caused by rheumatism. *n-* person with rheumatism.

rheumatic fever *n-* an infectious disease, especially of the young, marked by fever and swelling of the joints and often followed by serious heart disease.

rheu·ma·tism (rōō′ mə tĭz′ əm) *n-* 1 an acute, infectious disease, marked by fever and inflammation, swelling, stiffness, and pain in the joints. 2 any of various conditions marked by pains in the muscles, joints, etc. 3 rheumatic fever.

Rh factor (är′ ăch′) *n-* any of several antigens transmitted by genes and occurring on the surface of the red blood cells in most people. People with these antigens are termed **Rh positive**, and those without, **Rh negative**. When Rh-positive and Rh-negative bloods come into contact, severe and usually fatal reactions occur.

rhine·stone (rīn′ stōn′) *n-* colorless paste gem made to imitate a diamond and used in costume jewelry. *as modifier:* a rhinestone *brooch.*

Rhine wine (rīn) *n-* 1 any of several light, dry, still white wines produced from grapes grown along or near the Rhine. 2 any similar wine produced elsewhere.

rhi·no (rī′ nŏ) *n-* [*pl.* **rhi·nos**] rhinoceros.

rhi·noc·er·os (rī nŏs′ ər əs) *n-* any of several massive, plant-eating mammals of Africa and Asia, having a thick skin and three toes on each foot. The African rhinos have two horns on the nose, and the main Asian varieties have one.

African rhinoceros up to 15 ft long

rhi·zome (rī′ zŏm′) *n-* an underground, rootlike stem that grows horizontally and is often thickened with stored food.

Rho·de·si·an man (rŏ dēzh′ ən) *n-* a kind of Neanderthal man, known from fossil remains found in 1921 in Northern Rhodesia (now Zambia).

rho·di·um (rŏ′ dē əm) *n-* a hard, grayish-white metal element similar to platinum; and used to electroplate silver and jewelry. Symbol Rh, At. No. 45, At. Wt. 102.905.

rho·do·den·dron (rŏ′ də dĕn′ drən) *n-* any of various shrubs with glossy, evergreen leaves and large clusters of brilliantly colored flowers.

Rhododendron

rhom·boid (rŏm′ boid′) *n-* a parallelogram with oblique angles whose adjacent sides are of unequal lengths.

rhom·bus (rŏm′ bəs) *n-* parallelogram with oblique angles and all sides of equal length.

rhu·barb (rōō′ bärb′) *n-* 1 plant related to the buckwheats, with large green leaves and long, fleshy, reddish stems or stalks. 2 the stalks of this plant, used for sauce and for pie filling. 3 a medicine made from the roots of certain varieties of rhubarb. 4 *Slang* quarrel, especially one among players in a ball game.

Rhombus

rick (rĭk) *n-* outdoor stack of hay or straw. *vt-* to pile or heap into a stack.

rick·ets (rĭk′ əts) *n-* disease occurring in infants and young children, caused chiefly by a deficiency of vitamin D in the diet or from lack of sunlight, and marked by a softening of the bones and consequent deformity.

rick·et·tsi·a (rĭ kĕt′ sē ə) *n-* [*pl.* **rick·et·tsi·ae** (-sē ē) or **rick·et·tsi·as**] any of a group of parasitic, true bacteria that are slightly larger than viruses, and can grow only in living cells. They cause typhus, Rocky Mountain spotted fever, etc.

rife (rīf) *adj-* widespread: *Gossip is rife in the town.*
     rife with full of: *The village was rife with gossip.*

rode (rŏd) *p.t.* of **ride**. *Hom-* road.

ro·dent (rŏ′ dənt) *n-* any member of a large order of gnawing mammals (**Rodentia**) with a single pair of strong upper incisors. Rats, mice, squirrels, and beavers are all rodents. *as modifier:* Mice have rodent *teeth.*

ro·de·o (rŏ′ dē ō′, *also* rŏ dā′ ō) *n-* [*pl.* **ro·de·os**] 1 a show where cowboys compete in horseback riding, roping cattle, etc. 2 a roundup of cattle.

roe (rŏ) *n-* eggs of fish, especially when enclosed in an ovarian membrane. [from Middle English *rowne*, from Old Norse *hrogn*.] *Hom-* ¹row, ²row.

roe (rŏ) *n-* [*pl.* **roe** or **roes**] small deer found in Europe and western Asia. Also **roe deer**. [from Old English *rã*, "spotted," from earlier *rãha*.] *Hom-* ¹row, ²row.

roe·buck (rŏ′ bŭk′) *n-* [*pl.* **roe·buck** or **roe·bucks**] male roe deer.

roent·gen (rĕnt′ gən, rŭnt′ jən) *Physics n-* unit of X-ray radiation or gamma radiation.

Roentgen ray *n-* X ray.

rog·er (rŏj′ ər) *interj-* message received and understood.

rogue (rŏg) *n-* 1 dishonest person; cheat. 2 one, who plays pranks or teases; mischievous one. 3 solitary, often vicious animal living apart from the herd. *as modifier:* a rogue *trick;* a rogue *elephant.*

ro·guer·y (rŏ′ gə rē) *n-* [*pl.* **ro·guer·ies**] 1 dishonest practices; cheating. 2 playfully mischievous behavior.

rogues' gallery *n-* collection of the photographs of persons arrested as criminals, kept by the police.

ro·guish (rŏ′ gĭsh) *adj-* 1 mischievous; playful: *a roguish smile.* 2 *Archaic* dishonest; rascally. —*adv-* ro′ guish·ly. *n-* ro′ guish·ness.

roil (roil) *vt-* 1 to stir up sediment in water or other liquids. 2 to irritate; vex.

roil·y (roi′ lē) *adj-* [**roil·i·er**, **roil·i·est**] full of sediment; muddy: *the roily waters of the lake.*

roi·ster (roi′ stər) *vi-* to act in a noisy or boisterous manner; carouse. —*n-* roist′ er·er.

Ro·land (rŏ′ lənd) *n-* in French romance, nephew of Charlemagne, hero of the wars against the Saracens.

role or **rôle** (rŏl) *n-* 1 part or character taken by an actor: the role of *Romeo.* 2 duty or function: *his role as president;* the role of *hormones in the body.* *Hom-* roll.

roll (rŏl) *vi-* 1 to move by turning over and over: *The ball rolled down the hill.* 2 to move on wheels or rollers: *The carriage rolled down the street.* 3 to form, when being wound, the shape of a ball or cylinder: *The cloth rolls easily.*

rope (rŏp) *n-* 1 large, strong cord made of twisted, smaller cords. 2 collection of things braided or twined together in a line or string; also, a festoon: *a rope of pearls;* ropes of *laurel.* 3 slimy or stringy thread formed in a liquid. 4 execution or death by hanging. 5 lasso; lariat. *vt-* [**roped**, **rop·ing**] 1 to fasten, bind, or tie with, or as if with, a rope: *We roped and tied his feet so he couldn't escape.* 2 to mark off or enclose by means of a rope: *to rope off a street.* 3 to lasso: *to rope a calf. vi-* to form stringy threads, as syrup does. —*n-* rop′ er.

Rope

     give (someone) rope to give someone freedom of action in the expectation that he will defeat himself by overdoing matters. **know the ropes** *Informal* 1 to know all the details of a job or procedure. 2 to be sophisticated or worldly-wise. **the end of one's rope** the point at which one reaches the end of one's resources or strength. **rope in** *Informal* to involve or persuade by trickery, enticement, etc.; take in; deceive.

rop·y (rŏ′ pē) *adj-* [**rop·i·er**, **rop·i·est**] 1 forming slimy threads; stringy: *a ropy paint;* ropy *syrup.* 2 like cords or rope. —*n-* rop′ i·ness.

Roque·fort (rŏk′ fərt) *n-* blue-veined cheese from ewe's milk, ripened in caves near Roquefort, France.

ror·qual (ror′ kwəl, rôr′-) *n-* finback whale.

Ror·schach test (ror′ shäk′, rôr′-) *n-* in psychology, a personality test in which a person is shown ten standardized ink blots and asked to tell what they suggest to him.

ro·sa·ry (rŏ′ zə rē) *n-* [*pl.* **ro·sa·ries**] 1 string of beads for counting and reciting a series of prayers. 2 series of prayers thus recited.

paper route. *vt-* [rout·ed, rout·ing] to send or forward by a certain road or way. *Hom-* root or rout.

rou·tine (rōō tēn´) *n-* usual or regular way of doing things: *the daily* routine *of classes and homework*. *adj-* (*also* rōō´tēn´) regular or usual; ordinary; customary.

rove (rōv) *vi-* [roved, rov·ing] to wander; go from place to place and not settle down: *to rove all over the world.* *vt-:* *to rove the plains.*

rov·er (rō´vər) *n-* 1 person who wanders. 2 pirate.

¹row (rō) *n-* 1 series of persons or things in a line, especially a straight line: *a row of beets; a row of seats.* 2 line of houses side by side on a street; also, the street. 3 street or neighborhood marked by one type of business or occupancy: *cannery* row; *publishers'* row. [from Old English rōw or rēw meaning "a line; series."] *Hom-* roe.
 hard row to hoe hard task.

²row (rō) *vt-* 1 to propel by means of oars. 2 to take or carry in a boat with oars: *The boatman* rowed *us up the river.* 3 of a boat, to use (a specific number of oars): *The barge* rowed *ten oars.* 4 to use (oars or rowers), especially in a race: *The crew* rowed *five new men.* 5 to participate in, or compete against, with oars: *to row a race; to row last year's winning crew.* *vi-* 1 to move a boat by means of oars: *John has learned to row.* 2 to be moved by means of oars: *The boat* rows *easily.* *n-* act of moving a boat by oars; also, a ride in a rowboat. [from Old English rōwan.] *Hom-* roe. *—n-* row´er.

³row (rou) *n-* 1 noisy argument or quarrel: *to have a row with one's neighbors.* 2 loud noise; disturbance; uproar. *vi-* to quarrel. [altered from **rouse**, of uncertain origin.]

row·an (rou´ən) *n-* 1 tree bearing large clusters of orange or red berries. 2 the berry of this tree.

row·boat (rō´bōt´) *n-* small boat moved in water by means of oars.

row·dy (rou´dē) *adj-* [row·di·er, row·di·est] noisy, rough, and disorderly: *a rowdy audience;* rowdy *behavior.* *n-* [*pl.* row·dies] rude and disorderly person. *—adv-* row´di·ly. *n-* row´di·ness. *adj-* row´dy·ish.

Rowboat

row·dy·ism (rou´dē iz´əm) *n-* disorderly conduct.

row·el (rou´əl) *n-* the small wheel of a spur. *vt-* to prick (a horse) with this.

Rowel

roy·al (roi´əl) *adj-* 1 of or having to do with kings or queens: *the royal family.* 2 like a king; regal: *He behaved with royal dignity.* 3 of or having to do with the government of a king or queen: *the royal navy.* 4 fit for a king; splendid: *a royal welcome.* *n-* small sail above the topgallant sail and under the skysail. *—adv-* roy´al·ly.

roy·al·ist (roi´ə list´) *n-* 1 believer in, and supporter of, government by a king. 2 Royalist (1) Cavalier. (2) Tory. *adj-:* *a royalist party.*

royal jelly *n-* white, concentrated food paste produced from pollen by the salivary glands of the worker honeybee and fed to larvae. Larvae that are fed royal jelly throughout their development become queen bees.

royal palm *n-* any of several tall, ornamental American palm trees, widely planted in tropical regions.

roy·al·ty (roi´əl tē) *n-* [*pl.* roy·al·ties] 1 kings, queens, and their families: *a play performed before royalty.* 2 position, power, or duties of kings or queens: *Crowns and scepters are symbols of* royalty. 3 kingly nature or quality. 4 payment made to the owner of a copyright or patent: *Publishers pay a* royalty *to an author on the copies of his books they sell.* 5 tax paid to the crown, such as a percentage of gold mined or minted.

run·a·round (rŭn´ə round´) *n-* 1 *Slang* evasive excuse, answer, etc., especially in response to a request or question. 2 in printing, column of type set narrower than usual to fit around an illustration.

run·a·way (rŭn´ə wā´) *n-* 1 person who runs away; a fugitive: *a runaway from home.* 2 a horse out of control. *adj-* 1 running away; out of control: *a runaway horse; his runaway spending.* 2 brought about by running away or eloping: *a runaway marriage.* 3 *Informal* won by a wide margin: *a runaway victory.*

rung (rŭng) *n-* rodlike step of a ladder, or a rod joining the legs of a chair. [from Old English hrung meaning "staff; rod; spar."] *Hom-* wrung.

Rungs

run-in (rŭn´ĭn´) *n-* argument; quarrel.

run·nel (rŭn´əl) *or* **run·let** (rŭn´lət) *n-* small stream; rivulet.

run-through (rŭn´thrōō´) *n-* summary or rehearsal.

run·way (rŭn´wā) *n-* 1 beaten path or way along which animals pass. 2 a paved or cleared strip where planes take off and land. 3 fenced place: *a runway for dogs.* 4 ramp which serves as an extension to a stage or platform; also, ramp which is built over stairs for the passage of wheeled vehicles.

ru·pee (rōō´pē) *n-* 1 unit of money in India, Pakistan, and Ceylon. 2 the coin representing this unit.

Runway

rup·ture (rŭp´chər) *n-* 1 a bursting or breaking apart: *a rupture of the appendix.* 2 a breaking off or interruption of friendly relations. 3 hernia. *vt-* [rup·tured, rup·tur·ing] 1 to burst or break apart. 2 to cause a hernia in. 3 to bring about a breach of (friendship). *vi-* to suffer a breach or break.

ru·ral (rōōr´əl) *adj-* of or having to do with the country, country life, or agriculture. *—adv-* ru´ral·ly.

rural free delivery *or* **rural delivery** *n-* free mail delivery in country districts.

ruse (rōōz, rōōs) *n-* a trick or plan intended to deceive.

¹rush (rŭsh) *vi-* 1 to move with speed; hurry: *The doctor* rushed *to his patient.* 2 to act quickly, often without enough thought: *They* rushed *into the new project.* *vt-* 1 to cause to move or act with great speed: *Please* rush *this package to the post office. They* rushed *troops to the battlefield.* 2 to do something quickly, often without enough care: *He* rushed *the job.* 3 to attack swiftly and in force: *The troops* rushed *the enemy's outpost.* 4 in fraternities and sororities, to entertain (a prospective member) in order to persuade him or her to join. 5 *Informal* to pay marked attention to; court. 6 in football, to advance (the ball) by carrying it. *n-* 1 a driving forward with eagerness and haste; sudden forward motion: *a rush of wind; the rush of a flood.* 2 hurry; bustle and excitement: *the rush of life in a big city.* 3 sudden movement of people; state of unusual activity: *the gold rush to California in 1849; the Christmas shopping rush.* 4 an attack; charge. 5 an unusual demand: *a rush on bonds.* 6 a rough-and-tumble contest between students from different classes. 7 in football, a play in which the ball is carried toward the goal. 8 rushes in motion pictures, the first prints of uncut and unedited film. *adj-* done with or requiring haste: *a rush job; a rush order.* [from Old English hryscan.] *—n-* rush´er.

²rush (rŭsh) *n-* any of certain marsh plants having hollow stems. The stems are often dried and used for making baskets, hats, chair seats, etc. [from Old English rysc.] *—adj-* rush´like´.

rush hour *n-* time of day when traffic or business is at its peak.

rush·y (rŭsh´ē) *adj-* [rush·i·er, rush·i·est] 1 full of or covered with rushes: *a rushy pond.* 2 like rushes.

Russ. 1 Russia. 2 Russian.

rus·set (rŭs´ət) *n-* 1 reddish-brown color. 2 homespun cloth of this color. 3 kind of winter apple with a rough, reddish-brown skin. *adj-:* *a russet leaf.*

Rus·sian (rŭsh´ən) *n-* 1 member of the dominant Slavic-speaking peoples of Russia or one of his descendants. 2 one of the Slavic languages of the Soviet Union, now the official language. *adj-:* *The* Russian *winters are long.*

Russian dressing *n-* mayonnaise to which chili sauce, pimientos, and chopped pickles have been added.

S

S, s (ĕs) *n-* [*pl.* **S's, s's**] the nineteenth letter of the English alphabet.

S symbol for sulfur.

-s or **-es** *word ending* **1** used to form the plural of nouns: *two hats; nine dresses.* **2** used to form the third person singular of verbs, indicating that he, she, or it is doing an action at the present time: *He works. She fixes.*

¹'s *word ending* used to form the possessive of singular nouns and of plural nouns not ending in "-s": *the man's hat. Jane's book.* For plurals that end in "-s" or "-es," the possessive is formed by adding an apostrophe to the noun: *the boys' dormitory; the churches' windows.*

²'s 1 is: *It's Tuesday.* **2** has: *He's gone.* **3** us: *Let's go.*

s. 1 second. **2** shilling. **3** south. **4** southern. **5** singular.

S. 1 south. **2** southern. **3** saint. **4** senate. **5** signor.

Sa symbol for samarium.

S.A. 1 Salvation Army. **2** Sociedad Anónima (Spanish for corporation). **3** Société Anonyme. (French for corporation). **4** South Africa. **5** South America. **6** South Australia.

Sab·bath (săb′ əth) *n-* day of rest and religious worship. The Sabbath is Sunday for most Christians. It is Saturday for Jews and some groups of Christians.

sab·bat·i·cal (sə băt′ l kəl) *adj-* **1** of, having to do with, or resembling the Sabbath. **2** bringing a period of rest that occurs at regular intervals: *a sabbatical trip.*

sabbatical leave or **sabbatical year** *n-* a year or half year off, awarded usually to a teacher every seven years.

sa·ber (sā′ bər) *n-* **1** cavalry sword with a long, one-edged, slightly curved blade. **2** light sword for fencing. *vt-* to cut, kill, or strike with a cavalry sword. Also **sabre.**

Saber

saber rattling *n-* threatening display of military might.

saber saw *n-* portable electric saw with the blade fixed and powered only at one end.

sa·ber·tooth (sā′ bər to͞oth′) *n-* any of various large prehistoric cats that had long, curved, upper canine teeth. Also **saber-toothed cat, saber-toothed tiger.**

Sa·bine (sā′ bīn′) *n-* **1** one of an ancient people of central Italy who were conquered and absorbed by the Romans in 290 B.C. **2** their language. *adj-: the Sabine women.*

sa·ble (sā′ bəl) *n-* **1** small, dark-brown mammal of northern Europe and Asia, related to the weasels. **2** the valuable fur of these animals. **3** the American

sad·dle·bag (săd′ əl băg′) *n-* pouch or bags attached to a saddle for carrying small articles.

saddle blanket or **sad·dle·cloth** (săd′ əl klŏth′) *n-* thick cloth placed on an animal under a saddle.

sad·dle·bow (săd′ əl bō′) *n-* the arched front part of a saddle.

sad·dler (săd′ lər) *n-* person who makes, repairs, or sells saddles, harnesses, etc.

sad·dler·y (săd′ lə rē) *n-* [*pl.* **sad·dler·ies**] **1** business or shop of a saddler. **2** articles made by a saddler.

saddle shoes *n-* light-colored sport shoes with a band or saddle of dark leather across the instep.

saddle soap *n-* a mild soap, usually containing neat's-foot oil, used to clean, soften, and preserve leather.

Sad·du·cee (săj′ ə sē′, săd′ yo͞o sē′) *n-* member of an ancient aristocratic Jewish sect that followed only the Mosaic law and rejected all other doctrines. They were directly opposed to the Pharisees in politics.

sad·i·ron (săd′ ī′ ərn) *n-* flatiron with two pointed ends and a removable handle.

sa·dism (sā′ dīz′ əm, săd′ īz′ əm) *n-* tendency of a person to get pleasure from hurting others. —*n-* **sad′ ist.**

sa·dis·tic (sə dĭs′ tĭk) *adj-* of, having to do with, or marked by sadism. —*adv-* **sa·dis′ ti·cal·ly.**

sa·fa·ri (sə fä′ rē, -fâr′ ē) *n-* hunting trip or expedition, especially in Africa.

safe-de·pos·it box (sāf′ də pŏz′ ət) *n-* fireproof box in the vault of a bank, rented to a person for storing securities, jewelry, and other valuables.

safe·guard (sāf′ gärd′) *vt-* to keep safe; keep from harm or danger; protect. *n-* person or thing that guards or protects; protection: *A dike is a safeguard against floods.*

safe·keep·ing (sāf′ kē′ pǐng) *n-* a keeping or being kept safe; protection: *Put it in the file for safekeeping.*

safe·ty (sāf′ tē) *n-* [*pl.* **safe·ties**] **1** freedom from danger, injury, or damage; security; protection. **2** device or catch for preventing accidents, as in a gun or machine. **3** in football (1) a two-point score made by the defensive team when a player of the offensive team, who is carrying the ball, is tackled on or behind his own goal line. (2) a defensive player who takes the position nearest to his own goal line. *as modifier: a safety pin; a safety valve.*

safety belt *n-* **1** strong belt or harness that fastens a person to a fixed object and prevents him from slipping and falling. **2** seat belt.

safety glass *n-* shatterproof glass made of two sheets of glass separated by a layer of transparent plastic.

safety match *n-* a match that will not light unless struck upon a special surface.

safety pin *n-* pin bent back on itself to form a spring, with its point held behind a guard.

safety razor *n-* razor with a replaceable blade and a guard to prevent serious cuts. For picture, see *razor.*

safety valve *n-* valve which permits some steam to escape from a boiler when the pressure is so high that an explosion might result. **2** outlet for repressed emotion.

saf·flow·er (săf′ lou′ ər) *n-* **1** Asiatic plant resembling the thistle, having yellowish-red flower heads and seeds that yield an edible oil. **2** the dried flower heads of this plant, used in medicine or as a red dye.

saf·fron (săf′ rən) *n-* **1** a variety of crocus that blooms in the fall. **2** bright orange-yellow dye or flavoring obtained from this flower. **3** (also **saffron yellow**) orange yellow. *adj-: a dish of saffron rice; saffron satin.*

Safflower

S. Afr. 1 South Africa. **2** South African.

sag (săg) *vi-* [**sagged, sag·ging**] **1** to bend or sink downward in the middle from pressure, weight, or lack of tension: *The clothesline sagged.* **2** to become weak; lose firmness; droop: *His spirits sagged.* **3** to lean to one side; become lopsided: *The door sags.* **4** to decline: *Stock prices sagged. Automobile production sagged because of the strike.* *n-* a drooping; a settling; also, the extent of drooping or sinking under weight or pressure.

sa·ga (sä′ gə) *n-* **1** medieval Norse legend or history of heroes or their families. **2** any tale of heroic deeds.

sa·ga·cious (sə gā′ shəs) *adj-* of keen intelligence; shrewd; having sound judgment: *a sagacious ruler.* —*adv-* **sa·ga′ cious·ly.** —*n-* **sa·ga′ cious·ness.**

sa·gac·i·ty (sə găs′ ə tē) *n-* sound judgment; shrewdness.

sag·a·more (săg′ ə môr′) *n-* an Algonquian Indian chief, usually ranking below a sachem.

¹sage (sāj) *adj-* [**sag·er, sag·est**] **1** wise; having good judgment; learned: *a sage magistrate.* **2** showing wisdom or keen judgment: *a sage reply; sage advice.* *n-* wise and venerable man. [from Old French, from Latin *sapiens,* from *sapere,* "to know."] —*adv-* **sage′ ly.** *n-* **sage′ ness.**

²sage (sāj) *n-* **1** plant related to the mints, with gray-green leaves used for flavoring foods. **2** sagebrush. [from Old French *sauge,* from Latin *salvia,* "well; healthy." (The plant was once thought to heal.)]

Sagebrush

sage·brush (sāj′ brŭsh′) *n-* low, woody shrub of the dry plains of western United States.

sage hen *n-* large grouse found on the dry plains of western United States.

Sag·it·tar·i·us (săj′ ə târ′ ē əs,) *n-* constellation thought to outline the figure of an archer.

sa·go (sā′ gō′) *n-* powdered starch obtained from the pith of East Indian palms (**sago palms**).

sa·hib (sä′ ĭb′, -hĭb′) *n-* Indian and Pakistani title or form of address for people of rank and, formerly, for Europeans, equivalent to "Master," "Mr.," or "sir."

sa·laam (sə läm´) *n-* 1 Oriental greeting which means "Peace." 2 low bow with the palm of the hand placed on the forehead. *vi-* to make a low, formal bow or salaam. *vt-* to greet with such a bow.

sal·a·ble (sā´ lə bəl) *adj-* such as can be sold: *a salable product.* —*n-* sal´a·ble·ness or sal´a·bil´i·ty.

sa·la·cious (sə lā´ shəs) *adj-* 1 lustful; lewd. 2 obscene; indecent: *a salacious remark.* —*adv-* sa·la´cious·ly. *n-* sa·la´cious·ness.

sal·ad (săl´ əd) *n-* cold preparation of lettuce or other vegetables, meat, fish, fruit, etc., usually served with a dressing. *as modifier:* a salad *bowl; a* salad *dressing.*

salad days *n-* days of youth and inexperience.

sal·a·man·der (săl´ ə mǎn´ dər) *n-* 1 amphibian with a smooth skin that looks much like a lizard and lives part or all of its life in water. Those on land hide in damp places. 2 mythical creature able to live in fire; hence, anything that can bear intense heat.

Salamander (mud puppy) about 12 in long

sa·la·mi (sə lä´ mē) *n-* sausage made of cooked, highly spiced pork or beef, or a mixture of the two.

sal ammoniac (săl´ ə mŏ´ nē ǎk´) *n-* white crystalline chloride of ammonia (NH_4Cl) used in dyeing, tanning, etc.

sal·a·ried (săl´ ə rēd´) *adj-* 1 getting a salary: *a salaried accountant.* 2 yielding a salary: *a salaried position.*

sal·a·ry (săl´ ə rē) *n-* [*pl.* sal·a·ries] fixed sum of money paid at regular intervals for work.

sale (sāl) *n-* 1 exchange of goods or property for money: *the sale of a house.* 2 an offering of goods at a reduced price: *a big January* sale. 3 chance to sell; market: *There is almost no* sale *for ice skates in the summer.* 5 sales (1) amount sold. (2) business of selling. **on sale** offered at a reduced price.

sale·a·ble (sā´ lə bəl) salable.

sales·clerk (sālz´ klûrk´) *n-* person who sells goods in a store. If this person is a young woman, she is called a **salesgirl**; if she is older, she is called a **saleslady**.

sales·man (sālz´ mən) *n-* [*pl.* sales·men] person who sells; especially, one who visits prospective customers as representative of a firm.

sales·man·ship (sālz´ mən shǐp´) *n-* skill or ability in selling.

sales tax *n-* tax which is calculated as a fixed percentage of the money received from sales of goods and services.

sales·wom·an (sālz´ woŏm´ ən) *n-* [*pl.* sales·wom·en] woman who sells; especially, one who sells merchandise in a store; saleslady.

sal·i·cyl·ate (sə lǐs´ ə lāt´) *n-* any salt or ester of salicylic acid.

sal·i·cyl·ic acid (săl´ ə sǐl´ ǐk) *n-* white, crystalline organic acid used as a food preservative and mild antiseptic and to make aspirin.

sa·li·ent (sā´ lē ənt, săl´ yənt) *adj-* 1 outstanding; notable: *the* salient *feature of a face;* the salient *point of an argument.* 2 projecting outward: *a salient angle.* 3 leaping; moving by jumps: *a salient fish.* 4 gushing; jetting up: *a salient fountain.* *n-* the part of a fortification, trench system, or battle line that projects farthest toward the enemy. —*adv-* sa´lient·ly.

sa·line (sā´ lǐn´, -lēn´) *adj-* of or having to do with salt or sodium chloride; salty. *n-* 1 solution containing a relatively large amount of sodium chloride and used extensively in medicine, biological experiments, etc. 2 any of the metallic salts.

sa·lin·i·ty (sə lǐn´ ə tē) *n-* 1 saltiness. 2 the measure of salt concentration in one liter of saline solution.

Salis·bur·y steak (sălz´ bûr´ ē, sōlz´-) *n-* finely ground beef to which cream, eggs, and bread crumbs are added before being shaped into patties for frying.

sa·li·va (sə lī´ və) *n-* colorless, watery fluid secreted by the salivary glands of the mouth. It contains an enzyme, ptyalin, which begins the digestion of starchy foods.

sal·i·var·y (săl´ ə věr´ ē) *adj-* of or producing saliva.

salivary gland *n-* any one of the three pairs of glands which secrete saliva into the mouth cavity.

sal·i·vate (săl´ ə vāt´) *vi-* [sal·i·vat·ed, sal·i·vat·ing] to secrete saliva. —*n-* sal´i·va´tion.

sal·low (săl´ ō) *adj-* of a pale, sickly, greenish-yellow color or complexion. —*n-* sal´low·ness. *adj-* sal´low·ish.

sal·ly (săl´ ē) *n-* [*pl.* sal·lies] 1 a sudden rushing forth; especially, a sortie of troops from a fortified place to attack the enemy. 2 bold verbal attack or outburst, especially a clever or witty one: *The two lawyers traded* sallies. *We enjoyed his impudent* sallies. 3 short trip; excursion. *vi-* [sal·lied, sal·ly·ing] 1 to rush out suddenly. 2 to go (forth or out); set out.

salm·on (săm´ ən) *n-* [*pl.* salm·on; salm·ons (kinds of salmon)] 1 any of various salt-water or fresh-water food fishes with silver scales and yellowish-pink flesh. 2 (also salmon pink) orange-pink color. *adj-:* a salmon *mousse; a dress of* salmon *velvet.*

Chinook salmon. 25 pounds or over

Sa·lo·me (sə lō´ mē) *n-* in the New Testament, the stepdaughter of Herod Antipas. She demanded and got the head of John the Baptist as a reward for her dancing.

sa·lon (sə lŏn´, *Fr.* så lôⁿ´) *n-* 1 large room for receiving and entertaining guests. 2 periodic gathering of noted persons, usually at the home of a distinguished woman. 3 an art gallery; also, an exhibition at such a gallery. 4 a small, stylish shop or store. 5 a beauty parlor.

sa·loon (sə loōn´) *n-* 1 place where alcoholic drinks are sold; bar; tavern. 2 large room or hall, especially on a passenger ship, where people gather.

sal·si·fy (săl´ sə fē´) *n-* plant grown for its root, which tastes like an oyster and is used as a vegetable; oyster plant.

sal soda (săl) *n-* sodium carbonate; washing soda.

salt (sôlt) *n-* 1 white substance, sodium chloride, found in sea water and mineral deposits and used to season and preserve food. 2 *Chemistry* any of a very large group of compounds formed when acids and bases react with each other. 3 anything which, like sodium chloride, gives flavor or character; savor; zest. 4 sharp wit; dry humor. 5 *Informal* sailor. 6 salts (1) Epsom salts. (2) smelling salts. *adj-* 1 flavored with, seasoned with, or containing sodium chloride: *a* salt *pork; pan of* salt *water.* 2 growing in water containing sodium chloride: *a* salt *plant.* 3 sharp; bitter. *vt-* 1 to season or preserve with sodium chloride: *Did you* salt *the potatoes?* 2 to flavor or add zest to. 3 to place a mineral, such as gold, throughout (a mine), in order to deceive someone.

salt of the earth those people thought to lead good and useful lives and to be models for others. **with a grain of salt** with doubt or reserve; with allowance for exaggeration. **worth one's salt** to be worthwhile or useful.

salt away (or **down**) 1 to preserve in brine: *to* salt down *meat.* 2 to store or keep; to save.

salt grass *n-* any of several grasses that grow on wet brackish areas or alkaline ground.

sal·tine (sôl´ tēn´) *n-* crisp cracker sprinkled with salt.

salt lick *n-* natural deposit of salt which animals lick.

salt·pe·ter or **salt·pe·tre** (sôlt´ pē´ tər) *n-* 1 potassium nitrate. 2 (usually **Chile saltpeter**) sodium nitrate.

salt water *n-* 1 ocean water. 2 water containing salt. *adj-* (**salt-water**): *a* salt-water *fish; a* salt-water *lake.*

salt·y (sôl´ tē) *adj-* [salt·i·er, salt·i·est] 1 full of or tasting of salt. 2 suggesting the sea: *a* salty *smell.* 3 witty; sharp. —*adv-* salt´i·ly. *n-* salt´i·ness.

sa·lu·bri·ous (sə loō´ brē əs) *adj-* promoting health; healthful: *a* salubrious *climate.* —*adv-* sa·lu´bri·ous·ly. *n-* sa·lu´bri·ous·ness.

sal·u·tar·y (săl´ yə těr´ ē) *adj-* 1 good for the health: *the* salutary *mountain air.* 2 bringing a good effect; beneficial: *some* salutary *advice.*

sal·u·ta·tion (săl´ yə tā´ shən) *n-* 1 a saluting or greeting; also, the words or the gestures used: *He waved his hand in* salutation *as we passed him.* 2 the opening words of a letter. Example: Dear Sir.

sal·u·ta·to·ri·an (sə loō´ tə tôr´ ē ən) *n-* student, usually ranking second in the graduating class, who delivers the salutatory oration at the commencement exercises.

sa·lu·ta·to·ry (sə loō´ tə tôr´ ē) *adj-* of, relating to, or expressing a greeting or salutation.

sa·lute (sə lo͞ot′) *n-* **1** act of respect or recognition; greeting: *He waved his good-morning salute.* **2** formal act of respect done in a set way, such as the raising of fingers to the forehead, the discharge of guns, or the lowering and raising again of a flag. *vt-* [sa·lut·ed, sa·lut·ing] **1** to greet with words or gestures. **2** to honor with a set act of respect. *vi-* to make a gesture of respect; especially, to raise one's fingers to the forehead.

Salute

sal·vage (săl′ vĭj) *n-* **1** rescue of a ship or cargo from wreck, fire, etc.; also, the rescue of any property from destruction. **2** the saved ship or property. **3** payment made to those who rescued the property. *vt-* [sal·vaged, sal·vag·ing] to save or rescue from destruction: *The ship sank but they salvaged the cargo.*

sal·va·tion (săl vā′ shən) *n-* **1** a saving or rescue, especially from evil, danger, or sin. **2** something that saves or rescues: *Her care was my salvation when I was sick.* **3** in various religions, a soul's acceptance by God and the receiving of a soul into heaven; redemption. *—adj-* **sal·va′ tion·al:** *a salvational procedure.*

Salvation Army *n-* a worldwide religious and charitable body founded by General William Booth in England in 1865.

¹salve (săv, säv) *n-* **1** soft greasy substance or ointment used on sores or wounds to heal or lessen pain. **2** something that calms and soothes: *The trip was a salve for his nervousness.* *vt-* [salved, salv·ing] to soothe: *Nothing could salve his grief.* [from Old English *sealf* or **salb.**]

²salve (sălv) *vt-* [salved, salv·ing] to salvage. [from Old French **salvage,** from Medieval Latin **salvatium,** from Latin **salvere** meaning "to save."]

sal·ve (săl′ vă) *Latin* hail. [from Late Latin **salvere** meaning "to be safe or healthy."]

sal·ver (săl′ vər) *n-* a serving tray, usually made of metal.

sal·vi·a (săl′ vē ə) *n-* any of several plants related to the mints; especially, a sage with scarlet blossoms.

same (sām) *adj-* identical; not different in any way: *We left at the same time. Others have made the same suggestion. These two are the same.* *n-* identical thing previously encountered or mentioned (always preceded by "the"): *Please give me more of the same. The same is true today.* *pron-* in archaic and legal use, person or thing previously mentioned: *He gave me the hammer, and I took same and hit the nail.*

all (or **just**) **the same** nevertheless: *He was frightened, but he jumped all the same.* **same here** *Informal* ditto. **the same** (used as an adverb) in a similar or identical way, degree, etc.: *She and I feel the same about it.*

same·ness (sām′ nəs) *n-* **1** likeness in nature or character; identity; similarity. **2** monotony.

sam·i·sen (săm′ ə sĕn′) *n-* musical instrument of Japan that has three strings and resembles the banjo.

sam·ite (săm′ ĭt′, sā′ mĭt′) *n-* rich, silk fabric of medieval times, generally interwoven with gold or silver. *as modifier:* *a samite gown.*

Sa·mo·an (sə mō′ ən) *adj-* of or relating to the islands of Samoa, or to their inhabitants. *n-* **1** a native of Samoa. **2** the language of these people.

Samovar

sam·o·var (săm′ ə vär′) *n-* metal urn with a heating tube, used especially in Russia to heat water for making tea.

samp (sămp) *n-* coarsely ground hominy; also, a porridge of this. [American word from the Algonquian name.]

sam·pan (săm′ păn′) *n-* light, flat-bottomed boat with one sail, rowed from the stern, used along the coasts and on the rivers of China and Japan.

Sampan

sam·ple (săm′ pəl) *n-* a part that shows what the whole is like; an example; a specimen: *a sample of the artist's work.*

sandwich man *n-* **1** *Informal* person who carries two attached boards, one slung before him and the other behind, to advertise or picket a place of business. **2** person who makes or sells sandwiches.

sand·wort (sănd′ wərt) *n-* any of several low herbs, usually tufted, that grow in sandy terrain.

sand·y (săn′ dē) *adj-* [sand·i·er, sand·i·est] **1** made of, filled with, or like sand. **2** reddish yellow: *His sandy hair is too light to be called red.* *—n-* **sand′ i·ness.**

sane (sān) *adj-* [san·er, san·est] **1** sound and healthy in mind. **2** sensible; rational: *a sane approach to a problem.* *Hom-* **seine.** *—adv-* **sane′ ly.** *n-* **sane′ ness.**

sang (săng) *p.t.* of **sing.**

sang-froid (sän frwä′) *French n-* calmness under trying circumstances; composure.

san·gui·nar·y (săng′ gwə nĕr′ ē) *adj-* **1** attended with or accompanied by bloodshed: *a sanguinary battle.* **2** cruel; bloodthirsty: *a sanguinary pirate.*

san·guine (săng′ gwən) *adj-* **1** having an active blood circulation; hence, full of vitality; vivacious: *a sanguine disposition.* **2** ardent; hopeful; confident: *His outlook is sanguine.* **3** having somewhat the color of blood; ruddy: *a sanguine complexion.* *—adv-* **san′ guine·ly.**

san·guin·i·ty (săng gwĭn′ ə tē) *n-* condition of being sanguine.

San·he·drin (săn hĕd′ rən, -hē′ drən) *n-* in the time of Christ, the supreme council and judicial court of the Jews, presided over by the high priest.

san·i·tar·i·an (săn′ ə târ′ ē ən) *n-* person whose occupation is sanitation and public health.

san·i·tar·i·um (săn′ ə târ′ ē əm) *n-* sanatorium.

san·i·tar·y (săn′ ə tĕr′ ē) *adj-* **1** having to do with health; hygienic: *effective sanitary laws.* **2** free from dirt and disease: *a sanitary kitchen.* *—adv-* **san′ i·tar′ i·ly.**

san·i·ta·tion (săn′ ə tā′ shən) *n-* method and practice of bringing about sanitary conditions that protect health; hygiene. *as modifier:* *a sanitation engineer.*

san·i·tize (săn′ ə tīz′) *vt-* [san·i·tized, san·i·tiz·ing] to make (something) sanitary: *to sanitize a hospital room.*

san·i·ty (săn′ ə tē) *n-* **1** soundness of mind; mental balance or health: *Did he lose his sanity?* **2** sensibleness; reasonableness: *His decision displays sanity.*

San Jo·se scale (hō zā′) *n-* scale insect that is very injurious to various fruit trees.

sank (săngk) *p.t.* of **sink.**

sans (sănz, *Fr.* sä') *prep-* without.

San·skrit (săn′ skrĭt′) *n-* the ancient sacred language of the Hindus of India. It is the oldest Indo-European language of which written records exist. *adj-* *a Sanskrit scholar.* Also **San′ scrit.**

sans sou·ci (sän so͞o sē′) *French* gay and easy; carefree.

San·ta (săn′ tə, sän′ tə) *Italian, Spanish, & Portuguese* female saint.

San·ta Claus (săn′ tə klôz′) *n-* the jolly white-bearded old man in a red suit who personifies the spirit of Christmas. Often identified with St. Nicholas.

Santa Ger·tru·dis (gər tro͞o′ dəs) *n-* breed of cherry-red beef cattle developed in southern United States by crossbreeding cattle from India (for heat tolerance and resistance to disease) with shorthorn cattle (for good beef and the ability to put on flesh).

sap (săp) *n-* **1** juice that circulates through the tissues of trees and plants and keeps them alive. **2** any vital or health-promoting liquid constituent of an organism; hence, vigor or vitality. **3** *Slang* stupid or foolish person.

sa·rong (sə rông′) *n-* style of skirt with the hem pulled up at the front, worn by men and women of the Malay Archipelago and other islands of the Pacific.

sar·sa·pa·ri·la (săs′ pə rĭl′ ə, sär′ sə pə-) *n-* **1** any of various tropical American plants, the roots of which are used as medicine or for flavoring. **2** soda water flavored with extract of sarsaparilla.

sar·tor·i·al (sär tôr′ ē əl) *adj-* of or relating to tailoring or to men's clothes: *his sartorial elegance.* *—adv-* **sar·tor′ i·al·ly.**

sash (săsh) *n-* broad band of cloth or ribbon worn around the waist, or often across one shoulder as part of a uniform or as a decoration. [from Old English

shash, from Arabic **shâsh,** "a length of muslim cloth."]

sash (săsh) *n-* the framework which holds the glass in a window. [from earlier English **sashes,** from French **chassis,** from Old French **chasse,** "casket for relics; chest; ²case."]

sa·shay (să shā') *Informal vi-* 1 to go or go about in a vigorous and showy way. 2 to move rapidly sideways in dancing, with the same foot always leading. [American word from French **chassé** meaning "a gliding dance step."] *Hom-* sachet.

Sask. Saskatchewan.

sas·sa·fras (săs' ə frăs') *n-* 1 tree related to the laurels and having aromatic roots, leaves, and flowers. 2 root bark of this tree, used in medicine and for flavoring. [American word from Spanish **sasafras.**]

sas·sy (săs' ē) *Informal adj-* [sas·si·er, sas·si·est] saucy.

sat (săt) *p.t.* and *p.p.* of sit.

Sat. Saturday.

Sa·tan (sā' tan) *n-* the Devil.

sa·tan·ic (să tăn' ĭk) *adj-* having to do with Satan; hence, devilish; evil: *a satanic plot.* —*adv-* sa·tan' i·cal·ly.

satch·el (săch' əl) *n-* a small suitcase or briefcase.

sate (sāt) *vt-* [sat·ed, sat·ing] to satiate.

sa·teen (să tēn') *n-* cotton or woolen fabric with a glossy finish similar to that of satin.

sat·el·lite (săt' ə lĭt') *n-* 1 a moon, planet of the solar system, or other heavenly body that moves in an orbit about a body more massive than itself. 2 man-made device sent by rocket into an orbit about the earth or some other body. 3 country that is officially independent but actually under the control or very strong influence of another. 4 member of a retinue; steady attendant: *the actress and her satellites.*

sat·i·rize (săt' ə rīz') *vt-* [sat·i·rized, sat·i·riz·ing] to subject to satire: *He satirized Victorian values.*

sat·is·fac·tion (săt' ĭs făk' shən) *n-* 1 condition of being pleased; contentment: *The cat purred with satisfaction over its bowl of milk.* 2 source of pleasure or contentment. 3 compensation or getting even; reparation.

sat·is·fac·to·ry (săt' ĭs făk' tə rē) *adj-* meeting needs, hopes, or requirements; sufficient; adequate. —*adv-* sat·is·fac' to·ri·ly. *n-* sat' is·fac' to·ri·ness.

sat·is·fy (săt' ĭs fī') *vt-* [sat·is·fied, sat·is·fy·ing] 1 to meet (a desire or need); to content; gratify: *That satisfied my hunger.* 2 to convince: *We satisfied the police that we had nothing to do with the accident.* 3 to fulfill. 4 to pay in full; make good: *to satisfy a claim.* vi- to give satisfaction or gratification. —*adv-* sat' is·fy' ing·ly.

sa·trap (sā' trăp', să'-) *n-* governor of a province in ancient Persia; hence, any secondary ruler or chief, especially a tyrannical one.

sa·trap·y (sā' trə pē, să'-) *n-* [*pl.* sa·trap·ies] office or jurisdiction of a satrap.

sat·u·rate (săch' ə rāt') *vt-* [sat·u·rat·ed, sat·u·rat·ing] 1 to soak through and through: *The rain saturated my clothing.* 2 to fill or cover completely: *They saturated the market with the product.* 3 *Chemistry* to concentrate (a solution) until no more of the solute can be dissolved.

sat·u·rat·ed (săch' ə rā' təd) *Chemistry adj-* 1 of a solution, containing all of a certain substance that can be dissolved in the solvent. 2 of an organic compound, having most or all the valence bonds of its carbon atoms attached to other atoms, and hence not available for further combination.

saw·fish (sò' fĭsh') *n-* any of various large fishes related to the rays and having a long, flat snout with toothlike spines on each edge.

saw·horse (sò' hòrs', -hôrs') *n-* frame for supporting wood for sawing, usually consisting of a horizontal bar with two spreading legs at each end.

saw·mill (sò' mĭl') *n-* place where logs are sawed into lumber by machine.

sawn (sòn) *p.p.* of ¹saw.

saw·yer (sò' yər) *n-* person whose occupation is the sawing of logs or timber.

sax (săks) *n- Informal* saxophone.

sax·horn (săks' hòrn', -hôrn') *n-* any of a group of brass musical wind instruments with valves.

sax·i·frage (săk' sə frĭj, -frāj') *n-* any of a genus of low-growing plants with white, red, or yellow flowers.

Sax·on (săk' sən) *n-* 1 member of a Germanic people who inhabited northern Germany and, together with the Angles and Jutes, invaded and conquered England in the fifth and sixth centuries A.D. 2 native of Saxony; also, the dialect of German spoken in Saxony. *adj-* 1 of or relating to the Germanic people who invaded England in the fifth and sixth centuries A.D. 2 of or relating to modern Saxony, its inhabitants, or its dialect.

sax·o·phone (săk' sə fōn') *n-* wind instrument consisting of a sharply bent metal tube with keys, and a reed mouthpiece. —*n-* sax' o·phon' ist.

Saxophone

say (sā) *vt-* [said, (sĕd), say·ing] 1 to utter; speak: *He said only six words.* 2 to assert; declare (takes only a clause as object): *I say that you are wrong.* 3 to repeat; recite: *Claire said her prayers.* 4 to estimate; assume: *I would say he's worth a million dollars.* 5 to mean; communicate (takes only a clause as object): *These tracks say that a bear has passed by here.* *n-* 1 chance or right to express an opinion: *Give him his say.* *interj-* 1 used to attract attention, express surprise, etc: "Say! *Look at that!"* 2 meaning "I offer as an example (or estimate or assumption)": *He's worth,* say, *half a million dollars.* —*n-* say' er.

goes without saying is too obvious to need mention.

that is to say in other words.

say·ing (sā' ĭng) *n-* 1 something said: *one of Mark Twain's famous sayings.* 2 proverb: *an old saying of my aunt.*

says (sĕz) form of say used with "he," "she," "it," or singular noun subjects, in the present tense.

say-so (sā' sō') *Informal n-* 1 bare statement: *That's just his say-so.* 2 authority to make a decision.

Sb symbol for antimony.

S.B. Bachelor of Science

Sc symbol for scandium.

sc. scene.

S.C. 1 South Carolina. 2 Supreme Court. 3 Security Council.

scab (skăb) *n-* 1 crust of dried blood and serum that forms over a sore or wound while it heals. 2 *Informal* worker who accepts a lower wage than a union worker; also, one who takes a striker's job.

scalp (skălp) *n-* 1 the skin at the top of the head, usually covered by hair. *vt-* 1 to cut off or tear off the scalp or part of it. 2 *Informal* to buy (theater tickets or the like) and then sell at exorbitant prices. —*n-* scalp' er.

scarf (skärf) *n-* [*pl.* scarfs or scarves (skärvz)] 1 long piece of cloth worn about the shoulders or neck, or over the head, for warmth or decoration. 2 long strip of cloth used to cover tables, dressers, or other furniture. [from Old French **escarpe,** from Old Norse **skreppa** of the same meaning.]

²**scarf** (skärf) *n-* [*pl.* scarves] 1 (also scarf joint) joint by which two pieces of wood are connected lengthwise to make one piece, the ends being cut or grooved so as to fit into each other. 2 the cut or grooved end of a piece of wood used to form such a joint. *vt-* 1 to unite with such a joint. 2 to groove (wood) for such a joint.

Scarf joints

scarf·pin (skärf' pĭn') *n-* ornamental pin on a scarf.

scar·i·fi·ca·tion (skăr' ə fə kā' shən) *n-* 1 act of scarifying or scratching. 2 scratch or scratches: *the scarifications on a rock surface.*

scar·i·fy (skăr' ə fī') *vt-* [scar·i·fied, scar·i·fy·ing] 1 to scratch or make slight cuts in. 2 to criticize harshly; lacerate; flay. 3 to loosen or break up the surface of: *to scarify a roadbed.*

scar·la·ti·na (skăr′ lə tē′ nə) *n-* scarlet fever, especially a mild form of it.

scar·let (skär′ lət) *n-* vivid red color. *adj-*: *a scarlet dress.*

scarlet fever *n-* acute, contagious streptococcus disease, whose symptoms are vomiting, sore throat, high fever, and a bright-red skin rash.

scarp (skärp) *n-* 1 steep slope or cliff; escarpment. 2 steep wall or ditch around a fortification. *vt-* to cause to slope steeply: *The waves scarped the cliffs.*

scarves (skärvz) *pl.* of **scarf.**

scar·y (skâr′ ē) *Informal adj-* [scar·i·er, scar·i·est] 1 causing fear; frightening: *a scary movie.* 2 easily scared; timid: *a scary pony.*

scat (skăt) *Informal interj-* go away quickly!

scath·ing (skā′ thĭng) *adj-* bitterly adverse; denunciatory: *a scathing criticism.* —*adv-* **scath′ ing·ly.**

scat·ter (skăt′ ər) *vt-* 1 to fling about in all directions; throw here and there: *to scatter rubbish all over a picnic ground.* 2 to drive in different directions; disperse: *The police scattered the mob.* *vi-* to go in different directions: *The crowd scattered.* *n-* a scattering. —*n-* **scat′ ter·er.**

scat·ter·brain (skăt′ ər brān′) *n-* person incapable of serious or concentrated thinking; giddy, heedless person. —*adj-* **scat′ ter·brained′:** *a scatterbrained scheme.*

scat·ter·ing (skăt′ ər ĭng) *n-* 1 small, scattered number of persons or things; sparse group: *a scattering of voters.* 2 *Physics* irregular or diffuse reflection, refraction, or dispersion of waves or particles, caused by collisions with other particles or waves.

scav·en·ger (skăv′ ən jər) *n-* any of various animals, such as hyenas, crabs, and vultures, that eat waste matter and spoiled food.

sce·nar·i·o (sə nĕr′ ē ō′, -när′ ē ō′) *n-* [*pl.* **sce·nar·i·os**] 1 plot summary of a play. 2 the script for a motion picture, including dialogue, acting and camera directions; shooting script.

sce·nar·ist (sə nĕr′ ĭst, -när′ ĭst) *n-* writer of movie scenarios.

scene (sēn) *n-* 1 place of an action or event; locale: *the scene of heavy fighting.* 2 setting of a play, opera, or story: *The scene of the novel is prewar Poland.* 3 division of an act in a dramatic work: *Act II, scene 3 of "Hamlet."* 4 episode or incident in a play, opera, or story: *the storm scene in "King Lear."* 5 landscape: *a lush tropical scene.* 6 display of anger or other strong feeling: *to make a scene in a restaurant.* *Hom-* seen.

behind the scenes not directly in front of a theater audience; hence, out of public view; in private. **come on the scene** to arrive; begin to take part in something.

scen·er·y (sē′ nə rē) *n-* 1 general view of a landscape: *The scenery in the Alps is beautiful.* 2 the backdrops, platforms, canvas-covered frames, etc., that make up the setting of a stage performance.

sce·nic (sē′ nĭk, sĕn′ ĭk) *adj-* 1 of or related to natural scenery; picturesque: *the scenic delights of the mountain trail.* 2 having to do with stage effects or stage scenery.

scent (sĕnt) *n-* 1 odor; smell: *These roses have a delightful scent.* 2 odor left by an animal: *The hounds picked up the scent of the fox.* 3 sense of smell: *Hounds hunt by their keen scent.* 4 hint or clue by which something is recognized or followed: *the scent of danger.* 5 perfume: *a bottle of scent.* *vt-* 1 to recognize by smelling: *The hounds scented a fox.* 2 to get a hint of; become aware of: *The reporter scented a story.* 3 to fill with an odor; perfume: *Lilacs scent the air. Homs-* cent, sent. —*adj-* **scent′less.**

scep·ter (sĕp′ tər) *n-* 1 ornamental rod or staff held in ceremonies by a ruler as a sign of authority and power. 2 royal rank or power. Also **scep′ tre.**

scep·tic (skĕp′ tĭk) *n-* skeptic. —*adj-* **scep′ ti·cal.** *n-* **scep′ ti·cism.**

sched·ule (skĕj′ ōol, -əl) *n-* 1 list of events or procedures arranged in chronological order: *a radio schedule; a factory's production schedule.* 2 any ordered list or catalogue: *a schedule of shipping rates.* 3 transportation timetable: *a train schedule.* 4 group of things to be done; agenda: *a doctor with a very heavy schedule.* *vt-* [sched·uled, sched·ul·ing] 1 to enter in a schedule: *The bus line scheduled a new time of departure.* 2 to plan, for a particular time: *He scheduled the meeting for today.* **on schedule** at the planned or proper time; on time.

Sche·her·a·zade (shə hĕr′ ə zäd′) *n-* in the "Arabian Nights," the Sultan's bride whose life was spared because of her unequaled art of storytelling.

sche·ma (skē′ mə) *n-* [*pl.* **sche·ma·ta** (-mə tə)] outline or diagram showing something broadly or generally, without details.

sche·mat·ic (skĭ măt′ ĭk) *adj-* showing something in outline or plan, and not as it appears really or finally: *a schematic drawing.* *n-* diagram showing the parts, values, and connections of an electric or electronic device by the use of accepted symbols. —*adv-* **sche·mat′ i·cal·ly.**

scheme (skēm) *n-* 1 a plan, design, or system to be followed in doing something: *a scheme for building a new highway.* 2 underhanded plot: *a scheme to overthrow the government.* 3 outline sketch or diagram; schema: *the scheme of a missile's electrical system.* 4 arrangement or design; layout: *the scheme of a living room.* *vt-* [schemed, schem·ing] to plan, especially in an underhanded manner; plot: *to scheme a way to escape.* *vi-*: *He schemed for many years.* —*n-* **schem′ er.**

scher·zo (skĕrt′ sō) *Music n-* [*pl.* **scher·zos** or **scher·zi** (-sē)] lively part, usually the third movement, of many symphonic and chamber works.

Schick Test (shĭk) *n-* skin test that shows whether a person is immune to diphtheria. If the skin is inflamed after injection of a small amount of toxin, the person is not immune.

schism (skĭz′ əm) *n-* 1 division or split within a religious group; also, the offense of causing such a division. 2 group or sect formed by such a division.

schis·mat·ic (skĭz măt′ ĭk) *adj-* of, related to, or causing a schism: *a schismatic faction.* *n-* person who advocates or takes part in a schism.

schist (shĭst) *n-* type of metamorphic rock that contains layers of mica, graphite, hornblende, or other minerals.

schis·to·some (shĭs′ tə sōm′, skĭs′-) *n-* any of a large group of parasitic flatworms that are the cause of many diseases of the liver, intestines, blood, and bladder.

schiz·oid (skĭt′ soid′) *adj-* 1 resembling schizophrenia: *a schizoid disorder.* 2 showing a tendency toward schizophrenia: *a schizoid personality.* *n-* person who shows a tendency toward schizophrenia.

schiz·o·phre·ni·a (skĭt′ sə frē′ nē ə, -frēn′ yə) *n-* any of a group of severe mental diseases marked by withdrawal into a stupor, splitting of the personality, hallucinations and delusions, lack of contact with reality, etc.

schiz·o·phren·ic (skĭt′ sə frĕn′ ĭk) *adj-* of or having to do with schizophrenia: *a schizophrenic symptom.* *n-* person suffering from schizophrenia.

schmaltz (shmälts) *Slang n-* excessive sentimentality or ornateness, especially in music or art.

schnapps or **schnaps** (shnäps) *n-* any strong alcoholic liquor, especially Dutch or German.

schol·ar (skŏl′ ər) *n-* 1 person having thorough and expert knowledge in one or more fields of learning, especially in the humanities; also, one doing careful research in such a field: *a Shakespeare scholar.* 2 person going to school; student; pupil. 3 person holding a grant to allow him to continue his studies.

schol·ar·ly (skŏl′ ər lē) *adj-* 1 of, related to, or containing the work of a learned, careful, and thorough expert or experts: *a scholarly paper.* 2 learned; studious; erudite: *a scholarly newspaper man.* —*n-* **schol′ ar·li·ness.**

schol·ar·ship (skŏl′ ər shĭp) *n-* 1 knowledge gained through long study, especially by a person with thorough and expert knowledge in some field of learning. 2 thorough research and careful methods by such a learned person. 3 money or aid given to a deserving student or scholar to allow him to continue his studies.

scho·las·tic (skə lăs′ tĭk) *adj-* 1 having to do with schools, teachers, studies, or students; academic: *the high scholastic standing of our school.* 2 of or related to scholasticism. *n-* in the Middle Ages, philosopher or theologian whose teachings were based on the doctrines of scholasticism; schoolman. —*adv-* **scho·las′ ti·cal·ly.**

scho·las·ti·cism (skə lăs′ tə sĭz′ əm) *n-* system of philosophy that developed in Europe during the Middle Ages as a means of reconciling Greek philosophy, especially that of Aristotle, with the teachings of the church fathers.

¹**school** (skool) *n-* **1** any institution for learning, especially below the level of college. **2** the building or buildings of such an institution. **3** group of pupils at one place of learning: *The entire school will go to the track meet.* **4** time or session of instruction: *to have no school because of the snowstorm.* **5** group of persons influenced by the same teacher or body of ideas; also, the doctrines or practices of such a group: *the impressionist school of painting.* **6** division of a university given over to one branch of learning: *Does your university have a law school? as modifier:* a school *cafeteria. vt-* **1** to educate; teach: *to school someone in biology.* **2** to discipline: *to school yourself in self-control.* [from Old English **scōl**, from Latin *schola*, from Greek *scholé.*]

²**school** (skool) *n-* large group of fish that swims or feeds together; shoal. [from a earlier Dutch word of the same spelling, and related to ²**shoal.**]

school age *n-* age, often fixed by law, at which a child begins to attend school; also, the period of life when a child is attending school or is required to do so. *as modifier* (school-age): *a school-age child.*

school-bag (skool' bǎg') *n-* bag or case for carrying a student's books and supplies.

school board *n-* group of persons in charge of a local public school system; board of education.

school-book (skool' book') *n-* textbook used in grade schools or high schools.

school-boy (skool' boi') *n-* boy who attends school.

school-fel-low (skool' fěl' ō) *n-* schoolmate.

school-girl (skool' gûrl') *n-* girl who attends school.

school-house (skool' hous') *n-* building, especially a one-room or other small building, where school is held.

school-ing (skool' ling) *n-* training and instruction, especially in school; education.

school-man (skool' mǝn) *n-* [*pl.* **school-men**] a scholastic of the Middle Ages.

school-mas-ter (skool' mǎs' tǝr) *chiefly Brit. n-* man who teaches in a school. *n- fem.* **school' mis' tress.**

school-mate (skool' mǎt') *n-* companion at school.

school-room (skool' room') *n-* room where students are taught; classroom.

school-teach-er (skool' tē' chǝr) *n-* person who teaches in school, especially below the college level.

school-work (skool' wûrk') *n-* lesson or lessons assigned to a student.

school-yard (skool' yärd') *n-* playground of a school.

school year *n-* that part of the year, from about September to about June, when school is in session.

schoon-er (skoo' nǝr) *n-* **1** sailing vessel having two or more masts and a fore-and-aft rig. In a two-masted schooner the foremast is always the shorter. For picture, see *sailboat.* **2** *Informal* large beer glass.

schot-tische (shǒt' ĭsh) *n-* round dance similar to the polka; also, the music for this dance.

schuss (shoos) *n-* in skiing, a high-speed run down a straight, steep course; also, the course itself. *vi-: They all schussed for home. vt-: to schuss a slope.*

schwa (shwä) *n-* **1** phonetic symbol [ǝ] for various indistinct vowel sounds that occur in many unstressed syllables in English, such as the sound of *a* in *about, e* in *spoken, i* in *pencil, o* in *atom, u* in *circus.* **2** any of these sounds.

sci. **1** science. **2** scientific.

sci-at-ic (sī ǎt' ĭk) *adj-* **1** of or relating to the sciatic nerve. **2** of or relating to the hipbone.

sci-at-i-ca (sī ǎt' ĭ kǝ) *n-* pain along the sciatic nerve, caused by injury or inflammation.

sciatic nerve *n-* large nerve that, with its branches, extends from the lower back through the hip and back of the thigh and down the back of the leg to the foot.

sci-ence (sī' ǝns) *n-* **1** the study of the physical universe and all things in it, pursued chiefly because of a desire or need to explain them and conducted according to the scientific method. **2** any branch of such study: *the science of physics; the science of anthropology.* **3** any systematic study: *the science of theology.* **4** knowledge and skill in any subject, sport, etc.: *the science of boxing. as modifier: a science course.*

science fiction *n-* type of fiction, often set in the future or on another world, that deals chiefly with the effect of a highly developed science and technology on man.

sci-en-tif-ic (sī' ǝn tǐf' ĭk) *adj-* **1** of or relating to science or the methods of science: *a scientific instrument.* **2** based on facts or logical ideas developed from facts: *a scientific attitude.* —*adv-* **sci' en-tif' i-cal-ly.**

scientific method *n-* method of obtaining knowledge, based on careful observation, analytical thinking, and controlled experimentation. In general, it follows this pattern: a) the gathering of pertinent information on a specific problem, b) the formulation of a tentative hypothesis concerning the problem, c) the testing of the hypothesis through controlled experimentation, and d) the rejection of the hypothesis and the formulation and testing of a new one, or the acceptance of the hypothesis as a tentative conclusion

scientific notation *n-* **1** the recording of scientific data by means of systems of symbols that are briefer and more precise than words and can be used by scientists of all nations. **2** any such system, such as the notation used in astronomy.

sci-en-tist (sī' ǝn tĭst) *n-* **1** person trained or skilled in some branch of science and engaged in it as a profession. **2** **Scientist** Christian Scientist.

scim-i-tar (sĭm' ǝ tǝr) *n-* Oriental sword with a curved blade formerly used by soldiers of the Middle East.

Scimitar

scin-til-la (sĭn tĭl' ǝ) *n-* scarcely detectable amount; particle; trace: *not a scintilla of evidence.*

scin-til-late (sĭn' tǝ lāt') *vi-* [**scin-til-lat-ed, scin-til-lat-ing**] to sparkle or glitter; flash: *The sword scintillated in the sun. His speech scintillates with humor. vt-: That novel scintillates wit on almost every page.*

scin-til-la-tion (sĭn' tǝ lā' shǝn) *n-* **1** a scintillating; the scintillation of the stars. **2** a spark or flash of light.

scintillation counter *Physics n-* device for measuring the intensity of ionizing radiation by counting the scintillations caused when an ionizing particle strikes a phosphorescent material in the instrument. Also **scintillation detector.**

sci-on (sī' ǝn) *n-* **1** shoot or branch cut from a plant for rooting or grafting; cutting. **2** descendant or heir, especially of a wealthy or noble family.

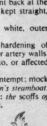

scis-sor (sĭz' ǝr) *vt-* to cut with scissors.

scis-sors (sĭz' ǝrz) *n-* (takes plural verb) cutting tool with pivoted double blades that slip tightly beside one another in closing and cut with a shearing action; shears. Also **pair of scissors** (takes singular verb).

Scissors

scissors kick *n-* swimming kick performed usually with the side stroke, in which one leg is bent back at the knee, the other is thrust forward and kept straight, then both are brought together sharply.

scle-ra (sklîr' ǝ) *n-* the tough, opaque, white, outer covering of the eyeball.

scle-ro-sis (sklǝ rō' sǝs) *n-* abnormal hardening of tissues, especially in the nervous system or artery walls.

scle-rot-ic (sklǝ rŏt' ĭk) *adj-* of, relating to, or affected by sclerosis.

scoff (skŏf, skôf) *vi-* to express scorn or contempt; mock or jeer (at): *Many people scoffed at Fulton's steamboat. n-* expression of scorn or contempt; jeer: *the scoffs of the mob.* —*n-* **scoff' er.** *adv-* **scoff' ing-ly.**

scoff-law (skŏf' lô', skôf-) *n-* person who treats the law with disdain; especially, a person who habitually flouts traffic laws by ignoring summonses.

scold (skōld) *vt-* to speak sharply to; rebuke; chide; reprove: *to scold someone for being late. vi-* to chatter angrily: *The frightened monkeys began to scold. n-* quarrelsome woman; shrew. —*n-* **scold' er.**

scol-lop (skŏl' ǝp, skôl'-) *n-* scallop.

Sconce

sconce (skŏns) *n-* ornamental wall bracket for holding a candle or electric light.

scone (skōn, skŏn) *n-* **1** Scottish batter cake of oatmeal, barley, or wheat, baked on a griddle.

scoop (skōōp) *n-* 1 any of various shovellike tools that are used to take up flour, sugar, coal, or other loose material. 2 the bucket of a dredge or power shovel. 3 (also **scoop′ ful**′) amount held by such a tool or bucket. 4 dipping movement: *Harvey caught the minnow with a scoop of the hand.* 5 *Informal* a news story published first, before rival newspapers carry it. *vt-* 1 to take up with or as if with a shovel: *to scoop fish into a net.* 2 to dig or hollow out with or as if with a shovel: *to scoop holes in the sand.* 3 *Informal* to beat (a rival newspaper, reporter, etc.) in publishing a story.

Scoop

scoot (skōōt) *Informal* *vi-* to run or walk swiftly; dart quickly, especially in getting away from someone or something: *He scooted away when he saw me coming.*

scoot·er (skōō′ tər) *n-* 1 toy vehicle consisting of a board slung between two aligned wheels and equipped with an upright steering bar. 2 motor scooter.

¹**scope** (skōp) *n-* 1 range of understanding, outlook, or ability: *a task in my scope.* 2 area covered; extent: *The scope of his travels includes Europe and America.* 3 freedom or opportunity: *He has been given enough scope in his work to do as he pleases.* [from Italian **scopo** meaning "goal; purpose," from Latin **scopus**, from Greek **skopos**, "watcher."]

Scooter

²**scope** (skōp) *Informal* *n-* any of various optical or viewing instruments, such as a telescope, microscope, or oscilloscope. *as modifier:* *a scope reading.* [from **-scope**.]

-scope *combining form* instrument for viewing or examining: *telescope* (device for viewing things at a distance). [from Greek *-skopeion*, "apparatus for viewing."]

sco·pol·a·mine (skə pŏl′ ə mēn′) *n-* drug extracted from several plants related to the potato and used as a sedative and truth serum.

scor·bu·tic (skôr byōō′ tĭk) *adj-* of, related to, or having scurvy: *a scorbutic symptom.*

scorch (skôrch, skôrch) *vt-* 1 to burn the surface of; discolor by burning: *I scorched a shirt when I ironed it.* 2 to wither or dry up by heat: *The sun scorched the grass.* 3 to critize harshly. *n-* slight burn.

scorch·er (skôr′ chər, skôr′-) *Informal* *n-* very hot day.

scorch·ing (skôr′ chĭng, skôr′-) *adj-* 1 very hot; burning: *a scorching day.* 2 severely critical; caustic; biting: *a scorching remark.* —*adv-* **scorch′ ing·ly.**

score (skôr) *n-* 1 record of points won in a game: *What was the final score in the football game?* 2 grade in a test; rating. 3 written copy of music; also, the music as distinct from the words of an opera or musical comedy. 4 obligation; debt; injury; grudge: *to settle a score.* 5 set of twenty: *a score of years.* 6 **scores** large unspecified number: *There were scores of people.* *as determiner* (always preceded by another determiner): *There are two score deer here but many score there.* *vt-* [**scored, scor·ing**] 1 to cut notches in. 2 to mark down the points in (a game); keep account of by marking down. 3 to arrange (music) in a certain way; orchestrate; compose: *to score a piece for three violins.* 4 to win (points) in a game: *I scored five points over my opponent.* 5 *Informal* to criticize harshly; excoriate; scourge: *The candidate scored his opponent.* 6 in baseball, to cause (a base runner) to reach home plate safely: *His hit scored the runner from second.* *vi-* 1 to win points in a game. 2 to achieve a success or advantage: *to score in an argument.* —*adj-* **score′ less.** *n-* **scor′ er.**

keep score to keep a record of points won in a game.

know the score *Slang* to be aware of what is happening about one; be in the know. **on that score** regarding that matter. **on the score that** on account of; because.

score·board (skôr′ bôrd′) *n-* in sports, a large board that shows the score of a game and other information.

score·card (skôr′ kärd′) *n-* in sports, a card for recording the score of a game.

score·keep·er (skôr′ kē′ pər) *n-* person, usually an official, who keeps score during a game.

sco·ri·a (skôr′ ē ə) *n-* 1 rough and glassy basalt rock having bubbles and holes and formed when lava cools very quickly. 2 slag from the smelting of ore.

scorn (skôrn, skôrn) *n-* 1 feeling that a person or thing is mean or worthy of contempt; disdain: *to have scorn for a coward.* 2 object of contempt: *He was the scorn of the neighborhood.* *vt-* to treat or reject with contempt; disdain: *She scorned his small gift.* —*n-* **scorn′ er.**

scorn·ful (skôrn fəl, skôrn′-) *adj-* feeling or showing great disapproval, contempt, or disdain: *She was scornful of us.* —*adv-* **scorn′ ful·ly.** *n-* **scorn′ ful·ness.**

Scor·pi·o (skôr′ pē ō, skôr′-) *n-* southern constellation thought to outline the figure of a scorpion.

scor·pi·on (skôr′ pē ən, skôr′-) *n-* animal related to the spiders, having a slender body, pincers, and a sting at the end of its tail.

Scot (skŏt) *n-* 1 native or inhabitant of Scotland, or a descendant of such a person. 2 member of a Gaelic people of northern Ireland who settled in Scotland.

Scorpion.
.ξ—8 in long

Scot. 1 Scotch. 2 Scotland. 3 Scottish.

scotch (skŏch) *vt-* 1 to stamp out, suppress, or hinder; crush: *to scotch a revolution; to scotch a rumor.* 2 to wound or injure so as render harmless: *to scotch a snake.*

Scotch (skŏch) *n-* 1 (also **Scotch whiskey**) whiskey made in Scotland from malted barley. 2 **the Scotch** (takes plural verb) the Scottish. —*adj-* Scottish.

▶The Scottish dislike the term Scotch when applied to themselves.

Scotch-Irish (skŏch′ Ī′ rĭsh) *n-* 1 the people of northern Ireland, descended from Scottish settlers. 2 people of such stock who emigrated to the United States before 1846, and their descendants. *adj-:* *the Scotch-Irish settlers of the Cumberlands.*

Scotch·man (skŏch′ mən) *n-* [*pl.* **Scotch·men**] Scot.

Scotch terrier or **Scottish terrier** *n-* any of a breed of terrier that originated in Scotland, with short legs, square muzzle, and rough, wiry hair; scottie.

sco·ter (skō′ tər) *n-* any of several large sea ducks found in the north; coot.

scot-free (skŏt′ frē′) *adj-* free from punishment or loss; safe: *The defendant went scot-free.*

Scotland Yard *n-* headquarters of the London police, and especially of the detective force (Criminal Investigation Division).

Scots (skŏts) *adj-* Scottish. *n-* (takes singular verb) the English language as spoken and written by the Scottish.

Scots·man (skŏts′ mən) *n-* [*pl.* **Scots·men**] Scot.

Scot·ti·cism (skŏt′ ə sĭz′ əm) *n-* Scottish word or idiom.

scot·tie (skŏt′ ē) *Informal* *n-* Scotch terrier.

Scot·tish (skŏt′ ĭsh) *adj-* of or relating to the Scots, their language, customs, land, etc.; Scots: *the Scottish highlands.* *n-* 1 the English language as spoken and written by the people of Scotland; Scots. 2 **the Scottish** (takes plural verb) the people of Scotland collectively.

Scottish Gaelic *n-* the Gaelic dialects of Scotland. *adj-* (**Scottish-Gaelic**): *a Scottish-Gaelic poem.* Also **Scots Gaelic.**

scoun·drel (skoun′ drəl) *n-* person of bad character; rascal; rogue.

scoun·drel·ly (skoun′ drə lē) *adj-* 1 having the character of a scoundrel: *a scoundrelly man.* 2 typical of a scoundrel: *a scoundrelly deed.*

¹**scour** (skour) *vt-* 1 to clean by rubbing hard: *to scour a pot with steel wool.* 2 to wear away by rubbing: *The stream scoured a new bed during the rains.* *n-* a cleaning by hard rubbing: *I gave the kitchen floor a good scour.* [from Medieval Dutch **schuren**, from Old French **escurer** meaning "scour; clean," from Latin **excūrāre**, "take good care of; clean off."] —*n-* **scour′ er.**

²**scour** (skour) *vt-* to look over carefully and minutely; search thoroughly: *to scour the woods for a lost child.* [from Old French **escourre**, from Latin **excurrere**, "to run out; make a (military) excursion; sally."]

scourge (skûrj) *n-* 1 a whip. 2 person or thing that causes pain, torment, or trouble: *war, the scourge of man.* *vt-* [**scourged, scourg·ing**] 1 to whip. 2 to devastate; afflict: *a plague that scourges a country.* 3 to criticize severely

scout (skout) *n-* 1 person sent out to get information, especially during a war. 2 person engaged in discovering new talent, especially in entertainment or sports. 3 (also **Scout**) member of the Boy Scouts or of the Girl Scouts. 4 *Informal* (also **good scout**) good fellow; friend; nice guy. *vt-* to go out to gather information about: *One squad scouted the area.* *vi-* 1 to take part in the activities of the Boy Scouts or Girl Scouts. 2 to go in search of something: *You'd better scout for wood before dark.* [from Old French *escoute*, "spy; listener," from *escouter*, "to listen," from Late Latin *ascultāre*.]

scout (skout) *vt-* to scoff at; dismiss with contempt: *He scouted any objection to his plan.* [from Old Norse *skūta* meaning "taunts; shot out," related to **shoot**.]

scout·ing (skou'tĭng) *n-* the activities of scouts, especially of the Boy Scouts or of the Girl Scouts.

scout·mas·ter (skout'măs'tər) *n-* man who leads a troop of Boy Scouts.

scow (skou) *n-* boat with a flat bottom and square ends, used for carrying garbage, gravel, or other heavy loads.

Scow

scowl (skoul) *n-* a wrinkling of the forehead in anger or displeasure. *vi-* *Jesse scowled at his bad grade.* *vt-*: *to scowl displeasure.* *—n- scowl'er.*

scrab·ble (skrăb'əl) *vi-* [scrab·bled, scrab·bling] to work hard against heavy odds or in very unpromising conditions: *The pioneers had to scrabble for a living.*

Scowl

scrag (skrăg) *n-* neck; especially, the lean end of a neck of mutton or veal. *vt-* [scragged, scrag·ging] 1 to wring the neck of. 2 to seize by the neck.

scrag·gly (skrăg'lē) *adj-* [scrag·gli·er, scrag·gli·est] 1 unkempt; shaggy: *a scraggly beard.* 2 jagged; irregular: *a scraggly cliff.*

scrag·gy (skrăg'ē) *adj-* [scrag·gi·er, scrag·gi·est] 1 lean and bony; scrawny. 2 jagged; rough.

scram (skrăm) *Slang interj-* leave quickly! get out of here at once! *vi-* [scrammed, scram·ming] to leave quickly.

scram·ble (skrăm'bəl) *vi-* [scram·bled, scram·bling] 1 to force one's way by the use of hands and feet; crawl: *to scramble up a rock;* *to scramble through the underbrush.* 2 to struggle or fight to get something: *They scrambled for pennies in the street.* 3 *Slang* to take off quickly in fighter planes in order to intercept an enemy air attack. *vt-* 1 to mix (the whites and yolks of eggs) and fry. 2 to mix up: *He scrambled the letters.* 3 in communications, to distort (speech sounds) by electrical means in order to produce a signal that cannot be understood. *n-* 1 hard climb: *It was a scramble to reach the top of the hill.* 2 confused struggle: *There was a scramble at the store during the bargain day sale.*

scram·bler (skrăm'blər) *n-* person or device that scrambles.

scrap (skrăp) *n-* 1 small piece; bit: *a scrap of lace;* *a scrap of evidence.* 2 broken, worn-out, or useless material; junk: *The foundry bought six carloads of scrap.* 3 scraps rejected or leftover food. *as modifier: a dealer in scrap metal;* *a load of scrap iron;* scrap par··. *vt-* [scrapped, scrap·ping] to discard; throw away: *to scrap worn-out machinery.* [from Old Norse *skrap* meaning "scrapings."]

scrap (skrăp) *Slang n-* fight; quarrel. *vi-* [scrapped, scrap·ping] to fight or quarrel. [a variant of **scrape**.] *—n- scrap'per.*

scrap·book (skrăp'book') *n-* book with blank pages in which clippings, photographs, etc., may be pasted.

scrape (skrāp) *vt-* [scraped, scrap·ing] 1 to push or strip away (paint, dirt, rust, etc.) by forcing a blade or other tool edgewise across a surface. 2 to remove something from in this way: *to scrape walls.* 3 to grind or graze harshly against: *The board scraped my skin.* *vi-* 1 to make, or move with, a scratching sound: *The chain scraped along the ground.* 2 to pass or squeeze (by or through) with difficulty: *The two cars managed to scrape by without touching.*

something. 2 harsh or grating sound: *the scrape of her fingernail on glass.* 3 difficult or embarrassing situation: scrape along to manage to live, but with difficulty. scrape up (or together) to gather; accumulate.

scrap·er (skrā'pər) *n-* person or thing that scrapes; especially, any of various tools or machines used to remove paint, varnish, or similar covering.

scrap heap *n-* heap of scrap or junk; place where used or unwanted things are thrown; junk pile.

scrap·ple (skrăp'əl) *n-* dish of pork scraps boiled together with corn meal or flour, allowed to set, and sliced and fried.

WALL
FLOOR
Scrapers

scrap·py (skrăp'ē) *adj-* [scrap·pi·er, scrap·pi·est] made up of scraps or bits; not coherent and complete: *a scrappy report.* [from **scrap.**]

scrap·py (skrăp'ē) *Slang adj-* [scrap·pi·er, scrap·pi·est] 1 full of fighting spirit; aggressive. 2 given to fighting or quarreling; quarrelsome. [from **scrap.**]

scratch (skrăch) *vt-* 1 to mark or tear the surface of with something rough or pointed: *to scratch the polished table.* 2 to mark or write with a sharp instrument: *Bob scratched his name on the wall.* 3 to dig or scrape with claws or nails: *He scratched his ear.* 4 *Informal* to cancel: *The weather caused them to scratch the flight.* *vi-* 1 to dig or scrape with claws or nails. 2 relieve itching by scraping the skin: *That dog is always scratching.* 3 to become marked or scraped: *That surface scratches easily.* 4 to make a scraping sound: *Chalk scratches on the blackboard.* *n-* 1 mark left by scraping or tearing something: *a scratch on furniture;* *a scratch on one's cheek.* 2 harsh, scraping sound: *the scratch of a pen.* *—n- scratch'er.*
from scratch 1 from the beginning. 2 from nothing.
up to scratch *Informal* at the normal or standard level.

scratch line *n-* the take-off line that may not be crossed by a contestant in the broad jump, javelin throw, etc.

scratch pad *n-* pad containing blank **scratch paper** for jotting down memos and similar notes.

scratch sheet *n-* daily racing publication that provides information about horses scheduled to compete that day, including past performances, jockeys, odds, etc.

scratch test *n-* 1 *Medicine* (1) test made to determine allergic sensitivity by introducing various allergens into scratches in the skin. (2) test for the presence of tuberculosis, glanders, leprosy, tinea, or certain other diseases, made by introducing the toxin in a scratch in the skin. 2 test of the hardness of a material, made by scratching it with other minerals of known hardness under controlled pressure.

scratch·y (skrăch'ē) *adj-* [scratch·i·er, scratch·i·est] 1 irritating; itchy: *a scratchy sweater.* 2 making a harsh, scraping sound; grating: *a scratchy phonograph record.* *—adv- scratch'i·ly.* *n- scratch'i·ness.*

scrawl (skrôl) *vt-* to write or draw hastily, carelessly, or awkwardly: *to scrawl one's name on a wall.* *n-*: *I can hardly read his scrawl.* *—n- scrawl'er.* *adj- scrawl'y* [scrawl·i·er, scrawl·i·est]: *a scrawly handwriting.*

scraw·ny (skrô'nē) *adj-* [scraw·ni·er, scraw·ni·est] lean; skinny.

scream (skrēm) *vi-* to give a loud, shrill, piercing cry, especially from fear or pain: *She screamed when she saw the mouse.* *vt-*: *She screamed her name.* *n-* 1 loud, shrill, piercing cry: *to utter a scream.* 2 *Informal* person, thing, or situation that provokes laughter or ridicule.

scream·er (skrē'mər) *n-* 1 person who screams. 2 any of various large South American birds related to the ducks and having a raucous cry.

scream·ing (skrē'mĭng) *adj-* 1 uttering screams: *a screaming baby.* 2 sensational; startling: *a screaming headline.* *—adv- scream'ing·ly.*

screech (skrēch) *n-* harsh, piercing cry or sound: *the screech of brakes.* *vi-* to utter a piercing cry: *An owl screeched.* *vt-*: *He screeched a reply.* *—n- screech'er.*

screech owl *n-* any of various small owls of North America, with hornlike tufts of feathers and a shrill cry.

screech·y (skrē'chē) *adj-* [screech·i·er, screech·i·est] harsh and piercing; shrill: *a screechy voice.*

screen (skrēn) *n-* 1 frame covered with fine net or mesh of wire or plastic, used in doors and windows to keep out insects. 2 something that hides or conceals: *a screen of trees; a smoke* screen. 3 partition or frame of folding panels. 4 a surface on which motion pictures or slides are shown; also, the surface of a television set or radar upon which images appear. 5 **the screen** (also **the silver screen**) motion pictures as an art and industry: *a play adapted for the* screen. 6 coarse wire mesh set in a frame, used in sifting or grading. *vt-* 1 to shelter; shield: *to* screen *one's eyes with an eyeshade.* 2 to sift. 3 to show (a motion picture). 4 to examine in order to classify or choose: *to* screen *applicants for a job.* —*n-* screen′er.

Window screen   Fireplace screen

screen·ing (skrē′nĭng) *n-* 1 examination in order to classify or choose: *a* screening *for a job.* 2 showing of a motion picture, to a select audience. 3 use of a screen to sift out particles of a certain size.

screen·ings (skrē′nĭngz) *n- pl.* material separated out by a sieve or screen.

screen·play (skrēn′plā′) *n-* story created for a movie.

screen test *n-* motion-picture scene or scenes made to test a person being considered for a role.

screw·ball (skrōo′bòl′) *n-* 1 in baseball, a pitch thrown by a right-handed pitcher that curves toward a right-handed batter, or one delivered with the left hand that curves toward a left-handed batter. 2 *Slang* eccentric or odd person.

screw·driv·er (skrōo′drī′vər) *n-* tool with a tip that fits into the slot or head of a screw and is used to turn it.

screw·eye (skrōo′ī′) *n-* ring with a projecting screw for fixing it solidly in place.

screw pine *n-* any of various tropical plants with stiltlike roots and narrow, spirally arranged leaves.

screw propeller *n-* device consisting of two or more thin and usually rounded blades set or molded on a hub at such an angle that a thrust is produced when the propeller turns, used underwater to drive boats.

screw thread *n-* spiral ridge running around a cylinder to form a screw.

scrib·ble (skrĭb′əl) *vt-* [scrib·bled, scrib·bling] to write hastily and carelessly: *She* scribbled *her name.* *vi-*: *He* scribbled *on a pad.* *n-* hasty, careless piece of writing.

scrib·bler (skrĭb′lər) *n-* 1 person who scribbles. 2 petty, untalented writer.

scribe (skrĭb) *n-* 1 person who copied manuscripts before the invention of printing presses. 2 formerly, a clerk or secretary. 3 among the ancient Jews, a teacher of the law. *vt-* [scribed, scrib·ing] 1 to score (a line, mark, etc.) with a scriber. 2 to mark (metal, wood, etc.) with a scriber.

scrib·er (skrī′bər) *n-* sharp tool for scribing.

scrim (skrĭm) *n-* loosely woven fabric of cotton or linen.

scrim·mage (skrĭm′ĭj) *n-* 1 rough and confused struggle; tussle: *a scrimmage over the ball.* 2 in football, the action that takes place after the ball is put into play by snapping it back; also, a practice game between members of the same team or between rival teams. *vi-* [scrim·maged, scrim·mag·ing] to engage in a football scrimmage: *We'll* scrimmage *on Saturday.*

scrimp (skrĭmp) *vi-* to be very economical or frugal; skimp; stint: *He* scrimps *on food.* *vt-*: *to* scrimp *cloth.*

scrimp·y (skrĭm′pē) *adj-* [scrimp·i·er, scrimp·i·est] scanty; skimpy. —*adv-* scrimp′i·ly. *n-* scrimp′i·ness.

scrim·shaw (skrĭm′shò′) *n-* 1 carved or engraved ornamental articles of bone, ivory, shell, etc.; especially, such articles made from whalebone by American whalers in the 19th century. 2 the art and practice of carving whalebone and making such articles. *vt-*: *He* scrimshaws *ivory.* *vi-*: *He* scrimshaws *on long voyages.*

scrip (skrĭp) *n-* 1 any of various certificates, often issued in place of money, indicating that the bearer is entitled to receive goods or services. 2 certificate for a part of a share of stock or a bond.

Scrip·tur·al or **scrip·tur·al** (skrĭp′chər əl) *adj-* of or relating to the Scriptures. —*adv-* scrip′tur·al·ly.

Scrip·ture (skrĭp′chər) *n-* 1 (also **the Scriptures** or **the Holy Scriptures**) the books of the Old and New Testament, and often the Apocrypha. 2 **scriptures** any sacred writing.

scriv·e·ner (skrĭv′ə nər) *Archaic n-* clerk; scribe.

scrod (skrŏd) *n-* young cod, especially one split to cook.

scrof·u·la (skrŏf′yə lə) *n-* tubercular infection of the lymph glands, and sometimes of the bones and joints, producing abscesses and fistulas. —*adj-* scrof′u·lous: *a* scrofulous *skin.*

scroll (skrōl) *n-* 1 book handwritten on a long strip of paper or parchment that a reader may roll up as he reads. 2 curved ornament. —*adj-* scroll′-like′.

Scrolls

scroll saw *n-* saw with a narrow blade for cutting thin wood in intricate, ornamental patterns.

scroll·work (skrōl′wûrk′) *n-* ornamental work of scroll-like patterns; especially, such work made with a scroll saw.

Scrooge (skrōoj) *n-* the miserly old man in Dickens' "A Christmas Carol"; hence, any miser.

scro·tum (skrō′təm) *n-* [*pl.* scro·ta (-tə) or scro·tums] in male mammals, the pouch containing the testes and their accessory organs.

scrounge (skrounj) *Slang vt- & vi-* [scrounged, scroung·ing] 1 to hunt up; scare up; forage (usually followed by "around" or "up"). 2 to beg; mooch. *n-* person who mooches; sponge.

¹**scrub** (skrŭb) *vt-* [scrubbed, scrub·bing] 1 to wash or clean by hard rubbing or brushing: *to* scrub *a floor.* 2 *Slang* to cancel: *The weather caused them to* scrub *the flight.* 3 to cleanse impurities from (a gas). *vi-* to clean oneself thoroughly with soap and a brush; especially, among surgeons, to cleanse the hands and arms before an operation. *n-*: *She gave the floor a* scrub. [from Middle English **scrobben**, probably of Scandinavian origin.]

²**scrub** (skrŭb) *n-* 1 any animal or plant that is undersized or inferior in growth or quality. 2 player on a second or inferior team: *The varsity practiced against the* scrubs. 3 stunted shrubs, bushes, or trees: *The rabbit ran into the* scrub. *as modifier: a member of the* scrub *team; a thick cover of* scrub *growth.* [probably from Danish **skrub** meaning "brushwood," and related to **shrub**.]

scrub·ber (skrŭb′ər) *n-* person or thing that scrubs; especially, an apparatus for freeing gas of impurities.

scrub·by (skrŭb′ē) *adj-* [scrub·bi·er, scrub·bi·est] 1 covered with scrub or brushwood: *a* scrubby *field.* 2 stunted: *a* scrubby *tree.* 3 shabby; paltry.

scruff (skrŭf) *n-* back of the neck; nape.

scrump·tious (skrŭmp′shəs) *Slang adj-* splendid; excellent; delightful; delicious.

scrunch (skrŭnch) *vt-* to crush or crumple; crunch. *vi-* to make, or walk with, a crunching sound: *He* scrunched *through the deep snow.* *n-* crunching sound.

scru·ple (skrōo′pəl) *n-* feeling of uneasiness, doubt, or uncertainty arising from one's conscience: *I had* scruples *about missing class.* *vi-* [scru·pled, scru·pling] to hesitate or be stopped by conscience or unwillingness (always in the negative, and usually followed by an infinitive or "about"): *He did not* scruple *to take his sister's share of the money. They did not* scruple *about abandoning us.*

scru·pu·lous (skrōo′pyə ləs) *adj-* strict; conscientious: *He has a* scrupulous *regard for the truth.* —*adv-* scru′pu·lous·ly. *n-* scru′pu·lous·ness.

scru·ti·nize (skrōo′tə nīz′) *vt-* [scru·ti·nized, scru·ti·niz·ing] to examine closely or minutely: *The police* scrutinized *the fingerprints.* —*n-* scru′ti·niz′er.

sea (sē) *n*- 1 the body of salt water that covers most of the earth's surface; ocean.

sea legs *n*- *pl.* ability to adapt oneself to the pitching and rolling motion of a ship.

²**seal·er** (sē′ lər) *n*- 1 person, device, or material that closes, seals, packages, makes watertight or airtight, etc. 2 paint applied to unfinished surfaces to prevent subsequent coats of paint, varnish, etc., from sinking in or being absorbed unevenly. 3 official who certifies that certain standards have been met. [from ²seal.]

sea level *n*- position of the surface of the ocean when it is halfway between high tide and low tide. The positions of all other land on the earth, including the bottoms of seas, are measured above or below sea level. For picture, see *elevation.*

sealing wax *n*- kind of wax that softens when heated and hardens quickly on cooling and is used for sealing letters, packages, etc.

sea lion *n*- large seal that lives in the Pacific Ocean.

seal·skin (sēl′ skĭn′) *n*- 1 skin or fur of a fur seal. 2 garment made of it. *as modifier:* a sealskin *coat.*

seam (sēm) *n*- 1 line made when two pieces of material are sewn, welded, or otherwise joined together. 2 wrinkle, welt, scar, or furrow: *The seam of an old cut crossed his cheek.* 3 layer of mineral in the earth: *A seam of quartz runs through the cliff.* *vt*- 1 to join together, especially by sewing: *to seam a dress.* 2 to mark with scars and furrows: *Wind and water had seamed the old seaman's face.* *Hom-* seem. *—adj-* seam′ less.

sea·man (sē′ mən) *n*- [*pl.* sea·men] 1 sailor. 2 in the Navy and Coast Guard, an enlisted man who ranks below a petty officer and above a recruit. *Hom-* semen. *—adj-* sea′ man·like′.

sea·man·ship (sē′ mən shĭp′) *n*- skill in sailing.

sea mew *n*- gull; especially, one of the common European gulls.

sea·mount (sē′ mount′) *n*- in geology, an isolated, undersea mountain that does not reach sea level.

seam·stress (sēm′ strəs) *n*- woman who sews for a living.

seam·y (sē′ mē) *adj*- [seam·i·er, seam·i·est] 1 having seams. 2 showing the rough, inner sides of seams. *—n- seam′ i·ness.*

the seamy side the worst, roughest side.

sé·ance (sā′ äns′) *n*- meeting of persons to receive spiritualistic messages.

sea otter *n*- large, nearly extinct otter having a valuable dark-brown fur and found along the North Pacific.

sea·plane (sē′ plān′) *n*- airplane designed to land on and take off from water; hydroplane.

sea·port (sē′ pôrt′) *n*- 1 port or harbor for ocean vessels. 2 town or city containing such a port or harbor.

sea power *n*- 1 nation having a powerful navy. 2 naval strength

sear (sēr) *vt*- 1 to dry up; wither: *A hot summer has seared the crops this year.* 2 to burn the surface of; scorch: *to sear a steak.* 3 to damage and leave a scar: *The tragedy had seared his mind.* *adj-* Archaic withered; dried up. *n-* mark made by burning. *Hom-* seer, sere.

search (sûrch) *vt*- 1 to examine carefully for something hidden or concealed: *They searched the room. He searched the prisoner for weapons.* 2 to look deeply into; probe: *to search one's heart. n-* a seeking or looking for a person or thing; investigation. *—n- search′ er.*

in search of looking for; trying to find.

search out to find or learn by searching.

search·ing (sûr′ chĭng) *adj-* sharply penetrating; scrutinizing: *a searching look. —adv- search′ ing·ly.*

search·light (sûrch′ lĭt′) *n*- large, powerful electric light, the beam of which may be turned in any direction.

search warrant *n*- written order giving a peace officer the authority to search for stolen goods, suspected lawbreakers, concealed weapons, etc.

sea room *n*- space at sea needed for maneuvering or changing the position of a ship.

sea rover *n*- a pirate; also, a pirate ship.

sea·scape (sē′ skāp′) *n*- 1 any picture showing a scene at sea. 2 view of the sea or ocean.

sea·shell (sē′ shĕl′) *n*- the shell of any sea mollusk.

sea·shore (sē′ shôr′) *n*- land bordering the sea; seacoast.

sea·sick (sē′ sĭk′) *adj-* suffering from illness or nausea caused by the motion of a ship. *—n- sea′ sick′ ness.*

sea·side (sē′ sīd′) *n*- land bordering the sea; seashore. *as modifier:* a seaside *cottage.*

sea snake *n*- any of several venomous, fish-eating snakes related to the cobras and found in warm parts of the Indian and Pacific oceans.

sea·son (sē′ zən) *n*- 1 any of the four divisions of the year (spring, summer, autumn, winter). 2 appropriate or proper time: *There is a season for everything.* 3 time of year associated with a special activity: *the opera season. vt*- 1 to make tasty by adding seasoning. 2 to bring to the best state for use or survival; toughen; mature: *to season timber; to season troops by hardship.* 3 to make agreeable; add interest to: *to season a lecture with pleasant anecdotes. vi*- to become fit for use: *Timber seasons well in the open air. —n- sea′ son·er.*

for a season for a while. *in good season* in good time for something; early enough. *in season* 1 available and fresh for use as food: *Oysters are in season now.* 2 legally subject to be hunted or caught: *Pheasants are in season for another month.* 3 at the proper or right time. *in and out of season* at all times. *out of season* not in season.

sea·son·a·ble (sē′ zə nə bəl) *adj-* 1 occurring or coming in good time: *his seasonable advice.* 2 in keeping with the season: *the seasonable weather. —n- sea′ son·a·ble·ness. adv- sea′ son·a·bly.*

▶Should not be confused with SEASONAL.

sea·son·al (sē′ zə nəl) *adj-* relating to or influenced by certain periods of the year: *a seasonal disease; seasonal rates; seasonal labor. —adv- sea′ son·al·ly.*

▶Should not be confused with SEASONABLE.

sea·son·ing (sē′ zən ĭng) *n*- 1 ingredient or ingredients, such as salt, pepper, and spices or herbs, added to food to flavor it. 2 anything that adds interest, variety, etc.

sea squirt *n*- any of various small sea animals having a leathery covering that contracts its soft body and causes it to squirt out jets of water.

seat (sēt) *n*- 1 place to sit, such as a chair, stool, or bench. 2 the part of a chair, stool, or bench on which one sits. 3 the part of the body on which one sits, or the part of a garment covering it: *the seat of one's trousers.* 4 place where anything is situated: *the seat of government.* 5 mansion or estate, especially in the country. 6 the position and rights of a member; membership: *a seat in Congress; a seat on the stock exchange.* 7 chair or space on a bench for a spectator: *three seats for a play.* 8 manner of sitting, as in riding a horse. 9 part or surface supporting another part or surface: *a valve seat.*

sec·re·tar·i·at (sĕk′ rə tĕr′ ē ət) *n*- 1 the official position of a secretary. 2 office where a secretary carries on his business, preserves records, etc. 3 secretarial staff. 4 government department headed by a secretary.

sec·re·tar·y (sĕk′ rə tĕr′ ē) *n*- [*pl.* sec·re·tar·ies] 1 someone who writes letters and keeps records for a person, company, etc. 2 government official in charge of a department and usually belonging to the chief executive's cabinet: *the Secretary of Labor.* 3 writing desk with an upper section for books. *—adj- sec′ re·tar′ i·al.*

secretary bird *n*- large, long-legged, South African bird that feeds on snakes and other reptiles and has long feathers suggesting pens stuck behind the ear.

sec·re·tar·y-gen·er·al (sĕk′ rə tĕr′ ē jĕn′ ər əl) *n*- [*pl.* sec·re·tar·ies-gen·er·al] chief administrative or executive officer.

Secretary bird

sec·re·tar·y·ship (sĕk′ rə tĕr′ ē shĭp′) *n*- term of office, position, or work of a secretary.

se·crete (sĭ krēt′) *vt*- [se·cret·ed, se·cret·ing] 1 of living things, to produce and give off (a secretion): *Glands secrete hormones. Flowers secrete nectar.* 2 to hide; put in a secret place: *Squirrels secrete nuts and acorns.*

seem·ing (sē' mǐng) *adj-* having an appearance which may or may not be true; apparent: *her seeming indignation*; seeming *neglect*. *n-* appearance; show; especially, false show. —*adv-* seem' ing·ly.

seem·ly (sēm' lē) *adj-* [seem·li·er, seem·li·est] fit or becoming to the circumstances; decent; proper: *her seemly behavior*. —*n-* seem' li·ness.

seen (sēn) *p.p.* of **see**. *Hom-* scene.

seep (sēp) *vi-* to leak slowly through small openings; ooze: *Water seeps into our cellar*. *n-* small spring, or a place where water, oil, or other liquid oozes from the ground.

seep·age (sē' pǐj) *n-* 1 a slow leaking through; ooze; percolation. 2 fluid or the amount of fluid that oozes.

seer (sēr) *n-* person supposed to have prophetic sight into the future. *Homs-* sear, sere. —*n- fem.* seer' ess.

seer·suck·er (sēr' sŭk' ər) *n-* thin fabric of cotton, linen, nylon, rayon, etc., usually having alternating stripes and a crinkled or puckered surface.

see·saw (sē' sò') *n-* 1 board balanced on a central support, the ends of which alternately rise and fall as riders on the ends shift their weight. 2 pastime enjoyed on such a board. 3 any up-and-down or to-and-fro movement. *as modifier: a seesaw motion*. *vi-* 1 to ride a seesaw. 2 to fluctuate: *The game seesawed back and forth until the home team won*

Seesaw

seethe (sēth) *vi-* [seethed, seeth·ing] 1 to move with a boiling, bubbling motion: *The flood seethed through town*. 2 to be violently moved or agitated: *I seethed with anger*.

Segment of a line

seg·ment (sĕg' mənt) *n-* 1 any of the structurally similar parts into which an object naturally separates or is divided: *a segment of an orange*; *the segments of a worm*; *the last segment of a plot*. 2 *Mathematics* (1) a line segment. (2) part of a circle bound by an arc and a chord. (3) solid formed when two parallel planes cut through a sphere. *vt-* to divide into parts.

Segment

seg·ment·ed (sĕg' měn' təd) *adj-* 1 divided into segments: *a segmented leaf*. 2 of a cell, divided by segmentation: *a segmented ovum*.

Segment of a circle

seg·men·ta·tion (sĕg' mən tā' shən) *n-* 1 a dividing or being divided into segments. 2 *Biology* division of a fertilized egg cell into a number of cells.

se·go (sē' gō) *n-* [*pl.* se·gos] bulb of the sego lily.

sego lily *n-* plant of the lily family, having white, trumpet-shaped flowers. It is common in western United States. [American word from the Ute Indian language.]

seg·re·gate (sĕg' rə gāt') *vt-* [seg·re·gat·ed, seg·ra·gat·ing] 1 to separate from others; isolate; set apart: *to segregate people who have been exposed to a disease*. 2 to set apart because of race or color.

Sego lily

seg·re·gat·ed (sĕg' rə gā' təd) *adj-* of or relating to segregation, especially of races: *a segregated school*.

seg·re·ga·tion (sĕg' rə gā' shən) *n-* 1 a separation from others; a setting apart: *The doctor ordered the segregation of unvaccinated students*. 2 a separation of one race from other races, especially in public places.

seg·re·ga·tion·ist (sĕg' rə gā' shən ĭst) *n-* person who practices or is in favor of racial segregation.

sei·gneur (sā nyŏr' *Fr.* sā nyŭr') *n-* 1 lord; noble. 2 formerly, feudal lord; lord of a manor. 3 title of respect equivalent to "Sir." Also sei' gnior.

sel·dom (sĕl' dəm) *adv-* hardly ever; rarely.

self-pol·li·na·tion (sĕlf' pŏl ə nā' shən) *n-* transfer of pollen from anthers to pistils of the same flower.

self-pos·sessed (sĕlf' pə zĕst') *adj-* having self-possession; calm; poised. —*adv-* self'-pos·ses' sed·ly.

self-pos·ses·sion (sĕlf' pə zĕsh' ən) *n-* control over one's feelings; composure; calmness; poise.

self-praise (sĕlf' prāz') *n-* praise of oneself.

self-pres·er·va·tion (sĕlf' prĕz' er vā' shən) *n-* 1 a keeping of oneself from harm or danger. 2 the urge, regarded as an instinct, to protect oneself when danger threatens.

self-pride (sĕlf' prīd') *n-* pride in oneself.

self-pro·pelled (sĕlf' prə pĕld') *adj-* 1 containing within itself its own means of propulsion; propelled by itself: *a self-propelled missile*. 2 of artillery, mounted on and fired from a truck or tractor.

self-pro·tec·tion (sĕlf' prə tĕk' shən) *n-* self-defense.

self-re·cord·ing (sĕlf' rĭ kòr' dĭng, -kôr' dĭng) *adj-* making an automatic record; self-registering.

self-reg·is·ter·ing (sĕlf' rĕj' ĭs tər ĭng) *adj-* registering or recording automatically: *a self-registering thermometer*.

self-reg·u·lat·ing (sĕlf' rĕg' yə lā' tǐng) *adj-* regulating or correcting itself: *a self-regulating guidance system*.

self-re·li·ance (sĕlf' rĭ lī' əns) *n-* dependence on or confidence in one's own resources, ability, or judgment. —*adj-* self'-re·li' ant. *adv-* self'-re·li' ant·ly.

self-re·proach (sĕlf' rĭ prōch') *n-* reproach, blame, or accusation of oneself. —*adj-* self'-re·proach' ing. *adv-* self'-re·proach' ing·ly.

self-re·spect (sĕlf' rĭ spĕkt') *n-* proper regard for oneself; self-esteem: *He had too much self-respect to tell a lie*. —*adj-* self'-re·spect' ing.

self-re·straint (sĕlf' rĭ strānt') *n-* control of one's impulses or desires by force of will; self-control. —*adj-* self'-re·strained'.

self-right·eous (sĕlf' rī' chəs) *adj-* convinced of the superiority of one's morals; morally vain: *a self-righteous prude*. —*adv-* self'-right' eous·ly. *n-* self'-right' eous·ness.

self-ris·ing (sĕlf' rī' zǐng) *adj-* rising by itself; especially, rising without the addition of baking powder, leaven, etc.: *a self-rising batter*.

self-sac·ri·fice (sĕlf' săk' rə fīs') *n-* sacrifice or subordination of one's personal interests or welfare for the sake of duty, another's happiness, etc. —*adj-* self'-sac' ri·fic' ing. *adv-* self'-sac' ri·fic' ing·ly.

self-same (sĕlf' sām') *adj-* the very same; identical.

self-sat·is·fac·tion (sĕlf' săt' ĭs făk' shən) *n-* excessive satisfaction with oneself and one's actions, position, etc.

self-sat·is·fied (sĕlf' săt' ĭs fīd') *adj-* entirely pleased with oneself and one's actions; complacent.

self-seek·ing (sĕlf' sē' kĭng) *n-* a looking out for one's own interests; selfishness. *adj-: He is a self-seeking hypocrite*. —*n-* self'-seek' er.

self-ser·vice (sĕlf' sûr' vəs) *n-* a serving of oneself in a restaurant, store, etc. *adj-: That is a self-service store*.

self-start·er (sĕlf' stär' tər) *n-* automatic or partly automatic device, such as an electric motor, for starting an internal-combustion engine.

self-styled (sĕlf' stīld') *adj-* given a specific name or designation by oneself alone: *a self-styled cook*.

self-suf·fi·cient (sĕlf' sə fĭsh' ənt) *adj-* 1 needing no help from others: *a self-sufficient community*. 2 having undue confidence in oneself; self-confident. —*n-* self'-suf·fi' cien·cy. *adv-* self'-suf·fi' cient·ly.

self-sup·port (sĕlf' sə pòrt') *n-* financial support of oneself or itself without outside help. —*adj-* self'-sup·port' ing: *a self-supporting institution*.

self-sus·tain·ing (sĕlf' sə stā' nǐng) *adj-* maintaining oneself or itself without outside help; self-supporting.

self-taught (sĕlf' tòt') *adj-* self-educated.

self-treat·ment (sĕlf' trēt' mənt) *n-* treatment of one's own disease or injury without medical supervision.

self-un·der·stand·ing (sĕlf' ŭn' dər stăn' dǐng) *n-* knowledge of one's own character, abilities, etc.

self-will (sĕlf' wǐl') *n-* insistence on having one's own way; stubbornness; obstinacy. —*adj-* self'-willed'.

Sen·e·ca (sĕn′ə kə) *n-* [*pl.* **Sen·e·cas**, also **Sen·e·ca**] one of the largest Iroquoian tribes that formed the Five Nations confederacy. *adj-: the Seneca clans.*

sen·es·chal (sĕn′ə shəl) *n-* official in medieval times who managed the castle of a lord.

se·nile (sĕn′īl′, sē′nīl′) *adj-* in a state of or showing senility: *a senile man; senile forgetfulness.*

se·nil·i·ty (sĭ nĭl′ə tē) *n-* state of infirmity, usually mental, associated with old age; dotage.

sen·ior (sēn′yər) *n-* 1 person who is older or higher in rank. 2 student in his last year of high school or college. *adj-* 1 older or oldest (used after the name of a father when the father and son have the same name). *Abbr.* Sr.: *Thomas Cox,* Sr. 2 higher in rank or position; longer in office: *the senior senator from Utah.* 3 having to do with the final year in high school or college.

senior high school *n-* school comprising the last three years of high school.

se·nior·i·ty (sēn yôr′ə tē, sēn yŏr′·) *n-* priority because of age, rank, or length of service.

sen·na (sĕn′ə) *n-* 1 any of several related plants, some of which have leaves and pods used in making medicine. 2 the medicine from these plants, used as a laxative.

se·ñor (sān yôr′) *Spanish* 1 title of courtesy equivalent to "Mr." or "sir." 2 a gentleman.

se·ño·ra (sān yôr′ə) *Spanish* 1 title of courtesy equivalent to "Mrs." or "Madam." 2 a lady.

se·ño·ri·ta (sān′yôrē′tə) *Spanish* 1 title of courtesy equivalent to "Miss." 2 a young lady.

sen·sa·tion (sĕn sā′shən) *n-* 1 a feeling through the senses: *a sensation of hearing; a sensation of cold.* 2 a mental or emotional feeling: *a sensation of dread.* 3 an arousing or exciting of the senses or feelings: *It was a great sensation to see the Grand Canyon.* 4 general excitement and interest: *His play created a sensation.*

sen·sa·tion·al (sĕn sā′shən əl) *adj-* 1 having to do with the senses. 2 thrilling; startling; extraordinary. 3 causing intense feeling, shock, thrill, etc.: *a sensational movie.* —*adv-* **sen·sa′tion·al·ly.**

sen·sa·tion·al·ism (sĕn sā′shən ə lĭz′əm) *n-* sensational writing or language intended to please vulgar taste. —*n-* **sen·sa′tion·al·ist.**

sense (sĕns) *n-* 1 any one of the physical powers by which an individual perceives the outside world or his own bodily changes. The five senses generally recognized are hearing, sight, smell, taste, and touch. 2 bodily feeling; sensation: *a sense of cold; a sense of pain.* 3 understanding; judgment; practical intelligence or wisdom: *He shows a great deal of sense.* 4 keen awareness; appreciation: *a sense of humor.* 5 meaning of a word or statement: *I don't intend it in that sense.* 6 (often **senses**) clear or sound mental faculties or mind; normal ability to think: *He came to his senses.* 7 that which is wise, sound, intelligent, or sensible: *to talk sense.* *as modifier: a sense organ; sense perception.* *vt-* [sensed, sens·ing] 1 to feel or be conscious of: *I sensed the danger.* 2 *Informal* to understand.

  in a sense from one aspect; looking at it one way: *What he says, is, in a sense, true.* **make sense** to be logical; to have a meaning that can be understood.

sense·less (sĕns′ləs) *adj-* 1 without the power of feeling; unconscious: *The ball hit him and knocked him senseless.* 2 without meaning or sense; stupid; foolish: *a senseless argument.* —*adv-* **sense′less·ly.** *n-* **sense′less·ness.**

sense of humor *n-* ability to see and enjoy the absurd or amusing: *He has no sense of humor.*

sen·si·tiv·i·ty (sĕn′sə tĭv′ə tē) *n-* [*pl.* **sen·si·tiv·i·ties**] 1 condition of being sensitive. 2 *Biology* (1) ability of an organism or sense organ to respond to a stimulus. (2) degree of responsiveness to stimulation. 3 in electricity, degree to which a receiving set reacts to incoming radio waves. 4 in photography, degree to which a photographic plate, film, etc., responds to light.

sen·si·tize (sĕn′sə tīz′) *vt-* [sen·si·tized, sen·si·tiz·ing] 1 to make sensitive or responsive. 2 of a photographic plate or film, to make susceptible to the action of light, X rays, etc. 3 to make (the cells of the body) hypersensitive to some foreign substance, so that its presence will cause a typical reaction. —*n-* **sen′si·tiz′er.**

sen·sor (sĕn′sôr′, -sər) *n-* instrument or device, such as a photoelectric cell, designed to receive and respond to a physical stimulus and transmit a resulting impulse for interpretation or measurement or for operating a control

sen·so·ry (sĕn′sə rē) *adj-* 1 of or relating to the senses or sensation: *a sensory impression.* 2 conveying sense impulses: *a sensory nerve.*

sensory nerve *n-* nerve that conveys impulses from the sense organs to the spinal cord or brain.

sen·su·al (sĕn′shŏŏ əl) *adj-* 1 having to do with or associated with the pleasures of the body; not mental or spiritual: *a sensual life.* 2 indulging in the pleasures of the body, especially sexual pleasure. 3 appealing to sexual pleasure; voluptuous; fleshy. 4 sensuous. —*adv-* **sen′su·al·ly.** *n-* **sen′su·al′i·ty.**

  ►Both **sensual** and **sensuous** refer to the senses. **sensual** suggests something gross or excessive or lewd. **sensuous** suggests something more delicate and refined.

sen·su·al·ist (sĕn′shŏŏ ə lĭst) *n-* person who indulges in sensual pleasure.

sen·su·ous (sĕn′shŏŏ əs) *adj-* 1 having to do with or appealing to the senses: *his sensuous music.* 2 resembling sensation or sense imagery: *her sensuous narration of the poem.* 3 readily responding to sense impression or the pleasures to be received through the senses. —*adv-* **sen′su·ous·ly.** *n-* **sen′su·ous·ness.**

  ►For usage note see **sensual.**

sent (sĕnt) *p.t.* and *p.p.* of **send.** *Homs-* cent, scent.

sentence (sĕn′təns) *n-* 1 *Grammar* group of words that is separate from any other grammatical construction, consists of at least one subject with its predicate, and

se·quoi·a (sĭ kwoi′ə) *n-* 1 the redwood. 2 the big tree. [American word from the name of the Cherokee chief, Sikwayi, who invented the Cherokee system of writing.]

se·ra (sēr′ə) *pl.* of **serum.**

se·ragl·io (sə rǎl′yō, -rāl′yō) *n-* harem.

se·ra·pe (sə rä′pē) *n-* wool blanket, often in bright colors, worn by Mexican men around the shoulders; sarape. [American word from Mexican Spanish.]

ser·aph (sĕr′əf) *n-* [*pl.* **ser·aphs** or **ser·a·phim** (-ə fĭm′)] one of the highest order of angels.

se·raph·ic (sə răf′ĭk) *adj-* 1 of or having to do with a seraph. 2 angelic; heavenly. —*adv-* **se·raph′i·cal·ly.**

sere (sēr) *adj-* withered; dried up: *the sere leaves of autumn. Homs-* sear, seer.

ser·e·nade (sĕr′ə nād′) *n-* 1 music sung or played at night, usually beneath a lady's window and in her honor. 2 musical composition for small orchestra, resembling a suite. 3 a singing or playing of such music. *vt-* [ser·e·nad·ed, ser·e·nad·ing] to sing or play such music to: *Let's go serenade the girls.* —*n-* **ser′e·nad′er.**

ser·en·dip·i·ty (sĕr′ən dĭp′ə tē) *n-* 1 lucky knack of finding important things by accident. 2 an instance of such a knack or discovery. —*adj-* **ser′en·dip′i·tous.**

se·rene (sə rēn′) *adj-* 1 calm; peaceful: *a serene sea; a serene disposition.* 2 **Serene** title for certain rulers, preceded by "His": *His Serene Highness.* —*adv-* **se·rene′ly.**

se·ren·i·ty (sə rēn′ə tē) *n-* calmness; peacefulness; also, composure: *The noise did not disturb her serenity.*

serf (sûrf) *n-* 1 in the Middle Ages, a person who could not leave the land he worked on and who was usually sold with it. 2 a slave. *Hom-* surf.

serf·dom (sûrf′dəm) *n-* 1 condition of being a serf. 2 condition of servitude; slavery.

serge (sûrj) *n-* woolen material woven with slanting ribs, used for clothing. *as modifier: a pair of serge trousers. Hom-* surge.

ser·geant (sär′jənt) *n-* 1 in the Army and Marine Corps, a noncommissioned officer who ranks below a warrant officer and above a corporal. 2 in the Air Force, a noncommissioned officer who ranks below a warrant officer and above an airman. 3 officer ranking below a lieutenant in a police department, fire department, etc.

sergeant at arms *n-* [*pl.* **sergeants at arms**] officer of a legislative or other official group, who is responsible for keeping order at meetings.

sergeant major *n-* in the Army and Marine Corps, a noncommissioned officer who ranks below a warrant officer but above all other noncommissioned officers.

¹set·tle (sĕt′ əl) *vt-* [**set·tled, set·tling**] **1** to put in order. **2** to put (something) firmly or evenly in place. **3** to relieve discomfort or tension in: *Knitting* settled *her nerves.* **4** to cause to sink or subside: *The rain* settled *the dust.* **5** to make impurities or dregs sink: *He* settled *the coffee.* **6** to adjust or decide finally; agree upon: *He* settled *the argument. We* settled *the price.* **7** to pay. **8** to populate; colonize. *vi-* **1** to sink gradually: *Dust* settled *on the piano.* **2** to sink slightly so as to become more firmly or evenly based: *A new house* settles *after a few years.* **3** to come to rest: *The parakeet* settled *on my finger.* **4** to make one's home: *We* settled *in a distant town.* **5** to compose oneself; make oneself comfortable: *Dad* settled *in his easy chair.* **6** to pay a bill (often followed by "up"). [from Old English *setlan* meaning "to fix; take a seat," from *setl,* "²**settle,**" and *sahtlian,* "to reconcile."]

settle down 1 to settle in a specific place or in a fixed way of life. **2** to begin to act or work in an orderly fashion.

settle on (or **upon**) in law, to give someone possession of money or property.

²set·tle (sĕt′ əl) *n-* old-fashioned, long, wooden seat with arms and a high, straight back. [from Old English *setl* meaning "a seat," and related to *sit* and **¹set.**]

set·tle·ment (sĕt′ əl mənt) *n-* **1** group of dwellings; town, village: *a* settlement *on the banks of the river.* **2** the deciding of a disagreement or legal conflict, especially about money or property: *The two parties reached a* settlement. *We made a* settlement *out of court.* **3** a settling of a new region: *They encourage the* settlement *of the Yukon.* **4** property or money given as a legal gift: *a large marriage* settlement. **5** settlement house.

settlement house *n-* community house, often in the poorer section of a city, which gives instruction, recreation, and advice to people in the section.

set·tler (sĕt′ lər) *n-* person who makes his home in a new, or newly developed, country; colonist.

set-to (sĕt′ tōō′) *n-* [*pl.* **set-tos**] quarrel; fight.

set-up (sĕt′ ŭp′) *n-* **1** structure or plan of an organization. **2** state of things; situation: *He explained the* setup *to us before we attacked.* **3** silverware, napkin, etc., arranged for serving a meal to one person. **4** a glass, ice, soda water, etc., to which whiskey or other liquor is added to make a drink. **5** *Informal* fight, contest, etc., which one side is certain to lose; also, the losing side or person.

sev·en (sĕv′ ən) *n-* **1** amount or quantity that is one greater than 6. **2** *Mathematics* (1) the cardinal number that is the sum of 6 and 1. (2) numeral such as 7 that represents this cardinal number. *as determiner* (traditionally called adjective or pronoun): *There are* seven *sticks here and* seven *there.*

sev·en·fold (sĕv′ ən fōld′) *adj-* **1** seven times as many or as much. **2** having seven parts. *adv-: The machine increased production* sevenfold.

Seven Seas *n- pl.* the oceans of the world: the North Atlantic, South Atlantic, North Pacific, South Pacific, Indian, Arctic, and (formerly) the Antarctic.

sev·en·teen (sĕv′ ən tēn′) *n-* **1** amount or quantity that is one greater than 16. **2** *Mathematics* (1) the cardinal number that is the sum of 16 and 1. (2) a numeral such as `17 that represents this cardinal number. *as determiner* (traditionally called adjective or pronoun): *There are* seventeen *trees here and* seventeen *there.*

sharp·er (shär′ pər) *n-* swindler or cheat: *a card* sharper.

sharp·ie (shär′ pē) *n-* **1** long, pointed, flat-bottomed boat having a centerboard and usually two masts, each carrying a triangular sail. **2** *Slang* unusually alert, keen person.

sharp·shoot·er (shärp′ shōō′ tər) *n-* excellent marksman, especially with a rifle.

sharp·sight·ed (shärp′ sī′ təd) *adj-* **1** having keen vision. **2** sharp-witted.

sharp-wit·ted (shärp′ wĭt′ əd) *adj-* having a keen, astute, or agile mind; acute: *a* sharp-witted *lawyer.*

shat·ter (shăt′ ər) *vt-* **1** to break or smash suddenly into small pieces, as by a blow or fall: *to* shatter *a window.* **2** to ruin; destroy: *to* shatter *hope.* *vi-: A glass* shattered.

shat·ter·proof (shăt′ ər prōōf′) *adj-* made so as not to shatter: *a* shatterproof *glass.*

shave (shāv) *vt-* [**shaved, shaved** or **shav·en, shav·ing**] **1** to cut off (hair) with a razor; also, to cut off hair from (the face, etc.) with a razor. **2** to cut thin slices from: *to* shave *a ham.* **3** to pass very close to; graze. *vi-* to remove hair with a razor: *He* shaves *twice a day. n-* **1** a cutting off of hair with a razor. **2** (usually **close shave**) a grazing or passing very close; also, a narrow escape.

shav·er (shā′ vər) *n-* **1** person or thing that shaves: *an electric* shaver. **2** *Informal* young fellow; youth.

shav·ing (shā′ vĭng) *n-* very thin slice of wood, metal, etc., cut off by a plane or similar tool; paring.

shawl (shôl) *n-* large piece of cloth worn over the shoulders or head, especially by women.

Shaw·nee (shô′ nē) *n-* [*pl.* **Shaw·nees,** also **Shaw·nee**] one of a tribe of Algonquian Indians, who formerly lived in the Cumberland River basin and now live in Oklahoma. *adj-: a* Shawnee *arrow.*

shay (shā) *n-* light, horse-drawn carriage; chaise.

she (shē) *pron-* (used as a singular subject in the third person) **1** female person or animal, that has been named or is being pointed out: *Where is Jane? She is upstairs. And what is* she *doing on the front porch?* **2** thing, thought of as a female: *Being a strong ship,* she *rode out the hurricane.* **3** any female (often followed by "who" or "that"): *They said that* she *who is chosen queen will have a screen test. n-* a female: *Is that rabbit a* she *or a* he*? as modifier:* a she-*rabbit.*

sheaf (shēf) *n-* [*pl.* **sheaves** (shēvz)] **1** bundle of cut grain tied in the middle. **2** bundle of things: *a* sheaf *of arrows.*

Sheaf

shear (shēr) *vt-* [**sheared, sheared** or **shorn** (shôrn), **shear·ing**] **1** to clip off (wool, hair, etc.) with shears or clippers: *to* shear *wool.* **2** to remove wool or hair from, with shears or clippers: *to* shear *a lamb.* **3** to slice (often followed by "off"): *It* sheared *off a wall. vi-* to break in a crosswise direction. *n- Physics* of a solid body under stress, displacement of two or more sections of it in opposite, crosswise directions by equal and opposite forces, as when rivets break crosswise in the failure of a riveted joint. *Hom-* sheer. **—n- shear′ er.**

shears (shērz) *n-* (takes plural verb) any of various kinds of large scissors for shearing sheep or cutting cloth, sheet metal, etc. Also **pair of shears** (takes singular verb).

sheath (shēth) *n-* [*pl.* **sheaths** (shēthz, shēths)] **1** protective covering or envelope: *The caterpillar wound a silken* sheath *about itself.* **2** close-fitting case for a sword or dagger; scabbard. *vt-* to sheathe.

sheathe (shēth) *vt-* [**sheathed, sheath·ing**] **1** to put into a scabbard or sheath: *to* sheathe *a sword.* **2** to enclose or cover fo protection: *to* sheathe *a roof with tin.*

Sheath

sheath·ing (shē′ thĭng, -thĭng) *n-* something that encases, covers, or protects, such as the copper casing on a ship's hull or the protective boarding on the outside of a frame house; also, the material used.

sheath knife *n-* knife with a fixed blade, designed to be worn on a belt in a sheath.

¹sheave (shēv) *vt-* [**sheaved, sheav·ing**] to gather and bind into bundles or sheaves: *to* sheave *wheat.* [from **sheaf,** from Old English *sceaf,* and related to **shove.**]

²sheave (shĭv, shēv) *n-* grooved wheel turning in a frame and used with a rope for raising weights; pulley. [variant form of **shive,** from Middle English *schēve.*]

sheaves (shēvz) *pl.* of **sheaf.**

She·ba (shē′ bə), **Queen of** *n-* in the Old Testament, a queen who visited King Solomon to find out for herself about his reputed wisdom.

she·bang (shə băng′) *Slang n-* business; concern; affair.

¹shed (shĕd) *vt-* [**shed, shed·ding**] **1** to pour out; let fall: *to* shed *tears.* **2** to cause to flow: *The war* shed *the blood of thousands.* **3** to pour forth; spread about: *The moon* shed *its light on us.* **4** to throw off; get rid of: *He* shed *his troubles as a duck* sheds *water.* **5** to cast away; let fall: *Our snake* sheds *its skin. vi-* to give off a covering: *The cat is starting to* shed. [from Old English *sc(e)ādan* meaning "to separate; cut apart."]

She·ol (shē′ ōl′, shē′ ōl′) *n-* in the Old Testament, the abode of departed spirits in the depths of the earth; the underworld or Hades.

shep·herd (shĕp′ ərd) *n-* 1 person who takes care of sheep. 2 minister, priest or other religious leader. *vt-* to take care of; guide; lead: *to shepherd students through a museum. n- fem.* **shep′herd·ess.**

sher·bet (shûr′ bət) *n-* frozen dessert made of fruit juices with water, milk, gelatin, etc.

sherd (shârd, *also* shûrd) shard.

she·rif (shə rēf′) *n-* a descendant of Mohammed through Fatima, his daughter; hence, a person of aristocratic birth in the Muslim world. Also **she·reef′, sha·rif′.**

sher·iff (shĕr′ if) *n-* chief law-enforcing officer of a county.

Sher·lock Holmes (shûr′ lŏk′ hōlmz) *n-* fictional detective created by Sir Arthur Conan Doyle.

sher·ry (shĕr′ ē) *n-* [*pl.* **sher·ries**] strong wine, light yellow to brown in color, originally made in Spain.

she's (shēz) 1 she is. 2 she has (auxiliary verb only).

Shet·land pony (shĕt′ lənd) *n-* one of a breed of small, shaggy ponies, originally from the Shetland Islands.

Shetland wool *n-* fine, loosely twisted yarn spun from the undercoat of Shetland sheep.

shew (shō) *Archaic* show.

shib·bo·leth (shĭb′ ə ləth) *n-* 1 custom or usage considered to identify members of a certain group. 2 party slogan or watchword.

shied (shīd) *p.t. & pp.* of **shy.**

shield (shēld) *n-* 1 leather- or metal-covered protective piece of armor once carried on the arm by soldiers. 2 anything that, or anyone who, protects: *Vaccination is a shield against smallpox.* 3 thing shaped like a soldier's shield. 4 movable barrier which protects miners or tunnel workers from a cave-in. 5 safety screen, as for moving machine parts. 6 plastic-lined cloth cover for the inside of the armhole of a garment to prevent soiling by perspiration. 7 in geology, a large portion of the earth's crust that has not been severely folded or distorted, but only gently warped. 8 in physics and electronics, any device or structure used to exclude or hold in unwanted radiations. A shield can be a metal box, a woven outer covering on a wire, a large and thick wall of lead, etc. *vt-* 1 to protect: *This tent will shield you against wind.* 2 to provide with a device that excludes or holds in unwanted radiation.

MEDIEVAL

GREEK

ROMAN

Shields

shi·er (shī′ ər) *compar.* of **shy.**

shies (shīz) form of the verb **shy** used with "he," "she," "it," or singular noun subjects in the present tense.

shi·est (shī′ əst) *superl.* of **shy.**

shift (shĭft) *vt-* to move from one person, place, or position to another: *to shift the blame; to shift a bundle from one hand to the other. vi-* 1 to change position or direction: *The load shifted.* 2 to change gears in a car. *n-* 1 a move from one person, place, position, to another; change: *a shift in jobs; a shift in ideas; a shift in the weather.* 2 group of people working at one time; also, the time during which the group works: *a night shift in a factory.* 3 trick; indirect method; expedient: *Tom tried every shift he could think of to avoid work.* 4 woman's dress, loosely fitted and with straight lines; also, formerly, a woman's undergarment. 5 gearshift. —*n-* **shift′ er.**

make shift to make do (with) what is available.

shift for oneself to make one's own way.

shift·less (shĭft′ləs) *adj-* without motivation or initiative; lazy; worthless. —*adv-* **shift′ less·ly.** *n-* **shift′ less·ness.**

shift·y (shĭf′ tē) *adj-* [**shift·i·er, shift·i·est**] 1 evasive; tricky; sly: *a shifty reply.* 2 capable; resourceful. —*adv-* **shift′ i·ly.** *n-* **shift′ i·ness.**

shi·kar (shik är′) *n-* in India, a wild-animal hunt.

shi·ka·ri (shik är′ ē) *n-* in India, a professional big-game hunter or guide.

shil·le·lagh or **shil·la·lah** (shə lā′ lē) *Irish n-* strong cudgel or club.

shil·ling (shĭl′ ing) *n-* unit of money in Great Britain, equal to twelve pence or one twentieth of a pound; also, a silver coin of this value.

shil·ly-shal·ly (shĭl′ ē shăl′ ē) *vi-* [**shil·ly-shal·lied, shil·ly-shal·ly·ing**] to hesitate; be indecisive; vacillate.

shim (shĭm) *n-* thin piece of metal, stone, or other material, used to adjust the fit of a machine part or structural member in a building.

shim·mer (shĭm′ ər) *vi-* to shine with a wavering light; glimmer: *Moonlight shimmers on the lake. n-* wavering light; sheen: *the shimmer of satin.* —*adj-* **shim′ mer·y.**

shim·my (shĭm′ ē) *n-* [*pl.* **shim·mies**] 1 a wiggling or shaking back and forth: *a shimmy in the front wheel.* 2 dance in which the body is moved in such a manner. *vi-* [**shim·mied, shim·my·ing**]: *The wheel shimmied.*

shin (shĭn) *n-* the forepart of the leg between the ankle and the knee. *vi-* [**shinned, shin·ning**] to climb with alternate grips of knees and hands: *Percy shinned up the tree. vt-: to shin a tree.*

Shin

shin·bone (shĭn′ bōn′) *n-* tibia.

shin·dig (shĭn′ dig′) *Slang n-* noisy party.

shine (shīn) *vi-* [**shone** (shōn) or **shined, shin·ing**] 1 to give off or reflect light or radiance; gleam: *The sun shone. His face shone with joy.* 2 to be best; excel: *Jenny shines in foreign languages. vt-* to cause to give forth a glow or luster; polish: *to shine silverware; to shine shoes. n-* 1 glow; radiance; luster: *the shine of new money.* 2 a polishing; especially, a polishing of shoes. 3 sunshine: *come rain or shine.*

take a shine to *Slang* to develop a liking for.

shine up to *Slang* to make friends with.

shin·er (shī′ nər) *n-* 1 person or thing that shines or polishes. 2 *Slang* black eye. 3 any of various small, silvery, fresh-water fishes related to the minnows.

¹**shin·gle** (shĭng′ gəl) *n-* 1 one of the thin, wedge-shaped boards placed on buildings in overlapping rows. 2 small signboard hung outside the office of a doctor, lawyer, etc. *vt-* [**shin·gled, shin·gling**] 1 to place shingles on (a building). 2 to cut (a woman's hair) short from the back of the head downward. [from Middle English **shindle,** from Latin **scindula** from **scindere,** "to split."]

Shingles

hang out (one's) shingle to establish oneself in a business or profession.

²**shin·gle** (shĭng′ gəl) *n-* rounded seashore pebbles, coarser than ordinary gravel; also, a beach or other area covered with such pebbles. [from Norwegian **singla,** "make a ringing sound," from **singa,** "sing." The meaning arises from the sound of walking or riding on gravel.]

shin·gles (shĭng′ gəlz) *n-* (takes singular or plural verb) painful skin disease caused by a virus and marked by small sores and blisters along the path of a nerve.

short·age (shôr′ tij, shôr′-) *n-* 1 amount lacking to complete anything: *There is a shortage of $50 in his bank account.* 2 too small a quantity to satisfy a need.

short·bread (shôrt′ brĕd′, shôrt′-) *n-* rich, crumbly cake or flat cookie made with much shortening.

short·cake (shôrt′ kāk′, shôrt′-) *n-* slightly sweetened biscuit or sponge cake, usually served with crushed berries as a dessert.

short–change (shôrt′ chānj′, shôrt′-) *Informal vt-* [**short-changed, short-chang·ing**] 1 to give less change than is due to (someone). 2 to fail to give what is rightfully due; cheat: *A lax teacher may short-change his students.*

short circuit *n-* electrical circuit, usually made by accident, in which the current flows to the ground or to the negative side of the source without passing through a resistance, motor, appliance, etc. Short circuits cause sparks and fire, and they damage equipment. *vt-* (**short-circuit**): *Too much power short-circuited the transformer. vi-: The whole power system short-circuited.*

short·com·ing (shôrt′ kŭm′ ing, shôrt′-) *n-* defect or deficiency; fault.

short cut *n-* route or method shorter than the regular one: *a short cut across the field; a short cut to success.*

short·en (shôr′ tən, shôr′-) *vt-* 1 to make shorter: *Mother shortened her coat.* 2 to add shortening to (cake or pastry dough). *vi-* to become shorter.

shut·ter·bug (shŭt′ ər bŭg′) *Slang n-* person who is enthusiastic about photography.

shut·tle (shŭt′ əl) *n-* 1 in weaving, an instrument in the shape of a cigar that carries the thread from side to side. 2 sewing machine device that holds thread and carries it back and forth to an upper thread to make a stitch. 3 anything that moves back and forth in a similar way; especially, a transport system that makes short trips back and forth between two points. *vt-* [**shut·tled, shut·tling**] to move back and forth frequently: *They shuttled Jim from job to job. vi-: He shuttled between jobs.*

shut·tle·cock (shŭt′ əl kŏk′) *n-* small cork ball with feathers or plastic imitation feathers, used in badminton.

Shuttlecock

¹**shy** (shī) *adj-* [**shi·er** or **shy·er, shi·est** or **shy·est**] 1 timid; bashful; self-conscious: *He was shy because it was his first day at school.* 2 *Informal* having a shortage of; short. *vi-* [**shied, shy·ing**] to jump; start; draw back quickly: *The horse shied at the car.* [from Old English scĕoh.] —*adv-* shy′ly. *n-* shy′ness. **fight shy of** to avoid; evade.

²**shy** (shī) *vt-* [**shied, shy·ing**] to throw with a sudden movement; to fling: *He shied a stone into the water. n-* [*pl.* **shies**] sudden throw; fling. [of uncertain origin.]

Shy·lock (shī′ lŏk′) *n-* in Shakespeare's "Merchant of Venice," a revengeful moneylender who requires a pound of flesh as a pledge for a loan to his enemy, Antonio.

shy·ster (shī′ stər) *Slang n-* sly and unscrupulous person in the practice of a profession, especially law.

¹**si** (sē) *Music n-* the seventh note of a musical scale. Also ti. [from Italian **si,** from the first letters of Latin **Sancte Ioannes,** "Saint John."] *Homs-* sea, see.

²**si** (sē) *adv-* word for "yes" in Spanish, Italian, and sometimes French.

Si symbol for silicon.

Si·a·mese (sī′ ə mēz′) *n-* native or inhabitant of Siam (now Thailand), its people, or their language. *adj-: in Siamese history.*

Siamese cat *n-* short-haired, blue-eyed cat with a fawn-colored body that is darker at the tips of the tail, feet, ears, and face. For picture, see *cat.*

Siamese twins *n- pl.* twins born joined together.

sib·i·lant (sĭb′ ə lənt) *n-* 1 consonant made by producing a hissing sound. 2 symbol for this consonant, such as "s," or "z." *adj-* 1 of or relating to such consonants. 2 hissing: *the sibilant sounds of a snake.* —*n-* sib′ i·lance.

sib·ling (sĭb′ lĭng) *n-* 1 brother or sister. 2 **siblings** brothers and sisters.

sib·yl (sĭb′ əl) *n-* 1 in ancient Greece and Rome, a woman who could foretell the future. 2 any prophetess.

¹**sic** (sĭk) *Latin* thus; so, placed in brackets after a quoted statement to show that, in spite of an obvious error, it is reproduced exactly. Example: "a yung [sic] man." *Hom-* sick.

²**sic** (sĭk) *vt-* [**sicked, sick·ing**] 1 to attack (used as a command to a dog): *Rover, sic him!* 2 to urge to attack: *He sicked a dog on us.* Also **sick.** [variant of **seek.**]

sick (sĭk) *adj-* [**sick·er, sick·est**] 1 ill; in poor health: *He's in bed,* sick. 2 vomiting or feeling as if one is going to vomit; nauseated: *Bus rides make him* sick. 3 greatly troubled or annoyed; disgusted: *It makes me* sick *to think of what he has done.* 4 annoyed and tired (of): *I'm* sick *of this weather.* 5 mentally ill or emotionally unbalanced; also, morbid; gruesome; macabre: *a sick mind; a sick joke; sick humor. Hom-* sic.

sick bay *n-* the hospital on a ship.

sick·bed (sĭk′ bĕd′) *n-* bed to which a sick person is confined.

sick·en (sĭk′ ən) *vt-* to make ill; also, to make disgusted: *The odor sickened her. vi-: She sickened at the thought.*

sick·en·ing (sĭk′ ən ĭng) *adj-* causing nausea or disgust; revolting: *a sickening odor.* —*adv-* sick′ en·ing·ly.

sick·room (sĭk′ rōōm′) *n-* room to which a sick person is confined.

sic tran·sit glo·ri·a mun·di (sĭk trăn′ sĭt glôr′ ē ə mŭn′ dĭ, -mōōn′ dē) *Latin* thus passes away the glory of this world.

sight·ly (sīt′ lē) *adj-* [**sight·li·er, sight·li·est**] pleasing to the eye; attractive. —*n-* sight′ li·ness.

sight·see·ing (sīt′ sē′ ĭng) *n-* a visiting of places of interest: *I love sightseeing in Paris. as modifier: a sightseeing trip.* —*n-* sight′ se′ er.

sign (sīn) *n-* 1 a lettered board or plate giving the name of a business, information, etc.: *a shoemaker's* sign; *a road* sign. 2 a mark or character that stands for a thing or an idea; symbol: *The Cross is the* sign *of the Christian religion.* 3 something by which something else is made known; indication or indicator: *His gift was a* sign *of his love. This skin rash is a* sign *of an allergy.* 4 motion or gesture used instead of words to express some wish, thought, or command: *The policeman gave a* sign *to the driver to stop.* 5 omen; portent. 6 anything left by an animal showing where it was; trail; trace; scent: *There were deer* signs *in the woods.* 7 one of the 12 equal divisions of the zodiac, or its symbol. 8 *Mathematics* (1) symbol used to indicate a mathematical operation such as addition or multiplication, as [+] or [×]. (2) symbol that represents a certain relation between two or more quantities, as [<] (less than) or [>] (greater than). (3) one of two symbols [+] (plus) or [—] (minus) that precedes a numeral or a variable and indicates, respectively, a positive or a negative value. *vt-* 1 to write (one's name) as a signature. 2 to write one's name at the end of: *to* sign *a letter.* 3 to hire by getting the signature of: *The foreman* signed *another carpenter.* 4 to guarantee to be genuine by putting one's signature, initials, or mark on: *to* sign *a check; to* sign *a work of art. vi-* 1 to write one's signature: *He* signed *on the dotted line.* 2 to motion; signal: *He* signed *for them to approach.* 3 to agree to the terms of a contract by putting one's signature to it: *The ballplayer* signed *for the next season. Hom-* sine. —*n-* sign′ er.

sign away to waive or renounce (a right, claim, etc.) by or as if by putting one's signature on a document.

sign off to announce the end of a radio or television program and stop broadcasting for the day.

sign on to agree to work for someone.

sig·nal (sĭg′ nəl) *n-* 1 sign agreed upon for sending information, instructions, notice of danger, etc.: *a train* signal; *a fire* signal; *a* signal *of distress.* 2 something that brings about action: *The shout of "Fire!" was a* signal *for panic.* 3 in radio, television, radar, etc., the modulation of an electromagnetic wave or electric current that transmits a sound, image, or message; also, the wave or current itself. 4 **signals** in football, numbers called out by the quarterback in announcing the play or as an indication of the instant it should start. *as modifier: a signal light. adj-* remarkable; extraordinary; memorable: *The affair was a* signal *success. vt-* to communicate with, inform, or notify by signs: *The captain* signaled *us to come to. vi-: I* signaled *for help.*

signal flag *n-* flag of special design that represents a letter of the alphabet, a numeral, or a message; also, a flag used for signaling by waving or holding it in certain positions.

sig·nal·ize (sĭg′ nə līz′) *vt-* [**sig·nal·ized, sig·nal·iz·ing**] to make noteworthy or prominent; mark; distinguish; characterize: *Poets* signalized *the reign of Elizabeth I.*

sig·nal·ly (sĭg′ nə lē) *adv-* in a remarkable or striking manner; notably: *The meeting hall was* signally *quiet.*

sig·na·tor·y (sĭg′ nə tôr′ ē) *n-* [*pl.* **sig·na·tor·ies**] person or nation that has signed an official document such as a treaty, charter, etc. *adj-* having to do with or bound by the terms of such a document: *the* signatory *powers.*

sign·board (sīn′ bôrd′) *n-* board with a sign, advertisement, or notice on it.

sig·net (sĭg′ nət) *n-* a seal; official stamp.

signet ring *n-* finger ring bearing a signet, formerly used for sealing letters and other documents.

sig·nif·i·cance (sĭg nĭf′ ə kəns) *n-* 1 meaning; sense: *I don't understand the* significance *of your remark.* 2 importance: *an event of great* significance *in history.*

sig·nif·i·cant (sĭg nĭf′ ə kənt) *adj-* 1 important; notable: *a significant improvement.* 2 having a special meaning; expressive; suggestive. —*adv-* sig·nif′ i·cant·ly.

Sis·y·phus (sis′ə fəs) *n-* in Greek mythology, a greedy king of Corinth who in Hades was condemned forever to roll uphill a huge stone that always rolled back down.

sit (sĭt) *vi-* [**sat** (săt), **sit·ting**] 1 to rest one's weight on the lower part of the body; be seated: *He sits in an easy chair after supper.* 2 to perch or roost, as a bird does. 3 to cover eggs to be hatched, as a hen does. 4 to have place or position; be situated: *The trunk sits on the floor. The island sits in the harbor.* 5 to occupy a seat as a member of a council or assembly: *to sit in the state legislature.* 6 to meet or be in session: *The court will sit next week.* 7 to press or weigh: *His duties sat heavily on him.* 8 to pose or model: *to sit for a portrait.* 9 to fit or suit: *Her jacket doesn't sit well in the shoulders.* *vt-* 1 to seat: *He sat the boy down and gave him a lecture.* 2 to maintain the proper position on (a riding animal): *He sits a horse well.*

sit down 1 to take a seat. 2 to begin a siege.

sit in on to take part in; participate in.

sit on (or **upon**) 1 to meet in judgment on. 2 to be a member of: *to sit on a jury or committee.*

sit out 1 to remain seated during: *to sit out a dance.* 2 to wait through; endure: *to sit out a storm.*

sit up 1 to raise the body to an upright sitting position: *to sit up in bed.* 2 to pay attention: *His great speed made the other players sit up and watch.* 3 to stay up past one's usual bedtime.

►The principal forms of SIT are SIT, SAT, SAT. *We sat for a long time. She sat her baby on the sofa.* Do not confuse this with SET, which has a different meaning.

sit-down strike (sit′doun′ strīk′) *n-* strike during which workers remain in their place of employment until an agreement is reached.

site (sīt) *n-* 1 place where something is or was situated: *the site of the battle.* 2 area set aside for a particular purpose: *the building site.* *Homs-* cite, sight.

sit-in (sit′ ĭn′) *n-* a protest demonstration in which people sit down in a public place and refuse to leave.

sit·ter (sit′ ər) *n-* 1 person who sits, especially in a seat or for a portrait. 2 baby sitter. 3 hen that sits on eggs to hatch them.

sit·ting (sit′ĭng) *n-* 1 session or meeting of a court, legislature, etc. 2 period of posing or act of posing: *a sitting for a portrait.* 3 group of eggs for hatching.

at one sitting at one time; without a break.

sitting duck *Informal n-* any easy target, like a duck sitting still on the water.

sitting room *n-* living room; parlor.

sit·u·ate (sĭch′ŏŏ āt′) *vt-* [**sit·u·at·ed, sit·u·at·ing**] to place in a location; locate: *Where will you situate the new factory?*

sit·u·at·ed (sĭch′ŏŏ ā′təd) *adj-* 1 placed; located: *a properly situated fort.* 2 living in a certain condition or at a certain level with respect to wealth, social standing, etc.: *He is comfortably situated financially.*

sit·u·a·tion (sĭch′ŏŏ ā′shən) *n-* 1 place; location. 2 circumstances; state of affairs: *an amusing situation.* 3 job; position. —*adj-* sit′u·a′tion·al.

situation comedy *n-* comedy in which the characters are placed in amusing or ridiculous predicaments, often highly improbable.

sit-up (sit′ ŭp′) *n-* conditioning exercise done by lying flat on the back and raising the head and trunk to an upright position repeatedly.

Si·va (sē′ və, shē′-) Shiva.

six (sĭks) *n-* 1 amount or quantity that is one greater than 5. 2 *Mathematics* (1) the cardinal number that is the sum of 5 and 1. (2) a numeral such as 6 that represents this cardinal number. *as determiner* (traditionally called adjective or pronoun): *There are six boxes here and six there.*

six·pence (sĭks′ pəns) *n-* small British silver coin worth half a shilling.

six-shoot·er (sĭks′ shŏŏ′ tər) *Informal n-* revolver that can fire six bullets without reloading.

six·teen (sĭks′ tēn′) *n-* 1 amount or quantity that is one greater than 15. 2 *Mathematics* (1) the cardinal number that is the sum of 15 and 1. (2) a numeral such as 16 that represents this cardinal number. *as determiner* (traditionally called adjective or pronoun): *There are sixteen persons here and sixteen there.*

six·teenth (sĭks′ tēnth′) *adj-* 1 next after fifteenth. 2 the ordinal of 16; 16th. *n-* 1 the next after the fifteenth; 16th. 2 one of sixteen equal parts of a whole or group. 3 the last term in the name of a fraction having a denominator of 16: *1/16 is one* sixteenth.

sixteenth note *Music n-* note held one sixteenth as long as a whole note. For picture, see *note.*

sixth (sĭksth) *adj-* 1 next after fifth. 2 the ordinal of 6; 6th. *n-* 1 the next after the fifth; 6th. 2 one of six equal parts of a whole or group. 3 the last term in the name of a fraction having a denominator of 6: *1/6 is one* sixth. 4 *Music* an interval of six tones on the scale counting the extremes, as from C to A, and the harmonic combination of these tones. *adv-: He called my name* sixth.

sixth·ly (sĭksth′ lē) *adv-* as sixth in a series.

sixth sense *n-* acute power of perception, regarded as a sense independent of the five senses; intuition.

six·ti·eth (sĭks′ tē əth) *adj-* 1 next after fifty-ninth. 2 the ordinal of 60; 60th. *n-* 1 the next after the fifty-ninth; 60th. 2 one of sixty equal parts of a whole or group. 3 the last term in the name of a fraction having a denominator of 60: *1/60 is one* sixtieth.

six·ty (sĭks′ tē) *n-* [*pl.* **six·ties**] 1 amount or quantity that is one greater than 59. 2 *Mathematics* (1) the cardinal number that is the sum of 59 and 1. (2) a numeral such as 60 that represents this cardinal number. *as determiner* (traditionally called adjective or pronoun): *There are sixty boxes here and sixty there.*

like sixty *Informal* very fast: *He ran like sixty.*

siz·a·ble or **size·a·ble** (sī′ zə bəl) *adj-* of considerable size, amount, or quantity; fairly large: *a sizable business; a sizable profit.* —*adv-* siz′a·bly or size′a·bly. *n-* siz′a·ble·ness or size′a·ble·ness.

¹**size** (sīz) *n-* 1 amount of height, width, or thickness of a thing; dimensions: *the size of a hat, room, or tire.* 2 largeness or smallness; bulk: *Notice the size of that spider.* 3 a measure showing how large something is: *What size is that dress?* 4 *Informal* actual fact; truth: *That's the size of it.* *vt-* [**sized, siz·ing**] 1 to arrange in order of bulk, height, volume, or extent. 2 to make or shape to certain dimensions. [from a shortened form of Middle English *assize* meaning "that which is fixed," from Late Latin *assisa,* "an assembly or sitting; judges."]

of a size of the same size.

size up 1 to form an opinion of; estimate; judge: *She sized him up carefully.* 2 to meet certain standards.

►For usage note see SIZED.

²**size** (sīz) *n-* (also **siz′ ing**) any of various thin pastes or glues used to glaze paper, cloth, walls, etc., or make them heavier. *vt-* [**sized, siz·ing**] to cover or treat with this type of paste or glue. [from Old French *sise,* from *assise,* or from earlier Italian *siza.*]

skimp·y (skĭm′ pē) *adj-* [**skimp·i·er, skimp·i·est**] scanty; inadequate: *I had a very skimpy breakfast.* —*adv-* skimp′i·ly. *n-* skimp′i·ness.

skin (skĭn) *n-* 1 outer covering of the body in man and animals. 2 pelt or hide of an animal after it is removed from the body: *a rug made of the skin of a tiger.* 3 rind of a fruit: *orange skin; banana skin.* 4 any thin covering that surrounds completely: *the skin of a frankfurter.* 5 container made of skin for liquids such as wine or water. *as modifier: a skin disease.* *vt-* [**skinned, skin·ning**] 1 to remove the covering of (an animal or bird): *to skin a rabbit.* 2 to scrape: *to skin a knee in a fall.* 3 *Slang* to defraud. —*adj-* skin′ less.

have a thick skin to be insensitive; be difficult to hurt by rebuke, criticism, or unkindness. **have a thin skin** to be sensitive; be easily hurt by rebuke, unkindness, or criticism. **mere skin and bones** extremely thin or skinny. **save one's skin** to escape with one's life. **the skin of one's teeth** a narrow margin.

skin-deep (skĭn′ dēp′) *adj-* 1 on the surface of the skin: *a skin-deep cut.* 2 superficial: *Her beauty is skin-deep.*

EPIDERMIS

PAPILLA

DERMIS

SWEAT GLAND

HAIR FOLLICLE

BLOOD VESSEL

Human skin, cross section

sleeping porch *n-* porch or veranda, often on an upper story, that is open to the air on one or more sides and arranged to permit sleeping.

sleeping sickness *n-* disease of the central nervous system characterized by dizziness and often death. It is caused by a trypanosome and is transmitted by the bite of the tsetse fly, common in tropical Africa.

sleep·less (slēp′ləs) *adj-* 1 without sleep: *a sleepless night.* 2 constantly active; restless: *the sleepless sea.* —*adv-* **sleep′less·ly.** *n-* **sleep′less·ness.**

sleep·walk·er (slēp′wó′ kər) *n-* person who walks in his sleep; somnambulist. —*n-* **sleep′walk′ing.**

sleep·y (slē′ pē) *adj-* [**sleep·i·er, sleep·i·est**] 1 drowsy; ready for sleep. 2 inactive: *a sleepy village.* —*adv-* **sleep′i·ly.** *n-* **sleep′i·ness.**

sleep·y·head (slē′ pē hĕd′) *n-* sleepy person.

sleet (slēt) *n-* frozen or partially frozen rain. *vi-* to fall from the air as frozen or partially frozen rain. —*adj-* **sleet′ y.** *n-* **sleet′ i·ness.**

sleeve (slēv) *n-* 1 that part of a garment which covers the arm. 2 tubular part of a machine, designed to fit over another part. —*adj-* **sleeved.** *adj-* **sleeve′less.**
up one's sleeve ready for use when needed.

sleigh (slā) *n-* vehicle on runners, used on snow or ice. *vi-* to travel by or ride in such a vehicle. *Hom-* slay.

sleigh·ing (slā′ ĭng) *n-* 1 a riding or traveling in a sleigh. 2 condition of the snow or ice which admits of the use of sleighs.

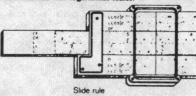
Sleigh

sleight (slīt) *n-* 1 dexterity or skill. 2 artful trick; especially, a trick done so expertly and quickly as to deceive the eye. *Hom-* slight.

sleight of hand *n-* tricks or skill of a juggler or magician; legerdemain.

slen·der (slĕn′ dər) *adj-* [**slen·der·er, slen·der·est**] 1 slim; thin: *a slender figure.* 2 weak; slight: *a slender possibility.* —*adv-* **slen′der·ly.** *n-* **slen′der·ness.**

slen·der·ize (slĕn′ də rīz′) *vt-* [**slen·der·ized, slen·der·iz·ing**] to make slender: *a diet to slenderize the figure.*

slept (slĕpt) *p.t. & p.p.* of **sleep.**

sleuth (slōōth) *n-* detective. *vi-* to act as a detective.

sleuth·hound (slōōth′ hound′) *n-* bloodhound.

¹slew (slōō) *p.t.* of **slay.**

²slew (slōō) *Informal n-* a great number; a lot of. [American word probably from Irish *sluagh,* "a crowd."]

³slew (slōō) **¹slue.** [of uncertain origin.]

slice (slīs) *n-* 1 flat section cut from something: *a slice of bread.* 2 in golf, a ball's path of flight curving to the right away from a right-handed player; also, stroke that causes this. 3 *chiefly Brit.* a flat-bladed food server. *vt-* [**sliced, slic·ing**] 1 to cut into thin, flat pieces; also, to cut with or as if with a knife: *He sliced the roast. The destroyer sliced the waves.* 2 to cut (a thin, flat piece) from a big piece: *He sliced off a piece of meat.* 3 of a right-handed golfer, to hit (a ball) so that it curves to the right. *vi-* in golf, to make such a stroke. —*n-* **slic′er.**

slick (slĭk) *adj-* [**slick·er, slick·est**] 1 smooth and glossy: *a slick paper.* 2 smooth and silky in speech and manner; tricky; also, ingenious; cleverly done, said, or devised; skillful: *a slick salesman.* 3 slippery. 4 *Slang* excellent; very good. *n-* 1 smooth place or spot, especially an oil-covered area on a surface of water. 2 a magazine printed on glossy paper. *vt-* to smooth down; make glossy. —*adv-* **slick′ly.** *n-* **slick′ness.**
slick up *Informal* to make smart or neat; spruce up.

slick·er (slĭk′ ər) *n-* 1 long, loose waterproof coat made of oiled or varnished cloth. 2 *Informal* clever, devious person.

slide (slīd) *vi-* [**slid** (slĭd), **slid** or **slid·den** (slĭd′ ən), **slid·ing**] 1 to move smoothly along on a surface. 2 to move quietly or without being seen: *The cat slid back into the room.* 3 to lose one's foothold; shift from a position; slip: *The plate slid from her hands.* 4 to pass gradually: *The days slid by during vacation.* 5 to back-slide. *vt-* to cause to move smoothly: *to slide a drawer*

into a chest. *n-* 1 smooth move; glide. 2 any smooth surface, either flat or sloping, on which a person or thing may move: *a slide in a playground.* 3 piece of glass on which one puts objects to examine them under a microscope. 4 transparent picture that can be projected on a screen or wall. 5 mass of earth, rock, snow, etc., that falls down a steep slope; avalanche: *a rock slide.*
let slide to let go by; postpone.
slide over to pass over quickly.

slide fastener *n-* zipper.

slide projector *n-* device that projects photographic slides on a screen or wall.

slid·er (slī′ dər) *n-* 1 person who slides; also, sliding thing. 2 any of several North American terrapins.

slide rule *n-* instrument for quick mathematical computation, consisting of a ruler with a sliding central part, both marked with logarithmic scales.

Slide rule

slid·ing (slī′ dĭng) *adj-* 1 moving in or as if in a groove: *a sliding door.* 2 varying with changing conditions: *a sliding scale of wages.*

slight (slīt) *adj-* [**slight·er, slight·est**] 1 slender; thin. 2 not important: *a slight error.* 3 small in amount or degree: *a slight hope; a slight trace of gas.* *n-* a show of disrespect or neglect; snub. *vt-* 1 to insult: *They slighted Dotty by not inviting her.* 2 to pay little attention to: *Jack's football practice caused him to slight his studies.* *Hom-* sleight. —*n-* **slight′ness.**

slight·ing (slī′ tĭng) *adj-* showing indifference or discourtesy; disparaging: *to speak in slighting terms; a slighting remark.* —*adv-* **slight′ing·ly.**

slight·ly (slīt′ lē) *adv-* 1 to a small or unimportant degree: *I am slightly ill.* 2 slenderly: *She is very slightly built.*

sli·ly (slī′ lē) *adv-* in a sly manner; slyly.

slim (slĭm) *adj-* [**slim·mer, slim·mest**] 1 slender; thin: *a slim figure.* 2 slight or scant; also, insufficient: *a slim excuse.* *vt-* [**slimmed, slim·ming**] to make slender: *Her new dress slims her waist.* *vi-* (often followed by "down") to become slimmer: *She ought to slim down.* —*adv-* **slim′ ly.** *n-* **slim′ ness.**

slime (slīm) *n-* 1 soft, slippery mud. 2 any sticky, slippery, or unpleasant substance; filth. 3 sticky substance given off by certain animals, such as snails.

slot (slŏt) *n-* 1 straight, narrow opening or channel; slit. 2 hole designed to receive a door bolt or machine part; hence, any suitable opening. *vt-* [**slot·ted, slot·ting**] to cut a slit or slits in.

sloth (slŏth, slôth, slōth) *n-* 1 extreme laziness; dislike of effort. 2 any of various slow-moving mammals of South and Central America that live in trees and cling upside down to the branches.

sloth bear *n-* black bear of Ceylon and India that feeds chiefly on fruit and honey.

sloth·ful (slŏth′ fəl, slôth′-, slōth′-) *adj-* very lazy; slow to act. —*adv-* **sloth′ful·ly.** *n-* **sloth′ful·ness.**

Two-toed sloth, about 2 ft long

slot machine *n-* 1 gambling machine worked by inserting a coin into a slot. 2 vending machine.

slouch (slouch) *vi-* 1 to act with slow, loose-jointed movements; shamble: *Leon slouched lazily to school.* 2 to stand or sit with the back curved and the shoulders drooping: *Marie slouched in her chair.* *n-* 1 drooping, loose-jointed posture: *to walk with a slouch.* 2 person who habitually acts in this manner.
no slouch (at) very good (at).

snare drum *n-* small drum the lower head of which has catgut strings that rattle when the upper head is struck.

¹**snarl** (snärl) *n-* 1 angry or vicious growl with the teeth exposed. 2 angry, rough tone of voice. *vi-* 1 to show the teeth and make a growling noise: *Rover snarled at the strangers.* 2 to speak in a rough, angry tone of voice: *Mr. Jones snarled at the noisy children. vt-* to utter in a rough, angry way; growl out: *He snarled commands.* [from earlier English *snar,* probably from a Germanic imitation of the sound.] *—n- snarl′ er. adv- snarl′ ing·ly.*

²**snarl** (snärl) *n-* 1 tangle; knot: *a snarl in one's hair.* 2 any disordered, chaotic condition: *Traffic here is in a continual snarl. vt-* to tangle or entangle: *The kitten snarled the ball of wool. Unexpected visitors snarled our plans. vi-: The wool snarled.* [probably from ¹**snare**.]

¹**snarl·y** (snär′ lē) *adj-* [snarl·i·er, snarl·i·est] ill-tempered; growly. [from ¹**snarl**.]

²**snarl·y** (snär′ lē) *adj-* [snarl·i·er, snarl·i·est] full of snarls. [from ²**snarl**.]

snatch (snăch) *vt-* to grab or try to grab suddenly or rudely; seize: *to snatch a purse; to snatch victory from defeat. n-* 1 quick, grabbing motion: *to make a snatch at a rope.* 2 small piece, bit, or period of time: *a snatch of music; to sleep in snatches. —n- snatch′ er.*

snatch at to make a quick, grasping motion toward.

snatch·y (snăch′ ē) *adj-* [snatch·i·er, snatch·i·est] not continuous; interrupted; irregular.

sneak (snēk) *vi-* 1 to move or go in a secret or sly way; slink: *She sneaked into the house after everyone was asleep.* 2 to act in a sly or furtive way: *Why do you sneak instead of acting openly? vt-* to take in a furtive way; steal. *n-* 1 sly, underhanded person. 2 a stealthy and surreptitious movement. *as modifier: a sneak attack.*

sneak·ers (snē′ kərz) *Informal n-* pl. canvas shoes with rubber soles, used for sports.

sneak·ing (snē′ kĭng) *adj-* 1 sly and underhanded; furtive: *a sneaking glance.* 2 not openly acknowledged; unavowed; secret: *a sneaking ambition to act; a sneaking suspicion that he is right. —adv- sneak′ ing·ly.*

sneak thief *n-* petty thief who steals without using force.

sneak·y (snē′ kē) *adj-* [sneak·i·er, sneak·i·est] sly, stealthy and furtive; also, underhanded. *—adv- sneak′ i·ly. n- sneak′ i·ness.*

sneer (snēr) *n-* 1 look of contempt or scorn made by slightly curling the upper lip. 2 contemptuous or scornful remark: *I have had enough of his sneers. vi-: She sneered at his offer to help. vt-: He sneered his disfavor. —n- sneer′ er. adv- sneer′ ing·ly.*

sneeze (snēz) *n-* sudden, explosive burst of breath through the mouth and nostrils. *vi-* [sneezed, sneez·ing]: *The dust made her sneeze. —n- sneez′ er.*

not to be sneezed at *Informal* not to be scorned.

snell (snĕl) *n-* short piece of leader whipped on a fishhook to attach it to a line. *—adj- snelled.*

snick·er (snĭk′ ər) *n-* sly laugh indicating scorn, disrespect, or amusement; giggle; titter. *vi-: Tom snickered at Fred's clumsy movements.* Also **snigger.**

snide (snīd) *adj-* [snid·er, snid·est] slyly malicious or disparaging; nasty. *—adv- snide′ ly. n- snide′ ness.*

sniff (snĭf) *vi-* 1 to draw air through the nostrils in short breaths that can be heard: *I sniffed but couldn't smell a thing.* 2 to express contempt by, or by such a breath: *She sniffed at my attempt to be funny.* 3 to breathe in; inhale: *He sniffed the morning air.* 2 to test by means of odor; smell: *to sniff expensive perfume.* 3 to detect or recognize; perceive: *to sniff danger; to sniff a revolt. n-* 1 short intake of air that can be heard; also, the sound made by this. 2 act of smelling: *a sniff of perfume.*

snip·py (snĭp′ ē) *adj-* [snip·pi·er, snip·pi·est] *Informal* 1 short and curt in speaking; snappy. 2 saucy and impertinent. Also **snip′ pet·y.** *—adv- snip′ pi·ness.*

snitch (snĭch) *Informal vt-* to steal; swipe. *vi-* to tattle or inform (on) someone.

sniv·el (snĭv′ əl) *vi-* 1 to complain in a weak, tearful manner. 2 to run at the nose; snuffle. *—n- sniv′ el·er.*

snob (snŏb) *n-* 1 person who values wealth and social position above all else, and scorns or patronizes those who do not have them. 2 someone who thinks himself better than others in some way: *an intellectual snob.*

snob·ber·y (snŏb′ ə rē) *n-* conduct of a snob.

snob·bish (snŏb′ ĭsh) *adj-* of or like a snob. *—adv- snob′ bish·ly. n- snob′ bish·ness.*

snood (snŏŏd) *n-* coarse net for holding a woman's hair.

snook (snŏŏk) *n-* [*pl.* **snook; snooks** (kinds of snook)] large game and food fish of warm seas.

snoop (snŏŏp) *vi-* to search in a sneaky way; pry: *He snooped through my desk when I wasn't home. n- Informal* (also **snoop′ er**) person who pries.

snoot·y (snŏŏ′ tē) *Informal adj-* [snoot·i·er, snoot·i·est] haughty; snobbish. *—adv- snoot′ i·ly. n- snoot′ i·ness.*

snooze (snŏŏz) *Informal vi-* [snoozed, snooz·ing] to doze; take a nap. *n-* nap; doze.

snore (snôr) *vi-* [snored, snor·ing] to breathe with a hoarse noise while sleeping. *n-* noisy, hoarse breathing of a sleeping person.

snor·kel (snôr′ kəl, snôr′-) *n-* 1 on submarines, a system of tubes to take air in and out while the submarine is submerged. 2 J-shaped tube, worn by swimmers to permit breathing while the face is under water. *vi-* to swim with such a tube to observe marine life.

snort (snôrt, snôrt) *n-* harsh noise made by forcing air out through the nostrils. *vi-* 1 to make such a noise. 2 to express anger or contempt by a harsh nasal sound: *He snorted with rage. vt-* to utter with a harsh nasal sound: *He snorted his answer to me. —n- snort′ er.*

snout (snout) *n-* 1 projecting nose, and sometimes mouth and jaws, of an animal; muzzle: *a pig's snout.* 2 something, such as a nozzle, that resembles this.

snow (snō) *n-* 1 groups of ice crystals matted together to form flattened, feathery flakes as a result of slow crystallization of water vapor at a temperature less than 32°. 2 such flakes while still falling, or an accumulation of them lying on the ground. 3 a fall of snow, or a

so·ci·e·ty (sə sī′ ə tē) *n-* [*pl.* **so·ci·e·ties**] 1 community of people living together at a particular time and place; also, all people collectively: *The police exist to protect society.* 2 persons joined together for a common aim. 3 class of people of wealth and fashion; also, their activities: *She reports on society for the newspaper.* 4 company; companionship: *We missed his society after he moved away. as modifier: a society column.*

Society of Friends *n-* dissenting Christian sect founded in England by George Fox around 1650. It stresses "Inner Light," rejects outer rites and ceremonies, and opposes war. Also known as **Quakers.**

Society of Jesus *n-* the Roman Catholic religious order of Jesuits founded by St. Ignatius of Loyola in 1534.

so·ci·o·e·co·nom·ic (sō′ sē ō ĕk′ ə nŏm′ ĭk, sō′ shē ō-) *adj-* of or having to do with a combination of social and economic matters: *Poverty is a socio-economic problem.*

so·ci·ol·o·gist (sō′ sē ŏl′ ə jĭst, so′ shē-) *n-* person trained in sociology and engaged in it as a profession.

so·ci·ol·o·gy (sō′ sē ŏl′ ə jē, sō′ shē-) *n-* the social science that deals with human society, including its development, forms, and relationships. *—adj- so′ ci·o·log′ i·cal* (-ə lŏj′ ĭ kəl). *adv- so′ ci·o·log′ i·cal·ly.*

¹**sock** (sŏk) *n-* short stocking reaching above the ankle but below the knee. [from Old English *socc,* from Latin *soccus* meaning "light shoe; comedian's buskin."]

²**sock** (sŏk) *Slang vt-* to hit or strike with the fist; punch. *n-* a blow with the fist; punch. [of uncertain origin.]

sock·et (sŏk′ ət) *n-* a hollow into which something is fitted, fastened, or secured: *the socket of the eye.*

So·crat·ic (sə krăt′ ĭk) *adj-* of or relating to Socrates or to his method of teaching. *n-* follower of Socrates.

sod (sŏd) *n-* 1 layer of soil containing grass and its roots; turf. 2 piece of this, usually cut square. *vt-* [sod·ded, sod·ding] to cover with sod: *to sod a path.*

ELECTRIC LAMP

CURTAIN ROD

Sockets

soda fountain *n-* 1 counter, often in a drug store, at which soda water, soft drinks, ice cream, sandwiches, etc., are prepared and sold. 2 apparatus with faucets for dispensing soda water.

¹-some *suffix* (used to form adjectives) **1** showing a tendency to: *venture*some; *tire*some. **2** rather or somewhat: *blithe*some; *light*some. [from Old-English -sum, and related to **some** and **same**.]

²-some *suffix* (used to form nouns) specific group of: *a four*some. [from **some**.]

³-some (sŏm) *combining form* body: *chromo*some. [from Greek *sōma* meaning "body."]

some·bod·y (sŭm′bŏd′ē, -bŭd′ē) *pron-* some person; someone: *I think somebody has borrowed my umbrella.* *n-* [pl. **some·bod·ies**] an important person: *Having that new car makes her think she is somebody.*

some·day (sŭm′dā′) *adv-* on some future day; also, at some future time: *We will talk someday soon.*

some·how (sŭm′hou′) *adv-* **1** in one way or another; in some way: *We'll get home somehow.* **2** for some reason or other: *I somehow don't like the candidate.*

some·one (sŭm′wŭn′) *pron-* some person; somebody.

som·er·sault (sŭm′ər sŏlt′) *vi-* to leap, roll, or dive and turn head over heels. *n-* such a leap, roll, or dive. Also **som′er·set′** (-sĕt′).

some·thing (sŭm′thĭng′) *pron-* **1** particular thing not specified: *The baby wants something to play with.* **2** thing not definitely known or understood: *There is something strange about that house.* *n-* a person or thing of importance: *It's something to own property.* *adv-* somewhat; rather: *You look something like him.*   **something of** somewhat of.

some·time (sŭm′tīm′) *adv-* at a time or date not known or exactly indicated: *The trains stopped running sometime last year.* *adj-* former: *a sometime football star.*

some·times (sŭm′tīmz′) *adv-* now and then; from time to time; once in a while: *We go there sometimes.*

some·way or **some way** (sŭm′wā′) *adv-* in an unspecified manner; somehow: *I'll get there someway.*

some·what (sŭm′hwăt, -hwət′) *adv-* to some extent; in some degree; rather: *She is somewhat lazy.* *pron-* Archaic something.   **somewhat of** having some of the characteristics of: *It was somewhat of a surprise to see him.*

some·where (sŭm′hwâr′) *adv-* **1** in, at, or to some place not known or named: *I've left my gloves somewhere.* **2** sometime: *I'll be there somewhere around nine.*

som·nam·bu·lism (sŏm năm′byə lĭz′əm) *n-* active behavior, resembling many of the activities of the waking state, carried on by a sleeping person; sleepwalking.   *—n-* **som′nam′bu·list**.

som·no·lence (sŏm′nə ləns) *n-* sleepiness; drowsiness.

som·no·lent (sŏm′nə lənt) *adj-* **1** sleepy; drowsy; heavy with sleep. **2** tending to cause sleep; also, marked by quiet, lazy peace: *the somnolent drone of the engines.*

son (sŭn) *n-* **1** boy or man in relation to his parents. **2** male descendant: *the sons of Jacob.* **3** male who is representative of or closely related to a nation, cause, etc.: *a true son of France.* **4** the Son Jesus Christ.

so·nar (sō′när′) *n-* device that detects and locates objects under water by means of sound waves reflected back from them. *as modifier:* *a sonar reading.* [shortened from *sound navigation and ranging.*]

so·na·ta (sə nä′tə) *Music n-* composition in three or four movements, usually for one or two instruments.

song (sŏng) *n-* **1** music produced by the human voice. **2** particular set of words sung to a melody; also, the

song·bird (sŏng′bûrd′) *n-* bird that sings, such as a canary, thrush, or nightingale.

song·book (sŏng′bŏŏk′) *n-* book of songs.

song·less (sŏng′ləs) *adj-* **1** unable to sing: *a songless bird.* **2** devoid of song; without singing.

Song of Solomon or **Song of Songs** *n-* twenty-second book of the Old Testament. In the CCD Bible, the **Canticle of Canticles**.

song sparrow *n-* singing sparrow of eastern United States, having a streaked breast with one large spot.

song·ster (sŏng′stər) *n-* **1** singing bird. **2** man who sings. **3** writer of songs or poetry. *—n- fem.* **song′ stress**.

son·ic (sŏn′ĭk) *adj-* **1** of, having to do with, or caused by sound: *a sonic vibration.* **2** at or near the speed of sound: *a sonic airplane flight.*

sonic barrier *n-* sudden increase in drag on an aircraft as it approaches the speed of sound; sound barrier.

sonic boom *n-* noise caused by a convergence of shock waves from an airplane traveling at or above the speed of sound.

son-in-law (sŭn′ In lô′) *n-* [pl. **sons-in-law**] husband of one's daughter.

son·net (sŏn′ət) *n-* fourteen-line poem usually having ten-syllable lines, and consisting of either three quatrains and a couplet (**Shakespearean sonnet**) or an octave and a sestet (**Italian sonnet**).

son·net·eer (sŏn′ə tēr′) *n-* person who writes sonnets.

son·ny (sŭn′ē) *Informal n-* little boy (used as a form of address). [from sonny.]

so·nor·i·ty (sə nôr′ə tē, sə nŏr′-) *n-* [pl. **so·nor·i·ties**] **1** depth, fullness, and richness of tone: *the sonority of the bass section; the sonority of his verse.* **2** word or phrase rendered in such tones: *a speech full of sonorities.*

so·no·rous (sə nôr′əs, sŏn′ər əs) *adj-* having sonority: *a sonorous voice.* *—adv-* **so·nor′ous·ly** or **son′or·ous·ly**.

soon (sōōn) *adv-* [**soon·er, soon·est**] **1** in a short time from now; before long: *We shall soon be having snow.* **2** shortly; quickly: *They left soon after five o'clock.* **3** at a time earlier than expected: *You came so soon!*   **as soon** as willingly; as readily: *I'd as soon leave as not.*

soot (sŏŏt, sŭt, sōōt) *n-* black powder, mostly of carbon, that forms when organic material is burned. *vt-* to cover or smear with such a powder. *Hom-* suit.

sooth (sōōth) *Archaic n-* truth. *adj-* true; real. *—adv-* **sooth′ly**.

soothe (sōōth) *vt-* [**soothed, sooth·ing**] **1** to make quiet and calm; to comfort: *to soothe a restless patient.* **2** to make less painful; relieve: *The salve soothed Eric's earache.* *—n-* **sooth′er**. *adv-* **sooth′ing·ly**.

sooth·say·er (sōōth′sā′ər) *n-* person who claims to have the power of foretelling the future; fortuneteller.   *—n-* **sooth′say′ing**.

soot·y (sŏŏt′ē, sŭt′ē, sōō′tē) *adj-* [**soot·i·er, soot·i·est**] **1** relating to or covered with soot. **2** dusky; black: *a sooty sky.* *—adv-* **soot′i·ly**. *n-* **soot′i·ness**.

sop (sŏp) *n-* **1** anything soaked, dipped, or softened in a liquid, such as bread in broth. **2** something given to pacify: *a sop to injured feelings.* *vt-* [**sopped, sop·ping**] **1** to dip or soak. **2** to wet; make soaking wet: *The rain sopped him.* **3** to soak up.

south·west·er·ly (south′wĕs′tər lē, sou wĕs′-) *adj-* **1** generally toward the southwest: *a southwesterly direction.* **2** of winds, generally from the southwest: *a southwesterly breeze.* *adv-* generally southwestward.

south·west·ern (south′wĕs′tərn) *adj-* located in or to the southwest: *the southwestern part of the state.*

South·west·ern·er (south′wĕs′tər nər) *n-* native or inhabitant of the southwestern part of the United States.

south·west·ward (south′wĕst′wərd) *adj-* toward the southwest: *a southwestward flight of birds.* *adv-* (also **south′west′wards**): *We walked southwestward.*

sou·ve·nir (sōō′və nēr′) *n-* something kept as a reminder of a person, place, or event; keepsake.

sou'west·er (sou wĕs′tər) southwester.

sov·er·eign (sŏv′rən) *n-* **1** a ruler or supreme power, such as a king, emperor, or other monarch; also, a governing body or state having supreme authority. **2** British gold coin equal to one pound sterling but no longer in use. *adj-* **1** supreme; highest: *A king holds sovereign power in a monarchy.* **2** having independent power; free: *a sovereign state.* **3** most effective; greatest; best: *a sovereign remedy.*

sov·er·eign·ty (sŏv′rən tē, sŭv′-) *n-* [pl. **sov·er·eign·ties**] **1** supreme power: *In a monarchy sovereignty rests with the king, but in a democracy it rests with the people.* **2** independent political power; power or right of self-government. **3** sovereign state or nation.

so·viet (sō′vē ĕt′, sŏv′ē ət) *n-* **1** (often **Soviet**) any of various councils or governing bodies of the U.S.S.R. which are elected by the people, and which send delegates to the higher congresses. **2 Supreme Soviet** the highest legislative body of the Soviet Union. **3 Soviets** the people of the U.S.S.R. or its political and military leaders. *adj-* of or relating to the U.S.S.R.

spear (spêr) *n-* blade or sprout of a plant: *a spear of grass.* [altered from ¹**spire** by influence of ¹**spear.**]

spear·fish (spêr' fĭsh´) *n-* [*pl.* **spear·fish; spear·fish·es** (kinds of spearfish)] either of two kinds of ocean fishes related to marlins and having slender, sharp bills.

spear·head (spêr' hĕd´) *n-* 1 point of a spear. 2 leading person or group in an endeavor, especially in a military attack. *vt-* to take the lead in (an attack, campaign, etc.): *George spearheaded the drive for a new library.*

spear·man (spêr' mən) *n-* [*pl.* **spear·men**] person, especially a soldier, armed with a spear.

spear·mint (spêr' mĭnt´) *n-* common garden mint, with leaves shaped like a spearhead.

spe·cial (spĕsh' əl) *adj-* 1 distinct from all others; unique as a group: *Surgery requires special skills.* 2 designed for a particular purpose: *a special course of study.* 3 out of the ordinary; unusual: *a special holiday; a special favor.* 4 highly esteemed: *a special friend. n- Informal* something not of the ordinary kind, especially something made, sold, or published. —*adv-* **spe·cial·ly.**

special delivery *n-* the delivery of mail by special messenger in advance of regular delivery for an extra fee; also, a piece of mail delivered this way. *adv-: Send it special delivery.*

spe·cial·ist (spĕsh' əl ĭst) *n-* person who devotes himself to a particular branch of study, business, etc.; especially, a doctor who devotes himself to one field of medicine.

spe·ci·al·i·ty (spĕsh' ē ăl' ə tē) *n-* [*pl.* **spe·ci·al·i·ties**] 1 way or respect in which something is special. 2 specialty.

spe·cial·ize (spĕsh' ə lĭz´) *vt-* [**spe·cial·ized, spe·cial·iz·ing**] 1 to concentrate on a particular action or course of study: *The doctor specializes in surgery.* 2 *Biology* to become adapted to a special environment or for some special function; evolve in a special way. *vt-* to apply, modify, or adapt for a specific use or purpose: *He specialized his studies.* —*n-* **spe·cial·i·za´tion.**

spell (spĕl) *n-* 1 any period of time: *a hot spell; a dry spell.* 2 a turn at work to relieve another: *He took a spell at the wheel.* 3 attack of bodily or mental disorder: *a fainting spell. vt-* [**spelled, spell·ing**] to take the place of someone; alternate with: *Let me spell you at the oars.* [From Old English **spelian,** "act for another."]

spell·bind (spĕl' bīnd´) *vt-* [**spell·bound, spell·bind·ing**] to hold as by a spell; fascinate. —*n-* **spell´ bind´ er.**

spell·bound (spĕl' bound´) *adj-* held as if by a spell.

spell·er (spĕl' ər) *n-* 1 person who spells: *He is a poor speller.* 2 book for teaching students how to spell.

spell·ing (spĕl' ĭng) *n-* 1 the act of forming words with letters. 2 the way in which a particular word is spelled. *as modifier: a spelling book; a spelling lesson.*

spelling bee *n-* contest in spelling.

spelt (spĕlt) *chiefly Brit. p.t. & p.p.* of ¹**spell.**

spend (spĕnd) *vt-* [**spent, spend·ing**] 1 to pay out or expend: *to spend money.* 2 to use up; wear out; exhaust; squander: *He spent his energy working on wild schemes.* 3 to pass (time): *He spent the summer at the beach. vi-* to expend money or other possessions: *He loves to spend.* —*n-* **spend´ er.**

spend·ing (spĕn' dĭng) *n-* the paying out of money, especially by a government or public agency.

spend·thrift (spĕnd' thrĭft´) *n-* person who spends money carelessly; squanderer. *adj-* wasteful.

spent (spĕnt) *p.t. & p.p.* of **spend.** *adj-* 1 exhausted; worn-out. 2 without force: *a spent arrow.*

sperm (spûrm) *n-* 1 male fertilizing fluid; semen. 2 male reproductive cell; spermatozoön.

sper·ma·ce·ti (spûr´ mə sĕt´ ē) *n-* fatty substance found in the head of sperm whales and used in making candles and ointments.

sper·ma·to·phyte (spər măt´ ə fīt´) *n-* any seed plant, such as a conifer or a flowering plant, all of which were formerly classified together in a single major group (Spermatophyta).

sper·ma·to·zo·ön (spər măt´ ə zō´ ən, spûr´ mə tə-) *n-* [*pl.* **sper·ma·to·zo·a** (-zō´ ə)] in animals, the male reproductive cell, usually having independent movement by means of a long tail.

sperm oil *n-* oil from the blubber of the sperm whale.

sperm whale *n-* large whale that secretes spermaceti in a large cavity in the head.

spew (spyo͞o) *vi-* 1 to come out in a flow or gush: *Oil spewed all over the ground.* 2 to vomit. *vt-* to cast forth; eject; emit: *The volcano spews lava.* —*n-* **spew´ er.**

sp. gr. specific gravity.

sphag·num (sfăg´ nəm) *n-* any of a group of pale-gray plants related to the mosses, found in bogs, and used widely for potting plants and in surgical dressings.

sphere (sfēr) *n-* 1 geometric solid with a surface that is everywhere the same distance from a center point; ball; globe. 2 place, field, or extent of a person's knowledge, activity, etc.: *When he talks about music he is outside his sphere.* 3 *Astronomy* the celestial sphere. 4 celestial body, such as a planet. 5 in ancient astronomy, any of the revolving, spherical, crystalline shells in which the heavenly bodies were supposed to be set.

spher·i·cal (sfēr´ ĭ kəl, sfĕr´-) *adj-* 1 having the shape of a sphere. 2 of or relating to a sphere or spheres: *He is studying spherical geometry.* —*adv-* **spher´ i·cal·ly.**

sphe·ric·i·ty (sfēr ĭs´ ə tē) *n-* [*pl.* **sphe·ric·i·ties**] condition of being spherical or nearly spherical; roundness.

sphe·roid (sfēr´ oid´, sfĕr´-) *n-* a solid similar to a sphere but not having the same diameter in all directions.

sphinc·ter (sfĭngk´ tər) *n-* circular muscle that closes off a passage or opening in the body when contracted.

sphinx (sfĭngks) *n-* [*pl.* **sphinx·es**] 1 in Egyptian and Greek legend, a monster with a human head and a lion's body. 2 statue of such a monster. 3 **the Sphinx** such a statue at Giza, Egypt. 4 secretive, mysterious person.

The sphinx at Giza

sphyg·mo·ma·nom·e·ter (sfĭg´ mō´ mə nŏm´ ə tər) *n-* instrument for measuring the blood pressure.

spice (spīs) *n-* 1 aromatic vegetable substance such as ginger, cinnamon, nutmeg, pepper, used to flavor food. 2 that which gives added interest or zest: *His wit added spice to the conversation.* 3 pungent or fragrant odor. *as modifier: a spice merchant; the spice trade;* spice *shelf. vt-* [**spiced, spic·ing**] to season or flavor.

spice·bush (spīs´ bo͞osh´) *n-* aromatic shrub related to the laurel and bearing small, clustered yellow flowers.

spick-and-span (spĭk´ ən spăn´) *adj-* neat and clean.

spic·ule (spĭk´ yo͞ol´) *n-* 1 small, pointed, hard body, needlelike or branched, such as those in the skeletons of many sponges. 2 in astronomy, one of the various small jets of hot gas in the chromosphere of the sun, which leap outward and last for only a brief period of time.

spic·y (spī´ sē) *adj-* [**spic·i·er, spic·i·est**] 1 containing, flavored with, or fragrant with spice. 2 like spice: *a spicy taste.* 3 spirited; witty: *a spicy conversation.* 4 somewhat scandalous. —*adv-* **spic´ i·ly.** *n-* **spic´ i·ness.**

spi·der (spī´ dər) *n-* any of many kinds of small, eight-legged animals, most of which can spin silken threads for egg-cases and webs, and many of which secrete venom for paralyzing or killing their prey. —*adj-* **spi´ der·y.** *adj-* **spi´ der·like´.**

spi·der·web (spī´ dər wĕb´) *n-* silken web spun by a spider to catch insects.

Garden spider.
1/2–3/4 in. across

spied (spīd) *p.t. & p.p.* of **spy.**

spiel (spēl) *Slang n-* noisy talk; speech; harangue.

spies (spīz) 1 plural of the noun **spy.** 2 form of the verb **spy** used with "he," "she," "it," or singular noun subjects, in the present tense.

sponge bath *n-* bath taken by washing with a sponge or cloth outside of a bathtub or shower.

sponge cake *n-* light, spongy cake made of flour, eggs, sugar, etc., but no shortening.

spong·er (spŭn´ jər) *n-* 1 *Informal* person who lives off others; parasite.

spon·sor·ship (spŏn′ sər shĭp′) *n-* the position, functions, or duties of a sponsor.

spon·ta·ne·ous (spŏn tā′ nē əs) *adj-* 1 arising or acting from a natural impulse: *a spontaneous burst of applause.* 2 produced by internal forces rather than by an external cause: *a spontaneous growth;* spontaneous *combustion.* —*adv-* spon·ta′ ne·ous·ly. *n-* spon·ta′ ne·ous·ness or spon′ ta·ne′ i·ty (spŏn′ tən ē′ ə tĕ, -ă′ ə tĕ).

spontaneous combustion *n-* a burning or ignition without the application of external heat. It results from the accumulation of heat by slow oxidation.

spoof (spōōf) *Informal vt-* to treat or mimic in a humorous and satirical manner; parody; burlesque. *n-* parody of a person or thing; take-off. —*n-* spoof′ er.

spook (spōōk) *n-* ghost; spirit; specter. *vt- Informal* to frighten; startle; scare: *The falling leaf* spooked *my horse.*

spook·y (spōō′ kē) *Informal adj-* [spook·i·er, spook·i·est] 1 of, having to do with, or suggesting spooks: *a spooky castle.* 2 nervous: *a spooky herd.* —*n-* spook′ i·ness.

spool (spōōl) *n-* 1 cylindrical piece of wood with flaring ends on which thread may be wound. 2 anything in the shape of a cylinder that is used in a like way; reel: *a spool of motion picture film.* 3 quantity of thread, wire, etc., held by such a cylinder; also, the cylinder and the material upon it. *vt-* to wind (thread, wire, etc.) on a cylinder.

Spool

spoon (spōōn) *n-* 1 a utensil with a small shallow bowl at the end of a handle, used in preparing, serving, or eating food. 2 (also **spoon′ ful**) amount such a utensil will hold when full. 3 something resembling this utensil, such as an oar with a curved blade or a metal fishing lure. 4 golf club with a wooden head that gives more lift than a brassie. *vt-* to take up with or as if with a spoon. *vi- Informal* to kiss, embrace, etc., as lovers do.

spoon·bill (spōōn′ bĭl′) *n-* any of various wading birds related to the ibises, with long legs and a broad bill.

spoon bread *n-* soft bread, made from milk, eggs, shortening, and cornmeal, and served with a spoon.

spoon·drift (spōōn′ drĭft′) *n-* spindrift.

spoon·er·ism (spōō′ nə rĭz′ əm) *n-* accidental interchange of sounds, usually the first, in two or more words. Example: *"She kissed like an angry hat,"* for *"She hissed like an angry cat."* [from Reverend W. A. Spooner.]

spoon-feed (spōōn′ fēd′) *vt-* [spoon-fed, spoon-feed·ing] 1 to feed with a spoon. 2 to spoil; pamper. 3 to teach or give out information in such a way as to leave no room for independent thought or action.

spoor (spōōr) *n-* a track, scent, or trail, especially of a wild animal. *vt-* to track: *The hunters* spoored *the boar through the woods. vi-: The pup can* spoor *well already.*

spo·rad·ic (spə răd′ ĭk) *adj-* 1 appearing or happening from time to time; occasional: *a few* sporadic *outbreaks of violence.* 2 appearing singly; widely separated from others: *the* sporadic *occurrence of a plant.* 3 of a disease, occurring in a few cases only; not epidemic. —*adv-* spo·rad′ i·cal·ly.

spo·ran·gi·um (spə răn′ jē əm) *n-* [*pl.* spo·ran·gi·a (-ə)] sac in which asexual spores are produced in algae, ferns, fungi, etc. Also *spore case.*

ˉpore (spôr) *n-* 1 in plants, a very small reproductive bᴜʟy. 2 in bacteria, a kind of inactive cell

spor·ran (spôr′ ən, spŏr′-) *n-* large purse or pouch worn in front of a Highland man's kilt.

sport (spôrt) *n-* 1 game, pastime, or contest that requires a reasonable amount of physical activity along with individual skill: *Skiing, tennis, and billiards are all* sports. 2 amusement; fun: *Mother teased us in* sport. 3 *Informal* unselfish companion. 4 *Informal* person who plays fair and is a good loser. 5 *Informal* person interested in sporting events, especially to bet on them. 6 *Biology* animal or plant which exhibits a spontaneous variation from the usual or normal type. *vi-* 1 to play or frolic; trifle. 2 to participate in a sporting event. 3 *Biology* to exhibit suddenly or spontaneously a variation from the normal type; mutate. *vt-* to show off in public; wear: *Bob* sported *a new hat on Sunday. as modifier* (also **sports**): *a* sport *shirt; a* sport *jacket;* sports *page.*

make sport of to make fun of; ridicule.

sport·ing (spôr′ tĭng) *adj-* 1 engaged or interested in sports: *The athlete belonged to a* sporting *crowd.* 2 playing fair and willing to be a good loser: *The children were taught to be* sporting *in their games.* 3 having to do with sports. 4 risky but offering a reasonable chance for success: *a* sporting *chance.* —*adv-* sport′ ing·ly.

spor·tive (spôr′ tĭv) *adj-* frolicsome; playful: *his* sportive *humor.* —*adv-* spor′ tive·ly. *n-* spor′ tive·ness.

sports car or **sport car** *n-* small, low automobile, usually a two-seat convertible, built for high speeds.

sports·cast (spôrts′ kăst′) *n-* radio or television broadcast of a sports event.

sports·man (spôrts′ mən) *n-* [*pl.* sports·men] 1 person who takes part in sports, such as hunting and fishing, etc. 2 person who plays fair or is honorable. —*n- fem.* sports′ wom′ an. *adj-* sports′ man·like′.

sports·man·ship (spôrts′ mən shĭp′) *n-* 1 behavior expected of a sportsman, such as fair play or good grace in defeat. 2 skill in or liking for sports.

sports·wear (spôrts′ wâr′) *n-* casual clothes.

sports·writ·er (spôrts′ rī′ tər) *n-* person who writes about sports for a magazine or newspaper.

sport·y (spôr′ tē) *Informal adj-* [sport·i·er, sport·i·est] 1 relating to or characteristic of a sport or sportsman. 2 loud; showy; flashy: *a* sporty *suit.* —*adv-* sport′ i·ly. *n-* sport′ i·ness.

spot (spŏt) *n-* 1 blot or mark; discolored place or stain; patch: *a grease* spot; *a* spot *of white on the black dog.* 2 a blemish: *a* spot *on the family name.* 3 locality, place, or area: *We can picnic in this* spot. 4 *Informal* particular position or situation: *They have a good* spot *on the program.* 5 *Brit.* small amount: *a* spot *of tea. vt-* [spot·ted, spot·ting] 1 to cause to become marked or stained; discolor; stain. 2 to disgrace; mar; blemish. 3 to place at a designated location: *to* spot *a billiard ball.* 4 *Informal* to recognize; detect: *He* spotted *the guilty man. vi-* to become marked or stained.

hit the spot *Informal* to be just what was needed or desired. **in a spot** *Informal* in trouble; in a bad situation. **on the spot** 1 at once; immediately. 2 on or at the place mentioned. 3 *Informal* in trouble; in a bad situation. 4 *Informal* in a position where a true answer, explanation, or effective solution must be given.

spring beauty *n-* any of several delicate wild plants related to the purslane, having white or pink flowers.

spring·board (spring′ bôrd′) *n-* 1 a flexible board that gives added height or spring to a jump; diving board. 2 something that gives a good start.

spring·bok (spring′ bŏk′) *n-* small South African animal resembling the gazelle, noted for its grace.

springer spaniel *n-* any of various medium-sized, spotted spaniels. For picture, see *spaniel.*

spring fever *n-* the feeling of laziness or restlessness that people have during the first warm sunny spring days.

spring·house (spring′ hous′) *n-* small building located over a cold-water spring and used for storing food.

spring-load·ed (spring′ lō′ dəd) *adj-* loaded or having force applied to by means of a spring.

spring peeper *n-* small tree toad that breeds in ponds and produces a chirping sound on spring evenings.

spring·tide (spring′ tīd′) *n-* springtime.

spring tide *n-* very high tide that occurs near the full moon and the new moon.

spring·time (spring′ tīm′) *n-* season of spring.

spring wheat *n-* wheat that is planted in the spring and ripens the same summer.

spring·y (spring′ ē) *adj-* [spring·i·er, spring·i·est] able to spring back; elastic; flexible; full of spring. —*adv-* spring′ i·ly. *n-* spring′ i·ness.

sprin·kle (spring′ kəl) *vt-* [sprin·kled, sprin·kling] 1 to spray with small drops of water: *You'll have to* sprinkle *the garden today.* 2 to scatter in small drops or particles: *The child* sprinkled *sand on the floor. vt-* to rain lightly. *n-* 1 a light rain. 2 small amount of something.

sprin·kler (spring′ klər) *n-* 1 any of various devices for sprinkling lawns, roads, etc., with water or other fluids. 2 one of the outlets of a sprinkler system.

sprinkler system *n-* 1 automatic system for putting out fires inside a building.

spruce (sprōōs) *adj-* [spruc·er, spruc·est] neat; tidy; trim. *vt-* [spruced, spruc·ing] to make neat and tidy (usually followed by "up"): *She* spruced *up the room. vi-* to make oneself neat (usually followed by "up"): *She will* spruce *up before going home.* [from earlier spruce **leather** meaning "Prussian leather," and related to ¹spruce.] —*adv-* spruce′ly. *n-* spruce′ness.

sprung (sprŭng) *p.t. & p.p. of* spring.

spry (sprī) *adj-* [spry·er or spri·er, spry·est or spri·est] active and nimble: *The old lady is very* spry *for her age.* —*adv-* spry′ly. *n-* spry′ness.

spud (spŭd) *n-* 1 sharp, narrow spade, especially for digging up weeds with large roots. 2 *Informal* potato. *vt-* [spud·ded, spud·ding] to dig with such a spade. *vi-* to begin the drilling of an oil well; cut through the soft upper strata with a special bit.

spume (spyōōm) *n-* foam; froth; scum. *vi-* [spumed, spum·ing] to foam; froth. —*adj-* spum′y.

spu·mo·ni or **spu·mo·ne** (spə mō′ nē) *n-* Italian frozen dessert resembling a mousse, usually made with ice cream arranged in layers of different colors or flavors and often containing dried fruits and nuts.

spun (spŭn) *p.t. & p.p. of* spin.

spun glass *n-* Fiberglas.

spunk (spŭngk) *Informal n-* courage; spirit.

spunk·y (spŭng′ kē) *adj-* [spunk·i·er, spunk·i·est] courageous; spirited. —*adv-* spunk′i·ly. *n-* spunk′i·ness.

spur (spûr) *n-* 1 metal frame with pricking point or points, fitted to a rider's boot heel, with which to urge on his horse; hence, anything that urges to action; incentive: *He offered a prize as a spur to good work.* 2 sharp, horny spine on a rooster's leg; also, anything of similar shape. 3 ridge of hills at an angle with a main ridge. 4 short railroad line connected with the main line at only one end. *vt-* [spurred, spur·ring] to urge (a horse) with a special pricking device; hence, to urge; goad: *Fear* spurred *him. vi-* to goad a horse or oneself to special effort (usually followed by "on").

Spur

on the spur of the moment without any planning; on impulse. **win one's spurs** to gain distinction or honor.

spu·ri·ous (spyŏŏr′ ē əs, spōŏr′-) *adj-* not genuine; false. —*adv-* spu′ri·ous·ly. *n-* spu′ri·ous·ness.

spurn (spûrn) *vt-* 1 to push away, as with the foot. 2 to turn down with scorn.

spurred (spûrd) *adj-* wearing or having a spur or spurs.

spurt (spûrt) *n-* 1 sudden gush of liquid. 2 sudden increase: *a spurt of activity; a spurt of speed. vi-* 1 to gush forth suddenly in streams: *Blood* spurted *from the open wound.* 2 to have a short burst of energy or activity; increase greatly: *Sales* spurted *greatly before Christmas. vt-* to throw or force out in a stream; squirt: *The wound* spurted *blood.* Also **spirt.**

sput·ter (spŭt′ ər) *n-* 1 noise like spitting or spluttering.

sprite (sprīt) *n-* fairy, elf, or goblin.

sprit·sail (sprĭt′ səl, -sāl′) *n-* fore-and-aft sail extended by a sprit.

sprock·et (sprŏk′ ət) *n-* 1 any of the teeth on a chain-driven cogwheel. 2 (also **sprocket wheel**) the wheel itself.

SPROCKETS

Sprocket wheel

sprout (sprout) *vi-* 1 to start to grow; to put forth buds or shoots: *The cabbages* sprouted. 2 to grow quickly; shoot up: *Gas stations* sprouted *along the new highway. vt-*: *The rain and warm weather* sprouted *the flowers. n-* 1 a beginning growth; a bud; a shoot. 2 **sprouts** brussels sprouts.

spruce (sprōōs) *n-* 1 any of various pointed evergreen trees related to the pines and bearing cones and short, thick needles. 2 the wood of this tree, used for lumber and paper pulp. 3 any of various related trees.

Red spruce.
twig and cone

squish·y (skwĭsh′ ē) *Informal adj-* [squish·i·er, squish·i·est] 1 easily squashed; mushy. 2 soft and wet.

Sr symbol for strontium.

Sr. 1 senior. 2 sister. 3 señor.

SS or **S.S.** steamship.

SSE or **S.S.E.** south-southeast.

SSR or **S.S.R.** Soviet Socialist Republic.

SSW or **S.S.W.** south-southwest.

St. 1 saint. 2 street. 3 strait.

stab (stăb) *vt-* [stabbed, stab·bing] 1 to pierce with any pointed instrument or weapon. 2 to hurt the feelings of, by treachery, harsh words, or the like: *The children's jeers* stabbed *Tony to the heart. vi-* 1 to make a jabbing motion. 2 to wound a person's feelings. *n-* 1 piercing wound made by something pointed. 2 jabbing motion; jab; thrust. —*n-* stab′ber.

have (or **make**) **a stab at** to make an effort at; try.

Sta·bat Ma·ter (stä′ bät′ mä′ tər, -mä′ tər) *n-* thirteenth-century Latin hymn recounting the suffering of the Virgin Mary at the Crucifixion. 2 any of several musical settings to this narrative.

sta·bil·i·ty (stə bĭl′ ə tē) *n-* condition of being stable.

sta·bi·lize (stā′ bə līz′) *vt-* [sta·bi·lized, sta·bi·liz·ing] to make or keep stable. —*n-* sta′ bi·li·za′ tion.

sta·bi·liz·er (stā′ bə līz′ ər) *n-* 1 the fixed crosswise airfoil at the tail of an airplane, to which the elevators are attached. 2 any of various devices, consisting of or controlled by a gyroscope, that reduce the rolling of a ship. 3 *Chemistry* substance used to prevent unwanted changes in a compound. 4 any person or thing that stabilizes.

sta·ble (stā′ bəl) *n-* 1 building in which animals, especially horses, are kept. 2 a group of horses under a single ownership: *The prince had a large racing* stable. *vt-* [sta·bled, sta·bling] to put or keep in such a building: *We* stable *our horses here.* [from Old French **estable,** from Latin **stabulum** meaning "a standing place for animals," from **stāre,** "to stand (firm)."]

sta·ble (stā′ bəl) *adj-* 1 not likely to change; durable. 2 not shaky or shifting: *a stable platform; a stable foundation.* 3 regular and predictable in behavior; not erratic; steady: *a stable personality.* 4 *Chemistry* of chemical compounds, not easily decomposed. 5 *Physics* of an atom or nucleus, not capable of spontaneous change. [from Latin **stabilis** meaning "firm; steady," from **stāre,** "to stand (firm)."] —*adv-* sta′ bly.

sta·ble·man (stā′ bəl mən, -măn′) *n-* [*pl.* sta·ble·men] person who works in a stable; hostler; groom. If this person is a boy, he is called a **stableboy.**

stac·ca·to (stə kä′ tō′) *adj- & adv-* 1 *Music* performed or to be performed in an abrupt, clear-cut manner with each note detached from the note that precedes or follows it. 2 abrupt; disconnected: *a staccato remark. n-* [*pl.* stac·ca·tos] note or passage performed in this manner.

Stacks of guns

stack (stăk) *n-* 1 a large, round pile: *a stack of straw.* 2 neat, orderly pile: *a stack of magazines.* 3 tall chimney; smokestack. 4 set of open bookshelves. 5 **stacks** part of a library where most books are stored on shelves. 6 conical stand of three or more rifles with their muzzles together. 7 *Informal* (often **stacks**) large amount or number. *vt-* 1 to pile neatly; heap up. 2 *Slang* to arrange dishonestly.

sta·di·um (stā′ dē əm) *n-* [*pl.* sta·di·ums or sta·di·a (-dē ə)] 1 field for athletic contests, surrounded or partially surrounded by permanent tiers of seats. 2 in ancient Greece, a unit of measurement usually equal to about 607 feet; also, a course for foot races with sloping banks of seats on both sides.

staff (stăf) *n-* [*pl.* staffs or staves (stāvz)] 1 long cane or stick, used for walking or defense: *a shepherd's* staff. 2 a rod as a sign of authority: *a bishop's* staff.

Staff

(3) in the armed forces, group of officers without combat duties or command but assisting a commander in his executive and administrative duties. **6** *Music* [*pl.* **staffs**] set of five lines and the spaces between them on which music is written. *vt-* to provide with or hire workers.

Stag, about 6 ft. high at shoulder

stag (stăg) *n-* **1** the full-grown male of some kinds of deer. **2** man who attends a social function unaccompanied by a woman. **3** social gathering where only men are present. *as modifier:* a stag *party*.

go stag to attend a social function unaccompanied by a woman.

stage (stāj) *n-* **1** raised platform or other part of a theater on which a play or other performance is acted. **2** the **stage** profession of acting. **3** place or field of action; scene: *Europe has been the stage for many important battles.* **4** degree, phase, or period of development, growth, advancement, etc.: *He has reached an important stage in his career.* **5** stagecoach. *as modifier:* a stage *career.* *vt-* [staged, stag·ing] to prepare or produce for theatrical performance: *to stage an opera.*

stage-coach (stāj′kōch′) *n-* in former times, a closed, horse-drawn coach that ran on a regular schedule and carried passengers, mail, and baggage.

Stagecoach

stage-craft (stāj′krăft′) *n-* art or skill of creating or preparing works for performance in the theater.

stage fright *n-* feeling of fear or panic sometimes experienced by a person who is about to face an audience.

stage-hand (stāj′hănd′) *n-* worker in a theater who moves scenery, operates lights, raises the curtain, etc.

stage-struck (stāj′strŭk′) *adj-* fascinated by the life of the theater; especially, very eager to become an actor.

stall (stôl) *Informal vt-* to delay, put off, or keep waiting by means of excuses, postponements, etc.: *to stall one's creditors because of lack of cash.* *vi-:* *Stop stalling and pay up!* *n-* excuse or pretext intended to prevent or delay an action or outcome. [from a variant of earlier *stale* meaning "decoy," from Old French *estale.*]

stal·lion (stăl′yən) *n-* male horse that has not been castrated.

stal·wart (stôl′wərt) *adj-* **1** strong and sturdy. **2** courageous and steady: *a stalwart fighter for liberty.* *n-* **1** strong or brave person. **2** firm, loyal supporter or partisan. *—adv-* **stal′wart·ly.** *n-* **stal′wart·ness.**

sta·men (stā′mən) *n-* pollen-bearing organ of a flower, consisting of an anther supported by a filament. For picture, see *flower.*

stam·i·na (stăm′ə nə) *n-* power of endurance; strength.

stam·i·nate (stăm′ə nət, stā′mə nət, -nāt′) *adj-* having stamens; especially, having stamens but not pistils.

stam·mer (stăm′ər) *vi-* to hesitate, falter, or repeat sounds or syllables in speaking: *He stammers when he is embarrased.* *vt-:* *He stammered an apology.* *n-:* *He speaks with a stammer.* *—n-* **stam′mer·er.** *adv-* **stam′mer·ing·ly:** *He speaks stammeringly.*

stamp (stămp) *n-* **1** object, such as a die, carved block, or piece of rubber, that is pressed against something to make a mark. **2** mark made by pressing such an object into or against a surface. **3** small piece of paper sold by the government and stuck on a letter, package, document, etc., to show that a fee or tax has been paid: *a postage stamp; a revenue stamp.* **4** downward blow

with the sole of the foot, a die, or a marker. **5** characteristic mark or impression: *His manners show the stamp of breeding.* **6** special quality: *Men of his stamp are rare.* *vt-* **1** to mark with a design or impression by, or as if by, means of a die or other device that is pressed against something: *He stamped the paper with a seal.* **2** to put a postage stamp or similar official paper on: *to stamp a letter.* **3** to set (one's foot, hoof, etc.) down heavily and sharply. **4** to strike or trample with the bottom of the foot: *to stamp the ground impatiently.* **5** to mark; indicate: *His manners stamp him as a man of good breeding.* **6** to shape or cut by pressure of a die or similar device: *to stamp automobile parts.* **7** to crush or grind (ore, rock, etc.) into powder. *vi-* **1** to set down the foot with a heavy, forceful motion: *He stamped on the ground.* **2** to walk with heavy, noisy steps.

stamp out 1 to put out (a fire) by trampling it. **2** to put an end to by forceful action: *to stamp out crime.*

stam·pede (stăm pēd′) *n-* **1** sudden, wild running away, as of a herd of animals. **2** any sudden rush or movement of a crowd: *a stampede for the exit.* *vt-* [stam·ped·ed, stam·ped·ing] to cause to panic and run wildly: *to stampede a crowd.* *vi-:* *The crowd stampeded.*

stance (stăns) *n-* **1** manner of standing; posture. **2** in baseball or golf, the position taken by a player as he prepares to strike the ball.

stanch (stônch, stănch) *vt-* **1** to stop the flow of: *to stanch blood from a wound.* **2** to stop the flow of blood from: *to stanch a wound.* [from Old French *estanchier,* from Late Latin *stancāre,* from Latin *stagnāre* meaning "cease to flow."] *—n-* **stanch′er.**

stanch (stônch, stănch) *adj-* [stanch·er, stanch·est] staunch. [from ¹stanch, "not leaky."] *—adv-* **stanch′ly.**

stan·chion (stăn′chən) *n-* **1** upright post or support, as in a window. **2** framework placed around an animal's neck to confine it in a stall. *vt-:* *to stanchion a window; to stanchion a cow.*

stand (stănd) *vi-* [stood (stŏŏd), stand·ing] **1** to rest on the feet, or on other supporting part or parts, in an upright position: *We stood in the sun all day. The broom stood in a corner.* **2** to rise to a position: *Please stand when I call your name.* **3** to be situated: *Our house stands on the top of the hill.* **4** to remain in one place or position: *The pile of rubbish stood in the yard for days.* **5** to be in a certain position, condition, or attitude: *to stand acquitted of a crime; to stand prepared for action.* **6** to occupy a place or position relative to others: *to stand first in line; to stand high in one's class.* **7** to remain firm or in force: *The rule stands.* **8** to take a position in defense or support of someone or something: *to stand behind a candidate; to stand for law and order.* *vt-* **1** to set in an upright position: *to stand books on a shelf.* **2** to bear; endure; tolerate: *She cannot stand the cold. I can't stand that noise!* **3** to remain firm against; withstand: *Flimsy materials cannot stand heavy pressure.* **4** to be subjected to; undergo: *to stand a heavy penalty; to stand trial.* **5** to pay for: *to stand the expenses of a party.* *n-* **1** stop or halt, especially to maintain a position or offer resistance: *The retreating army made a stand at the river.* **2** place or post in which one remains erect. **3** a position or attitude in regard to something: *What is your stand on this question?* **4** rack, pedestal, or small table for holding or supporting something: *a music stand; a plant stand.* **5** booth or counter from which something is sold: *a fruit stand; a cigar stand.* **6** platform or similar raised structure for a special purpose: *the witness stand in a courtroom.* **7** group of upright growing plants: *a stand of maples; a stand of wheat.* **8** stands outdoor seats in tiers; grandstand.

Plant stand

stand a chance to be likely to succeed.

stand by 1 to give support to; aid. **2** to wait in readiness.

stand for 1 to take the place of; represent; symbolize: *"U.S." stands for "United States."* **2** to put up with; tolerate: *I won't stand for such nonsense!*

stand in for to take the place of, or be ready to take the place of: *to stand in for a sick actor.*

stand off to repel (an attack, enemy, etc.).

stand on 1 to be based on. 2 to insist firmly on.

stand out 1 to project; protrude: *figures that stand out from a background.* 2 to be outstanding or noticeable.

stand over to stand near in order to watch closely.

stand up 1 to withstand wear, stress, etc. 2 *Slang* to fail deliberately to keep an appointment or date with.

stand up for to be firm or loyal in support of.

stand up to to face or fight with courage.

stan·dard (stăn′dərd) *n-* 1 generally accepted level or example of excellence, considered as a basis of comparison. 2 established measure of weight, length, value, etc. 3 flag, banner, or figure used as an emblem: *a naval* standard. 4 upright support: *a lamp on a tall* standard. *adj-* 1 conforming to or serving as a basis or model for measurement, value, comparison, etc.: *a* standard *mile;* standard *time.* 2 of recognized excellence or authority: *a standard reference work.* 3 widely used or practiced, and considered generally acceptable by those whose judgment is regarded as authoritative: *to speak standard English.*

standard conditions *n-* a temperature of 0°C (**standard temperature**) and a pressure of 760 mm (**standard pressure**), used for making many scientific measurements.

stan·dard·ize (stăn′dər dīz′) *vt-* [**stan·dard·ized, stan·dard·iz·ing**] 1 to make uniform or standard in size, quality, etc.: *to standardize automobile parts.* 2 to regulate or test by a standard: *to standardize a pressure gauge.* —*n-* **stan′dard·i·za′tion.**

standard of living *n-* degree to which the economic needs or wants of a person or group are satisfied. A country has a **high standard of living** when the amount of goods per person is comparatively high, and a **low standard of living** when this amount is low.

standard time *n-* system of keeping time in 24 time zones, east and west, around the earth. All clocks in one time zone are set one hour ahead of the next time zone to the west. The seven time zones used throughout the United States are (from east to west): Eastern, Central, Mountain, Pacific, Yukon, Alaska (same as Hawaii), and Bering.

stand·by (stănd′bī′) *n-* [*pl.* **stand·bys**] person or thing ready to be called on or used in an emergency.

stand·ee (stăn′dē′) *n-* person who must stand on a bus, at a play, etc., because he hasn't a seat.

stand-in (stănd′ĭn′) *n-* in motion pictures and television, a person who takes the place of an actor while equipment is being adjusted or during hazardous scenes; hence, anyone who substitutes for another.

stand·ing (stăn′dĭng) *n-* 1 relative position or rank: *What is his* standing *in his high school class?* 2 repute; good name: *a man of* standing *in his profession.* 3 duration: *a habit of long* standing.

standing army *n-* army that is permanently prepared for action, especially during times of peace.

standing room *n-* room or space available for standees.

stand·off (stănd′ôf′, -ŏf′) *n-* 1 deadlock; tie. 2 condition in which one set of circumstances, facts, etc., counterbalances or offsets another. 3 cold, distant behavior.

stand·off·ish (stănd′ôf′ĭsh, -ŏf′ĭsh) *adj-* coldly distant; reserved; aloof. —*n-* **stand′off′ish·ness.**

stand·pipe (stănd′pīp′) *n-* vertical pipe or high tower into which water is pumped to provide pressure in the water system of an apartment house, factory, etc.

stand·point (stănd′point′) *n-* basis or standard from which things are considered or judged; point of view.

stand·still (stănd′stĭl′) *n-* stop; halt.

stank (stăngk) *p.t.* of **stink**.

stan·nic (stăn′ĭk) *adj-* of or containing tin, especially in compounds where it has a valence of four.

stan·nous (stăn′əs) *adj-* of or containing tin, especially in compounds where it has a valence of two.

stan·za (stăn′zə) *n-* part of a poem consisting of an organized group of lines, often having the same rhyme scheme and meter as the other parts of the same poem.

staph·y·lo·coc·cus (stăf′ə lō kŏk′əs) *n-* [*pl.* **staph·y·lo·coc·ci** (-kŏk′sī′, -kŏk′sē)] any of various spherical bacteria that usually form irregularly shaped clusters.

sta·ple (stā′pəl) *n-* 1 small, U-shaped piece of metal driven into wood or similar material to fasten wires, a hook, bolt, etc. 2 thin, bracket-shaped piece of wire pressed into papers, cloth, leather, etc., as a fastening device. *vt-* [**sta·pled, sta·pling**]: *Please* staple *the card to the large sheet.* [from Old English **stapol** meaning "pillar; post; a step."]

for WOOD

for PAPER

Staples

sta·ple (stā′pəl) *n-* 1 principal product of a place. 2 very important or major element: *The election was the* staple *of conversation.* 3 raw material for manufacture. 4 fiber of cotton, wool, flax, etc., before it is spun or twisted into thread. 5 something produced regularly and in large amounts because of constant need or demand: *Sugar is a* staple. *as modifier: a* staple *product; a* staple *topic.* [from Old Dutch **stapel** meaning "a post; support."]

sta·pler (stā′plər) *n-* device used to press staples into paper, cardboard, cloth, etc.

star (stär) *n-* 1 any heavenly body visible from the earth as an apparently fixed point of light in the clear night sky. 2 *Astronomy* any of the gaseous heavenly bodies of great mass that shine by their own light, as distinguished from comets, meteors, nebulae, plants, and satellites. The stars are at such a distance from the earth that they appear as points of light, and most can be seen only with the aid of a telescope. 3 figure, usually with five or six points, that represents or resembles one of these bodies. 4 asterisk. 5 any of the heavenly bodies supposedly having an influence on human events; hence, fate; destiny: *It was not in our* stars *to win today.* 6 any person who is outstanding in his field; especially, a leading actor or actress. *as modifier: a* star *shape; a* star *performer.* *vi-* [**starred, star·ring**] to appear in a leading role: *My favorite actor* stars *in that play.* *vt-* 1 to mark or adorn with a star or stars. 2 to present or feature in a leading role. —*adj-* **star′less.** *adj-* **star′like.**

Stars

star·board (stär′bərd) *n-* the right side of a ship or boat as one faces the bow (for picture, see *aft*). *adj-* on or moving toward this side: *a* starboard *cabin; a* starboard *breeze.* *adv-: Move* starboard *a little.*

starch (stärch) *n-* 1 white, odorless, tasteless carbohydrate that is an important source of nourishment. It is present in most plants and is especially plentiful in grain and potatoes. 2 commercial preparation of this substance, used to stiffen cloth. 3 *Informal* energy; vigor; stamina. *vt-* to stiffen with commercial starch: *to* starch *a shirt.*

starch·y (stär′chē) *adj-* [**starch·i·er, starch·i·est**] 1 containing much starch: *Potatoes are a* starchy *food.* 2 stiffened with starch: *a* starchy *collar.* 3 stiff and formal in manner; not friendly. —*n-* **starch′i·ness.**

stare (stâr) *vi-* [**stared, star·ing**] 1 to look or gaze intently or fixedly with wide open eyes, because of surprise, curiosity, etc.: *to* stare *at a strange sight.* 2 to show brightly or conspicuously; glare: *Bright colors* stared *from the gaudy paintings.* *vt-* to affect in some way with a fixed, intent look: *She* stared *him into silence.* *n-* fixed gaze with wide-open eyes. *Hom-* stair. —*n-* **star′er.**

stare down (or **out of countenance**) to make uneasy by staring.

stare (one) in the face to be right in front of one's eyes; be perfectly plain and clear.

star·fish (stär′fĭsh′) *n-* [*pl.* **star·fish; star·fish·es** (kinds of starfish)] any of various star-shaped sea animals with five or more arms.

Starfish
3–5 in. across

star·gaze (stär′gāz′) *vi-* [**star·gazed, star·gaz·ing**] 1 to gaze or look at the stars, especially because one is interested in astronomy or astrology. 2 to daydream. —*n-* **star′gaz′er.**

stark (stärk) *adj-* [**stark·er, stark·est**] 1 unadorned; bare. 2 bleak; desolate; barren: *a stark scene.* 3 sheer; utter; absolute: *She was speechless with stark terror.* 4 rigid: *to be stark with cold.* *adv-* completely; totally: *He is stark blind.* —*adv-* **stark′ly.** *n-* **stark′ness.**

star·let (stär′lət) *Informal n-* young motion-picture actress who has small roles but receives much publicity.

star·light (stär′līt′) *n-* light given by the stars.

star·ling (stär′lĭng) *n-* any of various birds with dark, glossy, iridescent feathers that are speckled in winter.

star·lit (stär′lĭt′) *adj-* lighted by the stars: *a starlit evening.*

star-of-Beth·le·hem (stär′ əv bĕth′ lĭ hĕm′) *n-* plant related to the lilies, with clusters of star-shaped white flowers and narrow leaves.

Starling, about 8 1/2 in. long

star of Bethlehem *n-* large star which, according to the New Testament, guided the Magi to the manger of Jesus in Bethlehem.

Star of David *n-* six-pointed star, used as the symbol of Judaism and Israel.

star·ry (stär′ē) *adj-* [**star·ri·er, star·ri·est**] 1 showing or having many stars: *a starry sky; a starry night.* 2 shining like stars; sparkling; bright: *her starry eyes.* 3 shaped like a star. —*n-* **star′ri·ness.**

star·ry-eyed (stär′ē īd′) *adj-* looking on the bright side of things; naively trusting and optimistic.

Stars and Bars *n-* (takes singular or plural verb) first flag of the Confederacy, having three bars of alternating red and white and a blue field with white stars in a circle, each star representing a seceded State.

Stars and Stripes *n-* (takes singular or plural verb) the flag of the United States, with thirteen alternating red and white stripes representing the original colonies and, in the upper left corner, a blue field covered with white stars representing each State.

Star-Span·gled Banner (stär spăng′gəld) *n-* 1 the Stars and Stripes. 2 the national anthem of the United States, the words of which were written by Francis Scott Key in 1814.

start (stärt) *vi-* 1 to begin to go somewhere or do something; set out: *to start on a journey; to start in a new business.* 2 to have a beginning; commence: *Classes start at nine o'clock.* 3 to make a sudden, involuntary movement of surprise, pain, shock, etc.: *He started at a loud noise.* 4 to spring or leap forth suddenly: *The rabbit started from the underbrush.* 5 of a nail, screw, etc., to become loosened. *vt-* 1 to put into operation or action; set going: *to start a clock.* 2 to bring into being; originate: *to start a rumor; to start an argument.* 3 to begin; commence: *to start a course in French.* 4 to cause or help to begin an enterprise or activity: *to start a friend in business; to start a traveler on the right road.* 5 to enter in a contest, game, etc.: *to start a horse in a race.* 6 to rouse into motion, especially from a place of concealment; flush: *to start a rabbit from its burrow.* 7 to cause (a nail, screw, etc.) to loosen. *n-* 1 beginning. 2 sudden involuntary movement: *a start of surprise; to wake with a start.* 3 lead or advantage: *He has a start of two miles over the others.* 4 assistance or opportunity in beginning an activity or enterprise: *to give someone a start in a new career.* 5 brief spurt of motion or activity.

    to start with as a beginning; in the first place.

start·er (stär′tər) *n-* 1 person or thing that starts an activity or undertaking: *He was a slow starter, but he soon caught up with the others.* 2 device that sets a machine or engine in operation; self-starter. 3 person who gives the signal for the start of a race. 4 person who dispatches buses, taxicabs, etc., according to a schedule.

starting point *n-* place from which something or someone starts out: *the starting point of a journey.*

star·tle (stär′tal) *vt-* [**star·tled, star·tling**] 1 to cause to move suddenly in surprise, alarm, etc.: *That loud noise startled me.* 2 to fill with surprise or alarm; shock: *Her boldness startles me.* *vi-:* *She startles easily.*

star·tling (stärt′lĭng) *adj-* causing alarm or surprise; shocking; astonishing: *a startling discovery.* —*adv-* **star′tling·ly:** *a startlingly loud noise.*

star·va·tion (stär vā′shən) *n-* a starving or being starved.

starve (stärv) *vi-* [**starved, starv·ing**] 1 to die or suffer from lack of food. 2 *Informal* to be very hungry: *I ate a light lunch, and now I'm starving!* *vt-* to cause to die, suffer, weaken, etc., from lack of food: *to starve a prisoner to death; to starve the enemy into submission.*

    starve for to have great need for; long for; hunger.

starve·ling (stärv′lĭng) *n-* person, animal, or plant that is thin or weak from lack of nourishment. *as modifier:* *a starveling poet.*

state (stāt) *n-* 1 condition of a person or thing: *a state of good health; a state of confusion.* 2 excited mental or emotional condition: *She is in such a state today!* 3 body of people united under one government; commonwealth; nation. 4 powers, organization, government, or territory of such a body of people: *to defend one's state; to surround a state.* 5 (often **State**) one of the main political and geographical subdivisions of the United States and certain other nations. 6 dignity and great ceremony; pomp: *to receive an ambassador in state. as modifier:* *a state document; a state dinner.* *vt-* [**stat·ed, stat·ing**] to express in words; declare; set forth: *to state an opinion.*

    lie in state of a distinguished person, to be on public and formal display before burial.

state bank *n-* 1 bank owned or operated by a sovereign state. 2 (often **State Bank**) bank chartered and regulated by the State in which it is located. See also *national bank.*

state·craft (stāt′krăft′) *n-* art or skill of managing the political affairs of a nation; statesmanship.

stat·ed (stā′təd) *adj-* 1 fixed; regular: *a stated amount.* 2 announced; declared: *his stated motives.*

state·hood (stāt′hŏŏd′) *n-* condition of being a state; especially, official standing as one of the States of the United States of America: *Alaska was admitted to statehood in 1959.*

State·house or **state·house** (stāt′hous′) *n-* building in which the business of a State legislature is conducted; State capitol. Also **State House.**

state·less (stāt′ləs) *adj-* having no officially recognized nationality; lacking citizenship in any country: *a stateless immigrant.* —*n-* **state′less·ness.**

state·ly (stāt′lē) *adj-* [**state·li·er, state·li·est**] having a grand manner or appearance; impressive; dignified: *a stately walk; a stately palace.* —*n-* **state′li·ness.**

state·ment (stāt′mənt) *n-* 1 act of stating or declaring something; declaration: *his statement of the facts.* 2 something stated in speech or writing: *All these statements are correct.* 3 organized report or summary, especially on financial matters: *a bank statement.*

State police *n-* 1 police force under the jurisdiction of a State rather than that of a city or local municipality. 2 national police force of a totalitarian government.

state·room (stāt′rōōm′) *n-* luxurious bedroom or private suite on a passenger ship or railroad car.

state·side (stāt′sīd′) *Informal adj-* of, located in, or directed toward the continental United States, as *consteer.*

steer (stēr) *n-* young, castrated male of domestic cattle, especially when raised for beef. [from Old English *stēor* meaning "heavy" as applied to beasts.]

steer·age (stēr′ĭj) *n-* formerly, the part of a ship set aside for passengers paying the lowest rates.

steer·age·way (stēr′ĭj wā′) *n-* minimum forward speed to permit a boat to be steered.

steering committee *n-* legislative committee that determines the order in which bills will be considered.

steering wheel *n-* wheel for steering a car, ship, etc.

steg·o·sau·rus (stĕg′ə sôr′əs) *n-* [*pl.* **steg·o·sau·rus·es** or **steg·o·sau·ri** (-rī)] large dinosaur of the Jurassic period, having a small head and a double row of pointed bony plates along its back. For picture, see *dinosaur.*

stein (stīn) *n-* 1 large beer mug. 2 amount held by it.

ste·la (stē′lə) *n-* [*pl.* **ste·lae** (-lē)] upright stone slab, often carved and used in ancient times as a grave marker or monument.

¹still (stĭl) *adj-* [still·er, still·est] 1 without movement; motionless: *Please stand still.* 2 quiet; silent: *Please be still while she is talking.* 3 calm or tranquil: *a still night.* *vt-* to make quiet; calm: *Mother stilled the baby by giving him a rattle.* *adv-* 1 in spite of that; nevertheless: *Tim's toothache grew worse; still he didn't complain.* 2 even; yet: *You may be tall but your brother is still taller.* *n-* 1 stillness; tranquillity: *in the still of the night.* 2 still photograph. [from Old English **stille** meaning "quiet" as in a stall, and related to **stall.**]

²still (stĭl) *n-* 1 any of various apparatus for distilling liquids by evaporation and condensation, used especially for making strong alcoholic liquors. 2 distillery. [from earlier **still** meaning "to distill," from Latin *stillare,* "to drop or drip," from *stilla,* "a drop."]

still·birth (stĭl' bûrth') *n-* birth of a dead child; also, the dead child.

still·born (stĭl' bôrn') *adj-* dead at the time of birth.

still life *n-* painting or photograph of inanimate objects.

still·ness (stĭl' nəs) *n-* absence of sound or motion; calm: *the stillness of the sea; the stillness of the night.*

still photograph *n-* single photograph; especially, a photograph taken by a **still camera,** designed to take pictures one at a time and not rapidly enough to produce a series of photographs for a motion picture.

stilt (stĭlt) *n-* 1 one of a pair of long poles, each with a block on which a person may stand and walk at a distance above the ground. 2 one of the posts used to support a house, dock, or other structure above land or water. —*adj-* **stilt' like'.**

stilt·ed (stĭl' təd) *adj-* 1 stiffly formal; pompous: *a play with stilted dialogue.* 2 supported by slender props.

stim·u·lant (stĭm' yə lənt) *n-* 1 drug, beverage, etc., that arouses, quickens, or intensifies the senses or bodily functions. 2 anything that urges or spurs one on; stimulus: *Money was his major stimulant.*

stim·u·late (stĭm' yə lāt') *vt-* [stim·u·lat·ed, stim·u·lat·ing] 1 to quicken; arouse to greater activity: *Brisk walking stimulates the circulation.* 2 to excite; stir up: *This book has stimulated my interest.* 3 to act as a stimulus to (a sense organ, nerve, certain pattern of behavior, etc.): *Light stimulates the retina.* —*n-* **stim' u·la' tion.** *n-* **stim' u·la' tor:** *Walking is a good stimulator of the circulation.*

stim·u·lus (stĭm' yə ləs) *n-* [*pl.* **stim·u·li** (-lī, -lē)] anything that stimulates; especially, anything that causes a response in the nervous system, sensory system, feelings, etc., of a person or other organism.

sting (stĭng) *vi-* [stung (stŭng), sting·ing] 1 of certain animals and plants, to prick with a sharp organ that injects poison: *Bees, scorpions, and sting rays can sting.* 2 to cause a sharp pain or hurt, either to the body or the feelings: *Alcohol stings when put on a wound. His harsh words stung.* 3 to be sharply painful; smart: *This finger stings. Our eyes stung.* *vt-* 1 of certain animals and plants, to inject poison into by means of a sharp organ: *A hornet stung my brother.* 2 to incite to action by taunts or reproaches: *The harsh speech stung them to action.* *n-* 1 sharp organ used by certain animals and plants to inject poison. 2 act of wounding with such an organ; also, such a wound. 3 sharp, burning pain, either of the body or the feelings; smart. 4 a taunt, reproach, etc., that incites one to action. —*adv-* **sting' ing·ly.** *adj-* **sting' less.**

sting·a·ree (stĭng' ə rē') *n-* sting ray.

sting·er (stĭng' ər) *n-* 1 person, animal, or thing that stings. 2 the organ of a bee, scorpion, etc., that stings. 3 *Informal* sharp, stinging remark or blow.

sting ray *n-* any of several large tropical fish having a broad, flat body and a tail armed with bony spines that can inflict severe wounds. Also **sting' ray'.**

stin·gy (stĭn' jē) *adj-* [stin·gi·er, stin·gi·est] 1 reluctant to give, lend, or spend. 2 scanty; skimpy: *a stingy helping of food.* —*adv-* **stin' gi·ly.** *n-* **stin' gi·ness.**

stink (stĭngk) *vi-* [stank (stăngk) or stunk (stŭngk), stunk, stink·ing] 1 to give off a disgusting odor: *Garbage stinks.* 2 *Slang* to be extremely bad in character, worth, or quality. *n-* 1 disgusting odor: *the stink of spoiled fish.* 2 *Slang* moral outrage; scandal.

stink·bug (stĭnk' bŭg') *n-* any of various broad, flat bugs that emit an unpleasant odor.

stink·er (stĭng' kər) *n-* 1 any of several large sea birds that emit an offensive odor. 2 *Slang* person or thing that is extremely offensive or irritating.

stink·weed (stĭngk' wēd') *n-* any of various plants such as the jimson weed, having a strong, offensive scent.

stink·y (stĭng' kē) *Informal adj-* [stink·i·er, stink·i·est] 1 having a bad smell; smelly. 2 hateful; offensive. 3 of inferior quality.

stint (stĭnt) *vt-* to be frugal or sparing with; skimp: *to stint an allowance.* *vi-* : *Don't stint during your vacation.* *n-* chore; task assigned: *My stint is washing dishes.* **without stint** without sparing: *to give without stint.*

stipe (stīp) *n-* in botany, a stem or support, especially one supporting a pistil or one of the fronds of a fern.

sti·pend (stī' pənd) *n-* fixed pay or allowance; especially, the amount paid to a scholarship student.

stip·ple (stĭp' əl) *vt-* [stip·pled, stip·pling] to draw, paint, or engrave by means of dots or light touches rather than lines. *n-* art or method of drawing, painting, or engraving in such a way; also, the effect so produced.

stip·u·late (stĭp' yə lāt') *vt-* [stip·u·lat·ed, stip·u·lat·ing] to arrange or settle definitely; specify as part of an agreement: *He stipulated that he be paid in advance.*

stip·u·la·tion (stĭp' yə lā' shən) *n-* specific condition or requirement in a contract or agreement.

stip·ule (stĭp' yōōl) *n-* in some plants, either of two small appendages at the base of the leaf or petiole. —*adj-* **stip' uled'.**

stir (stûr) *vt-* [stirred, stir·ring] 1 to set in motion; move: *A light breeze stirred the leaves.* 2 to mix or rearrange with a moving implement: *to stir one's coffee; to stir the fire with a poker.* 3 to rouse or excite; provoke; incite (often followed by "up"): *to stir men to revolt; stir one's heart; to stir up trouble.* *vi-* 1 to move: *The leaves stirred in the trees. He would not stir from his chair.* 2 to be mixed by a moving implement: *This cake stirs easily.* 3 to be roused or excited: *Pity stirred in his heart.* 4 to be active or begin to show signs of activity: *Is anything stirring in town?* *n-* 1 slight movement: *There was a stir in the woods.* 2 a mixing: *Give the soup a stir.* 3 excitement; commotion. —*n-* **stir' rer.**

stir·ring (stûr' ĭng) *adj-* rousing; exciting; thrilling. —*adv-* **stir' ring·ly.**

stir·rup (stûr' əp) *n-* 1 one of a pair of metal or wooden loops hung from the side of a saddle to hold a rider's foot. 2 (also **stirrup bone**) the inner one of the three tiny, sound-transmitting bones of the middle ear (for picture, see ¹*ear*).

stirrup cup *n-* 1 cup of liquor given to a rider about to depart. 2 any farewell drink.

stitch (stĭch) *n-* 1 complete movement of a threaded needle in and out of material.

stitch·ing (stĭch' ĭng) *n-* series or arrangement of stitches.

stoat (stōt) *n-* the ermine, especially in its summer coat of reddish brown.

stock (stŏk) *n-* 1 a supply; store: *Jones' store has a large stock of goods.* 2 livestock. 3 raw or basic material: *A ham bone is stock for soup.* 4 liquid in which meat, and sometimes vegetables, has been cooked. It is often used as the basis for various soups. 5 trunk or stump of a tree, or stem of a plant. 6 ancestry. 7 an ethnic group; race. 8 shares in a business: *Mr. White owns most of the company's stock.* 9 shoulder piece of a firearm or crossbow

Stilts

Stirrup

Stocks

stock·ade (stŏk ād´) *n-*
1 strong defensive fence
made of tall, closely set posts
with sharpened tops, much
used around frontier forts
and animal pens; palisade.
2 the area or buildings enclosed by such a fence. 3 in
the Army, Marines, and Air
Force, a prison for service
personnel. *vt-* [stock·ad·ed,
stock·ad·ing] to surround or
defend with a stockade.

Stockade

stock·bro·ker (stŏk´ brō´ kər) *n-* person who buys and
sells stocks or securities for others.

stock car *n-* standard automobile adjusted for racing.

stock clerk *n-* person who is responsible for supplies
in a stockroom.

stock company *n-* 1 corporation whose capital is
divided into shares of stock. 2 theatrical company that
is more or less permanently associated with one management and presents a repertoire of plays.

stock exchange *n-* 1 place where stocks and bonds are
bought and sold. 2 association of stockbrokers engaged
in the business of buying and selling stocks.

stock·hold·er (stŏk´ hōl´ dər) *n-* person who owns stock
or shares in a company; shareholder.

stock·ing (stŏk´ ǐng) *n-* close-fitting woven or knit covering for the foot and leg.

stocking cap *n-* long, tapered knitted cap with a tassel
or pompon at the end, usually worn in winter.

stock in trade *n-* 1 merchandise that a store has ready
for sale. 2 most effective skill or quality; resources:
The quick joke was his stock in trade.

stock·man (stŏk´ mən) *n-* [*pl.* stock·men] person who
owns, raises, or is in charge of livestock.

stock market *n-* 1 trade in stocks and bonds; also, the
prices at which these are selling. 2 stock exchange.

stock·pile (stŏk´ pīl´) *n-* reserve supply of materials,
food, etc., to be used during a shortage. *vt-* [stock·piled,
stock·pil·ing] to store a reserve supply of.

stock·room (stŏk´ rōōm´) *n-* place where a business
stores its supplies.

stock split *n-* the exchange by a business of two shares
of its stock for each share held by a stockholder.

stock-still (stŏk´ stǐl´) *adj-* completely motionless.

stock·y (stŏk´ ē) *adj-* [stock·i·er, stock·i·est] short, solid,
and sturdy in build. —*adv-* stock´i·ly. *n-* stock´i·ness.

stom·ach (stŭm´ ək) *n-* 1 pouchlike part of the alimentary canal, between the esophagus and the duodenum
in man and other vertebrates, that secretes the gastric
juices and has an important digestive function. For
picture, see *intestine.* 2 ability to endure or enjoy: *She
has no stomach for a quarrel. vt-* to endure; tolerate:
I could not stomach his rudeness.

stom·ach·er (stŭm´ ə kər) *n-* formerly, the part of a
woman's dress covering the stomach and chest.

stomp (stŏmp) *vt-* to tread heavily upon; stamp: *to
stomp the ground. vi-*: *He stomped hard on the floor.
n-* jazz dance featuring a lively, heavy step.

stone (stōn) *n-* 1 hard mineral body; rock. 2 mineral
matter which makes up such bodies of any size. 3 precious stone; gem. 4 something like a stone in looks or
hardness: *a cherry stone; a gallstone; a kidney stone.
vt-* [stoned, ston·ing] 1 to remove stones from: *to stone
cherries.* 2 to throw stones at; especially, to put to
death by throwing stones at. *adj-* 1 made of rock:
a stone house. 2 made of stoneware.

Stone Age *n-* the earliest known period in human
culture, in which implements were made of stone.

stone-blind (stōn´ blīnd´) *adj-* completely blind.

stone-cut·ter (stōn´ kŭt´ ər) *n-* person or machine that
cuts stone or prepares it for use.

stone-deaf (stōn´ děf´) *adj-* completely deaf.

Stone·henge (stōn´ hěnj´) *n-* prehistoric monument in
southern England, north of Salisbury, consisting of a
group of thirty huge, rough-cut stones dating back
approximately to 1848 B.C.

stone·ma·son (stōn´ mā´ sən) *n-* person whose work is
to cut, prepare, and lay stones for walls, buildings, etc.

stone·ware (stōn´ wâr´) *n-* coarse, glazed pottery containing clay, sand, and flint.

stone·work (stōn´ wûrk´) *n-* 1 stone structure or part
of it; masonry. 2 process of working in stone. —*n-*
stone´work·er.

ston·y (stō´ nē) *adj-* [ston·i·er, ston·i·est] 1 covered with
stones: *a stony beach.* 2 like stone; cold, hard, or rigid:
a stony look. —*adv-* ston´i·ly. *n-* ston´i·ness.

stood (stŏŏd) *p.t. & p.p.* of stand.

stooge (stōōj) *Informal n-* 1 actor who is the foil for a
comedian. 2 person who unquestioningly carries out
the wishes of another.

stool (stōōl) *n-* 1 seat on a
long leg or legs, sometimes
with a low back. 2 backless
and armless seat with short
legs: *a milking stool.* 3 low
rest for the feet. 4 feces.

stool pigeon *n-* 1 pigeon
used as a decoy to help trap
other pigeons. 2 *Slang*
person who informs on criminals for the police.

Stools

stoop (stōōp) *vi-* 1 to lean down with back and shoulders
bent: *He had to stoop to pick up the box.* 2 to stand or
walk in this way: *He stooped when he was tired.* 3 to
degrade or lower oneself: *She would not stoop to gossip.*
4 to pounce or swoop down, as a bird on prey. *n-* 1 a
leaning down. 2 bent posture: *He stood with a stoop.*
[from Old English *stupian.*] *Hom-* stoup.

stoop (stōōp) *n-* porch, platform, or stairway at the
entrance of a house. [American word from Dutch
stoep meaning "a high step at the door."] *Hom-* stoup.

stop (stŏp) *vt-* [stopped, stop·ping] 1 to halt the motion,
action, or progress of: *to stop a car; to stop a rumor; to
stop a revolt.* 2 to hold back; hinder; restrain (often
followed by "from"): *to stop him from leaving.* 3 to
close up; fill in: *to stop a bottle; to stop a wound.* 4 to
obstruct; block (often followed by "up"): *to stop up a
channel.* 5 *Informal* in boxing, to defeat, especially by a
knockout. 6 *Music* to press (a string) or close (a finger
hole) so as to produce the desired pitch. *vi-* 1 to halt or
cease: *The car stopped at the gas station. He stopped
in the middle of his speech.* 2 to stay: *We are stopping
at my sister's house overnight.*

stop·gap (stŏp´ găp´) *n-* something that closes an opening; hence, a temporary substitute. *as modifier-* a
stopgap *job.*

stop·light (stŏp´ līt´) *n-* 1 traffic light 2 light on the rear
of a car or truck, that lights when the driver brakes.

stop·o·ver (stŏp´ ō´ vər) *n-* brief stay in a place, in the
course of a journey; also, a place used as a waiting point.

stop·page (stŏp´ ǐj) *n-* 1 act of stopping; stop; halt:
a work stoppage. 2 obstruction; block: *a stoppage in
the nasal passages.*

stop·per (stŏp´ ər) *n-* 1 plug or cork used to close an
opening in a bottle, sink, etc. 2 person or thing that
stops or deters some action or movement; check. *vt-*:
He stoppered *the bottle tightly.*

stop·ple (stŏp´ əl) *n-* plug; stopper, *vt-* [stop·pled, stop·
pling] to close with, or as if with, a stopper.

stop·watch (stŏp´ wŏch´) *n-* watch with a hand that
indicates fractions of a second and can be started or
stopped instantly by pressing a button.

stor·age (stôr´ ǐj) *n-* 1 a keeping or reserving of goods in
a safe place: *the storage of furniture in a warehouse.*
2 place for storing or state of being stored: *My piano is
in storage.* 3 the cost of keeping goods in a warehouse
or other place for storing: *Can you pay the storage on
your piano?* 4 part of an electronic computer that stores
information; memory. *as modifier-* a storage *bin.*

storage battery *n-* set of electrical cells that can
change chemical energy into direct-current electrical
energy and vice versa.

store (stôr) *n-* 1 place where goods are kept and sold: *a
grocery store; a department store.* 2 supply gathered
together; fund: *a store of acorns; a store of wisdom.*

stric·ture (strĭk′chər) *n-* **1** severe criticism or blame; censure: *I resent this* stricture *on my conduct.* **2** thing that limits, confines, or restricts; restraint. **3** abnormal narrowing of a passage; constriction.

stride (strĭd) *vi-* [strode (strōd), strid·den (strĭd′ən), strid·ing] to walk with long steps: *to stride along the beach. vt-* to sit or stand with one leg on either side of something; straddle; bestride: *to stride a horse. n-* long step or steps: *a steady* stride. —*n-* strid′er.

hit one's stride to reach one's peak of performance.

take in stride to deal with or handle without great fuss.

stri·den·cy (strī′dən sē) *n-* shrill and penetrating quality: *a* stridency *of tone.* Also **stri′dence.**

stri·dent (strī′dənt) *adj-* harsh; grating; shrill: *a* strident *tone.* —*adv-* stri′dent·ly.

strife (strīf) *n-* **1** a conflict; struggle: *the* strife *of battle.* **2** discord; contention: *the* strife *over a will.*

strike (strĭk) *vt-* [struck (strŭk), struck or strick·en (strĭk′ən), strik·ing] **1** to hit: *The ball* struck *the ground.* **2** to deliver a blow against: *to* strike *the floor with one's foot.* **3** to afflict or affect by disease, emotion, etc.: *An epidemic* struck *the town.* **4** to make an impression on: *The idea* struck *us as absurd.* **5** to produce by stamping or printing: *to* strike *a gold medal.* **6** to make burn by friction: *to* strike *a match.* **7** to sound: *The clock is* striking *the hour.* **8** to discover luckily or in a sudden manner: *The miner* struck *gold.* **9** to reach; make; conclude: *The shopkeeper* struck *a bargain with the customer.* **10** to cross out; cancel: *to* strike *a word from the minutes of the meeting.* **11** to stop work at (a factory, shop, etc.) in order to get more pay, better working conditions, etc. **12** of a venomous snake, to bite (someone or something) with a violent lunge: *The cobra* struck *him on the ankle.* **13** to take down and pack: *to* strike *a tent; to* strike *camp. vi-* **1** to deal a quick blow or thrust; make an attack: *The army* struck *in two places at once.* **2** to hit; collide; become stranded: *The ship* struck *on the reef.* **3** to proceed: *They* struck *into the woods.* **4** to sound, as a bell or clock. **5** to cease working in order to gain better pay, working conditions, etc. **6** of a venomous snake, to bite with a violent lunge: *The rattler coiled and* struck. *n-* **1** a stopping of work in order to gain more pay or better working conditions. **2** in baseball, a tally against the batter, scored either when he swings at a pitch and misses, or allows a pitch to pass through the strike zone, or fouls a ball when he has fewer than two such tallies against him, or hits a foul tip which the catcher holds, when he already has two such tallies against him. **3** a lucky discovery, especially of oil or ore; hence, any sudden success: *a gold* strike; *a lucky* strike. **4** in fishing, a hard bite.

on strike not working, because of a stoppage called in order to improve pay, working conditions, etc.

strike home to deliver a well-aimed and effective blow.

strike it rich to earn or produce wealth suddenly.

strike off to make (something) quickly but well.

strike out **1** in baseball, of a batter, to have three strikes recorded against him, and therefore be called out. **2** of a baseball pitcher, to cause a batter to strike out.

strike up to begin: *We* struck up *a friendship.*

strike·bound (strĭk′bound′) *adj-* closed by a strike.

strike·break·er (strĭk′brā′kər) *n-* worker hired to take the place of one out on strike.

strike·out (strĭk′out′) *n-* in baseball, an out caused by three strikes charged against the batter. *as modifier: the league's* strikeout *record.*

strik·er (strī′kər) *n-* **1** worker who ceases working as a protest against existing wages and working conditions or as a means of securing improvements in them. **2** person or thing that strikes. **3** in the U.S. Navy, a seaman training for a petty officer's rating.

strike zone *n-* in baseball, the rectangular area above home plate, as wide as the plate itself and as high as the distance between the batter's knees and armpits, through which a pitch must pass to be called a strike, if the batter does not swing.

strik·ing (strī′kĭng) *adj-* very noticeable; claiming attention; attractive: *a* striking *example of efficiency;*

string (strĭng) *n-* **1** thin cord or twine. **2** anything used to tie something: *an apron* string. **3** set of things arranged on a cord: *a* string *of beads.* **4** series or line of something: *a* string *of lanterns; a* string *of cars.* **5** wire or catgut cord for a musical instrument. **6** *Informal* team or part of a team: *I was on the first* string *in football.* **7** strings (1) section of an orchestra composed of stringed instruments. (2) *Informal* accompanying conditions: *The grant had a great many* strings *attached. vt-* [strung (strŭng), string·ing] **1** to put on a cord: *to* string *beads for a necklace.* **2** to furnish with cords: *to* string *a racket; to* string *a guitar.* **3** to pull the tough fibers off the edges of (vegetables). —*adj-* string′less. *adj-* string′like′.

have two strings to (one's) bow to have more than one possibility of action or response. pull strings to use special influence in order to get something done.

string along with to cooperate with; play along with.

string out **1** to extend. **2** to space out in a line.

string up **1** to hang. **2** *Informal* to execute by hanging.

string bean *n-* **1** kind of bean grown for its edible pods. **2** the pod itself. **3** *Slang* very tall and thin person.

stringed instrument *n-* musical instrument fitted with strings, such as a guitar, violin, or harp.

strin·gent (strĭn′jənt) *adj-* strict; rigid; severe in requirements; exacting, as a law: *a stringent standard; a* stringent *rule.* —*n-* strin′gen·cy. *adv-* strin′gent·ly.

string·er (strĭng′ər) *n-* **1** person or thing that strings. **2** in a building, airplane, boat, bridge, etc., a long timber or member connecting uprights or crosspieces.

string·y (strĭng′ē) *adj-* [string·i·er, string·i·est] **1** like string. **2** full of fibers: *a* stringy *piece of meat.* —*n-* string′i·ness.

¹strip (strĭp) *vt-* [stripped, strip·ping] **1** to remove (a covering); peel: *to* strip *wallpaper from a wall.* **2** to rob: *The invaders* stripped *the country of its treasures. vi-* to undress: *The boys* stripped *and went swimming.* [from Old English (be)strypan, "to plunder."] —*n-* strip′per.

²strip (strĭp) *n-* **1** long, narrow, flat piece. **2** place for airplanes to land and take off; also, a road or street. **3** comic strip. [from ¹strip, and influenced by stripe.]

strip cropping *n-* planting crops in strips that alternate with strips of grass or hay and run across the slope of the land, to reduce erosion.

stripe (strīp) *n-* **1** band or streak: *a tiger's* stripes; *a suit with a narrow black* stripe. **2** *Military Informal* a chevron. **3** sort or kind: *They are persons of the same* stripe. **4** blow with a whip or rod: *They gave the thief ten* stripes. **5** stripes prison uniform having broad horizontal bands, usually of black and white. *vt-* [striped, strip·ing] to mark with bands or streaks.

striped (strīpt, *also* strī′pəd) *adj-* marked with or made in stripes: *a small, striped snake.*

striped bass *n-* large sea bass with horizontal stripes on the sides and valued as food and game. Also strip′er.

strip·ling (strĭp′lĭng) *n-* boy between youth and manhood.

strive (strīv) *vi-* [strove (strōv), striv·en (strĭv′ən), striv·ing] **1** to try hard; make an effort: *You must* strive *for better marks.* **2** to struggle; battle: *to* strive *against a gale.*

sty·mie (stī′mē) *n-* in golf, the position of a ball on the putting green when it lies directly between the hole and the ball of the person who must putt next. *vt-* [sty·mied, sty·my·ing] to obstruct by playing a ball into this position; hence, to block so that one is unable to move.

styp·tic (stĭp′tĭk) *adj-* able to stop or check bleeding, especially by contracting the opened blood vessels. *n-: Alum is a* styptic.

sty·rene (stī′rēn′) *n-* an organic compound (C_8H_8) that is a constituent of one kind of synthetic rubber.

Styx (stĭks) *n-* in Greek mythology, the principal river of the underworld.

sua·sion (swā′zhən) *n-* persuasion. —*adj-* sua′sive. *adv-* sua′sive·ly. *n-* sua′sive·ness.

suave (swäv) *adj-* [suav·er, suav·est] bland, smooth, and winningly pleasant in manner. —*adv-* suave′ly. *n-* suav′i·ty or suave′ness.

sub·cu·ta·ne·ous (sŭb′kyoo tā′nē əs) *adj-* beneath the surface of the skin: *a* subcutaneous *inflammation.* —*adv-* sub′cu·ta′ne·ous·ly: *to inject* subcutaneously.

sub·stan·tive (sŭb′stən tĭv′) *adj-* 1 having independent and permanent substance or reality. 2 *Grammar* used as or functioning as a noun: *a substantive clause.* 3 substantial. *n-* noun or group of words used as a noun. —*adv-* sub′stan·tive·ly.

sub·sta·tion (sŭb′stā′ shən) *n-* station which is subsidiary to a main one, especially in an electrical power system.

sub·sti·tute (sŭb′ stə tōōt′, -tyōōt′) *n-* 1 person replacing another; one acting instead of another: *You will be my substitute for three days.* 2 thing that is used instead of something else. *vt-* [sub·sti·tut·ed, sub·sti·tut·ing] to use in place of another: *Let's substitute sugar for honey in the recipe.* *vi-*: *Do you think sugar will substitute for honey?*

sub·sti·tu·tion (sŭb′ stə tōō′shən, -tyōō′shən) *n-* the putting of a person or thing in the place of another: *the substitution of honey for sugar in a recipe.* *as modifier*: *Do you know the new substitution rules?*

sub·stra·tum (sŭb′ strā′ təm, -străt′ əm) *n-* [*pl.* sub·stra·ta] 1 an underlying layer: *sand on a substratum of gravel.* 2 thing that forms the groundwork or support of some other structure; foundation: *Education is the substratum of culture.*

sub·struc·ture (sŭb′ strŭk′ chər) *n-* 1 structure, such as a building foundation, which supports another structure. 2 bed of soil, gravel, etc., that supports railroad tracks.

sub·ter·fuge (sŭb′ tər fyōōj′) *n-* scheme, excuse, or trick by which one seeks to escape from a difficulty.

sub·ter·ra·ne·an (sŭb′ tə rā′ nē ən) *adj-* 1 below the surface of the earth; underground: *a subterranean river.* 2 hidden; out of sight; secret: *a subterranean maneuver.*

sub·tile (sŭt′ əl, sŭb′ təl) *adj-* [sub·til·er, sub·til·est] 1 of fluids, extremely thin and tenuous; delicate and rarefied; lacking density: *This antifreeze is very subtile, and easily leaks out.* 2 subtle. *Hom-* subtile.

sub·ti·tle (sŭb′ tǐ′ təl) *n-* 1 second title under a main title of a book, essay, poem, etc. 2 translation of words spoken in a motion picture, printed at the bottom of the frames for persons who do not know the language being spoken. *vt-* [sub·ti·tled, sub·ti·tling]: *I subtitled my story "How to Avoid Leaping Crocodiles."*

sub·tle (sŭt′ əl) *adj-* [sub·tier, sub·tlest] 1 delicate; fine: *to make a subtle distinction; the subtle difference in two shades of blue.* 2 difficult to understand the meaning of; elusive: *It was hard to tell from her subtle smile what she meant.* 3 able to understand or make fine differences of meaning; discerning: *a subtle mind; a subtle wit.* 4 underhanded; crafty; sly: *a subtle trick to outwit another.* *Hom-* subtile. —*n-* sub′tle·ness. *adv-* sub′tly.

sub·tle·ty (sŭt′ əl tē) *n-* [*pl.* sub·tle·ties] 1 quality of being subtle; discernment; keenness or delicacy of mind. 2 something subtle; especially, a finely drawn distinction: *I cannot follow the subtleties of your argument.*

sub·top·ic (sŭb′ tŏp′ ĭk) *n-* a division of the subject under the main topic.

sub·tract (səb trăkt′) *vt-* to deduct (one number or quantity) from another: *If you subtract 3 from 6, you have 3.* *vi-*: *to learn to subtract.* —*n-* sub·tract′ er.

sub·trac·tion (səb trăk′shən) *n-* 1 *Mathematics* operation that is the opposite of addition; also, operation or process of computing the difference between two numbers. 2 a taking away or deducting. 3 something subtracted.

sub·trac·tive (səb trăk′tĭv) *adj-* of, relating to, or involving subtraction.

sub·tra·hend (sŭb′trə hĕnd′) *Mathematics n-* the number that is subtracted from another given number. Example: In 8 − 6 = 2, the subtrahend is 6. See also *minuend.*

sub·urb (sŭb′ ûrb′) *n-* 1 residential district that lies close to a large city: *to live in a suburb and work in the city.* 2 the suburbs (1) all of the residential districts near a city: *to live in the suburbs near Chicago.* (2) such districts in general, regarded as a type of society: *the average income of the suburbs.*

sub·ur·ban (sə bûr′ bən) *adj-* of or having to do with a suburb: *a suburban community.*

sub·ur·ban·ite (sə bûr′ bə nīt′) *n-* person who lives in the suburbs.

sub·urb·i·a (sə bûr′ bē ə) *n-* suburbs and suburbanites, collectively; also, the special habits, viewpoints, interests, etc., of suburbs and suburbanites.

sub·ver·sion (səb vûr′ zhən) *n-* 1 a gradual undermining and destroying of something: *Your ideas will bring about the subversion of all we have worked for.* 2 activity aimed at such ends: *to combat subversion in government.*

sub·ver·sive (səb vûr′ sĭv, -zĭv) *adj-* having the aim or effect of subverting something: *a subversive doctrine.* *n-* person who subverts. —*adv-* sub·ver′sive·ly. *n-* sub·ver′sive·ness.

sub·vert (səb vûrt′) *vt-* to undermine or overthrow, especially in a gradual or insidious way: *to subvert a government; to subvert a principle.* —*n-* sub·vert′ er.

sub·way (sŭb′ wā′) *n-* 1 underground electric railway. 2 underground passage: *a subway under the street.* *as modifier*: *a subway train; a subway conductor.*

suc·ceed (sək sēd′) *vi-* 1 to gain or accomplish one's aim or purpose; to do extremely well: *Jim is a person who is bound to succeed in life.* 2 to be the heir or follow next in line (to an office, title, or property): *Queen Elizabeth succeeded to the throne when her father died.* *vt-* to come directly after: *Dawn succeeded night.*

suc·cess (sək sĕs′) *n-* 1 favorable result; good outcome; triumph: *Hard work is often the surest means of success.* 2 person or thing that succeeds. 3 degree of achievement (in gaining a desired result): *What success did you have in persuading him?* 4 gain of wealth, fame, etc.

suc·cess·ful (sək sĕs′ fəl) *adj-* 1 having or meeting with success; gaining what is desired or aimed at; turning out favorably. 2 fortunate and prosperous: *Dick's father is a successful lawyer.* —*adv-* suc·cess′ful·ly.

suc·ces·sion (sək sĕsh′ ən) *n-* 1 the coming of one after another in unbroken order; series; sequence: *a long succession of happy days.* 2 the taking over of another's office, title, or property through legal right or inheritance: *the succession to the throne.* 3 system by which rank, an office, etc., changes hands. 4 series of descendants; heirs.

in succession one after another.

suc·ces·sive (sək sĕs′ ĭv) *adj-* following one after the other without interruption; consecutive: *Last spring our baseball team won six successive games.* —*adv-* suc·ces′sive·ly.

suc·ces·sor (sək sĕs′ ər) *n-* person or thing that succeeds another; especially, a person who succeeds to an office, rank or property.

suc·cinct (sək sĭngkt′) *adj-* clearly expressed in a very few words; concise; terse; exactly to the point. —*adv-* suc·cinct′ly. *n-* suc·cinct′ ness.

suc·cor (sŭk′ ər) *vt-* to give needed help; aid. *n-* aid or relief given. *Hom-* sucker.

suc·co·tash (sŭk′ ə tăsh′) *n-* corn and beans, usually lima beans, cooked together.

sul·ly (sŭl′ē, sŏŏl′-) *vt-* [sul·lied, sul·ly·ing] to tarnish or soil; dirty or stain: *He sullied my reputation.*

sul·phate (sŭl′ fāt′, sŏŏl′-) sulfate.

sul·phide (sŭl′ fīd′, sŏŏl′-) sulfide.

sul·phur (sŭl′ fər, sŏŏl′-) sulfur.

sul·tan or **Sul·tan** (sŭl′ tən, sŏŏl′-) *n-* in certain Muslim countries, the ruler or governor.

sul·tan·a (səl tăn′ ə) *n-* 1 wife, daughter, mother, or sister of a sultan. 2 variety of seedless grapes valued for raisins and wine.

sul·tan·ate (sŭl′ tə năt′, sŏŏl′-) *n-* rule, rank, or territory of a sultan.

sul·try (sŭl′ trē, sŏŏl′-) *adj-* [sul·tri·er, sul·tri·est] hot, close, and moist; oppressive: *The jungle has a sultry climate.* —*adv-* sul′tri·ly. *n-* sul′tri·ness.

sum (sŭm) *n-* 1 total of two or more numbers, things, or quantities; whole: *The grocer adds the prices of items sold to find the sum the customer must pay.* 2 result obtained by addition: *He added 2 and 3 and 4 to get the sum of 9.* 3 *chiefly Brit.* problem in arithmetic. 4 amount of money: *the sum of five dollars.* 5 summary; essence; substance: *That book contains the sum of 50 years of thought.* *vi-* [summed, sum·ming] *chiefly Brit.* to do simple arithmetic. *Hom-* some.

swaddling clothes *n-* strips of cloth formerly used to wrap around a newborn baby, to prevent it from moving too much.

swag (swăg) *Slang n-* stolen goods or money; loot.

swag·ger (swăg′ər) *vi-* 1 to strut about and act in a showy or overbearing manner. 2 to boast noisily; bluster. *n-* 1 an overbearing walk or way of acting. 2 noisy boasting; bluster. —*n-* **swag′ger·er.** *adv-* **swag′ger·ing·ly:** *He moved swaggeringly down the street.*

swagger stick *n-* light cane carried by army officers.

Swa·hi·li (swä hē′lē) *n-* a Bantu language with some Arabic elements, used widely in commerce and in government circles of East Africa and in the Congo.

swain (swān) *n-* 1 *Archaic* country youth. 2 young male lover (used humorously).

¹**swal·low** (swŏl′ō) *vt-* 1 to transfer (food, drink, etc.) from the mouth to the stomach through the throat: *to swallow a piece of bread.* 2 to take in; absorb: *Expenses swallowed the profits.* 3 to take up completely and make disappear; engulf: *Darkness swallowed the fugitives.* 4 to believe or accept without question: *to swallow a story.* 5 to hold back; refrain from expressing: *to swallow one's pride; to swallow anger.* 6 to accept without protest; endure: *to swallow an insult.* 7 to take back; retract: *to swallow one's words.* *vi-* to perform the act of taking down food or liquid: *He had a sore throat and couldn't swallow.* *n-* 1 act of transferring food, drink, etc., from the mouth to the stomach through the throat. 2 amount so transferred at one time: *a swallow of water.* 3 space between the grooved edge of the wheel and the frame of a pulley, through which the rope passes. [from Old English *swelgan* meaning "to swallow; engulf."] —*n-* **swal′low·er.**

²**swal·low** (swŏl′ō) *n-* any of various slender, migratory birds with a long, forked tail and pointed wings, admired for swift, graceful flight. [from Old English *swalwe.*]

Barn swallow, about 5 in. long

swal·low·tail (swŏl′ō tāl′) *n-* 1 tail of a swallow; also, any similar deeply forked tail. 2 any of various large butterflies having the hind wing extended so as to suggest a tail. 3 (also **swallow-tailed coat**) *Informal* tails; tailcoat.

swam (swăm) *p.t.* of **swim.**

swa·mi (swä′mē) *n-* [*pl.* **swa·mis**] 1 Hindu title of respect, equivalent to "Master," "lord." 2 Hindu teacher, especially of religion; pundit.

swamp (swŏmp) *n-* low, spongy land soaked with water, often having a growth of trees, but unfit for cultivation; marsh; bog. *as modifier:* *a swamp boat; swamp fever.* *vt-* 1 to fill with water or cause to sink by flooding: *The big wave swamped the boat.* 2 to overwhelm: *Christmas mail swamped the post office.* *vi-* to tip so as to be flooded: *The boat swamped.* —*adj-* **swamp′ish.**

swamp·y (swŏm′pē) *adj-* [**swamp·i·er, swamp·i·est**] like a swamp; muddy; marshy; also, filled with swamps.

swan (swŏn) *n-* any of various large, usually white, swimming birds having very long, curved necks, admired for their grace on the water. See also **cygnet.** *as modifier:* *a swan feather.* —*adj-* **swan′like′.**

Swan, about 5 ft. long

¹**syn·di·cate** (sĭn′də kāt′) *vt-* [**syn·di·cat·ed, syn·di·cat·ing**] 1 to manage as or combine into a syndicate: *to syndicate a group of newspapers.* 2 to publish in a number of newspapers or magazines at the same time: *to syndicate a comic strip.* —*n-* **syn′di·ca′tion.**

²**syn·di·cate** (sĭn′dĭ kət) *n-* combination of companies or persons formed to pursue a business enterprise.

syn·od (sĭn′nəd) *n-* 1 church council or meeting. 2 any assembly or council. —*adj-* **syn′od·al.**

syn·o·nym (sĭn′ə nĭm′) *n-* word or phrase having the same or almost the same meaning as another word or phrase. A synonym for "happy" is "glad."

syn·on·y·mous (sə nŏn′ə məs) *adj-* similar or nearly similar in meaning. —*adv-* **syn·on′y·mous·ly.**

syn·op·sis (sĭ nŏp′səs) *n-* [*pl.* **syn·op·ses** (-sēz′)] condensed statement of a book, speech, or similar work; summary: *a one-page synopsis of a novel.*

syn·op·tic (sĭ nŏp′tĭk) *adj-* in a condensed form.

syn·tac·tic (sĭn tăk′tĭk) or **syn·tac·ti·cal** (-tĭ kəl) *Grammar adj-* of or relating to syntax: *a syntactic rule.* —*adv-* **syn·tac′ti·cal·ly.**

syn·tax (sĭn′tăks′) *Grammar n-* the relationship or arrangement of words into larger constructions, such as phrases, clauses, and sentences; also, the part of grammar that treats of this.

syn·the·sis (sĭn′thə səs) *n-* [*pl.* **syn·the·ses** (-sēz′)] 1 a combining of separate elements or parts to make a new form or whole. 2 a whole made of parts or elements combined: *His philosophy is a synthesis of old and new ideas.* 3 *Chemistry* the production of a compound by the union of two or more elements, radicals, or simpler compounds, especially by industrial or laboratory methods: *the synthesis of a new drug.*

syn·the·size (sĭn′thə sīz′) *vt-* [**syn·the·sized, syn·the·siz·ing**] to combine into a new form or whole; also, to make by combining separate parts or elements: *to synthesize rubber.*

syn·thet·ic (sĭn thĕt′ĭk) *adj-* 1 of, relating to, or using synthesis: *a synthetic manufacturing process.* 2 made by a combination of chemicals similar to those of which a natural product is composed; man-made: *nylon, rayon, and other* synthetic *fibers; synthetic rubber.* 3 not spontaneous; artificial. *n-* man-made substance formed by combining chemicals. —*adv-* **syn·thet′i·cal·ly.**

syph·i·lis (sĭf′ə ləs) *n-* contagious venereal disease, usually affecting first the genitals, second the skin, and third the bones, viscera, brain, and spinal cord.

syph·i·lit·ic (sĭf′ə lĭt′ĭk) *adj-* relating to or affected with syphilis. *n-* person affected with syphilis.

sy·rin·ga (sə rĭng′gə) *n-* mock orange.

sy·ringe (sə rĭnj′, sĭr′ĭnj) *n-* 1 narrow tube with a rubber bulb or plunger at one end for drawing in and discharging liquid. It is used for injecting fluid into the body, cleaning wounds, etc. 2 hypodermic syringe. —*vt-* [**sy·ringed, sy·ring·ing**] to cleanse with a syringe: *to syringe the ears.*

syr·inx (sĭr′ĭngks′) *n-* [**syr·in·ges** (-ĭn jēz′) or **sy·rinx·es**] 1 the song organ of birds, located at the lower end of the windpipe. 2 in anatomy, Eustachian tube. 3 panpipe.

syr·up (sûr′əp, sĭr′-) *n-* any of various thick, sweet liquids. Also **sirup.** —*adj-* **syr′up·like′** or **syr′up·y.**

sys·tem (sĭs′təm) *n-* 1 a group or combination of parts or units functioning together as a whole according to some common law or purpose: *the solar system; a railroad system.* 2 in physiology, a combination of parts of the body that work together and are dependent on one another: *the circulatory system; the digestive system.* 3 set of facts, rules, laws, etc., organized so as to make up a body of knowledge or a way of doing something: *a system of government; a system of education.* 4 orderly method of doing things; routine: *Hugh has a system for his day's work.* 5 bodily and mental makeup: *One's system can stand just so much.*

sys·tem·at·ic (sĭs′tə măt′ĭk) or **sys·tem·at·i·cal** (-ĭ kəl) *adj-* 1 arranged or carried on according to a system: *a systematic survey of population growth.* 2 careful and orderly in one's work or habits; methodical: *a systematic worker.* —*adv-* **sys′tem·at′i·cal·ly.**

sys·tem·a·tize (sĭs′tə mə tīz′) *vt-* [**sys·tem·a·tized, sys·tem·a·tiz·ing**] to arrange or organize according to a system or regular method. —*n-* **sys′tem·a·ti·za′tion, sys′tem·a·tiz′er.**

sys·tem·ic (sĭ stĕm′ĭk) *Medicine adj-* of, relating to, or affecting the body as a whole: *a systemic infection.* —*adv-* **sys·tem′i·cal·ly.**

sys·to·le (sĭs′tə lē) *n-* rhythmic contraction of the heart, especially of the ventricles, that forces the blood to circulate. See also **diastole.**

sys·tol·ic (sĭs tŏl′ĭk) *adj-* measured during, or having to do with, the stage of systole: *the systolic blood pressure*

T

T, t (tē) *n-* [*pl.* **T's, t's**] the twentieth letter of the English alphabet.

to a T perfectly; with precision.

T temperature (on the Kelvin scale).

T. 1 Tuesday. 2 Territory. 3 Township. 4 tablespoon.

t. 1 teaspoon. 2 temperature. 3 tenor. 4 ton.

Ta symbol for tantalum.

tab (tăb) *n-* 1 small projection on a file card or on the edge of a page for indexing purposes; also, any device used to bring special attention to something. 2 little loop or tag on a garment for lifting or hanging it, or on package for pulling it open or closing it.

ta-bor (tā′bər) *n-* in former times, a small drum beaten with one hand by a piper to accompany himself.

tab-u-lar (tăb′yə lər) *adj-* 1 arranged in a table, list, or column: *a tabular report.* 2 having a broad, flat top: *a tabular region.* —*adv-* **tab′u-lar-ly.**

tab-u-late (tăb′yə lāt′) *vt-* [**tab-u-lat-ed, tab-u-lat-ing**] to arrange in a table, list, or other systematic outline: *to tabulate election returns.* —*n-* **tab′u-la′tion.**

tab-u-la-tor (tăb′yə lā′tər) *n-* 1 typewriter device that automatically shifts the carriage to preset positions. 2 any of various office machines used for tabulating data.

ta-chis-to-scope (tə kĭs′tə skōp′) *n-* an instrument that displays visual images on a screen very briefly. It is used to study perception and attention and also to improve reading speed.

ta-chom-e-ter (tă kŏm′ə tər, tə-) *n-* an instrument for measuring the speed of rotation of an engine shaft.

tac-it (tăs′ĭt) *adj-* not spoken or written down, but nevertheless implied: *a tacit agreement.* —*adv-* **tac′it-ly.**

tac-i-turn (tăs′ə tûrn′) *adj-* silent or reserved; not inclined to talk: *a taciturn scholar.* —*n-* **tac′i-turn′i-ty.** *adv-* **tac′i-turn′ly.**

tack (tăk) *n-* 1 small, sharp-pointed nail with a broad, flat head. 2 in sailing ships, (1) a rope for lashing down the lower forward corner of certain sails; also, the corner of the sail so held down. (2) the direction of a ship as determined by the position of her sails. (3) change in a ship's direction to take advantage of side winds. 3 one's course of action: *His thoughts went off on a new tack.* 4 a simple stitch, often used as a temporary fastening. *vt-* 1 to fasten with tacks: *to tack a carpet; to tack a bow to a dress.* 2 to attach: *to tack a note to a report.* 3 to change the direction of (a sailboat) by turning into and across the wind in order to go indirectly toward one's destination; also, to navigate (a sailboat) in a zig-zag course toward one's destination, because the wind is against one. *vi-* 1 to sail in a zig-zag course. 2 to suddenly change one's course of action or attitude; veer. —*n-* **tack′er.**

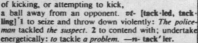
Tacks

tack-le (tăk′əl) *n-* 1 any act of seizing violently, usually with intent to subdue. 2 in football, (1) an attempt to seize and stop and, usually, throw to the ground an opponent who is running with the ball. (2) one of the two players in the line position between guard and end; also, the position itself. 3 the special equipment or gear for a job or sport: *fishing* tackle. 4 system of pulleys and ropes used for lifting and lowering weights; especially, on a boat or ship, the pulleys and ropes for managing sails and spars, taking on cargo, etc. 5 in soccer, the act of kicking, or attempting to kick, a ball away from an opponent. *vt-* [**tack-led, tack-ling**] 1 to seize and throw down violently: *The policeman tackled the suspect.* 2 to contend with; undertake energetically: *to tackle a problem.* —*n-* **tack′ler.**

Single and double tackles

tack-y (tăk′ē) *adj-* [**tack-i-er, tack-i-est**] slightly sticky: *the tacky surface of a freshly painted wall.* [from **tack.**]

tack-y (tăk′ē) *Informal adj-* [**tack-i-er, tack-i-est**] 1 shabby; seedy. 2 cheap and showy; gaudy. [American word of uncertain origin.]

tac-o-nite (tăk′ə nīt′) *n-* a low-grade iron ore.

tail-coat (tail′kōt′) *n-* man's swallow-tailed coat, worn as part of a full-dress suit; tails.

tailed (tāld) *adj-* having a tail, usually of a specified length or kind: *a tailed ape; a bushy-tailed deer.*

tail-first (tāl′fûrst′) or **tail-fore-most** (tāl′fôr′mōst′) *adv-* with the rear end first.

tail-gate (tāl′gāt′) *n-* panel at the rear end of a truck, station wagon, or cart, hinged at the bottom and let down for loading and unloading. *vi-* [**tail-gat-ed, tail-gat-ing**] *Informal* to drive dangerously close to the rear of another vehicle.

tail gun *n-* defensive machine gun mounted in the tail of a bomber or other military aircraft. —*n-* **tail′ gun′ ner.**

tail light *n-* warning light, usually red, that is mounted at the rear of a vehicle.

tai-lor (tā′lər) *n-* person who repairs or alters clothing; also, a person who makes clothing, especially to order. *vt-* 1 to repair, alter, or make (clothing): *to tailor a suit.* 2 to make, design, or adapt for a special purpose: *to tailor a law to the needs of society.*

tai-lor-ing (tā′lər ĭng) *n-* 1 the occupation or business of a tailor; also, the workmanship of a tailor: *a suit that shows fine tailoring.* 2 a making, designing, or adapting of something for a special purpose.

tai-lor-made (tā′lər mād′) *adj-* 1 made by a tailor. 2 made or fitted to one's particular needs or circumstances; made-to-order: *a tailor-made apartment.*

tail-piece (tāl′pēs′) *n-* 1 something added at the end. 2 flat piece of wood at the wider end of a violin or similar instrument, to which the strings are attached.

tail pipe *n-* exhaust pipe of a gasoline engine.

tail-race (tāl′rās′) *n-* channel for carrying used water away from a water wheel.

tails (tālz) *n- pl.* 1 man's swallow-tailed coat; tailcoat. 2 the full-dress suit of which it is part.

tail-spin (tāl′spĭn′) *n-* downward spiral movement of an airplane performing a stunt or out of control, in which the tail forms a wider circle than the nose.

tail wind *n-* wind blowing in the same general direction as that of a moving airplane or ship.

taint (tānt) *vt-* 1 to cause to spoil or infect; contaminate; pollute: *One bad apple can taint a whole barrel.* 2 to stain or blemish. *n-* blemish: *a taint on his character.*

take (tāk) *vt-* [**took** (tŏŏk), **tak-en, tak-ing**] 1 to get hold of; grasp: *He took the child's hand.* 2 seize by force; capture: *The Indians took the fort.* 3 to get or obtain: *We took the apartment. Our team took first prize.* 4 to subscribe to: *We take two morning papers.* 5 to accept: *Please take this gift. Jack took the bad news calmly.* 6 to remove or subtract (usually followed by "away"): *Mom took away the dishes.* 7 to select; choose: *You may take any hat.* 8 to eat, drink, or inhale: *Jack took the medicine.* 9 to lead: *This road takes you to town.* 10 to carry or convey: *I will take your trunk to the attic.* 11 to require; need: *Your hat takes my fancy.* 13 to travel by means of: *Mary took a plane to Boston.* 14 to make (an image or recording): *Frank took my picture.* 15 to feel; experience: *I take pride in my work.* 16 to engage in doing or making: *I took a walk.* 17 to conduct; escort: *I took my aunt to lunch.* 18 to consider; regard: *We took him to be intelligent.* 19 to react to or accept in the proper way: *The silk took the dye.* 20 to come upon: *I took him by surprise.* 21 *Grammar* to require as part of the construction or usage: *The verb takes an object.* 22 to determine by means of examination or a measuring instrument: *The nurse took my temperature.* 23 in baseball, of a batter, to allow (a pitch) to pass by without swinging at it. 24 *Informal* to cheat; deceive.

take amiss to be offended by.

take back to withdraw: *Ed would not take back the insult.*

take care to be careful.

take care of 1 to give care to. 2 to attend to.

take down 1 to tear down. 2 to take apart; dismantle. 3 *Informal* to make less proud; humble.

take effect to become effective.

take for to mistake for: *I took him for an actor.*

take ill to become sick.

tan·bark (tăn′bärk′) *n-* any of various barks rich in tannic acid, which, after the acid has been removed, is used in making soft surfaces, as in circus rings.

tan·dem (tăn′dəm) *adv-* one behind another. *adj-* arranged in this way: *a pair of* tandem *bicycle seats. n-* 1 bicycle for two or more persons with seats placed one behind the other. 2 pair of horses harnessed one behind the other; also, a two-wheeled carriage pulled by such a file of horses.

tang (tăng) *n-* 1 strong, sharp taste, smell, or flavor: *a* tang *of ginger.* 2 faint suggestion; tinge. 3 the part of a knife, sword, fork, etc., that goes into the handle.

tan·gent (tăn′jənt) *n-* 1 *Mathematics* straight line that touches a curve at only one point. For picture, see *circle.* 2 *Mathematics* of an acute angle in a right triangle, the ratio of the side opposite to the acute angle and the side adjacent to it. 3 an abrupt and unplanned change of course in thought or discussion; digression: *He tried to concentrate, but his mind kept flying off on a* tangent. *adj-* 1 touching a curve or surface at only one point and not intersecting the curve or surface: *a* tangent *line.* 2 touching at one point but not intersecting: *two* tangent *circles.*

tan·gen·tial (tăn jĕn′shəl) *adj-* 1 *Mathematics* of, related to, or in the direction of a tangent. 2 only slightly related or relevant to a subject: *a* tangential *comment.* —*adv-* tan·gen′tial·ly.

tan·ge·rine (tăn′jə rēn′) *n-* 1 small, reddish-yellow, sweet orange with a loose skin somewhat thinner than that of an orange. 2 reddish-orange color. *adj-: some* tangerine *juice; a* tangerine *scarf.*

tan·gi·ble (tăn′jə bəl) *adj-* 1 such as can be touched or felt by the touch: *a* tangible *object, not an illusion.* 2 real; definite: *Tom's visit was* tangible *proof of his friendship.* 3 in economics, having physical or material substance; also, such as can be accurately appraised: *A house is* tangible *property. n-* tangibles material assets.

tan·gle (tăng′gəl) *vt-* [tan·gled, tan·gling] to knot or twist so as to make difficult to unravel; entangle: *to* tangle *strands of yarn. vi-* 1 to become entangled: *The ropes* tangled *around the beams.* 2 *Informal* to argue or fight: *They* tangled *over political differences. n-* 1 knotted or twisted mass; hence, any confused condition: *a* tangle *of opposing stories.* 2 *Informal* argument or fight.

tan·gly (tăng′glē) *adj-* [tan·gli·er, tan·gli·est] full of tangles; entangled; snarled.

tan·go (tăng′gō) *n-* [*pl.* tan·gos] modern ballroom dance of Latin-American origin, with gliding steps and deliberate poses; also, the music for this dance.

tan·gy (tăng′ē) *adj-* [tang·i·er, tang·i·est] having a strong, sharp taste or smell; pungent.

Army tank with water tank in background

tank (tăngk) *n-* 1 any large container for liquids or gas: *a water* tank; *an oil* tank. 2 (often tank′ful′) amount that fills a tank; amount held by a tank. 3 large armored combat vehicle carrying guns and moving on caterpillar treads. *vt-* to put, store, or process in a tank.

tan·ning (tăn′ing) *n-* 1 process or business of making hides into leather. 2 *Informal* a whipping.

tan·nish (tăn′əsh) *adj-* somewhat tan.

tan·sy (tăn′zē) *n-* [*pl.* tan·sies] any of various strong-smelling herbs with small clusters of yellow flowers.

tan·ta·lize (tăn′tə līz′) *vt-* [tan·ta·lized, tan·ta·liz·ing] to tease or torment by being out of reach or showing something that is out of reach. —*n-* tan′ta·liz′er. *adv-* tan′ta·liz′ing·ly.

tar (tär) *Informal n-* sailor. [from tarpaulin.]

tar·an·tel·la (tär′ən tĕl′ə) *n-* lively Italian dance, once thought to cure the bite of the tarantula; also, the music for this dance.

ta·ran·tu·la (tə răn′chə lə) *n-* [*pl.* ta·ran·tu·las or ta·ran·tu·lae (-lē)] any of various large, hairy spiders found throughout tropical and semitropical areas of America and Europe. Tarantulas have a painful, but not dangerous, bite.

Tarantula, body about 3 1/2 in. long

Ta·ras·can (tä rä skän′) *n-* [*pl.* Ta·ras·cans, also Ta·ras·can] one of an important Mexican Indian people of southwestern Mexico. *adj-: the* Tarascan *empire.*

tar·dy (tär′dē) *adj-* [tar·di·er, tar·di·est] 1 not on time; late: *the* tardy *arrival of the train.* 2 slow: *a* tardy *growth of plants.* —*adv-* tar′di·ly. *n-* tar′di·ness.

tare (târ) *n-* 1 vetch. 2 the seed of this plant. 3 in the Bible, a harmful weed that grows among wheat. [from a shortened form of earlier tare-etch, from Middle English tare meaning "the darnel."] *Hom-* ²tear.

tare (târ) *n-* allowance of weight made to the purchaser by deducting the weight of the container. *vt-* [tared, tar·ing] to weigh (a container) in order to determine the weight to be deducted. [from French tare, "a loss in value," from Spanish tara, "an allowance in weight," from Arabic tarha, "thing thrown away."] *Hom-* ²tear.

tar·get (tär′gət) *n-* 1 something to be shot at or attacked, such as a series of painted circles one within the other, aimed at in archery, or the objective of a bombing raid. 2 something to work or strive for; goal; aim. 3 any object of insult, ridicule, or similar treatment: *A man in public life is always a* target *for criticism. as modifier: a* target *date;* target *practice.*

Target

tar·iff (tăr′if) *n-* 1 list of duties or taxes placed by a government on goods entering or leaving a country. 2 the tax or duty levied according to such a list or schedule: *There is a* tariff *on Swiss watches.* 3 any list or scale of rates or charges. *as modifier: new* tariff *laws.*

tar·mac (tär′măk′) *chiefly Brit. & Canadian n-* 1 tarmacadam road or runway. 2 **Tarmac** *Trademark* special preparation used for tarmacadam pavement.

tar·mac·ad·am (tär′mə kăd′əm) *n-* pavement consisting largely of pebbles held together by various tars; also, a mixture of such tars that is ready to use.

tarn (tärn) *n-* small mountain lake or pool.

tar·nish (tär′nish) *vi-* to lose brightness; become dull: *Silver* tarnishes *rapidly in this climate. vt-* to stain: *Egg yolk* tarnishes *silver. Slander* tarnished *his reputation. n-* 1 loss of brightness; dullness. 2 a stain; blemish. 3 a film of oxide or sulfide that stains some metal substances.

tar·nish·a·ble (tär′nish ə bəl) *adj-* such as can be tarnished or easily tarnished: *a* tarnishable *silver bowl.*

ta·ro (tär′ō) *n-* [*pl.* ta·ros] any of several tropical plants cultivated for their edible starchy roots; also, the root of such a plant. *as modifier: a* taro *farm.*

tar·pau·lin (tär pô′lən) *n-* heavy, waterproofed canvas or cloth, used as a protective covering. Also **tarp.**

tar·pon (tär′pən) *n-* large, silvery game fish found throughout the Caribbean Sea and slightly north.

Tb symbol for terbium.

TB or **T.B.** tuberculosis. Also **t.b.**

T-bar (tē′bär′) *n-* T-shaped bar hung top down from the cable of a ski lift so that two skiers can be carried up the slope by leaning back against the crosspiece. *as modifier: a* T-bar *lift; a* T-bar *tow.*

tbs. or **tbsp.** tablespoon; tablespoons.

Tc symbol for technetium.

Te symbol for tellurium.

tea (tē) n- 1 shrub with pointed leaves and white flowers, grown mainly in Asia and Africa. 2 the dried leaves of this shrub. 3 drink made from soaking these leaves in hot water. 4 similar drink made from leaves or meat extract: *sage* tea; *beef* tea. 5 late afternoon meal or party at which hot tea is served. *as modifier: a* tea *merchant.* Homs- tee, ti.

tea bag n- porous sack of tea leaves on a string, dipped into hot water to brew a small amount of tea.

teach (tēch) vt- [taught (tôt), tôt), teach·ing] 1 to instruct; educate: *to* teach *a pupil.* 2 to give instruction in: *Mr. Bean* teaches *history and sports.* 3 to help to learn: *Experience* taught *me to work carefully.* vt- to give instruction: *She* taught *for many years.*
▶Avoid using LEARN when you mean TEACH: *The teacher* teaches. *The learner* learns. Do not say: *He learned his son a lesson.* Say instead: *He taught his son a lesson.*

teach·a·ble (tē′chə bəl) adj- 1 such as can learn by being taught: *a teachable child.* 2 such as can be taught. —n- teach′a·ble·ness or teach′a·bil′i·ty.

teach·er (tē′chər) n- person who teaches; especially, a person whose profession is teaching.

teach·ing (tē′chĭng) n- 1 work of one who teaches; profession of a teacher. 2 something which is taught.

tea·cup (tē′kŭp′) n- 1 cup in which tea is served. 2 (also tea′cup·ful′) amount that such a cup holds.

tea·house (tē′hous′) n- in the Orient, a public place that serves tea and light meals; also, in Japan, a small garden house where tea is served with great ceremony.

teak (tēk) n- 1 tall East Indian tree, the leaves of which yield a red dye. 2 hard, durable timber of this tree, used in the making of ships and furniture. *as modifier: a* teak *table;* teak *decks.* Also teak′wood′.

tea·ket·tle (tē′kĕt′əl) n- covered kettle with a spout in which water is boiled.

teal (tēl) n- any of several kinds of small river or marsh ducks of central and eastern United States and Canada.

team (tēm) n- 1 group of people who make up one side in an athletic game or other contest; also, group of people who work together for any purpose: *a team of architects.* 2 two or more

Blue-winged teal.
about 16 in. long

horses, oxen, or other animals harnessed together to a plow, carriage, etc. *as modifier: a team effort; good* team *spirit.* vi- to join in a group: *Bill* teamed *with his friends.* vt- 1 to join (animals) together: *to* team *horses.* 2 to transport with animals: *to* team *logs.* Hom- teem.

team·mate (tēm′māt′) n- fellow member of a team.

team·ster (tēm′stər) n- 1 driver of a team of animals. 2 truck driver.

team·work (tēm′wûrk′) n- common effort of a group of people working together; cooperation.

tea·pot (tē′pŏt′) n- covered vessel with a spout and handle, for brewing and serving tea.

Teapot

tear (têr) n- drop of salty fluid from the eye, especially while crying. [from Old English *tēar.*] Hom- tier.
in tears crying; weeping: *She walked away in tears.*

teeth (tēth) n- pl. of tooth.

teethe (tēth) vi- [teethed, teeth·ing] to cut, grow, or develop teeth: *The infant is just beginning to* teethe.

tee·to·tal (tē′tō′tal) adj- 1 entire; total. 2 relating to total abstinence from alcoholic beverages.

tee·to·tal·er (tē′tō′tə lər) n- person who advocates total abstinence from alcoholic beverages.

teg·u·ment (tĕg′yə mənt) n- natural outer covering, such as the human skin or animal hide or shell.

tem·po·ral (tĕm′pər əl) adj- 1 limited in time: *a* temporal *phase.* 2 relating to the world; earthly: *a* temporal *concern.* 3 Grammar expressing time: *a* temporal *clause.* [from Middle English, from Latin temporalis, from tempor-, and tempus, "time."]

tem·por·al (tĕm′pər əl) adj- pertaining to parts of the head behind the eyes at the sides, either external or internal, such as the bones at the sides and base of the skull, and muscles and blood vessels in this region. [from Late Latin temporalis, from Latin tempora meaning "the temples (of the head)."]

tem·po·rar·y (tĕm′pə rĕr′ē) adj- continuing for or meant for a limited time only; not permanent; *a* temporary *job.* —adv- tem′po·rar′i·ly. n- tem′po·rar′i·ness.

temporary star nova.

tem·po·rize (tĕm′pə rīz′) vi- [tem·po·rized, tem·po·riz·ing] 1 to yield temporarily to current public opinion or circumstances: *The candidate* temporized *about several issues.* 2 to adopt a policy of delay; also, be evasive to gain time. —n- tem′po·ri·za′tion. n- tem′po·riz′er.

tempt (tĕmpt) vt- 1 to persuade or try to persuade to do something, especially something wrong or evil: *Hunger* tempts *some to steal.* 2 to lure; entice: *The bargains at the sale* tempted *her.* 3 to provoke or defy: *to* tempt *fate.*

temp·ta·tion (tĕmp tā′shən) n- 1 a tempting: *the temptation of a weak person by bad companions.* 2 condition of being tempted: *I try to avoid* temptation. 3 something that tempts: *That candy's a* temptation.

tempt·er (tĕmp′tər) n- 1 person who tempts. 2 the Tempter Satan; the Devil —n- fem. tempt′ress.

tempt·ing (tĕmp′tĭng) adj- alluring; attractive; seductive: *a tempting idea.* —adv- tempt′ing·ly.

ten (tĕn) n- 1 amount or quantity that is one greater than 9. 2 Mathematics (1) the cardinal number that is the sum of 9 and 1. (2) numeral such as 10 that represents this cardinal number. *as determiner* (traditionally called adjective or pronoun): *There are* ten *books here and* ten *there.*

ten·a·ble (tĕn′ə bəl) adj- such as can be held, defended, etc.: *a* tenable *viewpoint; a* tenable *fortress.* —n- ten′a·bil′i·ty. adv- ten′a·bly.

te·na·cious (tə nā′shəs) adj- 1 tight and unyielding: *a* tenacious *grip on the rope; a* tenacious *hold on life.* 2 holding or keeping hold very tightly: *He has a* tenacious *memory. He is as* tenacious *as a bulldog when he gets an idea.* —adv- te·na′cious·ly. n- te·na′cious·ness.

te·nac·i·ty (tə năs′ə tē) n- condition of being tenacious.

ten·an·cy (tĕn′ən sē) n- [pl. ten·an·cies] occupancy or use of land or buildings on the payment of rent to the owner; also, the length of such use or occupancy.

ten·ant (tĕn′ənt) n- 1 person who pays rent for the use of property. 2 any occupant or inhabitant: *The deer and fox are* tenants *of the woods.* 3 tenant farmer. vt- to occupy; inhabit. —adj- ten′ant·less.

tenant farmer n- farmer who rents, works, and usually lives on land belonging to someone else; especially, a sharecropper.

ten·ant·ry (tĕn′ən trē) n- [pl. ten·ant·ries] 1 condition of being a tenant. 2 the entire group of tenants occupying land and houses on one estate.

Ten Commandments n- in the Bible, the ten laws given to Moses by God.

tend (tĕnd) vi- 1 to be inclined in action or thought: *He* tends *to follow the ideas of his parents.* 2 to be likely to have a certain result: *Ill health* tends *to make some people grumpy.*

ten·der·heart·ed (tĕn′dər här′təd) adj- readily touched by the pain, grief, or love of others; compassionate; sympathetic.

ten·der·ize (tĕn′də rīz′) vt- [ten·der·ized, ten·der·iz·ing] to make (meat) softer and easier to chew, by pounding, marinating, or treating with enzymes.

ten·der·iz·er (tĕn′də rī′zər) n- liquid or powder, usually containing an enzyme from papaya juice, sprinkled on meat before cooking in order to tenderize it.

tensile strength n- the greatest stretching force that can be applied to a material without breaking it. It is expressed in pounds per square inch.

ter·ra·pin (tĕr′ ə pĭn) *n-* 1 any of various kinds of web-footed turtles of North and Central America having shells (covered with horny shields. 2 the flesh of some such turtles, prized as food.

ter·rar·i·um (tə rär′ ē əm) *n-* [*pl.* **ter·rar·i·ums** or **ter·rar·i·a** (-ē ə)] an enclosure like a dry aquarium for growing plants indoors or keeping small land animals such as toads or lizards.

Diamondback terrapin, 7–8 in. long

ter·res·tri·al (tə rĕs′ trē əl) *adj-* 1 of or relating to the planet Earth: *In his study of space science, he forgot terrestrial matters.* 2 consisting of land; not water or air: *the terrestrial surface of the earth.* 3 living on or in the ground. —*adv-* **ter·res′ tri·al·ly.**

ter·ri·ble (tĕr′ ə bəl) *adj-* 1 causing terror; dreadful; awful: *a terrible hurricane.* 2 distressing; causing sorrow: *a terrible accident.* 3 severe; causing extreme discomfort: *The heat was terrible last week.* 4 very bad; unpleasant: *a terrible book.* —*adv-* **ter′ ri·bly.**

ter·ri·er (tĕr′ ē ər) *n-* any of several kinds of small, active, intelligent dogs, such as the Airedale, Scotch, or Welsh terriers, once used to hunt small game.

ter·ri·fic (tə rĭf′ ĭk) *adj-* 1 arousing great fear or dread; terrible; appalling; alarming: *A terrific tornado almost destroyed the town.* 2 excessive; great: *The Presidency places a man under a terrific strain.* 3 *Slang* wonderful; marvelous; extremely good. —*adv-* **ter·rif′ i·cal·ly.**

Airedale terrier, 23 in. high

ter·ri·fy (tĕr′ ə fī′) *vt-* [ter·ri·fied, ter·ri·fy·ing] to cause great alarm to; frighten: *Airplane trips terrify her.* —*a/v-* **ter′ ri·fy·ing·ly:** *The slope was terrifyingly steep.*

ter·ri·to·ri·al (tĕr′ ə tôr′ ē əl) *adj-* of or having to do with a territory. —*adv-* **ter′ ri·tor′ i·al·ly.**

ter·ri·to·ry (tĕr′ ə tôr′ ē) *n-* [*pl.* **ter·ri·to·ries**] 1 large area of land; district or region. 2 an extent of land and water under the jurisdiction of a government or sovereign state: *The Northwest Territories is a territory of Canada.* 3 district alloted to a salesman or agent: *Tom's territory is outside Boston.* 4 land or space regarded by a person or animal as its special domain.

ter·ror (tĕr′ ər) *n-* 1 overwhelming fear; fright: *She has a terror of the dark.* 2 person or thing which terrifies or fills with fear or dread: *My cat is a terror to the dog next door.* 3 *Informal* annoying or mischievous person.

ter·ror·ism (tĕr′ ə rĭz′ əm) *n-* the committing of violent and terrifying acts for political purposes or to frighten a population into submission.

ter·ror·ist (tĕr′ ə rĭst) *n-* person who believes in or practices terrorism. —*adj-* **ter′ ror·is′ tic.**

ter·ror·i·za·tion (tĕr′ ər ə zā′ shən) *n-* a terrorizing.

ter·ror·ize (tĕr′ ə rīz′) *vt-* [ter·ror·ized, ter·ror·iz·ing] 1 to fill with terror by threats or acts of cruelty; terrify. 2 to control or dominate by terroristic means.

ter·ror·strick·en (tĕr′ ər strĭk′ ən) *adj-* in a state of extreme fright or intimidation.

ter·ry cloth (tĕr′ ē) *n-* cotton fabric woven with a deep pile with the loops uncut. *adj-* **(terry-cloth):** *a terrycloth robe.*

Tex·as leaguer (tĕk′ səs) *n-* in baseball, a short fly ball that falls safely between the infield and outfield.

Texas Ranger *n-* member of the State police of Texas.

text (tĕkst) *n-* 1 the main body of writing in a book or on a printed page, as distinguished from the notes and illustrations. 2 a passage of the Bible taken as the theme of a sermon. 3 theme; subject: *the text of a speech.* 4 textbook. 5 printed or written version of something: *Which text of the Bible do you use?*

text·book (tĕkst′ bŏŏk′) *n-* book written for the teaching

tex·tu·al (tĕks′ chŏŏ əl) *adj-* of or relating to a text or texts: *a textual error.* —*adv-* **tex′ tu·al·ly.**

thank (thăngk) *vt-* to say that one is grateful to; express or show gratitude to: *I will thank him myself for the book.* **have (oneself) to thank** to be solely to blame.

thank·ful (thăngk′ fəl) *adj-* feeling or showing gratitude or thanks; grateful: *I am thankful for this good weather.* —*adv-* **thank′ ful·ly.** *n-* **thank′ ful·ness.**

thank·less (thăngk′ ləs) *adj-* 1 not appreciated; unrewarding: *a thankless task.* 2 showing no appreciation; ungrateful. —*adv-* **thank′ less·ly.** *n-* **thank′ less·ness.**

thanks (thăngks) *interj-* thank you. *n- pl.* gratitude or an expression of gratitude.
   thanks to owing or due to; because of: *It was thanks to him that things went so well.*

thanks·giv·ing (thăngks′ gĭv′ ĭng) *n-* expression of gratitude or thanks; a prayer expressing thanks. *as modifier:* *a thanksgiving prayer.*

Thanks·giv·ing (thăngks′ gĭv′ ĭng) or **Thanksgiving Day** *n-* in the United States, the fourth Thursday in November, a day set apart for giving thanks to God. Thanksgiving was first celebrated by the Pilgrims at Plymouth in 1621. *as modifier:* *his Thanksgiving dinner.*

that (thăt) *determiner* (traditionally called demonstrative adjective or demonstrative pronoun) [*pl.* **those** thōz] 1 thing or person at a distance: *This is the house I was talking about, not that one.* 2 indicating a thing or person at a distance or already mentioned: *Give the papers to that boy over there.* 3 something already mentioned or pointed out: *Do I have to tell you that again?* 4 the other, as in contrast with this: *This is a nicer ring than that (ring).* 5 indicating the degree or amount previously mentioned or pointed out: *She lost the race by that much. She can walk that far.* *pron-* (relative pronoun) 1 who; whom; which: *the book that was here.* 2 in, on, or at which: *the years that he was gone.* 3 for which: *the reason that he came.* *conj-* 1 used to introduce clauses that can function as subjects, objects, and modifiers: *He said, "That I must go is certain." I know that he is there. We are sure that it is true. I'll look everywhere that I can.* 2 used to introduce clauses of purpose: *Work hard, that you may prosper.* 3 used to introduce subordinate clauses of result: *I am so sleepy that I can hardly see.* 4 used to introduce an expression of desire: *Oh, that what you say were true!*
   at that at a given moment: *And, at that, she left.* **in that** 1 as far as a certain thing is concerned: *He said it was pink, and in that he was right.* 2 since; because: *He cannot, in that he has not the tools.*

thatch (thăch) *n-* 1 straw, reeds or the like, used to cover a roof. 2 roof of such material: *Mice made their nests in the thatch.* 3 something that looks like thatch, such as thick, ragged hair. *vt-* to put thatch on.

Thatched cottage

that's (thăts) 1 that is. 2 that has.

thaw (thȯ) *vi-* 1 to melt: *The ice thawed in the warm room.* 2 to become friendlier or less formal: *The guests thawed when the birthday party got under way.* *vt-* to cause to melt; also, to bring to a temperature above the freezing point: *The sun will thaw the snow. Thaw the turkey before you cook it.* *n-* a melting of ice; also, weather warm enough to melt ice: *The thaw came late this spring.*

the (thə; thē before vowels) *definite article* 1 pointing out a specific or known person or thing

theirs (thârz) *pron-* (possessive pronoun) thing or things belonging to them: *The book is theirs but you may borrow it. That car of theirs is worn out.* *Hom-* there's.

the·ism (thē′ ĭz′ əm) *n-* 1 belief in the existence of a god or gods. 2 belief in a personal God as the creator and supreme ruler of the universe. —*n-* **the′ ist.** *adj-* **the·is′ tic.**

them (thĕm) *pron-* objective case of they: *I heard them singing.*

then (thĕn) *adv-* 1 at that time: *We were working then, but now we are resting.* 2 after that: *Eat dinner and then go to bed.*

ther·a·pist (thĕr′ə pĭst) *n-* person who gives therapy.

ther·a·py (thĕr′ə pē) *n-* [*pl.* **ther·a·pies**] the treatment of physical or mental disease or injury; also, a particular treatment or kind of treatment.

there (thĕr) *adv-* 1 in that or at that place: *Put it there, not here.* 2 to or toward that place; thither: *I can walk there in an hour.* 3 on that point; in that matter: *I disagree with you there.* *pron-* 1 that place or point: *I just came from there. Please read up to there.* 2 word of no meaning used to introduce a statement that something exists or is true: *I told him that there were two solutions. There is a new car outside.* 3 used as a vague intensifying substitute for a person's name or for "you": *Hello, there! Stop talking, there!* *interj-* exclamation of defiance, joy, sympathy, etc.: *I won't do it, so there! There, you did it!* There, there, *don't cry.* **Homs-** their, they're. **all there** normally intelligent; sane: *He's not all there.*
▶For usage note see HERE.

there·a·bouts (thăr′ə bouts′) *adv-* close to that time, place, degree, etc.: *We will come at six or thereabouts. They lived in Boston or thereabouts. He earned five thousand a year or thereabouts.* Also **there′a·bout′**.

there·af·ter (thăr ăf′tər) *adv-* from that time or place on; after that; afterwards: *For the first few days they came on time, but not thereafter.*

there·at (thăr′ ăt′) *adv-* 1 for that reason; therefore: *He was not invited, and was sad thereat.* 2 at that point; thereupon: *She made a bow, and thereat left.*

there·by (thăr′ bī′) *adv-* by that means: *She gave the dog a bone, thereby stopping his barking.*

there·for (thăr′ fôr′, -fôr′) *adv-* for that, this, or it: *They gave money for a hospital and the equipment therefor.* **Hom-** therefore.

there·fore (thăr′ fôr′) *adv-* for that reason; on account of that; hence: *He was sick and therefore missed three days.* **Hom-** therefor.

there·from (thăr′ frŭm′, -frŏm′) *adv-* from this; from that; from it: *The project was financed by investment and the income therefrom.*

there·in (thăr ĭn′) *adv-* 1 in this or that place; in it: *The house and all the furniture therein are for sale.* 2 in that respect: *I thought him honest, but therein I was wrong.*

there·of (thăr′ ŭv′, -ŏv′) *adv-* 1 of this; of that: *When he saw the wine, he drank thereof.* 2 from this or that cause: *He gobbled up the green fruit and became sick thereof.*

there·on (thăr ŏn′, -ŏn′) *adv-* on that place or thing: *the table and all the silver thereon.*

there's (thărz) there is. **Hom-** theirs.

there·to (thăr tōō′) *adv-* 1 to it; to that: *He locked the box and lost the key thereto.* 2 *Archaic* moreover; also.

there·un·der (thăr′ ŭn′ dər) *adv-* under that, it, or them.

there·un·to (thăr ŭn′tōō) *adv-* thereto.

there·up·on (thăr′ə pŏn′, -pŏn′) *adv-* 1 upon that; at once; immediately after: *The teacher said, "Ready," and thereupon Matilda began to read.* 2 thereon.

there·with (thăr′ wĭth′, -wĭth′) *adv-* 1 with it; with that; with this: *He received a diploma and all the privileges connected therewith.* 2 thereupon: *Our host said, "Good-by," and therewith we left.*

there·with·al (thăr′ wĭth ôl′) *Archaic adv-* 1 therewith; with that, it, or them. 2 at the same time; forthwith. 3 over and above; in addition.

therm- or **thermo-** *combining form:* heat: a therm*ionic radio tube;* a thermo*meter.* [from Greek **thérmē** meaning "heat," and from **thermos,** "hot."]

ther·mal (thûr′ məl) *adj-* 1 of or relating to heat: *a thermal unit.* 2 hot or warm: *a thermal bath. n-* a current of air moving upward because it is warmer than surrounding air.

thick·en (thĭk′ ən) *vt-* to make thick or thicker: *Mother thickened the gravy with flour. vi-* 1 to become thicker: *The woods thickened as we pushed into them.* 2 to become more complicated or intricate: *The plot thickened.*

thick·en·er (thĭk′ ən ər) *n-* 1 something added to a substance to make it thicker; thickening: *Put some thickener in that soup.* 2 person that thickens.

thick·en·ing (thĭk′ ən ĭng) *n-* 1 substance added to a liquid to thicken it. 2 a thickened place or part.

thin-skinned (thĭn′skĭnd′) *adj-* very sensitive to slights, insults, reproaches, etc.; easily hurt.

third (thûrd) *adj-* 1 next after second: *She was third in her class.* 2 ordinal of 3; 3rd: *He lives on Third Avenue. n-* 1 the next after the second; 3rd: *She was the third in line.* 2 one of three equal parts of a whole or a group: *He ate a third of the pie.* 3 the last term in the name of a common fraction having a denominator of 3: *1/3 is one third.* 4 the forward gear above second gear in a motor vehicle. 5 *Music* an interval of three tones on the scale counting the extremes, as from C to E, and the harmonic combination of these tones. 6 in baseball, third base: *He was out at third. adv-:* He spoke of you third.

third class *n-* 1 in U.S. postage, the class of mail that includes advertising and other printed matter, but not newspapers and magazines. 2 class of accomodations on trains, ships, etc., that is usually the least expensive and least comfortable. —*adj-* (**third-class**): *a third-class letter.* *adv-* (**third-class**): *to travel third-class.*

third degree *n- Informal* police interrogation of a prisoner which resorts to brutality in extracting a confession. *as modifier* (**third-degree**): *The detective used third-degree methods in questioning.*

third estate *n-* in former times, the common people, as distinguished from the nobility and the clergy.

third·ly (thûrd′ lē) *adv-* as third in a series.

third party *n-* 1 person other than the two main persons involved in a particular situation. 2 political party existing in addition to the major parties normally functioning in a two-party system.

third person *Grammar n-* 1 the form of the personal or possessive pronoun which stands for or refers to the person or persons, or the thing or things, spoken of. In English these forms are "he," "him," "his," "she," "her," "hers," "it," "its," "they," "them," "their," "theirs." 2 the form of the verb used with "he," "she," or "it," as "he sits," or with "they," as "they are."

third rail *n-* rail which runs parallel to the tracks of an electric railway and carries the electric current.

third-rate (thûrd′ rāt′) *adj-* 1 third in quality or rank. 2 very poor; quite inferior.

thirst (thûrst) *n-* 1 dry feeling in the mouth and throat caused by the need for something to drink. 2 strong desire; craving: *a thirst for praise. vi-* 1 to desire something to drink; to be thirsty. 2 to have a strong desire; have a craving: *to thirst for knowledge.*

thirst·y (thûr′ stē) *adj-* 1 feeling thirst. 2 without moisture; parched: *the thirsty garden.* 3 wanting something very much. 4 *Informal* producing thirst: *Digging is thirsty work.* —*adv-* **thirst′ i·ly.** *n-* **thirst′ i·ness.**

thir·teen (thûr′ tēn′) *n-* 1 amount or quantity that is one greater than 12. 2 *Mathematics* (1) the cardinal number that is the sum of 12 and 1. (2) a numeral such as 13 that represents this cardinal number. *as determiner* (traditionally called adjective or pronoun): *There are thirteen shirts here and thirteen there.*

thir·teenth (thûr′ tēnth′) *adj-* 1 next after twelfth. 2 the ordinal of 13; 13th. *n-* 1 the next after the twelfth; 13th. 2 one of thirteen equal parts of a whole or group. 3 the last term in the name of a fraction having a denominator of 13: *1/13 is one thirteenth.*

thir·ti·eth (thûr′ tē əth) *adj-* 1 next after twenty-ninth. 2 the ordinal of 30; 30th. *n-* the next after the twenty-ninth; 30th. 2 one of thirty equal parts of a whole or group. 3 the last term in the name of a fraction having a denominator of 30: *1/30 is one thirtieth.*

thir·ty (thûr′ tē) *n-* [*pl.* **thir·ties**] 1 amount or quantity that is one greater than 29. 2 *Mathematics* (1) the cardinal number that is the sum of 29 and 1.

thorn·y (thôr′ nē, thôr′-) *adj-* [**thorn·i·er, thorn·i·est**] 1 covered with thorns; spiny. 2 annoying; difficult; perplexing: *a thorny problem.* —*n-* **thorn′ i·ness.**

thor·ough (thûr′ ō) *adj-* 1 complete; to the fullest degree: *a thorough success.* 2 accurate; careful; exhaustive: *a thorough job of research.* 3 absolute; in every way. —*adv-* **thor′ ough·ly.** *n-* **thor′ ough·ness.**

thor·ough·bred (thûr′ ə brĕd′) *n-* 1 an animal of pure breed: *That dog is a thoroughbred.*

thrash (thrăsh) *vt-* 1 to beat or flog. 2 to thresh.
  thrash about to move or toss restlessly or violently.
  thrash out to discuss thoroughly.
  thrash over to go over again and again: *She thrashed the matter over in her mind.*

thrash·er (thrăsh′ ər) *n-* 1 person who thrashes. 2 brown thrasher. 3 thresher.

thrash·ing (thrăsh′ ing) *n-* 1 beating; flogging. 2 threshing.

thread (thrĕd) *n-* 1 thin, twisted strand of silk, cotton, wool, etc., from which cloth is woven or with which things are sewed. 2 any similar fiber or filament: *the threads of a spiderweb.* 3 something running through and connecting the parts of anything: *I can't follow the thread of his story.* 4 the spiral ridge of a screw or nut. *vt-* 1 to put a thread through: *to thread a needle; to thread beads.* 2 to provide with, or as with, a spiral ridge: *to thread a screw.* 3 to pass through (something difficult or perplexing): *They threaded their way through narrow streets.* —*adj-* **thread′ like′**. *n-* **thread′ er**.

Thread

  thread (one's) way to go with care and difficulty: *We threaded our way through the reefs.*

thread·bare (thrĕd′ bâr′) *adj-* 1 worn down to the threads; shabby: *a threadbare carpet; a threadbare suit.* 2 worn out; trite: *a threadbare joke.*

thread·y (thrĕd′ ē) *adj-* [**thread·i·er, thread·i·est**] 1 consisting of or covered with fibers or filaments: *a thready root.* 2 of liquids, forming threads; viscid. 3 resembling a thread in thinness or weakness: *a thready voice; a thready pulse.* —*n-* **thread′ i·ness**.

threat (thrĕt) *n-* 1 expression of an intention to hurt or punish: *I took his statement as a threat.* 2 a warning of unpleasantness or evil to come: *the threat of war.*

threat·en (thrĕt′ ən) *vt-* 1 to offer a threat to: *He threatened me.* 2 to announce as a threat; make a threat of: *They threaten war.* 3 to be a warning of: *The sky threatens rain. vi-* to give warning of itself; be about to happen: *A storm threatens. Disaster threatens.* —*n-* **threat′ en·er**. *adv-* **threat′ en·ing·ly**.

three (thrē) *n-* 1 amount or quantity that is one greater than two; 3. 2 *Mathematics* (1) the cardinal number that is the sum of 2 and 1. (2) a numeral such as 3 that represents this cardinal number. *as determiner* (traditionally called adjective or pronoun): *There are three coats here and* three *there.*

three-base hit *n-* in baseball, a triple. Also **three′ bag′ ger** (thrē′ băg′ ər).

three-di·men·sion·al (thrē′ də mĕn′ shən əl) *adj-* 1 of, having, or relating to the three dimensions of space. 2 giving an illusion of depth and perspective: *a method of taking three-dimensional photographs.*

three·fold (thrē′ fōld′) *adj-* 1 three times as many or as much. 2 having three parts: *Our trip served a threefold purpose. adv-*: *He increased his earnings threefold.*

three·pence (thrĭp′ əns) *n-* small British coin equal to three British pennies.

three·pen·ny (thrĭp′ ə nē) *Brit. adj-* 1 costing or worth threepence. 2 of little value; poor.

Three R's *n- pl.* reading, writing, and arithmetic.

three·score (thrē′ skôr′) *determiner-* (traditionally called adjective) three times twenty; sixty: *He lived threescore years.*

three·some (thrē′ səm) *n-* 1 group of three persons or things. 2 golf match in which two players, using one ball and taking turns hole by hole, compete with a single player.

thun·der·head (thŭn′ dər hĕd′) *n-* round mass of cumulus clouds, usually dark with shining white edges, often seen before a thunderstorm.

thun·der·ous (thŭn′ der əs) *adj-* full of or like thunder: *a thunderous applause.* —*adv-* **thun′ der·ous·ly**.

thun·der·show·er (thŭn′ dər shou′ ər) *n-* brief fall of rain, accompanied by thunder and lightning.

thun·der·storm (thŭn′ dər stôrm′, -stôrm′) *n-* storm of lightning, thunder, and usually rain.

tick (tĭk) *Brit. Informal n-* credit: *He has* tick *at the tobacconist's.* [contracted from **ticket.**] *Hom-* tic.

tick·er (tĭk′ ər) *n-* 1 something that ticks. 2 telegraphic instrument that prints stock quotations or news on a paper tape. 3 *Informal* the heart.

ticker tape *n-* paper tape on which a telegraphic ticker records information.

ticker-tape parade *n-* procession in honor of some hero or distinguished person, who rides in an open car and is showered with ticker tape and torn paper.

tick·et (tĭk′ ĭt) *n-* 1 slip of paper or card that allows the holder certain privileges, such as transportation, entrance to amusements, etc. 2 small tag or label stating the price, size, etc., of goods. 3 list of candidates offered by a particular party, group, or faction, to be voted upon by the public: *the* Liberal *ticket; the* Democratic *ticket.* 4 summons issued to a person alleged to have violated a traffic law: *a ticket for speeding. as modifier: the ticket booth at a theater. vt-* 1 to mark or identify with a tag or label. 2 to issue a traffic summons to.

tick fever *n-* any of several diseases that are transmitted by the bite of a tick.

tick·ing (tĭk′ ing) *n-* strong, closely woven cloth, usually striped, used to cover mattresses and pillows; tick.

tick·le (tĭk′ əl) *vt-* [**tick·led, tick·ling**] 1 to touch in a light way, producing a tingling sensation and usually causing laughter. 2 to please or amuse; delight: *The idea tickled me. vi-* to feel a tingling sensation: *My nose tickles. n-* a tingling or itching, or the touch causing this sensation.

tick·ler (tĭk′ lər) *n-* 1 person or thing that tickles. 2 card index, memorandum book, or any other automatic reminder to bring matters to timely attention.

tick·lish (tĭk′ lĭsh) *adj-* 1 easily aroused to laughter, squirming, etc., by light touches on the skin. 2 delicate or risky to handle: *a ticklish problem.* 3 easily upset or irritated; sensitive: *She is ticklish on the subject of waste.* —*adv-* **tick′ lish·ly**. *n-* **tick′ lish·ness**.

tick-tack-toe (tĭk′ tăk tō′) *n-* game in which two players alternately put crosses or circles in a block of nine squares, trying to get three of the same marks in a line before the opponent does.

tid·al (tī′ dəl) *adj-* 1 of, relating to, or resembling a tide or tides: *the tidal rhythm; a tidal movement of the earth's crust.* 2 holding water that is moved by the tides: *a tidal river.* 3 caused by a tide or tides: *a tidal current.*

tidal wave *n-* 1 one of a series of enormous and usually destructive ocean waves produced by undersea earthquakes or oceanic volcanic explosions; tsunami. 2 any widespread movement or exhibition of strong emotion, opinion, feeling, etc.: *a tidal wave of popular opposition.*

tid·bit (tĭd′ bĭt′) *n-* small, choice bit of anything: *a tidbit of cake; a tidbit of gossip.* Also **titbit.**

tid·dly·winks (tĭd′ lē wĭngks′) *n-* game in which players try to snap small disks into a cup by pressing their edges with larger disks.

tide (tīd) *n-* 1 rhythmic rising and falling of ocean waters, with high water occurring about every twelve hours at any given place, caused by the gravitational pull of the moon and sun. Much less noticeable tides occur in seas and large lakes. 2 anything that rises and falls or ebbs and floods in a similar way: *a tide of immigrants.* 3 *Archaic* time. *as modifier: a tide gauge; tide table; tide chart. Hom-* tied. —*adj-* **tide′ less**.
  turn the tide to change to the opposite condition.
  tide over to enable (one or someone) to manage.

tight·en (tī′ tən) *vt-* to draw or make tight: *to tighten a screw. vi-: The rope tightened.*

tight-fist·ed (tīt′ fĭs′ təd) *Informal adj-* stingy.

tight-lipped (tīt′ lĭpt′) *adj-* 1 having the lips closed tightly. 2 silent; secretive.

tight·rope (tīt′ rōp′) *n-* tightly stretched rope or cable on which acrobats walk and balance themselves while performing; highwire. *as modifier: a tightrope act; tightrope walker.* Also **tight′ wire′** (tīt′ wīar′).

time exposure *n-* in photography, a long exposure not made automatically by the shutter of the camera; also, a picture made by such an exposure.

tin·type (tĭn′ tĭp′) *n-* photograph made on a sensitized metal plate.

tin·ware (tĭn′ wâr′) *n-* articles made of tin plate.

ti·ny (tī′ nē) *adj-* [ti·ni·er, ti·ni·est] very small; wee.

-tion See *-ion, -ation, -ition.*

tip (tĭp) *n-* 1 point or end of anything: *the tip of my finger.* 2 small piece or part attached to the end of a thing: *Shoelaces have metal tips.* 3 foul tip. *vt-* [tipped, tip·ping] 1 to place a point on: *to tip an arrow with steel.* 2 in baseball, to hit (the ball) with a glancing blow. [probably from Germanic **tip**, probably related to ¹**tap**.]

tip (tĭp) *vt-* [tipped, tip·ping] 1 to slant or tilt; raise at one end or side: *to tip a table.* 2 to raise (one's hat) in greeting. *vi-* to assume a slant or tilt: *His chair tipped dangerously.* [probably altered from ¹**tip** having the original special sense of "pushing the tip over."]
tip over to overturn: *to tip over a vase.*

tip (tĭp) *n-* 1 sum of money given to a waiter, cab driver, etc., for services. 2 bit of private, helpful information: *a tip on the stock market.* *vt-* [tipped, tip·ping] to give a small fee to for services: *He tipped the waiter.* *vi-* : *He tips generously.* [of unknown origin.] —*n-* tip′per.
tip off *Informal* to give private, helpful information to: *He tipped me off on the coming sale.*

ti·pi (tē′ pē′) tepee.

tip-off (tĭp′ ôf′, -ŏf′) *Informal n-* 1 warning or hint. 2 unplanned disclosure of one's secret purpose.

tipped (tĭpt) *adj-* having a tip or point: *a tipped pole.* [from ¹**tip**.]

tipped (tĭpt) *adj-* tilted. [from ²**tip**.]

tip·pet (tĭp′ ət) *n-* 1 neck scarf or shoulder cape that hangs down in front. 2 in the Anglican communion, a long scarf worn by the clergy.

tip·ple (tĭp′ əl) *t t-* [tip·pled, tip·pling] to drink (liquor) habitually but in small amounts. *vi-* : *They are tippling at the tavern.* —*n-* tip′ pler.

tip·ster (tĭp′ stər) *n-* person who gives or sells tips, especially for betting on horse races.

tip·sy (tĭp′ sē) *adj-* [tip·si·er, tip·si·est] slightly drunk. —*adv-* tip′ si·ly. *n-* tip′ si·ness.

tip·toe (tĭp′ tō′) *vi-* [tip·toed, tip·toe·ing] to walk or stand on the tips of one's toes; hence, to walk softly.
on tiptoe 1 on the tips of one's toes. 2 cautiously; softly. 3 eagerly; expectantly: *She waited on tiptoe.*

tip-top (tĭp′ tŏp′) *n-* highest point: *At the tiptop of the crag was an eagle's nest.* *adj- Informal* very fine; excellent; first-rate: *The snow was tiptop for skiing.*

ti·rade (tī′ rād′, tə rād′) *n-* long, violent, usually abusive speech; harangue.

tire (tīər) *vt-* [tired, tir·ing] to fatigue in body, mind, or spirit: *The work quickly tired me.* *vi-* : *He tires easily.* [from Old English **teorian**.]

tire (tīər) *n-* band of metal or rubber, or a circular, air-filled rubber tube, around the rim of a wheel. [from Middle English, a shortened form of **attire**, "the covering (of a wheel)".] —*adj-* tired: *a rubber-tired wheel.*

tired (tīərd) *adj-* exhausted; weary; fatigued. —*adv-* tired′ ly. *n-* tired′ ness.

tire·less (tīər′ ləs) *adj-* not easily fatigued; untiring: *a tireless worker.* —*adv-* tire′ less·ly. *n-* tire′ less·ness.

tire·some (tīər′ səm) *adj-* boring; wearying; tedious: *a tiresome day.* —*adv-* tire′ some·ly. *n-* tire′ some·ness.

ti·ro (tī′ rō) tyro.

'tis (tĭz) *Archaic* it is.

tis·sue (tĭsh′ ōō) *n-* 1 the cells and connecting parts that make up any part of an animal or plant: *muscle tissue.* 2 thin, gauzy cloth. 3 soft, thin paper used chiefly as a handkerchief. 4 web or network: *a tissue of lies.* as *modifier:* extensive tissue *damage;* tissue *paper.*

tithe·ing (tī′ thĭng) *n-* 1 a paying or taking of tithes. 2 amount that is taken or set apart as a tithe.

ti·tian (tĭsh′ ən) *n-* golden-red color. *adj-* : *a titian wig.*

tit·il·late (tĭt′ ə lāt′) *vt-* [tit·il·lat·ed, tit·il·lat·ing] to arouse or excite in a pleasurable way: *to titillate one's fancy.* —*n-* tit′ il·la′ tion.

tit·i·vate (tĭt′ ə vāt′) *Informal vt-* [tit·i·vat·ed, tit·i·vat·ing] to dress up; spruce up. —*n-* tit′ i·va′ tion.

ti·tled (tī′ təld) *adj-* having a title of nobility.

to·bog·gan (tə bŏg′ ən) *n-* long, flat sled without runners and with a curved end. *vi-* : *to toboggan downhill.*

toc·sin (tŏk′ sən) *n-* bell or other signal for sounding an alarm. *Hom-* toxin.

to·day or **to-day** (tə dā′) *n-* the present day: *the menu for today; the writers of today.* *adv-* 1 on the present day: *We will go to the movies today.* 2 in these times; in this particular age: *Many people have television today.*

Toboggan

tod·dle (tŏd′ əl) *vi-* [tod·dled, tod·dling] to walk with short, uncertain steps, as a baby does.

tod·dler (tŏd′ lər) *Informal n-* young child; baby.

tod·dy (tŏd′ ē) *n-* [pl. tod·dies] 1 drink made of the sap of certain palm trees of East India; also, the sap of such palms. 2 drink made of liquor, hot water, and sugar.

to-do (tə dōō′) *Informal n-* bustle or stir; fuss: *a great to-do about nothing.*

toe (tō) *n-* 1 one of the separate digits or divisions of the foot. 2 the fore part of the foot or of any foot covering: *the toe of his shoe.* 3 any of various things resembling a toe: *the toe of Italy.* *vt-* 1 to provide with a toe: *She toed the socks.* 2 to drive at a slant, such as a nail; also, to attach by nails driven slantwise: *to toe a beam.* *vi-* to hold the toes in a given way: *to toe in or out. Hom-* tow.
on (one's) toes physically or mentally alert.
to toe the line (or the mark) 1 to put the tip of the foot on the starting line of a race. 2 to conform to the rules.

toed (tōd) *adj-* having a certain type or number of toes: *pigeon-toed; three-toed sloth. Hom-* toad.

toe·nail (tō′ nāl′) *n-* 1 nail growing on a toe. 2 nail driven slantwise. *vt-* to fasten by such nails.

tof·fee (tôf′ ē, tŏf′-) *n-* candy made of sugar and butter, boiled until it thickens, and then poured into a dish to cool and harden. Also **tof′fy.**

tog (tŏg) *Informal vt-* [togged, tog·ging] to dress, especially in one's finery (often followed by "out" or "up"): *He togged himself out for dinner.*

to·ga (tō′ gə) *n-* 1 in ancient Rome, a loose outer garment consisting of an elaborately draped piece of woolen cloth with the wearer's rank shown by the color of its border. 2 robe or gown characteristic of certain professions: *academic toga.*

to·geth·er (tōō gĕth′ ər) *adv-* 1 in one gathering, company, or association; with each other: *We live together in one house.* 2 in or into contact or union: *to mix flour and water together; to come together.* 3 without a break; continuously: *We marched for three days together.* 4 at the same time; simultaneously: *All the cannon went off together.* 5 in or into agreement: *Let's get together on a plan.*
together with as well as; in addition to.

Toga

tog·ger·y (tŏg′ ə rē) *Informal n-* clothing.

tog·gle (tŏg′ əl) *n-* 1 oblong button for a coat, usually inserted through a loop instead of a buttonhole. 2 any crosspiece, such as a bolt or rod, that is attached to a rope or chain and used for fastening or tightening. *vt-* [tog·gled, tog·gling] to fasten or furnish with a toggle.

toggle bolt *n-* bolt with a pivoted, winglike anchor that closes parallel to the bolt when entering a hole in a wall, and then opens up behind the wall to anchor the bolt.

toggle switch *n-* electric switch having a projecting lever whose movement through a small arc opens or closes a circuit.

toi·let·ry (toi′ lə trē) *n-* [pl. toi·let·ries] any of various articles, such as soap, toothpaste, or deodorant, used in washing or grooming oneself.

toilet water *n-* fragrant liquid that is milder than perfume and is used in the bath or on the skin.

toil·some (toil′ səm) *adj-* laborious; tiresome.

toil·worn (toil′ wôrn′) *adj-* fatigued or worn out by hard work.

to·ken (tō′ kən) *n-* 1 sign, mark, or symbol.

toll (tōl) *vt-* to cause (a bell) to sound with regular and continuous strokes. *vi-*: *The church bells* toll *every Sunday. n-* the sound made by the regular striking of a bell. [from Middle English **tollen** meaning "to sound a bell by pulling; pull."]

toll·booth (tōl' bōōth') *n-* booth where tolls are paid.

toll·gate (tōl' gāt') *n-* gate on a bridge or road, at which tolls are paid.

toll·house (tōl' hous') *n-* booth where tolls are paid.

toll·keep·er (tōl' kē' pər) *n-* person who collects tolls at a tollgate.

Tol·tec (tōl' těk, tōl'-) *n-* [*pl.* **Tol·tecs,** also **Tol·tec**] member of a highly civilized Indian people of central Mexico, between 900 and 1200 A.D., who influenced both the Aztecs and the Mayans. *adj-* (also **Tol·tec' an**): *the* Toltec *ruins.*

tol·u·ene (tōl' yŏō ěn') *n-* hydrocarbon (C₆H₅CH₃) related to benzene, obtained from coal tars, and used in the manufacture of dyes and explosives.

tom or **Tom** (tŏm) *n-* the male of certain animals, especially cats and birds.

tom·a·hawk (tŏm' ə hók') *n-* American Indian ax that was used as a weapon and a tool. *vt-* to strike or kill with such an ax. [American word from Algonquian.]

Tomahawk

to·ma·to (tə mā' tō, -mä' tō) *n-* [*pl.* **to·ma·toes**] 1 red or yellow juicy fruit of a garden plant of the nightshade family, widely eaten as a vegetable. 2 the plant bearing this fruit. [American word from American Spanish **tomate,** from Nahuatl Indian **tomatl.**]

tomb (tōōm) *n-* grave or vault for the dead.

tom·boy (tŏm' boi') *n-* lively, noisy girl who behaves like a boy.

tomb·stone (tōōm' stōn') *n-* stone placed over or at the head of a grave, usually bearing the dead person's name and dates of birth and death; gravestone; headstone.

tom·cat (tŏm' kăt') *n-* male cat.

tome (tōm) *n-* large, heavy, and usually scholarly book.

tom·fool·er·y (tŏm fōō' lə rē) *n-* [*pl.* **tom·fool·er·ies**] foolish conduct; nonsense; silliness.

tom·my·rot (tŏm' ē rŏt') *Informal n-* utter nonsense.

to·mor·row (tə mŏr' ō, -môr' ō) *n-* 1 the day after today: *Is* tomorrow *a holiday?* 2 the future: *space systems of* tomorrow. *adv-* on the day after today: *My mother will roast a turkey* tomorrow.

Tom Thumb *n-* in English fables, a dwarf who was no bigger than his father's thumb.

tom-tom (tŏm' tŏm') *n-* kind of drum, usually beaten with the hands. *as modifier:* a tom-tom *beat.*

ton (tŭn) *n-* 1 unit of weight; specifically, the **short ton** of 2,000 pounds, of the United States and Canada; the **long ton** of 2,240 pounds, of Great Britain; or the **metric ton** of 2,204.6 pounds. 2 unit of measure of the displacement of a ship, equal to 35 cubic feet, the amount of sea water that weighs about 2,240 pounds. 3 unit of measure for ship's cargo, equal to 40 cubic feet. 4 unit of measure of the internal capacity of ships, equal to 100 cubic feet. *Hom-* tun.

ton·al (tō' nəl) *adj-* of or relating to tone or tonality.

to·nal·i·ty (tə năl' ə tē) *n-* [*pl.* **to·nal·i·ties**] 1 *Music* melodic and harmonic relationships in a composition; also, the principle of key relationship between scales. 2 the scheme of hues or shades of color in a painting.

tone (tōn) *n-* 1 vocal or musical sound; also, its quality: *the quiet* tones *of a harp.*

tope (tōp) *vi-* [**toped, top·ing**] to drink alcoholic liquor frequently through the day. *Hom-* taupe. **—top' er.**

top-flight (tŏp' flīt') *Informal adj-* excellent; superior.

top·gal·lant (tə găl' ənt, tŏp-) *adj-* relating to or naming the spars, sails, and rigging of a ship that are next above the topmasts and topsails, and are usually the highest.

top hat *n-* man's black or gray hat having a tall, roundish crown, worn on formal occasions. Also **high hat.**

top-heav·y (tŏp' hěv' ē) *adj-* heavier at the top than at the bottom; improperly balanced.

top·ic (tŏp' ĭk) *n-* subject of a discussion, speech, argument, composition, etc.

to·pol·o·gy (tə pŏl' ə jē) *n-* branch of mathematics that studies those properties of geometric figures that do not change when the figures are stretched, twisted, or otherwise distorted without cutting or folding.

top·ping (tŏp' ĭng) *n-* anything that forms a top; especially, whipped cream placed on the top of cake or dessert.

top·ple (tŏp' əl) *vi-* [**top·pled, top·pling**] 1 to fall headlong; tumble: *The tree* toppled. 2 to collapse; be overthrown: *The government* toppled. *vt-:* *to* topple *a tower.*

tops (tŏps) *Informal adj-* top-notch; excellent; first-rate.

top·sail (tŏp' səl, -sāl') *n-* 1 the second and third sails above the deck of a full square-rigged vessel. 2 the sail above the upper gaff of a fore-and-aft rigged vessel. *as modifier:* a topsail *yard.*

top-se·cret (tŏp' sē' krət) *adj-* secret to all but the highest officials: *a top-secret missile program.*

top sergeant *Informal n-* first sergeant.

top·side (tŏp' sīd') *adv-* on deck: *He's stationed* topside. Also **top' sides'.**

top·soil (tŏp' soil') *n-* top or upper part of the soil; especially, the fertile surface layer of soil.

top·sy-tur·vy (tŏp' sē tûr' vē) *adj-* 1 upside down. 2 confused and disordered: *a topsy-turvy situation. adv-: The boat turned* topsy-turvy.

toque (tōk) *n-* woman's close-fitting, small hat without a brim.

to·rah (tōr' ə) *n-* 1 in Judaism, the whole body of religious thought and literature. 2 **Torah** the first five books of the Old Testament; Pentateuch. 3 leather or parchment scroll containing this.

torch (tôrch, tŏrch) *n-* 1 flaming light consisting of a stick of resinous wood, bundle of rushes, etc., burning at one end. 2 any of various devices that give off a hot flame: *a plumber's* torch. 3 anything that inspires, enlightens, etc.: *the* torch *of science.* 4 *chiefly Brit.* flashlight.

Torch of liberty

carry a torch for to continue to love.

torch bearer *n-* 1 person who carries a torch. 2 person who gives inspiration.

torch·light (tôrch' līt', tŏrch'-) *n-* light given by torches. *as modifier:* a torchlight *assembly.*

torch singer *n-* person who sings sad songs of unrequited love or yearning, called **torch songs.**

tore (tôr) *p.t.* of **tear.**

to·re·a·dor (tôr' ē ə dôr', -dôr') *Informal n-* a bullfighter.

to·re·ro (tō rā' rō) *Spanish n-* [*pl.* **to·re·ros**] bullfighter, especially one fighting on foot.

to·ri·i (tôr' ē ē) *n-* the gateway of a Japanese Shinto temple or shrine, consisting of two upright posts supporting a concave lintel with a straight crossbeam below it.

Torii

tor·ment (tôr měnt') *vt-* 1 to inflict severe physical or mental pain on; torture: *to* torment *a captive.* 2 to annoy or harass; vex: *He* tormented *her with complaints.*

tor·ment (tôr' měnt', tôr'-) *n-* 1 extreme mental or physical suffering; great pain; agony: *suffering the torments of jealous rage.* 2 something that causes suffering or pain: *His reckless driving was her* torment.

tor·men·tor or **tor·men·ter** (tôr měn' tər) *n-* person or thing that torments; torturer.

town (toun) *n-* 1 group of houses and buildings, larger than a village but smaller than a city. 2 the city as opposed to the country. 3 the people of a community. 4 township. 5 business or shopping district: *She went to* town. *as modifier:* a town *hall;* town *clerk.*

go to town *Slang* to do anything exuberantly and well. **on the town** *Slang* out for an enjoyable evening.

town clerk *n-* public officer who keeps the town records.

town crier *n-* formerly, an officer who made public announcements in the streets of a town or village.

town hall *n-* building where public meetings are held and town offices are located.

town meeting *n-* 1 under a form of direct democratic government now used chiefly in parts of New England,

tra·di·tion·al (trə dĭsh′ ən əl) *adj-* 1 having to do with tales, beliefs, customs, etc., handed down from generation to generation. 2 established by long usage: customary —*adv-* tra·di′tion·al·ly.

tra·duce (trə dōōs′, -dyōōs′) *vt-* [tra·duced, tra·duc·ing] to harm the good name of. —*n-* tra·duc′ er.

traf·fic (trăf′ ĭk) *n-* 1 movement of people, goods, and vehicles from place to place: *The traffic on city streets is a problem.* 2 the transportation business done by a railway, steamship line, etc., carrying persons or goods. 3 trade; business: *the traffic in stolen goods. as modifier:* *a traffic jam. vi-* [traf·ficked, traf·fick·ing] to trade or deal: *to traffic in cotton.* —*n-* traf′ fick·er.

traffic circle *n-* circular intersection around which all traffic flows counterclockwise.

traffic light *n-* signal light that, by showing various colors, directs the flow of traffic.

trag·a·canth (trăg′ ə kănth) *n-* gum tragacanth.

tra·ge·di·an (trə jē′ dē ən) *n-* 1 writer of tragedies. 2 actor who plays tragic parts. —*n- fem.* tra·ge′di· enne′ (-də ĕn′).

trag·e·dy (trăj′ ə dē) *n-* [*pl.* trag·e·dies] 1 sad event, especially one that involves death; disaster. 2 in dramatic literature, a serious play with an unhappy ending, arousing pity or terror by the misfortunes that befall the principal characters. 3 such plays as a group.

trag·ic (trăj′ ĭk) *adj-* 1 very sad; disastrous: *a tragic accident.* 2 of or having to do with tragedy: *a tragic drama.* Also **trag′ i·cal.** —*adv-* trag′ i·cal·ly.

trag·i·com·e·dy (trăj′ ĭ kŏm′ ə dē) *n-* [*pl.* trag·i· com·e·dies] 1 a play containing both tragic and comic scenes, especially one that has generally gloomy or tragic events but ends happily for the main characters. 2 a situation or event blending tragic and comic elements. —*adj-* trag′ i·com′ ic (-kŏm′ ĭk): *a tragicomic scene.*

trail (trāl) *n-* 1 path through woods or wild country: *After the blizzard we couldn't find the trail.* 2 scent or footprints left by a moving person or animal; track: *The dog followed the trail of the rabbit.* 3 a stream of people, dust, rubbish, etc., behind something moving: *The train left a trail of smoke. vt-* 1 to follow the path or footprints of. 2 to pull along or behind: *to trail a wagon.* 3 to bring along as a burden or hindrance: *I trailed my younger brothers with me. vi-* 1 to fall or hang down so as to sweep along the ground: *Her dress trailed in the mud.* 2 to move in a long and straggling line: *They trailed home one by one.* 3 to lag behind; be last. 4 to grow to some length: *The bush trailed along the fence.*

trail·blaz·er (trāl′ blā′ zər) *n-* 1 person who marks a trail for others. 2 a leader in new ventures; pioneer.

trail·er (trā′ lər) *n-* 1 person, animal, or thing that follows behind. 2 van for carrying loads, which is hooked to any vehicle. 3 vehicle with living quarters that can be hauled from place to place by a car. 4 a trailing plant or vine. 5 short film with scenes from a coming picture, used to advertise. *as modifier:* *a trailer camp.*

train (trān) *n-* 1 a connected line of railroad cars with or without an engine attached. 2 a group of people or things traveling together: *wagon train.* 3 a connected series of ideas, events, etc.: *a train of thought.* 4 group of attendants; retinue. 5 an extension of a lady's skirt that trails behind her.

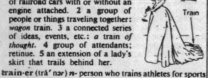

Train

train·er (trā′ nər) *n-* person who trains athletes for sports contests, horses for racing, animals for the circus, etc.

train·ing (trā′ nĭng) *n-* 1 instruction for some occupation: *Have you had training as a nurse?* 2 course of exercise, diet, etc., for an athlete. 3 good condition maintained by following such a course: *I am out of training. as modifier:* *a training school; a training ship.*

train·load (trān′ lōd′) *n-* total amount of passengers or total amount of freight a train can hold.

train·man (trān′ mən) *n-* [*pl.* train·men] person who works on a train and assists the conductor; especially, a brakeman.

train oil *n-* oil obtained from the blubber of whales and other sea animals.

traipse (trāps) *Informal vi-* [traipsed, traips·ing] to walk about idly or aimlessly; ramble.

trait (trāt) *n-* feature or characteristic, especially of personality: *Kindness and generosity are fine traits.*

trai·tor (trā′ tər) *n-* person who betrays his country, a cause, a friend, etc. —*n- fem.* trai′ tress.

trai·tor·ous (trā′ tər əs) *adj-* 1 of or like a traitor; treacherous. 2 of or having to do with treason: *a traitorous act.* —*adv-* trai′ tor·ous·ly.

tra·jec·to·ry (trə jĕk′ tə rē) *n-* path of an object moving through space, such as the path of a bullet.

tram (trăm) *n-* 1 kind of coal wagon used in mines. 2 *chiefly Brit.* streetcar.

tram·mel (trăm′ əl) *n-* 1 net used for catching birds, fish, etc. 2 a shackle or fetter for teaching a horse to amble. 3 trammels anything that hinders progress, action, or freedom. 4 an S-shaped hook from which pots are hung in a fireplace. *vt-* 1 to hamper or hinder; shackle. 2 to catch in a net.

tramp (trămp) *n-* 1 the sound of heavy steps: *I heard the tramp of soldiers.* 2 a walk or hike: *a tramp through the woods.* 3 man who goes about on foot doing odd jobs or begging; vagabond. 4 freight steamer that has no regular schedule but picks up cargo wherever it can. *as modifier:* *a tramp ship; a tramp dog. vi-* 1 to walk with heavy steps; trudge: *He tramped upstairs. He tramped home, tired after a day's hike.* 2 to travel or wander about as a vagabond. *vt-* 1 to step on heavily and repeatedly; tread: *The peasants tramp the grapes in making wine.* 2 to walk over; roam about. —*n-* tramp′ er.

tram·ple (trăm′ pəl) *vt-* [tram·pled, tram·pling] to tramp on; stamp on; crush: *The cows trampled my flower bed. vi-* to walk with heavy steps; stamp. *n-* the sound of tramping or stamping. —*n-* tram′ pler.

tram·po·lin or **tram·po·line** (trăm′ pə lĭn′, -lən) *n-* sheet of canvas or other strong material stretched tightly on a frame, used by acrobats as a springboard.

tram·way (trăm′ wā′) *n-* 1 *chiefly Brit.* streetcar line; also, streetcar. 2 road or track for heavy hauling; especially, a railway in a mine.

trance (trăns) *n-* 1 an unconscious state like sleep. 2 a daze; daydream: *The music put him in a trance.*

tran·quil (trăng′ kwəl) *adj-* 1 free from mental tension or strain; serene: *a tranquil mind.* 2 free from disturbance or tumult: *a tranquil country scene; tranquil waters.*

tran·quil·ize (trăng′ kwə lĭz′) *vt-* [tran·quil·ized, tran· quil·iz·ing] to make tranquil; especially, to reduce anxiety in (a patient) by use of drugs.

tran·quil·iz·er (trăng′ kwə lī′ zər) *n-* any of a group of drugs that tend to make a person calm and relaxed.

tran·quil·li·ty or **tran·quil·i·ty** (trăng′ kwĭl′ ə tē) *n-* a being tranquil; calmness; peacefulness; serenity.

trans- *prefix* 1 across; over; beyond: trans*atlantic.* 2 above and beyond: trans*sonic;* trans*uranium.* 3 with a complete change: trans*form.*

trans. 1 transitive. 2 transpose. 3 translated. 4 translator. 5 translation. 6 transportation. 7 transverse.

trans·act (trăn′ săkt′, -zăkt′) *vt-* to carry on; perform; complete (business, negotiations, etc.): *to transact a deal.* —*n-* trans·ac′ tor: *a transactor of shady business.*

trans·ac·tion (trăn′ săk′ shən, -zăk′ shən) *n-* 1 the management of any business or affair. 2 business deal: *This transaction involves a lot of money.* 3 transactions report, especially the published report, of the proceedings of a meeting of a society, organization, etc.

trans·at·lan·tic (trănz′ ət lăn′ ĭk, trăns′-) *adj-* 1 going across the Atlantic: *a transatlantic flight.* 2 on the other side of the Atlantic.

tran·scend (trăn′ sĕnd′) *vt-* 1 to rise above or go beyond; exceed: *Miracles transcend human knowledge.* 2 to excel; surpass: *His ability transcends mine.*

tran·scend·ent (trăn′ sĕn′ dənt) *adj-* 1 surpassing or rising above the usual; extraordinary: *the transcendent joys of childhood.* 2 transcendental. —*adv-* tran· scend′ ent·ly.

tran·scen·den·tal (trăn′ sən děn′ təl) *adj-* of or relating to eternity, infinity, absolute love, perfect joy, and other matters outside the world of ordinary sense experience; also, relating to philosophers or a philosophy dealing chiefly with such matters. —*adv-* tran′ scen·den′ tal·ly.

trans·con·ti·nen·tal (trăns′ kŏn tə nĕn′ təl) *n-* 1 going across a continent: *a transcontinental flight from New York to Los Angeles.* 2 on the other side of a continent.

tran·scribe (trăn′ skrīb′) *vt-* [tran·scribed, tran·scrib·ing] 1 to copy in writing: *T..e medieval monks transcribed many ancient manuscripts.* 2 to make a copy of (short-hand notes, dictation, etc.) on a typewriter or in long-hand. 3 to record (a radio program, commercial, etc.) for broadcast at a later date. 4 *Music* to arrange or adapt (music) for an instrument or voice other than that for which it was originally intended. —*n-* tran·scrib′ er.

tran·script (trăn′ skrĭpt′) *n-* 1 written, typewritten, or printed copy. 2 an exact official copy, especially of a student's academic record.

tran·scrip·tion (trăn′ skrĭp′ shən) *n-* 1 a transcribing or copying. 2 written copy; transcript. 3 *Music* arrangement or adaptation of a composition to suit a voice or instrument other than that for which it was written. 4 (also **electrical transcription**) a recording of a radio program, performance, etc., made for broadcast later.

trans·duc·er (trăns′ dōō′ sər, -dyōō′ sər) *n-* device that transforms one form of energy into another.

tran·sept (trăn′ sĕpt′) *n-* in churches that have the shape of a cross, the section that forms the transverse cross-piece; also, either of the two projecting ends of this part.

trans·fer (trăns′ fûr′) *vt-* [trans·ferred, trans·fer·ring] 1 to carry or remove from one person or place to another. 2 to give ownership of (something) to another: *to transfer a piece of land.*

trans·gres·sion (trăns′ grĕsh′ ən, trănz′-) *n-* a transgressing; violation of a law, rule, boundary, etc.; especially, a sin.

tran·ship (trăn′ shĭp′) *vt-* [tran·shipped, tran·ship·ping] to transship. —*n-* tran·ship′ ment.

tran·sient (trăn′ shənt) *adj-* 1 not permanent; brief; passing: *Her joy was transient.* 2 stopping for a short time: *a transient guest at the hotel.* *n-* visitor or boarder who remains only for a short time: *a hotel for transients.* —*n-* tran′ sience (-shəns) or tran′ sien·cy (-shən sē): *the transiency of life.* *adv-* trans′ ient·ly.

tran·sis·tor (trăn′ zĭs′ tər, -sĭs′ tər) *n-* small electronic device made of semiconductors such as germanium or silicon and used as a substitute for a vacuum tube in controlling or amplifying an electric current. *as modifier: a transistor radio; a transistor circuit.*

tran·sit (trăn′ sĭt, -zĭt) *n-* 1 a passing through or over; passage: *a rapid transit.* 2 a carrying from one point to another: *The tomatoes were spoiled in transit.* 3 public system of transportation including buses, subways, etc. 4 transition; change. 5 surveyor's instrument consisting of a telescope, a leveling device, and two scales for measuring horizontal and vertical angles; theodolite. 6 *Astronomy* (1) passage of a celestial body across a meridian. (2) passage of one celestial body in front of another as seen from the earth. *vt-* to pass through or over. *as modifier: the transit system; a transit strike.*

tran·si·tion (trăn′ zĭsh′ ən) *n-* 1 the passing from one place, period, state, subject, or the like, to another; change: *the transition from boyhood to manhood; the transition to the next paragraph.* 2 *Music* (1) abrupt change from one key to another. (2) passage serving to join two themes or sections more important than itself.

tran·si·tion·al (trăn′ zĭsh′ ən əl) *adj-* of or having to do with transition; intermediate: *a transitional period in history.* —*adv-* tran′ si′ tion·al·ly.

tran·si·tive (trăn′ sə tĭv, -zə tĭv) *Grammar adj-* of verbs, having an object. Examples: *John rode his bicycle down the street.* ("His bicycle" is the object of the verb "rode.") *I hope that you will come.* ("That you will come" is the object of the verb "hope.") *n-*: *That verb is a transitive.* —*adv-* tran′ si·tive·ly. *n-* tran′ si·tive·ness.

tran·si·tor·y (trăn′ sə tôr′ ē, trăn′ zə-) *adj-* lasting but a short time; brief; quickly passing. —*n-* tran′ si·to·ri·ness.

trans·late (trăns′ lāt′, trănz′ lāt′) *vt-* [trans·lat·ed, trans·lat·ing] 1 to change from one language into another. 2 to put into different words or express in a different manner: *He translated the theory of atomic power into language I could understand.* 3 to move from one place, condition, or position to another. *vi-* 1 to be adaptable for translation: *His novels translate easily.* 2 to act as a translator: *He translates for the French Embassy.* —*adj-* trans·lat′ a·ble.

trans·la·tion (trăns′ lā′ shən, trănz′-) *n-* 1 the changing of something written or spoken from one language to another; a translating: *The United Nations has a large staff for translation.* 2 result of translating: *three translations of a book.* 3 in mechanics, the movement of a body in one direction without rotation.

trans·la·tor (trăns′ lā′ tər, trănz′-) *n-* person who translates from one language into another; interpreter.

trans·lu·cence (trăns′ lōō′ səns, trănz′-) or **trans·lu·cen·cy** (-sən sē) *n-* the quality of being translucent.

trans·lu·cent (trăns′ lōō′ sənt, trănz′-) *adj-* letting light pass through, but not allowing images to be clearly seen on the other side. —*adv-* trans·lu′ cent·ly.

trav·el·er (trăv′ əl ər) *n-* person who travels.

trav·eled (trăv′ əld) *adj-* 1 having traveled widely. 2 used by many travelers: *a heavily traveled road.*

trav·e·logue or **trav·e·log** (trăv′ ə lòg′, -lŏg′) *n-* 1 a lecture about a journey, usually illustrated by films, slides, or pictures. 2 motion picture of a region.

trav·erse (trăv′ ərs) *n-* 1 something lying across something else, such as a crossbar or a rung of a ladder. 2 a crossing; also, route or path across. 3 zigzag course made by a sailing ship due to contrary winds, or by a skier on a steep slope. 3 communicating gallery across a building. 4 mound of earth, bags, etc., that protects a trench. 5 in surveying, a single line established across a plot of ground. *vt-* (also tra vûrs′) [trav·ersed, trav·ers·ing] 1 to pass over, across, or through: *They traversed the swamp safely.* 2 to move forward and backward over; cross and recross: *The beams of the searchlight traversed the sky.* 3 to lie or extend across: *A bridge traverses the stream.* *vi-* 1 to walk or move across; move back and forth or in a zigzag manner: *The skier traversed down the mountain.* 2 to turn; swivel. —*adj-* trav′ ers·a·ble. *n-* trav′ ers·er.

traverse rod (trăv′ ərs) *n-* metal rod or track for curtains or draperies, having a pulley mechanism for drawing them.

trav·es·ty (trăv′ ə stē) *n-* [*pl.* trav·es·ties] 1 any deliberate imitation with intent to ridicule; burlesque; parody 2 any likeness that is fantastic or ridiculous. *vt-* [trav·es·tied, trav·es·ty·ing] to burlesque or parody.

tra·vois (trə voi′, trăv′ oi′) *n-* [*pl.* tra·vois (-voiz′) or tra·vois·es (-voiz′ əz)] primitive sled formerly used by Plains Indians and consisting of a platform or netting supported by two long poles, the forward ends of which are fastened to a horse or dog, while the rear ends trail along the ground. Also **tra·voise** (-voiz′). [from Canadian French, from travail, "a brake."]

Horse pulling a travois

trawl (trôl) *n-* 1 large baglike net dragged behind a boat in catching fish. 2 long fishing line to which are attached many short lines with hooks. *as modifier: a trawl net; trawl line.* *vi-* to fish with a trawl.

trawl·er (trô′ lər) *n-* 1 person who fishes with a trawl. 2 boat used in trawling.

tray (trā) *n-* flat receptacle of wood, metal, etc., with a raised edge or rim, used for carrying, holding, or displaying articles. *as modifier: a tray shop.* *Hom-* trey.

treach·er·ous (trĕch′ ər əs) *adj-* 1 betraying a trust; traitorous; disloyal: *The treacherous servant spied on his employer.* 2 not to be trusted in spite of appearances; deceptive; unreliable: *a treacherous current in a quiet river.* —*adv-* treach′ er·ous·ly. *n-* treach′ er·ous·ness.

treach·er·y (trĕch'ə rē) *n-* [*pl.* **treach·er·ies**] betrayal of faith or confidence; disloyal conduct.

trea·cle (trē'kəl) *Brit. n-* molasses.

tread (trĕd) *vt-* [trod, trod·den or trod, tread·ing] 1 to walk on, over, or along: *He trod the moors all night.* 2 to press beneath the foot. 3 to make by walking or trampling: *to tread a path through the woods. vi-* 1 to step or walk: *You should tread carefully here.*

treb·ly (trĕb'lē) *adv-* in three ways or threefold: *He was trebly tormented: by illness, poverty, and a nagging wife.*

tree (trē) *n-* 1 large plant with a woody trunk that has branches bearing leaves. 2 shrub or bush resembling a tree: *a rose tree.* 3 piece of wood used for a particular purpose: *a shoe tree; a hat tree. vt-* [treed, tree·ing] to chase up a tree. —*adj-* **tree'less.** *adj-* **tree' like'.**

BARK
VASCULAR LAYER
CORK LAYER
CORK CAMBIUM
HEARTWOOD
SAPWOOD (CONDUCTING TISSUE)

Cross-section of tree trunk

up a tree *Informal* in a situation from which there is no apparent escape; also, in an embarrassing position.

tree farm *n-* forest area managed for the commercial production of trees.

tree fern *n-* large tropical fern with a woody stem.

tree toad *n-* any of various amphibians that are related to toads and frogs and live in trees. Also **tree frog.**

tree·top (trē'tŏp') *n-* highest part of a tree; also, the part of the tree near the top.

tre·foil (trē'oil', trē'foil') *n-* 1 any three-leafed plant, such as clover. 2 ornament resembling a cloverleaf.

trek (trĕk) *vi-* [trekked, trek·king] among the early Boers of South Africa, to make a journey by ox wagon; hence, to travel slowly and with great difficulty: *The Boers trekked across the veldt. n-* journey; also, a migration: *the trek to the West.* —*n-* **trek'ker.**

trel·lis (trĕl'əs) *n-* ornamental framework, used as support for vines or other creeping plants. It is usually made of small wood strips, crossed and widely spaced. *vt-* to fasten or support on a trellis: *to trellis a climbing rose.*

Trellis

trem·a·tode (trĕm'ə tōd') *n-* a parasitic flatworm or fluke, such as the liver flukes and blood flukes.

trem·ble (trĕm'bəl) *vi-* [trem·bled, trem·bling] 1 to shake or shiver, as from fear or cold; shudder. 2 to quaver, as a voice. *n-* involuntary shaking; shudder. —*n-* **trem'bler.** *adv-* **trem'bling·ly.**

trem·bly (trĕm'blē) *adj-* trembling; shaking.

tre·men·dous (trə mĕn'dəs) *adj-* 1 huge; vast; enormous. 2 of enormous value or importance; extraordinary: *a tremendous idea.* 3 *Informal* wonderful. —*adv-* **tre·men'dous·ly.** *n-* **tre·men'dous·ness.**

trem·o·lo (trĕm'ə lō) *Music n-* [*pl.* **trem·o·los**] 1 rapid repetition of a tone or tones by a vocalist or instrumentalist in order to produce a tremulous effect. 2 vibrato.

tre·mor (trĕm'ər, trē'mər) *n-* 1 a shaking; quivering. 2 thrill of emotion; shiver: *a tremor of anxiety.*

trem·u·lous (trĕm'yə ləs) *adj-* 1 quivering, shaking, or trembling: *a voice tremulous with fear.* 2 nervous or fearful; timid: *The young actress was tremulous as the curtain went up.* —*adv-* **trem'u·lous·ly.** *n-* **trem'u·lous·ness.**

trench (trĕnch) *n-* 1 long, narrow furrow in the earth. 2 deep ditch used as a protection for troops in combat. *vt-* to dig ditches in: *to trench a field for drainage.*

trench·ant (trĕn'chənt) *adj-* sharp and forceful; keen; also, biting or caustic: *a trenchant remark.* —*n-* **trench'an·cy.** *adv-* **trench'ant·ly.**

trench coat *n-* loose, belted, double-breasted raincoat.

trench·er (trĕn'chər) *n-* in former times, a wooden plate or platter on which food was carved or served. [from Old French *trencheor*, "something to cut with."]

trench·er (trĕn'chər) *n-* person who digs trenches or ditches. [from **trench.**]

trick·er·y (trĭk'ə rē) *n-* [*pl.* **trick·er·ies**] the use of tricks; deception; fraud; cheating.

trig·o·no·met·ric (trĭg'ə nə mĕ'trĭk) *adj-* having to do with trigonometry. —*adv-* **trig'o·no·met'ri·cal·ly.**

trigonometric function *n-* any of various functions of an angle, or its subtended arc, that consists of a variable ratio between two sides of a right triangle which contains the angle as an acute angle. The ratio varies with the size of the angle. The most commonly used trigonometric functions are the sine, cosine, and tangent.

trig·o·nom·e·try (trĭg'ə nŏm'ə trē) *n-* branch of mathematics that is based on the relations between the sides and angles of triangles.

tri·graph (trī'grăf') *n-* group of three letters representing one sound, such as "eau" in "beauty."

tri·lat·er·al (trī'lăt'ər əl) *adj-* 1 participated in by three sides or parties: *a trilateral agreement.* 2 three-sided.

tri·lin·gual (trī'lĭng'gwəl) *adj-* 1 written or expressed in three languages: *a trilingual edition.* 2 fluent in three languages: *a trilingual person.*

trill (trĭl) *n-* 1 *Music* trembling sound made by a rapid alternation of notes between a tone or half-tone apart. 2 similar sound, such as the warble of a bird. *vt-* to sing, play, or speak with a trill: *to trill a musical passage; to trill an "r." vi-:* *The birds trilled gaily.*

tril·lion (trĭl'yən) *n-* in the United States, a thousand billion (1,000,000,000,000); in Great Britain, a million million (1,000,000,000,000,000,000).

tril·lionth (trĭl'yənth) *adj-* 1 last in a series of a trillion. 2 ordinal of 1,000,000,000,000. *n-* 1 last in a series of a trillion. 2 one of a trillion equal parts of a whole or group. 3 last term in the name of a common fraction having a denominator of 1,000,000,000,000, or of the corresponding decimal fraction, .000000000001.

tril·li·um (trĭl'ē əm) *n-* any of various plants of the lily family, having three leaves with one large flower in the middle.

tri·lo·bate (trī'lō'bāt') *adj-* having three lobes: *a trilobate leaf.*

tri·lo·bite (trī'lə bīt') *n-* any of a class of extinct arthropods that were abundant in the Cambrian period and died out at the close of the Paleozoic era. Their nearest living relative is the horseshoe crab.

Trillium

tril·o·gy (trĭl'ə jē) *n-* [*pl.* **tril·o·gies**] series of three dramas, novels, or musical compositions, each complete in itself but forming a unified whole by reason of theme, subject matter, or treatment.

trim (trĭm) *vt-* [trimmed, trim·ming] 1 to make orderly, neat, and tidy by cutting, clipping, etc.: *to trim hair; to trim a hedge.* 2 to decorate; adorn: *to trim a coat with fur; to trim the Christmas tree.* 3 to balance (a vessel) by arranging cargo, etc.; also, to adjust (sails and yards) in position for sailing. 4 *Informal* to defeat; also, to cheat or victimize: *We trimmed our opponents by a good score. The salesman trimmed the tourist. n-* 1 order; proper condition: *They kept the business in trim. The old man wanted to keep in trim.* 2 woodwork of a building around the windows, doors, etc. 3 of a vessel, fitness for sailing; also, its position in the water. *adj-* [trim·mer, trim·mest] in good order or condition; neat: *a trim lawn; a trim figure.* —*adv-* **trim'ly.** *n-* **trim'mer.** *n-* **trim'ness.**

trim·ming (trĭm'ĭng) *n-* 1 decoration or ornament, especially on clothes: *the trimming on a hat.* 2 **trim·mings** (1) parts removed by cutting off the edges: *the trimmings of meat.* (2) the side dishes of a meal: *roast goose with its trimmings.* 3 *Informal* severe beating.

tri·month·ly (trī'mŭnth'lē) *adj-* occurring every three months: *a trimonthly meeting.*

tri·ni·tro·tol·u·ene (trī'nī'trō tŏl'yōo ēn') *a* very stable compound ($C_6H_2CH_3(NO_2)_3$), used chiefly as a high explosive; TNT. Also **tri·ni'tro·tol'u·ol.**

Trin·i·ty (trĭn'ə tē) *n-* 1 *Theology* the union of the Father, Son, and Holy Spirit in one divine being. 2 **trinity** [*pl.* **trin·i·ties**] any union of three in one: *triad.*

trin·ket (trĭng'kət) *n-* 1 small ornament or jewel. 2 toy.

tri·ode (trī'ōd') *n-* vacuum tube with three electrodes (anode, cathode, and grid).

trip (trĭp) *n-* 1 journey; voyage: *He took a flying trip to Brazil.* 2 stumble: *a trip on the stairs.* 3 slip; mistake or error. *vi-* [tripped, trip·ping] 1 to stumble: *He tripped on the dais.* 2 to make a mistake; err: *He tripped on the arithmetic test.* *vt-* 1 to cause to stumble (often followed by "up"): *The toy on the floor tripped him up.* 2 to catch in an error, falsehood, etc. (often followed by "up"): *He tripped him up with that question.* 3 to release, as by pulling a catch or trigger: *to trip an animal trap.*

tri·par·tite (trī pär′ tĭt′, trī′-) *adj-* 1 in three parts, such as a three-leaf clover; also, having three similar parts or copies. 2 made or existing among three persons or groups: *a tripartite agreement.*

tripe (trīp) *n-* 1 part of the stomach of an ox or cow, used for food. 2 *Informal* anything worthless or foolish.

trip hammer *n-* large power hammer that is hoisted into the air and then suddenly allowed to drop by a tripping device, delivering regular and heavy blows.

tri·ple (trĭp′ əl) *adj-* 1 having three parts; threefold: *a triple picture frame.* 2 three times as much or as many: *to charge a triple price.* *n-* 1 an amount three times as much or as many: *In that shop you pay triple for everything you buy.* 2 in baseball, a hit on which the batter reaches third base; three-base hit. *vt-* [tri·pled, tri·pling] to make or cause to be three times as much or as many: *to triple the output of work; to triple the value of the property.* *vi-* 1 to become three times as much or as many. 2 in baseball, to get a three-base hit.

triple play *n-* in baseball, a play in which three outs are made.

trip·let (trĭp′ lət) *n-* any one of three children born at one birth; also, any set of three things.

triple threat *n-* in football, a player who is good at running, kicking, and passing. *as modifier: a triple-threat back.*

¹**trip·li·cate** (trĭp′ lĭ kət) *adj-* threefold; made in sets of three: *a triplicate record.* *n-* something identical with two others; also, three identical things.

²**trip·li·cate** (trĭp′ lĭ kāt′) *vt-* [trip·li·cat·ed, trip·li·cat·ing] to reproduce three identical copies of: *to triplicate the letter.*

trip·ly (trĭp′ lē) *adv-* in a triple amount or degree; trebly.

tri·pod (trī′ pŏd′) *n-* 1 support or stand with three legs, as for a camera or gun. 2 any article with three legs, such as a stool.

trip·per (trĭp′ ər) *n-* releasing device or mechanism, such as one for operating a railroad signal.

Tripod

tri·sect (trī′ sĕkt′) *vt-* to cut or divide into three parts; especially, in geometry, to divide into three equal parts. *—n-* tri′sec′ tion.

tri·syl·la·ble (trī′ sĭl′ ə bəl) *n-* word made up of three syllables. *—adj-* tri′ syl·lab′ ic.

trite (trīt) *adj-* stale from too frequent use; commonplace: *such a trite expression.* *—adv-* trite′ ly. *n-* trite′ ness.

trit·i·um (trĭt′ ē əm, trĭsh′-) *n-* isotope of hydrogen containing two neutrons in addition to the proton in its atomic nucleus.

tri·ton (trī′ tən) *n-* 1 any of various large sea snails with long, spiraled shells. 2 Triton in Greek mythology, a demigod of the sea, son of Poseidon, generally pictured as part man and part dolphin and blowing a shell trumpet to calm the sea.

tri·umph (trī′ əmf) *n-* 1 victory; conquest; achievement; success: *the triumph of knowledge.* 2 in ancient Rome, a spectacular parade and celebration in honor of a returning victorious general and his army. 3 joy or acclaim over success, victory, etc. (often preceded by "in"): *There were shouts of triumph. He sat in triumph.* *vi-* 1 to be victorious or successful: *to triumph over great odds.* 2 to exult about victory or success: *to triumph over one's captives.*

tri·um·phal (trī ŭm′ fəl) *adj-* done or made in celebration or memory of a victory or triumph: *a triumphal feast; a triumphal arch.*

tri·um·phant (trī ŭm′ fənt) *adj-* 1 victorious: *a triumphant army.* 2 rejoicing or showing elation over having been successful or victorious: *a triumphant march.* *—adv-* tri·um′ phant·ly.

tri·um·vir (trī ŭm′ vər) *n-* [*pl.* tri·um·virs or tri·um·vi·ri (-və rē)] one of three persons who together govern a state; especially, in ancient Rome, one of the three ruling magistrates of the republic.

tri·um·vi·rate (trī ŭm′ və rət, -rət) *n-* 1 government by triumvirs. 2 group or association of three: *a triumvirate of friends.*

triv·et (trĭv′ ət) *n-* 1 three-legged stand for holding a kettle near or over an open fire. 2 short-legged metal plate on which to set hot dishes.

triv·i·a (trĭv′ ē ə) *n- pl.* (takes singular or plural verb) petty matters; trifles: *preoccupied with trivia.*

triv·i·al (trĭv′ ē əl) *adj-* 1 insignificant; unimportant; of little value; paltry: *a trivial remark.* 2 ordinary; commonplace: *the trivial tasks of everyday life.* 3 occupied or concerned with trifles: *He was a trivial person.* *—adv- triv′ i·al·ly.*

triv·i·al·i·ty (trĭv′ ē ăl′ ə tē) *n-* [*pl.* triv·i·al·i·ties] 1 insignificance; pettiness. 2 insignificant matter.

tri·week·ly (trī′ wēk′ lē) *adj-* 1 done or occurring three times a week. 2 done or occurring every third week: *a triweekly magazine.* *adv-: They published it triweekly.* *n-* publication that appears three times a week or every third week.

-trix *suffix* (used to form feminine nouns from masculine nouns ending in -tor): *aviatrix.*

tro·che (trō′ kē) *n-* medicated lozenge. *Hom-* trochee.

trod (trŏd) *p.t. & p.p.* of **tread.**

trod·den (trŏd′ ən) *p.p.* of **tread.**

trog·lo·dyte (trŏg′ lə dīt′) *n-* 1 dweller in a cave; especially, a prehistoric caveman. 2 recluse; hermit.

troi·ka (troi′ kə) *n-* Russian carriage drawn by three horses abreast; also, the horses.

Troi·lus (troi′ ləs) *n-* 1 in Greek mythology, a son of Priam, slain by Achilles. 2 in medieval legend, the lover of the faithless Cressida.

Tro·jan (trō′ jən) *n-* 1 inhabitant of ancient Troy. 2 fearless and industrious person. *adj-* of or relating to ancient Troy: *the Trojan women.*

Trojan horse *n-* 1 huge wooden horse built by the Greeks and filled with Greek warriors, which the Trojans were tricked into taking within Troy's walls. 2 any treacherous person, group, or plot that destroys from within.

Trojan War *n-* the ten-year conflict between the Greeks and the Trojans, caused by the abduction of Helen.

¹**troll** (trōl) *vi-* to fish by dragging the line through the water from a moving boat: *to troll for striped bass.* *vt- Music* to sing the parts of in succession, with different parts sung by different voices, as in a round: *They trolled "Three Blind Mice."* [from Old French *troller* meaning "to ramble; run without plan; run around in circles," from earlier *trauler,* probably Germanic.]

²**troll** (trōl) *n-* in Scandinavian folklore, an ugly giant or, in later tales, an impish dwarf who was supposed to live in caves, hills, and such places. [probably Old Norse.]

trol·ley (trŏl′ ē) *n-* [*pl.* trol·leys] 1 grooved wheel at the end of a pole on a streetcar, which makes contact with an overhead electric wire. 2 trolley car. 3 wheeled carriage, basket, etc., that runs suspended from an overhead track. *as modifier: a trolley wire.*

Electric trolley

trolley bus *n-* bus that is propelled electrically by current picked up from an overhead wire by a trolley.

trolley car *n-* electric streetcar that gets its power through a trolley.

trol·lop (trŏl′ əp) *n-* prostitute.

trom·bone (trŏm′ bōn′, trŏm bōn′) *n-* brass instrument of the trumpet family. A **slide trombone** changes tone by means of the U-shaped tube; a **valve trombone** changes tone by means of valves. *—n-* trom·bon′ ist.

tro·phy (trō′ fē) *n-* [*pl.* **tro·phies**] 1 something captured in battle and kept as a token of victory, such as a gun or flag. 2 any token of achievement; prize: *a tennis trophy.*

trop·ic (trŏp′ ĭk) *n-* 1 the tropic of Cancer or the tropic of Capricorn. 2 the **tropics** or the **Tropics** the region between the tropic of Cancer and the tropic of Capricorn.

North and South Tropics

trop·i·cal (trŏp′ ĭ kəl) *adj-* of or like the tropics: *a tropical climate; a tropical plant.* —*adv-* **trop′ i·cal·ly.**

tropical year *n-* the interval of time between consecutive passages of the sun through the vernal equinox, containing 365 days, 5 hours, 48 minutes, and 46 seconds, astronomical year.

tropic of Cancer *n-* the parallel of latitude around the earth at about 23½ °N, the northernmost parallel at which the sun is ever directly overhead.

tropic of Capricorn *n-* the parallel of latitude around the earth at about 23½ °S, the southernmost parallel at which the sun is ever directly overhead.

tro·pism (trō′ pĭz əm, trŏp′ ĭz-) *n-* growth movements in plants, or reflex movements in some simple animals, in response to an outside stimulus.

trop·o·pause (trō′ pə pòz′) *n-* the boundary layer of the earth's atmosphere between the troposphere and the stratosphere.

tro·po·sphere (trō′ pə sfêr′, trŏp′ ə-) *n-* the layer of the atmosphere nearest the earth, extending to a height of about seven miles and having air currents, varying temperatures, and clouds.

trot (trŏt) *n-* 1 jogging gait of a horse when the right front foot and the left hind foot are raised first, and then the other two feet. A trot is faster than a walk but slower than a canter or gallop. 2 a jogging run: *The children came at a trot. vi-* [**trot·ted, trot·ting**] 1 to move with a jogging gait or run: *The horses* trotted *to the fence. The boy* trotted *to his mother's side. vt-: He* trotted *his horse.* **trot out** *Informal* to exhibit for approval or inspection.

troth (trŏth, trôth) *Archaic n-* faith, loyalty, or truth. **plight one's troth** to pledge one's word to marry.

trot·ter (trŏt′ ər) *n-* person or horse that trots.

trou·ba·dour (trōō′ bə dôr′) *n-* one of a number of lyric poets who flourished from the 11th through the 13th centuries in southern France and northern Italy; hence, any singer of love songs.

trou·ble (trŭb′ əl) *n-* 1 disturbance; commotion: *The police rushed to the scene of* trouble. 2 distress; worry: *He is having money* troubles. 3 inconvenience; effort; bother: *Please don't go to any* trouble *for me.* 4 difficulty: *the* trouble *with your plan; in* trouble *at home.* 5 ailment: *heart* trouble; *stomach* trouble. *vt-* [**trou·bled, trou·bling**] 1 to worry or distress: *His debts* troubled *him.* 2 to inconvenience; bother: *May I* trouble *you for a loan? vi-* to take pains; bother: *Don't* trouble *to apologize.*

trou·ble·mak·er (trŭb′ əl mā′ kər) *n-* person who constantly causes trouble, usually intentionally.

trou·ble·shoot·er (trŭb′ əl shōō′ tər) *n-* 1 person who seeks out difficulties or failures in industrial equipment and repairs them. 2 person adept at resolving disputes, such as those in labor-management relations.

trou·ble·some (trŭb′ əl səm) *adj-* 1 causing trouble; annoying: *a* troublesome *child.* 2 hard to handle or solve; difficult: *a* troublesome *problem.* —*adv-* **trou′ ble·some·ly.** *n-* **trou′ ble·some·ness.**

trou·blous (trŭb′ ləs) *adj-* full of or bringing trouble and distress: *these* troublous *times.*

trough (trŏf, trôf, *also* trŏth) *n-* 1 long, narrow container to hold water or food for animals. 2 similar container for kneading dough or washing ore. 3 uncovered gutter for draining water. 4 hollow or depression, such as between waves or hills: *gulls floating in the* troughs *of the sea.* 5 in meteorology , a region of low atmospheric pressure between two regions of higher pressure.

trout (trout) *n-* [*pl.* **trout; trouts** (kinds of trout)] any of a group of food or game fishes of the salmon family, such as the brook trout or rainbow trout, found chiefly in cold, fresh waters.

Brook trout, about 1 ft long

trout lily *n-* the dogtooth violet.

trove (trōv) *n-* something that has been found: *a treasure* trove.

trow (trō) *Archaic vi-* to suppose; believe; think.

trow·el (trou′ əl) *n-* small, short-handled tool, used by masons, plasterers, and gardeners.

troy weight *n-* system of weights for precious metals and gems, in which twelve ounces equal one pound.

GARDEN

MASON'S

Trowels

tru·ant (trōō′ ənt) *n-* person who shirks his work or duty; especially, a boy or girl who stays away from school without permission. *adj-* idle; errant: *a* truant *worker.* —*n-* **tru′ an·cy.** **play truant** to stay away from school or work.

truant officer *n-* official of a public school system who investigates cases of truancy.

truce (trōōs) *n-* temporary lull or rest; especially, a temporary suspension of fighting, brought about by mutual agreement during a war.

¹**truck** (trŭk) *vt-* *Archaic* to barter or trade. *n-* 1 garden vegetables raised for market. 2 *Informal* trash; rubbish. [from Old French **troquer** meaning "to barter."] **have no truck with** *Informal* to have no dealings with.

²**truck** (trŭk) *n-* 1 large vehicle for carrying heavy loads: *an oil* truck. 2 small vehicle operated by hand or motor and used for carrying loads in a factory, on a wharf, etc. 3 group of wheels and their frame at each end of a railroad car. *vt-* to move or carry by truck: *He* trucked *the goods to Chicago. vi-* to drive a truck or otherwise work at trucking. [from Latin **trochus** meaning "iron hoop; wheel."]

Hand truck

truck·le (trŭk′ əl) *vi-* [**truck·led, truck·ling**] 1 to yield without opposition to the will of another; be subservient (to). 2 to roll on casters. *vt-* to cause to move on casters. —*n-* **truck′ ler.**

truc·u·lent (trŭk′ yə lənt, trōō′ kyə-) *adj-* 1 ready to attack; fierce or savage; ferocious; belligerent: *a* truculent *warrior.* 2 harsh; scathing: *a* truculent *satire.* —*n-* **truc′ u·lence** or **truc′ u·len·cy.** *adv-* **truc′ u·lent·ly.**

trudge (trŭj) *vi-* [**trudged, trudg·ing**] to walk steadily and wearily: *He* trudged *home after the day's work. n-* 1 long, tiring walk: *a* trudge *to the station.* —*n-* **trudg′ er.**

true (trōō) *adj-* [**tru·er, tru·est**] 1 according to fact; not false: *She gives a* true *account of what happened.* 2 loyal; faithful: *to be* true *to one's word.* 3 real; genuine: *a* true *gentleman;* true *gold.* 4 corresponding to a standard or type; correct; exact: *a* true *color; a* true *copy.* 5 rightful; legitimate: *the* true *heir to the throne. adv-* 1 truly; truthfully: *He spoke* true. 2 accurately: *The arrow sped* true *to the mark. vt-* [**trued, tru·ing** *or* **true·ing**] to make accurate; adjust: *to* true *a door frame.* **come true** to become a realized fact.

true bill *n-* in law, an indictment endorsed by a grand jury as being supported by enough evidence to justify prosecution.

true-blue (trōō′ blōō′) *adj-* faithful; loyal.

true north *n-* direction toward the North Pole. See also **magnetic north.**

truf·fle (trŭf′ əl) *n-* any of various potato-shaped fungi that grow underground and are highly prized as food.

tru·ism (trōō′ ĭz′ əm) *n-* obvious and self-evident truth; commonplace: *"You can only die once" is a* truism.

tru·ly (trōō′ lē) *adv-* 1 in a true manner; faithfully: *Please answer* truly. 2 really; indeed: *I am* truly *sorry.*

tsa·ri·na (tsä rē′ nə, zä-) czarina.

tset·se fly (tsĕt′ sē, tĕt′-) *n-* any of several kinds of bloodsucking flies of southern Africa, one of which is a carrier of the germs of sleeping sickness. Others transmit animal diseases. Also **tset′ se.**

T-shirt (tē′ shûrt′) *n-* light, collarless, short-sleeved sport shirt or undershirt.

tsp. teaspoon.

T square (tē′ skwär′) *n-* ruler with a cross bar at one end that slides along the edge of a drawing board.

tsu·na·mi (soo näm′ ē, tsoo-) *Japanese n-* tidal wave.

Tu. Tuesday.

T square

tub (tŭb) *n-* 1 large, round vessel used to hold water for washing clothes, bathing, etc. 2 bathtub. 3 *chiefly Brit.* bath. 4 container for holding butter, lard, etc. 5 the amount a tub holds: *a large tub of butter.* 6 *Informal* unwieldy or run-down ship. *vi-* [tubbed, tub·bing] to take a bath.

Tub

tu·ba (tōō′ bə, tyōō′-) *n-* large, deep-toned brass instrument.

tub·by (tŭb′ ē) *adj-* [tub·bier, tub·biest] 1 short and fat. 2 dull or flat in sound. *—n-* tub′ bi·ness.

tube (tōōb, tyōōb) *n-* 1 hollow cylinder that is longer than it is wide, used for holding or conveying various substances, especially liquids and gases; also, a similar structure in animals and plants: *the bronchial tubes.* 2 soft container for toothpaste, glue, etc., from which the contents are removed by squeezing. 3 tunnel for an electric railroad. 4 electron tube. 5 inner tube. *—adj- tube′ less. adj- tube′ like*.

Tuba

tu·ber (tōō′ bər, tyōō′-) *n-* 1 thick, often edible, part of an underground stem, such as the potato, bearing small eyes: 2 *Medicine* rounded swelling; tubercle.

twill (twĭl) *n-* 1 a weave of cloth that shows diagonal lines or ribs on the surface. 2 fabric woven with such ribs. *as modifier:* *a twill cloth; pair of twill trousers.* *vt-* to weave (cloth) so as to show diagonal lines or ribs.

twin (twĭn) *n-* 1 either of two children or animals born at one birth. 2 one of two persons or things that are very much alike: *This vase is the twin of that one.* *adj-* 1 born at the same time: *The girls are twin sisters.* 2 forming or being one of a closely connected pair: *a twin peak.* *vi-* [twinned, twin·ning] to give birth to twins.

twine (twīn) *n-* 1 strong, twisted string or thread made up of two or more strands. 2 a twist or tangle. *vt-* [twined, twin·ing] 1 to twist together; wind: *to twine flowers into a garland.* 2 to make by twisting or coiling: *to twine a garland.* 3 to encircle: *to twine ribbons around a pole.* *vi-:* *The vine twines over the porch.*

twinge (twĭnj) *n-* sudden, sharp pain of body or mind: *a muscular twinge; a twinge of conscience.* *vi-* [twinged, twing·ing] to feel a sudden, sharp pain.

twin·kle (twĭng′ kəl) *vi-* [twin·kled, twin·kling] 1 to shine with a light that comes and goes in flashes; flicker: *The stars twinkled above.* 2 to sparkle: *Her eyes twinkled.*

twit (twĭt) *vt-* [twit·ted, twit·ting] to tease in a good-natured way, especially by reminding of a mistake.

twitch (twĭch) *vt-* 1 to move in a quick, jerky manner: *He nervously twitched his fingers.* 2 to pull at suddenly; jerk: *Impatiently she twitched the cloth from the table.* *vi-:* *Her face twitched.* *n-* 1 brief, involuntary spasm of a muscle: *a facial twitch.* 2 short pull or jerk.

twit·ter (twĭt′ ər) *vi-* to make a series of short, sharp sounds; chirp: *The canary twittered in its cage.* *n-* 1 rapid series of short, sharp sounds; a chirping. 2 state of restless, nervous excitement; flutter.

two-pen·ny (tŭp′ ə nē) *Brit. adj-* 1 having the value of twopence. 2 commonplace; trifling; cheap.

two-ply (tōō′ plī′) *adj-* 1 made of two strands or layers of material. 2 of cloth, made of two separate webs woven into each other: *a two-ply carpet.*

two-score (tōō′ skôr′) *(traditionally called adjective or pronoun)* two times twenty; forty.

two-seat·er (tōō′ sē′ tər) *n-* airplane, car, etc., having seats for two passengers.

two-some (tōō′ səm) *n-* 1 two persons together. 2 game, dance, etc., for two persons.

two-star (tōō′ stär′) *adj-* having the two stars of a major general or rear admiral as insignia of rank.

two-step (tōō′ stĕp′) *n-* 1 ballroom dance in march or polka tempo performed with sliding steps. 2 music for such a dance.

two-time (tōō′ tīm′) *vt-* [two-timed, two-tim·ing] *Slang* to deceive; be unfaithful to. *—n-* two′-tim′ er.

two-way (tōō′ wā′) *adj-* 1 having or allowing movement in two directions: *a two-way street.* 2 able to transmit and receive: *a two-way radio.*

¹**-ty** *suffix* (used to form nouns) state, condition, or quality: *loyalty; royalty.* [ultimately from Latin *-tas* and *-tatis.*]

²**-ty** *suffix* (used to form some cardinal numerals) multiplied by ten: *sixty; ninety.* [from Old English *-tig.*]

ty·coon (tī kōōn′) *Informal n-* rich and powerful industrialist or financier.

ty·ing (tī′ ĭng) *pres. p.* of **tie**.

tyke (tīk) *n-* 1 *Informal* a child, especially a mischievous one. 2 mongrel dog; cur.

tym·pa·ni (tĭm′ pə nē) *n- pl.* kettledrums, especially those in a symphony orchestra. *—n-* tym′ pa·nist.

tym·pan·ic (tĭm′ păn′ ĭk) *adj-* 1 like a drum or drumhead. 2 having to do with the eardrum.

tympanic membrane *n-* membrane between the outer and middle ear, often called the eardrum.

tym·pa·num (tĭm′ pə nəm) *n-* [*pl.* tym·pa·na (-nə) or tym·pa·nums] middle ear; also, less correctly, eardrum.

type (tīp) *n-* 1 person or thing having the features that set apart a group or class; typical example: *Charles Dickens's characters are types of middle-class English life.* 2 group of persons or things that share common traits; kind; sort: *Men of that type like fast cars.* 3 *Biology* group or division of animals or plants having a common structure or form. 4 piece of metal with a raised letter or figure on one surface, used in printing or as part of a typewriter. 5 impression made from such pieces: *a line of italic type. as modifier: a type size; a type face.* *vt-* [typed, typ·ing] 1 to write on a typewriter: *to type a letter.* 2 to classify: *The director typed the actor for comic parts.* *vi-:* *She types at the rate of 60 words a minute.*

▶TYPE generally means "kind," and careful writers and speakers do not use TYPE as a modifier unless referring to printing type. Avoid saying: *this type airplane; that type person.* It is correct to say: *this type of airplane; that type of person.*

ROMAN
ITALIC
BOLD-FACE

Type and type faces

type metal *n-* an alloy of lead, tin, and antimony, used for casting printing type.

type·script (tīp′ skrĭpt′) *n-* manuscript prepared by typewriter.

type·set·ter (tīp′ sĕt′ ər) *n-* person or machine that arranges type for printing. *—n-* type′ set′ ting.

typ·i·cal (tĭp′ ĭ kəl) *adj-* 1 having the traits of its kind but no other notable features; representing a whole group: *a typical high school library; a typical suburban community.* 2 such as can be expected from knowing the type or group; characteristic: *He gave one of his typical answers.* *—adv-* typ′ i·cal·ly. *n-* typ′ i·cal·ness.

typ·i·fy (tĭp′ ə fī′) *vt-* [typ·i·fied, typ·i·fy·ing] 1 to be typical of; represent: *The cat typifies a family of animals.* 2 to symbolize: *The lamb typifies meekness.*

U

U or **u** (yōō) *n-* [*pl.* **U's, u's**] 1 the 21st letter of the English alphabet. 2 anything shaped like this letter.

U symbol for uranium.

u·biq·ui·tous (yōō bĭk' wĭ təs) *adj-* being, or seeming to be, everywhere at the same time. —*adv-* **u·biq' ui·tous·ly.** *n-* **u·biq' ui·tous·ness** or **u·biq' ui·ty.**

U-boat (yōō' bōt') *n-* German submarine. *as modifier:* *a U-boat attack; U-boat fleet.*

ud·der (ŭd' ər) *n-* sac that hangs down between the hind legs of a cow, ewe, she-goat, etc., and holds one or more milk-producing glands, each with its own teat.

UFO or **ufo** unidentified flying object.

ugh (ŏō, û, ŭg, ᴜᴋʜ, or various other grunts) *interj-* exclamation of distaste or sound made when one is hit.

ug·ly (ŭg' lē) *adj-* [**ug·li·er, ug·li·est**] 1 very unpleasant to the sight: *an ugly face.* 2 disagreeable: *an ugly task.* 3 threatening; dangerous: *an ugly sky.* 4 cross; quarrelsome: *an ugly mood.* 5 morally repulsive: *an ugly deed.*—*n-* **ug' li·ness.**

UHF or **uhf** ultrahigh frequency.

U.K. United Kingdom.

u·kase (yōō kās', ōō kās', -kāz') *n-* 1 in Russia under the czars, an imperial decree taking effect as law. 2 any official ruling or decree.

u·ku·le·le (yōō' kə lā' lē) *n-* any of several kinds of small, four-stringed musical instruments of the guitar type. [American word from Hawaiian.]

Ukulele

ul·cer (ŭl' sər, ŏōl'-) *n-* open sore or wound on the surface of the skin or mucous membrane, which causes a gradual destruction of the tissue; hence, any condition or influence that corrupts or destroys: *Poverty is an ulcer in our society.*

ul·cer·ate (ŭl' sə rāt', ŏōl'-) *vt-* [**ul·cer·at·ed, ul·cer·at·ing**] to form an ulcer; become ulcerous: *His stomach lining ulcerated.* —*n-* **ul' cer·a' tion.**

ul·cer·ous (ŭl' sər əs, ŏōl'-) *adj-* 1 marked or affected by an ulcer or ulcers: *an ulcerous area of skin.* 2 ulcerated: *an ulcerous sore.*

ul·na (ŭl' nə, ŏōl'-) *n-* [*pl.* **ul·nae** (-nē)] the inner and larger of the two bones of the forearm. —*adj-* **ul' nar:** *an ulnar fracture.*

ul·ster (ŭl' stər, ŏōl'-) *n-* long, loose overcoat, often with a belt.

ult. 1 ultimate. 2 ultimately. 3 ultimo.

ul·te·ri·or (ŭl' tēr' ē ər, ŏōl'-) *adj-* 1 beyond what is expressed or admitted; deliberately not mentioned: *an ulterior motive.* 2 farther off; more remote: *the ulterior regions of the country.* —*adv-* **ul' te' ri·or·ly.**

ul·ti·ma (ŭl' tə mə, ŏōl'-) *n-* last syllable of a word.

ul·ti·mate (ŭl' tə mət, ŏōl'-) *adj-* 1 final; last: *his ultimate goal; the ultimate result of one's actions.* 2 basic; fundamental: *some ultimate truths.* 3 farthest known or imagined in time past or future: *his ultimate ancestors.* *n-* the final or last state or degree: *the ultimate in style.*

ul·ti·mate·ly (ŭl' tə mət lē, ŏōl'-) *adv-* at the beginning or end.

un·aid·ed (ŭn' ā' dəd) *adj-* not aided; without help.

un·al·ter·a·ble (ŭn' ŏl' tər ə bəl) *adj-* such as cannot be altered or changed. —*adv-* **un' al' ter·a·bly.**

un·al·tered (ŭn' ŏl' tərd) *adj-* not altered or changed: *an unaltered policy.*

un-A·mer·i·can (ŭn' ə mĕr' ĭ kən) *adj-* not American in beliefs, actions, or attitudes; especially, not loyal to the American government or ideals.

u·na·nim·i·ty (yōō' nə nĭm' ə tē) *n-* complete agreement in opinion.

u·nan·i·mous (yōō nǎn' ə məs) *adj-* 1 united in a single opinion; agreeing: *We were unanimous in our approval.* 2 showing complete agreement: *a unanimous vote.* —*adv-* **u·nan' i·mous·ly.** *n-* **u·nan' i·mous·ness.**

un·an·swer·a·ble (ŭn' ǎn' sər ə bəl) *adj-* such as cannot be answered or disproved: *an unanswerable letter.*

un·ap·pe·tiz·ing (ŭn' ǎp' ə tī' zĭng) *adj-* not appetizing, especially to the taste.

un·ap·proach·a·ble (ŭn' ə prō' chə bəl) *adj-* 1 such as cannot be approached or reached: *The mountain peak is unapproachable in winter.* 2 not easy to know or deal with; unfriendly; cool: *The principal seemed to be unapproachable.* —*adv-* **un' ap·proach'a·bly.** *n-* **un' ap·proach'a·ble·ness.**

un·armed (ŭn' ärmd') *adj-* not armed; lacking weapons; defenseless.

un·as·sail·a·ble (ŭn' ə sā' lə bəl) *adj-* such as cannot be assailed, attacked, or disputed: *an unassailable defense; an unassailable reputation.* —*adv-* **un' as·sail'a·bly.**

un·as·sum·ing (ŭn' ə sōō' mĭng) *adj-* modest; retiring; not given to pushing oneself forward. —*adv-* **un' as·sum' ing·ly.** *n-* **un' as·sum' ing·ness.**

un·at·tached (ŭn' ə tǎcht') *adj-* 1 not attached or connected: *an unattached house.* 2 not married or engaged to be married. 3 *Military* not assigned to a company or regiment. 4 in track meets, competing on one's own, not as a member of any athletic organization. 5 in law, not taken or held under legal process.

un·at·tend·ed (ŭn' ə tĕn' dəd) *adj-* 1 without an escort; alone: *Mrs. Roberts is going to the concert unattended.* 2 receiving no attention or care; without supervision.

un·a·vail·ing (ŭn' ə vā' lĭng) *adj-* without result or effect; useless; futile: *Her calls for help were unavailing.* —*adv-* **un' a·vail' ing·ly.**

un·a·void·a·ble (ŭn' ə voi' də bəl) *adj-* such as cannot be avoided; inevitable: *an unavoidable delay.* —*adv-* **un' a·void' a·bly.** *n-* **un' a·void' a·ble·ness.**

un·a·ware (ŭn' ə wâr') *adj-* not aware or conscious: *They were unaware of danger.*

un·a·wares (ŭn' ə wârz') *adv-* 1 without being aware: *He walked into the surprise party unawares.* 2 by surprise: *You came upon me unawares.*

un·bal·anced (ŭn' bǎl' ənst) *adj-* 1 not in balance; out of equilibrium: *The scales were unbalanced.* 2 not adjusted as to be even in credit and debit: *an unbalanced account; an unbalanced budget.* 3 not sound mentally; partly insane: *an unbalanced mind.* 4 in football, having more players on one side of the center than on the other: *an unbalanced line.*

un·bar (ŭn' bär') *vt-* [**un·barred, un·bar·ring**] to remove a bar or bars from; open; unlock: *to unbar a door.*

un·bear·a·ble (ŭn' bâr' ə bəl) *adj-* such as cannot be borne; impossible to endure; intolerable: *an unbearable pain; unbearable suspense.* —*adv-* **un' bear' a·bly.**

un·beat·a·ble (ŭn' bē' tə bəl) *adj-* such as cannot be surpassed or defeated; invincible: *an unbeatable team.*

un·beat·en (ŭn' bē' tən) *adj-* 1 never beaten or surpassed: *an unbeaten team or player; an unbeaten record.* 2 never walked over; untrodden: *an unbeaten path.*

un·be·com·ing (ŭn' bĭ kŭm' ĭng) *adj-* 1 not suitable or fit; improper; unworthy: *their unbecoming conduct.* 2 not suited to one's appearance; not flattering: *an unbecoming hat.* —*adv-* **un' be·com' ing·ly.**

un·be·known (ŭn' bĭ nōn') or **un·be·knownst** (ŭn' bĭ nōnst') *adj-* unknown; not known of: *an unbeknown poet.* *adv-* in an unknown or unnoticed way; unknown (to): *He stole into the room unbeknownst to us.*

un·be·lief (ŭn' bĭ lēf') *n-* lack of positive belief or faith; especially, refusal to accept the teachings of religion.

un·be·liev·a·ble (ŭn' bĭ lē' və bəl) *adj-* such as cannot be believed; incredible: *an unbelievable story; unbelievable cruelty.* —*adv-* **un' be·liev' a·bly.**

un·be·liev·er (ŭn' bĭ lē' vər) *n-* 1 person who lacks faith; doubter. 2 person who refuses to accept the teachings of any religion.

un·be·liev·ing (ŭn' bĭ lē' vĭng) *adj-* 1 not believing; doubting; incredulous. 2 not accepting religious teachings. —*adv-* **un' be·liev' ing·ly.**

un·bend (ŭn' bĕnd') *vt-* [**un·bent, un·bend·ing**] 1 to straighten: *to unbend a crooked nail; to unbend one's legs after a long ride.* 2 to unfasten (a sail) from a spar. 3 to free from strain; relax: *to unbend the mind.* *vi-* 1 to become straight. 2 to become less formal or stiff; relax: *After a little while, he unbent and joined the party.*

un·bleached (ŭn' blēcht') *adj-* not bleached: *a yard of unbleached muslin; a sack of unbleached flour.*

un·blem·ished (ŭn' blĕm' ĭsht) *adj*- without a blemish, spot, or stain; spotless; pure: *an unblemished life.*

un·blush·ing (ŭn' blŭsh' ĭng) *adj*- 1 not blushing; not embarrassed. 2 not ashamed or timid; bold: *an unblushing offer of a bribe.* —*adv*- un' **blush' ing·ly.**

un·bolt (ŭn' bōlt') *vt*- to unlock (a door, gate, etc.) by pulling back the bolt; unbar.

un·born (ŭn' bôrn') *adj*- not yet born; still to come; future: *Generations of unborn children will hear of him.*

un·bos·om (ŭn' bŏŏz' əm) *vt*- to bring out (something one knows or feels but has not revealed); reveal: *to unbosom a secret.* *vi*- to free one's mind by telling one's thoughts.

unbosom (oneself) to tell (one's) thoughts, feelings, or secrets.

un·bound (ŭn' bound') *adj*- 1 not tied; free: *The unbound pony galloped across the field.* 2 not confined or limited: *a man unbound by custom.* 3 having pages not fastened together or not bound between covers.

un·bound·ed (ŭn' boun' dəd) *adj*- without limits; boundless; measureless: *a universe of unbounded space.*

un·bowed (ŭn' boud') *adj*- 1 not bowed or bent: *The old man was dignified and unbowed.* 2 not conquered; still erect and proud, though defeated.

un·bri·dled (ŭn' brī' dəld) *adj*- 1 not fastened with a bridle. 2 not restrained: *an unbridled tongue.*

un·bro·ken (ŭn' brō' kən) *adj*- 1 not broken; not damaged: *an unbroken toy.* 2 without interruption: *an unbroken dry spell.* 3 not tamed or trained: *an unbroken colt.* 4 not beaten or surpassed: *an unbroken record.*

un·buck·le (ŭn' bŭk' əl) *vt*- [un·buck·led, un·buck·ling] to undo or unfasten the buckle of: *to unbuckle a belt.*

un·bur·den (ŭn' bûr' dən) *vt*- 1 to rid of a load; ease: *He unburdened his horse after the long ride.* 2 to relieve of a burden: *He unburdened himself of a secret.*

un·but·ton (ŭn' bŭt' ən) *vt*- to unfasten the button or buttons of; open: *to unbutton a coat.*

un·called-for (ŭn' kôld' fôr', -fôr') *adj*- not needed; out of place; improper: *an uncalled-for remark.*

un·can·ny (ŭn' kăn' ē) *adj*- [un·can·nier, un·can·ni·est] 1 not to be explained by reason: *his uncanny knowledge of my past.* 2 mysterious; strange; weird: *an uncanny atmosphere.* —*adv*- un' **can' ni·ly.** *n*- un' **can' ni·ness.**

un·cap (ŭn' kăp') *vt*- [un·capped, un·cap·ping] to remove the cap, covering, or lid from: *to uncap a bottle.*

un·ceas·ing (ŭn' sē' sĭng) *adj*- without a stop; continuous: *an unceasing din.* —*adv*- un' **ceas' ing·ly.**

un·cer·e·mo·ni·ous (ŭn' sĕr' ə mō' nē əs) *adj*- 1 without any formality; informal: *an unceremonious visit; an unceremonious conference.* 2 without the usual courtesy; abrupt: *an unceremonious dismissal.* —*adv*- un' **cer' e·mo' ni·ous·ly.** *n*- un' **cer' e·mo' ni·ous·ness.**

un·cer·tain (ŭn' sûr' tən) *adj*- 1 not certain; not sure; doubtful: *to be uncertain of the answer to a question; butter of uncertain quality.* 2 not regular, dependable, or predictable: *the uncertain weather of early spring.* 3 not steady or firm: *an uncertain support or step.* 4 changing; fluctuating; variable: *the uncertain tide; uncertain prices.* —*adv*- un' **cer' tain·ly.** *n*- un' **cer' tain·ness.**

un·cer·tain·ty (ŭn' sûr' tən tē) *n*- [*pl.* un·cer·tain·ties] 1 lack of certainty; doubt: *There was some uncertainty about the date.* 2 uncertain or doubtful matter.

un·chain (ŭn' chān') *vt*- to unfasten the chain of; let loose; set free: *to unchain a door; unchain a dog.*

un·change·a·ble (ŭn' chān' jə bəl) *adj*- such as cannot be changed; unlikely to change or be changed: *His honesty is unchangeable.* —*adv*- un' **change' a·bly.** *n*- un' **change' a·ble·ness.**

un·char·i·ta·ble (ŭn' chăr' ə tə bəl) *adj*- 1 not charitable or generous to persons in need. 2 not kind in judging others or in dealing with others; harsh: *an uncharitable remark; uncharitable criticism.* —*adv*- un' **char' i·ta·bly.** *n*- un' **char' i·ta·ble·ness.**

un·chaste (ŭn' chāst') *adj*- not chaste or morally pure; not virtuous; lewd: *her unchaste behavior; an unchaste remark.* —*adv*- un' **chaste' ly.** *n*- un' **chaste' ness.**

un·checked (ŭn' chĕkt') *adj*- not held back or controlled; not restrained: *an unchecked flood.*

un·chris·tian (ŭn' krĭs' chən) *adj*- 1 not of the Christian religion. 2 not in keeping with the Christian religion: *an unchristian custom or practice.* 3 not kind or charitable: *an unchristian act or remark.*

un·ci·al (ŭn' chəl) *adj*- having to do with characters or letters found in manuscripts from the fourth to about the ninth century, which resembled modern capital letters but were more rounded. *n*- 1 character or letter of this kind. 2 manuscript written in such characters or letters.

un·civ·il (ŭn' sĭv' əl) *adj*- not civil or courteous; impolite; rude: *an uncivil letter.* —*adv*- un' **civ' il·ly.**

un·civ·i·lized (ŭn' sĭv' ə līzd) *adj*- not civilized; barbaric: *an uncivilized manner; uncivilized tribes.*

un·clad (ŭn' klăd') *adj*- without clothes; naked.

unc·tion (ŭngk' shən) *n*- 1 act of anointing as a rite of consecration. 2 an ointment; hence, anything soothing. 3 excessive and insincere courtesy; a smooth, oily manner. See also *extreme unction.*

unc·tu·ous (ŭng' chŏŏ əs) *adj*- 1 oily; smooth. 2 insincerely courteous or suave: *an unctuous manner.* —*adv*- unc' **tu·ous·ly.** *n*- unc' **tu·ous·ness.**

un·cul·ti·vat·ed (ŭn' kŭl' tə vā' təd) *adj*- 1 not tilled; not cultivated for production of food. 2 not developed; not practiced; neglected: *an uncultivated talent for art.* 3 uncivilized; not refined by education.

un·curl (ŭn' kûrl') *vt*- to straighten out: *The rain uncurled her hair.* *vi*-: *Her hair uncurled in the rain.*

un·cut (ŭn' kŭt') *adj*- 1 not cut down, cut off, or cut apart: *an uncut forest; uncut flowers; an uncut ham.* 2 not shortened or reduced in size, length, etc.: *an uncut novel or motion picture.* 3 having the edges untrimmed, so that the pages cannot be turned one at a time until they are slit apart. 4 unchanged by cutting, polishing, etc.: *an uncut diamond.*

un·daunt·ed (ŭn' dòn' təd) *adj*- not afraid or fearful; bold. —*adv*- un' **daunt' ed·ly.**

un·de·ceive (ŭn' dĭ sēv') *vt*- [un·de·ceived, un·de·ceiv·ing] to free from error or a mistaken idea or belief: *I thought it was a diamond, until the jeweler undeceived me.*

un·de·cid·ed (ŭn' dĭ sī' dəd) *adj*- 1 not yet decided or settled: *The question of moving to the country is still undecided.* 2 not having made up one's mind; wavering; vacillating: *We are undecided about what to do.* —*adv*- un' **de·cid' ed·ly.**

un·de·filed (ŭn' dĭ fīld') *adj*- 1 not soiled or contaminated. 2 not dishonored: *his undefiled name.*

un·de·mon·stra·tive (ŭn' dĭ mòn' strə tĭv) *adj*- reserved in showing one's feelings. —*adv*- un' **de·mon' stra·tive·ly.** *n*- un' **de·mon' stra·tive·ness.**

un·de·ni·a·ble (ŭn' dĭ nī' ə bəl) *adj*- not to be denied; true or real beyond doubt; obvious: *You may not like him but his good looks are undeniable.*

un·de·ni·a·bly (ŭn' dĭ nī' ə blē) *adv*- without doubt; truly; certainly.

un·der (ŭn' dər) *prep*- 1 in, to, or at a place or position directly below or beneath the surface of: *slippers under the bed; a picnic under the trees.* 2 concealed by; behind: *flowers under the leaves of a tree; to live under an assumed name.* 3 lower than (another) in rank, importance, value, etc.: *a rank under that of captain.* 4 less than (another) in amount, size, age, weight, etc.: *a price under two dollars; children under ten years of age.* 5 subject to the action or effect of: *to be under another's influence; under treatment by a doctor.* 6 subjected to; dominated by: *They suffer under a tyrant. He is under great strain.* 7 guided by; directed by: *He learned under great teachers.* 8 because of: *He refused under the circumstances.* 9 in conformity with; bound by: *to live under the laws of the land; under oath.* 10 during the time or rule of: *England under Queen Elizabeth.* *adv*- beneath or inside a surface: *The current sucked him under. She turned the hem under.* *adj*- 1 situated beneath something or on a lower surface: *the under surface of a leaf.* 2 lower in rank: *an under officer.*

go under to meet defeat or downfall; fail; be ruined.

un·der·car·riage (ŭn' dər kăr' ĭj) *n*- 1 framework that supports an automobile, railroad train, etc., from below. 2 the landing gear of an airplane.

un·der·ex·pose (ŭn′dər ĕk spōz′) *vt-* [un·der·ex·posed, un·der·ex·pos·ing] to expose (a photographic film, plate, etc.) to light for less than the usual or required amount of time. **—n-** un′der·ex·po′sure.

un·der·feed (ŭn′dər fēd′) *vt-* [un·der·fed, un·der·feed·ing] to give insufficient nourishment to.

un·der·foot (ŭn′dər foot′) *adv-* 1 beneath the feet; on the ground: *It is* muddy underfoot. 2 in the way; in danger of being stepped on: *That puppy is* underfoot.

un·der·gar·ment (ŭn′dər gär′mənt) *n-* garment worn under one's outer clothing.

un·der·go (ŭn′dər gō′) *vt-* [un·der·went, un·der·gone, un·der·go·ing] to be subjected to; go through; experience: *to* undergo *changes; to* undergo *hardships.*

un·der·grad·u·ate (ŭn′dər grăj′ōō ət) *n-* college or university student who has not yet received a bachelor's degree. *as modifier: an* undergraduate *student.*

un·der·ground (ŭn′dər ground′) *adj-* 1 situated, operating, or done beneath the surface of the earth: *an* underground *passage;* underground *excavations for a tunnel.* 2 acting or carried on in secret: *an* underground *system of spying. adv- (also* ŭn′dər ground′) 1 beneath the surface of the earth: *Miners work* underground. 2 in a secret place or by means of secret methods: *The spies worked* underground. *n-* 1 something situated under the ground, such as a space or passage. 2 secret group working against established authority. 3 *Brit.* subway.

un·der·grown (ŭn′dər grōn′) *adj-* below normal size.

un·der·growth (ŭn′dər grōth′) *n-* plants, bushes, vines, etc., growing thickly under trees or taller plants.

un·der·hand (ŭn′dər hănd′) *adj-* 1 not open or honest; secret and deceitful: *He used* underhand *methods to get ahead.* 2 in baseball, tennis, etc., done with or using a motion in which the hand and elbow are moved forward and are kept lower than the level of the shoulder: *an* underhand *pitch. adv-: to throw* underhand.

un·der·hand·ed (ŭn′dər hăn′dəd) *adj-* not open and aboveboard; deceptive and unfair; underhand. **—adv-** un′der·hand′ed·ly. *n-* un′der·hand′ed·ness.

un·der·lie (ŭn′dər lī′) *vt-* [un·der·lay, un·der·lain, un·der·ly·ing] 1 to lie or be under (something). 2 to be at the bottom of: *What motives* underlie *his actions?*

¹**un·der·line** (ŭn′dər līn′) *vt-* [un·der·lined, un·der·lin·ing] 1 to draw a line under. 2 to emphasize.

²**un·der·line** (ŭn′dər līn′) *n-* line placed under a word, phrase, etc., especially for emphasis.

un·der·ling (ŭn′dər lĭng) *n-* person having an inferior rank or position; subordinate.

un·der·lin·ing (ŭn′dər lī′nĭng) *n-* lines drawn under words, usually for emphasis.

un·der·ly·ing (ŭn′dər lī′ĭng) *adj-* 1 lying beneath another layer, surface, etc.: *The* underlying *soil is rocky.* 2 basic; essential: *the* underlying *causes.*

un·der·mine (ŭn′dər mīn′) *vt-* [un·der·mined, un·der·min·ing] 1 to dig a hollow or tunnel under; dig beneath. 2 to weaken by wearing away the base of: *The flood* undermined *our house.* 3 to work secretly against; injure by underhand methods: *to* undermine *a man's authority.* 4 to destroy gradually; weaken; impair: *Lack of sleep can* undermine *one's health.*

un·der·most (ŭn′dər mōst′) *adj-* lowest in place or position: *the* undermost *layer.*

un·der·neath (ŭn′dər nēth′) *prep-* (considered an adverb when the object is clearly implied but not expressed) under; beneath; below: *plants* underneath *the snow; to hide something* underneath *a pile of papers.*

un·der·pass (ŭn′dər păs′) *n-* road or passage that goes under a highway, bridge, etc.

un·der·pay (ŭn′dər pā′) *vt-* [un·der·paid, un·der·pay·ing] to give insufficient pay to: *He* underpays *his workers.*

un·der·pin·ning (ŭn′dər pĭn′ĭng) *n-* part or structure that supports a building or wall from below; hence, any support or prop.

un·der·priv·i·leged (ŭn′dər prĭv′ə lĭjd) *adj-* lacking opportunities or advantages because of poverty, poor education, poor health, neglect, etc.

un·der·pro·duc·tion (ŭn′dər prə dŭk′shən) *n-* production that falls short of what is normal or required.

un·der·rate (ŭn′dər răt′) *vt-* [un·der·rat·ed, un·der·rat·ing] to place too low an estimate or value upon.

un·der·score (ŭn′dər skōr′) *vt-* [un·der·scored, un·der·scor·ing] 1 to draw a line under; underline. 2 to give emphasis to.

un·der·score (ŭn′dər skōr′) *n-* an underline.

un·der·sea (ŭn′dər sē′) *adj-* existing or taking place beneath the surface of the sea: *an* undersea *exploration.*

un·der·sea (ŭn′dər sē′) *or* **un·der·seas** (-sēz′) *adv-* beneath the surface of the sea.

un·der·sec·re·tar·y (ŭn′dər sĕk′rə tĕr′ē) *n-* [*pl.* un·der·sec·re·tar·ies] government official who ranks next below a secretary: *an* Undersecretary *of State.*

un·der·sell (ŭn′dər sĕl′) *vt-* [un·der·sold, un·der·sel·ling] to sell at a lower price than (a competitor).

un·der·shirt (ŭn′dər shûrt′) *n-* close-fitting undergarment for the upper part of the body.

un·der·shoot (ŭn′dər shōōt′) *vt-* [un·der·shot, un·der·shoot·ing] 1 to miss (a target) by shooting short of it. 2 of an airplane, to land short of the runway, landing field, etc.).

un·der·shot (ŭn′dər shŏt′) *adj-* of the lower jaw, projecting beyond the upper jaw; also, having such a jaw.

undershot wheel *n-* water wheel driven by water passing beneath it.

un·der·side (ŭn′dər sīd′) *n-* the lower side or surface of something: *the* underside *of a leaf.*

un·der·signed (ŭn′dər sīnd′) *adj-* signed at the end of a document, letter, etc.: *the* undersigned *names.* *n-* the undersigned person or persons who have signed a document.

Undershot wheel

un·der·sized (ŭn′dər sīzd′) *adj-* smaller than the usual or normal size: *an* undersized *portion of cake.*

un·der·skirt (ŭn′dər skûrt′) *n-* skirt worn under an outer skirt and sometimes showing beneath it.

un·der·slung (ŭn′dər slŭng′) *adj-* of an automobile, having the supporting springs of the chassis attached to the underside of the axle.

un·der·stand (ŭn′dər stănd′) *vt-* [un·der·stood, un·der·stand·ing] (in senses 1 and 5 considered intransitive when the direct object is implied but not expressed) 1 to know or grasp the meaning of; comprehend: *They don't* understand *that.* 2 to have thorough knowledge of; be familiar with: *She* understands *French. He* understands *his business.* 3 to perceive clearly; recognize: *to* understand *the consequences of one's actions.* 4 to accept as a fact; have been told; believe: *I* understand *he will come tomorrow.* 5 to have a sympathetic attitude toward: *My parents don't* understand *me.*

un·dreamed-of (ŭn′drēmd′ŏv′, -ŭv′) *adj-* not imagined or considered possible: *an* undreamed-of *opportunity.* Also un′dreamt′-of′ (ŭn′drĕmt′-).

¹**un·dress** (ŭn′drĕs′) *vi-* to take off one's clothes. *vt-* to remove the clothing of: *to* undress *a doll. n-* 1 casual or informal clothing. 2 a being incompletely clothed: *in a state of* undress.

²**un·dress** (ŭn′drĕs′) *adj-* not intended for formal wear: *an* undress *uniform.*

un·due (ŭn′dōō′, -dyōō′) *adj-* 1 more than necessary; excessive: *He pays* undue *attention to trifles.* 2 not right or proper: *an* undue *disregard for authority.*

un·du·lant fever (ŭn′dyə lənt) *n-* disease characterized by recurring attacks of fever, swelling of the joints, and general bodily pain. It is caused by certain bacteria, and is transmitted to human beings chiefly through the milk of animals infected with the disease.

un·du·late (ŭn′dyə lāt′) *vi-* [un·du·lat·ed, un·du·lat·ing] 1 to move in waves, or in a wavelike, curving way; also, to form waves; have a rippling surface or appearance: *The wheat field* undulated *in the breeze.* *vt-* to cause to form waves or move with a wavelike motion. **—n-** un′du·la′tion. *adj-* un′du·la·tor′y (-lə tôr′ē).

un·du·ly (ŭn′dōō′lē, -dyōō′lē) *adv-* in an undue manner; unnecessarily: *He is* unduly *nervous.*

un·dy·ing (ŭn′dī′ĭng) *adj-* lasting or supposedly lasting forever; everlasting; eternal: *his* undying *devotion.*

un·fail·ing (ŭn′ fā′ lĭng) *adj-* 1 not failing or likely to fail; inexhaustible: *an unfailing water supply.* 2 constant; reliable: *an unfailing friend.* —*adv-* un′ fail′ ing·ly.

un·fair (ŭn′ fâr′) *adj-* 1 not fair; unjust: *an unfair wage.* 2 not fairly matched or balanced: *an unfair contest.* —*adv-* un′ fair′ ly. *n-* un′ fair′ ness.

un·faith·ful (ŭn′ fāth′ fəl) *adj-* 1 not faithful; false to a promise or duty; disloyal: *an unfaithful friend.* 2 not accurate or reliable: *an unfaithful version of the facts.* —*adv-* un′ faith′ ful·ly. *n-* un′ faith′ ful·ness.

un·fal·ter·ing (ŭn′ fôl′ tər ĭng) *adj-* not faltering; steady; steadfast. —*adv-* un′ fal′ ter·ing·ly.

un·fa·mil·iar (ŭn′ fə mĭl′ yər) *adj-* 1 not familiar; not well known: *an unfamiliar face.* 2 not acquainted: *to be unfamiliar with a language.* —*n-* un′ fa·mil′ i·ar′ i·ty (· mĭl′ ē är′ ə te, -ĕr′ ə tē). *adv-* un′ fa·mil′ iar·ly.

un·fas·ten (ŭn′ făs′ ən) *vt-* to undo the fastening of; untie; loosen: *He unfastened the chain.* *vi-*: *This chain unfastens easily.*

un·fath·om·a·ble (ŭn′ făth′ əm ə bəl) *adj-* 1 too deep to measure. 2 impossible to understand or explain.

un·fath·omed (ŭn′ făth′ əmd) *adj-* 1 not fathomed; not measured for depth: *the unfathomed waters.* 2 not understood or explained: *an unfathomed secret.*

un·fa·vor·a·ble (ŭn′ fā′ vər ə bəl) *adj-* 1 not favorable; not helpful in producing good results: *They work under unfavorable conditions.* 2 disapproving; opposing; adverse: *an unfavorable opinion.* —*n-* un′ fa′ vor·a·ble·ness. *adv-* un′ fa′ vor·a·bly.

un·feel·ing (ŭn′ fē′ lĭng) *adj-* 1 pitiless; hard-hearted; cruel: *an unfeeling person.* 2 lacking feeling or sensation. —*adv-* un′ feel′ ing·ly. *n-* un′ feel′ ing·ness.

un·feigned (ŭn′ fānd′) *adj-* not feigned; sincere; genuine: *his unfeigned enthusiasm.* —*adv-* un′ feign′ ed·ly.

un·fet·ter (ŭn′ fĕt′ ər) *vt-* to set free.

un·fin·ished (ŭn′ fĭn′ ĭsht) *adj-* 1 not finished; not complete: *an unfinished story*; unfinished business. 2 left in the rough state; not smoothed, varnished, or painted: *an unfinished piece of furniture.* 3 of fabrics, not processed after weaving: *an unfinished woolen cloth.*

un·fit (ŭn′ fĭt′) *adj-* 1 lacking fitness; not suitable because of some lack or shortcoming: *clothes unfit for this climate; a man unfit for high office.* 2 in poor physical or emotional condition. *vt-* to make unsuitable; disqualify: *His bad record unfits him for the job.* —*n-* un′ fit′ ness.

un·flag·ging (ŭn′ flăg′ ĭng) *adj-* not flagging; untiring: *his unflagging enthusiasm.* —*adv-* un′ flag′ ging·ly.

un·fledged (ŭn′ flĕjd′) *adj-* 1 of a young bird, lacking feathers needed for flight. 2 lacking experience.

un·flinch·ing (ŭn′ flĭn′ chĭng) *adj-* not flinching; unyielding in the face of danger, pain, or disagreeable duty; steadfast; resolute. —*adv-* un′ flinch′ ing·ly.

un·fold (ŭn′ fōld′) *vt-* 1 to open the folds of; spread open: *She unfolded the towel.* 2 to reveal by degrees: *The spy unfolded the details of his plan.* *vi-* 1 to become open, as the petals of a flower do. 2 to develop so as to be seen or known: *The plot of the story unfolded gradually.*

un·fore·seen (ŭn′ fôr sēn′.) *adj-* not foreseen; not counted on or provided for; unexpected.

un·for·get·ta·ble (ŭn′ fər gĕt′ ə bəl) *adj-* not likely to be forgotten; memorable. —*adv-* un′ for·get′ ta·bly.

un·formed (ŭn′ fôrmd′) *adj-* 1 not formed; not given definite shape: *an unformed mass of clay.* 2 not fully developed: *an unformed mind; unformed plans.*

un·for·tu·nate (ŭn′ fôr′ chə nət, ŭn′ fôr′-) *adj-* 1 lacking good fortune; unlucky: *an unfortunate person.* 2 unsuccessful; disastrous: *an unfortunate business venture.* 3 badly chosen; unsuitable; regrettable: *an unfortunate remark.* *n-* unlucky and unhappy person. —*adv-* un′ for′ tu·nate·ly.

un·found·ed (ŭn′ foun′ dəd) *adj-* lacking a sound basis; not backed by facts or evidence: *an unfounded hope.*

un·friend·ly (ŭn′ frĕnd′ lē) *adj-* [un·friend·li·er, un·friend·li·est] 1 not friendly; hostile. 2 not favorable; not pleasant: *an unfriendly climate.* —*n-* un′ friend′ li·ness.

un·frock (ŭn′ frŏk′) *vt-* to expel (a priest) from the clergy by official authority.

un·fruit·ful (ŭn′ frōōt′ fəl) *adj-* 1 not fruitful; not producing fruit or offspring; barren.

un·furl (ŭn′ fûrl′) *vt-* to unroll; spread out: *to unfurl sails.* *vi-*: *The flag unfurled in the breeze.*

un·fur·nished (ŭn′ fûr′ nĭsht) *adj-* not furnished; without furniture: *an unfurnished apartment.*

un·gain·ly (ŭn′ gān′ lē) *adj-* [un·gain·li·er, un·gain·li·est] awkward; clumsy. —*n-* un′ gain′ li·ness.

un·gen·er·ous (ŭn′ jĕn′ ər əs) *adj-* 1 not generous; not bountiful; stingy. 2 lacking kindness or sympathy; unfeeling; mean. —*n-* un′ gen′ er·ous·ness.

un·god·ly (ŭn′ gŏd′ lē) *adj-* [un·god·li·er, un·god·li·est] 1 lacking reverence for God or established religion; impious. 2 unholy; sinful; wicked. 3 *Informal* highly unsuitable; outrageous. —*n-* un′ god′ li·ness.

un·gov·ern·a·ble (ŭn′ gŭv′ ər nə bəl) *adj-* such as cannot be governed or restrained; uncontrollable; unruly: *an ungovernable temper.* —*adv-* un′ gov′ ern·a·bly.

un·grace·ful (ŭn′ grās′ fəl) *adj-* lacking grace; clumsy; awkward. —*adv-* un′ grace′ ful·ly. *n-* un′ grace′ ful·ness.

un·gra·cious (ŭn′ grā′ shəs) *adj-* lacking graciousness; rude. —*adv-* un′ gra′ cious·ly. *n-* un′ gra′ cious·ness.

un·grate·ful (ŭn′ grāt′ fəl) *adj-* 1 lacking gratitude; not thankful or appreciative. 2 causing discomfort or displeasure; disagreeable: *an ungrateful task.* —*adv-* un′ grate′ ful·ly. *n-* un′ grate′ ful·ness.

un·ground·ed (ŭn′ groun′ dəd) *adj-* 1 having no sound basis; unfounded: *his ungrounded fears.* 2 lacking instruction or information; untaught: *He is ungrounded*

u·ni·lat·er·al (yōō′ nə lăt′ ər əl) *adj-* 1 of or undertaken by one party or person only: *a unilateral decision.* 2 *Biology* affecting but one side of an animal, organ, etc. —*adv-* u′ ni·lat′ er·al·ly.

un·im·ag·i·na·ble (ŭn′ ĭ măj′ ə nə bəl) *adj-* such as cannot be imagined; inconceivable: *an unimaginable distance.* —*adv-* un′ im·ag′ i·na·bly.

un·im·ag·i·na·tive (ŭn′ ĭ măj′ ə nə tĭv′) *adj-* lacking imagination; prosaic. —*adv-* un′ im·ag′ i·na·tive′ ly.

un·im·peach·a·ble (ŭn′ ĭm pēch′ ə bəl) *adj-* too good and honest to be reasonably doubted: *a man of unimpeachable character.* —*adv-* un′ im·peach′ a·bly.

un·in·hab·it·ed (ŭn′ ĭn hăb′ ə təd) *adj-* not inhabited; having no inhabitants: *an uninhabited island.*

un·in·hib·it·ed (ŭn′ ĭn hĭb′ ə təd) *adj-* lacking inhibitions; free and relaxed in behavior, often more so than is socially acceptable. —*adv-* un′ in·hib′ it·ed·ly.

un·in·jured (ŭn′ ĭn′ jərd) *adj-* not injured; unharmed.

un·in·spired (ŭn′ ĭn spïrd′) *adj-* lacking inspiration or creative originality; dull.

un·in·tel·li·gent (ŭn′ ĭn tĕl′ ə jənt) *adj-* lacking intelligence; unwise; stupid. —*adv-* un′ in·tel′ li·gent·ly.

un·in·tel·li·gi·ble (ŭn′ ĭn tĕl′ ə jə bəl) *adj-* not intelligible; impossible to understand or make out: *an unintelligible scrawl.* —*adv-* un′ in·tel′ li·gi·bly.

un·in·ter·est·ed (ŭn′ ĭn′ tə rĕs′ təd) *adj-* not interested or curious; indifferent.

▶For usage note see DISINTERESTED.

un·in·ter·rupt·ed (ŭn′ ĭn′ tə rŭp′ təd) *adj-* having no interruption; continuous. —*adv-* un′ in′ ter·rup′ ted·ly.

un·ion (yōōn′ yən) *n-* 1 a uniting or being united; combination: *the union of church and state.* 2 the Union (1) the United States of America. (2) those States that remained under the Federal government during the Civil War. 3 league or association formed to protect or promote a common interest: *a labor union.* 4 partnership or association in marriage: *a long and happy union.* 5 harmony; agreement: *a union of like minds.* 6 coupling device for connecting pipes or rods. 7 part of a flag that stands for the joining of states or parts, and that appears in the upper corner near the flagstaff. A blue square covered with stars forms the union of the U.S. flag. 8 *Mathematics* set made up of all the elements of a pair of sets, without duplication of any element belonging to both of them. *as modifier*: *the Union forces; a union member.*

union shop *n-* factory or other business in which all workers must be or become union members.

u·nique (yōō nēk′) *adj-* 1 alone of its kind; different from all others: *The platypus is unique among animals.*

U·ni·ver·sal·ism (yōō′ nə vûr′ sə lĭz′ əm) *n-* the beliefs and practices of the Universalists.

U·ni·ver·sal·ist (yōō′ nə vûr′ sə lĭst) *n-* member of a religious denomination that stresses the salvation of all souls and the complete triumph of good over evil. The Universalists are now officially affiliated with the Unitarians. *adj-: a* Universalist *congregation.*

u·ni·ver·sal·i·ty (yōō′ nə vûr′ săl′ ə tē) *n-* [*pl.* **u·ni·ver·sal·i·ties**] universal presence, application, or truth: *the* universality *of the custom of marriage.*

universal joint *n-* in an engine, a joint or coupling between two shafts that allows torque to be transmitted when the shafts are not in line.

Universal joint

universal time mean time.

u·ni·verse (yōō′ nə vûrs′) *n-*
1 the whole system of existing material things; all creation; the cosmos. 2 mankind: *I proclaim my views to the whole* universe. 3 in logic, all objects, collectively, that are under consideration at one time.

u·ni·ver·si·ty (yōō′ nə vûr′ sə tē) *n-* [*pl.* **u·ni·ver·si·ties**] institution for higher learning which offers advanced degrees and usually has a liberal arts college, a graduate school, and colleges of education, law, medicine, engineering, etc. *as modifier:* the university *bookstore.*

un·just (ŭn′ jŭst′) *adj-* not just; unfair. —*adv-* un′ just′ ly. *n-* un′ just′ ness.

un·jus·ti·fi·a·ble (ŭn′ jŭs′ tə fī′ ə bəl) *adj-* such as cannot be justified. —*adv-* un′ jus′ ti·fi′ a·bly.

un·kempt (ŭn′ kĕmpt′) *adj-* 1 not combed: *to have* unkempt *hair.* 2 sloppy; untidy. 3 unpolished; rough.

un·kind (ŭn′ kīnd′) *adj-* [un·kind·er, un·kind·est] not kind or sympathetic; harsh; cruel. —*adv-* un′ kind′ ly. *n-* un′ kind′ ness.

un·know·a·ble (ŭn′ nō′ ə bəl) *adj-* such as cannot be known.

un·know·ing (ŭn′ nō′ ĭng) *adj-* not knowing: *an* unknowing *accomplice in a crime.* —*adv-* un′ know′ ing·ly.

un·known (ŭn′ nōn′) *adj-* 1 strange; unfamiliar; not in one's knowledge: *The book you speak of is* unknown *to me.* 2 not discovered: *He was shipwrecked on an* unknown *island. n-* person or thing not known.

un·lace (ŭn′ lās′) *vt-* [un·laced, un·lac·ing] to unfasten; loosen (something held together with laces).

un·latch (ŭn′ lăch′) *vt-* to open the latch of.

un·law·ful (ŭn′ lô′ fəl) *adj-* 1 against the law; illegal: *Driving above the speed limit is* unlawful. 2 breaking moral law; wrongful; sinful: *It is* unlawful *to hate.* —*adv-* un′ law′ ful·ly. *n-* un′ law′ ful·ness.

un·learn (ŭn′ lûrn′) *vt-* to forget or not do (something which one has previously learned): *to* unlearn *a habit.*

¹**un·learn·ed** (ŭn′ lûr′ nəd) *adj-* 1 not educated; ignorant; without schooling. 2 betraying lack of knowledge: *an* unlearned *comment.*

²**un·learned** (ŭn′ lûrnd′) *adj-* not learned by experience or study: *Blinking is an* unlearned *reflex.*

un·leash (ŭn′ lēsh′) *vt-* 1 to remove the leash from: *Don't* unleash *the dog.* 2 to release (something destructive) as if from a leash: *The storm* unleashed *its fury.*

un·leav·ened (ŭn′ lĕv′ ənd) *adj-* not leavened; especially, made without yeast.

un·less (ŭn lĕs′) *conj-* in all cases except that; except if: *The snow will melt* unless *the weather gets colder.*
►Should not be confused with WITHOUT.

un·let·tered (ŭn′ lĕt′ ərd) *adj-* not able to read or write.

un·like (ŭn′ līk′) *adj-* having no resemblance; different: *They contributed* unlike *amounts. prep-* 1 not typical or characteristic of: *How* unlike *Jack to forget to lock up!* 2 in a manner different from; not becoming: *behavior* unlike *a soldier.* —*n-* un′ like′ ness.

un·like·ly (ŭn′ līk′ lē) *adj-* [un·like·li·er, un·like·li·est] 1 not likely; not believable; not probable: *a most* unlikely *story; an* unlikely *event.* 2 not likely to succeed: *Jack is* unlikely *material for the team.* —*n-* un′ like′ li·ness.

un·looked-for (ŭn′ lŏŏkt′ fôr′, -fôr′) *adj-* not expected: *an* unlooked-for *happiness.*

un·loose (ŭn′ lŏŏs′) *vt-* [un·loosed, un·loos·ing] 1 to let go; unfasten: *He* unloosed *his grip on the branch.* 2 to set free; release. Also un′ loos′ en.

un·love·ly (ŭn′ lŭv′ lē) *adj-* [un·love·li·er, un·love·li·est] 1 not attractive or pleasing to the eye: *an* unlovely *color.* 2 unpleasant; disagreeable: *an* unlovely *episode.* —*n-* un′ love′ li·ness.

un·luck·y (ŭn′ lŭk′ ē) *adj-* [un·luck·i·er, un·luck·i·est] 1 not lucky; not fortunate: *an* unlucky *gambler; an* unlucky *choice.* 2 bringing bad luck: *Many people consider 13 an* unlucky *number.* 3 bringing trouble: *an* unlucky *day.* —*adv-* un′ luck′ i·ly. *n-* un′ luck′ i·ness.

un·made (ŭn′ mād′) *adj-* not made up or put in order.

un·man (ŭn′ măn′) *vt-* [un·manned, un·man·ning] 1 to rob of courage, virility, or strength. 2 *Archaic* to deprive of men: *to* unman *a ship.*

un·pop·u·lar (ŭn′ pŏp′ yə lər) *adj-* not generally liked. —*n-* un′ pop′ u·lar′ i·ty. *adv-* un′ pop′ u·lar·ly.

un·prac·ticed or **un·prac·tised** (ŭn′ prăk′ tĭst) *adj-* 1 not practiced; not put into practice. 2 unskilled; not expert: *an* unpracticed *beginner.*

un·prec·e·dent·ed (ŭn′ prĕs′ ə dĕn′ təd) *adj-* not done before; having no precedent: *an* unprecedented *voyage.* —*adv-* un′ prec′ e·dent′ ed·ly.

un·pre·dict·a·ble (ŭn′ prĭ dĭk′ tə bəl) *adj-* not predictable. —*adv-* un′ pre·dict′ a·bly.

un·prej·u·diced (ŭn′ prĕj′ ə dĭst) *adj-* not prejudiced; not biased; fair.

un·pre·med·i·tat·ed (ŭn′ prĭ mĕd′ ə tā′ təd) *adj-* not premeditated; not planned.

un·pre·pared (ŭn′ prĭ pârd′) *adj-* 1 not prepared: *an* unprepared *pupil.* 2 done without preparation; not arranged beforehand. 3 not equipped; not ready: *He was* unprepared *for college.*

un·pre·ten·tious (ŭn′ prĭ tĕn′ shəs) *adj-* not pretentious; not showy. —*adv-* un′ pre·ten′ tious·ly. *n-* un′ pre·ten′ tious·ness.

un·prin·ci·pled (ŭn′ prĭn′ sə pəld) *adj-* without moral principles; unscrupulous.

un·print·a·ble (ŭn′ prĭn′ tə bəl) *adj-* not suited for publication: *That story is* unprintable.

un·pro·fes·sion·al (ŭn′ prə fĕsh′ ən əl) *adj-* 1 not consistent with the rules or standards of a profession: *his* unprofessional *conduct.* 2 spoken or done by one outside a profession. —*adv-* un′ pro·fes′ sion·al·ly.

un·prof·it·a·ble (ŭn′ prŏf′ ə tə bəl) *adj-* not profitable; useless. —*adv-* un′ prof′ it·a·bly.

un·qual·i·fied (ŭn′ kwŏl′ə fīd′) *adj-* 1 lacking the proper qualifications; unfit: *She is* unqualified *for the job.* 2 lacking legal authority; not legally suited: *He is* unqualified *to vote.* 3 absolute. —*adv-* un′ qual′ i·fied′ ly.

un·quench·a·ble (ŭn′ kwĕn′ chə bəl) *adj-* not quenchable: *my* unquenchable *thirst.*

un·ques·tion·a·ble (ŭn′ kwĕs′ chən ə bəl) *adj-* beyond question; indisputable. —*adv-* un′ ques′ tion·a·bly.

un·ques·tioned (ŭn′ kwĕs′ chənd) *adj-* not questioned; indisputable: *his* unquestioned *loyalty.*

un·ques·tion·ing (ŭn′ kwĕs′ chən ĭng) *adj-* not questioning; without any doubt or reservation: *his* unquestioning *love.*

un·qui·et (ŭn′ kwī′ ət) *adj-* 1 disturbed, especially by fear or anxiety: *an* unquiet *mind.* 2 restless, turbulent, or stormy. —*adv-* un′ qui′ et·ly. *n-* un′ qui′ et·ness.

un·quote (ŭn′ kwōt′) *interj-* the quotation ends here.

un·rav·el (ŭn′ răv′ əl) *vt-* 1 to undo; separate a thread or threads from: *Mother* unraveled *the sweater and used the wool for something else.* 2 to untangle: *I* unraveled *the ball of yarn.* 3 to solve: *to* unravel *a mystery. vi-: The sock* unraveled *at the heel.*

un·read (ŭn′ rĕd′) *adj-* 1 not read: *an* unread *script.* 2 uneducated: *an* unread *man.*

un·read·y (ŭn′ rĕd′ ē) *adj-* not ready; not prepared. —*n-* un′ read′ i·ness.

un·re·al (ŭn′ rē′ əl, -rēl′) *adj-* not real; imaginary; fantastic; artificial. *Hom-* unreel. —*n-* un′ re·al′ i·ty.

un·rea·son·a·ble (ŭn′ rē′ zən ə bəl) *adj-* 1 not rational or reasonable; without good sense or sound judgment: *an* unreasonable *person; an* unreasonable *request.*

un·re·served (ŭn′rĭ zûrvd′) *adj-* 1 not held in reserve. 2 frank; outspoken. —*adv-* un′re·serv′ed·ly.

un·rest (ŭn′rĕst′) *n-* restlessness; anxiety; dissatisfaction: *Injustice and poverty cause social unrest.*

un·re·strained (ŭn′rĭ strānd′) *adj-* not restrained; not held back: unchecked: *Our joy was unrestrained.* —*adv-* un′re·strain′ed·ly.

un·right·eous (ŭn′rī′chəs) *adj-* 1 not righteous; not just. 2 wicked; sinful. —*adv-* un′right′eous·ly. *n-* un′right′eous·ness.

un·ripe (ŭn′rīp′) *adj-* 1 not ripe; immature. 2 not ready or prepared: *He was unripe for promotion.*

un·ri·valed or **un·ri·valled** (ŭn′rī′vəld) *adj-* having no rival; unequaled: *an unrivaled reputation.*

un·roll (ŭn′rōl′) *vt-* 1 to unfold and spread out: *to unroll a carpet.* 2 to make known; display; reveal: *The book unrolled the story of Captain Cook's voyages. vt-: The carpet unrolled. We listened as the story unrolled.*

un·ruf·fled (ŭn′rŭf′əld) *adj-* 1 smooth: *an unruffled pond.* 2 not disturbed or upset: *his unruffled calm.*

un·ruled (ŭn′rōōld′) *adj-* 1 having no ruled lines; entirely blank: *a sheet of unruled paper.* 2 ungoverned.

un·ru·ly (ŭn′rōō′lē) *adj-* [un·ru·li·er, un·ru·li·est] not obeying; difficult to control: *an unruly child; an unruly disposition.* —*n-* un′ru′li·ness.

un·sad·dle (ŭn′săd′əl) *vt-* [un·sad·dled, un·sad·dling] 1 to remove the saddle from (a horse, etc.). 2 to cause to fall out of a saddle; unhorse.

un·safe (ŭn′sāf′) *adj-* not safe; dangerous; insecure: *an unsafe bridge.*

un·said (ŭn′sĕd′) *adj-* not said or spoken; thought but not expressed: *Some things are better left unsaid.*

un·san·i·tar·y (ŭn′săn′ə tĕr′ē) *adj-* not sanitary; unclean; unhealthy. —*adv-* un′san′i·tar′i·ly. *n-* un′san′i·tar′i·ness.

▶Should not be confused with INSANITARY.

un·sat·is·fac·to·ry (ŭn′săt′ĭs făk′tə rē) *adj-* not satisfactory; not satisfying or fulfilling a requirement; disappointing: *an unsatisfactory answer to a question; an unsatisfactory experience.* —*adv-* un′sat′is·fac′to·ri·ly.

un·sat·is·fied (ŭn′săt′ĭs fīd′) *adj-* not satisfied, fulfilled, or relieved: *an unsatisfied hunger.*

un·sat·u·rat·ed (ŭn′săch′ə rā′təd) *adj-* not saturated. See *saturated.*

unsaturated fat *n-* a fat in which many of the carbon atoms share two electrons with adjacent carbon atoms. Most vegetable and fish oils are unsaturated.

un·sa·vor·y (ŭn′sā′və rē) *adj-* 1 lacking taste or seasoning. 2 disagreeable to taste or smell. 3 morally bad. Also, *Brit.,* un′sa′vour·y. —*n-* un′sa′vor·i·ness.

un·say (ŭn′sā′) *vt-* [un·said, un·say·ing] to cancel or retract (something that has been said).

un·scathed (ŭn′skāth̸d′) *adj-* uninjured; not hurt.

un·sci·en·tif·ic (ŭn′sī′ən tĭf′ĭk) *adj-* not done in a scientific way or supported by good evidence: *an unscientific inquiry.* —*adv-* un′sci′en·tif′i·cal·ly.

un·scram·ble (ŭn′skrăm′bəl) *vt-* [un·scram·bled, un·scram·bling] 1 to make clear; resolve. 2 to untangle; put in order. 3 to put (a scrambled message) back into plain language.

un·screw (ŭn′skrōō′) *vt-* 1 to take out or remove the screw or screws from: *to unscrew the hinges of a door.* 2 to remove by turning on threads: *to unscrew the top of a jar. vt-: The top of the jar unscrews easily.*

un·scru·pu·lous (ŭn′skrōō′pyə ləs) *adj-* without moral principles; unprincipled: *an unscrupulous scoundrel.* —*adv-* un′scru′pu·lous·ly. *n-* un′scru′pu·lous·ness.

un·seal (ŭn′sēl′) *vt-* 1 to remove or break the seal of. 2 to open (something that has been tightly shut).

un·search·a·ble (ŭn′sûr′chə bəl) *adj-* such as cannot be found by searching; hidden; mysterious.

un·sea·son·a·ble (ŭn′sē′zən ə bəl) *adj-* 1 out of season. 2 coming at an ill-chosen time; untimely: *an unseasonable request.* —*n-* un′sea′son·a·ble·ness. *adv-* un′sea′son·a·bly.

un·seat (ŭn′sēt′) *vt-* 1 to throw or remove (someone) from a seat; unhorse: *The horse unseated his rider.* 2 to remove (someone) from an official position; depose.

un·seem·ly (ŭn′sēm′lē) *adj-* [un·seem·li·er, un·seem·li·est] not proper; unfitting: *It is unseemly to gossip about one's neighbors.* —*n-* un′seem′li·ness.

un·seen (ŭn′sēn′) *adj-* 1 unnoticed: *He entered unseen.* 2 invisible: *an unseen presence in the room.*

un·self·ish (ŭn′sĕl′fĭsh) *adj-* not selfish; generous: *her unselfish attention to the patients in the hospital.* —*adv-* un′self′ish·ly. *n-* un′self′ish·ness.

un·set·tle (ŭn′sĕt′əl) *vt-* [un·set·tled, un·set·tling] 1 to disturb; upset; make restless or nervous: *The news unsettled him.* 2 to move; loosen; displace.

un·set·tled (ŭn′sĕt′əld) *adj-* 1 not decided or determined: *an unsettled question.* 2 without order or stability; disturbed: *The country was in an unsettled condition for many months after the revolution.* 3 not paid or disposed of: *an unsettled debt.* 4 not populated or inhabited: *an unsettled land.* 5 uncertain; changeable: *an unsettled temper; unsettled weather.*

un·shack·le (ŭn′shăk′əl) *vt-* [un·shack·led, un·shack·ling] 1 to release by opening a shackle. 2 to set free; unfetter: *They unshackled the rescued prisoners.*

un·shak·a·ble (ŭn′shā′kə bəl) *adj-* firm; determined.

un·tan·gle (ŭn′tăng′gəl) *vt-* [un·tan·gled, un·tan·gling] 1 to take out knots or snarls from: *to untangle yarn.* 2 clear up; explain: *to untangle a mystery.*

un·taught (ŭn′tôt′) *adj-* 1 not taught or educated; ignorant: *an untaught backwoodsman.* 2 learned without instruction; natural: *an untaught skill in drawing.*

un·think·ing (ŭn′thĭngk′ĭng) *adj-* 1 not thinking; careless; inconsiderate. 2 without the power of thought. —*adv-* un′think′ing·ly.

un·thought-of (ŭn′thôt′ ŭv, -ŏv′) *adj-* not thought of; not conceived of; unimagined.

un·thread·ed (ŭn′thrĕd′əd) *adj-* 1 not threaded. 2 not having threads.

un·ti·dy (ŭn′tī′dē) *adj-* [un·ti·di·er, un·ti·di·est] not tidy; sloppy. —*adv-* un′ti′di·ly. *n-* un′ti′di·ness.

un·tie (ŭn′tī′) *vt-* [un·tied, un·ty·ing] 1 to undo or loosen (something that has been tied); open (a knot or bow): *He untied his shoelaces and removed his shoes.* 2 to set loose: *He untied the horse and let it wander. vt-* to become unfastened: *His laces untied.*

un·til (ən tĭl′) *prep-* 1 up to the time of: *We shall wait for you until ten o'clock.* 2 before (used after a negative): *He did not go until dawn. conj-* 1 up to the time that: *We shall wait until you arrive.* 2 up to the place, or degree, that: *He talked until he was hoarse.* 3 before (used after a negative): *Don't leave until noon.*

un·time·ly (ŭn′tīm′lē) *adj-* 1 happening at an unsuitable time: *an untimely request for a favor.* 2 happening too soon or before the usual time: *An early snow put an untimely end to autumn. adv-* inopportunely; too soon. —*n-* un′time′li·ness.

un·tir·ing (ŭn′tīr′ĭng) *adj-* not growing tired or weary; tireless: *her untiring efforts.* —*adv-* un′tir′ing·ly.

un·to (ŭn′tōō) *Archaic prep-* to: *Give unto each his due.*

un·told (ŭn′tōld′) *adj-* 1 not told; not revealed: *an untold story.* 2 countless; innumerable: *the untold stars in the sky.*

un·touch·a·ble (ŭn′tŭch′ə bəl) *adj-* 1 such as cannot be touched, reached, or affected. 2 such as must not be touched. 3 disgusting or defiling to the touch. *n-* In India, a member of the lowest hereditary caste of Hindu belief, thought to defile or contaminate members of the higher castes even by touch. Distinctions and disabilities based on caste are now illegal.

un·touched (ŭn′tŭcht′) *adj-* not having been touched or affected: *a sleepy old town untouched by modern life.*

un·to·ward (ŭn′tôrd′) *adj-* 1 inconvenient; unfortunate: *an untoward meeting.* 2 unbecoming; uncouth: *We disliked his untoward rudeness to the stranger.* 3 hard to manage; stubborn; wayward: *an untoward child.* —*adv-* un′toward′ly. *n-* un′toward′ness.

un·tried (ŭn′trīd′) *adj-* 1 not tried; not tested: *Mother has many untried recipes.* 2 without a court trial.

un·trod (ŭn′trŏd′) *adj-* not having been trodden or walked upon; hence, unfrequented: *an untrod path.*

un·wea·ried (ŭn′wēr′ēd) *adj-* 1 not weary; not tired: *He was unwearied despite the trip.* 2 tireless; untiring.

un·wel·come (ŭn′wĕl′kəm) *adj-* not welcome; not received with pleasure; not desired: *an unwelcome guest.*

un·well (ŭn′wĕl′) *adj-* not well; sick; ill.

un·wept (ŭn′wĕpt′) *adj-* 1 not mourned for, as a dead person. 2 not shed, as tears.

un·whole·some (ŭn′hōl′səm) *adj-* 1 not good for the mind or body; unhealthy: *an unwholesome food.* 2 morally harmful: *his unwholesome companions.* 3 appearing unhealthy: *an unwholesome complexion.* —*adv-* **un′whole′some·ly.** *n-* **un′whole′some·ness.**

un·wield·y (ŭn′wēl′dē) *adj-* [**un·wield·i·er, un·wield·i·est**] hard to handle or manage; bulky; clumsy: *an unwieldy sofa.* —*n-* **un′wield′i·ness.**

un·will·ing (ŭn′wĭl′ĭng) *adj-* not willing; reluctant: *The taxi driver was an unwilling accomplice in the bank robbery.* —*adv-* **un′will′ing·ly.** *n-* **un′will′ing·ness.**

un·wind (ŭn′wīnd′) *vt-* [**un·wound, un·wind·ing**] 1 to wind (rope, ribbon, wire, etc.) off a reel or coil: *He unwound ten feet of cable.* 2 to straighten: *He unwound the twisted wire.* *vi-* 1 to uncoil: *The cable unwound from the reel.* 2 to become free from anxiety, tension, etc.; relax: *He needs a vacation to unwind.* 3 to be revealed little by little: *The tale unwound.*

un·wise (ŭn′wīz′) *adj-* not wise; not sensible; foolish: *an unwise decision.* —*adv-* **un′wise′ly.**

un·wit·ting (ŭn′wĭt′ĭng) *adj-* not conscious or intentional: *an unwitting insult.* —*adv-* **un′wit′ting·ly.**

un·wont·ed (ŭn′wŭn′tăd, -wōn′tăd) *adj-* not usual; infrequent; not customary: *His unwonted gaiety surprised us all.* —*adv-* **un′wont′ed·ly.** *n-* **un′wont′ed·ness.**

un·work·a·ble (ŭn′wûr′kə bəl) *adj-* 1 such as cannot be successfully applied or effected; impracticable: *an unworkable scheme.* 2 inoperable: *an unworkable switch.* 3 unsolvable: *an unworkable chess problem.*

un·world·ly (ŭn′wûrld′lē) *adj-* 1 free from worldly or material interests; spiritually minded: *He was a solitary, unworldly man.* 2 not of the world; unearthly: *an unworldly melody.* —*n-* **un′world′li·ness.**

un·wor·thy (ŭn′wûr′thē) *adj-* [**un·wor·thi·er, un·wor·thi·est**] 1 not worthy; not deserving; lacking merit (usually followed by "of"): *This is unworthy of you.* 2 not deserving respect; not suitable: *his unworthy conduct.* —*adv-* **un′wor′thi·ly.** *n-* **un′wor′thi·ness.**

un·wound (ŭn′wound′) *p.t. & p.p.* of **unwind.**

un·wrap (ŭn′răp′) *vt-* [**un·wrapped, un·wrap·ping**] to take the covering or wrapper off: *to unwrap a package.* *vi-*: *The parcel unwrapped in the mail.*

un·writ·ten (ŭn′rĭt′ən) *adj-* not expressed in writing; well known and understood, but not written down: *the unwritten legends of the tribe; an unwritten law.*

unwritten law *n-* 1 common law as distinguished from written or statute law. 2 rule of conduct based on public sentiment or custom, but not recognized legally.

un·yield·ing (ŭn′yēl′dĭng) *adj-* firm; resolute; not yielding or giving way. —*adv-* **un′yield′ing·ly.**

un·yoke (ŭn′yōk′) *vt-* [**un·yoked, un·yok·ing**] 1 to free from a yoke: *to unyoke oxen.* 2 to separate (things held together by or as if by a yoke): *to unyoke two ideas.*

un·zip (ŭn′zĭp′) *vt-* [**un·zipped, un·zip·ping**] to open by means of a zipper: *to unzip a valise.*

up (ŭp) *adv-* 1 from a lower to a higher place, position, etc.; away from the center of the earth: *to go up in an elevator; to throw a ball up.* 2 at a higher place: *He put it up on the shelf.* 3 from less to more; to a higher degree or to a higher position on a scale: *Prices go up. He climbed up on the social ladder.* 4 in an erect position; on one's feet: *He sat up. Please stand up.* 5 out of bed: *He isn't up yet.* 6 entirely; thoroughly: *Eat up your dinner. He broke the toy up.* 7 into being or action; into notice or consideration: *I must bring up an unpleasant subject.* 8 in or into a condition of equality; even: *He doesn't come up to her in skill. He can't catch up. The score is now 10 up.* 9 away; aside; in reserve: *We stored up all we could.* 10 in the sky; above the horizon: *The sun is up.* 11 comparatively high; higher than the average: *The river is up today. Our spirits were up.* 12 of time, at an end; finished: *The hour is up.* 13 especially keen and well prepared: *He is up in algebra. The singers were all up for that performance.* 14 ahead of an opponent: *Our team is now five up in the game.* 15 in baseball, at bat: *The catcher is up.* *adj-* leading, moving, or sloping toward a higher place or position: *the up escalator; the up curve.* *prep-* 1 from a lower to a higher place on or in: *We walked up the hill. They pushed it up the tube.* 2 to, toward, at, or near the top of: *I climbed up the tree.* 3 along: *He walked up the road toward the next farm.* 4 of streams, toward the source: *They paddled up the river.* 5 toward the north on, or along: *They sailed up the coast.* *vt-* [**upped, up·ping**] *Informal* to increase or cause to increase: *They upped their prices.* *n- Informal* an increase: *an up in prices.*

all up with the end or finish of, especially the final defeat of. **on the up and up** sincere; honest: *The offer was on the up and up.* **up against** having to fight or contend with. **up against it** in a difficult situation: *When the car stalled we were really up against it.* **up for** 1 being voted on or considered for: *He is up for governor.* 2 on trial for. **up on** well-informed on: *He is up on world politics.* **ups and downs** alternate good and bad luck, spirits, condition, etc. **up to** 1 doing; engaged in: *What's he up to?* 2 depending on the will or action of: *What we do is up to you.*

up-and-com·ing (ŭp′ən kŭm′ĭng) *adj-* doing well and likely to succeed; promising.

up-and-down (ŭp′ən doun′) *adj-* 1 having an alternate rising and falling rhythm. 2 perpendicular; vertical.

up·beat (ŭp′bēt′) *n-* 1 *Music* (1) an unaccented beat in a measure, especially the final beat. (2) note or several notes preceding the first accent of a piece of music. *adj- Slang* cheerful; joyous; optimistic.

up·braid (ŭp′brād′) *vt-* to scold severely; blame: *She upbraided him for rudeness.* —*adv-* **up′braid′ing·lv.**

up·bring·ing (ŭp′brĭng′ĭng) *n-* training during childhood and youth; way a person is raised; rearing.

up-coun·try (ŭp′kŭn′trē) *Informal n-* the interior or remote parts of a country. *adj-*: *an up-country town; an up-country boy.* *adv-*: *They traveled up-country.*

up·date (ŭp′dāt′) *vt-* [**up·dat·ed, up·dat·ing**] to bring up to date by adding new material or revising to accord with recent events: *to update a dictionary.*

up·draft (ŭp′drăft′) *n-* upward movement of air or some other gas.

up·end (ŭp′ĕnd′) *vt-* to set or place on end: *The collision upended one car.* *vi-*: *The car upended.*

up·grade (ŭp′grād′) *n-* an upward slope, especially in a road or railroad. *vt-* [**up·grad·ed, up·grad·ing**] to raise or improve in rank, quality, status, etc.: *to upgrade an employee; to upgrade a product.*

on the upgrade improving.

up·heav·al (ŭp′hē′vəl) *n-* 1 sudden great and violent change in conditions: *The revolution caused a great upheaval in Cuba.* 2 great pushing upward or heaving from below: *an upheaval of the earth's crust.*

up·hill (ŭp′hĭl′) *adv-* upward on a slope; toward the top of a hill: *They ran uphill.* *adj-* 1 sloping upward; going up a hill: *an uphill path.* 2 difficult; arduous.

up·hold (ŭp′hōld′) *vt-* [**up·held, up·hold·ing**] 1 to give support to; back: *She upheld his opinions.* 2 to hold up; support: *Marble columns uphold the roof.* 3 to refuse to set aside; confirm. —*n-* **up′hold′er.**

up·hol·ster (ŭp′hōl′stər) *vt-* to supply (the frames of chairs, sofas, and other seats) with webbing, stuffing, fabric, etc. —*n-* **up′hol′ster·er.**

up·hol·ster·y (ŭp′hōl′stə rē) *n-* 1 materials used for upholstering. 2 art or business of upholstering. *as modifier: an upholstery shop; upholstery tools.*

up·keep (ŭp′kēp′) *n-* the work and cost of keeping something in good order and repair; maintenance: *I am in charge of upkeep. The upkeep of the park is too high.*

up·land (ŭp′lănd, -lānd′) *n-* (also **up′lands′**) any region that is moderately higher than the land around it. *adj-*: *an upland farm.* See also **highland.**

¹up·lift (ŭp′lĭft′) *vt-* 1 to raise; elevate. 2 to improve the condition of, especially socially or morally.

²up·lift (ŭp′lĭft′) *n-* 1 a raising: *a mountain chain formed by the uplift of a plain.* 2 moral or spiritual improvement: *books devoted to uplift.* 3 something raised.

up·most (ŭp′mōst′) *adj-* uppermost.

up·stream (ŭp′strēm′) *adv-* toward the source of a stream; against the current. *adj-:* *an upstream village.*

¹up·surge (ŭp′sûrj′) *n-* a sudden rise or rising.

²up·surge (ŭp′sûrj′) *vi-* [up·surged, up·surg·ing] to rise up suddenly.

up·swing (ŭp′swing′) *n-* 1 a swinging upward: *the upswing of a golf club.* 2 rise; increase.

up·take (ŭp′tāk′) *n-* a taking up or into; intake.
    on the uptake *Informal* with regard to understanding or catching an idea: *George is very quick on the uptake.*

up·thrust (ŭp′thrŭst′) *n-* 1 a thrusting upward. 2 in geology, an upward lift, usually violent, of part of the earth's crust.

up-to-date (ŭp′tə dāt′) *adj-* 1 up to the present in records, information, etc.: *an up-to-date medical book.* 2 in the current fashion: *an up-to-date hair style.*

up·town (ŭp′toun′) *adj-* having to do with the northern or more northern part of a town or city: *an uptown resident. adv-* (often ŭp′ town′) in or toward that part of town: *Are you going* uptown?

up·trend (ŭp′trĕnd′) *n-* a rising trend; especially, an improvement in economic matters.

up·turn (ŭp′tûrn′) *n-* an upward turn: especially, a change for the better: *an upturn in one's fortunes.*

up·ward (ŭp′wərd) *adj-* moving from a lower to a higher level: *the upward flight of a bird. adv-* (also **up′wards**) from a lower to a higher level or condition: *The climbers struggled upward. n-* indefinite additional number or quantity: *I was ill for six months and* upward.
    upward or **upwards**) **of** in total over; more than.

up·well (ŭp′wĕl′) *vi-* to surge up; flow upward.

up·wind (ŭp′wĭnd′) *adv-* in the direction from which the wind blows; into the wind: *to stand upwind from a fire; to shout upwind. adj-: an upwind position.*

u·ra·ni·um (yŏŏr ā′nē əm) *n-* white metal element that is the heaviest natural element, with three naturally occurring isotopes and a number of artificial ones, used in atomic reactors and bombs. Compounds are used in coloring glazes and porcelains. Symbol U, At. No. 92, At. Wt. 238.03.

uranium 235 *n-* the naturally occurring isotope of uranium which emits neutrons and thus can start a chain reaction.

uranium 238 *n-* the most abundant naturally occurring isotope of uranium.

U·ra·nus (yŏŏr ā′nəs) *n-* 1 in Greek mythology, the father of the Titans and the Cyclopes. 2 the third largest planet in the solar system, seventh in order of distance from the sun.

ur·ban (ûr′bən) *adj-* having to do with, living in, or located in a city or town; not rural: *an urban resident.*

ur·bane (ûr bān′) *adj-* courteous and refined in manner. —*adv-* **ur·bane′ly.** *n-* **ur·ban′i·ty** (ər băn′ə tē).

ur·ban·ize (ûr′bə nīz′) *vi-* [ur·ban·ized, ur·ban·iz·ing] to become urban or more urban: *American society continues to urbanize. vt-: Machines are urbanizing our population.* —*n-* **ur′ban·i·za′tion.**

ur·chin (ûr′chĭn) *n-* 1 impudent or mischievous child, especially an impisl. city child. 2 sea urchin.

Ur·du (ûr′dōō′) *n-* language related to Hindi and Sanskrit and spoken by the Muslims of Pakistan and India. Urdu is the official language of Pakistan.

-ure *suffix* (used to form nouns from verbs) action; state; result: *seizure; mixture.*

u·re·a (yŏŏr ē′ə) *n-* white, highly soluble, crystalline compound [CO (NH₂)₂], found in the urine of mammals and also produced synthetically. It is used in fertilizers and medicine, and in the making of plastics.

u·re·mi·a (yŏŏr ē′mē ə) *n-* poisoned condition of the blood resulting from the presence of waste products that should be eliminated in the urine. —*adj-* **u·re′mic.**

u·re·mic poisoning (yŏŏr ē′mĭk) *n-* uremia.

u·re·ter (yŏŏr ē′tər) *n-* one of a pair of tubes in animals through which the urine passes from a kidney to the bladder or cloaca.

u·re·thra (yŏŏr ē′thrə) *n-* the duct or canal through which urine is discharged from the bladder. —*adj-* **u·re′thral.**

urge (ûrj) *vt-* [urged, urg·ing] 1 to plead with; persuade: *His friends urged him to accept the job.* 2 to encourage, drive, or force onward: *The jockey urged his horse forward.* 3 to speak earnestly for; recommend strongly: *He urged exercise to maintain good health. n-* strong impulse: *He felt the urge to travel.*

ur·gen·cy (ûr′jən sē) *n-* [*pl.* **ur·gen·cies**] condition of being urgent: *the urgency of our need.*

ur·gent (ûr′jənt) *adj-* 1 calling for immediate action or attention; pressing: *There was an urgent message waiting for him at his office.* 2 insistent; desperate: *an urgent plea.* —*adv-* **ur′gent·ly.**

u·ric (yŏŏr′ĭk) *adj-* of, relating to, or derived from urine.

uric acid *n-* white, odorless, almost insoluble compound found in small quantities in the urine of mammals; the chief constituent of the urine of birds and reptiles.

u·ri·nal (yŏŏr′ə nəl) *n-* 1 room or enclosure with facilities for urinating; also, an upright wall fixture used for this purpose. 2 glass receptacle for urine.

u·ri·nal·y·sis (yŏŏr′ə năl′ə səs) *Medicine n-* [*pl.* **u·ri·nal·y·ses** (-sēz′)] chemical analysis of the urine.

u·ri·nar·y (yŏŏr′ə nĕr′ē) *adj-* of or relating to urine, or to the organs concerned with urine.

u·ri·nate (yŏŏr′ə nāt′) *vi-* [u·ri·nat·ed, u·ri·nat·ing] to pass urine. —*n-* **u′ri·na′tion.**

u·rine (yŏŏr′ĭn) *n-* fluid given off by the kidneys and discharged from the bladder as waste.

urn (ûrn) *n-* 1 vase, especially one with a foot or a pedestal. 2 such a container, or one of another shape, used for the ashes of cremated persons. 3 large container for holding and serving a warm beverage. *Hom-* earn.

Decorative urn

Ur·sa Ma·jor (ûr′sə mā′jər) *n-* constellation thought to outline the figure of a bear; Great Bear. Ursa Major is one of the brightest constellations in the northern sky and contains the Big Dipper.

Ur·sa Mi·nor (ûr′sə mī′nər) *n-* northern constellation of eight stars thought to outline the figure of a bear; Little Bear. Because the seven brightest stars in Ursa Minor form the Little Dipper, the two are often confused.

Coffee urn

us (ŭs) *pron-* objective case of **we.**

U.S. or **US** United States.

U.S.A. or **USA** United States of America.

us·a·ble (yŏŏ′zə bəl) *adj-* such as can be used; fit to be used: *a usable tool.* —*n-* **us′a·bil′i·ty** or **us′a·ble·ness.**

USAF or **U.S.A.F.** United States Air Force.

us·age (yŏŏ′sĭj) *n-* 1 all the ways in which the words, grammatical forms and combinations, etc.

u·ter·ine (yŏŏ′tər ən, -tə rīn′) *adj-* 1 of or relating to the uterus or womb. 2 born of the same mother, but by a different father: *two uterine brothers.*

u·ter·us (yŏŏ′tər əs) *n-* [*pl.* **u·ter·i** (-tər ē, -ī)] 1 hollow, pear-shaped organ of a female mammal, in which the young are carried and nourished before birth; womb. 2 in zoology, a corresponding part in various animals other than mammals, which serves as a resting place for the eggs or young during all or part of their development.

U·ther (yŏŏ′thər) *n-* legendary king of Britain; father of King Arthur. Also **U′ther Pen′drag′on** (pĕn′drăg′ən).

u·til·i·tar·i·an (yŏŏ tĭl′ə târ′ē ən) *adj-* 1 useful and practical; having utility: *The new building is utilitarian, but rather ugly.* 2 of or relating to utilitarianism: *a utilitarian view of economics. n-* person who tends toward or is an advocate of utilitarianism.

u·til·i·tar·i·an·ism (yŏŏ tĭl′ə târ′ē ə nĭz′əm) *n-* philosophical doctrine that an act or thing is good insofar as it is useful and effects the greatest happiness of the greatest number.

u·til·i·ty (yŏŏ tĭl′ə tē) *n-* [*pl.* **u·til·i·ties**] 1 usefulness. 2 useful object: *A kitchen cabinet is a utility.* 3 public utility. 4 **utilities** the stocks of public utilities. *as modifier: a side of* utility *beef.*

V

V, v (vē) *n-* [*pl.* **V's, v's**] **1** the 22nd letter of the English alphabet. **2** Roman numeral for five.

v volt; voltage.

V symbol for vanadium.

v. **1** verb. **2** verse. **3** versus. **4** vice-. **5** volt; voltage.

V-1 (vē' wŭn') *n-* buzz bomb.

V-2 (vē' tōō') *n-* rocket-propelled guided missile used by Germany in World War II; rocket bomb.

VA or **V.A.** **1** Veterans Administration. **2** vice admiral.

Va. Virginia.

va·can·cy (vā' kən sē) *n-* [*pl.* **va·can·cies**] **1** unoccupied place or position: *a vacancy in the new office building.* **2** empty space; void. **3** condition of being empty or unoccupied: *the vacancy of his mind.*

va·cant (vā' kənt) *adj-* **1** empty; unoccupied: *a vacant building lot; a vacant job; a vacant house.* **2** showing lack of understanding or unawareness of surroundings: *a vacant stare.* —*adv-* **va' cant·ly.** *n-* **va' cant·ness.**

va·cate (vā' kāt') *vt-* [**va·cat·ed, va·cat·ing**] **1** to make empty; move out of (a house, apartment, etc.). **2** to give up (an office, position, etc.).

va·ca·tion (vā kā' shən) *n-* **1** period of time granted to an employee in which he can rest, travel, etc. **2** period of time in which school courses are suspended: *Their vacation was from July to September.* **3** pleasure trip or visit. *as modifier:* *a vacation trip out West.* *vi-* to spend a period of rest and recreation: *We vacationed in the mountains.* —*n-* **va·ca' tion·er** or **va·ca' tion·ist.**

vac·ci·nate (văk' sə nāt') *vt-* [**vac·ci·nat·ed, vac·ci·nat·ing**] to introduce vaccine into (a person or animal) to prevent certain diseases, such as smallpox or polio.

vac·ci·na·tion (văk' sə nā' shən) *n-* **1** act or process of vaccinating. **2** sore or scar caused by vaccinating.

vac·cine (văk sēn', văk' sēn') *n-* preparation containing killed or weakened germs of a disease, introduced into the body to make it resistant to attacks of that disease.

vac·il·late (văs' ə lāt') *vi-* [**vac·il·lat·ed, vac·il·lat·ing**] to waver back and forth in forming an opinion or making a decision: *He vacillated until we lost all interest in his opinion.* —*n-* **vac' il·la' tion.**

va·cu·i·ty (vā kyōō' ə tē, və-) *n-* [*pl.* **va·cu·i·ties**] **1** condition of being vacuous. **2** something vacuous.

vac·u·ole (văk' yōō ōl') *Biology n-* **1** one of the spaces scattered through the cytoplasm of a cell and containing a watery fluid. For picture, see **cell.** **2** very small cavity in the tissues of an organism, containing fluid or air.

vac·u·ous (văk' yōō əs) *adj-* **1** completely empty; void; vacant. **2** stupid; imbecilic: *a vacuous look; a vacuous mind.* **3** silly; inane: *a vacuous remark.*

vac·u·um (văk' yōō əm, văk' yōōm') *n-* **1** partial or complete absence of air and all other matter in a space; especially, such emptiness in a container from which air has been pumped out. **2** ignorance or lack of concern about facts, events, other people, etc.: *An artist should not live in a vacuum.* **3** vacuum cleaner. *as modifier:* *a vacuum pump.* *vt-* to use a vacuum cleaner on.

vacuum bottle *n-* **1** glass container made of two bottles, one inside the other, with a vacuum between them. **2** such a container and a metal or plastic covering, used to keep substances hot or cold; Thermos bottle.

vacuum cleaner *n-* electrical appliance for cleaning by means of suction which draws dirt into a bag.

vain·glo·ry (vān' glôr' ē) *n-* excessive and boastful pride.

vain·ly (vān' lē) *adv-* **1** in a conceited or self-satisfied manner: *She vainly paraded before her mirror.* **2** without success; fruitlessly; in vain.

val·ance (văl' əns) *n-* **1** short drapery hung around or on the framework or canopy of a bed. **2** short drapery, or wood or metal frame, hung at the top of a window.

vale (vāl) *Archaic n-* valley. *Hom-* veil.

val·e·dic·tor·i·an (văl' ə dĭk' tôr' ē ən) *n-* person who makes a farewell address; especially, a member of a graduating class in school or college who is usually chosen because he is highest in academic standing.

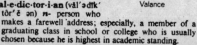

Valance

val·et (vă lā', văl' ət) *n-* **1** man who acts as a personal servant to another, taking care of his clothes and other personal items. **2** hotel employee who performs various services for guests.

val·e·tu·di·nar·i·an (văl' ə tōō' də nềr' ē ən, văl' ə tyōō'-) *n-* person who is in chronic bad health; especially, one who is preoccupied with his condition. *adj-* having to do with such a person.

Val·hal·la (văl hăl' ə) *n-* in Norse mythology, the great hall of Odin, into which heroes slain in battle were brought by the Valkyries.

val·iant (văl' yənt) *adj-* showing great bravery; courageous; heroic: *a valiant knight; a valiant act.* —*adv-* **val' iant·ly.** *n-* **val' iant·ness.**

val·id (văl' ĭd) *adj-* **1** based on facts; legitimate; acceptable: *He had a valid excuse for missing the meeting.* **2** acceptable in a court of law; binding: *The judge said the rumor was not valid evidence.* —*n-* **va·lid' i·ty** (və lĭd' ə tē). *adv-* **val' id·ly.**

val·i·date (văl' ə dāt') *vt-* [**val·i·dat·ed, val·i·dat·ing**] to ratify; make valid; confirm.

va·lise (və lēs') *n-* traveling case used for carrying clothes or other personal possessions; suitcase.

Val·ky·rie (văl kĕr' ē) *n-* in Norse mythology, one of Odin's warlike maidens who chose the fallen heroes from the battlefield and carried them to Valhalla.

val·ley (văl' ē) *n-* **1** lowland area between mountains or hills. **2** all the land drained by a river system: *the Tennessee Valley.*

val·or (văl' ər) *n-* great courage, especially in battle.

val·or·ous (văl' ər əs) *adj-* brave; fearless; courageous. —*adv-* **val' or·ous·ly.**

valse (vŏls) *n-* a waltz, especially one for the concert hall.

val·u·a·ble (văl' yōō ə bəl, -yə bəl) *adj-* **1** highly prized; held in esteem; very useful: *Joe was a valuable member of the team.* **2** costing much money; worth a great deal: *Her diamonds were very valuable.* *n-* **valuables** possessions having special value, especially jewelry, money, securities, precious heirlooms, etc. —*adv-* **val' u·a·bly.**

val·u·a·tion (văl' yōō ā' shən) *n-* **1** act of estimating the worth of something. **2** estimated worth or price.

val·ue (văl' yōō) *n-* **1** quality that makes a thing worth having: *The ring has a sentimental value.*

vam·pire (văm' pīr') *n-* **1** corpse that is superstitiously believed to rise from its grave at night and suck the blood of sleeping persons. **2** person who insidiously preys on others; especially, a vamp. **3** vampire bat.

vampire bat *n-* any of several kinds of tropical American bats that feed on fresh blood sucked from animals.

van (văn) *n-* front part of an army, fleet, etc.; hence, the position of those who lead a movement, cause, etc.: *He was in the van of all reform.* [from **vanguard**, from

va·nil·la (və nĭl' ə) *n-* **1** tropical American climbing plant related to the orchids. **2** (usually **vanilla bean**) the pod or bean of this plant, used to make a flavoring extract.

va·nil·lin (văn' ə lən, və nĭl'-) *n-* the essential oil ($C_8H_8O_3$), extracted from the vanilla bean, and used for flavoring and in perfumes.

van·ish (văn' ĭsh) *vi-* **1** to be removed from sight; disappear from view: *The ship vanished in the fog as we watched.* **2** to cease to be; depart forever: *Dinosaurs have vanished. All hope vanished.* —*n-* **van' ish·er.**

vanishing cream *n-* face cream, less oily than cold cream, used as a softener or a makeup foundation.

vanishing point *n-* **1** in perspective, the point where receding parallel lines seem to meet. **2** point at which something disappears.

van·i·ty (văn' ə tē) *n-* [*pl.* **van·i·ties**] **1** excessive pride in one's appearance or abilities; conceit. **2** a lack of usefulness, worth, or effect: *the vanity of trying to reason with him.* **3** dressing table. **4** vanity case.

vanity case *n-* **1** small, flat case containing a mirror, face powder etc.; compact. **2** small suitcase or handbag for carrying cosmetics.

van·quish (văng' kwĭsh) *vt-* to defeat thoroughly; conquer. —*n-* **van' quish·er.**

van·tage (văn' tĭj) *n-* **1** superior position; advantage. **2** in tennis, first point scored after deuce; advantage.

var·i·ant (vâr′ē ənt, văr′-) *adj-* having or showing variation; differing from another or others of the same kind or class: *a variant spelling of a word. n-* something that differs from another thing in form, though both are essentially the same: *"Rime" is a variant of "rhyme."*

var·i·a·tion (vâr′ē ā′shən, văr′-) *n-* 1 a varying or change; also, the amount of such change: *We can expect a variation of 10 degrees in temperature tonight.* 2 difference: *a variation in color between two napkins; a variation of several dollars in price.* 3 form or version (of something) that differs from the original version: *a new variation of an old song.* 4 *Music* the repeating of a single tune or theme with changes that vary, and often elaborate it.

var·i·col·ored (văr′ə kŭl′ərd, vâr′-) *adj-* spotted, streaked, or marked with various colors.

var·i·cose (văr′ə kōs′) *adj-* abnormally or irregularly swollen or dilated: *a varicose vein.*

var·ied (vâr′ēd, văr′-) *adj-* 1 having different shapes, forms, colors, sizes, etc.: *The town has houses of varied appearance.* 2 of many sorts or kinds; full of variety: *a varied collection of pictures; a varied career.* 3 altered.

var·i·e·gate (vâr′ē ə gāt′, văr′-) *vt-* [var·i·e·gat·ed, var·i·e·gat·ing] 1 to change the appearance of, by marking with different colors; streak; spot. 2 to give variety to; make varied. —*n-* var′i·e·ga′tion.

var·i·e·gat·ed (vâr′ē ə gā′təd, văr′-) *adj-* 1 having marks, streaks, or patches of different colors: *a variegated marble.* 2 marked by variety; diversified.

va·ri·e·ty (və rī′ə tē) *n-* [*pl.* va·ri·e·ties] 1 lack of sameness or monotony; change; diversity: *She had great variety in her daily activities.* 2 assortment of many different kinds: *a large variety of candy.* 3 kind; type; sort: *a new variety of popular song.* 4 *Biology* subdivision of species; group which distinctly differs from a typical member of a species; subspecies; also, a variation of any kind within a species.

variety show *n-* theatrical performance consisting of many short and different acts or numbers.

variety store *n-* store that sells assorted merchandise.

var·i·form (vâr′ə form′, văr′-) *adj-* having various forms: *many variform corals.*

var·i·ous (vâr′ē əs, văr′-) *adj-* 1 of different kinds: *Beverly received various gifts on her birthday.* 2 several; many and different: *Roses are of various colors.* —*adv-* var′i·ous·ly. *n-* var′i·ous·ness.

var·si·ty (vär′sə tē) *n-* [*pl.* var·si·ties] team that represents a school or college in interscholastic activities. *as modifier:* *the varsity teams.*

var·y (vâr′ē, văr′ē) *vi-* [var·ied, var·y·ing] 1 to change; be or become different: *Weather varies from day to day.* 2 *Mathematics* of one term, to assume different values under different conditions. *vt-* to cause to alter: *She varies the appearance of the room by rearranging the furniture.* —*adv-* var′y·ing·ly.

vas·cu·lar (văs′kyə lər) *adj-* pertaining to or consisting of plant or animal systems that transport fluids, such as the vessels of plants which carry water, and the blood and lymph vessels of animals.

vase (vās, vāz, väz) *n-* ornamental container of glass, pottery, etc., often used as a flower holder. —*adj-* vase′like′.

Vas·e·line (văs′ə lēn′) *n-* trademark name for petroleum jelly and certain other pharmaceutical preparations. Also **vaseline.**

vas·sal (văs′el) *n-* 1 in the feudal system, person who placed himself under the protection of a lord or master, and in return rendered homage and service; person who held land under feudal tenure. 2 a servant; retainer. *as modifier:* *a vassal state.*

Vase

veg·e·tate (vĕj′ə tāt′) *vi-* [veg·e·tat·ed, veg·e·tat·ing] 1 to grow as a plant does; hence, to lead an idle, unthinking existence. 2 of a wart, pimple, etc., to grow abnormally.

veil·ing (vā′lĭng) *n-* 1 thin, gauzy material used for veils. 2 a veil.

vein (vān) *n-* 1 blood vessel in which blood flows toward the heart. 2 one of the vascular ribs in a leaf, which also acts as a support. 3 one of the branching supports of an insect's wing. 4 in geology, strip of color or ore in a rock. 5 a strain; streak: *A vein of humor ran through the book.* *Homs-* vain, vane. —*adj-* veined. *adj-* vein′less. *adj-* vein′like′.

Veins of a leaf

vein·ing (vā′nĭng) *n-* system or pattern of veins.

veld or **veldt** (vĕlt, fĕlt) *n-* in South Africa, open pasture land or thinly wooded country.

vel·lum (vĕl′əm) *n-* 1 thin, smooth, tanned skin, usually of a calf, once used as writing paper but now used for covers of expensive books; fine parchment. 2 writing paper imitating this. *as modifier:* *a vellum binding.*

ve·loc·i·pede (və lŏs′ə pēd′) *n-* 1 a child's tricycle. 2 an early form of the bicycle or tricycle.

ve·loc·i·ty (və lŏs′ə tē) *Physics n-* [*pl.* ve·loc·i·ties] 1 rate of change of position in a given direction; the distance a moving object travels with respect to time. Velocity is a vector quantity having both magnitude (speed) and direction. 2 speed.

ve·lour or **ve·lours** (və lŏor′, -lŏorz′) *n-* [*pl.* ve·lours], soft, smooth, closely woven cotton or woolen fabric having a short, thick pile like that of velvet. *as modifier:* *a velour shirt; velour pillows.*

ve·lum (vē′ləm) *n-* [*pl.* ve·la (-lə)] 1 *Biology* a thin membranous covering or partition. 2 the soft palate.

vel·vet (vĕl′vət) *n-* 1 fine, closely woven fabric of silk, cotton, rayon, etc., with either a silk or cotton backing and a short, thick, soft nap or pile. 2 anything resembling the feel and softness of such a fabric. 3 the fuzzy, thin skin on the growing antler of a deer. *as modifier:* *a velvet evening gown; the velvet darkness of a summer sky.*

vel·vet·een (vĕl′və tēn′) *n-* cotton material with a short pile like velvet. *as modifier:* *a velveteen dress.*

vel·vet·y (vĕl′və tē) *adj-* 1 of a texture like velvet to the touch. 2 soft and mellow to sight, hearing, or taste.

ve·nal (vē′nəl) *adj-* 1 ready or willing to be bribed: *a venal judge.* 2 obtained or influenced by a bribe; corrupt: *his venal services.* —*adv-* ve′nal·ly.

ve·nal·i·ty (vī nâl′ə tē) *n-* [*pl.* ve·nal·i·ties] willingness to cheapen one's talents or services for gain.

ve·na·tion (və nā′shən, vē-) *n-* system or pattern of veins: *the venation of an insect's wing.*

vend (vĕnd) *vt-* to sell, offer for sale; peddle.

ven·det·ta (vĕn dĕt′ə) *n-* feud between two families, carried on by murder for vengeance.

vending machine *n-* machine operated by the insertion of a coin into a slot, used for selling merchandise.

ven·dor or **vend·er** (vĕn′dər) *n-* seller of goods.

ve·neer (və nēr′) *n-* 1 thin layer of fine wood used to overlay the surface of furniture. 2 thin layer of tile or brick, covering a coarser building material: *a building with a brick veneer.* 3 any of the thin sheets of wood glued together to form plywood.

ve·ni·re (və nī′rē, -nēr′ē) *n-* in law, a legal writ to a sheriff for the summoning of a jury to a court trial.

ve·ni·re·man (və nī′rē mən, -nēr′ē mən) *n-* person who has been summoned to serve on a jury by a venire.

ven·i·son (vĕn′ə sən, -zən) *n-* the flesh of a deer, used as food. *as modifier:* *a venison stew.*

Venn diagram (vĕn) *Mathematics n-* diagram in which regions, usually circular, are used to represent relations and operations in the algebra of sets.

ven·om (vĕn′əm) *n-* 1 the poisonous fluid injected by the bite of some snakes or by the sting or bite of scorpions and some insects. 2 spite; ill will; malice: *Her comment had a trace of venom.* —*adj-* ven′om·less.

ven·om·ous (vĕn′əm əs) *adj-* 1 secreting venom; also, capable of giving a poisonous bite or sting; poisonous: *a venomous snake.* 2 full of spite or malice: *a venomous tongue.* —*adv-* ven′om·ous·ly. *n-* ven′om·ous·ness.

ven·ti·late (věn′ tə lāt′) *vt-* [ven·ti·lat·ed, ven·ti·lat·ing] 1 to bring fresh air into and drive stale air out of; to air: *Open the windows and* ventilate *the room.* 2 to bring out (a subject) for public examination and discussion: *The plans for the new park were* ventilated *in the newspapers.* 3 to supply with an escape for air, gas, etc.

ven·ti·la·tion (věn′ tə lā′ shən) *n-* a ventilating; especially, the supplying and circulation of fresh air: *the* ventilation *in a room. as modifier: á* ventilation *system.*

ven·ti·la·tor (věn′ tə lā′ tər) *n-* any device for admitting, exhausting, or circulating air, such as an opening, a fan, or an air-conditioning unit.

ven·tral (věn′ trəl) *adj-* relating to, or situated on or near, the belly of an animal: *the* ventral *fins of a fish.*

ven·tri·cle (věn′ trĭ kəl) *n-* either of the two lower chambers of the heart which receive blood from the auricles and transmit it to the arteries. For picture, see *heart.*

ven·tril·o·quism (věn trĭl′ ə kwĭz′ əm) *n-* the art of producing voice sounds so that they seem to come from another person or a distance. —*n-* ven·tril′ o·quist.

ven·ture (věn′ chər) *n-* course of action or undertaking that contains some risk: *a* venture *into a wilderness; a mining* venture; *a new business* venture. *vt-* [ven·tured, ven·tur·ing]. 1 to hazard; dare to say or do: *She* ventured *an opinion on the candidate.* 2 to risk; stake. *vi-* to take a risk; dare. —*n-* ven′ tur·er.

at a venture without any particular aim or purpose; at hazard; offhand.

ven·ture·some (věn′ chər səm) *adj-* 1 willing to take risks; daring: *The* venturesome *boy was rescued from the mountain.* 2 involving risk, hazard, danger, etc.: *a* venturesome *experiment.* —*adv-* ven′ ture·some·ly. *n-* ven′ ture·some·ness.

Ven·tu·ri tube (věn tŏor′ ē) *n-* short tube having a constriction in the middle, used for measuring the rate of flow of fluids. It can be used to measure airspeed.

ven·tur·ous (věn′ chər əs) *adj-* venturesome. —*adv-* ven′ tur·ous·ly. *n-* ven′ tur·ous·ness.

ven·ue (věn′ yōō′) *n-* in law, the place where the alleged events occurred that caused the lawsuit; also, the place from which the jury must be drawn and where the case must be tried.

Ve·nus (vē′ nəs) *n-* 1 the most brilliant planet in our solar system, as seen from the earth, second in order of distance from the sun. 2 in Roman mythology, goddess of beauty and love, identified with Greek Aphrodite.

Ve·nus's-fly·trap (vē′ nə səz flī′ trăp′) *n-* plant with small, white flowers and leaves tipped with bristly extensions that can close together and trap insects.

Venus'flytrap

ve·ra·cious (və rā′ shəs) *adj-* 1 habitually telling the truth; truthful. 2 true; reliable: *a* veracious *report.* Hom- voracious. —*adv-* ve·ra′ cious·ly. *n-* ve·ra′ cious·ness.

ve·rac·i·ty (və răs′ ə tē) *n-* [*pl.* ve·rac·i·ties] 1 truthfulness; honesty. 2 accuracy; exactness: *the* veracity *of a news report.* 3 something true; truth. Hom- voracity.

ve·ran·da or **ve·ran·dah** (və răn′ də) *n-* porch, especially a covered one of some length.

Veranda

ver·dant (vûr′ dənt) *adj-* 1 covered with fresh green grass or foliage; fresh; green: *a* verdant *landscape.* 2 unsophisticated: *a* verdant *lad.* —*adv-* ver′ dant·ly

ver·dict (vûr′ dĭkt) *n-* decision or judgment, especially one made by a jury in a court trial.

ver·di·gris (vûr′ də grēs′, -grĭs′) *n-* 1 greenish patina or crust that collects on the surface of copper or brass after long exposure to air. 2 green or bluish-green poisonous pigment produced by the action of acetic acid on copper.

ver·dure (vûr′ jər) *n-* 1 greenness or freshness, especially of grass and growing plants.

ver·i·fy (věr′ ə fī′) *vt-* [ver·i·fied, ver·i·fy·ing] 1 to check or test the correctness or accuracy of: *Science* verifies *its theories by experiments.* 2 to check the truth of; confirm: *to* verify *a statement.* —*n-* ver′ i·fi′ er.

ver·i·ly (věr′ ə lē) *Archaic adv-* truly; really; in fact.

ver·i·si·mil·i·tude (věr′ ə sə mĭl′ ə tōōd′, -tyōōd′) *n-* closeness or similarity to truth.

ver·i·ta·ble (věr′ ə tə bəl) *adj-* true; genuine: *a* veritable *genius.* —*adv-* ver′ i·ta·bly. *n-* ver′ i·ta·ble·ness.

ver·i·ty (věr′ ə tē) *n-* [*pl.* ver·i·ties] 1 truth and accuracy: *the* verity *of her version of the story.* 2 something true; truth; fact: *the student's search for* verities. 3 honesty.

ver·mi·cel·li (vûr′ mə chěl′ ē, -sěl′ ē) *n-* food similar to spaghetti but with thinner strands.

ver·mi·cide (vûr′ mə sīd′) *n-* substance that kills worms; especially, a drug for killing intestinal worms.

ver·mic·u·lite (vər mĭk′ yə līt′) *n-* mineral similar to mica, occurring in masses easily split into thin plates, and used in insulating materials.

ver·mi·form (vûr′ mə fôrm′, -fôrm′) *adj-* worm-shaped.

vermiform appendix *n-* appendix.

ver·mil·ion (vər mĭl′ yən) *n-* 1 bright-red pigment, especially one consisting of mercuric sulfide. 2 bright-red color. *adj-: a* vermilion *dye.* Also **vermillion.**

ver·min (vûr′ mĭn) *n-* [*pl.* ver·min] unpleasant or harmful insects and small animals: *The house was overrun with* vermin. —*adj-* ver′ min·ous: *a* verminous *hovel.*

ver·mouth (vûr′ mōōth′) *n-* kind of alcoholic liquor made from white wine flavored with herbs.

ver·nac·u·lar (vər năk′ yə lər) *n-* 1 native language of a particular country, region, etc., that is used in common everyday speech. 2 fashion of speech among the people of a particular business or profession; jargon: *the* vernacular *of the stage.* *adj-* 1 of or relating to the language of a particular country, region, etc., that is naturally spoken by the people: *the* vernacular *speech of the Georgia Sea Islands.* 2 using the informal spoken language of a particular place; colloquial rather than literary: *a* vernacular *poet.* 3 of or relating to a common term or name rather than a scientific one.

ver·nal (vûr′ nəl) *adj-* 1 having to do with or appearing in the spring: *the* vernal *breezes.* 2 like the spring; hence, youthful.

vernal equinox *n-* 1 the point at which the center of the sun crosses the celestial equator from south to north. 2 the time at which this occurs, about March 21, when day and night are of equal length.

ver·ni·er (vûr′ nē ər) *n-* 1 small, auxiliary scale made to slide along a main scale, by which tenths of the smallest subdivision of the fixed scale can be read. 2 device designed to make very fine adjustments in the setting of an instrument.

¹**ve·ron·i·ca** (və rŏn′ ĭ kə) *n-* speedwell. [from modern Latin used in scientific writing, and related to ²**veronica.**]

²**ve·ron·i·ca** (və rŏn′ ĭ kə) *n-* 1 a picture of Jesus Christ's face said to have been miraculously impressed on a cloth handed to him by Saint Veronica to wipe the perspiration from his face on his way to Calvary; also, the cloth having this picture. 2 any cloth or handkerchief having a representation of Christ's face. [from the name of a Medieval Latin saint, from Late Latin **veraiconica** meaning "characterized by the true image," from vera, "true," and Latin **icon** (**icon**), "image."]

ver·sa·tile (vûr′ sə təl) *adj-* able to do many things; having many abilities: *The* versatile *actor could play any role.* —*adv-* ver′ sa·tile·ly. *n-* ver′ sa·til′ i·ty.

ver·sion (vûr′ zhən) *n-* 1 account or description from one point of view: *This is his* version *of the accident.* 2 a particular translation or edition (of a written work): *the King James* version *of the Bible.* 3 an adaptation (of a literary work): *a film* version *of a play.*

ver·sus (vûr′ səs) *Latin* 1 against: *Harvard* versus *Yale.* 2 as the alternative of: *democracy* versus *dictatorship.*

ver·te·bra (vûr′ tə brə) *n-* [*pl.* ver·te·brae (-brē, -brä) or ver·te·bras] any one of the individual bones making up the spinal column.

ver·te·bral (vûr′ tə brəl) *adj-* having to do with, resembling, or composed of vertebrae.

ves·per (věs′ pər) *n-* 1 bell that calls to vespers; also, an evening prayer service. 2 **Vesper** evening star or Hesperus; especially, the planet Venus as the evening star. *as modifier: a* vesper *service;* vesper *hymns.*

ves·pers or **Ves·pers** (věs′ pərz) *n- pl.* the sixth of the canonical hours; a late-afternoon religious service.

ves·sel (věs′ əl) *n-* 1 hollow container for holding something, especially a liquid. 2 boat larger than a rowboat; ship. 3 tube or canal that transports or contains a body fluid, such as the blood or lymph. 4 tube that transports water in a plant.

vest (věst) *n-* 1 man's sleeveless jacket worn over a shirt and under a coat, reaching usually to the waist in back and below it in front; waistcoat. 2 an undershirt. *vt-* 1 to clothe or endow (with authority, power, or the like): *The church* vests *its bishops with certain powers.*
2 to put into the care of: *They* vest *the authority in their president.* 3 to robe or clothe. *vi-* 1 to rest or reside (in) or devolve (upon) some person, group, etc.: *In this country, executive power vests in the president.* 2 to robe oneself for a ceremony. —*adj-* vest′less.

Ves·ta (věs′ tə) *n-* in Roman mythology, the goddess of the hearth and the hearth fire.

ves·tal (věs′ təl) *adj-* 1 of or having to do with the Roman goddess Vesta, or to the virgins who served in her temple; hence, suitable to a virgin or nun; chaste. *n-* 1 (also **vestal virgin**) one of the six virgin priestesses who tended the sacred fire in the temple of Vesta. 2 a virgin; also, a nun.

vest·ed (věs′ təd) *adj-* 1 dressed, especially in priestly or other ceremonial garments. 2 in law, marked by rights established by law; not subject to contingency or suspension; fixed: *his* vested *interests.*

vest·ee (věs tē′) *n-* small vest or a piece of material forming a V-shaped front, worn with a dress or jacket.

ves·ti·bule (věs′ tə byōōl′) *n-* 1 small entrance hall to a building or room. 2 enclosed platform of a railway passenger car.

ves·tige (věs′ tĭj) *n-* 1 trace, sign, or mark left of something: *Not a* vestige *of the original paint was to be seen.* 2 *Biology* a structure or organ reduced and simplified in the course of evolution from a larger and functional ancestral form, until it has lost its original function.

ves·ti·gi·al (vě stĭj′ē əl) *adj-* having the nature of a vestige. —*adv-* ves·ti·gi′al·ly.

vest·ment (věst′ mənt) *n-* robe; gown; garment, especially an official or ceremonial garment, or one worn by a clergyman performing religious rites.

vest-pock·et (věst′ pŏk′ ət) *adj-* suitable for or able to fit into a vest pocket; hence, small; compact.

ves·try (věs′ trē) *n-* [*pl.* **ves·tries**] 1 room in a church where the clergy put on their vestments or where such vestments and other sacred articles are kept. 2 room in a church used for Sunday school, a chapel, etc. 3 in the Anglican and Protestant Episcopal churches, a body of men who direct the affairs of a parish. —*n-* ves′try·man.

ves·ture (věs′ chər) *n-* 1 clothing; garments. 2 a covering.

¹vet (vět) *Informal n-* veterinarian.

²vet (vět) *Informal n-* veteran.

vetch (věch) *n-* any of various climbing vines related to the peas, often used as fodder.

vet·er·an (vět′ ər ən) *n-* 1 person who has done active military service: *His father is a* veteran *of both World Wars.* 2 one who is experienced from long practice and service: *a* veteran *of the stage. as modifier: a* veteran *society;* veteran *benefits;* veteran *troops; a* veteran *actor.*

view·point (vyōō′ point′) *n-* way of looking at things; point of view; standpoint.

vi·ges·i·mal (vĭ jěs′ ə məl) *adj-* 1 twentieth. 2 of or having to do with twenty. 3 progressing by twenties: *a* vigesimal *system of counting.*

vig·il (vĭj′ əl) *n-* 1 a keeping awake for the purpose of watching or protecting: *to keep* vigil *over a sick person.* 2 **vigils** (1) religious devotions in the evening or nighttime

vin·di·cate (vĭn′ də kāt′) *vt-* [**vin·di·cat·ed, vin·di·cat·ing**] 1 to clear of suspected guilt or wrongdoing; absolve: *to* vindicate *someone under arrest.* 2 to show to be true or right against opposition; uphold: *to* vindicate *an action.* 3 to justify: *His brave acts* vindicated *their faith in him.* —*n-* vin′di·ca′tion. *n-* vin′di·ca′tor.

vin·dic·tive (vĭn dĭk′ tĭv) *adj-* filled with a desire for revenge; spiteful and malicious: *a* vindictive *attack.* —*adv-* vin·dic′tive·ly. *n-* vin·dic′tive·ness.

vine (vīn) *n-* 1 any plant, such as ivy or honeysuckle, with a long stem that trails along the ground or climbs upward by fastening its tendrils to a support. 2 the stem of such a plant.

vin·e·gar (vĭn′ ə gər) *n-* sour liquid, consisting largely of acetic acid produced by the fermentation of wine, cider, etc., used to flavor or preserve food. —*adj-* vin′e·gar·y.

vinegar eel *n-* minute worm commonly found in vinegar or other fermenting liquids.

vine·yard (vĭn′ yərd) *n-* land used for the cultivation of grapes.

vin·tage (vĭn′ tĭj) *n-* 1 wine made from the grapes of a particular region in a particular year. 2 group or crop of anything: *That's a play of an old* vintage. *adj-* 1 of high quality; choice: *a* vintage *crop.* 2 out-of-date.

vint·ner (vĭnt′ nər) *n-* wine merchant.

vin·y (vī′ nē) *adj-* [**vin·i·er, vin·i·est**] 1 of, relating to, or like vines: *a* viny *plant.* 2 covered with vines.

vi·nyl (vī′ nəl) *n-* a monovalent radical that is the ethylene molecule minus one atom of hydrogen. Various vinyl compounds are used in plastics, resins, and synthetic fibers. *as modifier: a* vinyl *floor.*

Vi·nyl·ite (vī′ nə līt′) *n-* trademark name for a synthetic, thermoplastic substance used to make phonograph records, protective coatings, etc. Also **vinylite.**

vinyl resin or **vinyl plastic** *n-* any of various durable resins or plastics obtained by the polymerization of vinyl compounds.

vi·ol (vī′ əl) *n-* 1 any of various stringed instruments played with the bow that were used mainly in the 16th and 17th centuries, after which time they were replaced by the violin family. 2 **bass viol; double bass.** *Hom-* vial.

¹vi·o·la (vē ō′ lə) *n-* stringed instrument of the violin family, somewhat larger and deeper in tone than the violin. [from Italian and Spanish *viola* and *viol.*]

²vi·o·la (vī ō′ lə, vī′ ə lə) *n-* johnny jump-up. [from Latin *violet.*]

vi·o·late (vī′ ə lāt′) *vt-* [**vi·o·lat·ed, vi·o·lat·ing**] 1 to disregard; break: *to* violate *a treaty; to* violate *a law.* 2 to disturb: *to* violate *silence.* 3 to profane: *to* violate *a shrine.* 4 to rape. —*n-* vi′o·la′tor.

vi·o·la·tion (vī′ ə lā′ shən) *n-* 1 a breaking of a law, treaty, promise, etc.; infringement. 2 interruption or disturbance: *a* violation *of privacy.* 3 a profaning; desecration: *a* violation *of the court's dignity.* 4 rape.

vi·o·lence (vī′ ə ləns) *n-* 1 physical force, usually resulting in harm: *an act of* violence; *the* violence *of a storm.* 2 intensity; passion: *the* violence *of his rage.* 3 damage; outrage: *The deer did* violence *to my garden by tramping through it.*

vi·o·lent (vī′ ə lənt) *adj-* 1 marked by or resulting from the use of physical force: *a* violent *blow on the head; a* violent *death.* 2 having or showing strong feeling; passionate; intense: *his* violent *temper.* 3 extreme or severe: *a* violent *storm.* —*adv-* vi′o·lent·ly.

Common violet

VIP or **V.I.P.** very important person.

vi·per (vī′ pər) *n-* 1 any of a group of Old World poisonous snakes with hollow front fangs and, usually, heavy bodies. 2 **pit viper.** 3 evil, treacherous person.

vi·per·ine (vī′ pə rēn′) *n-* 1 belonging to the viper family. 2 resembling a viper in being swiftly venomous.

vi·per·ous (vī′ pər əs) *adj-* 1 of or relating to vipers. 2 malignant; venomous; viperine. —*adv-* vi′per·ous·ly.

vi·ra·go (və rä′ gō′, vĭr′ ə gō′) *n-* [*pl.* **vi·ra·gos, vi·ra·goes**] quarrelsome, ill-tempered woman; scold.

vi·ral (vī′ rəl) *adj-* of, related to, or caused by a virus.

vir·tu·o·so (vûr′ chŏō ō′ sō) *n-* [*pl.* vir·to·o·sos, vir·tu·o·si (-sē)] 1 person who is skilled in the technique of an art; especially, a person skilled in a musical art, such as playing the violin. 2 person who has a cultivated taste for, or knowledge of, artistic excellence; connoisseur. —*n-* vir′tu·os′i·ty (-ŏs′ ə tē): *his* musical *virtuosity.*

vir·tu·ous (vûr′ chŏō əs) *adj-* 1 having moral excellence. 2 chaste. —*adv-* vir′tu·ous·ly. *n-* vir′tu·ous·ness.

vir·u·lent (vĭr′ ə lənt, -yə lənt) *adj-* 1 poisonous; deadly: *a* virulent *disease.* 2 extremely hostile: *a* virulent *child.* 3 malicious; intensely bitter: *his* virulent *abuse.* —*n-* vir′u·lence. *adv-* vir′u·lent·ly.

vi·rus (vī′ rəs) *n-* [*pl.* vi·rus·es] 1 a form of matter that is smaller than bacteria but larger than molecules, and consists of a protein coat surrounding a core of either RNA or DNA. Viruses reproduce themselves only in living cells, and cause measles, mumps, smallpox, etc. 2 anything poisonous to the mind or spirit: *the* virus *of hate.* 3 venom. *as modifier:* a virus *infection.*

vi·sa (vē′ zə) *n-* official endorsement made on a passport of one country by an authority of another country, to permit the bearer to enter the country from which the endorsement was obtained. *vt-* [vi·saed, vi·sa·ing] to mark (a passport) with a visa.

vis·age (vĭz′ lj) *n-* 1 the face. 2 appearance; aspect.

vis·cer·a (vĭs′ər ə) *n-* *pl.* [*sing.* vis·cus (vĭs′kəs)] the organs, such as the stomach, liver, and intestines, found in the large cavity of the body of an animal. —*adj-* vis′cer·al. *adv-* vis′cer·al·ly.

vis·cid (vĭs′ ld) *adj-* 1 sticky; gluelike. 2 of certain leaves, covered with a sticky substance.

vis·cose (vĭs′ kōs′) *n-* substance produced by treating cellulose with caustic soda and other chemicals, and used in making rayon, cellophane, etc.

vis·cos·i·ty (vĭs kŏs′ə tē) *n-* 1 quality of being viscous; stickiness. 2 *Physics* property of a fluid that causes it to offer resistance to flow because of forces that hold together its molecules; the internal friction of a fluid.

vis·count (vī′ kount′) *n-* nobleman of a rank below an earl or count and above a baron.

vis·count·ess (vī′ koun′ təs) *n-* 1 wife or widow of a viscount. 2 woman who has the rank of viscount.

vis·cous (vĭs′ kəs) *adj-* 1 thick and sticky; gluelike. 2 having relatively high viscosity.

vise (vīs) *n-* any of various devices with two jaws that are tightened by turning a screw, used to hold objects firmly while work is being done to them. *Hom-* vice.

Vish·nu (vĭsh′ nōō′) *n-* Hindu deity, the second member of the Hindu trinity, associated with Brahma and Shiva.

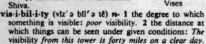
Vises

vis·i·bil·i·ty (vĭz′ ə bĭl′ə tē) *n-* 1 the degree to which something is visible: *poor* visibility. 2 the distance at which things can be seen under given conditions: *The* visibility *from this tower is forty miles on a clear day.*

vis·i·ble (vĭz′ ə bəl) *adj-* 1 such as can be seen: *In the fog my* hand was not visible *before my face.* 2 clear; apparent; perceptible: *He has no* visible *income.*

vis·i·tant (vĭz′ ə tənt) *n-* 1 visitor, especially one regarded as coming from a strange or supernatural place. 2 migratory bird that appears in an area at intervals for a time.

vis·it·a·tion (vĭz′ ə tā′ shən) *n-* 1 visit. 2 reward or punishment from God, especially, a severe affliction. 3 Visitation in the New Testament, the visit of Mary to her cousin, Elizabeth, before the birth of the latter's son, John the Baptist; also, the holy day, July 2, commemorating this visit.

visiting card *n-* small card bearing a person's name, used when making a visit. Also calling card.

visiting fireman *Informal n-* visitor to a large city, who makes incidental calls on friends there.

visiting teacher *n-* officer of a public school system who visits the homes of students in order to instruct sick students, enforce attendance, and attempt to solve various emotional and social problems affecting a student's work.

vi·tal·i·ty (vī tăl′ ə tē) *n-* [*pl.* vi·tal·i·ties] 1 strength; liveliness; energy. 2 ability to keep on living or existing: *the* vitality *of our nation.*

vi·tal·ize (vī′ tə līz′) *vt-* [vi·tal·ized, vi·tal·iz·ing] to fill with life or vigor. —*n-* vi′ tal·i·za′ tion.

vital statistics *n- pl.* statistics of births, deaths, and other factors concerning population increase and decrease.

vi·ta·min (vī′ tə mən) *n-* any of a class of complex organic compounds that are present in foods in minute quantities and which are necessary to the health and normal growth of most living organisms. *as modifier:* a vitamin *deficiency;* vitamin *pill.*

vitamin A *n-* any of a small group of fat-soluble vitamins made by animal cells from the carotene of plants. Vitamin A is also found in fish-liver oils and dairy products. Lack of this vitamin causes night blindness.

vitamin B *n-* original name for the vitamin B complex, before it was known to contain many different vitamins.

vitamin B₁ *n-* vitamin that is essential to the normal functioning of the nervous system; thiamine. It is found in the outer covering of various grains, in milk, in liver, and in kidneys. Lack of this vitamin causes beriberi.

vitamin B₂ *n-* vitamin that is essential to the normal functioning of the body cells; riboflavin. It is found in milk, meats, etc., and lack of it causes abnormalities of the skin and eyes.

vitamin B₆ *n-* vitamin that is important in metabolism; pyridoxine. It is found in meat and the husks of some grains. Lack of it causes dermatitis and convulsions.

vitamin B₁₂ *n-* vitamin that is important in the synthesis of nucleic acid. It is found in liver, and lack of it causes pernicious anemia.

vitamin B complex *n-* group of water-soluble vitamins found together in foodstuffs such as yeast and liver. Biotin, vitamin B₁, vitamin B₂, vitamin B₆, vitamin B₁₂, nicotinic acid, and pantothenic acid are parts of the vitamin B complex.

vitamin C *n-* vitamin that is found in most fruits, especially citrus fruits, and vegetables; ascorbic acid. Lack of it causes scurvy.

vitamin D *n-* vitamin found in fish-liver oils, fish, eggs, and specially prepared milk; viosterol. Lack of it causes rickets.

vitamin E *n-* vitamin that prevents sterility and muscular dystrophy in experimental animals, and is found in wheat germ and leafy vegetables.

vitamin G *n-* vitamin B₂.

vitamin H *n-* biotin.

vitamin K *n-* any of a small group of vitamins that are vital to the clotting of blood. They are present in green, leafy vegetables and in tomatoes.

vitamin P *n-* group of substances, no longer considered vitamins, that help to keep the capillaries healthy.

vi·ti·ate (vĭsh′ē āt′) *vt-* [vi·ti·at·ed, vi·ti·at·ing] 1 to make worthless; invalidate: *to* vitiate *a ballot.* 2 to impair the quality of; debase; contaminate: *The escaping gas* vitiated *the air.* —*n-* vi′ ti·a′ tion.

vit·re·ous (vī′ trē əs) *adj-* 1 of, like, or obtained from glass: *a* vitreous *rock.* 2 of or related to the vitreous humor.

vitreous humor *n-* jellylike, transparent substance that fills the space between the lens and the retina of the eye.

vit·ri·fy (vī′ trə fī′) *vt-* [vit·ri·fied, vit·ri·fy·ing] to change into glass or a glassy substance by the action of heat: *The nuclear explosion* vitrified *the sand.* *vi- The* sand *vitrified.* —*n-* vit′ ri·fi·ca′ tion (vī′ trə fə kā′ shən).

vi·va·cious (vī vā′ shəs, vĭ-) *adj-* lively; gay; high-spirited. —*adv-* vi·va′ cious·ly. *n-* vi·va′ cious·ness.

vi·vac·i·ty (vī vǎs′ə tē, vĭ-) *n-* gaiety; liveliness; high spirits; vivaciousness.

vi·var·i·um (vī vâr′ ē əm, vĭ vêr′-) *n-* [*pl.* vi·var·i·a (-, or vi·var·i·ums) place, such as a zoo or aquarium, for duplicating natural habitats for live animals.

vive (vēv) *French* long live! (used as a shout of acclaim).

viv·id (vĭv′ ld) *adj-* 1 bright; intense: *a* vivid *red.* 2 lifelike; convincing: *a* vivid *description of a circus.* 3 lively; active: *a* vivid *imagination.* 4 sharp and clear; distinct: *a* vivid *recollection.* —*adv-* viv′ id·ly. *n-* viv′ id·ness.

voice box *n-* larynx.

voiced (voist) *adj-* 1 having a voice; also, expressed by the voice: *a voiced protest.* 2 made entirely or partly by the vibration of the vocal cords: *All vowels in English are voiced. The consonant "d" is a voiced consonant.*

voice·less (vois' ləs) *adj-* 1 having no voice; mute; silent: *his voiceless anger.* 2 made without vibration of the vocal cords: *"P," "t," and "k" are voiceless consonants.* —*adv-* **voice' less·ly.**

Voice of America *n-* international U.S. government radio service that broadcasts programs in English and in foreign languages in order to acquaint other peoples with U.S. activities, goals, and policy.

void (void) *adj-* 1 in law, not having any force; not valid: *The will was declared void by the court.* 2 *Archaic* empty. 3 *Archaic* without effect; useless. *n-* 1 empty space; vacuum: *to fill a void.* 2 feeling of emptiness or loss: *His death left a void in our hearts. vt-* 1 in law, to cancel or annul; invalidate: *to void a contract.* 2 to empty; discharge. —*adv-* **void' a·ble.** *n-* **void' er.**

void of lacking in; devoid of: *He is void of humor.*

voile (voil) *n-* sheer fabric made of cotton, silk, wool, or synthetics, used for summer dresses or for curtains.

vol. volume.

vol·a·tile (vŏl' ə təl) *adj-* 1 easy or quick to evaporate; readily turning into vapor at a relatively low temperature: *Gasoline is a volatile liquid.* 2 changeable; fickle; lively; lighthearted: *a volatile disposition.* 3 unstable; shaky; explosive: *a volatile political situation.* —*n-* **vol' a·til' i·ty** (-ə tĭl' ə tē).

vol·can·ic (vŏl kăn' ĭk) *adj-* 1 of, like, or produced by a volcano: *high volcanic peaks.* 2 violent; explosive.

vol·can·ism (vŏl' kə nĭz' əm) *n-* the phenomena of volcanoes and volcanic action. Also **vulcanism.**

vol·ca·no (vŏl kā' nō) *n-* [*pl.* **vol·ca·noes** or **vol·ca·nos**] 1 an opening in the earth's crust, which is generally surrounded by a mass of ejected material forming a hill or mountain, and from which molten rock, ashes, steam are or have been expelled.

Alaskan volcano

2 the hill or mountain so formed, called "active" when in eruption, "dormant" during a long cessation of activity, or "extinct" when eruptions are believed to have ceased permanently.

vol·ca·nol·o·gy (vŏl' kə nŏl' ə jē) *n-* the scientific study of volcanoes and volcanic phenomena. —*adj-* **vol' can·o·log' i·cal** (vŏl' kə nə lŏj' ĭ kəl) *n-* **vol' ca·nol' o·gist.**

vole (vŏl) *n-* any of various rodents similar to rats and mice but usually having shorter tails.

Vole

vo·li·tion (və lĭsh' ən) *n-* act of willingly or freely choosing something; also, one's power of willing: *He came of his own volition.* —*adj-* **vo·li' tion·al.** *adv-* **vo·li' tion·al·ly.**

vol·ley (vŏl' ē) *n-* [*pl.* **vol·leys**] 1 flight or discharge of many bullets or other missiles at the same time: *a volley of arrows.* 2 any burst of a number of things at once. 3 in tennis, a return of the ball before it touches the ground. 4 in soccer, a kick at a ball before it touches the ground. *vt-* [**vol·leyed, vol·ley·ing**] 1 to be discharged all at once: *Guns volleyed to his left.* 2 in tennis, soccer, and badminton, to return the ball or shuttlecock before it touches the ground.

vol·ley·ball (vŏl' ē bôl') *n-* 1 game in which two teams attempt to bat a large ball back and forth across a high net with their hands without letting the ball touch the ground. 2 the ball used in this game.

vom·it (vŏm' ĭt) *vi-* 1 to discharge the contents of the stomach through the mouth; throw up. 2 to be discharged with violence: *Lava vomited out. vt-: He vomited his food. n-* matter thrown up by the stomach.

voo·doo (vōō' dōō) *n-* form of religious worship mixed with sorcery, of West African origin, but now practiced chiefly in Haiti. 2 person who worships or practices voodoo.

vul·can·ize (vŭl' kə nīz', vōōl' -) *vt-* [**vul·can·ized, vul·can·iz·ing**] to toughen (rubber) by treatment with sulfur or other chemicals under heat and pressure. —*n-* **vul' can·i·za' tion.** *n-* **vul' can·iz' er.**

vul·ca·nol·o·gy (vŭl' kə nŏl' ə jē, vōōl' -) volcanology.

Vulg. Vulgate.

vul·gar (vŭl' gər, vōōl' -) *adj-* 1 showing bad taste; crude; coarse: *a vulgar person; a vulgar joke.* 2 of the common people: *the vulgar tongue.* —*adv-* **vul' gar·ly.**

vul·gar·i·an (vəl gâr' ē ən) *n-* vulgar person.

vul·gar·ism (vŭl' gə rĭz' əm, vōōl' -) *n-* 1 word or expression used chiefly by uneducated persons, and not considered part of the formal or informal standard vocabulary. 2 vulgarity.

vul·gar·i·ty (vəl găr' ə tē, -gĕr' ə tē) *n-* [*pl.* **vul·gar·i·ties**] behavior or speech showing a lack of refinement, delicacy, or good taste.

vul·gar·ize (vŭl' gə rīz', vōōl' -) *vt-* [**vul·gar·ized, vul·gar·iz·ing**] 1 to make coarse, cheap, or low. 2 to make (a difficult and specialized study, book, etc.) easy and simple enough for general understanding: *This author skillfully vulgarizes nuclear physics.* —*n-* **vul' gar·iz' er.**

vul·gar·i·za·tion (vŭl' gə rə zā' shən, vōōl' -) *n-* 1 a vulgarizing: *the vulgarization of manners; the vulgarization of a philosophical treatise.* 2 something vulgarized.

Vul·gate (vŭl' gāt', vōōl' -) *n-* 1 the authorized Latin version of the Bible used in the Roman Catholic Church. 2 **vulgate** (1) the common or accepted version of any writing. (2) the ordinary language of the masses, partly made up of slang and vulgarisms; vernacular.

vul·ner·a·ble (vŭl' nər ə bəl, vōōl' -) *adj-* 1 open to or not safe against attack and ruin; not invincible: *a vulnerable outpost; a vulnerable reputation.* 2 such as can easily be wounded or hurt: *His feelings are very vulnerable.* —*n-* **vul' ner·a·bil' i·ty.** *adv-* **vul' ner·a·bly.**

vulnerable to easily hurt or conquered by; open to: *He is vulnerable to ridicule.*

vul·pine (vŭl' pīn', vōōl' -) *adj-* 1 of or relating to a fox or foxes. 2 crafty; cunning; sly; foxy.

vul·ture (vŭl' chər, vōōl' -) *n-* 1 any of various large, bald-headed birds of prey, related to the hawks and eagles, that feed chiefly on dead and decaying flesh. 2 grasping and merciless person who profits from misfortunes and disasters of other persons.

Vulture (California condor), about 4 ft long

vul·va (vŭl' və, vōōl' -) *n-* the external parts of the female sex organs.

vy·ing (vī' ĭng) *pres. p.* of **vie.**

W

W, w (dŭb′ əl yŏŏ′) *n-* [*pl.* **W's, w's**] the 23rd letter of the English alphabet.

W symbol for tungsten.

W or **w** **1** watt; watts. **2** west; western.

w. **1** width; wide. **2** week. **3** with. **4** weight. **5** west; western. **6** *Physics* work.

W. **1** Wednesday. **2** Wales; Welsh. **3** west; western.

wab·ble (wŏb′ əl) wobble. **—***adj-* **wab′ bly.**

WAC or **W.A.C.** (wăk) Women's Army Corps.

wack·y (wăk′ ē) *Slang adj-* [**wack·i·er, wack·i·est**] slightly insane in an amusing way. **—***adv-* **wack′ i·ly.** *n-* **wack′ i·ness.**

wad (wŏd) *n-* **1** tight mass of soft material, especially one squeezed into an opening. **2** *Slang* fat roll of paper money; also, a large amount of money. *vt-* [**wad·ded, wad·ding**] **1** to pack or squeeze into a tight mass: *to*

war·fare (wôr′ fâr′) *n-* the waging of war; especially, fighting between armed forces.

war hawk *n-* warmonger; especially, an American of about 1812 who demanded war with Great Britain.

war·head (wôr′ hĕd′) *n-* front part of a guided missile or torpedo, containing the explosive charge.

war·horse (wôr′ hôrs′, -hôrs′) *n-* **1** horse used in battle; charger. **2** *Informal* person who is deeply experienced and very dependable; veteran.

war·i·ly (wâr′ ə lē) *adv-* in a very cautious manner.

war·i·ness (wâr′ ē nəs) *n-* caution; distrust; suspicion.

war·like (wôr′ līk′) *adj-* **1** fond of fighting; quick to fight: *a warlike people.* **2** hostile; threatening war: *The chief sent a warlike challenge to the neighboring tribe.* **3** of or relating to war; military.

war·lock (wôr′ lŏk′) *n-* sorcerer; wizard.

war·lord (wôr′ lôrd′, -lôrd′) *n-* powerful military chief who rules a region despotically.

warm (wôrm) *adj-* [**warm·er, warm·est**] **1** having or giving off a moderate degree of heat; more hot than cold: *Hawaii has a warm climate. I drink warm milk at bedtime.* **2** keeping the heat in: *a warm blanket.* **3** affectionate; enthusiastic: *a warm greeting.* **4** excited; heated; brisk: *The debate aroused warm interest.* **5** of colors, suggesting warmth, as red, orange, or yellow: *Her dress was a warm shade of brown.* **6** *Informal* near something being looked for or guessed at: *That's not it, but you're warm. vt-* **1** to make slightly hot (often followed by "up"): *Mother warmed the milk.* **2** to make eager, excited, friendly, etc.: *The thought of seeing the family again warmed my heart. vi-* **1** to become slightly hot: *The rolls warmed in the oven.* **2** to become friendly or approving (to or toward) some person or thing. **—***adv-* **warm′ ly.** *n-* **warm′ ness.**

warm up **1** to run a gasoline engine or other device until it is at operating temperature. **2** to exercise or practice briefly before entering a game, contest, etc.: *The new pitcher is warming up.* **3** to make or become more friendly, interested, etc.

warm-blood·ed (wôrm′ blŭd′ əd) *adj-* **1** having warm blood and a steady body temperature not depending greatly on the temperature of the environment: *Mammals are warm-blooded.* **2** very affectionate or excitable.

warm·er (wôr′ mər) *n-* appliance or container used for warming something.

warm front *n-* the forward edge of an advancing mass of warm air.

warm-heart·ed (wôrm′ här′ təd) *adj-* **1** affectionate; friendly; kind. **2** ardent; eager; enthusiastic. **—***n-* **warm′ -heart′ ed·ness.**

warming pan *n-* large, long-handled, covered pan for holding live coals, formerly used to warm beds by passing it between the sheets.

war·mon·ger (wôr′ mŏng′ gər, -mŭng′ ər) *n-* person or group which favors or tries to provoke war; war hawk.

warmth (wôrmth) *n-* condition of being warm.

warm-up (wôrm′ ŭp′) *n-* **1** act of practicing or exercising to get one's body, voice, etc., ready for activity or performance. **2** act of running an engine or other device up to operating temperature. **3** act of entertaining and relaxing a studio audience before a television program. *as modifier: a few warm-up pitches.*

---

hurricane. **2** to give advance notice; to inform. **3** to admonish; counsel; advise: *I warned you not to swim out that far.* **4** to notify; signal: *Her look warned us it was time to leave.* **—***n-* **warn′ er.** *adv-* **warn′ ing·ly.**

warn·ing (wôr′ nĭng) *n-* **1** notice of danger or unpleasantness: *He had plenty of warning.* **2** act or thing that gives such notice: *This letter is a warning.*

War of 1812 *n-* the war between the United States and Great Britain from 1812 to 1815.

War of Independence *n-* the American Revolution.

warp (wôrp) *n-* **1** the lengthwise threads of a woven cloth through which woof threads are woven. **2** bend; twist: *Dampness gave the board a bad warp.* **3** mental twist: *Worry had given his mind a strange warp.* **4** heavy rope or cable used for hauling ships to or from a dock or mooring. *vt-* **1** to twist or bend: *The hot sun had warped the shingles.* **2** to twist mentally: *Bias warped the man's thinking.* **3** to haul (a ship) to or from a dock or mooring. *vi-* to become twisted or bent: *The planks warped.*

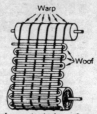

Warp / Woof

war paint *n-* **1** paint applied to the face and body by American Indians as a ceremonial decoration before going to war. **2** *Slang* a woman's makeup.

war·path (wôr′ păth′) *n-* route taken by American Indians on a warlike expedition.

on the warpath **1** at war or ready for war. **2** angry; ready for a fight.

war·plane (wôr′ plān′) *n-* airplane designed for military use, especially for combat.

war·rant (wôr′ ənt, wŏr′-) *n-* **1** official paper or writ that gives authority to do something, especially, to make an arrest or to search or seize property; legal authorization. **2** that which gives a right; justification: *What warrant have you to say such a thing?* **3** certificate of appointment issued to a warrant officer. *vt-* **1** to justify; give sufficient grounds for: *The crime warranted a severe punishment.* **2** to guarantee; promise: *The manufacturer warranted the product as genuine.* **3** to authorize; empower, especially legally. **4** to state with confidence: *I warrant that he will come.*

war·rant·a·ble (wôr′ ən tə bəl, wŏr′-) *adj-* such as can be warranted: *a warrantable product.* **—***n-* **war′ rant·a·ble·ness.** *adv-* **war′ rant·a·bly.**

warrant officer *n-* in the Army, Air Force, Navy, Marine Corps, and Coast Guard, an officer who ranks between the highest noncommissioned officer and the lowest commissioned officer, and whose authority is granted by a warrant.

war·ran·tor (wôr′ ən tər′, wôr′-) *n-* in law, person who gives or makes a warranty to another.

war·ran·ty (wôr′ ən tē, wôr′-) *n-* [*pl.* **war·ran·ties**] **1** a guarantee. **2** authorization; warrant.

war·ren (wôr′ ən, wŏr′-) *n-* **1** a place in which small animals, especially rabbits, breed or are numerous. **2** game enclosure for small animals. **3** slum.

war·ri·or (wôr′ ē ər) *n-* man experienced in fighting; soldier.

war·ship (wôr′ shĭp′) *n-* ship built and armed for war.

wart (wôrt) *n-* a small, usually hard lump on the skin or on a plant, caused by a virus infection.

watch·band (wŏch′ bănd′, wŏch′-) *n-* strap or bracelet for a wristwatch.

watch·dog (wŏch′ dŏg′, wŏch′-) *n-* **1** dog kept or trained to guard property. **2** person or organization acting as a guardian against loss, theft, inefficiency, etc.

watch·er (wŏch′ ər, wŏ′ chər) *n-* person who watches.

watch fire *n-* fire kept burning as a signal or for the use of a guard or watcher.

watch·ful (wŏch′ fəl, wŏch′-) *adj-* wide-awake; vigilant; on the watch. **—***adv-* **watch′ ful·ly.** *n-* **watch′ ful·ness.**

watch·mak·er (wŏch′ mā′ kər) *n-* person who makes or repairs watches. **—***n-* **watch′ mak′ ing.**

watch·man (wŏch′mən, wŏch′-) n- [pl. **watch·men**] person whose duty it is to watch and guard; especially, a person hired to guard property at night.

watch·tow·er (wŏch′tou′ər, wŏch′-) n- tower from which a guard or sentinel keeps watch.

watch·word (wŏch′wûrd′, wŏch′-) n- 1 a rallying cry; slogan: *The watchword is Liberty.* 2 password.

wa·ter (wô′ tər, wŏt′ər) n- 1 colorless, tasteless, odorless liquid compound of hydrogen and oxygen (H_2O) that freezes at 32 degrees F. or 0 degrees C. and boils at 212 degrees F. or 100 degrees C. under standard pressure. 2 lake, river, ocean, or other body of this liquid: *We crossed the water by ferry.* 3 any liquid containing or resembling water: *soda* water; *toilet* water. 4 kind of wavy, shiny pattern given to some fabrics or metals. *as modifier:* a water *pipe*; water *sports.* vt- 1 to moisten, sprinkle, or cover with water: *to water the lawn.* 2 to provide with a supply of water: *to water an oil tanker.* 3 to irrigate: *The Columbia River waters a large valley.* 4 to give drinking water to (an animal): *to water horses.* 5 to dilute with water: *to water wine.* 6 in finance, to issue (shares of stock) without a corresponding increase in assets. 7 to give a shiny, wavy pattern to: *to water silk.* vi- 1 to secrete tears: *His eyes watered in the smog.* 2 to salivate. 3 of animals, to drink water: *The elephants water at the river.* —n- wa′ter·er. adj- wa′ter·less.

above water out of trouble. **by water** by ship: *to travel by water.* **hold water** 1 to be true, valid, and logical: *Your theory doesn't hold water.* 2 to stop or steady a small boat by holding the oars or paddles steady in the water. **in hot water** in trouble: *He's in hot water with his parents.* **keep (one's) head above water** to stay in control of a situation. **of the first water** of the first class.

water bag n- 1 bag for holding water. 2 the second stomach of a camel or a related animal.

water beetle n- any of several fresh-water beetles with fringed legs for swimming.

water bird n- bird that swims or lives near water.

water blister n- blister filled with lymph.

wa·ter·borne (wô′ tər bôrn′, wŏt′ ər-) adj- 1 floating on water. 2 carried by water; transported by ship.

wa·ter·buck (wô′ tər bŭk′, wŏt′ ər-) n- [pl. **wa·ter·buck** or **wa·ter·bucks**] either of two large African antelopes, found near water.

water buffalo n- common, wide-horned buffalo of Asia, often domesticated for its milk and used as a draft animal; water ox; carabao.

water bug n- 1 Croton bug. 2 any of various bugs that propel themselves through the water with their legs.

water chestnut n- 1 water plant with an edible nutlike fruit. 2 the fruit of this plant.

water closet n- toilet; bathroom.

water color n- 1 paint that is mixed with water instead of oil. 2 painting done with this kind of paint or pigment. 3 art of painting with water colors. *as modifier* (**water-color**): *a water-color portrait.*

water cooler n- device that cools and dispenses water.

wa·ter·course (wô′ tər kôrs′, wŏt′ ər-) n- 1 stream of water, such as a brook or river. 2 channel for water.

wa·ter·craft (wô′ tər krăft′, wŏt′ ər-) n- [pl. **wa·ter·craft**] any boat or ship; also, ships or boats collectively.

wa·ter·cress (wô′ tər krĕs′, wŏt′ ər-) n- green water plant of the mustard family with crisp leaves, used in salads.

water cure n- 1 the treatment of diseases by use of water, either as baths or internally. 2 *Informal* method of torturing by forcing water down someone's throat.

water cycle n- the continuous process by which water moves from the earth to the atmosphere by evaporation and then returns to the earth by precipitation.

wat·tle (wŏt′ əl) n- 1 twig or rod easily bent; also, a framework of pliant rods. 2 material made of pliant twigs twisted together and used for walls, fences, etc. 3 wattles rods used in a roof to support thatch made of straw. 4 fold of loose red flesh under the throat of certain birds or reptiles. vt- [wat·tled, wat·tling] 1 to twist or interweave (twigs or rods) into a framework, fence, etc. 2 to cover or fence in with rods.

wat·tled (wŏt′ əld) adj- 1 made or built with wattles. 2 of a bird, snake, etc., having a wattle.

wave (wāv) n- 1 rise and swell on the surface of a body of water: *an ocean* wave. 2 something resembling this in shape or movement. 3 increase or surge of something: *a wave of anger; a heat wave.* 4 *Physics* (1) any periodic or cyclic vibration produced in and propagated through a medium. (2) an electromagnetic wave. vi- [wave, wav·ing] 1 to move up and down or back and forth: *The flag waved in the breeze.* 2 to signal by such motion: *He waved to us.* 3 to form into ripples: *Her hair waves easily.* vt-: *to wave a flag; to wave good-by; to wave one's hair.* Hom- waive. —adj- wave′ like′.

wave·length (wāv′ lĕngth′) *Physics* n- distance between any two corresponding points on a wave, measured along the line of travel of the wave.

wa·ver (wā′ vər) vi- 1 to hesitate; be undecided: *She wavered over choosing the present.* 2 to flicker; tremble. 3 to sway back and forth. 4 to fail or begin to give way: *The sick man's mind wavered.* n- a flickering, trembling, or shaking. —n- wa′ ver·er. adv- wa′ ver·ing·ly.

WAVES or **W.A.V.E.S.** (wāvz) corps of women in the U.S. Navy, including all women except nurses. Officially, **Women in the U.S. Navy.** [from the former name, *Women Appointed for Voluntary Emergency Service.*]

wav·y (wā′ vē) adj- [wav·i·er, wav·i·est] 1 moving to and fro in waves or swells. 2 full of waves or curves. —adv- wav′ i·ly. n- wav′ i·ness.

Wavy lines

¹**wax** (wăks) n- 1 sticky, yellowish substance made by bees, from which the honeycomb is built; beeswax. 2 any of several substances somewhat resembling this: *a sealing* wax; *paraffin* wax. 3 compound containing wax for giving a luster to floors, furniture, etc. vt- to polish or coat with this. *as modifier:* a wax *fruit.* [from Old English weax, "beeswax."] —adj- wax′ like′.

²**wax** (wăks) vi- 1 to increase in apparent size, power, degree, etc., as the moon does as it approaches fullness. 2 to grow; become increasingly: *He waxed talkative after dinner.* [from Old English weaxan, "to grow."]

wax bean n- yellow string bean.

wax·en (wăk′ sən) adj- 1 made of wax. 2 like wax in appearance, consistency, etc.; soft; plastic. 3 pallid.

wax myrtle n- any of several slender, evergreen shrubs or trees of eastern United States that bear wax-covered berries from which candle wax is obtained; bayberry.

wax paper n- paper coated with wax that repels water, grease, etc.

wax·wing (wăks′ wing′) n- crested gray and brown bird with a yellow tail band and head, red, waxy tips on some of its wing feathers; cedarbird; cedar waxwing.

Cedar waxwing

wax·work (wăks′ wûrk′) n- 1 modeled work in wax. 2 waxworks collection of wax figures of persons, usually life-size representations of historical characters .

wax·y (wăk′ sē) adj- [wax·i·er, wax·i·est] 1 resembling wax. 2 made of, or coated with, wax. —n- wax′ i·ness.

way·bill (wā′ bil′) n- paper containing shipping instructions for goods carried by train or steamer.

way·far·er (wā′ fâr′ ər) n- traveler, especially one who travels on foot.

way·far·ing (wā′ fâr′ ing) n- traveling, especially on foot. *as modifier:* a wayfaring *man.*

way·lay (wā′ lā′) vt- [way·laid, way·lay·ing] 1 to lie in wait for and attack; ambush. 2 to wait for and stop (a person) by surprise: *The fans waylaid the actress to ask for her autograph.* —n- way′ lay′ er.

weath·er·ing (wĕth′ ər ing) n- 1 in geology, the physical and chemical process by which surface rock is broken down into fragments by the action of rain, snow, carbon dioxide, and other atmospheric agents. 2 similar process by which any object exposed to the weather undergoes changes in color, texture, or form.

weath·er·man (wĕth′ ər măn′) n- [pl. **weath·er·men**] person who forecasts the weather. 2 person who works for the Weather Bureau.

we'll (wĕl) we shall; we will. *Homs-* weal, wheel.

well-ad·vised (wĕl′ od vīzd′) *adj-* 1 acting with wisdom; judicious; prudent: *She would be well-advised to follow the instructions.* 2 showing careful planning; based upon wise counsel: *a well-advised action.*

well-ap·point·ed (wĕl′ ə poin′ tǝd) *adj-* properly equipped or furnished: *a well-appointed ship.*

well-a·way (wĕl′ ə wā′) or **well-a·day** (wĕl′ ə dā′) *Archaic interj-* exclamation of grief or sorrow; alas.

well-bal·anced (wĕl′ băl′ ǝnst) *adj-* 1 balanced evenly; properly regulated or adjusted: *a well-balanced budget.* 2 having good judgment; sensible; reasonable; sound.

well-be·ing (wĕl′ bē′ ĭng) *n-* general health and happiness; welfare.

well-born (wĕl′ bôrn′) *adj-* 1 born into a good family. 2 in former times, of noble birth.

well-bred (wĕl′ brĕd′) *adj-* 1 having or showing good breeding; of good family; having good manners. 2 of animals, bred of good stock: *a well-bred spaniel.*

well-con·tent (wĕl′ kǝn tĕnt′) *adj-* completely happy or pleased.

well-dis·posed (wĕl′ dĭ spōzd′) *adj-* 1 inclined to be friendly, kind, etc. 2 receptive to an idea, plan, etc.

well-done (wĕl′ dŭn′) *adj-* 1 done with skill and thoroughness. 2 cooked thoroughly, as meat.

well-fa·vored (wĕl′ fā′ vǝrd) *adj-* handsome; pretty.

well-fixed (wĕl′ fĭkst′) *Informal adj-* having lots of money; wealthy.

well-found (wĕl′ found′) *adj-* well equipped or provided; well-appointed: *a well-found ship.*

well-found·ed (wĕl′ foun′ dǝd) *adj-* founded on good reasoning or on facts: *a well-founded suspicion.*

well-groomed (wĕl′ grōomd′) *adj-* 1 carefully dressed; neat and tidy. 2 carefully cared for; curried and combed.

well-ground·ed (wĕl′ groun′ dǝd) *adj-* 1 well instructed in fundamental principles. 2 well-founded.

well-hand·led (wĕl′ hăn′ dǝld) *adj-* managed with capability and efficiency.

well-head (wĕl′ hĕd′) *n-* fountainhead; source.

well-heeled (wĕl′ hēld′) *Informal adj-* having a good amount of money; rich.

well-in·formed (wĕl′ ĭn fôrmd′, -fôrmd′) *adj-* 1 having complete knowledge of one subject. 2 having considerable knowledge of many subjects, especially current events.

well-in·ten·tioned (wĕl′ ĭn tĕn′ shǝnd) *adj-* having good intentions; well-meaning.

well-knit (wĕl′ nĭt′) *adj-* strongly and firmly jointed, constructed, formed, etc.: *a well-knit argument.*

well-known (wĕl′ nōn′) *adj-* generally recognized; widely known; famous: *a well-known actor.*

well-man·nered (wĕl′ măn′ ǝrd) *adj-* having or displaying good manners; polite.

well-mean·ing (wĕl′ mē′ nĭng) *adj-* showing or having good intentions; intending well.

well-nigh (wĕl′ nī′) *adv-* very nearly; almost: *He was well-nigh exhausted.*

well-off (wĕl′ ŏf′, -ôf′) *adj-* in a favorable condition; especially, wealthy; prosperous.

well-or·dered (wĕl′ ôr′ dǝrd, -ôr′ dǝrd) *adj-* arranged or set up so as to run smoothly; carefully ordered.

well-pre·served (wĕl′ prĭ zûrvd′) *adj-* in good condition or having a good appearance in spite of age: *a well-preserved monument; a well-preserved woman.*

well-read (wĕl′ rĕd′) *adj-* having read many books on many subjects; having read much.

well-set (wĕl′ sĕt′) *adj-* 1 properly built; firmly set up. 2 strongly built: *a well-set person.*

well-spo·ken (wĕl′ spō′ kǝn) *adj-* 1 skillfully said. 2 accustomed to speak with accuracy and refinement.

well-spring (wĕl′ sprĭng′) *n-* 1 a flow of water issuing from the earth; spring. 2 source of a never-failing supply: *He is a wellspring of ideas.*

well-thought-of (wĕl′ thŏt′ ǝv, -ŏv′) *adj-* having a good reputation; esteemed.

well-timed (wĕl′ tīmd′) *adj-* done or said at the right time; timely.

well-wish·er (wĕl′ wĭsh′ ǝr) *n-* person who has kind feelings for another person, a cause, etc.

well-worn (wĕl′ wôrn′) *adj-* 1 showing much wear or use: *a well-worn rug.* 2 trite; banal: *a well-worn joke.*

welsh (wĕlsh) *Slang vt-* 1 to cheat by avoiding payment of a bet or other debt (usually followed by "on"). 2 to fail to fulfill an obligation; go back on (usually followed by "on"). Also **welch.** —*n-* **welsh′ er.**

Welsh (wĕlsh) *adj-* of or relating to Wales, its people, or their language. *n-* 1 the language spoken in Wales. 2 the Welsh the people of Wales, collectively.

Welsh·man (wĕlsh′ mǝn) *n-* [*pl.* **Welsh·men**] a native or citizen of Wales. —*n- fem.* **Welsh′ wom′ an.**

Welsh rabbit *n-* a dish of melted, seasoned cheese cooked with milk and ale or beer, served on toast or crackers. Erroneously called **Welsh rarebit.**

Welsh terrier *n-* one of a breed of black-and-tan terriers that resemble Airedales but are smaller. They were developed for hunting in Wales.

welt (wĕlt) *n-* 1 narrow strip of leather joining the sole and upper part of a shoe; also, a strip of cloth stitched to a seam, border, or edge in order to reinforce or trim it. 2 swelling on the skin caused by a blow. *vt-* to secure with a strip of leather or cloth.

wel·ter (wĕl′ tǝr) *vi-* 1 to tumble around or lie soaked in something wet, such as mud or slush; wallow. 2 to rise and fall with violent tossing, as waves do during a storm. *n-* 1 a violent tossing. 2 state of confusion.

wel·ter·weight (wĕl′ tǝr wāt′) *n-* boxer or wrestler whose fighting weight is usually 136 to 147 pounds.

wen (wĕn) *n-* a benign tumor consisting of a cyst filled with fatty secretions from the skin. *Hom-* when.

wench (wĕnch) *n-* 1 girl or young woman (used humorously). 2 *Archaic* young peasant woman; also, a maid.

wend (wĕnd) *vt-* to go or proceed on (one's way): *The caravan wended its way across the desert.*

went (wĕnt) *p.t.* of **go.**

wept (wĕpt) *p.t. & p.p.* of **weep.**

were (wûr) form of **be** used with "you," "we," "they," and plural noun subjects in the past tense. *Hom-* whir. **as it were** as if it were so; so to speak.

whip·cord (hwĭp′ kôrd′, -kôrd′) *n-* 1 sturdy, tightly twisted cord, often used for whiplashes. 2 cord of catgut. 3 closely woven worsted fabric with diagonal ribs.

whip graft *n-* type of plant graft made by fitting part of a twig to a slit that has been cut in the stock.

whip hand *n-* the hand that holds the whip in riding or driving; hence, advantage; control.

whip·lash (hwĭp′ lăsh′) *n-* 1 the striking part, or lash, of a whip. 2 injury of the spinal cord in the area of the neck and lower part of the brain, caused by a violent snapping, as in an automobile collision.

whipped cream *n-* cream beaten into a froth.

whip·per·snap·per (hwĭp′ ǝr snăp′ ǝr) *n-* insolent and arrogant person, especially a young person.

whip·pet (hwĭp′ ǝt) *n-* small, fleet dog resembling a greyhound, used especially for racing.

whip·ping (hwĭp′ ĭng) *n-* 1 a beating. 2 a cord binding at the end of a rope.

whipping boy *n-* formerly, a person who served as companion to a nobleman and was punished for the latter's misdeeds; hence, anyone blamed for another.

whip·saw (hwĭp′ sô′) *n-* narrow, tapering saw about six feet long, set in a frame and operated by one or two persons. *vt-* [whip·sawed, whip·sawed or whip·sawn, whip·saw·ing]: *to* whipsaw *wood.*

whir (hwûr) *vi-* [whirred, whir·ring] to revolve or move rapidly with a whizzing or buzzing sound: *The helicopter* whirred. *n-* such a sound. Also, *Brit.,* **whirr.** *Hom-* were.

whirl (hwûrl) *vi-* 1 to turn around and around rapidly; spin. 2 to move swiftly: *She* whirled *angrily out of the room. vt-* to give a spinning motion to: *The wind* whirled *people's hats away. n-* 1 spinning movement: *the whirl of a falling leaf.* 2 bewilderment; confusion of mind. 3 hectic, bustling activity. *Hom-* whorl. —*n-* **whirl′ er.**

whirl·i·gig (hwûr′ lǝ gĭg′) *n-* 1 child's toy that spins or whirls. 2 merry-go-round. 3 anything that turns or whirls around rapidly; also, a whirling motion.

whirl·pool (hwûrl′ pōol′) *n-* swift, circling current of water, with a central depression into which floating objects are drawn; vortex.

wild-eyed (wīld′īd′) *adj-* staring wildly, as if from fear, anger, or other intense emotion: *a wild-eyed mob.*

wild·fire (wīld′ fīr′) *n-* fire that spreads very rapidly and is difficult to extinguish.

wild flower *n-* 1 the flower of any uncultivated plant found in fields, woods, etc. 2 the plant itself.

wild fowl *n-* wild birds hunted as game, such as wild geese and ducks, partridges, pheasants, and quail.

wild-goose chase (wīld′ gōōs′) *n-* useless pursuit or fruitless attempt.

wild·ing (wīl′dĭng) *n-* wild plant or its fruit; especially, a wild apple or crab apple. *as modifier: a wilding tree.*

wild·life (wīld′ līf′) *n-* wild living things; especially, wild animals. *as modifier: a wildlife preserve.*

wild oat *n-* a tall grass that grows like a weed in fields and resembles the cultivated oat.

  sow (one's) wild oats to do foolish or socially unacceptable things as a youth, before settling down.

wild pitch *n-* in baseball, an error charged against the pitcher when he throws a ball that the catcher cannot reach, and allows one or more base runners to advance.

wild rice *n-* the grain of a North American water grass, regarded as superior to rice and served as a delicacy.

Wild West *n-* western United States in the late 19th century, the land of cowboys and Indians. This period and its adventures were formerly celebrated in the traveling **Wild West show**, a spectacle like a circus.

wild·wood (wīld′ wōōd′) *n-* forest in its natural state. *as modifier: a wildwood scene; wildwood flower.*

wile (wīl) *n-* clever or crafty trick or words, intended to deceive or lure: *She used her wiles to get him to do as she wanted. vt-* [**wiled, wil·ing**] to obtain by trickery: *She wiled the secret from him. Hom-* while.

wil·i·ness (wī′ lē nəs) *n-* craftiness; slyness; foxiness.

wood alcohol *n-* methyl alcohol.

wood·bine (wōōd′ bīn′) *n-* any of several climbing vines, such as the Virginia creeper or a European plant related to the honeysuckle.

wood·block (wōōd′ blŏk′) *n-* 1 solid block of wood, especially one in which letters or designs are carved to produce an engraving. 2 a print, illustration, etc., made from this. *as modifier: a woodblock engraving.*

wood·carv·ing (wōōd′ kär′ vĭng) *n-* 1 art or process of carving in wood. 2 a carving made in wood. —*n-* wood′ carv′ er.

wood·chuck (wōōd′ chŭk′) *n-* chunky, brown or grayish burrowing animal related to the squirrels and found in eastern North America; ground hog; marmot.

wood·cock (wōōd′ kŏk′) *n-* chunky, brown, short-legged game bird with a very long, pointed bill and a short, stubby tail.

wood·craft (wōōd′ krăft′) *n-* 1 skill and knowledge in anything pertaining to the woods, such as camping, hunting, forestry, etc. 2 skill in woodwork or in carving and making objects from wood.

Woodchuck.
16 – 18 in long

wood·cut (wōōd′ kŭt′) *n-* 1 block of wood for printing designs or illustrations, in which the parts that will not print are cut away from the surface. 2 a print or illustration made from this. *as modifier: a woodcut print.* See also **wood engraving.**

wood·cut·ter (wōōd′ kŭt′ ər) *n-* person who cuts wood or fells trees. —*n-* wood′ cut′ ting.

wood·ed (wōōd′ əd) *adj-* having many trees.

wood·en (wōōd′ ən) *adj-* 1 made of wood: *a wooden bucket.* 2 stiff; awkward: *the wooden gestures of a bad actor.* 3 lacking spirit or warmth; dull: *a wooden smile.* —*adv-* wood′ en·ly. *n-* wood′ en·ness.

wood engraving *n-* 1 block of wood for printing illustrations, in which an engraving of fine lines and tones is cut into the end grain with a graver. 2 illustration made from this. 3 the art of making such blocks or illustrations. See also **woodcut.** —*n-* wood engraver.

wood lot *n-* 1 piece of land having a stand of trees that are cut for firewood or other uses. 2 tree farm.

wool·en (wōōl′ ən) *adj-* 1 made of wool. 2 of or having to do with wool or things made of wool: *the woolen trade. n-* **woolens** fabrics or garments made of wool.

wool·gath·er (wōōl′ găth′ ər) *vi-* to indulge in idle dreaming. —*n-* wool′ gath′ er·er.

wool·ly (wōōl′ ē) *adj-* [**wool·li·er, wool·li·est**] 1 consisting of or resembling wool: *a woolly fabric.* 2 covered with wool or a similar fuzzy material: *a woolly lamb; a woolly toy.* 3 not clear; confused; vague: *a woolly mind. n-* (usually **woollies**) clothing, especially underwear, made of wool. Also **wool′ y.** —*n-* wool′ li·ness.

  wild and woolly resembling the early frontier life of western United States; rough and uncivilized.

woolly bear *n-* fuzzy, black-and-brown caterpillar of the tiger moth.

wool·pack (wōōl′ păk′) *n-* bale or bundle of wool enclosed in a wrapper of canvas, burlap, etc.; also, the wrapper itself.

woo·zy (wōō′ zē, wōōz′ ē) *Informal adj-* [**woo·zi·er, woo·zi·est**] dazed and confused; dizzy; befuddled. —*adv-* woo′ zi·ly. *n-* woo′ zi·ness.

Worces·ter·shire sauce (wōōs′ tər shər) *n-* spicy sauce containing soy, vinegar, etc., originally made in Worcester, England, and used especially with meats.

word (wûrd) *n-* 1 a sound or a combination of sounds meaning a certain thing, feeling, idea, etc., and forming a grammatical part of speech. 2 written or printed representation of such a sound. 3 a brief expression; remark: *a word of warning.* 4 promise; guarantee. 5 news; information. 6 command; order: *the word to go ahead.* 7 password; slogan: *Let the word be: "On they come."* 8 **words** (1) talk; conversation: *He is not given to words.* (2) language used in anger or reproach: *They had words yesterday.* 9 **the Word** (1) Christ considered as the expression of the Divine Intelligence and as the mediator between God and men. (2) the Scriptures. *vt-* to say or write with words: *to word a message.*

  be as good as (one's) word to keep (one's) word or promise. **break (one's) word** to fail to keep (one's) word or promise. **by word of mouth** by speech, not by writing; orally. **eat (one's) words** to take back something (one) has said. **have a word with** to have a brief talk with. **have words with** to argue angrily with. **in a word** briefly; in short. **in so many words** precisely and plainly; exactly. **man of his word** person who keeps his word or promise. **take a person at his word** to take a person's words literally and deal with him accordingly. **take the words out of (one's) mouth** to say what (one) was just about to say (oneself). **word for word** entirely, and in the very words: *to repeat a message word for word.*

writ·ing (rī′ tĭng) *n-* 1 anything that is written, such as a letter, document, manuscript, or inscription. 2 handwriting; penmanship: *He couldn't make out her writing.* 3 manner of expressing oneself in writing; literary style: *His writing is crisp and concise.* 4 occupation of a writer or author: *He chose writing as a career.* 5 **writings** novels, plays, or other literary works: *the writings of Mark Twain.*

writ·ten (rĭt′ ən) *p.p.* of **write.** *adj-* 1 produced by writing. 2 clearly seen, as if displayed by writing: *Grief is written on his face.*

wrong (rŏng) *adj-* 1 not morally right or just; wicked; unlawful. 2 not according to fact; incorrect: *The answer is wrong.* 3 out of order; amiss: *The clock is wrong.* 4 not according to the rules: *the wrong way to handle a machine.* 5 unsuitable; inappropriate: *the wrong bolt; the wrong thing to say.* 6 not meant to be showing, arranged, or located in this way: *The glove is wrong side out. The tube is wrong end up. n-* 1 that which is contrary to moral right, fact, principles, etc.; evil; injury; crime: *to know right from wrong.* 2 an act of injustice; pain unjustly inflicted: *to suffer wrongs. adv-* in a wrong manner, direction, position, etc: *You've got it all wrong. vt-* to treat unjustly; harm; violate the rights of: *He wronged his neighbor by making an unjust accusation.* —*adv-* wrong′ ly. *n-* wrong′ ness.

  go wrong 1 to turn out badly. 2 to go astray morally; turn out badly. **in the wrong** mistaken; guilty.

X

X, x (ĕks) [*pl.* **X's, x's**] **1** the 24th letter of the English alphabet. **2** Roman numeral for ten. **3** sign used in multiplication. **4** symbol used to represent an unknown quantity, factor, etc. **5** mark used in diagrams, maps, and charts to point out something. **6** symbol used in letters and notes to indicate a kiss.

x-axis (ĕks′ ăk′ sɐs) *Mathematics* **n-** the horizontal (or first) axis in a Cartesian co-ordinate system. For picture, see *abscissa*.

X chromosome See *sex chromosome*.

xe·bec (zē′ bĕk′) **n-** three-masted sailing ship with long overhanging bow and stern, formerly used by pirates.

xe·non (zē′ nŏn′) **n-** heavy, colorless, inert gaseous element that is present in the air in minute quantities. Symbol Xe, At. No. 54, At. Wt. 131.3.

xen·o·phobe (zĕn′ ə fōb′) **n-** person with xenophobia.

xen·o·pho·bi·a (zĕn′ ə fō′ bē ə) **n-** fear or hatred of foreigners or strangers.

xe·ro·phyte (zēr′ ə fīt′) **n-** any of various desert plants, such as the cactus, sagebrush, yucca, and agave, that store up water or give off very little to the air. **—adj-** xe′ ro·phyt′ ic (-fĭt′ ĭk).

Xmas (krĭs′ məs) Christmas.

X ray n- 1 electromagnetic radiation of high penetrating power and extremely short wavelength, ranging from about a hundredth of an angstrom to about 10 angstroms. X rays are produced by bombarding a substance with high-velocity electrons, and are used to photograph the interior of objects opaque to visible light. **2** instrument that produces such rays. **3** photograph made by such rays. *as modifier* (X-ray): *an* X-ray *examination.* *vt-* (X-ray): *The doctor* X-rayed *my chest.*

xy·lem (zī′ ləm) **n-** in botany, one of the inner, fleshy tissues that conduct water in most plants.

Xylophone

xy·lo·phone (zī′ lə fōn′) **n-** musical instrument made of strips of wood that give off different tones when struck with wooden hammers.

Y

Y, y (wī) [*pl.* **Y's, y's**] the 25th letter of the English alphabet.

Y symbol for yttrium.

¹-y *suffix* (used to form adjectives) **1** having; full of: *a dirty floor.* **2** inclined to; tending to: *a sleepy child; a rainy day.* **3** somewhat; rather: *a chilly morning; a salty cracker.* [from Middle English -y and -ie.]

²-y *suffix* (used to form nouns) quality or condition: *honesty; victory.* [from Middle English -ie, from Old English -ig.]

³-y *suffix* (used to form nouns) **1** small; tiny: *sonny.* **2** endearing or familiar name or term: *Daddy; aunty.* [from Old French -ie, from Latin -ia.]

y. **1** yard. **2** year.

yacht (yŏt) **n-** any of various sailing or engine-driven vessels for pleasure cruises or racing. *as modifier:* a yacht *race.*

yacht·ing (yŏt′ ĭng) **n-** the sport or practice of sailing or racing in a yacht.

yachts·man (yŏts′ mən) **n-** [*pl.* **yachts·men**] person who owns or sails a yacht.

Ya·hoo (yä′ hōō′, yä-) **n-** in Swift's "Gulliver's Travels," any of the nasty creatures having the form and vices of man.

¹yak (yăk) **n-** long-haired ox of Central Asia and Tibet, often domesticated and used as a beast of burden. [from Tibetan *ghyag*.]

Yak, about 6 ft. high at shoulder

²yak (yăk) *Slang* **vi-** [**yakked, yak·king**] **1** to chatter noisily or incessantly. **2** to laugh boisterously. [from an imitation of the sound used chiefly in comic strips.]

yam (yăm) **n- 1** any of various climbing tropical plants with a fleshy, starchy, edible root; also, the root of any of these plants. **2** kind of sweet potato.

yank (yăngk) *Informal* **vt-** to pull with a sudden, quick movement; jerk: *to yank a coat from a hook.* **vi-** *He* yanked *at the rope.* **n-:** *She gave the yarn a* yank.

Yank (yăngk) *Informal* **n-** Yankee.

Yan·kee (yăng′ kē) **n- 1** person who is a native of the New England States. **2** native of the United States, especially of a northern State. **3** Union soldier in the Civil War.

Yankee Doodle n- humorous song popular during the American Revolution and still one of the national airs of the United States.

yap (yăp) **n- 1** a sharp, shrill bark. **2** *Slang* the mouth. **vi-** [**yapped, yap·ping**] **1** to bark sharply; yelp. **2** *Slang* to talk noisily or foolishly; jabber.

Ya·qui (yä′ kē) **n-** [*pl.* **Ya·quis,** also **Ya·qui**] **1** member of an Indian people of northern Mexico. **2** the language of these people. **adj-:** *a* Yaqui *custom.*

¹yard (yärd) **n- 1** standard measure of length, equal to 3 feet or 36 inches. **2** one of the crosspieces on a ship's mast used to support sails. [from Old English *gerd* meaning "rod; measure."]

Yards

²yard (yärd) **n- 1** enclosed or partially enclosed space adjoining a house, barn, school, or other building. **2** space, usually partly enclosed, used for some special work or occupation: *railway* yard; *lumber* yard; *navy* yard. *as modifier:* a yard *boss.* [from Old English *geard*.]

yard·age (yär′ dĭj) **n-** amount as measured in yards: *the* yardage *gained by a football team.*

yard·arm (yärd′ ärm′) **n-** either side of a yard that supports a square sail.

yard·man (yärd′ mən) **n-** [*pl.* **yard·men**] man who works in a railroad or lumber yard.

yard·mas·ter (yärd′ măs′ tər) **n-** official in charge of a railroad yard.

yard·stick (yärd′ stĭk′) **n- 1** flat stick a yard long, used for measuring. **2** any standard used for measuring or comparing: *Honesty is a yardstick of a man's worth.*

yar·mul·ke (yä′ məl kə) **n-** skullcap worn by Jewish men in the synagogue, and by some Orthodox Jews at all times.

yarn (yärn) **n- 1** spun thread, especially a heavy woolen thread for knitting or crocheting. **2** *Informal* exaggerated tale or story: *a sailor's* yarns.

yar·row (yăr′ ō) **n-** strongly scented plant with clusters of small white flowers and finely divided leaves.

yaw (yò) **vi- 1** of a ship, to turn unintentionally from a steady course; veer. **2** of an airplane or projectile, to swing to the right or left along a flight path. **n-** any of such, or similar, movements; also, the amount of such a movement.

yawl (yòl) **n- 1** sailboat with the mainmast well forward and a smaller mast far aft. For picture, see *sailboat.* **2** ship's small boat, usually rowed by four or six men.

yawn (yòn, yŏn) **vi- 1** to open the mouth wide with a deep breath because of sleepiness, fatigue, or boredom. **2** to be wide open; gape: *The chasm* yawned *below.* **vt-** to utter with a yawn: *He* yawned *his reply.* **n-:** *The young boy's* yawns *told us he was growing very sleepy.* **Hom-** yon.

yaws (yòz) **n-** *pl.* contagious skin disease of certain tropical regions.

y-axis (wī′ ăk′ səs) *Mathematics* *n-* the vertical (or second) axis in a Cartesian co-ordinate system. For picture, see *abscissa*.

Yb symbol for ytterbium.

Y chromosome See *sex chromosome*.

y·clept or **y·cleped** (ē klĕpt′) *Archaic adj-* called; named.

yd. yard.

¹ye (yē) *pron-* old, poetic, or religious form of **you** (used always as a subject). [from Old English **gē**.]

²ye (thə, *also* yē) archaic spelling of **the**. [from the runic character **þ** for "th." Early printers misread the character as "y."]

yea (yā) *adv- Archaic* **1** yes. **2** indeed; truly. *n-* affirmative reply or vote: *The yeas outnumbered the nays.*

year (yēr) *n-* **1** length of time it takes the earth to revolve once around the sun, equal to 12 months, or 365 days, 5 hours, 48 minutes, and 46 seconds. **2** period of twelve consecutive months starting at any time: *within a year.* **3** period of time, usually less than a year, spent in some particular activity: *the school year.* **4 years** (1) age: *Mr. Jones is on in years.* (2) time; especially, a long time: *That happened years ago.*

year after year every year. **year by year** with each succeeding year; each year. **year in, year out** from one year to the next; always; continuously.

year·book (yēr′ book′) *n-* **1** book published annually, giving information about the previous year. **2** school publication containing photographs of, and information about, a graduating class.

year·ling (yēr′ ling) *n-* animal between one and two years old. *as modifier:* *a yearling colt.*

year·long (yēr′ lông′) *adj-* lasting or continuing for a full year: *a yearlong religious observance.*

year·ly (yēr′ lē) *adj-* **1** once a year or every year; annual: *a yearly vacation.* **2** for a year; annual: *a yearly salary.* *adv-* once a year; annually: *a celebration that occurs yearly.*

yearn (yûrn) *vi-* **1** to feel a deep desire or longing; pine: *to yearn for home.* **2** to be filled with pity or compassion; have sympathy: *to yearn for the oppressed.*

yearn·ing (yûr′ nĭng) *n-* deep, tender desire; longing: *a yearning for one's country.* **—adv-** yearn′ ing·ly.

yeast (yēst) *n-* any of various fungi that ferment sugars into ethyl alcohol and carbon dioxide. Yeast is used in making beer and wine and in raising bread.

yeast cake *n-* yeast mixed with starch and pressed into a small cake, used in brewing and baking.

yeast·y (yēs′ tē) *adj-* [yeast·i·er, yeast·i·est] **1** of, resembling, or containing yeast. **2** frothy; foamy: *the yeasty scum on the waves.* **3** filled with change, growth, or ferment: *the yeasty years of his boyhood.*

yegg (yĕg) *Slang n-* burglar or safe cracker.

yell (yĕl) *n-* **1** a sharp, loud cry, as of pain, rage, or terror; shriek. **2** shout or cheer by a crowd, as at a school game. *vi-:* *He yelled in pain.* *vt-:* *I yelled a command.*

yel·low (yĕl′ ō) *n-* **1** the color of lemons, sunflowers, and buttercups. Yellow is between orange and green in the spectrum. **2** something, or a part of something, that has this color, especially the yolk of an egg. *adj-* [yel·low·er, yel·low·est] **1** having this color: *a yellow sash.* **2** cowardly; dishonorable: *The boy has a yellow streak.* **3** concerned with scandal and other sensationalism rather than fact: *a yellow newspaper.* *vt-:* *Time yellowed the pages.* *vi-:* *The books yellowed with age.* **—n-** yel′ low·ness.

yel·low·bird (yĕl′ ō bûrd′) *n-* any of various yellow birds, such as the American goldfinch or yellow warbler.

yellow daisy *n-* the black-eyed Susan.

yellow fever *n-* acute virus disease of tropical regions, transmitted by the bite of an infected mosquito and marked by fever, chills, stomach pains, and jaundice.

yel·low·ham·mer (yĕl′ ō hăm′ ər) *n-* **1** the flicker, a woodpecker of North America. **2** European finch, the male of which has bright-yellow markings.

yel·low·ish (yĕl′ ō ĭsh) *adj-* somewhat yellow.

yellow jacket *n-* any of several small American wasps having bright yellow markings.

yellow pine *n-* **1** any of various American pines having a hard, yellowish wood; especially, a pine found in the South and valued as a source of turpentine. **2** the wood of any of these pines.

yel·low·throat (yĕl′ ō thrōt′) *n-* any of various American warblers.

yellow warbler *n-* small, bright-yellow warbler of the southern United States.

yelp (yĕlp) *n-* a sharp bark or cry, especially in pain: *the yelp of a hurt puppy.* *vi-:* *The dog yelped when the cat bit it.*

¹yen (yĕn) *n-* basic unit of money in Japan. [from Japanese, from Chinese **yuan** meaning "round; a dollar."]

²yen (yĕn) *Informal n-* deep desire or longing. [American word of uncertain origin.]

yeo·man (yō′ mən) *n-* [*pl.* **yeo·men**] **1** in the Navy and Coast Guard, a petty officer who does clerical duty. **2** in England, a small farmer who owns his own land. **3 Yeoman of the Guard** member of the bodyguard of the British royal family.

yeo·man·ry (yō′ mən rē) *n-* **1** yeomen of England collectively. **2** in Great Britain, formerly a volunteer cavalry force, now part of the territorial army.

yeoman's service *n-* exceptionally good or loyal service or support.

yes (yĕs) *adv-* **1** expression of affirmation, agreement, or assent; opposite of "no": *Are you coming? Yes, I am. Come here at once! Yes, sir. Yes, that's the man.* **2** more than that; even more: *It is very cold, yes, freezing.* *n-* [*pl.* **yes·es** or **yes·ses**] **1** reply in the affirmative: *Answer with a simple "yes" or "no."* **2** affirmative vote or voter: *The yeses win the vote.*

ye·shi·vah (yə shē′ və) *n-* **1** seminary for the training of Orthodox rabbis. **2** Jewish parochial school. **3** school for Talmudic study. Also **ye·shi′ va.**

yes·man (yĕs′ măn^) *Informal n-* [*pl.* **yes·men**] person who agrees with every opinion or proposal of a superior without criticism; toady.

yester- *prefix* any time before the present day: *yesterday; yesteryear.*

yes·ter·day (yĕs′ tər dē, -dā) *n-* **1** day before today. *He has been with us since yesterday.* **2** recent past: *the fashions of yesterday.* *adv-* **1** on the day before today: *We finished painting the house yesterday.* **2** recently: *Janey was in pigtails only yesterday.*

yes·ter·year (yĕs′ tər yēr′) *n-* **1** last year. **2** the recent past: *the heroes of yesteryear.*

yet (yĕt) *adv-* **1** up to this time; up to a particular time: *Nothing has happened yet.* **2** now; at the present time: *You can't leave yet.* **3** still; as before: *There is yet a faint chance.* **4** at some future time; eventually: *Henry may yet learn to ride a bicycle.* **5** in addition; besides: *There is much work yet to be done.* **6** after the long amount of time that has passed: *Haven't you finished*

you're (yŏŏr, yŏr) you are. *Homs-* yore, your.

yours (yŏŏrz, yŏrz) *pron-* (possessive pronoun) thing or things belonging to you: *Is this yours? That is no business of yours.*

your·self (yŏŏr′ sĕlf′, yŏr′-, yər-) *pron-* [*pl.* **your·selves** (-sĕlvz′)] **1** (reflexive form of **you**) your own self: *You are fooling yourself.* **2** your normal or true self: *You are not yourself when angry.* **3** intensive form of **you:** *You yourself should go to see him.*

yours truly formal phrase used before the signature in closing a letter. *pron- Informal* I or me.

youth (yŏŏth) *n-* [*pl.* **youths** (yŏŏths, yŏŏthz)] **1** a being young: *the energy of youth.* **2** period between childhood and maturity. **3** early stage in the growth or development of anything: *in our country's youth.* **4** young man. **5** young people: *the youth of a nation.*

youth·ful (yŏŏth′ fəl) *adj-* **1** young; not old. **2** of or like a young person; fresh or vigorous: *his youthful spirit; the new, youthful styles.* **—adv-** youth′ ful·ly. *n-* youth′ ful·ness.

Yo·yo (yō′ yō′) *n-* trademark name for a toy, consisting of a grooved disk attached to one end of a string upon which it can be made to spin up and down.

Y.P.S.C.E. Young People's Society of Christian Endeavor.

Z

Z, z (zē) [*pl.* **Z's, z's**] the 26th letter of the English alphabet.

Zach·a·ri·ah (zăk′ ə rī′ ə) *n-* the father of St. John the Baptist. In the CCD Bible, **Zach′ a·rī′ a.**

za·ny (zā′ nē) *n-* [*pl.* **za·nies**] in old comedies, a clown or acrobat who mimicked the principal actors; hence, a stupid person; fool. *adj-* [**za·ni·er, za·ni·est**] comical in a crazy, outlandish way; ludicrous: *the zany antics of a circus clown.*

Za·po·tec (zăp′ ə tĕk′) *n-* [*pl.* **Za·po·tecs,** also **Za·po·tec**] 1 member of an Indian people of southern Mexico. 2 the language of these people. —*adj-* **Za′ po·tec′ an.**

zeal (zēl) *n-* eagerness; enthusiasm; earnestness: *patriotic zeal; his zeal for work.*

zeal·ot (zĕl′ ət) *n-* person of too great zeal; fanatic: *He is a zealot who can tolerate no religion but his own.*

zeal·ot·ry (zĕl′ ə trē) *n-* excessive zeal; fanaticism.

zeal·ous (zĕl′ əs) *adj-* eager; enthusiastic: *Nathan Hale was a zealous patriot.* —*adv-* **zeal′ ous·ly.** *n-* **zeal′ ous·ness.**

Zebra. 4–5 ft high at shoulder

ze·bra (zē′ brə) *n-* wild African animal of the horse family, marked with black and white stripes.

ze·bu (zē′ byōō′, -bōō′) *n-* domesticated ox of Asia and East Africa, having a large hump on its shoulders.

zed (zĕd) *Brit. n-* the letter Z or z.

Zen Buddhism (zĕn) *n-* form of Japanese Buddhism introduced in the 12th century from China, that seeks truth

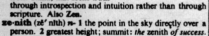

Zebu

through introspection and intuition rather than through scripture. Also **Zen.**

ze·nith (zē′ nĭth) *n-* 1 the point in the sky directly over a person. 2 greatest height; summit: *the zenith of success.*

zo·ol·o·gist (zō ŏl′ ə jĭst) *n-* person trained or skilled in the science of zoology and engaged in it as a profession.

zo·ol·o·gy (zō ŏl′ ə jē) *n-* 1 the scientific study of animal life. 2 the animal life of a region; fauna. *as modifier:* *a zoology textbook.*

zoom (zōōm) *vi-* 1 to make, or move with, a humming or buzzing sound: *The car zoomed past me.* 2 to take a sudden upward course in an airplane. *vt-* to cause (an airplane) to take a sudden upward course.

zoom lens *n-* in photography and television, a lens that permits continuous changes in focal length and image size without losing focus.

zo·o·phyte (zō′ ə fīt′) *n-* marine animal, such as a sea anenome or coral, that resembles a plant in appearance or manner of growth.

Zo·ro·as·tri·an (zôr′ ō ăs′ trē ən) *n-* disciple of Zoroaster or follower of Zoroastrianism. *adj-:* *the Zoroastrian doctrines.*

Zo·ro·as·tri·an·ism (zôr′ ō ăs′ trē ə nĭz′ əm) *n-* the religious system founded by Zoroaster in Persia around 1000 B.C., based on the belief that there are two creative powers, good and evil, and that the good would triumph over evil in life after death.

Zou·ave (zōō äv′, zwäv) *n-* 1 member of certain French infantry regiments, originally made up of Algerians known for their bravery and colorful uniforms. 2 in the Civil War, a member of a Union volunteer regiment that imitated the dress of the French Zouaves.

zounds (zoundz) *Archaic interj-* mild oath, meaning "God's wounds."

Zr symbol for zirconium.

zuc·chi·ni (zōō kē′ nē) *n-* type of green summer squash, shaped like a cucumber.

Zu·lu (zōō′ lōō) *n-* [*pl.* **Zu·lus** or **Zu·lu**] 1 member of a south African Bantu people. 2 the language spoken by these people. *adj-:* *Most Zulu villages are laid out in circles.*

Zu·ñi (zōō′ nyē; zōōn′ ē) *n-* [*pl.* **Zu·ñis** or **Zu·ñi**] 1 one of a tribe of pueblo-dwelling Indians who are still living in New Mexico. 2 the language of these people. *adj-:* *handsome Zuñi silver jewelry.*

WEIGHTS AND MEASURES

APOTHECARIES' WEIGHT

20 grains	1 scruple
3 scruples	1 dram
8 drams	1 ounce
12 ounces	1 pound

Ounce and pound are the same as in Troy Weight.

AVOIRDUPOIS WEIGHT

27 11/32 grains	1 dram
16 drams	1 ounce
16 ounces	1 pound
25 pounds	1 quarter
4 quarters	1 cwt.
2,000 pounds	1 short ton
2,240 pounds	1 long ton

TROY WEIGHT

24 grains	1 pwt.
20 pwt.	1 ounce
12 ounces	1 pound

Used for weighing gold, silver and jewels.

CLOTH MEASURE

2¼ inches	1 nail
4 nails	1 quarter
4 quarters	1 yard

CUBIC MEASURE

1,728 cubic inches	1 cubic foot
27 cubic feet	1 cubic yard
128 cubic feet	1 cord (wood)
40 cubic feet	1 ton (shipping)
2,150.42 cubic inches	1 standard bu.
231 cubic inches	1 U. S. standard gal.
1 cubic foot	about 4/5 of a bushel

DRY MEASURE

2 pints	1 quart
8 quarts	1 peck
4 pecks	1 bushel
36 bushels	1 chaldron

LIQUID MEASURE

4 gills	1 pint
2 pints	1 quart
4 quarts	1 gallon
31½ gallons	1 barrel
2 barrels	1 hogshead

LONG MEASURE

12 inches	1 foot
3 feet	1 yard
5½ yards	1 rod
40 rods	1 furlong
8 furlongs	1 sta. mile
3 miles	1 league

MARINERS' MEASURE

6 feet	1 fathom
120 fathoms	1 cable length

7½ cable lengths	1 mile
5,280 feet	1 statute mile
6,080.2 feet	1 nautical mile

SQUARE MEASURE

144 sq. inches	1 sq. ft.
9 sq. ft.	1 sq. yard
30¼ sq. yards	1 sq. rod
40 sq. rods	1 rood
4 roods	1 acre
640 acres	1 sq. mile

SURVEYORS' MEASURE

7.92 inches	1 link
25 links	1 rod
4 rods	1 chain
10 sq. chains or 160 sq. rods	1 acre
640 acres	1 sq. mile
36 sq. miles (6 miles sq.)	1 township

TIME MEASURE

60 seconds	1 minute
60 minutes	1 hour
24 hours	1 day
7 days	1 week
28, 29, 30 or 31 days	1 cal. month
30 days	1 month .. in comp. interest
365 days	1 year .. 366 days 1 lp. yr.

MISCELLANEOUS

3 inches	1 palm
4 inches	1 hand
6 inches	1 span
18 inches	1 cubit
21.8 inches	1 Bible cubit
2½ feet	1 military pace

METRIC EQUIVALENTS

Linear Measure

1 centimeter	0.3937 inches
1 inch	2.54 centimeters
1 decimeter	3.937 in.... 0.328 foot
1 foot	3.048 decimeters
1 meter	39.37 inches ... 1.0936 yds.
1 yard	0.9144 meter
1 dekameter	1.9884 rods
1 rod	0.5029 dekameter
1 kilometer	0.621 mile
1 mile	1.609 kilometers

Square Measure

1 square centimeter	0.1550 sq. inches
1 square inch	6.452 square centimeters
1 square decimeter	0.1076 square foot
1 square foot	9.2903 square dec.
1 square meter	1.196 square yds.
1 square yard	0.8361 square meter
1 acre	160 square rods
1 square rod	0.00625 acre

WEIGHTS AND MEASURES

1 hectare ....2.47 acres
1 acre ....0.4047 hectare
1 square kilometer ....0.386 sq. mile
1 square mile ....2.59 sq. kilometers

Measure of Volume

1 cubic centimeter ....0.061 cu. inch.
1 cubic inch ....16.39 cubic cent.
1 cubic decimeter ....0.0353 cubic foot
1 cubic foot ....28.317 cubic dec.
1 cubic meter ....1.308 cubic yards
1 cubic yard ....0.7646 cubic meter
1 stere ....0.2759 cord
1 cord ....3.624 steres
1 liter ....0.908 qt. dry ...1.0567 qts. liq.
1 quart dry ....1.101 liters
1 quart liquid ....0.9463 liter
1 dekaliter ....2.6417 gals.... 1.135 pecks
1 gallon ....0.3785 dekaliter
1 peck ....0.881 dekaliter
1 hektoliter ....2.8375 bushels
1 bushel ....0.3524 hektoliter

Weights

1 gram ....0.03527 ounce
1 ounce ....28.35 grams
1 kilogram ....2.2046 pounds
1 pound ....0.4536 kilogram
1 metric ton ....0.98421 English ton
1 English ton ....1.016 metric ton

APPROXIMATE METRIC EQUIVALENTS

1 decimeter :.......................4 inches
1 liter ....1.06 quarts liquid, 0.9 qt. dry
1 meter ....1.1 yards
1 kilometer ....⅝ of a mile
1 hektoliter ....2⅝ bushels
1 hectare ....2½ acres
1 kilogram ....2 1/5 pounds
1 stere, or cubic meter .. ..¼ of a cord
1 metric ton .... 2,204.6 pounds

TEMPERATURES

	Fahrenheit
Milk	Freezes 30° above Zero
Water	Freezes 32° above Zero
Olive Oil	Freezes 36° above Zero
Wines	Freeze 20° above Zero
Vinegar	Freezes 28° above Zero
Alcohol	Boils at 173° above Zero
Water	Boils at 212° above Zero
Petrol. (av.)	Boils at 306° above Zero
Blood Heat	98.4° above Zero
Eggs Hatch	104° above Zero

To find diameter of a circle multiply circumference by .31831.

To find circumference of a circle multiply diameter by 3.1416.

To find area of a circle multiply square of diameter by .7854.

To find surface of a ball multiply square of diameter by 3.1416.

To find side of an equal square multiply diameter by .8862.

To find cubic inches in a ball multiply cube of diameter by .5236.

Doubling the diameter of a pipe increases its capacity four times.

Double riveting is from 16 to 20% stronger than single.

One cubic foot of anthracite coal weighs about 58 lbs.

One cubic foot of bituminous coal weighs from 47 to 50 lbs.

One ton of coal is equivalent to two cords of wood for steam purposes.

There are nine square feet of heating surface to each square foot of grate surface.

Each nominal horse power boiler requires 30 to 35 pounds of water per hour.

To sharpen dull files lay them in diluted sulphuric acid until they are eaten deep enough.

A horse power is equivalent to raising 33,000 pounds one foot per minute or 550 pounds one foot per second.

The average consumption of coal for steam boilers is 12 pounds per hour for each sq. foot of grate surface.

To find the pressure in pounds per square inch of a column of water multiply the height of the column in feet by .434.

Steam rising from water at its boiling point (212 degrees) has a pressure equal to the atmosphere (14.7 pounds to the square inch).

DECIMAL EQUIVALENTS

Drill	Equivalent	Drill	Equivalent	Drill	Equivalent	Drill	Equivalent	Drill	Equivalent
1/16	.0625	53/64	.8281	1 19/32	1.5938	2 23/64	2.3594	3 1/4	3.2500
5/64	.07813	27/32	.8438	1 39/64	1.6094	2 3/8	2.3750	3 9/32	3.2813
3/32	.09375	55/64	.8594	1 5/8	1.6250	2 25/64	2.3906	3 5/16	3.3125
7/64	.10938	7/8	.8750	1 41/64	1.6406	2 13/32	2.4063	3 11/32	3.3438
1/8	.125	57/64	.8906	1 21/32	1.6563	2 27/64	2.4219	3 3/8	3.3750
9/64	.14063	29/32	.9063	1 43/64	1.6719	2 7/16	2.4375	3 13/32	3.4063
5/32	.15625	59/64	.9219	1 11/16	1.6875	2 29/64	2.4531	3 7/16	3.4375
11/64	.17188	15/16	.9375	1 45/64	1.7031	2 15/32	2.4688	3 15/32	3.4688
3/16	.1875	61/64	.9531	1 23/32	1.7188	2 31/64	2.4844	3 1/2	3.5000
13/64	.20313	31/32	.9688	1 47/64	1.7344	2 1/2	2.5000	3 17/32	3.5313
7/32	.21875	63/64	.9844	1 3/4	1.7500	2 33/64	2.5156	3 9/16	3.5625
15/64	.23438	1	1.0000	1 49/64	1.7656	2 17/32	2.5313	3 19/32	3.5938
1/4	.25	1 1/64	1.0156	1 25/32	1.7813	2 35/64	2.5469	3 5/8	3.6250
17/64	.26563	1 1/32	1.0313	1 51/64	1.7969	2 9/16	2.5625	3 21/32	3.6563
9/32	.28125	1 3/64	1.0469	1 13/16	1.8125	2 37/64	2.5781	3 11/16	3.6875
19/64	.29688	1 1/16	1.0625	1 53/64	1.8281	2 19/32	2.5938	3 23/32	3.7188
5/16	.3125	1 5/64	1.0781	1 27/32	1.8438	2 39/64	2.6094	3 3/4	3.7500
21/64	.32813	1 3/32	1.0938	1 55/64	1.8594	2 5/8	2.6250	3 25/32	3.7813
11/32	.34375	1 7/64	1.1094	1 7/8	1.8750	2 41/64	2.6406	3 13/16	3.8125
23/64	.35938	1 1/8	1.1250	1 57/64	1.8906	2 21/32	2.6563	3 27/32	3.8438
3/8	.375	1 9/64	1.1406	1 29/32	1.9063	2 43/64	2.6719	3 7/8	3.8750
25/64	.39063	1 5/32	1.1563	1 59/64	1.9219	2 11/16	2.6875	3 29/32	3.9063
13/32	.40625	1 11/64	1.1719	1 15/16	1.9375	2 45/64	2.7031	3 15/16	3.9375
27/64	.42188	1 3/16	1.1875	1 61/64	1.9531	2 23/32	2.7188	3 31/32	3.9688
7/16	.4375	1 13/64	1.2031	1 31/32	1.9688	2 47/64	2.7344	4	4.0000
29/64	.45313	1 7/32	1.2188	1 63/64	1.9844	2 3/4	2.7500	4 1/16	4.0625
15/32	.46875	1 15/64	1.2344	2	2.0000	2 49/64	2.7656	4 1/8	4.1250
31/64	.48438	1 1/4	1.2500	2 1/64	2.0156	2 25/32	2.7813	4 3/16	4.1875
1/2	.50	1 17/64	1.2656	2 1/32	2.0313	2 51/64	2.7969	4 1/4	4.2500
33/64	.51563	1 9/32	1.2813	2 3/64	2.0469	2 13/16	2.8125	4 5/16	4.3125
17/32	.53125	1 19/64	1.2969	2 1/16	2.0625	2 53/64	2.8281	4 3/8	4.3750
35/64	.54688	1 5/16	1.3125	2 5/64	2.0781	2 27/32	2.8438	4 7/16	4.4375
9/16	.5625	1 21/64	1.3281	2 3/32	2.0938	2 55/64	2.8594	4 1/2	4.5000
37/64	.57813	1 11/32	1.3438	2 7/64	2.1094	2 7/8	2.8750	4 9/16	4.5625
19/22	.59375	1 23/64	1.3594	2 1/8	2.1250	2 57/64	2.8906	4 5/8	4.6250
39/64	.60938	1 3/8	1.3750	2 9/64	2.1406	2 29/32	2.9063	4 11/16	4.6875
5/8	.6250	1 25/64	1.3906	2 5/32	2.1563	2 59/64	2.9219	4 3/4	4.7500
41/64	.6406	1 13/32	1.4063	2 11/64	2.1719	2 15/16	2.9375	4 13/16	4.8125
21/32	.6563	1 27/64	1.4219	2 3/16	2.1875	2 61/64	2.9531	4 7/8	4.8750
43/64	.6719	1 7/16	1.4375	2 13/64	2.2031	2 31/32	2.9688	4 15/16	4.9375
11/16	.6875	1 29/64	1.4531	2 7/32	2.2188	2 63/64	2.9844	5	5.0000
45/64	.7031	1 15/32	1.4688	2 15/64	2.2344	3	3.0000	5 1/8	5.1250
23/32	.7188	1 31/64	1.4844	2 1/4	2.2500	3 1/32	3.0313	5 1/4	5.2500
47/64	.7344	1 1/2	1.5000	2 17/64	2.2656	3 1/16	3.0625	5 3/8	5.3750
3/4	.7500	1 33/64	1.5156	2 9/32	2.2813	3 3/32	3.0938	5 1/2	5.5000
49/64	.7656	1 17/32	1.5313	2 19/64	2.2969	3 1/8	3.1250	5 5/8	5.6250
25/32	.7813	1 35/64	1.5469	2 5/16	2.3125	3 5/32	3.1563	5 3/4	5.7500
51/64	.7969	1 9/16	1.5625	2 21/64	2.3281	3 3/16	3.1875	5 7/8	5.8750
13/16	.8125	1 37/64	1.5781	2 11/32	2.3438	3 7/32	3.2188	6	6.0000

To find diameter of a circle multiply circumference by .31831.

To find circumference of a circle multiply diameter by 3.1416.

To find area of a circle multiply square of diameter by .7854.

To find surface of a ball multiply square of diameter by 3.1416.

To find side of a square multiply diagonal by .707.

To find cubic inches in a ball multiply cube of diameter by .5236.

Doubling the diameter of a pipe increases its capacity four times.

Double riveting is from 16 to 20% stronger than single.

One cubic foot of anthracite coal weighs about 58 lbs.

One cubic foot of bituminous coal weighs from 47 to 50 lbs.

One ton of coal is equivalent to two cords of wood for steam purposes.

There are nine square feet of heating surface to each square foot of grate surface.

Each nominal horse power boiler requires 30 to 35 pounds of water per hour.

To sharpen dull files lay them in diluted sulphuric acid until they are eaten deep enough.

A horse power is equivalent to raising 33,000 pounds one foot per minute or 550 pounds one foot per second.

The average consumption of coal for steam boilers is 12 pounds per hour for each sq. foot of grate surface.

To find the pressure in pounds per square inch of a column of water multiply the height of the column in feet by .434.

Steam rising from water at its boiling point (212 degrees) has a pressure equal to the atmosphere (14.7 pounds to the square inch).

DIMENSIONS OF THE WORLD

Equatorial Diameter	7,926.68 Miles
Polar Diameter	7,899.99 Miles
Difference	26.69 Miles
Mean Diameter	7,918.00 Miles
Equatorial Circumference	24,902.37 Miles
Meridional Circumference	24,860.44 Miles
Difference	41.83 Miles
Area of Surface	196,950,284 Square Miles
Water Area	139,950,284 Square Miles
Land Area	57,000,000 Square Miles
Volume of Land	29,300,000 Cubic Miles
Volume of Water	320,000,000 Cubic Miles

DIMENSIONS OF CONTINENTS

Africa	11,500,000 Square Miles
Asia	17,000,000 Square Miles
Europe	3,750,000 Square Miles
North America	8,000,000 Square Miles
Oceania	4,000,000 Square Miles
Polar Regions	6,205,000 Square Miles
South America	6,800,000 Square Miles

The latest estimates of the earth's area place the fertile regions at 33,000,000 square miles, steppes at 19,000,000 miles; deserts at 5,000,000 square miles.

Asia, the largest continent, is about 6,000 miles from East to West, and over 5,300 miles from North to South. Africa is 5,000 miles from North to South. Europe is 2,400 miles from North to South, and 3,300 miles from East to West. South America is 4,600 miles from North to South and 3,200 miles from East to West. North America is 4,900 miles from North to South and over 4,000 miles from East to West.

AREAS AND DEPTHS OF THE OCEAN

Oceans	Area (Square Miles)	Greatest Depth (Feet)
Pacific	68,634,000	30,000
Atlantic	41,321,000	27,366
Indian	29,340,000	18,582
Antarctic	7,500,000	25,200
Arctic	4,000,000	9,000

WEATHER WISDOM

SUNSET COLORS — A gray, lowering sunset, or one where the sky is green or yellowish green, indicates rain. A red sunrise, with clouds lowering later in the morning, also indicates rain.

HALO (Sun Dogs) — By halo we mean the large circles, or parts of circles, about the sun or moon. A halo occurring after fine weather indicates a storm.

RAINBOWS — A morning rainbow is regarded as a sign of rain; an evening rainbow of fair weather.

SKY COLOR — A deep-blue color of the sky, even when seen through clouds, indicates fair weather; a growing whiteness, an approaching storm.

Signs of the Zodiac

 ARIES, *The Ram*
March 21st - April 19th

 TAURUS, *The Bull*
April 20th - May 20th

 GEMINI, *The Twins*
May 21st - June 20th

 CANCER, *The Crab*
June 21st - July 22nd

 LEO, *The Lion*
July 23rd - August 22nd

 VIRGO, *The Virgin*
August 23rd - September 23rd

 LIBRA, *The Balance*
September 24th - October 23rd

 SCORPIO, *The Scorpion*
October 24th - November 21st

 SAGITTARIUS, *The Archer*
November 22nd - December 21st

 CAPRICORN, *The Goat*
December 22nd - January 19th

 AQUARIUS, *The Water Bearer*
January 20th - February 18th

 PISCES, *The Fish*
February 19th - March 20th

Birthstones and Flowers

BIRTHSTONES	MONTH	FLOWERS
Garnet	January	Snowdrop
Amethyst	February	Primrose
Bloodstone, Aquamarine	March	Violet
Diamond	April	Daisy
Emerald	May	Hawthorne
Pearl, Alexandrite	June	Honeysuckle
Ruby	July	Water Lily
Sardonyx, Peridot	August	Poppy
Sapphire	September	Morning Glory
Opal, Tourmaline	October	Hops
Topaz	November	Chrysanthemum
Turquoise, Zircon	December	Holly

Traditional Wedding Anniversary Gifts

1. Paper
2. Cotton
3. Leather
4. Silk, Flowers
5. Wooden
6. Garnet, Iron, Candy
7. Woolen, Copper
8. Bronze, Pottery
9. Topaz, Willow, Pottery
10. Tin, Aluminum

12. Linen, Silk
15. Crystal
20. China
25. Silver
30. Pearl
35. Coral, Jade
40. Ruby
45. Sapphire
50. Golden
60. Diamond
75. Diamond

NOTES